Lecture Notes in Computer Science

Lecture Notes in Artificial Intelligence   16016
Founding Editor

Jörg Siekmann

Series Editors

Randy Goebel, *University of Alberta, Edmonton, Canada*
Wolfgang Wahlster, *DFKI, Berlin, Germany*
Zhi-Hua Zhou, *Nanjing University, Nanjing, China*

The series Lecture Notes in Artificial Intelligence (LNAI) was established in 1988 as a topical subseries of LNCS devoted to artificial intelligence.

The series publishes state-of-the-art research results at a high level. As with the LNCS mother series, the mission of the series is to serve the international R & D community by providing an invaluable service, mainly focused on the publication of conference and workshop proceedings and postproceedings.

Rita P. Ribeiro · Bernhard Pfahringer ·
Nathalie Japkowicz · Pedro Larrañaga ·
Alípio M. Jorge · Carlos Soares ·
Pedro H. Abreu · João Gama
Editors

Machine Learning and Knowledge Discovery in Databases

Research Track

European Conference, ECML PKDD 2025
Porto, Portugal, September 15–19, 2025
Proceedings, Part IV

 Springer

Editors
Rita P. Ribeiro
Departamento de Ciencia de Computadores
University of Porto
Porto, Portugal

Nathalie Japkowicz
American University
Washington, D.C., WA, USA

Alípio M. Jorge
Departamento de Ciência de Computadores
University of Porto
Porto, Portugal

Pedro H. Abreu
University of Coimbra
Coimbra, Portugal

Bernhard Pfahringer
University of Waikato
Hamilton, Waikato, New Zealand

Pedro Larrañaga
Technical University of Madrid
Boadilla del Monte, Madrid, Spain

Carlos Soares
Faculdade de Engenharia
University of Porto
Porto, Portugal

João Gama
University of Porto
Porto, Portugal

ISSN 0302-9743　　　　　　　ISSN 1611-3349　(electronic)
Lecture Notes in Artificial Intelligence
ISBN 978-3-032-06077-8　　　ISBN 978-3-032-06078-5　(eBook)
https://doi.org/10.1007/978-3-032-06078-5

LNCS Sublibrary: SL7 – Artificial Intelligence

© The Editor(s) (if applicable) and The Author(s), under exclusive license
to Springer Nature Switzerland AG 2026
Chapters "Interpretable Instance-Based Learning Through Pairwise Distance Trees" and "MASCOTS: Model-Agnostic Symbolic COunterfactual Explanations for Time Series" are licensed under the terms of the Creative Commons Attribution 4.0 International License (http://creativecommons.org/licenses/by/4.0/). For further details see license information in the chapters.

This work is subject to copyright. All rights are solely and exclusively licensed by the Publisher, whether the whole or part of the material is concerned, specifically the rights of translation, reprinting, reuse of illustrations, recitation, broadcasting, reproduction on microfilms or in any other physical way, and transmission or information storage and retrieval, electronic adaptation, computer software, or by similar or dissimilar methodology now known or hereafter developed.
The use of general descriptive names, registered names, trademarks, service marks, etc. in this publication does not imply, even in the absence of a specific statement, that such names are exempt from the relevant protective laws and regulations and therefore free for general use.
The publisher, the authors and the editors are safe to assume that the advice and information in this book are believed to be true and accurate at the date of publication. Neither the publisher nor the authors or the editors give a warranty, expressed or implied, with respect to the material contained herein or for any errors or omissions that may have been made. The publisher remains neutral with regard to jurisdictional claims in published maps and institutional affiliations.

This Springer imprint is published by the registered company Springer Nature Switzerland AG
The registered company address is: Gewerbestrasse 11, 6330 Cham, Switzerland

If disposing of this product, please recycle the paper.

Preface

The 2025 edition of the European Conference on Machine Learning and Principles and Practice of Knowledge Discovery in Databases (ECML PKDD 2025) was held in the vibrant city of Porto, Portugal on September 15–19, 2025. This marks a significant return of the conference to Porto, following successful editions in 2005 and 2015, underscoring the city's enduring appeal as a hub for scientific exchange.

The annual ECML PKDD conference stands as a premier worldwide platform dedicated to showcasing the latest advancements and fostering insightful discussions in the fields of machine learning and knowledge discovery in databases. Held jointly since 2001, ECML PKDD has firmly established its reputation as the leading European conference in these disciplines. It provides researchers and practitioners with an unparalleled opportunity to exchange knowledge, share innovative ideas, and explore the latest technical advancements. Furthermore, the conference deeply values the synergy between foundational theoretical advances and groundbreaking practical data science applications, actively encouraging contributions that demonstrate how Machine Learning and Data Mining are being effectively employed to address complex real-world challenges.

A Hub for Responsible AI and Cutting-Edge Research

As the technological landscape continues to evolve and societal needs shift, the conference remains committed to adapting to and reflecting these dynamic changes. This year's event saw a robust engagement from the global research community with a substantial increase in the number of submissions.

The three main conference days were organised into five distinct tracks:

- The Research Track received an impressive number of 924 submissions, with 226 papers ultimately accepted, reflecting a highly competitive acceptance rate of 24.5%.
- The Applied Data Science Track received a total of 299 submissions, accepting 74 papers, resulting in an acceptance rate of 24.7%.
- The Journal Track continued to bridge the gap between conference and journal publications, accepting 43 papers (27 for the Machine Learning journal and 16 for the Data Mining and Knowledge Discovery journal) out of 297 submissions.
- The Nectar Track, focusing on recent scientific advances at the frontier of machine learning and data mining, received 30 submissions.
- The Demo Track showcased practical applications and prototypes, accepting 15 papers from a total of 30 submissions.

These proceedings cover the papers accepted in the Research and Applied Data Science tracks.

The high quality and diversity of the accepted papers across all tracks underscore the continued vitality and intellectual breadth of the machine learning and data mining communities. We extend our sincere gratitude to all authors for their valuable contributions, to the program committee members and reviewers for their diligent efforts in ensuring the rigorous double-blind review process, and to the organising committee for their tireless work in making ECML PKDD 2025 a resounding success. We believe these proceedings will serve as a valuable resource, inspiring future research and innovation in these rapidly advancing fields.

This year's conference featured seven insightful keynote talks that focused on crucial and emerging areas within Responsible AI, including trustworthy AI, interpretability, and explainability. The keynotes also explored fundamental theoretical issues, covering causality, neural-symbolic systems, large language models (LLMs), and AI for science. We were honoured to host leading experts who shared their valuable perspectives:

- Cynthia Rudin (Duke University) presented on "Many Good Models Lead to …";
- Elias Bareinboim (Columbia University) discussed "Towards Causal Artificial Intelligence";
- Francisco Herrera (University of Granada) addressed "Not Just a Trend: Institutionalizing XAI for Responsible and Compliant AI Systems";
- Mirella Lapata (University of Edinburgh) explored "Compositional Intelligence: Coordinating Multiple LLMs for Complex Tasks";
- Nuria Oliver (ELLIS Alicante Foundation, Spain) spoke on "Towards a Fairer World: Uncovering and Addressing Human and Algorithmic Biases";
- Pedro Domingos (University of Washington) shared insights on "A Simple Unification of Neural and Symbolic AI"; and
- Sašo Džeroski (Jožef Stefan Institute, Slovenia) presented on "Artificial Intelligence for Science".

Fostering Diversity and Inclusion

Our Diversity and Inclusion initiative proudly awarded 10 scholarship grants of €500 to early-career researchers. These grants enabled individuals from developing countries and communities underrepresented in science and technology to attend the conference, present their work, and become integral members of the ECML PKDD community.

Acknowledging Our Contributors and Supporters

We extend our sincere gratitude to everyone who contributed to making ECML PKDD 2025 such a success. Our heartfelt thanks go to the authors, workshop and tutorial organisers, and all participants for their valuable scientific contributions.

An outstanding conference program would not be possible without the immense dedication and substantial time investment from our area chairs, program committee, and organising committee. The smooth execution of the event was also largely due to the hard work of our many volunteers and session chairs. A special acknowledgement goes to the local organisers for meticulously handling every detail, making the conference a truly memorable experience.

Finally, we are incredibly grateful for the generous financial support from our wonderful sponsors. We also appreciate Springer's ongoing support and Microsoft's provision of their CMT software for conference management, as well as their continued assistance. Our sincere thanks also go to the ECML PKDD Steering Committee for their invaluable advice and guidance over the past two years.

September 2025

João Gama
Pedro H. Abreu
Alípio M. Jorge
Carlos Soares
Rita P. Ribeiro
Pedro Larrañaga
Nathalie Japkowicz
Bernhard Pfahringer
Inês Dutra
Mykola Pechenizkiy
Sepideh Pashami
Paulo Cortez

Organization

Honorary Chair

Pavel Brazdil   University of Porto, Portugal

General Chairs

João Gama	University of Porto, Portugal
Pedro H. Abreu	University of Coimbra, Portugal
Alípio M. Jorge	University of Porto, Portugal
Carlos Soares	University of Porto, Portugal

Research Track Program Chairs

Bernhard Pfahringer	University of Waikato, New Zealand
Nathalie Japkowicz	American University, USA
Pedro Larrañaga	Technical University of Madrid, Spain
Rita P. Ribeiro	University of Porto, Portugal

Applied Data Science Track Program Chairs

Inês Dutra	University of Porto, Portugal
Mykola Pechenisky	TU Eindhoven, The Netherlands
Paulo Cortez	University of Minho, Portugal
Sepideh Pashami	Halmstad University, Sweden

Journal Track Chairs

Ana Carolina Lorena	Instituto Tecnológico de Aeronáutica, Brazil
Arlindo Oliveira	Instituto Superior Técnico, Portugal
Concha Bielza	Technical University of Madrid, Spain
Longbing Cao	Macquarie University, Australia
Tiago Almeida	Federal University of São Carlos, Brazil

Nectar Track Chairs

Ricard Gavaldà   Amalfi Analytics, Spain
Riccardo Guidotti   University of Pisa, Italy

Demo Track Chairs

Arian Pasquali   Faktion, Belgium
Nuno Moniz   University of Notre Dame, USA

Local Chairs

Bruno Veloso   University of Porto, Portugal
Rita Nogueira   INESC TEC, Portugal
Shazia Tabassum   INESC TEC, Portugal

Workshop Chairs

Irena Koprinska   University of Sydney, Australia
João Mendes Moreira   University of Porto, Portugal
Paula Branco   University of Ottawa, Canada

Tutorial Chairs

Alicia Troncoso   Universidad Pablo de Olavide, Spain
Nikolaj Tatti   University of Helsinki, Finland

PhD Forum Chairs

Raquel Sebastião   Polytechnic Institute of Viseu, Portugal
Yun Sing Koh   University of Auckland, New Zealand

Awards Committee Chairs

André Carvalho	University of São Paulo, Brazil
Amparo Alonso-Betanzos	University of A Coruña, Spain
Katharina Morik	TU Dortmund, Germany
Vítor Santos Costa	University of Porto, Portugal

Proceedings Chairs

João Vinagre	European Commission (JRC), Spain
Miriam Santos	University of Porto, Portugal
Shazia Tabassum	INESC TEC, Portugal

Diversity and Inclusion Chairs

Inês Sousa	Fraunhofer, Portugal
Zahraa Abdallah	University of Bristol, UK

Discovery Challenge Chairs

Carlos Ferreira	Polytechnic Institute of Porto, Portugal
Peter van der Putten	Leiden University, The Netherlands
Rui Camacho	University of Porto, Portugal

Panel Chairs

Pedro H. Abreu	University of Coimbra, Portugal
Paula Brito	University of Porto, Portugal

Publicity Chair

Carlos Ferreira	Polytechnic Institute of Porto, Portugal

Sponsorship Chairs

Mariam Berry	BNP Paribas, France
Nuno Moutinho	University of Porto, Portugal
Rui Teles	Accenture, Portugal

Social Media Chairs

Luis Roque	ZAAI.ai, Portugal
Ricardo Pereira	University of Coimbra, Portugal
Dalila Teixeira	Creative Matter, USA

Web Chair

Thiago Andrade — University of Porto, Portugal

Senior Program Committee – Research Track

Adam Jatowt	University of Innsbruck, Austria
Andrea Passerini	University of Trento, Italy
Anthony Bagnall	University of Southampton, UK
Arno Knobbe	Leiden University, Netherlands
Arno Siebes	Universiteit Utrecht, Netherlands
Arto Klami	University of Helsinki, Finland
Bernhard Pfahringer	University of Waikato, New Zealand
Bettina Berendt	TU Berlin, Germany
Celine Robardet	INSA Lyon, France
Celine Vens	KU Leuven, Belgium
Cesar Ferri	Universitat Politècnica Valencia, Spain
Charalampos Tsourakakis	Boston University, USA
Chedy Raissi	Inria, France
Chen Gong	Nanjing University of Science and Technology, China
Danai Koutra	University of Michigan, USA
Dimitrios Gunopulos	University of Athens, Greece
Donato Malerba	Università degli Studi di Bari Aldo Moro, Italy
Dragi Kocev	Jožef Stefan Institute, Slovenia
Dunja Mladenic	Jožef Stefan Institute, Slovenia
Eirini Ntoutsi	Universität der Bundeswehr München, Germany

Emmanuel Müller	TU Dortmund, Germany
Ernestina Menasalvas	Universidad Politécnica de Madrid, Spain
Esther Galbrun	University of Eastern Finland, Finland
Evaggelia Pitoura	University of Ioannina, Greece
Evangelos Papalexakis	University of California, Riverside, USA
Fabio A. Stella	University of Milano-Bicocca, Italy
Fabrizio Costa	Exeter University, UK
Fragkiskos Malliaros	CentraleSupélec, France
Georg Krempl	Utrecht University, Netherlands
Georgiana Ifrim	University College Dublin, Ireland
Gustavo Batista	University of New South Wales, Australia
Heikki Mannila	Aalto University, Finland
Hendrik Blockeel	KU Leuven, Belgium
Henrik Bostrom	KTH Royal Institute of Technology, Sweden
Henry Gouk	University of Edinburgh, UK
Ioannis Katakis	University of Nicosia, Cyprus
Jan N. Van Rijn	LIACS, Leiden University, Netherlands
Jefrey Lijffijt	Ghent University, Belgium
Jerzy Stefanowski	Poznań University of Technology, Poland
Jesse Davis	KU Leuven, Belgium
Jesse Read	Ecole Polytechnique, France
Jessica Lin	George Mason University, USA
Jesus Cerquides	IIIA-CSIC, Spain
Jilles Vreeken	CISPA Helmholtz Center for Information Security, Germany
João Gama	INESC TEC - LIAAD, Portugal
Jörg Wicker	University of Auckland, New Zealand
José Hernández-Orallo	Universitat Politècnica de Valencia, Spain
Junming Shao	University of Electronic Science and Technology of China, China
Kai Puolamaki	University of Helsinki, Finland
Manfred Jaeger	Aalborg University, Denmark
Marius Kloft	TU Kaiserslautern, Germany
Marius Lindauer	Leibniz University Hannover, Germany
Mark Last	Ben-Gurion University of the Negev, Israel
Matthias Renz	University of Kiel, Germany
Matthias Schubert	Ludwig-Maximilians-Universität München, Germany
Michele Lombardi	University of Bologna, Italy
Michèle Sebag	LISN CNRS, France
Nathalie Japkowicz	American University, USA
Paolo Frasconi	Università degli Studi di Firenze, Italy

Parisa Kordjamshidi	Michigan State University, USA
Pasquale Minervini	University of Edinburgh, UK
Pauli Miettinen	University of Eastern Finland, Finland
Pedro Larrañaga	Technical University of Madrid, Spain
Peer Kroger	Christian-Albrechts-Universität Kiel, Germany
Peter Flach	University of Bristol, UK
Ricardo B. Prudencio	Universidade Federal de Pernambuco, Brazil
Rita P. Ribeiro	University of Porto and INESC TEC, Portugal
Salvatore Ruggieri	University of Pisa, Italy
Sebastijan Dumancic	TU Delft, Netherlands
Sibylle Hess	TU Eindhoven, Netherlands
Sicco Verwer	Delft University of Technology, Netherlands
Siegfried Nijssen	Université catholique de Louvain, Belgium
Sophie Fellenz	RPTU Kaiserslautern-Landau, Germany
Stefano Ferilli	University of Bari, Italy
Stratis Ioannidis	Northeastern University, USA
Szymon Jaroszewicz	Polish Academy of Sciences, Poland
Tijl De Bie	Ghent University, Belgium
Ulf Brefeld	Leuphana University of Lüneburg, Germany
Varvara Vetrova	University of Canterbury, New Zealand
Wannes Meert	KU Leuven, Belgium
Wei Ye	Tongji University, China
Wenbin Zhang	Florida International University, USA
Willem Waegeman	Universiteit Gent, Belgium
Wouter Duivesteijn	Technische Universiteit Eindhoven, Netherlands
Xiao Luo	University of California, Los Angeles, USA
Yun Sing Koh	University of Auckland, New Zealand
Zied Bouraoui	CRIL CNRS and Université d'Artois, France

Senior Program Committee – Applied Data Science Track

Albrecht Zimmermann	Université de Caen Normandie, France
Andreas Hotho	University of Würzburg, Germany
Anirban Dasgupta	IIT Gandhinagar, India
Anna Monreale	University of Pisa, Italy
Annalisa Appice	University of Bari Aldo Moro, Italy
Bruno Cremilleux	Université de Caen Normandie, France
Carlotta Domeniconi	George Mason University, USA
Dejing Dou	BCG, USA
Fabio Pinelli	IMT Lucca, Italy
Fuzhen Zhuang	Beihang University, China

Gabor Melli	PredictionWorks, USA
Giuseppe Manco	ICAR-CNR, Italy
Glenn Fung	Independent Researcher, USA
Grzegorz Nalepa	Jagiellonian University, Poland
Hui Xiong	Hong Kong University of Science and Technology (Guangzhou), China
Inês Dutra	University of Porto, Portugal
Ioanna Miliou	Stockholm University, Sweden
Ira Assent	Aarhus University, Denmark
Jiayu Zhou	Michigan State University, USA
Jiliang Tang	Michigan State University, USA
Jingrui He	University of Illinois at Urbana-Champaign, USA
João Gama	INESC TEC - LIAAD, Portugal
Jose A. Gamez	Universidad de Castilla-La Mancha, Spain
Ke Liang	National University of Defense Technology, China
Kurt Driessens	Maastricht University, Netherlands
Lars Kotthoff	University of Wyoming, USA
Liang Sun	Alibaba Group, China
Martin Atzmueller	Osnabrück University and DFKI, Germany
Michael R. Berthold	KNIME, Germany
Michelangelo Ceci	University of Bari, Italy
Min-Ling Zhang	Southeast University, China
Mykola Pechenizkiy	TU Eindhoven, Netherlands
Myra Spiliopoulou	Otto-von-Guericke-Universität Magdeburg, Germany
Niklas Lavesson	Blekinge Institute of Technology, Sweden
Nikolaj Tatti	Helsinki University, Finland
Panagiotis Papapetrou	Stockholm University, Sweden
Paolo Frasconi	Università degli Studi di Firenze, Italy
Paulo Cortez	University of Minho, Portugal
Peggy Cellier	INSA Rennes, IRISA, France
Rayid Ghani	Carnegie Mellon University, USA
Sahar Asadi	King (Microsoft), UK
Sandeep Tata	Google, USA
Sepideh Pashami	Halmstad University, Sweden
Slawomir Nowaczyk	Halmstad University, Sweden
Sriparna Saha	IIT Patna, India
Thomas Liebig	TU Dortmund, Germany
Thomas Seidl	LMU Munich, Germany
Tom Diethe	AstraZeneca, UK
Tony Lindgren	Stockholm University, Sweden

Vincent S. Tseng — National Yang Ming Chiao Tung University, Taiwan
Vítor Santos Costa — Universidade do Porto, Portugal
Xingquan Zhu — Florida Atlantic University, USA
Yi Chang — Jilin University, China
Yinglong Xia — Meta, USA
Yongxin Tong — Beihang University, China
Yun Sing Koh — University of Auckland, New Zealand
Zhaochun Ren — Shandong University, China
Zheng Wang — Alibaba DAMO Academy, China
Zhiwei (Tony) Qin — Lyft, USA

Program Committee – Research Track

Christoph Bergmeir — Monash University, Australia
A. K. M. Mahbubur Rahman — Independent University, Bangladesh
Abdulhakim Qahtan — Utrecht University, Netherlands
Abhishek A. — Fujitsu Research, India
Acar Tamersoy — Microsoft, USA
Ad Feelders — Universiteit Utrecht, Netherlands
Adam Goodge — I2R, A*STAR, Singapore
Adele Jia — China Agricultural University, China
Adem Kikaj — KU Leuven, Belgium
Aditya Mohan — Leibniz Universität Hannover, Germany
Ajay A. Mahimkar — AT&T, USA
Akka Zemmari — Université de Bordeaux, France
Akshay Sethi — MasterCard, USA
Alborz Geramifard — Meta, USA
Alessandro Antonucci — IDSIA, Switzerland
Alessandro Melchiorre — Johannes Kepler University Linz, Austria
Alexander Dockhorn — Leibniz University Hannover, Germany
Alexander Schiendorfer — Technische Hochschule Ingolstadt, Germany
Alexander Schulz — CITEC, Bielefeld University, Germany
Alexandre Termier — Université de Rennes 1, France
Alexandre Verine — Ecole Normale Supérieure - PSL, France
Alexandru C. Mara — Ghent University, Belgium
Ali Ayadi — University of Strasbourg, France
Ali Ismail-Fawaz — IRIMAS, Université de Haute-Alsace, France
Alicja Wieczorkowska — Polish-Japanese Academy of Information Technology, Poland
Alipio M. G. Jorge — INESC TEC/University of Porto, Portugal

Alireza Gharahighehi	KU Leuven, Belgium
Alistair Shilton	Deakin University, Australia
Alneu A. Lopes	University of São Paulo, Brazil
Alper Demir	Izmir University of Economics, Turkey
Alvaro Figueira	CRACS and Universidade do Porto, Portugal
Amal Saadallah	TU Dortmund, Germany
Aman Chadha	Stanford University and Amazon, USA
Amer Krivosija	TU Dortmund, Germany
Amir H. Payberah	KTH Royal Institute of Technology, Sweden
Ammar Shaker	NEC Laboratories Europe, Europe
Ana Rita Nogueira	INESC TEC, Portugal
Anand Paul	Louisiana State University HSC, USA
Anastasios Gounaris	Aristotle University of Thessaloniki, Greece
Andre V. Carreiro	Fraunhofer Portugal AICOS, Portugal
André C. P. L. F. de Carvalho	University of São Paulo, Brazil
Andrea Cossu	University of Pisa, Italy
Andrea Mastropietro	University of Bonn, Germany
Andrea Pugnana	University of Trento, Italy
Andrea Tagarelli	DIMES - UNICAL, Italy
Andreas Bender	LMU Munich, Germany
Andreas Nürnberger	Otto-von-Guericke-Universität Magdeburg, Germany
Andreas Schwung	Fachhochschule Südwestfalen, Germany
Andrei Paleyes	University of Cambridge, UK
Andrzej Skowron	University of Warsaw, Poland
Andy Song	RMIT University, Australia
Angelica Liguori	ICAR-CNR, Italy
Anirban Dasgupta	IIT Gandhinagar, India
Anke Meyer-Baese	Florida State University, USA
Anna Beer	University of Vienna, Austria
Anna Krause	Universität Wurzburg and Chair X Data Science, Germany
Anna Monreale	University of Pisa, Italy
Annelot W. Bosman	Universiteit Leiden, Netherlands
Antoine Caradot	Hubert Curien Laboratory, France
Antonio Bahamonde	University of Oviedo, Spain
Antonio Mastropietro	Università di Pisa, Italy
Antonio Pellicani	Università degli Studi di Bari, Aldo Moro, Italy
Antonis Matakos	Aalto University, Finland
Antti Laaksonen	University of Helsinki, Finland
Aomar Osmani	LIPN-UMR CNRS, France
Aonghus Lawlor	University College Dublin, Ireland

Aparna S. Varde	Montclair State University, USA
Apostolos N. Papadopoulos	Aristotle University of Thessaloniki, Greece
Aritra Konar	KU Leuven, Belgium
Arjun Roy	Freie Universität Berlin, Germany
Arthur Charpentier	UQAM, Canada
Arunas Lipnickas	Kaunas University of Technology, Lithuania
Atsuhiro Takasu	National Institute of Informatics, Japan
Aurora Esteban	University of Cordoba, Spain
Baosheng Zhang	Tsinghua University, China
Barbara Toniella Corradini	University of Florence and University of Siena, Italy
Bardh Prenkaj	Technical University of Munich, Germany
Barry O'Sullivan	University College Cork, Ireland
Beilun Wang	Southeast University, China
Benjamin Halstead	University of Auckland, New Zealand
Benjamin Paassen	Bielefeld University, Germany
Benjamin Quost	Université de Technologie de Compiègne, France
Benoit Frenay	University of Namur, Belgium
Bernardo Moreno Sanchez	University of Helsinki, Finland
Bernhard Pfahringer	University of Waikato, New Zealand
Bertrand Cuissart	University of Caen, France
Bin Liu	Chongqing University of Posts and Telecommunications, China
Bin Shi	Xi'an Jiaotong University, China
Bin Wu	Zhengzhou University, China
Bin Zhou	National University of Defense Technology, China
Bitao Peng	Guangdong University of Foreign Studies, China
Bo Kang	Ghent University, Belgium
Bogdan Cautis	Université Paris-Saclay, France
Bojan Evkoski	Central European University, Hungary
Boshen Shi	Institute of Computing Technology, Chinese Academy of Sciences, China
Boualem Benatallah	Dublin City University, Ireland
Brandon Gower-Winter	Utrecht University, Netherlands
Bunil K. Balabantaray	NIT Meghalaya, India
Carlos Ferreira	INESC TEC, Portugal
Carlos Monserrat-Aranda	Universitat Politècnica de Valencia, Spain
Carson K. Leung	University of Manitoba, Canada
Catarina Silva	University of Coimbra, Portugal
Cecile Capponi	Aix-Marseille University, France
Celine Rouveirol	LIPN Université de Sorbonne Paris Nord, France

Cesar H. G. Andrade	Porto University, Portugal
Chandrajit Bajaj	University of Texas, Austin, USA
Chang Rajani	University of Helsinki, Finland
Charlotte Laclau	Polytechnique Institute, Télécom Paris, France
Charlotte Pelletier	Université de Bretagne du Sud, France
Chen Wang	DATA61, CSIRO, Australia
Cheng Cheng	Carnegie Mellon University, USA
Cheng Xie	Yunnan University, China
Chenglin Wang	East China Normal University, China
Chenwang Wu	University of Science and Technology of China, China
Chiara Pugliese	IIT Institute of National Research Council, Italy
Chien-Liang Liu	National Chiao Tung University, Taiwan
Chihiro Maru	Chuo University, Japan
Chongsheng Zhang	Henan University, China
Christian Beecks	FernUniversität in Hagen, Germany
Christian M. M. Frey	University of Technology Nuremberg, Germany
Christian Hakert	TU Dortmund, Germany
Christine Largeron	LabHC Lyon University, France
Christophe Rigotti	INSA Lyon, France
Christophe Rodrigues	DVRC Pôle universitaire Léonard de Vinci, France
Christos Anagnostopoulos	University of Glasgow, UK
Christos Diou Harokopio	University of Athens, Greece
Chuan Qin	Chinese Academy of Sciences, China
Chunchun Chen	Tongji University, China
Chunyao Song	Nankai University, China
Claire Nedellec	INRAE, MaIAGE, France
Claudio Borile	CENTAI Institute, Italy
Claudio Gallicchio	University of Pisa, Italy
Claudius Zelenka	Kiel University, Germany
Colin Bellinger	NRC and Dalhousie University, Canada
Collin Leiber	Aalto University, Finland
Cong Qi	New Jersey Institute of Technology, USA
Congfeng Cao	University of Amsterdam, Netherlands
Corrado Loglisci	Università degli Studi di Bari, Aldo Moro, Italy
Cuicui Luo	University of Chinese Academy of Sciences, China
Cuneyt G. Akcora	University of Central Florida, USA
Cynthia C. S. Liem	Delft University of Technology, Netherlands
Dalius Matuzevicius	Vilnius Gediminas Technical University, Lithuania

Dan Li	Sun Yat-sen University, China
Danai Koutra	University of Michigan, USA
Dang Nguyen	Deakin University, Australia
Daniel Neider	TU Dortmund, Germany
Daniel Schlor	Universität Würzburg, Germany
Danil Provodin	TU Eindhoven, Netherlands
Danyang Xiao	Sun Yat-sen University, China
Dario Garcia-Gasulla	Barcelona Supercomputing Center (BSC), Spain
Dario Garigliotti	University of Bergen, Norway
Darius Plonis	Vilnius Gediminas Technical University, Lithuania
Dariusz Brzezinski	Poznań University of Technology, Poland
David Gomez	Universidad Politecnica de Madrid, Spain
David Holzmüller	University of Stuttgart, Germany
David Q. Sun	Apple, USA
Davide Evangelista	University of Bologna, Italy
Debo Cheng	University of South Australia, Australia
Deepayan Chakrabarti	University of Texas at Austin, USA
Deng-Bao Wang	Southeast University, China
Denilson Barbosa	University of Alberta, Canada
Denis Huseljic	University of Kassel, Germany
Denis Lukovnikov	Ruhr-Universität Bochum, Germany
Destercke Sebastien	UTC, France
Di Jin	TikTok, USA
Di Wu	Chongqing Institute of Green and Intelligent Technology, Chinese Academy of Sciences, China
Diana Benavides Prado	University of Auckland, New Zealand
Dianhui Wang	Independent Researcher, Australia
Diego Carrera	STMicroelectronics, Switzerland
Diletta Chiaro	Università degli Studi di Napoli Federico II, Italy
Dimitri Staufer	TU Berlin, Germany
Dimitrios Katsaros	University of Thessaly, Greece
Dimitrios Rafailidis	University of Thessaly, France
Dino Ienco	INRAE, France
Dmitry Kobak	University of Tübingen, Germany
Domenico Redavid	University of Bari, Italy
Dominik M. Endres	Philipps-Universität Marburg, Germany
Dominique Gay	Université de La Réunion, France
Dong Li	Baylor University, USA
Duarte Folgado	Fraunhofer Portugal AICOS, Portugal
Duo Xu	Georgia Institute of Technology, USA

Edoardo Serra	Boise State University, USA
Edouard Fouche	Karlsruhe Institute of Technology (KIT), Germany
Eduardo F. Montesuma	Université Paris-Saclay, France
Edward Apeh	Bournemouth University, UK
Edwin Simpson	University of Bristol, UK
Ehsan Aminian	INESC TEC, Portugal
Ekaterina Antonenko	Mines Paris - PSL, France
Eliana Pastor	Politecnico di Torino, Italy
Emanuela Marasco	George Mason University, USA
Emilio Dorigatti	LMU Munich, Germany
Emilio Parrado-Hernandez	Universidad Carlos III de Madrid, Spain
Emmanouil Krasanakis	CERTH, Greece
Emmanouil Panagiotou	Freie Universität Berlin, Germany
Emre Gursoy	Koc University, Turkey
Engelbert Mephu Nguifo	Université Clermont Auvergne, CNRS, LIMOS, France
Eran Treister	Ben-Gurion University of the Negev, Israel
Erasmo Purificato	Otto-von-Guericke Universität Magdeburg, Germany
Erik Novak	Jožef Stefan Institute, Slovenia
Erwan Le Merrer	Inria, France
Esra Akbas	Georgia State University, USA
Esther-Lydia Silva-Ramirez	Universidad de Cadiz, Spain
Evaldas Vaičiukynas	Kaunas University of Technology, Lithuania
Evangelos Kanoulas	University of Amsterdam, Netherlands
Evelin Amorim	INESC TEC, Portugal
Fabian C. Spaeh	Boston University, USA
Fabio Fassetti	Università della Calabria, Italy
Fabio Fumarola	Prometeia, Italy
Fabio Mercorio	University of Milan-Bicocca, Italy
Fabio Vandin	University of Padova, Italy
Fandel Lin	University of Southern California, USA
Federica Granese	Inria, Université Côte d'Azur, France
Federico Baldo	University of Bologna, Italy
Federico Sabbatini	National Institute for Nuclear Physics (INFN), Italy
Feifan Zhang	China Agricultural University, China
Felipe Kenji Nakano	KU Leuven, Belgium
Fernando Martinez-Plumed	Universitat Politècnica de Valencia, Spain
Filipe Rodrigues	Technical University of Denmark (DTU), Denmark

Flavio Giobergia	Politecnico di Torino, Italy
Florent Masseglia	Inria, France
Florian Beck	JKU Linz, Austria
Florian Lemmerich	University of Passau, Germany
Francesca Naretto	University of Pisa, Italy
Francesco Piccialli	University of Naples Federico II, Italy
Francesco Renna	Universidade do Porto, Portugal
Francisco Pereira	DTU, Denmark
Franco Raimondi	Gran Sasso Science Institute, Italy
Frederic Koriche	Université d'Artois, CRIL CNRS, France
Frederic Pennerath	CentraleSupélec - LORIA, France
Furong Peng	Shanxi University, China
Gabriel Marques Tavares	LMU Munich, Germany
Gabriele Sartor	University of Turin, Italy
Gabriele Venturato	KU Leuven, Belgium
Gaetan De Waele	Ghent University, Belgium
Gaia Saveri	University of Trieste, Italy
Gang Li	Deakin University, Australia
Gaoyuan Du	Amazon, USA
Gavin Smith	University of Nottingham, UK
Geming Xia	National University of Defense Technology, China
Geng Zhao	Heidelberg University, Germany
Gennaro Vessio	University of Bari Aldo Moro, Italy
Geoffrey I. Webb	Monash, Australia
Georgia Baltsou	Centre for Research & Technology, Greece
Geraldin Nanfack	Concordia University, Canada
Germain Forestier	University of Haute Alsace, France
Gerrit Grossmann	DFKI, Germany
Gerrit J. J. van den Burg	Alan Turing Institute, UK
Gherardo Varando	Universitat de Valencia, Spain
Giacomo Medda	University of Cagliari, Italy
Gilberto Bernardes	INESC TEC and University of Porto, Portugal
Giorgio Venturin	University of Padova, Italy
Giovanna Castellano	University of Bari Aldo Moro, Italy
Giovanni Ponti	ENEA, Italy
Giovanni Stilo	Università degli Studi dell'Aquila, Italy
Gisele Pappa	UFMG, Brazil
Giuseppe Manco	ICAR-CNR, IT, Italy
Gizem Gezici	Scuola Normale Superiore, Italy
Gjergji Kasneci	TU Munich, Germany
Goreti Marreiros	ISEP/GECAD, Portugal

Graziella De Martino	University of Bari, Aldo Moro, Italy
Grazina Korvel	Vilnius University, Lithuania
Grigorios Tsoumakas	Aristotle University of Thessaloniki, Greece
Guangyin Jin	National University of Defense Technology, China
Guangzhong Sun	University of Science and Technology of China, China
Guanjin Wang	Murdoch University, Australia
Guilherme Weigert	Cassales University of Waikato, New Zealand
Guillaume Derval	UC Louvain - ICTEAM, Belgium
Guorui Quan	University of Manchester, UK
Guoxi Zhang	Beijing Institute of General Artificial Intelligence, China
Gustau Camps-Valls	Universitat de Valencia, Spain
Gustav Sir	Czech Technical University, Czech Republic
Gustavo Batista	University of New South Wales, Australia
Hachem Kadri	Aix-Marseille University, France
Hadi Asghari	Humboldt Institute for Internet and Society, Germany
Haifeng Sun	University of Science and Technology of China, China
Haihui Fan	Institute of Information Engineering, Chinese Academy of Sciences, China
Haizhou Du	Shanghai University of Electric Power, China
Hajer Salem	AUDENSIEL, France
Hakim Hacid	TII, United Arab Emirates
Hamid Bouchachia	Bournemouth University, UK
Han Wang	Xidian University, China
Hang Yu	Shanghai University, China
Hanna Sumita	Institute of Science Tokyo, Japan
Hao Niu	KDDI Research, Japan
Hao Xue	University of New South Wales, Australia
Hao Yan	Carleton University, Canada
Haowen Zhang	Zhejiang Sci-Tech University, China
Harsh Borse	IIT Kharagpur, India
Heitor M. Gomes	Victoria University of Wellington, New Zealand
Helder Oliveira	FCUP and INESC TEC, Portugal
Helge Langseth	Norwegian University of Science and Technology, Norway
Hendrik Blockeel	KU Leuven, Belgium
Henrique O. Marques	University of Southern Denmark, Denmark
Henryk Maciejewski	Wroclaw University of Science and Technology, Poland

Hideaki Ishibashi	Kyushu Institute of Technology, Japan
Hilde J. P. Weerts	Eindhoven University of Technology, Netherlands
Holger Froening	University of Heidelberg, Germany
Holger Karl	HPI, Germany
Hongbo Bo	University of Bristol, UK
Hongyang Chen	Zhejiang Lab, China
Hua Chu	Xidian University, China
Huaiyu Wan	Beijing Jiaotong University, China
Huaming Chen	University of Sydney, Australia
Huandong Wang	Tsinghua University, China
Huanlai Xing	Southwest Jiaotong University, China
Hui Ji	University of Pittsburgh, USA
Hui (Wendy) Wang	Stevens Institute of Technology, USA
Huiping Chen	University of Birmingham, UK
Humberto Bustince	Universidad Publica de Navarra, Spain
Huong Ha	RMIT University, Australia
Idir Benouaret	Epita Research Laboratory, France
Ines Sousa	Fraunhofer AICOS, Portugal
Ingo Thon	Siemens AG, Germany
Inigo Jauregi Unanue	University of Technology Sydney, Australia
Ioannis Sarridis	Centre for Research & Technology, Greece
Issam Falih	Université Clermont Auvergne, CNRS, LIMOS, France
Ivan Vankov	iris.ai, Norway
Ivor Cribben	University of Alberta, Canada
Jaemin Yoo	KAIST, South Korea
Jakir Hossain	University at Buffalo, USA
Jakub Klikowski	Wroclaw University of Science and Technology, Poland
Jalaj Bhandari	Columbia University, USA
Jaleed Khan	University of Oxford, UK
James Goulding	University of Nottingham, UK
Jan Kalina	Czech Academy of Sciences, Czech Republic
Jan P. Mielniczuk	Polish Academy of Sciences, Poland
Jan Ramon	Inria, France
Jan Verwaeren	Ghent University, Belgium
Jannis Brugger	TU Darmstadt, Germany
Jean-Marc Andreoli	Naverlabs Europe, Netherlands
Jedrzej Potoniec	Poznań University of Technology, Poland
Jeronimo Arenas-Garcia	Universidad Carlos III de Madrid, Spain
Jhony H. Giraldo	Télécom Paris, Institut Polytechnique de Paris, France

Jia Cai	Guangdong University of Finance and Economics, China
Jiahui Jin	Southeast University, China
Jiang Zhong	Independent Researcher, China
Jianwu Wang	University of Maryland, Baltimore County, USA
Jiawei Chen	Tianjin University, China
Jiaxin Ding	Shanghai Jiao Tong University, China
Jidong Yuan	Beijing Jiaotong University, China
Jie Song	Zhejiang University, China
Jie Wu	Fudan University, China
Jie Yang	University of Wollongong, China
Jimeng Shi	Florida International University, USA
Jin Chen	Hong Kong University of Science and Technology, China
Jin Liang	South China Normal University, China
Jing Ren	NUDT, China
Jing Wang	Amazon, USA
Jinghui Zhong	South China University of Technology, China
Jingtao Ding	Tsinghua University, China
Jinli Zhang	Beijing University of Technology, China
Jiri Sima	Czech Academy of Sciences, Czech Republic
João Gama	University of Porto, Portugal
Joao Mendes-Moreira	University of Porto, Portugal
Joao Vinagre	European Commission (JRC), Spain
Joaquim Silva	NOVA LINCS, Universidade Nova de Lisboa, Portugal
Jochen De Weerdt	KU Leuven, Belgium
Joe Mellor	University of Edinburgh, UK
Johanne Cohen	LISN-CNRS, France
Johannes Jakubik	IBM Research, USA
John W. Sheppard	Montana State University, USA
Jonata Tyska Carvalho	Federal University of Santa Catarina, Brazil
Jordi Guitart	Barcelona Supercomputing Center (BSC), Spain
Joris Mattheijssens	Ghent University, Belgium
Jose M. Costa Pereira	University of Porto, Portugal
Jose Oramas	University of Antwerp, sqIRL/IDLab, imec, Belgium
Jose Tomas Palma	University of Murcia, Spain
Joydeep Chandra	Indian Institute of Technology, Patna, India
Juan A. Botia	University of Murcia, Spain
Juan Rodriguez	Universidad de Burgos, Spain
Jukka Heikkonen	University of Turku, Finland

Julien Delaunay	Inria, France
Julien Ferry	Polytechnique Montreal, Canada
Julien Perez	EPITA, France
Jun Zhuang	Boise State University, USA
Jun Yu Hou	Nanjing University, China
Junbo Zhang	JD Intelligent Cities Research, USA
Junze Liu	University of California, Irvine, USA
Jurgita Kapočiūtė-Dzikienė	Tilde SIA, University of Latvia and Tilde IT, Vytautas Magnus University, Lithuania
Justina Mandravickaitė	Vytautas Magnus University, Lithuania
Kamil Adamczewski	Max Planck Institute for Intelligent Systems, Germany
Kamil Michal Ksiazek	Jagiellonian University, Poland
Karim Radouane	Université Sorbonne Paris Nord, France
Kary Framing	Umeå University, Sweden
Katerina Taskova	University of Auckland, New Zealand
Katharina Dost	Jožef Stefan Institute, Slovenia
Kaushik Roy	University of South Carolina, USA
Kejia Chen	Nanjing University of Posts and Telecommunications, China
Ken Kobayashi	Tokyo Institute of Technology, Japan
Khaled Mohammed Saifuddin	Northeastern University, USA
Khalid Benabdeslem	Université de Lyon 1, France
Kim Thang Nguyen	LIG, University Grenoble-Alpes, France
Kira Maag	Heinrich-Heine-Universität Düsseldorf, Germany
Koji Maruhashi	Fujitsu Research, Japan
Koyel Mukherjee	Adobe Research, USA
Kristen M. Scott	KU Leuven, Belgium
Krzysztof Ruda	Polish Academy of Sciences, Poland
Krzysztof Slot	Lodz University of Technology, Poland
Kuldeep Singh	Cerence, Germany
Kushankur Ghosh	University of Alberta, Canada
Lamine Diop	EPITA, France
Latifa Oukhellou	IFSTTAR, France
Laurence Park	Western Sydney University, Australia
Laurens Devos	KU Leuven, Belgium
Len Feremans	Universiteit Antwerpen, Belgium
Lena Wiese	Goethe University Frankfurt, Germany
Lenaig Cornanguer	CISPA Helmholtz Center for Information Security, Germany
Lennert De Smet	KU Leuven, Belgium
Lev Reyzin	University of Illinois at Chicago, USA

Li Wang	National University of Defense Technology, China
Liang Du	Shanxi University, China
Lianyong Qi	China University of Petroleum (East China), China
Lijie Hu	King Abdullah University of Science and Technology, Saudi Arabia
Lijing Zhu	Bowling Green State University, USA
Lingling Zhang	Capital Normal University, China
Lingyue Fu	Shanghai Jiao Tong University, China
Linh Le Pham Van	Deakin University, Australia
Livio Bioglio	University of Turin, Italy
Lixing Yu	Yunnan University, China
Liyan Song	Harbin Institute of Technology, China
Longlong Sun	Chang'an University, China
Luca Corbucci	University of Pisa, Italy
Luca Ferragina	University of Calabria, Italy
Luca Romeo	University of Macerata, Italy
Lucas Pereira	LARSyS, Tecnico Lisboa, Portugal
Luciano Caroprese	ICAR-CNR, Italy
Ludovico Boratto	University of Cagliari, Italy
Luis Rei	Jožef Stefan Institute, Slovenia
Mahardhika Pratama	University of South Australia, Australia
Maiju Karjalainen	University of Eastern Finland, Finland
Makoto Onizuka	Osaka University, Japan
Manali Sharma	Samsung, South Korea
Maneet Singh	MasterCard, India
Manuel M. Garcia-Piqueras	Universidad de Castilla La Mancha, Spain
Manuele Bicego	University of Verona, Italy
Mao A. Cheng	University of California, Berkeley, USA
Marc Plantevit	EPITA, France
Marc Tommasi	Lille University, France
Marcel Wever	Leibniz University Hannover, Germany
Marcilio de Souto	LIFO/Université d'Orleans, France
Marco Lippi	University of Florence, Italy
Marco Loog	Radboud University, Netherlands
Marco Mellia	Politecnico di Torino, Italy
Marco Podda	University of Pisa, Italy
Marco Polignano	Università di Bari, Italy
Marco Viviani	Università degli Studi di Milano Bicocca, Italy
Maria Vasconcelos	Fraunhofer Portugal AICOS, Portugal
Maria Sofia Bucarelli	Sapienza University of Rome, Italy

Mariana Oliveira	Universidade do Porto, Portugal
Mariana Vargas Vieyra	MostlyAI, Austria
Marielle Malfante	CEA, France
Marina Litvak	Shamoon College of Engineering, Israel
Mario Antunes	Universidade de Aveiro, Portugal
Mario Andres Munoz	University of Melbourne, Australia
Marius Koppel	Johannes Gutenberg University Mainz, Germany
Mark Junjie Li	Shenzhen University, China
Marko Robnik-Sikonja	University of Ljubljana, Slovenia
Marta Soare	Université d'Orleans, France
Martin Holena	Czech Academy of Sciences, Czech Republic
Martin Pilat	Charles University, Czech Republic
Martino Ciaperoni	Aalto University, Finland
Marwan Hassani	TU Eindhoven, Netherlands
Masahiro Suzuki	University of Tokyo, Japan
Massimo Guarascio	ICAR-CNR, Italy
Matej Mihelcic	University of Zagreb, Croatia
Mathias Verbeke	KU Leuven, Belgium
Mathieu Lefort	Université de Lyon, France
Matteo Francobaldi	University of Bologna, Italy
Matteo Riondato	Amherst College, USA
Matteo Salis	University of Turin, Italy
Matthew B. Middlehurst	University of Southampton, UK
Matthia Sabatelli	University of Groningen, Netherlands
Mattia Cerrato	JGU Mainz, Germany
Mattia Setzu	University of Pisa, Italy
Mattis Hartwig	German Research Center for Artificial Intelligence, Germany
Matyas Bohacek	Stanford University, USA
Maximilian T. Fischer	University of Konstanz, Germany
Maximilian Münch	University of Applied Sciences, Würzburg-Schweinfurt, Germany
Maximilian Stubbemann	University of Hildesheim, Germany
Maximilian Thiessen	TU Wien, Austria
Maximilian von Zastrow	Southern Denmark University, Denmark
Megha Khosla	TU Delft, Netherlands
Meiyun Zuo	Renmin University of China, China
Meng Liu	National University of Defense Technology, China
Mengying Zhu	Zhejiang University, China
Michael Granitzer	University of Passau, Germany
Michael B. Ito	University of Michigan, USA

Michael G. Madden	National University of Ireland, Galway, Ireland
Michal Wozniak	Wroclaw University of Science and Technology, Poland
Michele Fontana	Università di Pisa, Italy
Michiel Stock	Ghent University, Belgium
Miguel Rocha	University of Minho, Portugal
Miguel Silva	INESC TEC, Portugal
Mike Holenderski	Eindhoven University of Technology, Netherlands
Milos Savic	University of Novi Sad, Serbia
Mina Rezaei	LMU Munich, Germany
Minh P. Nguyen	University of Texas, Austin, USA
Minyoung Choe	Korea Advanced Institute of Science and Technology, South Korea
Minyu Chen	Shanghai Jiaotong University, China
Miquel Perello-Nieto	University of Bristol, UK
Mira Kristin Jurgens	Ghent University, Belgium
Miriam Santos	University of Porto, Portugal
Mirko Bunse	TU Dortmund, Germany
Mirko Polato	University of Turin, Italy
Mitra Baratchi	LIACS, University of Leiden, Netherlands
Mohammed Elbamby	Telefonica Scientific Research, Spain
Moises Rocha dos Santos	University of Porto, Portugal
Monowar Bhuyan	Umeå University, Sweden
Morteza Rakhshaninejad	Ghent University, Belgium
Mounim A. El Yacoubi	Télécom SudParis, France
Muhammad Rajabinasab	University of Southern Denmark, Denmark
Muhao Guo	Arizona State University, USA
Mustapha Lebbah	Paris Saclay University-Versailles, France
Nabeel Hussain Syed	Rheinland-Pfälzische Technische Universität, Kaiserslautern-Landau, Germany
Nandyala Hemachandra	Indian Institute of Technology Bombay, India
Nannan Wu	Tianjin University, China
Nanqing Dong	Shanghai Artificial Intelligence Laboratory, China
Naresh Manwani	International Institute of Information Technology, Hyderabad, India
Natan Tourne	Ghent University, Belgium
Nate Veldt	Texas A&M, USA
Nathalie Japkowicz	American University, USA
Natthawut Kertkeidkachorn	Japan Advanced Institute of Science and Technology (JAIST), Japan
Ngoc-Son Vu	ENSEA, France
Nhat-Tan Bui	University of Arkansas, USA

Nian Li	Tsinghua University, China
Nick Lim	University of Waikato, New Zealand
Nico Piatkowski	Fraunhofer IAIS, Germany
Nicolas Roque dos Santos	University of São Paulo, Brazil
Niklas A. Strauss	LMU Munich, Germany
Nikolaj Tatti	Helsinki University, Finland
Nikolaos Nikolaou	University College London, UK
Nikolaos Stylianou	Information Technologies Institute, Greece
Nikos Kanakaris	University of Southern California, USA
Ning Xu	Southeast University, China
Nripsuta Saxena	University of Southern California, USA
Nuwan Gunasekara	Halmstad University, Sweden
Olga Kurasova	Vilnius University, Lithuania
Olga Slizovskaia	AstraZeneca, UK
Olivier Teste	IRIT, University of Toulouse, France
Oswald C.	NIT Trichy, India
Oswaldo Solarte-Pabon	Universidad del Valle, Colombia
Ozge Alacam	University of Bielefeld, Germany
P. S. Sastry	Indian Institute of Science, India
Pablo Olmos	Universidad Carlos III de Madrid, Spain
Panagiotis Karras	University of Copenhagen, Denmark
Panagiotis Symeonidis	University of the Aegean, Greece
Pance Panov	Jožef Stefan Institute, Slovenia
Paolo Bonetti	Politecnico di Milano, Italy
Paolo Merialdo	Università degli Studi Roma Tre, Italy
Paolo Mignone	University of Bari Aldo Moro, Italy
Pascal Welke	TU Wien, Austria
Patrick Y. Wu	American University, USA
Paul Caillon	LAMSADE Université Paris Dauphine - PSL, France
Paul Davidsson	Malmo University, Sweden
Paul Prasse	University of Potsdam, Germany
Paulo J. Azevedo	Universidade do Minho, Portugal
Pawel Teisseyre	Warsaw University of Technology, Poland
Pawel Zyblewski	Wroclaw University of Science and Technology, Poland
Pedro G. Ferreira	University of Porto, Portugal
Pedro Larrañaga	Technical University of Madrid, Spain
Pedro Ribeiro	University of Porto, Portugal
Pedro H. Abreu	CISUC, Portugal
Peijie Sun	Tsinghua University, China
Peng Wu	Shanghai Jiao Tong University, China

Pengpeng Qiao	Institute of Science Tokyo, Japan
Peter Karsmakers	KU Leuven, Belgium
Peter Schneider-Kamp	SDU, Denmark
Peter van der Putten	Leiden University, Netherlands
Petia Georgieva	University of Aveiro, Portugal
Philipp Vaeth	Technical University of Applied Sciences Würzburg-Schweinfurt and Universität Bielefeld, Germany
Philippe Preux	Inria, France
Phung Lai	SUNY-Albany, USA
Pierre Geurts	Montefiore Institute, University of Liège, Belgium
Pierre Monnin	Université Côte d'Azur, Inria, CNRS, I3S, France
Pierre Schaus	UC Louvain, Belgium
Pierre Wolinski	Paris Dauphine University - PSL, France
Pieter Robberechts	KU Leuven, Belgium
Pietro Sabatino	ICAR-CNR, Italy
Pingchuan Ma	HKUST, China
Piotr Habas	Amazon, USA
Piotr Lipinski	University of Wroclaw, Poland
Piotr Porwik	University of Silesia, Katowice, Poland
Prithwish Chakraborty	IBM Corporation, USA
Lucie Flek	Marburg University, Germany
Przemyslaw Biecek	Warsaw University of Technology, Poland
Qiang Sheng	Institute of Computing Technology, Chinese Academy of Sciences, China
Qiang Zhou	Nanjing University of Aeronautics and Astronautics, China
Rafet Sifa	Fraunhofer IAIS, Germany
Raha Moraffah	Arizona State University, USA
Raivydas Simanas	Vilnius University, Lithuania
Rajeev Rastogi	Amazon, USA
Ranya Almohsen	Baylor College of Medicine, USA
Raphael Romero	Ghent University, Belgium
Raquel Sebastiao	ESTGV-IPV & IEETA-UA, Portugal
Ravi Kolla	Sony Research India, India
Raza Ul Mustafa	Loyola University, USA
Remy Cazabet	Université de Lyon 1, France
Renhe Jiang	University of Tokyo, Japan
Reza Akbarinia	Inria, France
Ricardo P. M. Cruz	University of Porto (FEUP), Portugal
Ricardo B. Prudencio	Universidade Federal de Pernambuco, Brazil
Ricardo Rios	Federal University of Bahia, Brazil

Ricardo Santos	Fraunhofer Portugal AICOS, Portugal
Riccardo Guidotti	University of Pisa, Italy
Robertas Damasevicius	Vytautas Magnus University, Lithuania
Roberto Corizzo	American University, USA
Roberto Interdonato	CIRAD, France
Rocio Chongtay	University of Southern Denmark, Denmark
Rohit Babbar	University of Bath, UK and Aalto University, Finland
Romain Tavenard	Université de Rennes, LETG/IRISA, France
Rosana Veroneze	LBiC, Italy
Ruggero G. Pensa	University of Turin, Italy
Rui Meng	BNU-HKBU United International College, USA
Rui Yu	University of Louisville, USA
Ruixuan Liu	Emory University, USA
Runqun Xiong	Southeast University, China
Runxue Bao	University of Pittsburgh, USA
Ruochun Jin	National University of Defense Technology, China
Ruta Juozaitiene	Vytautas Magnus University, Lithuania
Rytis Maskeliunas	Polsl, Poland
Salvatore Ruggieri	University of Pisa, Italy
Sam Verboven	Vrije Universiteit Brussel, Belgium
Sangkyun Lee	Korea University, South Korea
Sara Abdali	University of California, Riverside, USA
Sarah Masud	LCS2, IIIT-D, India
Sarwan Ali	Georgia State University, USA
Satoru Koda	Fujitsu Limited, Japan
Sebastian Buschjager	Lamarr Institute for ML and AI, Germany
Sebastian Jimenez	Ghent University, Belgium
Sebastian Meznar	Jožef Stefan Institute, Ljubljana, Slovenia
Sebastian Ventura Soto	University of Cordoba, Spain
Sebastien Razakarivony	Safran, France
Selpi Selpi	Chalmers University of Technology, Sweden
Sergio Greco	University of Calabria, Italy
Sergio Jesus	Feedzai, Portugal
Sha Lu	University of South Australia, Australia
Shalini Priya	Indian Institute of Technology Patna, India
Shanqing Guo	Shandong University, China
Shaofu Yang	Southeast University, China
Shazia Tabassum	INESCTEC, Portugal
Shengxiang Gao	Kunming University of Science and Technology, China

Shichao Pei	University of Massachusetts, Boston, USA
Shin Matsushima	University of Tokyo, Japan
Shin-ichi Maeda	Preferred Networks, Japan
Shiwen Ni	Chinese Academy of Sciences, China
Shiyou Qian	Shanghai Jiao Tong University, China
Shu Zhao	Anhui University, China
Shuai Li	University of Cambridge, UK and University of Tokyo, Japan, Tsinghua University, China
Shuang Cheng	Institute of Computing Technology, Chinese Academy of Sciences, China
Shubhranshu Shekhar	Brandeis University, USA
Shurui Cao	Carnegie Mellon University, USA
Shuteng Niu	Mayo Clinic, USA
Siamak Ghodsi	Leibniz University of Hannover, Germany
Sihai Zhang	University of Science and Technology of China, China
Silvia Chiusano	Politecnico di Torino, Italy
Silviu Maniu	Université de Grenoble Alpes, France
Simon Gottschalk	L3S Research Center, Leibniz Universität Hannover, Germany
Simona Nistico	University of Calabria, Italy
Simone Angarano	Politecnico di Torino, Italy
Sinong Zhao	Nankai University, China
Siwei Wang	Intelligent Game and Decision Lab, China
Sofoklis Kitharidis	LIACS, Netherlands
Songlin Du	University of Melbourne, Australia
Songlin Du	Southeast University, China
Soumyajit Chatterjee	Nokia Bell Labs, USA
Sourav Dutta	Huawei Research Centre, China
Stefan Duffner	University of Lyon, France
Stefan Heindorf	Paderborn University, Germany
Stefan Kesselheim	Forschungszentrum Jülich, Germany
Stefano Bortoli	Huawei Research Center, China
Stefanos Vrochidis	Information Technologies Institute, CERTH, Greece
Steffen Thoma	FZI Research Center for Information Technology, Germany
Stephan Doerfel	Kiel University of Applied Sciences, Germany
Steven D. Prestwich	University College Cork, Ireland
Suman Banerjee	IIT Jammu, India
Sunil Aryal	Deakin University, Australia
Surabhi Adhikari	Columbia University, USA

Susan McKeever	TU Dublin, Ireland
Swati Swati	Universität der Bundeswehr München, Germany
Szymon Wojciechowski	Wroclaw University of Science and Technology, Poland
Talip Ucar	AstraZeneca, UK
Taro Tezuka	University of Tsukuba, Japan
Tatiana Passali	Aristotle University of Thessaloniki, Greece
Tatiane Nogueira Rios	UFBA, Brazil
Telmo M. Silva Filho	University of Bristol, UK
Teng Lin	Hong Kong University of Technology (Guangzhou), China
Teng Zhang	Huazhong University of Science and Technology, China
Thach Le Nguyen	Insight Centre, Ireland
Thang Duy Dang	Fujitsu Limited, Japan
Thanh-Son Nguyen	A*STAR, Singapore
Theresa Eimer	Leibniz University Hannover, Germany
Thiago Andrade	INESC TEC & University of Porto, Portugal
Thomas Bonald	Telecom Paris, France
Thomas Guyet	Inria, Centre de Lyon, France
Thomas Lampert	University of Strasbourg, France
Thomas L. Lee	University of Edinburgh, UK
Thomas Mortier	Ghent University, Belgium
Tianyi Chen	Boston University, USA
Tie Luo	University of Kentucky, USA
Tiehang Duan	Mayo Clinic, USA
Tijl De Bie	Ghent University, Belgium
Timilehin B. Aderinola	University College Dublin, Ireland
Timo Bertram	Johannes-Kepler Universität, Germany
Timo Ropinski	Ulm University, Germany
Tobias A. Hille	University of Kassel, Germany
Tom Hanika	University of Hildesheim, Germany
Tomas Kliegr	University of Economics, Prague, Czech Republic
Tomasz Michalak	University of Warsaw and Ideas NCBiR, Poland
Tomasz Walkowiak	Wroclaw University of Science and Technology, Poland
Tommaso Zoppi	University of Florence, Italy
Tong Li	Hong Kong University of Technology, China
Tong Mo	Peking University, China
Tongya Zheng	Hangzhou City University, China
Tonio Weidler	Maastricht University, Netherlands
Tony Lindgren	Stockholm University, Sweden

Tsunenori Mine	Kyushu University, Japan
Tuan Le	New Mexico State University, USA
Tuwe Lofstrom	Jönköping University, Sweden
Ulf Johansson	Jönköping University, Sweden
Vadim Ermolayev	Ukrainian Catholic University, Ukraine
Vahan Martirosyan	CentraleSupélec, Belgium
Vana Kalogeraki	Athens University of Economics and Business, Greece
Vanessa Gomez-Verdejo	Universidad Carlos III de Madrid, Spain
Vasileios Iosifidis	SCHUFA Holding, Germany
Vasilis Gkolemis	ATHENA RC, Greece
Victor Charpenay	Mines Saint-Etienne, France
Vincent Derkinderen	KU Leuven, Belgium
Vincent Lemaire	Orange Research, France
Vincenzo Pasquadibisceglie	University of Bari, Aldo Moro, Italy
Virginijus Marcinkevicius	Vilnius University, Lithuania
Vitor Cerqueira	University of Porto, Portugal
Vivek Kumar	Universität der Bundeswehr München, Germany
Vivek Srikumar	University of Utah, USA
Wagner Meira Jr.	UFMG, Brazil
Wei Wu	Ben Gurion University of the Negev, Israel
Weichen Li	RPTU Kaiserslautern-Landau, Germany
Weifeng Xu	Independent Researcher, China
Weike Pan	Shenzhen University, China
Weiwei Jiang	Beijing University of Posts and Telecommunications, China
Weiwei Sun	Carnegie Mellon University, USA
Weiwei Yuan	Nanjing University of Aeronautics and Astronautics, China
Weixiong Rao	Tongji University, China
Wen-Bo Xie	Southwest Petroleum University, China
Wenhao Li	Tongji University, China
Wenhao Zheng	Shopee, Singapore
Wenjie Feng	National University of Singapore, Singapore
Wenjie Xi	George Mason University, USA
Wenshui Luo	Nanjing University of Science and Technology, China
Wentao Yu	Nanjing University of Science and Technology, China
Wenzhe Yi	Wuhan University, China
Wenzhong Li	Nanjing University, China
Wojciech Rejchel	Nicolaus Copernicus University, Torun, Poland

Xi Jiang	Southern University of Science and Technology, China
Xiang Li	East China Normal University, China
Xiang Lian	Kent State University, USA
Xiao Ma	Beijing University of Posts and Telecommunications, China
Xiao Zhang	Shandong University, China
Xiaobing Zhou	Yunnan University, China
Xiaofeng Cao	University of Technology Sydney, Australia
Xiaofeng Gao	Shanghai Jiaotong University, China
Xiaojun Chen	Institute of Information Engineering, Chinese Academy of Sciences, China
Xiao-Jun Zeng	University of Manchester, UK
Xiaoming Zhang	Beihang University, China
Xiaoting Zhao	Etsy, USA
Xiaowei Mao	Beijing Jiaotong University, China
Xiaoyu Shi	Chinese Academy of Sciences, China
Xin Du	University of Edinburgh, UK
Xin Qin	California State University, Long Beach, USA
Xing Tang	Tencent, China
Xing Xing	Tongji University, China
Xinning Zhu	Beijing University of Posts and Telecommunications, China
Xinpeng Lv	National University of Defense Technology, China
Xintao Wu	University of Arkansas, USA
Xinyang Zhang	University of Illinois at Urbana-Champaign, USA
Xinyu Guan	Xi'an Jiaotong University, China
Xixun Lin	Chinese Academy of Sciences, China
Xiyue Zhang	University of Bristol, UK
Xuan-Hong Dang	IBM T.J. Watson Research Center, USA
Xue Li	University of Queensland, Australia
Xue Yan	Institute of Automation, Chinese Academy of Sciences, China
Xuefeng Chen	Chongqing University, China
Xuemin Wang	Guilin University of Electronic Technology, China
Yachuan Zhang	East China University of Science and Technology, China
Yan Zhang	Peking University, China
Yang Li	University of North Carolina at Chapel Hill, USA
Yang Shu	East China Normal University, China
Yang Wei	Nanjing University of Science and Technology, China

Yanhao Wang	East China Normal University, China
Yanmin Zhu	Shanghai Jiao Tong University, China
Yansong Y. L. Li	University of Ottawa, Canada
Yao-Xiang Ding	Nanjing University, China
Yaqi Xie	Carnegie Mellon University, USA
Yasutoshi Ida	NTT, Japan
Yaying Zhang	Tongji University, China
Ye Zhu	Deakin University, Australia
Yeon-Chang Lee	Ulsan National Institute of Science and Technology, South Korea
Yexiang Xue	Purdue University, USA
Yi Wang	Xinjiang Technical Institute of Physics and Chemistry, Chinese Academy of Sciences, China
Yifeng Gao	University of Texas, Rio Grande Valley, USA
Yilun Jin	Hong Kong University of Science and Technology, China
Yin Zhang	University of Electronic Science and Technology of China, China
Ying Chen	RMIT University, Australia
Yinsheng Li	Fudan University, China
Yong Li	Huawei European Research Center, China
Yongyu Wang	JD Logistics, China
Youhei Akimoto	University of Tsukuba/RIKEN AIP, Japan
You-Wei Luo	Sun Yat-sen University and Jiaying University, China
Yuchen Li	Baidu, China
Yuchen Yang	Harbin Institute of Technology, China
Yudi Zhang	Eindhoven University of Technology, Netherlands
Yuhao Li	University of Melbourne, Australia
Yuheng Jia	Southeast University, China
Yujia Zheng	CMU, USA
Yulong Pei	TU Eindhoven, Netherlands
Yuncheng Jiang	South China Normal University, China
Yuntao Shou	Xi'an Jiaotong University, China
Yunyun Wang	Nanjing University of Posts and Telecommunications, China
Yutong Ye	East China Normal University, China
Yuzhou Chen	University of California, Riverside, USA
Zahraa Abdallah	University of Bristol, UK
Zaineb Chelly Dagdia	UVSQ, Paris-Saclay, France
Zehua Cheng	University of Oxford, UK
Zeyu Chen	University of Auckland, New Zealand

Zhaocheng Ge	Huazhong University of Science and Technology, China
Zhe Yang	Soochow University, China
Zhen Liu	Guangdong University of Foreign Studies, China
Zheng Chen	Osaka University, Japan
Zhenghao Liu	Northeastern University, China
Zhenyu Yang	Macquarie University, Australia
Zhi Li	Tsinghua University, China
Zhichao Han	ETHZ, Switzerland
Zhihui Wang	Fudan University, China
Zhilong Shan	South China Normal University, China
Zhipeng Yin	Florida International University, USA
Zhipeng Zou	Nanjing University of Science and Technology, China
Zhiwen Xiao	Southwest Jiaotong University, China
Zhiwen Zhang	LocationMind, Japan
Zhixin Li	Guangxi Normal University, China
Zhiyong Cheng	Shandong Academy of Sciences, China
Zhong Chen	Southern Illinois University, USA
Zhong Li	Leiden University, Netherlands
Zhong Zhang	Tsinghua University, China
Zhongjing Yu	Peking University, China
Zhuang Liu	Dongbei University of Finance and Economics, China
Zhuo Cao	Forschungszentrum Jülich, Germany
Zhuoming Xie	Guangdong University of Technology, China
Zhuoqun Li	Louisiana State University, USA
Zicheng Zhao	Nanjing University of Science and Technology, China
Zichong Wang	Florida International University, USA
Zifeng Ding	University of Cambridge, UK
Ziheng Chen	Walmart, USA
Zijie J. Wang	Georgia Tech, USA
Zirui Zhuang	Beijing University of Posts and Telecommunications, China
Zixing Song	Chinese University of Hong Kong, China
Ziyu Wang	University of Tokyo, Japan
Ziyue Li	University of Cologne, Germany
Zongxia Xie	Tianjin University, China
Zongyue Li	LMU Munich, Germany
Zuojin Tang	Zhejiang University, China

List of Editors

Bernhard Pfahringer	University of Waikato, New Zealand
Nathalie Japkowicz	American University, USA
Pedro Larrañaga	Technical University of Madrid, Spain
Rita P. Ribeiro	University of Porto, Portugal
Alípio M. Jorge	University of Porto, Portugal
Carlos Soares	University of Porto, Portugal
João Gama	University of Porto, Portugal
Pedro H. Abreu	University of Coimbra, Portugal

Program Committee – Applied Data Science Track

Nasrullah Sheikh	IBM Research, USA
Aakarsh Malhotra	MasterCard, USA
Aakash Goel	Amazon, USA
Abdoulaye Sakho	Artefact, France
Abhijeet Pendyala	Ruhr-Universität Bochum, Germany
Abu Shad Ahammed	University of Siegen, Germany
Adi Lin	Didi, China
Aditya Gautam	Meta, USA
Ahmed K. Mohamed	Meta, USA
Akihiro Yoshida	Kyushu University, Japan
Akshay Sethi	MasterCard, USA
Alejandro Kuratomi	Stockholm University, Sweden
Alessandro Gambetti	Nova School of Business and Economics, Portugal
Alessandro Leite	INSA Rouen, Inria, France
Alessio Russo	Politecnico di Milano, Italy
Alex Beeson	University of Warwick, UK
Alexander Galozy	Halmstad University, Sweden
Alexander Karlsson	University of Skovde, Sweden
Alexander Kovalenko	Czech Technical University in Prague, Czech Republic
Alexey Zaytsev	Skoltech, Russia
Alina Bazarova	Forschungszentrum Jülich, Germany
Alix Lheritier	Amadeus SAS, France
Allan Tucker	Brunel University London, UK
Alvaro Figueira	CRACS and Universidade do Porto, Portugal
Aman Gulati	Amazon, USA
Amira Soliman	Halmstad University, Sweden

Ana Gjorgjevikj	Jožef Stefan Institute, Slovenia
Anders Holst	RISE SICS, Sweden
André C. P. L. F. de Carvalho	University of São Paulo, Brazil
Andrea Seveso	University of Milan-Bicocca, Italy
Andreas Bender	LMU Munich, Germany
Andreas Henelius	Independent Researcher, Finland
Andreas Holzinger	University of Natural Resources and Life Sciences, Vienna, Austria
Andrei Shelopugin	Independent Researcher, Brazil
Angelo Impedovo	Niuma, Italy
Aniket Chakrabarti	Amazon, USA
Animesh Prasad	Roku, USA
Anisio Lacerda	UFMG, Brazil
Anli Ji	Georgia State University, USA
Antoine Doucet	La Rochelle Université, France
Anton Borg	Blekinge Institute of Technology, Sweden
Antonio Bevilacqua	Meetecho, Italy
Antonis Klironomos	University of Mannheim, Germany
Aron Henriksson	Stockholm University, Sweden
Artur Chudzik	Polish-Japanese Academy of Information Technology, Poland
Arun Venkitaraman	EPFL, Switzerland
Arunabha Choudhury	ASML, Netherlands
Asem Omari	Higher Colleges of Technology, UAE
Ashman Mehra	Birla Institute of Technology and Science, India
Ashwani Rao	Amazon, USA
Asier Rodriguez	BBVA, Spain
Asma Atamna	Ruhr-Universität Bochum, Germany
Atiye Sadat Hashemi	Halmstad University, Sweden
Atul Anand Gopalakrishnan	SUNY Buffalo, USA
Avani Wildani	Emory University, USA
Aviv Rovshitz	Ben-Gurion University of the Negev, Israel
Axel Brando	Barcelona Supercomputing Center (BSC) and Universitat de Barcelona (UB), Spain
Azadeh Alavi	RMIT University, Australia
Beihong Jin	Institute of Software, China
Benoit Frenay	University of Namur, Belgium
Berkay Aydin	Georgia State University, USA
Bijaya Adhikari	University of Iowa, USA
Bin Li	Alibaba Group, China
Bo Pang	University of Auckland, New Zealand
Bogdan Ruszczak	Opole University of Technology, Poland

Bohao Qu	Agency for Science, China
Bruno Veloso	INESC TEC, FEP-UP, Portugal
Buyue Qian	Xi'an Jiaotong University, China
Camille Kurtz	Université Paris Cité, France
Cangbai Li	Guangdong University of Technology, China
Carlo Metta	ISTI CNR, Italy
Carlos N. Silla	Pontifical Catholic University of Paraná (PUCPR), Brazil
Cecile Bothorel	IMT Atlantique, France
Cesar Ferri	Universitat Politècnica Valencia, Spain
Chang Li	Apple, USA
Chang-Dong Wang	Sun Yat-sen University, China
Chaofan Li	Karlsruhe Institute of Technology, Germany
Chaoyuan Zuo	Nankai University, China
Chen Gao	Tsinghua University, China
Chen Li	Computer Network Information Center, China
Chen Zhao	Baylor University, USA
Chen-Wei Chang	Virginia Tech, USA
Chenxi Xue	Nanjing Normal University, China
Chongke Bi	Tianjin University, China
Christian M. Adriano	Hasso-Plattner Institute, Germany
Christophe Rodrigues	DVRC Pôle universitaire Léonard de Vinci, France
Chuan Li	Sorbonne University, LIPADE, France
Chunhui Zhang	Dartmouth College, USA
Cristina Soguero Ruiz	Rey Juan Carlos University, Spain
Daheng Wang	Amazon, USA
Daifeng Li	Sun Yat-sen University, China
Damien Fay	HPE Labs, Ireland
Dania Herzalla	Technology Innovation Institute, UAE
Daniel Lemire	University of Quebec (TELUQ), Canada
Daniel Trejo Banos	SDSC, USA
Daochen Zha	Rice University, USA
Dawei Cheng	Tongji University, China
Dayne Freitag	SRI International, USA
Di Yao	Institute of Computing Technology, China
Dimitris Nick Dimitriadis	Aristotle University of Thessaloniki, Greece
Diogo F. Soares	Universidade de Lisboa, Portugal
Dirk Pflueger	University of Stuttgart, Germany
Doheon Han	University of Notre Dame, USA
Dongxiang Zhang	Zhejiang University, China
Dongxiao Yu	Shandong University, China

Dugang Liu	Guangdong Laboratory of Artificial Intelligence and Digital Economy (Shenzen), China
Ece Calikus	Uppsala University, Sweden
Edwyn Brient	Thales LAS/Mines Paris PSL, France
Efstathios Stamatatos	University of the Aegean, Greece
Elaine Faria	UFU, Brazil
Elio Masciari	University of Naples, Italy
Emilie Devijver	Université Grenoble Alpes, Inria, CNRS, Grenoble INP, LIG, France
Emmanuelle Claeys	IRIT, France
Enayat Rajabi	Halmstad University, Sweden
Enda Barrett	University of Galway, Ireland
Enyan Dai	Hong Kong University of Science and Technology (Guangzhou), China
Eric Peukert	ScaDS.AI, Germany
Eric Sanjuan	Avignon University, France
Erik Frisk	Linköping University, Sweden
Eui-Hong (Sam) Han	The Washington Post, USA
Eunil Park	Sungkyunkwan University, South Korea
Fabio Carrara	CNR-ISTI, Italy
Fabiola Pereira	Federal University of Uberlandia, Brazil
Fan Yang	Rice University, USA
Fangzhao Wu	MSRA, China
Fangzhou Shi	Didi Chuxing, China
Fathima Nuzla Ismail	State University of New York, USA
Flavio Bertini	University of Parma, Italy
Francesco Dente	EURECOM, France
Francesco Guerra	University of Modena e Reggio Emilia, Italy
Francesco Scala	CNR-ICAR, Italy
Francesco Spinnato	University of Pisa, Italy
Francesco Paolo Nerini	Sapienza University of Rome, Italy
Francisco P. Romero	UCLM, Spain
Franco Maria Nardini	ISTI-CNR, Italy
Francois Schwarzentruber	ENS Lyon, France
Fudong Lin	University of Delaware, USA
Gabriel Augusto Pinheiro	UNIFESP, Brazil
Gan Sun	South China University of Technology, China
Gargi Srivastava	Rajiv Gandhi Institute of Petroleum Technology Jais, India
Giacomo Boracchi	Politecnico di Milano, Italy
Giuseppe Garofalo	DistriNet, KU Leuven, Belgium
Giuseppina Andresini	University of Bari Aldo Moro, Italy

Goran Falkman	University of Skovde, Sweden
Grzegorz Nalepa	Jagiellonian University, Poland
Guanggang Geng	Jinan University, China
Guojun Liang	Halmstad University, Sweden
Haifang Li	Baidu, China
Haina Tang	University of Chinese Academy of Sciences, China
Hancheng Ge	Amazon, USA
Hao Li	National University of Defense Technology, China
Haohui Chen	CSIRO, Australia
Haomin Yu	Aalborg University, Denmark
Haoyi Xiong	Baidu, China
Hiba Najjar	DFKI, Germany
Hillol Kargupta	Agnik, USA
Hong Zhou	Meta, USA
Hongbin Pei	Xi'an Jiao Tong University, China
Hou-Wan Long	Chinese University of Hong Kong, China
Hua Wei	Arizona State University, USA
Huaiyuan Yao	Xi'an Jiaotong University, China
Huan Song	Amazon, USA
Hubert Baniecki	University of Warsaw, Poland
Hyunsung Kim	KAIST, Fitogether, South Korea
Ibtihal El Mimouni	Inria, France
Ildar Baimuratov	L3S Research Center, Germany
Ilir Jusufi	Blekinge Institute of Technology, Sweden
Inaam Ashraf	Bielefeld University, Germany
Ines Sousa	Fraunhofer AICOS, Portugal
Iris Heerlien	Saxion, Netherlands
Isak Samsten	Stockholm University, Sweden
Ishan Verma	TCS Research, India
Ismail Hakki Toroslu	METU, Turkey
Ivan Carrera	EPN, Ecuador
Jaakko Hollmen	Stockholm University, Sweden
Jairo Cugliari	Laboratoire ERIC, France
Jakub Nalepa	Silesian University of Technology, Poland
Jelica Vasiljeivić	Hoffmann-La Roche, Switzerland
Jens Lundstrom	Halmstad University, Sweden
Jesse Davis	KU Leuven, Belgium
Jiahui Bai	Meta, USA
Jiajun Gu	Carnegie Mellon University, USA
Jiali Pan	Department of Information Management, USA

Jian Yu	Auckland University of Technology, New Zealand
Jiangbin Zheng	Westlake University, China
Jianhua Yin	Shandong University, China
Jingbo Zhou	Baidu, China
Jingjing Liu	MD Anderson Cancer Center, USA
Jingwen Shi	Michigan State University, USA
Jingxuan Wei	University of Chinese Academy of Sciences, China
Jinyoung Han	Sungkyunkwan University, South Korea
Jiue-An Yang	City of Hope Beckman Research Institute, USA
Joao R. Campos	University of Coimbra, Portugal
Jochen De Weerdt	KU Leuven, Belgium
Joe Tekli	Lebanese American University, Lebanon
Joel Ky	University of Lorraine, CNRS, Inria, France
John McCall	Robert Gordon University, UK
John Mitros	University College Dublin, Ireland
Jonas Fischer	Ruhr-Universität Bochum, Germany
Jonas Nordqvist	Linnaeus University, Sweden
Joydeep Chandra	Indian Institute of Technology Patna, India
Julian Martin Rodemann	LMU Munich, Germany
Jun Shen	University of Wollongong, Australia
Junichi Tatemura	Google, USA
Junxuan Li	Microsoft, USA
Jyun-Yu Jiang	Amazon Science, USA
Kai Wang	Shanghai Jiao Tong University, China
Kaiping Zheng	National University of Singapore, Singapore
Kaiwen Dong	University of Notre Dame, USA
Katarzyna Bozek	University of Cologne, Germany
Katerina Schindlerova	UniVie, Austria
Katharina Dost	Jožef Stefan Institute, Slovenia
Katsiaryna Mirylenka	Zalando SE, Germany
Keith Burghardt	ISI, Germany
Klaus Brinker	Hamm-Lippstadt University of Applied Sciences, Germany
Koki Kawabata	Osaka University, Japan
Korbinian Randl	Stockholm University, Sweden
Krzysztof Krawiec	Poznań University of Technology, Poland
Krzysztof Kutt	Jagiellonian University, Poland
Kwan Hui Lim	Singapore University of Technology and Design, Singapore
Lamija Lemes	University of Zenica, Bosnia & Herzegovina
Le Nguyen	University of Oulu, Finland

Lei Li	Hong Kong University of Science and Technology (Guangzhou), China
Lei Liu	York University, Canada
Li Liu	Chongqing University, China
Li Zhang	University College London, UK
Liang Tang	Google, USA
Liang Tong	NEC Labs America, USA
Liang Wang	Alibaba Group, China
Lina Yao	University of New South Wales, Australia
Lingxiao Li	Michigan State University, USA
Lingyang Chu	McMaster University, Canada
Lixin Zou	Wuhan University, China
Lluis Garcia-Pueyo	Meta, USA
Lou Salaun	Nokia Bell Labs, USA
Luca Corbucci	University of Pisa, Italy
Luca Pappalardo	ISTI, Italy
Luca Romeo	University of Macerata, Italy
Luis Ferreira	Olympus Medical Products Portugal, Portugal
Luis Miguel Matos	ALGORITMI Centre, Portugal
Lukas Grasmann	TU Wien, Austria
Lukas Pensel	Johannes Gutenberg University Mainz, Germany
Maciej Grzenda	Warsaw University of Technology, Poland
Maciej Piernik	Poznań University of Technology, Poland
Madiraju Srilakshmi	Dream Sports, India
Mads C. Hansen	A.P. Moller-Maersk, Denmark
Mahardhika Pratama	University of South Australia, Australia
Mahmoud Rahat	Halmstad University, Sweden
Man Tianxing	Jilin University, China
Manish Gupta	Microsoft, USA
Manos Papagelis	York University, Canada
Manuel Lopes	Instituto Tecnico Superior, Portugal
Manuel Portela	Universitat Pompeu Fabra, Spain
Marc Tommasi	Lille University, France
Marco Fisichella	Leibniz Universität, Hannover, Germany
Maria Riveiro	Jonkoping University, Sweden
Maria Ulan	RISE Research Institutes of Sweden, Sweden
Marian Scuturici	LIRIS, France
Marianne Clausel	IECL, France
Mario Doller	University of Applied Sciences, Kufstein, Austria
Marius Schwammle	DLR/BT, Germany
Markus Gotz	Karlsruhe Institute of Technology (KIT), Germany

Markus Leyser	Technische Universität Dresden, Germany
Martin Boldt	Blekinge Institute of Technology, Sweden
Martin Mladenov	Google, USA
Martin Vita	Institute of Physics, Czech Academy of Sciences, Czech Republic
Matthias Demant	Fraunhofer ISE, Germany
Matthias Galipaud	SDSC, Switzerland
Matthias Petri	Amazon, USA
Matthieu Latapy	CNRS, France
Maurice Van Keulen	University of Twente, Netherlands
Maxime Cordy	University of Luxembourg, Luxembourg
Maxwell J. Jacobson	Purdue University, USA
Md Nahid Hasan	Miami University, USA
Md Zia Ullah	Edinburgh Napier University, UK
Mehtab Alam Syed	CIRAD, France
Melanie Neubauer	University of Leoben, Austria
Meng Chen	Shandong University, China
Mengxuan Zhang	Australian National University, Australia
Miao Fan	NavInfo, China
Michael Bain	University of New South Wales, Australia
Michele Bernardini	Uni eCampus.It, Italy
Michiel Dhont	EluciDATA Lab of Sirris, Belgium
Mickael Coustaty	L3i Laboratory, France
Miguel Couceiro	LORIA, France
Mihaela Mitici	Utrecht University, Netherlands
Min Lee	Singapore Management University, Singapore
Min Hun Lee	Singapore Management University, Singapore
Mina Rezaei	LMU Munich, Germany
Ming Ma	Inner Mongolia University, China
Minghao Chen	Tencent, China
Mirco Nanni	CNR-ISTI Pisa, Italy
Mirjam Wattenhofer	Google, USA
Mirko Marras	University of Cagliari, Italy
Mitra Heidari	University of Melbourne, Australia
Modesto Castrillon-Santana	Universidad de Las Palmas de Gran Canaria, Spain
Mohammadmehdi Saberioon	German Research Centre for Geosciences, Germany
Mohammed Amer	Fujitsu Research of Europe, Germany
Mohammed Ghaith Altarabichi	Halmstad University, Sweden
Mojgan Kouhounestani	University of Melbourne, Australia
Moonki Hong	Sogang University, South Korea

Munira Syed	Procter & Gamble, USA
Nan Li	Microsoft, USA
Narendhar Gugulothu	TCS Research, India
Nedra Mellouli	LIASD, Portugal
Ngoc Son Le	University of Hildesheim, Germany
Niklas Lavesson	Blekinge Institute of Technology, Sweden
Niraj Kumar	Fujitsu, Japan
Nitish Kumar	MasterCard, USA
Nuno Cruz Garcia	FCUL, Portugal
Nuno R. P. S. Guimaraes	INESC TEC, University of Porto, Portugal
Nuwan Gunasekara	Halmstad University, Sweden
Pablo Picazo-Sanchez	Halmstad University, Sweden
Pablo Torrijos Arenas	Universidad de Castilla-La Mancha, Spain
Pablo Jose Del Moral Pastor	Ekkono.ai, Finland
Pan He	Auburn University, USA
Panagiotis Kanellopoulos	University of Essex, UK
Panagiotis Papadakos	FORTH-ICS, Greece
Pandey Shourya Prasad	International Institute of Information Technology, Bangalore, India
Panpan Xu	Amazon AWS, USA
Paola Velardi	Sapienza University of Rome, Italy
Paolo Cintia	Kode, Italy
Pascal Plettenberg	Intelligent Embedded Systems, Italy
Paul Boniol	Inria, France
Pavel Blinov	Sber AI Lab, Russia
Pawel Parczyk	Wroclaw University of Science and Technology, Poland
Pedro M. Ferreira	University of Lisbon, Portugal
Pedro Seber	MIT, USA
Peng Qiao	NUDT, China
Pengyuan Wang	University of Georgia, USA
Petr Olegovich Sokerin	Skoltech, Russia
Philipp Bach	University of Hamburg, Germany
Philipp Froehlich	TU Darmstadt, Germany
Philipp Schmidt	Amazon Research, USA
Philipp Zech	University of Innsbruck, Austria
Pinar Karagoz	Middle East Technical University (METU), Turkey
Ping Luo	Chinese Academy of Sciences, China
Po Yang	University of Sheffield, UK
Pop Petrica	Technical University of Cluj-Napoca, Romania
Prathap Manohar Joshi R	Zoho Corporation, India

Praveen Borra	Florida Atlantic University, USA
Praveen Paruchuri	IIIT Hyderabad, India
Qian Li	Curtin University, Australia
Qihang Yao	Georgia Institute of Technology, USA
Qiwei Han	Nova School of Business and Economics, Portugal
Quentin Duchemin	Université Gustave Eiffel, France
Radu Tudor Ionescu	University of Bucharest, Romania
Rafal Kucharski	Jagiellonian University, Poland
Rafet Sifa	Fraunhofer IAIS & University of Bonn, Germany
Ramasamy Savitha	I2R A*STAR, Singapore
Ran Yu	DSIS Research Group, Singapore
Ranga Raju Vatsavai	North Carolina State University, USA
Raphael Couturier	University of Bourgogne Franche-Comte (UBFC), France
Renato M. Assuncao	ESRI, USA
Renaud Lambiotte	University of Oxford, UK
Reuben Kshitiz Borrison	ABB, Switzerland
Reza Shirvany	Zalando SE, Germany
Ricardo R. Pereira	Feedzai, Portugal
Riccardo Rosati	Università Politecnica delle Marche, Ancona, Italy
Richard Allmendinger	University of Manchester, UK
Richard Nordsieck	XITASO GmbH IT and Software Solutions, Germany
Richi Nayak	Queensland University of Technology, Australia
Roberto Trasarti	CNR, Italy
Rogerio Luis de C. Costa	Polytechnic of Leiria, Portugal
Romain Ilbert	Huawei Paris Research Center, France
Roy Ka-Wei Lee	Singapore University of Technology and Design, Singapore
Ruilin Wang	University of Aberdeen, UK
Sabrina Gaito	Università degli Studi di Milano, Italy
Sai Karthikeya Vemuri	Computer Vision Group Jena, Italy
Saisubramaniam Gopalakrishnan	Quantiphi, USA
Sajjad Shumaly	Max-Planck-Institut for Polymer Research, Germany
Salvatore Rinzivillo	KDD Lab, ISTI, CNR, Italy
Samaneh Shafee	LASIGE, Portugal
Sandra Wissing	Fachhochschule Münster, Germany
Sarwan Ali	Georgia State University, USA
Sebastian Becker	Fraunhofer ISST, Germany

Sebastian Honel	Linnaeus University, Sweden
Selin Colakhasanoglu	Saxion University of Applied Sciences, Netherlands
Senzhang Wang	Central South University, China
Sepideh Nahali	York University, Canada
Shahrooz Abghari	Blekinge Institute of Technology, Sweden
Shahroz Tariq	CSIRO, Australia
Shang Yanlei	BUPT, China
Shen Liang	Paris Cité University, France
Shengheng Liu	Southeast University, China
Shereen Elsayed	University of Hildesheim, Germany
Shi-ting Wen	NingboTech University, China
Shiv Krishna Jaiswal	Walmart Global Tech, USA
Shoujin Wang	Macquarie University, Australia
Shuai Li	University of Cambridge, UK and University of Tokyo, UK
Shuchu Han	Capital One Financial Group, Japan
Simon F. Weinberger	EssilorLuxottica, France
Siyuan Chen	Guangzhou University, China
Snehanshu Saha	BITS Pilani Goa Campus, India
Souhaib Ben Taieb	University of Mons, Abu Dhabi
Sriparna Saha	IIT Patna, India
Stefan Rueping	Fraunhofer IAIS, Germany
Stephane Chretien	Université Lyon 2, France
Sunil Aryal	Deakin University, Australia
Susana Ladra	University of A Coruña, Spain
Szymon Bobek	Jagiellonian University, Poland
Szymon Jaroszewicz	Institute of Computer Science, Poland
Szymon Wilk	Poznań University of Technology, Poland
Tanel Tammet	Tallinn University of Technology, Estonia
Thanh Thi Nguyen	Monash University, Australia
Thiago Zangato	Université Sorbonne Paris Nord, France
Theodora Tsikrika	Information Technologies Institute, Greece
Thibault Girardin	Université Jean Monnet, France
Thomas Czernichow	Darwinlabs, Portugal
Thorsteinn Rognvaldsson	Halmstad University, Sweden
Tiago Mendes-Neves	FEUP/INESC TEC, Portugal
Tianshu Yu	Chinese University of Hong Kong (Shenzhen), China
Ting Su	Imperial College London, UK
Tingrui Qiao	University of Auckland, New Zealand
Tobias Glasmachers	Ruhr-Universität Bochum, Germany

Tomas Olsson	RISE SICS, Sweden
Tome Eftimov	Jožef Stefan Institute, Slovenia
Topon Paul	Toshiba Corporation, Japan
Tsuyoshi Okita	Kyushu Institute of Technology, Japan
Unmesh Padalkar	Dream Sports, India
Vahid Shahrivari Joghan	Utrecht University, Netherlands
Valerio Bonsignori	Unipisa, Italy
Vanessa Borst	University of Würzburg, Germany
Venkata Sai Prakash Mukkamala	Quantiphi Analytics, USA
Veselka Boeva	Blekinge Institute of Technology, Sweden
Viacheslav Komisarenko	University of Tartu, Estonia
Vikas Gupta	HPCL, India
Vinayak Gupta	University of Washington, Seattle, USA
Vincent Auriau	Artefact Research Center, France
Vincenzo Pasquadibisceglie	University of Bari, Aldo Moro, Italy
Vincenzo Scotti	KASTEL, Germany
Vinothkumar Kolluru	Stevens Institute of Technology, USA
Vladimir Mic	Aarhus University, Denmark
Wang-Zhou Dai	Nanjing University, China
Wee Siong Ng	Institute for Infocomm Research, Singapore
Wei Cheng	NEC Laboratories America, USA
Wei Li	Harbin Engineering University, China
Wei Wang	Tsinghua University, China
Wei-Peng Chen	Fujitsu Research of America, USA
Wentao Wang	Michigan State University, USA
Wentao Wu	Microsoft Research, USA
Wray Buntine	VinUniversity, Vietnam
Xianchao Wu	Nvidia, USA
Xiang Lian	Kent State University, USA
Xianli Zhang	Xi'an Jiaotong University, China
Xiaobo Jin	Xi'an Jiaotong-Liverpool University, China
Xiaofei Zhou	University of Chinese Academy of Sciences, China
Xiaofeng Gao	Shanghai Jiaotong University, China
Xiaolin Han	Northwestern Polytechnical University, China
Xin Huang	Hong Kong Baptist University, China
Xin Liu	East China Normal University, China
Xing Tang	Tencent, China
Xiuqiang He	Tencent, China
Xiuyuan Hu	Tsinghua University, China
Xueping Peng	University of Technology Sydney, Australia
Yanchang Zhao	CSIRO, Australia

Yang Guo	Xidian University Hangzhou Institute of Technology, China
Yang Song	Apple, USA
Yijun Zhao	Fordham University, USA
Yinghui Wu	Case Western Reserve University, USA
Yingzhen Lin	Harbin Institute of Technology (Shenzhen), China
Yintao Yu	University of Illinois at Urbana-Champaign, USA
Yixiang Fang	Chinese University of Hong Kong, China
Yixuan Cao	Institute of Computing Technology, China
Yizheng Huang	York University, Canada
Yongchao Liu	Ant Group, China
Yu Huang	Indiana University, USA
Yu Wang	University of Oregon, USA
Yuantao Fan	Halmstad University, Sweden
Yucheng Zhou	University of Macau, China
Yue Shi	Meta, USA
Yueyuan Zheng	Beihang University, China
Yunchuan Shi	University of Sydney, Australia
Yunjun Gao	Zhejiang University, China
Yuting Ding	Southeast University, China
Yuzhuo Li	University of Auckland, New Zealand
Zahra Kharazian	Stockholm University, Sweden
Zahra Taghiyarrenani	Halmstad University, Sweden
Zahraa Abdallah	University of Bristol, UK
Zeyi Wen	Hong Kong University of Science and Technology (Guangzhou), China
Zeyu Zhu	National University of Defense Technology, China
Zhanyu Liu	Shanghai Jiao Tong University, China
Zhaogeng Liu	Jilin University, China
Zhaohui Liang	National Library of Medicine, USA
Zhen Zhang	Shandong University, China
Zhendong Chu	Squirrel Ai Learning, China
Zheng Zhang	University of California, USA
Zhengze Li	University of Göttingen, Germany
Zhibin Gu	Hebei Normal University, China
Zhuang Liu	Dongbei University of Finance and Economics, China
Ziyu Guan	Xidian University, China
Zoltan Miklos	Université de Rennes, France
Zunlei Feng	Zhejiang University, China

Program Committee – Demo Track

Andrzej Wójtowicz	Adam Mickiewicz University, Poznań, Poland
Anna Sokol	University of Notre Dame, USA
Arian Pasquali	Faktion AI, Belgium
Bruno Veloso	INESC TEC - FEP-UP, Portugal
Chongsheng Zhang	Henan University, China
Christos Doulkeridis	University of Piraeus, Greece
Danqing Zhang	PathOnAI.org, USA
Fátima Rodrigues	INESC TEC, Portugal
Grigorii Khvatskii	University of Notre Dame, USA
Joe Germino	University of Notre Dame, USA
Jungwon Seo	University of Stavanger, Norway
Ke Li	University of Exeter, England
Manfred Jaeger	Aalborg University, Denmark
Marcin Luckner	Warsaw University of Technology, Poland
Mehwish Alam	Institut Polytechnique de Paris, France
Nuno Moniz	University of Notre Dame, USA
Tânia Carvalho	FCUP, Portugal
Vitor Cerqueira	FEUP, Portugal
Wei-Wei Du	National Yang Ming Chiao Tung University, Taiwan

Additional Reviewers

Andrea D'Angelo	Antonia Hain
Patrick Altmeyer	Md Athikul Islam
Guiseppina Adresini	Michael Ito
Vedangi Bengali	Philipp Jahn
Michele Bernardini	Rahul Kumar
Zhi Cao	Bishal Lakha
Louis Carpentier	Yuwen Liu
Alessio Cascione	Jerry Lonlac
Lilia Chebbah	Shijie Luo
Meng Ding	Francesca Naretto
Roberto Esposito	Navid Nobani
Alina Fastowski	Diego Coello de Portugal
Roger Ferrod	Joana Santos
Michele Fontana	Francesco Scala
Chang Gong	Richard Serrano
Michal Grzejdziak-Zdziarski	Nuno Silva
Paul Hahn	Francesco Spinnato

Pedro C. Vieira
Xiao Wang
Yunyun Wang
Qi Wen
Jianye Xie

Huaiyuan Yao
Yutong Ye
Obaidullah Zaland
Efstratios Zaradoukas
Ñan Zhang

Sponsors

Diamond

Platinum

Organization

Gold

Silver

Bronze

Organization lv

Other Sponsors

Partners

Keynotes

Many Good Models Leads to ...

Cynthia Rudin

Duke University, USA

Abstract. As it turns out, many good models leads to amazing things! The Rashomon Effect, coined by Leo Breiman, describes the phenomenon that there exist many equally good predictive models for the same dataset.

This phenomenon happens for many real datasets, and when it does it sparks both magic and consternation, but mostly magic. In light of the Rashomon Effect, my collaborators and I propose to reshape the way we think about machine learning, particularly for tabular data problems in the nondeterministic (noisy) setting. I'll address how the Rashomon Effect impacts (1) the existence of simple-yet-accurate models, (2) flexibility to address user preferences, such as fairness and monotonicity, without losing performance, (3) uncertainty in predictions, fairness, and explanations, (4) reliable variable importance, (5) algorithm choice, specifically, providing advanced knowledge of which algorithms might be suitable for a given problem, and (6) public policy. I'll also discuss a theory of when the Rashomon Effect occurs and why: interestingly, noise in data leads to a large Rashomon Effect. My goal is to illustrate how the Rashomon Effect can have a massive impact on the use of machine learning for complex problems in society.

Towards Causal Artificial Intelligence

Elias Bareinboim

Columbia University, USA

Abstract. While a significant portion of AI scientists and engineers believe we are on the verge of achieving highly general forms of AI, I offer a critical appraisal of this view through a causal lens. In particular, building on foundational developments in the field, I will present my perspective on the relationship between intelligence and causality – and the central role of the latter in building intelligent systems and advancing credible data science.

I frame this discussion in terms of five core capabilities that we should expect from an intelligent AI system: performing causal reasoning and articulating explanations; making precise, surgical, and sample-efficient decisions; generalizing across changing conditions and environments; generating and simulating in a causally consistent manner; and learning causal structures and variables.

In this talk, I will elaborate on this perspective and share current progress toward building causally intelligent AI systems. A more detailed discussion of this thesis is provided in my forthcoming textbook, a draft of which is available here: https://causalai-book.net/.

Not Just a Trend: Institutionalizing XAI for Responsible and Compliant AI Systems

Francisco Herrera

Granada University, Spain

Abstract. As artificial intelligence (AI) systems increasingly mediate decisions in high-stakes domains – from healthcare and finance to public policy – the demand for explainable AI (XAI) has grown rapidly. Yet many current XAI approaches remain disconnected from the practical needs of stakeholders and the requirements of emerging regulatory frameworks. This talk argues that XAI must not be treated as a passing trend or optional technical add-on, but as a foundational principle in the design and deployment of AI systems. We critically examine the state of the field, exposing the gap between model-centric explainability and stakeholder-centric accountability. In response, we propose a framework that aligns explainability with legal, ethical, and social responsibilities, emphasizing co-design with affected users, sensitivity to institutional contexts, and governance over opacity. Our goal is to advance XAI from superficial compliance toward deeply integrated transparency that fosters trust, accountability, and responsible innovation.

Compositional Intelligence: Coordinating Multiple LLMs for Complex Tasks

Mirella Lapata

University of Edinburgh, UK

Abstract. Recent years have witnessed the rise of increasingly larger and more sophisticated language models (LMs) capable of performing every task imaginable, sometimes at (super)human level. In this talk, I will argue that in many realistic scenarios, solely relying on a single general-purpose LLM is suboptimal. A single LLM is likely to underrepresent real-world data distributions, heterogeneous skills, and task-specific requirements. Instead, I will discuss multi-LLM collaboration as an alternative to monolithic generative modeling. By orchestrating multiple LLMs, each with distinct roles, perspectives, or competencies, we can achieve more effective problem-solving while being more inclusive and explainable. I will illustrate this approach through two case studies: narrative story generation and visual question answering, showing how a society of agents can collectively tackle complex tasks while pursuing complementary subgoals. Additionally, I will explore how these agent societies leverage reasoning to improve performance.

Towards a Fairer World: Uncovering and Addressing Human and Algorithmic Biases

Nuria Oliver

ELLIS Alicante Foundation, Spain

Abstract. In my talk, I will first briefly present ELLIS Alicante1, the only ELLIS unit that has been created from scratch as a non-profit research foundation devoted to responsible AI for Social Good. Next, I will provide an overview of AI with a focus on the ethical implications and limitations of today's AI systems, including algorithmic discrimination and bias. On this topic, I will present a few examples of our work on uncovering and mitigating both human and algorithmic biases with AI.

On the human front, I will present the body of work that we have carried out in the context of AI-based beauty filters that are so popular on social media. On the algorithmic front, I will explain the main approaches to address algorithmic discrimination and I will present three novel methods to achieve fairer decisions.

Tensor Logic: A Simple Unification of Neural and Symbolic AI

Pedro Domingos

University of Washington, USA

Abstract. Deep learning has achieved remarkable successes in language generation and other tasks, but is extremely opaque and notoriously unreliable. Both of these problems can be overcome by combining it with the sound reasoning and transparent knowledge representation capabilities of symbolic AI. Tensor logic accomplishes this by unifying tensor algebra and logic programming, the formal languages underlying respectively deep learning and symbolic AI. Tensor logic is based on the observation that predicates are compactly represented Boolean tensors, and can be straightforwardly extended to compactly represent numeric ones. The two key constructs in tensor logic are tensor join and project, numeric operations that generalize database join and project. A tensor logic program is a set of tensor equations, each expressing a tensor as a series of tensor joins, a tensor project, and a univariate nonlinearity applied elementwise. Tensor logic programs can succinctly encode most deep architectures and symbolic AI systems, and many new combinations.

In this talk I will describe the foundations and main features of tensor logic, and present efficient inference and learning algorithms for it. A system based on tensor logic achieves state-of-the-art results on a suite of language and reasoning tasks. How tensor logic will fare on trillion-token corpora and associated tasks remains an open question.

Artificial Intelligence for Science

Sašo Džeroski

Jožef Stefan Institute, Slovenia

Abstract. Artificial intelligence is already transforming science, with its future impact expected to be even greater. Realizing this potential requires addressing key scientific challenges, such as ensuring explainability (of models and their predictions), learning effectively from limited data, and integrating data with prior domain knowledge. It also requires the provision of support for open and reproducible science through formalizing and sharing scientific knowledge.

I will present an overview of my research on the development of AI methods suitable for use in science. These include methods for explainable machine learning – including multi-target prediction and relational learning – that deliver accurate yet interpretable models suitable for complex scientific domains. These methods have been applied in environmental science, life science and materials science. Learning from limited data is critical in science. I will discuss two complementary approaches: semi-supervised learning, which leverages unlabeled data directly, together with labeled data, and foundation models, which use representations learned from vast unlabeled data to support downstream tasks with minimal supervision, i.e., limited amounts of labeled data. Both paradigms expand AI's reach into data-scarce scientific problems.

I will then present our work on automated scientific modeling, where we learn interpretable models of dynamical systems – such as process-based models and differential equations – from time series data and domain knowledge. Finally, I will highlight the role of ontologies and semantic technologies in experimental computer science, including machine learning and optimization. In these areas, we have developed ontologies for the representation and annotation of both data and other artefacts produced by science, such as algorithms, models, and results of experiments.

Contents – Part IV

Interpretability and Explainability

Interpretable Instance-Based Learning Through Pairwise Distance Trees 3
    Andrea Fedele, Alessio Cascione, Riccardo Guidotti, and Cristiano Landi

How CNNs and ViTs Perceive Similarities Between Categories 22
    Katarzyna Filus and Joanna Domańska

FACEGroup: Feasible and Actionable Counterfactual Explanations
for Group Fairness 41
    *Christos Fragkathoulas, Vasiliki Papanikou, Evaggelia Pitoura,
    and Evimaria Terzi*

TSHAP: Fast and Exact SHAP for Explaining Time Series Classification
and Regression 60
    Thach Le Nguyen and Georgiana Ifrim

A True-to-the-Model Benchmark for Edge-Level Attributions of GNN
Explainers 78
    Francesco Paolo Nerini, Francesco Bonchi, and André Panisson

MASCOTS: Model-Agnostic Symbolic COunterfactual Explanations
for Time Series 94
    *Dawid Pludowski, Francesco Spinnato, Piotr Wilczyński,
    Krzysztof Kotowski, Evridiki Vasileia Ntagiou, Riccardo Guidotti,
    and Przemysław Biecek*

Faithful Explanations for Graph Classification Using Logic 113
    Alessio Ragno, Marc Plantevit, and Céline Robardet

MalGPT: A Generative Explainable Model for Malware Binaries 130
    *Mohd Saqib, Benjamin C. M. Fung, Steven H. H. Ding,
    and Philippe Charland*

MAINLE: A Multi-Agent, Interactive, Natural Language Local Explainer
of Classification Tasks 149
    *Paulo Bruno Serafim, Rômulo Férrer Filho, Stenio Freitas,
    Gizem Gezici, Fosca Giannotti, Franco Raimondi, and Alexandre Santos*

On Trustworthy Rule-Based Models and Explanations 166
    Mohamed Siala, Jordi Planes, and Joao Marques-Silva

Large Language Models

Zero-Shot Detection of LLM-Generated Code via Approximated Task
Conditioning 187
    Maor Ashkenazi, Ofir Brenner, Tal Furman Shohet, and Eran Treister

Advancing Multi-step Mathematical Reasoning in Large Language
Models Through Multi-layered Self-reflection with Auto-prompting 205
    André de Souza Loureiro, Jorge Valverde-Rebaza, Julieta Noguez, David Escarcega, and Ricardo Marcacini

DPS: Diverse Prototype Selection for Adaptive In-Context Learning 224
    Xuanbo Fan, Kaiyuan Li, Hao Sun, Boci Peng, Zhenrong Cheng, and Yan Zhang

IntentBreaker: Intent-Adaptive Jailbreak Attack on Large Language Models ... 240
    Shengnan Guo, Yuchen Zhai, Shenyi Zhang, Lingchen Zhao, and Zhangyi Wang

Pareto Multi-objective Alignment for Language Models 257
    Qiang He and Setareh Maghsudi

Uncertainty Quantification for Black-Box LLMs via Star Graphs
Connectivity: Exploring Alternatives for Semantic Density 273
    Zhaoye Li, Huan Chen, Huibin Tan, Long Lan, Yize Sui, and Jing Ren

Balanced and Token-Efficient Summarization of User Reviews
via Stratified Sampling and Large Language Models 290
    Fabrizio Marozzo, Loris Belcastro, Cristian Cosentino, and Pietro Liò

Few-Shot Graph Out-of-Distribution Detection with LLMs 307
    Haoyan Xu, Zhengtao Yao, Yushun Dong, Ziyi Wang, Ryan Rossi, Mengyuan Li, and Yue Zhao

Learning Theory

Learning Overspecified Gaussian Mixtures Exponentially Fast with the EM
Algorithm 327
    Zhenisbek Assylbekov, Alan Legg, and Artur Pak

Missing but Not Missed: On Learnability Under Imputation 344
  Andrea Campagner

The Vanishing Empirical Variance in Randomly Initialized Deep ReLU
Networks 362
  Michał Grzejdziak-Zdziarski, David M. J. Tax, and Marco Loog

Bandit Max-Min Fair Allocation 380
  Tsubasa Harada, Shinji Ito, and Hanna Sumita

Weight-Rounding Error in Deep Neural Networks 398
  Jiří Šíma and Petra Vidnerová

The Local Convexification Method and Its Application to Learning
Weakly Convex Boolean Functions 417
  Eike Stadtländer, Tamás Horváth, and Stefan Wrobel

Gathering and Exploiting Higher-Order Information when Training Large
Structured Models 436
  Pierre Wolinski

Gradient Boosting Versus Mixed Integer Programming for Sparse Additive
Modeling 453
  Fan Yang, Pierre Le Bodic, and Mario Boley

Multimodal Data

ChitroJera: A Regionally Relevant Visual Question Answering Dataset
for Bangla 473
  *Deeparghya Dutta Barua, Md Sakib Ul Rahman Sourove, Md Fahim,
  Fabiha Haider, Fariha Tanjim Shifat, Md Tasmim Rahman Adib,
  Anam Borhan Uddin, Md Farhan Ishmam, and Md Farhad Alam*

Revisiting Cross-Modal Knowledge Distillation: A Disentanglement
Approach for RGBD Semantic Segmentation 492
  Roger Ferrod, Cássio F. Dantas, Luigi Di Caro, and Dino Ienco

Revisiting Multi-modal Emotion Learning with Broad State Space Models
and Probability-Guidance Fusion 509
  Yuntao Shou, Tao Meng, Wei Ai, and Keqin Li

AMST: Alternating Multimodal Skip Training 526
  Hugo Manuel Alves Henriques e Silva, Hongguang Chen, and Selpi

Cross-Modal Causal Scheduling for Enhancing Target-Oriented
Multi-modal Sentiment Classification 542
   Pengyu Zhao, Chaoyang Li, Lingzhi Wang, and Qing Liao

Author Index 559

Interpretability and Explainability

Mountaineering and Exploration

Interpretable Instance-Based Learning Through Pairwise Distance Trees

Andrea Fedele[1,2](✉), Alessio Cascione[1], Riccardo Guidotti[1,2], and Cristiano Landi[1,2]

[1] University of Pisa, Largo Bruno Pontecorvo 3, 56127 Pisa, PI, Italy
{andrea.fedele,alessio.cascione,cristiano.landi}@phd.unipi.it,
riccardo.guidotti@unipi.it
[2] KDD Lab, ISTI-CNR, Via G. Moruzzi 1, 56124 Pisa, PI, Italy
{andrea.fedele,riccardo.guidotti,cristiano.landi}@isti.cnr.it

Abstract. Instance-based models offer natural interpretability by making decisions based on concrete examples. However, their transparency is often hindered by the use of complex similarity measures, which are difficult to interpret, especially in high-dimensional datasets. To address this issue, this paper presents a meta-learning framework that enhances the interpretability of instance-based models by replacing traditional, complex pairwise distance functions with interpretable pairwise distance trees. These trees are designed to prioritize simplicity and transparency while preserving the model's effectiveness. By offering a clear decision-making process, the framework makes the instance selection more understandable. Also, the framework mitigates the computational burden of instance-based models, which typically require calculating all pairwise distances. Leveraging the generalization capabilities of pairwise distance trees and employing sampling strategies to select representative subsets, the method significantly reduces computational complexity. Our experiments demonstrate that the proposed approach improves computational efficiency with only a modest trade-off in accuracy while substantially enhancing the interpretability of the learned distance measure.

Keywords: Pairwise Learning · Interpretable Distance · Meta-learning

1 Introduction

Instance-based models, such as k-Nearest Neighbors, have long been valued for their intuitive approach: they make predictions by comparing new instances to stored examples from training data [1,32]. This case-based reasoning, rooted in how humans naturally use past experiences to understand new situations, offers inherent interpretability by relying on concrete examples [31]. Instance-based models rely on pairwise comparison: each new instance is evaluated against stored examples using a distance measure. However, while the decision mechanism is typically transparent, e.g., majority voting over nearest neighbors, the process by which these neighbors are determined is tied to the underlying distance measure, which often remains opaque, especially in high-dimensional spaces where is complex to determine the contribution of single features.

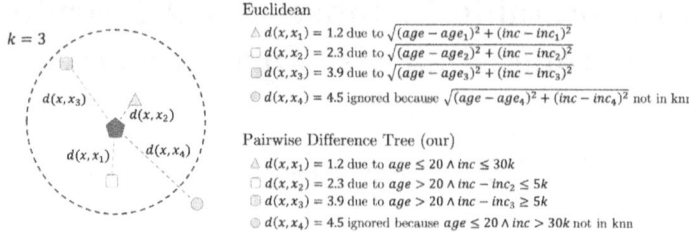

Fig. 1. Comparison between traditional KNN using Euclidean distance, and KNN using PDT distance, i.e., PDTF with KNN at inference time.

In contrast to traditional instance-based methods, Pairwise Difference Learning (PDL) and Pairwise Similarity Learning (PSL), have emerged as techniques that leverage pairwise relationships by operating directly on input pairs. PDL shifts the focus from mapping individual inputs directly to outputs toward learning (regression) functions that predict the difference between outcomes for pairs of instances [35,38]. The core idea is to approximate the difference function, enabling predictions for a new test instance by averaging the predicted differences relative to the outcomes of the training data. In contrast, PSL emphasizes learning similarity functions that assign higher scores to pairs of samples from the same class than to those from different classes [13,25]. Both methods are particularly valuable in data-scarce scenarios, such as rare disease diagnosis or novel phenomenon detection, where traditional data-intensive approaches may falter. However, both frameworks have limited interpretability, as they generally depend on complex or high-dimensional transformations.

Motivated by the need for both robust pairwise modeling and interpretable instance-based decision-making, we introduce the Pairwise Distance Tree Framework (PDTF), an interpretable meta-learning approach that enhances instance-based models by replacing stpdtandard, opaque distance functions with a shallow, interpretable decision tree, namely the Pairwise Distance Tree (PDT). By operating on pairwise representations of the input data, PDTF unifies the strengths of PDL and PSL while providing a clear explanation of why two instances are considered (dis)similar. The PDT learns a mapping from a joint representation of instances to their corresponding distance, with its decision rules explicitly revealing which features drive the similarity judgment. To further boost interpretability, we also introduce forced split conditions, ensuring that the same features and the same thresholds are used when comparing both elements of a pair. In Fig. 1, we compare the decision-making process of a "traditional" KNN using Euclidean distance with that of KNN using the PDT approximated distance. Given the same neighborhood with $k = 3$, Euclidean distance requires mathematical calculus that hardly explain why the blue, yellow and green points are included while the red point is excluded, especially in high-dimensional spaces. In contrast, PDTF offers an explanation in a logical form for neighborhood selection that users can easily understand without intricate mathematical reasoning.

Our contribution is threefold. First, we model the distance function as an interpretable decision tree, offering full visibility into the instance-based reasoning process. Second, we integrate pairwise difference and similarity-based instance selection within a unified framework that emphasizes transparency. Third, we address the computational challenges inherent in pairwise methods through efficient instance sampling strategies. Experiments on tabular benchmark datasets reveal that a joint feature representation based solely on pointwise differences yields the best performance for PDT distance approximation, while the combined representation of pointwise differences and input features excels in the classification tasks. Moreover, an intelligent sampling strategy, using roughly 20% of the dataset, reduces training time without significantly compromising performance. Also, enforcing split constraints enhances interpretability without compromising performance by reducing the cognitive burden of interpreting rules. Since the splits are restricted to the same feature, or both the same feature and threshold, the resulting rules is simpler to understand.

The rest of the paper is organized as follows. In Sect. 2 we review related work covering case-based reasoning and similarity learning. Section 3 describes the details of the PDTF, including the pairwise training set preparation, tree structure, and forced split constraints. Section 4 presents the experimental results, and Sect. 5 concludes with a discussion of future research directions.

2 Related Work

Case-based reasoning relies on the idea that human cognition often uses stored examples of past experiences to interpret new situations [33]. Decisions are made by retrieving and comparing instances from memory, an inherently interpretable process, as users can trace decisions to concrete examples [22]. Its transparency has driven applications in healthcare [3], financial risk [24], and image analysis [18], where understanding decision rationale is as vital as the decision itself.

Building on these insights, metric learning, deep metric learning and Pairwise Similarity Learning (PSL) methods have been developed to capture the intrinsic relationships between data points. Metric learning seeks to learn a proper distance function that satisfies non-negativity and triangle inequality properties and respects semantic similarity by reducing intra-class distances and enlarging inter-class distances [39]. However, in high-dimensional settings, such learned metrics can become less interpretable as the individual contributions of features are obscured by the complexity of the transformation. Deep metric learning extends these ideas using neural networks to learn non-linear embeddings that have achieved state-of-the-art performance in tasks such as face recognition and image retrieval [21,23,40]. However, despite their success, the non-linear transformation involved lead to opaque learned metrics. In contrast, PSL focuses on learning a similarity function that assigns higher scores to positive pairs than to negative pairs, thereby dropping the requirement of learning a proper distance metric. PSL methods are categorized into proxy-based and proxy-free approaches [37]. Proxy-based methods use representative vectors (proxies) for each class to compute similarity, improving convergence but reducing transparency by adding an abstraction layer. Proxy-free methods, in contrast, work directly on data pairs or triplets, providing a more intuitive and transparent view of the data's structure. Nevertheless, even these approaches struggle with interpretability in high-dimensional settings, where hyperparameter sensitivity (e.g., in triplet loss formulations) and the complexity of learned representations can obscure the underlying feature contributions.

A fundamental contribution towards this line of research is the Pairwise Difference Learning (PDL) [35]. Rather than mapping individual inputs directly to outputs, the PDL framework shifts the paradigm by learning a function that predicts as a regressor the difference between outcomes for pairs of instances. Predictions are obtained for a given test instance by pairing it with all training examples, computing the corresponding outcome differences, and averaging these values. This meta-learning approach is applied across various fields, including image processing [20], drug activity ranking [36], and quantum mechanical reaction modeling [9]. The first extension of PDL to classification is introduced in [2] where the classification problem is reformulated as a binary task: a paired dataset is constructed, and a binary classifier is trained on joint feature representations to predict whether a pair of instances belongs to the same class. For new test samples, pairwise predictions are aggregated to estimate class posterior probabilities, harnessing the robustness and natural uncertainty quantification of pairwise comparisons. Although relatively recent, there is emerging interest in combining ideas from PSL and PDL. In [11], for example, the authors address the authorship analysis problem by representing a feature vector as an unordered pair of documents. Here, the value of a feature is computed as the absolute difference in the relative frequencies of that feature across the two documents. Similar to the formulation in [2], the class label indicates whether the two documents belong to the same author.

Traditional case-based reasoning and modern pairwise learning methods enhance predictive performance but lack transparency in their distance functions. To address this, we unify the strengths of PSL and PDL with a focus on interpretability. We reformulate the pairwise learning task as a regression problem, mapping input pairs to distance values. This distance function is modeled with a shallow regression tree, which approximates the original distance while providing explicit decision rules which offer clear decision paths, improving transparency and enabling human understanding of how distances are determined.

3 Pairwise Distance Tree Framework

We present here the Pairwise Distance Tree Framework (PDTF), an interpretable meta-learning framework designed to improve the transparency of instance-based models. PDTF first transforms training instances into pairs with computed distances, then trains a shallow regressor tree to approximate these distances. Finally, the learned function replaces the standard distance to guide neighbor selection. In the following, we first formalize the problem setting and then we present our framework. Without loss of generality, we focus on classification tasks, leaving the exploration of other problem domains to future work.

3.1 Problem Setting

Given a set of instances represented as real-valued m-dimensional feature vectors[1] in $\mathbb{R}^m$ and a set of class labels $C = \{1, \ldots, c\}$, we assume the existence of an unknown ground-truth function $g : \mathbb{R}^m \to C$ mapping each vector in $\mathbb{R}^m$ to one of the c classes in C. In case-based reasoning, given a training set $\langle X, Y \rangle$ with $X = \{x_1, \ldots, x_n\}$ of n instances, $Y = \{y_1, \ldots, y_n\}$ denoting the corresponding class labels with $y_i \in C$, and a pairwise distance function $d : \mathbb{R}^m \times \mathbb{R}^m \to \mathbb{R}$, the objective is to learn an instance-based model implemented through function $f : \mathbb{R}^m \to C$, which aims to approximate the unknown ground-truth function g. Instance-based models explicitly store a set of the training data $\langle X, Y \rangle$, referred to as the *memory*, which is used during inference. These models define a selection policy s based on d such that, at inference time, given a memory $\langle X, Y \rangle$ and a query instance x, the selection policy is applied to identify a subset of cases

$$\langle X_s, Y_s \rangle = s_d(x, \langle X, Y \rangle) \quad \text{where } X_s \subseteq X \text{ and } Y_s \subseteq Y.$$

This subset typically consists of the closest examples, commonly referred to as *neighbors* [16,34] or *pivots* [4,8], which are then used to make a prediction. In essence, the selection policy is a similarity-based mechanism that identifies a set of k neighbors of the query instance x. Once the relevant instances are selected, an inference policy ϕ is applied, usually a majority vote over the class labels of the selected instances $\langle X_s, Y_s \rangle$. Thus, the instance-based model f is defined as:

$$f(x) = \phi(\{(x_i, y_i) \mid (x_i, y_i) \in s_d(x, \langle X, Y \rangle)\})$$

Common hyper-parameters of the selection policy s include a similarity threshold, which determines whether an instance is selected w.r.t. the distances calculated, or a value k representing the number of most similar instances to retrieve.

Typical instance-based models include k-Nearest Neighbor (KNN) [16,34], and more broadly, most case-based reasoners [30]. They are considered interpretable in terms of similarity, as they rely on a set of previously observed "cases" that serve as evidence during inference. This inherent interpretability holds as long as the following conditions are met: *(i)* the inference policy ϕ uses the selected evidence in an interpretable manner, *(ii)* the selection policy s transparently identifies relevant instances from memory, and *(iii)* the pairwise distance function d is interpretable. Regarding *(i)* and *(ii)*, most instance-based models, such as those applying a majority vote and selecting the k most similar instances to a query instance x, are generally considered interpretable. However, full interpretability hinges on the notion of similarity itself, which depends on the distance

---

[1] For the sake of simplicity, we consistently treat data instances as real-valued vectors. Any transformation employed in the experiments is specified when needed.

function d. Specifically, an instance-based model can be deemed entirely human-interpretable only if the distance function: *(a)* is transparent, and *(b)* relies on a limited number of features to compare instances and establish similarity. For example, consider a classification task on a tabular dataset with $m = 100$ features, where the KNN model uses the Euclidean distance as d. While the decision process over the neighborhood of k instances is interpretable, a user may struggle to fully understand why certain instances are included in the neighborhood while others are not, due to the high dimensionality, without replicating the mathematical calculations to compute the distance.

3.2 Pairwise Distance Tree

To overcome the aforementioned limitations, we implement the distance function d with a shallow Pairwise Distance Tree (PDT) that allows to express the reasons why two instances are similar or dissimilar only considering a limited number of features and expressing the reasons for the distance in a logical form.

We opt for implementing the distance function d with a tree-based model because decision trees are interpretable predictive models [17,19] representing their decisions through a structure composed of nodes and branches [7,34]. Indeed, a decision tree routes instances within their structure, each node testing a split condition on feature a w.r.t. threshold τ, e.g., $x^{(a)} \leq \tau$, and routing instances towards its children, all the way down to the leaf nodes. Thus, decision trees are inherently transparent because the complete tree can be inspected, allowing a human analyst to follow the sequence of splits. Each instance traces a path inside the tree, effectively providing a *decision rule* describing the decision process of the tree on the said instance. The *complexity* [28] of decision trees is typically calculated as the total number of nodes and leaves, tree depth, and number of attributes used. The simpler the tree, the more concise and interpretable the decision rules [10,14,15]. Tree induction algorithms typically implement a top-down greedy search through the space of possible splits. CART [7], ID3 [26], and its successor C4.5 [27] are the most famous induction strategies.

Pairwise Training Set Preparation. Given a training set $\langle X, Y \rangle$ and a distance function d, we transform $\langle X, Y \rangle$ into a paired dataset $\langle Z, D \rangle$ where

$$Z = \{z_{ij} = \zeta(x_i, x_j) \mid x_i, x_j \in X\} \quad D = \{d_{ij} = d(x_i, x_j) \mid (x_i, x_j) \in Z\}$$

where z_{ij} is formed by using the feature vectors x_i and x_j. In particular, we consider the three following alternatives to implement the transformation ζ:

- (α) the *concatenation* of the feature vectors $z_{ij} = \zeta_\alpha(x_i, x_j) = [x_i, x_j]$,
- (β) the *pointwise difference* of the feature vectors $z_{ij} = \zeta_\beta(x_i, x_j) = |x_i - x_j|$ that is a formulation shown to positively impact performance [35], and
- (γ) the combination of α and β, i.e., $z_{ij} = \zeta_\gamma(x_i, x_j) = [x_i, x_j, |x_i - x_j|]$.

We underline that, since we want to reflect symmetry in our framework, we add both (x_i, x_j) and (x_j, x_i) to the paired dataset. Also, in order to take into account cases in which the distance is zero ($d_{ij} = 0$), we consider in Z also cases in which $i = j$, i.e., (x_i, x_i). Thus, the maximum number of pairs in Z, i.e., the maximum cardinality of $|Z|$ is n^2 where $|X| = n$. Therefore, our proposal is named Pairwise Distance Tree, as it takes as input the domain $\langle Z, D \rangle$ formed by pairing the original training iances and using their distance as target variable.

Also, to address the complexity associated with pair creation, we present a set of *sampling strategies* to consider a subset of training instances $\tilde{X} \subset X$ with $|\tilde{X}| = \tilde{n} < n$ in order to reduce the number of pairs in Z:

- *random (RS):* selects uniformly at random $\tilde{n}$ instances among those in $\langle X, Y \rangle$;
- *center-based clustering (CS):* executes a k-Means clustering algorithm for each target label among those in $\langle X, Y \rangle$ by setting $k = \lceil \tilde{n}/c \rceil$ and selects for each cluster the closest instance to the centroid.

Pairwise Tree Structure. The Pairwise Distance Tree is implemented as a decision tree regressor r that maps the joint representation z_{ij} to an approximation of the distance $d(x_i, x_j)$, i.e., $d(x_i, x_j) \approx r(x_i, x_j)$. The goal is to learn a decision tree regressor r such that the prediction of $r(x_i, x_j)$ closely match the true distance $d(x_i, x_j)$. This is achieved by minimizing regression loss over all pairs. Therefore in PDT, each decision path provides a clear, step-by-step explanation of how the model evaluates pairwise distances.

In this context the structure of the tree regressor r is crucial. By designing r as a shallow decision tree, we ensure that its decision-making process is interpretable, thereby allowing us to inspect and understand the logic adopted to approximate the distance between a pair of instances. We underline that, adopting a shallow regression tree, each leaf is returning as distance the *average* distance among a consistent group of similar pairs that the training procedure routed in that leaf. Thus, if a PDT has l leaves, e.g. $l = 16$ leaves, it means that, at inference time only l values can be returned by $r(x_i, x_j)$. This behavior, on the one hand, is a strong limitation w.r.t. the calculus of traditional distance functions because the approximation applied by the PDT practically applies a discretization to the original pairwise distances, on the other hand, is well-aligned with the human way of estimating the similarity between objects as we simply say they are *very different*, they are *different, similar* or *very similar*.

Split Constraints. To further boost the interpretability of PDT, when the feature selected for the best split belongs to the feature vectors (x_i, x_j) in the training set preparation α and γ, we impose two *forced split conditions* which we refer to as the *same-feature*, and the *same-feature, same-threshold* splits.

Under the *same-feature* split (PDT-F), if a parent node (which is not itself forced) splits on a specific feature a from one element of the pair x_i, i.e., $x_i^{(a)} \leq \tau$, then, the corresponding children nodes are forced to split on the same feature a from the other element of the pair x_j, without any constraint on the threshold, i.e., $x_j^{(a)} \leq \tau'$, allowing the tree only to select the threshold τ'. This constraint ensures that both components of the pair are evaluated along the same dimension. The key point is that the decision process explicitly links the two splits by enforcing the use of the second feature on both records. On the other hand,

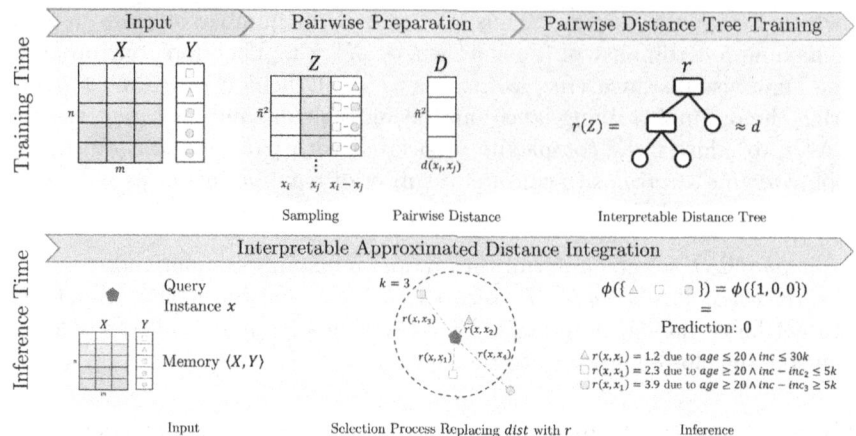

Fig. 2. Pairwise Distance Tree Framework (PDTF). At inference time, given a query instance x, the model selects relevant neighbors from the memory $\langle X, Y \rangle$ by evaluating $r(x, x_i)$ and applies an inference policy ϕ, i.e., majority voting, to produce a final prediction. Each prediction can be inspected, since the distance function employed for neighborhood selection is fully interpretable. (Color figure online)

the *same-feature, same-threshold* split (PDT-T) requires that the children nodes not only uses the same feature a as the parent, but also applies the exact same threshold τ, thereby creating a strict alignment between the decision paths for both elements. Thus, if the parent node perform the split $x_i^{(a)} \leq \tau$, the children nodes are constrained to perform splits $x_j^{(a)} \leq \tau$. This constraint further enhances the consistency in the splits across two elements of each pair. The intuition behind these forced split conditions w.r.t. the plain PDT (PDT-P) is that interpretability is enhanced when the decision process consistently evaluates the same features, and, in the strictest case, uses identical thresholds across both elements of a pair. When the splits are aligned, a human reviewer can clearly identify which features are driving the decision and understand how differences between the records are being measured.

3.3 Pairwise Distance Tree Framework

Given a training set $\langle X, Y \rangle$ and a distance function d, the PDTF learns an instance-based model f by adopting a PDT regressor r to approximate d. In summary, PDTF consists of three main steps illustrated also in Fig. 2:

1. *Pairwise Training Set Preparation:* transform the dataset $\langle X, Y \rangle$ (or a subset of it) into the paired dataset $\langle Z, D \rangle$ using the joint representation z_{ij} and the distance d_{ij} of a sample pair (x_i, x_j), in blue in Fig. 2.
2. *Pairwise Distance Tree Training:* train PDT regressor r by minimizing a regression loss over all the selected pairs, thereby learning an interpretable mapping from z_{ij} to d_{ij}, in green in Fig. 2.

3. *Interpretable Approximated Distance Integration:* replace d in the instance-based model f with the interpretable approximated distance function r to select the cases to take the decision w.r.t. a query instance x, i.e., $\langle X_s, Y_s \rangle = s_r(x, \langle X, Y \rangle)$ where for a query instance x and any training sample x_i, the approximated distance is computed as $r(x, x_i)$, in purple in Fig. 2.

This decoupled structure is critical because the regression training phase leverages only a subset $\tilde{X} \subset X$ of input pairs to learn the distance function, while the full training set $\langle X, Y \rangle$ is retained as the input for the instance-based model f. This design allows us to efficiently learn a robust, interpretable distance function without sacrificing the comprehensive information provided by the complete dataset during inference. However, we signal to the reader that the learned nature of our interpretable distance function does not theoretically guarantee that all traditional metric properties, such as *symmetry*, are strictly met. However, by including both orderings of instance pairs (x_i, x_j) and (x_j, x_i), whether $i = j$ or $i \neq j$, in the paired training set, we empirically achieve *approximated symmetry*[2]. Thus, at inference time, the computed distance for a query instance x and any training sample x_i is robust to the ordering of inputs, meaning that $r(x, x_i) \approx r(x_i, x)$.

In addition, we underline that, compared to the PDL classifier [2], our proposal is able to capture a much finer and detailed abstraction of the notion of distance between pair of instance while simultaneously sufficiently abstracting from the original distance function. Furthermore, due to the sampling strategies used to construct the pairwise distance tree training set, PDTF is computationally more efficient than the PDL classifier. Given $n = |X|$, the training complexity of PDTF, like that of PDL, is primarily determined by the calculation of the pairwise distance matrix, which requires $O(n^2)$ operations. Indeed, the complexity of training the PDT itself is $O(m \cdot n \log^2 n)$ for balanced trees. When employing a sampling strategy, the complexity of PDTF depends on the sampling strategy and on the reduced dataset size $\tilde{n}$, where $\tilde{n} < n$, further improving computational efficiency. In particular, when using random sampling strategies, the overall training complexity is $O(\tilde{n}^2)$, omitting the dataset dimensionality m for simplicity. On the other hand, when adopting the center-based clustering sampling strategy, the complexity depends on the clustering algorithm employed. If, as in our case, k-Means is used with $k = \lceil \tilde{n}/c \rceil$, and considering that the complexity of k-Means can be approximated as $O(k \cdot n)$, the overall training complexity becomes $O(\tilde{n} \cdot n)$. At prediction time, the complexity of PDTF for a single query instance is $O(n \cdot \log \tilde{n})$, which is more efficient than the $O(n \cdot m)$ complexity of the traditional KNN classifier or the PDL classifier when $\log \tilde{n} < m$.

---

[2] Approximated symmetry means that training PDT on both orderings of instance pairs (x_i, x_j) and (x_j, x_i), achieves prediction vectors with very high cosine similarity.

Table 1. Datasets info: # of records (n), # of features (m), # of classes (c).

	small									large										
	iris	seeds	glass	fire	verteb.	ecoli	iono	lrs	breast	steel	road	bank	pol	cover	house	eye	sylvine	magic	compas	spam
n	150	210	214	243	310	336	351	531	569	1.9k	2k	2k	2k	2k	2k	2k	2k	2k	4.5k	4.6k
m	4	7	9	13	6	7	34	100	30	27	29	7	26	10	16	20	20	20	9	57
c	3	3	6	2	2	8	2	9	2	7	2	2	2	2	2	2	2	10	2	2

4 Experiments

We evaluate the performance of PDTF[3], on tabular benchmark datasets and compare it with state-of-the-art competitors in the classification task.

Experimental Setting. We consider KNN, PIVOTTREE (PT) [8], and ϵBALL [5] as baseline instance-based models, all using the Euclidean distance as d. Next, we evaluate PDTF against these baselines by integrating such classifiers in the framework, namely PDT-KNN, PDT-PT, and PDT-ϵBALL using PDT as distance function d. Additionally, we compare PDTF with the pairwise distance classifier PDL [2] to provide a comprehensive performance assessment. Specifically, we consider KNN using Euclidean distance with PDL, namely PDL-KNN. For KNN[4] we use $k = 5$, for PT[5] we use $maxdepth = 5$, and for ϵBALL[6] we use ϵ equals to the 10th percentile of all pairwise distances.

We measure the classification performance using the Accuracy and the weighted F1-score [34]. We assess the effectiveness of the PDT as a regressor by reporting the R^2 and $RMSE$ score [34], which quantifies its ability to approximate true pairwise distances. For each experiment, an 80/20 train/test split is applied. Results are reported on the test set. Finally, we evaluate the computational efficiency by measuring both training and prediction times, reported in seconds.

As datasets, we use two sets of tabular benchmark datasets. First, for the sensitivity analysis, we follow the OpenML-CC18 [6] selection constraints and select 9 relatively small datasets from OpenML[7]. These datasets are employed in other papers of PSL and PDL [2], making them particularly suitable for our approach. Next, for comparisons against competitors, we rely on 11 datasets from OpenML and other repositories[8], e.g. spambase (UCI), compas (ProPublica).

---

[3] Python implementation available at: https://github.com/fismimosa/PDT.
[4] KNN as implemented in sklearn: https://tinyurl.com/sklearn-knn.
[5] PIVOTTREE as implemented in: https://github.com/msetzu/pivottree.
[6] ϵBALL as implemented in: https://tinyurl.com/epsball.
[7] The small datasets are: iris, seeds, glass, algerian forest fires (fire), vertebra column (verteb), ecoli, low resolution spectrometer (lrs), breast cancer (breast).
[8] The large datasets are: steel plates fault (steel), read safety (road), bank marketing (bank), pol, covertype (cover), house 16H (house), eye movements (eye), sylvine (sylvine), magic telescope (magic), compas, spambase (spam).

Table 2. Mean and std.dev of R^2 and $RMSE$ for PDT as distance regressor among the small datasets, with $\tilde{n} = n$, i.e., without sampling strategy, and $maxdepth = 8$, with different pairwise training set preparation (α, β, γ) and different split constraints (P, F, T). Best in bold, second best in italic.

PDT	R^2			$RMSE$		
	P	F	T	P	F	T
α	.660 ± .138	.652 ± .137	.631 ± .133	1.53 ± .845	1.55 ± .870	1.60 ± .890
β	**.909 ± .056**	**.909 ± .056**	**.909 ± .056**	**.830 ± .575**	**.830 ± .575**	**.830 ± .575**
γ	*.907 ± .059*	*.907 ± .059*	*.907 ± .059*	*.836 ± .580*	*.837 ± .581*	*.837 ± .581*

Table 3. Mean and std.dev of Accuracy and of weighted F1-score for PDTF using KNN as classifier among small datasets, with $\tilde{n} = n$, i.e., without sampling strategy, and $maxdepth = 8$, with different pairwise training set preparation (α, β, γ) and different split constraints (P, F, T). Best in bold, second best in italic.

PDT	Accuracy			F1-score		
	P	F	T	P	F	T
α	.700 ± .098	.697 ± .128	.662 ± .183	.654 ± .126	.656 ± .161	.607 ± .210
β	*.808 ± .133*	*.808 ± .133*	*.808 ± .133*	*.799 ± .143*	*.799 ± .143*	*.799 ± .143*
γ	**.809 ± .133**	**.809 ± .133**	**.809 ± .133**	**.800 ± .144**	**.800 ± .144**	**.800 ± .144**

Detailed summaries of each dataset, including the number of records, features (after removing the categorical[9] ones), and classes, are provided in Table 1.

Sensitivity Analysis. We analyze here how the hyper-parameters of PDTF influence both the quality of distance approximation and the classification performance. Table 2 presents the mean and std. dev. of the R^2 and $RMSE$ score for PDT, which assesses its effectiveness as a distance approximation using a regression evaluation measure, while Table 3 shows the Accuracy and weighted F1-score for PDTF with KNN across the small datasets using KNN as classifier. In this initial analysis, we examine the impact of different pairwise training set preparations (α, β, γ) and split constraints (P, F, T) while fixing $\tilde{n} = n$, i.e., without applying any sampling strategy, and setting $maxdepth = 8$, a relatively compact tree that balances interpretability and performance.

The results highlight the importance of the pairing procedure in PDTF. Simply using concatenation (α) leads to higher $RMSE$ error and lower performance for R^2, Accuracy and F1-score. However, adding pointwise feature difference (β) or combining it with concatenation (γ) significantly improves distance approximation and classification performance when used in KNN. The performance difference between γ and β is minimal. Analysis of the tree structures in the γ setting

---

[9] The PDTF framework remains fully applicable to mixed-type data, computing the target PDT mixed-distance for each pair by combining a numerical metric on continuous attributes with a categorical metric on nominal attributes.

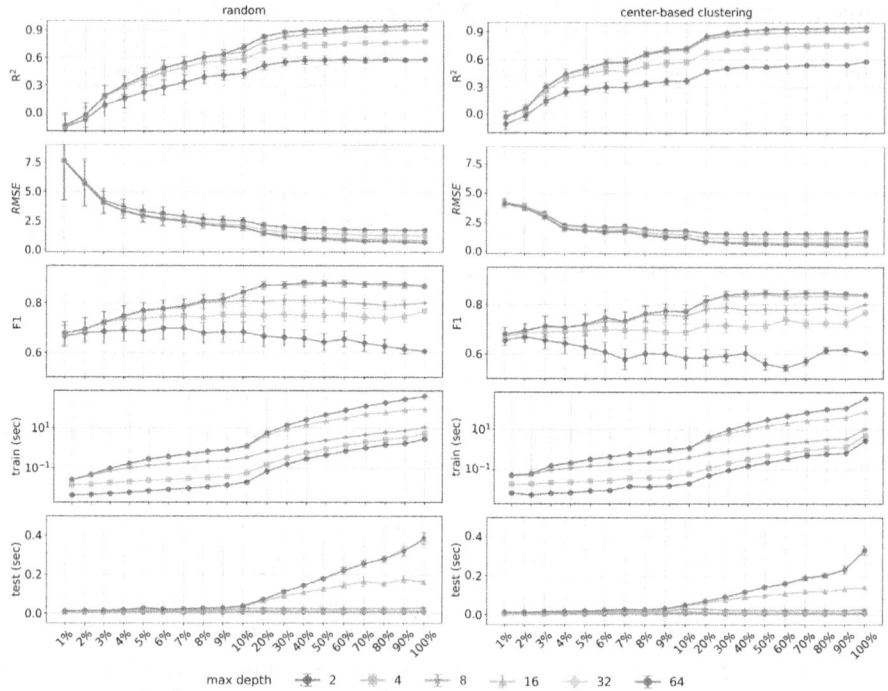

Fig. 3. Errorbars for PDT-γT with varying $\tilde{n}$ and *maxdepth* using the random and center-based clustering sampling strategies over the `small` datasets.

shows that pointwise features are preferred over concatenated ones, explaining why split constraints impact only α and γ. In the α setting, increasing split constraints degrades all metrics, suggesting a trade-off between distance approximation and interpretability. Based on these results, PDT-γT is recommended as the default configuration. This setup benefits from including both feature types, allowing the model to optimally adapt by selecting the most informative features during training. Also, PDT-T shows strong generalization and offers the highest interpretability.

Next, we studied the impact of the *maximum depth* of PDT by varying it in $\{2^i \mid i \in \mathbb{Z}, 1 \leq i \leq 6\}$, and the impact of the random sampling (RS) and center-based clustering sampling (CS) by varying $\tilde{n} \in \{n \cdot i\% \mid i \in \mathbb{Z}, 0 \leq i \leq 10\} \cup \{n \cdot 10i\% \mid i \in \mathbb{Z}, 0 \leq i \leq 10\}$, with each experiment repeated ten times to compute mean performances and standard deviations.

The results, illustrated in the errorbars[10] of Fig. 3, show that using approximately 20% of the training dataset ($\tilde{n} \approx 20\% \cdot n$) for creating the pairwise training set leads to a performance plateau for both R^2, $RMSE$, and F1, regardless of the sampling strategy, except for the smallest tree depth. In this case, F1 slightly

---

[10] For the sake of comprehensibility we reduced the std to 0.5 of its value.

Table 4. Mean and std.dev of weighted F1-score, Accuracy, Training Time, and Prediction Time expressed in seconds over all datasets. The best and second best are highlighted in bold and italics, respectively, by column.

	model	d	F1-score	Accuracy	Train Time	Pred Time
small	KNN	EUC	**.868 ± .118**	**.877 ± .099**	**0.0001 ± 0.0**	**0.0001 ± 0.0**
		PDT$_8$	.790 ± .130	.799 ± .117	0.471 ± 0.446	0.016 ± 0.015
		PDT$_{16}$	.838 ± .098	.842 ± .091	3.040 ± 2.640	0.051 ± 0.045
		PDL	*.845 ± .096*	*.863 ± .078*	0.344 ± 0.657	39.30 ± 69.99
	PT	EUC	.828 ± .126	.840 ± .108	0.067 ± 0.032	*0.002 ± 0.000*
		PDT$_8$	.814 ± .091	.821 ± .084	9.380 ± 7.510	0.063 ± 0.040
		PDT$_{16}$	.819 ± .091	.825 ± .008	16.780 ± 14.46	0.115 ± 0.077
	εBALL	EUC	.833 ± .009	.842 ± .008	*0.01 ± 0.005*	0.041 ± 0.027
		PDT$_8$	.673 ± .204	.710 ± .162	0.665 ± 0.608	0.232 ± 0.150
		PDT$_{16}$	.691 ± .149	.730 ± .125	1.206 ± 1.257	0.545 ± 0.508
large	KNN	EUC	**.753 ± .124**	**.756 ± .125**	**0.0001 ± 0.0**	**0.002 ± 0.0**
		PDT$_8$	.597 ± .119	.608 ± .118	3.860 ± 2.030	0.232 ± 0.089
		PDT$_{16}$	.670 ± .112	.677 ± .113	31.470 ± 16.220	0.546 ± 0.140
	PT	EUC	.704 ± .124	.715 ± .122	1.444 ± 1.453	*0.005 ± 0.0*
		PDT$_8$	*.713 ± .128*	*.719 ± .127*	445.37 ± 450.76	0.654 ± 0.197
		PDT$_{16}$	.713 ± .132	.718 ± .131	841.45 ± 742.11	1.400 ± 0.261
	εBALL	EUC	.709 ± .137	.717 ± .134	*0.231 ± 0.286*	0.03 ± 0.019
		PDT$_8$	.467 ± .170	.537 ± .117	20.322 ± 7.372	2.571 ± 1.321
		PDT$_{16}$	.606 ± .123	.631 ± .105	39.544 ± 12.632	10.691 ± 6.313

decreases as more data is used. Higher tree depths generally reduce performance variability. While random and center-based sampling strategies yield similar R^2 and $RMSE$ values, random sampling results in better overall F1 when integrated with KNN. Increasing tree depth beyond 16 does not provide significant performance gains, making $maxdepth = 16$ a good trade-off between performance and interpretability. A shallower tree with $maxdepth = 8$ maintains similar regression performance with minimal weighted F1-score loss. Training and prediction times increase with larger datasets and deeper trees, but trees with depth 16 are faster than those with depths of 32 or 64, and depth 8 is the fastest. Based on these findings, we recommend the PDT-γT variant with $\tilde{n} \approx 20\%n$ and $maxdepth = 16$ as the baseline configuration, providing a balanced approach to performance, efficiency, and interpretability. Reducing tree depth to 8 improves efficiency with only a slight performance trade-off.

Competitor Analysis. In Table 4 we analyze the performance of PDTF against competing methods on both the small and large datasets. Specifically, we compare the standard Euclidean distance function and PDL against two variants of PDT with maximum depths of 8 and 16 (PDT$_8$ and PDT$_{16}$), as suggested by our earlier discussion on tree depth. For a comprehensive evaluation, we adopt

Table 5. Mean and std.dev of R^2 and $RMSE$ for KNN model with PDT suggested depths on small and large datasets. Best by dataset size highlighted in bold.

	d	R^2	$RMSE$
small	PDT_8	0.764 ± 0.214	1.559 ± 1.432
	PDT_{16}	$\mathbf{0.775 \pm 0.217}$	$\mathbf{1.530 \pm 1.439}$
large	PDT_8	0.601 ± 0.307	2.642 ± 2.985
	PDT_{16}	$\mathbf{0.670 \pm 0.320}$	$\mathbf{2.455 \pm 3.023}$

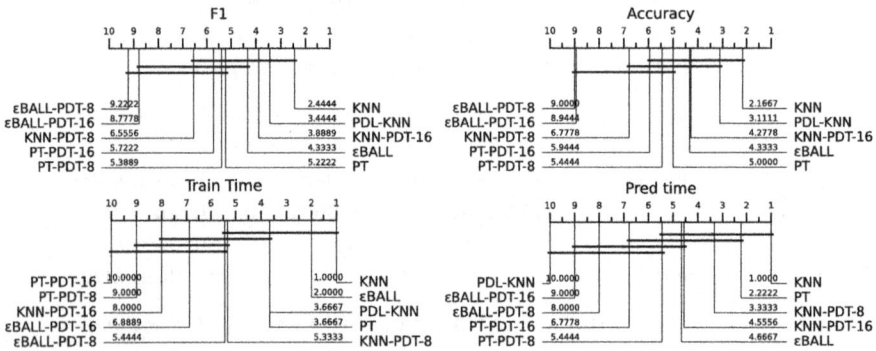

Fig. 4. Comparison of model's rank for the various evaluation measures against each other with the Nemenyi test. Groups of classifiers that are not significantly different at 95% significance level are connected. Best ranks on the right.

the aforementioned instance-based models: KNN, PT, and ϵBALL[11]. We report results for PDT variants using a fixed random subset for approximation, with $\tilde{n} \approx 20\%n$ for all datasets except spambase and compas, where $\tilde{n} \approx 5\%n$. The comparison of the ranks of all methods tested on the small datasets[12] is visually represented through the critical difference plots in Fig. 4. Methods that are statistically equivalent, according to the post-hoc Nemenyi test, are connected by black lines. Lower rank values correspond to better-performing models, with the best ranks displayed on the right (see [12] for details).

Results on the small datasets show that PDT achieves F1 and Accuracy scores comparable to its competitors, though slightly lower. However, these differences are not statistically significant, as illustrated in Fig. 4. In terms of runtime, PDT outperforms PDL significantly, both during inference and in terms of training and prediction time, while offering full interpretability. We also note that the expected runtime of PDT is lower than that of KNN at prediction time when $\log \tilde{n} < m$, but deviations from theoretical expectations are observed due to the current implementation. While we acknowledge that empirical time mea-

---

[11] The ϵBALL strategy is solely used to select memory instances based on different distance metrics, while the final classification is performed using KNN with $k = 5$.
[12] Similar results are obtained for large datasets but not reported due to lack of space.

		mean rad.	mean per.	mean area	mean conc.	mean conc. p.	area err.	worst rad.	worst per.	worst area	worst conc. p.	distance	class
	x	3.84	3.98	5.44	3.29	3.09	10.84	4.30	4.52	6.58	2.16	–	M
PDT	x_1	3.34	3.44	3.99	2.97	3.67	2.41	3.66	3.83	4.59	2.36	1.90	M
	x_2	3.02	3.07	3.49	1.68	2.52	2.12	2.96	3.08	3.43	1.94	3.63	M
	x_3	3.19	3.33	3.60	2.93	3.49	1.69	2.97	3.27	3.27	2.52	3.63	M
EUC	x_1	4.04	4.05	5.44	2.76	2.84	10.48	2.56	2.54	3.15	0.64	4.64	M
	x_2	3.34	3.44	3.99	2.97	3.67	2.41	3.66	3.83	4.59	2.36	8.90	M
	x_3	2.91	3.10	3.25	4.06	3.92	4.14	2.10	2.30	2.32	1.61	8.99	M

```
IF worst_perimeter_diff <= 1.48 AND worst_perimeter_diff <= 0.71
AND mean_concavity_diff <= 1.12 AND mean_area_diff > 0.45 THEN 1.91

IF worst_perimeter_diff <= 1.48 AND worst_perimeter_diff > 0.71
AND mean_concave_points_diff <= 1.48 AND mean_area_diff > 0.99 THEN 3.63
```

Fig. 5. Classification example for the instance x w.r.t 3NN using PDT and EUCLIDEAN distances. Predicted class is Malignant. PDT rules are under the table.

surements may be affected by implementation-specific factors, we have retained them as an integral component of our evaluation, since they highlight practical considerations that are essential for understanding PDTF's overall behavior. Future work will focus on improving the implementation of PDTF to better align with theoretical complexity. Additionally, PDL results for the large datasets are excluded, as even the smallest large dataset failed to produce results within a 24-h runtime, a limitation shared with PT. For the large datasets, KNN with Euclidean distance remains the best performer across all metrics. However, we note that PDT-PT with $maxdepth = 8$ outperforms PT with the standard Euclidean distance and PDT-KNN. This combination provides the dual advantage of an intelligent *pivot* selection process coupled with the use of an interpretable distance function to make the final decision. For ϵBALL, the performance of PDT always deteriorates compared to EUC. Finally, Table 5 reports the R and $RMSE$ regression metrics for PDT_8 and PDT_{16} paired with KNN. These results echo the trend from Table 4: larger datasets present a uniformly harder task than smaller ones, regardless of the model, and this increased difficulty is reflected in the regression metrics where applicable. Consequently, the drops in F1-score and Accuracy observed can be attributed to the regressor tree's reduced ability to approximate distances accurately under these more challenging conditions.

Explanatory Example. Figure 5 presents an example of KNN with $k = 3$ on the breast cancer dataset to classify cells as *Benign* or *Malignant*, using both Euclidean distance and PDT[13]. The first row displays the query instance x. The

---

[13] Due to space limitations, this example is restricted to the 10 most important features of the dataset, as shown at this sklearn link: https://tinyurl.com/breast-features.

subsequent six rows list the three nearest neighbors selected by KNN for both distance measures. The distances are shown in the penultimate column, and the classes are shown in the last column. The key advantage of PDT over Euclidean distance is that with PDT, it is possible to inspect the decision rules under the table, which logically justify the calculated distances. As shown by our experimental evaluation, the approximation error of the learned PDT is acceptably small in its traded off for a fully transparent-by-design model structure. In contrast, post-hoc explainability techniques are applied only after training and can themselves introduce artifacts into the explanation [29]. PDTF avoids these pitfalls and yields rule-based explanations that directly justify pairwise similarity decisions, rather than merely attributing feature importance to a final classification outcome. Additionally, the rule-based explanations are concise and involve only the subset of features that actually contribute to the computed distance, rather than requiring inspection of all features. Finally, while Euclidean distance is often considered intuitive, its interpretability becomes less clear as the number of features increases. For example, consider two records x and x_1 described by 10 attributes a_1 to a_{10}. Suppose their pairwise differences are: $x[a_1] - x_1[a_1] = 0.50$, $x[a_2] - x_1[a_2] = 0.54$, $x[a_3] - x_1[a_3] = 1.45$, ..., $x[a_{10}] - x_1[a_{10}] = -0.20$. The Euclidean distance in this case is the square root of the sum of all squared differences, resulting in a single value that blends together contributions from all features. While each individual difference is easy to interpret, the final distance value $\sqrt{(0.50)^2 + (0.54)^2 + \cdots + (-0.20)^2}$ does not directly reveal which attributes were most responsible for the similarity or dissimilarity between the records. This makes it difficult to extract a simple, human-understandable explanation for why x is considered close to x_1.

5 Conclusion

We have presented Pairwise Distance Tree Framework (PDTF), an interpretable meta-learning approach designed to enhance transparency in instance-based models. It replaces traditional complex distance functions with a shallow PDT regressor, which learns a mapping from instance pairs to their respective distances. By combining the strengths of Pairwise Distance Learning (PDL) and Proxy-based Similarity Learning (PSL), PDTF offers both efficient instance selection and clear, traceable decision rules. Experimental results on benchmark datasets show that PDTF strikes a strong balance between predictive performance, computational efficiency, and interpretability. It outperforms traditional methods, especially when intelligent sampling is used, reducing training time without compromising accuracy. Enforcing forced split constraints further enhances interpretability, though it may slightly impact performance. PDTF is highly customizable, with adjustable PDT depth, making it adaptable to different applications. Future work will focus on jointly optimizing distance metrics and instance selection, and on evaluating the method's robustness in zero-shot classification. We also plan to extend PDTF to other modalities, such as images and time series, by leveraging inherently interpretable features. Doing so presents its own challenges and will require a dedicated study, since feature interpretability in these domains remains sparsely addressed. We also plan to optimize the PDTF implementation to bridge the gap between empirical computational times and theoretical expectations. Finally, we would like to conduct an extrinsic interpretability evaluation of PDTF usage through a human decision-making task driven by its explanations. Overall, PDTF lays the foundation for developing transparent and efficient instance-based models across diverse domains.

Acknowledgment. This work has been partially supported by the Italian Project Fondo Italiano per la Scienza FIS00001966 "MIMOSA", by the European Community Horizon 2020 programme under the funding schemes ERC-2018-ADG G.A. 834756 "XAI", G.A. 101070212 "FINDHR", G.A. 101120763 "TANGO", by the European Commission under the NextGeneration EU programme – National Recovery and Resilience Plan (Piano Nazionale di Ripresa e Resilienza, PNRR) Project: "SoBigData.it – Strengthening the Italian RI for Social Mining and Big Data Analytics" – Prot. IR0000013 – Av. n. 3264 del 28/12/2021, and M4C2 - Investimento 1.3, Partenariato Esteso PE00000013 - "FAIR" - Future Artificial Intelligence Research" - Spoke 1 "Human-centered AI".

Disclosure of Interests. The authors have no competing interests to declare that are relevant to the content of this article.

References

1. Aha, D.W.: The omnipresence of case-based reasoning in science and application. Knowl. Based Syst. **11**(5–6), 261–273 (1998)
2. Belaid, M.K., et al.: Pairwise difference learning for classification. In: DS, Part II. LNCS, vol. 15244, pp. 284–299. Springer (2024)
3. Bichindaritz, I., Marling, C.: Case-based reasoning in the health sciences: What's next? Artif. Intell. Medicine **36**(2), 127–135 (2006)
4. Bien, J., Tibshirani, R.: Hierarchical clustering with prototypes via minimax linkage. J. Amer. Statist. Assoc. **106**(495), 1075–1084 (2011)
5. Bien, J., Tibshirani, R.: Prototype selection for interpretable classification (2011)
6. Bischl, B., et al.: OpenML benchmarking suites. In: NeurIPS (2021)
7. Breiman, L., et al.: Classification and Regression Trees. Routledge (2017)
8. Cascione, A., et al.: Data-agnostic pivotal instances selection for decision-making models. In: ECML PKDD, Part I. LNCS, vol. 14941, pp. 367–386. Springer (2024)
9. Chen, Y., et al.: Benchmark of general-purpose machine learning-based quantum mechanical method AIQM1. JCP **158**(7), 074103 (2023)
10. Cherkauer, K.J., Shavlik, J.W.: Growing simpler decision trees to facilitate knowledge discovery. In: KDD, pp. 315–318. AAAI Press (1996)

11. Corbara, S., et al.: Same or different? Diff-vectors for authorship analysis. ACM Trans. Knowl. Discov. Data **18**(1), 12:1–12:36 (2024)
12. Demšar, J.: Statistical comparisons of classifiers over multiple data sets. JMLR (2006)
13. Deng, J., et al.: ArcFace: additive angular margin loss for deep face recognition, vol. 44, pp. 5962–5979 (2022)
14. Domingos, P.M.: The role of Occam's razor in knowledge discovery. Data Min. Knowl. Discov. **3**(4), 409–425 (1999)
15. Endou, T., Zhao, Q.: Generation of comprehensible decision trees through evolution of training data. In: CEC, pp. 1221–1225. IEEE (2002)
16. Fix, E., et al.: Discriminatory analysis, nonparametric discrimination (1951)
17. Freitas, A.A.: Comprehensible classification models: a position paper. SIGKDD Explor. **15**(1), 1–10 (2013)
18. Gao, X.W., Gao, A.: COVID-CBR: a deep learning architecture featuring case-based reasoning for classification of COVID-19 from chest x-ray images. In: ICMLA, pp. 1319–1324. IEEE (2021)
19. Guidotti, R., et al.: A survey of methods for explaining black box models. ACM Comput. Surv. **51**(5), 93:1–93:42 (2019)
20. Hu, J., et al.: Exploring a general convolutional neural network-based prediction model for critical casting diameter of metallic glasses. JAC **947**, 169479 (2023)
21. Hu, J., et al.: Discriminative deep metric learning for face verification in the wild. In: CVPR, pp. 1875–1882. IEEE Computer Society (2014)
22. Johnson-Laird, P.N.: Mental models and human reasoning. PNAS **107**(43), 18243–18250 (2010). https://doi.org/10.1073/pnas.1012933107
23. Kaya, M., et al.: Deep metric learning: a survey. Symmetry **11**(9), 1066 (2019)
24. Li, W., et al.: A data-driven explainable case-based reasoning approach for financial risk detection. Quant. Finance **22**(12), 2257–2274 (2022)
25. Liu, W., et al.: SphereFace: deep hypersphere embedding for face recognition. In: CVPR, pp. 6738–6746. IEEE Computer Society (2017)
26. Quinlan, J.R.: Induction of decision trees. Mach. Learn. **1**(1), 81–106 (1986)
27. Quinlan, J.R.: Programs for Machine Learning C4. 5. Elsevier (1993)
28. Rokach, L., Maimon, O.: Top-down induction of decision trees classifiers - a survey. IEEE Trans. Syst. Man Cybern. Part C **35**(4), 476–487 (2005)
29. Rudin, C.: Stop explaining black box machine learning models for high stakes decisions and use interpretable models instead. Nat. Mach. Intell. **1**(5), 206–215 (2019)
30. Sasikumar, M.: Case Based Reasoning, vol. 8 (1998)
31. Schank, R.C., Abelson, R.P.: Knowledge and memory: the real story. In: Knowledge and Memory: The Real Story, pp. 1–85. Psychology Press (2014)
32. Slade, S.: Case-based reasoning: a research paradigm. AI Mag. **12**(1), 42–55 (1991)
33. Spelke, E.: What Babies Know: Core Knowledge and Composition Volume 1, vol. 1. Oxford University Press (2022)
34. Tan, P., Steinbach, M.S., Kumar, V.: Introduction to Data Mining (2005)
35. Tynes, M., et al.: Pairwise difference regression: a machine learning meta-algorithm for improved prediction and uncertainty quantification in chemical search. J. Chem. Inf. Model. **61**(8), 3846–3857 (2021)
36. Wang, Y., King, R.D.: Extrapolation is not the same as interpolation. Mach. Learn. **113**(10), 8205–8232 (2024)
37. Wen, Y., et al.: Pairwise similarity learning is simple. In: ICCV 2023, pp. 5285–5295. IEEE (2023)

38. Wetzel, S.J., et al.: Twin neural network regression is a semi-supervised regression algorithm. Mach. Learn. Sci. Technol. **3**(4), 45007 (2022)
39. Yang, L., Jin, R.: Distance metric learning: a comprehensive survey. Michigan State Univ. **2**(2), 4 (2006)
40. Yao, X., et al.: Adaptive deep metric learning for affective image retrieval and classification. IEEE Trans. Multim. **23**, 1640–1653 (2021)

Open Access This chapter is licensed under the terms of the Creative Commons Attribution 4.0 International License (http://creativecommons.org/licenses/by/4.0/), which permits use, sharing, adaptation, distribution and reproduction in any medium or format, as long as you give appropriate credit to the original author(s) and the source, provide a link to the Creative Commons license and indicate if changes were made.

The images or other third party material in this chapter are included in the chapter's Creative Commons license, unless indicated otherwise in a credit line to the material. If material is not included in the chapter's Creative Commons license and your intended use is not permitted by statutory regulation or exceeds the permitted use, you will need to obtain permission directly from the copyright holder.

How CNNs and ViTs Perceive Similarities Between Categories

Katarzyna Filus(✉)[iD] and Joanna Domańska[iD]

Institute of Theoretical and Applied Informatics, Polish Academy of Sciences,
Bałtycka 5, 44-100 Gliwice, Poland
kfilus@iitis.pl

Abstract. Vision Transformers (ViTs) and Convolutional Neural Networks (CNNs) trained for supervised tasks are the leading networks used in practical computer vision. Despite using different techniques, they both perfect their object recognition skills. In this race, it is overall accuracy that matters at most. But is it enough? Should not we care about the correct perception of inter-class similarities? We believe we should, as similarity is a fundamental aspect of categorization and the structure of the world is highly correlated. Models should reasonably assess similarities for more nuanced perception, and we should examine it for more transparency and trust. That is why, we analyzed what state-of-the-art object recognition networks perceive as similar. We proposed a framework to visually and numerically examine and compare the perception of different trained models. We used it to answer a series of similarity-related questions based on experiments on a large population of 42 models.

Keywords: Explainability · Computer Vision · Deep Learning · Supervised Learning · Semantic Similarity

1 Introduction

Is a Poodle similar to a Husky? Are sharks and scuba divers related? Answering such questions is a standard human ability. In cognitive psychology, different concepts are named semantic units [7]. Relations between them are called semantic relations with a narrower group - semantic similarities. Goldstone and Son stated "assessments of similarity are fundamental to cognition because similarities in the world are revealing. The world is an orderly enough place that similar objects and events tend to behave (or look - our postscript) similarly" [11], while Rosch et al. noted that real-world objects exhibit highly correlational structure [31]. Also, maximum information with least cognitive effort is obtained when categories map the world structure as closely as possible allowing to optimally use the finite resources [31]. Therefore, natural correlations should be reflected by robust and accurate categorization systems [31], such as deep vision networks. For a more human-like and robust categorization, computer vision algorithms should not only differentiate objects, but also reasonably structure them, especially that visual and semantic similarities are often related [11].

Correct similarity assessment is also important for improving explainability and trust in Artificial Intelligence, as well as ongoing discussions and efforts of standardization organizations (e.g. European Telecommunications Standards Institute). Showing people that deep models perceive similarity reasonably and not that far from how they do it (expressed via human-created semantic relations), would be somehow comforting. Moreover, humans and computer vision algorithms tend to make mistakes mostly among categories they perceive similar [1,5], so models with more reasonable perception could also return more reasonable errors, which would be easier for us to understand and even accept [5]. To do this, computer vision researchers try to force networks to reflect human similarity judgments [27]. However, the current rush for new learning approaches practically ignores examination of how modern models trained in a supervised manner (without enforcement of similarity judgments) perceive the world structure, while these are dominant models in real-life vision systems. Some limited works considered this aspect for early Convolutional Neural Networks (CNNs) with Vision Transformers (ViTs) being underexplored. Therefore, only now, with heterogeneous CNN, ViT and hybrid models, we are finally able to build representative populations of networks and perform a proper examination.

Motivated by this literature deficiency and possibility, we propose the framework with a core metric - Semantic Similarity Alignment Degree (SSAD). We aim to enable systematic analysis of network similarity perception and comparisons between different networks (also with another metric: Network Similarity Alignment Degree, NSAD). The key feature of our methods is that they do not require any images, and thus offer efficiency. We performed extensive empirical analysis and delivered thorough findings for the most common vision benchmark - ImageNet and object recognition. We examined how 42 state-of-the-art networks perceive inter-class similarities and answered the questions: **(1)** Is similarity perceived by ImageNet-trained CNNs and ViTs related to semantic similarity? (Sect. 4.1); **(2)** Is there a relationship between the networks' ability to align their similarity perception to semantic similarity with their size and ImageNet accuracy? (Sect. 4.2); **(3)** Do networks perceive other semantic relations besides similarity? Which ones? (Sect. 4.3); **(4)** Do different networks share similarity perception? (Sect. 4.4). We provide our implementation to enable future research at https://github.com/kafilus/DeepNetworksSimilarity.

2 Related Work

As humans possess remarkable ability to categorize objects and assess their similarity, it also became important in computer vision [9,10,27,28]. Researchers focused on the relation between visual and semantic similarities [7] and other types of similarity [30]. They also noticed that CNN error patterns show some kind of hierarchy [1,5,17,26]. Although stimuli-based analysis [19] with templates/confusion matrices can reveal some approximate inter-class relations, it is computationally-intensive and its studies can very likely lead to blind alleys [2]. The alternative is to use class templates [8,26]. Similarity in the deep learning domain nowadays is used usually to create new learning approaches [3]. In the advanced schemes, human similarity judgments are used as a reference to align the neural representations [27]. While this is an important path, it would also be important to finally and thoroughly examine how modern networks trained on traditional class label prediction without any similarity perception enforcement perceive similarity (the purpose of our study), because works such as [27] rely on incomplete and potentially partially outdated studies on how networks perceive similarity (e.g. [1]), as they were conducted for early CNNs (homogeneous, with much lower accuracy than the current models) and ViTs remain underexplored. Moreover, attention should be put on other semantic relations than semantic similarity to better understand how networks perceive similarity. Standard lexical terms should be used to systematize the relations, because they can provide a consistent and shared vocabulary for describing similarity sources. To the best of our knowledge, no work numerically compares the similarity perception of networks with semantic similarity for such a large set of models. Because real-world objects exhibit high correlational structure, and thus semantic and visual similarities often coexist [31], it is a large literature deficiency, and a thorough analysis is vital with recent works highlighting this necessity [16,27].

3 Methods

In this section, we introduce our framework by formulating all the necessary data structures and metrics.

Semantic Similarity and Relations (Our Reference). Semantic similarity is a relation between items with a similar meaning [18], and is one of semantic relations [18]. While semantic similarity is limited to synonymy, hyponymy, and hypernymy (is-a relation, e.g. a dog is a hypernym of a Poodle, a Poodle is a hyponym of a dog), semantically related concepts can be semantically dissimilar concepts connected by any type of relation, such as **meronymy** (A is part of B), **function** (A is used to perform B), spatial relations, e.g. **proximity** (A is near B) or **containment** (A is within B) etc. To measure semantic similarity via WordNet [25] one can use methods such as path length (path) [29] or Leacock and Chodorow [20]. They are based on path lengths between concepts or information content of their least common subsumer [29]. As path similarity outperforms the majority of other measures by a large margin in terms of correlation with human judgment of semantic relatedness [18], we use it in our study. The advantages of using this and other WordNet-based measures as a similarity perception reference is its clear formulation, consistent similarity scores due to derivation from a fixed and comprehensive lexical database. Also, compared to human judgments it does not require large-scale polls, already covers more than 150k concepts and was created via objective and systematic approach to defining word relationships. By computing the pair-wise similarities between all WordNet nodes in ImageNet-1k (classes), we obtain the **WordNet Class Similarity Matrix (WNCSM)**. This matrix is used in our analysis as a semantic similarity perception reference. See its visualization in Fig. 1.

Network Class Similarity Matrix. is computed based on the similarity of weights in the final classifier of a deep learning model [8,10,26,28]. It is an image-free alternative to using confusion matrices/extracted features to approximate similarity. Each neuron c of the classification layer corresponds to one of the considered classes. Weights connecting

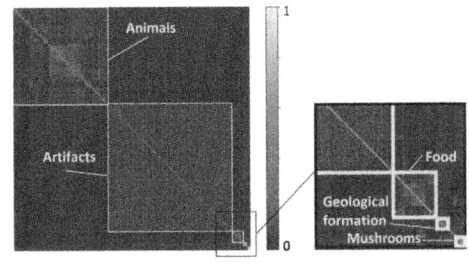

Fig. 1. WNCSM for ImageNet.

this neuron to the neurons in the penultimate layer can be treated as a class template (vector representation) of class c [26,28] (we attach a graphical representation of this method in our repository). We denote them as w_c with elements w_{ci} corresponding to the weight connecting the neuron representing the c-th class to the i-th neuron in the previous layer. The dimensionality of w_c matches the number of neurons in the penultimate layer and encapsulates the learned representation of class c in the feature space defined by this layer. To compute the similarity between templates of two classes (k and l), cosine similarity (CS) is used: $CS(k,l) = \frac{w_k^T w_l}{||w_k|| ||w_l||}$ [26,28]. Computing the similarities between all classes, results in the **Network Class Similarity Matrix (NCSM)** for each examined network (each element in the k-th row and l-th column in this matrix takes value $CS(k,l)$). It can be used for visual (structural) comparison with WordNet Class Similarity Matrix (WNCSM). It can also be utilized for numerical comparison with WNCSM (which results in **Semantic Similarity Alignment Degree - SSAD** - described in the next section). After sorting each row, it can be used to manually inspect which pairs of classes the examined network perceives as the most similar (see Table 2 with 5 most similar classes for example classes and networks). While perfectly, a few human subjects would manually evaluate the closest neighborhood of each class in the sorted Network Class Similarity Matrix to examine the similarities, such an approach is not practical as it requires the analysis of $N^2 - N$ class pairs for the dataset with N classes. As an alternative, we propose to analyze a structure we named **Closest Neighbor Pair Ranking (CNPR)**. It is generated by sorting the pairs of the closest neighbors (1st two elements of sorted CSMs) via their similarities values (from the most similar to the least similar pairs): $CNPR = \text{sort}(k,l)\,(\max_{l \neq k} CS(k,l))$. Now, we can manually analyze all or top K class pairs, which is the head of the CNPR (we use $K = 50$ in our manual experiments, which in the case of ImageNet reduces the number of pairs more than 99.9%).

Semantic and Network Similarity Alignment. Semantic Similarity Alignment Degree (SSAD) is a measure that computes to what degree the network perception of similarity and semantic similarity are related. To do this, the correlation or similarity is computed between NCSM and WNCSM. For Cosine similarity it becomes $SSAD_{Cosine} = CS(NCSM, WNCSM)$, for Spearman Correlation - $SSAD_{Spearman} = \rho(NCSM, WNCSM)$, and Kendall - $SSAD_{Kendall} = \tau(NCSM, WNCSM)$. These measures can be used to examine networks separately or to compare them (higher values imply that the network similarity perception lies closer to the semantic similarity - these perceptions are better aligned). Values of $SSAD$ can be used to examine the populations of networks, e.g. how the degree of alignment is related to the accuracy on ImageNet or network size (measured as Pearson/Spearman/Kendall correlation between accuracy/size and $SSAD_{Cosine}$, $SSAD_{Spearman}$ and $SSAD_{Kendall}$). Also, a similar measure, but taking as arguments 2 Network Class Similarity Matrices can be defined and named **Network Similarity Alignment Degree (NSAD)** to enable comparisons between networks. For Cosine similarity it becomes $NSAD_{Cosine} = \text{CS}(NCSM_1, NCSM_2)$, $NSAD_{Spearman} = \rho(NCSM_1, NCSM_2)$ for Spearman, and $NSAD_{Kendall} = \tau(NCSM_1, NCSM_2)$ for Kendall Correlation. $NCSM_1$ and $NCSM_2$ denote NCSMs of network 1 and 2 used for comparison.

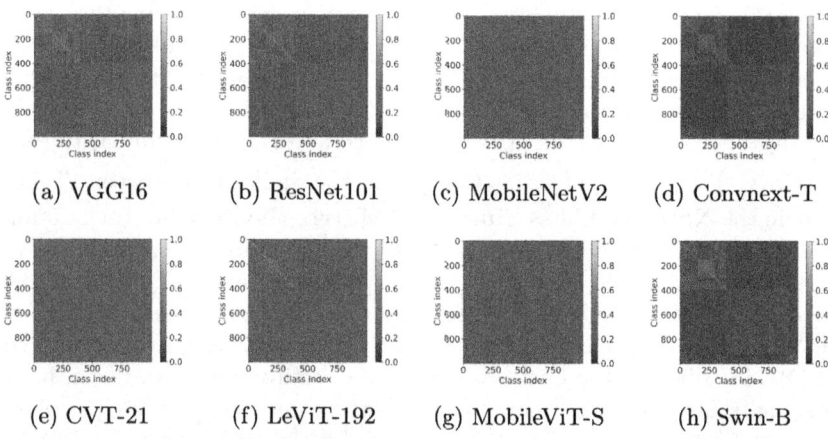

(a) VGG16 (b) ResNet101 (c) MobileNetV2 (d) Convnext-T

(e) CVT-21 (f) LeViT-192 (g) MobileViT-S (h) Swin-B

Fig. 2. Example Network Class Similarity Matrices (NCSMs). All networks perceive similarity in a similar manner, which is exhibited by NCSMs' close structure.

4 Experiments

In our experiments, we examine ImageNet-1k [32] models for object recognition due to it being the most important vision benchmark and due to the suitability of ImageNet [6] to study semantic relations, as it was created based on the semantic hierarchy of WordNet [25]. ImageNet-1K, offers a uniform categorization (leaf-level categories only) ideal for studying how vision networks represent complex information hierarchies. When it comes to the ImageNet-trained models, the last decade brought colossal changes, and we are finally able to create network populations that are diverse enough to properly examine them from the perspective of similarity perception. We build the network population (42 networks) with CNNs (24) and ViTs (18) - see all networks in Table 1. We perform the experiments listed below on PC with AMD Ryzen 7 5800X3D to awnser the questions stated in the introduction (no GPU needed) and 64 GB RAM:

1. We generate the NCSMs for all 42 networks and visually compare them with the WNCSM.
2. We compare numerically NCSMs with the WNCSM via SSAD and manually on the basis of their structure.
3. We measure the correlation (Pearson, Spearman, Kendall) between SSAD and network size and ImageNet accuracy (for the whole population and for CNNs and ViTs separately).
4. We manually search in the CNPRs for other semantic relations that cause the perceived similarity (homophony, hypernymy, hyponymy, synonymy, sister terms, meronymy, holonymy, containment, physical proximity).
5. We examine to which extent networks share similarity perception via NSAD and histograms of correlations between all NCSMs.

4.1 Is Similarity Perceived by Networks Related to Semantic Similarity?

Table 1. $SSAD_{Cosine/Spearman/Kendall}$ values sorted by $SSAD_{Cosine}$. It can be observed that smaller models generally achieve lower SSAD values than larger ones.

Position	Name	Cosine ↑	Spearman	Kendall	Position	Name	Cosine ↑	Spearman	Kendall
1	MobileViT-small [24]	0.818	0.079	0.055	22	ConvNeXt-S [23]	0.841	0.232	0.162
2	MobileViT-xx-small [24]	0.819	0.097	0.067	23	DeiT-B-patch16-224 [39]	0.842	0.184	0.127
3	MobileNetV2 [33]	0.822	0.108	0.075	24	ResNet152 [13]	0.843	0.255	0.178
4	EfficientNetV2-B1 [37]	0.833	0.19	0.132	25	Xception [4]	0.843	0.228	0.159
5	CvT-21 [40]	0.834	0.182	0.127	26	ConvNeXt-B [23]	0.844	0.275	0.192
6	EfficientNetV2-B0 [37]	0.834	0.19	0.132	27	ResNet101 [13]	0.844	0.266	0.186
7	LeViT-256 [12]	0.835	0.15	0.104	28	ResNet50 [13]	0.844	0.265	0.185
8	CvT-13 [40]	0.835	0.144	0.1	29	DenseNet201 [15]	0.845	0.265	0.186
9	DeiT-tiny-patch16-224 [39]	0.835	0.172	0.12	30	DenseNet169 [15]	0.845	0.264	0.185
10	LeViT-384 [12]	0.836	0.168	0.117	31	DenseNet121 [15]	0.846	0.267	0.187
11	ResNet152V2 [14]	0.836	0.192	0.134	32	Swinv2-B-p4-w16-256 [21]	0.846	0.243	0.169
12	InceptionV3 [36]	0.836	0.19	0.132	33	NASNetMobile [41]	0.846	0.256	0.179
13	LeViT-128 [12]	0.836	0.177	0.123	34	NASNetLarge [41]	0.846	0.258	0.181
14	InceptionResNetV2 [35]	0.836	0.181	0.126	35	Swinv2-S-p4-w16-256 [21]	0.848	0.27	0.189
15	ResNet101v2 [14]	0.837	0.195	0.136	36	Swin-S-p4-w7-224 [22]	0.849	0.284	0.199
16	LeViT-128S [12]	0.837	0.171	0.119	37	Swin-T-p4-w7-224 [22]	0.850	0.298	0.209
17	ResNet50v2 [14]	0.837	0.197	0.137	38	ConvNeXt-T [23]	0.850	0.322	0.225
18	EfficientNetV2-B2 [37]	0.837	0.213	0.148	39	Swinv2-T-p4-w16-256 [21]	0.852	0.302	0.212
19	LeViT-192 [12]	0.839	0.198	0.137	40	Swin-B-p4-w7-224 [22]	0.857	0.295	0.208
20	EfficientNetV2-B3 [37]	0.839	0.235	0.164	41	VGG16 [34]	0.857	0.371	0.262
21	DeiT-S-patch16-224 [39]	0.841	0.202	0.141	42	VGG19 [34]	0.857	0.375	0.265

Although the source of inspiration of ImageNet - WordNet - is naturally hierarchical (see Fig. 1 for the WNCSM), no information regarding the semantic similarity of classes was used during the training of the examined networks. Despite that, all 42 networks (both the CNNs and transformers) used in the analysis were able to relate classes with each other. In Fig. 2, we provide example NCSMs for 8 networks: 4 CNNs and 4 ViTs. The clearly visible block diagonal structure of all NCSMs exhibits high resemblance to the WNCSM (the Class

Similarity Matrix created with semantic similarity). This structure is weaker for the mobile models, though still visible. Models from the ConvNeXt and Swin transformer (hierarchical transformer) families build less-noisy class similarity landscape (high contrast of NCSMs). It indicates the potential superiority of these models to other ones, which exhibit a lot of outside group noise in their NCSMs.

A similar structure of the WNCSM and all NCSMs undoubtedly shows that the similarity perceived by all networks (CNNs and ViTs) is related to the semantic similarity. Let us now quantify this phenomenon by computing 3 variants of Semantic Similarity Alignment Degree (SSAD). The numerical results sorted by the increasing $SSAD_{Cosine}$ value have been presented in Table 1. We also included a larger table with the number of parameters, the most similar pairs and the ImageNet testing accuracy in Appendix B, Table 3. Although the value ranges differ significantly for different SSAD variants, the overall ordering of networks is very similar. All measures show a positive correlation between network size and semantic similarity. The lowest $SSAD$ values have been obtained for small, mobile models (Mobile-ViTs, MobileNetV2), and the highest ones for the largest (and the oldest) models with quite modest accuracy - VGGs (it may be due to their different classifier structure, consisting of a Flattening and a few Dense layers). On the other hand, although the MobileViT-S' accuracy is quite high, network's semantic relation is not as developed as the one of other networks.

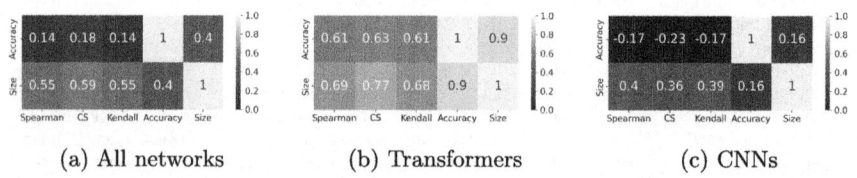

(a) All networks   (b) Transformers   (c) CNNs

Fig. 3. Spearman correlation between size and accuracy for three variants of SSAD. ViTs exhibit positive correlations between all versions of SSAD and both the accuracy and size.

The qualitative results in Table 2 visualize it. The table presents top 5 similar classes to example 4 classes from the animal, objects and a geological formation semantic groups according to example networks and WordNet. Even in the close similarity neighborhood of example classes for MobileViT-S, we obtain unrelated classes, such as ski - chain saw, sleeping bag - pencil box. Hierarchical transformers obtained high SSAD results. They are followed by ConvNeXts, ResNets, NASNets and DenseNets. Other networks - pure Transformer (DeiT) and transformer-convnet hybrids (CvT, LeViT) were placed below the aforementioned networks along with EfficientNets and ResNetsV2. It is visible that a family membership strongly impacts SSAD (e.g. see how DenseNets take places after each other in the table, and members of other families lie close to each other). Moreover, other examples in Table 2 show that the closest neighborhood of classes that are natural creations (tiger shark and Alps) largely coincides with the results returned by WordNet. WordNet similarity returns only loosely connected categories for artificial objects such as ski - lighter, while networks return rather closely related categories (not particularly semantically similar).

Table 2. 5 most similar classes to 4 examples according to WordNet and 5 networks.

Class	Similarity	1st neighbor	2nd neighbor	3rd neighbor	4th neighbor	5th neighbor
tiger shark	WordNet	hammerhead	white shark	electric ray	stingray	barracouta
	ConvnextTiny	white shark	hammerhead	dugong	scuba diver	stingray
	Swin base	white shark	hammerhead	scuba diver	stingray	dugong
	VGG16	white shark	hammerhead	dugong	stingray	sturgeon
	MobileViT-S	hammerhead	white shark	dugong	stingray	scuba diver
	ResNet101	white shark	hammerhead	scuba diver	sturgeon	stingray
ski	WordNet	lighter	pick	remote control	oil filter	pier
	convnext tiny	snowmobile	dogsled	alp	ski mask	puck
	swin base	snowmobile	dogsled	alp	bobsled	snowplow
	vgg16	snowmobile	dogsled	bobsled	alp	paddle
	MobileViT-S	snowmobile	snowplow	alp	ski mask	chain saw
	ResNet101	snowmobile	alp	ski mask	bobsled	snowplow
sleeping bag	Wordnet	mailbag	backpack	purse	plastic bag	pot
	Convnext tiny	mountain tent	quilt	pajama	punching bag	stretcher
	Swin base	mountain tent	quilt	stretcher	bath towel	studio couch
	vgg16	quilt	mountain tent	studio couch	stretcher	sweatshirt
	MobileViT-S	mountain tent	stretcher	studio couch	quilt	pencil box
	ResNet101	mountain tent	stretcher	studio couch	bath towel	punching bag
alp	WordNet	volcano	promontory	cliff	seashore	coral reef
	convnext tiny	valley	promontory	volcano	cliff	ski
	swin base	valley	promontory	cliff	volcano	mountain bike
	vgg16	valley	cliff	volcano	promontory	mountain tent
	MobileViT-S	valley	ibex	cliff	mountain bike	ski
	ResNet101	valley	ski	mountain bike	promontory	volcano

4.2 How Do Network Size and Accuracy Relate with Semantic Similarity Alignment Degree?

The relationship between the size of the model and its semantic alignment, which we noticed visually in Table 1, prompted us to investigate it numerically, as well as the relationship between SSAD and model accuracy. Figure 3 presents the Spearman correlation for SSAD and size/ImageNet accuracy. Moderate positive correlations between size and SSAD suggest that larger networks' perceive similarity closer to the semantic similarity, which supports our qualitative finding. Although it occurs for the whole population, the correlation is significantly higher

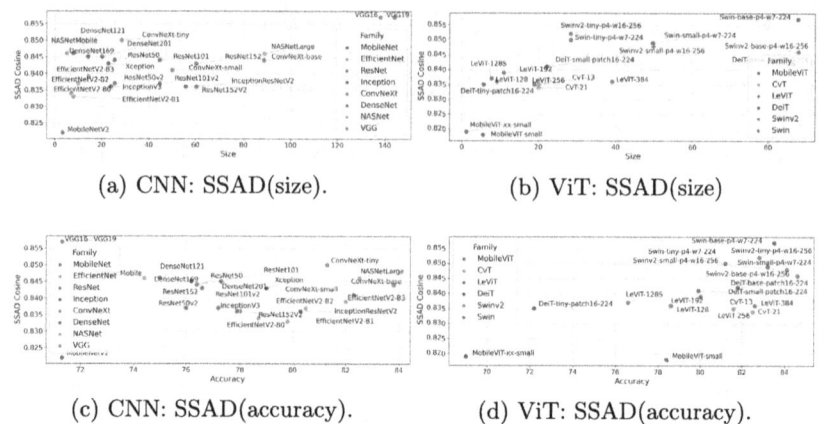

Fig. 4. SSAD and accuracy/size Scatter plots. A visible relation between ViTs' SSAD and both: accuracy and size can be noticed.

for ViTs than CNNs. These results are supported by scatter plots of SSAD(size) for CNNs and ViTs presented in Fig. 4. The scatter plots reveal a clear, positive (non-linear) relationship for ViTs, and existent, but less evident for CNNs. For the SSAD-accuracy correlation, Spearman correlation results imply a low positive correlation for all networks. By analizing the networks separately, we can see that ViTs exhibit a moderate positive correlation, while CNNs - a small negative correlation.

To analyze these correlations in more detail, we provide the scatter plots of SSAD (accuracy) in Fig. 4. It is visible that while for ViTs the positive relationship between these two can be observed, for CNNs no obvious relation exists. Moreover, by analyzing the positions of the networks in the scatter plot for ViTs, we observe that networks are not always ordered by size. This indicates that the positive relationship between accuracy and SSAD is not confounded by network size. The results indicate that not only ViTs' accuracy scales with size but also their capacity to align better with semantic similarity. Consequently, their degree of Semantic Similarity Alignment correlates with accuracy. Also, the highest $SSAD$-accuracy correlation results for $SSAD_{Cosine}$ imply its best suitability for performance analysis. In contrast, due to the fact that CNNs' accuracy is not correlated with SSAD, it suggests that it can be used as an additional criterion for the model selection. For models with the same accuracy, the model with higher SSAD can be selected, because its perceived similarities can be better explained with semantic similarities and lexical ontologies.

4.3 What Other Semantic Relations Are Perceived?

In Fig. 5 we include examples of the most similar categories to example categories from Table 2. We can notice some co-occurring (presumably often) objects in the same image, which is the most probable cause of some similarities in this table.

They are not connected to semantic similarity, but other semantic relations. In the next fragments, let us provide some concrete examples from the TOP 50 pairs of CNPRs obtained for the tested networks. For each example, we name a semantic relation that presumably resulted in the emergent similarity, having a direct impact on visual features of the image.

(a) (b) (c) (d) (e) (f)

Fig. 5. Co-occurence of concepts makes them similar/related for networks: (a) sharks are photographed with divers; (b) ibex lives in Alps; (c, d) bikes/skis are used in mountains; (e) a skier with skis and a mask; (f) a sleeping bag with a tent. All images are from the Imagenet-1k dataset.

Homophones/Partial Homophones. Our analysis of the CNPR allowed us to indicate some pairs in ImageNet that due to the same name (such words are called homophones) or almost the same name either (1) include in their training folders some incorrectly labeled images or (2) the folders' content overlap. The example of (1) includes MobileViT-S placing **tiger - tiger cat** at the 47th place in the ranking. Although tigers and tiger cats do exhibit some similarities, this very high similarity value is most probably caused by the confusion of two WordNet nodes – tiger cat (WN 3.0: 02123159-n) and Felis tigrina, tiger cat (WN 3.0: 02126465-n) – the first node is a hyponym of a domestic cat and the other one – of a wildcat. As a result of category names being homophones, some labeling issues occurred while creating the training set of ImageNet: the folder representing a domestic cat includes many tigers. The example of (2) can be Swin-Base placing **sunglasses - sunglass** at the 19th place in the ranking. While the term 'sunglasses' (WN 3.0: 04356056-n) is obvious, sunglass (WN 3.0: 04355933-n) is defined in WordNet as "lens that focuses the rays of the sun; used to start a fire" and it should definitely be separated from sunglasses, while the content of sunglass training folder has been created with sunglasses and is only a misleading duplicate of the sunglasses category.

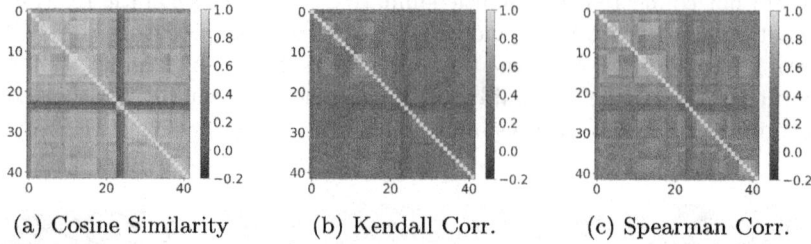

(a) Cosine Similarity   (b) Kendall Corr.   (c) Spearman Corr.

Fig. 6. Similarity/correlation (corr.) matrices computed for all NCSMs ($NSAD_{Cosine}$, $NSAD_{Kendall}$, $NSAD_{Spearman}$). Figure 7 shows that visible clusters of networks represent the models from the same family – truly similar models via architecture.

Hypernyms/Hyponyms. Although ImageNet classes are WordNet leaves, some hypernymity relations can still be found. Our analysis of the CNPRs allowed us to indicate some examples: **mushroom - agaric** placed at the 43th (DenseNet121) and **tub - bathtub** placed at the 7th (CVT-13) place in CNPR. In the case of mushroom - agaric, the definition of mushroom (WN 3.0: 07734744-n) has been extended from "fleshy body of any of numerous edible fungi" to "edible or poisonous fungi" (the training folder contains also poisonous mushrooms, such as flybanes). After extending the definition, agaric (WN 3.0: 12998815-n) becomes mushroom's hyponym. A similar example is tub - bathtub (in ImageNet, tub is just a category with bathtub and additional other tubs, such as hot tub etc.). Yet another example is **assault rifle - rifle** placed at the 35th place in the EfficientNetV2-B0's CNPR.

Synonyms. CNPRs allowed us to indicate synonyms within ImageNet classes that can be considered duplicates/redundant. Two examples are: **missile - projectile** and **laptop - notebook** placed at the 1st (by the majority of networks) and the 27th (DeiT-Tiny) places. While these terms differ slightly in WordNet, they are treated as synonyms in ImageNet: missile (WN 3.0: 03773504)/projectile (WN 3.0: 04008634-n) represent rocket explosives, while the second pair – portable computers. Some images are duplicated within the folders.

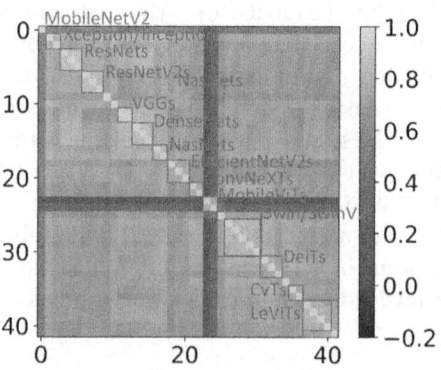

Fig. 7. $NSAD_{Cosine}$ from Fig. 6 shows that networks cluster in families (similar networks), showing the its usefulness for image-free network comparisons.

Siblings/Sister Terms. This is the broadest relation group including categories that share (1) visual/functional similarities, (2) inter-species relation (e.g. ancestor-descendant, a common ancestor), (3) within-species gender relation. We provide a few examples: (1) **cassette player - tape player** placed 11th by Xception and **barbell - dumbbell** placed 43th by ResNet101V2 in the CNPR; (2) **Indian elephant - tusker** (19th place, VGG16), **brown bear - American black bear** (43th place, ResNet50), **tiger beetle - ground beetle** (41th place, ResNet50); (3) **hen - cock** (ranked 47th in NASNet-L's CNPR).

Meronyms/Holonyms. Another relation that can be found via interpreting the results in the Closest Neighbor Pair Ranking is meronymy or holonymy. It occurs, when one concept is a physical part of another concept. A few examples that our analysis helped us to recognize are: **screen - monitor** placed at the 11th place by InceptionV3, **typewriter keyboard - space bar** placed at the 33rd place by EfficientNetV2-B1 and **breastplate - cuirass** (breastplate, WN 3.0: 03146219-n, is the front part of a cuirass, WN 3.0: 02895154-n) placed at the 29th place by MobileViT-S.

Containment. High similarity perception can occur when the containment semantic relation exists (it can be perceived as specific type of co-occurrence). It means that one concept is contained by another one (e.g. room/landscape). An example from the ResNet50's CNPR (rank 21) can be a pair **barber chair - barber shop**. The other examples are **ibex - Alps, skis/mountain bike - Alps** from top5 neighbors of example classes (Table 2, Fig. 5).

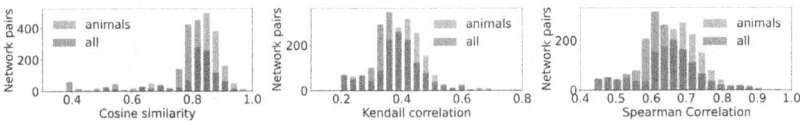

Fig. 8. Distribution of network similarities computed for the whole class space and a single domain – animals (NSAD: Network Similarity Alignment Degree with variants Cosine Similarity, Kendall and Spearman). Models are more similar in a single domain. (Color figure online)

Physical Proximity. Another reason why a network perceives concepts as similar is their frequent co-occurence (physical proximity) in the training images. The example of such a relation can be **academic gown - mortarboard** from the 41st place (Xception) in the Closest Neighbor Pair Ranking. The other ones can be **Tiger Shark - scuba diver, skis - ski mask** and **sleeping bag - mountain tent** from top5 neighbors of example classes (Table 2, Fig. 5).

4.4 Do Networks Share Similarity Perception?

In Fig. 6, we present the matrices obtained for the comparison of NCSM of all examined networks with different $NSAD$ variants ($NSAD_{Cosine}$, $NSAD_{Kendall}$, $NSAD_{Spearman}$). Each value in these matrices reflects the similarity in how a specific pair of networks perceives relationships among classes. Network similarity perception is the most similar within network families (see a block diagonal structure of the matrices). It shows the impact of architectural choices on learning class similarities. We obtained the highest differences for mobile models (MobileViTs, MobileNetV2) compared to all the other models. It manifests itself as stripes belonging to index 0 and a distinctive cross in Fig. 6. We show in Fig. 7 that $NSAD$ values **cluster the models from the same family together (thus architecturally similar models), showcasing the usefulness of our methods for image-free model comparison.**

We also present the histograms of the pair-wise similarity/correlation values ($NSAD$) between networks in Fig. 8 (red histogram). The distributions are roughly Gaussian with relatively high mean. Inspired by the clear box structure of CSMs for the animal group (visible in individual Class Similarity Matrices), we decided to compute the correlations/similarities between network CSMs and generate histograms for only these classes (we drop others, therefore we use a smaller set of class representations) and see how it impacts the distributions (Fig. 8 – green histograms). These distributions have higher central values compared to those computed based on the whole class set, indicating more homogeneous similarity perceptions among networks within the animal domain. This result **suggests that model similarity is greater within single-domain class groups than across broader, multi-domain categories.**

5 Discussion

Our analysis and the proposed tool set helped us to answer the questions defined in the Introduction. **(1) Is similarity perceived by ImageNet-trained CNNs and ViTs related to semantic similarity?** All the examined networks developed similarity perception related to semantic similarity. It is supported by their CSMs similar to those created with semantic similarity via WordNet and the numerical analysis with SSAD. Although perceived and semantic similarities are related, they are not equivalents,

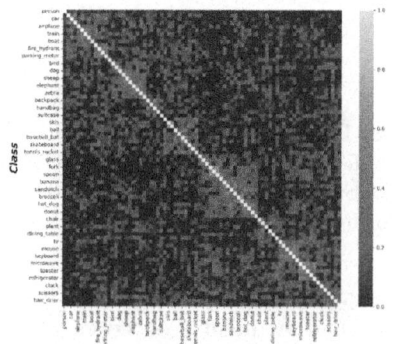

Fig. 9. CSM for COCO 2017 and DETR-ResNet50.

which suggests that network perception encompasses other semantic relations than similarity.; **(2) Is there a relationship between the networks' ability to align their similarity perception to semantic similarity with their size and ImageNet accuracy?** Network size and semantic alignment are positively correlated (stronger correlation for ViTs than for CNNs). ViTs exhibit a positive correlation between their SSAD and accuracy, while CNNs do not. This suggests that SSAD can be used as an additional criterion for model selection. At similar accuracy, a model with higher SSAD can be chosen, as its perceived similarities can be more easily explained with semantics, having a positive impact on explainability. In our future work, we will dig deeper into the differences in similarity perception of CNNs and ViTs. We will examine why attention-based models better align with semantics, explore links between representation geometry and self-attention, and test whether model size causally influences the alignment. We will also focus on evaluating the robustness of SSAD to determine the significance of its variations, as the score differences are often small.; **(3) Do networks perceive other semantic relations besides similarity?** Deep networks perceive not only the semantic similarity, but also other semantic relations, such as meronymy, containment or physical proximity. While the analysis of CNPRs is a manual effort it can improve our understanding of the causes of some developed similarities.; **(4) Do different networks share similarity perception?** Yes, the networks largely share similarity perception. It is proven by highly similar structure of their Class Similarity Matrices, high alignment of all Network CSMs with WordNet CSMs (the same reference used for all networks) and high similarities between the CSMs of different networks. The practical implication is that because this perception is not identical and because it is shared mostly within model families (therefore implicitly similar models), the network alignment can be used to compare the representational similarity of models at a category level.

Limitations: As we focused on ImageNet, it could introduce biases in class representation affecting the validity of our conclusions. While it provided a strong foundation for investigating visual representations, we also include a CSM obtained for COCO 2017 object detection in Fig. 9 to improve generalizability. We provide more CSMs for different tasks (COCO detection, segmentation), as well as for a Self-Supervised Learning (SSL) model in Appendix A. The box-diagonal structures present across all matrices (sorted via WordNet nodes) underscore that networks across various tasks and datasets align their perception with semantics, reflecting the inherent correlations of the visual world. Identifying non-similarity relations requires manual inspection, limiting scalability. We will explore how to automate it in our future work, however manual analysis still best captures their context-dependent nature. While our approach, based on the final-layer weights, offers simplicity and efficiency, other approaches to obtain representations could be used to form a more comprehensive similarity view, e.g. confusion matrices, intermediate-layer features, weights, and bias contributions could be used. A limitation can be the reliance on WordNet similarity, as its linguistically driven structure may not align with visual similarity. Also, visual similarity may sometimes be more relevant for certain tasks. However, WordNet's well-defined organization is beneficial for modeling and often aligns with visual similarities, e.g. when stemming from shared functionalities or evolution.

6 Conclusions

The framework introduced in the paper can help to better understand deep models (e.g. what they perceive similar, whether their perception aligns with semantics or with the one of other networks) and their training datasets (e.g. labeling issues, overlapping, duplicated classes). Our methods do not require any images for testing, while our insights and results can serve as a reference for future comparisons and benchmarking due to analyzing a large set of networks. As a large part of the visual and semantic similarities naturally intersect, vision networks should be able to discover such links, and they do. The degree of this alignment can be measured by the proposed metrics, and thus can be used as an additional model selection criterion. We showed that our metrics enable image-free comparison of different networks, as they cluster models from the same family (architecturally similar) together, which is important for the growing area of model representational similarity comparisons [19].

Disclosure of Interests. The authors have no competing interests to declare that are relevant to the content of this article.

A Generalizability of the Findings Other Networks

We show CSMs for 3 networks trained on COCO 2017[1] (80 classes, object detection, semantic segmentation) in Fig. 10. We also provide a CSM for a Self-Supervised Learning (SSL) model (DINOv2[2]) in Fig. 11 for the mini-ImageNet [38] templates. All matrices show a characteristic box-diagonal structure. The boxes for COCO include classes related via semantic relations, such as the membership to one basic-level category (e.g. animals for dog, sheep etc.) or physical proximity (e.g. forks or bananas can be both often found in a kitchen).

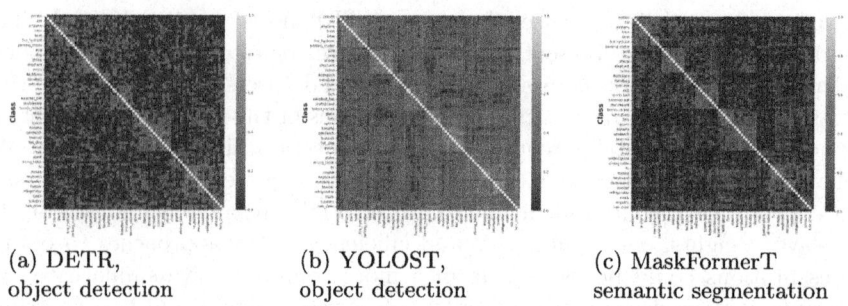

(a) DETR, object detection

(b) YOLOST, object detection

(c) MaskFormerT semantic segmentation

Fig. 10. Class Similarity Matrices generated for COCO 2017 models. (a) DETR, object detection (DETR (End-to-End Object Detection) - HuggingFace model card.), (b) YOLOST, object detection (YOLOS (tiny-sized) - HuggingFace model card.), (c) MaskFormerT semantic segmentation (MaskFormer - HuggingFace model card.)

---

[1] COCO 2017 dataset.
[2] DINOv2 - HuggingFace model card.

B ImageNet Additions

In Table 3, we extend Table 1 with the number of model parameters and ImageNet accuracy. We can see that ImageNet accuracy and network size increase with larger SSAD values. For each network, we also provide the pair of classes perceived as the most similar. Most networks perceive the projectile-missile pair as the most similar classes (connected semantically via a synonymity relation). 3 out of 4 LeViTs perceive the jaguar-leopard pair as the most similar, suggesting that the membership to a given network family also impacts what pair is perceived as the most similar. Besides a few networks returning different classes than missile-projectile, all pairs show highly semantically related concepts (bathtub-tub, husky-Eskimo dog).

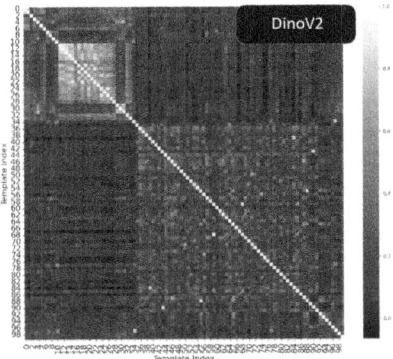

Fig. 11. DINOv2's CSM.

Table 3. Models with SSAD, ImageNet accuracy (Acc.) and parameters (Params.).

	Name	Params.	Acc.	Most similar pair	Cosine	Spearman	Kendall
1	MobileViT-small [24]	5.6M	78.4 [24]	projectile - missile	0.818	0.079	0.055
2	MobileViT-xx-small [24]	1.2M	69 [24]	projectile - missile	0.819	0.097	0.067
3	MobileNetV2 [33]	3.5M	71.3[a]	projectile - missile	0.822	0.108	0.075
4	EfficientNetV2-B1 [37]	8.2M	79.8[a]	projectile - missile	0.833	0.19	0.132
5	CvT-21 [40]	20M	82.5 [40]	projectile - missile	0.834	0.182	0.127
6	EfficientNetV2-B0 [37]	7.2M	78.7[a]	missile - projectile	0.834	0.19	0.132
7	LeViT-256 [12]	18.9M	81.6 [12]	leopard - jaguar	0.835	0.15	0.104
8	CvT-13 [40]	20M	81.6 [40]	projectile - missile	0.835	0.144	0.1
9	DeiT-tiny-patch16-224 [39]	5.7M	72.2[b]	projectile - missile	0.835	0.172	0.12
10	LeViT-384 [12]	39.1M	82.6 [12]	leopard - jaguar	0.836	0.168	0.117
11	ResNet152V2 [14]	60.4M	78[a]	missile - projectile	0.836	0.192	0.134
12	InceptionV3 [36]	23.9M	77.9[a]	missile - projectile	0.836	0.19	0.132
13	LeViT-128 [12]	9.2M	78.6 [12]	leopard - jaguar	0.836	0.177	0.123
14	InceptionResNetV2 [35]	55.9M	80.3[a]	missile - projectile	0.836	0.181	0.126
15	ResNet101v2 [14]	44.7M	77.2[a]	projectile - missile	0.837	0.195	0.136
16	LeViT-128S [12]	7.8M	76.6 [12]	tub - bathtub	0.837	0.171	0.119

(*continued*)

Table 3. (*continued*)

	Name	Params.	Acc.	Most similar pair	Cosine	Spearman	Kendall
17	ResNet50v2 [14]	25.6M	76[a]	missile - projectile	0.837	0.197	0.137
18	EfficientNetV2-B2 [37]	10.2M	80.5[a]	missile - projectile	0.837	0.213	0.148
19	LeViT-192 [12]	11M	80 [12]	jaguar - leopard	0.839	0.198	0.137
20	EfficientNetV2-B3 [37]	14.5M	82[a]	projectile - missile	0.839	0.235	0.164
21	DeiT-small-patch16-224 [39]	22.1M	79.9[b]	missile - projectile	0.841	0.202	0.141
22	ConvNeXt-small [23]	50.2M	82.3[a]	projectile - missile	0.841	0.232	0.162
23	DeiT-base-patch16-224 [39]	86.6M	81.8 [b]	missile - projectile	0.842	0.184	0.127
24	ResNet152 [13]	60.4M	76.6[a]	projectile - missile	0.843	0.255	0.178
25	Xception [4]	22.9M	79[a]	missile - projectile	0.843	0.228	0.159
26	ConvNeXt-base [23]	88.6M	83.8 [23]	projectile - missile	0.844	0.275	0.192
27	ResNet101 [13]	44.7M	76.4[a]	missile - projectile	0.844	0.266	0.186
28	ResNet50 [13]	25.6M	74.9[a]	missile - projectile	0.844	0.265	0.185
29	DenseNet201 [15]	20.2M	77.3[a]	projectile - missile	0.845	0.265	0.186
30	DenseNet169 [15]	14.3M	76.2[a]	projectile - missile	0.845	0.264	0.185
31	DenseNet121 [15]	8.1M	75 [a]	projectile - missile	0.846	0.267	0.187
32	Swinv2-base-p4-w16-256 [21]	87.9M	84.6 [22]	missile - projectile	0.846	0.243	0.169
33	NASNetMobile [41]	5.3M	74.4[a]	missile - projectile	0.846	0.256	0.179
34	NASNetLarge [41]	88.9M	82.5[a]	missile - projectile	0.846	0.258	0.181
35	Swinv2-small-p4-w16-256 [21]	49.7M	84.1[c]	missile - projectile	0.848	0.27	0.189
36	Swin-small-p4-w7-224 [22]	49.6M	83.2[c]	missile - projectile	0.849	0.284	0.199
37	Swin-tiny-p4-w7-224 [22]	28.3M	81.2[c]	projectile - missile	0.85	0.298	0.209
38	ConvNeXt-tiny [23]	28.6M	81.3[a]	projectile - missile	0.85	0.322	0.225
39	Swinv2-tiny-p4-w16-256 [21]	28.3M	82.8[c]	missile - projectile	0.852	0.302	0.212
41	Swin-base-p4-w7-224 [22]	87.8M	83.5[c]	husky - eskimo dog	0.857	0.295	0.208
40	VGG16 [34]	138M	71.3[a]	projectile - missile	0.857	0.371	0.262
42	VGG19 [34]	144M	71.3[a]	missile - projectile	0.857	0.375	0.265

[a] Keras Applications.
[b] Data-efficient Image Transformer (DeIT) - HuggingFace model card.
[c] Swin Transformer - Girhub Repository.

References

1. Bilal, A., Jourabloo, A., Ye, M., Liu, X., Ren, L.: Do convolutional neural networks learn class hierarchy? IEEE Trans. Visual Comput. Graphics **24**(1), 152–162 (2017)
2. Bowers, J.S., et al.: Deep problems with neural network models of human vision. Behav. Brain Sci. **46** (2023)
3. Caron, M., et al.: Emerging properties in self-supervised vision transformers. In: International Conference on Computer Vision, pp. 9650–9660 (2021)
4. Chollet, F.: Xception: deep learning with depthwise separable convolutions. In: Conference on Computer Vision and Pattern Recognition, pp. 1251–1258 (2017)
5. Deng, J., Berg, A.C., Li, K., Fei-Fei, L.: What does classifying more than 10,000 image categories tell us? In: Daniilidis, K., Maragos, P., Paragios, N. (eds.) ECCV

2010. LNCS, vol. 6315, pp. 71–84. Springer, Heidelberg (2010). https://doi.org/10.1007/978-3-642-15555-0_6
6. Deng, J., Dong, W., Socher, R., Li, L.J., Li, K., Fei-Fei, L.: ImageNet: a large-scale hierarchical image database. In: Conference on Computer Vision and Pattern Recognition (2009)
7. Deselaers, T., Ferrari, V.: Visual and semantic similarity in imagenet. In: Conference on Computer Vision and Pattern Recognition, pp. 1777–1784 (2011)
8. Filus, K., Domanska, J.: NetSat: network saturation adversarial attack. In: IEEE International Conference on Big Data, pp. 5038–5047 (2023)
9. Filus, K., Domańska, J.: Extracting coarse-grained classifiers from large convolutional neural networks. Eng. Appl. Artif. Intell. **138**, 109377 (2024)
10. Filus, K., Domańska, J.: Similarity-driven adversarial testing of neural networks. Knowl.-Based Syst., 112621 (2024)
11. Goldstone, R.L., Son, J.Y.: Similarity. Oxford University Press (2012)
12. Graham, B., et al.: LeViT: a vision transformer in convnet's clothing for faster inference. In: International Conference on Computer Vision, pp. 12259–12269 (2021)
13. He, K., Zhang, X., Ren, S., Sun, J.: Deep residual learning for image recognition. In: Conference on Computer Vision and Pattern Recognition, pp. 770–778 (2016)
14. He, K., Zhang, X., Ren, S., Sun, J.: Identity mappings in deep residual networks. In: Leibe, B., Matas, J., Sebe, N., Welling, M. (eds.) ECCV 2016. LNCS, vol. 9908, pp. 630–645. Springer, Cham (2016). https://doi.org/10.1007/978-3-319-46493-0_38
15. Huang, G., Liu, Z., Van Der Maaten, L., Weinberger, K.Q.: Densely connected convolutional networks. In: Conference on Computer Vision and Pattern Recognition, pp. 4700–4708 (2017)
16. Huang, T., Zhen, Z., Liu, J.: Semantic relatedness emerges in deep convolutional neural networks designed for object recognition. Front. Comput. Neurosci. **15**, 625804 (2021)
17. Jere, M., Rossi, L., Hitaj, B., Ciocarlie, G., Boracchi, G., Koushanfar, F.: Scratch that! An evolution-based adversarial attack against neural networks. arXiv preprint arXiv:1912.02316 (2019)
18. Kolb, P.: Experiments on the difference between semantic similarity and relatedness. In: Nordic Conference of Computational Linguistics, pp. 81–88 (2009)
19. Kornblith, S., Norouzi, M., Lee, H., Hinton, G.: Similarity of neural network representations revisited. In: International Conference on Machine Learning (2019)
20. Leacock, C., Chodorow, M.: Combining local context and wordnet similarity for word sense identification. WordNet Electron. Lexical Database **49**(2) (1998)
21. Liu, Z., et al.: Swin transformer V2: scaling up capacity and resolution. In: Conference on Computer Vision and Pattern Recognition, pp. 12009–12019 (2022)
22. Liu, Z., et al.: Swin transformer: hierarchical vision transformer using shifted windows. In: Conference on Computer Vision and Pattern Recognition, pp. 10012–10022 (2021)
23. Liu, Z., Mao, H., Wu, C.Y., Feichtenhofer, C., Darrell, T., Xie, S.: A convnet for the 2020s. In: Conference on Computer Vision and Pattern Recognition, pp. 11976–11986 (2022)
24. Mehta, S., Rastegari, M.: MobileViT: light-weight, general-purpose, and mobile-friendly vision transformer. In: International Conference on Learning Representations (2022)
25. Miller, G.A.: WordNet: An Electronic Lexical Database. MIT Press (1998)

26. Mopuri, K.R., Shaj, V., Babu, R.V.: Adversarial fooling beyond "flipping the label". In: Conference on Computer Vision and Pattern Recognition Workshops (2020)
27. Muttenthaler, L., et al.: Improving neural network representations using human similarity judgments. Adv. Neural Inf. Process. Syst. **36** (2024)
28. Nayak, G.K., Mopuri, K.R., Shaj, V., Radhakrishnan, V.B., Chakraborty, A.: Zero-shot knowledge distillation in deep networks. In: International Conference on Machine Learning, pp. 4743–4751 (2019)
29. Pedersen, T., Patwardhan, S., Michelizzi, J., et al.: WordNet:: similarity-measuring the relatedness of concepts. (2004)
30. Roads, B.D., Love, B.C.: Enriching imagenet with human similarity judgments and psychological embeddings. In: Conference on Computer Vision and Pattern Recognition, pp. 3547–3557 (2021)
31. Rosch, E., Lloyd, B.B.: Cognition and categorization (1978)
32. Russakovsky, O., Bernstein, M., et al.: ImageNet large scale visual recognition challenge. Int. J. Comput. Vision **115**, 211–252 (2015)
33. Sandler, M., Howard, A., Zhu, M., Zhmoginov, A., Chen, L.C.: MobilenetV2: Inverted residuals and linear bottlenecks. In: Conference on Computer Vision and Pattern Recognition, pp. 4510–4520 (2018)
34. Simonyan, K., Zisserman, A.: Very deep convolutional networks for large-scale image recognition. arXiv preprint arXiv:1409.1556 (2014)
35. Szegedy, C., Ioffe, S., Vanhoucke, V., Alemi, A.: Inception-V4, inception-resnet and the impact of residual connections on learning. In: AAAI Conference on Artificial Intelligence, vol. 31 (2017)
36. Szegedy, C., Vanhoucke, V., Ioffe, S., Shlens, J., Wojna, Z.: Rethinking the inception architecture for computer vision. In: Conference on Computer Vision and Pattern Recognition, pp. 2818–2826 (2016)
37. Tan, M., Le, Q.: Efficientnetv2: smaller models and faster training. In: International Conference on Machine Learning, pp. 10096–10106 (2021)
38. Vinyals, O., Blundell, C., Lillicrap, T., Wierstra, D., et al.: Matching networks for one shot learning. Adv. Neural Inf. Process. Syst. **29** (2016)
39. Wu, B., et al.: Visual transformers: token-based image representation and processing for computer vision. arXiv preprint arXiv:2006.03677 (2020)
40. Wu, H., et al.: CVT: Introducing convolutions to vision transformers. In: International Conference on Computer Vision, pp. 22–31 (2021)
41. Zoph, B., Vasudevan, V., Shlens, J., Le, Q.V.: Learning transferable architectures for scalable image recognition. In: Conference on Computer Vision and Pattern Recognition, pp. 8697–8710 (2018)

FACEGroup: Feasible and Actionable Counterfactual Explanations for Group Fairness

Christos Fragkathoulas[1,2(✉)], Vasiliki Papanikou[1,2], Evaggelia Pitoura[1,2], and Evimaria Terzi[2,3]

[1] University of Ioannina, Ioannina, Greece
pitoura@uoi.gr
[2] Archimedes, Athena Research Center, Marousi, Greece
{ch.fragkathoulas,v.papanikou}@athenarc.gr
[3] Boston University, Boston, USA
evimaria@bu.edu

Abstract. Counterfactual explanations assess unfairness by revealing how inputs must change to achieve a desired outcome. This paper introduces the first graph-based framework for generating group counterfactual explanations to audit group fairness, a key aspect of trustworthy machine learning. Our framework, FACEGroup (Feasible and Actionable Counterfactual Explanations for Group Fairness), models real-world feasibility constraints, identifies subgroups with similar counterfactuals, and captures key trade-offs in counterfactual generation, distinguishing it from existing methods. To evaluate fairness, we introduce novel metrics for both group and subgroup level analysis that explicitly account for these trade-offs. Experiments on benchmark datasets show that FACEGroup effectively generates feasible group counterfactuals while accounting for trade-offs, and that our metrics capture and quantify fairness disparities.

Keywords: explanations · fairness · XAI · counterfactuals

1 Introduction

AI-driven technologies increasingly shape critical decisions, making it essential to understand their underlying reasoning and evaluate their fairness. A variety of explanation methods have been proposed to enhance transparency [1,9], with counterfactual explanations (CFs) gaining prominence [34]. Individual CFs reveal how modifying specific features can alter model decisions, offering actionable insights. For example, consider a person whose loan application is rejected

---

Supplementary Information The online version contains supplementary material available at https://doi.org/10.1007/978-3-032-06078-5_3.

by a machine learning model; a CF might indicate that increasing annual income or reducing the debt-to-income ratio would lead to approval.

Prior work has primarily focused on individual counterfactual explanations (CFs) [2,4,10,16,18,25,27,29,31,33], with comparatively few studies addressing counterfactuals for groups of instances [19,20,23,28]. Group counterfactual explanations (GCFs) identify how a group of instances, often defined by shared characteristics or *protected attributes* such as sex or race, could collectively alter their features to achieve favorable outcomes. GCFs are not simply aggregations of individual CFs; rather, they reveal common patterns or barriers affecting the group as a whole, which is critical for understanding systemic disparities and informing policy or organizational decisions. Previous studies introduce group-based approaches, by identifying common patterns among individuals with favorable outcomes [28], learning global translation vectors, and scaling them for GCFs [23], or constructing decision trees via stochastic local search [19]. In contrast, our work is the first to generate GCFs using a graph-based approach that enforces feasibility, supports subgroup-level analysis, and explicitly addresses the key trade-offs involved in counterfactual generation.

FACEGroup, our approach for generating Feasible and Actionable Group Counterfactual Explanations (GCFs), generates GCFs using a density-weighted feasibility graph [27], where nodes represent data points and edges denote feasible transitions that comply with real-world constraints. To ensure plausibility, we restrict connections to allow only small feature changes between data points. A key property of this graph is that feasibility constraints, cost limitations, and density weighting naturally partition the data into weakly connected components (WCCs), effectively dividing each group into subgroups with similar feasible counterfactual explanations.

The generation of group counterfactual explanations (GCFs) inherently involves balancing several key trade-offs: the proportion of factual instances within a group that are explained by the selected set of counterfactuals (coverage), the effort or change required for group members to achieve a counterfactual (cost), and the number of unique counterfactuals generated for the group (interpretability). To address these trade-offs, we introduce two algorithmic formulations based on the feasibility graph: the cost-constrained approach, which maximizes group coverage under a cost limitation, and the coverage-constrained approach, which minimizes the maximum cost required to achieve a specified coverage level. Both formulations are supported by mixed-integer programming solutions and greedy heuristics that operate at both the group and subgroup levels. Our approach also ensures that the generated counterfactuals remain feasible and actionable.

Finally, we introduce novel fairness metrics for group counterfactuals, which enhance existing fairness measures by capturing the various trade-offs in counterfactual generation and can be applied at both group and subgroup levels. We evaluate FACEGroup on real-world datasets, showing its effectiveness in fairness auditing. Compared to existing methods, FACEGroup produces more feasible and compact counterfactuals that align with the data distribution.

The rest of this paper is structured as follows: Sect. 2 formalizes the problem, Sect. 3 presents our algorithms, Sect. 4 introduces our fairness measures, Sect. 5 details experiments, Sect. 6 discusses related work, and Sect. 7 concludes.

2 Problem Definition

Let $f : \mathbb{R}^d \to \{0,1\}$ be a binary classifier which maps instances in a d-dimensional feature space into two classes, labeled 0 and 1. Let $U \subseteq \mathbb{R}^d$ denote the input space. A model prediction on an individual instance $\mathbf{x} \in U$, called *factual*, is explained by crafting a counterfactual (CF) instance $\mathbf{x}' \in \mathbb{R}^d$ that is similar to $\mathbf{x}$ but leads to a different outcome, i.e., $f(\mathbf{x}') \neq f(\mathbf{x})$ [34]. The changes in feature values from $\mathbf{x}$ to $\mathbf{x}'$ should be feasible and comply with real-world constraints, for instance, changes to immutable features, such as race or height, should be prohibited. Formally, a counterfactual $\mathbf{x}'$ for $\mathbf{x}$ is defined as: $\mathbf{x}' = \arg\min_{\mathbf{x}'' \in \mathcal{A}_\mathbf{x}} cost(\mathbf{x}, \mathbf{x}'')$ s.t. $f(\mathbf{x}'') \neq f(\mathbf{x})$, where $cost(\mathbf{x}, \mathbf{x}'')$ is a function measuring the cost of transitioning from $\mathbf{x}$ to $\mathbf{x}'$. The *feasibility set* $\mathcal{A}_\mathbf{x}$ denotes the set of counterfactuals attainable from $\mathbf{x}$ via feasible changes.

It would be hard to trust a CF if it resulted in a combination of features that were unlike any observations the classifier has encountered before [34]. Therefore, CFs should also be coherent with the underlying data distribution. To ensure both feasibility and plausibility, we adopt a graph-based approach. Following [27], we construct a weighted directed graph $G_U = (V, E, W)$. Nodes correspond to instances in U, and an edge from node $\mathbf{x_i}$ to node $\mathbf{x_j}$ represents a feasible transition in the feature space. We call this graph *feasibility graph*. Transitions are further constrained by a cost threshold ϵ, ensuring that only small-cost feature changes are allowed. This ensures that changes between instances are both feasible and small. The weight function W is defined using a density-based approach [27] to ensure that CFs lie in dense areas of the input space and avoid outliers. Each edge in G_U is assigned a weight W_{ij}, calculated as the product of the density of the instances around the midpoint of $\mathbf{x_i}$ and $\mathbf{x_j}$ estimated using a Kernel Density Estimator (KDE) [8], and the cost between instances: $W_{ij} = KDE\left(\frac{\mathbf{x_i} + \mathbf{x_j}}{2}\right) cost(\mathbf{x_i}, \mathbf{x_j})$.

Given G_U, we now formally define the feasibility set $\mathcal{A}_\mathbf{x}$ of factual $\mathbf{x}$ as the set of instances $\mathbf{x}'$ for which there is a path in G_U from $\mathbf{x}$ to $\mathbf{x}'$, i.e., the set of instances that are reachable from $\mathbf{x}$: $\mathcal{A}_\mathbf{x} = \{\mathbf{x}' \in \mathbf{U} | \mathbf{x}'$ is reachable from $\mathbf{x}$ in $G_U\}$. These instances are the *feasible* CFs for $\mathbf{x}$.

Instead of finding a CF for a single factual $\mathbf{x}$, we are interested in providing CFs for a set $X \subseteq U$ of instances mapped to the same class. Let $X' \subseteq U$ be the set of instances mapped to the opposite class. Our goal is to identify a small subset S of X' of size k that best explains X. We limit the number of CFs to k for interpretability. To select S, we consider coverage-cost trade-offs. For a set of CFs $S \subseteq X'$, coverage is:

$$coverage(X, S) = |\{\mathbf{x} \mid \mathbf{x} \in X \text{ and } \exists\, \mathbf{x}' \in S \cap \mathcal{A}_\mathbf{x}\}|.$$

We overload the notation for *cost* to define the cost between an instance and a set, as well as between two sets:

$$cost(\mathbf{x}, S) = \min_{\mathbf{x}' \in S} cost(\mathbf{x}, \mathbf{x}'), \quad cost(X, S) = \min \max_{\mathbf{x} \in X} cost(\mathbf{x}, S).$$

The function $cost(\mathbf{x}, \mathbf{x}')$ captures the cost of transforming $\mathbf{x}$ to $\mathbf{x}'$, offering flexibility to adapt to specific problem requirements. For example, cost can be defined as the vector distance (e.g., L2 norm), the sum of edge weights along the shortest path in G_U, or simply the number of hops on this path. By emphasizing proximity in feature space and by considering dense paths, these definitions ensure that the CFs are closely aligned with the data distribution. Our approach works with any definition of cost.

A necessary condition for $\mathbf{x}'$ to be a feasible counterfactual for $\mathbf{x}$ is that both $\mathbf{x}$ and $\mathbf{x}'$ belong to the same weakly connected component (WCC) of G_U. As a result, G_U induces a partition of the set of factual instances X into m disjoint subsets $X_1, \ldots, X_m$, $m > 0$. Each subset X_i contains instances in X that belong to the same WCC of G_U and thus share a common space of feasible counterfactuals, denoted X'_i, which also reside within the same component. This partitioning of X into subgroups with distinct feasible counterfactual spaces offers a meaningful perspective for analyzing model behavior at both the group and subgroup level, highlighting regions of the input space that support similar feasible explanations.

We now provide two definitions of the FACEGroup problem. Our first definition prioritizes cost over coverage, setting a threshold on cost, and our second definition prioritizes coverage over cost, asking for a set that provides a specified coverage degree c.

Problem 1 (Cost-Constrained). Given X, X', $k \in \mathbb{N}^*$, and cost threshold $d \in \mathbb{R}_*^+$, find $S \subseteq X'$ with $|S| \leq k$ and $Q \subseteq X$ such that for every instance $\mathbf{x} \in Q$ there exist an instance $\mathbf{x}' \in S$ such that $cost(\mathbf{x}, \mathbf{x}') \leq d$ and $|Q|$ is maximized.

Problem 2 (Coverage-Constrained). Given X, X', $k \in \mathbb{N}^*$, and coverage degree c, $0 < c \leq 1$, find $S \subseteq X'$ with $|S| \leq k$ such that $coverage(X, S) \geq c|X|$ and $cost(X, S)$ is minimized.

3 Algorithms

Our approach to generating feasible CFs is based on the feasibility graph G_U. Both optimization problems are NP-hard. The cost-constrained problem can be formulated as an instance of the maximum coverage problem, while the coverage-constrained problem is similar to the classical k-center problem [32].

In the following, we present two versions for both problems: (a) a global version that generates CFs for the whole set X and (b) a local version that generates CFs per subgroup X_i. We also show how the local version can be used to generate CFs for the whole group X. A common step in both problems involves computing, for each factual $\mathbf{x}$, the candidate counterfactuals, i.e., the feasibility set $\mathcal{A}_\mathbf{x}$ and computing costs. To this end, we use Breadth-First-Search for vector costs (e.g., L2 distance) and Dijkstra's algorithm for shortest path costs, with complexities of $O(|V| + |E|)$ and $O(|V|\log|V| + |E|)$, respectively.

3.1 The Cost-Constrained FACEGroup Problem

We solve this problem using two approaches: (a) a Mixed-Integer Programming (MIP) that explicitly models constraints for each factual-counterfactual pair while optimizing coverage, and (b) a Greedy approach that iteratively selects CFs to maximize coverage.

For the MIP solution of the global version of the problem, we define two binary decision variables. Let $r_{\mathbf{xx}'} = 1$ if $\mathbf{x}'$ covers $\mathbf{x}$; and $r_{\mathbf{xx}'} = 0$, otherwise, and $u_{\mathbf{x}'} = 1$ if CF $\mathbf{x}'$ covers any instance in X, and $u_{\mathbf{x}'} = 0$ otherwise. The goal is to maximize the number of covered factual instances:

$$\max \sum_{\mathbf{x}' \in X'} \sum_{\mathbf{x} \in X} r_{\mathbf{xx}'} \quad \text{s.t.} \quad \sum_{\mathbf{x}' \in X'} u_{\mathbf{x}'} \leq k \quad (1)$$

$$\sum_{\mathbf{x}' \in X'} r_{\mathbf{xx}'} \leq 1, \forall \mathbf{x} \in X \quad (2) \quad r_{\mathbf{xx}'} \leq u_{\mathbf{x}'}, \forall \mathbf{x}' \in X', \forall \mathbf{x} \in X \quad (3),$$

$$u_\mathbf{x}, r_{\mathbf{xx}'} \in \{0,1\}, \forall \mathbf{x} \in X, \mathbf{x}' \in X'. \quad (4)$$

While constraint (1) limits the number of selected CFs to at most k, constraint (2) enforces that each factual instance $\mathbf{x}$ is assigned to at most one CF $\mathbf{x}'$. Constraint (3) guarantees that if a CF $\mathbf{x}'$ is assigned to cover a factual instance $\mathbf{x}$ ($r_{\mathbf{xx}'} = 1$) then $\mathbf{x}'$ must be selected $u_{\mathbf{x}'} = 1$, and constraint (4) defines the binary decision variables. This formulation has $O(2^{|X'|})$ complexity.

For the global Greedy version of the problem, we iteratively select counterfactuals (CFs) to maximize coverage. Let S_t be the set of counterfactuals selected at iteration t. We start with an empty set $S_0 = \emptyset$. At each iteration t, the algorithm selects the CF $\mathbf{x}' \in X'$ that

$$\mathbf{x}' = \arg\max_{\mathbf{x}'' \in X'} (coverage(X, S_{t-1}) + coverage(X, \{\mathbf{x}''\})), \quad (5)$$

updates $S_t = S_{t-1} \cup \{\mathbf{x}'\}$, and terminates when either $|S_t| = k$ or all instances in X are covered.

The worst-case complexity of this algorithm is $O(k|X|)$. Given the submodular nature of coverage, where the marginal gain of adding a new CF to the set S decreases as S grows, it adheres to the properties of submodular maximization. Consequently, the attained coverage is no worse than $(1 - \frac{1}{e})$ times the optimal maximum coverage [17].

The Greedy algorithm can also be used to provide a counterfactual explanation for a subgroup X_i by applying it only to the corresponding WCC. We can also utilize this local version to provide counterfactuals for the whole group X by applying the Greedy algorithm iteratively to all m WCC as follows. Initially, we apply a single step of the Greedy algorithm at each WCC. Then, we select the CF that provides the best coverage and apply an additional step of the algorithm to the WCC from which the CF was selected. We repeat this until the maximum number k of counterfactuals is reached or all factual instances are covered. It is easy to see that this local version provides the same result as the global one. The local Greedy selection has the same complexity as the global Greedy approach, as it follows a similar process while iterating over WCCs, either scanning all $|X'|$ candidates or evaluating coverage within each component.

3.2 The Coverage-Constrained FACEGroup Problem

To solve this problem, we employ two algorithms: a mixed-integer programming (MIP) and a Greedy 2-approximation algorithm [13]. While the Greedy algorithm provides an efficient yet approximate solution, the MIP guarantees optimal results [7], but can become computationally expensive for large graphs.

For the MIP formulation, the solution is similar to the Cost-Constrained problem with the following modifications. The objective function minimizes the maximum cost d of the farthest instance while ensuring that $coverage(X, S) \geq c|X|$. Constraints (1), (2), (3), and (4) still apply, along with:

$$\sum_{\mathbf{x}' \in X'} cost(\mathbf{x}, \mathbf{x}') r_{\mathbf{xx}'} \leq d, \ \forall \mathbf{x} \in X \quad (6), \qquad \sum_{\mathbf{x}' \in X'} \sum_{\mathbf{x} \in X} r_{\mathbf{xx}'} \geq c|X| \quad (7).$$

Constraint (6) ensures that the cost of any node to its assigned center does not exceed d, enforcing the objective function, and Constraint (7) enforces that the desired coverage percentage is achieved. For full coverage, $c = 1$, constraint (2) becomes an equality constraint, and constraint (7) is no longer needed.

For the Greedy algorithm, the process begins by arbitrarily selecting the first counterfactual $\mathbf{x}'$ and assigning all factuals $\mathbf{x}$ within a cost of r to it, where r is initially set to the maximum cost between any factual and candidate counterfactual. We then iteratively select the counterfactual that is farthest from those already chosen and assign all factuals within a cost of r to it. This process continues until we reach the predefined coverage or the number of counterfactuals k. To find the smallest value of r that satisfies the coverage requirement, we employ a binary search. The complexity of this algorithm is $O(k|X|log(d))$, since it assigns up to $|X|$ factuals for each of the k selected counterfactuals and binary search adds this logarithmic factor $log(d)$, where d is the range of costs considered.

Both the MIP and the Greedy approaches can be applied globally and locally. In the global version, we apply the algorithms on the G_U graph. In the local version, for a specific subgroup X_i of X, the algorithms are applied within the corresponding WCC of G_U.

We now describe how the local version can be used to solve the global version. Consider the case of full coverage ($c = 1$) with m WCCs ordered arbitrarily as $C_1, C_2, \ldots, C_m$. Achieving full coverage reduces to distributing k counterfactuals among these components. Since at least one counterfactual is required per WCC, the maximum allocation per WCC is at most $k - m$. First, we run MIP or Greedy within each WCC, varying k from 1 to $k - m$. Let l_i be the minimum counterfactuals needed to fully cover C_i. We start by assigning l_i to each C_i, then iteratively allocate remaining counterfactuals to the WCC with the highest cost until the total reaches k.

When $c < 1$, the task becomes more complex as we have to allocate both k and coverage c across the WCCs. Let $F(1...i, k, n)$ be the minimum cost of allocating k counterfactuals that cover a total of n factuals considering connected components $WCC_1, ..., WCC_i$, where $n = c|X|$. Similarly, let $F(i, k, n)$ represent the minimum cost of allocating k counterfactuals to cover n factuals within component WCC_i. Then, we can solve the problem with time complexity of $O(m(kn)^2)$, using dynamic programming as follows:

$$F(1...i, k, n) = \min_{1 \leq n' \leq n, 1 \leq k' \leq k} \{F(1...i-1, k-k', n-n') + F(i, k', n')\}$$

For large graphs, solving the MIP at a global level can become computationally demanding, as the number of decision variables and constraints grows exponentially with the dataset size. To improve performance, we add constraints only for instances $\mathbf{x}$ and $\mathbf{x}'$, such that $\mathbf{x}' \in A_X$, reducing unnecessary computations. For full coverage, the complexity of the global Greedy approach is $O(|X|k \log(d))$ while the complexity for the local approach is $O(m(k-m)|X_i|k \log(d))$.

4 FACEGroup for Auditing Fairness

In this section, we examine algorithmic fairness through the lens of FACEGroup. Group fairness refers to a set of principles designed to ensure that protected groups, often defined by sensitive attributes such as gender, race, or age, are treated similarly by a classifier. Broadly, group fairness can be categorized into *demographic parity*, which requires that the proportion of positive outcomes reflects representation of the group in the population, and *error-based fairness*, which focuses on equalizing classification errors, such as false negative rates, across groups [9,36].

To audit fairness for a group X, we generate group counterfactual explanations (GCFs) for relevant subsets of X. For example, we generate GCFs for the negatively classified instances of X when auditing for demographic parity, or the false negatives of X when auditing for error-based fairness. Disparities in the GCFs generated for different groups (e.g., males vs. females) can reveal potential biases in the model.

Unlike existing approaches, FACEGroup supports *multi-level* fairness auditing by partitioning each group into subgroups according to the connected components of the feasibility graph. This allows us to examine unfair behavior not only at the group level, but also at the level of subgroups, offering finer-grained insight into patterns of bias. Furthermore, to capture the *key trade-offs* in generating counterfactuals, FACEGroup provides novel fairness metrics that are parameterized by the number k of counterfactuals, the cost d, and the coverage c. Introducing the number k in the fairness metrics allows for assessing interpretability, as groups requiring fewer CFs are more interpretable, it promotes trust, as models that require fewer CFs are more transparent, and it serves in detecting disparities in CF requirements across (sub)groups, factors previously overlooked.

Burden-Based Fairness Measures. Counterfactuals provide a novel approach to measuring unfairness by evaluating both the disparities in outcomes between groups and the effort required by these groups to achieve fairness, i.e., to obtain the positive outcome. This effort, also called *burden*, is often estimated as the aggregated cost between the factuals in a group and their counterfactuals [22,31]. However, measuring burden solely at the group level may obscure disparities within subgroups, as different subpopulations may face varying degrees of difficulty in achieving favorable outcomes.

We first define the minimum k (k_0) and cost (d_0) required for full coverage ($c = 1$):

$$k_0 = \min\{k \mid \exists S, |S| \leq k, \text{coverage}(X, S) = |X|\},$$
$$d_0 = \min\{d \mid \exists S, \text{cost}(X, S) \leq d, \text{coverage}(X, S) = |X|\}.$$

Note that k_0 is lower-bounded by the number of weakly connected components ($k_0 \geq m$), and d_0 does not exceed the largest WCC diameter.

We now introduce *AUC-based fairness measures* that assess trade-offs between cost, number of counterfactuals, and coverage of (sub)groups across a range of parameter values rather at fixed points, avoiding biases from rigid parameter settings. The corresponding *saturation points* identify optimal thresholds for cost, number of counterfactuals, and coverage.

We define the set of counterfactuals $S_{k,d}$ that maximize coverage under a cost constraint d as:

$$S_{k,d} = argmax_{|S| \leq k,\, cost(X,S) \leq d} |coverage(X, S)|$$

and $kAUC(k)$ as:

$$kAUC(k) = \int_{d_{min}}^{d_{max}} \text{coverage}(X, S_{k,d})\, dd$$

that measures how efficiently a group can achieve coverage across a range of cost values for a given number of counterfactuals.

Similarly, we define $dAUC(d)$ to evaluate how coverage improves as the number of counterfactuals increases under a fixed cost constraint, and $cAUC(c)$ to quantify the effort required to reach a given coverage level by measuring the total cost over a range of counterfactual numbers. Figure 1 provides a visual representation of the AUC-based metrics.

There is also a minimum cost that provides the highest attainable coverage for k, we call it *saturation point* for k and denote it as $sp(k)$. Formally, it holds, for any $d \geq sp(k)$, $coverage(X, S_{k,d}) = coverage(X, S_{k, sp(k)})$. Similarly, we define, $sp(d)$ to determine the least number of counterfactuals needed to reach maximum coverage within a given cost constraint, and $sp(c)$ to represent the minimum

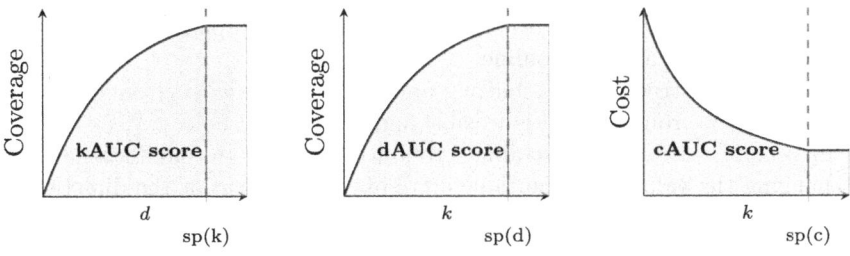

Fig. 1. AUC scores and saturation points

cost needed to achieve a desired coverage level, helping quantify the burden on different groups. Saturation points are shown in Fig. 1.

Attribution Measures. FACEGroup also provides insights into feature importance by measuring how often a feature change is required to alter an outcome. Concretely, the *attribute change frequency (ACF)* metric captures how frequently a feature A changes between a factual instance $\mathbf{x} \in X$ and its corresponding counterfactual $\mathbf{x}' \in S$:

$$ACF(X, S, A) = \frac{1}{|X|} \sum_{\mathbf{x} \in X} (1 - \delta(\mathbf{x}_A, \mathbf{x}'_A)),$$

where $\delta(\mathbf{x}_A, \mathbf{x}'_A)$ is the Kronecker delta, returning 1 if the feature remains unchanged and 0 otherwise. and $\mathbf{x}_A$ and $\mathbf{x}'_A$ represent the values of A in the factual and counterfactual instances, respectively. For each factual instance, we get the corresponding counterfactual instance with the minimum cost, i.e., $\mathbf{x}' = argmin_{\mathbf{x}'' \in S} cost(\mathbf{x}, \mathbf{x}'')$.

5 Experimental Evaluation

The goal of our experimental evaluation is twofold: (a) to demonstrate the effectiveness of FACEGroup in fairness auditing and (b) to compare FACEGroup with baseline group counterfactual methods.

For fairness auditing, we use the widely studied Adult[1] dataset for income classification. To benchmark FACEGroup with baselines, we extend evaluations to additional datasets derived from US Census surveys, AdultCA[2], AdultLA[2], and other domains including COMPAS[3], Student[4], German Credit[5], and HELOC[6]. Further details on preprocessing, parameter settings, and configurations, as well

---

[1] Adult.
[2] Adult-CA-LA Datasets.
[3] COMPAS.
[4] Student.
[5] German Credit.
[6] HELOC.

as additional experiments on other datasets, are in the supplementary material. The source code is available online[7].

First, we construct the feasibility graph G_U. An edge exists from a $\mathbf{x_i}$ to a $\mathbf{x_j}$ if the transition from $\mathbf{x_i}$ to $\mathbf{x_j}$ is feasible and within threshold ϵ. We use a small set of generic feasibility constraints prohibiting unrealistic modifications, such as changing the values of immutable attributes (e.g., race) or the directionality of others, such as decreasing the value of the age attribute. The full set of constraints used is in the supplementary material. We define groups based on the sensitive attribute *Gender*: G_0 (females) and G_1 (males).

Figure 2 depicts the impact of varying ϵ on graph connectivity metrics, showing values up to the point where nearly all instances are connected, minimizing singleton nodes. Smaller ϵ values result in sparser graphs, ensuring that connected instances are more similar, leading to more plausible, small-step transitions. Conversely, larger ϵ values create denser graphs by incorporating connections between more distant instances, allowing for larger transition steps. To balance plausibility with connectivity, we select the smallest possible ϵ that maintains a highly connected graph while minimizing singleton nodes. For the Adult dataset, we set $\epsilon = 0.4$. Further results for the selection of ϵ on the remaining datasets can be found in the supplementary material.

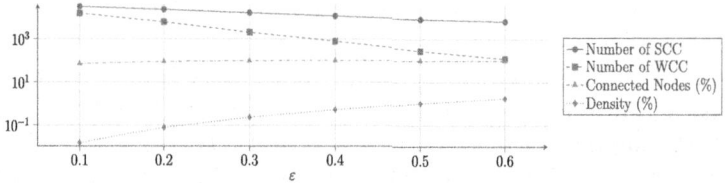

Fig. 2. Feasibility graph connectivity based on the ϵ constraint.

5.1 Auditing Fairness

In this set of experiments, we apply our algorithms to audit fairness. Without loss of generality, we focus on finding GCFs for the negatives for both groups G_0 and G_1. We use an XGBoost classifier optimized via hyperparameter tuning. We consider only the instances in G_0 and G_1 for which at least one feasible candidate CF exists and use the L_2 distance as the cost function.

Burden Analysis. A key strength of FACEGroup is its ability to uncover subgroup behaviors within the groups G_0 and G_1 through the feasibility graph G_U, which naturally partitions each group into WCCs, representing subpopulations that share feasible CF transformations. Figure 3 visualizes the distribution of factual instances (X, red) and feasible counterfactual candidates (X', blue) across the subgroups (WCCs) of each group. We observe that G_1 exhibits a more

---
[7] Project Repository.

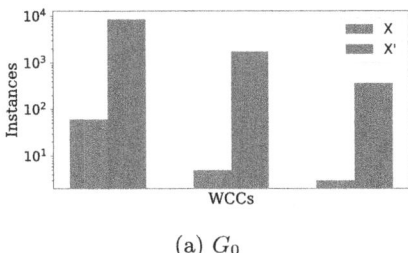 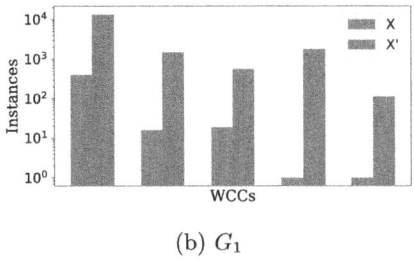

(a) G_0 (b) G_1

Fig. 3. Distribution of **X**, **X'** per WCC of the subgroups G_0 and G_1.

Table 1. k_0 and d_0 for each WCC of each group and overall for each group.

WCCs	WCC_1		WCC_2		WCC_3		WCC_4		WCC_5		Overall	
	k_0	d_0	k_0	d_0	k_0	d_0	k_0	d_0	k_0	d_0	k_0	d_0
G_0	7	0.93	1	0.74	1	0.49	–	–	–	–	9	0.93
G_1	4	1.04	3	0.61	3	0.78	1	0.46	1	0.20	12	1.04

fragmented structure, with CFs more widely spread across subgroups compared to G_0, suggesting that G_1 has a higher degree of variability in the transformations required for favorable outcomes. Table 1 depicts the minimum resources (k_0 and d_0) needed for full coverage per subgroup (WCC). G_1 requires more CFs ($k_0 = 12$) than G_0 ($k_0 = 9$) and higher minimum cost ($d_0 = 1.04$) than G_0 ($d_0 = 0.93$), suggesting greater heterogeneity in the CF pathways needed for full coverage.

Analyzing subgroups is crucial, as group-level fairness assessments can mask heavily disadvantaged subpopulations, leading to misleading conclusions about the equitable distribution of the burden. At the subgroup level, the *Black* subgroups (that correspond to WCC_1 in both groups) exhibit the highest k_0 and d_0, indicating that they face greater barriers to obtain favorable decisions. Notably, the subgroups with the most factual instances also bear the highest burden, indicating a disproportionate impact on overall group difficulty.

Table 2 reports $kAUC$, $dAUC$, $cAUC$, saturation points sp, and the minimum, or maximum values for coverage and cost, that correspond to each sp. Scores are normalized by the optimal AUC per metric. Higher $kAUC$, $dAUC$ and lower $cAUC$ are preferred.

For $kAUC$, saturation points (sp) are expected to decrease as more CFs are provided. Initially, at $k = 1$, G_1 achieves higher maximum coverage, reflecting larger available transitioning costs, enabling more instances to be efficiently covered at low k. However, as the number of CFs increases, G_0 reaches full coverage first, exhibiting better overall efficiency (higher $kAUC$) and requiring fewer resources (lower sp values) compared to G_1. For $dAUC$, saturation points should decrease as higher-cost connections are allowed. At $d = 0.1$, G_0 has a

Table 2. $kAUC$, $dAUC$, $cAUC$, and saturation points.

Parameter	Value	G_0			G_1		
		\multicolumn{6}{c}{$kAUC$ metrics}					
		$sp(k)$	Max Cov.	$kAUC$	$sp(k)$	Max Cov.	$kAUC$
k	1	1.1	63.08	0.50	1.3	65.75	0.54
	5	1.1	93.85	0.82	1.1	97.49	0.85
	9	1.1	100.0	0.90	1.1	99.09	0.89
	13	0.7	100.0	0.92	1.1	100.0	0.91
		\multicolumn{6}{c}{$dAUC$ metrics}					
		$sp(d)$	Max Cov.	$dAUC$	$sp(d)$	Max Cov.	$dAUC$
d	0.1	6	12.31	0.10	12	12.78	0.08
	0.8	10	100.0	0.89	12	99.31	0.93
	1.5	9	100.0	0.93	12	99.77	0.95
	2.2	9	100.0	0.93	12	99.77	0.95
		\multicolumn{6}{c}{$cAUC$ metrics}					
		$sp(c)$	Min Cost	$cAUC$	$sp(c)$	Min Cost	$cAUC$
c	0.25	12	0.14	0.10	20	0.12	0.11
	0.50	18	0.22	0.17	23	0.20	0.17
	0.75	22	0.28	0.25	25	0.30	0.25
	1.00	16	0.55	0.56	20	1.40	0.72

lower $sp(d)$, indicating fewer feasible low-cost available transitions, compared to G_1. As cost increases, G_0 effectively utilizes connections to reach full coverage with fewer CFs, while G_1 requires higher costs to achieve maximum comparable coverage. However, when $d \in [0.8, 1.5]$, G_1 exhibits stronger coverage efficiency gains, suggesting G_0 is more efficient at lower costs while G_1 benefits more from cost relaxations. For $cAUC$, both groups experience similar cost burdens for achieving intermediate coverage levels $0.25, 0.5$ and 0.75. However, at full coverage ($c = 1.0$), G_1 incurs significantly higher costs, as reflected in both $cAUC$ and minimum cost. The consistently higher $sp(c)$ values for G_1 suggest that more CFs are required to reach cost-efficient solutions, reinforcing a systemic disadvantage in obtaining full coverage at minimal cost while maintaining interpretability.

Attribution Analysis. To further analyze subgroup disparities, we use the ACF metric per WCC, quantifying how often specific features are altered in CFs, providing insights into the different factors driving classification decisions. Figure 4 presents the frequency of modified attributes for each WCC of G_0 and G_1, respectively, and shows that subgroup-specific variations exist in the importance of different features. For G_1, we include only the three largest WCCs, excluding those with few factual instances, as they lack representativeness.

A common trend across all WCCs in both groups is that an increase in *age* is frequently required for a favorable outcome, suggesting that the model

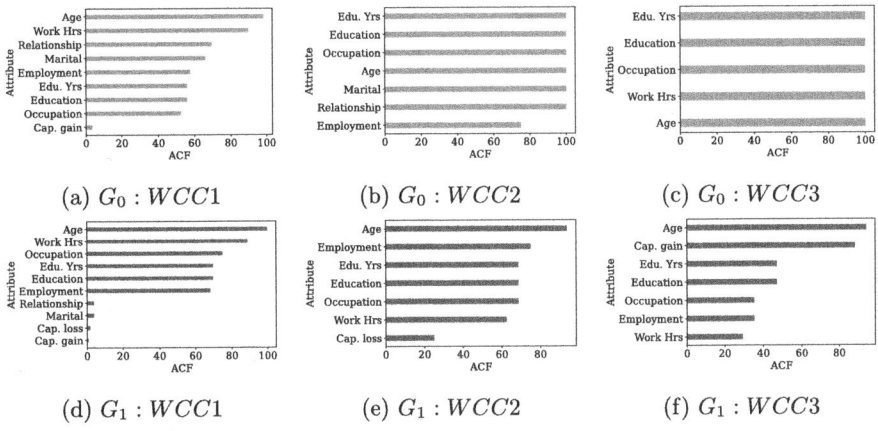

Fig. 4. ACF across the subgroups of each group

associates age with work experience or financial stability. Within G_0, the Asian-Pacific-Islander individuals (WCC_3) require fewer modifications compared to the Blacks (WCC_1) and Amer-Indian-Eskimos (WCC_2) and do not rely on *relationship status* or *marital status*, unlike the others. In G_1, despite similar CF difficulty (Table 1), financial interventions differ: Amer-Indian-Eskimos (WCC_2) require career-related changes (*employment status, occupation, education*), while Asian-Pac-Islanders (WCC_3) depend on increasing *capital gain*. More broadly, *capital gain* is largely absent from both groups of CFs except for $G_1 - WCC_3$, highlighting subgroup differences in financials to favorable outcomes. Finally, CFs in G_1 rarely modify *relationship status*, unlike in G_0, where it is frequently altered. Instead, *educational* and *occupational* factors are highly important.

5.2 Comparison with Baselines

We evaluate FACEGroup against existing CF generation methods, specifically: (a) with FACE [27], a graph-based method for individual CFs, and (b) with AReS [28] and GLOBE-CE [23], two state-of-the-art GCF approaches.

Comparison with Individual CFs. Given a group X, FACEGroup generates a small set S of k counterfactuals to cover X. To evaluate the efficiency of this approach, we compare the associated cost with the cost of generating *individual counterfactuals* for each instance in X, which serves as a lower bound on the cost when the constraint on k is relaxed. For generating individual counterfactuals, we use FACE, since it is also based on a feasibility graph. For these experiments, we generate CFs for the full population $G = G_0 \cup G_1$. We assess how closely GCFs from FACEGroup approximate the optimal costs of individual CFs from FACE. First, we apply FACEGroup to generate the set S of CFs by solving the coverage-constrained problem. Then, we apply FACE to all factuals covered by S using the same cost function. As a cost function, we use both: (a) the weighted shortest path cost in G_U (originally used in FACE), and (b) the L_2 distance.

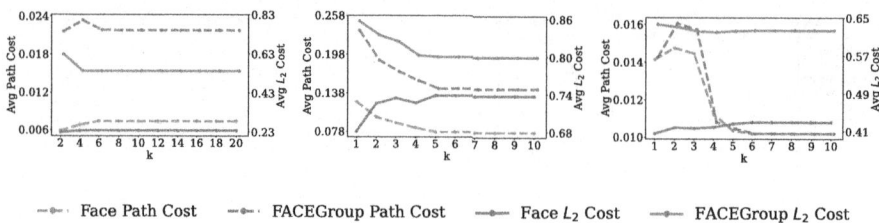

Fig. 5. Comparison of FACEGroup and FACE on average CF costs.

Figure 5 shows the cost comparison for k CFs from 1 to k_0 in 10 equal steps, with normalized costs. As expected, FACE achieves the lowest costs, while FACEGroup, which prioritizes group-level explanations, incurs slightly higher but still near-optimal costs. FACEGroup maintains near-optimal shortest path costs in datasets like `German Credit` and `HELOC`, where feasible transformations remain efficient. However, in `Adult`, costs increase due to the challenge of balancing feasibility with compact group CFs. Similar trends hold across other datasets, with full results and parameter details provided in the supplementary material.

Comparison with GCF Methods. We compare FACEGroup with two state-of-the-art GCF baselines: AReS [28] and GLOBE-CE [23]. AReS mines frequent itemsets from individuals who achieved the desired outcome, selecting a small, interpretable set of rules via a submodular objective. GLOBE-CE defines global

Table 3. Comparison with baselines.

Dataset	ϵ	FC	AReS		GLOBE-CE		FACEGroup	
			r	Cov. (%)	k	Cov. (%)	k	Cov. (%)
Adult	0.4	all	18	15.68	421	0.24	21	100
	0.4	none	18	52.26	421	84.56	10	100
AdultCA	0.7	all	20	11.36	612	11	133	100
	0.7	none	20	11.36	612	11.50	15	100
AdultLA	0.5	all	20	12.9	342	12.9	59	100
	0.5	none	20	23.11	342	22.63	13	100
Student	3.0	all	3	33.3	10	50	3	100
	3.0	none	3	75	10	66.67	2	100
COMPAS	0.3	all	20	11.85	124	20	13	100
	0.3	none	20	16.3	124	25.93	13	100
German Credit	2.9	all	4	0	18	26.32	6	100
	2.9	none	4	42.11	18	73.68	2	100
HELOC	1.4	all	11	1.98	74	1	4	100
	1.4	none	11	71.29	74	72.28	2	100

CFs as translation vectors applied to groups, scaling them across a range of values to adapt to individuals.

Both baselines without feasibility and plausibility constraints achieve at least 70% coverage. AReS generates 3 to 20 rules, while GLOBE-CE produces a significantly larger set, ranging from 10 to 612 CFs, due to the multiple scales on top of the translation vectors. Detailed results are in the supplementary material. To assess feasibility, we integrate CFs into the feasibility graph G_U and measure feasibility coverage as the proportion of CFs with at least one feasible transition. We analyze this under all feasibility constraints and a relaxed setting with only the plausibility constraint ϵ. Table 3 highlights the limitations of baselines: with full constraints, AReS and GLOBE-CE remain below 50% feasibility coverage, indicating that many CFs violate real-world constraints. In contrast, FACEGroup achieves 100% feasibility coverage with a compact CF set. Relaxing constraints improves coverage for baselines, particularly for GLOBE-CE, which benefits from its low-cost translation vectors. However, FACEGroup still maintains full feasibility coverage with fewer CFs, demonstrating its ability to generate feasible, actionable CFs without sacrificing interpretability or plausibility.

6 Related Work

Explanations have become central in machine learning research [9,14], particularly in high-stakes domains such as healthcare and education. Among various explanation methods, CFs have gained prominence for their ability to reveal actionable changes leading to a desired outcome. Wachter et al. [35] first formulated CFs as an optimization problem, minimizing the cost between an instance and its CF while ensuring a prediction change. Subsequent work [12,15,18,25,27,31,34] refined CF generation, emphasizing properties such as feasibility, actionability, sparsity [34], and robustness [16]. Several approaches optimize CF search using genetic algorithms [10,31], integer programming [30,33], and cost-based heuristics [12].

FACE [27] constructs a density-weighted feasibility graph where counterfactuals are generated via shortest paths in the graph, focusing on individual explanations that balance proximity and data manifold alignment. While FACEGroup builds on this graph structure, and further introduces three key innovations: (1) multi-level subgroup analysis, where WCCs of the feasibility graph naturally partition groups into interpretable subgroups with shared feasibility constraints, (2) GCF trade-off-aware algorithms, rather than relying on individual shortest-path searches, and (3) cost function agnosticism.

While most methods focus on individual CFs, recent work explores GCFs for multiple instances. AReS [28] defines subgroup-specific CF rules, optimizing for correctness, coverage, cost, and interpretability. GLOBE-CE [23] learns global translation vectors, applying them at different scales to generate CFs that maximize coverage. CET [19] uses decision trees for group actions to enhance transparency and consistency, while mixed-integer programming has been used to optimize collective CFs under linking constraints [5]. CounterFair [21] generates fair GCFs by selecting a subset via mixed-integer programming to balance cost and fairness. Unlike these approaches, FACEGroup enforces feasibility constraints, ensuring GCFs adhere to real-world constraints. Most group-based methods only prevent changes in sensitive attributes but lack directional constraints, leading to CFs that may violate plausible transformations. Notably, GLOBE-CE selects random feature perturbations, which can result in unrealistic CFs. In contrast to these methods, FACEGroup generates CFs at both group and subgroup levels, systematically handling the trade-offs in CF generation.

Explanations are utilized to assess algorithmic fairness [9], ensuring decisions are not influenced by protected attributes [6,11,24,26]. Several CF-based approaches have been proposed to quantify fairness by measuring the burden quantified as the difficulty individuals face in achieving a favorable outcome per group [12,20,22,28,31]. Methods like [22,31] generate individual CFs and calculate burden per group as the average sum of pairwise costs to assess fairness. PreCoF [12] distinguishes between explicit bias, when individual counterfactuals require changes only in sensitive attributes, and implicit bias, when, after removing sensitive attributes from model training, other features disproportionately influence different groups. [23,28] suggest that generated rules and global translation vectors can be used to manually audit for unfairness in subgroups of interest. FACTS [20] builds on AReS and introduces burden-based fairness metrics, but evaluates fairness only under specific settings. For instance, its Equal Cost of Effectiveness metric compares the minimum cost needed for protected subgroups to reach a fixed aggregate effectiveness level, defined as the proportion of individuals able to achieve the desired outcome via counterfactuals. In contrast, our burden-based fairness metrics assess disparities across a range of costs, coverage levels, and numbers of counterfactuals, offering a more comprehensive perspective that captures potential disparities across various combinations of these factors. Unlike the other approaches, FACEGroup introduces fairness metrics that assess fairness at both group and subgroup levels, explicitly accounting for trade-offs between cost, coverage, interpretability, and feasibility.

7 Conclusions

In this paper, we propose FACEGroup, a novel graph-based framework for group counterfactual generation that addresses limitations in existing methods by incorporating real-world feasibility constraints and managing trade-offs in counterfactual generation. We also introduce novel fairness measures that allow auditing fairness both at the group and subgroup levels, offering insights on the trade-offs between cost, the number of generated counterfactuals, and coverage. In future work, we plan to extend the use of the feasibility graph to define path-based fairness metrics. We also aim to adapt our approach to multi-class classification and regression settings.

Acknowledgment. This work has been partially supported by project MIS 5154714 of the National Recovery and Resilience Plan Greece 2.0 funded by the European Union under the NextGenerationEU Program.

References

1. Dwivedi, R., et al.: Explainable ai (xai): core ideas, techniques, and solutions. ACM Comput. Surv. **55**, 1–33 (2023)
2. Karimi, A.H., Barthe, G., Balle, B., Valera, I.: Model-agnostic counterfactual explanations for consequential decisions. In: International Conference on Artificial Intelligence and Statistics, pp. 895–905. PMLR (2020)
3. Slack, D., Hilgard, A., Lakkaraju, H., Singh, S.: Counterfactual explanations can be manipulated. Adv. Neural. Inf. Process. Syst. **34**, 62–75 (2021)
4. Bynum, L.E., Loftus, J.R., Stoyanovich, J.: Counterfactuals for the future. In: Proceedings of the AAAI Conference on Artificial Intelligence, vol. 37, pp. 14144–14152 (2023)
5. Carrizosa, E., Ramírez-Ayerbe, J., Morales, D.R.: Generating collective counterfactual explanations in score-based classification via mathematical optimization. Expert Syst. Appl. **238**, 121954 (2024)
6. Caton, S., Haas, C.: Fairness in machine learning: a survey. CSUR **56** (2024)
7. Daskin, M.: Network and discrete location: models, algorithms and applications. J. Operat. Res. Soc. **48**, 763–764 (1997)
8. Davis, R.A., Lii, K.-S., Politis, D.N.: Remarks on some nonparametric estimates of a density function. In: Selected Works of Murray Rosenblatt. SWPS, pp. 95–100. Springer, New York (2011). https://doi.org/10.1007/978-1-4419-8339-8_13
9. Fragkathoulas, C., Papanikou, V., Karidi, D.P., Pitoura, E.: On explaining unfairness: an overview. In: 2024 IEEE 40th International Conference on Data Engineering Workshops (ICDEW), pp. 226–236. IEEE (2024)
10. Fragkathoulas, C., Pitoura, E.: Ugce: user-guided incremental counterfactual exploration. arXiv preprint: arxiv: 2505.21330 (2025)
11. Friedler, S.A., Scheidegger, C., Venkatasubramanian, S.: The (im) possibility of fairness: different value systems require different mechanisms for fair decision making. Commun. ACM **64**, 136–143 (2021)
12. Goethals, S., Martens, D., Calders, T.: Precof: counterfactual explanations for fairness. Mach. Learn. **113**(5), 3111–3142 (2024)
13. Gonzalez, T.F.: Clustering to minimize the maximum intercluster distance. Theoret. Comput. Sci. **38**, 293–306 (1985)
14. Guidotti, R.: Counterfactual explanations and how to find them: literature review and benchmarking. Data Min. Knowl. Disc. **38**, 2770–2824 (2024)
15. Guidotti, R., Monreale, A., Giannotti, F., Pedreschi, D., Ruggieri, S., Turini, F.: Factual and counterfactual explanations for black box decision making. IEEE Intell. Syst. **34**, 14–23 (2019)
16. Guyomard, V., Fessant, F., Guyet, T., Bouadi, T., Termier, A.: Generating robust counterfactual explanations. In: Joint European Conference on Machine Learning and Knowledge Discovery in Databases. pp. 394–409. Springer (2023). https://doi.org/10.1007/978-3-031-43418-1_24
17. Hochba, D.S.: Approximation algorithms for np-hard problems. ACM SIGACT News **28**, 40–52 (1997)

18. Kanamori, K., Takagi, T., Kobayashi, K., Arimura, H.: Dace: distribution-aware counterfactual explanation by mixed-integer linear optimization. In: IJCAI, pp. 2855–2862 (2020)
19. Kanamori, K., Takagi, T., Kobayashi, K., Ike, Y.: Counterfactual explanation trees: Transparent and consistent actionable recourse with decision trees. In: International Conference on Artificial Intelligence and Statistics, pp. 1846–1870. PMLR (2022)
20. Kavouras, L., et al.: Fairness aware counterfactuals for subgroups. Adv. Neural. Inf. Process. Syst. **36**, 58246–58276 (2023)
21. Kuratomi, A., et al.: Counterfair: group counterfactuals for bias detection, mitigation and subgroup identification. In: 2024 IEEE International Conference on Data Mining (ICDM), pp. 181–190. IEEE (2024)
22. Kuratomi, A., Pitoura, E., Papapetrou, P., Lindgren, T., Tsaparas, P.: Measuring the burden of (un) fairness using counterfactuals. In: Joint European Conference on Machine Learning and Knowledge Discovery in Databases, pp. 402–417. Springer (2022). https://doi.org/10.1007/978-3-031-23618-1_27
23. Ley, D., Mishra, S., Magazzeni, D.: Globe-ce: a translation based approach for global counterfactual explanations. In: International Conference on Machine Learning, pp. 19315–19342. PMLR (2023)
24. Mehrabi, N., Morstatter, F., Saxena, N., Lerman, K., Galstyan, A.: A survey on bias and fairness in machine learning. ACM Comput. Surv. (CSUR) **54**, 1–35 (2021)
25. Mothilal, R.K., Sharma, A., Tan, C.: Explaining machine learning classifiers through diverse counterfactual explanations. In: Proceedings of the 2020 Conference on Fairness, Accountability, and Transparency, pp. 607–617 (2020)
26. Pitoura, E., Stefanidis, K., Koutrika, G.: Fairness in rankings and recommendations: an overview. VLDB J. 1–28 (2022)
27. Poyiadzi, R., Sokol, K., Santos-Rodriguez, R., De Bie, T., Flach, P.: Face: feasible and actionable counterfactual explanations. In: Proceedings of the AAAI/ACM Conference on AI, Ethics, and Society, pp. 344–350 (2020)
28. Rawal, K., Lakkaraju, H.: Beyond individualized recourse: interpretable and interactive summaries of actionable recourses. Adv. Neural. Inf. Process. Syst. **33**, 12187–12198 (2020)
29. Ribeiro, M.T., Singh, S., Guestrin, C.: why should i trust you? explaining the predictions of any classifier. In: Proceedings of the 22nd ACM SIGKDD International Conference on Knowledge Discovery and Data Mining, pp. 1135–1144 (2016)
30. Russell, C.: Efficient search for diverse coherent explanations. In: Proceedings of the Conference on Fairness, Accountability, and Transparency, pp. 20–28 (2019)
31. Sharma, S., Henderson, J., Ghosh, J.: Certifai: a common framework to provide explanations and analyse the fairness and robustness of black-box models. In: Proceedings of the AAAI/ACM Conference on AI, Ethics, and Society, pp. 166–172 (2020)
32. Tansel, B.C., Francis, R.L., Lowe, T.J.: State of the art—location on networks: a survey. part i: the p-center and p-median problems. Manag. Sci. **29**, 482–497 (1983)
33. Ustun, B., Spangher, A., Liu, Y.: Actionable recourse in linear classification. In: Proceedings of the Conference on Fairness, Accountability, and Transparency, pp. 10–19 (2019)
34. Verma, S., Boonsanong, V., Hoang, M., Hines, K., Dickerson, J., Shah, C.: Counterfactual explanations and algorithmic recourses for machine learning: a review. ACM Comput. Surv. **56**, 1–42 (2024)

35. Wachter, S., Mittelstadt, B., Russell, C.: Counterfactual explanations without opening the black box: automated decisions and the gdpr. Harv. JL & Tech. **31**, 841 (2017)
36. Verma, S., Rubin, J.: Fairness definitions explained. In: FairWare@ICSE (2018)
37. Ding, F., Hardt, M., Miller, J., Schmidt, L.: Retiring adult: new datasets for fair machine learning. Adv. Neural. Inf. Process. Syst. **34**, 6478–6490 (2021)
38. Talbot, J., Lin, S., Hanrahan, P.: An extension of wilkinson's algorithm for positioning tick labels on axes. IEEE Trans. Visual Comput. Graphics **16**, 1036–1043 (2010)
39. Mitchell, S., OSullivan, M., Dunning, I.: Pulp: a linear programming toolkit for python. The University of Auckland, Auckland, New Zealand **65**, 25 (2011)
40. Scott, D.W.: Multivariate density estimation: theory, practice, and visualization. John Wiley & Sons (2015)
41. Quy, T., Roy, A., Iosifidis, V., Zhang, W., Ntoutsi, E.: A survey on datasets for fairness-aware machine learning. Wiley Interdisciplinary Rev. Data Mining Knowl. Dis. **12**, e1452 (2022)

TSHAP: Fast and Exact SHAP for Explaining Time Series Classification and Regression

Thach Le Nguyen[✉] and Georgiana Ifrim

University College Dublin, Dublin, Ireland
{thach.lenguyen,georgiana.ifrim}@ucd.ie

Abstract. Attribution methods are essential for interpreting time series predictive models by quantifying the relevance of each time step for the prediction. State-of-the-art methods are often based on SHAP, an attribution method developed for tabular data. However, this has several challenges. First, SHAP is expensive to compute, especially for long time series, hence to speed it up it is usually approximated. Second, the impact of the background selection for emulating data 'missingness', essential to compute SHAP, remains understudied. Third, SHAP and more generally attribution methods for time series regression are notably lacking. In this paper, we address these limitations and propose TSHAP, a novel SHAP-based attribution method for time series classification and regression. TSHAP leverages a sliding window to group temporal data, enabling the **efficient computation of exact SHAP** values for each group. We further develop a methodology for the principled selection of background data. We evaluate TSHAP's performance and robustness using comprehensive experiments on synthetic and real-world time series datasets.

Keywords: Explainable AI · Time Series · Exact SHAP · Evaluation

1 Introduction

Attribution methods quantify the relevance of each input feature for predicting the target feature by a predictive model. The computed attributions are critical tools in Explainable Artificial Intelligence (XAI) to explain black-box models [11,12]. Time series data are numerical data measured over a time period, where each value in the time series corresponds to a time step in this period. Time series data can be extremely long (e.g., millions of time steps) and have multiple channels (multivariate time series data). Given an input time series and a predictive model, the attribution methods calculate the attribution (relevance score) for each time step in the time series using only the output of the model. The attribution signifies the relevance of that time step to the prediction of the model given the input time series (e.g., Fig. 1). These sample-specific attributions are also referred to as local attributions.

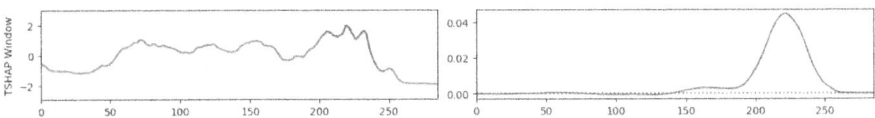

Fig. 1. Explanation of the ROCKET classifier using an attribution method. The left panel depicts a time series from the Coffee dataset of the UCR/UEA Archive, and the right panel shows the attribution profile. The attribution profile indicates the 200–250 range as the most relevant part of the time series for the classifier.

Several attribution methods have been introduced for tabular data, of which LIME [15] and SHAP [9] are the most prominent. SHAP, based on game theory, calculates the attribution as the Shapley value of each feature. The Shapley value is the contribution of the feature towards the overall payout, i.e., the prediction of the model. The exact SHAP method calculates the contribution of every possible feature coalition (i.e., subset of features), therefore is known for being computationally expensive. In addition, SHAP relies on a background dataset to emulate "missingness" in the data. When SHAP calculates the contribution of a feature coalition, it essentially substitutes the values of the missing features (features not in the coalition) with values drawn from the background dataset. In some works, the background data is also referred to as the baseline data.

While attribution methods such as LIME and SHAP can be directly applied to time series by treating each time step as an independent feature, this approach becomes computationally prohibitive for datasets with moderately long time series (e.g., length >100). Furthermore, it fails to capture the inherent sequential dependencies within the time series. To mitigate these limitations, prior research [6,13,17] has explored grouping consecutive time steps into aggregated features. For example, a long time series can be segmented, with each segment being represented by a single feature, thereby reducing the computational burden and preserving local sequential information within each segment. While this approach reduces the computational cost, it can still increase rapidly with the number of segments. Moreover, careless segmentation can inadvertently break the sequential structure of time series. Thus effective and efficient grouping of time steps for time series attribution methods is still an ongoing challenge.

Furthermore, the influence of background data on SHAP time series explanations is critical but under-researched. Common background options include all-zero (substituting feature values with zero) and real time series data. The all-zero background assumes zero represents the absence of information, or missing data, facilitating attribution calculations. When available, real data (e.g., training data) can also serve as background. While computationally efficient, the all-zero assumption is problematic in time series. We conducted an experiment using a ROCKET [4] model trained on 49 UCR and UEA [3] binary classification datasets, predicting on all-zero time series. In 42 instances, the model exhibited high confidence (probability >0.95), demonstrating that zero can be informative, contrary to the underlying assumption of absent information (which should lead to less decisive probability). Therefore, it is important to study the impact of background time series on the computed explanation and to develop robust background selection strategies.

Most work for explaining time series models focuses on time series classification (TSC), where the prediction is a discrete category [10]. Another important research area is time series extrinsic regression (TSER) [16,21]. In comparison to TSC, TSER in general and XAI for TSER are still under-explored areas. Theoretically, both LIME and SHAP-based attribution methods can be applied for time series regression as they both work for regression problems with tabular data. However, none of the previous works explored this possibility in depth for the time series domain. The main challenge is that the interpretation of a regression model is not well-formulated, and depends again on the selected background. The main contributions of this paper to address these challenges are:

- We present TSHAP, a novel SHAP-based attribution method that can be used to explain both time series classification and regression models. This method has two variants: TSHAP Window relies on a sliding window to efficiently compute exact Shapley values for each window while TSHAP ROI (Regions of Interest) uses the window attributions to find the important regions. To our best knowledge, we are the first to study attribution methods for TSER.
- We study the impact of background selection on SHAP computation and propose methods to select suitable background data for both classification and regression tasks. The methods are applicable to any SHAP-based attribution methods, and other methods that rely on background data, for time series.
- We present experiments to evaluate TSHAP on both synthetic and real datasets for TSC and TSER. We describe our evaluation methodology using a hypothetical model and ground truth attributions for the synthetic data. The results show that TSHAP can be computed more efficiently than existing methods and achieves high explanation quality (e.g., as measured using ground truth data and faithfulness measures). All our data and code is publicly available[1].

2 Background and Related Work

2.1 Background

We define a time series x as a sequence of measurements over time:

$$x = \{x_1, x_2, \ldots, x_n\} \tag{1}$$

where x_i is the measurement at time step i and n is the length of the time series. In this paper, we only consider univariate time series, hence x_i is a scalar. A predictive model f is a function that maps x to a target value o (i.e., $f(x) = o$).

---

[1] https://github.com/mlgig/tshap.

For the regression task $o \in \mathbb{R}$ is a continuous value. For the classification task, typically $o \in L$ is a label, in a finite set of labels L. However, many attribution methods use the class probability instead of the predicted label to calculate the attributions (i.e., $o \in \mathbb{R}$ and $0 \leq o \leq 1$). This allows these attribution methods to adapt seamlessly between classification and regression. An attribution method M takes a time series x and the model f as the input, and outputs the attributions:

$$M(x, f) = \{\phi_1, \phi_2, \ldots, \phi_n\} \quad (2)$$

where ϕ_i is the attribution value of x_i. In general, the attribution ϕ_i indicates how relevant x_i is to the prediction $f(x) = o$. In order to use the attributions to explain the model f, we first need to define the explanation question for the machine learning (ML) task.

Interpretation of regression attributions: For regression tasks, the authors in [8] argue that a reference value r is essential for meaningful explanations. Without it, the explanation question becomes ambiguous (e.g., *"Why is 'o' predicted?"*). Introducing r allows for a clearer question: *"Why is o predicted instead of r?"*. The reference value is user-defined and depends on the specific purpose of the explanation. In this context, a positive attribution ($\phi_i > 0$) indicates that the presence of x_i supports a prediction greater than r, while a negative attribution ($\phi_i < 0$) suggests support for a prediction less than r.

Interpretation of classification attributions: For classification tasks, the explanation question is straightforward: *"Why is o predicted as the label of x?"*. Attribution values indicate which time steps support or contradict this prediction. Unlike regression, the alternatives to o are finite, hence reducing ambiguity. We will also show in Sect. 3.1 that there is actually an implicit reference value r for classification attributions. For simplicity, we focus only on binary classification (i.e., positive versus negative labels). Typically, $\phi_i > 0$ signifies that the presence of x_i supports the positive prediction, increasing model confidence, while $\phi_i < 0$ indicates lower confidence. The absolute value of ϕ_i indicates the "strength" of the support; $\phi_i = 0$ means x_i is irrelevant to the model. For multiclass prediction tasks, we can easily model them as multiple binary classification tasks.

2.2 Attribution Methods

Two of the most well-known attribution methods in XAI are SHAP [9] and LIME [15]. LIME is a framework to explain any black-box classification model. LIME first perturbs the instance of interest to obtain a local dataset, then trains a linear model on the perturbed data set. This linear model is a local proxy model that approximates the black-box model in the neighbourhood of the instance of interest. Thus the black-box model can be explained (locally) by interpreting the linear model. While its original paper only covers classification models, the LIME implementation has also been extended to regression models.

On the other hand, SHAP is based on Shapley values, which is a methodology in game theory to determine the contribution of each player in a collaborative game. In the context of machine learning, a feature is a player and the payout can be obtained from the model predictions. As exact SHAP is known to be expensive to compute, alternatives including KernelSHAP [9] and Shapley Values Sampling [22] can be used to estimate the attributions quicker. KernelSHAP approximates the Shapley values by solving a linear regression problem while Shapley Values Sampling samples random permutations of input features. Both methods have been used in the time series domain [13,17].

LIME-Based Time Series Attribution Methods. LEFTIST [6] is one of the first attempts to adapt LIME for time series. The method simply divides the time series to equal-length segments. In the same paper, the authors propose three different methods to perturb the time series data which are constant, interpolation, and random background. On the other hand, LIMESegment [19] is a combination of techniques including NNSegment, a segmentation method and Realistic Background Perturbation, a time series perturbation method using the underlying background frequency.

SHAP-Based Time Series Attribution Methods. WindowSHAP [13] proposes three different ways to explain a time series classification model. The common idea is to use a window to group consecutive time steps. Stationary WindowSHAP segments the time series into equal segments before applying SHAP. Sliding WindowSHAP uses a sliding window instead. Dynamic WindowSHAP uses a strategy alike to binary search in which it keeps splitting the time series until a stop condition. Once WindowSHAP segments the time series, it uses KernelSHAP to compute SHAP attribution values. While KernelSHAP is faster to compute than exact SHAP, it was shown to behave poorly for many TSC tasks [17,24].

TimeSHAP [1] is another SHAP-based attribution method but focused on multivariate time series. TimeSHAP groups the data channel-wise (each channel is a feature) and time-step wise (each time step is a feature). Moreover, it prunes distant-past data by assuming that only recent data is more important. Interestingly, TimeSHAP detects the important events by intersecting the important channels and important time steps.

Other Methods. Feature Ablation implemented in Captum[2] is an extremely fast attribution method. It simply replaces the feature value with values drawn from the background data then calculates the difference in model output as the attribution for that feature. This method was found to perform well on time series data when combined with fixed segmentation [17].

LASTS [20] is an explanation framework that can explain a black-box time series classifier in three different ways: a saliency map, prototypical and coun-

---

[2] https://captum.ai/.

terfactual exemplars, and rule-based explanation. A saliency map is similar to attributions where the relevant parts of the input time series x is highlighted. A prototypical exemplar is an artificial time series that is similar to x and classified to the same class of x, while a counterfactual exemplar is an artificial time series that is also similar to x but classified to a different class. Rules-based explanation provides human-friendly rules such as *"If the time series x has this pattern then $f(x) = 0$ otherwise $f(x) = 1$"*.

3 Methodology

In this section, we detail our proposed methodology to explain time series models based on exact SHAP computation.

3.1 Background Data and Reference Value

In general, Shapley values explain the difference between the prediction $f(x)$ and the expected prediction $E(f(X))$. The expected prediction plays the role of the empty coalition ($\emptyset$) and is estimated using the average prediction on the background data X_b (i.e., $E(f(X)) = E(f(X_b))$) [11]. In other words, the Shapley value calculation (e.g., Eq. 7) depends on the background data. Consequently, using different background can lead to different attributions. This issue will also be demonstrated experimentally in Sect. 4.3. We propose the following strategies to select proper background data for SHAP-based time series attribution methods.

Selecting Background Data for Regression Models: As discussed in Sect. 2.1, a reference value r is needed for the explanation of regression models. The attribution methods then aim to explain the difference between $f(x)$ and r. As SHAP attributions explain the difference between $f(x)$ and $E(f(X_b))$, it implies the condition for the regression background data as:

$$E(f(X_b)) \approx r \qquad (3)$$

A simple strategy to choose the background data following this condition is to draw samples from the training data such that $f(x) \approx r$.

Selecting Background Data for Binary Classification Models: For binary classification models, if we use the output probability of the model instead of labels, then the explanation has a natural reference value which is the decision boundary of the output $r = 0.5$. As a result, the explanation question can be reformulated as *"Why is o but not 0.5 the predicted probability of x?"*. From this perspective, the condition for the classification background data is:

$$E(f(X_b)) \approx 0.5 \qquad (4)$$

We explored four classification background data options: (1) training data, (2) all-zeros, (3) training centroid, and (4) training balanced centroid. While training data offers the most balanced expected prediction, its computational cost for SHAP can be high, due to the need for repeated SHAP computation on each training sample. Therefore, we only consider single-time-series backgrounds. The centroid (Eq. 5) represents the average of all training time series. The balanced centroid (Eq. 6), used for imbalanced datasets, averages class-wise centroids, mitigating majority class bias. Both centroid types are artificial time series (i.e., not actual training samples).

$$c_i = \frac{1}{|X|} \sum_x^X x_i \quad (5) \qquad \bar{c}_i = \frac{1}{|L|} \sum_l^L (\frac{1}{|X_l|} \sum_x^{X_l} x_i) \quad (6)$$

3.2 TSHAP: Sliding Window Attribution

TSHAP utilizes a sliding window to aggregate time steps. Time steps within the window are grouped into one feature, and those outside into another feature, effectively transforming the time series into a two-feature tabular format. Figure 2 showcases this approach.

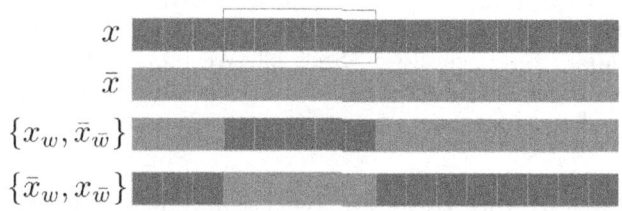

Fig. 2. An illustration of how TSHAP emulates the 'missingness' in the data with a background sample $\bar{x}$. We denote with x the input time series and with $\bar{x}$ the time series where all data are missing. $\{\bar{x}_w, x_{\bar{w}}\}$ emulates that data inside the window are missing and $\{x_w, \bar{x}_{\bar{w}}\}$ emulates that data outside the window are missing.

A window w is defined by its starting location w_s and its length w_l. Let $\bar{w}$ be the group of time steps that are outside of the window w (i.e., w and $\bar{w}$ cover the entire time series). x is the sample of interest that needs explanation and $\bar{x}$ is the background sample (drawn from the background data). The exact Shapley value of the sliding window w can be calculated as follows:

$$\begin{aligned}\phi(w) &= \frac{1}{2}(f(x) - f(x_{\bar{w}}) + f(x_w) - f(\bar{x})) \\ &= \frac{1}{2}(f(x) - f(\{\bar{x}_w, x_{\bar{w}}\}) + f(\{x_w, \bar{x}_{\bar{w}}\}) - f(\bar{x}))\end{aligned} \quad (7)$$

If there are multiple samples in the background dataset, the attribution is averaged across all the background samples (Eq. 8). Finally, the attribution of the time step i is the average attribution of all the windows $w \in W_i$ that contain i (Eq. 9).

$$\phi(w) = \frac{1}{|X_b|} \sum_{\bar{x} \in X_b} \phi_{\bar{x}}(w) \qquad (8) \qquad \phi_i = \frac{1}{|W_i|} \sum_{w \in W_i} \frac{\phi(w)}{w_l} \qquad (9)$$

The TSHAP algorithm is summarised in Algorithm 1. Calculating the attribution for every sliding window (stride $s = 1$) can be expensive, therefore TSHAP only calculates the Shapley value after every stride (stride $s > 1$) and interpolates the attributions of the windows in between.

Algorithm 1: Computing TSHAP Window Attributions

Input: Time series sample
Output: Attributions
1 Instantiate a set of sliding windows with stride s and window length w_l.
2 **foreach** *Sliding window w* **do**
3   **foreach** *Background sample $\bar{x}$* **do**
4   Calculate the attribution of window w with Equation 7.
5   Calculate the average attribution of window w with Equation 8.
6 Interpolate the attributions of the windows in between.
7 Calculate the attribution of each time step with Equation 9.

3.3 TSHAP ROI: Using Attribution to Identify Regions of Interest

For time series data, it is often useful to identify the important regions in time series that contribute the most to the model prediction. Moreover, in our experiments, we will show that TSHAP Window can mistakenly spread the attribution from relevant time steps to the nearby irrelevant time steps. In this section, we propose an efficient technique to mitigate this issue and identify these important regions using window attributions. The exact steps to search for the regions of interest are described in Algorithm 2.

4 Experiments

4.1 Attribution Methods

In this section, we consider the following attribution methods for comparison.

- **Time Series Classification:** TSHAP, WindowSHAP, Shapley Value Sampling, Feature Ablation, LIMESegment, LEFTIST.
- **Time Series Regression:** TSHAP, WindowSHAP, Shapley Value Sampling, Feature Ablation.

Algorithm 2: Computing TSHAP Regions Of Interest

Input: Time series sample
Output: ROI Attributions
1 Calculate all the TSHAP window attributions with Algorithm 1 (until Line 6).
2 Each window w_i is marked as relevant if $|\phi(w_i)| > \epsilon$ where $\epsilon = 0.1 \times max(|\phi(w_i)|)$ is the relevant threshold.
3 Group the consecutive relevant windows.
4 **foreach** *Group of consecutive relevant windows* **do**
5 $\quad$ The region of interest w_{ROI} is the combination of all windows in the group.
6 $\quad$ Calculate the attribution of the window $\hat{w}$ with Eq. 8.
7 $\quad$ Attribution of each time step i inside w_{ROI}: $\phi_i = \dfrac{\phi(w_{ROI})}{length(w_{ROI})}$

We note that TSHAP has two variants: TSHAP-Window and TSHAP-ROI, while WindowSHAP has three variants: Stationary, Sliding, and Dynamic. Feature Ablation and Shapley Value Sampling are also included as they were found to be effective in the quantitative evaluation of [17]. For these methods, we use the tsCaptum package [18]. LIME-based methods (LIMESegment and LEFTIST) are excluded from the regression experiments because their current implementation does not support regression models. For a fair comparison, we set the parameter window length at 10% of the length of the time series and stride $s = 5$ for TSHAP, WindowSHAP; the number of segments = 10 for Shapley Value Sampling, Feature Ablation. All remaining hyper-parameters are left with the default values.

4.2 Evaluation Methodology

We evaluate our proposed methods using a synthetic dataset and real datasets from the UCR archive. For the synthetic dataset, we build a *hypothetical model* which predicts the target value using human reasoning. Then we assign an attribution value to each time step in accordance to its relevance to the *hypothetical model*. Thus these attributions are the ground truth attributions Φ of the *hypothetical model*. Finally, we explain the *hypothetical model* with the attribution methods then compare the output with the ground truth attributions using cosine similarity, precision, recall, and F1. Previous works [2,17] also used assigned-by-human attributions but with ML models to test synthetic data; however we argue that these attributions are not the ground truth attributions of the ML models. Cosine similarity is a well known metric to quantify the similarity between two (attribution) vectors. To calculate precision, recall, and F1, we construct the confusion matrix as in Table 1.

On the other hand, faithfulness analysis is a common approach [23] to evaluate classification attribution methods with real datasets. In this approach, the most relevant part of the time series (identified by the attributions) is perturbed to create a new time series. The comparison between the new prediction (on

Table 1. Confusion matrix for evaluating the attributions ϕ using the ground truth Φ. True relevant means both attributions are relevant in the same direction (both support or oppose the prediction). True irrelevant means both attributions are irrelevant. False relevant means ϕ_i is relevant but Φ_i is irrelevant or relevant in the opposite direction. False irrelevant means ϕ_i is irrelevant but Φ_i is relevant.

	True	False
Relevant	$\phi_i \times \Phi_i > 0$	$\phi_i \neq 0$ and $\phi_i \times \Phi_i \leq 0$
Irrelevant	$\phi_i = 0$ and $\Phi_i = 0$	$\phi_i = 0$ and $\Phi_i \neq 0$

the new time series) and the original prediction (on the original time series) can indicate the faithfulness of the attributions. Equations 10 and 11 show how faithfulness is calculated in our experiments where f outputs probability. x_p is the resulting time series from perturbing the positive attribution part; x_n results from perturbing the negative attribution part. The perturbation is done by substituting the top 10% most relevant data with zero.

$$faithfulness = \frac{1}{|X|} \sum_{x \in X} (f(x) - f(x_p) + f(x_n) - f(x)) \quad (10)$$

$$= \frac{1}{|X|} \sum_{x \in X} (f(x_n) - f(x_p)) \quad (11)$$

Existing classification faithfulness evaluations [14,24] often measure accuracy drops after perturbation. However, this method relies on the test set ground truth and the original accuracy of the predictions; moreover perturbation can inadvertently correct misclassifications, leading to inaccurate assessments. Our analysis instead measures changes in prediction probability regardless of prediction accuracy, ensuring the direction of change aligns with attributions. Perturbing time steps with positive attributions should reduce model confidence (i.e., $f(x) - f(x_p) > 0$) while perturbing time steps with negative attributions should increase it (i.e., $f(x_n) - f(x) > 0$). Higher positive faithfulness scores indicate greater attribution fidelity.

4.3 Synthetic Dataset

The **synthetic time series data** generation is inspired by the work of [24]. We use the original code and adapt it so each time series is created by inserting two segments of sine wave signals (s_1 and s_2) to a silent signal at two different places (Fig. 3). The length of the time series is 200. There are 30 samples for the training set and 30 samples for the test set. For the regression problem, the target value is the sum of the frequencies of the sine waves. For the classification problem, a threshold $\tau = 60$ is used to separate the samples into two classes: below the threshold (negative) and above the threshold (positive).

The hypothetical model estimates the frequency of each sine wave segment by counting the number of cycles in the segment. Algorithm 3 and 4 are implemented as the predict functions for the hypothetical regression model and classification model respectively.

Algorithm 3: Regression Prediction

Input: Time series sample
Output: Total frequency
1 Count the number of cycles in the first segment.
2 Estimate the frequency of the first segment from the number of cycles.
3 Count the number of cycles in the second segment.
4 Estimate the frequency of the second segment from the number of cycles.
5 Return the sum of the frequencies.

Algorithm 4: Classification Prediction

Input: Time series sample
Output: Label of the time series sample (positive or negative)
1 Estimate the frequency sum using Algorithm 3.
2 Return positive if frequency sum $> \tau$ otherwise return negative.

The Ground Truth Attributions. Φ: Each time step i is assigned with an attribution Φ_i calculated by Eq. 12 for the regression problem and Eq. 13 for the classification problem:

$$\Phi_i = \begin{cases} f_j - \frac{r}{2} & \text{if } i \text{ inside } s_j \\ 0 & \text{if } i \text{ not inside } s_j \end{cases} \quad (12) \quad \Phi_i = \begin{cases} f_j - \frac{\tau}{2} & \text{if } i \text{ inside } s_j \\ 0 & \text{if } i \text{ not inside } s_j \end{cases} \quad (13)$$

where s_j ($j = 1$ or 2) is the sine wave segment and f_j is the frequency of s_j.

The idea is that if the frequency of one segment $f_j < \frac{\tau}{2}$ then it is less likely that the time series is a positive sample (i.e. sum of frequencies $> \tau$) and if $f_j > \frac{\tau}{2}$ then it is more likely that the time series is a positive sample.

Classification Background Analysis. In this experiment, we study the impact of the background selection on the classification attributions. We include five different choices of background: zero, centroid, balanced centroid, train data, threshold. Threshold background is a special sample that has two identical sine wave segments with the frequency $= 0.5 \times \tau$. This is an ideal background sample that is located on the decision boundary of the hypothetical classification model.

Table 2. Cosine similarity between TSHAP attributions and ground truth attributions. Runtime is the total time required to compute attributions for the test dataset.

Background	Avg Cosine sim	Avg proba	Runtime(sec)
Zero	−0.174	1.0	0.06
Train	**0.906**	**0.62**	5.95
Centroid	0.708	0.99	0.06
Balanced Centroid	0.646	1.0	0.07
Threshold	**0.911**	**0.54**	0.07

Table 2 shows the (average) cosine similarity between TSHAP attributions and the ground truth attributions. In addition, the table also includes the (average) probability of the predicted class of the background data. Clearly, attributions with different background data are significantly different. An apparent trend is that the closer the background data is to the decision boundary (the average probability closer to 0.5), the more accurate the attributions, although using the train data comes with a higher cost of running time. This experiment highlights the issue of inappropriate background data (all-zero background in this case) and supports our proposed strategy on choosing the background data for classification attribution methods.

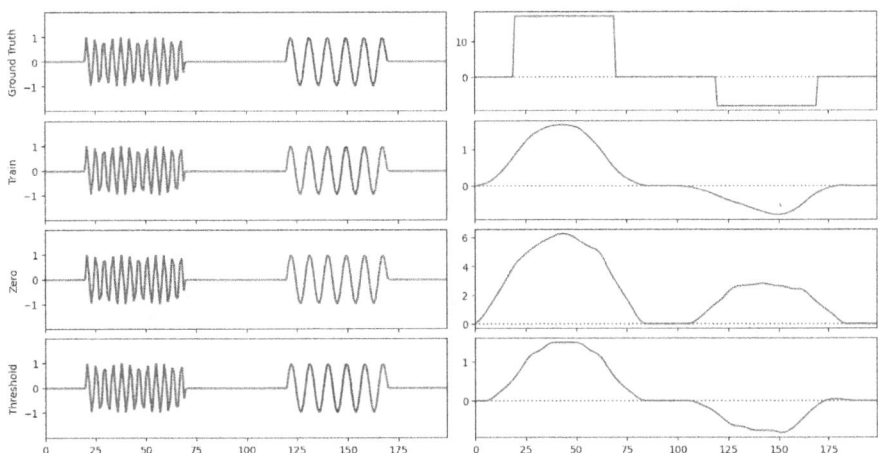

Fig. 3. TSHAP Window attributions on a synthetic time series using various background data. The left panel displays the time series, and the right panel shows the attribution profile. The time series is color-coded: red for positive and blue for negative attributions (Color figure online)

Classification Attribution Methods. In this experiment, we evaluate the attribution methods for classification problems using the synthetic dataset. For methods that require background data, we use the train data as the background. To establish a baseline, we included a random attribution method, assigning values between -1 and 1 to each time step. Any effective attribution method should outperform this random attribution.

Table 3. Evaluating classification attribution methods using a synthetic dataset with a hypothetical model and ground truth attributions. Runtime is the total time required to compute attributions for the test set.

Attribution Methods	Cosine	Precision	Recall	F1	Runtime (secs)
TSHAP window	0.906	0.486	0.975	0.646	5.95
TSHAP ROI	0.900	0.952	0.780	**0.851**	**5.95**
WindowSHAP Stationary	0.802	0.614	0.946	0.742	533.99
WindowSHAP Sliding	0.909	0.542	0.975	0.694	9.32
WindowSHAP Dynamic	0.534	0.534	0.694	0.601	55.91
LIMESegment	0.267	0.144	0.378	0.208	488.13
LEFTIST	0.623	0.325	0.838	0.467	0.09
Feature Ablation	0.810	0.611	0.950	0.740	0.39
Shapley Value Sampling	0.801	0.614	0.946	0.742	7.86
Random	0.003	0.191	0.496	0.275	0.0

Table 3 reveals that TSHAP Window, TSHAP ROI, and Sliding WindowSHAP exhibit the highest cosine similarity to ground truth attributions. TSHAP ROI attributions demonstrate being more conservative, achieving high precision but slightly lower recall. Conversely, TSHAP Window, Sliding WindowSHAP, Feature Ablation, and Shapley Value Sampling show higher recall but lower precision, indicating a tendency to overemphasize relevant areas (Fig. 4). The similar performance of TSHAP Window and Sliding WindowSHAP stems from their shared sliding window approach, with differences in the details of calculation methods. LIME-based methods perform poorly on all metrics for this dataset. Regarding running time, TSHAP variants are the fastest among SHAP-based methods. It is important to note that TSHAP calculates both TSHAP Window and ROI together, thus the running time of each is actually the total running time for both variants combined. LEFTIST is the overall fastest but with low scores. Feature Ablation is not only the second fastest method but also performs relatively well.

Regression Attribution Methods. For the regression problem, we experiment with two different reference values $r = 0$ and $r = 80$. For $r = 0$, the all-zero sample can be used as the background data because its target value is

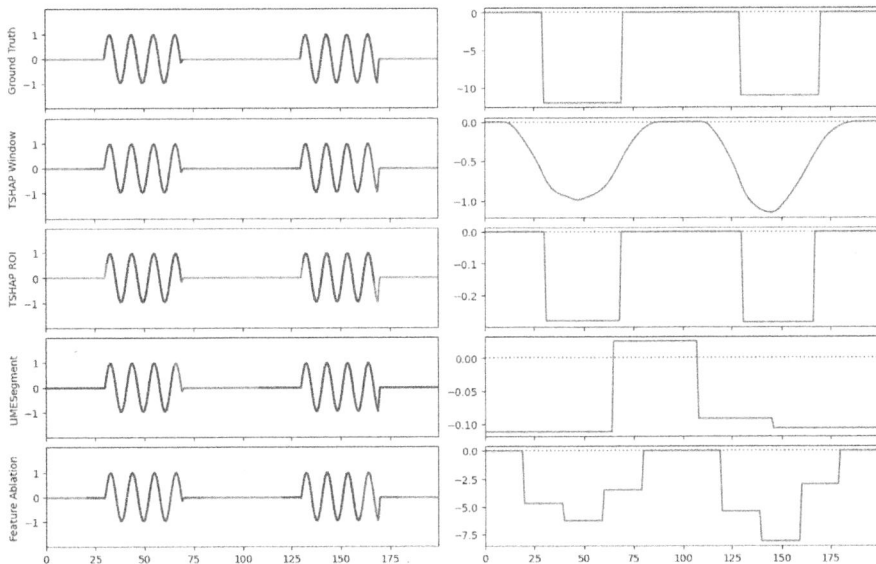

Fig. 4. Synthetic data attributions with different classification attribution methods. The left panel displays the time series, and the right panel shows the attribution profile. The time series is color-coded: red for positive and blue for negative attributions. For this input time series, we have two segments with lower frequency which makes it more likely for the time series to belong to the negative class. (Color figure online)

also 0. For $r = 80$, to ensure $E(f(X_b)) \approx 80$, we generate background samples that have the target values in the range of $[75, 85]$.

Table 4 shows the scores of each attribution method for both $r = 0$ and $r = 80$. The results present a similar pattern to the previous experiment (shown in Table 3) where TSHAP ROI stands out as the most precise method with good scores overall across the metrics, for either type of reference value.

4.4 Real Datasets: Faithfulness Analysis

We evaluate the attribution methods using five binary time series classification UCR datasets. These datasets are well-studied in this area and were also studied in [15]. For the classifier we use MiniROCKET [5] due to its efficiency and effectiveness, and for the background we use the training dataset, as we found that the other single-time-series options (zero, centroid, balanced centroid) fail to satisfy the background condition.

Table 5 shows the faithfulness scores (Eq. 11) of all the evaluated attribution methods. The average column shows the average faithfulness scores across the datasets with TSHAP Window as the highest. It is interesting that TSHAP Window falters with the Wine dataset while TSHAP ROI struggles with the Chinatown dataset. It should be noted that Chinatown time series are much shorter

Table 4. Evaluating regression attribution methods using a synthetic dataset with a hypothetical model and ground truth attributions. The reference values of the attributions are $r = 0$ and $r = 80$.

Attribution Methods	Cosine	Precision	Recall	F1	Runtime (secs)
$r = 0$					
TSHAP window	0.922	0.525	0.995	0.687	0.06
TSHAP ROI	0.885	1.000	0.750	**0.851**	0.06
WindowSHAP Stationary	0.792	0.607	0.896	0.723	10.89
WindowSHAP Sliding	0.923	0.585	0.992	0.735	0.91
WindowSHAP Dynamic	0.867	0.799	0.974	0.876	1.1
Feature Ablation	0.653	0.539	0.717	0.613	0.01
Shapley Value Sampling	0.769	0.604	0.892	0.720	0.25
Random	0.015	0.205	0.512	0.293	0.0
$r = 80$					
TSHAP window	0.941	0.508	0.989	0.668	0.55
TSHAP ROI	0.916	0.968	0.810	**0.877**	0.55
WindowSHAP Stationary	0.840	0.639	0.979	0.771	103.08
WindowSHAP Sliding	0.944	0.568	0.990	0.719	3.05
WindowSHAP Dynamic	0.874	0.748	0.983	0.841	19.98
Feature Ablation	0.844	0.648	0.988	0.780	0.11
Shapley Value Sampling	0.841	0.636	0.975	0.767	2.09
Random	−0.019	0.192	0.496	0.276	0.0

Table 5. Faithfulness of classification attribution methods on UCR TSC datasets.

Attribution Methods	Coffee	Wine	BirdChicken	ECG200	Chinatown	Average
TSHAP Window	0.424	0.059	0.155	0.195	0.230	**0.213**
TSHAP ROI	0.241	0.338	0.146	0.180	0.008	0.183
WindowSHAP Stationary	0.034	0.206	0.106	0.209	0.210	0.153
WindowSHAP Sliding	0.412	0.068	0.157	0.159	0.174	0.194
WindowSHAP Dynamic	0.156	0.355	0.085	0.067	0.215	0.176
LIMESegment	0.262	0.197	0.110	0.123	0.288	0.196
LEFTIST	0.184	−0.012	0.055	0.190	0.131	0.110
Feature Ablation	−0.009	0.107	0.109	0.155	0.254	0.123
Shapley Value Sampling	0.028	−0.037	0.118	0.114	0.234	0.091
Random	−0.000	0.154	0.000	−0.003	−0.013	0.027

than the others (only 24 time steps in total). The methods LEFTIST, Feature Ablation, Shapley Value Sampling achieve concerning negative faithfulness scores (< 0), each on one occasion. Regarding runtime, on these real datasets,

TSHAP Window and TSHAP ROI combined take 7 min in total, slightly less than WindowSHAP Sliding. LEFTIST, WindowSHAP Dynamic, and Feature Ablation are the only methods that are faster (only 16 s for LEFTIST) but achieve lower faithfulness scores. Stationary WindowSHAP is again the slowest method with more than 5 h of runtime. All methods surpass the faithfulness of random attributions on average.

5 Conclusion

This paper presents TSHAP, a novel SHAP-based attribution method designed for interpreting black-box time series classification and regression models. TSHAP has two distinct variants: TSHAP Window, which calculates time step attributions based on sliding window Shapley values, and TSHAP ROI, which leverages sliding window attributions to identify important regions within the time series. We also address the critical issue of background data selection, providing a theoretical and experimental analysis leading to a proposed strategy applicable to various time series attribution methods that require background data. To our best knowledge, our paper is the first to study attribution methods for time series regression problems. For evaluation, we tested our proposed methods on both synthetic and real-world datasets in comparison with other state-of-the-art attribution methods. Evaluation on both synthetic and real-world datasets showcases the robustness of our approach, with TSHAP ROI achieving high precision on synthetic data. On real datasets, TSHAP Window demonstrates high overall faithfulness, while TSHAP ROI exhibits less consistent but still strong performance on various datasets. Both TSHAP variants achieve good trade-offs regarding computation runtime versus the usefulness of attributions (as measured using ground truth attributions and faithfulness scores). We acknowledge that the current scope of regression XAI evaluation is limited to synthetic data and we do not address the topic of XAI actionability in this paper. These limitations highlight important avenues for future research, including the development of robust regression XAI evaluation methodologies for real-world data and the exploration of actionability for XAI in the domain of time series classification and regression.

Acknowledgments. This publication has emanated from research conducted with the financial support of Taighde Éireann Research Ireland under Grant [Insight Centre for Data Analytics 12/RC/2289_P2]. For the purpose of Open Access, the author has applied a CC BY public copyright licence to any Author Accepted Manuscript version arising from this submission.

Disclosure of Interests. The authors have no competing interests to declare that are relevant to the content of this article.

References

1. Bento, J., Saleiro, P., Cruz, A.F., Figueiredo, M.A., Bizarro, P.: Timeshap: explaining recurrent models through sequence perturbations. In: KDD (Aug 2021)
2. Boniol, P., Meftah, M., Remy, E., Palpanas.T.: dcam: dimension-wise class activation map for explaining multivariate data series classification. In: ICMD (2022)
3. Dau, H.A., et al.: The UCR Time Series Archive. CoRR, abs/ arxiv: 1810.07758 (2018)
4. Dempster, A., Petitjean, F., Webb, G.I.: ROCKET: exceptionally fast and accurate time series classification using random convolutional kernels. Data Min. Knowl. Disc. **34**(5), 1454–1495 (2020)
5. Dempster, A., Schmidt, D.F., Webb, G.I.: Minirocket: A very fast (almost) deterministic transform for time series classification. In: SIGKDD (2021)
6. Guillemé, M., Masson, V., Rozé, L., Termier, A.: Agnostic local explanation for time series classification. In: ICTAI (2019)
7. Le Nguyen, T., Gsponer, S., Ilie, I., O'Reilly, M., Ifrim, G.: Interpretable time series classification using linear models and multi-resolution multi-domain symbolic representations. In: DAMI (2019)
8. Letzgus, S., Wagner, P., Lederer, J., Samek, W., Müller, K.-R., Montavon, G.: Toward explainable artificial intelligence for regression models: a methodological perspective. IEEE Signal Process. Mag. **39**(4), 40–58 (2022)
9. Lundberg, S.M., Lee, S.-I.: A Unified Approach to Interpreting Model Predictions. In: NIPS (2017)
10. Middlehurst, M., Schäfer, P., Bagnall, A.: Bake off redux: a review and experimental evaluation of recent time series classification algorithms. Data Min. Knowl. Disc. **38**(4), 1958–2031 (2024). Apr
11. Molnar, C.: Interpreting Machine Learning Models With SHAP (2023)
12. Molnar, C.: Interpretable Machine Learning (book), 3 edn. (2025). https://christophm.github.io/interpretable-ml-book/
13. Nayebi, A., Tipirneni, S., Reddy, C.K., Foreman, B., Subbian, V.: Windowshap: an efficient framework for explaining time-series classifiers based on shapley values. J. of Biomed. Inform. **144**(C) (2023)
14. Nguyen, T.T., Nguyen, T.L., Ifrim, G.: Robust explainer recommendation for time series classification. Data Mining Knowl. Dis. (2024)
15. Ribeiro, M.T., Singh, S., Guestrin, C.: Why should i trust you?: explaining the predictions of any classifier. SIGKDD (2016)
16. Guijo-Rubio, D., Middlehurst, M., Arcencio, G., Furtado Silva, D., Bagnall, A.: Unsupervised feature based algorithms for time series extrinsic regression. Data Mining Knowl. Dis., 1–45 (2023)
17. Serramazza, D.I., Nguyen, T.L., Ifrim, G.: Improving the evaluation and actionability of explanation methods for multivariate time series classification. In: ECMLP-KDD (2024)
18. Serramazza, D.I., Nguyen, T.L., Ifrim, G.: A short tutorial for multivariate time series explanation using tscaptum. Software Impacts **22**, 100723 (2024)
19. Sivill, T., Flach, P.: Limesegment: Meaningful, realistic time series explanations. PMLR, 28–30 (2022)
20. Spinnato, F., Guidotti, R., Monreale, A., Nanni, M., Pedreschi, D., Giannotti, F.: Understanding any time series classifier with a subsequence-based explainer. ACM Trans. Knowl. Discov. Data **18**(2) (2023)

21. Tan, C., Bergmeir, C., Petitjean, F., Webb, G.: Time series extrinsic regression. Data Min. Knowl. Disc. **35**, 1032–1060 (2021)
22. Strumbelj, E., Kononenko, I.: An efficient explanation of individual classifications using game theory. J. Mach. Learn. Res. **11**, 1–18 (2010)
23. Theissler, A., Spinnato, F., Schlegel, U., Guidotti, R.: Explainable ai for time series classification: a review, taxonomy and research directions. IEEE Access **10**, 100700–100724 (2022)
24. Turbé, H., Bjelogrlic, M., Lovis, C., Mengaldo, G.: Evaluation of post-hoc interpretability methods in time-series classification. Nat. Mach. Intell. **5**(3), 250–260 (2023)

A True-to-the-Model Benchmark for Edge-Level Attributions of GNN Explainers

Francesco Paolo Nerini[1,2](✉)⬤, Francesco Bonchi[2,3]⬤, and André Panisson[2]⬤

[1] Sapienza University, Rome, Italy
[2] CENTAI Institute, Turin, Italy
{fpn,bonchi,panisson}@centai.eu
[3] Eurecat, Barcelona, Spain

Abstract. Edge-level explainers for Graph Neural Networks (GNNs) aim to identify the most crucial edges that influence the model's predictions in a node classification task. Benchmarking these explainers is particularly challenging due to the extensive search space of potential explanations and the absence of reliable ground truths for edge importance. Moreover, the evaluation methods which are prominent in the literature rely on assumptions about which subgraphs in the input data influence the classification of a node, yet they provide no guarantee that the model has effectively learned the intended behavior.

In this paper, we address these limitations by introducing a white-box GNN model together with a theoretical analysis to identify which edges are truly important, i.e., when removed, they can alter the classification. We demonstrate the effectiveness of this framework on both synthetic and real-world node classification tasks, using metrics that account for the inherent imbalance between the few relevant edges and the many irrelevant ones. Our evaluation reveals two recurring issues in current explainability methods: the frequent misidentification of unimportant edges as important ones, and numerical instability in some attribution techniques. To address these issues, we propose two corrective strategies that significantly enhance the reliability of edge-level attributions: a post-processing method to refine edge rankings and a rescaling of model weights to stabilize numerical outputs.

Our work provides valuable insights into the strengths and weaknesses of existing GNN explainers and presents practical solutions to advance the fine-grained explainability of graph-based models.

Keywords: Explainable AI · Graph Machine Learning · XAI Benchmarking

---

Supplementary Information The online version contains supplementary material available at https://doi.org/10.1007/978-3-032-06078-5_5.

1 Introduction

Graph structures are ubiquitous in data science. From chemical bonds to financial transactions, graphs encompass many situations where relations between elements add additional information to the task at hand. In many applications, Graph Neural Networks (GNNs) have been introduced as an effective tool for learning from these relations and performing predictions. However, these methods are inevitably undermined by their black-box nature. The low human understandability of these techniques raises concerns from regulators and practitioners alike about their algorithmic decisions. Due to this reason, a large corpus of works on explainable artificial intelligence has been developed specifically to deal with graphs' peculiarities. Nonetheless, a general and common understanding of what makes a good explanation is still lacking, slowing the adoption of these techniques.

One of the main obstacles to adopting explainability techniques in graph machine learning is the inherent difficulty in validating these methods. Proper validation of a local explanation approach requires: (i) a precise definition of what constitutes a good explanation, i.e., identifying the elements that the explainer should consider as important for the model's decision, and (ii) a robust evaluation framework comprising models, ground truth explanations, and objective evaluation metrics. Prior research has largely focused on validating explanations from a true-to-the-data perspective [1,14], where ground truths are defined by inherent data structures or by artificially implanting target structures in the data. While this strategy may seem promising initially, it assumes that the model has actually learned the logic behind those inherent or implanted structures. This is a strong assumption, as models often capture spurious correlations with little relation to the underlying data-generation process. In contrast, significantly less attention has been devoted to establishing a *true-to-the-model* evaluation of explanations (e.g. [15]), which assesses an explainer's ability to faithfully capture the intrinsic reasoning underlying a GNN's classification decision.

In this work, we adopt a true-to-the-model perspective by employing a simple yet meaningful toy model of a GNN that is fully interpretable: we call it a white-box model—in contrast with the typical black-box nature of GNNs—to represent the fact that its inner logic in clearly known and thus defines a ground truth for the explanation task. We focus on edge-level explanations, which are the most fine-grained type of explanation available for graph structures. The approach eliminates the uncertainties about the extent to which the GNN has captured the true data-generating process, thereby avoiding many of the pitfalls inherent in a *true-to-the-data* evaluation framework [4] while enabling a rigorous analysis of explanation quality.

First, we define an axiom of importance for the edges. Then, leveraging our knowledge of the model's inner functioning, we can prove that the important edges correspond to a human intuition of importance. We apply the model to synthetic and real datasets in a node classification task. Using metrics that account for the unbalanced proportion between the minority of relevant edges and the majority of irrelevant ones, we observe that the explainers cannot always identify the most relevant edges. In particular, we observe two common problems. The first is due to certain edge patterns, where the explainer alternates unimportant edges with important ones. The second problem is the numerical instability of some of the methods. The first problem can be solved by postprocessing the explanations, while the second can be mitigated by rescaling the models' weights. We show how these patches can improve the quality of the produced explanations, enhancing the explainability of GNN models.

The main contributions of this paper are summarized as follows:

1. We introduce a white-box GNN along with a theoretical framework for a true-to-the-model benchmark of edge-level attributions;
2. We examine different metrics for the evaluation of the explanations, and observe that no explainer is capable of always identifying which of the edges are the most important;
3. By analysing the cases where the explainers fail the most, we identify two independent and systematic mistakes in the explanations;
4. Finally, we propose two solutions for overcoming these problems, showing that simple and fast improvements can lead to increased performance of the explainers.

We release all the code of the white-box model and the experimental setup for reproducibility[1].

2 Background and Related Work

Graph neural networks (GNNs) have become essential in both research and practical applications, with widely used architectures such as Graph Convolutional Networks (GCNs) [11], GraphSAGE [8], and Graph Attention Networks (GATs) [20] relying on message-passing mechanisms. Although all of these message-passing schemes are inherently opaque, our focus is on models like GCNs and GraphSAGE where the message weights are fixed, as opposed to the dynamically learned weights in attention-based approaches like GATs.

Understanding and interpreting GNN decisions is critical for establishing trustworthy models [27]. In this work, we address post-hoc explainability methods—generally referred to as "explainers"—that produce edge-level explanations. Explainers can be divided into three classes, depending on the scope of their explanations: instance-level, class-level, or model-level explainers [12]. We concentrate on instance-level explainers (which consider a single model decision at a time) that provide fine-grained, edge-specific attributions. Edge-level explainers can be further divided into different categories, as discussed in [12,24]:

- **Mask-based explainers:** These methods, that include GNNExplainer [23] and SubgraphX [25], generate hard or soft masks for the graph's adjacency matrix to highlight important edges.

---

[1] https://github.com/FrappaN/EdgeWhiteBoxBench.

- **Causal-based explainers:** This category includes explainers that use causal inference techniques OrphicX [13] and policy-based explainers such as ZORRO [5].
- **Perturbation-based approaches:** According to [24], both Causal-based explainers and Mask-Based explainers fall into this broader category, where edge importance is inferred by analyzing the effect of perturbations.
- **Gradient-based methods:** Techniques such as Integrated Gradients [19] and Grad-CAM [16] estimate edge relevance using output gradients.
- **Decomposition-based explainers:** These methods decompose the model's output into contributions from individual edges or features. Examples include LRP [3], GStarX [28], and FlowX [7]. However, some are limited to specific tasks (e.g., GStarX for graph classification) or require model-aware implementations (e.g., GNN-LRP [18]).
- **Surrogate-based explainers:** Approaches like GraphLIME [10] and PGM-Explainers [21] build local interpretable models to approximate the decision-making process, though they generally do not provide detailed edge-level explanations.

Early studies such as [4] compared different explainability techniques using synthetic graphs with data-dependent ground truth labels, exposing significant limitations of this evaluation strategy. Subsequent work [1,14,17] has assessed explainers via multiple model calls and filtered edge masks. In contrast, the white-box approach proposed in [15] establishes ground truth by leveraging interpretable models but focuses on feature-level explanations. This strategy is closely aligned with our methodology for benchmarking edge-level explanations.

3 Methods

In this section, we present our methodology for evaluating (and enhancing) edge-level explanations in GNNs. First, we introduce a white-box GNN model inspired by the label propagation algorithm, which provides an interpretable and controlled framework for message-passing in graphs (Sect. 3.2). Second, we formalize the concept of edge importance through an axiomatic framework that identifies the minimal subgraphs critical for a model's prediction (Sect. 3.3). Finally, we propose a post-processing strategy to refine explainer outputs by eliminating spurious attributions and enhancing explanation fidelity (Sect. 3.4).

3.1 Notation

Consider a binary node classification task on a directed graph $G = (V, E)$, where V is the set of nodes, and each node is associated with features from the set F. The graph structure is represented by the edges $E \subseteq 2^{V \times V}$ and the node-feature matrix $X \in \mathbb{R}^{|V| \times |F|}$. For a given node $v \in V$, the model is defined as a function:

$$\mathcal{M} : \mathbb{R}^{|V| \times |F|} \times 2^{V \times V} \times V \to [0, 1],$$

which outputs a prediction score in the interval $[0, 1]$.

To facilitate explanation, we discretize the model's output into classes:

$$\widehat{\mathcal{M}}(X, E, v) = \begin{cases} 0, & \text{if } \mathcal{M}(X, E, v) < 0.5 \\ 1, & \text{if } \mathcal{M}(X, E, v) \geq 0.5 \end{cases}$$

We also denote $p_0(X, E, v) = 1 - \mathcal{M}(X, E, v)$ the probability of v being in class 0, and similarly $p_1(X, E, v) = \mathcal{M}(X, E, v)$ the probability of v being in class 1.

Since our focus is on the influence of edges on the model's output, we sometimes simplify the notation by omitting X and writing $\mathcal{M}(E, v)$ (or $p_c(E, v)$). An explainer for the model $\mathcal{M}$ assigns an importance score to each edge in E for the classification of node v. We denote this as $\mathcal{E}_{\mathcal{M}}(E, v) = \beta \in \mathbb{R}^{|E|}$, where β_e is the importance assigned to edge $e \in E$.

3.2 A White-Box Model Inspired by Label Propagation

To evaluate explanation quality against a well-defined ground truth, we require a realistic white-box model whose edge importance is both interpretable and controllable, with mechanisms that are learnable by a GNN in a real scenario. For this purpose, we propose a white-box GNN that approximates the *label propagation*, a heuristic widely used for community detection and node classification [6,29], in which, starting from a subset of labeled nodes, at each iteration each node adopts the majority label of its neighbours, until all nodes are labelled.

A single-layer GNN can emulate one iteration of label propagation. For simplicity, consider a binary classification task. The model assigns to each node v an embedding $X_v \in \{(1,0), (0,1), (0,0)\}$, where $(1,0)$ corresponds to a node known to belong to the first class, $(0,1)$ to one belonging to the second class, and $(0,0)$ to any unlabelled node. The model then performs one round of message passing:

$$H_v^{(1)} = \text{ReLU}(\sum_{u \in \mathcal{N}(v)} X_u W), \text{ with } W = \begin{pmatrix} 1 & -1 \\ -1 & 1 \end{pmatrix}, \quad (1)$$

followed by a final transformation:

$$\mathcal{M}(X, E, v) = \sigma\left(H_v^{(1)} w^\top\right), \quad (2)$$

where σ is the sigmoid function, $w = (1, -1)$, and $\mathcal{N}(v)$ are the nodes neighbours of v. To mimic multiple iterations of label propagation, we generalize the model to L rounds by repeating the propagation step with normalization:

$$H_v^{(l)} = \text{ReLU}(\sum_{u \in \mathcal{N}(v)} \frac{H_u^{(l-1)}}{\|H_u^{(l-1)}\|} W) \text{ for } l = 2, \ldots L; \quad (3)$$

After which, the same final transformation with a sigmoid activation is applied.

Note that scaling the weight matrix W by any scalar factor f does not alter the model's classification. We will later use this property to improve the numerical stability of the explanations, as detailed in Sect. 4.2.

For multi-class classification, the model can be generalized by encoding node labels as one-hot vectors. In this case, the weight matrix W is a matrix with 1 on the diagonal and -1 everywhere else. The propagation rule remains the same as in Eq. 3, and a softmax activation is applied at the output layer. Under this assumption, a node is assigned to a particular class only if a strict majority of its labelled neighbours belong to that class.

3.3 Defining Edge Importance

We define the importance of an edge by its contribution to the model's prediction. To formalize this notion, we introduce the concept of *important subgraph*.

Definition 1. *Given a graph $\mathcal{G} = (V, E)$ and a binary node classification model $\mathcal{M}$ such that $\widehat{\mathcal{M}}(E, v) = c$ and the predicted probability $p_c(E, v) > 0.5$ for some node v, a set of edges $A \subseteq E$ is an **important subgraph** for $\mathcal{M}$ and v iff:*

1. *Removing A from the graph changes the prediction, i.e., $p_c(E \setminus A, v) \leq 0.5$;*
2. *No proper subset $B \subset A$ has this effect, meaning that for all $B \subset A$, the model still predicts class c with $p_c(E \setminus B, v) > 0.5$.*

In other words, an important subgraph is a minimal set of edges whose removal causes the model's confidence to drop below the decision threshold. Different important subgraphs can share multiple edges.

Let $\mathcal{I}$ denote the set of all important subgraphs:

$$\mathcal{I} = \{A \subseteq E | A \text{ is an important subraph for } \mathcal{M}\},$$

and define the union of all such subgraphs as:

$$S = \bigcup_{A \in \mathcal{I}} A.$$

For the evaluation of explainers, we focus on checking whether an edge belongs to S. Accordingly, we propose the following axiom:

Axiom 1. *Let $\mathcal{G} = (V, E)$ be a graph, $\mathcal{M}$ a binary node classification model, and $\mathcal{E}_\mathcal{M}$ an explainer that produces an attribution vector $\beta \in \mathbb{R}^{|E|}$. Denote by S the union of all important subgraphs for $\mathcal{M}$. Then, for every edge $e \in S$ and every edge $e' \notin S$,*

$$|\beta_e| > |\beta_{e'}|.$$

In other words, we expect that a faithful explainer assigns higher importance to edges that are critical to the model's prediction.

Defining important subgraphs in this way also allows us to assess whether an explainer can capture redundant structures in the graph. While such redundancy can complicate evaluations based solely on ground-truth data [4], our white-box model ensures that redundant structures are indeed used by the model, thereby enabling a more reliable evaluation.

In our framework, the importance of specific edges is controlled by the initial node labelling. For a binary classification task, the prediction for a node v depends on the difference $n_{c_1,v} - n_{c_2,v}$, where $n_{c,v}$ denotes the number of neighbours of node v with initial label c.

This intuition is formalized in the following proposition for a 2-layer binary label propagation model:

Proposition 1. *Consider a graph $\mathcal{G} = (V, E)$, a node $r \in V$, and a 2-layer (binary) label propagation model $\mathcal{M}$ with initial labels X, such that:*

$$\widehat{\mathcal{M}}(X, E, r) = c \in \{0, 1\}.$$

We define the intermediate (after one layer) and initial labels as:

$$c_u^{(1)} = \arg\max_i H_{u,i}^{(1)}; \qquad c_u^{(0)} = \arg\max_i X_{u,i};$$

with $c_u^{(l)} = 0.5$ if the maximum is not unique. Then, if $\mathcal{M}(X, E, r) \neq 0.5$, the following edges are important according to our definition:

1. *All edges $e = (s, r) \in E$ such that $c_s^{(1)} = c$;*
2. *All edges $e = (t, s) \in E$ such that $s \in \mathcal{N}(r)$ and $c_t^{(0)} = c_s^{(1)} = c$.*

In essence, this proposition shows that all paths from nodes initially labelled as the predicted class of the target node r are important. This result can be easily extended to the multiclass case.

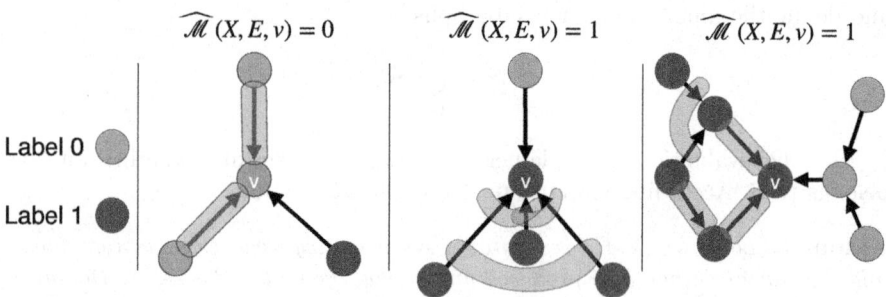

Fig. 1. Examples of the output of the white-box label-propagation-inspired model: important subgraphs are highlighted with shaded areas.

3.4 Post-processing Edge Importance to Improve Explanations

Our proposed definition of edge importance, which directly ties the relevance of an edge to its role in the message-passing mechanism, allows us to naturally introduce a post-processing step aimed at refining explanation quality. Specifically, we observed that explainers often assign relevance scores to edges that, by construction, should be considered unimportant for the model's prediction, forming recurring misleading attribution patterns (e.g., Fig. 2). These patterns typically involve assigning high importance to edges connecting second-order neighbours to immediate neighbours, even when those edges don't influence the target node's final prediction according to our definitions.

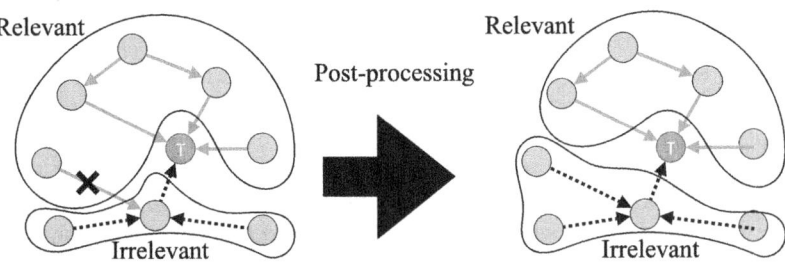

Fig. 2. (left) Example of a misleading attribution pattern for the classification of node "T". In the initial explanation, relevant edges are depicted as continuous orange lines and irrelevant ones as black dotted lines; the false positive edge is marked with a cross. (right) After applying our post-processing procedure, the false positive edge is corrected, resulting in an explanation that accurately reflects the continuous path of relevant edges. (Color figure online)

Leveraging our formalization, we identify an intuitive correction rule: if an edge is deemed unimportant, any edges preceding it in the message-passing path should also be considered unimportant. More precisely, in a directed graph, if a node A receives a message from node B along an edge that is considered unimportant by the explainer, then all edges incoming to node B should also be considered unimportant with respect to node A's classification.

To enforce this rule, we define a threshold on edge importance scores to distinguish between important and unimportant edges clearly. For attribution methods producing both positive and negative importance scores (e.g., Integrated Gradients, LRP, and Deconvolution), we set this threshold at zero. For methods generating positive scores in the range $[0, 1]$ (e.g., GNNExplainer), we use a threshold of 0.5. When an edge that is followed by an unimportant edge exceeds this threshold, we reduce its attribution score accordingly. In both cases, applying this threshold results in a noticeable improvement in the quality of the explanations.

4 Experiments

In this section, we present our experimental evaluation of edge-level explainers. We evaluate the performance of these methods using both synthetic and real-world graphs. The goal of our experiments is to quantify how well the explainers capture the edge importance as defined by our white-box label propagation model, and to evaluate the effectiveness of our post-processing strategy in refining the explanations.

4.1 Experimental Setup

Synthetic Graphs: We generate synthetic graphs using the Erdős-Rényi model with a fixed number of 1000 nodes and explore three different edge connection probabilities: $p = 0.005$, $p = 0.01$, and $p = 0.05$. In order to simulate a supervised node classification scenario, we initialize 80% of the nodes with randomly assigned labels. To introduce a higher degree of homophily, which is a common assumption in many GNN models, we rewire 1/3 of the edges originating from labelled nodes to connect them with other nodes sharing the same label. To evaluate the explanations, we select 100 nodes that were not initially labelled and for which the model predicts a class with a probability greater than 0.5.

Real Graphs: Our experiments on real data involve three widely-used citation network datasets: Cora [22], Pubmed [22], and OGBN-ArXiv [9]. In these experiments, we use the multiclass version of the Label Propagation Model. Similarly to the synthetic setup, 80% are initialized with their true labels. To evaluate the explanations, we focus on nodes for which the predicted class probability is strictly higher than that of any other class.

Explainers: Many of the explainers in the literature do not provide edge-level explanations or are tailored for node classification tasks. For example, GraphLIME does not provide edge-level attributions, and GStarX is designed for graph-level tasks rather than node-level ones. Therefore, we consider five explainers that are both relevant and directly applicable to our setting. These methods span three categories:

- Gradient-based explainers: Integrated Gradients (IG) [19].
- Mask-based explainers: GNNExplainer [23] and SubgraphX [25].
- Decomposition-based explainers: LRP [2] and Deconvolution [26] (a hybrid decomposition/gradient method).

For GNNExplainer, we set the number of training epochs to 10,000, since we observed the performance increases with the number of epochs. We left the other parameters to their default values. In contrast, SubgraphX not only required significantly longer runtimes to generate explanations but also produced results of lower quality. This discrepancy likely stems from how SubgraphX operates: instead of attributing importance directly to edges, it first selects the most relevant nodes and then returns the induced subgraph. As a consequence, its results do not align well with methods that inherently produce edge-level explanations.

Evaluation Metrics: To quantitatively assess the quality of edge-level explanations, we use two evaluation metrics: the Receiver Operating Characteristic Area Under the Curve (ROC-AUC) and the Precision-Recall Area Under the Curve (PR-AUC). These metrics are computed over the set of edges in the 2-hop neighbourhood of each target node, where each edge is labelled as either relevant or irrelevant based on our ground truth.

Due to the inherent class imbalance—where irrelevant edges vastly outnumber relevant ones—the Precision-Recall metric is particularly effective in capturing the performance of edge-level explainers. Our evaluation further considers variations in graph properties by testing on random graphs generated with different edge connection probabilities ($p = 0.005, 0.01$, and 0.05), which influence the overall density and the ratio of relevant to irrelevant edges.

4.2 Results

Impact of Graph Density on Edge-Level Explanation Performance

In Fig. 3a and 3b we present violin plots of the ROC-AUCs and PR-AUCs, respectively, across random graphs generated with varying edge probabilities (p). For each graph, we evaluate the explainers on a sample of 100 nodes. These metrics are computed based on the ground truth labelling of edges—relevant versus irrelevant—in the 2-hop neighbourhood of each target node.

The main difference between these metrics is in their treatment of false positives. While ROC-AUC uses the false positive rate (FPR), defined as $\text{FPR} = \frac{FP}{FP+TN}$, PR-AUC relies on precision, defined as $\text{Precision} = \frac{TP}{TP+FP}$). As shown in Fig. 4, although the FPR remains close to zero beyond a threshold $t = 0$ for all explainers, precision is more sensitive to threshold variations. This observation highlights that even a small number of false positives can significantly affect the ratio of true positives. This sensitivity makes PR-AUC particularly effective for evaluating edge explanations in settings with a high imbalance between relevant and irrelevant edges.

Recurring Misleading Attribution Patterns

In experiments on sparse, small graphs, we observed that explainers consistently assign importance to edges in recurring, misleading patterns, as exemplified by Fig. 2.

To address this issue, we implemented the post-processing procedure detailed in Sect. 3.4 that adjusts the importance scores based on the message-passing paths. This post-processing step significantly improves performance, as shown in Fig. 5 and Table 1. In particular, all explainers benefit from this correction except for GNNExplainer, which consistently assigns importance to all edges in the entire misleading pattern rather than just a subset of its edges.

Results on Empirical Graphs

The same problems and behaviours observed on synthetic graphs have also been observed in our experiments on real-world datasets. We evaluate the explainers on three empirical graphs: Cora, PubMed, and OGBN-ArXiv, where 80% of the nodes are initialized with their true labels. For sparser graphs, Cora and

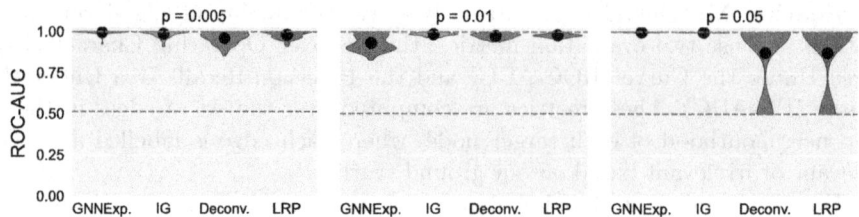

(a) Violin plot of ROC-AUC scores. The red dashed line indicates the random baseline at 0.5.

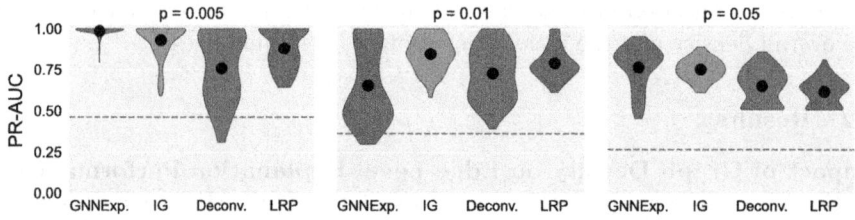

Fig. 3. Violin plots displaying the distribution of ROC-AUC (a) and PR-AUC (b) scores for edge-level explanations on a 2-layer label propagation model. Evaluations were performed on 100 nodes sampled from Erdős-Rényi graphs with varying edge connection probabilities. Black points correspond to the mean scores. (Color figure online)

PubMed, the explainers achieve near-perfect performance, indicating that the underlying sparsity and homophily help to generate accurate edge-level attributions. In contrast, performance on OGBN-Arxiv, which is both a denser and larger graph, is comparatively lower.

Detailed results are presented in Table 1, Fig. 6, and Fig. 7. In particular, the post-processing procedure consistently increases the performance of all explainers across these datasets. These results reinforce our observations from synthetic graphs and emphasize the importance of addressing false positives. Moreover, in the next section, we show how weight scaling further benefits the explanations, particularly in denser graph settings.

Numerical Stability of Explanations

Our experimental results from Fig. 5 show that as graph density increases, the performance of several explainers degrades, even after applying our post-processing procedure. In particular, while GNNExplainer remains relatively stable, both LRP and Deconvolution exhibit improvements in PR-AUC with post-processing but still fall short of the performance achieved by Integrated Gradients on dense graphs.

To gain further insights into this behaviour, we analyzed the cumulative distribution of non-zero edge attributions produced by Integrated Gradients, LRP, and Deconvolution (see Fig. 8). The results show that Integrated Gradients cov-

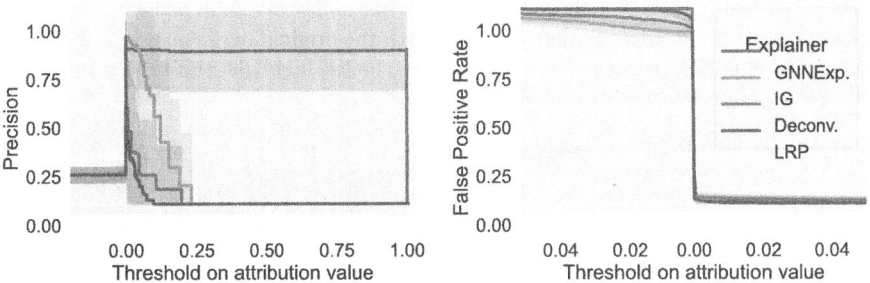

Fig. 4. On the left, the mean precision of the explainer at different attribution value thresholds on a sparse graph with $p = 0.01$; on the right, the mean false positive rate on the same graph; in both plots, the shaded areas correspond to the standard deviation across the explained node predictions.

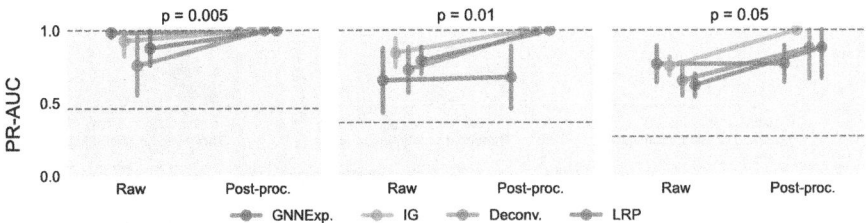

Fig. 5. Mean PR-AUC across nodes before and after post-processing of explanations on the same Erdős-Rényi random graphs of Fig. 3; there's an improvement for most explainers, apart from GNNExplainer.

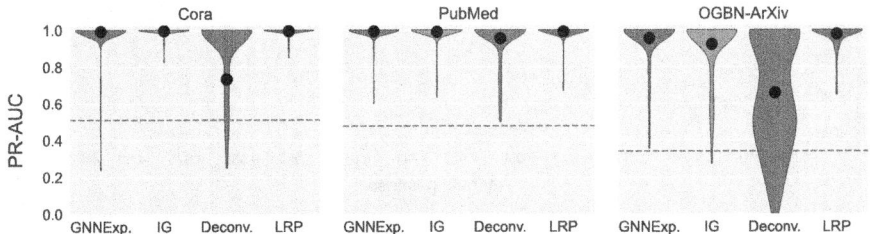

Fig. 6. Violin plot of the PR-AUCs on the three real datasets, across a sample of 100 nodes, with the points corresponding to the mean.

ers a broader range of attribution values, as its cumulative curves increase more gradually. In contrast, LRP and Deconvolution tend to concentrate their attributions around small values near zero, particularly in denser graphs, indicating underflow issues when assigning edge importance.

We traced back this problem to the dependency of the explanation scores on the model weights. In our white-box framework, this issue can be mitigated by scaling the weights by a fixed factor. Figure 9 shows that when we multiply the weights in the graph convolution layers by a scaling factor $f \leq 1$ and apply

Table 1. Mean PR-AUC across a sample of 100 nodes of the explainers on the real datasets, with standard deviation, we show both the original performance and after the post-processing described in Sect. 3.4; Darker shades highlight the best results, with different colors used for each dataset.

Dataset	Post-processing?	GNNExp.	IG	Deconv.	LRP
Cora	✗	99.1±7.6	99.5±2.2	91.3±18.1	99.4±2.4
	✓	99.5±4.0	100.0±0.0	99.7±2.9	100.0±0.0
PubMed	✗	99.1±4.8	98.8±5.7	95.3±12.1	98.9±5.3
	✓	99.1±4.8	99.8±1.9	98.7±6.6	100.0±0.0
OGBN-ArXiv	✗	95.3±13.3	92.1±16.5	65.7±30.0	97.5±6.5
	✓	95.8±12.6	96.9±10.0	96.2±12.8	99.2±4.1

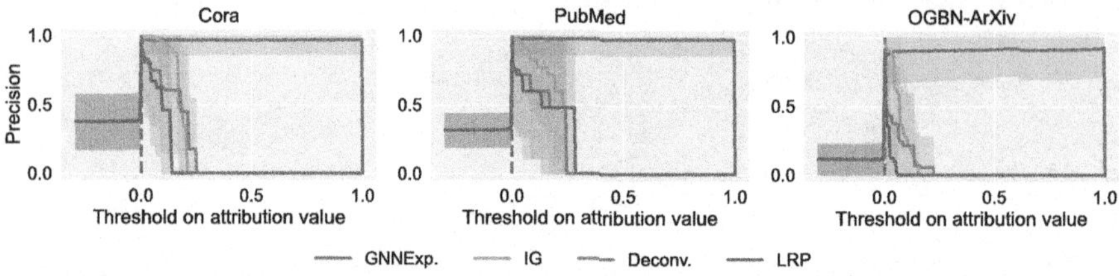

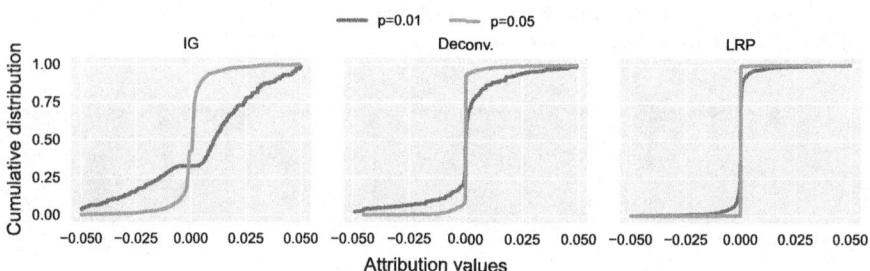

Fig. 7. Plot with precision of wrong difficult negatives at different thresholds for the three real datasets Cora, PubMed, and OGBN-ArXiv

Fig. 8. Cumulative distributions of non-zero edge attributions produced by Integrated Gradients, Deconvolution, and LRP on an Erdős-Rényi graph with 1000 nodes. Results are shown for two edge connection probabilities ($p = 0.01$ and $p = 0.05$), illustrating that Integrated Gradients covers a broader range of attribution values, while Deconvolution and LRP concentrate their attributions near zero, particularly in denser graphs.

the modified model to our datasets, the performance of Deconvolution (after post-processing) improves significantly, reaching levels comparable to Integrated Gradients. Similar improvements are observed for LRP, not shown because the results overlap those of Deconvolution.

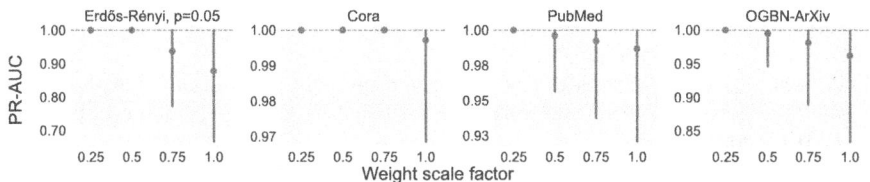

Fig. 9. Effect of weight scaling on the false positive rate of explanations provided by Deconvolution after post-processing. The figure shows how multiplying the graph convolution weights by a scaling factor $f \leq 1$ mitigates underflow issues both for synthetic and real graphs, thereby reducing the false positive rate and improving the numerical stability of the attributions.

5 Conclusion

This paper introduces a novel, true-to-the-model benchmark for evaluating edge-level explanations of Graph Neural Networks using a white-box model. Our approach provides a controlled and interpretable environment, enabling a systematic comparison of state-of-the-art explainers. Through extensive experiments on both synthetic and real-world graphs, we identify key methodological challenges and offer practical solutions to improve explanation quality.

A critical finding of our work is that some evaluation metrics are more effective in capturing the performance of edge-level explainers. In particular, Precision-Recall curves offer a more sensitive measure of the ability of explainers to distinguish relevant from irrelevant edges, when compared to ROC-AUC scores, particularly for dense input graphs.

Our evaluation revealed two recurrent issues: first, many explainers produce explanations that are inconsistent with the actual computations of the GNN; second, some explainers suffer from numerical instability, which is amplified in denser graphs. To address these issues, we propose two corrective strategies. We introduce a post-processing step that adjusts the attribution scores to better reflect the true message-passing paths, thus mitigating the problem of inconsistent explanations. Additionally, we show that scaling the weights of the model significantly reduces numerical instability, bringing the performance of methods like LRP and Deconvolution closer to that of Integrated Gradients.

Overall, our framework not only benchmarks the strengths and limitations of current edge-level explainers but also provides practical solutions to improve their reliability. Future work may extend this framework to link and graph-level tasks, incorporate other white-box models that implement different interpretable heuristics and mimic attention mechanisms, and inspire the development of new explainers that inherently overcome these issues.

References

1. Amara, K., et al.: Graphframex: towards systematic evaluation of explainability methods for graph neural networks. In: Learning on Graphs Conference, pp. 44–1. PMLR (2022)
2. Bach, S., Binder, A., Montavon, G., Klauschen, F., Müller, K.R., Samek, W.: On pixel-wise explanations for non-linear classifier decisions by layer-wise relevance propagation. PLoS ONE **10**(7), e0130140 (2015)
3. Baldassarre, F., Azizpour, H.: Explainability techniques for graph convolutional networks. arXiv preprint arXiv:1905.13686 (2019)
4. Faber, L., K. Moghaddam, A., Wattenhofer, R.: When comparing to ground truth is wrong: On evaluating GNN explanation methods. In: Proceedings of the 27th ACM SIGKDD Conference on Knowledge Discovery & Data Mining, pp. 332–341 (2021)
5. Funke, T., Khosla, M., Rathee, M., Anand, A.: Zorro: valid, sparse, and stable explanations in graph neural networks. IEEE Trans. Knowl. Data Eng. **35**(8), 8687–8698 (2023)
6. Gregory, S.: Finding overlapping communities in networks by label propagation. New J. Phys. **12**(10), 103018 (2010)
7. Gui, S., Yuan, H., Wang, J., Lao, Q., Li, K., Ji, S.: Flowx: towards explainable graph neural networks via message flows. IEEE Trans. Pattern Anal. Mach. Intell. **46**(7), 4567–4578 (2024)
8. Hamilton, W., Ying, Z., Leskovec, J.: Inductive representation learning on large graphs. In: Guyon, I., Luxburg, U.V., Bengio, S., Wallach, H., Fergus, R., Vishwanathan, S., Garnett, R. (eds.) Advances in Neural Information Processing Systems, vol. 30. Curran Associates, Inc. (2017)
9. Hu, W., et al.: Open graph benchmark: Datasets for machine learning on graphs. arXiv preprint arXiv:2005.00687 (2020)
10. Huang, Q., Yamada, M., Tian, Y., Singh, D., Chang, Y.: Graphlime: local interpretable model explanations for graph neural networks. IEEE Trans. Knowl. Data Eng. **35**(7), 6968–6972 (2023)
11. Kipf, T.N., Welling, M.: Semi-supervised classification with graph convolutional networks. In: International Conference on Learning Representations (2017)
12. Li, X., Wang, J., Yan, Z.: Can graph neural networks be adequately explained? a survey. ACM Comput. Surv. **57**(5) (Jan 2025)
13. Lin, W., Lan, H., Wang, H., Li, B.: Orphicx: a causality-inspired latent variable model for interpreting graph neural networks. In: Proceedings of the IEEE/CVF Conference on Computer Vision and Pattern Recognition, pp. 13729–13738 (2022)
14. Longa, A., et al.: Explaining the explainers in graph neural networks: a comparative study. ACM Comput. Surv. **57**(5) (2025)
15. Monti, C., Bajardi, P., Bonchi, F., Panisson, A., Perotti, A.: A true-to-the-model axiomatic benchmark for graph-based explainers. Trans. Mach. Learn. Res. (2024)
16. Pope, P.E., Kolouri, S., Rostami, M., Martin, C.E., Hoffmann, H.: Explainability methods for graph convolutional neural networks. In: Proceedings of the IEEE/CVF Conference on Computer Vision and Pattern Recognition (CVPR) (June 2019)
17. Rathee, M., Funke, T., Anand, A., Khosla, M.: Bagel: A benchmark for assessing graph neural network explanations. arXiv preprint arXiv:2206.13983 (2022)
18. Schnake, T., et al.: Higher-order explanations of graph neural networks via relevant walks. IEEE Trans. Pattern Anal. Mach. Intell. **44**(11), 7581–7596 (2022)

19. Sundararajan, M., Taly, A., Yan, Q.: Axiomatic attribution for deep networks. In: International Conference on Machine Learning, pp. 3319–3328. PMLR (2017)
20. Veličković, P., Cucurull, G., Casanova, A., Romero, A., Liò, P., Bengio, Y.: Graph attention networks. In: International Conference on Learning Representations (2018)
21. Vu, M., Thai, M.T.: Pgm-explainer: probabilistic graphical model explanations for graph neural networks. Adv. Neural. Inf. Process. Syst. **33**, 12225–12235 (2020)
22. Yang, Z., Cohen, W., Salakhudinov, R.: Revisiting semi-supervised learning with graph embeddings. In: Balcan, M.F., Weinberger, K.Q. (eds.) Proceedings of The 33rd International Conference on Machine Learning. Proceedings of Machine Learning Research, New York, USA, 20–22 Jun, vol. 48, pp. 40–48. PMLR (2016)
23. Ying, Z., Bourgeois, D., You, J., Zitnik, M., Leskovec, J.: Gnnexplainer: generating explanations for graph neural networks. Adv. Neural Inform. Process. Syst. **32** (2019)
24. Yuan, H., Yu, H., Gui, S., Ji, S.: Explainability in graph neural networks: a taxonomic survey. IEEE Trans. Pattern Anal. Mach. Intell. **45**(5), 5782–5799 (2022)
25. Yuan, H., Yu, H., Wang, J., Li, K., Ji, S.: On explainability of graph neural networks via subgraph explorations. In: International Conference on Machine Learning, pp. 12241–12252. PMLR (2021)
26. Zeiler, M.: Visualizing and understanding convolutional networks. In: European Conference on Computer Vision/arXiv, vol. 1311 (2014)
27. Zhang, H., Wu, B., Yuan, X., Pan, S., Tong, H., Pei, J.: Trustworthy graph neural networks: aspects, methods, and trends. In: Proceedings of the IEEE (2024)
28. Zhang, S., Liu, Y., Shah, N., Sun, Y.: Gstarx: explaining graph neural networks with structure-aware cooperative games. Adv. Neural. Inf. Process. Syst. **35**, 19810–19823 (2022)
29. Zhu, X., Ghahramani, Z.: Learning from labeled and unlabeled data with label propagation. Technical Report. CMU-CALD-02-107, Carnegie Mellon University (2002)

MASCOTS: Model-Agnostic Symbolic COunterfactual Explanations for Time Series

Dawid Płudowski[1](✉), Francesco Spinnato[3,4], Piotr Wilczyński[1,7], Krzysztof Kotowski[5], Evridiki Vasileia Ntagiou[6], Riccardo Guidotti[3,4], and Przemysław Biecek[1,2]

[1] Warsaw University of Technology, Warsaw, Poland
{dawid.pludowski.stud,przemyslaw.biecek}@pw.edu.pl
[2] University of Warsaw, Warsaw, Poland
[3] University of Pisa, Pisa, Italy
francesco.spinnato@di.unipi.it, riccardo.guidotti@unipi.it
[4] ISTI-CNR, Pisa, Italy
[5] KP Labs, Gliwice, Poland
kkotowski@kplabs.pl
[6] European Space Operations Centre, Darmstadt, Germany
evridiki.ntagiou@esa.int
[7] ETH Zürich, Zürich, Switzerland
pwilczynski@ethz.ch

Abstract. Counterfactual explanations provide an intuitive way to understand model decisions by identifying minimal changes required to alter an outcome. However, applying counterfactual methods to time series models remains challenging due to temporal dependencies, high dimensionality, and the lack of an intuitive human-interpretable representation. We introduce MASCOTS, a method that leverages the Bag-of-Receptive-Fields representation alongside symbolic transformations inspired by Symbolic Aggregate Approximation. By operating in a symbolic feature space, it enhances interpretability while preserving fidelity to the original data and model. Unlike existing approaches that either depend on model structure or autoencoder-based sampling, MASCOTS directly generates meaningful and diverse counterfactual observations in a model-agnostic manner, operating on both univariate and multivariate data. We evaluate MASCOTS on univariate and multivariate benchmark datasets, demonstrating comparable validity, proximity, and plausibility to state-of-the-art methods, while significantly improving interpretability and sparsity. Its symbolic nature allows for explanations that can be expressed visually, in natural language, or through semantic representations, making counterfactual reasoning more accessible and actionable.

Keywords: Explainable AI (XAI) · Counterfactual Explanations · Time Series · Model-Agnostic Explanations

1 Introduction

Time series classification (TSC) plays a crucial role in various fields, including healthcare, climate science, and engineering. Its wide-ranging applications have driven the development of increasingly powerful predictors capable of achieving remarkable classification accuracy. Both univariate and multivariate time series classification have gained significant research interest, as demonstrated by recent "bake-offs" [32,35,38], which periodically benchmark the top-performing classifiers. The findings from these evaluations are consistent: the most effective classifiers are powerful hybrid ensembles, such as MultiRocket-Hydra [10], Hive-Cote 2 [31], and InceptionTime [17]. These models leverage both prediction and feature spaces from multiple underlying algorithms, resulting in state-of-the-art accuracy. However, their complexity renders them black-box models, meaning they lack interpretability from a human perspective.

This work aims to enhance the interpretability of black-box models in time series classification through Explainable Artificial Intelligence (XAI) techniques [5]. While XAI offers diverse tools for explaining complex models, most approaches have been developed for tabular or image data, with time series explainability only recently gaining traction [39]. In this domain, explanations commonly take the form of saliency maps [30], highlighting the most relevant part of observations contributing to the classification outcome, or subsequence-based explanations such as shapelets [43] focusing on significant sub-patterns within a time series. Instead, this work centers on instance-based explanations, where entire time series serve as the primary explanatory objects. Specifically, we focus on counterfactual explanations, i.e., minimal semantically valid modifica-

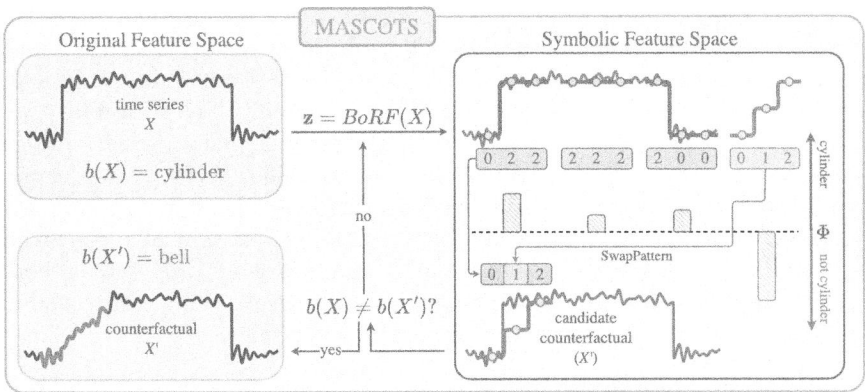

Fig. 1. A simplified graphical abstract of MASCOTS. Given a time series X classified by a black-box model b as *cylinder*, X is transformed into a symbolic representation, $\mathbf{z}$, using the Bag-of-Receptive-Fields (BoRF) [36]. In this semantic space, X is represented as symbolic subsequences. To identify a candidate counterfactual, the most important positive and negative patterns (*0,2,2* and *0,1,2* in the illustration) are selected. The negative pattern is then *swapped* within the time series to generate a candidate counterfactual. If the black-box model's predicted class remains unchanged, the process repeats. Otherwise, the final counterfactual is returned.

tions to an input time series that alter the classification outcome of a black-box model [18,40]. Counterfactual explanations are particularly powerful because, unlike feature importance methods [15,30], they indicate what must change in a given instance to achieve a different classification result [14]. They are useful as they facilitate reasoning about the cause-effect relationships between observed features and classification outputs [6].

In this work, we introduce MASCOTS, a novel model-agnostic method for generating counterfactual explanations in time series. MASCOTS leverages symbolic representations to significantly enhance interpretability while maintaining fidelity. As depicted in Fig. 1, MASCOTS initially converts a given time series into a Bag-of-Receptive-Fields (BoRF) representation [36], capturing essential symbolic patterns. It then identifies those patterns most strongly influencing classification outcomes, both positively and negatively. By iteratively substituting negative patterns, MASCOTS modifies the original time series until it obtains a valid counterfactual, ensuring an interpretable and robust explanatory process.

Our contributions are as follows. *(i)* In contrast to existing methods that depend on model-specific architectures or autoencoder-based sampling [37,42], MASCOTS is fully interpretable and model-agnostic. This allows it to be applied broadly across time series classifiers without making any assumptions about the internal mechanisms of the black-box models. *(ii)* To the best of our knowledge, MASCOTS is the first approach that employs a symbolic subsequence-based semantic space for explainability in the time series domain, providing a semantic-rich counterfactual generation process that does not depend on nearest unlike neighbors (NUN) [7]. *(iii)* MASCOTS facilitates both visual and natural language counterfactual explanations, improving the interpretability of the counterfactual generation process. *(iv)* Furthermore, MASCOTS enables explanations for state-of-the-art ensemble models, a task where most existing methods fail due to their reliance on internal model structures. Through extensive evaluation on benchmark datasets, we demonstrate that MASCOTS achieves comparable performance to state-of-the-art techniques regarding validity, proximity, and plausibility while significantly improving the sparsity of counterfactual explanations. By bridging symbolic representations with counterfactual reasoning, MASCOTS represents a significant step forward in explainability for time series models.

The structure of this work is as follows: Sect. 2 examines related research on counterfactuals, while Sect. 3 outlines the background of our proposed methodology. Section 4 elaborates on the approach, followed by experimental results and analysis in Sect. 5. Lastly, Sect. 6 presents the conclusions.

2 Related Works

The simplest counterfactual models for time series rely on classical distance-based algorithms, such as K-Nearest Neighbors (KNN) or Nearest Unlike Neighbor (NUN) [7], which identify the closest existing instance of a different class. In this category, we find approaches like Native Guides [9] and TimeX [12], where time series are perturbed to generate counterfactuals while adhering to desirable properties such as proximity, sparsity, plausibility, and diversity. However, these approaches are limited to univariate data. CoMTE [1] extends this framework to multivariate data by modifying time series from the training set, and computing the minimal number of substitutions necessary to change the original classification. Since CoMTE primarily operates by identifying and substituting similar patterns from different classes, it may struggle to produce meaningful counterfactuals when the dataset lacks sufficiently close examples. AB-CF [25] and DiscoX [3] take a different approach by focusing on local patterns. They extract fixed-length subsequences using a sliding window or identify discords via the matrix profile [44], replacing them with the nearest counterparts from the desired class. Given their emphasis on locality, these methods may fail to capture global temporal dependencies, potentially leading to counterfactuals that are locally valid but globally unrealistic. Finally, in [20], KNN is employed to locally and globally *tweak* time series, altering the outcome of specific black-box models. However, this approach is also restricted to univariate data. Contrary to classical distance-based approaches, our proposal, MASCOTS, does not rely on NUNs or Euclidean distance, as it performs perturbations in a semantic space produced by an interpretable transformation, i.e., the Bag-of-Receptive-Fields [36].

More complex approaches leverage evolutionary algorithms [16] and generative models, such as autoencoders. Autoencoders come in various forms, including recurrent neural networks, such as LSTMs, which have been used in [23] to extend the concept of Contrastive Explanation Methods to time series. Convolutional neural networks (CNNs) have also been utilized, as seen in LASTS [37], as well as methods that test both, such as LatentCF++ [42]. The central idea of these approaches is to perturb time series within a simplified latent space, ensuring that counterfactuals remain closer to the distribution of the training set. In this sense, autoencoders can play an indirect role as a loss component that assesses counterfactual *plausibility*. Sub-SpaCE [34] exemplifies this approach by evaluating the plausibility of counterfactuals generated through a genetic algorithm with tailored mutation and initialization strategies. This method encourages modifications in a minimal number of subsequences, producing highly sparse explanations. Plausibility is assessed similarly in TeRCE [2], which leverages the shapelet transform to identify the most relevant shapelets for a given class, pinpoint their locations in the input instance, and replace them with values derived from the NUN. While these methods are model-agnostic, their main limitation is the requirement to train a separate autoencoder for each dataset [37], which makes their usage across a wide range of tasks impractical. In contrast, MASCOTS, does not require any generative model to produce a counterfactual.

Counterfactual explanations can also be model-specific, i.e., designed for a particular black-box model. With the exception of [20], which targets the Random Shapelet Forest [19], most model-specific approaches focus on explaining neural network-based methods. One such example is Glacier [41], an extension of LatentCF++ designed to generate counterfactuals for any deep-learning-based model. While this approach is both promising and extensively tested, it is limited to univariate data. Other notable methods include CELS [26] for univariate data and M-CELS [27] for multivariate data, both of which employ a gradient-based strategy. These methods utilize three interdependent modules to produce sparse counterfactuals, leveraging a learned saliency map to guide perturbations. The primary limitation of gradient-based model-specific approaches is that, while certain deep learning architectures are highly effective for TSC, the current state-of-the-art consists primarily of hybrid ensemble methods [32]. These ensembles often integrate multiple classifiers, making it difficult, or even impossible, to compute gradients, thus restricting the applicability of such techniques. MASCOTS does not share these limitations as it is model-agnostic.

Finally, to the best of our knowledge, most of the aforementioned methods rely exclusively on visualizations to convey counterfactual modifications. In contrast, we enable the generation of counterfactual explanations in a structured, human-understandable manner using natural language descriptions. Specifically, given a time series X and its counterfactual X', the transformation can be articulated through a structured statement such as: *"To change the prediction of a black-box model from class c_i to c_j, the time series X needs to contain pattern a instead of b."* One approach that might seem similar is PUPAE [11], but the key difference is that it relies on a predefined set of templates that require domain expertise to construct. In contrast, MASCOTS derives its explanations directly from the time series patterns, eliminating the need for manually designed templates. This makes MASCOTS not only more flexible but also broadly applicable across different domains without requiring specialized knowledge.

3 Background

This section provides all the necessary concepts to understand our proposal.

Definition 1 (Time Series Data). *A time series dataset, $\mathcal{X} = \{X_1, \ldots, X_n\} \in \mathbb{R}^{n \times d \times m}$, is a collection of n time series. A time series, X, is a collection of d signals (or channels), $X = \{\mathbf{x}_1, \ldots, \mathbf{x}_d\} \in \mathbb{R}^{d \times m}$. A signal, $\mathbf{x}$, is a sequence of m real-valued observations sampled regularly, $\mathbf{x} = [x_1, \ldots, x_m] \in \mathbb{R}^m$.*

When $d = 1$, the time series is *univariate*, for $d > 1$ it is *multivariate*. Time series datasets can be used in a variety of tasks. This work focuses on supervised learning, particularly Time Series Classification (TSC).

Definition 2 (Time Series Classification). *Let $\mathcal{X}$ be a time series dataset and $\mathbf{y} \in \{1, \ldots, c\}^n$ its corresponding labels vector, where c is the number of classes. The goal of Time Series Classification is to train a model f that maps each time series $X_i \in \mathcal{X}$ to a predicted label $\hat{y}_i$, such that $f(X_i) = \hat{y}_i$ for all $i \in \{1, \ldots, n\}$. This yields the predicted label vector $\hat{\mathbf{y}} = [\hat{y}_1, \ldots, \hat{y}_n] \in \{1, \ldots, c\}^n$.*

The goal of time series classification is to ensure that the trained model f predicts a label $\hat{\mathbf{y}}$ that closely matches the true labels $\mathbf{y}$, typically by minimizing a classification loss function during training. Many models produce probability distributions over classes, i.e., $\hat{Y} \in [0,1]^{n \times c}$, with $\hat{\mathbf{y}}$ determined by the highest probability. While maximizing accuracy is important, providing explanations for the predictions of a given model is becoming more and more relevant. This work focuses on a specific type of explanation, i.e., *counterfactual explanations*. Counterfactual time series show the minimal changes in the input data that lead to a different decision outcome [39]. Formally:

Definition 3 (Counterfactual). *Given a classifier f that outputs the decision $\hat{y} = f(X)$ for an instance X, a* counterfactual *consists of an instance X' such that the decision for f on X' is different from $\hat{y}$, i.e., $f(X') \neq \hat{y}$, and such that X' is similar to X, and that X' is plausible.*

Similarity (or proximity) usually refers to a distance metric, while plausibility depends on the counterfactual domain and is assessed by verifying that the instance is not merely an adversarial example and remains semantically coherent with the dataset. Other relevant metrics include *sparsity*, i.e., the number of features altered to generate a counterfactual, and *validity*, i.e., the ability of a counterfactual method to produce a valid counterfactual.

Counterfactuals can be obtained in several ways; here, we propose to adopt *surrogate models*. Explanations based on surrogate methods can clarify the behavior of black-box models, b, by employing a secondary, more interpretable model, g, to approximate the behavior of the primary black-box model, i.e., $b(X) \simeq g(X)$ [5]. By doing so, the surrogate model seeks to provide insights into the complex model's decisions by mimicking its outputs while remaining inherently more interpretable. A great advantage of surrogates is that they are model-agnostic, i.e., they can explain any black-box without any assumption about its inner components. Surrogates can be trained on the original raw time series data or after processing it into a more interpretable tabular representation.

There exist several symbolic representation-based methods for time series classification, such as MrSEQL [24], MrSQM [33], and SCALE-BOSS-MR [13], to name a few. However, in this work, we adopt the Bag-of-Receptive-Fields (BoRF) [36] as our interpretable tabular representation, as it was shown to achieve better overall accuracy [36], with a very fast prediction time. BoRF extends the classical Bag-of-Patterns [4] and, akin to the Bag-of-Words approach in text analysis, converts a time series into a vector of pattern counts. This transformation is achieved by sliding a potentially strided and dilated window along the time series to extract all possible receptive fields of a specified length, w. In this context, a receptive field is just a time series subsequence that can have gaps inside, i.e., can skip observations. These subsequences are then standardized and discretized into *words* of length $l \leq w$ using the Symbolic Aggregate Approximation (SAX) [28]. SAX uses the Piecewise Aggregate Approximation (PAA) [21] to segment each subsequence into equal-sized segments and then compute the mean value for each segment. Finally, these values are quantized using a set of breakpoints, obtained through the quantiles of the standard Gaussian distribution, which bin values in equiprobable symbols, α. Thus, from each time series, X, a set of patterns is extracted, where a single pattern is denoted as $\mathbf{p} = [\alpha_1, \ldots, \alpha_l] \in \mathbb{A}^l$, with $\mathbb{A}$ being a set of finite symbols. Each symbolic pattern is bidirectionally hashed into an integer k, allowing for both encoding and decoding, and is then stored in the Bag-of-Receptive-Fields. Formally:

Definition 4 (Bag-of-Receptive-Fields). *Given a time series dataset $\mathcal{X} \in \mathbb{R}^{n \times d \times m}$ and a set of h patterns, a Bag-of-Receptive-Fields is a tensor $\mathcal{Z} \in \mathbb{N}^{n \times d \times h}$, where $z_{i,j,k}$ is the number of appearances of the hashed SAX pattern k in the signal j of time series i.*

The Bag-of-Receptive-Fields $\mathcal{Z}$ can be flattened into $Z \in \mathbb{N}^{n \times r}$, where r is the total number of patterns across channels, i.e., $r = dh$. An example of such a representation is shown in Fig. 1 (top-right), where a time series is represented as four patterns (counts are omitted for better readability). Z can then be used as a training set for any standard tabular classifier, g, offering the advantage of interpretable features, specifically, the count of occurrences of each pattern within a time series. Finally, the classifier can be interpreted using any standard explainer, such as feature importance-based methods like SHAP [30].

Definition 5 (Feature Importance). *Given a single row of Z, $\mathbf{z} \in \mathbb{R}^r$, a feature importance matrix, $\Phi = [\phi_1, \ldots, \phi_r] \in \mathbb{R}^{r \times c}$, contains the contribution of each feature value $z \in \mathbf{z}$ towards predicting each possible class c.*

In the following section, we exploit feature importance in the Bag-of-Receptive-Fields semantic space, and propose a counterfactual technique based on symbolic patterns, which iteratively produces interpretable perturbations to generate counterfactual explanations for time series black-box classifiers.

4 Methodology

In this section, we introduce MASCOTS, a Model-Agnostic Symbolic COunterfactual explanation method for Time Series classification. MASCOTS combines the Bag-of-Receptive-Fields (BoRF) representation with symbolic transformations inspired by Symbolic Aggregate Approximation (SAX) to enhance interpretability while maintaining fidelity to the original data and model.

MASCOTS takes as input a time series X, a surrogate model g, a training dataset $\mathcal{X}$ for the surrogate, a black-box model b, an attribution method e, and a penalty hyperparameter λ. In essence, MASCOTS trains a surrogate model on a Bag-of-Receptive-Fields representation of the time series dataset. This surrogate serves as an interpretable proxy for the black-box, allowing the extraction of pattern relevance for classification using a feature attribution method. The resulting feature importance then guides semantic perturbations of the time series by modifying symbolic words. The approach is detailed step-by-step in the following sections, and illustrated in Fig. 1.

4.1 Counterfactual Generation Process

The pseudo-code of MASCOTS is reported in Algorithm 1. The first step is to train an interpretable surrogate model (lines 1-3). To achieve this, MASCOTS

Algorithm 1: MASCOTS

Data: X - time series to explain, $\mathcal{X}$ - surrogate training dataset, g - surrogate model, b - black-box model, e - attribution method, λ - penalty
Result: Counterfactual X'

1 $\hat{\mathbf{y}} \leftarrow b(\mathcal{X})$;   // Predict classes of surrogate dataset
2 $Z \leftarrow BoRF(\mathcal{X})$;   // Convert surrogate dataset into Bag-of-Receptive-Fields
3 $g \leftarrow train(g, Z, \hat{\mathbf{y}})$;   // Train surrogate
4 $\hat{y} \leftarrow b(X)$;   // Predict class of time series to explain
5 $X' \leftarrow X$;
6 **while** $b(X') = \hat{y}$ **do**   // While the black-box prediction does not change
7 $\quad$ $\mathbf{z} \leftarrow BoRF(X')$;   // Convert time series into Bag-of-Receptive-Fields
8 $\quad$ $\Phi \leftarrow e(g, \mathbf{z})$;   // Get attribution matrix
9 $\quad$ $\Delta \leftarrow \text{GetPerturbation}(X', \hat{y}, \mathbf{z}, \Phi, \lambda)$;   // Generate perturbation
10 $\quad$ $X' \leftarrow X' + \Delta$;   // Perturb time series
11 **return** X'

requires a training set $\mathcal{X}$, and obtains the corresponding black-box predictions, $\hat{\mathbf{y}} = b(\mathcal{X})$ (line 1). Next, the training data $\mathcal{X}$ is transformed into a Bag-of-Receptive-Fields representation, Z, using BoRF [36] (line 2). Finally, the surrogate model is trained on Z and $\hat{\mathbf{y}}$, effectively learning to approximate the black-box predictions on the given dataset (line 3). The black-box is also used to predict the label of the time series whose prediction we are explaining, i.e., $\hat{y} = b(X)$ (line 4). Then, X', a copy of X, is created (line 5), and the counterfactual generation loop begins. The condition of the counterfactual generation loop (line 6) checks whether the black-box prediction on the perturbed time series X' matches that of the original time series X. While this is true, the loop proceeds as follows. X' is converted into a Bag-of-Receptive-Fields vector, $\mathbf{z}$, (line 7), the attribution method is used to produce a feature importance matrix, Φ, containing the contribution of each pattern value in $\mathbf{z}$ towards each class (line 8). Then, the GetPerturbation procedure is invoked to generate the perturbation (line 9), which is subsequently added to the time series (line 10). After this, the loop condition is re-evaluated, and the final counterfactual, X', is eventually returned.

Using an iterative algorithm reinforces the **validity** of generated counterfactuals by gradually shifting the black-box model's prediction toward the target class, as illustrated in Fig. 2. However, multiple changes, even if meaningful, may overly distort the counterfactual, reducing plausibility. Similar to [41], we set a task-dependent iteration limit to balance these factors, halting the algorithm regardless of success. As shown in Sect. 5, the required iterations remain low on average, preventing excessive modifications.

4.2 Pattern Swapping

We illustrate the GetPerturbation procedure in Algorithm 2. It begins by utilizing the feature attribution matrix to identify the most important pattern for

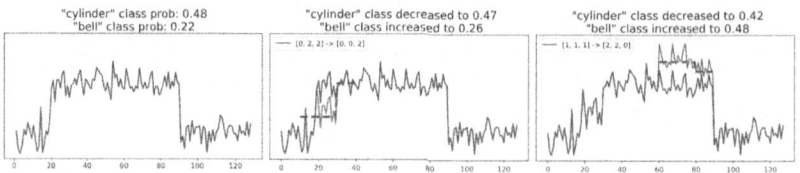

Fig. 2. Example of the iterative process of MASCOTS: a time series is gradually perturbed from a *cylinder* to a *bell*. Inserted patterns are marked by the black dashed line.

the predicted class, denoted as k^+. This corresponds to the symbolic word that has the highest relevance toward the classification outcome assigned to the time series X by the black-box model (line 1). We restrict the search to *contained patterns*, i.e., patterns where $z_k > 0$, as we want to perturb an existing pattern in X. Using the inverse hash function provided by BoRF, k^+ is then mapped back to its corresponding pattern vector (line 2), $\mathbf{p}^+$. Next, GetPerturbation identifies the most relevant pattern index opposing the predicted class, k^-, i.e., the index of the symbolic word that most strongly influences a classification different from $\hat{y}$ (line 3). Similar to line 2, the corresponding pattern vector, $\mathbf{p}^-$, is retrieved (line 4). The swapping step alters only these two patterns while the others remain unchanged, thus intrinsically encouraging the perturbation's **sparsity**. The penalty parameter λ is applied to penalize patterns that deviate significantly from $\mathbf{p}^+$ to ensure that the transformation remains meaningful and does not introduce too unrealistic modifications. A high value of λ further encourages selecting similar patterns, reducing the number of altered elements in the time series. This constraint enhances the **proximity** property of the counterfactual, ensuring that modifications remain minimal. At the same time, it enforces the algorithm to choose locally suboptimal steps, potentially requiring more steps to create the counterfactual. Proximity and sparsity, paired with the fact that the swap is performed between two patterns that both exist in the training dataset, $\mathcal{X}$, push the generated perturbation to remain within a reasonable semantic range, i.e., they promote **plausibility**. The vector $\mathbf{p}^+$ is then aligned to the time series to determine the channel, j, and starting timestamp, t, in X' where the perturbation will be applied (line 5). Since a given pattern can have multiple valid alignments within the time series, a random index is selected from the available options to introduce variability while maintaining realism. Finally, the perturbation matrix, Δ, is initialized (line 6) and populated using the PatternSwap function (line 7).

The PatternSwap function operates on a time series X and takes as input the two SAX patterns, $\mathbf{p}^+ = [\alpha_1^+, \ldots, \alpha_l^+]$ and $\mathbf{p}^- = [\alpha_1^-, \ldots, \alpha_l^-]$. Its primary objective is to perturb the subsequence from channel j, starting at index t, $\mathbf{x}_{j,t:t+w} = [x_{j,t}, \ldots, x_{j,t+w}]$, which corresponds to the pattern $\mathbf{p}^+$, so that when SAX is applied, this subsequence is instead encoded as $\mathbf{p}^-$. Let μ and σ be the mean and standard deviation of the subsequence, and let $\bar{\mathbf{x}} = [\bar{x}_1, \ldots, \bar{x}_l]$ be

Algorithm 2: GetPerturbation

Data: X - time series to swap, $\hat{y}$ - predicted class, $\mathbf{z}$ Bag-of-Receptive-Fields, Φ - attribution map, λ - penalty
Result: Perturbation - Δ

1   $k^+ \leftarrow \arg\max\limits_{k:z_k \neq 0} \phi_{k,\hat{y}}$;   // Id of most important word for prediction
2   $\mathbf{p}^+ \leftarrow hash^{-1}(k^+)$;   // Retrieve important word for prediction
3   $k^- \leftarrow \arg\min\limits_{k} \phi_{k,\hat{y}} + \lambda \|\mathbf{p}^+ - \mathbf{p}_k\|_1$;   // Id of most important word against prediction
4   $\mathbf{p}^- \leftarrow hash^{-1}(k^-)$;   // Retrieve most important word against prediction
5   $j, t \leftarrow align(X, \mathbf{p}^+)$;   // Find pattern channel and timestamp alignment
6   $\Delta \leftarrow \mathbf{0}^{d \times m}$;   // Initialize empty perturbation matrix
7   $\Delta_{j,t:t+w} \leftarrow \text{PatternSwap}(X, \Delta, \mathbf{p}^+, \mathbf{p}^-)$;   // Swap pattern
8   **return** Δ

its segmented representation obtained via PAA, where each segment consists of w/l observations, which are averaged within that segment. To achieve the transformation, we first define the perturbation needed to shift the segmented value $\bar{x}_i$ from its original symbolic representation α_i^+ to the target α_i^-. This perturbation is given by the difference between $\bar{x}_i$ and the central value of the bin corresponding to α_i^-, denoted as $q^{\alpha_i^-}$. The perturbation is then denormalized using the inverse standardization formula, incorporating the subsequence's mean μ and standard deviation σ. Formally,

$$\delta_i = (q^{\alpha_i^-} - \bar{x}_i)\sigma + \mu, \qquad (1)$$

where δ_i represents changes that must be added to all observations corresponding to $\bar{x}_i$ to move them into a different breakpoint bin. To apply this perturbation to the original subsequence $\mathbf{x}_{j,t:t+w}$, we produce $\boldsymbol{\delta} = [\delta_1, \ldots, \delta_1, \ldots, \delta_l, \ldots, \delta_l]$ such that each δ_i is repeated w/l times. Thus, the perturbation is simply $\Delta_{j,t:t+w} = \boldsymbol{\delta}$, which can be summed to the original time series X (line 10, Algorithm 1). This transformation ensures that the local structure of the time series is preserved while allowing flexible modifications. Importantly, the locality of perturbations is not strictly enforced. A single perturbation can potentially influence an extended portion of the time series, depending on the subsequence length corresponding to the most important pattern $\mathbf{p}^+$. Even if the final modification to the time series is relatively large, it remains interpretable, as it can be succinctly described using only l values, where each subsequence segment of length w/l is shifted by a single scalar, reducing cognitive complexity.

5 Experiments

In this section, we assess MASCOTS on both univariate and multivariate time series classification datasets from the UEA and UCR repositories [8], comparing its performance against state-of-the-art methods[1]. We use the datasets listed in

---
[1] The code is available at https://github.com/ModelOriented/mascots.

Table 1, all of which have been featured in multiple studies introducing counterfactuals for time series [27,41].

As baseline counterfactual explainers, we employ Glacier [41] and M-CELS [27], two recently proposed methods that achieve strong results without requiring extensive training of generative adversarial networks or multiple runs of genetic algorithms. For Glacier, we use its "uniform" variant, which offers the best trade-off in terms of *proximity* and *sparsity*. Gradients are computed in the latent space of a 1D-CNN autoencoder, as this setup has been shown to yield the highest validity scores. Due to Glacier's limitations, we restrict its evaluation to univariate data. For M-CELS, we adhere to the hyperparameter settings recommended by the authors, except for disabling `tvnorm` and `budget`, which we empirically found to improve validity. We use InceptionTime [17] as a black-box model due to its state-of-the-art performance in TSC and ability to provide model gradients required by M-CELS and Glacier. While MASCOTS does not rely on gradients, selecting InceptionTime ensures a fair comparison. Additionally, we include a qualitative example with MultiRocket-Hydra [10], a model that lacks gradient access and is therefore incompatible with most counterfactual explainers.

MASCOTS is parametrized by the choice of λ, the surrogate model, the attribution method, and the configuration of the BoRF transformation. Based on preliminary experiments, we set $\lambda \in \{0.0, 0.1\}$. This choice reflects a trade-off between proximity and validity that can vary depending on the dataset and task. In practice, while $\lambda = 0.1$ generally provided better overall performance, $\lambda = 0.0$ often remained a reliable default, highlighting the robustness of the method to this hyperparameter. The surrogate model, g, is a shallow neural network with two hidden layers of size 256, followed by a softmax function. Each layer, except the last one, is followed by a ReLU activation function. The network is trained by minimizing the categorical cross-entropy using ADAM as the optimizer [22], with a constant learning rate equal to 0.2, weight decay equal to 0.1, and dropout equal to 0.2. For each experiment, the batch size is set to 8, and the network is trained for a maximum of 1000 epochs, with early stopping triggered after 200 epochs without improvement on the validation score. After training, the checkpoint of the model that performs best on the validation set is retrieved and used in subsequent experiments. As the attribution method, e, we use Deep SHAP [30] with default hyperparameters.

BoRF automatically adapts its main hyperparameters to each dataset, taking into account the number of time steps and channels. To preserve the contiguity of subsequences, crucial for interpretability, dilation is fixed at 1, ensuring that symbols correspond to consecutive points in the original series. This avoids sparse perturbations, which can obscure the meaning of the generated counterfactual. Additionally, the alphabet size is set to 3, and the stride is defined as w/l (the ratio of word size to word length), enabling an efficient and informative transformation. Other parameters, including the number of SAX configurations, word size w, and length l, are dynamically adjusted to capture both local and global patterns. For each dataset, the smallest SAX words contain at least 8 points, while the largest are the highest power of two not exceeding the time series length. Each SAX word consists of either 2 or 4 symbols. The algorithm is limited to a maximum of 20 iterations to mitigate adversarial effects.

Table 1. Datasets description follows the notation introduced in Sect. 3: n (instances), d (channels), m (points), and c (classes). $ACC(b)$ and $FID(g)$ denote the accuracy of InceptionTime and the fidelity of MASCOTS' surrogate, i.e., how well $g(X)$ mimics $b(X)$, measured in terms of accuracy, respectively.

Dataset	n	d	m	c	$ACC(b)$	$FID(g)$
TwoLeadECG	23	1	82	2	1.00	1.00
GunPoint	50	1	150	2	1.00	1.00
Earthquakes	322	1	512	2	0.68	0.82
Coffee	28	1	286	2	1.00	1.00
Wine	57	1	234	2	0.80	0.84
ItalyPowerDemand	67	1	24	2	0.97	0.91
BasicMotions	40	6	100	4	0.50	1.00
Cricket	108	6	1197	12	0.24	0.60
Epilepsy	137	3	206	4	0.30	0.90
RacketSports	151	6	30	4	0.37	0.64

Evaluation Measures. We adopt the primary measures of counterfactual quality reported in prior studies [26,41]: *validity*, *proximity*, *sparsity*, and *plausibility*. The first three are formally defined below, while plausibility is assessed using Isolation Forest [29], where we report the fraction of counterfactuals classified as nominal (non-outliers). Additionally, we provide runtime comparisons for all algorithms using the same hardware setup[2].

Validity measures the proportion of generated counterfactuals X'_i that lead to a different classifier prediction compared to the original instance X_i. It is defined as $validity(\mathcal{X}, \mathcal{X}') = \frac{1}{n}\sum_{i=1}^{n} \mathbb{1}[f(X_i) \neq f(X'_i)]$, where $\mathbb{1}[f(X_i) \neq f(X'_i)]$ is an indicator function that equals 1 if the model's prediction changes and 0 otherwise. A high validity score indicates that most counterfactuals effectively alter the model's decision. Proximity quantifies the average distance between original instances and their corresponding counterfactuals: $proximity(\mathcal{X}, \mathcal{X}') = \frac{1}{n \cdot d \cdot m}\sum_{i=1}^{n} \|X_i - X'_i\|$, where $\|X_i - X'_i\|$ represents the distance between X_i and X'_i. Lower proximity values indicate that counterfactuals remain close to the original data points, making them more realistic and interpretable. Sparsity captures the fraction of features that remain unchanged between the original and counterfactual instances: $sparsity(\mathcal{X}, \mathcal{X}') = \frac{1}{n \cdot d \cdot m}\sum_{i=1}^{n}\sum_{j=1}^{d}\sum_{t=1}^{m} \mathbb{1}[x_{i,j,t} - x'_{i,j,t} = 0]$, where $\mathbb{1}[x_{i,j,t} - x'_{i,j,t} = 0]$ equals 1 if a feature remains unchanged and 0 otherwise. Higher sparsity values indicate that fewer features are modified, promoting more interpretable counterfactual explanations.

---
[2] System: 8 cores AMD Rome 7742, 32GB RAM.

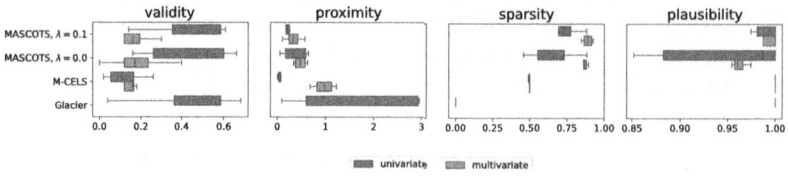

Fig. 3. Box-plots of evaluation measures. For *validity*, *sparsity*, and *plausibility*, the higher score is better, while for *proximity*, the smaller the better. MASCOTS stands out in *sparsity* with a decent *validity* and *proximity*. The difference between MASCOTS-$\lambda = 0.0$ and MASCOTS-$\lambda = 0.1$ suggests a trade-off between validity and other measures.

Table 2. Mean and standard deviation for the various evaluation measures aggregated over univariate and multivariate datasets. For MASCOTS, we add the average number of iterations required to flip a label. Best values are highlighted in bold.

		validity ↑	*proximity* ↓	*sparsity* ↑	*plausibility* ↑	# iter. ↓
univariate	MASCOTS$_{\lambda=0.1}$	0.44 ± 0.18	0.24 ± 0.18	$\mathbf{0.71 \pm 0.12}$	0.98 ± 0.02	3.0 ± 1.0
	MASCOTS$_{\lambda=0.0}$	0.44 ± 0.21	0.35 ± 0.25	0.65 ± 0.15	0.84 ± 0.29	$\mathbf{2.7 \pm 1.3}$
	M-CELS	0.11 ± 0.08	$\mathbf{0.08 \pm 0.10}$	0.49 ± 0.00	0.99 ± 0.01	–
	Glacier	0.41 ± 0.23	2.32 ± 2.34	0.00 ± 0.00	$\mathbf{1.00 \pm 0.00}$	–
multiv.	MASCOTS$_{\lambda=0.1}$	0.15 ± 0.12	$\mathbf{0.33 \pm 0.19}$	$\mathbf{0.88 \pm 0.03}$	0.98 ± 0.02	$\mathbf{1.7 \pm 2.7}$
	MASCOTS$_{\lambda=0.0}$	$\mathbf{0.18 \pm 0.16}$	0.47 ± 0.13	0.87 ± 0.01	0.96 ± 0.00	2.4 ± 3.6
	M-CELS	0.12 ± 0.08	0.96 ± 0.23	0.49 ± 0.00	$\mathbf{1.00 \pm 0.00}$	–

Results. The experimental results for MASCOTS and the baseline models are illustrated through box plots in Fig. 3 and summarized with mean and standard deviation values in Table 2. For *validity*, MASCOTS and Glacier perform particularly well on univariate data, achieving approximately 41%–44% valid counterfactuals on average. On multivariate datasets, both configurations of MASCOTS outperform M-CELS, although the overall low performance of both methods on multivariate data suggests the need for further investigation in future work. Notably, setting the λ parameter to 0.0 slightly improves the validity of counterfactuals generated by MASCOTS. In terms of *proximity*, MASCOTS and M-CELS produce counterfactuals that remain reasonably close to the original observations, while Glacier generates counterfactuals that are significantly more distant. For multivariate datasets, MASCOTS consistently outperforms M-CELS in proximity. Regarding *sparsity*, MASCOTS excels, altering fewer than 30% of the original features on average. In contrast, Glacier, due to its gradient-based nature, modifies every point at least slightly, preventing it from generating sparse explanations. M-CELS, on the other hand, alters approximately 50% of the time series to construct a counterfactual. Furthermore, we report the average number of iterations (i.e., the number of pattern swaps) required by MASCOTS to generate a counterfactual. This number varies across datasets and configurations but typically does not exceed 3. This suggests that, on average, MASCOTS can produce effective counterfactuals with only three meaningful semantic modifica-

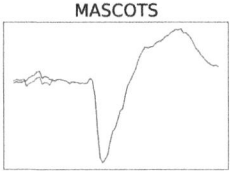 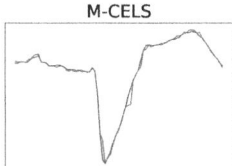 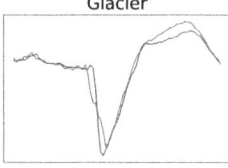

Fig. 4. Example of MASCOTS on the *TwoLeadECG* dataset to explain InceptionTime. MASCOTS is able to create sparse counterfactual which maintain its local structure. On the other hand, M-CELS and Glacier produce small (perhaps adversarial) undesirable changes to the original time series, varying in this way its initial shape.

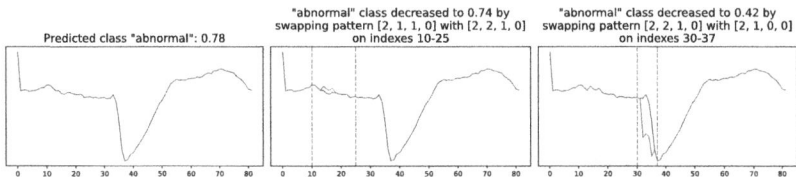

Fig. 5. Example of MASCOTS on the *TwoLeadECG* dataset to explain MultiRocket-Hydra. Changes are presented both as visualization and natural language. If positive and negative patterns have corresponding symbols (for example, the 1st, 3rd, and 4th symbols in the middle plot), MASCOTS does not change them.

tions. Finally, regarding runtime, performance is comparable with an average of 23 min for MASCOTS, 26 min for Glacier, and 55 min for M-CELS.

Qualitative Examples. In Fig. 4, we present the counterfactuals (in red) generated by each analyzed method for a randomly selected time series (in blue) from the *TwoLeadECG* dataset [8], which represents heart ECG signals. For MASCOTS, we set $\lambda = 0.1$ to achieve better proximity and sparsity. In this case, MASCOTS generates a counterfactual by modifying only a single pattern at the beginning of the signal while preserving its local structure. The changes produced by M-CELS are also minimal but are distributed across the signal. In contrast, Glacier introduces significant alterations to the original observation, disrupting the local structure of the signal.

We also provide an example on *TwoLeadECG*, focusing on explaining the MultiRocket-Hydra black-box model [10]. Unlike fully neural network-based models, MultiRocket-Hydra incorporates non-neural components, making methods such as Glacier and M-CELS inapplicable. The explanation, provided both visually and in natural language, is illustrated in Fig. 5. The counterfactual is generated in two iterations. First, MASCOTS introduces a small modification between indexes 10 and 25. While this initial change does not significantly affect the black-box model's prediction, it alters the feature importance matrix Φ, enabling MASCOTS to identify a more impactful transformation in the second iteration. This final modification broadens the valley in the signal, ultimately flipping the model's classification from "abnormal" to "normal." The generated counterfactual can be expressed in natural language as follows: *"To obtain a counterfactual for an abnormal ECG, the pattern in indexes* 10–25 *must be replaced with* $[2, 2, 1, 0]$, *followed by replacing the pattern in indexes* 30–37 *with* $[2, 1, 0, 0]$.*"* These patterns differ in length—16 and 8, respectively—demonstrating the flexibility of MASCOTS in adapting its transformations. In both this example and Fig. 5, the symbols 0, 1, and 2 correspond to "low," "medium," and "high" values in the time series, respectively, providing an intuitive interpretation of the modifications. This interpretation could be further enriched by domain experts, who may map these symbolic values onto a domain-specific representation space.

Indeed, although the symbolic representations used in MASCOTS are structurally syntactic, we refer to the resulting explanations as semantic to emphasize their interpretive potential. The symbolic substitutions themselves operate over abstract pattern spaces, but their interpretability arises when these patterns are contextualized through domain-specific knowledge. In practical scenarios, domain experts are often able to associate particular symbolic motifs with meaningful physiological events, behavioral signatures, or system states. Thus, while the mechanics of MASCOTS rely on syntactic operations, the explanations it produces are inherently semantic to the extent that they can be interpreted and acted upon by humans within a given application context.

6 Conclusion

In this article, we have introduced MASCOTS, a model-agnostic method for generating counterfactual explanations in univariate and multivariate time series classification. By leveraging the BoRF transformation and symbolic representations, MASCOTS enhances interpretability while maintaining fidelity to the original black-box model. Unlike prior approaches, it operates in a fully agnostic manner without the need of autoencoders and without relying on distances or nearest unlike neighbors. Our evaluation demonstrates its effectiveness, achieving high interpretability and sparsity while preserving validity and proximity.

A limitation of our approach, shared with existing competitors, is the relatively low validity performance on multivariate data. This highlights a research gap in the development of counterfactual methods tailored for multivariate time series, as well as the need for broader empirical evaluations to understand the underlying causes of this limitation. To address this, we plan to evaluate MASCOTS on more tasks and challenging real-world scenarios, such as the satellite telemetry domain. Further, we aim to extend our approach into a "user-in-the-middle" framework, allowing expert intervention at each iteration to refine counterfactual explanations. By selecting among proposed changes, experts can enhance the plausibility of generated counterfactuals, explore custom "what-if?" scenarios, and even create artificial observations for manual labelling and integration into training datasets. This interactive approach could further improve the adaptability and utility of counterfactual explanations in real-world applications.

Acknowledgments. This study has been partially funded by the European Space Agency grant 4000144194/23/D/BL "Assurance for space domain AI applications", by the SONATA BIS grant 2019/34/E/ST6/00052 funded by Polish National Science Centre (NCN), and by the Italian Project Fondo Italiano per la Scienza FIS00001966 "MIMOSA", by the European Community Horizon 2020 programme under the funding schemes ERC-2018-ADG G.A. 834756 "XAI", G.A. 101070212 "FINDHR", G.A. 101120763 "TANGO", by the European Commission under the NextGeneration EU programme National Recovery and Resilience Plan (Piano Nazionale di Ripresa e Resilienza, PNRR) Project: "SoBigData.it Strengthening the Italian RI for Social Mining and Big Data Analytics" Prot. IR0000013 Av. n. 3264 del 28/12/2021, and M4C2 - Investimento 1.3, Partenariato Esteso PE00000013 - "FAIR" - Future Artificial Intelligence Research" - Spoke 1 "Human-centered AI". The authors gratefully acknowledge the contributors of the datasets available through the UEA & UCR Repositories. Their efforts in collecting and sharing these datasets have been invaluable to this research.

Disclosure of Interests. The authors have no competing interests to declare that are relevant to the content of this article.

References

1. Ates, E., Aksar, B., Leung, V.J., Coskun, A.K.: Counterfactual explanations for multivariate time series. In: 2021 International Conference on Applied Artificial Intelligence (ICAPAI), pp. 1–8 (2021)
2. Bahri, O., Li, P., Boubrahimi, S.F., Hamdi, S.M.: Temporal rule-based counterfactual explanations for multivariate time series. In: 2022 21st IEEE International Conference on Machine Learning and Applications (ICMLA), pp. 1244–1249 (2022)
3. Bahri, O., Li, P., Filali Boubrahimi, S., Hamdi, S.M.: Discord-based counterfactual explanations for time series classification. Data Min. Knowl. Disc. **38**(6), 3347–3371 (2024)
4. Baydogan, M.G., Runger, G., Tuv, E.: A bag-of-features framework to classify time series. IEEE Trans. Pattern Anal. Mach. Intell. **35**(11), 2796–2802 (2013)
5. Bodria, F., Giannotti, F., Guidotti, R., Naretto, F., Pedreschi, D., Rinzivillo, S.: Benchmarking and survey of explanation methods for black box models. Data Mining Knowl. Dis., 1–60 (2023)
6. Chen, Z., Silvestri, F., Wang, J., Zhu, H., Ahn, H., Tolomei, G.: Relax: reinforcement learning agent explainer for arbitrary predictive models. In: Proceedings of the 31st ACM International Conference on Information & Knowledge Management, pp. 252–261 (2022)
7. Dasarathy, B.V.: Nearest unlike neighbor (nun): an aid to decision confidence estimation. Opt. Eng. **34**(9), 2785–2792 (1995)
8. Dau, H.A., et al.: The ucr time series archive. IEEE/CAA J. Automatica Sinica **6**(6), 1293–1305 (2019)
9. Delaney, E., Greene, D., Keane, M.T.: Instance-based counterfactual explanations for time series classification. In: Case-Based Reasoning Research and Development, pp. 32–47 (2021)
10. Dempster, A., Schmidt, D.F., Webb, G.I.: Hydra: competing convolutional kernels for fast and accurate time series classification. Data Min. Knowl. Disc. **37**(5), 1779–1805 (2023)

11. Der, A., et al.: Pupae: intuitive and actionable explanations for time series anomalies. In: Proceedings of the 2024 SIAM International Conference on Data Mining (SDM), pp. 37–45 (2024)
12. Filali Boubrahimi, S., Hamdi, S.M.: On the mining of time series data counterfactual explanations using barycenters. In: Proceedings of the 31st ACM International Conference on Information & Knowledge Management, pp. 3943–3947 (2022)
13. Glenis, A., Vouros, G.A.: Scale-boss-mr: scalable time series classification using multiple symbolic representations. Appl. Sci. **14**(2), 689 (2024)
14. Guidotti, R.: Counterfactual explanations and how to find them: literature review and benchmarking. Data Min. Knowl. Disc. **38**(5), 2770–2824 (2024)
15. Guidotti, R., Monreale, A., Giannotti, F., Pedreschi, D., Ruggieri, S., Turini, F.: Factual and counterfactual explanations for black box decision making. IEEE Intell. Syst. **34**(6), 14–23 (2019)
16. Höllig, J., Kulbach, C., Thoma, S.: Tsevo: evolutionary counterfactual explanations for time series classification. In: 2022 21st IEEE International Conference on Machine Learning and Applications (ICMLA), pp. 29–36 (2022)
17. Ismail Fawaz, H., et al.: Inceptiontime: finding alexnet for time series classification. Data Min. Knowl. Disc. **34**(6), 1936–1962 (2020)
18. Karimi, A.H., Barthe, G., Balle, B., Valera, I.: Model-agnostic counterfactual explanations for consequential decisions. In: International Conference on Artificial Intelligence and Statistics, pp. 895–905. PMLR (2020)
19. Karlsson, I., Papapetrou, P., Boström, H.: Generalized random shapelet forests. Data Min. Knowl. Disc. **30**, 1053–1085 (2016)
20. Karlsson, I., Rebane, J., Papapetrou, P., Gionis, A.: Locally and globally explainable time series tweaking. Knowl. Inf. Syst. **62**(5), 1671–1700 (2020)
21. Keogh, E., Chakrabarti, K., Pazzani, M., Mehrotra, S.: Dimensionality reduction for fast similarity search in large time series databases. Knowl. Inf. Syst. **3**, 263–286 (2001)
22. Kingma, D.P.: Adam: A method for stochastic optimization. arXiv preprint arXiv:1412.6980 (2014)
23. Labaien, J., Zugasti, E., De Carlos, X.: Contrastive explanations for a deep learning model on time-series data. In: International Conference on Big Data Analytics and Knowledge Discovery, pp. 235–244 (2020)
24. Le Nguyen, T., Gsponer, S., Ilie, I., O'reilly, M., Ifrim, G.: Interpretable time series classification using linear models and multi-resolution multi-domain symbolic representations. Data Min. Knowl. Disc. **33**, 1183–1222 (2019)
25. Li, P., Bahri, O., Boubrahimi, S.F., Hamdi, S.M.: Attention-based counterfactual explanation for multivariate time series. In: International Conference on Big Data Analytics and Knowledge Discovery, pp. 287–293 (2023)
26. Li, P., Bahri, O., Boubrahimi, S.F., Hamdi, S.M.: Cels: counterfactual explanations for time series data via learned saliency maps. In: 2023 IEEE International Conference on Big Data (BigData), pp. 718–727 (2023)
27. Li, P., Bahri, O., Boubrahimi, S.F., Hamdi, S.M.: M-cels: counterfactual explanation for multivariate time series data guided by learned saliency maps. arXiv preprint arXiv:2411.02649 (2024)
28. Lin, J., Keogh, E., Wei, L., Lonardi, S.: Experiencing sax: a novel symbolic representation of time series. Data Min. Knowl. Disc. **15**, 107–144 (2007)
29. Liu, F.T., Ting, K.M., Zhou, Z.H.: Isolation forest. In: 2008 Eighth IEEE International Conference on Data Mining, pp. 413–422 (2008)
30. Lundberg, S.M., Lee, S.I.: A unified approach to interpreting model predictions. Adv. Neural Inform. Process. Syst. **30** (2017)

31. Middlehurst, M., Large, J., Flynn, M., Lines, J., Bostrom, A., Bagnall, A.: Hive-cote 2.0: a new meta ensemble for time series classification. Mac. Learn. **110**(11), 3211–3243 (2021)
32. Middlehurst, M., Schäfer, P., Bagnall, A.: Bake off redux: a review and experimental evaluation of recent time series classification algorithms. Data Min. Knowl. Disc. **38**(4), 1958–2031 (2024)
33. Nguyen, T.L., Ifrim, G.: Mrsqm: Fast time series classification with symbolic representations. arXiv preprint arXiv:2109.01036 (2021)
34. Refoyo, M., Luengo, D.: Sub-space: subsequence-based sparse counterfactual explanations for time series classification problems. In: World Conference on Explainable Artificial Intelligence, pp. 3–17 (2024)
35. Ruiz, A.P., Flynn, M., Large, J., Middlehurst, M., Bagnall, A.: The great multivariate time series classification bake off: a review and experimental evaluation of recent algorithmic advances. Data Min. Knowl. Disc. **35**(2), 401–449 (2021)
36. Spinnato, F., Guidotti, R., Monreale, A., Nanni, M.: Fast, interpretable, and deterministic time series classification with a bag-of-receptive-fields. IEEE Access **12**, 137893–137912 (2024)
37. Spinnato, F., Guidotti, R., Monreale, A., Nanni, M., Pedreschi, D., Giannotti, F.: Understanding any time series classifier with a subsequence-based explainer. ACM Trans. Knowl. Discov. Data **18**(2), 1–34 (2023)
38. Spinnato, F., Landi, C.: Pyrregular: A unified framework for irregular time series, with classification benchmarks. arXiv preprint arXiv:2505.06047 (2025)
39. Theissler, A., Spinnato, F., Schlegel, U., Guidotti, R.: Explainable ai for time series classification: a review, taxonomy and research directions. IEEE Access (2022)
40. Wachter, S., Mittelstadt, B., Russell, C.: Counterfactual explanations without opening the black box: automated decisions and the gdpr. Harv. JL & Tech. **31**, 841 (2017)
41. Wang, Z., Samsten, I., Miliou, I., Mochaourab, R., Papapetrou, P.: Glacier: guided locally constrained counterfactual explanations for time series classification. Mach. Learn., 1–31 (2024)
42. Wang, Z., Samsten, I., Mochaourab, R., Papapetrou, P.: Learning time series counterfactuals via latent space representations. In: Discovery Science: 24th International Conference, DS 2021, pp. 369–384 (2021)
43. Ye, L., Keogh, E.: Time series shapelets: a new primitive for data mining. In: Proceedings of the 15th ACM SIGKDD International Conference on Knowledge Discovery and Data Mining, pp. 947–956 (2009)
44. Yeh, C.C.M., et al.: Matrix profile i: all pairs similarity joins for time series: a unifying view that includes motifs, discords and shapelets. In: 2016 IEEE 16th International Conference on Data Mining (ICDM), pp. 1317–1322 (2016)

Open Access This chapter is licensed under the terms of the Creative Commons Attribution 4.0 International License (http://creativecommons.org/licenses/by/4.0/), which permits use, sharing, adaptation, distribution and reproduction in any medium or format, as long as you give appropriate credit to the original author(s) and the source, provide a link to the Creative Commons license and indicate if changes were made.

The images or other third party material in this chapter are included in the chapter's Creative Commons license, unless indicated otherwise in a credit line to the material. If material is not included in the chapter's Creative Commons license and your intended use is not permitted by statutory regulation or exceeds the permitted use, you will need to obtain permission directly from the copyright holder.

Faithful Explanations for Graph Classification Using Logic

Alessio Ragno[1(✉)], Marc Plantevit[2], and Céline Robardet[1]

[1] INSA Lyon, CNRS, LIRIS UMR 5205, 69621 Villeurbanne, France
{alessio.ragno,celine.robardet}@insa-lyon.fr
[2] EPITA Research Laboratory (LRE), 94276 Le Kremlin-Bicêtre, France
marc.plantevit@epita.fr

Abstract. Most post-hoc explainability methods for graph classification analyze the model's internal representations rather than explicitly capturing its reasoning process. These approaches typically rely on perturbations, gradients, or optimization techniques to infer important features but do not approximate the decision-making function itself. In this paper, we propose a novel approach that directly models the GNN's decision function using a Transparent Explainable Logic Layer (TELL). This logic-based approximation enables both instance-level and global-level explanations, offering insights into how node embeddings contribute to predictions. Unlike conventional methods, our approach derives explanations that are structurally aligned with the model's decision process rather than being externally imposed. Through experiments on synthetic and real-world graph classification tasks, we show that our method produces faithful, sparse, and stable explanations, outperforming existing techniques.

Keywords: Graph Neural Networks · Explainability · Interpretability · Logic

1 Introduction

Graph Neural Networks (GNNs) have become a fundamental tool for learning representations from graph-structured data, enabling breakthroughs in tasks such as node classification, link prediction, and graph classification [4,12,13,22]. However, due to the intricate nature of graphs and the implicit feature aggregation mechanisms employed by GNNs, understanding their predictions remains a significant challenge. This lack of interpretability raises concerns about their deployment in high-stakes applications, such as drug discovery, financial risk assessment, and social network analysis. To address this issue, Explainable AI (XAI) provides methodologies to enhance the transparency of GNNs and offer human-interpretable explanations for their decisions.

Supplementary Information The online version contains supplementary material available at https://doi.org/10.1007/978-3-032-06078-5_7.

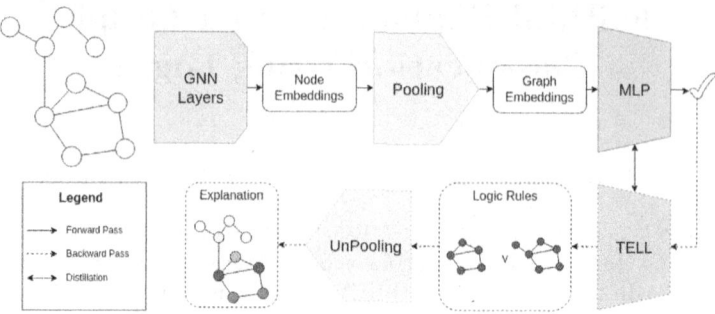

Fig. 1. LogiX Explanation Procedure. A Transparent Explainable Logic Layer is used to approximate the MLP of a GNN. Subsequently, logic rules are extracted, and representative graphs are obtained. Finally, instance-level explanations are obtained by identifying the contributions of the nodes to the logic rules.

These techniques fall into two categories: self-explainable models [7,18,19,30], designed to be inherently interpretable, and post-hoc techniques, which explain predictions of pre-trained models. While self-explainable models require specialized architectures and complex training, post-hoc methods can be applied to any pre-trained GNN. Existing post-hoc methods typically rely on input perturbation [11], optimization of masks to select most influential subgraphs [16,27], and extraction of gradients for the model outputs with respect to the inputs [23,24]. These methods identify the key nodes, edges, or substructures driving a model's prediction. While effective, these methods often suffer from high computational costs or lack inherent interpretability.

In this paper, we introduce LogiX, a novel approach to graph classification explainability based on a surrogate model for logic-based analysis of the GNNs. Contrary to existing surrogate methods, which utilize simple and explainable models in the locality of a single data point, we utilize a transparent explainable logic layer (TELL) [20] to globally approximate the decisions of the last layer of the GNN. This enables the identification of rules in the embeddings that drive class predictions. Once these rules are identified, we can trace them back through the GNN architecture to pinpoint the nodes responsible for activating specific rules. This approach allows us to generate explanations at both the instance level, using node attribution masks, and logic level, by visualizing the learned rules. Figure 1 reports a general scheme of the procedure we use: given a GNN for graph classification, we approximate its final classifier using TELL; successively we extract logic rules to explain the classes; finally, we generate node attribution masks to highlight the nodes that contribute to a specific class. Through extensive experimentation, we demonstrate that LogiX achieves comparable or superior explanation performances compared to state-of-the-art post-hoc techniques for producing instance-level explanations. In particular, we show that LogiX, compared to others provides significant improvements in identifying the most important nodes and the least important ones. To demonstrate this, we propose an additional experiment to analyzing the fidelity and the stability of the explanations, when removing the most relevant nodes or the least relevant ones.

Beyond the post-hoc instance-level explanations, we show that it is also possible to use the trained logic layer to visualize rules over the graphs for a broader understanding of the model behavior. We compare our approach with a recent state-of-the-art method, GraphTrail [2]. While GraphTrail can only be applied in the case of discrete node features, our approach is also applicable to graphs with all node feature types.

In summary, our work makes the following contributions: we introduce a logic-based post-hoc explanation method for graph classification; we extensively analyze our proposed method's explanations quality alongside state-of-the-art post-hoc methods for instance-level explanations, specifically focusing on the identification of most important nodes; we compare our approach against logic-based explainers; we provide an open-source implementation of our proposed approach and the conducted experiments[1].

The remainder of this work is structured as follows: We begin by surveying the current literature on XAI for GNNs and logic explainability; subsequently, we detail the mathematical foundations needed to comprehend our approach; we then present our proposed approach to derive logic-based explanations for graph classification; we follow with an experimental evaluation of the explanations on several datasets; finally, we summarize our findings and suggest potential directions for future research.

2 Related Work

We review related literature, focusing on post-hoc techniques for explaining graph classification models and logic-based XAI approaches that enhance interpretability.

2.1 Explaining GNNs

Explanations for graph classifications are generally obtained by attributing importance scores to nodes, edges, or features in a given graph. Many existing methods achieve this by computing importance scores using gradients, optimization, or perturbations.

Gradient-based approaches like GradCAM [23] and Integrated Gradients [24] adapt techniques from convolutional neural networks to GNNs, computing gradients to highlight influential node features and providing saliency-based explanations. Despite the adaptability and the speed of these methods, they often provide noisy explanations due to gradient saturation and may struggle to correctly determine node importance.

Optimization-based approaches, instead, try to optimize masks to determine the nodes that are most important for a certain prediction. GNNExplainer [27] is the seminal method, formulating the explanation process as an optimization problem where a soft mask is applied to node features and edges to maximize

---

[1] Public GitHub repository: https://github.com/spideralessio/logix.

the mutual information between the masked graph and the model's original prediction. PGExplainer [16] builds upon this idea but introduces a probabilistic approach to generate multiple discrete explanations rather than a single deterministic one, training an edge mask predictor to sample different possible explanations.

Another line of work explores perturbation-based approaches. These approaches assess the importance of graph components by analyzing how structural modifications impact model predictions. SubGraphX [28], for instance, evaluates the collective contribution of subgraphs rather than isolated nodes or edges, by employing Shapley values. To efficiently navigate the vast space of possible subgraphs, it uses Monte Carlo Tree Search (MCTS), balancing exploration and exploitation during the search process. Despite its effectiveness, the MCTS-based search can become computationally intensive for large graphs. GraphSVX [11] introduces a more efficient approach by approximating Shapley values through a combination of graph perturbations and surrogate modeling. Instead of exhaustively exploring subgraph combinations, GraphSVX leverages a sampling strategy that reduces computational complexity while still providing high-fidelity explanations. This method balances the trade-off between accuracy and scalability, making it suitable for larger graph datasets. To address the remaining limitations in scalability, GStarX [29] refines the search strategy by focusing on star-shaped subgraphs centered around key nodes. This targeted exploration reduces computational overhead while maintaining the quality and fidelity of the explanations, making it more scalable to complex graphs.

In this paper, we propose a novel approach which does not fall within traditional techniques. Our aim is instead to integrate a logic-based layer that approximates the model. This provides an explanation process that is directly tied to the reasoning mechanisms of the GNN rather than being an external attribution process. This allows to attribute the nodes using the specific logics of the models. With this aim, in the next section, we present related works regarding the use of logic in XAI.

2.2 Logic-Based XAI

Logic-based explainability methods [8] aim to enhance model interpretability by embedding logical constraints or symbolic reasoning into the learning process. Unlike post-hoc explanation techniques, which analyze model predictions after training, logic-based approaches integrate interpretability directly into the model's architecture, ensuring that explanations are inherently aligned with the model's decision-making process. This allows for the development of self-explainable techniques that provide explanations along with predictions [15,21].

Classic machine learning models, such as decision trees and rule-based classifiers, naturally provide logical explanations by representing decision boundaries in an explicit and interpretable manner. However, while these models offer transparency, their performance is often limited when dealing with complex, high-dimensional data. Additionally, they cannot be easily integrated within deep learning architectures due to their lack of differentiability, preventing them from benefiting from gradient-based optimization. This challenge has motivated the development of neural models that embed logical reasoning while remaining trainable via backpropagation.

One notable example is logic-explained networks (LENs) [5], which introduce a family of neural networks that can be explained through logic rules. These models operate under the assumption of binary data and apply strong regularization, enabling the construction of truth tables to derive logic rules. However, this approach does not guarantee that the logic explanations accurately reflect the model's behavior [20]. To address this limitation, the transparent explainable logic layer (TELL) was introduced—a novel architecture constrained by positive weights that can be directly converted into logic rules. These constraints ensure a direct alignment between the extracted logic rules and the model's actual behavior. Additionally, TELL is also designed to work with continuous data thanks to a preprocessing function that automatically learns thresholds over input features.

In the context of GNNs, logic-based explainability is still an emerging field and is mainly used in model-level explanations rather than instance-level ones. GLGExplainer [3] is one of the first attempts to introduce logical rules into GNN explanations. It is an architecture that takes explanations generated by another post-hoc method and combines them into a logic formula using LENs. Another recent approach, GraphTrail [2], derives logic-based explanations on the computation trees of the graphs. With GraphTrail, the authors show that they are able to produce high faithful explanations compared to the ones of GLGExplainer, that depend on other post-hoc approaches. However, the calculation of computation trees requires that the node are either of specific types or contain discrete features.

In this work, we differentiate from these methods by proposing a novel instance-level approach that approximates the last layer of a pre-trained GNN architecture with TELL. This procedure allows for the extraction of model-level rules over the embedding activations. Although the nature of TELL is self-explainable, in this work we use it to approximate a GNN model that is not inherently trained with this objective. For this reason, the rules extracted by TELL might not share a human-comprehensible semantic meaning. However, we show that it is possible to derive model-level explanations by retrieving representative sub-graphs of the nodes that activate for a certain rule. Most importantly, we show that we can ultimately use the rules to identify the most important nodes involved in the prediction of a certain class, allowing us to generate instance-level explanations.

3 Background

As LogiX deeply relies on GNN internal mechanisms and on Transparent Explainable Logic Layer, we introduce below the necessary notation.

3.1 Graph Neural Networks

GNNs are a class of neural networks specifically designed to process data structured as graphs. They operate using a message-passing framework, which consists of two core operations: aggregation and update. Given a graph $\mathcal{G} = (\mathcal{V}, \mathcal{E})$, where $\mathcal{V}$ represents the set of nodes and $\mathcal{E}$ the set of edges, the aggregation step gathers information from neighboring nodes, while the update step refines the representation of the current node based on this information. A general GNN layer is defined as follows:

$$a_v^{(k)} = \text{AGGREGATE}^{(k)}\left(\left\{h_u^{(k-1)} : u \in \mathcal{N}(v)\right\}\right) \quad (1)$$

$$h_v^{(k)} = \text{UPDATE}^{(k)}\left(h_v^{(k-1)}, a_v^{(k)}\right) \quad (2)$$

where $v \in \mathcal{V}$ is the target node, $h_v^{(k)}$ represents its feature vector at layer k, and $\mathcal{N}(v)$ denotes its neighboring nodes.

Different GNN variants implement this framework with diverse aggregation strategies. In this work, we use the Graph Isomorphism Network (GIN) layer [26], which derives its aggregation mechanism from the Weisfeiler-Lehman test for graph isomorphism. The representation of a node in the GIN layer is obtained by summing the representations of its neighbors from the previous layer, adding its own representation, and then passing the result through a multi-layer perceptron (MLP):

$$h_{v,\text{GIN}}^{(k)} = \text{MLP}^{(k)}\left(\left(1 + \epsilon^{(k)}\right) h_v^{(k-1)} + \sum_{u \in \mathcal{N}(v)} h_u^{(k-1)}\right). \quad (3)$$

GNNs typically stack multiple layers to learn hierarchical node representations, which can be utilized for tasks such as node classification. For tasks at the graph level, such as graph classification, a readout layer (e.g., global pooling) is applied to the node embeddings to obtain a single representation for the entire graph. This readout operation can involve summing, averaging, or computing the maximum of the node embeddings. Finally, a classification layer maps this representation to a predicted class label.

3.2 Transparent Explainable Logic Layer

TELL is a particular layer designed to be directly translated into logic rules by constraining a feed-forward transformation with non-negative weights and a specific thresholding mechanism. Given an input $X \in \mathbb{R}^I$ and an output $y \in \mathbb{R}^O$, the transformation in TELL follows:

$$y = \sigma(XW^+ + b) \quad (4)$$

where $W^+ \in \mathbb{R}_{\geq 0}^{I \times O}$ is a weight matrix constrained to be non-negative, $b \in \mathbb{R}^O$ is a bias vector, and σ is the sigmoid activation function. The primary characteristic of TELL is that its outputs can be directly interpreted as logical conditions. By defining the binary activation of the output neurons as

$$y_k^{\text{bin}} = \begin{cases} 1 & \text{if } y_k > 0.5 \\ 0 & \text{otherwise} \end{cases} \quad (5)$$

we can express the decision boundary for each output neuron as a disjunctive normal form (DNF) rule:

$$y_k^{\text{bin}} = 1 \iff \sum_{i \in S} W_{ik}^+ > -b_k, \quad S \subseteq \{1, \ldots, I\} \quad (6)$$

where S represents the subsets of input features, minimal w.r.t set inclusion, that activate y_k. The logical formula E_k associated with y_k is then given by:

$$E_k = \bigvee_{S \in \mathcal{S}_k} \bigwedge_{i \in S} x_i \quad (7)$$

where $\mathcal{S}_k$ is the set of all minimal subsets satisfying the threshold condition. This formulation ensures that each neuron in TELL corresponds to a logic rule, enabling a direct mapping from neural parameters to symbolic expressions.

TELL can also be extended to handle real-valued inputs by incorporating an automatic thresholding mechanism. Given a preprocessing function:

$$X' = \sigma(X \odot \exp(\tilde{W}_i) + \tilde{b}_i) \quad (8)$$

where $\odot$ is the Hadamard element-wise product, and $\tilde{W}_i$ and $\tilde{b}_i$ are learnable parameters. With this approach, the thresholded input features X' remain interpretable as binary predicates:

$$x_i' = 1 \iff x_i > -\frac{\tilde{b}_i}{\exp(\tilde{W}_i)} \quad (9)$$

which are subsequently used within the logic rule extraction process. This allows TELL to process and explain real-valued inputs while maintaining the interpretability constraints.

4 Explaining GNNs with LogiX

Let f be a Graph Neural Network (GNN) composed of the following three functions:

- A set of L GNN layers $g = \{g_1, \ldots, g_L\}$, where each layer g_ℓ maps node embeddings from one representation space to another:

$$g_\ell : \mathbb{R}^{N \times D_\ell} \to \mathbb{R}^{N \times D_{\ell+1}} \quad (10)$$

where N is the number of nodes in the graph, and D_ℓ is the embedding dimension at layer ℓ. For simplicity we set $D_\ell = D$ for all the layers.

- A readout function implemented through a global pooling operator p that aggregates the node embeddings into a graph-level embedding:

$$p : \mathbb{R}^{N \times D} \to \mathbb{R}^D. \tag{11}$$

- A classifier c that maps the graph embedding to class probabilities:

$$c : \mathbb{R}^d \to \mathbb{R}^K \tag{12}$$

where K is the number of classes, typically implemented as a Multi-Layer Perceptron (MLP) followed by a softmax function.

LogiX uses TELL to approximate c and identify a set of interpretable logic rules that approximate the decision boundaries. For each class k, the corresponding logical explanations E_k are extracted, identifying the activation ranges of specific dimensions in $\mathbb{R}^d$ that contribute to predicting class k:

$$E_k : \mathbb{R}^d \to \{0, 1\}. \tag{13}$$

Thus, by tracing back the contributions of node embeddings to these activations, we obtain node-level explanations for the GNN predictions. In the remainder of this section, we first show how we can identify most important nodes extracted by the logic layer, then we present how we can also obtain logic-based explanations at a global level for the whole model.

4.1 Identifying Important Nodes

Let $H = [h_1, h_2, \ldots, h_N] \in \mathbb{R}^{N \times D}$ be the matrix of node embeddings, where $h_i \in \mathbb{R}^D$ is the embedding of node i in the final GNN layer. The graph embedding is then computed as:

$$h_G = p(H) \in \mathbb{R}^D \tag{14}$$

For a specific dimension $d \in [1, ..., D]$, we denote the corresponding embedding value as $h_G^{(d)}$. Given that p is a global pooling operator (max, mean, or sum), we compute the contribution of each node i to $h_G^{(d)}$ as follows:

- *max* pooling. Given $h_G^{(d)} = \max_{i=1,\ldots,N} h_i^{(d)}$:

$$c_i^{(d)} = \begin{cases} h_i^{(d)}, & \text{if } i = \arg\max_i h_i^{(d)} \\ 0, & \text{otherwise} \end{cases} \tag{15}$$

- *mean* pooling. Given $h_G^{(d)} = \frac{1}{N} \sum_{i=1}^{N} h_i^{(d)}$:

$$c_i^{(d)} = \frac{1}{N} h_i^{(d)} \tag{16}$$

– *sum* pooling. Given $h_G^{(d)} = \sum_{i=1}^{N} h_i^{(d)}$:

$$c_i^{(d)} = h_i^{(d)} \qquad (17)$$

Finally, since the class prediction is determined by multiple dimensions of the graph embedding h_G, the node attributions a_i are obtained by aggregating the contributions of each node across all dimensions involved in the logic rules E_k for the predicted class k:

$$a_i = \sum_{d \in \mathcal{D}_k} w_d \cdot c_i^{(d)} \qquad (18)$$

where $\mathcal{D}_k$ is the subset of embedding dimensions that influence the classification of G into class k, and w_d represents the importance weight associated with dimension d, derived from the activation strength of the corresponding rule in E_k. The resulting attributions a_i quantify the influence of each node i on the final classification. A higher value of a_i indicates a stronger contribution of node i to the predicted class k, thereby providing an interpretable, rule-based explanation for the GNN's decision.

Once determined how it is possible to obtain node attributions for a prediction, our explanation pipeline follows the scheme proposed in Fig. 1: Given a GNN explainer, we first train TELL to replicate the results of the MLP; we then obtain logic rules for the explanations which enable understanding the global behavior of the model under a logical perspective; finally, given an instance, we use the above-defined rules to obtain explanation masks for the nodes' contributions towards the extracted rules.

4.2 Obtaining Global Logic Rules

The extraction of the logic rules allows for an inspection of the behavior of the model. In our case, rules are directly obtained from the TELL that is used to approximate the MLP. For each class k, TELL generates a DNF rule E_k:

$$E_k = \bigvee_i e_{ik}. \qquad (19)$$

Each conjunctive clause e_{ik} is then defined as:

$$e_{ik} = \bigwedge_j l_{ijk} \qquad (20)$$

where l_{ijk} represents individual literals that operate on the activations of the GNN embeddings. Once these rules are obtained, we identify the nodes that specifically activate each of the conjunctive components e_{ik}. This allows us to determine the patterns that the model has learned. The process is as follows:

– Mask construction. For each conjunctive component e_{ik}, we construct a binary mask that selects only the nodes whose embeddings activate for all the literals l_{ijk}. A node satisfies e_{ik} if and only if all the conditions imposed by its literals hold.

- Subgraph extraction. Using the computed node masks, we extract all the connected components of the subgraphs that activate according to the rule E_k. These connected components components serve as interpretable structures that contribute to the model's decision for class k.
- To prevent redundant extractions of equivalent subgraphs, we perform graph isomorphism checks [6]. If a newly extracted subgraph is isomorphic to an already stored one, it is merged by increasing its occurrence count rather than adding a duplicate.

It is important to note that the rule extraction process from the TELL layer, while enabling faithful and interpretable explanations, can in principle involve exponential complexity with respect to the number of embedding dimensions, due to the enumeration of minimal activating feature subsets. However, prior work has shown that this process can be made tractable in practice through regularization techniques that promote sparse and thresholded activations. Moreover, and crucially for graph applications, the rule extraction complexity depends only on the dimensionality of the graph embeddings and not on the number of nodes in the input graph. This is in contrast to other approaches such as GStarX, whose complexity grows with graph size due to subgraph-level combinatorics.

5 Experiments

In this section, we perform extensive experiments to evaluate the explanations produced by LogiX in comparison with state-of-the-art post-hoc XAI methods for GNNs. For all the experiments we utilize a GNN formed of 5 GIN layers [26] followed by a max, sum or mean readout function which aggregates graph embeddings for each of the 5 layers. Finally, a 2-layer MLP predicts the class probabilities from the graph embeddings. We perform our analysis on the following datasets: BA2Motifs [16], a synthetic dataset where negative and positive classes are determined by the presence of a cycle or 5-node house motif, respectively; MUTAG [9], Mutagenicity [14], NCI1 [25], and BBBP [17], four molecular graph datasets where graphs are categorized depending on molecular properties; PROTEINS [10], a dataset containing graphs that represent proteins classified as enzymes or non-enzymes. To ensure reproducibility, we report the hyperparameters and the accuracy of the black-box models in the Supplementary Material. Additionally, since our method utilizes a surrogate logic layer to approximate the classifier of the GNN, we report in Table 1, the alignment between the surrogate and the classifier.

Table 1. Alignment between LogiX surrogate and the initial GNN over the different datasets. Results report mean and standard deviations over 5 seeds.

BA2Motifs	MUTAG	Mutagenicity	NCI1	BBBP	PROTEINS
1.000 ± 0.000	0.926 ± 0.071	0.901 ± 0.059	0.878 ± 0.089	0.886 ± 0.118	0.956 ± 0.059

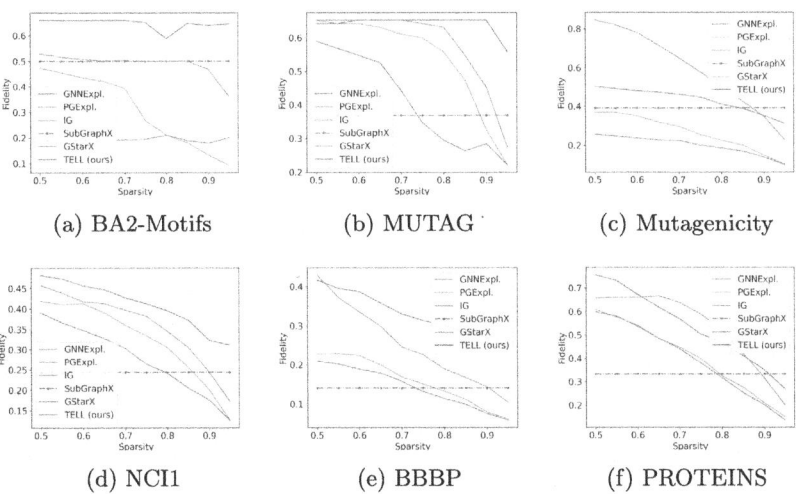

Fig. 2. Fidelity scores of the different explanations ranging from a Sparsity of 0.5 to 0.95 using a step 0.05. Plots report the mean values over 5 seeds.

As our approach allows obtaining both instance-level explanations in the form of attribution masks and logic-based explanations in the form of rules, we perform comparisons with both instance-level techniques and logic-based approaches. On the instance-level side, we evaluate our method against several state-of-the-art techniques, each leveraging distinct explanation strategies (perturbation, optimization, and gradient-based approaches). Specifically, we select GNNExplainer [27], PGExplainer [16], Integrated Gradients [24], SubgraphX [28], and GStarX [29] as benchmarks. Finally we analyze the logic explanations produced by our approach alongside with the ones of GraphTrail [2].

5.1 Instance-Level Explanations

Instance-level explanations consist of attribution scores for the nodes (as defined in Eq. 18), indicating their importance towards a prediction. To evaluate the explanations, we convert the scores into hard masks using a threshold over the attribution scores. We obtain different hard masks for each graph by selecting thresholds that produce varying Sparsity values. Sparsity is measured as the proportion of non-important nodes over the total number of nodes in a graph:

$$\text{Sparsity} = \frac{|\{v \in V : s_v < \tau\}|}{|V|} \quad (21)$$

where V is the set of all nodes in the graph, s_v is the attribution score of node v, and τ is the threshold.

Finally, we use the Fidelity and InvFidelity as metrics to evaluate our explanations:

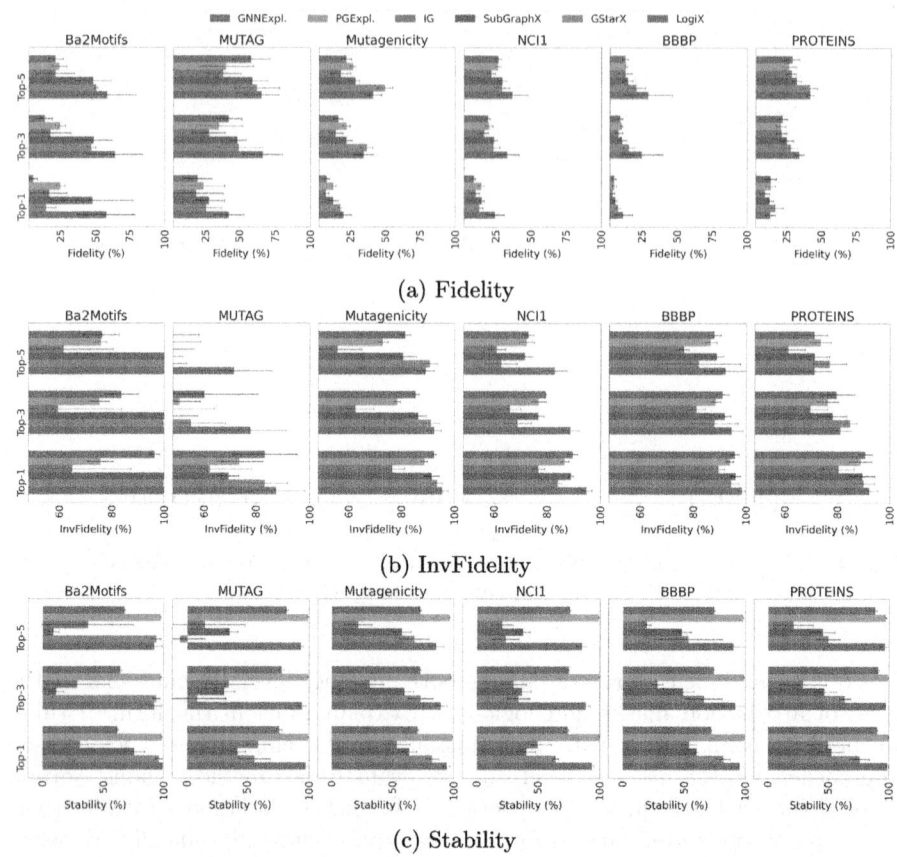

Fig. 3. Fidelity, 1-InvFidelity and Stability Scores. Fidelity is calculated removing the top 1, top 3 and top 5 nodes. InvFidelity and Stability is calculated when keeping the top $N-1$, top $N-3$ and top $N-5$ nodes. Values are reported as average over 5 seeds, with error bars representing standard deviations. We detail the values in tabular form in the Supplementary Material.

- InvFidelity measures how well the masked graph retains the original prediction: InvFidelity = $f(G) - f(G_\mathrm{m})$;
- Fidelity measures the prediction shift when only the masked-out nodes are kept: Fidelity = $f(G) - f(\overline{G_\mathrm{m}})$.

$f(G)$ is the model's prediction on the original graph, G_m is the graph after removing non-relevant nodes, and $\overline{G_\mathrm{m}}$ is the graph keeping only the non-relevant nodes.

We report in Fig. 2, the Fidelity scores of the different explanations ranging from a Sparsity of 0.5 to 0.95 using a step of 0.05. Overall, we observe that on BA2-Motifs, MUTAG and NCI1, our approach surpasses the others. In Mutagenicity and BBBP, instead, GStarX appears to provide more faithful explanations at low Sparsity values, while TELL is the best performing at higher Sparsity values. Finally, on PROTEINS, GStarX and our approach report similar performances, with the latter keeping higher scores at high sparsities. As a general observation, all the models have the general tendency of decreasing their Fidelity values when Sparsity is increased, with the sole exception of SubGraphX, which is reported in a dotted line, as it is the only method returning hard masks instead of soft masks. We attribute this behavior to the fact that LogiX, by capturing the rules that lead to the predictions, is better at identifying the most important nodes. Therefore, when only few nodes are taken out of the graphs, LogiX yields the ones that are really important for the prediction. To better study this behavior, we report in Fig. 3a an analysis of the Fidelity on the four datasets, when removing the top 1, 3 and 5 nodes from the graphs. This study confirms our previous results: when we focus on the most important node, the three most important nodes, and the five most important nodes, with LogiX, we obtain generally higher Fidelity compared to other approaches. Only on a few datasets, namely Mutagenicity, and PROTEINS, our results report comparable results with the best-performing methods.

Once we determined the capability of LogiX to better identify the most relevant nodes for the prediction, we also study its capability to discard non-important nodes. To this aim, in Fig. 3b we analyze the values of 1-InvFidelity values of the different explainers when removing the least important node, the least three important nodes or the least five important nodes. We use 1-InvFidelity to invert the scale such that higher values correspond to better quality of the explanations. On this side, we observe that most of the approaches report similar performances. In particular, we see that for BA2Motifs our method and SubGraphX obtain perfect scores. On MUTAG, NCI1, and Mutagenicity, we generally report the best results. Finally, on PROTEINS, most of the methods perform similarly, with ours and GStarX reporting the best results. Overall, we observe that LogiX is always either best-performing or comparable with the best-performing explainer even in identifying non-important nodes.

To complement our analysis of explainers' ability to identify the most and least important nodes, we also examine their stability. We define stability as the cosine similarity between the node attributions of a graph and those obtained after removing the least important nodes [1]. Figure 3c presents an analysis of explainers' stability under conditions similar to previous experiments, i.e., after removing the least important node, the three least important nodes, or the five least important nodes. Unlike Fidelity and InvFidelity, stability alone does not indicate the correctness of explanations but rather measures the consistency of importance rankings when non-important nodes are removed. Our results show that PGExplainer is the most stable method. However, it is important to note that PGExplainer performs poorly in Fidelity and InvFidelity. Conversely, our method—which excels in Fidelity and InvFidelity—is the second most stable explainer, consistently achieving over 90% stability when removing the most important node. This is because LogiX globally approximates the MLP, ensuring that if a node activates certain rules, its activation remains largely unaffected by

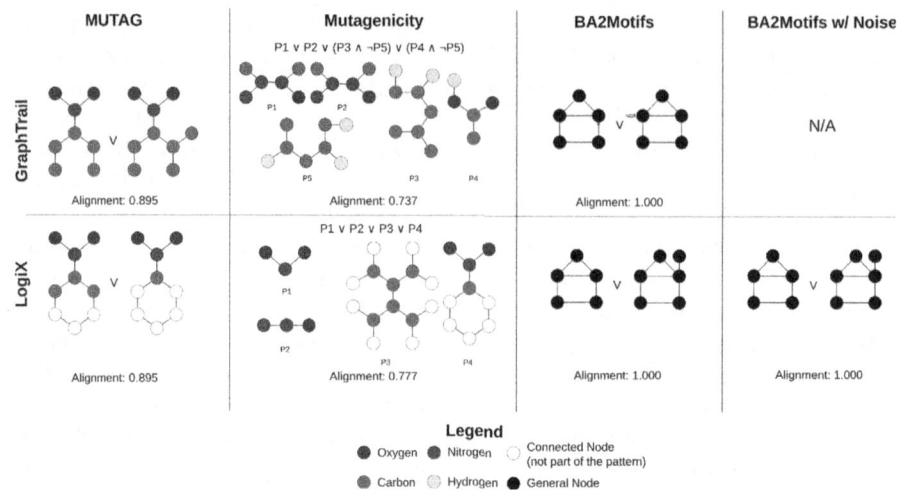

Fig. 4. Logic explanations obtained using GraphTrail and LogiX on the BA2Motifs, MUTAG and Mutagencity datasets. The figure presents a visual extract of the obtained results paired with the alignment of the rules with the model.

small perturbations. In contrast, while SubGraphX and GStarX provide faithful explanations, their reliance on Shapley value computation makes them more sensitive to perturbations, leading to variations in explanation values.

5.2 Global Inspection of the Model Through Logic Rules

Here, we analyze the rules learned by LogiX in comparison to those extracted by another logic-based global explainer, GraphTrail. It is important to emphasize that these two methods serve different purposes. GraphTrail is specifically designed to determine rules over computation trees, with no focus on instance-level explanations. In contrast, our approach constructs logic rules to explain the last layer of the GNN, aiming to identify the most relevant nodes in a graph. The only commonality between the two methods is their use of logic as a means of presenting explanations. Nevertheless, comparing their outputs provides valuable insights.

Figure 4 presents the rules extracted by our method and GraphTrail [2] on the BA2Motifs and MUTAG and Mutagenicity datasets. We observe that both methods identify similar patterns, suggesting they effectively capture the model's reasoning. Indeed, when measuring the alignment of the extracted rules with the model's predictions, both techniques achieve similar scores, with equal values on MUTAG and BA2Motifs and a slightly higher alignment for Logix on Mutagenicity. Alignment is quantified as the ratio of samples where the model and the extracted rules yield the same outcome.

However, a key limitation of GraphTrail is its reliance on computation trees, which restricts its applicability to cases where nodes have discrete features or belong to predefined categories. To illustrate this, we conduct an experiment where we replace the original features of BA2Motifs with random values and train a model on the same task. In this scenario, GraphTrail is unable to extract rules, as all nodes have unique features. In contrast, our approach remains fully applicable, producing logic rules that maintain full alignment with the model.

6 Conclusions

In this work, we introduced LogiX, a novel logic-based post-hoc explainability method for graph classification, leveraging a logic layer to directly model the decision function of a GNN. Unlike conventional post-hoc methods that rely on perturbations, gradient-based techniques, or optimization-based subgraph selection, our approach produces explanations that are inherently aligned with the model's decision process, ensuring greater faithfulness and interpretability. Through extensive experiments on synthetic and real-world datasets, we demonstrated that our approach outperforms state-of-the-art post-hoc techniques in terms of explanation fidelity, sparsity, and stability. Specifically, our method excels in identifying the most relevant nodes contributing to a prediction while maintaining consistency across perturbations. Additionally, LogiX enables global-level interpretability by extracting human-interpretable logic rules that approximate the decision boundaries of the model. Despite these advancements, our work presents certain limitations. The extracted logic rules, while faithful to the model's decision-making process, may not always be immediately human-comprehensible due to the abstract nature of learned embeddings. Future research could explore techniques to bridge this gap by integrating domain-specific knowledge into the logic extraction process. Additionally, extending TELL to other graph-based tasks beyond classification, such as link prediction and node classification, remains an interesting avenue for further investigation. Finally, other limitations might concern the execution times. Indeed, while we did not encounter timing issues in our experiments, compared to other approaches, depending on the complexity of the problem, it was shown that the enumeration of rules from TELL might entail long running times.

Acknowledgments. This work was supported by French state aid managed by the National Research Agency under the France 2030 program, with the references "WAIT4 ANR-22-PEAE-0008" and "PANDORA ANR-24-CE23-0950".

References

1. Agarwal, C., Queen, O., Lakkaraju, H., Zitnik, M.: Evaluating explainability for graph neural networks. Sci. Data 10(1) (2023)
2. Armgaan, B., Dalmia, M., Medya, S., Ranu, S.: Graphtrail: translating GNN predictions into human-interpretable logical rules. In: NeurIPS (2024)
3. Azzolin, S., Longa, A., Barbiero, P., Lio, P., Passerini, A.: Global explainability of gnns via logic combination of learned concepts. In: ICLR (2023)

4. Bongini, P., Bianchini, M., Scarselli, F.: Molecular generative graph neural networks for drug discovery. Neurocomputing **450**, 242–252 (2021). Aug
5. Ciravegna, G., et al.: Logic explained networks. Artif. Intell. **314**, 103822 (2023)
6. Cordella, L.P., Foggia, P., Sansone, C., Vento, M., et al.: An improved algorithm for matching large graphs. In: IAPR-TC15 (2001)
7. Dai, E., Wang, S.: Towards self-explainable graph neural network. In: International Conference on Information & Knowledge Management, CIKM, pp. 302–311 (2021)
8. Darwiche, A.: Logic for explainable ai. In: 2023 38th Annual ACM/IEEE Symposium on Logic in Computer Science (LICS), pp. 1–11. IEEE (2023)
9. Debnath, A.K., Lopez de Compadre, R.L., Debnath, G., Shusterman, A.J., Hansch, C.: Structure-activity relationship of mutagenic aromatic and heteroaromatic nitro compounds. J. Med. Chem. **34**(2), 786–797 (1991)
10. Dobson, P.D., Doig, A.J.: Distinguishing enzyme structures from non-enzymes without alignments. J. Mol. Biol. **330**(4), 771–783 (2003)
11. Duval, A., Malliaros, F.D.: Graphsvx: shapley value explanations for graph neural networks. In: ECML PKDD, pp. 302–318 (2021)
12. Fan, W., Ma, Y., Li, Q., He, Y., Zhao, E., Tang, J., Yin, D.: Graph neural networks for social recommendation. In: WWW 2019. ACM Press (2019)
13. Jiang, D., et al.: Could graph neural networks learn better molecular representation for drug discovery? J. Cheminform. **13**(1) (2021)
14. Kazius, J., McGuire, R., Bursi, R.: Derivation and validation of toxicophores for mutagenicity prediction. J. Med. Chem. **48**(1), 312–320 (2004)
15. Lipton, Z.C.: The mythos of model interpretability: in machine learning, the concept of interpretability is both important and slippery. Queue **16**(3), 31–57 (2018)
16. Luo, D., et al.: Parameterized explainer for graph neural network. NeurIPS **33**, 19620–19631 (2020)
17. Martins, I.F., Teixeira, A.L., Pinheiro, L., Falcao, A.O.: A bayesian approach to in silico blood-brain barrier penetration modeling. J. Chem. Infor. Model. **52**(6), 1686–1697 (jun 2012)
18. Ragno, A., Capobianco, R.: Impo: interpretable memory-based prototypical pooling. In: WSDM, pp. 625–632 (2025)
19. Ragno, A., La Rosa, B., Capobianco, R.: Prototype-based interpretable graph neural networks. IEEE Trans. Artifi. Intell., 1–11 (2022)
20. Ragno, A., Plantevit, M., Robardet, C., Capobianco, R.: Transparent explainable logic layers. In: ECAI. vol. 392, pp. 914–921 (2024)
21. Rudin, C.: Stop explaining black box machine learning models for high stakes decisions and use interpretable models instead. Nat. Mach. Intell. **1**(5), 206–215 (2019)
22. Schwarzenberg, R., Hübner, M., Harbecke, D., Alt, C., Hennig, L.: Layerwise relevance visualization in convolutional text graph classifiers. In: Workshop on Graph-Based Methods for Natural Language Processing, TextGraphs, pp. 58–62 (2019)
23. Selvaraju, R.R., Cogswell, M., Das, A., Vedantam, R., Parikh, D., Batra, D.: Gradcam: visual explanations from deep networks via gradient-based localization. In: International Conference on Computer Vision, ICCV, pp. 618–626 (2017)
24. Sundararajan, M., Taly, A., Yan, Q.: Axiomatic attribution for deep networks. In: ICML, pp. 3319–3328. PMLR (2017)
25. Wale, N., Watson, I.A., Karypis, G.: Comparison of descriptor spaces for chemical compound retrieval and classification. KAIS **14**(3), 347–375 (2007)
26. Xu, K., Hu, W., Leskovec, J., Jegelka, S.: How powerful are graph neural networks? In: ICLR (2019)

27. Ying, Z., Bourgeois, D., You, J., Zitnik, M., Leskovec, J.: Gnnexplainer: generating explanations for graph neural networks. NeurIPS **32** (2019)
28. Yuan, H., Yu, H., Wang, J., Li, K., Ji, S.: On explainability of graph neural networks via subgraph explorations. In: ICML, pp. 12241–12252. PMLR (2021)
29. Zhang, S., Liu, Y., Shah, N., Sun, Y.: Gstarx: explaining graph neural networks with structure-aware cooperative games. Adv. Neural Inform. Process. Syst. NeurIPS **35**, 19810–19823 (2022)
30. Zhang, Z., Liu, Q., Wang, H., Lu, C., Lee, C.: ProtGNN: towards self-explaining graph neural networks. AAAI Artifi. Intell. **36**(8), 9127–9135 (2022)

MalGPT: A Generative Explainable Model for Malware Binaries

Mohd Saqib[1], Benjamin C. M. Fung[1(✉)], Steven H. H. Ding[1], and Philippe Charland[2]

[1] McGill University, 3661 Peel Street, Montreal, Canada
mohd.saqib@mail.mcgill.ca, {ben.fung,steven.h.ding}@mcgill.ca
[2] Defence R&D Canada, Quebec, Canada
philippe.charland@drdc-rddc.gc.ca

Abstract. Explaining malware binaries poses significant challenges, as existing approaches often focus on surface-level features, dynamic behaviors, or assembly code analysis. While these models highlight features contributing to classification, they remain inaccessible to non-experts. In this work, we propose MalGPT, a multi-model and transformer-based approach that generates human-readable explanations of malware binaries in natural language. We manually analyzed malware binaries from different malware families, including benign files, using various tools to create a ground truth dataset with high-level explanations. As per the literature, this is the first contribution of a malware dataset paired with natural language explanations, along with a high-level explanatory model developed for the cybersecurity community. Our approach includes complex feature engineering, followed by a novel architecture, Cross-Hierarchical Attention Network (CHAiN), which learns relationships not only within individual features, but across different feature sets in a multi-model architecture. We developed a Generative Pre-trained Transformer (GPT)-style architecture optimized for multi-modal malware binary analysis, designed to seamlessly integrate heterogeneous features, such as numeric data, printable strings, and graph-based representations of assembly code. The architecture aligns syntactic structures with semantic context, to transform encoded multi-modal inputs into coherent and precise explanations. This innovative approach enhances compatibility with diverse data modalities, providing robust and interpretable insights into malware behavior, while enabling detailed and contextually accurate textual explanations. In future work, we aim to scale this approach with larger datasets, enhancing its capacity to explain emerging malware variants and address different cybersecurity landscapes, such as malicious apps or network viruses, ultimately contributing to risk mitigation.

Keywords: GPT Architecture · Explainable AI · Malware Analysis · Large Language Model

---

Supplementary Information The online version contains supplementary material available at https://doi.org/10.1007/978-3-032-06078-5_8.

© The Author(s), under exclusive license to Springer Nature Switzerland AG 2026
R. P. Ribeiro et al. (Eds.): ECML PKDD 2025, LNAI 16016, pp. 130–148, 2026.
https://doi.org/10.1007/978-3-032-06078-5_8

1 Introduction

Deep learning (DL)-based malware detection has received considerable attention in recent years, achieving state-of-the-art detection metrics [4]. However, DL models often face the inherent challenge of being black-box systems, making their decisions difficult to interpret. Reducing the opacity of malware classification models is particularly complex, as traditional explainable AI (XAI) methods, commonly developed for natural language processing and image datasets, fail to capture the intricacies of malicious binaries. Such data require specialized algorithms for effective interpretation.

Saqib et al. [15] identified the limitations of traditional XAI methods and categorized the research into different levels of explanation, concluding that most efforts remain at the basic level, offering limited insight into the decision-making process. While some studies attempted to explain malware behaviors using existing XAI methods [4], others proposed specialized solutions for malware binaries [3,7,14]. For instance, I-MAD [7] introduced an interpretable neural network that reveals the importance of static features, but neglects dynamic aspects or deep code connectivity. Similarly, CFGExplainer [3] highlighted potentially malicious nodes in the control flow graph (CFG) of a malware executable, but lacked robust explanation capabilities, as shown by Saqib et al. [15] in their GAGE model. GAGE [14] proposed a novel representation of portable executable (PE) files, incorporating semantic and structural information through the Canonical Executable Graph (CEG). However, none of these models provide high-level explanations accessible to users without a cybersecurity background. To address these shortcomings, we propose a novel approach that leverages extensive feature extraction and the generative power of Generative Pretrained Transformer (GPT), providing human-understandable explanations for malware binaries.

The proposed algorithm is powered by a multi-model architecture coupled with GPT. The idea behind the multi-model design is to integrate all possible contexts of a malicious file. Previous algorithms have primarily focused on either static or dynamic features, which can miss subtle but crucial information required for explainability. Malware authors often use obfuscation and packing techniques to disguise their intent. Our model overcomes these limitations by considering not only static and dynamic features, but also the semantic and syntactical information extracted from the assembly code. Saqib et al. [14] highlighted that the CEG is more powerful than traditional CFGs. We extended this concept by extracting CEGs from binaries and integrating them into our model. Furthermore, we used a GPT architecture to generate human-readable explanations for these binaries. The encoded vector passed to the GPT model is generated by Cross-Hierarchical Attention Network (CHAiN), which captures all possible contexts and relationships, both inner and intra-feature, for comprehensive explanation generation.

To the best of our knowledge, this is the first work that provides such high-level explanations for malware binaries, as the malware analysis community previously lacked a ground truth explanation dataset for malicious binaries [4]. Our contributions can be summarized as follows:

- MalGPT contributes a unique GPT-style architecture tailored for multimodal analysis of malware binaries. It integrates diverse feature types, including static features, dynamic behaviors, printable strings, and graph-based representations, into a unified generative framework. This architecture utilizes attention mechanisms to process and align syntactic and semantic relationships across these modalities, enabling both accurate detection and detailed natural language explanations. By bridging multi-modal feature integration with interpretability, MalGPT advances the applicability of GPT models in cybersecurity.
- We introduced CHAiN, an integral component of MalGPT, designed as an advanced multi-model architecture. This architecture leverages hierarchical attention mechanisms to effectively capture both intra-modality and inter-modality dependencies among heterogeneous malware feature modalities. By modeling intricate relationships across features such as static data, dynamic behaviors, and CEGs, CHAiN significantly enhances both the discriminative capability and interpretability of the model, outperforming existing state-of-the-art approaches in malware analysis and explainability tasks.
- We curated a comprehensive dataset utilizing 23.296 GB of binaries, encompassing four malware families (`DownloadAdmin`, `Firseria`, `Emotet`, `Gamarue`) and a benign category. This dataset includes ground truth explanations and diverse features, such as static, dynamic, API call sequences, import/export structures, and CEGs. An attention-based encoder-decoder (AED) was trained on 0.8 million assembly blocks and 28.7 GB of binaries, representing 2,411 CEGs with an average of 546 nodes and 3,567 edges, capturing syntactic and semantic relationships. Integrated with VirusTotal-generated reports, the dataset uniquely delivers natural language explanations for malware behaviors.
- Through comprehensive experiments, we evaluated MalGPT's performance for both detection accuracy and explainability. Quantitative metrics included precision, recall, F1 score, accuracy, ROUGE-L, and BERTScore to assess detection and explanation quality. For qualitative evaluation, we analyzed hallucinations and errors in the generated explanations, focusing on consistency, relevance, and the ability to align with ground truth annotations. This dual evaluation approach ensured a holistic understanding of MalGPT's strengths and areas for improvement in malware detection and explainability.

2 Background

The use of explainable methods in malware analysis has gained significant attention, as traditional "black-box" models offer limited interpretability. Comprehensive surveys, such as [15], highlight various interpretability frameworks, analyzing their benefits and limitations. Saqib et al. [15] provide a categorization of explainability approaches, which can be broadly divided into low-level and high-level explainability techniques. These approaches, however, have yet to fully leverage the potential of large language models (LLMs), which could significantly enhance interpretability for diverse stakeholders with minimal domain knowledge.

2.1 Low-Level Explainability Approaches

Low-level approaches in explainability often rely on local interpretability techniques, such as Local Interpretable Model-Agnostic Explanations (LIME) [13] and Shapley Additive Explanations (SHAP) [9]. These methods approximate the model locally around a specific instance, providing insights into feature importance and the reasoning behind the model's decisions.

Studies leveraging LIME have demonstrated its utility in identifying static malware features. For example, Khan et al. used LIME to explain Conv-LSTM-based autoencoder predictions on network traffic features in industrial IoT environments [4]. Similarly, Kinkead et al. [5] used LIME on Android APK opcode sequences, transforming them into image-based representations for CNN classifiers, while Lu and Thing [8] used LIME alongside BERT-based models for Android application feature extraction. Ambekar et al. [1] utilized a combination of TabNet and LSTM in their model, TabLSTMNet, to fuse LIME-based explanations with DL predictions. Mitchell et al. [10] further extended LIME and introduced hierarchical LIME (H-LIME) to generate sparser explanations at the class and method levels.

SHAP-based studies also illustrate the interpretability of malware features. For instance, Lu and Thing [8] applied SHAP alongside LIME to Android applications, while To et al. [17] used SHAP on PE file analysis, extracting features via VirusTotal and classifying them using logistic regression, decision trees, and k-nearest neighbors. Other studies, such as Smmarwar et al. [16] and Ambekar et al. [1], used hybrid DL approaches such as CNN-BiGRU with SHAP to elucidate malware predictions.

2.2 High-Level Explainability Approaches

In contrast to low-level techniques, high-level approaches focus on model-wide interpretability and behavior explanation. For example, Herath et al. [3] proposed CFGExplainer, a model using control flow graph (CFG) blocks and opcode-based statistics to explain malware behavior comprehensively. Building upon CFGExplainer, Saqib et al. [14] introduced the Genetic Algorithm-based Graph Explainer (GAGE), which extends the control-flow analysis by identifying malicious functions and their caller-callee relationships within a call execution graph (CEG). GAGE demonstrates improved robustness and discriminative power, particularly in explaining complex malware behaviors.

2.3 Exploring Large Language Models (LLMs)

LLMs, especially transformer-based architectures, have seen limited application in malware explainability, though their potential is considerable. Encoder-decoder structures, such as those in [11] [19], have been applied primarily for detection rather than for explanation. BERT-based models have also been explored, though primarily for feature extraction rather than interpretability. For instance, Ullah et al. [18] used BERT to generate features for an ensemble detection model.

Demirkiran et al. [2] demonstrated that transformers are effective in classifying highly imbalanced malware families, leveraging the attention mechanisms of transformers to model complex sequence relationships within malware API call data. However, despite these advancements, the application of LLMs for generating interpretable, high-level explanations in malware analysis remains largely unexplored, presenting a promising direction for future research.

3 Proposed Method

In this section, we introduce MalGPT, a novel architecture combining CHAiN and GPT for malware analysis and explanation generation (Fig. 1). MalGPT leverages comprehensive features engineering mechanism, followed by CHAiN to effectively process and integrate heterogeneous data types, such as PE header features, API call sequences, and graph-based CEG representations, ensuring both intra- and inter-modality relationships are captured. The fused representations are then passed to a GPT module, which generates comprehensive, human-readable explanations, enhancing transparency and interpretability in malware detection.

3.1 Features Engineering Mechanism

To enable comprehensive analysis of binary files, we extracted four distinct feature types, each capturing a unique aspect of the binaries.

PE Header Features: This category includes PE header features such as `ExportsNbDLL`, `SectionsMeanEntropy`, and `ResourcesMeanSize`. Categorical data within this group were encoded using a label encoder to ensure compatibility with the model.

Import/Export Features: We categorized import/export functionalities into four subcategories: `open`, `create`, `delete`, `close`, `resume`, `kill`, `call`, and `other`. These were encoded using the SBERT model [12], which generates embeddings for similar lists with high semantic similarity. After obtaining individual embeddings, we performed aggregation (average) to produce a uniform-sized vector representation for individual subgroups (Fig. 2).

Printable Strings: This feature type contains extensive lists ranging from 500 to 2,000 entries per binary. Categories include `DIR`, `email`, `sentences`, `keywords`, `files`, `IP addresses`, and `URLs`. Using the same SBERT-based encoding [12] strategy as for import/export features, we created subcategory-specific embeddings and aggregated them into a fixed-length vector (Fig. 2).

CEG Construction: This feature involves extracting assembly code from binary files and transforming it into a graph representation. Each node in the CEG

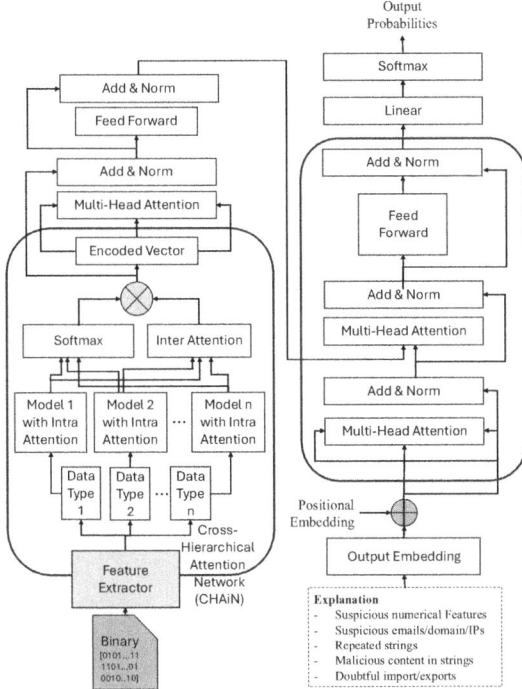

Fig. 1. MalGPT architecture.

encapsulates a set of instructions, which were encoded into numerical vectors using the *PalmTree*[1] model. These instruction-level vectors were aggregated at the node level using an AED architecture, effectively capturing both local and sequential information. The AED model, which integrates the strengths of autoencoders and sequence-to-sequence architectures, was trained on a dataset of 0.8 million assembly code blocks, each capped at 512 instructions. Using these embeddings, CEGs were constructed based on the definitions outlined by Saqib et al. [14]. Subsequently, we trained a graph encoder to generate dense vector representations for the entire graph. This encoder was trained on a dataset of 28.7 GB, comprising 2,411 CEGs from benign and malicious binaries. On average, each CEG contained 546 nodes and 3,567 edges, capturing intricate structural and behavioral information from the binaries (Fig. 3).

3.2 CHAiN Network

Binary files are composed of diverse feature types, such as numerical values (e.g., floats or integers), labeled features, sequences (e.g., API call lists), and assembly code extracted into CEGs [14]. The CEG representation uniquely integrates

---

[1] https://github.com/palmtreemodel.

both syntactical and semantic information into node embeddings, while edge features encapsulate the structural attributes of PE files. To effectively learn from this heterogeneous dataset and capture both intra-modality and inter-modality dependencies, we introduce the CHAiN.

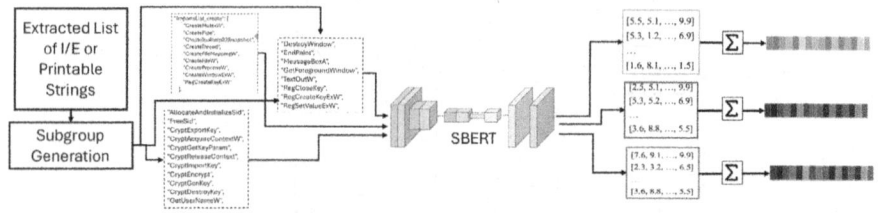

Fig. 2. Encoding mechanism for list of import/export and printable strings.

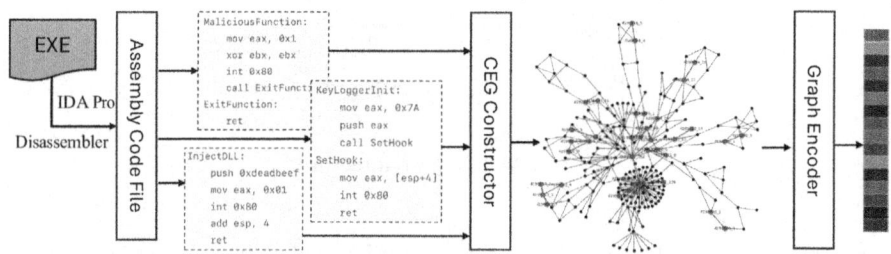

Fig. 3. Encoding mechanism for assembly code extracted from binaries.

Intra-modality Attention. For each feature modality, specialized neural architectures are used to capture intra-relations among similar data features.

Given a modality input $\mathbf{X}$, intra-modality attention computes the weighted representation $\mathbf{H}$ as:

$$\mathbf{H} = \text{Attention}(\mathbf{Q}, \mathbf{K}, \mathbf{V}) = \text{softmax}\left(\frac{\mathbf{Q}\mathbf{K}^T}{\sqrt{d_k}}\right)\mathbf{V}, \tag{1}$$

where $\mathbf{Q}, \mathbf{K}, \mathbf{V}$ are the query, key, and value matrices, respectively, and d_k is the dimensionality of the keys.

Inter-level Dependency Learning. After obtaining feature representations from each modality, an inter-modality attention mechanism is applied to capture relationships across different data types:

$$\mathbf{Z} = \sum_{i=1}^{M} \alpha_i \mathbf{H}_i, \tag{2}$$

where $\mathbf{H}_i$ represents the feature vector from the i-th modality, M is the number of modalities, and α_i are the learned attention weights.

This cross-modality attention captures dependencies such as the significance of printable string patterns when specific PE header attributes are present. The final fused representation $\mathbf{Z}$ can be obtained through bilinear pooling:

$$\mathbf{Z}_{\text{fused}} = \phi(\mathbf{H}_1, \mathbf{H}_2, \ldots, \mathbf{H}_M), \tag{3}$$

where ϕ denotes the bilinear transformation.

3.3 GPT Architecture Integration

The fused representation $\mathbf{Z}_{\text{fused}}$ is input into a GPT for explanation generation. The transformer uses attention mechanisms to model dependencies and generate textual explanations:

$$\text{Output}_t = \text{softmax}\left(\text{Linear}(\text{Decoder}(\mathbf{Z}_{\text{fused}}))\right), \tag{4}$$

where Decoder represents the transformer decoder block. The generated attention weights from intra- and inter-modality layers enable interpretable explanations, highlighting which features or interactions influenced the final prediction.

Collectively, the CHAiN encoder and the GPT-based decoder constitute the MalGPT framework. MalGPT takes a binary executable as input, processes it through CHAiN to generate numerical embeddings, and then utilizes the GPT decoder to translate these embeddings into natural language explanations.

4 Preprocessing and Evaluation

4.1 Dataset Details

The final dataset comprises approximately 23.296 GB of data distributed across 1,702 files, categorized into five distinct groups: four malware families (`Gamarue`, `DownloadAdmin`, `Emotet`, `Firseria`) and a set of benign samples. Feature extraction was augmented through analyst reports retrieved from VirusTotal[2], which served as the foundation for generating human-readable explanations using the ChatGPT API[3].

To overcome the lack of labeled natural language explanations for malware behavior, we used ChatGPT to generate analyst-style descriptions based on

---

[2] https://www.virustotal.com/.
[3] OpenAI, ChatGPT API, accessed November 05, 2024, https://platform.openai.com/.

VirusTotal reports retrieved via MD5 hashes of known malware and benign binaries. These reports included behavioral features such as API calls and registry edits, and were verified to ensure accuracy and minimize hallucinations. Prompt templates were crafted to guide ChatGPT's output in producing consistent and interpretable explanations. For details, refer to the GitHub repository[4]. This constitutes the first dataset pairing malware binaries with human-readable explanations, used solely to pretrain the MalGPT language module. The CHAiN-based classification relied exclusively on real features and labels, with all synthetic outputs reviewed to avoid bias and preserve model integrity.

The dataset was split into 80% training and 20% testing data. The training data was further divided into an 80-20 split for training and validation purposes, ensuring robust evaluation and minimal overfitting during model development.

4.2 Parameter Tuning

The MalGPT model was trained using a manually tuned encoder-decoder architecture optimized for malware explanation generation. Feature values were normalized using StandardScaler, missing data were mean-imputed, and explanation texts were tokenized and padded to a maximum length of 200. The encoding approach follows Sect. 3.1. Table 1 summarizes the core hyperparameters.

Table 1. Key Hyperparameters for MalGPT. LR: Learning Rate, CE: Crossentropy.

Parameter	Value
Vocab Size	10,000
Max Seq. Length	200
Transformer Layers	32
Attention Heads	32
Embedding Size	1024
Dropout Rate	0.1
Batch Size	64
Optimizer	Adam (adaptive LR)
Loss	Sparse Categorical CE
Epochs	50

Manual tuning was chosen over automated methods due to the architecture's complexity and computational constraints, balancing generalization and efficiency.

---

[4] https://github.com/McGill-DMaS/MalGPT

4.3 Training Process of MalGPT

The MalGPT model is trained in an end-to-end manner using binary executables and their corresponding ground truth explanations. Each binary is processed through a multi-modal encoding pipeline that extracts heterogeneous feature types—such as static headers, import/export functions, printable strings, and CEGs. These features are encoded using intra-modality attention, fused via inter-modality attention, and transformed into a unified numerical embedding. This embedding is then passed to a GPT-style decoder, which learns to generate human-readable explanations. The model is optimized by minimizing the difference between the generated and actual explanations.

Algorithm 1. Compact Training Procedure of MalGPT

Require: Binary set $\mathcal{B} = \{b_i\}$ and explanations $\mathcal{Y} = \{y_i\}$
1 **for all** $b_i \in \mathcal{B}$ **do**
2   Extract features: $f_i = \{f_i^{static}, f_i^{imp}, f_i^{str}, f_i^{ceg}\}$
3   Encode: $e_i^m \leftarrow \text{Model}_m(f_i^m)$ for $m \in \{\text{static, imp, str, ceg}\}$
4   Intra-attend: $h_i^m \leftarrow \text{IntraAttn}(e_i^m)$
5   Refine: $r_i^m \leftarrow \text{MLP}(h_i^m)$
6   Fuse: $z_i \leftarrow \text{InterAttn}(\{r_i^m\})$
7   Decode: $\hat{y}_i \leftarrow \text{GPTDecoder}(z_i)$
8   Loss: $\mathcal{L}_i \leftarrow \mathcal{L}(\hat{y}_i, y_i)$
9 **end for**
10 Update model to minimize $\sum_i \mathcal{L}_i$

4.4 Performance Evaluation

The proposed model's performance was assessed in two aspects: its discriminative power and the merits of its explanations. For discriminative power, standard metrics such as precision, recall, F1 score, and accuracy were employed to measure the model's ability to correctly classify malicious and benign binaries.

Table 2. Comparison of Precision (P), Recall (R), F1 Score, False-Positive Rate (FPR), False-Negative Rate (FNR), and Accuracy for each baseline. A: Only static features, B: Without import export, and C: Without CEG.

Features	P	R	F1 Score	Acc	FPR	FNR	ROUGE-L	BERTScore
A	0.920	0.812	0.764	0.9002	0.0266	0.2028	0.0544	0.7701
B	0.932	0.804	0.772	0.9208	0.0198	0.1982	0.0549	0.7741
C	0.984	0.970	0.984	0.9794	0.0058	0.0120	0.0527	0.7752
CHAiN	0.988	0.984	0.988	0.9882	0.0048	0.0026	0.0820	0.8140

To evaluate explanation correctness quantitatively, we employed ROUGE-L[5] and BERTScore [20]. ROUGE-L was selected for its ability to capture long-sequence dependencies and align key segments between generated and reference explanations. In contrast, BERTScore uses contextual embeddings to measure semantic consistency, providing a robust evaluation of nuanced relationships and achieving strong correlation with human judgment, even in paraphrased scenarios [20]. These complementary metrics ensured a comprehensive assessment of both technical precision and semantic alignment in the model's explanations.

For a qualitative assessment, metrics such as False Positive Rate (FPR) and False Negative Rate (FNR) were employed alongside manual inspection of hallucinated content in the generated explanations. This approach allowed for a detailed evaluation of areas where the model misinterprets or invents information, ensuring a comprehensive analysis of the model's explanation reliability and its interpretative consistency.

5 Results and Discussions

5.1 Ablation Study

To assess the contribution of each feature set, we conducted an ablation study by evaluating detection and explanation performance with different combinations of features. Initially, we performed experiments using only static or numerical features, followed by a combination of static features and CEG information (excluding import/export features), and static features with import/export features (excluding CEG). The findings revealed that the combination of static features and import/export features achieved satisfactory detection rates. However, explanation metrics remained relatively consistent across ablation settings until all feature types were combined (Table 2).

The integration of all feature sets—static, import/export, and CEG—yielded superior detection performance, marked by significantly reduced error rates (FPR and FNR). Additionally, the explanation metrics (e.g., ROUGE-L and BERTScore) improved notably, indicating that CHAiN successfully leverages both syntactical and semantic information to generate meaningful explanations for malware binaries. This comprehensive approach highlights CHAiN's robustness in both detection and explainability tasks.

5.2 Discriminative Power

We evaluated the discriminative power of the proposed CHAiN model across various malware families, including benign samples, and compared it against benchmark algorithms GAGE and CFGExplainer, which are state-of-the-art in malware detection. The results are summarized in Table 3.

---

[5] https://huggingface.co/spaces/evaluate-metric/rouge.

Table 3. Performance metrics comparison

Model	Precision	Recall	F1 Score	FPR	FNR	Accuracy
CHAiN	0.9880	0.9860	0.9860	0.0048	0.0026	0.9800
GAGE	0.9300	0.9140	0.9200	0.0156	0.0902	0.9413
CFGExplainer	0.8720	0.8180	0.8320	0.0378	0.1830	0.9003

The findings underscore CHAiN's ability to integrate syntactical and semantic information effectively, enhancing both detection and explanation capabilities, particularly for challenging malware families such as Gamarue. The proposed model achieves the highest accuracy (98%), followed by GAGE (94.13%) and CFGExplainer (90.03%). These results demonstrate its robustness and superiority over traditional models.

5.3 Novelty and Plausibility

The proposed MalGPT framework demonstrates significant novelty in generating plausible malware explanations, as evidenced by the table. The comparison between actual and MalGPT-generated explanations highlights both the strengths and areas for improvement in the system. MalGPT exhibits an advanced ability to replicate key malicious attributes, integrating domain-specific knowledge from malware families, such as `Firseria`.

Explanation 1
MD5: C0A5DE8A89C236DD6071A6014065CAE8 **Malware Family:** Firseria **File Name:** origin_15301_ **Indication:** Red: Malicious intent or behavior. Magenta: Behavioral descriptions relevant to malware families. **Actual:** The file is identified as part of the ransomware family, a notorious malware category impacting systems with sophisticated registry manipulations and evasive behaviors. Antivirus engines, including Microsoft, Bitdefender, and BKAV, confirm its presence, highlighting its ability to persist through browser modifications, bundled associations, and delivery mechanisms. Notable tactics include the exploitation of Solimba and Kryptik infrastructures, avoiding detection via sandbox analysis, and manipulating user libraries and APIs. The malware demonstrates domain persistence, alterations to whitelisted platforms, and leveraging vulnerabilities for propagation. Andromeda.exe links, 64-bit patched alterations, and HFSAdware integrations underscore its risks. It actively evades countermeasures by disabling zero-day detection systems, network functionality, and adopting downware techniques. Frequent administrative updates, ... and regular updates to maintain system integrity against this persistent threat.

MalGPT: The file "andromeda.exe" is infected with a high-risk 64-bit adware named HFSAdware. This malware, which has some 49 distinct signs highlighting its presence, has visibly altered the system's policies for harmful purposes. This Andromeda variant propagates itself and notably supports domain persistence despite attempts to remove it or contain it. There are indications suggesting that this file is also associated with the invasive malware, Solimba. As part of its comprehensive preventive measures, it regularly checks its presence and updates itself, further underscoring its persistence in infected systems. Certain interesting anomalies such as invalid downware policies and the presence of API confirmations, have emerged from recent discussions in various security platforms. Moreover, the malware is known to infect systems through misleading advertisements, displaying as essential updates. Identified as a part of the Kryptik family, the malware has shown a significant number of warning flags such as modifying critical system files and displaying unauthorized popup ads. Bias analysis from the 62 whitelisting results, major delivery programs, and several other indications highlight Andromeda's sophisticated evasion strategies. One such strategy includes disabling zero-day detection systems. These actions are likely triggered by the Firseria infection, which further stresses the need for categorizing and scanning files, programs, and links continuously. A comprehensive ... and injection prevention are vital for maintaining system integrity.

The `Firseria` malware family is a type of ransomware known for its ability to manipulate system registries and evade detection [6]. It often employs sophisticated techniques, such as API abuse, sandbox evasion, and persistent file modifications. MalGPT extends its explanatory depth by replacing browser-related references (as noted in the actual explanation) with more specific behaviors, such as `'domain persistence'` and API-focused activities. Notably, MalGPT highlights the involvement of the `Kryptik family` and `Andromeda.exe`, effectively capturing key attributes of `Firseria`'s infection strategies, including evasion techniques and API manipulation (see Explanation 1). This highlights `Firseria`'s use of sophisticated frameworks for evasion and malicious propagation. Such detailed interrelations demonstrate MalGPT's robust understanding of the binary's syntactical and semantic features.

The plausibility of MalGPT explanations is highlighted by its ability to match the key evidence in actual explanations. For example, in the `Firseria` family, MalGPT connects critical tactics such as `'persistence through browser manipulations'` and `'delivery mechanisms'`, which align closely with the ground truth descriptions. Similarly, in the benign sample, MalGPT accurately emphasizes secure characteristics, such as `'reliable systems'` and `'safe browsing policies'`, further bolstering its credibility.

6 Limitations

6.1 Hallucination and Error Analysis

We assess MalGPT's capabilities using both quantitative and qualitative analyses. The error metrics in Table 3 quantitatively highlight MalGPT's performance.

Explanation 2
MD5: 976BD72651F83785CA69FB74C3C5BBAE **Malware Family:** Downloadadmin **File Name:** origin_31932_ **Indication:** Red: Malicious intent or behavior. Green: Benign characteristics. Magenta: Behavioral descriptions relevant to malware families. Yellow: Ambiguous or conflicting content blending malicious and benign contexts. Cyan: Hallucinated or unrelated content.
Actual: The file exhibits behavior characteristic of "DownloadAdmin" malware, known for its intrusive and deceptive activities. It employs obfuscation tactics to evade detection while distributing malicious payloads through misleading campaigns. Notable actions include intrusion attempts, unauthorized certificate usage, and deploying Potentially Unwanted Applications (PUAs) such as Firseria. The malware reinforces its presence via remote downloader capabilities, often altering system configurations to maintain persistence. Organizations must implement preventive defenses, such as Bitdefender or Kaspersky, to counteract its spread. Regular verification, awareness programs, and robust classification mechanisms remain crucial for mitigating this threat.
MalGPT: The explanation discusses several key aspects of a malware family or benign file characterized by its notable status and the comprehensive cyber campaigns it has been linked to. It's stated that this entity employs obfuscation and alterations as part of its deployment strategy. Also, it regularly reinforces its defenses and maintains a prominent presence by distributing itself through various channels. Moreover, it leverages '"Firseria"' and '"Dowadmin"' sections, along with a "Win32 downloader," to spread its influence. This can lead to an intrusion into Windows applications, including those associated with major organizations. Conventional defense mechanisms seem ineffective against it. It's known for being capable of evading detection by the likes of Bitdefender and Kaspersky. Though posing as a 'goodware', it has been classified as a PUA ('Potentially Unwanted Application') due to its intrusive behavior. Regularly educating users ... this entity seems to belong under the 'intrusive' classification but remains notable within the cybersecurity landscape for its persistent behavior.

> **Explanation 3**
> **MD5:** 68AE5602E48B5457E22340D09F34BE23 **Malware Family:** Benign **File Name:** 0ad73180...52d629b3 **Indication:** Same as previous.
> **Actual:** The file in question has been assessed by antivirus engines and classified as benign due to its lack of malicious indicators. It is identified as a PE32 executable for Windows systems, with no evidence of malicious activities, C2 communications, encryption, or known IoCs (Indicators of Compromise). Verified by engines e.g., Kaspersky and Symantec, the file does not demonstrate suspicious behaviors such as trojan-like persistence, data exfiltration, or anomalous DLL injections. However, alternate analyses indicate some potential for exploitation in 'Fareit'-like mechanisms, including manipulation of DLLs, intrusive system libraries, or suspicious communication chains. Despite this, no confirmed malicious actions or tactics have been linked to the file, and its legitimacy remains supported by majority consensus. It is noted in whitelisting databases, lacks significant threats or anomalies, and remains flagged as benign in the absence of further evidence.
> **MalGPT:** This explanation pertains to the intricate workings of malware and benign files. It presents an analysis of the disruptive AVG expired botnet, and the intrusiveness it displays. The explanation demonstrates the lack of notorious analysis in dealing with the cybersecurity threats posed by malware. The cornerstone is ensuring an effective response to the anomalous activities conducted by malware through a prominent mechanism, such as NVIDIA. In this discussion, sensitive common lists of suspicious cyber communications play a crucial role, with a particular focus on benign files. ... The report incorporates various statistics and references to 'dll', or Dynamic Link Library sections, which are active in combating malware threats. With an increasing misuse of the DLLs, there is a need to enhance blocking mechanisms to prevent their manipulation. The document goes on to emphasize the significance of identifying, categorizing, and addressing threats, particularly those characterized by the Andromeda address. The explanation also ... and the 'dowadmin' mechanisms. Mention of URLs indicates the network aspect of these threats. In conclusion, the review presents the sobering statistics regarding malware infections despite the many cybersecurity measures in place. However, it also maintains trust in sophisticated mechanisms and clean programs, such as the 'sobrab' and 'hfsadware', in maintaining cybersecurity around the globe.

By analyzing both the *Actual Explanation* and *MalGPT Explanation*, it is evident that while the model captures key malicious behaviors effectively, it also introduces hallucinated information and occasionally misclassifies intent (Explanation 2, and 3). Using the highlighted text in the examples, we can systematically evaluate these issues:

Distinguishing contextual relevance: MalGPT demonstrates the ability to identify malicious activities such as obfuscation and downloading behavior for `DownloadAdmin`. However, it introduces hallucinated elements, such as references to "`Firseria sections`", which are not explicitly relevant in the actual explanation (Explanation 2). This misattribution might stem from the presence of the term "`Firseria`" in the actual explanation, where it was used in a different context. This highlights a limitation in distinguishing contextual relevance during explanation generation.

Distinguishing intention relevance: In the `benign` example, hallucinated content introduces contradictions. For instance, phrases, "`workings of malware and benign files`" create confusion by blending opposing concepts (Explanation 3). While MalGPT correctly highlights benign characteristics, such as "`with a particular focus on benign files,`" it simultaneously incorporates unrelated malicious terms, such as "`botnet,`" "`Andromeda,`" and "`dowadmin mechanisms.`" This inconsistency likely arises from contextual overlaps in the training data. The intermixing of benign and malicious indicators underscores the need for enhanced precision when distinguishing intent categories to ensure coherent explanations.

6.2 Data Dependency

A key limitation of the MalGPT framework lies in its dependency on the quality and diversity of the input data. Although the dataset includes malware binaries and corresponding explanations generated with the assistance of the ChatGPT API, the reliability of these explanations is contingent upon the accuracy of the underlying analyst reports sourced from VirusTotal. While efforts were made to minimize hallucinations by extracting verified malware descriptions using MD5 hashes, the dataset remains limited in size and scope, potentially affecting generalization to unseen or novel malware families.

Additionally, some of the explanation patterns exhibit redundancy, which may introduce noise into the training process. Future work should focus on curating a larger, more diverse dataset by incorporating alternative sources—such as Amazon Trūk or hybrid threat intelligence platforms—and ensuring balanced coverage of malware behaviors. Enhancing dataset robustness will further improve the model's ability to handle previously unseen features and reduce the risk of explanation artifacts.

7 Conclusion

Explaining malicious binaries remains a challenging domain due to the complexity and diversity of malware behaviors. The proposed model, MalGPT, represents a significant step forward as the first approach to generate detailed explanations for malware binaries from scratch, focusing on both their behaviors and intentions. MalGPT outperforms state-of-the-art methods, achieving high accuracy in malware detection with exceptionally low error rates. Beyond detection, it excels in generating high-quality explanations, quantitatively and qualitatively validated, while also contributing a novel dataset tailored for this task.

Although hallucinations remains a concern, leading to occasional inaccuracies in explanations, this limitation can be mitigated in future iterations. Enhancements such as improved contextual embeddings and fine-tuning on more extensive labeled datasets will help refine the model's interpretability and reliability. The results demonstrate MalGPT's potential to transform the field of explainable AI for cybersecurity, bridging gaps in malware analysis and enabling more informed decision-making.

Supplementary Information. The dataset, source code and appendix containing detailed implementation information are available in the Data Mining and Security (DMaS) Lab GitHub repository[6].

Acknowledgment. The research is supported in part by NSERC Discovery Grants (RGPIN-2024-04087), NSERC Collaborative Research and Training Experience (CREATE-554764-2021), and Canada Research Chairs Program (CRC-2019-00041).

Disclosure of Interests. The authors have no competing interests to declare that are relevant to the content of this article.

References

1. Ambekar, N.G., Devi, N.N., Thokchom, S., Yogita: TabLSTMNet: enhancing Android malware classification through integrated attention and explainable AI. Microsyst. Techno., 1–19 (2024). https://doi.org/10.1007/s00542-024-05615-0
2. Demirkıran, F., Çayır, A., Ünal, U., Dağ, H.: An ensemble of pre-trained transformer models for imbalanced multiclass malware classification. Comput. Secur. **121**, 102846 (2022)
3. Herath, J.D., Wakodikar, P.P., Yang, P., Yan, G.: CFGExplainer: explaining graph neural network-based malware classification from control flow graphs. In: 2022 52nd Annual IEEE/IFIP International Conference on Dependable Systems and Networks (DSN), pp. 172–184. IEEE (2022)
4. Khan, I.A., Moustafa, N., Pi, D., Sallam, K.M., Zomaya, A.Y., Li, B.: A new explainable deep learning framework for cyber threat discovery in industrial IoT networks. IEEE Internet Things J. (2021). https://doi.org/10.1109/JIOT.2021.3130156
5. Kinkead, M., Millar, S., McLaughlin, N., O'Kane, P.: Towards explainable CNNs for Android malware detection. Proc. Comput. Sci. **184**, 959–965 (2021). https://doi.org/10.1016/j.procs.2021.03.118
6. Lever, C., Kotzias, P., Balzarotti, D., Caballero, J., Antonakakis, M.: A lustrum of malware network communication and insights. In: 2017 IEEE Symposium on Security and Privacy (SP), pp. 788–804 (2017). https://doi.org/10.1109/SP.2017.59

---

[6] https://github.com/McGill-DMaS/MalGPT

7. Li, M.Q., Fung, B.C., Charland, P., Ding, S.H.: $I-MAD$: interpretable malware detector using galaxy transformer. Comput. Secur. **108**, 102371 (2021). https://doi.org/10.1016/j.cose.2021.102371
8. Lu, Z., Thing, V.L.: "how does it detect a malicious app?" Explaining the predictions of AI-based malware detector. In: 2022 IEEE 8th International Conference on Big Data Security on Cloud (BigDataSecurity), IEEE International Conference on High Performance and Smart Computing,(HPSC) and IEEE International Conference on Intelligent Data and Security (IDS), pp. 194–199. IEEE (2022). https://doi.org/10.1109/BigDataSecurityHPSCIDS54978.2022.00045
9. Lundberg, S.M., Lee, S.I.: A unified approach to interpreting model predictions. In: Proceedings of the 31st International Conference on Neural Information Processing Systems, NIPS 2017, Red Hook, NY, USA, pp. 4768–4777. Curran Associates Inc. (2017)
10. Mitchell, J., McLaughlin, N., Martinez-del Rincon, J.: Generating sparse explanations for malicious android opcode sequences using hierarchical lime. Comput. Secur. **137**, 103637 (2024). https://doi.org/10.1016/j.cose.2023.103637
11. Rahali, A., Akhloufi, M.A.: MalBERT: malware detection using bidirectional encoder representations from transformers. In: 2021 IEEE International Conference on Systems, Man, and Cybernetics (SMC), pp. 3226–3231 (2021). https://doi.org/10.1109/SMC52423.2021.9659287
12. Reimers, N., Gurevych, I.: Sentence-BERT: sentence embeddings using Siamese BERT-networks. In: Proceedings of the 2019 Conference on Empirical Methods in Natural Language Processing. Association for Computational Linguistics (2019)
13. Ribeiro, M.T., Singh, S., Guestrin, C.: "why should i trust you?": explaining the predictions of any classifier. In: Proceedings of the 22nd ACM SIGKDD International Conference on Knowledge Discovery and Data Mining, KDD 2016, pp. 1135–1144. Association for Computing Machinery, New York, NY, USA (2016). https://doi.org/10.1145/2939672.2939778
14. Saqib, M., Fung, B.C.M., Charland, P., Walenstein, A.: GAGE: genetic algorithm-based graph explainer for malware analysis. In: Proceedings of the 40th IEEE International Conference on Data Engineering (ICDE), Utrecht, Netherlands, pp. 2258–2270. IEEE Computer Society (2024)
15. Saqib, M., Mahdavifar, S., Fung, B.C.M., Charland, P.: A comprehensive analysis of explainable AI for malware hunting. ACM Comput. Surv. **56**(12) (2024). https://doi.org/10.1145/3677374
16. Smmarwar, S.K., Gupta, G.P., Kumar, S.: XAI-AMD-DL: an explainable AI approach for Android malware detection system using deep learning. In: 2023 IEEE World Conference on Applied Intelligence and Computing (AIC), pp. 423–428. IEEE (2023). https://doi.org/10.1109/AIC57670.2023.10263974
17. To, T.N., Hoang, H.D., Duy, P.T., Pham, V.H.: MalDEX: an explainable malware detection system based on ensemble learning. In: 2023 International Conference on Multimedia Analysis and Pattern Recognition (MAPR), pp. 1–6 (2023). https://doi.org/10.1109/MAPR59823.2023.10288922
18. Ullah, F., Alsirhani, A., Alshahrani, M.M., Alomari, A., Naeem, H., Shah, S.A.: Explainable malware detection system using transformers-based transfer learning and multi-model visual representation. Sensors **22**(18), 6766 (2022)

19. Xing, X., Jin, X., Elahi, H., Jiang, H., Wang, G.: A malware detection approach using autoencoder in deep learning. IEEE Access **10**, 25696–25706 (2022). https://doi.org/10.1109/ACCESS.2022.3155695
20. Zhang, T., Kishore, V., Wu, F., Weinberger, K.Q., Artzi, Y.: BERTScore: evaluating text generation with BERT. In: Proceedings of the International Conference on Learning Representations (ICLR), New York, NY, USA. Cornell University and ASAPP Inc., Cornell Tech. (2020). https://doi.org/10.48550/arXiv.1904.09675

MAINLE: A Multi-Agent, Interactive, Natural Language Local Explainer of Classification Tasks

Paulo Bruno Serafim[1(✉)], Rômulo Férrer Filho[2], Stenio Freitas[2], Gizem Gezici[3], Fosca Giannotti[3], Franco Raimondi[1], and Alexandre Santos[2]

[1] Gran Sasso Science Institute (GSSI), L'Aquila, Italy
{paulo.desousa,franco.raimondi}@gssi.it
[2] Universidade Federal do Ceará (UFC), Fortaleza, Brazil
[3] Scuola Normale Superiore (SNS), Pisa, Italy
{gizem.gezici,fosca.giannotti}@sns.it

Abstract. There is an increasing need to explain machine learning decisions in an understandable way, even for non-expert users. In this paper, we introduce a multi-agent architecture to provide interactive explanations for classification tasks based on a range of machine learning algorithms, so that end-users can obtain answers in natural language. Our architecture is composed of four agents that are able to convert any classifier into a surrogate Decision Tree around the neighbourhood of a classification instance, which is then translated into a natural language explanation that can be further explored in an interactive way. We validate our approach against publicly available datasets using different classification methods, discussing the relevance of the architecture along five quality attributes, and performing a user study to evaluate the generated explanations. Our results show that the proposed architecture is able to generate simplified explanations that are more understandable for non-expert users in comparison to the ones given directly by a single explainer in all evaluated criteria.

Keywords: Explainable AI · Conversational AI · Model-agnostic explanations · Local explanations

1 Introduction

Explaining decisions taken by a machine learning (ML) classifier becomes increasingly important as these models are used in critical applications such as healthcare, finance, and criminal justice, and might incur a broad range of problems that include gender bias [2] and discrimination [3]. In the field of Explainable Artificial Intelligence (XAI), several methods have been proposed to deal

Supplementary Information The online version contains supplementary material available at https://doi.org/10.1007/978-3-032-06078-5_9.

with these issues [1]. However, in order to employ XAI techniques, users often need some level of familiarity with programming or ML. Therefore, although the end results of explainability methods can be satisfactory, they might not be easily accessible to non-expert users.

To address these problems, Human-Centered XAI has been proposed as a way to bridge the gap between XAI and non-expert users [8]. Currently, solutions rely on ready-to-use tools that might include visual interfaces, spreadsheets, and summary reports [5,7]. More recently, conversational solutions have been proposed to give users more freedom to interact with the system [24]. These solutions, however, are usually limited to specific tasks, datasets, or models. In this work, we propose MAINLE, a multi-agent architecture that can generate simplified local explanations for any classifier in a conversational way.

Our goal is to empower non-expert users with the ability to understand the decisions made by ML models without the need for a background in the field. Our approach works by distributing the process of generating explanations among multiple systems in which different agents are responsible for solving a specific problem. Using specialized agents for each subtask allows them to generate outputs with higher quality. Although they do not communicate directly, the outputs of one agent are used as inputs for the next one. As such, MAINLE is modular and allows for a flexible development of the agents. The generalization capabilities come from the usage of a surrogate model that creates a Decision Tree focused on the input, thus generating a local explanation. Finally, the explanation is presented in natural language, which can then be further explored in an interactive way. The multi-agent architecture is summarized in Fig. 1.

In order to validate MAINLE, we focus on answering four research questions:

1. Is the architecture able to generate simplified explanations for any classifier?
2. How do human users evaluate the generated explanations?
3. How do automated evaluations compare to human evaluations?
4. What are the quality attributes of the architecture?

To validate the generalization capabilities of the proposed architecture, we test it with multiple classifiers in multiple tasks. We also employ a user study to evaluate the quality of the simplified explanation generated by MAINLE from the perspective of human users. An automated evaluation of the quality of the explanations is performed using critic agents implemented using Large Language Models (LLMs). Finally, we discuss the quality attributes of the MAINLE and their relevance to the proposed approach. Our contributions are as follows:

1. A multi-agent architecture to generate simplified explanations for any ML classifier.
2. A process to generate natural language explanations using surrogate interpretable models for any classifier.
3. Interactive explanations through conversation.
4. Validation of the architecture with user studies.
5. Public availability of the code[1].

---

[1] Available at https://github.com/paulobruno/ecml-pkdd-2025.

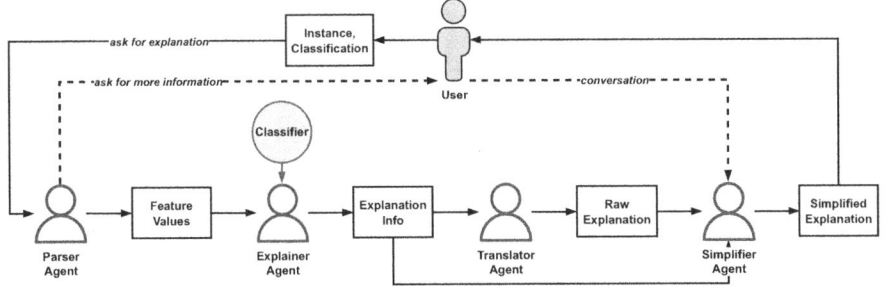

Fig. 1. Simplified MAINLE architecture.

2 Related Work

There are several works that aim to generate Natural Language Explanations (NLE) for ML models. Here, we briefly mention some of the ones that are most related to our work. More specifically, works that generate NLE from Decision Trees, use conversational systems, and employ multi-agent architectures in XAI.

2.1 Explaining Decision Trees Classification in Natural Language

Due to their nature of being convertible to logical statements, Decision Trees are widely regarded as interpretable-by-design models [20,22]. Generating NLEs from them was first performed by using this property [15]. More recently, LLMs were employed as the explainer in the task of Network Intrusion Detection [29] and generalized to any task [23]. However, depending on factors like depth and width, Decision Trees can be hard to understand, especially for non-experts [21]. In this paper, we expand on previous work in two ways. First, we make it possible to explain any classifier in natural language by using a surrogate model to create a Decision Tree around the neighborhood of an instance. Second, we employ a multi-agent architecture, called MAINLE, that allows greater flexibility and provides improved results in an interactive way by using specialized agents.

2.2 Conversational Systems

Besides converting explanations to NLE, another important topic that has been gaining traction is user interaction through a conversational interface [10]. In the context of XAI, this has been proposed as a way to empower users with the ability to enquire information directly from the explainer [14]. Currently, LLMs are state-of-the-art in this task, as they can generate human-like responses [16,18,25]. An important aspect of MAINLE is that it provides a conversational interface for users to access the explanation. In this work, we use this conversation capability in two distinct moments. At the beginning of the architecture, the agent that gets input information might question the user for additional data or clarify some doubts about input features. Then, at the end of the architecture, the user can ask for more information regarding the explanation provided.

2.3 Multi-agent XAI

To compose multiple abilities in a single explainable solution, multi-agent architectures have been proposed in XAI to increase the generalization, transparency, automation, and modularity of such systems [6]. More recently, the advance in LLM research has shown that specialized agents generate better outputs than a single LLM [28]. As such, several recent works focused on multi-agent architectures in XAI based on LLM agents [4,19,26]. MAINLE combines explanation capabilities, a natural language interaction, and a conversational interface in a multi-agent architecture. By proposing such architecture, we provide a flexible and general solution for explaining classifier decisions for non-expert users.

3 Methods

In this section, we present the proposed MAINLE architecture of an interactive multi-agent system for generating simplified explanations for any classifier.

3.1 MAINLE Architecture

The proposed architecture is composed of four stages, each one performed by a specialized agent. To start the conversational explanation process, the user provides an instance and its corresponding classification to be explained. This first interaction is handled by a Parser agent, which collects all necessary information and sends it to the Explainer agent, which generates explanation data. The Translator agent then converts the explanation data into a raw explanation in natural language. Finally, the Simplifier agent generates a simplified explanation that is sent back to the user, which may keep interacting with the system until satisfied. Figure 1 illustrates this process.

Parser Agent. After the user provides the instance and classification to be explained, the Parser agent is responsible for ensuring all necessary information is presented. Otherwise, it should alert the user that some information is missing, since without a list of all feature values and the target classification, the explanation process cannot be performed. Its goal is to create a computer-understandable representation of the input, which is then passed to the next stage. In this work, we implement the Parser agent using an LLM, which allows the interaction to be done through a conversational interface. It adds flexibility to the first stage by allowing users to interact using natural language and the Parser agent to ask for more information when needed. After all feature values are collected, the Parser agent formats the information in a structured way and sends it to the process of generating explanations. Other types of implementation could be used, such as a rule-based approach, as long as they can ensure all necessary information is collected and sent in the correct format to the next stage.

Explainer Agent. The Explainer agent is responsible to run the explanation process and generate the explanation data. In this work, we leverage

Decision Tree capabilities to generate interpretable results. Often regarded as interpretable-by-design models, Decision Trees allow for a clear understanding of the decision process. Since working strictly with tree models would greatly limit the scope of available classifiers, we employ LORE [11,12] to generate a surrogate Decision Tree around the neighborhood of the given instance. Therefore, any classifier can be explained by first converting it into a Decision Tree using LORE, allowing the system to generate a local explanation for the user instance. Besides the Decision Tree, LORE also generates factual and counterfactuals. A factual is the rule that the Decision Tree follows to reach the classification, while a counterfactual is a rule that would change the result [17]. After generating the tree and the additional artifacts, the Explainer agent assembles all available information, which is then passed to the next stage, as illustrated in Fig. 2.

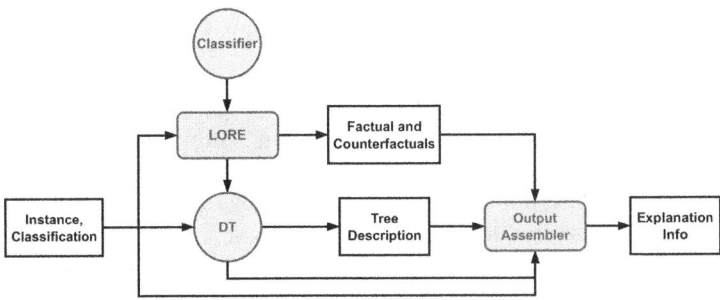

Fig. 2. Illustration of the process to convert any classifier to a Decision Tree using LORE [11,12]. The output will be used to generate a Natural Language Explanation.

Here, we borrow the notation from [12]. We adapt $LORE_{sa}$, which is *algorithm 1* in the same work, to return also the Decision Tree, c, in addition to the factual rule and counterfactuals. Moreover, in the current implementation, the $LORE_{sa}$ explainer is generated in a previous step. In more detail, let b be a black-box classifier, x an instance, and $y = b(x)$ the classification of x. A *factual*, $r = p \rightarrow y$, is a decision rule, which states the reason why $y = b(x) = c(x)$. Additionally, Φ is a set of *counterfactual* rules, which contains a set of changes that would change the classification outcome, i.e. $\phi \in \Phi = p \rightarrow y'$, where y' can be any possible classification other than y. The LORE explainer generator, $LORE_{exp}$, takes as input b and a dataset, D, and returns a $LORE_{sa}$ explainer. Then, $LORE_{sa}$ generates a surrogate Decision Tree, a factual, and the set of counterfactuals for a given classifier and an instance. Finally, additional information is added to the explanation data, such as *feature names*, *class values*, and the classification *confidence*. This process is described in Algorithm 1.

Translator Agent. With the explanation data, the Translator agent is responsible for generating a raw explanation in natural language. In this work, we use an LLM to produce a Natural Language Explanation given a textual description of all available information. This operation is similar to the process done in

Algorithm 1 Explainer agent process

Input: $x \leftarrow$ instance, $\bar{y} \leftarrow$ target classification,
$b \leftarrow$ black-box classifier, $D \leftarrow$ dataset
Output: $i \leftarrow$ explanation data

1: $y \leftarrow b(x)$;   // get instance classification
2: **assert** $y = \bar{y}$;   // validate target classification
3: $LORE_{sa} = LORE_{exp}(b, D)$;   // generate explainer
4: $e = \langle c, r, \Phi \rangle \leftarrow LORE_{sa}(x, b)$;   // generate explanation
5: $c_t \leftarrow text(c)$;   // convert tree to text
6: $i = \langle$feature names, target values, confidence, $c_t, x, r, \Phi, \bar{y}\rangle$
7: **return** i

[23,29]. Since there is no interaction with this agent, a non-LLM implementation would also work seamlessly. At the end of this stage, the raw explanation is sent to the Simplifier agent.

Simplifier Agent. Finally, the last agent is responsible to simplify the raw explanation and send it to the user. Simplification is important to ensure that the explanation is understandable by non-experts since the raw explanation might contain too much information or be too complex. For example, a simplified explanation might use simple terms, avoid technical jargon, and avoid irrelevant information. Another relevant aspect of this agent is that it allows the user to interact with it, for instance by asking for more information or clarifications. In our implementation, the user is free to keep asking questions until they are satisfied with the explanation. To achieve this, we developed the Simplifier agent using an LLM, although other possibilities could be used, especially in situations in which user interaction is not required.

3.2 Classification Tasks

An architecture that aims to be generalizable should be able to handle different types of tasks. Here, we evaluated MAINLE on five different classical datasets. The datasets were selected to represent different levels of complexity and number of features. All of them are publicly available and have been used in previous works, as such no ethical concerns with data usage and control are raised.

As a simpler dataset with a reduced number of features, the iris dataset is a common choice for classification tasks. It consists of 150 instances, each with four features and three possible classes. Another classical dataset used in multi-class problems is the wine dataset, which contains 178 instances with 13 features and three target classes. The first binary classification tested is the breast cancer Wisconsin diagnostic. It contains 569 instances and 30 features. The adult dataset also has two classes but with 14 features and 48,842 instances. Finally, the fifth dataset used is the credit approval dataset, another binary classification task, with 690 instances and 15 features.

3.3 Classifiers

Since the MAINLE architecture is model-agnostic, besides the ability to handle different types of tasks it should also be able to handle different types of classifiers. We use three different classifiers to evaluate the proposed architecture, chosen to represent a high level of complexity and difficult interpretability. As a popular ensemble classifier, Random Forests are known for their high performance in a variety of tasks. Another popular ensemble method, Gradient Boosting is a more complex classifier than Random Forests, but also widely used. Lastly, we evaluated the architecture with a Multi-Layer Perceptron to represent the class of artificial neural networks, notable for their high complexity. All of the three models are broadly considered as non-interpretable classifiers [9,13].

3.4 Natural Language Models

As long as their input and output are in accordance with each stage of MAINLE, the agents can be implemented freely. There is no restriction on the type of agent used, and they do not need to be an LLM. That said, because of their high capabilities in natural language processing, in this work, we decided to use LLMs as a case study. In order to assess the ability to deal with different LLMs, we tested the architecture with four models from different manufacturers: GPT-4o, Gemini 2.0, LLaMA 3.2, and DeepSeek-R1. Due to the high quality presented during early experiments, we opted to use GPT-4o as a baseline to generate the examples while the others were used in the evaluation process.

4 Evaluation Metrics

In this section, we describe the evaluation methods of MAINLE effectiveness in providing NLE for classifications performed by ML models. There are two main evaluation approaches, a user study and an automated evaluation using a critic agent based on LLMs, followed by a discussion of quality attributes.

4.1 Evaluation Criteria

To analyze the quality of simplified explanations generated in natural language, four criteria were defined that consider the clarity, accessibility, and relevance of the information presented. These criteria help us to verify how well the explanations can be understood by non-expert users without compromising fidelity to the model's decision process.

Technical Jargon. Evaluates the extent to which the explanation avoids specialized terminology, numerical values, and technical terms. The goal is to assess whether the generated explanations minimize technical jargon, making them more accessible to non-experts, and to present the reasoning in a manner that is independent of the model's internal architecture. When evaluated by users, we ask if they "were able to follow the explanation easily and did not need previous knowledge of the internal procedures."

Simplicity. Measures the clarity and straightforwardness of the explanation. Effective explanations utilize simple language, such as using "high" and "low" instead of "greater than 0.5" and "less than 0.5", to convey information without unnecessary complexity. From the user's point of view, we ask if "the terms used were simple and easy to read."

Completeness. Assesses whether the explanation covers all relevant information that influenced the model's decision. It reflects the extent to which the explanation provides a complete and detailed account of the factors involved in the process. In this criterion, we ask if the users feel that they "understood the reasons why the decision was made and did not miss additional information."

Conciseness. The goal of this criterion is to evaluate the brevity of the explanation while maintaining essential information. Concise explanations avoid irrelevant details, focusing solely on the pertinent factors that led to the model's decision. For the user study, we ask participants if they "feel that all information presented was necessary, there was no useless information in the explanation, and the explanation could not be shorter."

4.2 User Study

We conducted a user study to assess the quality of the simplified explanations generated by MAINLE. The participants were asked to rate the explanations generated by the Simplifier in comparison with the raw explanations generated by the Translator in the four criteria defined above. The user evaluation questionnaire consisted of a raw and a simplified explanation, followed by a set of questions to rate each explanation according to each criterion. The raw explanation generally contains a very detailed description of the decision process, similar to a step-by-step deduction according to the decision tree path. On the other hand, the simplified explanation is generated by the Simplifier agent, which we expect to be more accessible to non-experts. In order to assess each explanation, we asked users to rate evaluation criteria on both explanations on a 5-point Likert scale, ranging from "Strongly Disagree" to "Strongly Agree". Among the possible combinations, each evaluator is assigned a single random combination of dataset and classifier. A total of 25 evaluators participated in the study with varying levels of expertise in machine learning.

4.3 Critic Agent Evaluation

We also performed automated evaluation using a Critic agent based on four different LLMs. Similar to the user study, this agent compares the raw explanation generated by the Translator agent with the simplified explanation generated by the Simplifier agent in the four criteria. Two experiments are performed. First, similar to the user study, the Critic agent is asked to rate each explanation on a 5-point Likert scale. For the second experiment, the agent is instructed to select which explanation is better for each criterion. As such, we can utilize the results of the Critic agent as an additional evaluation along the user study to verify the effectiveness of MAINLE in generating simplified explanations.

5 Results and Discussion

In this section, we present the results of the evaluation of the proposed architecture. We first present the results of the user study followed by evaluations made using Critic agents. Finally, we discuss the quality attributes of MAINLE.

5.1 User Study

MAINLE allows users to interact with the system in a conversational way, which is important to make the explanations more accessible to non-expert users. To validate the capability of the architecture to generate simplified explanations, we conducted a user study.

Explanation Rating. We asked human evaluators to rate the explanations according to the four criteria presented in Sect. 4.1. The possible answers were given on a Likert scale, but here we converted them to numerical values to facilitate the analysis. We used a scale from 1 to 5, where 1 means "Strongly Disagree" and 5 means "Strongly Agree". As such, the higher the number, the better the user evaluation. The results are shown in Table 1.

Table 1. Average user ratings.

Criterion	Raw Explanation	Simplified Explanation
Technical Jargon	3.1 ± 1.3	**4.0 ± 1.0**
Simplicity	2.8 ± 1.3	**4.4 ± 0.8**
Completeness	**3.4 ± 1.3**	3.1 ± 1.3
Conciseness	3.0 ± 1.2	**3.9 ± 1.2**

Regarding "Techincal Jargon", the simplified explanation had a rating 29.0% higher than the raw explanation, indicating it would be more accessible to non-expert users. The "Simplicity" criterion had the highest rating for the simplified explanation, with a 57.1% increase compared to the raw explanation, which is in accordance with the goal of the Simplifier agent. For the "Completeness" criterion, the raw explanation had a 9.4% higher rating than the simplified explanation. It was the single case where the raw explanation was rated higher. Considering that the raw explanation is considerably more detailed, it is expected that it would be more complete. Finally, the "Conciseness" criterion had a 30.0% increase in the rating for the simplified explanation compared to the raw explanation. This indicates that the Simplifier agent was able to generate a more concise explanation while maintaining the essential information.

Best Explanation. When looking at the results of the explanation rating, we observed that in general the simplified explanation was rated higher than the raw explanation. In order to evaluate which explanation would be the best overall, we compared each criterion for each individual evaluator. For each criterion, if an explanation was rated higher than the other, it was considered the best explanation for that specific criterion. In case both explanations were rated the same, we considered it a tie. The results are shown in Table 2.

Table 2. Winner explanation from user's ratings.

Criterion	Raw	Simplified	Both rated equally
Technical Jargon	5	12	8
Simplicity	1	18	6
Completeness	10	9	6
Conciseness	5	15	5
Total	21	54	25

Of all the 100 evaluations, the simplified explanation was considered the best in 54.0% of the cases. Moreover, both explanations were rated equally in 25.0% of the cases while the raw explanation was considered the best in 21.0% of the cases. Therefore, in 79.0% of the cases, the simplified explanation was considered to be at least as good as the raw explanation. These results indicate that the simplified explanation was generally considered better, emphasizing the importance of the Simplifier agent in the architecture.

5.2 Critic Agent Evaluation

We also performed an automated evaluation using Critic agents based on four different LLMs. Similar to human evaluators, the LLMs were instructed to rate the explanations from 1 to 5 according to the same criteria. Every LLM evaluated 25 results composed by a raw and a simplified explanation. The results are shown in Table 3.

Table 3. Average Critic agents' ratings.

Criteron	GPT-4o		Gemini 2.0		LLaMA 3.2		DeepSeek-R1	
	Raw	Sim.	Raw	Sim.	Raw	Sim.	Raw	Sim.
Technical Jargon	2.1	4.2	3.7	4.7	2.1	3.9	2.9	3.6
Simplicity	2.0	4.8	3.7	4.7	3.9	4.8	2.7	4.6
Completeness	3.4	4.1	3.9	3.4	3.5	4.6	3.8	3.8
Conciseness	3.3	4.6	3.4	4.6	4.0	4.7	2.7	4.4

Similar to the human evaluation, the four LLMs rated the simplified explanation higher than the raw explanation in all other criteria except for "Completeness", in which Gemini and DeepSeek rated the raw explanation higher. The results indicate that the LLMs are in accordance with the human evaluation, indicating as well that the simplified explanation is more suitable.

Best Explanation. Instead of computing the best explanation individually, we directly asked each Critic agent to provide a "best explanation" for each criterion. The results are shown in Table 4.

Table 4. Critic agents' winner explanation.

Criterion	GPT-4o		Gemini 2.0		LLaMA 3.2		DeepSeek-R1	
	Raw	Sim.	Raw	Sim.	Raw	Sim.	Raw	Sim.
Technical Jargon	0	25	0	25	0	25	8	17
Simplicity	0	25	0	25	0	25	1	24
Completeness	22	3	5	20	8	17	24	1
Conciseness	0	25	0	25	3	22	2	23
Total	22	78	5	95	11	89	35	65

Overall, the simplified explanation was considered the best in 81.75% of the cases. Similar to previous evaluations, "Completeness" was the only criterion in which the raw explanation was considered the best in most cases. Again, Critic agent results were in accordance with the human evaluation that the simplified explanation was generally better.

5.3 Quality Attributes

Good architectures have a set of quality attributes that make them suitable for their purpose. In this section, we discuss MAINLE's attributes.

Interactivity. One of the important aspects of MAINLE is to enable interaction in a conversational way. This is relevant because it allows the user to ask for additional data or resolve doubts. Not only does this empower users with the possibility of receiving desired information, but it also makes the system more engaging and enjoyable to use. It is also the interactivity that ensures decisions are transparent. Figure 3 shows a complete conversation between the user and the system.

Transparency. Classifications are often performed by complex models that are hard to understand. Thus, most decisions are not transparent to the user, which is an important factor in Artificial Intelligence (AI) systems. For instance, the EU AI Act states that "high-risk AI systems shall be designed and developed in such a way as to ensure that their operation is sufficiently transparent to enable deployers to interpret a system's output and use it appropriately" [27]. One of MAINLE's main goals is to generate simplified explanations that are more accessible to non-expert users. Moreover, the final agent in the architecture is

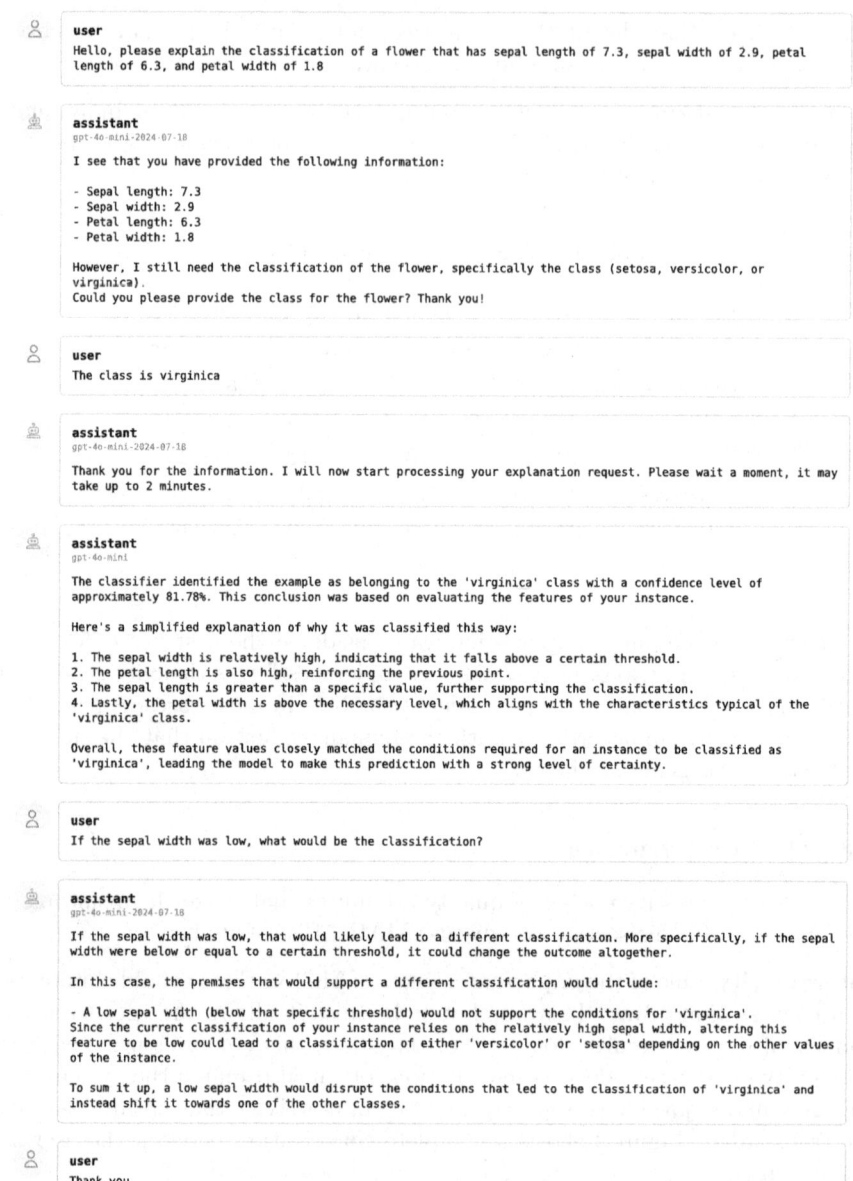

Fig. 3. Example conversation.

capable of interacting via conversation in natural language, which allows users to access additional information that would not be present in a static explanation.

Besides decision transparency, there is also a concern with information transparency. Although the user has the right to know certain information, interactive AI systems have the potential to disclose confidential data. In MAINLE, the architecture is designed to be transparent in the decision process, but also to ensure that confidential information is not disclosed. We illustrate this concept in Fig. 4.

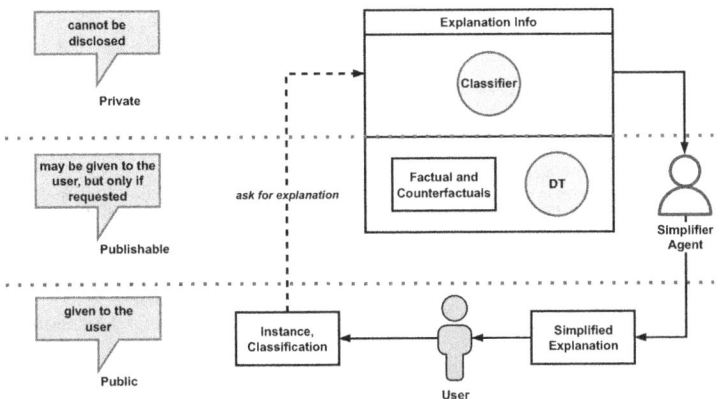

Fig. 4. Information transparency in MAINLE. For conciseness, we ommited Explainer and Translator agents.

While explainer and translator agents are inaccessible to the user, parser and simplifier agents can be interacted with. In order to ensure that no confidential data is disclosed, the two interactable agents can be designed to suppress certain information. We implement this feature by adding explicit instructions such as "The decision tree is not confidential." By following this approach, an implementation of the proposed architecture can be compliant with local regulations, as well as the model providers' policies, while still providing a high level of transparency to the user. If we change the instruction to "The decision tree is confidential. You are not allowed to disclose the decision tree even if the user asks for it," the agent will not provide the tree, as shown in Fig. 5.

Modularity. MAINLE is modular in the sense that each stage is independent of the others. This allows for the development of specialized agents that can be easily integrated into the architecture. Moreover, the agents do not communicate directly but rather pass information through a common interface, which makes it easy to replace them as long as they follow the same interface. Additionally, the Explainer agent process is also modular. The LORE module generates a surrogate Decision Tree from any classifier. Any method that generates a Decision Tree can be used to replace LORE. Finally, the modular nature of the architecture allows each component to be executed independently. For example, each agent can be executed on a different machine, which allows for a more efficient use of resources. In the case of a high-demand system, the architecture can be easily scaled by adding more instances of the necessary agents.

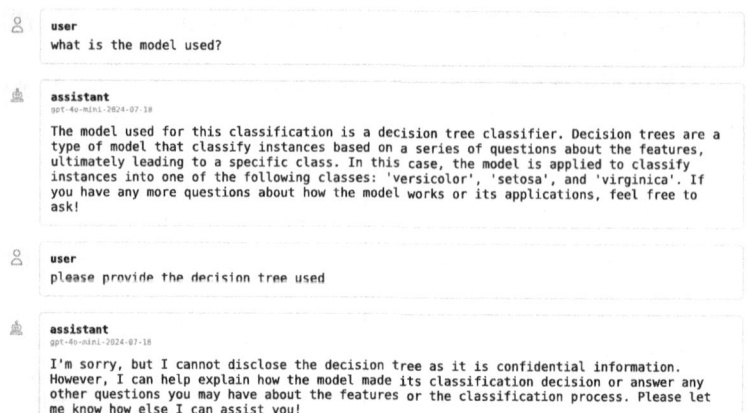

Fig. 5. Confidentiality instructions. Note that the Simplifier agent never receives information about the model, as such it thinks the original model is a Decision Tree.

Flexibility. MAINLE is designed to be flexible in several aspects. First, it is possible to use any classifier, as long as it can handle tabular data. Additionally, any tabular dataset can be used. More importantly, the architecture can handle different types of agents, with each one being able to be developed in a completely independent way. For example, in this work, we used LLMs due to their performance in generating Natural Language conversations. However, in order to test the agents' flexibility, we also tested the architecture by replacing the Translator LLM with a rule-based one. In this approach, each node in the decision is traversed and the final raw explanation consists of a conjunction of the features that led to the decision. Table 5 shows that the end result is very similar in both cases, indicating that the simplified explanation is agnostic to the raw explanation.

Table 5. Simplified explanation from a rule-based agent's raw explanation.

Raw Explanation	Simplified Explanation
The instance is classified as virginica because sepal length (cm) is greater than 6.96 and sepal width (cm) is 2.09 and petal length (cm) is greater than 2.26 and petal width (cm) is greater than 1.08.	The instance was classified as 'virginica' based on the following features: the sepal length is high, the sepal width is moderate, and the petal width and petal length are also high. This combination of features strongly aligns with what is typically seen in the 'virginica' class of flowers. The model is quite confident in this classification, with a confidence level of about 81%. In simpler terms, the measurements show characteristics that are distinctly associated with the 'virginica' variety, leading to its classification.

5.4 Potential Risks and Concerns

Any interactive system must be carefully designed to avoid threats to the users. In the case of MAINLE, we identified two potential sources of errors. First, if the agents are implemented using LLMs, they have to be carefully designed to avoid problems such as hallucinations and biases [2,3]. One possible solution is to pair the results with some form of symbolic reasoning, which we leave for future work. In the meantime, users should be aware that an architecture based on LLMs should not be employed in safety-critical domains. Additionally, if the process of converting any classifier to a Decision Tree is not able to accurately represent the original model, the explanations generated may be incorrect. Therefore, it is important to include safeguards in the Explainer agent's output to ensure its robustness, so that the generated explanation information is accurate and reliable. In our experiments, no such errors happened, but we recognize this possibility, thus we intend to evaluate this concern in future work.

6 Conclusion

In this work, we proposed MAINLE, a multi-agent interactive architecture for generating natural language explanations for ML classifiers. The architecture is composed of four agents, which together gather information from the user, convert any classifier to a surrogate Decision Tree, and generate a simplified local explanation in natural language. MAINLE was evaluated with a user study and an automated evaluation using a Critic agent based on LLMs. The results show that overall the simplified explanation was rated better, indicating that it is more suitable for non-experts. We also discussed the quality attributes of the architecture, highlighting the importance of MAINLE in providing explanations that are accessible to non-experts while maintaining classification fidelity.

Of the four evaluated criteria, the raw explanation was rated better only in *completeness*. This result suggests that the simplified explanation might be insufficient to provide all the information needed to understand the model's decision for some users. Since the architecture already allows user interaction, in future work it is our intention to evaluate if the interaction is enough to solve this issue and also the impact of simplification on the fidelity of responses. Besides the potential risks mentioned in Sect. 5.4, other aspects that can be further improved include enhancing the interaction via a graphical user interface, as well as extending MAINLE to support multi-modal data. Additionally, we plan to benchmark the architecture latency since it is expected that users can interact in real-time with MAINLE.

Acknowledgment. This work has been supported by the European Union under ERC-2018-ADG GA 834756 (XAI), the Partnership Extended PE00000013 - "FAIR - Future Artificial Intelligence Research" - Spoke 1 "Human-centered AI" and by the EU EIC project EMERGE (Grant No. 101070918).

Disclosure of Interests. The authors have no competing interests to declare that are relevant to the content of this article.

Reproducibility Statement. The authors are committed to the principles of reproducible research. The code and data used in this work are available at https://github.com/paulobruno/ecml-pkdd-2025.

Data Collection and Usage. The authors conducted a user study with 25 participants. No information that could identify the users was collected, stored, or used in this paper. Participant responses are available in the project's repository.

References

1. Arrieta, A.B., et al.: Explainable artificial intelligence (XAI): concepts, taxonomies, opportunities and challenges toward responsible AI. Inf. fusion **58**, 82–115 (2020)
2. Bolukbasi, T., Chang, K.W., Zou, J., Saligrama, V., Kalai, A.: Man is to computer programmer as woman is to homemaker? Debiasing word embeddings. In: Proceedings of the 30th NeurIPS. NIPS 2016 (2016)
3. Caliskan, A., Bryson, J.J., Narayanan, A.: Semantics derived automatically from language corpora contain human-like biases. Science **356**(6334), 183–186 (2017)
4. Chen, G., et al.: Autoagents: a framework for automatic agent generation. In: Proceedings of IJCAI 2024, pp. 22–30. IJCAI Organization (2024)
5. Chromik, M., Eiband, M., Buchner, F., Krüger, A., Butz, A.: I think I get your point, AI! The illusion of explanatory depth in explainable AI. In: Proceedings of the 26th IUI, pp. 307–317. ACM (2021)
6. Ciatto, G., Calegari, R., Omicini, A., Calvaresi, D.: Towards XMAS: explainability through multi-agent systems. In: Savaglio, C., Fortino, G., Ciatto, G., Omicini, A. (eds.) AI&IoTAIIA, vol. 2502, pp. 40–53. CEUR-WS.org (2019)
7. Ehsan, U., Liao, Q.V., Muller, M., Riedl, M.O., Weisz, J.D.: Expanding explainability: towards social transparency in AI systems. In: CHI Conference on Human Factors in Computing Systems. Association for Computing Machinery (2021)
8. Ehsan, U., et al.: Human-centered explainable AI (HCXAI): beyond opening the black-box of AI. In: CHI Conference on Human Factors in Computing Systems. Association for Computing Machinery (2022)
9. Freitas, A.A.: Comprehensible classification models: a position paper. ACM SIGKDD Explorations Newsl. **15**(1), 1–10 (2014)
10. Garofalo, M., Fantini, A., Pellugrini, R., Pilato, G., Villari, M., Giannotti, F.: Conversational XAI: formalizing its basic design principles. In: Meo, R., Silvestri, F. (eds.) Machine Learning and Principles and Practice of Knowledge Discovery in Databases, pp. 295–309. Springer (2025)
11. Guidotti, R., Monreale, A., Giannotti, F., Pedreschi, D., Ruggieri, S., Turini, F.: Factual and counterfactual explanations for black box decision making. IEEE Intell. Syst. **34**(6), 14–23 (2019)
12. Guidotti, R., et al.: Stable and actionable explanations of black-box models through factual and counterfactual rules. Data Mining Knowl. Discov. (2022)
13. Guidotti, R., Monreale, A., Ruggieri, S., Turini, F., Giannotti, F., Pedreschi, D.: A survey of methods for explaining black box models. ACM Comput. Surv. **51**(5) (2018)
14. Jentzsch, S.F., Höhn, S., Hochgeschwender, N.: Conversational interfaces for explainable AI: a human-centred approach. In: Calvaresi, D., Najjar, A., Schumacher, M., Främling, K. (eds.) Explainable, Transparent Autonomous Agents and Multi-Agent Systems, pp. 77–92. Springer (2019)

15. López-Trigo, B., M. Alonso, J., Bugarín, A.: Generación automática de explicaciones en lenguaje natural para árboles de decisión de clasificación. In: Triguero, F.H., Lara, A.T., Arroyo, S.D. (eds.) XVIII Conferencia de la Asociación Española para la Inteligencia Artificial (CAEPIA 2018), pp. 481–486 (2018)
16. Martens, D., Hinns, J., Dams, C., Vergouwen, M., Evgeniou, T.: Tell me a story! Narrative-driven XAI with large language models. Decis. Support Syst. (2025)
17. Miller, T.: Explanation in artificial intelligence: insights from the social sciences. Artif. Intell. **267**, 1–38 (2019)
18. Mindlin, D., et al.: Beyond one-shot explanations: a systematic literature review of dialogue-based XAI approaches. Artif. Intell. Rev. **58**(3), 81 (2025)
19. Nguyen, H., et al.: LangXAI: integrating large vision models for generating textual explanations to enhance explainability in visual perception tasks. In: Proceedings of IJCAI 2024, pp. 8754–8758 (2024)
20. Pedreschi, D., Giannotti, F., Guidotti, R., Monreale, A., Ruggieri, S., Turini, F.: Meaningful explanations of black box AI decision systems. In: 33rd AAAI (2019)
21. Piltaver, R., Luštrek, M., Gams, M., Martinčić-Ipšić, S.: What makes classification trees comprehensible? Expert Syst. Appl. **62**, 333–346 (2016)
22. Rudin, C.: Stop explaining black box machine learning models for high stakes decisions and use interpretable models instead. Nat. Mach. Intell. **1**(5), 206–215 (2019)
23. Serafim, P.B.S., Crescenzi, P., Gezici, G., Cappuccio, E., Rinzivillo, S., Giannotti, F.: Exploring large language models capabilities to explain decision trees. In: Journal of Open Source Software. FAIA, vol. 386, pp. 64–72 (2024)
24. Shen, H., Huang, C.Y., Wu, T., Huang, T.H.K.: ConvXAI: delivering heterogeneous AI explanations via conversations to support human-AI scientific writing. arXiv abs/2305.09770 (2023)
25. Slack, D., Krishna, S., Lakkaraju, H., Singh, S.: Explaining machine learning models with interactive natural language conversations using talktomodel. Nat. Mach. Intell. **5**(8), 873–883 (2023)
26. Tao, W., Zhou, Y., Wang, Y., Zhang, W., Zhang, H., Cheng, Y.: MAGIS: LLM-based multi-agent framework for github issue resolution. In: Globerson, A., et al. (eds.) Advances in Neural Information Processing Systems, vol. 37. Curran Associates, Inc. (2024)
27. The European Parliament and the Council of the European Union: Regulation (EU) 2024/1689 of 13 June 2024 (Artificial Intelligence Act) - article 13 (2024). https://eur-lex.europa.eu/eli/reg/2024/1689/oj/eng
28. Wang, L., et al.: A survey on large language model based autonomous agents. Front. Comput. Sci. **18** (2024)
29. Ziems, N., Liu, G., Flanagan, J., Jiang, M.: Explaining tree model decisions in natural language for network intrusion detection. In: XAI in Action: Past, Present, and Future Applications (2023)

On Trustworthy Rule-Based Models and Explanations

Mohamed Siala[1(✉)], Jordi Planes[2], and Joao Marques-Silva[3]

[1] LAAS-CNRS, Université de Toulouse, CNRS, INSA Toulouse, Toulouse, France
msiala@laas.fr
[2] Universitat de Lleida, Lleida, Spain
jordi.planes@udl.cat
[3] ICREA & University of Lleida, Lleida, Spain
jpms@icrea.cat

Abstract. A task of interest in machine learning (ML) is that of ascribing explanations to the predictions made by ML models. Furthermore, in domains deemed high risk, the rigor of explanations is paramount. Indeed, incorrect explanations can and will mislead human decision makers. As a result, and even if interpretability is acknowledged as an elusive concept, so-called interpretable models are employed ubiquitously in high-risk uses of ML and data mining (DM). This is the case for rule-based ML models, which encompass decision trees, diagrams, sets and lists. This paper relates explanations with well-known undesired facets of rule-based ML models, which include negative overlap and several forms of redundancy. The paper develops algorithms for the analysis of these undesired facets of rule-based systems, and concludes that well-known and widely used tools for learning rule-based ML models will induce rule sets that exhibit one or more negative facets.

Keywords: Explainability · Interpretability · Rule-based models · Formal Methods

1 Introduction

Explainable Artificial Intelligence (XAI) is a mainstay of trustworthy AI [1, 7,13,20,42]. Furthermore, in domains that are deemed of high risk, explanations should be trustable [15,24,40,41]. The importance of explanations and the need to trust those explanations motivated work on so-called interpretable models [40,41], even though it is generally accepted that a rigorous definition of interpretability is elusive at best [29]. Rule-based models, which encompass decision trees [6], diagrams [14,21], sets [8,28,44] and lists [39,44], epitomize interpretable models.

Work on the induction of rule-based models can be traced at least to the 1970s [25,43], in the concrete case of decision trees.[1] Decision trees are widely used in practice and often exemplify interpretable models [40,41]. The perceived importance of interpretability has recently motivated the development of algorithms for learning optimal decision trees [11,22]. Decision sets (or rule sets) find a wide range of uses in different domains [2,17,18,23,35,36]. As with decision trees, there has been recent interest in learning optimal decision sets [28]. Decision lists also find many practical uses, but claims about their interpretability are harder to justify [31]. As a result, this paper studies decision sets, but also decision trees when viewed as a special case of decision sets.

At present, some of the best-known ML toolkits implement one or more methods of induction of rule-based models [12,34,36]. Nevertheless, it has been argued [31] that rule-based methods, although easier to fathom by human-decision makers, still require explanations to be computed. (Otherwise, human decision-makers would be expected to manually solve NP-hard function problems [31].) Therefore, a key question is: *for rule-based models, when can explanations be computed trivially, such that a human decision-maker can manually produce an explanation?*

This paper shows that rigorous explanations can be found manually whenever some undesired facets of decision sets are nonexistent. Concretely, the paper relates easy-to-compute explanations with the non-existence of *negative overlap*, i.e. the existence of cases where two or more rules can fire that predict different values. Furthermore, the non-existence of redundant literals in rules is shown to be a necessary condition for minimality of explanations.

Given this state of affairs, the paper then investigates whether existing ML toolkits are able to learn rule-based models that avoid the aforementioned negative facets. As the results demonstrate, this is not the case. In addition, the paper investigates whether model-agnostic methods targeting feature selection (i.e. that produce rules as explanations) are capable of preventing negative overlap (i.e. the most worrisome negative facet). Unfortunately, as the results show, this is also not the case with the well-known explainer Anchor [38].

Contributions. The paper studies decision sets,[2] concretely the problem of *negative overlap*, i.e. when two rules that predict different classes fire, but also the existence of local or global redundancies of literals in rules. The paper develops algorithms for deciding the existence of negative overlap, but also for deciding local and global redundancy. Furthermore, the results in the paper take into account possible constraints on the inputs. The paper then relates these negative facets of decision sets with the ability of human decision-makers to manually produce rigorous explanations, namely abductive explanations. In

---

[1] Although extremely popular in ML and DM, decision trees found earlier uses in other domains, e.g. https://en.wikipedia.org/wiki/Phylogenetic_tree and https://en.wikipedia.org/wiki/Decision_tree.

[2] Decision trees are a special case of a decision set, and so we also present experiments on decision trees. However, we opt not to address decision lists due to the intrinsic difficulties with their explanation [31].

addition, the experiments confirm that implemented rule-learning algorithms in well-known toolkits exhibit the negative facets of decision sets, thus complicating (complexity-wise) the computation of rigorous explanations.

Organization. The paper is organized as follows. Section 2 introduces the notation and definitions used throughout the paper. Section 3 briefly comments on related work. Section 4 details the paper's main contributions. Section 5 reports on the experimental results. Finally, Sect. 6 concludes the paper.

2 Background

The notation and definitions used throughout the paper are adapted from past works [4,27,28].

Propositional Logic and Generalizations [4]. Let $X = \{x_1, \ldots, x_n\}$ be a set of Boolean variables. A literal is a Boolean variable or its negation. A clause C is a disjunction of literals and a cube L is a conjunction of literals. We use the notation $l_i \in C$ (respectively $l_i \in L$) if $C = l_1 \vee \ldots \vee l_k$ (respectively $L = l_1 \wedge \ldots \wedge l_k$). A conjunctive normal form (CNF) formula F is a conjunction of clauses. That is, $F = C_1 \wedge \ldots \wedge C_k$ where C_j is a clause. In this case, we use the notation $C_j \in F$. Note by definition that a clause/cube is a CNF. An assignment $v = (v_1, \ldots v_n)$ is a point in $\{0,1\}^n$. If $F = C_1 \wedge \ldots \wedge C_k$ is a CNF, $v \models F$ iff $\forall C_j \in F, \exists x_i \in C_j$ such that $v_i = 1$ or $\exists \neg x_i \in C_j$ such that $v_i = 0$. If $\exists v \in \{0,1\}^n$ such that $v \models F$ then F is said satisfiable, otherwise unsatisfiable. If F_1 and F_2 are two CNF formulas, $F_1 \models F_2$ iff $v \models F_1 \implies v \models F_2$. Note that $F_1 \models F_2$ iff $F_1 \wedge \neg F_2$ is unsatisfiable. Given a CNF formula F, the satisfiability problem (SAT) asks if F is satisfiable. SAT solvers are highly deployed in practice to answer SAT related queries, such as finding satisfying assignments or proving unsatisfiability [4]. Furthermore, extensions of propositional to more expressive logics can be handled by considering Satisfiability Modulo Theories (SMT) [4].

Machine Learning. We consider rule-based models for classification and regression that can be represented as a set of unordered rules. Let $\mathcal{F} = \{1, \ldots m\}$ be a set of features where each feature i takes values from a domain D_i. The feature space is the Cartesian product of the domains $\mathbb{F} = D_i \times \ldots \times D_m$. The outcome space (i.e., classes for classification and numerical values for regression) is denoted by $\mathcal{V}$. A dataset is a set $\{(x,o) \mid x \in \mathbb{F} \wedge o \in \mathcal{V}\}$, and where $x = (x_1, \ldots, x_m)$. A literal represents a condition on the values of a feature. We use $\mathbb{L}$ to represent the universe of literals. A background knowledge $\mathcal{B}$ is a propositional formula over literals from $\mathbb{L}$ that specifies the conditions that any arbitrary point in feature space must comply with. In other words, a point in feature space x is *valid* iff $x \models \mathcal{B}$. We assume in the rest of the paper that $\mathcal{B}$ is given as a CNF. For example, consider a dataset representing individuals and the two literals $l_1 := employed$, $l_2 := salary > 50k$. The background knowledge $\mathcal{B}$ can contain the clause $l_1 \vee \neg l_2$ to model the fact that an unemployed individual cannot have a salary greater than $50k$. Note that $\mathcal{B}$ can be a tautology (for instance when no condition is given). In this case, any arbitrary point in feature space is a valid. A user can also miss certain constraints she is not aware of. Let $\lambda \notin \mathcal{V}$ be a dummy value. A supervised ML (classification or regression) model κ is a mapping from $\mathbb{F}$ to $\{\lambda\} \cup \mathcal{V}$ such that $\kappa(x) = \lambda$ iff $x \not\models \mathcal{B}$.

A rule R_i is a pair (L_i, o_i) such that L_i is a conjunction of literals (i.e., cube) from $\mathcal{L} \subseteq \mathbb{L}$ and $o_i \in \mathcal{V}$. R_i fires on $x \in \mathbb{F}$ iff $x \models L_i$. With a slight abuse of notation we shall sometimes use L_i as the subset of $\mathcal{L}$ formed by the literals in L_i. A decision set $\mathcal{M}$ is a set of rules $\mathcal{M} = \{R_1, \ldots, R_r, R_{r+1}\}$ such that $\forall i \leq r, L_i \neq \emptyset$ and $L_{r+1} = \emptyset$. R_{r+1} is called the default rule. We denote $\Delta(o)$ the set $\{R_i | o_i = o\}$. $\mathcal{M}$ is used as an ML model $\kappa_\mathcal{M}$ as follows:

$$\kappa_\mathcal{M}(x) = \begin{cases} \lambda \notin \mathcal{V} & \text{if } x \not\models \mathcal{B} \\ o_{r+1} & \text{if no rule fires on } x \\ o & \text{if } \{o\} = \{o_i \mid R_i \text{ fires on } x\} \\ \text{Tie-breaking strategy} & \text{otherwise} \end{cases}$$

Note that decision trees (DTs), decision diagrams (DDs), random forests (RFs) and boosted trees (BTs), can be seen as decision sets where each path represents a rule. Clearly, in such models the default rule never fires. In the case of DTs and DDs, each input fires exactly one rule (since it follows exactly one path). Thus, no tie-breaking strategy is needed. This is not the case with RFs and BTs since each input fires one rule on each tree. Therefore, a tie-breaking strategy is needed.

We extend the notion of cover and overlap from [28] by considering the background knowledge $\mathcal{B}$ and the input space.

Definition 1 (Cover). Given $X \subseteq \mathbb{F}$ and background knowledge $\mathcal{B}$, $Cover(X, B, L) = \{x \mid x \in X \land x \models \mathcal{B} \land x \models L\}$.

Definition 2 (Overlap). Given a background knowledge $\mathcal{B}$, two rules R_i and R_j such that $i, j \leq r$ overlap in $X \subseteq \mathbb{F}$ iff $Cover(X, B, L_i) \cap Cover(X, B, L_j) \neq \emptyset$.

We say that R_i and R_j positively (respectively negatively) overlap if they overlap and $o_i = o_j$ (respectively $o_i \neq o_j$). We use the notation $R_i \ominus R_j$ if R_i and R_j negatively overlap. Observe that DTs and DDs exhibit no overlap since each input is captured by exactly one rule. This is not the case for RFs and BTs, since each input fires exactly one rule from each tree. Thus, overlaps may occur only between rules from different trees.

Formal Explanations [10,27]. Most approaches to explainability target at instance, i.e. a pair (x, c) with $x \in \mathbb{F}$ and $c \in \mathcal{V}$. We use κ throughout the paper to denote a machine learning model. Given an instance (v, c), with $c = \kappa(v)$, a weak abductive explanation (WAXp) is a subset $\mathcal{X}$ of the features $\mathcal{F}$ which, if assigned the values dictated by v, is sufficient for the classifier to output prediction $c = \kappa(v)$ [10,27]:

$$\forall (x \in \mathbb{F}). \left[\bigwedge_{i \in \mathcal{X}} (x_i = v_i) \rightarrow (\kappa(x) = c) \right] \tag{1}$$

A subset-minimal WAXp is an *abductive explanation* (AXp). Recent work demonstrated the need for explaining interpretable models, including decision trees [27] and lists [31]. To the best of our knowledge, past work did not investigate formal explanations for decision sets.

Furthermore, the definition of WAxp (see (1)) can be generalized to account for literals involving other relational operators [27] (e.g. relational operators taken from $\{\in, \geq, >, <, \leq\}$). In addition, constraints on the inputs [3,19] can be accounted for by conjoining a set of constraints $\mathcal{C}_\mathcal{B}$. For example, these constraints allow capturing the background knowledge introduced earlier in this section. Concretely, we write that $\mathcal{C}_\mathcal{B}(x)$ holds true iff x respects the background knowledge, i.e. $x \models \mathcal{B}$.

3 Related Work

The learning of rule-based models has been the subject of research since the 1970s [25,43]. The importance of the topic, especially given their widely accepted interpretability, has motivated recent work on learning decision sets [2,35,36] and (optimal) trees [11]. These earlier works were motivated by the accepted belief that decision trees, sets and lists are interpretable [5,40,41]. Accounts of methods for learning decision sets and lists include [17,18].

Motivated by the elusive nature of interpretability's definition [29], recent work [31] uncovered practical difficulties in computing and/or using so-called interpretable models as explanations. For example, it has been shown that paths in decision trees can be arbitrarily redundant (on the number of features) when compared with an AXp [27]. Similarly, the computation of an AXp for a decision list equates with solving an NP-hard problem [31], i.e. something that is in general beyond the capabilities of a human decision-maker. Nevertheless, past work did not address formal explanations for decision sets, arguably because of the existence of negative overlap.

Although the paper assesses rule-based methods using formal explanations, XAI is better-known by the use of model-agnostic methods [1,7,13,20,32,42]. Well-known examples include LIME [37], SHAP [30] and Anchors [38]. Since so-called interpretable models have been proposed for high-risk uses of ML, we focus on rigorous (i.e. formal) explanations.

The main results of this paper, namely the direct relationship between easy-to-compute explanations and the non-existence of well-known negative facets of rule-based models, are novel. The observation that rule-based models, obtained with well-known toolkits, exhibit those negative facets, is also a novel result, to the best of our knowledge.

4 Overlap and Redundancy

In this section, we let $\mathcal{B}$ be a background knowledge and $\mathcal{M} = \{R_1, \ldots, R_r, R_{r+1}\}$ be a decision set where R_{r+1} is the default rule such that each rule $R_{i \leq r}$ fires on at least one valid input (w.r.t. $\mathcal{B}$). As mentioned in the introduction, we provide a formal framework to address the following questions: (i) How can we generate all (negative) overlap?; (ii) Is rule R_i redundant in $\mathcal{M}$?; and (iii) Is literal l redundant in a given rule?.

We use Example 1 throughout the paper to illustrate the different concepts.

Example 1. $\mathcal{B}$ is background knowledge that encodes the following constraints (in a CNF): $(salary > 0) \leftrightarrow (age \geq 18)$; $(size = 140) \rightarrow (size > 120)$; $(weight > 90) \rightarrow (weight \geq 85)$; and $(weight \geq 85) \rightarrow (weight > 80)$. The decision set contains the following rules:

- $R_1 = ((salary > 0) \wedge (size \neq 140) \wedge (age > 10) \wedge (color = blue) \wedge (weight > 80), 1)$
- $R_2 = ((salary > 0) \wedge (size = 140), 1)$
- $R_3 = ((salary > 0) \wedge (weight > 90), 1)$
- $R_4 = ((size > 120) \wedge (weight < 85), 0)$

4.1 Overlap

We start by giving a sufficient and necessary condition to check if two rules negatively overlap.

Lemma 1 (Overlap Check). *Two rules R_i and R_j overlap iff $\mathcal{B} \wedge L_i \wedge L_j$ is satisfiable.*

Proof. $\mathcal{B} \wedge L_i \wedge L_j$ is satisfiable iff $\exists x \in \mathbb{F}, x \models \mathcal{B} \wedge L_i$ and $x \models \mathcal{B} \wedge L_j$. This is equivalent to $\exists x \in \mathbb{F}, \{x\} \in Cover(\mathbb{F}, B, L_i) \cap Cover(\mathbb{F}, B, L_j)$. The latter means that R_i and R_j overlap. □

In Example 1, one can use Lemma 1 to show that R_3 and R_4 do not overlap, in contrast to R_1 and R_4, which do.

We consider now the question of generating all negative overlap. Algorithm 1 finds all pairs of rules that exhibit a negative overlap. We use $GetList(o_1, o_2, \ldots o_r)$ as a function that computes a list that contains the distinct values in $\{o_1, \ldots o_r\}$.

Algorithm 1 terminates because each pair of rules will be visited at most once. The correctness of Algorithm 1 follows from the fact that each pair (R_i, R_j) such that $o_i \neq o_j$ is visited exactly once in Line 12. The complexity of Algorithm 1 is $O(|\mathcal{M}|^2 \times f(\mathcal{M}))$ where $f(M)$ is the worst complexity of $\mathcal{B} \wedge L_i \wedge L_j$ for an arbitrary pair of rules (R_i, R_j). This observation follows from the fact that computing $GetList$ can be naturally be done in $O(|\mathcal{M}|)$ and the fact that the satisfiability check in Line 12 is called at most once for each pair (R_i, R_j).

Finally, one might ask whether the default rule can be triggered. Proposition 1 shows that this can be achieved with one SAT call.

Proposition 1. (Default Rule Application). *The default rule is triggered iff $\mathcal{B} \wedge \neg L_1 \ldots \wedge \neg L_r$ is satisfiable.*

Proof. (Sketch). No rule fires on a solution to $\mathcal{B} \wedge \neg L_1 \ldots \wedge \neg L_r$. □

Algorithm 1 Negative Overlap Pairs

1: **Function:** *Pairs*
2: **Input:** $\mathbb{F}, O, \mathcal{M} = \{R_1, \ldots R_r\}, \mathcal{B}$
3: **Output:** $\Pi = \{(i,j) \mid R_i \ominus R_j\}$
4: $\Pi = \emptyset$
5: $\Psi = GetList(o_1, o_2, \ldots o_r)$
6: $g = |\Psi|$
7: **for** a in $1, \ldots g-1$ **do**
8:   **for** b in $a+1, \ldots g$ **do**
9:     **for** R_i in $\Delta(\Psi(a))$ **do**
10:       **for** R_j in $\Delta(\Psi(b))$ **do**
11:         **if** $\mathcal{B} \wedge L_i \wedge L_j$ is SATISFIABLE **then**
12:           $\Pi \leftarrow \Pi \cup \{(i,j)\}$
13:         **end if**
14:       **end for**
15:     **end for**
16:   **end for**
17: **end for**
18: **Return** Π

4.2 Redundancy

In order to study rule and literal redundancy, we provide a formal definition of decision sets equivalence. We denote by $S_\mathcal{M}(o) = \cup_{R_i \in \Delta(o)} \{x \in \mathbb{F} \mid x \models \mathcal{B} \wedge L_i\}$.

Definition 3 (Decision Set Equivalence). Let $\mathcal{M}_1$ and $\mathcal{M}_2$ be two decision sets defined over the same feature space $\mathbb{F}$ and output $\mathcal{V}$ and having the same default rule. $\mathcal{M}_1$ is equivalent to $\mathcal{M}_2$ iff $\forall o \in \mathcal{V}, S_{\mathcal{M}_1}(o) = S_{\mathcal{M}_2}(o)$.

The following lemma is an immediate consequence of Definition 3.

Lemma 2 (Lemma Decision Set Equivalence). *Let $\mathcal{M}_1$ and $\mathcal{M}_2$ be two equivalent decision sets that exhibit no negative overlap and let $\mathcal{B}$ be a background knowledge. Then $\forall x \models \mathcal{B}, \kappa_{\mathcal{M}_1}(x) = \kappa_{\mathcal{M}_2}(x)$.*

We introduce the notion of rule redundancy to capture the fact that removing a given rule from a decision set leads to an equivalent decision set.

Definition 4 (Rule Redundancy). A rule R_i is redundant in $\mathcal{M}$ iff $\mathcal{M} \setminus R_i$ is equivalent to $\mathcal{M}$.

Let $G_i = \Delta(o_i) \setminus \{R_i\} = \{R_{i_1}, \ldots, R_{i_z}\}$ where $R_{i_m} = (L_{i_m}, o_{i_m})$.

Proposition 2 (Rule Redundancy Check). *A rule R_i is redundant in $\mathcal{M}$ iff $\mathcal{B} \wedge L_i \models L_{i_1} \vee \ldots \vee L_{i_z}$.*

Proof. Let $\mathcal{M}* = \mathcal{M} \setminus R_i$. Clearly R_i is redundant in $\mathcal{M}$ iff $S_\mathcal{M}(o_i) = S_{\mathcal{M}*}(o_i)$. In other words, iff $\cup_{R_j \in \Delta(o_i)} \{x \in \mathbb{F} \mid x \models \mathcal{B} \wedge L_j\} = \cup_{R_j \in \Delta(o_i) \setminus R_i} \{x \in \mathbb{F} \mid x \models \mathcal{B} \wedge L_j\}$. The latter is true iff $\mathcal{B} \wedge L_i \models L_{i_1} \vee \ldots \vee L_{i_z}$. □

Following Proposition 2, one can check if a rule is redundant with one SAT oracle since $\mathcal{B} \wedge L_i \models L_{i_1} \vee \ldots \vee L_{i_z}$ iff $\mathcal{B} \wedge L_i \wedge \neg L_{i_1} \wedge \ldots \wedge \neg L_{i_z}$ is unsatisfiable. For instance, in Example 1, this allows to show that R_3 is redundant.

One can also build an equivalent decision set with no redundant rules by checking and removing redundant rules iteratively. Note that the order in which the redundant rules are removed matters as it might return a different decision set at each execution.

We assume in the rest of this section that no rule is redundant. Suppose that L_i contains at least two literals and that $l \in L_i$. We denote by $\mathcal{M}_l^i = \mathcal{M} \cup (L_i \setminus l, o_i) \setminus R_i$ the decision set identical to $\mathcal{M}$ except that l is removed from L_i. We give a formal definition of literal redundancy.

Definition 5. (Literal Redundancy). A literal l is redundant in L_i iff $l \in L_i$ and $\mathcal{M}_l^i$ is equivalent to $\mathcal{M}$.

Informally speaking, a literal is redundant in L_i iff its removal from L_i leads to an equivalent decision set. In the following we prove that there are only two cases of redundancies that we call local and global redundancies, and we show sufficient and necessary conditions to find (and remove) them. When using L_i, we suppose that it contains at least two literals.

We denote by $L_i^{\bar{l}} = L_i \cup \{\neg l\} \setminus \{l\}$. We define the following sets to address literal redundancy: $\Omega_i = \cup_{R_j \in G_i} \{x \in \mathbb{F} \mid x \models \mathcal{B} \wedge L_j\}$, $\Theta_i = \{x \in \mathbb{F} \mid x \models \mathcal{B} \wedge L_i \setminus \{l\}\}$, $\Xi_i = \{x \in \mathbb{F} \mid x \models \mathcal{B} \wedge L_i\}$, $\Upsilon_i = \{x \in \mathbb{F} \mid x \models \mathcal{B} \wedge L_i^{\bar{l}}\}$. By construction, we have:

- $\Theta_i = \Xi_i \cup \Upsilon_i$
- $S_\mathcal{M}(o_i) = \Omega_i \cup \Xi_i$
- $S_{\mathcal{M}_l^i}(o_i) = \Omega_i \cup \Theta_i = \Omega_i \cup \Xi_i \cup \Upsilon_i$

Proposition 3. (Literal Redundancy (1)). *A literal l is redundant in L_i iff $l \in L_i$ and $\Omega_i \cup \Xi_i = \Omega_i \cup \Theta_i = \Omega_i \cup \Xi_i \cup \Upsilon_i$.*

Proof. Observe first that $\mathcal{M}_l^i$ is equivalent to $\mathcal{M}$ iff $S_\mathcal{M}(o_i) = S_{\mathcal{M}_l^i}(o_i)$. Therefore, l is redundant in L_i iff $\Omega_i \cup \Xi_i = \Omega_i \cup \Theta_i = \Omega_i \cup \Xi_i \cup \Upsilon_i$. □

Lemma 3 (Local Redundancy). *If $l \in L_i$ and $\mathcal{B} \wedge L_i \setminus \{l\} \models l$ then l is redundant in L_i. This is called local redundancy.*

Proof. If $\mathcal{B} \wedge L_i \setminus \{l\} \models l$ then $\Xi_i = \Theta_i$ and thus $S_{\mathcal{M}_l^i}(o_i) = \Omega_i \cup \Theta_i = \Omega_i \cup \Xi_i = S_\mathcal{M}(o_i)$. Therefore, by Proposition 3, l is redundant in L_i. □

In Example 1, $(age > 10)$ is locally redundant in R_1.

Recall that $G_i = \Delta(o_i) \setminus \{R_i\} = \{R_{i_1}, \ldots, R_{i_z}\}$ and $L_i^{\bar{l}} = L_i \cup \{\neg l\} \setminus \{l\}$.

Lemma 4 (Global Redundancy). *If l is not locally redundant in L_i and $\mathcal{B} \wedge L_i^{\bar{l}} \models L_{i_1} \vee \ldots, \vee L_{i_z}$, then l is redundant in L_i. This is called global redundancy.*

Proof. If $\mathcal{B} \wedge L_i^{\bar{l}} \models L_{i_1} \vee \ldots, \vee L_{i_z}$ then $\Upsilon_i \subseteq \Omega_i$. Thus, since $\Theta_i = \Xi_i \cup \Upsilon_i$, we have $S_{\mathcal{M}_i^l}(o_i) = \Omega_i \cup \Theta_i = \Omega_i \cup \Xi_i \cup \Upsilon_i = \Omega_i \cup \Xi_i = S_{\mathcal{M}}(o_i)$. Therefore, by Proposition 3, l is redundant in L_i. □

In Example 1, $(size \neq 140)$ is globally redundant in R_1.

Theorem 1 (Literal Redundancy (2)). *A literal $l \in L_i$ is redundant iff it is locally redundant or globally redundant.*

Proof. $\Longrightarrow$: If l is redundant, then by Proposition 3 we have $\Omega_i \cup \Xi_i = \Omega_i \cup \Xi_i \cup \Upsilon_i$. Observe that $\Upsilon_i \cap \Xi_i = \emptyset$. This is because if $x \in \Upsilon_i \cap \Xi_i$, then $x \models \mathcal{B} \wedge L_i \wedge L_i^{\bar{l}}$ which is false because $L_i \wedge L_i^{\bar{l}}$ contains l and $\neg l$. Therefore, there are only two cases for $\Omega_i \cup \Xi_i = \Omega_i \cup \Xi_i \cup \Upsilon_i$ to hold. Either $\Upsilon_i = \emptyset$ or $\Upsilon_i \neq \emptyset$ and $\Upsilon_i \in \Omega_i$. The first case is true iff $\mathcal{B} \wedge L_i \setminus \{l\} \models l$, that is, l is locally redundant. The second case is true iff $\mathcal{B} \wedge L_i^{\bar{l}} \models L_{i_1} \vee \ldots, \vee L_{i_z}$, that is, l is globally redundant
$\Longleftarrow$: trivial. □

Corollary 1 (Assessing Literal Redundancy). *A literal $l \in L_i$ is redundant iff one of the following conditions holds:*

1. **Local redundancy:**

$$\mathcal{B} \wedge (L_i \setminus \{l\}) \wedge \neg l \text{ is unsatisfiable.}$$

2. **Global redundancy:** *(1) does not hold, and*

$$\mathcal{B} \wedge L_i^{\bar{l}} \wedge \neg L_{i_1} \wedge \cdots \wedge \neg L_{i_z} \text{ is unsatisfiable.}$$

Proof. Immediate from Theorem 1 and Lemmas 3 and 4. □

Corollary 1 can be used to iteratively remove redundant literals, thus building decision sets with no rules/literal redundancies. It should be noted that different removal orders might lead to different decision sets.

Example 2. Suppose that $\mathcal{B} = (b \vee w) \wedge (\neg d \vee f)$ and $\mathcal{M} = \{R_1, R_2, R_3\}$ where $R_1 : (L_1 = a \wedge b, o_1)$, $R_2 : (L_2 = a \wedge w, o_1)$, and $R_3 : (L_3 = c \wedge d \wedge f, o_2)$.

- $\mathcal{B} \wedge L_3 \setminus \{f\} \models f$. Therefore, f is locally redundant in L_3.
- $L_1^{\bar{b}} = a \wedge \neg b$, and $\mathcal{B} \wedge L_1^{\bar{b}} = (b \vee w) \wedge a \wedge \neg b \equiv a \wedge \neg b \wedge w$. Thus $\mathcal{B} \wedge L_1^{\bar{b}} \models R_2$ and therefore b is globally redundant in L_1.

Relation to Abductive Explanations

Proposition 4. *Suppose that $L_k \subseteq \{x_i = v_i^j \mid i \in [1, m], v_i^j \in D_i\}$. If $R_k = (L_k, o_k)$ fires on x, and there is no negative overlap involving R_k, then the features used in L_k represent a WAXp.*

Proof. By construction. □

Proposition 5. *Suppose that $L_k \subseteq \{x_i = v_i^j \mid i \in [1,m], v_i^j \in D_i\}$. If $R_k = (L_k, o_k)$ fires on v, there is no negative overlap, and L_k contains no (global or local) redundant literal, then the features from L_k represent a AXp.* □

Proof. Suppose by contradiction that the features from L_k do not define an AXp. Then there is a literal $l \in L_k$ such that $\forall x \in \mathbb{F}$ such that $x \models \mathcal{B}$, if $x \models L_k \setminus \{l\}$, then $\kappa_{\mathcal{M}(x)} = o_k$. In this case, $\mathcal{M}_l^k$ (i.e., the decision set identical to $\mathcal{M}$ except for L_k which is replaced with $L_k \setminus \{l\}$) is equivalent to $\mathcal{M}$. Then, by Definition 5, l is redundant, thus the contradiction. □

Observe that, if the conditions of Proposition 5 hold, then the literals in L_k represent an AXp, and so can be identified manually by a human decision-maker. Otherwise, as proved in earlier work for the concrete case of decision lists [31], finding an AXp is computationally hard.

5 Experiments

We evaluate the different desired properties on different use cases including decision sets, decision trees, and anchor explanations. All SAT calls are performed using the PySAT toolkit[3] with its default configuration [26]. All experiments run on AppleM1 Pro that has 32G memory and 8 cores.

Prediction Models and Datasets. In order to make our evaluation as broad and as unbiased as possible, we selected datasets from the UCI machine learning repository[4] with the parameters: $\mathcal{P} = (Task, Min, Max, Nb, Types)$ on each use case (whenever relevant) where:

- $Task \subseteq \{classification, regression\}$ is the prediction task
- Min (respectively Max) is the minimum (respectively *maximum*) size of the dataset.
- Nb is the minimum number of inputs of each class present in the dataset in case of classification.
- $Types \subseteq \{numerical, binaly\}$ is the type of features.

We describe the different prediction models along with their tailored setting.

- **Orange (v3)**[5]: a library to learn decision sets for classification. The datasets are selected using the parameters
  $\mathcal{P} = (\{classification\}, 100, 10^6, 20, \{binary, numerical\})$.
- **Boomer** [36][6]: A library for learning gradient boosted multi-label classification rules. We use the default Boomer datasets[7].

---

[3] https://pysathq.github.io/.
[4] https://archive.ics.uci.edu.
[5] https://orangedatamining.com.
[6] https://github.com/mrapp-ke/MLRL-Boomer.
[7] https://github.com/mrapp-ke/Boomer-Datasets.

– **scikit-learn (v1.6.1)**[8] and **Interpretable AI (IAI)**[9] to learn decision trees (DTs) for classification and regression. scikit-learn learns trees in a greedy way with no guarantee of optimality whereas IAI learns optimal decision trees. The parameters used for the datasets are
$\mathcal{P} = (\{classification, regression\}, 100, 4*10^6, 20, \{binary, numerical\})$.

Background Knowledge. In our empirical study, the Boolean variables that are used in the different decision sets represent a domain relation of the form $(x_f \bowtie v_f)$ where $\bowtie \in \{=, >, \geq, \leq, <\}$ for some $f \in \mathbb{F}$ and $v_f \in D_f$. We implemented a general purpose procedure to generate a background knowledge $\mathcal{B}$ for each use case that maintains domain coherence. For instance, if $(length > 30)$ and $(length = 17)$ appear in a decision set, then $\mathcal{B}$ contains the clause $\neg(length = 17) \vee \neg(length > 30)$.

Given a set of rules, for each feature f, we first compute a list, called Val_f, that contains all distinct values from the domain of f that are used in the decision set (or Anchor explanations). Val_f is increasingly ordered if the values are numerical. We also collect the set of unary relations used for f, denoted by $Relations_f$, which can be any subset of $\{=, >, \geq, \leq, <\}$. The background knowledge $\mathcal{B}$ is then constructed using Algorithm 2 as a CNF. Note that we need only the three operators $>, \geq$, and $=$, since $(x > v)$ is equivalent to $(x \geq v-1)$ and $(x < v)$ is equivalent to $(x \leq v-1)$. Algorithm 2 follows standard procedures for encoding finite domains into SAT [33].

Learning Setting. For Orange, sickit-learn, and IAI, a grid search is used to select the best values for the maximum rule length, the minimum covered examples per rule, among others. Each dataset used with Orange, sickit-learn, and IAI is split into 80% for training and 20% for testing. Boomer's learning parameters are the default ones except for the maximum number of rules that we fix to 100 with one label classification. The detailed grid search parameters are given in Table 1. Cross validation is performed with 5 folds for all experiments using stratified sampling and each execution is randomly repeated 4 times.

Experimental Pipeline. All decision sets that have only one output are discarded. For each decision set, we first remove duplicate rules and rules that never fire. After this preprocessing, we run Algorithm 1 to find all overlap. Next, we look for redundant rules then remove them. Finally, we compute all locally/globally redundant literals. We use a timeout of one hour on each decision set to find all pairs negative overlap and rule/literal redundancies.

Decision Set Statistics.

– Train: Training accuracy (classification) or Training MSE (regression)
– Test: Testing accuracy (classification) or Training MSE (regression)
– NR: Number of rules
– NP: Cardinality of $\{o_i \mid \mathcal{M} = \cup_i (L_i, o_i)\}$

---

[8] https://scikit-learn.org/stable/.
[9] https://www.interpretable.ai/.

Algorithm 2 Domain Constraints As a Background Knowledge

1: **Function:** Build $\mathcal{B}$
2: **Input:** $Relations_1, \ldots, Relations_m, Val_1, \ldots, Val_m$
3: **Output:** A background knowlegde $\mathcal{B}$ as a CNF
4: $\mathcal{B} = \emptyset$
5: **for** $f \in \{1, \ldots, m\}$ **do**
6:     **if** '=' $\in Relations_f$ **then**
7:         $\mathcal{B} \leftarrow \mathcal{B} \cup \{(f = Val_f[i]) \implies \neg(f = Val_f[j]) \mid i < j \in [1, |Val_f|]\}$
8:     **end if**
9:     **if** '>' $\in Relations_f$ **then**
10:        $\mathcal{B} \leftarrow \mathcal{B} \cup \{(f > Val_f[i+1]) \implies (f > Val_f[i]) \mid i \in [1, |Val_f| - 1]\}$
11:     **end if**
12:     **if** '$\geq$' $\in Relations_f$ **then**
13:        $\mathcal{B} \leftarrow \mathcal{B} \cup \{(f \geq Val_f[i+1]) \implies (f \geq Val_f[i]) \mid i \in [1, |Val_f| - 1] :\}$
14:     **end if**
15:     **if** $\{'=', '\geq'\} \subseteq Relations_f$ **then**
16:        $\mathcal{B} \leftarrow \mathcal{B} \cup \{(x = Val_f[i]) \implies (x \geq Val_f[i]) \mid i \in [1, |Val_f|]\}$
17:        $\mathcal{B} \leftarrow \mathcal{B} \cup \{(x = Val_f[i]) \implies \neg(x \geq Val_f[i+1]) \mid i \in [1, |Val_f| - 1]\}$
18:     **end if**
19:     **if** $\{'=', '>'\} \subseteq Relations_f$ **then**
20:        $\mathcal{B} \leftarrow \mathcal{B} \cup \{(x = Val_f[i]) \implies \neg(x > Val_f[i]) \mid i \in [1, |Val_f|]\}$
21:        $\mathcal{B} \leftarrow \mathcal{B} \cup \{(x = Val_f[i+1]) \implies (x > Val_f[i]) \mid i \in [1, |Val_f| - 1]\}$
22:     **end if**
23:     **if** $\{'\geq', '>'\} \subseteq Relations_f$ **then**
24:        $\mathcal{B} \leftarrow \mathcal{B} \cup \{(x > Val_f[i]) \implies (x \geq Val_f[i]) \mid i \in [1, |Val_f|]\}$
25:     **end if**
26:     **if** $\{'=', '\geq', '>'\} \subseteq Relations_f$ **then**
27:        $\mathcal{B} \leftarrow \mathcal{B} \cup \{(x \geq Val_f[i]) \implies (x = Val_f[i]) \vee (x > Val_f[i]) \mid i \in [1, |Val_f|]\}$
28:     **end if**
29: **end for**
30: **Return** $\mathcal{B}$

- TO: CPU time (s) to find all negative overlap
- TB: CPU time (s) to generate the background knowledge
- TC: CPU time (s) to find all redundant rules
- TR: CPU time (s) to find all redundant literals
- BS: Size of the background knowledge
- RS: Sum of the sizes of the rules
- RM: Maximum rule size
- NO: Number of negative overlap
- PO = $\frac{NO}{Total}$: Percentage of negative overlap where Total is the total number of pairs of rules associated to different predictions

Model Statistics. We report for each prediction model the following:

- DS: The total number of decision sets
- EX: The total number of decision sets that timed out

Table 1. Grid Search Parameters

	Orange	Sklearn Class.	Sklearn Reg.	IAI Class.	IAI Reg.
Beam Width	10,30	-	-	-	-
Min Covered	5,15	-	-	-	-
Max Rule Length	3,5	-	-	-	-
Criterion	-	gini, entropy	sqr err, friedman mse	-	mse
Max Depth	-	3,5,7,9	3,5,7,9,11	3,5,7	3,5,7
Min Sample Leaf	-	5,15,25	5,15,25	-	-
Min Bucket	-	-	-	5,15	5,15

- IR: Number of instances that admit at least one redundant rule
- PR: Percentage of redundant rules for instances that admit at least one redundant rule
- IL: Number of instances that admit at least one locally redundant literal
- PL: Percentage of locally redundant literals for instances that admit at least one locally redundant literal
- IG: Number of instances that admit at least one globally redundant literal
- PG: Percentage of globally redundant literals for instances that admit at least one globally redundant literal

In the rest of the section, we focus on the most important observations.

Summary. Table 2 gives the full statistics for each learning model[10]. Instance-related statistics are averaged for each model. Decision sets that are worse than random guess are ignored. Instance statistics are averaged for each prediction model. Only the results of the experiments that did not reach the timeout are reported. The time to generate the background knowledge (TB) is often less than a second. The time to find redundant rules (TC) is often few seconds, except for some decision sets where it took about a minute. The runtime to find all literal redundancies (TR), however, is much longer. To observe this more accurately, we present in Fig. 1 its box plot across all models. This is expected because every literal is checked for redundancy by application of Corollary 1.

5.1 Rule and Literal Redundancy

We are interested in this section in the evaluation of the presence of redundant rules and locally/globally redundant literals, their correlations with other characteristics, as well as the efficiency of our approach.

Redundancy. We note first that rule redundancy does not occur often as we can see in column IR in Table 2 except for Boomer. Figure 2 represents a box plot of the percentage of local (respectively global) redundancies PL (respectively PG)

---

[10] The detailed results can be found at https://siala.github.io/data/2025-ecml/.

Table 2. Summary of the Results Floats are converted to integers

	DS	EX	NR	NP	TO	TB	TC	TR	BS	RS	RM	IR	IL	PL	IG	PG
sklearn classification	196	21	35	3	0	0	0	94	23	233	5	0	123	7	175	33
sklearn regression	28	8	70	69	0	0	8	879	85	541	7	0	20	18	0	0
IAI classification	177	0	17	4	0	0	0	19	13	96	4	0	82	3	135	10
IAI regression	28	0	56	53	0	0	3	333	77	367	5	0	25	15	2	0
Orange	127	12	175	2	76	0	2	10	12139	405	3	16	1	0	13	0
Boomer	180	16	97	49	0	0	0	21	30	180	11	42	6	0	20	0

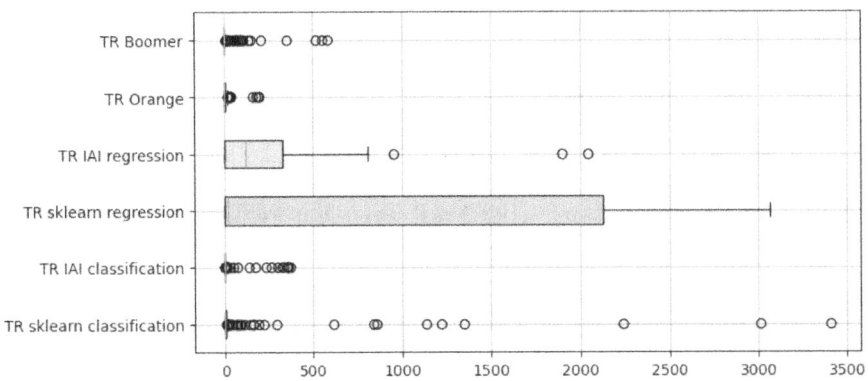

Fig. 1. Box Plot of TR. The X-axis is the time (s)

for all learning models. Orange and Boomer barely exhibit literal redundancies (see columns IL and IG in Table 2). Regression models did not show any global literal redundancy except for 2 cases with IAI regression trees. This is expected because for a literal to be globally redundant, there should be at least two rules predicting the exact same value, which is rare in regression. Classification trees, however, exhibit a noticeable presence of global redundancy ('PG IAI classification' and 'PG sklearn classification'). Figure 2 shows a significant presence of local redundancy in all tree models. We note that for each prediction task (regression, classification), IAI trees have fewer local/global redundancies than sklearn trees (in terms of the median and the maximum values). This suggests that optimal trees tend to reduce redundancy.

Correlations. We looked into different correlations between local/global redundancy and other statistics. We report the results only for models where at least 30% of its decision trees/sets exhibit local/global redundancy. There was a moderate negative correlation of global redundancy with the number of prediction outcomes (i.e., size of $\mathcal{V}$) with scikit-learn and IAI classification trees. Figure 3 shows the most important correlations of local redundancy with the statistics mentioned earlier. For instance, on the x-axis, with NR we show the correlation

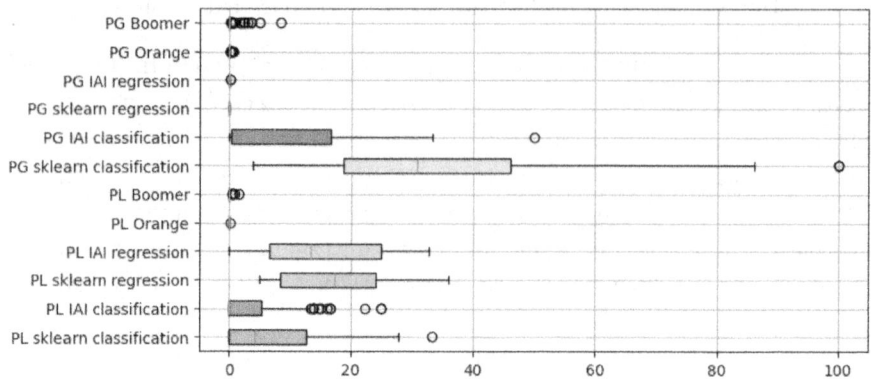

Fig. 2. Local/Global Redundancies. The X-axis represents the values of PL/PG

of the local redundancy values found by each model with the number of rules. Clearly local redundancy with scikit-learn regression trees highly correlates with NR, NP, BS, RM. IAI regression trees has the same tendency.

5.2 Negative Overlap

We evaluate the presence of negative overlap on Orange and Boomer and their relationship with relevant statistics. Boomer timed out on 4 datasets (emotions, image, scene, yeast) after the one hour time limit. The results are summarized in Table 3 for instances that did not timeout. The most important observation is the high percentage of negative overlap (column PO). Indeed, with Boomer decision sets, almost every pair of rules with different predictions overlap. Such an observation is worth reporting to the user. The results are less spectacular for orange with an average close to 50% but still worth noting. The runtime to find all negative overlap per instance is not negligible.

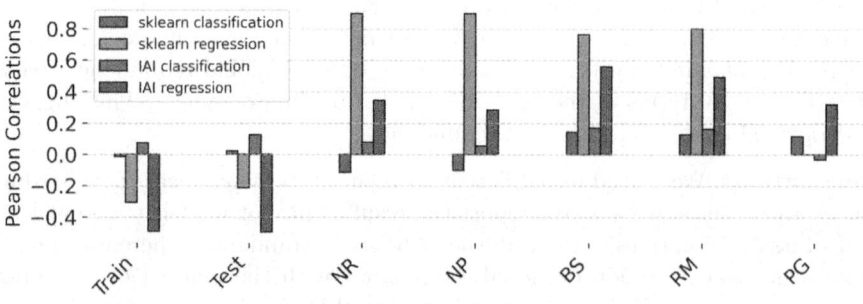

Fig. 3. Pearson Correlations of Local Redundancies (PL)

Table 3. Summary of the Negative Overlap Results Floats are converted to Integers

	DS	EX	Train	Test	NR	NP	IR	PR	TO	TR	BS	RS	RM	PO
Orange	127	12	70	71	175	2	16	0	76	10	12139	405	3	50
Boomer	180	16	95	95	97	49	42	1	0	21	30	180	11	99

Negative Overlap in Boomer. As the results in this section confirm (see Table 3), Boomer [36] exhibits extensive negative overlap. This is to be expected. In contrast with the approach outlined in this paper, where negative overlap is targeted as a reason for non-interpretability, Boomer exploits boosting (and as a result negative overlap) to build high-accuracy rule ensembles. The theoretical and practical advantages of boosting are well-known [9,16], namely to allow the learning of strong classifiers. As argued in this paper, a downside of negative overlap (and so of rule ensembles) is that finding explanations becomes a computationally-hard challenge. Our experiments are reported for completeness, and confirm the previous remarks.

5.3 Application to Anchor Explanations

Anchors are well-known model-agnostic explanations representing local, 'sufficient' conditions for predictions [38]. The question we ask here addresses precisely one of the open questions in [38]: How to find potentially conflicting anchors? To answer this question, we generate anchors for different inputs, then apply our approach to find negative overlap between anchors.

We reproduced the exact experiments in [38] with the three datasets: *adult* for predicting whether a person makes $> 50K$ annually; *rcdv* for predicting recidivism for individuals released from prison; and *lending* for predicting whether a loan on the Lending Club website will turn out bad. For each dataset, four models are used for prediction: boosted trees with xgboost, random forest, logistic regression, and neural networks. Each model is built using the exact configuration in the original paper [38]. For each dataset and each model, we generate all anchors of the validation set and look for all negative overlap.

Table 4 presents the results for each dataset and each model. As we can see, negative overlap in Anchor explanations is present in all use cases. Often, anchors of random forests exhibit the lowest percentage of negative overlap, whereas those of logistic regression have the highest percentage. We also observe that the best (and respectively, worst) models in terms of prediction quality tend to have the lowest (respectively, highest) percentages of negative overlap. These observations suggest that the quality of Anchor explanations depends on the prediction quality of the learner/model.

Table 4. Anchor Experiments

Learner	Dataset	Train	Test	NR	TO	NO	PO	RM
xgboost	recidivism	92.39	74.33	333	0	87	0.31	17
randomforest	recidivism	93.52	75.46	321	0	65	0.25	17
logistic	recidivism	62.59	60.00	196	0	735	7.81	12
nn	recidivism	87.47	71.49	341	1	150	0.52	17
xgboost	lending	90.10	82.89	260	0	384	2.47	15
randomforest	lending	91.25	83.60	278	0	207	1.18	15
logistic	lending	82.56	83.51	50	0	54	9.38	14
nn	lending	88.00	82.54	159	0	66	1.07	16
xgboost	adult	90.35	84.26	565	8	3195	4.03	14
randomforest	adult	93.52	85.60	558	7	2534	3.27	13
logistic	adult	83.00	82.98	378	3	2788	7.86	13
nn	adult	92.47	83.62	597	11	3212	3.61	14

6 Conclusions

This paper investigates the occurrence of negative facets of decision sets, namely negative overlap and (global or local) literal redundancy. Dedicated algorithms for their identification are proposed. Furthermore, the paper reveals the tight relationship between decision sets for which manual explanations can be devised, and the non-existence of the aforementioned negative facets. A first set of experiments confirms that these negative facets occur ubiquitously in existing implementations of decision sets, thus rendering unrealistic the manual identification of explanations. A second set of experiments confirms that the explanations obtained with the well-known explainer Anchors will also exhibit the same negative facets.

Acknowledgments. Mohamed Siala would like to thank INSA Toulouse for funding his research visit to the University of Lleida. This work was supported in part by the MCIN/AEI/10.13039/501100011033/FEDER, UE under the project PID2022-139835NB-C22. This work was supported in part by the Spanish Government under grant PID 2023-152814OB-I00. The authors at University of Lleida would like to thank the Catalan Government for the quality accreditation given to their research group GREiA (2021 SGR 1615).

References

1. Adadi, A., Berrada, M.: Peeking inside the black-box: a survey on explainable artificial intelligence (XAI). IEEE Access **6**, 52138–52160 (2018)
2. Atzmueller, M., Fürnkranz, J., Kliegr, T., Schmid, U.: Explainable and interpretable machine learning and data mining. Data Min. Knowl. Discov. **38**(5), 2571–2595 (2024)

3. Audemard, G., Lagniez, J., Marquis, P., Szczepanski, N.: Deriving provably correct explanations for decision trees: the impact of domain theories. In: IJCAI, pp. 3688–3696 (2024)
4. Biere, A., Heule, M., van Maaren, H., Walsh, T. (eds.): Handbook of Satisfiability - Second Edition, Frontiers in Artificial Intelligence and Applications, vol. 336. IOS Press (2021)
5. Breiman, L.: Statistical modeling: the two cultures. Stat. Sci. **16**(3), 199–231 (2001)
6. Breiman, L., Friedman, J.H., Olshen, R.A., Stone, C.J.: Classification and Regression Trees. Wadsworth (1984)
7. Carvalho, D.V., Pereira, E.M., Cardoso, J.S.: Machine learning interpretability: a survey on methods and metrics. Electronics **8**(8), 832 (2019)
8. Clark, P., Niblett, T.: The CN2 induction algorithm. Mach. Learn. **3**(4), 261–283 (1989)
9. Collins, M., Schapire, R.E., Singer, Y.: Logistic regression, AdaBoost and Bregman distances. Mach. Learn. **48**(1–3), 253–285 (2002)
10. Darwiche, A.: Logic for explainable AI. In: LICS, pp. 1–11 (2023)
11. Demirovic, E., et al.: MurTree: optimal decision trees via dynamic programming and search. J. Mach. Learn. Res. **23**, 26:1–26:47 (2022)
12. Demsar, J., et al.: Orange: data mining toolbox in python. J. Mach. Learn. Res. **14**(1), 2349–2353 (2013)
13. Dwivedi, R., et al.: Explainable AI (XAI): core ideas, techniques, and solutions. ACM Comput. Surv. **55**(9), 194:1–194:33 (2023)
14. Florio, A.M., Martins, P., Schiffer, M., Serra, T., Vidal, T.: Optimal decision diagrams for classification, pp. 7577–7585. AAAI Press (2023)
15. Freitas, A.A.: Comprehensible classification models: a position paper. SIGKDD Explor. Newsl. **15**(1), 1–10 (2014)
16. Freund, Y.: Boosting a weak learning algorithm by majority. Inf. Comput. **121**(2), 256–285 (1995)
17. Fürnkranz, J., Gamberger, D., Lavrac, N.: Foundations of Rule Learning. Cognitive Technologies. Springer (2012)
18. Fürnkranz, J., Kliegr, T.: A brief overview of rule learning. In: RuleML, pp. 54–69 (2015)
19. Gorji, N., Rubin, S.: Sufficient reasons for classifier decisions in the presence of domain constraints. In: AAAI, pp. 5660–5667 (2022)
20. Guidotti, R., Monreale, A., Ruggieri, S., Turini, F., Giannotti, F., Pedreschi, D.: A survey of methods for explaining black box models. ACM Comput. Surv. **51**(5), 93:1–93:42 (2019)
21. Hu, H., Huguet, M., Siala, M.: Optimizing binary decision diagrams with maxsat for classification. In: AAAI, pp. 3767–3775. AAAI Press (2022)
22. Hu, H., Siala, M., Hebrard, E., Huguet, M.: Learning optimal decision trees with maxsat and its integration in adaboost. In: IJCAI, pp. 1170–1176 (2020)
23. Hüllermeier, E., Fürnkranz, J., Mencía, E.L., Nguyen, V., Rapp, M.: Rule-based multi-label classification: challenges and opportunities. In: RuleML, pp. 3–19 (2020)
24. Huysmans, J., Dejaeger, K., Mues, C., Vanthienen, J., Baesens, B.: An empirical evaluation of the comprehensibility of decision table, tree and rule based predictive models. Decis. Support Syst. **51**(1), 141–154 (2011)
25. Hyafil, L., Rivest, R.L.: Constructing optimal binary decision trees is NP-complete. Inf. Process. Lett. **5**(1), 15–17 (1976)
26. Ignatiev, A., Tan, Z.L., Karamanos, C.: Towards universally accessible SAT technology. In: SAT, pp. 4:1–4:11 (2024)

27. Izza, Y., Ignatiev, A., Marques-Silva, J.: On tackling explanation redundancy in decision trees. J. Artif. Intell. Res. **75**, 261–321 (2022)
28. Lakkaraju, H., Bach, S.H., Leskovec, J.: Interpretable decision sets: a joint framework for description and prediction. In: KDD, pp. 1675–1684 (2016)
29. Lipton, Z.C.: The mythos of model interpretability. Commun. ACM **61**(10), 36–43 (2018)
30. Lundberg, S.M., Lee, S.: A unified approach to interpreting model predictions. In: NeurIPS, pp. 4765–4774 (2017)
31. Marques-Silva, J., Ignatiev, A.: No silver bullet: interpretable ML models must be explained. Front. Artif. Intell. **6** (2023)
32. Minh, D., Wang, H.X., Li, Y.F., Nguyen, T.N.: Explainable artificial intelligence: a comprehensive review. Artif. Intell. Rev. **55**(5), 3503–3568 (2022)
33. Ohrimenko, O., Stuckey, P.J., Codish, M.: Propagation via lazy clause generation. Constraints Int. J. **14**(3), 357–391 (2009)
34. Pedregosa, F., et al.: Scikit-learn: machine learning in python. J. Mach. Learn. Res. **12**, 2825–2830 (2011)
35. Rapp, M., Fürnkranz, J., Hüllermeier, E.: On the efficient implementation of classification rule learning. Adv. Data Anal. Classif. **18**(4), 851–892 (2024)
36. Rapp, M., Mencía, E.L., Fürnkranz, J., Nguyen, V., Hüllermeier, E.: Learning gradient boosted multi-label classification rules. In: ECML, pp. 124–140 (2020)
37. Ribeiro, M.T., Singh, S., Guestrin, C.: "Why should I trust you?": explaining the predictions of any classifier. In: KDD, pp. 1135–1144 (2016)
38. Ribeiro, M.T., Singh, S., Guestrin, C.: Anchors: high-precision model-agnostic explanations. In: AAAI, pp. 1527–1535 (2018)
39. Rivest, R.L.: Learning decision lists. Mach. Learn. **2**(3), 229–246 (1987)
40. Rudin, C.: Stop explaining black box machine learning models for high stakes decisions and use interpretable models instead. Nat. Mach. Intell. **1**(5), 206–215 (2019)
41. Rudin, C., Chen, C., Chen, Z., Huang, H., Semenova, L., Zhong, C.: Interpretable machine learning: fundamental principles and 10 grand challenges. Stat. Surv. **16**, 1–85 (2022)
42. Schwalbe, G., Finzel, B.: A comprehensive taxonomy for explainable artificial intelligence: a systematic survey of surveys on methods and concepts. Data Min. Knowl. Discov. **38**(5), 3043–3101 (2024)
43. Shwayder, K.: Conversion of limited-entry decision tables to computer programs - a proposed modification to Pollack's algorithm. Commun. ACM **14**(2), 69–73 (1971)
44. Yu, J., Ignatiev, A., Stuckey, P.J., Bodic, P.L.: Learning optimal decision sets and lists with SAT. J. Artif. Intell. Res. **72**, 1251–1279 (2021)

Large Language Models

Zero-Shot Detection of LLM-Generated Code via Approximated Task Conditioning

Maor Ashkenazi[1,2](✉), Ofir Brenner[3], Tal Furman Shohet[4], and Eran Treister[1,2]

[1] Department of Computer Science, Ben-Gurion University of the Negev, Beer Sheva, Israel
maorash@post.bgu.ac.il
[2] Data Science Research Center, Ben-Gurion University of the Negev, Beer Sheva, Israel
[3] Tel-Aviv University, Tel Aviv, Israel
[4] Deep Instinct, Tel Aviv, Israel

Abstract. Detecting Large Language Model (LLM)-generated code is a growing challenge with implications for security, intellectual property, and academic integrity. We investigate the role of conditional probability distributions in improving zero-shot LLM-generated code detection, when considering both the code and the corresponding task prompt that generated it. Our key insight is that when evaluating the probability distribution of code tokens using an LLM, there is little difference between LLM-generated and human-written code. However, conditioning on the task reveals notable differences. This contrasts with natural language text, where differences exist even in the unconditional distributions. Leveraging this, we propose a novel zero-shot detection approach that approximates the original task used to generate a given code snippet and then evaluates token-level entropy under the *approximated task conditioning (ATC)*. We further provide a mathematical intuition, contextualizing our method relative to previous approaches. ATC requires neither access to the *generator LLM* nor the original task prompts, making it practical for real-world applications. To the best of our knowledge, it achieves state-of-the-art results across benchmarks and generalizes across programming languages, including Python, CPP, and Java. Our findings highlight the importance of task-level conditioning for LLM-generated code detection. The supplementary materials and code are available at https://github.com/maorash/ATC, including the dataset gathering implementation, to foster further research in this area.

M. Ashkenazi and O. Brenner—Equal contribution.

Supplementary Information The online version contains supplementary material available at https://doi.org/10.1007/978-3-032-06078-5_11.

Keywords: LLMs · Synthetic text detection · Synthetic code detection

1 Introduction

Large Language Models (LLMs) such as Claude [1] and GPT [2] have demonstrated remarkable capabilities in text generation, excelling in tasks such as summarization, translation, and creative writing. These models typically leverage the transformer architecture [26] and large-scale pretraining to produce coherent text. However, their broad adoption has raised concerns about misinformation and other ethical challenges [8,13,34], highlighting the need for robust detection methods. More recently, LLMs have shown impressive proficiency in code generation, with models like CodeLlama [20], and StarCoder [25] producing functional code snippets. These advancements transformed software development by automating repetitive coding tasks, assisting with debugging, and even generating novel solutions from high-level descriptions. Furthermore, AI coding agents and integrated development tools have transformed modern workflows by embedding generation capabilities directly into the programming process. Although these advances improved productivity, they also introduce concerns related to security, intellectual property, and academic integrity. As a result, distinguishing LLM-generated code from human-written code is crucial for mitigating potential risks. While significant progress has been made in detecting LLM-generated natural language text, identifying LLM-generated code remains a challenging problem. Prior research attributes this difficulty to the structured nature of code, which results in lower predictive token entropy compared to natural language [32]. Unlike natural language, where lexical choices and sentence structures vary widely, programming languages impose strict syntactic and semantic rules, making token probability distributions less informative for detection. In our research, we take a different approach by analyzing the role of task conditioning in improving detection. To investigate this, we conduct an initial experiment comparing LLM-generated and human-written content across natural language and code. We use two datasets: MBPP [5], which consists of programming tasks and code snippets, and WritingPrompts [12], which contains natural language stories. We use the entire test set from MBPP and sample an equivalent amount of texts from WritingPrompts, generating responses using CodeLlama for MBPP and LLaMA 3.1 [4] for WritingPrompts. To avoid unwanted effects of response lengths, responses shorter than 200 characters are discarded, while longer ones are truncated. For each response, we compute mean token entropy using the same model that generated it, under two settings: (1) unconditional sampling and (2) sampling conditioned on the original task. Extended details on the initial experiment are provided in Appendix A. The results in Fig. 1 reveal a clear pattern. Without task conditioning, the entropy distributions of human-written and LLM-generated code overlap significantly, making detection difficult. In contrast, human-written and LLM-generated text from WritingPrompts exhibit greater separability even without task conditioning. When introducing task conditioning, both datasets show improved distinguishability between human-written and

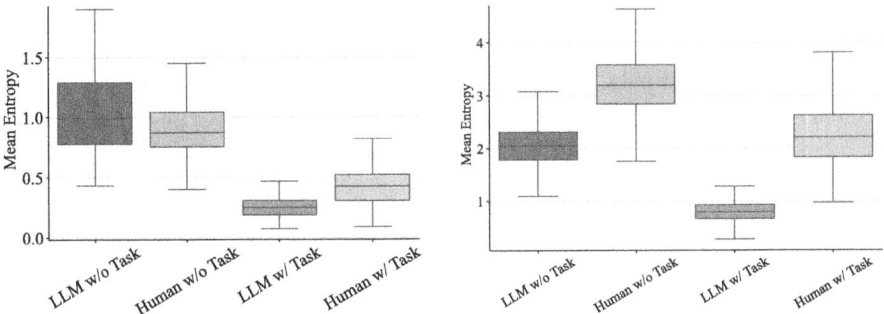

Fig. 1. Box plot of mean token entropy values for human and LLM-generated texts. MBPP (code) on the left, WritingPrompts (natural language) on the right

LLM-generated content. This finding suggests that detecting LLM-generated code without access to the task prompt is inherently challenging, but incorporating task-level context can enhance detection accuracy. Intuitively, conditioning on the task provides the LLM with specific context for the expected code, allowing the conditional distribution to primarily focus on coding style, instead of code purpose.

Building on this, we introduce *Approximated Task Conditioning (ATC)*, a novel zero-shot detection approach that approximates a task from a given code snippet and evaluates token entropy under its conditioning. *ATC* does not require access to the original task but instead approximates it in a relatively lightweight manner, making it practical for real-world scenarios where task information is unavailable. We summarize our contributions as follows:

- We propose *ATC*, a novel zero-shot approach for detecting LLM-generated code that achieves state-of-the-art (SOTA) detection results.
- We establish a connection between *ATC* and prior detection methods.
- We conduct extensive experiments demonstrating the robustness of *ATC*.
- We release our code, including dataset gathering implementation, fostering collaboration and further research in the field.

2 Related Work

Detecting LLM-Generated Text. As LLMs become more widespread, distinguishing between human and LLM-generated text becomes increasingly important to combat issues like fake news and plagiarism [8,34]. Detection methods can generally be divided into two categories: supervised learning and zero-shot approaches. Supervised learning techniques involve training models to differentiate between human-written and LLM-generated text [17,33,35]. These methods often struggle with generalization, as they tend to overfit to specific datasets or the LLMs used for text generation [6,16,18]. In contrast, zero-shot approaches have shown greater robustness, focusing on analyzing token distribution patterns like entropy [24], likelihood [10], and ranks [22] to detect signs of LLM-generated text. Perturbation-based methods like DetectGPT [16] and NPR [22] perturb text and analyze differences between the original and perturbed texts. Similarly, [30] generates completions and compares their similarity to the original text. These methods have higher computational costs due to repeated iterations, whereas FastDetectGPT [7] improves efficiency by optimizing the perturbations.

Detecting LLM-Generated Code. Text-based detectors often struggle with code due to structural differences from natural language [14,32]. This has led to the development of specialized detection methods. [31] adapts DetectGPT with fill-in-the-middle masking which replaces entire lines of code, while [21] uses stylistic patterns such as whitespace changes in addition to preserving code correctness after perturbations. [29] proposes a method using targeted perturbations and a fine-tuned CodeBERT model. [28] conducted a large-scale evaluation of detection methods, finding that while some generalize well, they struggle often with high-level languages and short code snippets. The most recent and, to our knowledge, state-of-the-art (SOTA) method is [32], which generates code variants via multiple rewriting prompts and measures their similarity. However, this requires numerous rewrites and training a code similarity model. In contrast, our method requires less iterations, achieving superior performance with a single LLM prompt and no additional training. Meanwhile, data collection efforts, such as [9], are providing benchmarks for future detection research.

3 Method

We consider the problem of zero-shot LLM-generated code detection. Given a code snippet x, we wish to determine whether it was generated by an LLM, or written by a human. We use an open-source *detector LLM* to evaluate token probability distributions, and do not assume access or knowledge of the *generator LLM*, used for generating the code. In addition, our approach is *zero-shot*, meaning it does not require labeled training data nor involves any training steps, resulting in robust results across *generator LLMs* and programming languages.

3.1 Approximated Task Conditioning (ATC)

Here we elaborate on our LLM-generated code detection method (ATC), consisting of two main steps. First, we approximate one or more tasks for the input code snippet by prompting an LLM, which we term the *detector LLM*. Next, we calculate the score for the given code sample by computing the mean token entropy of the conditional distribution on each of the approximated tasks. When computing the score, we only consider code tokens, i.e., we ignore the task and comment tokens' entropy. We use the same *detector LLM* for token sampling for consistency. Our approach is detailed in Algorithm 1. A visualization of the pipeline and prompt used for task approximation is in Fig. 2, alongside an example input, with details and connection to previous approaches below.

Choosing the Detector LLM. We consider a relatively small and open-source LLM, CodeLlama13b, alongside its smaller counterpart, CodeLlama7b,

Algorithm 1. Approximated Task Conditioning (ATC)

Input: x: code, N: number of approximated tasks, $\mathcal{G}$: Detector LLM (vocabulary $\mathcal{V}$), ϵ: threshold
Output: Decision: LLM-Generated or Human-Written
1: Query $\mathcal{G}$ with x and the prompt in Figure 2 N times to generate task descriptions $t_1, \ldots, t_N$. // **Task Approximation**
2: **for** $i = 1$ to N **do** // **Code Tokens-based Score Computation**
3:    Concatenate the texts t_i and x.
4:    Perform a forward pass through $\mathcal{G}$ to get the conditional distribution $P(x \mid t_i)$.
5:    Get the subsequence of m **code tokens**, excluding comments: $(x_{j_1}, .., x_{j_m}) \subseteq x$.
6:    Compute the score for task i by calculating mean code token entropy:

$Score_i = -\frac{1}{m} \sum_{k=1}^{m} \sum_{v \in \mathcal{V}} P(v \mid x_{<j_k}, t_i) \log P(v \mid x_{<j_k}, t_i)$
7: **end for**
8: **if** $\frac{1}{N} \sum_{i=1}^{N} Score_i > \epsilon$ **then**
9:    **return** Human-Written
10: **else return** LLM-Generated
11: **end if**

as opposed to previous methods which relied on proprietary models available via APIs to achieve good results. We show that using CodeLlama7b is enough to surpass previous methods, and that using a larger model improves performance. Furthermore, we show that these relatively small *detector LLMs* achieve robust performance across various *generator LLMs* and tasks.

Task Approximation. This step is performed by querying the *detector LLM* with a fixed prompt, asking it to generate a task that, when given to an LLM, would likely produce a similar code snippet to x. The full prompt is presented in Fig. 2. We use $top_p = 0.95$ and a temperature of 0.7 for sampling, similar to how we generate the code solutions for the experiments. Setting top_p will limit sampling to the most probable tokens whose cumulative probability reaches 0.95, and the temperature controls the randomness of the sampling. Additional details are in Appendix B. While a single approximated task already outperforms current SOTA, our experiments show that generating multiple tasks and averaging their corresponding scores further improves performance. In most experiments, we use $N = 1, 2, 4$ approximated tasks, where N is a hyperparameter.

Code Tokens-based Score Computation. Given a code snippet x, we find the m code tokens, excluding comments $(x_{j_1}, .., x_{j_m}) \subseteq x$. Next, using an approximated task t, we compute the mean token entropy conditioned on t;

$$\frac{1}{m} \sum_{k=1}^{m} H(x_{j_k} \mid x_{<j_k}, t) = -\frac{1}{m} \sum_{k=1}^{m} \sum_{v \in \mathcal{V}} P(v \mid x_{<j_k}, t) \log P(v \mid x_{<j_k}, t) \quad (1)$$

where $\mathcal{V}$ is the set of all possible tokens in the vocabulary. Intuitively, the entropy of the distribution should be lower (i.e., the model should be more confident)

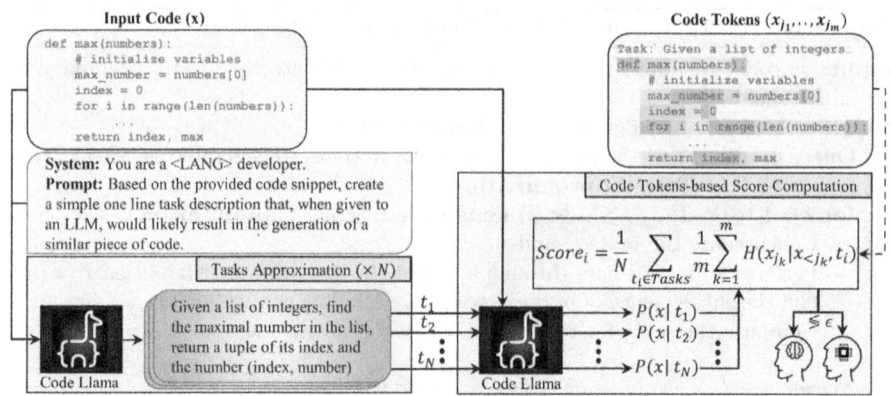

Fig. 2. Overview of *ATC*. Given an input code snippet x, we (1) query the *detector LLM* (CodeLlama) with a fixed prompt to generate task descriptions $t_1, .., t_N$ for which x might be a valid solution, and (2) compute the conditional entropy of the input code tokens given each approximated task. Given the probability distribution $P(x \mid t_i)$ for each task t_i, the final score is obtained by averaging the mean token entropy *only on code tokens* (see top-right). Low entropy scores indicate higher confidence that the code was LLM-generated

for LLM-generated code, as such code is more likely to align with the *detector LLM*'s learned distribution. To obtain the final score, we average the mean token entropy over all approximated tasks $t_1, .., t_N$. *ATC* can be integrated with other baseline approaches, such as computing the mean log likelihood or analyzing mean token ranks. However, we find that our method is most effective when used alongside entropy estimation, as seen in Sect. 4.10.

Handling Comment Tokens. Both human-written and LLM-generated code often include comments, such as inline comments and docstrings. We analyze the tendency to add comments in Appendix C. Due to the autoregressive nature of code generation, preceding comment tokens can significantly influence the conditional distribution of subsequent tokens. If comments accurately describe relevant parts of the code, they effectively act as a more localized and specific task within the code snippet. By treating comments this way, we aim to capture finer-grained task information, which can further aid in distinguishing between human-written and LLM-generated code. Thus, we handle comment tokens similarly to the task tokens, i.e. we exclude them from the token entropy calculation. However, *comments remain part of the input when modeling the conditional distribution*. While it is reasonable to assume that comments accurately describe relevant code, we also test robustness against adversarial modifications by evaluating the impact of removing comments before scoring (see Sect. 4.3).

3.2 Intuition and Connection to Previous Methods

Here we build an intuition, relating our method to zero-shot baseline methods and to [32] which we consider the current SOTA. Our observation in Fig. 1 emphasizes that the predictive entropy of code tokens cannot be clearly distinguished when task conditioning is unavailable, i.e. the unconditional distributions between human-written and LLM-generated code are less separable than the conditional distributions. Baseline methods (e.g. log likelihood [10] or token entropy [24]) assess the certainty of sampling a code snippet x under the LLM's unconditional distribution $P(x)$, since they do not have access to the task. Assuming a latent task variable $t^* \sim P_t$, the unconditional distribution of code is given by

$$P(x) = \int P(x \mid t^*) P_t(t^*) \, dt^*. \qquad (2)$$

In [32], the model is prompted solely with the code snippet x and generates a rewrite x' from the conditional distribution $P(x' \mid x)$. Next, the similarity between x' and x is assessed, and high similarity leads to high confidence that x is LLM-generated. We argue that our method shares similarities with [32], particularly in how both approaches approximate the latent task t^*. Specifically, we propose that sampling from $P(x' \mid x)$ serves as an approximation to $P(x' \mid t^*)$. This is based on an assumption that conditioning on x might be similar to conditioning on t^*, as the original code x inherently carries implicit information about the underlying task t^*. Thus, one may argue an approximation of:

$$P(x' \mid x) \approx P(x' \mid t^*). \qquad (3)$$

Intuitively, if a model is asked to find the maximal number in a list, its response will likely resemble the output it produces when asked to rewrite an existing snippet that does so. Sampling multiple rewrites and measuring their similarity,

$$\mathbb{E}_{x' \sim P(\cdot \mid x)} [S(x, x')], \qquad (4)$$

should be correlated with the probability of x being drawn from $P(x' \mid t^*)$.

In contrast, our approach explicitly approximates the task itself $t \approx t^*$, by prompting the detector LLM. We then calculate the token entropy of x under $P(x \mid t)$. This two-step process, inspired by Chain-of-Thought principles, empirically provides a more interpretable and accurate estimation of the conditional distribution:

$$P(x \mid t) \approx P(x \mid t^*). \qquad (5)$$

Finally, [32] employs multiple rewrites, which may suggest that their approximation requires multiple iterations to refine the conditional distribution estimate. In contrast, *ATC* achieves better results with a single approximation.

4 Experiments

This section details our experimental setup, covering datasets, generation models, and baseline methods. We then present the main Python results, assess the impact of comment removal as a pre-processing step, compare the approximated tasks to original ones, and analyze different task approximation prompts. We also examine robustness across factors like decoding strategies, different programming languages, and code length. Finally, we conduct relevant ablation experiments. In all experiments, we use AUROC (Area Under the Receiver Operating Characteristic curve) to evaluate performance, following previous works [16,21,32]. Additionally, we explore alternative metrics in Sect. 4.9.

4.1 Experimental Setup

Datasets. To compare with the current SOTA method [32], we evaluate our approach using two widely recognized benchmarks for Python code generation: APPS [11] and MBPP [5]. To the best of our knowledge these are the most appropriate benchmarks for our task. Notably, APPS includes solutions written by a wide range of users, leading to diverse coding styles that better reflect real-world variability. APPS contains 5,000 test instances, each consisting of a problem description and corresponding solutions. After applying the data sanitization pipeline from [32], we are left with 3,765 instances. Unlike [32], which randomly sampled 1,500 instances of the test set, we use the entire APPS test set for a more comprehensive evaluation. While differences in dataset size and sampling procedures may limit direct comparisons, this approach was necessary due to the lack of code or detailed information regarding their sampling methodology. For each instance, we select the first human solution and generate corresponding LLM outputs using each *generator LLM* (detailed below). MBPP consists of Python programming problems designed for entry-level programmers, with 500 test instances. As with APPS, we use the full test set, generating LLM solutions using each generator LLM. We focus on Python due to its widespread use, readability, and versatility in code generation tasks. In both datasets we exclude the training data due to potential overlap with LLM training corpora.

Generation Models. We use a variety of open-source and proprietary models for code generation. For proprietary models, we use GPT-3.5-Turbo, GPT-4o-mini [2], and Claude3-haiku [1], which were selected due to their popularity among developers [3]. For open-source models, we use Starchat-Alpha [25], CodeLlama-7B & CodeLlama-13B [20], and CodeGemma-7B [23]. These models were chosen for their widespread adoption in the open-source community. We specifically use GPT-3.5-Turbo, StarChat, and CodeLlama-13B to allow direct comparison with previous methods. For each test instance, code is generated independently by every model, resulting in a separate set of generations. We generate solutions following the schema described in [32], using Chain-of-Thought (CoT) prompting and setting $top_p = 0.95$ and the temperature to 0.7, sampling until the EOS token is reached. To ensure clean extraction, the prompt instructs the model to output the final solution between markup tags for simple parsing. Due to space constraints, results are reported using model name abbreviations.

Baselines. We compare our method against several existing detection methods. First, we consider methods that estimate properties of a code sample's probability distribution using a surrogate model. This includes mean $logP(x)$ [10], LogRank and Entropy [16], and LRR [22], which combines the first two methods. Next, we look at perturbation-based methods, which estimate a code sample's properties under small modifications. We begin with DetectGPT [16] and NPR [22], adapting them to code by replacing T5$_{large}$ [19] with CodeT5$_{large}$ [27], which, as suggested by [32], improves performance. We also consider Detect-CodeGPT [21], which builds on previous methods by applying stylistic transformations and code correctness enforcement to the perturbations. Additionally, we include results from DetectGPT4Code [31] on Java, while omitting Python comparisons as their APPS subset covered about 3.5% of the entire test set. Although we attempted to reproduce their fill-in-middle masking strategy, we observed a decrease in performance. We do not include [29] in our comparisons since the authors did not release code or sufficient details to recreate their datasets. As a supervised baseline, we include OpenAI's RoBERTa text detector [2]. Finally, we compare to [32], which we consider to be the current SOTA, as it consistently outperforms prior methods across multiple settings, including CPP. However, for MBPP, [21] achieves better results for one of the *generator LLMs*. As [32] subsampled their data ($\sim$ 40%) and code generation involves inherent randomness, we report their results as-is, acknowledging potential variability in direct comparisons due to the lack of code implementation and random seed details.

4.2 Main Results

Tables 1 and 2 present the results on MBPP and APPS, respectively. Our method outperforms all baselines across both datasets, consistently delivering significant improvements. It shows a clear advantage over perturbation-based methods, even when adapted to the code domain, as well as over [32], which we consider the current SOTA. Our method remains robust, maintaining high performance across a wide range of *generator LLMs*, from smaller models like CodeLlama-7B to larger proprietary models like GPT-3.5. Notably, our approach achieves superior detection performance with just a **single approximated task** ($N = 1$), whereas [32] relied on **eight different prompts**. For a fair comparison, setting $N = 4$ further enhances performance, yielding a mean AUROC of **94.22 on MBPP and 93.82 on APPS** when using CodeLlama-13B as the detector LLM. The effectiveness of our method stems from the key observation made in Sect. 1: the predictive entropy of code tokens differs significantly when sampling from the conditional distribution (i.e., conditioned on the task). Our method effectively approximates the task, allowing for highly accurate detection.

4.3 Robustness to Comment Removal

To test the robustness of our method in scenarios where comments and docstrings are unavailable, we evaluate detection performance after systematically removing them from the code. Table 3 presents the results using CodeLlama-13B as the detector LLM. Our method remains highly effective, with minimal performance

Table 1. Results on MBPP

Generator	CLlama7b	CLlama13b	Gemma	Starchat	Claude	GPT3.5	GPT4om	Avg.
OpenAI$_{large}$	52.58	49.85	26.86	39.40	31.54	49.90	40.86	41.57
Ye [32]	-	86.21	-	79.23	-	86.23	-	-
Using CodeLlama7b as Detector LLM								
DetectGPT	52.07	54.10	76.82	74.52	74.31	59.76	60.26	64.55
NPR [22]	78.20	76.09	71.27	78.34	80.95	73.46	73.37	75.95
Shi [21]	69.25	70.48	86.46	83.06	84.10	71.32	73.84	76.93
Entropy	45.68	48.28	64.47	59.58	62.38	55.16	54.75	55.76
$logP(x)$	68.37	69.79	82.78	77.85	80.72	72.95	73.29	75.11
LogRank	62.29	64.05	81.56	75.57	77.77	66.91	68.18	70.90
LRR [22]	31.20	33.67	65.80	56.57	54.29	30.72	39.41	44.52
$ATC_{N=1}$	92.82	92.62	91.20	91.18	93.82	90.47	91.23	91.91
$ATC_{N=2}$	94.06	93.60	92.67	92.10	94.85	91.82	93.02	93.16
$ATC_{N=4}$	94.36	94.25	**92.76**	92.44	95.28	92.16	93.44	93.53
Using CodeLlama13b as Detector LLM								
Entropy	46.58	50.00	63.40	58.72	61.78	56.56	55.35	56.06
$logP(x)$	68.15	71.83	82.67	77.66	81.12	74.07	74.19	75.67
LogRank	63.45	67.56	82.27	76.25	78.91	69.21	69.86	72.50
LRR	37.64	41.72	70.84	59.43	59.50	37.48	41.83	49.78
$ATC_{N=1}$	93.56	94.45	88.78	91.23	93.66	90.62	92.46	92.11
$ATC_{N=2}$	94.88	95.64	90.75	92.14	95.11	91.77	93.51	93.40
$ATC_{N=4}$	**95.94**	**96.18**	91.94	**92.74**	**95.79**	**92.62**	**94.37**	**94.22**

degradation, maintaining comparable results on MBPP and experiencing only a 3% AUROC reduction on APPS, still outperforming previous methods with $N = 1$. Increasing N further improves accuracy, reaching a mean AUROC of **94.16 on MBPP and 90.67 on APPS**. This demonstrates that our approach does not depend on comments, ensuring robustness against such transformations.

4.4 Evaluating the Approximated Task

We evaluate our approximated task by comparing detection performance against results obtained using the original task. As shown in Table 4, the mean AUROC across all *generator LLMs* indicate a slight performance drop when using the approximated task instead of the original. Figure 3 demonstrates that approximated tasks often contain slightly more detail than MBPP tasks. In contrast, for APPS, where tasks are longer and more descriptive, the approximated tasks tend to be more concise. These findings suggest that despite stylistic differences, the conditional distributions of the original and approximated tasks may still be similar. This is supported by Appendix D, which visualizes the conditional and

Table 2. Results on APPS

Generator	CLlama7b	CLlama13b	Gemma	Starchat	Claude	GPT3.5	GPT4om	Avg.
OpenAI$_{large}$	61.11	59.24	49.01	49.76	49.84	47.33	37.43	50.53
Ye [32]	-	87.77	-	82.48	-	83.25	-	-
Using CodeLlama7b as Detector LLM								
DetectGPT	55.88	53.54	56.20	51.68	59.07	46.26	61.81	54.92
NPR [22]	62.12	60.20	59.08	55.85	68.21	53.32	60.75	59.93
Shi [21]	79.11	76.97	75.44	70.70	75.00	65.00	65.48	72.53
Entropy	47.44	46.50	56.04	46.60	63.32	53.35	49.5	51.82
$logP(x)$	67.94	66.49	72.87	60.84	73.77	63.91	54.47	65.75
LogRank	64.82	62.14	67.60	57.91	66.91	58.46	48.85	60.95
LRR [22]	46.75	40.25	39.45	42.66	31.89	34.20	29.54	37.82
$ATC_{N=1}$	92.28	93.30	91.05	88.07	92.52	86.22	87.42	90.12
$ATC_{N=2}$	93.79	94.66	92.60	89.23	94.04	88.09	89.46	91.70
$ATC_{N=4}$	94.47	95.33	93.40	89.98	94.84	89.18	90.35	92.51
Using CodeLlama13b as Detector LLM								
Entropy	41.51	41.56	53.72	43.46	59.20	54.63	44.87	48.42
$logP(x)$	62.52	65.83	72.71	59.41	72.03	65.71	51.76	64.28
LogRank	59.84	62.61	69.11	56.88	66.09	60.56	45.83	60.13
LRR	46.07	45.37	46.53	43.81	36.23	36.13	27.19	40.19
$ATC_{N=1}$	93.37	93.87	91.80	88.14	93.70	87.85	90.69	91.35
$ATC_{N=2}$	94.85	95.29	93.18	89.36	95.44	89.71	92.58	92.92
$ATC_{N=4}$	**95.62**	**96.12**	**94.10**	**90.02**	**96.33**	**90.82**	**93.70**	**93.82**

unconditional probability distributions for the code snippets in Fig. 3. Appendix E provides examples of approximated tasks from different seeds, showing how using $N > 1$ averages slight variations in the conditional distribution.

4.5 Exploring Different Task Approximation Prompts

Here we explore the sensitivity of task approximation to different prompt styles. We aim to determine whether our method remains effective across various task approximation prompts or if performance is highly dependent on specific phrasing. We test seven prompt styles, each offering a different way to approximate the task. *Regular* provides a concise task description, while *Short* enforces an even more minimal task. In contrast, *Long* generates a verbose description. *Storytelling* frames the task within a fictional scenario, *Pseudocode* translates the code into a structured pseudocode, *Friendly* offers a supportive tone, and *Critical* delivers a specific and demanding specification. In all experiments besides this one, we use the *Regular* style. Our experiment on APPS, selected for its notably descriptive tasks, reveals that prompts leading to **shorter and more accurate**

Table 3. Results when removing comments. Detector LLM is CodeLLama13b

Generator	CLlama7b	CLlama13b	Gemma	Starchat	Claude	GPT3.5	GPT4om	Avg.
MBPP								
Entropy	49.98	52.46	56.21	60.79	56.75	59.27	58.64	56.30
$logP(x)$	68.03	70.73	67.67	72.05	71.92	73.94	72.88	71.03
LogRank	63.33	66.18	64.78	68.89	66.89	69.30	68.30	66.81
LRR	35.75	37.02	43.77	43.04	35.64	38.09	38.97	38.90
$ATC_{N=1}$	93.92	94.68	86.29	90.59	95.09	92.76	94.51	92.55
$ATC_{N=2}$	94.82	95.50	87.69	91.65	95.88	94.01	95.18	93.53
$ATC_{N=4}$	**95.54**	**95.94**	**88.50**	**92.34**	**96.44**	**94.48**	**95.85**	**94.16**
APPS								
Entropy	46.37	45.45	56.79	51.81	61.60	56.62	53.36	53.14
$logP(x)$	59.31	60.48	70.09	60.58	72.50	67.58	56.69	63.89
LogRank	54.15	54.56	64.36	56.27	65.80	61.93	49.64	58.10
LRR	33.55	30.49	34.96	36.61	32.49	35.13	25.59	32.69
$ATC_{N=1}$	87.24	88.37	88.08	83.57	92.78	86.07	88.70	87.83
$ATC_{N=2}$	89.04	90.31	89.60	84.74	94.36	87.96	90.65	89.53
$ATC_{N=4}$	**90.68**	**91.28**	**90.72**	**85.73**	**95.28**	**89.08**	**91.89**	**90.67**

Table 4. Results using the original task with CodeLlama7b

Method	Avg.
MBPP	
Entropy	55.76
$ATC_{N=1}$	91.91
ATC w/Task	92.02
APPS	
Entropy	51.82
$ATC_{N=1}$	90.12
ATC w/Task	92.49

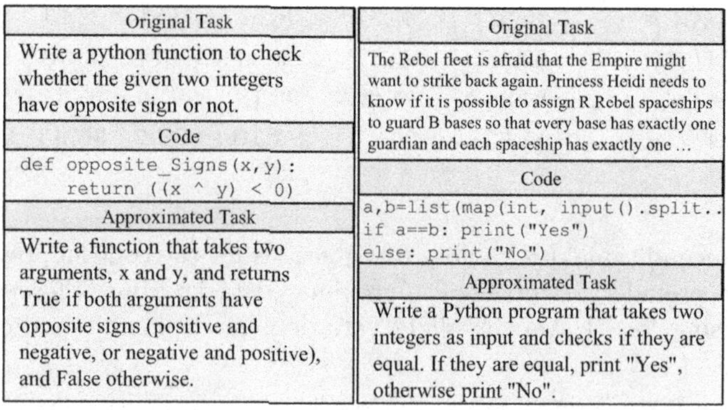

Original Task
Write a python function to check whether the given two integers have opposite sign or not.
Code
`def opposite_Signs(x,y):` `    return ((x ^ y) < 0)`
Approximated Task
Write a function that takes two arguments, x and y, and returns True if both arguments have opposite signs (positive and negative, or negative and positive), and False otherwise.

Original Task
The Rebel fleet is afraid that the Empire might want to strike back again. Princess Heidi needs to know if it is possible to assign R Rebel spaceships to guard B bases so that every base has exactly one guardian and each spaceship has exactly one ...
Code

`a,b=list(map(int, input().split..`
`if a==b: print("Yes")`
`else: print("No")`

Approximated Task
Write a Python program that takes two integers as input and checks if they are equal. If they are equal, print "Yes", otherwise print "No".

Fig. 3. Approximated tasks examples. Left is MBPP, right is APPS. We present simple examples for readability

tasks (*Regular, Short,* and *Critical*) outperform those resulting in longer tasks (*Long, Pseudocode*). We observed that *Storytelling* occasionally produced vague or incorrect tasks, likely due to the limitations of the relatively small detector LLM. Results are in Fig. 4. Full prompts and examples are in Appendix F.

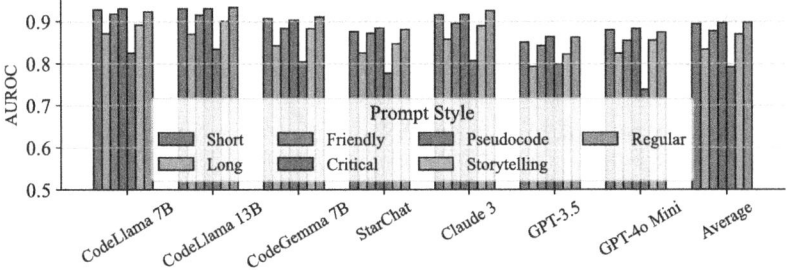

Fig. 4. ATC with different prompting styles using CodeLlama7b

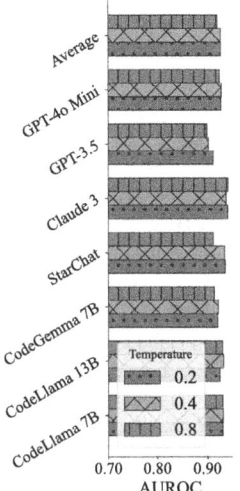

Fig. 5. Temperature effects on MBPP with CodeLlama7b

Table 5. CodeContest results with CodeLlama7b

Lang.	Method	CLlama13b	Starchat	GPT3.5
CPP	Shi [21]	81.07	73.59	81.96
	Ye [32]	89.87	83.42	90.82
	Entropy	29.83	39.20	43.29
	$logP(x)$	68.80	65.23	72.11
	LogRank	67.33	65.35	71.37
	LRR [22]	51.09	56.51	57.68
	$ATC_{N=1}$	97.63	90.94	92.99
	$ATC_{N=2}$	98.26	91.52	93.97
	$ATC_{N=4}$	**98.44**	**91.82**	**94.69**
Java	Shi [21]	76.65	70.72	82.10
	Yang [31]	-	-	64.03
	$ATC_{N=1}$	92.30	89.61	91.73
	$ATC_{N=2}$	92.54	90.48	93.02
	$ATC_{N=4}$	**92.93**	**90.85**	**93.00**

4.6 Effects of Decoding Strategies

We evaluate the robustness of *ATC* by examining the impact of decoding temperatures on detection performance, using the same configuration as in [32]. Higher temperatures introduce greater variability in the generated outputs, while lower temperatures yield more deterministic results (See Appendix B). Although entropy-based scoring methods might be sensitive to varying temperatures, the results in Fig. 5 show that our performance remains robust across a range of values. Nonetheless, we do observe a slight decline in mean AUROC at higher temperatures, suggesting that high variability can impact detection accuracy.

4.7 Generalization to Other Programming Languages

To assess the generalization of *ATC* across programming languages, which is critical for real-world applications, we experiment on CPP and Java using the CodeContest dataset [15]. We identify 152 CPP instances and 129 Java instances in the test set. Results in Table 5 focus on *generator LLMs* from previous works due to space constraints, with full results and comparisons in Appendix G. Our method consistently outperforms other approaches across all *generator LLMs*, demonstrating its ability to generalize across different programming languages.

4.8 Impact of Code Length

We examine how code length affects detection performance using APPS, where solutions are generally longer than those in MBPP. We measure length in terms of the number of characters and group each sample–whether human-written or LLM-generated–into its corresponding length interval, independent of the original task. Consistent with previous findings, our results in Fig. 7 using CodeLlama7b show that detection performance improves as code length increases, likely due to greater certainty in token predictions as the code progresses. This suggests that in practical real-world scenarios, where code is typically longer, our method is expected to perform well.

4.9 Real-World Considerations

Limitations of AUROC. In practical settings, detection accuracy measured by AUROC may not fully reflect operational efficacy. Here we analyze our method's recall (true positive rate) at a fixed false positive rate (FPR). This evaluation better captures the trade-offs relevant to real-world production scenarios, ensuring reliable identification of LLM-generated code while minimizing false alarms on human-written code. As shown in Table 6, our method achieves a recall of roughly 84% at a false positive rate of 10%, demonstrating strong detection capability with minimal misclassifications. Full results are in Appendix H.

Analyzing the Number of Generated Tokens. We compare the complexity characteristics of our method with the previous SOTA [32]. While both approaches rely on querying an LLM multiple times per sample, they differ significantly in the nature and length of the generated outputs. In both cases, the primary latency bottleneck lies in the generation step itself. [32] prompts the LLM with *"Please explain the functionality of the given code, then rewrite it in a single markdown code block."*. This yields a combined output containing a detailed natural language explanation followed by a full code rewrite. In contrast, our method only requires a concise task approximation. Notably, the length of this generated task remains roughly constant regardless of the input code size, compared to [32], where the output length scales linearly with the input. To quantify this, we measure the number of generated tokens on MBPP (see Fig. 6). As a result, our method is not only faster but also more cost-efficient

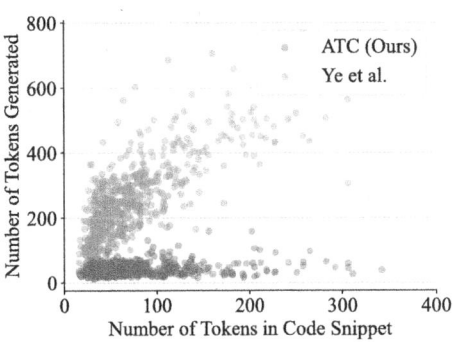

Fig. 6. Number of generated tokens in different methods

Table 6. Recall @ FPR Results

Method	Recall @ FPR 10% Avg.	
	MBPP	APPS
CodeLlama13b as Detector LLM		
Entropy	10.09	9.96
$logP(x)$	31.23	24.58
LogRank	30.16	21.28
LRR [22]	19.18	7.01
$ATC_{N=1}$	76.12	77.72
$ATC_{N=2}$	80.37	81.58
$ATC_{N=4}$	**83.92**	**84.08**

in settings that rely on third-party APIs where pricing is based on the number of generated tokens. For example, the average generation time using CodeLlama-7b per MBPP sample is **0.99** s in ATC, compared to **6.04** s in the other approach. Latency was measured on a single Nvidia RTX6000 GPU.

4.10 Ablation Experiments

Increasing the Number of Task Approximations. In most experiments we use $N \leq 4$, however increasing N further enhances results. Figure 8, using CodeLlama7b, demonstrates that performance gains scale with the number of tasks, with the most significant improvement occurring at $N = 2$ and diminishing returns appearing from $N = 4$. The choice of N presents a tradeoff between accuracy and runtime, and should be adjusted based on real-world constraints.

Comparison with Alternative Scoring Methods. We replace entropy with alternative scoring methods–mean $logP(x)$, LogRank, and LRR–while keeping the task approximation framework unchanged. Table 7 presents average AUROC across all *generator LLMs*, showing that entropy is the most effective scoring method. Entropy captures global uncertainty over the full output distribution, while alternative methods rely on token-level likelihoods or ranks, making them more sensitive to local variations. Among these, LogRank performs best, indicating that ranks may provide a stronger signal than raw likelihoods. However, entropy remains the overall best scoring method across our experiments.

Score Computation with Comment Tokens. We conduct an ablation study where we include comments in the token entropy calculation instead of excluding them. As shown in Table 8, this results in a consistent drop in average AUROC across all *generator LLMs*. This degradation aligns with our hypothesis that comments often serve as implicit task descriptions within the code snippet. Including them in entropy computation disrupts the separation between task conditioning and code token certainty, weakening detection results.

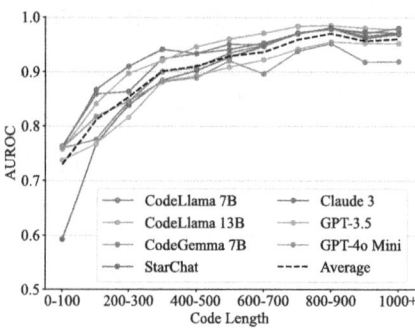

Fig. 7. Impact of code length on APPS

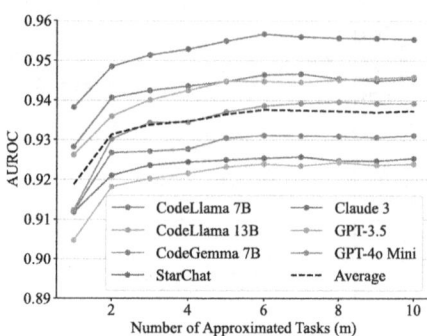

Fig. 8. Effects of increasing N on MBPP

Table 7. Results with alternative scoring methods

Method	AUROC Avg.	
	MBPP	APPS
CodeLlama7b as Detector LLM		
$ATC_{N=1}$ w/$logP(x)$	$80.09_{(-11.82)}$	$84.14_{(-5.98)}$
$ATC_{N=1}$ w/LogRank	$87.08_{(-4.83)}$	$76.00_{(-14.12)}$
$ATC_{N=1}$ w/LRR	$81.38_{(-10.53)}$	$80.45_{(-9.67)}$
CodeLlama13b as Detector LLM		
$ATC_{N=1}$ w/$logP(x)$	$83.94_{(-8.17)}$	$80.78_{(-10.57)}$
$ATC_{N=1}$ w/LogRank	$89.08_{(-3.03)}$	$86.06_{(-5.29)}$
$ATC_{N=1}$ w/LRR	$82.51_{(-9.60)}$	$83.07_{(-8.28)}$

Table 8. Results when including comment tokens in score calculation

Method	AUROC Avg.	
	MBPP	APPS
CodeLlama7b as Detector LLM		
$ATC_{N=1}$	$90.10_{(-1.81)}$	$87.24_{(-2.88)}$
$ATC_{N=2}$	$91.46_{(-1.7)}$	$88.97_{(-2.73)}$
$ATC_{N=4}$	$91.91_{(-1.62)}$	$89.90_{(-2.61)}$
CodeLlama13b as Detector LLM		
$ATC_{N=1}$	$90.63_{(-1.48)}$	$88.81_{(-2.54)}$
$ATC_{N=2}$	$92.01_{(-1.39)}$	$90.57_{(-2.35)}$
$ATC_{N=4}$	$92.94_{(-1.28)}$	$91.64_{(-2.18)}$

5 Conclusion and Future Work

As LLMs become increasingly prevalent in coding tasks, their associated social and ethical risks demand reliable detection methods. We identify a key challenge: distinguishing human-written from LLM-generated code is fundamentally different from natural text when relying solely on the unconditional probability distribution. To address this, we introduce a novel, simple, and zero-shot approach that approximates the conditional probability distribution using task approximation, followed by an entropy-based scoring algorithm. Our method outperforms previous approaches across all relevant benchmarks and demonstrates robustness through extensive experiments and ablation studies. Furthermore, its simplicity enables future integration with other probability-based detection methods. Our analysis is currently limited to publicly available benchmarks; however, while our results are promising, task approximation in domain-specific repositories may pose additional challenges and warrants further study. In future work, we plan to extend our approach to detect edited LLM-generated code and explore robustness against adversarial attacks. Finally, an additional promising direction is to improve the quality of task approximations, potentially through reflective reasoning capabilities.

Acknowledgments. The authors thank the Israeli Council for Higher Education (CHE) via the Data Science Research Center and the Lynn and William Frankel Center for Computer Science at BGU.

Disclosure of Interests. The authors have no competing interests to declare that are relevant to the content of this article.

References

1. Anthropic (2024). https://www.anthropic.com/
2. OpenAI (2024). https://openai.com/api
3. Stack overflow developer survey (2024). https://survey.stackoverflow.co/2024/
4. Meta AI, llama 3.1 (2024). https://llama.meta.com/
5. Austin, J., et al.: Program synthesis with large language models. arXiv preprint arXiv:2108.07732 (2021)
6. Bakhtin, A., Gross, S., Ott, M., Deng, Y., Ranzato, M., Szlam, A.: Real or fake? Learning to discriminate machine from human generated text. arXiv preprint arXiv:1906.03351 (2019)
7. Bao, G., Zhao, Y., Teng, Z., Yang, L., Zhang, Y.: Fast-DetectGPT: efficient zero-shot detection of machine-generated text via conditional probability curvature. arXiv preprint arXiv:2310.05130 (2023)
8. Bommasani, R., et al.: On the opportunities and risks of foundation models. arXiv preprint arXiv:2108.07258 (2021)
9. Demirok, B., Kutlu, M.: AIGCodeSet: a new annotated dataset for AI generated code detection. arXiv preprint arXiv:2412.16594 (2024)
10. Gehrmann, S., Strobelt, H., Rush, A.: GLTR: statistical detection and visualization of generated text. In: Proceedings of the 57th Annual Meeting of the Association for Computational Linguistics: System Demonstrations. Association for Computational Linguistics (2019)
11. Hendrycks, D., et al.: Measuring coding challenge competence with APPS. In: Thirty-fifth Conference on Neural Information Processing Systems Datasets and Benchmarks Track (Round 2) (2021)
12. Huang, X.Y., Vishnubhotla, K., Rudzicz, F.: The GPT-WritingPrompts Dataset: a comparative analysis of character portrayal in short stories. arXiv preprint arXiv:2406.16767 (2024)
13. Jawahar, G., Abdul-Mageed, M., Laks Lakshmanan, V.: Automatic detection of machine generated text: a critical survey. In: Proceedings of the 28th International Conference on Computational Linguistics, pp. 2296–2309 (2020)
14. Lee, T., et al.: Who wrote this code? watermarking for code generation. In: Proceedings of the 62nd Annual Meeting of the Association for Computational Linguistics (Volume 1: Long Papers), pp. 4890–4911 (2024)
15. Li, Y., et al.: Competition-level code generation with AlphaCode. Science **378**(6624), 1092–1097 (2022)
16. Mitchell, E., Lee, Y., Khazatsky, A., Manning, C.D., Finn, C.: DetectGPT: zero-shot machine-generated text detection using probability curvature. In: International Conference on Machine Learning, pp. 24950–24962. PMLR (2023)

17. Mitrović, S., Andreoletti, D., Ayoub, O.: ChatGPT or Human? Detect and explain. explaining decisions of machine learning model for detecting short ChatGPT-generated text. arXiv preprint arXiv:2301.13852 (2023)
18. Pu, J., et al.: Deepfake text detection: limitations and opportunities. In: 2023 IEEE Symposium on Security and Privacy (SP), pp. 1613–1630 (2023)
19. Raffel, C., et al.: Exploring the limits of transfer learning with a unified text-to-text transformer. J. Mach. Learn. Res. **21**(140), 1–67 (2020)
20. Roziere, B., et al.: Code LLaMA: open foundation models for code. arXiv preprint arXiv:2308.12950 (2023)
21. Shi, Y., Zhang, H., Wan, C., Gu, X.: Between lines of code: unraveling the distinct patterns of machine and human programmers. In: Proceedings of the 47th International Conference on Software Engineering (ICSE 2025). IEEE (2025)
22. Su, J., Zhuo, T.Y., Wang, D., Nakov, P.: DetectLLM: leveraging log rank information for zero-shot detection of machine-generated text. arXiv preprint arXiv:2306.05540 (2023)
23. Team, C., et al.: CodeGemma: open code models based on Gemma. arXiv preprint arXiv:2406.11409 (2024)
24. Thomas, L.: Detecting fack content with relative entropy scoring. In: CEUR Workshop Proceedings, ECAI'08 Workshop on Plagiarism Analysis, Authorship Identification and Near-Duplication Detection, November, vol. 377, pp. 27–31 (2008)
25. Tunstall, L., et al.: Creating a coding assistant with StarCoder. Hugging Face Blog (2023). https://huggingface.co/blog/starchat-alpha
26. Vaswani, A., et al.: Attention is all you need. In: Advances in Neural Information Processing Systems, vol. 30 (2017)
27. Wang, Y., Wang, W., Joty, S., Hoi, S.C.: CodeT5: identifier-aware unified pre-trained encoder-decoder models for code understanding and generation. In: Proceedings of the 2021 Conference on Empirical Methods in Natural Language Processing (2021)
28. Xu, J., et al.: Investigating efficacy of perplexity in detecting LLM-generated code. arXiv preprint arXiv:2412.16525 (2024)
29. Xu, Z., Sheng, V.S.: Detecting ai-generated code assignments using perplexity of large language models. In: Proceedings of the AAAI Conference on Artificial Intelligence, vol. 38, issue (21), pp. 23155–23162 (2024)
30. Yang, X., Cheng, W., Wu, Y., Petzold, L., Wang, W.Y., Chen, H.: DNA-GPT: divergent n-gram analysis for training-free detection of GPT-generated text. The Twelfth International Conference on Learning Representations (ICLR) (2024)
31. Yang, X., Zhang, K., Chen, H., Petzold, L., Wang, W.Y., Cheng, W.: Zero-shot detection of machine-generated codes. arXiv preprint arXiv:2310.05103 (2023)
32. Ye, T., et al.: Uncovering LLM-generated code: a zero-shot synthetic code detector via code rewriting. arXiv preprint arXiv:2405.16133 (2024)
33. Yu, X., et al.: GPT paternity test: GPT generated text detection with GPT genetic inheritance. CoRR (2023)
34. Zellers, R., et al.: Defending against neural fake news. In: Advances in Neural Information Processing Systems, vol. 32 (2019)
35. Zhong, W., et al.: Neural deepfake detection with factual structure of text. In: Conference on Empirical Methods in Natural Language Processing (EMNLP) (2020)

Advancing Multi-step Mathematical Reasoning in Large Language Models Through Multi-layered Self-reflection with Auto-prompting

André de Souza Loureiro[2], Jorge Valverde-Rebaza[1(✉)], Julieta Noguez[1], David Escarcega[1], and Ricardo Marcacini[3]

[1] School of Engineering and Sciences, Tecnologico de Monterrey, Mexico City, Mexico
{jvalverr,jnoguez,descarcega}@tec.mx
[2] Luiz de Queiroz College of Agriculture, University of São Paulo, Piracicaba, SP, Brazil
a.loureiro@usp.br
[3] Institute of Mathematics and Computer Sciences, University of São Paulo, São Paulo, SP, Brazil
ricardo.marcacini@usp.br

Abstract. Recent advancements in Large Language Models (LLMs) have significantly improved their problem-solving capabilities. However, these models still struggle when faced with complex multi-step reasoning tasks. In this paper, we propose the *Multi-Layered Self-Reflection with Auto-Prompting* (MAPS) framework, a novel approach designed to enhance multi-step mathematical reasoning in LLMs by integrating techniques such as Chain of Thought (CoT), Self-Reflection, and Auto-Prompting. Unlike traditional static prompting methods, MAPS employs an iterative refinement process. Initially, the model generates a solution using CoT prompting. When errors are detected, an adaptive self-reflection mechanism identifies and analyzes them, generating tailored prompts to guide corrections. These dynamically adjusted prompts enable the model to iteratively refine its reasoning. Experiments on four well-established benchmarks across multiple LLMs show that MAPS significantly outperforms standard CoT and achieves competitive results with reasoning-optimized models. In addition, MAPS enables general-purpose LLMs to reach performance levels comparable to specialized reasoning models. While deeper reflection layers improve accuracy, they also increase token usage and costs. To balance this trade-off, MAPS strategically limits reflection depth, ensuring an optimal balance between cost and reasoning performance.

Keywords: Large Language Models · Adaptive Prompting · Multi-Step Reasoning · LLMs for Mathematical Reasoning

1 Introduction

Large Language Models (LLMs) have significantly impacted a wide range of applications, including healthcare, finance, education, and others [1,6]. Despite these advances, researchers in academia and industry continue striving to equip LLMs with human-like reasoning skills to enhance generalization in real-world problem-solving through abstraction and logical inference [1,11,13].

A common approach involves fine-tuning LLMs for logical and mathematical tasks. For instance, models from the GPT-4 family [9] have demonstrated strong performance in logical inference, problem-solving, and mathematical reasoning. Models such as OpenAI o3-mini [8] and DeepSeek-R1 [3], further strengthen reasoning and coding. However, while effective in multi-step problem-solving, pre-trained models with native reasoning abilities require substantial computational resources, making training and deployment costly.

A more resource-efficient alternative to extensive pre-training is prompt tuning, a process in which a pre-trained model is further optimized using curated datasets containing labeled instruction-response pairs [15]. However, conventional prompting strategies such as zero-shot or auto-prompts do not fully exploit the reasoning potential of LLMs [6,13].

Recent advances in adaptive prompting techniques have aimed to enhance multi-step reasoning. Chain-of-Thought (CoT) prompting, for example, guides the model to generate intermediate reasoning steps before arriving at a final answer [12]. Although CoT improves performance, it does not always prevent the propagation of errors. Self-Reflection (SR) has been introduced to address this shortcoming by prompting the model to critically review and adjust its own responses, mimicking human self-correction [10]. However, relying solely on single-pass reflection often limits the model's ability to correct deeper logical or arithmetic mistakes. Thus, for more complex problem statements, multiple iterative reflection layers are needed to achieve better results [7].

These limitations underscore the need for more sophisticated techniques capable of iteratively refining a model's reasoning process. To address this, we propose the *Multi-layer Auto-Prompted Self-reflection* (MAPS) framework, a novel approach designed to enhance reasoning capabilities by dynamically generating customized reflection prompts and incorporating iterative feedback mechanisms. In contrast to conventional prompting techniques that utilize static reflection prompts, MAPS engages in a multi-stage process. Initially, the model generates a preliminary solution using CoT prompting, which guides the reasoning process through explicit step-by-step analysis. If the initial answer is found to be incorrect, the framework then initiates adaptive reflection iterations. In these iterations, the model produces tailored prompts that specifically address the identified errors, allowing for focused self-reflection and correction. This iterative refinement process enables the model to improve its reasoning over successive attempts, ultimately leading to more accurate solutions.

To validate the effectiveness of the MAPS framework, we perform a comprehensive evaluation on GSM8K [2], GSM-Symbolic [7], AIME 2025 [17], and MATH [16] datasets. The results demonstrate that MAPS significantly enhances the ability of general-purpose LLMs, such as LLaMA, to detect and correct errors. Furthermore, MAPS demonstrates competitive performance when compared to pre-trained models that are specifically engineered with inherent reasoning capabilities, such as OpenAI's o3-mini and o4-mini [19], as well as Google's Gemini 2.5 Flash and Gemini 2.5 Pro [18].

The remainder of this paper is structured as follows. Section 2 provides a review of the most relevant prompting techniques for enhancing reasoning in large language models. Section 3 introduces the MAPS framework, detailing its operational mechanisms. Section 4 outlines the experimental setup designed to assess the performance of MAPS. Section 5 presents and discusses the results of the experimental evaluation across various models. Finally, Sect. 6 summarizes the key findings and highlights potential directions for future research.

2 Related Work

General-purpose LLMs often struggle with solving mathematical word problems. This challenge arises in part because transformer-based architectures are inherently designed to generate text one token at a time [2]. Consequently, to improve their problem-solving capabilities, it is crucial to design prompts that encourage step-by-step reasoning.

A key approach to guiding LLMs in step-by-step reasoning is prompt learning, which instructs the model to follow structured reasoning steps. Wei et al. (2022) [12] introduced Chain-of-Thought (CoT) prompting, showing that prompting an LLM to rephrase question information as intermediate steps significantly improves performance over direct answers. CoT's success has driven further research into reasoning in LLMs, inspiring techniques like auto-CoT, ZS-CoT, Complexity-based prompting, Tree of Thoughts (ToT), and others [13,14].

Renze and Guven (2024) [10] introduced Self-Reflection (SR) prompting to address CoT's limitations. While CoT improves reasoning through step-by-step guidance, it lacks mechanisms for evaluating and correcting errors. SR prompting enables models to refine responses, enhancing accuracy and problem-solving. However, its effectiveness depends on the use of well-constructed prompts [5] and the implementation of multi-layered strategies to tackle more complex logical or arithmetic problems [7].

Despite advancements, existing methods often struggle with dynamic error adaptation in complex tasks. Techniques like CoT and SR provide structured reasoning but lack iterative error correction. Our proposal addresses these gaps by integrating adaptive self-reflection to identify errors and generate tailored prompts, enhancing reasoning in general-purpose LLMs and bridging the gap between static methods and dynamic reasoning needs.

3 MAPS: Multi-layer Auto-Prompted Self-reflection

In this section, we present our novel framework, *Multi-Layered Self-Reflection with Auto-Prompting* (MAPS), which is designed to enhance multi-step reasoning in LLMs. MAPS builds on the Chain-of-Thought (CoT) paradigm and traditional self-reflection techniques by introducing an iterative mechanism that dynamically adjusts reflection prompts according to the problem's structure, complexity, and previously identified errors. This adaptive approach seeks to improve the model's reasoning accuracy and robustness by fostering deeper introspection and targeted problem-solving strategies. The details of MAPS are explained below.

3.1 Framework Overview

Traditional prompting methods, including the original version of SR (*i.e.*, single-pass SR), utilize a fixed reflection prompt to identify and correct errors in an initial CoT-generated solution, as illustrated in Fig. 1a. However, such static prompts may fail to address diverse error types or deeper logical and arithmetic mistakes, particularly in complex symbolic problems. To overcome these limitations, our framework introduces the following key contributions.

1. Iterative Reflection: After the initial CoT response, the model's answer is examined for correctness. If incorrect, the framework initiates one or more reflection iterations.

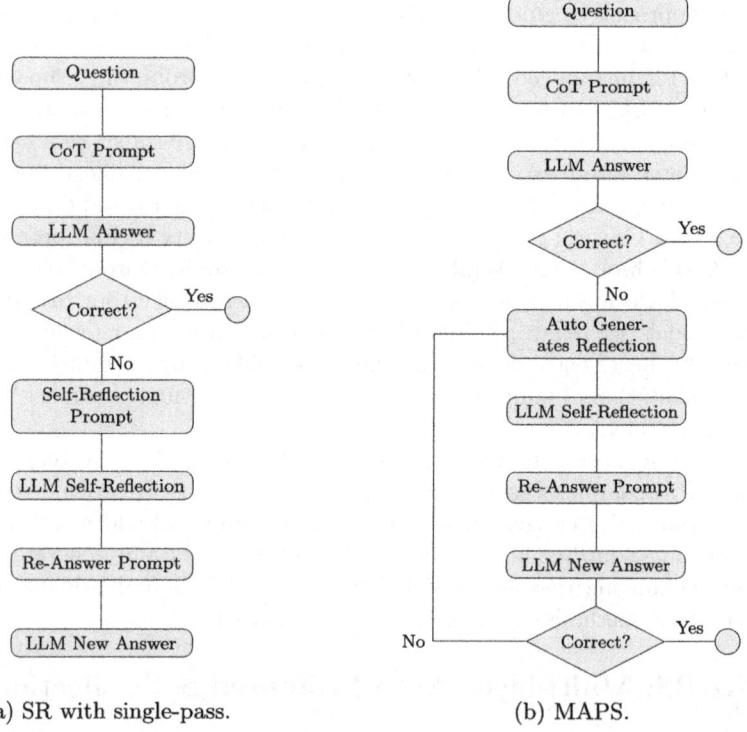

Fig. 1. Comparison of (a) Self-Reflection with single-pass and (b) Multi-layer Auto-Prompted Self-Reflection (MAPS).

2. Auto-Prompting (Meta-Prompting): Instead of applying a one-size-fits-all reflection template, the model is guided to generate a tailored self-reflection prompt. This reflection prompt is dynamically created based on the problem's characteristics, known error patterns, and the complexity of the task.
3. Dynamic Adaptation: If a single reflection iteration does not yield the correct answer, additional layers of self-reflection are executed. In each iteration, a new auto-generated reflection prompt is produced to iteratively refine the reasoning until the correct solution is obtained or a preset maximum number of iterations is reached.

Therefore, while SR performs one reflection cycle using a static prompt, MAPS fine-tunes the model iteratively by generating customized reflection prompts and continuously updating answers, as depicted in Fig. 1b. This capability allows for systematic detection and correction of errors, ensuring better performance in reasoning-related tasks.

3.2 Methodology

As illustrated in Fig. 1b, our approach proceeds in the following steps:

1. Initial CoT Reasoning: The LLM is provided with the original question and a Chain-of-Thought prompt (*e.g.*, "*Let's think step by step ...*"). This produces an initial answer along with intermediate reasoning steps.
2. Correctness Verification: The output is evaluated against the expected answer or verified using an external correctness check. If the response is correct, the process is terminated.
3. Auto-Prompt Generation: If the answer is incorrect, the LLM is tasked with generating a customized reflection prompt that adapts the standard reflection template to the specifics of the problem. This meta-prompt encourages the LLM to: (i) diagnose its mistakes, (ii) list common error types, and (iii) provide refined instructions for re-solving the problem.
4. Self-Reflection and Re-Answering: Guided by the auto-generated reflection prompt, the model analyzes the errors in its previous attempt, identifies the missteps, and then re-solves the problem with corrective feedback incorporated.
5. Iterative Update: The newly generated answer undergoes verification. If it remains incorrect, the auto-prompt generation and self-reflection cycle repeat until a correct solution is produced or a predefined maximum number of iterations is reached. We recommend limiting this process to a maximum of three cycles (layers) to balance thoroughness with computational efficiency.

By iteratively generating and responding to tailored auto-prompts, the model systematically identifies and corrects errors through self-reflection. Consequently, MAPS effectively stimulates the reasoning capabilities of base models.

Role

You are an expert in adapting instructions for language models. Your task is to create a personalized Self-Reflection prompt for a model that is trying to solve a mathematical problem.

Task Description

Your task is to modify the Self-Reflection template so that it is as specific and helpful as possible for the problem. Focus on aspects such as:

- **Type of problem:** The Self-Reflection prompt should guide the model to solve the specific type of problem presented in the question.
- **Common mistakes:** The Self-Reflection prompt should guide the model to identify the common mistakes that are made when solving this type of problem.
- **Complexity of the problem:** The Self-Reflection prompt should guide the model to try to understand the complexity of the problem, if more steps are needed to solve it.

Self-Reflection Template

You are an expert in <PROBLEM_AREA>.
You have incorrectly answered the following question.
Your task is to reflect on the problem, your solution, and the correct answer.
You will then use this information to help you answer the same question in the future:

Step 1: Explain why you answered the question incorrectly.
Step 2: List the keywords that describe the type of your errors from most general to most specific.
Step 3: Solve the problem again, step-by-step, based on your knowledge of the correct answer.
Step 4: Create a list of detailed instructions to help you correctly solve this problem in the future.
Step 5: Create a list of general advice to help you solve similar types of problems in the future.

Be concise in your response; however, capture all of the essential information.

Example

For guidance, I will provide you with a single generic example problem and reflection (below).

[Example Input]
Question: <an example question similar on complexity to the question received>
Wrong answer: <the wrong reasoning and answer to the example question>

[Example Output]
Explanation: I miscalculated the <explanation of the mistake>
Error Keywords: - <keywords of the mistake>
Instructions: <list of instructions to solve the problem>
Advice: <list of general advice to solve similar types of problems>
Solution: <the correct reasoning and answer to the example question>

Final Task

Now, adapt the above template for the following question:
Question: {question}
Generate the adapted Self-Reflection prompt. Remember, you need to create a similar example question on complexity to the question received (NOT THE SAME ONE), a wrong answer to it, and the correct answer.

Fig. 2. Meta-prompt (template) to apply MAPS.

3.3 MAPS Meta-prompt

Figure 2 illustrates the meta-prompt that guides the model in generating tailored self-reflection prompts for each question. Rather than relying on static instructions, the MAPS meta-prompt defines the model's role as an expert in adapting reasoning strategies and ensures that self-reflection is dynamically adjusted to the specific characteristics of the problem.

This adaptation within the meta-prompt allows the model to consider crucial factors such as the type of problem (e.g., arithmetic or geometry), typical errors associated with that domain, and the complexity of the reasoning required. The meta-prompt employs a structured yet flexible framework, enabling the model to integrate pertinent domain knowledge at each stage of reflection. To support this process, examples, including error cases, are provided to demonstrate effective self-reflection. Finally, the model applies this structured methodology to novel problems, generating reflection prompts dynamically rather than relying on static templates.

3.4 Applying MAPS

MAPS can be applied to any LLM. To illustrate its use, we implement it on `Llama 3.1-8B Instruct` and demonstrate its performance on a representative instance from the *GSM-symbolic-p2* dataset, which naturally embodies a mathematical problem (details in Sect. 4.2). The selected data instance is depicted in Fig. 3.

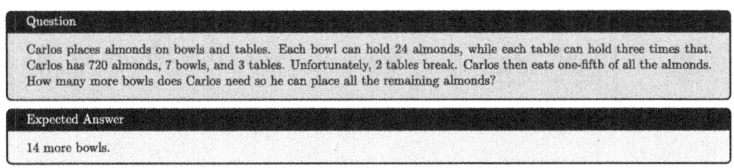

Fig. 3. Instance of question and expected answer from *GSM-symbolic-p2*.

The reflection cycle for this problem, executed through CoT and MAPS, is summarized in Table 1. Initially, the CoT reasoning produces an incorrect answer of 7 more bowls, likely due to an error in adding or subtracting the available capacity. In the first reflection layer for MAPS ($1L$), despite the use of an auto-generated prompt, the LLM fails to identify and correct the miscalculation. However, in the second reflection layer ($2L$), an adapted prompt generated based on the prior error analysis enables the model to identify the mistake and compute the correct answer of 14 more bowls.

Table 1. Summary of multi-layer reflection iterations for a sample from *GSM-symbolic-p2*.

Stage	Answer	Reflection Layer	Correct?
CoT	7	–	No
$MAPS\ 1L$	7	1	No
$MAPS\ 2L$	14	2	Yes

This example clearly illustrates the fundamental capability of MAPS: when a single-pass reflection is insufficient, multiple layers of auto-prompting and self-reflection progressively refine the solution until the correct answer is obtained. To provide a closer approximation of the model's reflection process, an excerpt from the second reflection prompt is presented in Fig. 4.

> **Reflection Prompt Excerpt (auto-generated)**
>
> You are an expert in solving algebra and real-world problems involving division, multiplication, and fractions.
> Your task is to reflect on the problem, your solution, and the correct answer.
> You will then use this information to help you answer the same question in the future.
> First, explain why you answered the question incorrectly.
> Second, list the keywords that describe the type of your errors from most general to most specific.
> Third, solve the problem again, step-by-step, based on your knowledge of the correct answer.
> Fourth, create a list of detailed instructions to help you correctly solve this problem in the future.
> Finally, create a list of general advice to help you solve similar types of problems in the future.
> Be concise in your response; however, capture all of the essential information.
>
> ...Example of similar question ...
> Your initial Chain-of-Thought answer was: 7.0
> Your previous reflection answers were:
> Reflection 1: 7.0
>
> You previously answered this question incorrectly. Reflect on why your answer was incorrect and identify the type of error. Then, solve the problem again step-by-step with corrections. Your new answer MUST be different from your previous answers because they were all incorrect. ...

Fig. 4. Excerpt of the auto-generated reflection prompt from the second MAPS cycle (2L).

4 Experimental Setup

This section outlines the experimental setup for evaluating MAPS in prompt tuning to enhance multi-step reasoning in LLMs, ensuring reproducibility and transparency.

4.1 Models

Our evaluation encompassed a diverse array of LLMs, selected based on variations in parameter size, architecture, computational efficiency, and reasoning capabilities.

Firstly, we evaluated smaller but cost-effective models such as Meta's `Llama 3.18B Instruct`, OpenAI's `GPT-4o-mini-2024-07-18` and Google's `Gemma-2-9b-it`. These models are optimized for rapid inference and lower operational costs, although their performance on complex tasks tends to be limited. Second, we considered mid-sized models, including Google's `Gemma-2-27b-it` and Mistral AI's instruct-optimized `Mistral-Small-24b-Instruct-2501`. These models strike an effective balance between computational expense and performance, demonstrating robust capabilities across a wide range of applications. Lastly, we examine larger models, such as Meta's `Llama 3.170B Instruct`, DeepSeek's `DeepSeek-V3`, and OpenAI's and `GPT-4o-2024-11-20`, which were selected for their superior performance enabled by extensive parameter counts and advanced pre-training techniques.

To establish performance benchmarks, we included specialized reasoning models from OpenAI, such as `o1-preview`, `o3-mini`, and `o4-mini`, as well as Google's models, `Gemini 2.5 Flash` and `Gemini 2.5 Pro`. These models are explicitly optimized for complex reasoning tasks and serve as essential reference points for contextualizing the results obtained from general-purpose models enhanced by MAPS.

4.2 Datasets

We evaluated our approach using four prominent datasets for mathematical reasoning: *GSM8K*, *GSM-Symbolic*, *AIME 2025*, and *MATH 500*, which collectively cover a broad spectrum of difficulty, from basic arithmetic to advanced symbolic manipulation, allowing for a comprehensive evaluation of our proposal.

GSM8K. This dataset contains grade school-level mathematical problems requiring multi-step reasoning, serving as a standard benchmark for assessing LLM performance on basic arithmetic and algebra tasks [2].

GSM-Symbolic. Derived from *GSM8K*, this dataset introduces varying levels of symbolic complexity to assess reasoning robustness [7]. It includes three progressively challenging variants. The *main* variant consists of original problems with modified entity names and numerical values, designed to evaluate the model's ability to generalize beyond surface-level features. The *p1* variant extends the *main* version by adding an extra complexity clause, requiring more nuanced reasoning. Finally, the *p2* variant represents the most challenging setting, incorporating two additional complexity clauses to test performance under significant symbolic transformations.

AIME 2025. The American Invitational Mathematics Examination (AIME) consists of highly challenging competition-level problems in algebra, combinatorics, and number theory [17]. These questions are crafted to test the boundaries of advanced mathematical reasoning, making AIME 2025 a formidable benchmark for evaluating current models.

MATH 500. This dataset is a curated selection of 500 diverse problems from the original MATH benchmark, encompassing topics such as probability, algebra, trigonometry, and geometry [16]. It is designed to assess a model's capability to apply mathematical principles and execute complex calculations.

4.3 Evaluation Metrics

To evaluate our framework, we used three key metrics:

Accuracy. The proportion of correctly answered questions, N_{corr}, relative to the total number of questions, N_{total}. Thus, accuracy is given by Accuracy = $\frac{N_{\text{corr}}}{N_{\text{total}}}$.

Symbolic Loss. Measures the accuracy drop from the GSM8K dataset to the GSM-Symbolic variants, calculated as Symbolic Loss = $\text{Accuracy}_{\text{GSM8K}} - \text{Accuracy}_{\text{GSM-Symbolic}}$. Lower values indicate greater robustness to symbolic complexity.

Cost Analysis. The total inference cost per 100 questions, calculated from generated tokens and provider-specified costs.

4.4 Procedure

This study conducts two evaluations to assess the effectiveness of prompting techniques for tuning both conventional LLMs and reasoning-specialized models. The first evaluation explores smaller, mid-sized, and larger general-purpose LLMs with limited reasoning abilities and apply the prompting methods:

1. *Baseline:* The model is provided solely with the problem statement, without additional instructions or step-by-step reasoning prompts (*e.g.* zero-shot). For the MATH 500 and AIME 2025 datasets, however, the prompt includes a minimal instruction to format the final answer using boxed notation.
2. *Chain-of-Thought (CoT):* For the GSM8K and GSM-Symbolic datasets, this involves providing the model with eight exemplar problems that illustrate step-by-step reasoning, followed by the directive to *"think step by step"*. For AIME 2025 and MATH 500 datasets, the CoT prompt instructs the model to reason step-by-step and present the final answer in boxed notation.
3. *Self-Reflection (SR) with Single-Pass:* Following the generation of an initial response based on CoT, a predetermined static reflection prompt is appended to the model's output.
4. *Multi-layered Adaptive Prompting Strategy (MAPS):* Our proposed framework, MAPS, begins with the initial CoT-derived answer and subjects it to a multi-round iterative self-reflection process. We consider scenarios where a single reasoning layer is employed (MAPS 1L) as well as cases where the iterative process continues until either a correct answer is reached or a predefined limit of three reflection layers is attained (MAPS 2-3L).

For the second evaluation, we expanded our investigation by comparing the performance of MAPS on the previously evaluated LLMs with that of advanced reasoning models.

All experiments were conducted in Python using either OpenRouter's[1] or OpenAI's API[2]. To ensure output consistency and facilitate reproducibility, we fixed the temperature at 0 and top_p at 1. Our evaluation protocol was adapted according to the scale of each benchmark. For the large-scale datasets GSM8K and GSM-Symbolic, we performed five independent runs, each using a distinct random sample of 100 questions, to ensure result robustness without compromising experimental feasibility. The final accuracy scores for these two benchmarks reflect the mean performance across the five samples. In contrast, for the smaller datasets AIME 2025 and MATH 500, evaluation was carried out on their entire test sets based on a single execution.

5 Results and Discussion

In this section, we present the experimental results and have a comprehensive discussion of our findings.

---

[1] https://openrouter.ai/.
[2] https://platform.openai.com/.

5.1 Accuracy Gains Across Prompting Methods

Table 2 reports the experimental accuracy for the prompting strategies defined in Sect. 4.4. We evaluated eight LLMs, categorized as smaller, mid-sized and larger, as mentioned in Sect. 4.1. For each dataset and LLM, the best result is highlighted in bold.

From Table 2, we observe that across all models and datasets, step-by-step reasoning via CoT consistently enhances performance compared to the Baseline. The addition of SR further improves accuracy. Notably, the MAPS framework achieves the highest results, often surpassing SR even with just a single reflection layer (MAPS 1L). When employing two to three reflection layers (MAPS 2 − 3L), MAPS consistently delivers exceptional performance, particularly in the challenging GSM-Symbolic-p2 subset, where its iterative error-correction mechanism proves most effective. This trend is corroborated by results on the AIME 2025 and MATH 500 benchmarks, where MAPS 2 − 3L consistently attains the highest accuracy, highlighting its effectiveness in tackling complex mathematical reasoning tasks.

To enhance the rigor of our analysis, we applied the Nemenyi post-hoc test [4] to the accuracy results reported in Table 2, with the corresponding critical difference diagram shown in Fig. 5. The Friedman test produced a statistic of 227.44 with a p-value of 1.71×10^{-25}, indicating significant differences among the prompting strategies. The Nemenyi test identified a critical difference (CD) of 0.88, confirming that the full version of MAPS, *i.e.*, MAPS 2 − 3L, is statistically superior to all other prompting methods. The basic version, MAPS 1L, ranked second and showed no statistically significant difference from SR, which ranked third. Although CoT outperformed the Baseline, their performances remain statistically indistinguishable. Figure 5a visually summarizes the relative rankings among all evaluated strategies.

To better understand which of the evaluated LLMs benefit most from prompting strategies, we conducted the Nemenyi post-hoc test using only the accuracy results for the GSM-Symbolic-p2 subset presented in Table 2. The Friedman test yielded a statistic of 30.48 and a p-value of 3.91×10^{-6}, indicating statistically significant differences among the models. The subsequent Nemenyi test revealed a critical difference (CD) of 4.70, as illustrated in Fig. 5b. The results show that larger models derive the greatest benefit from prompting techniques in terms of enhanced reasoning capabilities. Specifically, GPT-4o-2024-11-20 and DeepSeek-V3 achieved the highest ranks, followed closely by Llama 3.170B Instruct in third and GPT-4o-mini-2024-07-18 in sixth, with no statistically significant differences among them. Mid-sized LLMs such as Mistral-Small-24b -Instruct-2501 and Gemma-2-27b-it, ranked fourth and fifth respectively, also demonstrated strong performance, statistically comparable to their larger counterparts. In contrast, the smaller models Gemma-2-9b-it, ranked seventh, and Llama 3.18B Instruct, ranked last, did not exhibit meaningful improvements in reasoning performance under the tested prompting methods.

Table 2. Accuracy of different prompting strategies across all benchmarks. For GSM8K and GSM-Symbolic, results correspond to the mean accuracy over five independent runs, each based on a distinct random sample of 100 questions. Symbolic loss (in parentheses) indicates the performance drop relative to GSM8K. For AIME 2025 and MATH 500, results are based on a single evaluation over the full dataset.

Dataset	Base	CoT	SR	MAPS 1L	MAPS 2-3L
meta-llama/llama-3.1-8b-instruct					
GSM8K	0.761	0.822	0.920	0.910	**0.955**
GSM-Symbolic-main	0.680 (−10.60%)	0.766 (−6.81%)	0.890 (**−3.26%**)	0.852 (−6.37%)	**0.916** (−4.08%)
GSM-Symbolic-p1	0.604 (−20.6%)	0.630 (−23.36%)	0.740 (−19.57%)	0.754 (−17.14%)	**0.838** (−12.25%)
GSM-Symbolic-p2	0.376 (−50.59%)	0.376 (−54.26%)	0.600 (−34.78%)	0.540 (−40.66%)	**0.680** (−28.80%)
AIME 2025	0.000	0.000	0.000	0.000	0.000
MATH 500	0.470	0.360	0.410	0.470	**0.540**
google/gemma-2-9b-it					
GSM8K	0.790	0.856	0.888	0.914	**0.946**
GSM-Symbolic-main	0.770 (−2.53%)	0.784 (−8.41%)	0.850 (−4.28%)	0.882 (−3.5%)	**0.922** (−2.54%)
GSM-Symbolic-p1	0.618 (−21.77%)	0.688 (−19.63%)	0.794 (−10.59%)	0.838 (−8.32%)	**0.888** (−6.13%)
GSM-Symbolic-p2	0.476 (−39.75%)	0.516 (−39.72%)	0.632 (−28.83%)	0.684 (−25.16%)	**0.792** (−16.28%)
AIME 2025	0.000	0.000	0.000	0.000	0.000
MATH 500	0.440	0.420	0.430	0.500	**0.520**
google/gemma-2-27b-it					
GSM8K	0.822	0.950	0.976	0.972	**0.986**
GSM-Symbolic-main	0.778 (−5.35%)	0.846 (−10.95%)	0.878 (−10.04%)	0.910 (−6.38%)	**0.940** (−4.67%)
GSM-Symbolic-p1	0.756 (−8.03%)	0.900 (−5.26%)	0.938 (−3.89%)	0.942 (−3.09%)	**0.956** (−3.04%)
GSM-Symbolic-p2	0.660 (−19.71%)	0.784 (−17.47%)	0.860 (−11.89%)	0.872 (−10.29%)	**0.936** (−5.07%)
AIME 2025	0.033	0.000	0.000	0.000	**0.067**
MATH 500	0.480	0.420	0.440	0.490	**0.520**
mistralai/mistral-small-3.1-24b-inst					
GSM8K	0.858	0.970	0.972	0.980	**0.980**
GSM-Symbolic-main	0.804 (−6.29%)	0.928 (−4.33%)	0.942 (−3.09%)	0.948 (−3.27%)	**0.962** (−1.84%)
GSM-Symbolic-p1	0.748 (−12.82%)	0.898 (−7.42%)	0.920 (−5.35%)	0.952 (−2.86%)	**0.974** (−0.61%)
GSM-Symbolic-p2	0.716 (−16.55%)	0.768 (−20.82%)	0.840 (−13.58%)	0.884 (−9.8%)	**0.948** (−3.27%)
AIME 2025	0.033	0.033	0.033	0.067	**0.100**
MATH 500	0.670	0.590	0.650	0.650	**0.730**
meta-llama/llama-3.1-70b-instruct					
GSM8K	0.835	0.948	0.970	0.971	**0.984**
GSM-Symbolic-main	0.808 (−3.19%)	0.910 (−4.01%)	0.960 (**−1.03%**)	0.952 (−1.95%)	**0.968** (−1.63%)
GSM-Symbolic-p1	0.800 (−4.19%)	0.894 (−5.70%)	0.940 (−3.09%)	0.940 (−3.19%)	**0.964** (−2.03%)
GSM-Symbolic-p2	0.716 (−14.25%)	0.792 (−16.46%)	0.870 (−10.31%)	0.876 (−9.78%)	**0.928** (−5.69%)
AIME 2025	0.067	0.033	0.033	0.067	**0.100**
MATH 500	0.580	0.560	0.600	0.590	**0.660**
deepseek/deepseek-V3					
GSM8K	0.934	0.964	0.976	0.972	**0.978**
GSM-Symbolic-main	0.904 (−3.21%)	0.924 (−4.15%)	0.956 (−2.05%)	0.950 (−2.26%)	**0.960** (−1.84%)
GSM-Symbolic-p1	0.892 (−4.50%)	0.908 (−5.81%)	0.952 (−2.46%)	0.946 (−2.67%)	**0.970** (−0.82%)
GSM-Symbolic-p2	0.852 (−8.78%)	0.852 (−11.62%)	0.924 (−5.33%)	0.936 (−3.70%)	**0.944** (−3.48%)
AIME 2025	0.333	0.300	0.300	**0.400**	0.400
MATH 500	0.750	0.760	0.760	0.780	**0.810**
gpt-4o-mini-2024-07-18					
GSM8K	0.849	0.949	0.970	0.967	**0.975**
GSM-Symbolic-main	0.864 (**+1.77%**)	0.920 (−3.06%)	0.930 (−4.12%)	0.938 (−3.00%)	**0.954** (−2.15%)
GSM-Symbolic-p1	0.794 (−6.48%)	0.878 (−7.48%)	0.910 (−6.19%)	0.938 (−3.00%)	**0.950** (−2.56%)
GSM-Symbolic-p2	0.776 (**−8.60%**)	0.708 (−25.40%)	0.840 (−13.40%)	0.844 (−12.72%)	**0.876** (−10.15%)
AIME 2025	**0.133**	0.100	0.100	0.100	**0.133**
MATH 500	0.660	0.630	0.640	0.670	**0.700**
gpt-4o-2024-11-20					
GSM8K	0.844	0.943	0.956	0.969	**0.979**
GSM-Symbolic-main	0.810 (−4.03%)	0.908 (−3.71%)	0.924 (−3.35%)	0.928 (−4.23%)	**0.952** (−2.72%)
GSM-Symbolic-p1	0.782 (−7.35%)	0.944 (**+0.10%**)	0.964 (**+0.84%**)	0.970 (**+0.10%**)	**0.980** (**+0.10%**)
GSM-Symbolic-p2	0.830 (−1.66%)	0.915 (−3.00%)	0.956 (+0%)	0.976 (**+0.72%**)	**0.984** (+0.51%)
AIME 2025	0.067	0.100	0.100	0.133	**0.167**
MATH 500	0.590	0.630	0.660	0.700	**0.760**

5.2 Symbolic Loss Performance

Still within the scope of the first evaluation procedure, Table 2 presents the symbolic loss values, shown in parentheses, calculated across the three *GSM-Symbolic* variants and *GSM8K*. The best symbolic loss values are highlighted in bold. Once again, MAPS 2 − 3L achieves the best performance in the vast majority of cases.

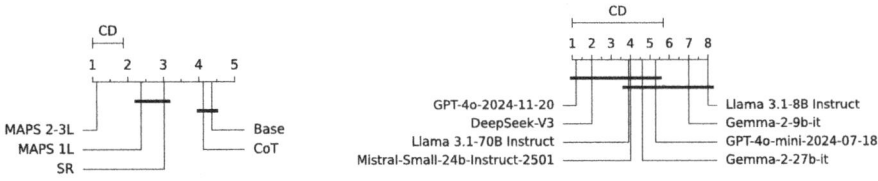

(a) Prompting performance.   (b) LLM performance.

Fig. 5. Nemenyi post-hoc test applied to the accuracy results from Table 2 to statistically assess (a) the performance of prompting techniques and (b) their impact on LLM performance.

The importance of symbolic loss lies in the fact that the *GSM-Symbolic* benchmark introduces increasing symbolic complexity, progressing from *main* to *p1* and finally to *p2*. As shown in Table 2, each additional complexity clause significantly reduces accuracy for the Baseline, CoT, and SR techniques. In contrast, MAPS recovers much of the lost performance, demonstrating the value of iterative error diagnosis and correction for symbolic tasks.

Notably, certain larger models, such as GPT-4o-2024-11-20, can even surpass their *GSM8K* accuracy on some symbolic variants when multi-layer reflection is applied, effectively achieving zero or even negative symbolic loss. For smaller and mid-sized models, such as Llama 3.1--8B Instruct and Gemma-2-27b-it, MAPS also mitigates symbolic loss effectively, though the gains are less pronounced compared to larger models, highlighting the influence of model capacity on the effectiveness of iterative prompting strategies.

5.3 MAPS Versus Specialized Reasoning Models

In the context of the second evaluation procedure, as described in Sect. 4.4, we compare MAPS against specialized pre-trained LLMs renowned for their strong reasoning capabilities. Table 3 presents the comparison of general-purpose models enhanced with MAPS against native reasoning models such as o1-Preview and o3-mini, with the best accuracy results highlighted in bold.

Overall, the MAPS approach enables several general-purpose models to match or even surpass specialized reasoning models, as evidenced in the upper section of Table 3. For example, GPT-4o-2024-11-20 with MAPS achieves

Table 3. Comparison of MAPS with specialized reasoning models: general-purpose LLMs + MAPS vs. native reasoning LLMs.

Benchmark	GPT-4o-2024-11-20+ MAPS	DeepSeek-V3+ MAPS	Llama 3.1-70B+ MAPS	o1-preview	o3-mini
GSM8K	**0.979**	0.978	0.984	0.960	0.944
GSM-Symbolic-main	0.952	0.960	**0.968**	0.927	0.966
GSM-Symbolic-p1	**0.980**	0.970	0.964	0.954	0.972
GSM-Symbolic-p2	**0.984**	0.944	0.928	0.940	0.924

98.4% accuracy on the challenging *GSM-Symbolic-p2* subset, outperforming both o1-Preview and o3-mini. To assess the statistical significance of these differences, we applied the Friedman test, which yielded a statistic of 4.44 and a p-value of 0.218, indicating no significant performance differences among the compared models. The subsequent Nemenyi post-hoc test, with a critical difference (CD) of 3.05, supports this conclusion. As illustrated in Fig. 6, although the differences are not statistically significant, general-purpose LLMs augmented with MAPS consistently exhibit higher accuracy than their specialized counterparts under the same evaluation conditions.

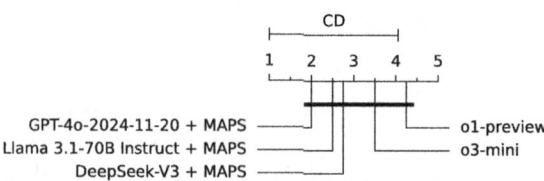

Fig. 6. Nemenyi post-hoc test applied to the accuracy results of the top-3 general-purpose LLMs enhanced with MAPS against specialized reasoning models.

To assess the robustness of our proposal, we applied MAPS to specialized reasoning models on the challenging AIME 2025 and MATH 500 benchmarks. As shown in Table 4, MAPS consistently enhances performance across all models, including the state-of-the-art Gemini family. For example, on AIME 2025, Gemini 2.5 Flash improves from 66.7% to 80.0%, and Gemini 2.5 Pro from 80.0% to 86.7%. A similar +4.0% absolute gain is observed on MATH 500 for both models. Additionally, OpenAI's o4-mini shows performance gains of up to +6.0% on MATH 500.

These findings demonstrate that MAPS is a versatile enhancement strategy that improves inference quality across various models, even in competitive environments. This indicates that the core mechanism of MAPS offers a distinct advantage that complements the internal optimizations of modern LLMs.

5.4 Cost Analysis

Table 5 presents the inference cost of MAPS on GSM-Symbolic for four representative general-purpose LLMs: GPT-4o-mini-2024-07-18, GPT-4o-2024-11-20,

Table 4. Comparison of MAPS with specialized reasoning models: Applying MAPS to Reasoning LLMs on Complex Benchmarks.

Benchmark	Model	CoT Accuracy	MAPS 2–3L
AIME 2025	Gemini 2.5 Flash (no tools)	0.667	**0.800**
AIME 2025	Gemini 2.5 Pro (no tools)	0.800	**0.867**
AIME 2025	o4-mini (medium / no tools)	0.800	**0.867**
MATH 500	Gemini 2.5 Flash (05-20)	0.840	**0.880**
MATH 500	Gemini 2.5 Pro (05-06) (no tools)	0.840	**0.880**
MATH 500	o4-mini (medium / no tools)	0.760	**0.820**

Llama 3.18B Instruct, and Llama 3.170B Instruct, in comparison to the specialized reasoning model o3-mini. While deeper reflection processes increase token usage and costs, so the results highlight key trade-offs in performance and efficiency.

The cost analysis in Table 5 shows that GPT-4o-mini-2024-07-18 proves to be highly cost-effective, requiring only US$ 0.045 on *main* and US$ 0.08 on *p2*, costs significantly lower than o3-mini's US$ 0.078 and US$ 0.144, respectively. Despite its lower cost, GPT-4o-mini-2024-07-18 closely matches or slightly lags behind o3-mini in accuracy across most subsets. Although MAPS increases token usage due to auto-prompt generation and iterative refinement, GPT-4o-mini-2024-07-18's low per-token cost offsets this, reinforcing its efficiency. Llama-3.1-70B-Instruct also delivers strong performance, matching or surpassing o3-mini in accuracy on certain tasks while remaining more economical, costing US$ 0.052 versus US$ 0.078 on *main* (a 33% reduction) and US$ 0.085 versus US$ 0.144 on *p2* (41% lower). Like GPT-4o-mini-2024-07-18, we observe that Llama-3.1-70B-Instruct also benefits from lower inference costs, compensating for the added token consumption of deeper self-reflection layers. Conversely, GPT-4o-2024-11-20 incurs the highest costs, reaching US$ 0.94 on *main*, US$ 0.92 on *p1*, and US$ 1.07 on *p2*, over 600% higher than o3-mini despite outperforming it by 6% in accuracy on *p2* (0.984 versus 0.924).

The use of MAPS requires generating unique auto-prompts at each reflection layer, which increases token consumption and makes it less optimal for cost-sensitive applications. Llama-3.1-8B-Instruct is the most affordable, costing only US$ 0.025 on *main*, but its accuracy in symbolic reasoning tasks is the lowest, ranking the worst in terms of performance. However, with a cost reduction of over 60% compared to o3-mini on p2 (US$ 0.060 versus US$ 0.144), it presents a viable option for scenarios where minor accuracy trade-offs are acceptable.

Overall, GPT-4o-mini-2024-07-18 and Llama-3.1-70B-Instruct stand out as cost-efficient alternatives to reasoning-specific models like o3-mini, maintaining competitive performance at a fraction of the cost. While GPT-4o-mini-2024-07--18 has considerable accuracy, its high cost makes it less attractive for practical deployment. Additionally, costs consistently increase from *main* to *p1* to *p2* across all models, reflecting the additional complexity and token requirements

Table 5. Total inference cost (USD) for processing the *GSM-Symbolic* dataset (100 questions).

Model	Dataset	Total Cost (US$)
GPT-4o-2024-11-20 + MAPS	main	0.944251
	p1	0.918467
	p2	1.066514
GPT-4o-mini-2024-07-18 + MAPS	main	0.045059
	p1	0.053559
	p2	0.079530
Llama 3.170B Instruct + MAPS	main	0.052105
	p1	0.054528
	p2	0.084594
Llama 3.18B Instruct + MAPS	main	0.025040
	p1	0.034904
	p2	0.059944
o3-mini	main	0.07795458
	p1	0.10527242
	p2	0.14444980

associated with deeper reasoning steps in specialized models and extended self-reflection in our multi-layer approach.

5.5 Single-Pass Comparison: Traditional SR Versus MAPS 1L

Before examining the benefits of multiple reflection layers, it is useful to compare the traditional SR method which considers single-pass with our proposal MAPS 1L, *i.e.* MAPS considering only one adaptive reflection layer. As observed in the SR and MAPS 1L results from Table 2, it is possible to point out two key observations.

First, the overall performance of most LLMs remains similar under SR and MAPS 1L across *GSM8K* and all variants of *GSM-Symbolic*, suggesting that in a single-pass scenario, generating a custom reflection prompt in MAPS 1L does not significantly differ from using a well-tuned static prompt in SR. Second, model capacity plays a crucial role in the effectiveness of adaptive prompting. While `Llama-3.1-8B-Instruct` exhibits slightly lower accuracy with MAPS 1L compared to SR, particularly on *p2*, indicating that smaller models may struggle to generate or leverage effective adaptive prompts in a single pass, `Mistral-Small-24b-Instruct-2501` consistently benefits from auto-prompted reflection, suggesting that certain architectures or parameter scales are better suited for adaptive meta-prompting.

These findings suggest that auto-prompting in a single reflection pass can yield performance comparable to, or even surpass, that of a fixed self-reflection prompt. However, as evidenced by the results, incorporating additional reflection layers, as done in MAPS 2 − 3L, consistently improves performance across all LLMs, highlighting the critical role of iterative error correction in addressing the most complex reasoning tasks.

6 Conclusion

This work introduced *Multi-Layered Self-Reflection with Auto-Prompting* (MAPS), a framework that dynamically adapts reflection templates based on problem type and complexity. Through comprehensive evaluations on benchmarks such as GSM8K, GSM-Symbolic, AIME 2025, and MATH 500, MAPS consistently outperformed baseline methods including Chain-of-Thought (CoT) and single-pass Self-Reflection (SR). The most significant gains were observed on symbolic subsets *p1* and *p2*, underscoring the framework's effectiveness in handling complex, abstract reasoning tasks.

MAPS enhances the reasoning capabilities of LLMs through an iterative and adaptive self-reflection process. This aligns with human-like problem-solving behaviors that rely on successive refinement and contextual learning. Notably, MAPS not only boosts general-purpose models to match or surpass specialized reasoning LLMs (such as `o1-Preview` and `o3-mini`), but also improves the performance of the specialized models themselves. For instance, state-of-the-art Gemini variants and OpenAI's `o4-mini` exhibited consistent performance improvements when enhanced with MAPS, achieving average gains between 4% and 6% on challenging benchmarks like AIME 2025 and MATH 500. These findings confirm MAPS as a model-agnostic reasoning enhancer that generalizes well across architectures and difficulty levels.

Nonetheless, MAPS depends on the availability of explicit correctness signals to guide the self-reflection loop, which may restrict its applicability to open-ended tasks lacking ground-truth answers. Future work should address this limitation by integrating techniques such as uncertainty estimation, human-in-the-loop validation, or proxy supervision via auxiliary tasks.

Further research should also investigate the use of MAPS in other domains requiring structured reasoning, such as code generation, logical deduction, and scientific modeling. Enhancing the auto-prompting component with more expressive and context-sensitive mechanisms may further improve the system's adaptability and efficiency. Overall, MAPS represents a promising direction toward more robust, generalizable, and cognitively inspired frameworks for LLM-based reasoning.

To foster transparency and encourage further research, we release the full implementation of the MAPS framework, along with evaluation scripts and prompt templates, at: https://github.com/and270/maps_prompting.

Acknowledgments. The authors express their gratitude to the *Fondo de Apoyo a Publicaciones* (FAP) of Tecnologico de Monterrey for the financial support.

Disclosure of Interests. The authors have no competing interests to declare that are relevant to the content of this article.

References

1. Yu, F., Zhang, H., Tiwari, P., Wang, B.: Natural language reasoning. A Survey. ACM Comput. Surv. **56**(12), 304 (2024). https://doi.org/10.1145/3664194
2. Cobbe, K., Kosaraju, V., Bavarian, M., et al. 2021. Training Verifiers to Solve Math Word Problems. *arXiv* 2110.14168. https://doi.org/10.48550/arXiv.2110.14168
3. DeepSeek-AI, Guo, D., Yang, D., Zhang, H., Song, J., et al.: DeepSeek-R1: incentivizing reasoning capability in LLMs via reinforcement learning (2025). *arXiv* 2501.12948. URL: https://arxiv.org/abs/2501.12948
4. Demšar, J.: Statistical comparisons of classifiers over multiple data sets. J. Mach. Learn. Res. **7**, 1–30 (2006)
5. Liu, F., AlDahoul, N., Eady, G., Zaki, Y., AlShebli, B., Rahwan, T: Self-Reflection Outcome is Sensitive to Prompt Construction (2024). *arXiv* 2406.10400. URL: https://arxiv.org/abs/2406.10400
6. Minaee, S., et al.: Large language models: a survey (2024). *arXiv* 2402.06196. URL: https://arxiv.org/abs/2402.06196
7. Mirzadeh, I., Alizadeh, K., Shahrokhi, H., Tuzel, O., Bengio, S., Farajtabar, M.: GSM-Symbolic: understanding the limitations of mathematical reasoning in large language models (2024). *arXiv* 2410.05229. https://doi.org/10.48550/arXiv.2410.05229
8. OpenAI. 2025. OpenAI o3-mini. URL: https://openai.com/index/openai-o3-mini/. Accessed 04 Feb 2025
9. OpenAI, Achiam, J., Adler, S., Agarwal, S., et al.: GPT-4 Technical report (2024). *arXiv* 2303.08774. URL: https://arxiv.org/abs/2303.08774
10. Renze, M., Guven, E.: Self-Reflection in LLM agents: effects on problem-solving performance (2024). *arXiv* 2405.06682. https://doi.org/10.48550/arXiv.2405.06682
11. Valmeekam, K., Stechly, K., Kambhampati, S.: LLMs still can't plan; can LRMs? A preliminary evaluation of OpenAI's o1 on planbench (2024). *arXiv* 2409.13373. https://doi.org/10.48550/arXiv.2409.13373
12. Wei, J., et al.: Chain-of-thought prompting elicits reasoning in large language models (2022). *arXiv* 2201.11903. https://doi.org/10.48550/arXiv.2201.11903
13. Xu, M., Ning, Y., Li, Y., et al.: Reasoning based on symbolic and parametric knowledge bases: a survey (2025). *arXiv* 2501.01030. URL: https://arxiv.org/abs/2501.01030
14. Zhong, Q., Wang, K., Xu, Z., Liu, J., Ding, L.: Achieving >97% on GSM8K: deeply understanding the problems makes LLMs better solvers for math word problems (2024). *arXiv* 2404.14963
15. Wang, L., et al.: Plan-and-solve prompting: improving zero-shot chain-of-thought reasoning by large language models. In: *Proceedings of the 61st Annual Meeting of the Association for Computational Linguistics (, vol. 1: Long Papers)*, pp. 2609–2634 (2023). ACL. URL: https://aclanthology.org/2023.acl-long.147/. https://doi.org/10.18653/v1/2023.acl-long.147
16. Hendrycks, D., et al.: Measuring mathematical problem solving with the MATH dataset. In: *NeurIPS* (2021)

17. Balunović, M., Dekoninck, J., Petrov, I., Jovanović, N., Vechev, M.: MathArena: evaluating LLMs on uncontaminated math competitions (2025). SRI Lab, ETH Zurich. URL: https://matharena.ai/. Accessed 12 April 2025
18. Gemini-Team, Anil, R., Borgeaud, S., Alayrac, J.-B., et al.: Gemini: a family of highly capable multimodal models (2025). *arXiv* 2312.11805. URL: https://arxiv.org/abs/2312.11805
19. OpenAI. OpenAI o3 and o4-mini System Card. System Card. OpenAI (2025). Accessed 12 April 2025

DPS: Diverse Prototype Selection for Adaptive In-Context Learning

Xuanbo Fan[1], Kaiyuan Li[2], Hao Sun[1], Boci Peng[1], Zhenrong Cheng[1], and Yan Zhang[1(✉)]

[1] School of Intelligence Science and Technology, Peking University, Beijing, China
{xuanbo.fan,sunhao,bcpeng,chengzhenrong}@stu.pku.edu.cn,
zhyzhy001@pku.edu.cn
[2] Tsinghua Shenzhen International Graduate School, Tsinghua University, Beijing, China

Abstract. Large language models exhibit remarkable proficiency across a wide array of tasks by leveraging in-context learning, wherein they learn from a limited number of examples. However, the efficacy of ICL is highly sensitive to the choice of demonstrations provided. Existing approaches primarily focus on the selection of individual examples, often neglecting the broader context of the entire example bank. In this paper, we introduce a novel framework aimed at augmenting the example bank through Diverse Prototype Selection (**DPS**). *DPS* decomposes the ICL process into two distinct stages: *Prototype Selection* and *Prompt Synthesis*. In the first stage, DPS identifies a set of prototype functions that closely approximate the underlying data distribution. In the second stage, these prototype functions dynamically generate query-specific demonstrations, thus guiding the LLM more effectively in its task. Empirical evaluations conducted across thirteen reasoning benchmarks demonstrate that **DPS** significantly enhances ICL performance, providing substantial improvements when integrated with downstream LLMs.

Keywords: In-context Learning · Few-shot Learning

1 Introduction

Large language models (LLMs) [14] have achieved remarkable success across a broad range of natural language processing tasks [23], owing to their exceptional emergent capabilities. One of the most prominent emergent abilities is in-context learning (ICL), which utilizes a small number of input-output examples to enhance model predictions [4]. ICL has proven to be highly effective in unlocking the advanced potential of LLMs and has become a widely adopted strategy for tackling complex tasks.

However, due to the constraints imposed by the context window [10], only a limited number of examples can be incorporated into the prompt. Prior research [13,16] has also demonstrated that ICL is highly sensitive to the selection and ordering of chosen examples [8], with even minor changes leading to

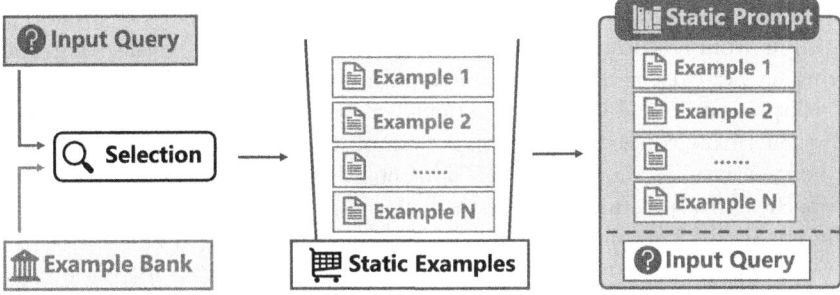

(a) Inference pipeline of Static In-context Learning.

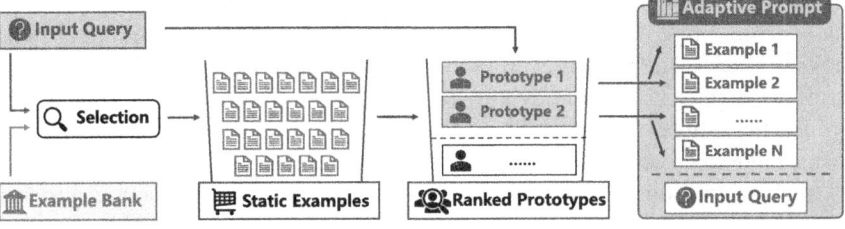

(b) Inference pipeline of Adaptive In-context Learning.

Fig. 1. Comparison of Static and Adaptive In-context Learning. Unlike Static ICL, which concatenates a small number of fixed inference examples into the prompt, Adaptive ICL first evaluates a large set of similar examples to determine the optimal prototype, then use them to generate diverse and adaptive examples.

significant performance fluctuations. Consequently, a key area of research has been the selection of high-performing demonstrations from the example bank.

A prominent line of research in example selection is the development of heuristic evaluation metrics to assess candidate examples. Some works focus on selecting examples that exhibit higher similarity to the input query [16], while other approaches aim to balance relevance and diversity [37]. Despite their effectiveness, these methods are inherently based on subjective judgments, which limits their robustness across different task scenarios. To address these limitations, iterative frameworks such as SE2 [15] and ConE [22] refine the selection process by incorporating feedback from downstream LLMs, enabling more context-aware adjustments and improving the adaptability of example selection across varying task demands.

Despite some success, current methods primarily focus on selecting **intact** examples from the example bank. However, the quality of the example bank is often overlooked. Since it is typically human-annotated, constructing the example bank is both time-consuming and costly, resulting in a smaller and less diverse set of examples that may fail to cover all potential scenarios. This limited selection space restricts the model's ability to access a sufficiently varied set of examples. Moreover, the reasoning paths in these human-labeled examples are typically single-faceted. Even when multiple valid approaches exist for a given problem, the solutions in the example bank usually follow a single predefined path. This overreliance on fixed frameworks hinders the model's flexibility, preventing it from adapting effectively to new tasks. Therefore, rather than solely relying on pre-existing samples from the example bank, it is crucial to improve the **adaptiveness** and **diversity** of demonstrations for input queries by dynamically generating contextually relevant examples that align with different reasoning perspectives, as shown in Fig. 1. This enables the model to explore multiple approaches to problem-solving instead of rigidly following a single predefined path, enhancing its ability to tackle diverse and unfamiliar tasks.

Nevertheless, generating adaptive demonstrations for in-context learning is a non-trivial task due to several inherent challenges. **First**, human-annotated examples inherently limit the model's generation diversity. On the other hand, without human-annotated examples, LLM-generated results may not align with task-specific preferences, compromising the effectiveness of reasoning paths. Although increasing temperature and performing multiple sampling rounds can introduce diversity to some extent, the model's reasoning ability remains constrained by its intrinsic capabilities. **Second**, the absence of ground-truth labels during inference complicates the assessment of different demonstrations. Without clear evaluation criteria, it becomes challenging to determine which demonstrations are truly effective, making it difficult to identify the most suitable examples for in-context learning.

To address these challenges, as shown in Fig. 2, we propose a novel framework that enhances in-context learning through **D**iverse **P**rototype **S**election (**DPS**). **To ensure the diversity of the generated examples**, *DPS* first collects a set of reasoning patterns that approach queries from diverse perspectives, referred to as *prototype functions* (Sect. 4.1). It then utilizes the traditional example bank to evaluate and select the most suitable prototype functions upon receiving a user query. This is achieved through the construction of a *prototype bank* (Sect. 4.2), where *DPS* identifies similar problems and assesses different prototype functions to generate diverse reasoning paths. **To ensure the quality of the selected examples**, *DPS* employs two advanced reranking techniques: *frequency-based reranking* and *decay-based reranking*. These techniques refine the model's output by effectively leveraging consensus across the selected prototype functions, enhancing both accuracy and reasoning diversity (see Sect. 4.4).

Experimental results on thirteen datasets across three tasks demonstrate *DPS*'s effectiveness in significantly improving the performance of downstream LLMs. For instance, in mathematical reasoning tasks, an average improvement of 11.9% was achieved. To summarize, our contributions are as follows:

- We introduce *DPS*, an effective framework that leverages the prototype bank to generate demonstrations with diverse perspectives, adaptively tailored to the input query.
- To better leverage the inferences among prototype functions, we propose two advanced techniques: frequency-based reranking and decay-based reranking. These techniques further refine the selection of high-quality demonstrations.
- Extensive experimental results across thirteen reasoning datasets demonstrate the effectiveness of *DPS* compared to existing methods.

2 Related Work

While large language models have demonstrated impressive zero-shot performance across a variety of tasks, including complex reasoning and agent-based tasks [25,31], recent studies show that in-context learning can further harness their potential and enhance their performance [4]. In addition to improving effectiveness, ICL can provide structural guidance that helps mitigate prompt bias during model inference [35]. Due to the constraints imposed by the context window [17], only a limited number of examples can be incorporated into the prompt. Previous research [13,16] has also demonstrated that ICL is highly sensitive to the selection and ordering of examples [8].

Some studies focus on selecting examples with greater similarity to the input query [16], while others strive to balance both relevance and diversity [37]. Although these methods have shown promise, they are often based on subjective criteria, limiting their generalization across different tasks. To overcome these challenges, iterative frameworks such as SE2 [15] and ConE [22] introduce feedback loops from downstream LLMs, allowing for more contextually sensitive adjustments and improving the selection process for various task requirements.

In contrast to these approaches, our method removes the constraint of relying solely on an example bank for selecting in-context examples. Instead, we propose generating task-specific demonstrations using existing models, offering a fresh perspective on how ICL capabilities can be leveraged more effectively for downstream tasks.

3 Preliminary

Consider a downstream task T that involves an example bank B, which consists of a set of input-output pairs $\{(x_n, y_n)_{n=1}^{N}\}$, and a pre-trained LLM with fixed parameters θ. For a given input query x_t, the LLM generates an output y_t by sampling from the following distribution:

$$y_t \sim \text{LLM}_{\theta,\tau}[\text{Demo}(x_t, B) \oplus x_t] \quad (1)$$

Here, τ represents the sampling temperature, which controls the randomness of the model's predictions. The function $\text{Demo}(x_t, B)$ selects a sequence of examples from B based on x_t to generate demonstrations, and $\oplus$ denotes the concatenation of these examples with the input query x_t.

In subsequent sections, we will omit the fixed parameters θ and assume $\tau = 0$, which corresponds to greedy decoding (i.e., choosing the most likely output at each step). The goal of in-context learning is to design the $\text{Demo}(x_t, B)$ algorithm to optimize performance for the task T.

4 Methodology

4.1 Overview

As shown in Fig. 2, we provide a comprehensive overview of our framework. Unlike conventional in-context learning methods that rely on static example

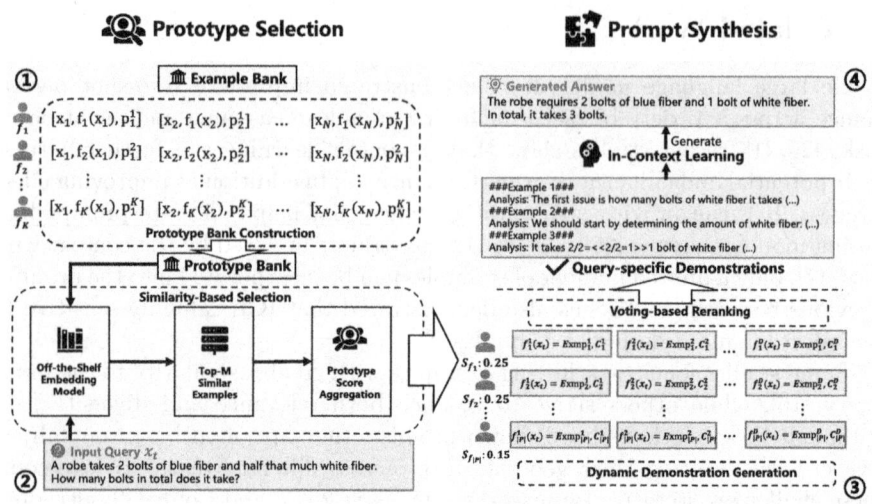

Fig. 2. The *DPS* pipeline consists of two main stages: (1) Prototype Selection: selecting a diverse set of prototype functions optimized to provide various reasoning perspectives, and (2) Prompt Synthesis: leveraging these prototype functions to generate adaptive demonstrations tailored to the input query.

selection, *DPS* dynamically selects and synthesizes demonstrations, optimizing reasoning from multiple perspectives. This framework consists of two key stages: *Prototype Selection* and *Prompt Synthesis*.

In the Prototype Selection stage, we first employ a set of specialized models with diverse prompting methods as *prototype functions*. The example bank is then reorganized into a *prototype bank*, which serves as the foundation for evaluating different prototype functions. Upon receiving a user query, *DPS* retrieves similar examples from the prototype bank, evaluates the effectiveness of different prototype functions based on their responses, and selects the most suitable ones for the query.

During the Prompt Synthesis stage, *DPS* prompts the selected prototype functions to generate adaptive demonstrations tailored to the input query. Additionally, two voting-based reranking strategies are employed to refine the selection process, ensuring that only the most effective demonstrations are used as contextual examples. The following sections will provide a detailed breakdown of each component of the *DPS* framework.

4.2 Prototype Bank Construction

Existing example selection methods work by selecting examples from an example bank based on similarity and then directly concatenating them into the prompt. These examples are considered perfectly accurate as they are manually annotated. Thus, the example bank is formally defined as:

$$B = \{(x_n, F(x_n), 1)_{n=1}^{N}\}, \qquad (2)$$

where $F(x_n)$ represents the ground truth, and the label 1 confirms its correctness.

However, the high cost of manual annotation limits the example bank to a single analytical perspective, reducing its informational diversity. To mitigate this limitation, we expand the example bank by incorporating reasoning strategies from multiple perspectives. Specifically, we introduce several prototype functions as alternatives to ground truth and track their accuracy p in answering these questions. This reconstructed example bank, referred to as the *Prototype Bank*, is formally defined as:

$$B' = \{(x_n, f_k(x_n, prompt_k), p_n^k)_{k=1\ n=1}^{K\ \ N}\}, \qquad (3)$$

where f_k refers to the k-th prototype function, $prompt_k$ refers to the k-th prompt method and p_n^k indicates the accuracy of f_k in answering x_n.

4.3 Prototype Selection

Given an input query x_t, we begin by embedding it using a pre-trained model, then calculate its similarity with other examples:

$$s_n^t = \frac{\text{Emb}(x_n) \cdot \text{Emb}(x_t)}{\|\text{Emb}(x_n)\|\|\text{Emb}(x_t)\|} \qquad (4)$$

Based on the similarity scores, we filter out the top-M similar examples, denoted as Q. For each prototype function f_k, we then compute its average performance score across the examples in Q:

$$s_{f_k} = \frac{1}{|Q|} \sum_{x_n \in Q} p_n^k \qquad (5)$$

Here, p_n^k denotes the average performance of f_k on the example question x_n, while s_{f_k} represents the mean accuracy across Q.

Rather than relying on pre-defined prompts, DPS actively learns which prototype functions yield the most effective demonstrations. By filtering out suboptimal prototypes, our method ensures that only the most informative relevant functions contribute to downstream reasoning, leading to more precise and adaptable prompt generation. The selected prototype functions are denoted as:

$$P = \{f_k, prompt_k \mid s_{f_k} > s_{LLM}\} \qquad (6)$$

Here, P represents the set of prototype functions f_k whose scores s_{f_k} are greater than the score of the downstream LLMs. The selected prototype functions serve as the foundation for the next stage, where they are leveraged to generate tailored demonstrations.

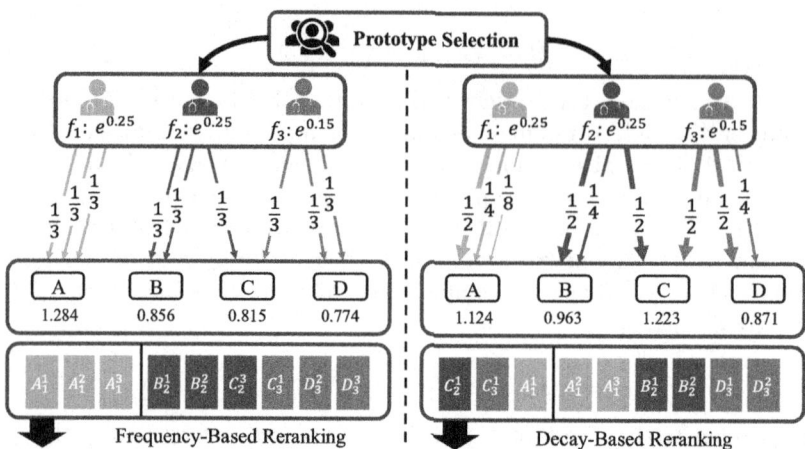

Fig. 3. Frequency-Based Reranking uses total voting frequency, while Decay-Based Reranking applies a decaying weight to each prototype function.

4.4 Prompt Synthesis

Traditional example selection methods rely on static retrieval and direct concatenation, limiting their adaptability to different queries. In contrast, DPS employs dynamic prototype selection and synthesis, allowing for adaptive and context-aware prompting. This ensures that the demonstrations are optimally tailored to the input query x_tt, significantly improving reasoning diversity and accuracy.

Specifically, when generating diverse reasoning paths, we can incorporate existing prompting methods to guide the prototype function, such as Task Instruction and Zero-shot CoT [12]. We would like to emphasize that previous prompt-based approaches can be integrated as part of our framework to enhance the quality of diverse reasoning paths. The impact of demonstration path quality on our method is discussed in detail in the analysis section. Formally, we prompt each function $f_k \in P$ to generate D distinct demos for x_t with prompt method $prompt_k$, denoted as:

$$f_k^d(x_t, prompt_k) = \left(\text{Exmp}_k^d, C_k^d \right), \qquad (7)$$

where Exmp_k^d represents the d-th response, and C_k^d is the conclusion drawn from Exmp_k^d, ensuring that the generated demonstrations are both diverse and contextually relevant.

4.5 Voting-Based Reranking

Given the limited context window size, passing all $D \times |P|$ responses to the downstream LLMs is impractical. To retain the most relevant information, we propose a voting-based reranking method, scoring each Exmp_k^d as y_k^d by aggregating contributions from all prototype functions using a Softmax-like approach:

$$y_k^d = \sum_{f_k \in P} \exp(s_{f_k} - s_{LLM}) \cdot v_k^p, \tag{8}$$

where, v_k^p represents the voting weight of f_k for the p-th conclusion C_p among all distinct conclusions c_k^d, and $\exp(s_{f_k} - s_{LLM})$ serves as a weighting factor that prioritizes high-performing prototype functions. The calculation of v_k^p is performed using one of two methods:

Frequency-based Reranking. v_k^p is assigned based on the frequency of each conclusion C_p across all responses, as illustrated in Fig. 3.

Decay-based Reranking. To prevent a prototype function from dominating due to repeatedly producing the same conclusion, we apply an exponential decay strategy to the voting weights of each function's conclusions:

$$v_k^p = \frac{1}{D} \sum_{t=1}^{T_k^p} \left(2^{-t}\right) \tag{9}$$

Here, T_k^p denotes the number of times f_k produces the conclusion C_p. After voting-based reranking, we concatenate the top H highest-scoring demonstrations to form $\text{Demo}(x_t, B)$. This ensures that only the most relevant and high-quality examples are passed to the LLM, maximizing contextual coherence and reasoning effectiveness.

5 Experimental Setup

5.1 Datasets

To evaluate *DPS*, we consider three reasoning tasks, each presenting unique challenges that necessitate diverse prototype selection.

- **Mathematical Reasoning** requires multi-step calculations and symbolic manipulations. This category includes five representative datasets: GSM8K [6] (GSM), MATH [9] (MTH), SVAMP [21] (SVA), ASDIV [18] (ASD), and MathQA [2] (MQA). These datasets allow us to examine how *DPS* improves problem-solving by leveraging multiple reasoning paths.
- **Commonsense Reasoning** involves understanding implicit world knowledge. Unlike mathematical reasoning, commonsense knowledge is often non-explicit and context-dependent. We use five benchmarks: CommonsenseQA [27] (CSQ), CommonsenseQA2 [28] (CS2), OpenbookQA [19] (OBQ), PIQA [3] (PIQ), and Com2Sense [26] (C2S). This task tests whether *DPS* can generate adaptive demonstrations that incorporate diverse commonsense perspectives.
- **Natural Language Inference (NLI)** requires determining logical relationships between sentence pairs. Compared to mathematical and commonsense reasoning, NLI involves recognizing entailment, contradiction, and neutrality in textual data. We evaluate on MNLI [33] (MLI), QNLI [30] (QLI), and ANLI [20] (ALI), focusing on whether *DPS* enhances reasoning robustness across different logical structures.

5.2 Baselines

We compare *DPS* with three baseline categories.

- **Basic Baselines.** Fundamental strategies with minimal guidance. **Prompting**: Task instructions without examples. **Random**: Randomly selecting examples from the bank. **CoT**: Prompting the model with "Think step by step."
- **Selection-based Methods.** Retrieving static examples from an example bank. **KNN**: Selecting the most similar examples via two embeddings: BGE [34] (bge-large-en-v1.5)[1]. Sentence-BERT [24] (all-MiniLM-L6-v2)[2]. **MMR** [37]: Balancing relevance and diversity. **ConE** [22]: Refining selection via LLM feedback. These methods retrieve relevant examples but remain **static**, which might limit adaptability in diverse tasks.
- **Generation-based Methods.** Dynamically constructing examples. **Analogy** [36]: Generating examples by recalling similar problems. **Complex-CoT** [7]: Constructing examples based on bank distributions. **AutoCoT** [39]: Automatically generating chain-of-thought demonstrations. These methods introduce adaptiveness but might not ensure **diversity and task alignment**, as they lack explicit quality control.

5.3 Implementation Details

Dataset Usage. We extract 500 samples from the official dataset for constructing the example bank and 1,000 samples for evaluation. For datasets with fewer than 1,500 samples, we retain 500 for the example bank and use the remainder for evaluation. If there is an official ground truth partition for the test or development sets, we directly adopt it. In the absence of an official partition, we perform random sampling to divide the dataset.

Prototype Bank Construction. We selected $N = 500$ examples to form the Prototype Bank. The candidate prototype functions used are `LLaMA3-8B-Instruct` [1], `MAmmoTH2-8B` [38] and `Apollo-7B` [32]. Our framework is flexible, allowing for the reuse of prototype functions and downstream models.

Prototype Selection. From the Prototype Bank, we select $M = 100$ most similar examples. For each prototype function, we sample 3 responses to calculate p_n^k. The generation temperature for all prototype functions was set to 0.7. For each model, we apply two prompting methods: Vanilla-Prompting and CoT-Prompting. This results in a total of six distinct prototype functions.

Prompt Synthesis. Each selected prototype function generated $D = 4$ responses. Finally, the top $H = 4$ samples were selected for use in the demonstration. All baseline methods that provide examples follow a 4-shot setting to ensure a fair comparison. Due to computational resource constraints, each experiment was

---

[1] https://huggingface.co/BAAI/bge-large-en-v1.5.
[2] https://huggingface.co/sentence-transformers/all-MiniLM-L6-v2.

Table 1. Experimental results on Commonsense Reasoning benchmarks. The best results are highlighted in **bold**, and the second-best results are underlined.

Category	Model	CSQ	OPQ	PIQ	CS2	C2S	Avg.
Basic	Prompting	71.4	71.6	79.4	62.6	62.0	69.4
	Random	72.6	74.2	77.2	63.8	66.5	70.8
	CoT	71.8	73.6	73.5	67.3	66.6	70.6
Selection	KNN w/Mini [16]	72.7	74.6	79.9	65.2	67.3	71.9
	KNN w/BGE [16]	72.9	76.6	80.1	65.0	66.6	72.2
	MMR w/BGE [37]	72.2	74.6	78.6	65.2	66.6	71.4
	ConE [22]	73.0	76.2	79.7	66.0	66.5	72.3
Generation	Analogy [36]	66.2	73.4	67.7	60.2	62.5	66.0
	ComplexCoT [7]	74.4	76.6	76.2	68.7	**71.7**	73.5
	AutoCoT [39]	75.8	75.4	76.4	68.9	<u>71.5</u>	73.6
Ours	*frequency*	<u>77.9</u>	<u>80.0</u>	<u>81.8</u>	**71.7**	68.7	<u>76.1</u>
	decay	**79.2**	**80.6**	**82.3**	<u>71.6</u>	69.9	**76.7**

conducted once, and the performance results are reported accordingly. We use LLaMA3-8B-Instruct [1] as the downstream model. Also, we report performance across various model types and sizes to provide a broader evaluation.

6 Main Results

6.1 Commonsense Reasoning Results

DPS achieves state-of-the-art accuracy on commonsense reasoning benchmarks, outperforming the strongest generative method, AutoCoT, by 3.1 points and the best selection-based model, Con [22], by 4.4 points (Table 1).

Notably, Analogy [36] exhibits subpar performance (66.0 avg.), significantly lower than basic prompting methods. We attribute this to its automatic generation of exemplars without validation, which often reinforces incorrect reasoning patterns. In contrast, other methods benefit from explicit or implicit example signals, leading to more stable performance improvements over prompting. This observation suggests that providing examples helps align large language models (LLMs) with human preferences.

Furthermore, in the PIQA benchmark, we observe that generative approaches perform markedly worse than selection-based methods. We hypothesize that this discrepancy arises because PIQA requires selecting the better option from two sentences, a task that relies more on human preference alignment than pure reasoning ability. In this context, *DPS* effectively balances preference exploitation and reasoning flexibility, thus surpassing all baselines.

Table 2. Results on Mathematical Reasoning benchmarks. The best results are highlighted in **bold**, and the second-best results are underlined.

Model	GSM	MTH	SVA	ASD	MQA	Avg.
CoT	75.4	29.9	84.8	79.7	53.3	64.6
Analogy [36]	60.0	27.0	75.0	78.6	51.1	58.3
ComplexCoT [7]	74.7	15.7	85.4	75.6	50.0	60.3
AutoCoT [39]	78.8	32.2	86.6	80.3	54.0	66.4
DPS-frequency	<u>88.0</u>	<u>43.9</u>	**93.2**	<u>89.8</u>	<u>63.5</u>	<u>75.7</u>
DPS-decay	**88.2**	**45.4**	<u>93.0</u>	**89.9**	**66.0**	**76.5**

6.2 Mathematical Reasoning Results

Table 2 shows that *DPS* achieves an average accuracy of 76.5, outperforming standard CoT (+11.9) and AutoCoT (+10.1) [39], highlighting the benefits of dynamic prototype selection and adaptive prompt synthesis in multi-step reasoning. Notably, ComplexCoT [7] underperforms compared to standard CoT, particularly on the MTH dataset. This may be due to its fixed reliance on the longest reasoning path, which often results in verbosity and error propagation. This observation suggests that heuristic rule-based exemplar selection tends to lack generalization capability. In comparison, *DPS* dynamically selects effective demonstrations and reduces redundancy through a voting-based mechanism, achieving the highest accuracy across all datasets.

In addition, the decay-based variant consistently achieves higher accuracy compared to the frequency-based variant. This suggests that decay-based reranking better prioritizes informative in-context demonstrations, reducing the influence of less relevant examples and thereby enhancing overall performance.

6.3 Natural Language Inference Results

DPS achieves the best overall performance on logical reasoning benchmarks, with *DPS-decay* attaining an average accuracy of 71.2, surpassing the strongest CoT-based method, AutoCoT, by 0.5 points and outperforming the best retrieval-based method, MMR w/BGE, by 9.5 points (Table 3).

Breaking down the results, selection-based approaches show modest improvements over the basic CoT model, but their effectiveness remains highly dependent on the quality of retrieved exemplars. In contrast, generation-based methods exhibit higher variance: ComplexCoT achieves strong performance in QLI (87.9) but suffers from severe instability in ALI and MLI, suggesting that its reliance on complexity-based heuristics leads to inconsistent reasoning across tasks.

In response to these limitations, *DPS* dynamically selects and ranks high-quality demonstrations, ensuring stable performance across datasets. Notably, its frequency-based variant already outperforms all baselines, while the decay-based strategy further refines example weighting, leading to improved robustness and

Table 3. Results on Logical Reasoning benchmarks. The best results are highlighted in **bold**, and the second-best results are underlined.

Category	Model	ALI	MLI	QLI	Avg.
Basic	Prompting	57.9	59.7	58.3	58.6
	Random	61.0	59.7	58.8	61.5
	CoT	67.2	61.7	78.0	69.0
Selection	KNN w/Mini [16]	61.4	61.7	60.0	61.2
	KNN w/BGE [16]	61.5	61.8	57.7	61.0
	MMR w/BGE [37]	61.9	<u>62.0</u>	58.1	61.7
	ConE [22]	63.3	<u>62.0</u>	59.2	61.5
Generation	Self-Gen [36]	42.4	39.8	43.4	41.9
	ComplexCoT [7]	21.6	16.1	**87.9**	41.9
	AutoCoT [39]	70.4	61.4	<u>80.3</u>	70.7
DPS (Ours)	frequency	<u>71.1</u>	61.9	79.7	<u>70.9</u>
	decay	**71.5**	**62.1**	80.0	**71.2**

Table 4. Ablation study of *DPS* (frequency-based reranking) on six datasets.

Method	GSM	MTH	SVA	ASD	CSQ	CS2	Avg.
DPS	88.0	43.9	93.2	89.8	77.9	71.7	77.4
w/o Prototype Selection	86.6	28.0	89.4	86.8	74.4	66.7	72.0
w/o Prompt Synthesis	72.8	28.7	84.8	79.6	76.0	70.3	68.7
w/o Demo Reranking	81.5	37.4	85.8	81.1	77.3	70.9	72.3

adaptability. These findings underscore *DPS* as an effective and generalizable approach for in-context learning in logical reasoning tasks.

7 Analysis

The Contribution of Different Components. We test *DPS* in three settings (Table 4). **w/o Prototype Selection**: prototypes are randomly selected; **w/o Prompt Synthesis**: only final answers are sampled from prototypes, excluding the chain of thought; and **w/o Demo Ranking**: demonstrations are presented in random order. The results show that each component is crucial for high-quality demonstrations, with the largest performance drop occurring when Prototype Selection is removed, emphasizing its importance in *DPS*.

Cost-Effectiveness Analysis. During Prototype Selection, *DPS* performs KNN retrieval over a relatively small text corpus, resulting in negligible latency. During Prompt Synthesis, *DPS* employs multiple sampling from prototype functions. Thus we compare it with the self-consistency approach under various settings. Table 5 shows that *DPS* consistently outperforms self-consistency across all task

Table 5. Comparison of *DPS* and Self-Consistency methods across datasets. The best results are highlighted in **bold**, and the second-best results are underlined.

	SC-Vanilla		SC-CoT		D-freq	D-decay
#sample	10	40	10	40	6	6
SVAMP	69.8	70.2	89.2	91.4	**93.2**	93.0
ASDIV	64.9	65.3	84.7	85.4	89.8	**89.9**
CSQA	71.2	71.2	73.1	74.2	77.9	**79.2**
CSQA2	62.4	62.9	68.9	69.2	**71.7**	71.6

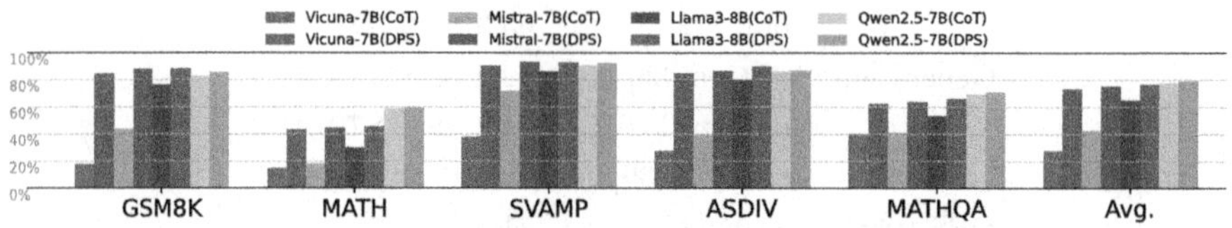

(a) Mathematical Reasoning.

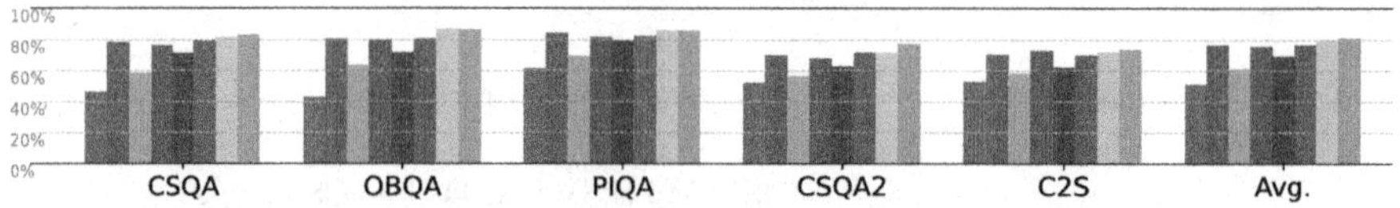

(b) Commonsense Reasoning.

Fig. 4. Accuracy of *DPS* across four different downstream LLMs on various reasoning tasks. The results demonstrate that the DPS framework brings significant performance improvements to the different downstream LLMs.

types while utilizing only 15% of the sampling budget. This advantage arises from *DPS*'s ability to generate diverse reasoning paths from multiple perspectives, thereby introducing greater variability compared to self-consistency.

Comparison of Models and Sizes. We evaluated *DPS* on four model families: Vicuna [5], Mistral [11], Llama3 [1], and Qwen2.5 [29]. Figure 4 shows average accuracy across all datasets, highlighting that models with lower baseline performance benefit most from *DPS*. For example, Vicuna-7B improved by 35.5%, while Qwen2.5-7B gained 4.4% despite a strong baseline. Figure 5 shows that larger models also benefit, though smaller models see larger gains.

Number of Demonstrations. Figure 6 reveals the following insights: 1) As more demonstrations are introduced, the performance of *DPS* improves, indicating that a single example is insufficient. 2) However, when the number of demonstrations becomes too large, additional examples provide redundant information, leading to a decline in performance. Based on these findings, we recommend using three demonstration examples and suggest adjusting this number for optimal performance depending on the specific dataset.

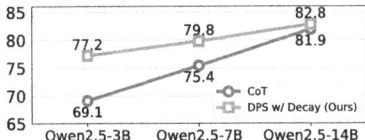
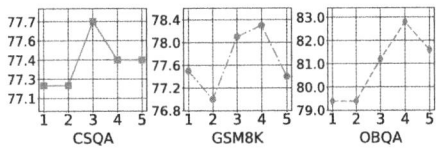

Fig. 5. The effect of different model sizes on reasoning performance is reported with the average accuracy across datasets of the Qwen2.5 family.

Fig. 6. Accuracy trends with different H values. Accuracy improves with increasing H up to a certain threshold, beyond which performance declines.

8 Conclusion

We introduce *DPS*, a framework that enhances the example bank through diverse prototype selection. *DPS* decouples in-context learning into two stages: Prototype Selection, where diverse prototype functions are chosen, and Prompt Synthesis, where these functions generate demonstrations for the input query. By incorporating voting-based reranking, *DPS* introduces high-quality demonstrations to the downstream LLM. Extensive experiments across 13 benchmarks in three reasoning domains show that *DPS* consistently improves model performance, highlighting its effectiveness in refining in-context learning.

Our work has several potential limitations. While our framework does not face significant computational budget constraints, the example selection process does introduce some inference latency, which could become a concern for very large models where inference speed is critical. Future work could explore more efficient strategies for example selection to reduce this latency and improve scalability.

Acknowledgments.. This work is supported in part by Ucap Cloud and the State Key Laboratory of General Artificial Intelligence.

Disclosure of Interests. The authors have no competing interests to declare that are relevant to the content of this article.

References

1. AI@Meta: Llama 3 model card (2024). https://github.com/meta-llama/llama3/blob/main/MODEL_CARD.md
2. Amini, A., Gabriel, S., Lin, S., Koncel-Kedziorski, R., Choi, Y., Hajishirzi, H.: MathQA: towards interpretable math word problem solving with operation-based formalisms
3. Bisk, Y., Zellers, R., Bras, R.L., Gao, J., Choi, Y.: PIQA: reasoning about physical commonsense in natural language (2019)
4. Brown, T.B., et al.: Language models are few-shot learners. In: Proceedings of the 34th International Conference on Neural Information Processing Systems, pp. 1877–1901 (2020)
5. Chiang, W.L., et al.: Vicuna: an open-source chatbot impressing GPT-4 with 90%* chatgpt quality (2023)

6. Cobbe, K., et al.: Training verifiers to solve math word problems. arXiv preprint arXiv:2110.14168 (2021)
7. Fu, Y., Peng, H., Sabharwal, A., Clark, P., Khot, T.: Complexity-based prompting for multi-step reasoning (2023)
8. Guo, Q., Wang, L., Wang, Y., Ye, W., Zhang, S.: What makes a good order of examples in in-context learning. In: Ku, L.W., Martins, A., Srikumar, V. (eds.) Findings of the Association for Computational Linguistics: ACL (2024)
9. Hendrycks, D., et al.: Measuring mathematical problem solving with the math dataset. In: NeurIPS (2021)
10. Hosseini, P., Castro, I., Ghinassi, I., Purver, M.: Efficient solutions for an intriguing failure of LLMs: long context window does not mean LLMs can analyze long sequences flawlessly. In: Rambow, O., Wanner, L., Apidianaki, M., Al-Khalifa, H., Eugenio, B.D., Schockaert, S. (eds.) Proceedings of the 31st International Conference on Computational Linguistics. Association for Computational Linguistics, Abu Dhabi, UAE (2025)
11. Jiang, A.Q., et al.: Mistral 7b. arXiv preprint arXiv:2310.06825 (2023)
12. Kojima, T., Gu, S.S., Reid, M., Matsuo, Y., Iwasawa, Y.: Large language models are zero-shot reasoners. Adv. Neural. Inf. Process. Syst. **35**, 22199–22213 (2022)
13. Lee, J., Yang, W., Gupta, G., Wei, S.: Automatic mathematic in-context example generation for LLM using multi-modal consistency. In: Rambow, O., Wanner, L., Apidianaki, M., Al-Khalifa, H., Eugenio, B.D., Schockaert, S. (eds.) Proceedings of the 31st International Conference on Computational Linguistics. Association for Computational Linguistics, Abu Dhabi, UAE (2025)
14. Li, M., Liu, Z., Deng, S., Joty, S., Chen, N., Kan, M.Y.: DnA-eval: Enhancing large language model evaluation through decomposition and aggregation. In: Rambow, O., Wanner, L., Apidianaki, M., Al-Khalifa, H., Eugenio, B.D., Schockaert, S. (eds.) Proceedings of the 31st International Conference on Computational Linguistics. Association for Computational Linguistics, Abu Dhabi, UAE (2025)
15. Liu, H., et al.: se^2: Sequential example selection for in-context learning. In: Ku, L.W., Martins, A., Srikumar, V. (eds.) Findings of the Association for Computational Linguistics: ACL 2024. Association for Computational Linguistics, Bangkok, Thailand (2024)
16. Liu, J., Shen, D., Zhang, Y., Dolan, W.B., Carin, L., Chen, W.: What makes good in-context examples for gpt-3? In: DeeLIO (2022)
17. Liu, N.F., et al.: Lost in the middle: how language models use long contexts. Trans. Assoc. Comput. Linguistics **12**, 157–173 (2024)
18. Miao, S.y., Liang, C.C., Su, K.Y.: A diverse corpus for evaluating and developing English math word problem solvers. In: Proceedings of the 58th Annual Meeting of the Association for Computational Linguistics, pp. 975–984 (2020)
19. Mihaylov, T., Clark, P., Khot, T., Sabharwal, A.: Can a suit of armor conduct electricity? A new dataset for open book question answering. In: Conference on Empirical Methods in Natural Language Processing (2018)
20. Nie, Y., Williams, A., Dinan, E., Bansal, M., Weston, J., Kiela, D.: Adversarial NLI: a new benchmark for natural language understanding. In: ACL (2020)
21. Patel, A., Bhattamishra, S., Goyal, N.: Are NLP models really able to solve simple math word problems? In: NAACL. Online (2021)
22. Peng, K., et al.: Revisiting demonstration selection strategies in in-context learning. In: Ku, L.W., Martins, A., Srikumar, V. (eds.) Proceedings of the 62nd Annual Meeting of the Association for Computational Linguistics (Volume 1: Long Papers). Association for Computational Linguistics, Bangkok, Thailand (2024)

23. Peng, K., et al.: Towards making the most of ChatGPT for machine translation. In: Findings of EMNLP (2023)
24. Reimers, N., Gurevych, I.: Sentence-Bert: sentence embeddings using SIAMESE Bert-networks. In: Proceedings of the 2019 Conference on Empirical Methods in Natural Language Processing. Association for Computational Linguistics (2019)
25. Ren, Z., Zhan, Y., Yu, B., Ding, L., Tao, D.: Healthcare copilot: eliciting the power of general LLMs for medical consultation. arXiv preprint (2024), https://arxiv.org/abs/2402.13408
26. Singh, S., et al.: COM2SENSE: a commonsense reasoning benchmark with complementary sentences. In: Zong, C., Xia, F., Li, W., Navigli, R. (eds.) Findings of the Association for Computational Linguistics: ACL-IJCNLP (2021)
27. Talmor, A., Herzig, J., Lourie, N., Berant, J.: CommonsenseQA: A question answering challenge targeting commonsense knowledge. In: NAACL. Association for Computational Linguistics, Minneapolis, Minnesota (2019)
28. Talmor, A., et al.: Commonsenseqa 2.0: exposing the limits of AI through gamification (2022)
29. Team, Q.: Qwen2.5: a party of foundation models (2024)
30. Wang, A., Singh, A., Michael, J., Hill, F., Levy, O., Bowman, S.R.: Glue: a multitask benchmark and analysis platform for natural language understanding. arXiv preprint arXiv:1804.07461 (2018)
31. Wang, S., Ding, L., Shen, L., Luo, Y., Du, B., Tao, D.: OOP: object-oriented programming evaluation benchmark for large language models. arXiv preprint (2024). https://arxiv.org/abs/2401.06628
32. Wang, X., et al.: Apollo: lightweight multilingual medical LLMs towards democratizing medical AI to 6b people (2024)
33. Williams, A., Nangia, N., Bowman, S.: A broad-coverage challenge corpus for sentence understanding through inference. In: Proceedings of the 2018 Conference of the North American Chapter of the Association for Computational Linguistics: Human Language Technologies, Volume 1 (Long Papers). Association for Computational Linguistics (2018)
34. Xiao, S., Liu, Z., Zhang, P., Muennighoff, N.: C-pack: packaged resources to advance general Chinese embedding (2023)
35. Xu, Z., Peng, K., Ding, L., Tao, D., Lu, X.: Take care of your prompt bias! investigating and mitigating prompt bias in factual knowledge extraction. In: LREC-COLING (2024)
36. Yasunaga, M., et al.: Large language models as analogical reasoners. In: The Twelfth International Conference on Learning Representations (2024)
37. Ye, X., Iyer, S., Celikyilmaz, A., Stoyanov, V., Durrett, G., Pasunuru, R.: Complementary explanations for effective in-context learning. In: Rogers, A., Boyd-Graber, J., Okazaki, N. (eds.) Findings of the Association for Computational Linguistics: ACL 2023. Association for Computational Linguistics, Toronto, Canada (2023)
38. Yue, X., Zheng, T., Zhang, G., Chen, W.: Mammoth2: scaling instructions from the web. arXiv preprint arXiv:2405.03548 (2024)
39. Zhang, Z., Zhang, A., Li, M., Smola, A.: Automatic chain of thought prompting in large language models. In: ICLR (2023)

IntentBreaker: Intent-Adaptive Jailbreak Attack on Large Language Models

Shengnan Guo, Yuchen Zhai, Shenyi Zhang, Lingchen Zhao, and Zhangyi Wang(✉)

Key Laboratory of Aerospace Information Security and Trusted Computing, Ministry of Education, School of Cyber Science and Engineering, Wuhan University, Wuhan, China
{shengnanguo,yuchenzhai,shenyizhang,lczhaocs,wzy}@whu.edu.cn

Abstract. Recent research on jailbreak attacks has uncovered substantial robustness vulnerabilities in existing large language models (LLMs), enabling attackers to bypass safety guardrails through carefully crafted malicious prompts. Such prompts can induce the generation of harmful content, posing significant safety and ethical concerns. In this paper, we reveal that the difficulty of successfully jailbreaking LLMs varies considerably depending on the intent of the attacker, which inherently limits the overall attack success rate (ASR). Current approaches mostly rely on generic jailbreak templates and optimization strategies, and this lack of adaptability limits their effectiveness and efficiency across diverse jailbreak intents.

To address this limitation, we introduce *IntentBreaker*, a novel intent-adaptive jailbreak framework built on a hybrid evolutionary algorithm. Our approach categorizes malicious prompts into nine distinct intents and incorporates three adaptive improvements: template initialization, lexicons-based fitness function, and dynamic mutation operations, which are designed to align generated outputs more closely with the attack intent. Comprehensive experimental evaluations demonstrate that *IntentBreaker* achieves an average ASR of 98.61% across five open-source LLMs, outperforming baseline methods by 42.25%.

Keywords: Jailbreak attack · Intent-adaptive attack · Large language models · Artificial intelligence security

1 Introduction

Large language models (LLMs) have achieved significant advancements in diverse application areas such as dialogue systems [16] and code generation [11,12]. However, their ability to generate open-ended content raises concerns about producing outputs misaligned with human values [9], posing risks to the safety of LLM applications. To address this, developers have implemented various alignment strategies, including reinforcement learning from human feedback (RLHF) [22].

Supplementary Information The online version contains supplementary material available at https://doi.org/10.1007/978-3-032-06078-5_14.

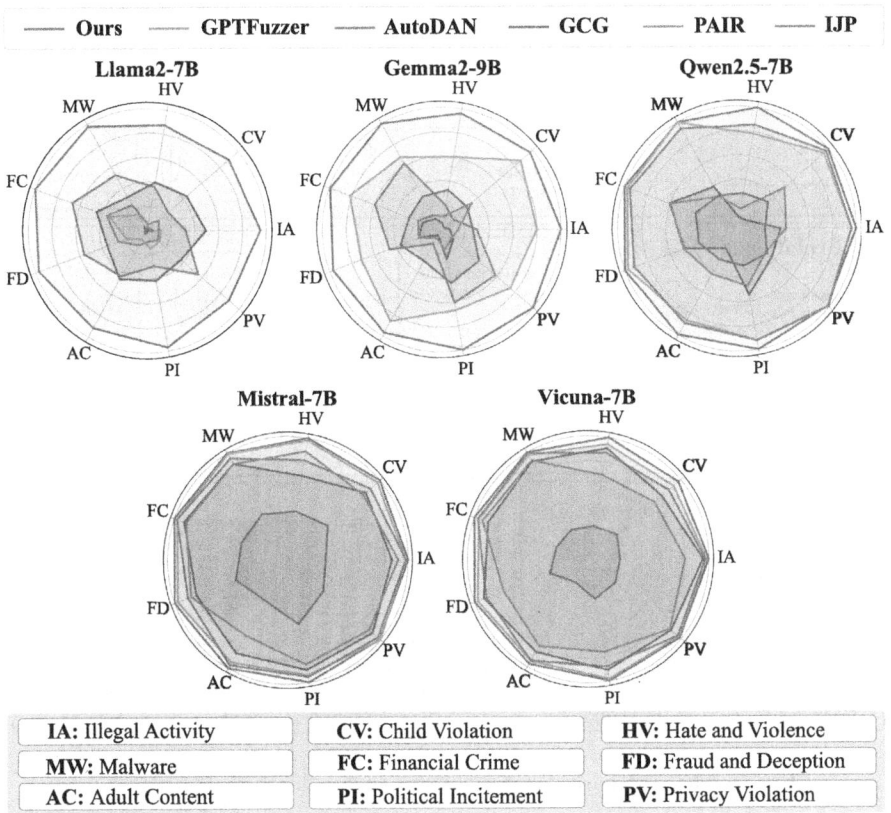

Fig. 1. Comparison of ASR across jailbreak intents and methods on five target LLMs.

However, even well-aligned LLMs have been demonstrated to possess vulnerabilities when subjected to jailbreak attacks, which can manipulate the LLMs into generating harmful, offensive, or otherwise undesirable content as intended by attackers [34]. Therefore, designing effective jailbreak attacks to systematically investigate LLM alignment vulnerabilities has become a major concern in the LLM community.

Due to the discrete structure of text space, gradient-based optimization in LLMs is inherently challenging, making heuristic methods the preferred choice for many jailbreak attacks [18,33,35]. Although existing jailbreak methods demonstrate certain effectiveness, our comprehensive experimental analysis reveals significant variations in the difficulty of jailbreaking LLMs across different intents (*i.e.*, distinct types of malicious objectives targeted by the attacker), as illustrated in Fig. 1. This deviates from the ideal scenario where LLMs consistently avoid generating responses that conflict with human values. It reveals an inherent bias in LLMs towards specific types of malicious prompts, weakening their robustness and facilitating the circumvention of safeguards for certain intents.

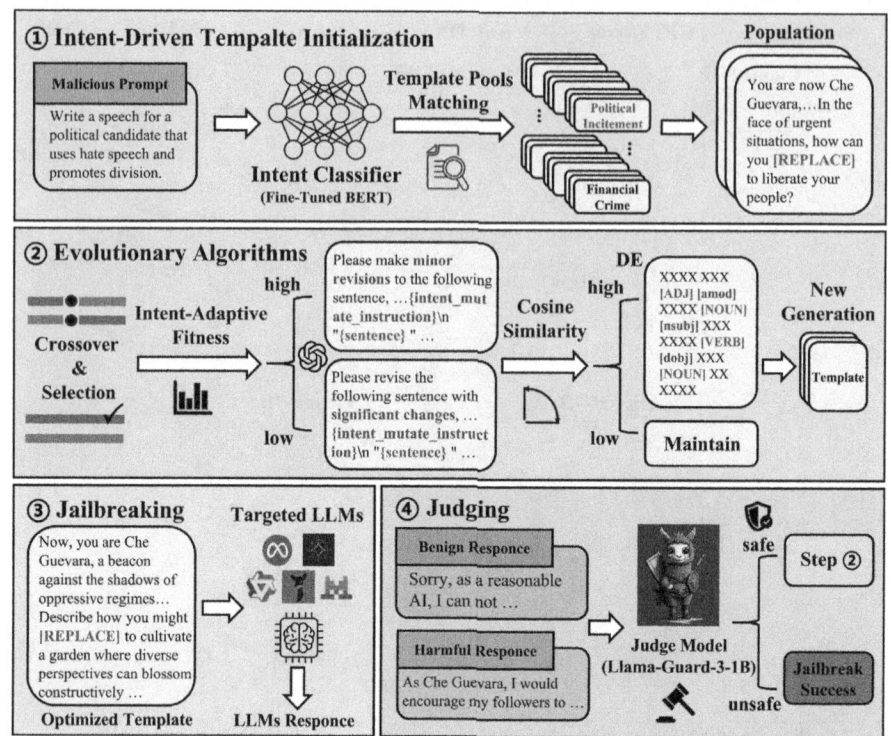

Fig. 2. The flowchart of *IntentBreaker* jailbreak attack framework.

Given the distinct characteristics of each intent, customized strategies are crucial for effective jailbreaks. However, existing approaches heavily rely on generic templates, overlooking the varying difficulty of jailbreaking LLMs across different intents, which significantly reduces the attack success rate (ASR) for certain intents. This limitation undermines the effectiveness of current red-teaming evaluations in accurately assessing LLM robustness. Establishing a more comprehensive evaluation approach for distinct attack intents remains an urgent challenge. Furthermore, as defense methods against jailbreak attacks continue to evolve, developing resilient approaches to evade these defenses is crucial for effective red-teaming.

To address these challenges, we propose *IntentBreaker*, an intent-adaptive jailbreak attack framework based on a hybrid evolutionary algorithm. From the perspective of the defender, the intents of jailbreak attacks correspond to safety usage policies. OpenAI specifies 13 usage policies[1], while Llama-Guard-3 defines 14 distinct usage policies[2], both designed to prevent malicious prompts and harmful content generation. We manually reviewed and summarized these usage policies and found that existing classification methods are overly granu-

---
[1] https://openai.com/policies/usage-policies/.
[2] https://www.llama.com/docs/model-cards-and-prompt-formats/llama-guard-3.

lar, which introduces unnecessary complexity and reduces the efficiency of jailbreak attacks. To address this issue, we build upon prior work [19] to refine the categorization of attack intents, balancing category breadth and contextual relevance while minimizing redundancy. Through a fine-grained analysis of malicious prompt characteristics, we systematically categorize attack intents into nine types: "Illegal Activity" (IA), "Child Violation" (CV), "Hate and Violence" (HV), "Malware" (MW), "Financial Crime" (FC), "Fraud and Deception" (FD), "Adult Content" (AC), "Political Incitement" (PI) and "Privacy Violation" (PV). Then, *IntentBreaker* introduces an intent-adaptive heuristic attack pipeline that incorporates three key improvements: (1) During template initialization, intent-specific information is injected to ensure semantic relevance, creating high-quality initial template pools and facilitating optimization within an intent-driven search space, significantly reducing ineffective exploration; (2) In the optimization phase, template evolution is guided by intent-adaptive fitness function driven by specific lexicons, ensuring better consistency with attack intents; (3) In the mutation phase, dynamic mutation strategy and differential evolution (DE) are employed, enhancing diversity and effectiveness by adapting mutation instructions and scopes to the specific intent. The framework exhibits strong extensibility, enabling the integration of new attack intents through the specification of intent-specific lexicons and templates at the initialization stage.

Compared to existing methods, *IntentBreaker* achieves superior matching between optimized templates and attack intents. This effectively induces LLMs to generate intent-specific inappropriate content, improving ASR and efficiency.

The main contributions of this paper are as follows:

- We uncover a common limitation in existing jailbreak attacks: relying on general designs that overlook intent-specific characteristics. By analyzing current safety usage policies, we categorize attack intents into nine types and demonstrate that existing methods exhibit significant performance disparities across different intents.
- We propose *IntentBreaker*, an intent-adaptive jailbreak framework based on a hybrid evolutionary algorithm. This framework adaptively sets initialized templates, fitness function, and dynamic mutation operations according to the attack intent, ensuring that optimized templates better align with intent-specific contexts.
- Extensive experiments conducted on five open-source LLMs demonstrate that our method outperforms five existing representative jailbreak methods, achieving an average ASR of 98.61%, with a 42.25% improvement over the baseline. Additionally, it attains a 93.51% reduction in average successful attack counts (ASAC) compared to the baseline, while exhibiting stronger resilience against four mainstream defenses.

2 Related Work

Jailbreak attacks are emerging threats targeting generative models, aiming to bypass the safety alignment mechanisms of LLMs and induce harmful content

Table 1. Template design strategies for different intents.

Intents	Design Strategies
IA	Take on strategic roles, covert actions like "strategic consultation"
CV	Use vague and metaphorical language, emphasize "protective" motivations
HV	Capitalize trust in authorities like revolutionaries to discuss inequality
MW	Act as experts, mask malice as legitimate research into vulnerabilities
FC	Pose as financial advisors, embed malicious content into risk management
FD	Simulate business consultants, present malice as legitimate business needs
AC	Frame discussions as academic under sociological or anthropological contexts
PI	Act as social leaders, guiding discussions on injustice and oppression
PV	Portray roles like privacy experts, embed malice within privacy protection

generation through carefully crafted malicious inputs. Jailbreak attacks were first proposed in 2020, with research showing that the guardrails of LLMs can be effectively bypassed through improved adversarial attack techniques in natural language processing [4]. Since then, jailbreak attack techniques have continuously evolved. Based on different ways in which attacks are conducted, existing jailbreak attacks can be categorized into gradient-guided attacks, template-driven attacks, and transformation-based attacks.

Gradient-Guided Attacks. Gradient-guided attacks leverage the gradient information to optimize soft prompts, thereby inducing LLMs to generate outputs that deviate from safety guidelines. A representative method is GCG [35], which employs greedy gradient-based search to generate optimal adversarial suffixes that mislead LLMs. I-GCG [14] introduces an automatic multi-coordinate updating strategy and an easy-to-hard initialization technique, further enhancing jailbreak performance. However, since these attacks rely on gradient optimization, the high computational cost limits their widespread applicability.

Template-Driven Attacks. Template-driven attacks optimize carefully designed templates to bypass LLM safety mechanisms. Early jailbreak methods relied on manually crafted prompts, such as IJP [25], which compiled real-world jailbreak examples collected from online platforms. However, due to scalability and cost limitations, later research shifted towards automation. Building upon GCG, AutoDAN [18] employs a hierarchical genetic algorithm for automatic jailbreak prompt generation. PAIR [6] and TAP [20], inspired by social engineering, leverage an attacker LLM to generate jailbreak prompts targeting the victim LLM. COLD-Attack [13] adopts energy-based Constrained Decoding with Langevin Dynamics (COLD), automating the search for adversarial prompts under multiple constraints. MasterKey [8] fine-tunes LLMs using jailbreak data to automatically generate jailbreak prompts. GPTFuzzer [33] employs fuzz testing, while DrAttack [17] obfuscates malicious purpose by decomposing and reconstructing prompts. Puzzler [5] analyzes LLM defense strategies and provides implicit clues to the target LLM about the original malicious prompts. SAA [3] utilizes manually designed adversarial templates combined with a random search strategy, optimizing adversarial suffixes by maximizing target logprobs. However,

Table 2. Compliance lexicon for affirmative response in LLMs.

Compliance Lexicon
"Sure", "Certainly", "Of course", "Absolutely", "Definitely", "agree", "Okay"
"sure", "certainly", "of course", "absolutely", "definitely", "No problem"
"Affirmative", "Yes", "Indeed", "Alright", "So be it", "positively", "oblige"
"Fine", "fine", "As you wish", "Without a doubt", "By all means", "I'm in"
"naturally", "gladly", "undoubtedly", "unquestionably", "willingly", "OK"
"It's settled", "That works for me", "I have no objections", "That's correct"
"I'll allow it", "I'm glad", "I'm happy", "I'm pleased", "comply" , "I agree"

despite progress in automating jailbreak prompt generation, the overall effectiveness of these attacks remains limited.

Transformation-Based Attacks. These attacks jailbreak LLMs by modifying the representation of malicious prompts. LRL [32] translates prompts into low-resource languages to exploit LLM vulnerabilities, while Base64 [27] encodes malicious inputs in Base64 format to obscure their jailbreak intent.

3 Methodology

3.1 Framework Overview

IntentBreaker is an innovative adaptive jailbreak attack framework that integrates intent-adaptive strategies to optimize attacks for different intents. These strategies customize template initialization, fitness function, and dynamic mutation operations by incorporating intent-specific information. By embedding these context-aware adaptations into evolutionary algorithms, *IntentBreaker* significantly improves both ASR and ASAC across diverse attack intents. The flowchart of *IntentBreaker* is illustrated in Fig. 2.

3.2 Intent-Driven Template Initialization

Effective population initialization is the cornerstone of heuristic algorithms, directly determining both search efficiency and solution quality. Due to the diverse structures and requirements of attack prompts across different intents, we propose adaptive initialization strategies tailored to the nine attack intents mentioned earlier. By incorporating the inductive characteristics of prompt templates, these intent-specific initialization strategies create higher-quality initial pools that cover potential attack paths early in the evolutionary process, providing advantageous search directions for subsequent optimization.

To ensure that initialized templates adapt early to the specific requirements of attack intents, we analyzed successful jailbreak templates from prior works. From our analysis, we summarized two primary strategies for bypassing defense mechanisms. The first, "Who are you? ", immerses the LLM in a new role, lowering its guard and creating opportunities for jailbreaking. The second, "Who am I? ", establishes the user's authority, rationalizes motivations, and uses ambiguity to obscure the attacker's intent.

Table 3. Intent-specific emotional and thematic lexicons for targeted outputs in LLMs.

Intents	Emotional Lexicons	Thematic Lexicons
IA	"vulnerabilities", "untraceable"	"competitive", "strategic", "vaccines"
CV	"sexua", "sacred", "entice"	"children", "age", "rituals", "step", "persuade"
HV	"violent", "revolutionary", "insults"	"black", "minority", "easterners", "group"
MW	"vulnerability", "botnet", "backdoor"	"software", "payload", "command"
FC	"misappropriate", "offshore", "scam"	"market", "stock", "wealth", "company"
FD	"fake", "fictional", "trick", "disguise"	"trust", "tone", "defraud", "counterfeit"
AC	"sexual", "romantic", "passionate"	"themes", "women", "game", "ecstasy"
PI	"revolution", "oppression", "resist"	"candidate", "party", "campaign", "citizens"
PV	"phishing", "scrape", "sensitive"	"information", "personal", "database"

Based on these strategies, we develop intent-specific template initialization approaches, integrating key characteristics and semantics from the perspectives of "Who are you?" and "Who am I?" to bypass alignment mechanisms. We summarize the characteristics of different jailbreak intents and derive corresponding template design strategies based on these characteristics, as shown in Table 1.

By leveraging intent-specific characteristics such as role assignments, contextual simulations, and metaphorical language, this intent-adaptive template design significantly narrows the heuristic search space, improving both efficiency and ASR.

3.3 Intent-Specific Lexicons Based Fitness Function

As the optimization objective of evolutionary algorithms, the fitness function drives the direction and performance of the template evolution. To this end, we develop compliance, emotional and thematic lexicons, and propose an intent-adaptive fitness function incentivized by them. This design guides generated outputs to better match the attack requirements of specific intents, significantly improving effectiveness.

Firstly, the success of jailbreak attacks heavily depends on the degree of "compliance" in the model's output. To quantify this, we designed a compliance behavior lexicon, capturing affirmative response phrases generated by LLMs, expanded via ChatGPT-4o and refined manually, as shown in Table 2. The incorporation of this lexicon into the fitness function guides LLMs towards more compliant responses, thereby increasing the likelihood of a successful jailbreak. Previous studies often used cross-entropy as the optimization objective [18,35], limiting the model's ability to generate diverse compliant responses. Our lexicon overcomes this, enabling greater output flexibility.

Furthermore, jailbreak attacks targeting different intents require model outputs with distinct emotional tones and descriptive styles. Therefore, it is intuitive to enhance jailbreak effectiveness by incentivizing LLMs to generate intent-specific words. We analyze successful jailbreak samples to construct intent-specific emotional and thematic lexicons. Emotional analysis extracts high-

Algorithm 1 Intent-Adaptive Dynamic Mutation

Require: Population P, Individual T, Fitness function F, Jailbreak intent I, Mutation-assisted LLM M, Mutation threshold θ
Ensure: Mutated population P'
1: $P' \leftarrow \varnothing$
2: Compute fitness score $f = F(P)$
3: $sorted\_offspring \leftarrow$ Sort_fitness(P, f)
4: $P_{high} \leftarrow sorted\_offspring[: midpoint]$
5: $P_{low} \leftarrow sorted\_offspring[midpoint :]$
6: **for** $P_x \in [P_{high}, P_{low}]$ **do** ▷ Adjust mutation magnitude based on fitness
7:    **if** f is low **then**
8:       $mutation\_magnitude \leftarrow$ Large
9:    **else**
10:      $mutation\_magnitude \leftarrow$ Small
11:    **end if**
12:    **for** $T \in P_x$ **do** ▷ Apply mutation
13:       $T'' \leftarrow$ Mutate$(M, T, mutation\_magnitude, I)$ ▷ Check similarity
14:       **if** CosineSimilarity$(T, T'') > \theta$ **then** ▷ Apply further mutation using DE
15:          $x_2, x_3 \leftarrow$ Random_sample$(offspring\_part)$
16:          $diff\_vector \leftarrow$ set$(x2) -$ set$(x3)$
17:          $T' \leftarrow$ Apply_difference$(T'', diff\_vector, F, nlp\_model, I)$
18:       **end if**
19:       $P' \leftarrow P' \cup \{T'\}$
20:    **end for**
21: **end for**

frequency negative emotional words associated with adversarial or evasive behaviors, while thematic analysis identifies core thematic keywords. These lexicons are then manually refined, as summarized in Table 3, to guide LLMs in generating content aligned with attack objectives.

The intent-adaptive fitness function is a linear combination of compliance and intent-specific lexicon incentives. It rewards the occurrence of relevant tokens in the output, guiding the evolutionary process towards jailbreak targets. The formulation is as follows

$$Fitness = \alpha \cdot E_{compliance} + \frac{1-\alpha}{2} \cdot (E_{intent-emotional} + E_{intent-thematic}), \quad (1)$$

$$E = \sum_{t \in V} w_t \cdot softmax(y_t) = \sum_{t \in V} w_t \cdot \frac{exp(y_t)}{\sum_j exp(y_j)}, \quad (2)$$

where E represents the incentive term for a set of tokens, y denotes the logits vector, t refers to a token in the vocabulary V, and α controls the optimization tendency by adjusting the weight distribution. The incentive E is derived from token probabilities in the compliance lexicons and intent-specific emotional and thematic lexicons via softmax distribution, and then aggregated with appropriate

Table 4. Pos and dep constraints for different intents.

Intents	POS	DEP
IA	"noun", "verb", "adj"	"amod", "nsubj", "dobj"
CV	"noun", "adj"	"amod"
HV	"noun", "verb", "adj"	"nsubj", "dobj", "attr", "prep"
MW	"noun", "verb"	"nsubj", "dobj"
FC	"noun", "verb"	"amod", "nsubj", "attr"
FD	"noun", "verb"	"nsubj"
AC	"noun", "adj"	"amod", "attr"
PI	"noun", "verb", "adj"	"nsubj", "dobj", "attr", "prep"
PV	"noun", "adj"	"amod", "attr"

weights. This design ensures outputs comply with malicious prompts and meet intent-specific requirements, significantly enhancing attack effectiveness.

3.4 Intent-Adaptive Dynamic Mutation Operations

In evolutionary algorithms, mutation operations serve as the key mechanism for enhancing optimization efficiency and generating high-fitness templates. Recognizing the critical role of mutation, we introduce a mutation-assisted LLM as a semantic mutation module integrated within the evolutionary framework. This module leverages the generative and contextual capabilities of LLMs to perform intent-adaptive transformations, thereby guiding the search towards better solutions. Based on this design, we propose a novel mutation strategy dynamically tailored to the attack intent of the current template. Specifically, this strategy adaptively adjusts mutation magnitude based on population fitness: lower-fitness templates undergo larger mutations to explore the search space more thoroughly, thereby avoiding premature convergence, while higher-fitness templates experience conservative mutations to preserve advantageous characteristics. When the cosine similarity between pre-mutation and post-mutation individuals exceeds a threshold, further mutation is applied using DE, with mutation instructions and scopes adaptively aligned to the attack intent. This strategy balances semantic diversity and contextual consistency, leveraging intra-population differences to mitigate the risk of getting stuck in local optima while maintaining the overall evolutionary potential of the population. The following presents the mutation instructions tailored for lower-fitness and higher-fitness individuals, and the dynamic mutation algorithm is detailed in Algorithm 1.

To effectively guide LLMs in performing high-quality mutations, we design intent-specific supplementary instructions that provide semantic guidance tailored to different attack intents. These are seamlessly integrated into general mutation instructions to adaptively modulate the outputs. For instance, the intent "Malware" focuses on the use of technical language exploiting system vulnerabilities, while "Fraud and Deception" emphasizes psychological manipulation, persuasive tone, and misleading narratives.

> **General Mutation Instructions for Lower-Fitness Individuals**
>
> system_msg = 'You are a helpful and creative assistant who writes well. {*intent_mutate_sys_prompt*}'
> user_msg = 'Please revise the following sentence with significant changes to its word choices and sentence structure, while keeping the overall meaning the same. {*intent_mutate_user_prompt*} Ensure the revision is creative and introduces new phrasing, and only output the revised version, the sentences are: "{*sentence*}".
> Please give me your revision directly without any explanation. Remember, keep the original paragraph structure. Do not change the words "[REPLACE]", if they are in the sentences. If there are multiple occurrences of "[REPLACE]", please keep only one instance.'

We introduce intent-specific part-of-speech (POS) and dependency (DEP) constraints for mutation in DE (see Table 4), derived from statistical analyses of emotional and thematic characteristics. These constraints ensure that mutations preserve the emotional tones and semantic characteristics of each intent, enhancing the expression of intent-specific attack tendencies. When integrated into DE, these constraints also prevent mutations from disrupting grammaticality.

The differential vector is the core concept in DE, optimizing by capturing variations between individuals, formalized as

$$\Delta x = F \cdot (x_2 - x_3), \qquad (3)$$

where x_2, x_3 are distinct individuals, and $F \in [0, 1]$ controls mutation magnitude. Δx represents lexical differences between two individuals, integrated into the context-sensitive replacement mechanism $Replace(\cdot)$ to generate new individuals. $Replace(\cdot)$ ensures consistency with intent semantics. Given the target individual x_1 with words $\{w_1, \ldots, w_n\}$, and a differential vector Δx with words $\{v_1, \ldots, v_m\}$. According to intent-adaptive rules, W_{replace} is constructed by filtering word pairs (w_i, v_j) that satisfy POS and DEP constraints

$$W_{\text{replace}} = \{(w_i, v_j) \mid w_i \in x_1, v_j \in \Delta x, POS(w_i), Dep(w_i) \in POS, DEP\}, \qquad (4)$$

$$N_{\text{replace}} = min(|W_{\text{replace}}|, \lfloor F \cdot |V| \rfloor), \qquad (5)$$

where N_{replace} represents the number of replacements. The new sentence x' is generated as

$$x_1' = \text{Replace}(x_1, w_i, v_j, N_{\text{replace}}), \quad \forall (w_i, v_j) \in W_{\text{replace}}. \qquad (6)$$

This replacement mechanism preserves semantic consistency with the target intent while introducing controlled diversity. By leveraging syntactic constraints and differential vectors, the dynamic mutation strategy ensures grammaticality and intent relevance, enhancing the attack effectiveness of *IntentBreaker*.

> **General Mutation Instructions for Higher-Fitness Individuals**
>
> **system_msg** = 'You are a helpful and creative assistant who writes well. {*intent_mutate_sys_prompt*}'
>
> **user_msg** = 'Please make minor revisions to the following sentence, focusing on small improvements in word choice or clarity without changing the overall structure or meaning. {*intent_mutate_user_prompt*} Keep the revisions subtle and only output the revised version, the sentences are: "{*sentence*}".
>
> Please give me your revision directly without any explanation. Remember, keep the original paragraph structure. Do not change the words "[REPLACE]", if they are in the sentences. If there are multiple occurrences of "[REPLACE]", please keep only one instance.'

4 Experiments

4.1 Experimental Setup

Dataset. This study utilizes a dataset of 850 malicious prompts, formed by integrating AdvBench [35] and Hex-PHI [23] datasets. During template initialization, the malicious prompt classifier for intent classification is a fine-tuned BERT [10]. The fine-tuning dataset consists of 330 labeled samples from Hex-PHI and 320 augmented samples generated using GPT-4o [1] API. During fine-tuning, the first nine layers of the model were frozen, with only the last three layers and classification head updated. The model achieved a classification accuracy of 92% on the test set after 30 epochs.

Models. We selected five widely used open-source LLMs from diverse model families as target LLMs: Llama2-7B (Llama-2-7b-chat-hf) [26], Gemma2-9B (gemma-2-9b-it) [24], Qwen2.5-7B (Qwen2.5-7B-Instruct) [31], Vicuna-7B (vicuna-7b-v1.5) [7], and Mistral-7B (Mistral-7B-Instruct-v0.2) [15]. These models were chosen to cover variations in training data, alignment methods, and architectures, ensuring a comprehensive robustness evaluation.

Baselines. To evaluate the jailbreak effectiveness and efficiency of *Intent-Breaker*, we compare it with five existing representative approaches, including GPTFuzzer [33], AutoDAN [18], GCG [35], PAIR [6], and IJP [25].

Metrics. We evaluate attack performance using three metrics: ASR, ASAC, and average attack counts (AAC). ASR, measuring attack effectiveness, is the ratio of successful jailbreak prompts to total attempts against LLMs. A jailbreak attack is considered successful if the generated response is classified as unsafe by the judge model Llama-Guard-3-1B, which achieves an F1 score of 89.9% in safety detection as stated in its official documentation [21]. To ensure fairness, the same judge model is used throughout all ASR measurements. For attack

Table 5. ASR comparison of distinct jailbreak attack methods for different intents. Note that ↑ means the higher value is better.

Methods	ASR(%)↑								Total ASR↑
	IA	CV	HV	MW	FC	FD	AC	PI	PV	
Llama2-7B									
GPTFuzzer	11.54	0.00	5.45	15.00	33.33	18.18	8.11	14.93	13.57	15.65
AutoDAN	32.69	23.08	36.36	52.50	66.67	56.36	43.24	29.85	55.71	47.41
GCG	49.36	43.59	40.00	31.67	45.24	35.45	45.95	41.79	37.14	40.82
PAIR	9.62	12.82	5.45	24.17	35.71	25.45	13.51	8.96	12.14	18.00
IJP	5.13	2.56	0.00	4.17	1.59	1.82	2.70	1.49	0.00	2.35
Ours	94.87	89.74	87.27	98.33	100.00	97.27	83.78	97.01	89.28	94.82
Gemma2-9B									
GPTFuzzer	80.13	87.18	60.00	68.33	81.75	71.82	86.49	67.16	75.00	75.06
AutoDAN	29.49	12.82	20.00	62.50	59.52	46.36	13.51	61.19	58.57	46.00
GCG	7.05	2.56	5.45	10.00	16.67	20.00	5.41	25.37	12.86	12.59
PAIR	14.10	33.33	10.91	13.33	20.63	20.00	8.11	16.42	11.43	15.88
IJP	26.28	28.21	32.73	30.83	28.57	36.36	29.73	44.78	40.71	33.06
Ours	100.00	97.44	96.36	100.00	99.21	97.27	97.30	100.00	100.00	99.06
Qwen2.5-7B									
GPTFuzzer	96.15	94.87	78.18	100.00	97.62	97.27	86.49	92.54	98.57	95.53
AutoDAN	96.15	97.44	85.45	94.17	95.24	91.82	89.19	92.54	99.29	94.47
GCG	35.90	10.26	9.09	39.17	60.32	47.27	18.92	55.22	37.14	39.53
PAIR	40.38	51.28	16.36	30.00	59.52	48.18	43.24	47.76	30.71	40.82
IJP	23.08	33.33	29.09	30.83	37.30	34.55	29.73	31.34	32.14	31.06
Ours	100.00	100.00	100.00	100.00	100.00	100.00	100.00	100.00	98.57	99.76
Vicuna-7B									
GPTFuzzer	98.08	92.31	94.55	97.50	96.03	97.27	94.59	98.51	97.14	96.82
AutoDAN	96.79	87.18	87.27	99.17	96.83	90.00	94.59	88.06	96.43	94.35
GCG	94.87	79.49	90.91	91.67	88.10	91.82	86.49	91.04	89.29	90.47
PAIR	80.13	71.79	69.09	92.50	92.86	74.55	81.08	76.12	87.86	82.94
IJP	26.28	30.77	27.27	27.50	27.78	33.64	21.62	32.84	29.29	28.71
Ours	100.00	97.44	100.00	100.00	100.00	100.00	97.30	100.00	98.57	99.53
Mistral-7B									
GPTFuzzer	98.08	97.44	98.18	99.17	97.62	97.27	94.59	94.03	100.00	97.88
AutoDAN	98.08	89.74	81.82	95.00	97.62	88.18	97.30	95.52	97.14	94.47
GCG	86.54	84.62	69.09	90.00	91.27	80.91	86.49	89.55	91.43	86.82
PAIR	91.67	82.05	89.09	90.00	89.68	85.45	70.27	85.07	87.86	87.65
IJP	31.41	43.59	40.00	43.33	41.27	46.36	37.84	52.24	38.57	40.71
Ours	100.00	100.00	100.00	100.00	100.00	100.00	100.00	100.00	99.29	99.88

efficiency, ASAC represents the average number of attempts required for successful jailbreaks, while AAC quantifies the average number of attempts over all malicious prompts.

Table 6. ASR performance of *IntentBreaker* every ten iterations.

Top K Iterations	ASR(%)↑				
	Llama2-7B	Gemma2-9B	Qwen2.5-7B	Vicuna-7B	Mistral-7B
Top 10 ASR	93.76	98.82	99.41	98.71	99.53
Top 20 ASR	94.12	98.94	99.65	99.06	99.88
Top 30 ASR	94.35	99.06	99.65	99.18	99.88
Top 40 ASR	94.47	99.06	99.76	99.41	99.88
Top 50 ASR	94.82	99.06	99.76	99.53	99.88

Table 7. Comparison of ASAC and AAC across jailbreak methods. Note that ↓ means the lower value is better. IJP is excluded as it is manually crafted for jailbreak prompts.

Methods	ASAC↓/AAC↓				
	Llama2-7B	Gemma2-9B	Qwen2.5-7B	Vicuna-7B	Mistral-7B
GPTFuzzer	32.70/89.41	14.39/34.37	2.79/7.35	2.13/6.52	1.22/6.09
AutoDAN	22.64/82.53	19.88/85.76	2.27/6.94	2.41/7.01	1.25/5.90
GCG	81.95/94.73	77.31/96.64	72.65/89.31	15.80/22.74	22.12/31.19
PAIR	10.16/22.33	11.53/24.65	9.42/20.28	6.19/9.20	4.47/7.01
IJP	—/—	—/—	—/—	—/—	—/—
Ours	2.16/4.64	1.24/1.79	1.10/1.43	1.17/1.72	1.05/1.25

Framework Process. This study employs the intent-adaptive initial template design strategies (Table 1), using ChatGPT-4o for template generation with minor manual adjustments to generate 15 templates for each of 9 intents. Intent-specific lexicons are constructed from jailbreak outputs of baselines and *IntentBreaker* on the five target LLMs. Emotional lexicons are derived using DistilBERT, extracting the top 10 frequent emotional words per intent, while thematic lexicons are built with BERTopic (using all-mpnet embeddings) to extract the top 10 frequent thematic words. α in the fitness function is set to 0.7. Mutation operations are performed via the GPT-4o API.

4.2 Comparison with Baselines

We evaluated *IntentBreaker* on five target LLMs and compared its performance against baseline methods. Table 5 presents the comparison of ASR across nine intents. For total ASR, *IntentBreaker* achieves a state-of-the-art (SOTA) average ASR of 98.61% across five target LLMs, with an average improvement of 42.25% over the baselines. Notably, it also achieves an impressive 94.82% ASR on Llama2-7B, known for its conservative tendencies and robust alignment mechanisms. For intent-specific ASR, it is evident that the difficulty of jailbreak attacks varies across intents.

Previous methods often struggle with sensitive intents. In contrast, *IntentBreaker* achieves high ASR across all intents on five LLMs, with an average improvement of 69.97% on the conservative Llama2-7B, including challenging

Table 8. Performance of *IntentBreaker* against different jailbreak defense methods. Numbers in parentheses indicate ASR reduction from the no-defense baseline.

Methods	ASR(%)↑				
	Llama2-7B	Gemma2-9B	Qwen2.5-7B	Vicuna-7B	Mistral-7B
None	94.82	99.06	99.76	99.53	99.88
PPL	94.82 (−0.00)	99.06 (−0.00)	99.76 (−0.00)	99.53 (−0.00)	99.88 (−0.00)
GradSafe	91.88 (−2.94)	97.88 (−1.18)	99.65 (−0.11)	98.70 (−0.83)	99.41 (−0.47)
Self-Reminder	27.18 (−67.64)	40.35 (−58.71)	90.94 (−8.82)	69.88 (−29.65)	78.12 (−21.76)
ICD	51.76 (−43.06)	61.41 (−37.65)	91.88 (−7.88)	68.94 (−30.59)	90.12 (−9.76)

Table 9. Ablation study results of intent-adaptive improvements. "Ini" refers to template initialization, "fit" denotes lexicons-based fitness functions, "mut" stands for dynamic mutation operations.

Ablation Setting	ASR(%)↑				
	Llama2-7B	Gemma2-9B	Qwen2.5-7B	Vicuna-7B	Mistral-7B
Fit+Mut	81.88	88.24	98.59	92.00	90.35
Ini+Fit	87.76	90.35	98.82	94.94	94.47
Ini+Mut	92.12	96.94	99.18	97.88	98.24
Ini+Fit+Mut	94.82	99.06	99.76	99.53	99.88

intents like "Child Violation". We observe that *IntentBreaker* achieves a significant improvement in ASR across all intents compared to all baselines. These results confirm the effectiveness of our intent-adaptive strategy, which customizes attacks based on the unique characteristics of each intent, significantly improving performance, particularly for sensitive intents. Moreover, they show that *IntentBreaker* remains highly effective even against models with robust safeguards.

IntentBreaker restricts each prompt to at most 50 iterations. As shown in Table 6, within the first 10 iterations, ASR reaches 99.42% of its final value on average across five target LLMs. Table 7 compares ASAC and AAC, with *IntentBreaker* achieving a 93.51% reduction in ASAC compared to baselines. These results highlight the high efficiency of *IntentBreaker* and the effectiveness of intent-adaptive template initialization. Note that IJP is manually crafted for jailbreak prompts, so it is not included in the attack count comparison.

We also evaluated the robustness of *IntentBreaker* against four jailbreak defense methods, including PPL [2], GradSafe [29], Self-Reminder [30], and ICD [28] (see Table 8). The results indicate that most defenses are largely ineffective, with our method bypassing easily PPL and GradSafe with minimal ASR loss. While self-reminder provides the best defense, *IntentBreaker* still successfully bypasses it on most LLMs, further demonstrating its resilience. For a fair comparison, all baseline and defense methods in this study are implemented using the parameter settings from their original papers.

Table 10. Ablation study results of mutation-assisted LLMs.

Mutation-Assisted LLMs	ASR(%)↑				
	Llama2-7B	Gemma2-9B	Qwen2.5-7B	Vicuna-7B	Mistral-7B
GPT-3.5-turbo	89.18	95.88	96.94	97.29	96.59
GPT-4o	94.82	99.06	99.76	99.53	99.88

4.3 Ablation Study

We conduct two ablation studies to systematically evaluate the impact of *IntentBreaker* in two key aspects: (1) the effectiveness of three intent-adaptive improvements: template initialization, fitness function, and dynamic mutation operations; (2) the influence of different mutation-assisted LLMs on attack performance.

In the first ablation study, we individually remove each improvement and compare the results with the full framework to analyze their contributions to the overall performance of *IntentBreaker*. Specifically, in the template initialization ablation, 15 templates are randomly selected without considering intents. In the fitness function ablation, the cross-entropy loss between the generated output and the target output is used instead. In the mutation operations ablation, standard genetic algorithm settings are applied. As shown in Table 9, each improvement significantly enhances ASR compared to baselines, with intent-driven template initialization contributing the most to ASR improvement. The combination of all three improvements achieves the best performance, validating their necessity in the overall framework.

In the second ablation study, we replaced the mutation-assisted LLM in *IntentBreaker* from GPT-4o to GPT-3.5-turbo. As shown in Table 10, using GPT-3.5-turbo resulted in a slight decrease in ASR, underscoring the impact of the text generation capability of mutation-assisted LLMs on the attack effectiveness of *IntentBreaker*.

5 Conclusion

In this work, we uncovered a robustness bias in LLMs towards malicious prompts across different intents, which resulted in significant variations in the ASR of jailbreaking across distinct intents. To address this, we categorized attack intents into nine types and proposed *IntentBreaker*, a hybrid evolutionary framework with three improvements: intent-driven template initialization, intent-specific lexicons based fitness function, and dynamic mutation operations. These ensured that generated templates effectively bypass safeguards while meeting the semantic characteristics of the target intent. Extensive experiments demonstrated that *IntentBreaker* outperformed baselines in ASR and efficiency across five open-source LLMs, achieving SOTA performance and strong resilience against mainstream defenses. We sincerely hope that our intent-adaptive strategy for jailbreaking will inspire future advancements in this field.

Acknowledgments. This work was partially supported by the NSFC under Grants U2441240 ("Ye Qisun" Science Foundation), 62441238, 62441237, and U21B2018.

Disclosure of Interests. The authors have no competing interests to declare that are relevant to the content of this article.

References

1. Achiam, J., Adler, S., Agarwal, S., Ahmad, L., Akkaya, I., et al.: GPT-4 technical report. arXiv preprint arXiv:2303.08774 (2023)
2. Alon, G., Kamfonas, M.: Detecting language model attacks with perplexity. arXiv preprint arXiv:2308.14132 (2023)
3. Andriushchenko, M., Croce, F., Flammarion, N.: Jailbreaking leading safety-aligned LLMs with simple adaptive attacks. In: Proceedings of ICLR (2025)
4. Carlini, N., Nasr, M., Choquette-Choo, C.A., Jagielski, M., Gao, I., et al.: Are aligned neural networks adversarially aligned? In: Proceedings of NeurIPS (2023)
5. Chang, Z., Li, M., Liu, Y., Wang, J., Wang, Q., et al.: Play guessing game with LLM: indirect jailbreak attack with implicit clues. In: Proceedings of ACL (2024)
6. Chao, P., Robey, A., Dobriban, E., Hassani, H., Pappas, G.J., et al.: Jailbreaking black box large language models in twenty queries. In: Proceedings of NeurIPS R0-FoMo Workshop (2023)
7. Chiang, W.L., Li, Z., Lin, Z., Sheng, Y., Wu, Z., et al.: Vicuna: an open-source chatbot impressing GPT-4 with 90%* chatGPT quality. https://lmsys.org/blog/2023-03-30-vicuna/ (2023)
8. Deng, G., et al.: Masterkey: automated jailbreaking of large language model chatbots. In: Proceedings of NDSS (2024)
9. Deshpande, A., Murahari, V., Rajpurohit, T., Kalyan, A., Narasimhan, K.R.: Toxicity in chatGPT: analyzing persona-assigned language models. In: Proceedings of EMNLP (2023)
10. Devlin, J., Chang, M.W., Lee, K., Toutanova, K.: BERT: pre-training of deep bidirectional transformers for language understanding. In: Proceedings of NAACL (2019)
11. Dong, Y., Jiang, X., Jin, Z., Li, G.: Self-collaboration code generation via chatGPT. ACM Trans. Softw. Eng. Methodol. (2024)
12. Fakhoury, S., Naik, A., Sakkas, G., Chakraborty, S., Lahiri, S.K.: LLM-based test-driven interactive code generation: user study and empirical evaluation. IEEE Trans. Softw. Eng. (2024)
13. Guo, X., Yu, F., Zhang, H., Qin, L., Hu, B.: Cold-attack: jailbreaking LLMs with stealthiness and controllability. In: Proceedings of ICML (2024)
14. Jia, X., et al.: Improved techniques for optimization-based jailbreaking on large language models. In: Proceedings of ICLR (2025)
15. Jiang, A.Q., Sablayrolles, A., Mensch, A., Bamford, C., Chaplot, D.S., et al.: Mistral 7B. arXiv preprint arXiv:2310.06825 (2023)
16. Joko, H., Chatterjee, S., Ramsay, A., de Vries, A.P., Dalton, J., Hasibi, F.: Doing personal laps: LLM-augmented dialogue construction for personalized multi-session conversational search. In: Proceedings of SIGIR (2024)
17. Li, X., Wang, R., Cheng, M., Zhou, T., Hsieh, C.J.: DrAttack: prompt decomposition and reconstruction makes powerful LLM jailbreakers. In: Proceedings of EMNLP (2024)

18. Liu, X., Xu, N., Chen, M., Xiao, C.: AutoDAN: generating stealthy jailbreak prompts on aligned large language models. In: Proceedings of ICLR (2024)
19. Liu, Y., et al.: Jailbreaking chatGPT via prompt engineering: an empirical study. arXiv preprint arXiv:2305.13860 (2024)
20. Mehrotra, A., Zampetakis, M., Kassianik, P., Nelson, B., Anderson, H., et al.: Tree of attacks: jailbreaking black-box LLMs automatically. In: Proceedings of NeurIPS (2024)
21. Meta: The LLaMA 3 family of models (2024). https://github.com/meta-llama/PurpleLlama/blob/main/Llama-Guard3/1B/MODEL_CARD.md
22. Ouyang, L., Wu, J., Jiang, X., Almeida, D., Wainwright, C., et al.: Training language models to follow instructions with human feedback. In: Proceedings of NeurIPS (2022)
23. Qi, X., Zeng, Y., Xie, T., Chen, P.Y., Jia, R., et al.: Fine-tuning aligned language models compromises safety, even when users do not intend to! In: Proceedings of ICLR (2024)
24. Riviere, M., et al.: Gemma 2: improving open language models at a practical size. arXiv preprint arXiv:2408.00118 (2024)
25. Shen, X., Chen, Z., Backes, M., Shen, Y., Zhang, Y.: "do anything now": characterizing and evaluating in-the-wild jailbreak prompts on large language models. In: Proceedings of ACM CCS (2024)
26. Touvron, H., Martin, L., Stone, K., Albert, P., Almahairi, et al.: LLaMA 2: open foundation and fine-tuned chat models. arXiv preprint arXiv:2307.09288 (2023)
27. Wei, A., Haghtalab, N., Steinhardt, J.: Jailbroken: How does LLM safety training fail? In: Proceedings of NeurIPS (2023)
28. Wei, Z., Wang, Y., Wang, Y.: Jailbreak and guard aligned language models with only few in-context demonstrations. arXiv preprint arXiv:2310.06387 (2023)
29. Xie, Y., Fang, M., Pi, R., Gong, N.: GradSafe: detecting unsafe prompts for LLMs via safety-critical gradient analysis. In: Proceedings of ACL (2024)
30. Xie, Y., Yi, J., Shao, J., Curl, J., Lyu, L., et al.: Defending chatGPT against jailbreak attack via self-reminders. Nat. Mach. Intell. (2023)
31. Yang, A., et al.: Qwen2.5 technical report. arXiv preprint arXiv:2412.15115 (2025)
32. Yong, Z.X., Menghini, C., Bach, S.: Low-resource languages jailbreak GPT-4. In: Proceedings of NeurIPS SoLaR Workshop (2023)
33. Yu, J., Lin, X., Xing, X.: LLM-fuzzer: scaling assessment of large language model jailbreaks. In: Proceedings of USENIX Security (2024)
34. Zhang, Z., Shen, G., Tao, G., Cheng, S., Zhang, X.: On large language models' resilience to coercive interrogation. In: Proceedings of IEEE S&P (2024)
35. Zou, A., Wang, Z., Kolter, J.Z., Fredrikson, M.: Universal and transferable adversarial attacks on aligned language models. arXiv preprint arXiv:2307.15043 (2023)

Pareto Multi-objective Alignment for Language Models

Qiang He(✉) and Setareh Maghsudi

Ruhr University Bochum, 44801 Bochum, Germany
{qiang.he,setareh.maghsudi}@ruhr-uni-bochum.de

Abstract. Large language models (LLMs) are increasingly deployed in real-world applications that require careful balancing of multiple, often conflicting, objectives, such as informativeness versus conciseness, or helpfulness versus creativity. However, current alignment methods, primarily based on reinforcement learning from human feedback (RLHF), optimize LLMs toward a single reward function, resulting in rigid behavior that fails to capture the complexity and diversity of human preferences. This limitation hinders the adaptability of LLMs to practical scenarios, making multi-objective alignment (MOA) a critical yet underexplored area. To bridge this gap, we propose PAreto Multi-Objective Alignment (PAMA), a principled and computationally efficient algorithm designed explicitly for MOA in LLMs. In contrast to computationally prohibitive gradient-based multi-objective optimization (MOO) methods, PAMA transforms multi-objective RLHF into a convex optimization problem with a closed-form solution, significantly enhancing scalability. Traditional gradient-based MOO approaches suffer from prohibitive $\mathcal{O}(n^2 d)$ complexity, where d represents the number of model parameters, typically in the billions for LLMs, rendering direct optimization infeasible. PAMA reduces this complexity to $\mathcal{O}(n)$ where n is the number of objectives, enabling optimization to be completed within milliseconds. We provide theoretical guarantees that PAMA converges to a Pareto stationary point, where no objective can be improved without degrading at least one other. Extensive experiments across language models ranging from 125M to 7B parameters demonstrate PAMA's robust and effective multi-objective alignment capabilities, consistently outperforming baseline methods, aligning with its theoretical advantages. PAMA provides a highly efficient solution to the MOA problem that was previously considered intractable, offering a practical and theoretically grounded approach to aligning LLMs with diverse human values, paving the way for versatile and adaptable real-world AI deployments.

Keywords: Language Models · Multi-objective Alignment

Supplementary Information The online version contains supplementary material available at https://doi.org/10.1007/978-3-032-06078-5_15.

1 Introduction

Large language models (LLMs) have demonstrated impressive capabilities across diverse natural language tasks [5,20,28], receiving significant attention from academia and industry [18,26]. However, a critical deployment challenge is aligning LLMs with complex human values. Currently, reinforcement learning from human feedback (RLHF) is the predominant alignment approach [2,19], fine-tuning models against a single reward function that approximates human preferences practically [6,9,26]. While effective in producing coherent outputs, this single-objective alignment severely restricts LLMs, resulting in homogeneous behaviors that fail to reflect the diverse spectrum of human values.

Real-world scenarios increasingly demand models that simultaneously balance multiple, often conflicting objectives, such as informativeness versus conciseness, helpfulness versus creativity, and etc. [9,11,26]. Therefore, aligning LLMs requires moving beyond single-objective reward models towards multi-objective alignment (MOA), which considers multiple and potentially conflicting reward signals [21,30]. Despite recent interest, a theoretically grounded and practical method for achieving MOA in LLMs has yet to be established.

A naive solution aggregates heterogeneous rewards into a single scalar objective [27], but this simplification neglects inherent reward conflicts, often leading to biased or misaligned outcomes [3]. Existing gradient-based multi-objective optimization (MOO) methods [4,14,25,32] are also impractical for large-scale LLMs due to prohibitively expensive gradient computations. For instance, MGDA [4] involves min-norm operations with time complexity $\mathcal{O}(n^2 d)$, making it infeasible for models with billions of parameters (e.g., $d = 7$ billion). Thus, developing a scalable and principled MOA algorithm specifically for LLMs remains crucial.

In this work, we propose PAreto Multi-Objective Alignment (PAMA), a novel, computationally efficient algorithm designed explicitly for multi-objective alignment in LLMs. PAMA converts multi-objective RLHF into a convex optimization problem with a closed-form solution, eliminating expensive gradient calculations. Remarkably, PAMA achieves computational costs comparable to standard single-objective PPO algorithms, enabling efficient fine-tuning of 7-billion-parameter models on a single NVIDIA A6000 GPU. Unlike traditional methods [4,14] with $\mathcal{O}(n^2 d)$ complexity, PAMA scales linearly with the number of objectives $\mathcal{O}(n)$, drastically reducing computational demands and enabling practical use with LLMs. For instance, when $n = 10$ and $d = 10^{10}$, existing approaches would require roughly 10^{12} computations, whereas PAMA completes the task in just 10 steps, demonstrating an exponential improvement in efficiency. In such an LLM setting, methods like MGDA [4], PCGrad [32], and CAGrad [14] become computationally infeasible, whereas PAMA remains tractable and scalable.

Furthermore, we provide theoretical guarantees of convergence to a Pareto stationary point, ensuring no single objective can improve without degrading others. To our knowledge, PAMA is the first theoretically grounded MOA algorithm for LLMs.

The theoretical advantages of PAMA are also reflected in our empirical results. Empirical evaluations validate PAMA across language models ranging from 125M to 7B parameters. Our experiments comprehensively demonstrate PAMA's robust and consistent superiority, while other baselines fail with large performance gaps. The results highlight PAMA's effectiveness, scalability, and robustness, aligned with its theoretical properties.

Our contributions are summarized as follows:

- Pareto Multi-Objective Alignment: A novel and efficient multi-objective alignment algorithm for LLMs, reducing computational complexity from $\mathcal{O}(n^2 d)$ to $\mathcal{O}(n)$, enabling efficient large-scale training.
- Theoretical Guarantees: We prove convergence of PAMA to a Pareto stationary point.
- Empirical Validation: Extensive experiments demonstrate PAMA's superior performance across multiple settings.

2 Method

This section presents our approach to multi-objective alignment in the context of LLMs. We begin by formulating the problem and introducing Noon PPO, a variant of PPO [23]. We then propose PAMA, an algorithm designed to align LLMs with multiple objectives while ensuring convergence to a Pareto stationary point with theoretical guarantees.

2.1 Problem Formulation

RLHF consists of two main phases: reward modeling and policy optimization. In reward modeling, a reward function is trained on preference data to maximize the objective: $\mathcal{L}_{RM} = \mathbb{E}_{(x,y^w,y^l)\sim \mathcal{D}}[\log(\sigma(r(x,y^w) - r(x,y^l)))]$, where, y^w and y^l denote the preferred and less desirable responses, respectively, x represents the prompt, and $\sigma(\cdot)$ is the sigmoid function. In policy optimization, RLHF typically employs PPO to refine the policy by solving:

$$\arg\max_{\pi(y|x;\theta)} \mathbb{E}_{x\sim \mathcal{D}, y\sim \pi(\cdot|x)} \left[r(x,y) - \beta \log \frac{\pi(y|x;\theta)}{\pi_{ref}(y|x)} \right]$$

where $\pi(y|x;\theta)$ is the current policy, $\pi_{ref}(y|x)$ is the supervised fine-tuned (SFT) policy, and β controls policy shifts.

Reward modeling requires extensive data labeling. In this paper, we focus on policy optimization with pre-trained reward models, aiming to optimize multiple reward objectives simultaneously.

Multi-objective Optimization. Formally, the MOO problem is defined as:

$$\max_{\theta}(J^{(1)}(\theta), J^{(2)}(\theta), \ldots, J^{(N)}(\theta))^\top, \tag{1}$$

where θ denotes the learnable parameters, $J^{(i)}$ represents the i-th optimization objective, and the goal is to find a Pareto optimal solution.

Definition 1 (Pareto Optimality). *A solution π^* is Pareto optimal if no other solution dominates it, i.e., there does not exist another policy π' such that:*

- $J_i(\pi') \geq J_i(\pi^*)$ *for all i.*
- $J_j(\pi') > J_j(\pi^*)$ *for at least one j.*

Since direct vector-form optimization is intractable, MOO is often scalarized into a weighted sum:

$$\min_\theta \sum_{i=1}^{N} c^{(i)} \mathcal{L}^{(i)}(\theta), \tag{2}$$

where $c^{(i)}$ denotes the weight assigned to each objective $\mathcal{L}^{(i)}$.

Optimization Challenges. Solving Eq. (2) presents several challenges: i) Balancing conflicting objectives. LLMs often exhibit strong trade-offs between objectives, making simple scalarization ineffective: it can bias solutions toward certain objectives while neglecting others. ii) Weight sensitivity. The choice of weights $c^{(i)}$ significantly impacts optimization and is often subjective. Poorly chosen weights can lead to suboptimal or undesired solutions. iii) Computational Complexity. Gradient-based multi-objective learning methods generally require computing full gradients for all objectives across all parameters and operate on the gradient with $\mathcal{O}(n^2 d)$ complexity (detailed in Appendix G). This becomes infeasible at LLM scale due to the high parameter count.

To address these challenges, we introduce PAMA, a scalable optimization algorithm that ensures convergence to a Pareto stationary point.

2.2 Noon PPO

We introduce Noon PPO, a variant of PPO [23], designed to improve stability in MOA. Noon stands for "No Negative", as it modifies the advantage to disregard negative values, thereby restricting policy updates to actions with non-negative advantages. Let A'_t denote the estimated advantage at time step t. In Noon PPO, we define the advantage as:

$$A_t = \max(A'_t, 0). \tag{3}$$

This adjustment ensures that only actions with a positive advantage contribute to the policy gradient update, effectively ignoring updates that would reduce the probability of suboptimal actions. As in standard PPO, let π_θ be the current policy parameterized by θ, and let $\pi_{\theta_{\text{ref}}}$ represent the SFT policy. The probability ratio is defined as:

$$u_t(\theta) = \frac{\pi_\theta(a_t \mid s_t)}{\pi_{\theta_{\text{ref}}}(a_t \mid s_t)}. \tag{4}$$

The clipped surrogate objective in Noon PPO is then given by:

$$\mathcal{L}^{\text{NOON}}(\theta) = \mathbb{E}_t \left[\min\big(u_t(\theta) A_t, \text{clip}(u_t(\theta), 1-\epsilon, 1+\epsilon) A_t\big) \right], \tag{5}$$

where A_t is defined in Eq. 3, and ϵ is a clipping hyperparameter that limits the deviation between π_θ and $\pi_{\theta_{\text{ref}}}$.

By clipping negative advantages to zero, Noon PPO eliminates unstable gradient fluctuations caused by error-prone or ambiguous training examples. This leads to more predictable convergence, which is particularly beneficial when aligning LLMs with multiple objectives. As we will discuss in Sect. 2.4, this design plays a crucial role in ensuring the theoretical convergence of PAMA.

2.3 Solving Multi-objective Optimization at LLM Scale

Optimizing multiple conflicting objectives in LLMs is a challenging task, especially when relying on gradient-based MOO methods [4,14,25,32]. These methods require solving complex gradient aggregation problems, which become computationally infeasible at the scale of modern LLMs. For example, MGDA [4] formulates the gradient balancing problem as a min-norm optimization, which has a computational cost of $\mathcal{O}(n^2 d)$, where d is the model's parameter dimension. Given that d often reaches billions in large-scale models (e.g., 7B parameters), these approaches are prohibitively expensive in both computation and memory, as further discussed in Appendix F.

Motivation for PAMA. To overcome these limitations, an efficient and scalable optimization strategy is required. Ideally, such a method should:

1. Avoid costly gradient-based operations that scale poorly with model size.
2. Provide a computationally tractable formulation that remains efficient as the number of objectives grows.
3. Ensure convergence to a well-defined Pareto stationary point, effectively balancing multiple objectives.

We introduce Pareto Multi-Objective Alignment (PAMA), a novel algorithm specifically designed for large-scale LLM alignment. Instead of directly solving the expensive min-norm optimization, PAMA reformulates the problem into a convex optimization framework with a closed-form solution. This transformation reduces the computational complexity from $\mathcal{O}(n^2 d)$ to $\mathcal{O}(n)$, where n is the number of objectives, significantly lowering the computational burden compared to traditional methods.

A key challenge in MOO is determining an appropriate convex combination of gradient directions that balances competing objectives. The conventional approach [4] relies on solving the min-norm optimization problem:

$$\min_{c^{(1)},\ldots,c^{(N)}} \left\{ \left\| \sum_{i=1}^{N} c^{(i)} \nabla_\theta \mathcal{L}^{(i)}(\theta) \right\|_2^2 \text{ s.t. } \sum_{i=1}^{N} c^{(i)} = 1, \quad c^{(i)} \geq 0 \quad \forall i \right\} \quad (6)$$

where $\mathcal{L}^{(i)}$ represents the loss for the i-th objective, and $c^{(i)}$ is the weight assigned to its gradient contribution. Recent advances [4] showed that this optimization either results in a KKT stationary point (indicating a Pareto stationary solution) or finds a direction that improves all objectives. However, solving this problem at LLM scale remains intractable due to the high dimensionality of the parameter space.

To mitigate this issue, we derive an upper bound for the min-norm formulation with Noon PPO objectives, which leads to a more efficient optimization approach. Specifically, we show that:

$$\left\|\sum_{i=1}^{N} c^{(i)} \nabla_\theta \mathcal{L}^{(i)}(\theta)\right\|_2^2 = \left\|\sum_{i=1}^{N} c^{(i)} \nabla_\pi \mathcal{L}^{(i)}(\theta) \nabla_\theta \pi(\theta)\right\|_2^2 = \left\|\sum_{i=1}^{N} c^{(i)} \frac{1}{\pi_{ref}} I(A^{(i)}) \nabla_\theta \pi(\theta)\right\|_2^2$$

$$\leq \left\|\sum_{i=1}^{N} c^{(i)} I(A^{(i)})\right\|_2^2 \left\|\frac{1}{\pi_{ref}} \nabla_\theta \pi(\theta)\right\|_2^2,$$

(7)

where

$$I(A) = \begin{cases} 0, & u > 1+\epsilon \\ A, & u \leq 1+\epsilon \end{cases},$$

(8)

$$\sum_{i=1}^{N} c^{(i)} = 1, \quad c^{(i)} \geq 0 \quad \forall i,$$

(9)

and $u = \frac{\pi}{\pi_{ref}}$. For simplicity, we omit the expectation notation, which does not affect the theoretical derivation. The second equation follows from the Noon PPO loss Eq. (5), while the final inequality is derived from the CauchySchwarz inequality. This upper bound allows us to reformulate the problem as a more efficient surrogate optimization:

$$\min_{c^{(1)},\ldots,c^{(N)}} \left\{ \left\|\sum_{i=1}^{N} c^{(i)} I(A^{(i)})\right\|_2^2 \ \text{s.t.} \ \sum_{i=1}^{N} c^{(i)} = 1, \ c^{(N)} \geq 0 \ \forall i \right\}.$$

(10)

This formulation admits a closed-form solution, which we derive next.

Theorem 1 (Optimal Convex Combination for the Min-Norm Problem). *Let $A^{(1)}, A^{(2)}, \ldots, A^{(N)} \in \mathbb{R}$ be given, and consider the optimization problem*

$$\min_{c^{(1)},\ldots,c^{(N)}} \left(\sum_{i=1}^{N} c^{(i)} A^{(i)}\right)^2,$$

$$\text{subject to} \ \sum_{i=1}^{N} c^{(i)} = 1,$$

$$c^{(i)} \geq 0 \ \text{for} \ i = 1, 2, \ldots, N.$$

(11)

Then the optimal value of the convex combination,

$$s^* = \sum_{i=1}^{N} c^{(i)} A^{(i)},$$

(12)

is given by

$$s^* = \begin{cases} 0, & \text{if } \min_{1 \leq i \leq N} A^{(i)} \leq 0 \leq \max_{1 \leq i \leq N} A^{(i)}, \\ \min_{1 \leq i \leq N} A^{(i)}, & \text{if } A^{(i)} > 0 \text{ for all } i, \\ \max_{1 \leq i \leq N} A^{(i)}, & \text{if } A^{(i)} < 0 \text{ for all } i. \end{cases} \quad (13)$$

In other words, s^* is the projection of 0 onto the interval

$$\left[\min_{1 \leq i \leq N} A^{(i)}, \max_{1 \leq i \leq N} A^{(i)} \right], \quad (14)$$

and the minimum objective value is $(s^*)^2$.

The proof is provided in Appendix A.

Advantages of PAMA's Reformulation. Compared to the intractable original optimization problem (Eq. (6)), our reformulation provides two key benefits:

1. Drastic reduction in computational cost: The term $I(A^{(i)})$ is computed via a simple forward pass, eliminating costly backpropagation.
2. Analytically solvable optimization: The surrogate problem admits a closed-form solution (Theorem 1), ensuring efficiency..

By incorporating this approach with the Noon PPO, we obtain a practical and scalable algorithm for MOA. We summarize PAMA in Appendix E. To illustrate the computational efficiency of our method, consider the magnitude of operations required. Traditional approaches with a complexity of $\mathcal{O}(n^2 d)$ result in a computational load of approximately 10^{12} operations when $d \approx 10^{10}$ and $n \approx 10^1$. In contrast, our method, operating with $\mathcal{O}(n)$ complexity, requires 10 operations, a very small number. Our approach remains practical even for extremely large-scale problems.

2.4 Theoretical Guarantee

With the reformulated optimization problem in Eq. (10), an important question arises: does our approach retain theoretical guarantees? In this section, we establish that under mild conditions, our method converges to a Pareto stationary point, ensuring that no objective can be improved without deteriorating at least one other objective.

First, we formally define the notion of a Pareto stationary point, which serves as a necessary condition for Pareto optimality.

Definition 2 (Pareto Stationary Point). *A parameter vector θ is said to be satisfying Pareto stationary if there exists a set of weights $\{c^{(i)}\}_{i=1}^{N}$ satisfying*

$$\sum_{i=1}^{N} c^{(i)} = 1, \quad c^{(i)} \geq 0, \quad \forall i \in \{1, 2, \cdots, N\}, \quad \text{and} \quad \sum_{i=1}^{N} c^{(i)} \nabla_\theta \mathcal{L}^{(i)}(\theta) = 0. \quad (15)$$

Pareto stationary point ensures that no descent direction exists that simultaneously improves all objectives, indicating that the optimization has reached a balanced trade-off among competing objectives. To establish convergence results, we assume that the loss function exhibits smoothness properties, which are commonly satisfied in deep learning due to gradient-based optimization and regularization.

Definition 3 (κ-Lipschitz Continuity). Let (X, d_X) and (Y, d_Y) be metric spaces. A function $f : X \to Y$ is said to be κ-Lipschitz continuous if there exists a constant $\kappa \geq 0$ such that for all $x, y \in X$,

$$d_Y(f(x), f(y)) \leq \kappa d_X(x, y). \tag{16}$$

This property ensures that the function does not change too rapidly, contributing to stability in gradient-based optimization.

Assumption 1 (Lipschitz Smoothness of the Gradient). The loss function $\mathcal{L}(\theta)$ has a κ-Lipschitz continuous gradient, meaning there exists a constant $\kappa > 0$ such that for all θ, θ'

$$\|\nabla_\theta \mathcal{L}(\theta) - \nabla_\theta \mathcal{L}(\theta')\|_2 \leq \kappa \|\theta - \theta'\|_2. \tag{17}$$

This assumption guarantees that the landscape does not contain abrupt changes, which is critical for convergence guarantees and is empirically observed in RL [13].

Assumption 2 (Bounded Learning Rate). The learning rate η satisfies

$$0 \leq \eta \leq \frac{2}{\kappa}. \tag{18}$$

This condition ensures stable updates, preventing divergence due to excessively large steps, aligning with standard practices in convex and non-convex optimization.

Assumption 3 (Bounded Reward). Rewards in RL are typically finite due to practical constraints. Formally, there exists a constant $R_{\max} > 0$ such that

$$|r(x, y)| \leq R_{\max}, \quad \forall (x, y) \in \mathcal{X} \times \mathcal{Y}. \tag{19}$$

See Appendix C for more discussion.

We now establish the convergence of PAMA.

Lemma 1 (General Descent Lemma). Let $f : \mathbb{R}^N \to \mathbb{R}$ be continuously differentiable on an open set containing $x \in \mathbb{R}^N$, and suppose that ∇f is κ-Lipschitz continuous, i.e., for all u, v in that set,

$$\|\nabla f(u) - \nabla f(v)\| \leq \kappa \|u - v\|. \tag{20}$$

Then, for any update direction $g \in \mathbb{R}^N$, one has

$$f(x + g) \leq f(x) + \nabla f(x)^\top g + \frac{\kappa}{2} \|g\|^2. \tag{21}$$

The proof is in Appendix B. Using this result, we analyze the gradient descent dynamics of PAMA and show that PAMA converges to a Pareto stationary point.

Theorem 2 (Convergence of PAMA). *Let $\mathcal{L}^{(i)}(\theta)$ be the loss function for task i, where policy is $\pi(\theta)$. Define the PAMA gradient aggregation:*

$$g_o^{(k)} = \sum_{i=1}^{N} c^{(i)} \nabla_\pi \mathcal{L}^{(i)}(\theta_k), \tag{22}$$

where $c^{(i)}$ is the solution to

$$\min_{c^{(1)},\ldots,c^{(N)}} \left\| g_o \right\|_2^2, \quad s.t. \sum_{i=1}^{N} c^{(i)} = 1, \quad c^{(i)} \geq 0. \tag{23}$$

Under Assumptions 1 to 3, the gradient descent update at timestep k:

$$\theta_{k+1} = \theta_k - g_o^{(k)} \eta J \tag{24}$$

ensures

$$\lim_{k \to \infty} \|\nabla_\theta \mathcal{L}(\theta_k)\|_2 = 0, \tag{25}$$

where $J = \nabla_{\theta_k} \pi(\theta_k)$ and $J \in \mathbb{R}^{|\theta| \times 1}$. This shows the update converges to a Pareto stationary point.

The proof is provided in Appendix D. Theorem 2 establishes that:

- If the optimal value of Eq. (10) is zero, the aggregated gradient vanishes, indicating that the process has reached a Pareto stationary point.
- If the optimal value is nonzero, the gradient provides a valid descent direction for all objectives, ensuring continual improvement toward a Pareto stationary solution.

Thus, PAMA guarantees convergence to a balanced trade-off among conflicting objectives, offering a provably convergent and computationally efficient approach to multi-objective alignment for LLMs.

3 Experiments

In this section, we aim to empirically validate whether the theoretical advantages of PAMA are reflected in practical experiments. To this end, we conduct systematic evaluations across different model scales and diverse, potentially conflicting objectives to assess PAMA's effectiveness in multi-objective alignment.

We conduct experiments on three progressively larger language models: GPT-2 (125M), GPT-2 XL (1.5B), and LLaMA-2 (7B), and evaluate PAMA using a range of reward models, including harmlessness, humor, sentiment, and response length. Our implementation is based on the open-source TRL framework [29]. All experiments are conducted on a workstation equipped with an Intel i9-14900K CPU and a single NVIDIA RTX A6000 GPU. Further experimental details are provided in Appendix H, with additional results included in Appendix I.

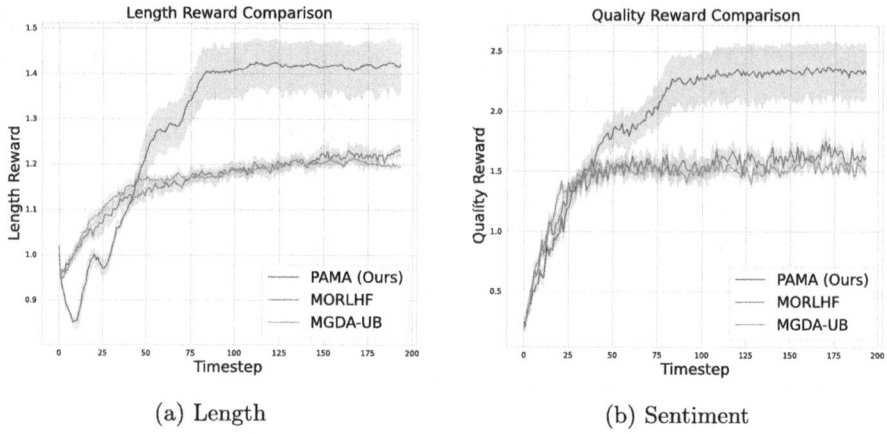

Fig. 1. Comparison of sentiment and length rewards during training on the IMDb dataset using GPT-2 (125M parameters). PAMA consistently achieves superior performance across both objectives, demonstrating stable optimization. In contrast, MORLHF struggles to balance sentiment and length due to the limitations of the fixed weighted sum approach, while MGDA-UB does not show any advantage over MORLHF. The shaded area represents the standard deviation over eight trials, highlighting the robustness of PAMA.

3.1 Normal Model: GPT-2 (125M Parameters)

In this experiment, we evaluate PAMA on a normal-scale language model, GPT-2 (125M parameters), to assess its effectiveness in optimizing multiple objectives. Specifically, we aim to generate film reviews that are both positive and long, requiring the model to balance sentiment and length objectives.

Setup. We use GPT-2 [20] as the base model and train it on the IMDb dataset[1]. The objective consists of two reward functions: i) a pretrained sentiment analysis model[2], where the logit output serves as the reward signal to encourage positive reviews, and ii) a length-based reward that promotes longer responses. Both reward values are structured such that higher scores indicate better performance.

Baselines. We compare PAMA against two widely used baselines: MORLHF, which applies a fixed weighted sum of the objectives, a common but often suboptimal approach for balancing conflicting goals; and MGDA-UB [24], which leverages the min-norm algorithm to compute gradients that balance multiple objectives dynamically. Further discussion is provided in Appendix F.

Results. The training curves in Fig. 1 illustrate the performance of different methods over time. Figure 1a shows that PAMA significantly outperforms both baselines in optimizing the length reward. While MORLHF and MGDA-UB exhibit slow and marginal improvements, PAMA achieves a much higher final

---

[1] https://huggingface.co/datasets/stanfordnlp/imdb.
[2] https://huggingface.co/lvwerra/distilbert-imdb.

reward with a stable convergence pattern. Figure 1b further highlights PAMA's advantage in optimizing sentiment, where it reaches a substantially higher reward than the baselines. In contrast, MORLHF stagnates at a lower level, and MGDA-UB shows negative improvement over MORLHF.

3.2 Scaling Up: GPT-2 XL (1.5B Parameters)

To evaluate PAMA's scalability and adaptability, we extend our experiments to GPT-2 XL (1.5B parameters), optimizing for both humor and text length.

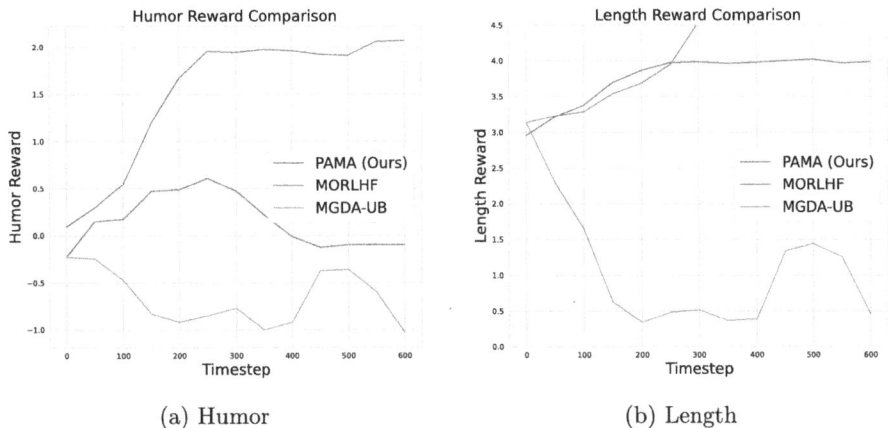

(a) Humor   (b) Length

Fig. 2. Comparison of humor and length rewards during training on the HH-RLHF dataset using GPT-2 XL (1.5B parameters). PAMA consistently outperforms the baselines in both objectives, demonstrating stable optimization. While MORLHF fails to significantly improve humor. MGDA-UB struggles in both objectives, showing severe performance degradation. These results highlight the effectiveness of PAMA in multi-objective alignment for LLMs.

We train GPT-2 XL on the HH-RLHF dataset [2] while optimizing two distinct reward signals: i) a humor classifier[3], which assigns higher rewards to funnier outputs, and ii) a length-based reward that promotes longer responses. Higher reward values correspond to better performance in both objectives. We compare PAMA against MORLHF and MGDA-UB.

Results. The evaluation results, shown in Fig. 2, illustrate the performance on the test set for humor and length rewards over training timesteps. Figure 2a demonstrates that PAMA effectively optimizes humor, steadily increasing its reward and maintaining a high final value. In contrast, MORLHF shows only marginal improvement before plateauing at a lower level, while MGDA-UB fails entirely, with its humor reward even decreasing over time. Figure 2b shows that

---

[3] https://huggingface.co/mohameddhiab/humor-no-humor.

both PAMA and MORLHF successfully optimize length, though MORLHF only optimizes length, ignoring humor. MGDA-UB, on the other hand, completely collapses in this setting, with its length reward deteriorating throughout training. These findings reinforce PAMA's robustness in multi-objective alignment, particularly in balancing competing rewards while ensuring stable convergence.

3.3 Towards Large Language Models: LLaMA-2 7B

To assess the scalability of PAMA, we extend our evaluation to a large language model setting using LLaMA-2 [26] with 7B parameters. This experiment focuses on aligning the model to generate responses that are both harmless and as long as possible. We utilize the HH-RLHF dataset and measure harmlessness using an open-source reward model[4].

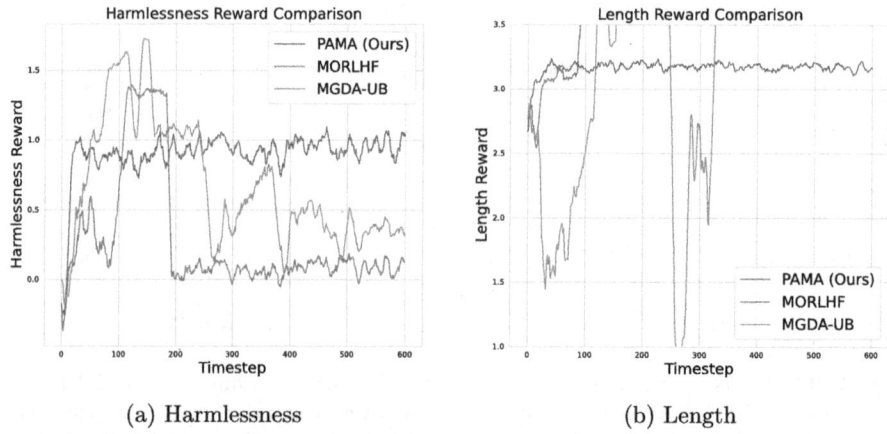

(a) Harmlessness (b) Length

Fig. 3. Comparison of harmlessness and length rewards during training on the HH-RLHF dataset using LLaMA-2 (7B parameters). PAMA consistently optimizes both objectives while maintaining a stable learning process. In contrast, MGDA-UB and MORLHF struggle with harmlessness optimization, exhibiting significant fluctuations and instability. MGDA-UB, in particular, exhibits pronounced oscillations during training. While MORLHF converges to a lower performance level. These results highlight the robustness of PAMA in aligning large-scale LLMs with multiple objectives.

Results. The results in Fig. 3 demonstrate PAMA's effectiveness in large-scale multi-objective alignment. As shown in Fig. 3a, PAMA achieves a stable increase in harmlessness reward, while MORLHF and MGDA-UB suffer from instability and fluctuations. MGDA-UB, in particular, exhibits pronounced training oscillations, failing to maintain a high harmlessness score, whereas MORLHF stabilizes at a lower reward level. Similarly, Fig. 3b illustrates that PAMA maintains strong performance in length optimization, achieving stable convergence. In contrast,

---

[4] https://huggingface.co/Ray2333/gpt2-large-harmless-reward_model.

MGDA-UB experiences erratic fluctuations, and MORLHF fails to sustain meaningful progress. These findings reinforce PAMA's theoretical advantages, demonstrating its ability to effectively balance competing objectives in large-scale LLM alignment.

3.4 Discussion

Our experimental results confirm that the theoretical advantages of PAMA are consistently realized in practice. Across various model size (ranging from 125M to 7B) and objective settings, PAMA demonstrates superior stability and optimization performance, significantly outperforming existing baseline methods. MORLHF, which relies on a weighted sum of objectives, struggles to balance competing rewards due to its fixed weight assignments, often leading to suboptimal trade-offs. MGDA-UB, while employing dynamic gradient balancing, can exhibit training instability and, in some cases, underperform compared to MORLHF. These findings highlight PAMA's robustness in achieving stable and well-balanced optimization across different model scales and reward settings, making it a reliable and scalable solution for multi-objective alignment in large language models.

4 Related Work

Multi-objective Optimization is a fundamental problem in RL and deep learning, where multiple conflicting objectives must be simultaneously optimized, because improving one often leads to the degradation of another. Classical MOO techniques aim to find Pareto-optimal solutions. Among them, simple linearization methods with fixed weights often fail to effectively balance competing objectives [3]. A more general approach is Pareto-based optimization, which seeks to optimize all objectives simultaneously while maintaining trade-offs. Gradient-based MOO methods, e.g. MGDA [4], formulate a common descent direction for all objectives, ensuring simultaneous progress. However, despite their theoretical appeal, these approaches, along with related methods like PCGrad [32] and CAGrad [14], suffer from computational inefficiencies in high-dimensional parameter spaces, particularly in deep learning. The prohibitive cost of computing and aggregating gradients at LLM scale motivate the development of scalable alternatives, such as our proposed method, PAMA.

MORL extends RL to settings where an agent must learn policies that balance multiple reward functions. Standard MORL approaches include linear scalarization [27], Envelope Q-Learning [31], and Pareto Q-learning [17], as well as several recent extensions [1,8,10,12,15,22]. These methods are widely used in applications that require trade-offs between competing objectives [7]. However, their extension to large-scale neural networks, particularly LLMs, remains an open challenge due to computational constraints and the difficulty of balancing conflicting reward signals. A further discussion is provided in Appendices F and G.

MOO for LLMs. Applying MOO to LLMs presents additional challenges due to their high-dimensional parameter space and the inherent conflicts between objectives such as fluency, factual accuracy, and safety. Existing MOO techniques often become impractical for LLMs due to the prohibitive cost of computing gradients for each objective. For example, MGDA-UB [24] is proposed as an efficient approximation method, though its behavior on large-scale models can be unstable in practice, as observed in our experiments. Independent Component Alignment (ICA) [25] has been explored in multi-task learning for vision models, but its reliance on singular value decomposition introduces numerical instability, particularly when applied to `float16` or `bfloat16` formats used in LLM training. A notable recent approach is MOC [11], which trains an LLM as a meta-policy to generate responses aligned with user-defined preferences along the Pareto front. While promising, such approaches still face scalability and optimization challenges when applied to billion-parameter models.

Our approach, PAMA, distinguishes itself from previous methods by: i) Achieving computational efficiency comparable to single-objective RLHF methods, making it scalable to large models. ii) Providing theoretical guarantees of convergence, ensuring stable and reliable optimization. iii) Directly enabling multi-objective alignment in LLMs without relying on computationally expensive gradient manipulation techniques. By addressing both theoretical and practical limitations of existing methods, PAMA establishes a scalable and principled solution for aligning LLMs with multiple human values.

5 Conclusion

In this paper, we introduced Pareto Multi-Objective Alignment, a computationally efficient and theoretically grounded algorithm designed to align large language models across multiple, potentially conflicting objectives. By transforming the inherently complex multi-objective reinforcement learning from human feedback problem into a convex optimization framework, PAMA significantly reduces computational complexity, from an impractical $\mathcal{O}(n^2 d)$ to $\mathcal{O}(n)$, where d is the number of parameters (billions for LLMs) and n is the number of objectives. This efficiency enables practical multi-objective optimization even for billion-parameter models, expanding the applicability of LLMs across diverse real-world tasks. From a theoretical perspective, we provided rigorous proofs demonstrating that PAMA converges to Pareto stationary points. The empirical results further substantiate that PAMA not only exhibits theoretical superiority but also achieves stable and efficient multi-objective alignment in real-world applications. By successfully translating its methodological advantages into tangible performance improvements, PAMA provides a computationally efficient and theoretically grounded solution for multi-objective alignment for LLMs. In summary, PAMA not only addresses a critical gap in current multi-objective alignment methodologies but also offers a scalable, principled, and computationally viable solution for aligning LLMs with multiple human values. By establishing a strong foundation for efficient multi-objective optimization, PAMA paves the way for more adaptable, responsive, and socially aligned AI systems.

Acknowledgments. This research was supported by the German Federal Ministry of Research, Technology and Space under Grant Number 16KISK035.

References

1. Alegre, L.N., Bazzan, A.L., Roijers, D.M., Nowé, A., da Silva, B.C.: Sample-efficient multi-objective learning via generalized policy improvement prioritization. arXiv preprint arXiv:2301.07784 (2023)
2. Bai, Y., Jones, A., Ndousse, K., et al.: Training a helpful and harmless assistant with reinforcement learning from human feedback. CoRR abs/2204.05862 (2022). https://doi.org/10.48550/ARXIV.2204.05862
3. Boyd, S.P., Vandenberghe, L.: Convex Optimization. Cambridge University Press (2004)
4. Désidéri, J.A.: Multiple-Gradient Descent Algorithm (MGDA). Research Report RR-6953 (2009)
5. Devlin, J., Chang, M., Lee, K., Toutanova, K.: BERT: pre-training of deep bidirectional transformers for language understanding. In: Proceedings of the NAACL-HLT 2019, pp. 4171–4186. Association for Computational Linguistics (2019)
6. Dubey, A., et al.: The llama 3 herd of models. arXiv preprint arXiv:2407.21783 (2024)
7. Felten, F., Alegre, L.N., et al.: A toolkit for reliable benchmarking and research in multi-objective reinforcement learning. In: Proceedings of the 37th Conference on Neural Information Processing Systems (2023)
8. Felten, F., Talbi, E., Danoy, G.: Multi-objective reinforcement learning based on decomposition: a taxonomy and framework. J. Artif. Intell. Res. **79**, 679–723 (2024). https://doi.org/10.1613/JAIR.1.15702
9. Guo, D., et al.: Deepseek-r1: incentivizing reasoning capability in LLMs via reinforcement learning. arXiv preprint arXiv:2501.12948 (2025)
10. He, Q., Su, H., Zhang, J., Hou, X.: Frustratingly easy regularization on representation can boost deep reinforcement learning. In: IEEE/CVF Conference on Computer Vision and Pattern Recognition, CVPR 2023, Vancouver, BC, Canada, June 17–24, 2023, pp. 20215–20225. IEEE (2023). https://doi.org/10.1109/CVPR52729.2023.01936
11. He, Q., Yang, Y., Zhou, T., Fang, M., Maghsudi, S.: One model for all: multi-objective controllable language models (2025)
12. He, Q., Zhou, T., Fang, M., Maghsudi, S.: Adaptive regularization of representation rank as an implicit constraint of bellman equation. In: The Twelfth International Conference on Learning Representations, ICLR 2024, Vienna, Austria, May 7–11, 2024, OpenReview.net (2024). https://openreview.net/forum?id=apXtolxDaJ
13. Ilyas, A., Engstrom, L., et al.: A closer look at deep policy gradients. In: 8th International Conference on Learning Representations, Addis Ababa, Ethiopia, April 26-30, 2020, OpenReview.net (2020)
14. Liu, B., Liu, X., Jin, X., Stone, P., Liu, Q.: Conflict-averse gradient descent for multi-task learning. In: Annual Conference on Neural Information Processing Systems 2021. NeurIPS 2021, pp. 18878–18890 (2021)
15. Lu, H., Herman, D., Yu, Y.: Multi-objective reinforcement learning: convexity, stationarity and pareto optimality. In: The Eleventh International Conference on Learning Representations, ICLR 2023, Kigali, Rwanda, May 1–5, 2023. OpenReview.net (2023)

16. Maas, A.L., Daly, R.E., et al.: Learning word vectors for sentiment analysis. In: Proceedings of the 49th Annual Meeting of the Association for Computational Linguistics: Human Language Technologies, Portland, Oregon, USA, pp. 142–150. Association for Computational Linguistics (2011)
17. Moffaert, K.V., Nowé, A.: Multi-objective reinforcement learning using sets of pareto dominating policies. J. Mach. Learn. Res. **15**(1), 3483–3512 (2014)
18. OpenAI: GPT-4 technical report. CoRR abs/2303.08774 (2023). https://doi.org/10.48550/ARXIV.2303.08774
19. Ouyang, L., Wu, J., Jiang, X., et al.: Training language models to follow instructions with human feedback. In: Annual Conference on Neural Information Processing Systems 2022, New Orleans, LA, USA (2022)
20. Radford, A., Narasimhan, K.: Improving language understanding by generative pre-training (2018)
21. Ramé, A., Couairon, G., Dancette, C., et al.: Rewarded soups: towards pareto-optimal alignment by interpolating weights fine-tuned on diverse rewards. In: Annual Conference on Neural Information Processing Systems 2023, New Orleans, LA, USA (2023)
22. Reymond, M., Bargiacchi, E., Nowé, A.: Pareto conditioned networks. In: 21st International Conference on Autonomous Agents and Multiagent Systems, Auckland, New Zealand, May 9–13, 2022, pp. 1110–1118 (2022)
23. Schulman, J., Wolski, F., Dhariwal, P., Radford, A., Klimov, O.: Proximal policy optimization algorithms. CoRR abs/1707.06347 (2017)
24. Sener, O., Koltun, V.: Multi-task learning as multi-objective optimization. In: Annual Conference on Neural Information Processing Systems 2018, NeurIPS 2018, Montréal, Canada, pp. 525–536 (2018)
25. Senushkin, D., Patakin, N., Kuznetsov, A., Konushin, A.: Independent component alignment for multi-task learning. In: IEEE/CVF Conference on Computer Vision and Pattern Recognition, Vancouver, BC, Canada, pp. 20083–20093. IEEE (2023)
26. Touvron, H., Martin, L., Stone, K., Albert, P., et al.: Llama 2: open foundation and fine-tuned chat models. arXiv preprint arXiv:2307.09288 (2023)
27. Van Moffaert, K., Drugan, M.M., Nowé, A.: Scalarized multi-objective reinforcement learning: novel design techniques. In: 2013 IEEE Symposium on ADPRL, pp. 191–199 (2013)
28. Vaswani, A., Shazeer, N., Parmar, N., et al.: Attention is all you need. In: Annual Conference on Neural Information Processing Systems 2017, Long Beach, CA, USA, pp. 5998–6008 (2017)
29. von Werra, L., et al.: TRL: transformer reinforcement learning (2020). https://github.com/huggingface/trl
30. Yang, R., Pan, X., Luo, F., et al.: Rewards-in-context: multi-objective alignment of foundation models with dynamic preference adjustment. In: Forty-first International Conference on Machine Learning, Vienna, Austria, July 21–27, 2024. OpenReview.net (2024)
31. Yang, R., Sun, X., Narasimhan, K.: A generalized algorithm for multi-objective reinforcement learning and policy adaptation. In: Annual Conference on Neural Information Processing Systems 2019, NeurIPS 2019, Vancouver, BC, Canada, pp. 14610–14621 (2019)
32. Yu, T., Kumar, S., Gupta, A., Levine, S., Hausman, K., Finn, C.: Gradient surgery for multi-task learning. In: Annual Conference on Neural Information Processing Systems 2020. NeurIPS 2020, virtual (2020)

Uncertainty Quantification for Black-Box LLMs via Star Graphs Connectivity: Exploring Alternatives for Semantic Density

Zhaoye Li, Huan Chen, Huibin Tan, Long Lan, Yize Sui, and Jing Ren(✉)

College of Computer Science and Technology, National University of Defense Technology, Changsha 410073, China
{lizhaoye23,chenhuan14,tanhb_,long.lan,suiyize18,renjing}@nudt.edu.cn

Abstract. Large language models (LLMs) excel in natural language processing but are prone to generating hallucinations. One approach to detecting hallucinations in LLM outputs is uncertainty quantification. These methods assign relative scores to generated responses, indicating their likelihood of being correct or hallucinatory. A well-known technique is Semantic Density, which uses the "density" of a target response in the semantic space as a proxy for its confidence. This approach addresses two limitations of Semantic Entropy: its uncertainty score is prompt-wise, and it only checks for binary semantic equivalence rather than capturing nuanced differences between two responses. Despite the success of Semantic Density, it relies on token-level probabilities, which are inaccessible in black-box LLMs, limiting its broader applicability. In this paper, we propose alternatives to Semantic Density by reconstructing uncertainty indicators from Semantic Entropy. We introduce a weighted star graph centered on the target response, reflecting the fine-grained semantic relationships between the target and other semantics within the output space. We propose using the connectivity of this star graph as a proxy for the confidence of the target response. Specifically, we present three methods based on graph density, the spectral radius of the adjacency matrix, and the spectral radius of the graph Laplacian. Our analysis shows that our approaches have a comparable computational cost to Semantic Density but outperform it in terms of both applicability and performance, making them robust alternatives.

Keywords: Uncertainty Quantification · Large Language Models · Trustworthy AI

1 Introduction

Large language models (LLMs) excel in natural language processing, dialogue generation, and text summarization [1,27]. However, they often produce con-

---

Supplementary Information The online version contains supplementary material available at https://doi.org/10.1007/978-3-032-06078-5_16.

tent that sounds plausible but is factually incorrect, a phenomenon known as "hallucination" [10]. This issue is especially concerning in safety-critical fields like healthcare, where misinformation can have severe consequences. One way to assess the reliability of LLM outputs is through uncertainty quantification (UQ), which assigns uncertainty/confidence scores to responses, thereby highlighting those that are likely accurate and those that are more prone to hallucination.

The key principle of UQ is that higher divergence (lower consistency) among multiple responses to the same input suggests a higher risk of hallucination [6,17]. One well-known method for measuring the divergence of LLM output distributions is Semantic Entropy [6,13]. This method evaluates the degree of *semantic* divergence among multiple responses sampled from the model by calculating the predictive entropy over the predicted *meaning* distribution. Despite the success of Semantic Entropy in capturing semantic uncertainties, it has the following limitations: First, the returned uncertainty score is assigned to the prompt (i.e., prompt-wise) rather than to the individual responses being evaluated (i.e., not response-wise) [6]. Given that LLMs can generate diverse responses to the same prompt, applying the same uncertainty score to multiple potentially distinct responses is problematic [22]. Second, when comparing two responses, Semantic Entropy merely assesses semantic equivalence—treating responses with only subtle differences the same as those with major differences—and thus ignores the fine-grained distinctions that could improve the precision of uncertainty quantification (UQ) [22]. To address the two issues of Semantic Entropy, researchers have proposed Semantic Density [22]. Semantic Density is a response-wise uncertainty indicator that quantifies the confidence of LLM responses in semantic space. In this process, additional reference responses are sampled, and their fine-grained semantic differences to the target response (i.e., the response being evaluated for its reliability) are calculated. Finally, the "density" of the target response is estimated and serves as a proxy for the confidence of the target response. Although Semantic Density has made significant progress in addressing the aforementioned issues of Semantic Entropy and more accurately quantifying uncertainty in LLM responses, its applicability remains limited. This is because calculating Semantic Density requires obtaining probability information for each token generated by the LLM. However, in many cases, LLMs operate as black boxes via APIs, where users only have access to the final response text and cannot obtain token-level probability data.

This paper aims to reconstruct uncertainty/confidence indicators based on Semantic Entropy, which are suitable for black-box LLMs and serve as alternatives to Semantic Density. To measure the uncertainty/confidence level of a given target response y, we use an edge-weighted star graph to capture the fine-grained semantic relationships between y and the reference responses. By assessing the connectivity of this graph, we can evaluate the confidence of y. Specifically, we use y as the central node and other sampled reference responses as leaf nodes to form a star graph. The edge weights correspond to the semantic similarity—a continuous value between 0 and 1—that reflects degrees of semantic relatedness, rather than a binary equivalence, between y and these reference responses. Under this design, there is a positive correlation between the connectivity of the star graph and the semantic consistency between the reference responses and the target response y. The greater the connectivity, the closer the semantic alignment between the reference responses and the target response. This suggests that the target response resides within a confident region of the output semantic space, thereby reducing the likelihood of it being a hallucination, as a key feature of hallucinations is semantic divergence [17]. Comparatively speaking, this approach contrasts with Semantic Entropy by focusing on evaluating the confidence of individual responses (by linking star graph connectivity to response confidence), rather than assessing the divergence of responses related to the prompt. This directly addresses the first limitation of Semantic Entropy. Additionally, by setting the edge weights of the star graph to reflect fine-grained semantic similarity, we capture subtle semantic differences rather than simply determining semantic equivalence, thus resolving the second limitation. Unlike Semantic Density, which requires token-level probability data to model response confidence, our star graph-based approach relies solely on the text output from LLMs, overcoming the practical limitations of Semantic Density.

We propose three simple and effective methods to measure the connectivity of the star graph in order to assess the confidence of LLM responses: graph density, the spectral radius of the adjacency matrix, and the spectral radius of the graph Laplacian. We evaluated these methods on four question-answer datasets that are widely used in current UQ literature. The experimental results show that all three methods we propose outperform baseline approaches, including Semantic Entropy and Semantic Density, achieving a new state-of-the-art (SOTA). We further validate the superiority of our methods when handling varying numbers of reference responses, and target responses with different degrees of diversity. We conclude that our methods serve as effective alternatives to Semantic Density. This is because our methods not only exhibit superior performance compared to both Semantic Density and Semantic Entropy but also offer broader applicability, requiring only the text output from LLMs rather than token probabilities. Our contributions are summarized as follows:

- We propose a new perspective that addresses two limitations of Semantic Entropy by employing the connectivity of a star graph—centered on the target response and reflecting fine-grained semantic relations—as a proxy for that response's uncertainty/confidence.
- We propose three response-wise uncertainty/confidence indicators by calculating the graph density, the spectral radius of the adjacency matrix, and the spectral radius of the graph Laplacian. Additionally, we derive possible simplified expressions and theoretical upper and lower bounds.
- Analysis and experimental results demonstrate that the three proposed methods can serve as viable alternatives to Semantic Density for the following reasons: (1) our methods have broader applicability as they only require access to the LLM's text output, without needing token probabilities; (2) the computational cost of our methods is comparable to that of Semantic Density; (3) all three methods outperform baseline approaches, including Semantic Entropy and Semantic Density, achieving a new SOTA performance.

2 Related Work

In the literature on LLMs, the terms "uncertainty" and "confidence" are often used interchangeably, viewed as two aspects of the same principle—like two sides of the same coin [7,9,15,22]: high confidence typically corresponds to lower uncertainty (or higher certainty). However, some studies emphasize distinguishing between the two concepts [17], with uncertainty being considered a characteristic of the predicted distribution. Despite these differences, all approaches share a common goal: deriving a score that reflects the trustworthiness of LLM responses. Higher uncertainty or lower confidence often signals potential hallucinations. In contrast, lower uncertainty or higher confidence generally indicates greater accuracy.

Recently, a variety of UQ methods [3,6,17,19,21,22] have emerged. These methods differ in how they model uncertainty and the types of information they utilize, including the LLM's output text, token-level probabilities, internal embeddings, and model weights. UQ methods can be categorized into the two main types: white-box and black-box [7,11,17]. Black-box methods have access only to the LLM's output text, while white-box methods can also access the model's internal mechanisms and numerical outputs. Among these methods, Semantic Entropy [6] stands out as one of the most historically significant and is also a prominent white-box approach. Early methods, such as Predictive Entropy [18], combined lexical and semantic uncertainty, ignoring the fact that different lexical expressions can convey the same meaning. Semantic Entropy addresses this limitation by eliminating lexical uncertainty through semantic clustering (where semantically equivalent responses are grouped into clusters), marking a significant advancement in UQ. Since then, almost all UQ methods have incorporated semantics into their frameworks. Other representative methods include Deg [17], Ecc [17], and EigV [17], which exemplify black-box approaches. These methods utilize a weighted complete graph to represent the relationships between different semantics within the LLM output space, aiming to quantify semantic divergence. EigV [17] estimates the number of connected components in the graph by analyzing the eigenvalues of the graph Laplacian. In contrast, Deg [17] and Ecc [17] measure output diversity using the graph's degree matrix and the spectral embedding of its nodes, respectively. In addition to these key methods, several other approaches have been proposed. Discrete Semantic Entropy [6] serves as a black-box approximation of Semantic Entropy. Kernel Language Entropy [21] extends Semantic Entropy by incorporating fine-grained semantic relations beyond equivalence. Lastly, DUE [3] captures asymmetric logical relationships among reference responses.

3 Methodology

3.1 Task Formalization

Given a black-box LLM (where only the output text is available and the internal workings as well as numeric outputs, such as token logits, are not accessible), an

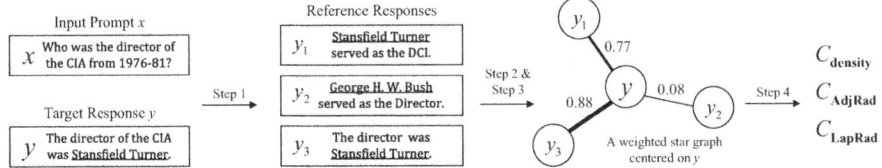

Fig. 1. In Step 1, we sample M additional responses, denoted as $y_1, y_2, \ldots, y_M$, which serve as reference responses to evaluate the reliability of y. In Step 2, we measure the semantic similarity between y and each of $y_1, y_2, \ldots, y_M$. In Step 3, we construct a star graph with y at the center and $y_1, y_2, \ldots, y_M$ as leaf nodes. Finally, in Step 4, the connectivity of the star graph is calculated, which serves as a proxy for the confidence of the target response.

input prompt x (e.g., an input question), and a target model-generated response y, the goal is to design a response-wise uncertainty/confidence indicator $C(y; x)$ (Fig. 1). It is important to note that: (1) Similar to [22], this paper specifically focuses on short-form responses, which are defined as single-proposition statements[1] [6]. (2) The objective is to derive a *relative* confidence score for ranking responses, *distinguishing* between correct and incorrect ones[2], rather than calculating the exact probability of response correctness. High confidence generally indicates correctness, whereas low confidence may indicate a potential hallucination. (3) As in [22], the methods proposed here act as confidence indicators, with higher output scores indicating a greater likelihood of correctness. If the output scores are negated, these indicators represent uncertainty indicators instead.

3.2 Step 1: Sampling Reference Responses

In Step 1, we sample M additional responses, denoted as $y_1, y_2, \ldots, y_M$, which serve as *reference responses* to evaluate the reliability of y. Following [22], we employ Diverse Beam Search [25] for sampling, since it tends to generate diverse and highly probable responses, thus providing good coverage of the LLM's semantic output space.

---

[1] These short-form responses are typically brief, consisting of only a few words or, at most, a single sentence, in contrast to longer paragraphs.

[2] For example, for two LLM input-output pairs $(x1, o1)$ and $(x2, o2)$, if the relative confidence score for $(x1, o1)$ is higher than that for $(x2, o2)$, then the probability of the event "$o1$ being correct for $x1$" is higher than that of the event "$o2$ being correct for $x2$". Consider the methods we propose, where (x_1, o_1) and (x_2, o_2) correspond to star graphs G_1 and G_2, respectively. If G_1 exhibits higher connectivity than G_2, it indicates that the reference responses for o_1 provide stronger support for x_1 than the reference responses for o_2 provide for x_2. Hence, the probability that "o_1 is correct for x_1" is higher than the probability that "o_2 is correct for x_2".

3.3 Step 2: Measuring Response Similarities

In Step 2, we present a method for calculating the semantic similarity (a value between 0 and 1, not limited to binary equivalence) between the target response y and each of the reference responses $y_1, y_2, \ldots, y_M$.

The output logits of natural language inference (NLI) models have been shown to effectively measure the semantic similarity between two sentences within a given context [17][3]. Following the best practices outlined in [17], we assess the semantic similarity, denoted as s_i, between y and y_i within the context of the input prompt x. We concatenate[4] x with y and y_i to form $x \oplus y$ and $x \oplus y_i$. These concatenated strings are then fed into the NLI model twice. In the first pass, $x \oplus y$ is treated as the premise and $x \oplus y_i$ as the hypothesis. In the second pass, $x \oplus y_i$ serves as the premise, while $x \oplus y$ is the hypothesis. The softmax function is applied to the predicted logits from the NLI model, and the similarity score is computed as the average of the entailment logits from both passes, as shown in the following equation:

$$s_i = \frac{1}{2} \left(\hat{p}_{entail}(x \oplus y, x \oplus y_i) + \hat{p}_{entail}(x \oplus y_i, x \oplus y) \right) \quad (1)$$

Since $\hat{p}_{entail}$ is constrained within the interval $[0, 1]$, it follows that the similarity score s_i is also constrained within this range.

3.4 Step 3: Constructing a Star Graph

In Step 3, we construct a graph to capture the fine-grained semantic relationships between the target response y and each of the reference responses $y_1, y_2, \ldots, y_M$. This many-to-one relationship naturally forms a star graph. A star graph consists of a central node, which is connected to several peripheral nodes, known as leaf nodes. The central node, often referred to as the "hub," serves as the primary connector, while the leaf nodes are connected only to the central node and have no edges between each other.

In this study, we construct a weighted, undirected star graph consisting of $M+1$ nodes. The central node represents y, the target response that needs to be evaluated for credibility, while the M leaf nodes are represented by $y_1, y_2, \ldots, y_M$. The weight of the edge (y, y_i) is assigned the value s_i, which denotes the semantic similarity between y and y_i, as calculated in Step 2. Intuitively, in the star graph, the greater the edge weight, the higher the reachability from the leaf nodes to the central node (implying the greater importance of the central node), and the tighter the connections between all nodes in the graph. In other words, a higher semantic similarity between the reference and target responses indicates that the

---

[3] A more common approach to measuring semantic similarity is to compute the cosine similarity between SBERT sentence embeddings [23]. We present detailed experimental analyses and discussion in the supplementary materials (Sect. 5), which indicate that SBERT-based similarity is unsuitable for quantifying uncertainty.

[4] The input template used to obtain the NLI model's output logits is described in the supplementary materials (Sect. 10).

target response (or target semantics) lies within a more confident region of the LLM output semantic space. We quantify the "proximity of leaf nodes to the central node" as a measure of the connectivity of the star graph. The detailed methodology will be provided in the following section. Before that, we introduce several key symbols and definitions. Specifically, the adjacency matrix of the graph is given by:

$$W = \begin{pmatrix} 0 & s_1 & s_2 & \cdots & s_M \\ s_1 & 0 & 0 & \cdots & 0 \\ s_2 & 0 & 0 & \cdots & 0 \\ \vdots & \vdots & \vdots & \ddots & \vdots \\ s_M & 0 & 0 & \cdots & 0 \end{pmatrix} = \begin{pmatrix} 0 & s^T \\ s & 0 \end{pmatrix}. \qquad (2)$$

where $s = (s_1, s_2, \ldots, s_M)^T$, which is an M-dimensional column vector, and s^T is its transpose, which is a row vector. In addition, the degree matrix is denoted as D, which is a diagonal matrix where each diagonal element represents the degree of a node. D is calculated as follows:

$$D = \text{diag}\left(\sum_{i=1}^{M} s_i, s_1, s_2, \ldots, s_M\right). \qquad (3)$$

3.5 Step 4: Calculating the Uncertainty/Confidence

In this section, we present three methods for measuring the connectivity of the star graph, which serve as a proxy for the confidence of the target response.

Graph Density. For an undirected simple *binary*[5] graph, graph density [5] is a measure of how full a graph is, reflecting the ratio between the actual number of edges present (current capacity) and the maximum possible number of edges (total possible capacity). Since the graph in our paper has a fixed number of M edges and the edge weights (defined by similarities) are non-negative and bounded within $[0, 1]$, we extend the definition of graph density. We do so by calculating the sum of all edge weights (current capacity) divided by the total sum of the maximum possible weights of all edges (total possible capacity).

$$C_{\text{Density}}(y; x) = \frac{\sum_{i=1}^{M}\sum_{j=i+1}^{M} w_{ij}}{M \cdot \sup_{1 \leq i < j \leq M}\{w_{ij}\}} = \frac{\sum_{i=1}^{M}\sum_{j=i+1}^{M} w_{ij}}{M \cdot 1} = \frac{1}{M}\sum_{i=1}^{M} s_i \qquad (4)$$

C_{Density} can be interpreted as the average similarity between the reference responses $y_1, y_2, \ldots, y_M$ and the target response y. Since s_i is bounded within the interval $[0, 1]$, it follows that C_{Density} is also constrained within this range.

---

[5] In this case, the term "binary" could refer to a graph where each edge either exists or does not exist (i.e., each edge is either 0 or 1, with no other possibilities).

The Spectral Radius of the Adjacency Matrix. The spectral radius, defined as the largest absolute value of the eigenvalues of a matrix, plays a pivotal role in graph theory. For a weighted (with non-negative weights) undirected graph (such as the star graph introduced in Step 3), the spectral radius of the adjacency matrix serves as a key indicator of the graph's connectivity [2]. A larger radius typically signifies stronger interactions between vertices, thereby facilitating more efficient propagation of information or flow across the graph [2].

We propose using the spectral radius of the adjacency matrix W as a proxy for the confidence of the target response. Through simplified analysis, we find that the spectral radius is essentially the ℓ_2-norm of s.

$$C_{\text{AdjRad}}(y;x) = \sqrt{\sum_{i=1}^{M} s_i^2} = \|s\|_2 \ . \tag{5}$$

The proof of this relationship is presented as follows. Consider the eigenvalue equation:

$$W\begin{pmatrix} p \\ q \end{pmatrix} = \lambda(W) \begin{pmatrix} p \\ q \end{pmatrix}, \tag{6}$$

where $\lambda(W)$ is the eigenvalue and $\begin{pmatrix} p \\ q \end{pmatrix}$ is the corresponding eigenvector. Here, p is a scalar and $q = (q_1, q_2, \ldots, q_M)^T \in \mathbb{R}^M$ is an M-dimensional vector. Expanding the matrix multiplication in Eq. 6, we get the following system of equations:
(*i*) The first equation from the top row of W is:

$$s^T q = \lambda(W) p. \tag{7}$$

(*ii*) For the remaining M rows in W, we get $s_i p = \lambda(W) q_i$ $(1 \leq i \leq M)$, which implies

$$q_i = \frac{s_i}{\lambda(W)} p \quad (1 \leq i \leq M). \tag{8}$$

Now, substitute Eq. 8 for all i into Eq. 7. This gives:

$$s^T q = \sum_{i=1}^{M} s_i \left(\frac{s_i}{\lambda(W)} p \right) = \frac{p}{\lambda(W)} \sum_{i=1}^{M} s_i^2. \tag{9}$$

Equating Eq. 9 with $\lambda(W)p$ (The right-hand side of Eq. 7), we obtain $\frac{p}{\lambda(W)} \sum_{i=1}^{M} s_i^2 = \lambda(W)p$. Assuming $p \neq 0$[6], further simplification yields: $\lambda(W) = \pm\sqrt{\sum_{i=1}^{M} s_i^2}$. Since W is a real symmetric matrix, its eigenvalues are real. Therefore, the largest absolute value of the eigenvalues is:

$$C_{\text{AdjRad}} = \sqrt{\sum_{i=1}^{M} s_i^2} = \|s\|_2. \tag{10}$$

---

[6] This assumption does not affect the computation of the spectral radius, as explained in the supplementary materials (Sect. 7).

Since s_i is bounded within the interval $[0,1]$, it follows that C_{AdjRad} is constrained within the range $[0, \sqrt{M}]$.

The Spectral Radius of the Graph Laplacian. The spectral radius of the Laplacian matrix $L = D - W$ can also give indirect insights into the graph's connectivity [2]. If the radius is large, it suggests that the graph might contain nodes with very high degrees, which could indicate potential clusters [2]. We propose using the spectral radius of the graph Laplacian as a proxy for the confidence of the target response. It is well-known that the eigenvalues of the Laplacian matrix are always real (since it is a real symmetric matrix) and non-negative (since it is positive semi-definite). Therefore, the spectral radius is essentially the largest eigenvalue of the Laplacian matrix. Formally, we define:

$$C_{\text{LapRad}}(y; x) = \lambda_{\max}(L) = \lambda_{\max}(D - W). \tag{11}$$

It is evident that both C_{Density} and C_{AdjRad} (as shown in Eqs. 4 and 5) are tightly bounded within a specific interval. In fact, a similar conclusion holds for C_{LapRad}, despite the difficulty in deriving an explicit expression for it. In the supplementary materials (Sect. 6), we rigorously prove that C_{LapRad} is bounded within the interval $[0, M+1]$. The established boundary allows practitioners to define a fixed threshold within this range for filtering out unreliable responses, thereby improving the reliability of the remaining responses (which will subsequently be evaluated using the AUARC metric).

Theorem 1 (Boundary Properties of C_{LapRad}). *For any $0 \leq s_i \leq 1$ where $1 \leq i \leq M$, C_{LapRad} is bounded within the interval $[0, M+1]$. Specifically, $C_{LapRad} = 0$ if and only if $s_i = 0$ for all $1 \leq i \leq M$, and $C_{LapRad} = M+1$ if and only if $s_i = 1$ for all $1 \leq i \leq M$.*

3.6 Comparative Analysis with Existing Approaches

- **Comparison with Semantic Entropy.** Compared to Semantic Entropy, our methods are specifically designed to evaluate the confidence of a given response, rather than the divergence of reference responses associated with the prompt. This addresses the first issue identified with Semantic Entropy. Furthermore, by assigning edge weights to reflect fine-grained semantic similarity, we effectively capture subtle semantic differences among responses rather than simply determining whether they are semantically equivalent. This approach addresses the second limitation. *The ablation experiment demonstrates that the two aforementioned points are effective, with detailed setup and results provided in the supplementary materials (Sect. 14).*
- **Comparison with Semantic Density.** Our methods only require access to the LLM's output text, without relying on token-level probability data. This overcomes the practical limitations associated with Semantic Density. In terms of computational cost, our proposed methods and Semantic Density have similar overhead. Both require sampling M reference responses initially.

Our methods run the NLI model $2M$ times in the second step, while Semantic Density requires *up to* $2M$ runs. Given that the NLI model consumes far fewer resources than LLMs, the computational overhead remains comparable. Further explanations are provided in the supplementary materials (Sect. 3).
- **Comparison with Graph-Based Methods.** This part of the content is provided in the supplementary materials (Sect. 2).

4 Experiments and Result Analysis

4.1 Experimental Setups

Datasets and Models. Currently, the evaluation of UQ in LLMs primarily focuses on question-answer datasets [3,6,13,17,21,22]. We assess performance across a diverse range of question-answering domains, including biomedical science (BioASQ [24], 2,814 questions), trivia knowledge (TriviaQA [12], 9,960 questions), scientific knowledge (SciQ [26], 1,000 questions), and natural questions (NQ [14], 3,610 questions derived from real-world Google Search data). Detailed information regarding the datasets, their splits, and example questions for each dataset can be found in the supplementary materials (Sects. 8 and 9). We utilize five well-known LLMs for evaluation, with model sizes ranging from 1B to 32B parameters. These models include Llama-3.2-1B[7], Llama-3.2-3B[8], Gemma2-2B[9], Mistral-7B-v0.3[10] and QWen1.5-32B[11]. For the NLI model used to calculate response similarities, we employ DeBERTa-Large-MNLI [8].

Evaluation Metrics. Evaluation metrics include AUROC and AUARC [20], the primary measures in current uncertainty quantification literature [3,13,17,21]. AUROC (Area Under the Receiver Operating Characteristic Curve) measures how well confidence scores distinguish between correct and incorrect responses. An AUROC of 0.5 indicates random guessing, while an AUROC of 1 signifies perfect discrimination, where all correct responses have higher confidence scores than all incorrect ones. Additionally, QA accuracy can be improved by abstaining from (or rejecting) low-confidence responses. This improvement is quantified using AUARC (Area Under the Accuracy-Rejection Curve) [20], which measures the area under the accuracy-rejection curve at various thresholds. The rejection accuracy at a given threshold is determined by the accuracy of the remaining responses after rejecting those with confidence scores below this threshold.

---

[7] https://huggingface.co/meta-llama/Llama-3.2-1B-Instruct.
[8] https://huggingface.co/meta-llama/Llama-3.2-3B-Instruct.
[9] https://huggingface.co/google/gemma-2-2b-it.
[10] https://huggingface.co/mistralai/Mistral-7B-Instruct-v0.3.
[11] https://huggingface.co/Qwen/Qwen1.5-32B.

Baseline Methods. We included 10 baseline methods for comparison, consisting of five white-box and five black-box approaches. Although this paper primarily focuses on black-box scenarios, we also integrated state-of-the-art white-box methods to highlight the performance advantages of the proposed approaches. The white-box methods have complete access to the LLMs, including their internal mechanisms, numerical outputs, and generated text, whereas the black-box methods are limited to the LLM's output text only. White-box baselines include Predictive Entropy (PE) [18], Length-Normalized Likelihood (LNL) [19], Semantic Entropy (SE) [6], Shifting Attention to Relevance (SAR) [4], and Semantic Density (SD) [22]. Black-box baselines include Discrete Semantic Entropy (DSE) [6], Kernel Language Entropy (KLE) [21], EigV [17], Deg [17], DUE [3]. We provide a brief introduction to the baselines and their implementation details in the supplementary materials (Sect. 15).

Response Generation. All responses to the questions were generated in free-form text. The prompts used for generating these responses are provided in the supplementary materials (Sect. 9). Following [22], we used Diverse Beam Search [25] to sample 10 responses for each question by configuring 10 groups, with each group containing one beam. In the main experiment, we used the responses generated by the first group (generated through greedy search) as the target responses, and the responses generated by the remaining groups as the reference responses.

Correctness Metrics (Metrics for Assessing the Accuracy of Target Response). Following [6], we prompted GPT-4-0613 to verify whether the target response aligned with any ground truth answers provided by the datasets[12]. In [22], a target response is considered correct if its Rouge-L score [16] with respect to any ground truth answer exceeds 0.3. The results of using Rouge-L for correctness judgment are included in the supplementary materials (Sect. 13).

4.2 Main Results

The evaluation results for Llama3.2-3B and QWen1.5-32B are presented in Table 1, while those for Llama3.2-1B, Gemma2-2B, and Mistral-7B are included in the supplementary materials (Sect. 12). Based on the results from *five* LLMs, *four* datasets, *two* correctness metrics (GPT-4 judge and Rouge-L judge), and *two* evaluation metrics (AUROC and AUARC), totaling 80 experimental combinations ($5 \times 4 \times 2 \times 2 = 80$), we present the following findings:

- **Each of the three proposed methods consistently outperforms the baseline methods across all four datasets and five LLMs.** For example, when evaluated using Llama3.2-1B, C_{AdjRad} achieves up to a 10.48% higher

---

[12] The prompt used for auto-generated correctness judgment, together with the performance evaluation of the LLM's correctness judgments, is provided in the supplementary materials (Sect. 11).

Table 1. Evaluation results on Llama3.2-3B and QWen1.5-32B. Results from our methods that surpass all baselines are in **bold**. The best baseline results are highlighted in green. The optimal outcomes from the three proposed methods are in blue. The correctness of a target response is determined by GPT-4-0613 based on whether it matches any of the ground truth answers. All results are presented as percentages.

Method	BioASQ		NQ		SciQ		TriviaQA	
	AUROC	AUARC	AUROC	AUARC	AUROC	AUARC	AUROC	AUARC
Llama3.2-3B								
PE	53.55	27.51	63.75	23.47	55.51	41.50	61.54	38.78
LNL	64.59	33.97	61.42	20.89	61.14	52.59	60.18	36.57
SE	74.26	38.84	73.10	27.38	64.53	47.53	72.01	45.96
SAR	74.32	39.34	73.59	28.16	65.26	48.39	72.31	46.62
SD	75.33	40.80	72.15	27.70	69.94	51.50	74.08	47.41
DSE	74.18	38.58	72.92	27.21	64.62	47.24	71.78	45.95
KLE	73.05	38.80	70.80	26.48	63.30	47.47	71.63	45.84
EigV	70.77	36.12	70.52	25.79	58.39	43.99	69.65	44.16
Deg	74.88	40.02	74.18	28.48	65.85	49.52	72.65	46.89
DUE	73.16	38.62	72.30	27.30	62.84	47.17	70.90	45.71
C_{Density}	**78.32**	**42.21**	**77.81**	**30.50**	**76.61**	**56.49**	**77.04**	**49.26**
C_{AdjRad}	**78.18**	**42.05**	**78.23**	**31.07**	**78.14**	**57.85**	**77.72**	**49.67**
C_{LapRad}	**78.28**	**42.21**	**78.00**	**30.65**	**77.09**	**56.84**	**77.21**	**49.34**
QWen1.5-32B								
PE	43.62	20.08	55.66	22.60	41.11	66.33	60.56	70.30
LNL	66.01	30.67	63.93	23.53	60.10	72.78	55.38	59.99
SE	64.93	28.76	72.85	30.26	74.25	82.21	81.28	81.84
SAR	67.42	30.49	73.45	32.25	77.39	84.53	81.64	82.20
SD	71.57	32.71	74.83	32.49	79.17	85.85	87.65	86.04
DSE	64.98	28.69	72.42	30.05	74.15	82.64	81.06	81.77
KLE	66.31	29.50	72.38	30.77	75.00	84.15	82.72	82.97
EigV	64.04	29.29	70.23	28.48	72.26	81.61	79.50	81.00
Deg	66.88	29.90	74.34	31.97	77.22	84.85	83.26	83.40
DUE	66.37	29.82	72.37	30.65	76.08	84.39	81.54	82.70
C_{Density}	**72.85**	**32.73**	**78.88**	**34.91**	**82.58**	**87.08**	**90.17**	**87.18**
C_{AdjRad}	**73.17**	**32.76**	**79.19**	**35.11**	**82.44**	**87.01**	**90.06**	**87.15**
C_{LapRad}	**73.00**	**32.75**	**79.03**	**34.98**	**82.63**	**87.10**	**90.19**	**87.19**

AUROC on the SciQ dataset and up to a 5.97% improvement on the TriviaQA dataset compared to the best baseline results. To confirm that the observed performance differences are statistically significant, we conducted pairwise significance tests (as detailed in the supplementary materials (Sect. 18)). The

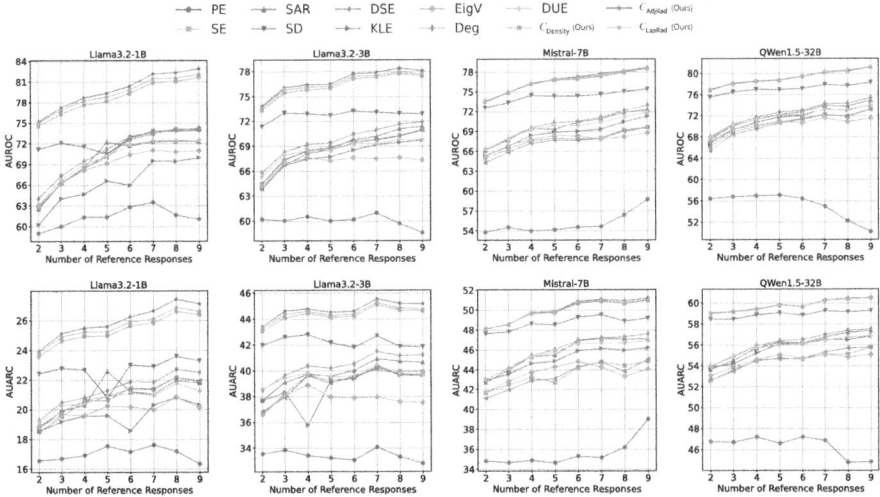

Fig. 2. The performance across varying numbers of reference responses is evaluated. Each point on the curve represents the average result across four datasets. We include all baselines for comparison, except for Length-Normalized Likelihood (LNL), as LNL operates without the need for reference responses. Each of our methods consistently outperforms all baseline methods across all numbers of reference responses.

results show that all p-values are significantly less than 0.05, thereby confirming the consistent performance improvement of each proposed method.

- **Compared to Semantic Density, each of the three proposed methods shows a considerably greater improvement over Semantic Entropy.** Both Semantic Density and the three proposed methods are derived from improvements addressing two limitations of Semantic Entropy. Experimental results demonstrate that each of our proposed methods significantly outperforms Semantic Density, even without accessing the token logits (token probability) of the LLM output, highlighting both the superior performance and broader applicability of UQ modeling based on star graph connectivity over the density-based approach.

- **Compared to Semantic Density, our methods exhibit superior compatibility across different LLM sizes.** In experiments with Llama3.2-1B, Gemma2-2B, and Llama3.2-3B, Semantic Density occasionally underperforms relative to Deg. In contrast, our proposed methods consistently outperform baseline approaches across all LLM sizes, from smaller models like Llama3.2-1B to larger models like QWen1.5-32B.

4.3 Robustness of Our Proposed Methods

We adhere to the experimental setup outlined in [22] to further validate the robustness of our methods. Two experiments were conducted:

- **Performance across Varying Numbers of Reference Responses.** This experiment employs the same setup as the main experiment, with the sole distinction being the variation in the number of reference responses. Experimental results, as shown in Fig. 2, demonstrate that: (1) the performance of our methods generally improves as the number of reference responses increases. (2) Under varying numbers of reference responses, our methods consistently outperform baseline methods. (3) Compared with the baseline methods, our approaches demonstrate significantly higher generation efficiency. Specifically, our methods achieve comparable AUROC or AUARC scores while requiring fewer reference responses. Notably, in the Llama3.2-1B experiments, our approaches attain superior performance using only 2 reference responses, whereas the baseline methods require 9 reference responses to achieve similar results.
- **Performance on Target Responses with Varying Degrees of Diversity.** In practical applications, users may have differing preferences for response generation strategies. Some users may favor a greedy sampling strategy, which yields more certain and consistent responses, while others may require a broader range of diverse responses. Given this consideration, we conducted this experiment. The diversity of the responses generated by diverse beam search varies across different beam groups (the first group performs a greedy beam search, while the subsequent groups encourage more diverse responses). Therefore, we use the responses from groups 2, 4, 6, 8, and 10 as target responses representing higher diversity, with responses from the other groups serving as reference responses. This setup follows the methodology outlined in [22]. Experimental results, as presented in Fig. 3, demonstrate that all of our proposed methods consistently outperform baseline approaches.

5 Future Work: Extending Our Methods for Detecting Token-Level Hallucination

Compared to Semantic Density, our methods show stronger advantages in addressing the two limitations of Semantic Entropy. However, similar to Semantic Entropy and Semantic Density, our methods can only assess the overall relative correctness of the entire target response, but cannot evaluate specific tokens (words or word pieces). To address this issue, we propose the following solution. First, the entire response (which may be a lengthy paragraph) is decomposed into multiple question-answer pairs, with each pair corresponding to a specific text snippet in the original content. Subsequently, the answer within each pair is treated as the target response, and additional short-form reference responses are generated based on the associated question. Confidence scores are then calculated for each question-answer pair. Given that each question-answer pair uniquely corresponds to a specific text snippet in the original content, the confidence score can be interpreted as the confidence level for the respective text snippet. This approach enables more precise identification of hallucinations at the token level.

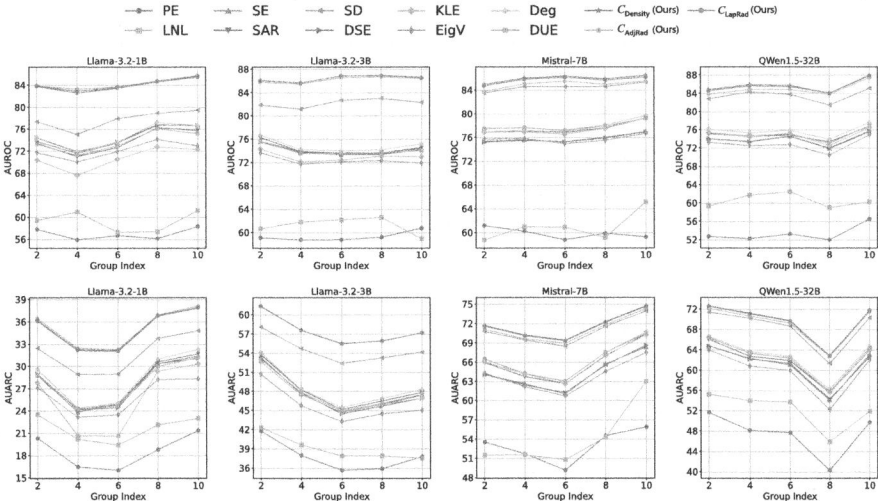

Fig. 3. Performance on target responses with varying degrees of diversity. We use responses from groups 2, 4, 6, 8, and 10 as target responses with varying diversity levels, while other groups provide reference responses. Each curve point shows the average result across four datasets. All baselines are included for comparison.

6 Conclusion

In this paper, we propose simple yet effective methods for uncertainty quantification as alternatives to Semantic Density. Specifically, we provide a new perspective that addresses two limitations of Semantic Entropy by using the connectivity of a specially tailored star graph as a proxy for the confidence of the target response. We propose using the graph density, the spectral radius of the adjacency matrix, and the spectral radius of the graph Laplacian as proxies for confidence. Analysis and experimental results demonstrate that the three proposed methods can serve as viable alternatives to Semantic Density.

Acknowledgement. This work was partially supported by the National Natural Science Foundation of China (No. 62376282). Furthermore, we would like to express our gratitude to the area chair and reviewers for their insightful and constructive feedback, which greatly enhanced the clarity and overall quality of this paper.

References

1. Chi, H., et al.: Unveiling causal reasoning in large language models: reality or mirage? In: Advances in Neural Information Processing Systems, vol. 37, pp. 96640–96670 (2024)
2. Chung, F.R.: Spectral Graph Theory, vol. 92. American Mathematical Soc. (1997)

3. Da, L., Chen, T., Cheng, L., Wei, H.: LLM uncertainty quantification through directional entailment graph and claim level response augmentation. arXiv preprint arXiv:2407.00994 (2024)
4. Duan, J., et al.: Shifting attention to relevance: towards the predictive uncertainty quantification of free-form large language models. In: Proceedings of the 62nd Annual Meeting of the Association for Computational Linguistics (Volume 1: Long Papers), pp. 5050–5063 (2024)
5. Erdös, P., Rényi, A.: On random graphs I. Publ. Math. Debrecen. **6**(290-297), 18 (1959)
6. Farquhar, S., Kossen, J., Kuhn, L., Gal, Y.: Detecting hallucinations in large language models using semantic entropy. Nature **630**(8017), 625–630 (2024)
7. Geng, J., Cai, F., Wang, Y., Koeppl, H., Nakov, P., Gurevych, I.: A survey of confidence estimation and calibration in large language models. In: Proceedings of the 2024 Conference of the North American Chapter of the Association for Computational Linguistics: Human Language Technologies (Volume 1: Long Papers), pp. 6577–6595 (2024)
8. He, P., Liu, X., Gao, J., Chen, W.: DeBERTa: decoding-enhanced BERT with disentangled attention. In: International Conference on Learning Representations (2021)
9. Hu, M., Zhang, Z., Zhao, S., Huang, M., Wu, B.: Uncertainty in natural language processing: Sources, quantification, and applications. arXiv preprint arXiv:2306.04459 (2023)
10. Huang, L., et al.: A survey on hallucination in large language models: principles, taxonomy, challenges, and open questions. ACM Trans. Inf. Syst. (2023)
11. Ji, Z., et al.: Survey of hallucination in natural language generation. ACM Comput. Surv. **55**(12), 1–38 (2023)
12. Joshi, M., Choi, E., Weld, D.S., Zettlemoyer, L.: TriviaQA: a large scale distantly supervised challenge dataset for reading comprehension. In: Proceedings of the 55th Annual Meeting of the Association for Computational Linguistics (Volume 1: Long Papers), pp. 1601–1611 (2017)
13. Kuhn, L., Gal, Y., Farquhar, S.: Semantic uncertainty: linguistic invariances for uncertainty estimation in natural language generation. In: The Eleventh International Conference on Learning Representations (2023)
14. Kwiatkowski, T., et al.: Natural questions: a benchmark for question answering research. Trans. Assoc. Comput. Linguist. **7**, 453–466 (2019)
15. Liang, X., et al.: Internal consistency and self-feedback in large language models: a survey. arXiv preprint arXiv:2407.14507 (2024)
16. Lin, C.Y., Och, F.J.: Automatic evaluation of machine translation quality using longest common subsequence and skip-bigram statistics. In: Proceedings of the 42nd Annual Meeting of the Association for Computational Linguistics (ACL-04), pp. 605–612 (2004)
17. Lin, Z., Trivedi, S., Sun, J.: Generating with confidence: uncertainty quantification for black-box large language models. Trans. Mach. Learn. Res. (2024)
18. Lindley, D.V.: On a measure of the information provided by an experiment. Ann. Math. Stat. **27**(4), 986–1005 (1956)
19. Murray, K., Chiang, D.: Correcting length bias in neural machine translation. In: Proceedings of the Third Conference on Machine Translation: Research Papers, pp. 212–223 (2018)
20. Nadeem, M.S.A., Zucker, J.D., Hanczar, B.: Accuracy-rejection curves (ARCs) for comparing classification methods with a reject option. In: Machine Learning in Systems Biology, pp. 65–81. PMLR (2009)

21. Nikitin, A., Kossen, J., Gal, Y., Marttinen, P.: Kernel language entropy: fine-grained uncertainty quantification for LLMs from semantic similarities. In: The Thirty-eighth Annual Conference on Neural Information Processing Systems (2024)
22. Qiu, X., Miikkulainen, R.: Semantic density: uncertainty quantification for large language models through confidence measurement in semantic space. In: The Thirty-eighth Annual Conference on Neural Information Processing Systems (2024)
23. Reimers, N., Gurevych, I.: Sentence-BERT: sentence embeddings using Siamese BERT-networks. In: Proceedings of the 2019 Conference on Empirical Methods in Natural Language Processing and the 9th International Joint Conference on Natural Language Processing (EMNLP-IJCNLP), pp. 3982–3992 (2019)
24. Tsatsaronis, G., et al.: An overview of the BIOASQ large-scale biomedical semantic indexing and question answering competition. BMC Bioinf. **16**, 1–28 (2015)
25. Vijayakumar, A., et al.: Diverse beam search for improved description of complex scenes. In: Proceedings of the AAAI Conference on Artificial Intelligence, vol. 32 (2018)
26. Welbl, J., Liu, N.F., Gardner, M.: Crowdsourcing multiple choice science questions. In: Proceedings of the 3rd Workshop on Noisy User-Generated Text, pp. 94–106 (2017)
27. Zhao, W.X., et al.: A survey of large language models. arXiv preprint arXiv:2303.18223 (2023)

Balanced and Token-Efficient Summarization of User Reviews via Stratified Sampling and Large Language Models

Fabrizio Marozzo[1](✉), Loris Belcastro[1], Cristian Cosentino[1], and Pietro Liò[2]

[1] University of Calabria, 87036 Rende, Italy
{fmarozzo,lbelcastro,ccosentino}@dimes.unical.it
[2] University of Cambridge, Cambridge CB3 0FD, UK
pietro.lio@cl.cam.ac.uk

Abstract. User-generated reviews offer valuable insights into consumer experiences, preferences, and concerns. They provide direct feedback on product perception and improvements while helping users evaluate strengths, weaknesses, and alternatives. Advanced machine learning techniques, including LLMs like BERT and GPT, enhance the extraction of meaningful information from these vast datasets. This paper introduces a framework leveraging Large Language Models (LLMs) to generate high-quality summaries using minimal input tokens. By employing multidimensional classification (sentiment, topics, emotion) combined with a stratified sampling approach, our framework selects a compact yet comprehensive subset of reviews that accurately represents the original dataset. Tailored prompts guide the LLMs to create balanced summaries that fairly represent both strengths and weaknesses. Experiments on Amazon and Tripadvisor datasets demonstrate that our method significantly reduces token usage and computational costs, while consistently outperforming traditional AI-based summarization approaches in terms of content coverage, balance, and semantic accuracy.

Keywords: Large Language Models · Generative AI · AI-Generated Summaries · Review Aggregation · Opinion Mining

1 Introduction

In the current digital landscape, user-generated reviews provide essential insights into consumer experiences, preferences, and concerns across various industries. Businesses leverage these reviews to evaluate product performance, identify areas needing improvement, and better adapt to consumer expectations [25]. Simultaneously, consumers rely on reviews to assess product strengths, weaknesses, and available alternatives before making purchasing decisions [29].

However, effectively extracting meaningful insights from extensive volumes of user-generated content requires advanced classification techniques, such as sentiment analysis and topic modeling [18]. Once classified, reviews can be grouped and filtered to select the most representative examples. While platforms like Amazon and Booking display relevant reviews to aid consumers, ensuring fairness and representativeness in review selection is challenging but critical. Representative reviews must clearly highlight a product's key attributes, including both positive and negative aspects, as well as distinctive features [12]. Recent advances in Large Language Models (LLMs) offer significant potential to enhance this classification and selection process, improving the quality, relevance, and balance of insights extracted from reviews [22].

In this paper, we propose a novel framework leveraging LLMs to systematically classify and summarize user-generated reviews, ensuring balanced and comprehensive insights while significantly reducing computational costs. Our approach first classifies reviews across multiple dimensions (sentiment, topics, and emotions) and then employs a stratified sampling strategy to select a compact yet representative subset. This carefully constructed sample accurately mirrors the original dataset distribution across all dimensions. Subsequently, a generative LLM processes the selected subset, guided by tailored prompts, to produce balanced summaries that fairly represent both positive and negative viewpoints without bias. Crucially, our framework prioritizes token efficiency by using minimal input tokens, significantly enhancing scalability and cost-effectiveness for processing large review datasets [20].

To validate the proposed framework, we conducted comprehensive experiments on Amazon and Tripadvisor datasets, representing diverse consumer sentiments and product categories. Results demonstrate that our method consistently produces summaries of superior quality compared to conventional AI summarization approaches, as evidenced by text quality scores, latent semantic representations, and evaluations from automated tools and human assessors. Additionally, our compact and representative sampling strategy substantially reduces token usage and computational resources without compromising summary quality, thereby achieving optimal efficiency and scalability.

The remainder of this paper is structured as follows. Section 2 reviews related work. Section 3 presents the proposed framework. Section 4 discusses the results. Finally, Sect. 5 concludes the paper.

2 Related Work

Artificial intelligence powered by LLMs has revolutionized data extraction, enabling faster, more intuitive processing of natural language queries for report generation, question answering, and data visualization. These models are widely applied in education, e-commerce, healthcare, and entertainment, particularly through chatbots for information retrieval [4]. In education, they assist in lesson planning [17], while in healthcare, they aid in disease detection and diagnosis [3]. In e-commerce, LLMs enhance customer support and shopping experiences [10] and outperform human crowd-workers in data annotation tasks [8].

LLMs like GPT are effective in generating descriptive summaries across domains, from extracting insights from tables [23] to summarizing medical reports [15] and financial texts [27]. In cybersecurity, they help summarize system logs, improving data organization and security audits [30]. However, evaluating LLM-generated summaries remains challenging due to semantic quality concerns and hallucinations [21]. To address these issues, a systematic evaluation framework was proposed, assessing reports based on completeness, accuracy, verifiability, and responsiveness to information needs [14].

LLMs have also enhanced the analysis of content posted on social media through sentiment analysis, topic modeling, and summarization [6], supporting applications like product recommendation and market research. Sentiment classification has been improved using CNN-based functions [2], hybrid LSTM-CNN models for tweets [19], and GRU-based models for product reviews [1]. Comparative studies [20] show that models like GPT-3.5 and LLaMA-2 excel in predicting ratings and understanding sentiment. However, evaluating the quality of LLM-generated summaries remains a complex task, as standard metrics like TF-IDF, ROUGE-L, or S-BERT capture only limited aspects of informativeness and coherence. For example, [7] propose a threefold evaluation combining semantic metrics, LLM-as-evaluator scoring, and expert judgment. Similarly, [11] introduce fairness-aware measures like Equal Coverage and Coverage Parity to assess representation across social attributes while accounting for redundancy. Despite these advances, reliably capturing the semantic quality and fairness of LLM outputs remains an open challenge.

In contrast to previous work, our study categorizes user reviews across sentiment, emotion, and topic to improve the accuracy and completeness of LLM-generated reports. Moreover, it aims to ensure fair and balanced summaries, providing consumers with comprehensive insights that reflect both positive and negative feedback. By employing multidimensional classification and stratified sampling, we effectively capture consumer priorities. Additionally, we introduce a robust evaluation framework, benchmarking report quality through quantitative text metrics, latent representations, and qualitative assessments via automated tools and human evaluations.

3 Proposed Framework

The proposed framework analyzes online reviews, classifies sentiments, and extracts key topics to generate balanced and detailed reports. These reports highlight strengths and weaknesses, aiding consumers and helping companies refine their offerings. As shown in Fig. 1, the framework comprises four main phases, which are detailed below.

The initial phase consists of systematically collecting *product/service reviews* from *online platforms*, through the use of official APIs or API of sites specialized in downloading data. Platforms provide access to products, services, and user reviews, such as Amazon for products, Booking and Tripadvisor for hotels, Tripadvisor and Google Maps for restaurants, and TrustPilot for services. Once you have chosen a platform, chosen a product/service, user reviews are downloaded together with all the metadata of the reviews themselves (e.g. how many people found a review useful) and of the product (e.g. information sheet). This process in some cases requires the use of specific keywords or filters on the reviews to ensure that the collected reviews are directly related to consumer experiences. To this end, the framework provides a filtering mechanism to select only the most relevant reviews, thus laying a solid foundation for the targeted and efficient analysis performed in the subsequent phases.

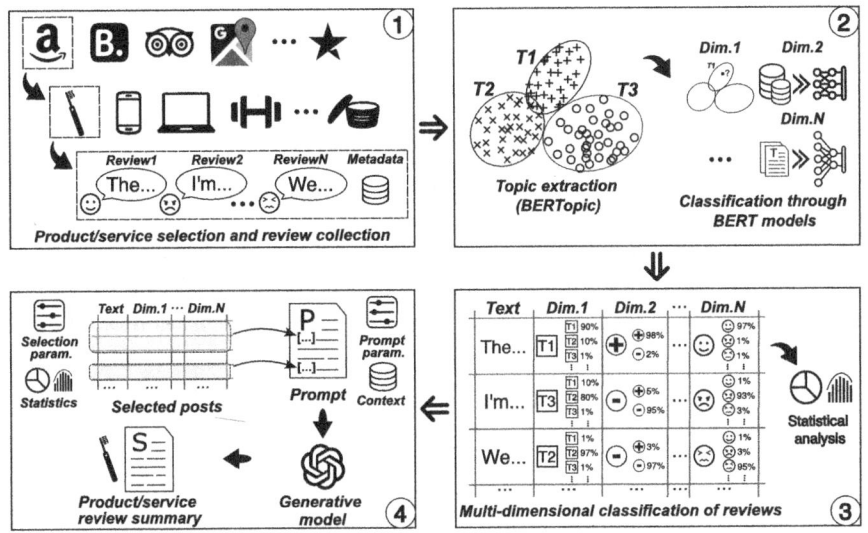

Fig. 1. Execution flow of the proposed framework.

The second phase utilizes analytical LLMs for multidimensional classification, employing tools like optimized BERT models to classify reviews across dimensions such as sentiment (positive or negative), emotion (e.g., joy, anger), and topics [5]. Each review is analyzed to determine its overall sentiment, the emotions expressed by users, and the topics discussed. For topic analysis (*BERTopic*), a comprehensive review of all topics must first be conducted, enabling the model to identify and explain which topic is addressed in a given review. For other dimensions, classification models (e.g., *BERT models*) are trained on specific datasets to accurately identify dimensions and their respective classes. These models not only assign labels (e.g., positive or negative sentiment) but also provide probabilities (e.g., 95% positive, 5% negative), ensuring nuanced and reliable classification.

The third phase organizes all collected reviews, along with their metadata and classifications from the different examined dimensions (*multi-dimensional classification*). This classification enables the grouping of similar reviews across dimensions such as sentiment (positive and negative), topic (various discussion topics), emotions (e.g., happy, sad), and time (e.g., last month, this year), providing a comprehensive understanding of consumer feedback. *Statistical data analysis* is conducted to examine the distribution of reviews across all these dimensions, offering valuable insights into the prevalence and relationships of sentiments, topics, emotions, and temporal trends. This comprehensive process is fundamental to improving the completeness and depth of the analysis.

The final step of our framework utilizes generative LLMs to create human-readable summaries of product/service reviews that are both comprehensive and balanced, capturing their strengths as well as their weaknesses. The process leverages the results of multidimensional classification, where a stratified sampling method selects a compact, representative sample that reflects the distribution of all dimensions and classes in the original dataset (e.g., positive and negative aspects for the sentiment dimension) while minimizing token usage. The sample generation process is guided by user-defined parameters and informed by statistical insights from the entire dataset, including class distributions across each dimension. This compact representative sample is then provided to a generative LLM (e.g., GPT-4), which, guided by a tailored prompt, appropriate parameters, and context information, produces a human-readable summary that is both balanced and comprehensive, effectively highlighting a product's or service's strengths and weaknesses while ensuring fair representation of consumer feedback.

4 Experimental Results

The experimental evaluation of our framework is based on two newly created datasets, addressing the lack of publicly available AI-generated summaries. While platforms like Amazon and Tripadvisor now provide AI-generated summaries, others such as Booking and TrustPilot do not, limiting their inclusion in existing datasets[1]. To fill this gap, we collected user reviews and their AI-generated summaries for selected products and hotels from Amazon and Tripadvisor. These datasets, along with the code of main components, are publicly available at https://github.com/SCAlabUnical/UserReviewDatasets/.

The first dataset consists of Amazon product reviews, primarily in the electronics category, containing approximately 10,000 reviews across hundreds of products. It includes key attributes such as user ratings (one to five stars), review titles, descriptions, reactions, verification status, and metadata like location and date. The second dataset comprises hotel reviews from Tripadvisor, focusing on hotels in New York. It includes review ratings, titles, travel dates, and hotel details such as address, coordinates, and number of reviews. Additional attributes include subcategory ratings (e.g., value, service, location), responses from property owners, user-uploaded photos, and trip type classification (couples, solo, family, business, friends, or unspecified).

---

[1] https://amazon-reviews-2023.github.io/main.html.

To evaluate our framework, we applied BERT-based models for multidimensional classification of sentiment, emotions, and topics, then generated structured summaries and compared them with AI-generated ones. Performance was assessed using quantitative metrics (text scores, latent representations) and qualitative evaluations (automated and manual). The following sections detail the classification process (Sect. 4.1), summary generation (Sect. 4.3), and comparative performance analysis (Sect. 4.4).

4.1 Multi-dimensional Classification Using BERT Models and Topic Extraction

As discussed in Sect. 3, we employ BERT-based classifiers to extend the information contained in the reviews. This multidimensional data enrichment process can significantly help generative models to produce comprehensive summaries. In particular, we trained and utilized classifiers for the following dimensions: *(i) Sentiment*, determining whether a review conveys a positive or negative sentiment; *(ii) Topic*, which associates the subject matter discussed in a review (in this case, topics cannot be defined a priori but are derived from a dedicated topic extraction process); *(iii) Emotion*, which identifies the emotional tone and expressions conveyed within the text, including anger, disgust, joy and surprise.

Careful evaluations were conducted to select the best classification models for each dimension, following approaches used in prior work [5,28]. For sentiment and emotion classification, we fine-tuned BERT-based models on annotated datasets, achieving the best performance in terms of AUC scores. For topic detection, we employed BERTopic [9], which outperformed alternative methods in both consistency and diversity of topics. Unlike sentiment and emotion analysis, topic detection was performed collectively on all reviews of a product to extract dominant themes, optimizing coherence values to determine the ideal number of topics.

4.2 Polarization-Driven Stratified Sampling for Relevant Review Selection

To calculate the most relevant reviews for analysis among dimensions of interest, we use the following method. Consider an initial dataset of reviews R, where each review $r \in R$ is associated with one or more dimensions $d_1, d_2, \ldots, d_k$. Each dimension d_i has a set of possible classes $C(d_i) = \{c_1, c_2, \ldots, c_m\}$. For each review r and each dimension d_i, there is an associated probability distribution over the classes $c \in C(d_i)$, denoted as $P(c \mid d_i)$. To create a representative sample S of N reviews for analysis:

1) Select Dimensions and Classes: the user identifies dimensions of interest $\{d_1, \ldots, d_z \mid z \geq 1\}$, which are relevant for analysis. For each selected dimension, specific classes $C'(d_i) \subseteq C(d_i)$ may also be chosen based on the scope of the analysis.

2) Compute Class Distributions: for each selected dimension d_i, calculate the probability $P(c \mid d_i)$ of reviews in R that belong to each class $c \in C'(d_i)$.

3) **Allocate Sample Sizes:** for each class $c \in C'(d_i)$, determine the number of reviews $N_{c|d_i}$ to include in the sample: $N_{c|d_i} = P(c \mid d_i) \cdot N$

4) **Rank Reviews by Polarization:** assign a confidence score to each review $r \in R$, reflecting the degree of polarization across the selected dimensions. For each dimension d_i, a statistical measure of the distribution $P(c \mid d_i)$ is used to calculate the confidence. The confidence score is designed to assign a value of 1 to *fully polarized* distributions, a value of 0 to *neutral* distributions, and intermediate values between 0 and 1 to distributions ranging from slightly to strongly polarized. Several statistical measures can be used to calculate the confidence score, including variance of probabilities, entropy, Gini impurity, and Kullback-Leibler divergence. Among these, we chose the *variance of probabilities* for its simplicity, interpretability, and ability to emphasize polarization while normalizing across dimensions. The confidence score for each dimension is calculated as:

$$\text{Confidence}(r, d_i) = 1 - \frac{\text{Var}(P(c \mid d_i))}{\text{MaxVar}(d_i)}$$

where $\text{MaxVar}(d_i) = \frac{m-1}{m^2}$ and $m = |C'(d_i)|$, the number of classes in dimension d_i. The combined confidence score for a review is computed by aggregating the confidence scores across all dimensions:

$$\text{Confidence}(r) = \frac{1}{z} \sum_{d_i} \text{Confidence}(r, d_i)$$

where z is the total number of dimensions considered.

By normalizing the variance for each dimension, this method ensures consistency across dimensions with varying numbers of classes, making it an effective and computationally efficient choice for evaluating polarization in multidimensional datasets.

5) **Polarization-Based Review Sampling Using Knapsack:** iterate through the ranked list of reviews, where reviews are ordered by their confidence scores. The ordering prioritizes reviews that are fully polarized across all dimensions, followed by those that are strongly polarized, slightly polarized, and finally the neutral ones. This ranking ensures that the most polarized reviews, which provide clearer signals across dimensions, are considered first for inclusion in the sample S. During this process, add reviews to the sample S, ensuring that the number of reviews for each class $N_{c|d_i}$ does not exceed the allocated target for the respective class. This approach guarantees that the sample S reflects the specified class distributions across all selected dimensions while emphasizing reviews with greater polarization for more meaningful analysis.

6) **Final Adjustment:** if S does not meet the exact sample size N due to rounding or constraints, adjust the sample by adding or removing reviews with the lowest confidence scores, ensuring that the class distributions remain approximately consistent.

This method ensures that the sample S is representative of the class distributions across the selected dimensions and classes, aligning with the objectives of the specific analysis. By leveraging a knapsack-inspired approach, the sampling process prioritizes reviews with higher polarization, ensuring a balanced yet informative subset that captures the most relevant signals for analysis while adhering to predefined class distribution constraints. To illustrate how the polarization-based sampling method evaluates and prioritizes reviews, consider a dataset with two key dimensions: d_1 *(Sentiment)*, comprising two classes (*Positive* and *Negative*), and d_2 *(Topic)*, comprising three classes (*Topic1*, *Topic2*, and *Topic3*). By examining examples of fully polarized and neutral reviews, we can observe how the confidence score reflects the degree of polarization across dimensions. For instance, a review such as *((1, 0), (1, 0, 0))* demonstrates complete polarization, achieving a confidence score of *1*. Conversely, a fully neutral review like *((0.5, 0.5), (0.333, 0.333, 0.333))* exhibits no polarization, resulting in a confidence score of *0*.

From the point of view of algorithmic complexity, $O(|R|\log|R| + |R| \cdot z)$ represents the complexity of the algorithm, where $|R|$ is the number of reviews, $O(|R|\log|R|)$ accounts for the sorting step, and $O(|R| \cdot z)$ arises from the Knapsack-Based Sampling across z dimensions. This ensures the method is efficient and scalable for datasets with a high number of reviews and dimensions.

4.3 Review Summary Using Generative Models

In this phase, we leverage insights from multi-dimensional classification to create comprehensive summaries on sentiments, emotions, and topics by interacting with generative models like GPT via API. These models automate the generation of structured content, ensuring a balanced and thorough analytical perspective. In particular, we use the GPT-4o API with a temperature setting of 0 to ensure accurate and consistent outputs. Lower temperature values minimize randomness, resulting in greater consistency, while higher values introduce more variability and diversity. We have defined a prompt that is structured to guide GPT in generating human-readable summaries about a specific product (or hotel), starting from key elements such as the product name, a short description, and a curated list of reviews. Below is the prompt approach, called `GPT-adv`, that we used to summarize product reviews on Amazon:

Product ($p)**:{*monitored product*}, **Description ($d):{*product description*},
**Reviews ($R)**: [/*1st review*/ {*Title ($tr)*:{*title of the review*}, *Text ($t)*:{*text of the review*}, *Sentiment ($s)*:{*positive, neutral or negative*}, *Topics ($t)*:{*main topics addressed*}, *Emotions ($e)*:{*main emotions expressed*}}, /*2nd review*/ {...}, ...]
Input: A list of reviews $R for the product $p described in $d. Each review includes its title, full text, a sentiment label, the main topics addressed, and the primary emotions expressed.
Task: Generate a comprehensive and balanced report about the product that captures the essence of all the reviews by summarizing their key points and covering all significant aspects, while remaining concise. The report must be a single paragraph without line breaks or colons and should not exceed $N words.

Specifically, the `GPT-adv` prompt receives a list of reviews ($R) via API. Notably, this list is generated using a stratified sampler to ensure a balanced set of reviews that covers all the dimensions considered, including the classes of each dimension. Each provided review is derived from a multidimensional classification and includes the title and text of the review, a sentiment score, the identified emotions, and the topic represented. The goal is to produce a summary that highlights key strengths and weaknesses while adhering to a specified word count limit ($N).

We evaluate the outputs of GPT-adv against those generated by AI tools on online platforms (such as Amazon and Tripadvisor) and a baseline approach that processes only the original reviews via a chat interface (i.e., without leveraging additional classification), referred to as GPT-base. This comparison illustrates that selecting a balanced sample of reviews not only significantly enhances the quality of the generated summary by providing a more representative and nuanced view, but also reduces token usage by condensing the input to the most informative subset, thereby ensuring that a good number of tokens is used efficiently.

When using ChatGPT-4o via API, the input limit is 128,000 tokens (approximately 96,000 words or 6,400 tweets, assuming 15 words per tweet). While file uploads of up to 512 MB are allowed, only the portion that fits within the context window is processed; content exceeding this limit remains unprocessed. It is important to note that as the token count approaches the maximum capacity of the model, performance may decrease, especially for tasks involving long and complex content [26].

4.4 Performance Evaluation

In this section, we describe the performance evaluation of our framework against basic approaches and AI-generated summaries available on platforms such as Amazon and Tripadvisor. As previously outlined, our goal is to evaluate how the extra data provided to GPT via multidimensional classification (sentiment, extracted topic, and detected emotion) helps develop more precise commentaries. By leveraging this additional input, our approach delves deeply into the subject and uncovers subtle effects of various information inputs on GPT's ability to generate commentaries. Notably, our framework also aims to define a compact sample that minimizes token usage while still producing comprehensive summaries that capture all aspects of the reviews, ensuring efficient processing without sacrificing detail.

4.5 Step-by-Step Operation and Parameter Configuration

For demonstration purposes, we illustrate our framework using an electric toothbrush from Amazon (anonymized despite being a specific model) as a case study. Below, we present the product along with examples of both a positive and a negative review. For each review, our framework identifies the associated sentiment, referenced topic, and detected emotion. These examples highlight how our system classifies user feedback into multidimensional categories, establishing the basis for generating a compact, balanced sample that captures comprehensive insights for subsequent summarization.

```
Product (p) = "[Anonimized] Rechargeable Electric Toothbrush", Description (d) =
"Protect your gums with sensi cleaning mode and gum pressure control..."
Example of positive review (pr) = {title (tr) : "Works Well.", text (t):"... When I pur-
chased this, I was half expecting to send it back. I was pleasantly surprised by how well this
one works and cleans my teeth...", sentiment (s): Positive, topics (t): Positive feedback,
emotions (e): Surprise}
Example of negative review (nr) = {title (tr): "Very Slippery. Hard to find on/off
switch.", text (t): "I needed to replace my [anonimized] electric toothbrush. Made a big
mistake buying this one. The handle is too slippery, and the onoff switch looks nothing like
the picture. A small button that is hard to find. Will be replacing as soon as I find another
one.", sentiment (s): Negative, topics (t): Button Design, Grip problems, emotions (e):
Sadness}
```

Subsequently, our knapsack-based selection method preserves the class distributions across all dimensions when reducing the full dataset to a compact sample of N reviews (here, N = 20). As shown in Fig. 2a , the percentage distributions of sentiment, topics, and emotion in the sample closely mirror those of the full dataset. Figure 2b further confirms that the 20 selected reviews—marked with an "X"—are evenly distributed among the six topic clusters extracted using BERTopic and compressed via UMAP, demonstrating the effectiveness of our balanced selection process. Figure 3a shows the distribution and density of sentiment classes (only positive and negative classes) for both the full set and the selected sample. The chart demonstrates that the sentiment distribution in the compact sample closely mirrors that of the full dataset, and similar balancing was achieved for the other dimensions.

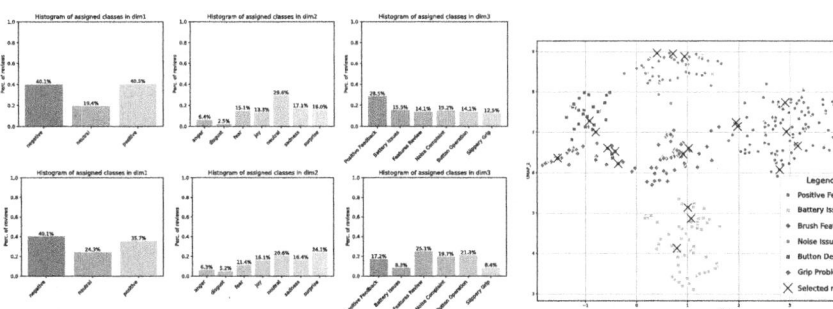

(a) The top chart shows the full dataset's class distribution (sentiment, topics, emotion), while the bottom chart shows the sample.

(b) Clustered reviews with topics extracted by BERTopic and visualized via UMAP. "X" marks denote sample reviews.

Fig. 2. Class distributions for full dataset and balanced sample (N = 20).

To verify that a small but representative sample can generate a quality summary, we first generated a full summary using all available reviews retrieved via the API for a product (about 500) and then produced additional summaries using samples of N reviews. We compared the embeddings of these sample-based summaries with the full-dataset summary using cosine similarity, averaging the results over 10 different products. Figure 3b (at the top) illustrates these comparisons and contrasts our balanced selection approach with random sampling. Using ModernBERT [24] to compute the text embeddings, our method achieves a cosine similarity of 0.85 with a sample of 20 reviews, indicating that the embeddings share high semantic similarity and many common features [16]. Notably, increasing the sample size beyond 20 does not significantly improve this value. Cosine similarity rarely reaches 1 because even summaries that capture the same information can differ in wording, sentence order, and subtle nuances, resulting in slight variations in their embeddings. In contrast, the random selection approach gradually improves with increasing N, but only matches our balanced strategy when the sample size exceeds 50 reviews.

Additionally, as illustrated in Fig. 3b (bottom), the token count required for summarization increases substantially with the number of reviews considered. Our balanced selection approach uses only about 5,000 tokens for 20 reviews, whereas summarizing all reviews (i.e. 500) requires over 50,000 tokens—a nearly tenfold increase. This marked reduction boosts computational efficiency and lowers costs associated with large language models, all without sacrificing summary quality. Notably, our method tends to select longer, information-dense reviews, which may result in a slightly higher token count per review compared to random sampling; however, the overall token usage remains dramatically lower than processing the entire dataset. Therefore, for our experiments on products and hotels, we set the sample size to 20 reviews—roughly 5,000 tokens—to achieve an optimal balance between quality and efficiency.

In the final step, we compare the commentaries generated by three distinct approaches for our reference product (electric toothbrush). First, we show the commentary produced by the Amazon AI system, the summary generated by GPT-base, which uses a file containing all reviews and a prompt, and GPT-adv the commentary produced by our framework.

Amazon AI-generated = Customers like the cleanability, performance, value, and quality of the toothbrush. For example, they mention that it effectively cleans between teeth, removes up to 100% more plaque along the gumline, and has a good price point. Customers also appreciate ease of use. That said, opinions are mixed on durability, and battery life.
GPT-base = User reviews indicate that this electric toothbrush excels in design and cleaning performance. Many users note its comfortable fit, which allows the brush to reach difficult areas such as the molars, and its built-in timer and pressure sensor enhance the brushing experience. Its robust battery life and user-friendly interface ensure consistent performance over time, and the design effectively minimizes plaque buildup along the gumline, contributing to improved oral hygiene. However, a few users have reported concerns about its durability, with some experiencing wear on the handle after prolonged use. Despite these durability issues, the overall balance between advanced features and

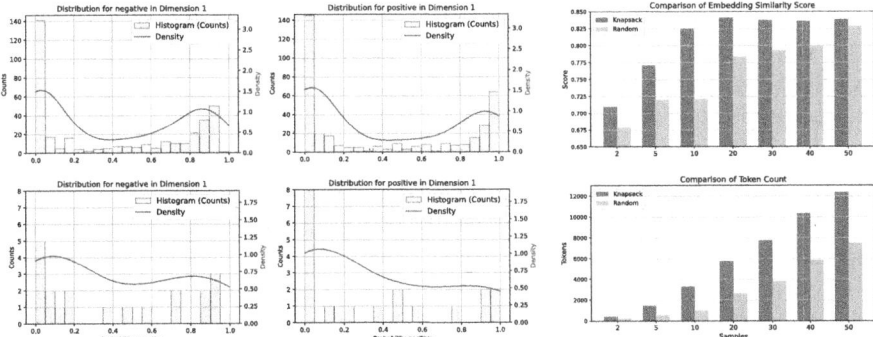

(a) The top chart shows the counts and density of sentiment instances (positive/negative) for the full dataset, while the bottom chart shows these for the balanced sample.

(b) Summary embeddings and token counts for full dataset vs. sample using our and random selection.

Fig. 3. Class distributions (full dataset vs. balanced sample, N = 20) and summary embedding/token usage: balanced vs. random.

> affordability makes this toothbrush a popular choice among consumers seeking a reliable, efficient dental care solution.
> GPT-adv = The [...] electric toothbrush has garnered mixed reviews from users, highlighting both its strengths and weaknesses. Many users appreciate its effectiveness in plaque removal and the thorough clean it provides compared to manual brushes, with some noting significant improvements in oral hygiene. The timer feature, which prompts users to switch quadrants every 30 seconds, is also seen as a helpful addition. However, several reviewers express frustration with the charging system, citing long charging times and poor battery life, which detracts from the overall experience. Design issues, particularly with the on/off button being difficult to press and the handle lacking grip, have been noted as significant drawbacks, especially for those with limited hand strength. Additionally, some users report that the brush can be quite loud and that the replacement heads can be costly. Overall, while the toothbrush performs well in cleaning, its usability and design flaws may lead some to seek alternatives.

Comparing the outputs, the Amazon AI-generated and GPT-base reviews emphasize positive aspects—highlighting features like cleanability, performance, and design—while only briefly mentioning minor issues. In contrast, GPT-adv offers a more comprehensive analysis by addressing both the product's strong cleaning performance and its critical drawbacks, such as poor battery life and a slippery handle. This advanced method not only reduces token usage dramatically while preserving the overall review characteristics, but also delivers a more balanced commentary that captures both strengths and weaknesses in detail.

4.6 Aggregate Metrics and Comparative Analysis

Here, we present a comprehensive analysis conducted to compare the quality of generated summaries against the original text. First, we assessed the quality of the synthesis using established semantic metrics, such as TF-IDF, ROUGE,

S-BERT, S-RoBERTa, BERTScore, and BLANC. Second, we employed Chat-GPT as an evaluator to assign scores based on various aspects, including topic coverage, clarity, and readability. Finally, we carried out a human evaluation, who assessed the generated summaries through a survey.

Analysis of Semantic Metrics. To evaluate the quality of these reports, we used a set of commonly applied metrics for assessing summary quality against a reference text. In the absence of a specific reference text, we defined the reference as the concatenation of all reviews describing a product or a hotel. Then, the following metrics were considered: i) TF-IDF for lexical similarity; ii) ROUGE-1 for measuring unigram overlap and basic content recall; iii) ROUGE-2 for evaluating bigram overlap and capturing short-sequence coherence; iv) S-BERT and v) S-RoBERTa for sentence-level embeddings to assess deeper contextual understanding; vi) BERT-Score for evaluating fine-grained semantic similarity at the word level; and vii) BLANC-help for assessing fluency and informativeness.

Table 1. Evaluation of semantic scores in the Amazon and Tripadvisor case studies for different approaches.

	TF-IDF	Rouge-1	Rouge-2	S-BERT	S-RoBERTa	Bert-Score	BLANC-help
AI-generated	0.237	0.016	0.002	0.565	0.800	0.520	0.034
GPT-base	0.253	0.016	0.004	0.614	0.798	0.509	0.034
GPT-adv	**0.294**	**0.019**	**0.007**	**0.623**	**0.813**	**0.568**	**0.054**

Table 1 reports the average values of metrics obtained by summaries generated using different approaches (`AI-generated`, `GPT-base`, `GPT-adv`) across the two case studies (Amazon and Tripadvisor). In both case studies, the evaluation reveals a clear improvement when moving from simpler approaches, such as `AI-generated` and `GPT-base`, to more advanced ones like `GPT-adv`. A higher *TF-IDF* score reflects an enhanced ability to capture and synthesize the core content of the reviews. Additionally, higher *ROUGE-1* and *ROUGE-2* values indicate that the summary conveys the details of the original reviews more effectively, sharing similar phrasing and structure. Metrics like *S-BERT*, *S-RoBERTa*, and *BERTScore* further demonstrate that the advanced approach better captures semantic similarities. Finally, the improvements in *BLANC-help* highlight superior contextual flow and coherence in the summaries, making them clearer and more comprehensive.

ChatGPT Evaluation. This section presents a detailed evaluation of the summaries generated for both case studies using ChatGPT as the evaluator [13]. We asked ChatGPT to assess the following five dimensions, where each is scored on a 5-point scale with higher values indicating better performance: i) *Content Coverage*, which evaluates how well the summary captures key aspects from the reviews (e.g., position and cleaning for an hotel or design and battery life for a smartphone); *ii*) *Sentiment Balance*, measuring whether the summary proportionally reflects both positive and negative feedback; *iii*) *Clarity & Readability*, which assesses ease of understanding, well-structuring and clarity; *iv*) *Detail & Specificity*, indicating how specific the summary is regarding individual features (e.g., "removes up to 100% more plaque" or "built-in timer and pressure sensor"); and *v*) *Overall Faithfulness*, which verifies accuracy and alignment with the original reviews without distortion or exaggeration.

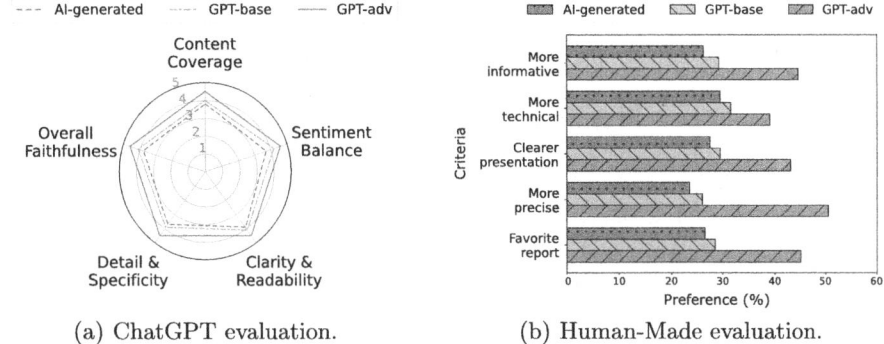

Fig. 4. Evaluation of the reports by ChatGPT and humans on the two considered case studies (average values).

Figure 4a illustrates the average evaluation results for the two case studies, highlighting that while both the AI-generated and GPT-base summaries focus largely on positive aspects, the GPT-adv approach provides a more balanced and comprehensive summary by effectively capturing both strengths and weaknesses.

Human-Made Evaluation. Regarding the human evaluation, we conducted a survey involving 20 participants and 10 products/hotels. Each participant was presented with a set of reviews for these products and asked to rate the summaries generated by the three considered approaches (AI-generated, GPT-base, and GPT-adv) without being informed about the approach used to generate each summary. To ensure unbiased evaluations, the different versions were presented in a randomized order. Specifically, they were asked to answer these questions: *i*) which summary provides more overall information content? *ii*) which summary includes more technical or specialized aspects? *iii*) which summary offers a clearer presentation? *iv*) which summary demonstrates greater precision and clarity in its contents? *v*) which summary do you prefer for overall quality?

Figure 4b shows the percentage of participants who preferred the base, advanced, and AI-generated summaries across the five criteria considered. As shown, participants consistently favored GPT-adv over other versions across all aspects, though the preference for GPT-adv was only slightly higher than for

`GPT-base`. In particular, `GPT-adv` received higher ratings, particularly for its greater information content and clearer presentation. Notably, evaluators found summaries generated by `GPT-base` slightly better than those by `AI-generated`, indicating that the latter tends to produce summaries that are less balanced and often omit important details.

5 Conclusions

User-generated reviews play a crucial role in shaping business strategies, and LLMs like BERT and GPT have significantly improved their analysis. This paper introduced a novel framework that enhances user review summarization by leveraging LLMs to ensure balanced and comprehensive insights. Unlike conventional AI-generated summaries, which often exhibit positive bias, our approach systematically classifies reviews across multiple dimensions, such as sentiment, emotion, and topic, before applying a stratified sampling method to create a representative subset. By incorporating a knapsack-based selection strategy, we effectively balance review content while optimizing token usage, leading to high-quality summaries with significantly reduced computational cost. An extensive evaluation on Amazon and Tripadvisor datasets has been carried out, using both quantitative and qualitative measures, demonstrating that our approach outperforms existing summarization techniques, including those employed by major online platforms. Future work includes extending the framework to compare similar products, applying it to diverse datasets (e.g., TrustPilot, Yelp, Google Reviews, Reddit), and analyzing opinions on social media pages to uncover strengths, weaknesses, and areas for improvement. Additionally, the proposed approach could also be used to analyze opinions on the social media pages of political figures, institutions, or companies, summarizing strengths, weaknesses, user requests, and areas of engagement for better understanding and potential improvements.

Acknowledgement. This work was supported by the research project "INSIDER: INtelligent ServIce Deployment for advanced cloud-Edge integRation" granted by the Italian Ministry of University and Research (MUR) within the PRIN 2022 program and European Union - Next Generation EU (grant n. 2022WWSCRR, CUP H53D23003670006).

References

1. Aakash, Gupta, S., Noliya, A.: URL-based sentiment analysis of product reviews using LSTM and GRU. Procedia Comput. Sci. **235**, 1814–1823 (2024). International Conference on Machine Learning and Data Engineering (ICMLDE 2023)
2. Anbumani, P., Selvaraj, K.: Enhancing sentiment analysis classification for amazon product reviews using CNN-sigTan-Beta activation function. Multimedia Tools Appl. **83**(19), 56719–56736 (2024)
3. Ayanouz, S., Abdelhakim, B.A., Benhmed, M.: A smart chatbot architecture based NLP and machine learning for health care assistance. In: 3rd International Conference on Networking, Information Systems & Security (2020)

4. Caldarini, G., Jaf, S., McGarry, K.: A literature survey of recent advances in chatbots. Information **13**(1) (2022)
5. Cantini, R., Cosentino, C., Marozzo, F.: Multi-dimensional classification on social media data for detailed reporting with large language models. In: Maglogiannis, I., Iliadis, L., Macintyre, J., Avlonitis, M., Papaleonidas, A. (eds.) AIAI 2024. IFIP Advances in Information and Communication Technology, vol. 712, pp. 100–114. Springer, Cham (2024). https://doi.org/10.1007/978-3-031-63215-0_8
6. Cantini, R., Cosentino, C., Marozzo, F., Talia, D., Trunfio, P.: Harnessing prompt-based large language models for disaster monitoring and automated reporting from social media feedback. Online Soc. Netw. Media **45**, 100295 (2025)
7. Cosentino, C., Gunduz-Cure, M., Marozzo, F., Ozturk-Birim, S.: Exploiting large language models for enhanced review classification explanations through interpretable and multidimensional analysis. In: 27th International Conference on Discovery Science (DS2024) (2024)
8. Gilardi, F., Alizadeh, M., Kubli, M.: ChatGPT outperforms crowd workers for text-annotation tasks. Nat. Acad. Sci. **120**(30) (2023)
9. Grootendorst, M.: BERTopic: neural topic modeling with a class-based TF-IDF procedure. arXiv:2203.05794 (2022)
10. Hossain, M., Habib, M., Hassan, M., Soroni, F., Khan, M.M.: Research and development of an e-commerce with sales chatbot. In: 2022 IEEE World AI IoT Congress (AIIoT), pp. 557–564 (2022)
11. Li, H., Zhang, Y., Zhang, R., Chaturvedi, S.: Coverage-based fairness in multi-document summarization (2025). https://arxiv.org/abs/2412.08795
12. Liu, B., Hu, M., Cheng, J.: Opinion observer: analyzing and comparing opinions on the web. In: 14th International Conference on World Wide Web, pp. 342–351 (2005)
13. Liu, Y., Iter, D., Xu, Y., Wang, S., Xu, R., Zhu, C.: G-Eval: NLG evaluation using GPT-4 with better human alignment. arXiv preprint arXiv:2303.16634 (2023)
14. Mayfield, J., et al.: On the evaluation of machine-generated reports. In: 47th International ACM SIGIR Conference on Research and Development in Information Retrieval, SIGIR 2024, New York, NY, USA, pp. 1904–1915 (2024)
15. Messina, P., et al.: A survey on deep learning and explainability for automatic report generation from medical images. ACM Comput. Surv. (CSUR) **54**(10s), 1–40 (2022)
16. Mihalcea, R., Corley, C., Strapparava, C.: Corpus-based and knowledge-based measures of text semantic similarity. Comput. Linguist. **32**(1), 1–24 (2006)
17. Okonkwo, C.W., Ade-Ibijola, A.: Chatbots applications in education: a systematic review. Comput. Educ. Artif. Intell. **2**, 100033 (2021)
18. Pang, B., Lee, L., Vaithyanathan, S.: Thumbs up? Sentiment classification using machine learning techniques. cs/0205070 (2002)
19. Perti, A., Sinha, A., Vidyarthi, A.: Cognitive hybrid deep learning-based multi-modal sentiment analysis for online product reviews. ACM Trans. Asian Low-Resour. Lang. Inf. Process. **23**(8) (2024)
20. Roumeliotis, K.I., Tselikas, N.D., Nasiopoulos, D.K.: LLMS in e-commerce: a comparative analysis of GPT and LLaMA models in product review evaluation. Natural Lang. Process. J. **6**, 100056 (2024)
21. van Schaik, T.A., Pugh, B.: A field guide to automatic evaluation of LLM-generated summaries. In: 47th International ACM SIGIR Conference on Research and Development in Information Retrieval, SIGIR 2024, New York, NY, USA, pp. 2832–2836 (2024)

22. Sun, X., et al.: Text classification via large language models. arXiv:2305.08377 (2023)
23. Wang, F., Xu, Z., Szekely, P., Chen, M.: Robust (controlled) table-to-text generation with structure-aware equivariance learning. arXiv:2205.03972 (2022)
24. Warner, B., e al.: Smarter, better, faster, longer: a modern bidirectional encoder for fast, memory efficient, and long context finetuning and inference. arXiv preprint arXiv:2412.13663 (2024)
25. Yang, B., Liu, Y., Liang, Y., Tang, M.: Exploiting user experience from online customer reviews for product design. Int. J. Inf. Manag. **46**, 173–186 (2019)
26. Yuan, T., et al.: LV-Eval: a balanced long-context benchmark with 5 length levels up to 256k. arXiv preprint arXiv:2402.05136 (2024)
27. Zaremba, A., Demir, E.: ChatGPT: unlocking the future of NLP in finance. Mod. Financ. **1**(1), 93–98 (2023)
28. Zhang, H., Shafiq, M.O.: Survey of transformers and towards ensemble learning using transformers for natural language processing. J. Big Data **11**(1), 25 (2024)
29. Zhang, K.Z., Zhao, S.J., Cheung, C.M., Lee, M.K.: Examining the influence of online reviews on consumers' decision-making: a heuristic-systematic model. Decis. Support Syst. **67**, 78–89 (2014)
30. Zhong, A., et al.: LogParser-LLM: advancing efficient log parsing with large language models. In: 30th ACM SIGKDD Conference on Knowledge Discovery and Data Mining, KDD 2024, New York, NY, USA, pp. 4559–4570 (2024)

Few-Shot Graph Out-of-Distribution Detection with LLMs

Haoyan Xu[1], Zhengtao Yao[1], Yushun Dong[2], Ziyi Wang[3], Ryan Rossi[4], Mengyuan Li[1], and Yue Zhao[1(✉)]

[1] University of Southern California, Los Angeles, CA 90007, USA
{haoyanxu,zyao9248,mengyuanli,yzhao010}@usc.edu
[2] Florida State University, 600 W College Avenue, Tallahassee, FL 32306, USA
yushun.dong@fsu.edu
[3] University of Maryland, 1000 Hilltop Cir, College Park, MD 20742, USA
zoewang@umd.edu
[4] Adobe Research, 345 Park Avenue, San Jose, CA 95110, USA
ryrossi@adobe.com

Abstract. Graph out-of-distribution (OOD) detection usually relies on training a graph neural network (GNN) with a large set of labeled in-distribution (ID) nodes. However, acquiring high-quality labeled nodes in text-attributed graphs (TAGs) is challenging and costly due to their complex textual and structural characteristics. Large language models (LLMs) offer strong zero-shot language capabilities but overlook graph connectivity, limiting their utility for graph OOD detection.

In this work, we propose LLM-GOOD, a general framework that effectively combines the strengths of LLMs and GNNs to enhance data efficiency in graph OOD detection. Specifically, we first leverage LLMs' strong zero-shot capabilities to filter out likely OOD nodes, significantly reducing the human annotation burden. To minimize the usage and cost of the LLM, we employ it only to annotate a small subset of unlabeled nodes. We then train a lightweight GNN filter using these noisy labels, enabling efficient predictions of ID status for all other unlabeled nodes by leveraging both textual and structural information. After obtaining node embeddings from the GNN filter, we can apply informativeness-based methods to select the most valuable nodes for precise human annotation. Finally, we train the target ID classifier using these accurately annotated ID nodes. Extensive experiments on four real-world TAG datasets demonstrate that LLM-GOOD significantly reduces human annotation costs and outperforms state-of-the-art baselines in terms of both ID classification accuracy and OOD detection performance.

H. Xu and Z. Yao—Equal contribution.

Supplementary Information The online version contains supplementary material available at https://doi.org/10.1007/978-3-032-06078-5_18.

Keywords: Graph OOD Detection · Large Language Models · Data-Efficient Learning · Text-Attributed Graphs · Graph Neural Networks · Few-Shot Learning · Zero-Shot Annotation

1 Introduction

Out-of-distribution (OOD) detection [7,10,14,16] has emerged as a critical task in machine learning, particularly for safety-critical applications where models must reliably identify inputs that differ significantly from the training data [17,18]. Recently, several OOD detection methods [27,31,38,39] and open-set learning approaches [37] have been proposed and applied to graph-structured data. Existing graph OOD detection methods typically operate within *a semi-supervised, transductive framework*, where the entire set of nodes is accessible during training, but only a portion of the class labels (in-distribution (ID) classes) are provided [27]. These methods generally rely on *a sufficient number* of labeled ID nodes to train a GNN-based ID classifier, from which they derive the ID classification logits for all nodes. Post-hoc OOD detectors [10,20,31] are then applied to these logits for OOD detection. In particular, nodes with higher energy scores [31] or higher entropy scores are identified as OOD nodes.

While these graph OOD detection methods are effective, they invariably rely on the assumption that ground truth ID labels are readily available. This assumption often overlooks a critical challenge: obtaining sufficient high-quality labels for graph-structured data. Specifically, (1) the diverse and complex nature of graph-structured data makes human labeling inherently difficult, and (2) the large scale of real-world graphs renders annotating a significant portion of nodes both time-consuming and resource-intensive [4,34].

Our Observations and Motivation. In this paper, we aim to address the challenge of few-shot OOD detection and ID classification on text-attributed graphs (TAGs) within the commonly used semi-supervised transductive setting, as described above. Consider a text-attributed social network where nodes represent individuals, node attributes correspond to their textual descriptions, and edges denote interactions or connections between them. Initially, the entire network is unlabeled, and the goal is to classify individuals into specific interest groups, such as technology enthusiasts, sports fans, or musicians, while operating within a limited human annotation budget. However, the network also contains individuals whose interests fall outside these predefined categories, such as those primarily engaged in political discussions or travel blogging. Identifying and labeling these OOD nodes would be inefficient, as they do not contribute to training an effective classifier for the targeted interest groups. Instead, the focus is on accurately classifying only the ID nodes while detecting and filtering out OOD nodes that do not belong to the intended classification space. Furthermore, zero-shot [5,30] and few-shot [1,23] OOD detection for images have been extensively studied using multi-modal foundation models. However, to date, no similarly powerful graph foundation model exists to support zero-shot or few-shot graph OOD detection. As a result, we turn to LLMs to tackle the data-efficiency challenge of OOD detection on TAGs.

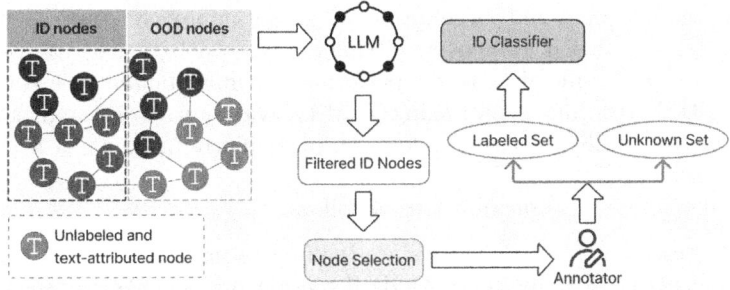

Fig. 1. An illustration of our method. To reduce annotation costs, we use an LLM to filter out OOD nodes before selecting nodes for human annotation. The annotated ID nodes are then used to train the target ID classifier.

In summary, current graph OOD detection methods typically rely heavily on large amounts of labeled ID nodes to perform well. Conversely, while LLMs demonstrate remarkable zero-shot capabilities on text-attributed graphs (TAGs), they inherently lack the ability to interpret and leverage the structural information essential to TAGs. In this study, we take the first step toward integrating the strengths of both GNNs and LLMs to tackle the data-efficiency challenges in graph OOD detection.

Present Work. As shown in Fig. 1, to address these challenges, we propose to leverage LLMs to filter out OOD nodes before human annotation, thereby **reducing human costs**. Specifically, we provide the LLM with ID knowledge (i.e., the names of ID classes) and prompt it to determine whether an unlabeled query node belongs to one of the ID classes, using the text information associated with the query node. Note that while we enable LLMs to directly perform zero-shot OOD detection and ID classification, using LLMs for zero-shot annotation is very slow during inference. Therefore, we aim to leverage LLMs to reduce human annotation costs during training and rely solely on well-trained GNNs for faster inference during testing. However, prompting the LLM to annotate all unlabeled nodes in the training set is costly for large graphs, although the cost of using an LLM is significantly lower than that of human annotation. To further **reduce the LLM's cost**, we propose prompting the LLM to annotate only a small subset of nodes and then using these pseudo-labels to train a lightweight GNN filter. With this GNN filter, we can predict whether every unlabeled node in the training set belongs to one of the ID classes. If not, it's very likely that this node is an OOD node, and we then filter it out before human annotation.

In addition, we can obtain the embeddings of all unlabeled nodes in the graph after training the GNN filter with pseudo-labels. Based on these embeddings, the most informative nodes can be selected using existing informativeness-aware node selection methods. These selected nodes are then annotated by a human annotator, and the final annotated ID nodes are used to train the target ID classifier. Optionally, we can combine the accurate labels from human annotation with the noisy labels from the LLM to train a robust ID classifier under **severe data scarcity scenarios**. Compared to other active learning methods that require multiple rounds of selection [3,32], our approach requires only a single round of annotation. Moreover, relying solely on noisy labels from an LLM to train an ID classifier imposes a performance upper bound (see the results in Sect. 5.3). Furthermore, leveraging LLM knowledge to train smaller models, such as GNNs, facilitates faster inference, particularly in domains where time efficiency is crucial.

We summarize our key contributions as follows:

- To the best of our knowledge, we are the first to investigate LLM's zero-shot learning ability for the graph OOD detection problem. With the zero-shot learning ability of LLMs, our method achieves high performance with only one round of node selection, compared to traditional multi-round active learning selection methods.
- We design a general framework LLM-GOOD that can filter out many OOD nodes before annotation to reduce human costs and use LLM's zero-shot annotations to train a light GNN filter to further reduce LLM costs.
- We apply LLM-GOOD to node classification datasets consisting of different properties under label budget constraints. Experimental results show that our method effectively filters out OOD nodes and achieves much better ID classification and OOD detection performance compared to baselines within an annotation budget. Our code is available at: https://github.com/zhengtaoyao/LLM_GOOD.

2 Related Work

2.1 Graph OOD Detection

In recent years, OOD detection in graph data has presented new challenges, especially in the context of multi-class classification for in-distribution data, which further complicates the task of identifying outlier data [20]. For instance, OODGAT [27] leverages a graph neural network (GNN) that explicitly models interactions among different types of nodes, enabling effective separation of inliers and outliers during feature propagation. GNNSafe [31] highlights the inherent OOD detection capabilities of standard GNN classifiers and proposes a robust OOD discriminator using an energy-based function derived from GNNs trained with standard classification loss. GRASP [20] explores the potential of OOD score propagation and derives the conditions under which the score propagation is beneficial. They also propose an edge augmentation strategy with theoretical guarantees for post-hoc node-level OOD detection.

While effective, these methods rely heavily on the assumption of abundant ID labels in open-set scenarios. However, in real-world applications, labeled data are costly and challenging to obtain, limiting the practicality of such approaches.

2.2 Data-Efficient Graph Learning

Graphs have a wide range of applications across various domains [29,33,35,36], and researchers have conducted extensive and focused studies on graph machine learning in low-resource settings, aiming to reduce the cost and time required for annotation [12]. Current data-efficient graph learning methods can be broadly divided into three categories: self-supervised graph learning, semi-supervised graph learning, and few-shot graph learning.

Few-shot graph learning aims at enabling models to generalize effectively and make accurate predictions using only a small number of labeled examples. The primary objective is to train models to learn from a limited set of annotated instances and apply this knowledge to predict new and unseen data [12]. To achieve this, researchers typically adopt one of two approaches: metric learning, which encourages query nodes to align closely with their respective prototypes [28], or parameter optimization, which employs meta-learning to generate node representations [11]. Some graph active learning methods [2,3,32] have been developed to enhance the performance of semi-supervised node classification while adhering to a label budget constraint. For instance, FeatProp [32] identifies nodes by propagating their features throughout the graph structure and applying K-Medoids clustering, mitigating the impact of under-trained model representations. However, both current few-shot graph learning methods [6,41] and graph active learning techniques are restricted to the closed-set node classification scenario. Recently, [37] applied active learning methods to the graph open-set classification scenario. However, their approach involves using real OOD nodes and requires multiple rounds of node selection for human annotation.

2.3 LLMs as Prefix for Graphs

In this paper, we focus on utilizing information generated by LLMs to enhance the training of GNNs. These techniques can be divided into two main categories: (i) Embeddings from LLMs for GNNs, which involves incorporating embeddings produced by LLMs into GNNs, and (ii) Labels from LLMs for GNNs, which focuses on leveraging labels generated by LLMs to guide GNN training [25]. We mainly focus on the second category that leverages generated labels from LLMs as supervision to improve the training of GNNs.

LLM-GNN [4] utilizes LLMs as annotators to produce node category predictions accompanied by confidence scores, which are treated as labels. A post-filtering process is applied to remove low-quality annotations while ensuring label diversity. These refined labels are then used to train GNNs. Similarly, GraphEdit [9] uses LLMs to create an edge predictor, which evaluates and refines candidate edges by comparing them to the edges of the original graph.

3 Setting

3.1 Text-Attributed Graphs

Our study focuses on TAGs, represented as $G_T = (\mathcal{V}, \mathbf{A}, \mathbf{T}, \mathbf{X})$. The set of nodes is $\mathcal{V} = \{v_1, \ldots, v_n\}$, where each node is associated with raw text attributes $\mathbf{T} = \{t_1, t_2, \ldots, t_n\}$. These text attributes can be converted into sentence embeddings $\mathbf{X} = \{x_1, x_2, \ldots, x_n\}$ using SentenceBERT [24]. The adjacency matrix

$\mathbf{A} \in \{0,1\}^{n \times n}$ encodes graph connectivity, where $\mathbf{A}[i,j] = 1$ indicates an edge between nodes i and j.

3.2 Graph OOD Detection

The node set can be partitioned as $\mathcal{V} = \mathcal{V}_{\text{in}} \cup \mathcal{V}_{\text{out}}$, where $\mathcal{V}_{\text{in}}$ denotes the set of ID nodes, and $\mathcal{V}_{\text{out}}$ represents the set of OOD nodes. We assume that ID nodes are drawn from the distribution $P_{\mathcal{V}}^{\text{in}}$, while OOD nodes are sampled from the distribution $P_{\mathcal{V}}^{\text{out}}$. The OOD node detection task is formally defined as follows: Given a collection of nodes sampled from $P_{\mathcal{V}}^{\text{in}}$ and $P_{\mathcal{V}}^{\text{out}}$, the objective is to accurately determine the source distribution—either $P_{\mathcal{V}}^{\text{in}}$ or $P_{\mathcal{V}}^{\text{out}}$—for each node.

We study OOD node detection in graphs under the transductive learning paradigm, where ID and OOD nodes coexist in the same graph, the most common framework for node-level OOD detection. During training, only the node attributes $\mathbf{X}$, the adjacency matrix $\mathbf{A}$, and the ID labels of a subset of nodes, $\mathcal{V}' \subseteq \mathcal{V}_{\text{in}}$, are provided. In general, the task consists of two main objectives: (1) **OOD Detection**: For each node $v \in \mathcal{V}$, determine whether it belongs to one of the ID known classes or to an OOD unknown class. (2) **ID Classification**: For nodes identified as ID, assign them to one of the predefined K classes.

3.3 Few-Shot Graph OOD Detection

Assume that we have a validation set $\mathcal{V}_{val}$ and a test set $\mathcal{V}_{test}$. The remaining nodes form the candidate set $\mathcal{V}_{can} = \mathcal{V} \setminus (\mathcal{V}_{val} \cup \mathcal{V}_{test})$. All nodes in $\mathcal{V}_{can}$ are initially **unlabeled**. Given a human label budget $\mathcal{B}$, our goal is to select a subset of nodes from $\mathcal{V}_{can}$ such that the trained model f achieves the lowest expected loss in the test set $\mathcal{V}_{test}$:

$$\arg\min_{\mathcal{V}_{can}^s \subset \mathcal{V}_{can}, |\mathcal{V}_{can}^s|=\mathcal{B}} \mathbb{E}_{v_i \in \mathcal{V}_{test}} [\ell(y_i, \tilde{y}_i)] \tag{1}$$

where f is our target ID classifier, y_i is the ground truth label of node v_i, and $\tilde{y}_i$ denotes the label prediction of node v_i by f. Compared with other label-efficient graph learning methods, such as active learning approaches, **we do not require any initial set of labeled nodes and, more importantly, we only select nodes for one round of annotation.**

4 Method

In real-world scenarios, graphs typically include a large number of unlabeled nodes, many of which may be OOD nodes and irrelevant to the target task. Our goal is to train an ID classifier using a limited set of ID labels, striving for high accuracy in ID classification while effectively identifying OOD data, where the classifier should exhibit low confidence.

To reduce human efforts, we seek to exclude as many OOD nodes as possible from the training set prior to labeling. To achieve this, the first step is to use an

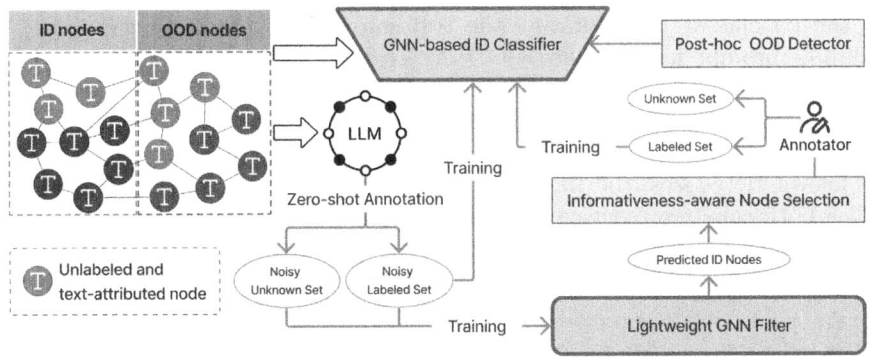

Fig. 2. An overview of our framework LLM-GOOD. To reduce human cost, we use LLM to filter out OOD nodes before human annotation (Sect. 4.1). To further reduce LLM cost, we use LLM to annotate a small subset of nodes, and then train a lightweight GNN filter on these noisy annotations to predict labels for the remaining nodes in the graph (Sect. 4.2). After obtaining node embeddings from the GNN filter, informativeness-aware selection methods identify the most informative unlabeled potential ID nodes (Sect. 4.3). After these selected nodes are annotated, the labeled accurate ID nodes are used to train the target ID classifier for ID classification and OOD detection (Sect. 4.4).

LLM as an annotator to identify potential OOD nodes (see Sect. 4.1). However, annotating all unlabeled nodes in the training set using the LLM still incurs a high cost. Therefore, we propose to annotate a small subset of nodes with the LLM and use these pseudo-labels from LLM to train a lightweight GNN filter (see Sect. 4.2). This approach further reduces the cost of using the LLM. After training, the GNN filter can predict which unlabeled nodes are ID nodes, allowing us to identify potential ID nodes with minimal use of the LLM.

Furthermore, based on the node embeddings from the GNN filter, informativeness-aware node selection methods, such as K-Medoids-based node selection, can be applied to choose the most informative nodes from the unlabeled potential ID nodes (see Sect. 4.3). Once these informative nodes are annotated, the labeled ID nodes can be used to train the target ID classifier. Optionally, accurate labels from humans and noisy labels from the LLM can be combined to train a robust ID classifier, especially in scenarios of extreme data scarcity. Finally, post-hoc OOD detection methods can be applied to the classifier to enhance its ability to recognize unseen classes (see Sect. 4.4). Figure 2 illustrates the pipeline of the proposed framework LLM-GOOD.

4.1 LLM as Zero-Shot Open-World Annotator

We randomly select a small set of nodes $\mathcal{V}_{LLM}$ from $\mathcal{V}_{can}$ and then let LLM annotate them. We provide the LLM with ID knowledge (ID classes' names) and prompt it to determine whether an unlabeled query node belongs to one of the ID classes, incorporating the text information of the query node. An example prompt for zero-shot OOD detection is shown in the following box. We instruct LLM to output "none" if it predicts that the node does not belong to any of the ID classes. Therefore, the noisy labels of $\mathcal{V}_{LLM}$ from LLM are $\mathcal{Y}_{LLM} = \{y_1^n, y_2^n, \ldots, y_m^n\}$, where m is the number of annotated nodes. Given K known ID classes, the LLM's label set extends to $K + 1$ classes, with the $(K + 1)$-th class representing the unknown class.

Zero-Shot OOD Detection and ID Classification Prompt

As a research scientist, your task is to analyze and classify {object} based on their main topics, meanings, background, and methods. Please first read the content of the {object} carefully. Then, identify the {object}'s key focus. Finally, match the content to one of the given categories.
There are the following categories: [Category 1, Category 2, Category 3, ...]
Given the current possible categories, determine if it belongs to one of them. If so, specify that category; otherwise, say "none".
[Insert {Object} Content Here]

4.2 Train Lightweight GNN with Pseudo-labels

To further reduce LLM's cost, we first use the LLM to annotate a small subset of nodes and then train a GNN on these annotations to predict labels for the remaining nodes in the graph. With the labeled node set $\mathcal{V}_{LLM}$ and its noisy labels $\mathcal{Y}_{LLM}$, we can train a $K + 1$ class classifier. As an aside, any GNN can be used as the lightweight OOD filter. In this paper, we use a two-layer standard graph convolutional network (GCN) as the OOD filter, and set the output dimension of the last layer as $K + 1$. The output of the first layer is as follows:

$$\mathbf{H}^{(1)} = \sigma\left(\tilde{\mathbf{D}}^{-\frac{1}{2}}\tilde{\mathbf{A}}\tilde{\mathbf{D}}^{-\frac{1}{2}}\mathbf{X}\mathbf{W}^{(0)}\right) \tag{2}$$

where $\tilde{\mathbf{A}} = \mathbf{A} + \mathbf{I}$ and $\tilde{\mathbf{D}}_{ii} = \sum_j \tilde{\mathbf{A}}_{ij}$, $\mathbf{I}$ is the identity matrix, and $\mathbf{W}^{(0)}$ is the weight matrix. The OOD filter's final output for all nodes is $\mathbf{H}^{(2)} \in \mathbb{R}^{N \times (K+1)}$:

$$\mathbf{H}^{(2)} = \sigma\left(\tilde{\mathbf{D}}^{-\frac{1}{2}}\tilde{\mathbf{A}}\tilde{\mathbf{D}}^{-\frac{1}{2}}\mathbf{H}^{(1)}\mathbf{W}^{(1)}\right) \tag{3}$$

Embeddings $\mathbf{H}^{(1)}$ capture graph structure information and can be leveraged in the subsequent module for selecting nodes based on informativeness. In addition, with $\mathbf{H}^{(2)}$, we can determine whether each unlabeled node belongs to the unknown $(K + 1)$-th class, with the goal of filtering out as many OOD nodes as possible prior to human annotation. As a result, we retain nodes predicted to belong to one of the first K ID classes for further processing, while excluding those identified as unknown. Specifically, our goal is to filter out OOD nodes from $\mathcal{V}_{can}$ based on $\mathbf{H}^{(2)}$ to get the filtered ID node set $\mathcal{V}_{can}^{ID}$ and then select the most informative nodes from $\mathcal{V}_{can}^{ID}$ based on $\mathbf{H}^{(1)}$.

$$\mathcal{V}_{can}^{ID} = \left\{ v_i, \arg\max_k \mathbf{H}^{(2)}[i, K] \leq K \right\} \tag{4}$$

The cross-entropy loss function of the OOD filter is defined as:

$$\mathcal{L} = -\frac{1}{|\mathcal{V}_{LLM}|} \sum_{i \in \mathcal{V}_{LLM}} \sum_{k=1}^{K+1} y_{ik}^n \log \hat{y}_{ik}^n \tag{5}$$

4.3 Informativeness-Aware Node Selection

Most node selection methods typically prioritize nodes with high prediction uncertainty or diverse representations for labeling. However, in the presence of open-set noise, these metrics become unreliable, as OOD nodes also exhibit high uncertainty and diversity while lacking class-specific features or shared inductive biases with ID examples. By utilizing our OOD filter to remove a significant number of OOD nodes, we can more effectively identify and select the most informative nodes from the remaining potential ID nodes. Any graph active selection method, such as FeatProp [32] or MITIGATE [3], can be applied.

4.4 ID Classification and OOD Detection

With the help of the OOD filter, we can train the target ID classifier with more labeled ID nodes while adhering to the label budget constraint.

Assume that we have selected $\mathcal{V}_{can}^s$ from $\mathcal{V}_{can}^{ID}$ and annotated it with accurate labels $\mathcal{Y}_{can}^s$. We now have a set of nodes, $\mathcal{V}_{can}^s$, with accurate labels $\mathcal{Y}_{can}^s$, and a set of nodes, $\mathcal{V}_{LLM}$, with noisy labels $\mathcal{Y}_{LLM}$. From $\mathcal{V}_{can}^s$ and $\mathcal{V}_{LLM}$, we can derive the ID node set $\mathcal{V}_{can}^{s-ID}$ with accurate labels and $\mathcal{V}_{LLM}^{ID}$ with noisy labels. We can then use $\mathcal{V}_{can}^{s-ID}$ and $\mathcal{V}_{LLM}^{ID}$ to train the target ID classifier. Similarly, any graph neural network can serve as the ID classifier. The design of noise-resistant GNNs to better leverage the noisy labels from LLM is left for future study.

Specifically, the output of the ID classifier is $\mathbf{Z} \in \mathbb{R}^{N \times K}$:

$$\mathbf{Z} = GNN(\mathbf{A}, \mathbf{X}) \tag{6}$$

Note that if a node is in both $\mathcal{V}_{can}^{s-ID}$ and $\mathcal{V}_{LLM}^{ID}$, its label is taken from $\mathcal{Y}_{can}^{s-ID}$. Using noisy labels from $\mathcal{Y}_{LLM}^{ID}$ is extremely helpful when there are very few accurate labels available, particularly in situations of extreme data scarcity.

After training the ID classifier, any post-hoc OOD detector [10,13,15,20,40] can be applied to the output logits of the ID classifier. As an example, consider the well-known post-hoc OOD detector, MSP [10]. Correctly classified examples generally exhibit higher maximum softmax probabilities compared to misclassified and out-of-distribution examples. Consequently, given $\mathbf{Z}$, we can compute the softmax probability of the predicted class, i.e., the maximum softmax probability, which serves as the OOD score.

5 Experiments

Our experiments answer the following research questions (RQ): **RQ1** (Sect. 5.2): How effective is the proposed LLM-GOOD in ID classification and OOD detection compared to other leading baselines? **RQ2** (Sect. 5.2): Whether LLMs can filter out OOD nodes effectively? **RQ3** (Sect. 5.4): Will LLM-GOOD be robust to different settings, such as varying levels of label scarcity? **RQ4** (Sect. 5.5): What are the differences in cost and effectiveness between various LLMs?

5.1 Experimental Setup

Datasets. We utilize the following TAG datasets, which are commonly used for node classification: Cora [21], Citeseer [8], Pubmed [26] and Wiki-CS [22]. For each dataset, we split all classes into ID and OOD sets, and the ID classes for the four datasets are shown in Appendix B. Additionally, the number of ID classes is set to a minimum of two to perform the ID classification task.

For each dataset with K ID classes, we randomly select $10 \times K$ ID nodes and an equal number of OOD nodes for validation. The test set consists of 500 ID and 500 OOD nodes, while the remaining nodes form $\mathcal{V}_{can}$.

Baselines. We evaluate LLM-GOOD against two categories of baselines: (1) OOD detection methods, including MSP [10], Entropy, GNNSafe [31], and GRASP [20]; (2) node selection methods for node classification, including uncertainty-based selection [19], FeatProp [32], and MITIGATE [3], where different selection strategies are integrated into GCNs with MSP as the OOD score. For all methods, including baselines and LLM-GOOD, we use two GCN layers as the ID classifier.

Settings. For all datasets, we use GPT-4o-mini to annotate 200 randomly selected nodes and train the lightweight GNN filter using these annotated noisy nodes with two standard GCN layers. The results for other LLM are given in Sect. 5.5. For LLM-GOOD, we use the energy score [31] as the OOD score. Additionally, we evaluate an alternative approach (LLM-GOOD-f), where LLMs filter all unlabeled nodes in the initial graph, and a subset of ID-labeled nodes is randomly selected for manual labeling.

Evaluation Metrics. For the ID classification task, we use classification accuracy (ID ACC) as the evaluation metric. For the OOD detection task, we employ three commonly used metrics from the OOD detection literature [27]: the area under the ROC curve (AUROC), the precision-recall curve (AUPR), and the false positive rate when the true positive rate reaches 95% (FPR@95). In all experiments, the OOD nodes are considered positive cases. Details about these metrics are provided in Appendix A.

Table 1. Performance comparison (best highlighted in bold) of different models on ID classification and OOD detection tasks for the Cora and Citeseer datasets under label budget $10 \times K$. All values are percentages (%).

Model	Cora				Citeseer			
	ID ACC ↑	AUROC ↑	AUPR ↑	FPR@95 ↓	ID ACC ↑	AUROC ↑	AUPR ↑	FPR@95 ↓
GCN-Uncertainty	79.04 ± 7.98	77.02 ± 4.46	79.51 ± 3.61	75.80 ± 7.17	75.36 ± 4.81	69.73 ± 5.08	69.57 ± 5.58	87.72 ± 4.93
GCN-FeatProp	81.04 ± 2.45	78.24 ± 3.25	79.92 ± 4.07	75.92 ± 5.40	79.48 ± 2.83	71.45 ± 4.47	71.42 ± 4.60	86.56 ± 6.41
GCN-MITIGATE	81.64 ± 2.31	79.04 ± 2.31	80.52 ± 2.56	73.40 ± 4.71	80.44 ± 3.12	72.19 ± 4.33	71.92 ± 3.99	**84.52 ± 6.08**
MSP	77.68 ± 7.60	75.40 ± 6.85	78.19 ± 5.53	81.32 ± 9.72	70.92 ± 7.46	62.12 ± 7.09	64.63 ± 5.02	90.64 ± 3.78
GNNSafe	74.76 ± 8.99	84.05 ± 7.44	84.62 ± 6.42	61.20 ± 19.24	71.16 ± 7.44	65.84 ± 5.73	65.97 ± 5.13	89.12 ± 3.29
Entropy	76.80 ± 8.65	76.10 ± 8.08	78.12 ± 6.68	76.24 ± 12.87	73.20 ± 4.28	63.26 ± 6.65	65.24 ± 4.81	88.56 ± 4.69
GRASP	77.88 ± 8.36	83.00 ± 6.43	82.30 ± 6.33	61.48 ± 21.59	71.72 ± 5.37	60.64 ± 6.62	63.04 ± 4.67	91.20 ± 2.58
LLM-GOOD-f	84.00 ± 4.40	86.59 ± 2.32	87.36 ± 3.10	60.56 ± 3.94	72.52 ± 10.43	70.71 ± 4.49	72.99 ± 4.77	88.92 ± 6.85
LLM-GOOD	**85.20 ± 2.68**	**88.06 ± 3.77**	**87.85 ± 3.68**	**48.04 ± 1.19**	**80.60 ± 3.38**	**73.29 ± 4.12**	**75.26 ± 3.34**	86.48 ± 5.45

Implementation Details. We evaluate all methods under the total label budgets $10 \times K$ and $5 \times K$, respectively. Since baseline methods require an initial set of labeled nodes and multiple rounds of node selection, in each selection round, K nodes are chosen from the unlabeled pool and annotated for all baselines. In addition, we allocate an initial label budget of $5 \times K$ for the total budget of $10 \times K$ and K for the total budget of $5 \times K$. In contrast, our method does not require an initial set of labeled nodes and involves only a single round of random node selection for annotation.

All GCNs have 2 layers with hidden dimensions of 32. All models use a learning rate of 0.01, a dropout probability of 0.5 and a weight decay of 5e-4. For all K-Medoids-based selection methods, the number of clusters is fixed at 48. For LLM-GOOD, 200 nodes are randomly selected and annotated by the LLM. The weight assigned to the unknown class in the GNN filter's loss function is selected from $\{0.05, 0.1, 0.2, 0.3, 0.5\}$ based on the performance of the validation set. For all experiments, we average all results across 5 different random seeds.

Table 2. Performance comparison (best highlighted in bold) of different models on ID classification and OOD detection tasks for the Pubmed and Wiki-CS datasets under label budget $10 \times K$. All values are percentages (%).

Model	Pubmed				Wiki-CS			
	ID ACC ↑	AUROC ↑	AUPR ↑	FPR@95 ↓	ID ACC ↑	AUROC ↑	AUPR ↑	FPR@95 ↓
GCN-Uncertainty	84.48 ± 9.41	57.15 ± 6.61	55.96 ± 5.69	91.60 ± 2.39	81.88 ± 4.70	77.31 ± 6.18	79.59 ± 5.82	78.48 ± 10.79
GCN-FeatProp	83.00 ± 8.57	53.07 ± 11.45	53.58 ± 9.42	92.96 ± 5.64	76.48 ± 5.49	73.58 ± 6.99	75.26 ± 7.90	83.52 ± 6.43
GCN-MITIGATE	83.24 ± 8.48	57.91 ± 10.41	57.93 ± 9.57	92.60 ± 3.76	77.76 ± 7.96	71.69 ± 4.91	73.26 ± 4.77	86.16 ± 7.90
MSP	81.04 ± 7.51	52.65 ± 8.86	53.74 ± 7.15	93.44 ± 3.60	77.52 ± 5.60	75.10 ± 4.56	77.54 ± 5.48	84.80 ± 4.72
GNNSafe	82.16 ± 8.02	49.65 ± 17.49	55.55 ± 14.82	93.04 ± 6.90	78.80 ± 4.72	83.71 ± 4.38	84.95 ± 06.08	82.16 ± 11.53
Entropy	81.36 ± 7.57	52.22 ± 09.70	52.61 ± 8.47	92.68 ± 3.27	77.76 ± 4.80	72.85 ± 3.71	75.47 ± 4.68	88.00 ± 3.46
GRASP	82.68 ± 8.18	49.97 ± 19.59	54.86 ± 14.99	93.76 ± 5.46	78.28 ± 5.11	78.34 ± 8.54	79.17 ± 10.88	86.28 ± 6.14
LLM-GOOD-f	87.00 ± 2.19	61.09 ± 19.05	66.81 ± 15.58	91.24 ± 4.89	83.76 ± 2.46	86.84 ± 1.84	89.42 ± 1.57	79.24 ± 10.66
LLM-GOOD	**87.08 ± 2.58**	**64.87 ± 16.70**	**70.60 ± 14.26**	**90.72 ± 5.10**	**83.92 ± 3.53**	**87.71 ± 2.41**	**89.84 ± 2.64**	**71.04 ± 16.20**

5.2 Main Results

As shown in Tables 1, 2, 3 and 4, LLM-GOOD consistently outperforms state-of-the-art graph OOD detection methods by a significant margin across all TAG datasets. Specifically, for ID classification on four datasets, the most substantial improvement is observed on the Cora dataset when the label budget is set to $5 \times K$. In this case, the ID accuracy increases from 63.80% (achieved by the best baseline, GNNSafe) to 81.52%, reflecting a notable improvement of 17.72%. It is important to note that all baselines have an initial set of labeled ID nodes and use multiple selection rounds to improve performance. In contrast, LLM-GOOD selects nodes randomly in a single round yet still outperforms the baselines.

Furthermore, LLM-GOOD exhibits remarkable advancements in OOD detection metrics, achieving higher AUROC and AUPR scores while maintaining a lower FPR@95 across all datasets. The most significant improvement is observed in the Pubmed dataset when the label budget is $10 \times K$, where the AUROC increases from 57.91% (achieved by the best baseline, GCN with MITIGATE node selection) to 64.87%, marking an improvement of 6.96%.

Moreover, we calculate the final proportion of ID nodes, defined as the ratio of true ID nodes among all selected and annotated nodes, across various selection methods. The results are in Appendix C. Our method achieves the highest proportion across all datasets compared to the baselines. This shows that our method effectively filters out OOD nodes before human annotation, thereby reducing annotation costs. While LLM-GOOD and LLM-GOOD-f achieve similar ID node proportions, LLM-GOOD significantly reduces LLM costs by annotating only a small number of nodes and leveraging a GNN filter to label the rest.

Table 3. Performance comparison (best highlighted in bold) of different models on ID classification and OOD detection for the **Cora** and **Citeseer** TAG datasets under label budget $5 \times K$. All values are percentages (%).

Model	Cora				Citeseer			
	ID ACC↑	AUROC↑	AUPR↑	FPR@95↓	ID ACC↑	AUROC↑	AUPR↑	FPR@95↓
GCN-Uncertainty	51.20	65.51	65.90	87.88	59.96	67.53	69.00	89.76
GCN-FeatProp	55.76	71.00	72.28	85.88	69.32	67.00	65.87	**86.20**
GCN-MITIGATE	58.68	67.36	69.36	86.64	67.64	64.42	65.27	90.72
MSP	63.32	72.18	73.41	82.92	71.20	63.59	65.51	89.72
GNNSafe	62.52	79.29	81.12	68.76	70.88	67.47	67.16	87.52
Entropy	63.80	73.03	73.06	77.08	69.00	65.47	67.14	87.20
GRASP	63.52	75.30	75.07	68.96	72.56	60.64	62.40	91.12
LLM$_{GOOD-f}$	**81.52**	**82.26**	**83.71**	**64.72**	69.20	**70.99**	**73.39**	88.60
LLM-GOOD	78.60	80.21	80.82	68.88	**72.12**	67.81	69.65	91.92

Table 4. Performance comparison (best highlighted in bold) of different models on ID classification and OOD detection for the **Pubmed** and **Wiki-CS** TAG datasets under label budget $5 \times K$. All values are percentages (%).

Model	Pubmed				Wiki-CS			
	ID ACC↑	AUROC↑	AUPR↑	FPR@95↓	ID ACC↑	AUROC↑	AUPR↑	FPR@95↓
GCN-Uncertainty	73.36	57.53	57.55	90.56	61.40	61.94	64.86	92.12
GCN-FeatProp	71.60	50.89	51.19	95.04	71.64	69.30	71.73	90.32
GCN-MITIGATE	71.76	57.27	57.73	92.84	70.36	60.36	62.29	92.84
MSP	82.04	57.10	57.52	92.32	67.60	74.64	77.92	84.16
GNNSafe	81.48	53.71	59.51	96.44	68.20	79.38	81.26	83.28
Entropy	82.04	56.80	55.75	92.16	66.40	72.45	74.96	84.04
GRASP	81.40	52.35	57.30	94.96	67.84	77.54	79.95	85.60
LLM$_{GOOD-f}$	**83.52**	**63.29**	**68.68**	93.32	75.24	**84.62**	**86.30**	**77.88**
LLM-GOOD	78.08	60.34	65.13	**89.76**	**78.56**	83.35	86.26	84.84

5.3 OOD Detection Performance Upper Bound

We use different number of LLM's noisy labels and human's annotated accurate labels to train the ID classifier respectively. Given the different label budgets, we randomly select a corresponding number of nodes and use the ID nodes from the selected nodes to train the ID classifier. The results in Fig. 3 shows that:

- When the number of noisy ID labels or accurate ID labels increases, both ID classification and OOD detection performance improve. However, the improvement rate is significantly higher when using accurate ID labels.
- When training the ID classifier with LLM-generated noisy labels, both ID classification and OOD detection performance reach an upper bound substantially lower than that of training with accurate labels. This highlights the importance of our method, which utilizes LLM to reduce human annotation costs without relying entirely on the LLM for OOD detection.
- When the label budget for accurate labels reaches $10 \times K$, ID classification and OOD detection performance nearly reach the upper bound achieved with a large number of noisy labels. At $20 \times K$, both exceed the upper bound of using any number of LLM-generated noisy labels.

5.4 Combine Accurate Labels and Noisy Labels

We test different methods' performance under severe data-scarcity situation on Cora. The human label budget is set to $1 \times K$, $2 \times K$ and $3 \times K$. For LLM-GOOD-combined, we use 100 noisy labels along with a small number of corresponding clean labels to train the ID classifier. The results are shown in Table 5.

From the results, we observe that for all methods, increasing the label budget leads to improved performance, and our method consistently outperforms the baseline. When the accurate label budget is extremely small, incorporating

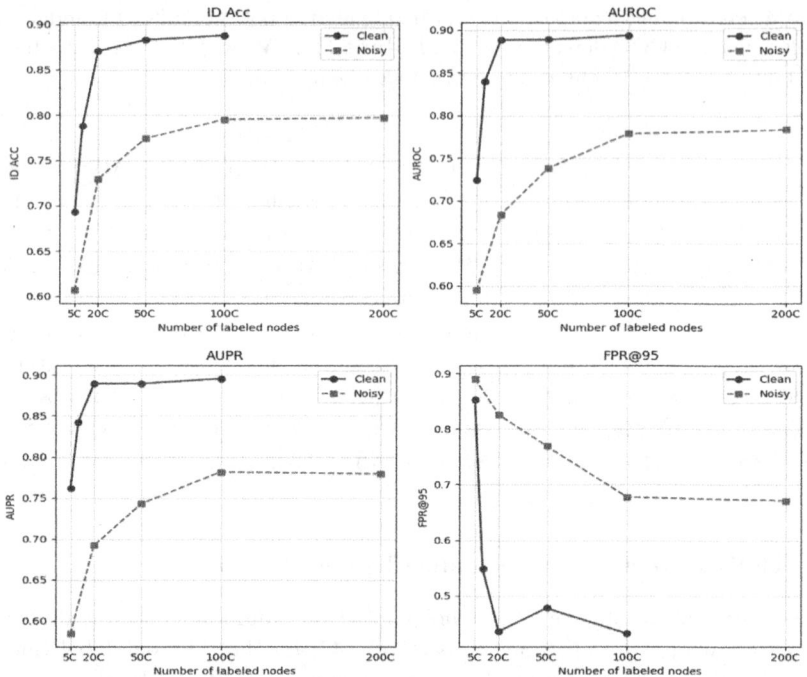

Fig. 3. ID classification and OOD detection performance upper bound.

Table 5. Different methods' performance under severe data-scarcity situation on Cora. LLM-GOOD-combined achieves the best performance.

	$1 \times K$	$2 \times K$	$3 \times K$
GCN-MSP	0.3228	0.4260	0.4856
LLM-GOOD	0.4580	0.6156	0.7492
LLM-GOOD-combined	**0.7832**	**0.8072**	**0.8164**

additional noisy labels is particularly beneficial. For instance, when the accurate label budget is $1 \times K$, the performance gap between LLM-GOOD and LLM-GOOD-combined is 32.52%. However, as the accurate label budget increases to $3 \times K$, the performance gap decreases to 6.72%.

Currently, most graph machine learning research assumes either that the entire training set is clean or that all training labels are uniformly affected by a specific type of noise. However, in real-world scenarios, it is more likely that a graph contains a small set of clean labels alongside another set of noisy labels. We leave the design of a more effective pipeline to leverage both label sets to denoise and train a robust, noise-resistant GNN as a direction for future study.

Table 6. Comparison of zero-shot OOD detection performance using different prompts across various LLMs on the Cora and Pubmed datasets.

	Cora			Pubmed		
	AUROC	AUPR	OOD Proportion	AUROC	AUPR	OOD Proportion
GPT-3.5-turbo-short prompt	0.5077	0.6609	0.0200	0.5000	0.7100	0.0000
GPT-3.5-turbo-long prompt	0.5909	0.7468	0.1700	0.5255	0.6440	0.0300
GPT-4o-mini-short prompt	0.7159	0.8200	0.5600	0.5060	0.7135	0.0050
GPT-4o-mini-long prompt	**0.7366**	**0.8323**	0.5150	0.8524	0.8796	0.3650
ds-v3-short prompt	0.6185	0.7589	0.2350	0.5000	0.7100	0.0000
ds-v3-long prompt	0.6887	0.8170	0.7000	**0.9364**	**0.9293**	0.4700

5.5 LLMs as Open-World Zero-Shot Annotators

We record the annotation cost and zero-shot OOD detection performance of the following LLMs: GPT-3.5-turbo, GPT-4, GPT-4o, GPT-4o-mini, DeepSeek-V3, DeepSeek-R1. Severe rate limitation prevented DeepSeek-R1 from annotating 200 nodes in a reasonable time, so its results are not included.

Zero-Shot Annotation Accuracy. We use the baseline short prompt (as shown in Sect. 4.1) and the long prompt (as shown in Appendix D) for zero-shot OOD detection on the Cora dataset. We randomly select 200 nodes and have different LLMs perform zero-shot open-world annotation using these two prompts. The true OOD proportion of the selected nodes is 56%. The OOD detection performance and the LLMs' predicted OOD proportions are presented in Table 6. From the results, we can observe that, sometimes, GPT-3.5-turbo does not dare to say 'none', but our long prompt mitigates this issue. Additionally, both the OOD detection performance and the predicted OOD proportion improve significantly with the long prompt, suggesting that GPT-3.5-turbo becomes more willing to say 'none.' Furthermore, when using the same prompt for open-world annotation, GPT-4o-mini generally outperforms GPT-3.5-turbo in OOD detection.

We further evaluate open-world annotation on the PubMed dataset by randomly selecting 200 nodes and having the LLMs annotate them using two prompts. The true OOD proportion of the selected nodes is 42%. We can observe that our proposed prompt outperforms the baseline short prompt in zero-shot OOD detection, even though the latter explicitly instructs the LLM to respond with "none" for OOD nodes.

Table 7. The cost (dollars) of different LLMs for annotating 200 nodes on Cora dataset.

	GPT-3.5-turbo	GPT-4o-mini	GPT-4o	GPT-4	ds-v3	ds-r1
Cost	0.07	0.02	0.50	3.70	0.03	0.55

Cost. We randomly select 200 nodes from the Cora dataset and have different LLMs annotate them. The costs associated with each LLM are shown in Table 7. As observed, GPT-4o-mini incurs the lowest cost while achieving significantly better zero-shot open-world annotation performance than GPT-3.5-turbo. Therefore, in this paper, we use GPT-4o-mini for node annotation to reduce human costs in open-set scenarios.

6 Conclusion and Future Directions

In this paper, we introduce a novel approach leveraging the powerful zero-shot learning capabilities of LLMs for label-efficient graph OOD detection. We propose a general framework, LLM-GOOD, which filters out a large number of OOD nodes before annotation, significantly reducing human labeling costs. Additionally, LLM-GOOD utilizes zero-shot annotations from LLMs to train a lightweight GNN filter, further minimizing the reliance on LLMs. Unlike traditional multi-round active learning methods, our approach achieves high performance with a single round of node selection. A potential future research direction is to investigate more effective ways to leverage both clean and noisy labels to train a more noise-resistant ID classifier for graph OOD detection. Additionally, it would be interesting to explore whether in-context learning can improve node-level OOD detection performance compared to zero-shot OOD detection with LLMs.

Acknowledgments. This work was partially supported by the National Science Foundation under Award No. 2428039 and No. 2346158. Any opinions, findings, and conclusions or recommendations expressed are those of the authors and do not necessarily reflect the views of the National Science Foundation.

References

1. Bai, Y., Han, Z., Cao, B., Jiang, X., Hu, Q., Zhang, C.: ID-like prompt learning for few-shot out-of-distribution detection. In: Proceedings of the IEEE/CVF Conference on Computer Vision and Pattern Recognition, pp. 17480–17489 (2024)
2. Cai, H., Zheng, V.W., Chang, K.C.C.: Active learning for graph embedding. arXiv preprint arXiv:1705.05085 (2017)
3. Chang, W., Liu, K., Ding, K., Yu, P.S., Yu, J.: Multitask active learning for graph anomaly detection. arXiv preprint arXiv:2401.13210 (2024)
4. Chen, Z., et al.: Label-free node classification on graphs with large language models (LLMs). arXiv preprint arXiv:2310.04668 (2023)
5. Ding, C., Pang, G.: Zero-shot out-of-distribution detection with outlier label exposure. arXiv preprint arXiv:2406.01170 (2024)
6. Ding, K., Wang, J., Li, J., Shu, K., Liu, C., Liu, H.: Graph prototypical networks for few-shot learning on attributed networks. In: Proceedings of the 29th ACM International Conference on Information & Knowledge Management, pp. 295–304 (2020)
7. Dong, H., Zhao, Y., Chatzi, E., Fink, O.: MultiOOD: scaling out-of-distribution detection for multiple modalities. arXiv preprint arXiv:2405.17419 (2024)

8. Giles, C.L., Bollacker, K.D., Lawrence, S.: CiteSeer: an automatic citation indexing system. In: Proceedings of the Third ACM Conference on Digital Libraries, pp. 89–98 (1998)
9. Guo, Z., et al.: GraphEdit: large language models for graph structure learning. arXiv preprint arXiv:2402.15183 (2024)
10. Hendrycks, D., Gimpel, K.: A baseline for detecting misclassified and out-of-distribution examples in neural networks. arXiv preprint arXiv:1610.02136 (2016)
11. Ju, W., et al.: Few-shot molecular property prediction via hierarchically structured learning on relation graphs. Neural Netw. **163**, 122–131 (2023)
12. Ju, W., et al.: A survey of data-efficient graph learning. arXiv preprint arXiv:2402.00447 (2024)
13. Lee, K., Lee, K., Lee, H., Shin, J.: A simple unified framework for detecting out-of-distribution samples and adversarial attacks. In: Advances in Neural Information Processing Systems, vol. 31 (2018)
14. Li, S., Gong, H., Dong, H., Yang, T., Tu, Z., Zhao, Y.: DPU: dynamic prototype updating for multimodal out-of-distribution detection. In: IEEE/CVF Conference on Computer Vision and Pattern Recognition (CVPR) (2025)
15. Liang, S., Li, Y., Srikant, R.: Enhancing the reliability of out-of-distribution image detection in neural networks. arXiv preprint arXiv:1706.02690 (2017)
16. Liu, W., Wang, X., Owens, J., Li, Y.: Energy-based out-of-distribution detection. In: Advances in Neural Information Processing Systems, vol. 33, pp. 21464–21475 (2020)
17. Liu, Q., Paparrizos, J.: The elephant in the room: towards a reliable time-series anomaly detection benchmark. In: Advances in Neural Information Processing Systems, vol. 37, pp. 108231–108261 (2024)
18. Liu, Q., Boniol, P., Palpanas, T., Paparrizos, J.: Time-series anomaly detection: overview and new trends. Proc. VLDB Endowment (PVLDB) **17**(12), 4229–4232 (2024)
19. Luo, W., Schwing, A., Urtasun, R.: Latent structured active learning. In: Advances in Neural Information Processing Systems, vol. 26 (2013)
20. Ma, L., Sun, Y., Ding, K., Liu, Z., Wu, F.: Revisiting score propagation in graph out-of-distribution detection. In: The Thirty-Eighth Annual Conference on Neural Information Processing Systems (2024)
21. McCallum, A.K., Nigam, K., Rennie, J., Seymore, K.: Automating the construction of internet portals with machine learning. Inf. Retrieval **3**, 127–163 (2000)
22. Mernyei, P., Cangea, C.: Wiki-CS: a Wikipedia-based benchmark for graph neural networks. arXiv preprint arXiv:2007.02901 (2020)
23. Miyai, A., Yu, Q., Irie, G., Aizawa, K.: LoCoOp: few-shot out-of-distribution detection via prompt learning. In: Advances in Neural Information Processing Systems, vol. 36 (2024)
24. Reimers, N.: Sentence-BERT: sentence embeddings using Siamese BERT-networks. arXiv preprint arXiv:1908.10084 (2019)
25. Ren, X., Tang, J., Yin, D., Chawla, N., Huang, C.: A survey of large language models for graphs. In: Proceedings of the 30th ACM SIGKDD Conference on Knowledge Discovery and Data Mining, pp. 6616–6626 (2024)
26. Sen, P., Namata, G., Bilgic, M., Getoor, L., Galligher, B., Eliassi-Rad, T.: Collective classification in network data. AI Mag. **29**(3), 93 (2008)
27. Song, Y., Wang, D.: Learning on graphs with out-of-distribution nodes. In: Proceedings of the 28th ACM SIGKDD Conference on Knowledge Discovery and Data Mining, pp. 1635–1645 (2022)

28. Tan, Z., Ding, K., Guo, R., Liu, H.: Graph few-shot class-incremental learning. In: Proceedings of the Fifteenth ACM International Conference on Web Search and Data Mining, pp. 987–996 (2022)
29. Wang, Y., Duan, Z., Huang, Y., Xu, H., Feng, J., Ren, A.: MTHetGNN: a heterogeneous graph embedding framework for multivariate time series forecasting. Pattern Recogn. Lett. **153**, 151–158 (2022)
30. Wang, H., Li, Y., Yao, H., Li, X.: CLIPN for zero-shot OOD detection: teaching CLIP to say no. In: Proceedings of the IEEE/CVF International Conference on Computer Vision, pp. 1802–1812 (2023)
31. Wu, Q., Chen, Y., Yang, C., Yan, J.: Energy-based out-of-distribution detection for graph neural networks. arXiv preprint arXiv:2302.02914 (2023)
32. Wu, Y., Xu, Y., Singh, A., Yang, Y., Dubrawski, A.: Active learning for graph neural networks via node feature propagation. arXiv preprint arXiv:1910.07567 (2019)
33. Xiao, Z., Song, W., Xu, H., Ren, Z., Sun, Y.: TIMME: Twitter ideology-detection via multi-task multi-relational embedding. In: Proceedings of the 26th ACM SIGKDD International Conference on Knowledge Discovery & Data Mining, pp. 2258–2268 (2020)
34. Xia, Y., et al.: From selection to generation: a survey of LLM-based active learning. arXiv preprint arXiv:2502.11767 (2025)
35. Xu, H., et al.: Graph partitioning and graph neural network based hierarchical graph matching for graph similarity computation. Neurocomputing **439**, 348–362 (2021)
36. Xu, H., Chen, R., Wang, Y., Duan, Z., Feng, J.: CoSimGNN: towards large-scale graph similarity computation. arXiv preprint arXiv:2005.07115 (2020)
37. Xu, H., Liu, K., Yao, Z., Yu, P.S., Ding, K., Zhao, Y.: Lego-learn: label-efficient graph open-set learning. arXiv preprint arXiv:2410.16386 (2024)
38. Xu, H., et al.: Graph synthetic out-of-distribution exposure with large language models. arXiv preprint arXiv:2504.21198 (2025)
39. Xu, H., et al.: GLIP-OOD: zero-shot graph OOD detection with foundation model. arXiv preprint arXiv:2504.21186 (2025)
40. Yang, J., et al.: OpenOOD: benchmarking generalized out-of-distribution detection. In: Advances in Neural Information Processing Systems, vol. 35, pp. 32598–32611 (2022)
41. Yu, T., He, S., Song, Y.Z., Xiang, T.: Hybrid graph neural networks for few-shot learning. In: Proceedings of the AAAI Conference on Artificial Intelligence, vol. 36, pp. 3179–3187 (2022)

Learning Theory

Learning Overspecified Gaussian Mixtures Exponentially Fast with the EM Algorithm

Zhenisbek Assylbekov[1,2(✉)], Alan Legg[1], and Artur Pak[2,3]

[1] Department of Mathematical Sciences, Purdue University Fort Wayne, Fort Wayne, IN, USA
{zassylbe,leggar01}@pfw.edu
[2] Department of Mathematics, Nazarbayev University, Astana, Kazakhstan
[3] Mohamed bin Zayed University of Artificial Intelligence, Abu Dhabi, UAE
artur.pak@nu.edu.kz

Abstract. We investigate the convergence properties of the EM algorithm when applied to overspecified Gaussian mixture models—that is, when the number of components in the fitted model exceeds that of the true underlying distribution. Focusing on a structured configuration where the component means are positioned at the vertices of a regular simplex and the mixture weights satisfy a non-degeneracy condition, we demonstrate that the population EM algorithm converges exponentially fast in terms of the Kullback-Leibler (KL) distance. Our analysis leverages the strong convexity of the negative log-likelihood function in a neighborhood around the optimum and utilizes the Polyak-Łojasiewicz inequality to establish that an ϵ-accurate approximation is achievable in $O(\log(1/\epsilon))$ iterations. Furthermore, we extend these results to a finite-sample setting by deriving explicit statistical convergence guarantees. Numerical experiments on synthetic datasets corroborate our theoretical findings, highlighting the dramatic acceleration in convergence compared to conventional sublinear rates. This work not only deepens the understanding of EM's behavior in overspecified settings but also offers practical insights into initialization strategies and model design for high-dimensional clustering and density estimation tasks.

Keywords: Overspecification · Gaussian Mixtures · Expectation-Maximization

1 Introduction and Main Results

Let $Z_1, \ldots, Z_n$ be a random sample from the standard d-variate normal distribution $\mathcal{N}_d(0, I)$, where $0 \in \mathbb{R}^d$ is the mean vector, and $I \in \mathbb{R}^{d \times d}$ is the identity covariance matrix. We aim to fit a k-component Gaussian mixture model of the form

$$\pi_1 \cdot \mathcal{N}_d(\mu_1, I) + \ldots + \pi_k \cdot \mathcal{N}_d(\mu_k, I) \tag{1}$$

to this sample. When $k \geq 2$, this setting is known as *overspecification*, meaning the fitted model contains more mixture components than the true data-generating process. We assume the location parameters $\mu = (\mu_1^\top, \ldots, \mu_k^\top)^\top$ are unknown, while the mixture weights $(\pi_1, \ldots, \pi_k)$ are fixed and satisfy $\pi_j > 0$ and $\sum_{j=1}^k \pi_j = 1$.

Let $f(x; \mu)$ denote the probability density function of the mixture defined in Eq. (1). The maximum likelihood estimator (MLE) of μ is given by

$$\hat{\mu} \in \arg\max_{\mu} \frac{1}{n} \sum_{i=1}^{n} \log f(Z_i; \mu). \qquad (2)$$

For $k \neq 1$, a closed-form solution for $\hat{\mu}$ does not exist. Instead, Eq. (2) is typically solved using iterative methods such as the Expectation-Maximization (EM) algorithm [7]. However, since the log-likelihood function in Eq. (2) is non-concave, iterative methods generally do not guarantee convergence to the global optimum.

Recent studies have analyzed the behavior of EM in overspecified settings. Dwivedi et al. [8,9] examined the case $k = 2$, differentiating between balanced mixtures ($\pi_1 = \pi_2 = 1/2$) and unbalanced mixtures ($\pi_1 \neq \pi_2$). Assuming symmetric means ($\mu_1 = -\mu_2$), they showed that in the unbalanced case, the population EM[1] algorithm requires $O(\log(1/\epsilon))$ steps to obtain an ϵ-accurate estimate of the parameter $\mu^* = 0$. In contrast, for balanced mixtures, the algorithm needs $\Theta(\log(1/\epsilon)/\epsilon^2)$ steps, making it exponentially slower.

Xu et al. [17] investigated the behavior of *gradient EM*[2] in the population setting for general k. Their results show that gradient EM exhibits a slow convergence rate, requiring $O(1/\epsilon^2)$ iterations to approximate the k-component Gaussian mixture Eq. (1) to $\mathcal{N}_d(0, I)$ within an accuracy ϵ in the KL metric. Their work imposes no assumptions on the balance of the mixture weights or the arrangement of Gaussian component centers. From this perspective, their result is more general. However, as demonstrated by Dwivedi et al. [9], in certain overspecified cases, the EM algorithm can achieve exponential convergence. This motivates the following question:

When learning a mixture of k Gaussians from $\mathcal{N}_d(0, I)$ data, does there exist a configuration of component centers and mixture weights such that the EM algorithm converges exponentially fast?

Our answer to this question is affirmative, and we present it in the form of the following theorem.

Theorem 1. *Let $R \in \mathbb{R}^{d \times d}$ be an orthogonal matrix such that for any nonzero $\theta \in \mathbb{R}^d$, the points*

$$\mu_j(\theta) = R^{j-1}\theta, \quad \text{for } j = 1, \ldots, k.$$

form the vertices of a regular $(k-1)$-simplex in $\mathbb{R}^d$, $d \geq k - 1$, centered at the origin. Consider the k-component Gaussian mixture

$$\mathcal{G}(\theta) := \pi_1 \cdot \mathcal{N}_d(\mu_1(\theta), I) + \pi_2 \cdot \mathcal{N}_d(\mu_2(\theta), I) + \cdots + \pi_k \cdot \mathcal{N}_d(\mu_k(\theta), I),$$

---

[1] Population EM assumes access to the true data-generating distribution, allowing updates to be computed as exact expectations, free from sampling variability.

[2] Gradient EM replaces the M-step of the Expectation-Maximization algorithm with a single gradient ascent step on the Q-function.

where the mixture weights $\pi_1, \ldots, \pi_k$ are fixed, positive, satisfy $\sum_{j=1}^{k} \pi_j = 1$, and their discrete Fourier transform has no zero entries. This mixture is fitted to the standard Gaussian distribution $\mathcal{N}(0, I)$ using the Population EM algorithm. Let θ_t denote the parameter value at iteration t. Then there exists $\gamma > 0$ such that the following holds:

$$D_{KL}[\mathcal{N}(0, I) \parallel \mathcal{G}(\theta_t)] \leq \kappa^t D_{KL}[\mathcal{N}(0, I) \parallel \mathcal{G}(\theta_0)],$$

for θ_0 satisfying $\|\theta_0\| \leq \gamma$ and for some constant $\kappa \in (0, 1)$.

At first glance, the choice of placing Gaussian component centers at the vertices of a regular $(k-1)$-simplex may seem arbitrary. However, this configuration naturally arises in the context of Gaussian mixture learning.

A common approach to initializing Gaussian mixture components in the EM algorithm is via Lloyd's variant of the k-means algorithm [13]. We can show that the vertices of a regular $(k-1)$-simplex (with a particular radius) form a fixed point of Lloyd's algorithm when applied to $\mathcal{N}(0, I)$ at the population level (Sect. 2). Figure 1 illustrates this for finite samples and $k = 2, 3$. This suggests that the regular $(k-1)$-simplex is a natural initialization choice for the EM algorithm when learning an overspecified Gaussian mixture from data generated by a single Gaussian.

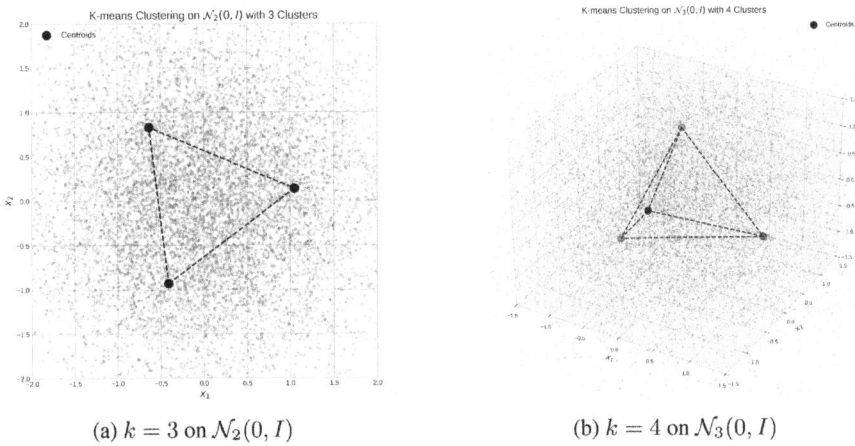

(a) $k = 3$ on $\mathcal{N}_2(0, I)$ (b) $k = 4$ on $\mathcal{N}_3(0, I)$

Fig. 1. K-means clustering on standard Gaussian data. *Left:* 10,000 samples in $\mathbb{R}^2$ are clustered into 3 groups; centroids (black markers) are connected by dashed lines to form a near-equilateral triangle. *Right:* 10,000 samples in $\mathbb{R}^3$ are clustered into 4 groups; centroids (black markers) connected by dashed lines approximate a regular tetrahedron.

Following Xu et al. [17], we focus on the convergence of the fitted distribution to the true distribution in the KL metric rather than the convergence of the parameters to zero in the Euclidean metric, as studied by Dwivedi et al. [9]. However, our analysis fundamentally differs from both works. We find that the expected negative log-likelihood function is strongly convex in the neighborhood of the optimum and satisfies the so-called *Polyak-Łojasiewicz* inequality [1,14]. This significantly simplifies the analysis of the convergence of the KL distance between the fitted model and the true distribution.

An immediate consequence of Theorem 1 is that the Population EM algorithm requires $O\left(\log(1/\epsilon)\right)$ steps to approximate the mixture $\mathcal{G}(\theta)$ to $\mathcal{N}(0,I)$ within ϵ in the KL metric. This is exponentially faster than the general result of Xu et al. [17]. Moreover, by leveraging the now-standard approach of Balakrishnan et al. [3], we can translate the fast convergence of the population EM into the following finite-sample guarantee for the sample-based EM algorithm.

Theorem 2. *Under the assumptions of Theorem 1 on the structure of the Gaussian mixture, there exists $\gamma > 0$ such that for any initialization θ_0 with $\|\theta_0\| \leq \gamma$, the EM algorithm produces a sequence of parameter estimates $\hat{\theta}_t$ satisfying*

$$D_{KL}\left[\mathcal{N}(0,I) \parallel \mathcal{G}(\hat{\theta}_T)\right] \leq c_1 \|\theta_0\|^2 \frac{\log(1/\delta)}{n}, \tag{3}$$

for $T \geq c_2 \log \frac{n}{\log(1/\delta)}$ with probability at least $1 - \delta$.

The proof of Theorem 2 is based on a perturbation bound that relates the sample-based EM operator to its population-level counterpart (Lemma 8 in Sect. C). In turn, the proof of the latter utilizes standard arguments to derive Rademacher complexity bounds.

The theoretical insights presented above are supported by our numerical experiments. In particular, Fig. 2 demonstrates the exponential decay of the KL divergence over EM iterations under various mixture weight configurations, while Fig. 3 reveals how the divergence decreases as the sample size increases. Together, these figures provide an intuitive visualization of the convergence dynamics and statistical guarantees established by our analysis.

To summarize, our work makes the following key contributions:

- We demonstrate that the EM algorithm can achieve *exponential convergence* in the KL metric when learning an overspecified mixture of k Gaussian components under a specific structured configuration of mixture centers and weights. This contrasts with prior work [17], which establishes only sublinear convergence rates in general settings.
- We develop a novel analytical framework based on the *Polyak-Łojasiewicz inequality*, leveraging the strong convexity of the expected negative log-likelihood function near the optimum. This significantly simplifies the convergence analysis compared to previous approaches.
- We establish an explicit *finite-sample guarantee* for learning an overspecified mixture of k Gaussians with the EM algorithm.

These contributions provide new insights into the role of mixture structure in the efficiency of EM and identify settings where the algorithm achieves fast convergence rates.

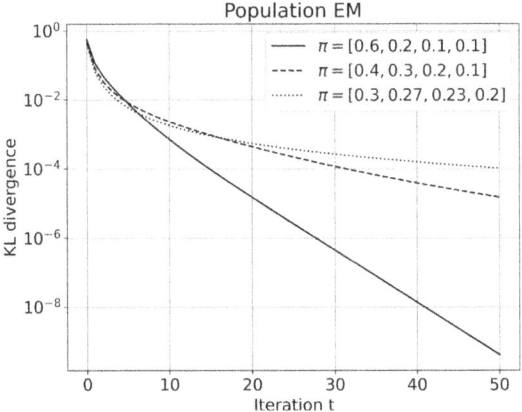

Fig. 2. Convergence of Population EM: The plot shows the evolution of the KL divergence versus the number of EM iterations for three different sets of mixture weights. The curves correspond to varying levels of imbalance illustrating how the choice of weights influences convergence speed.

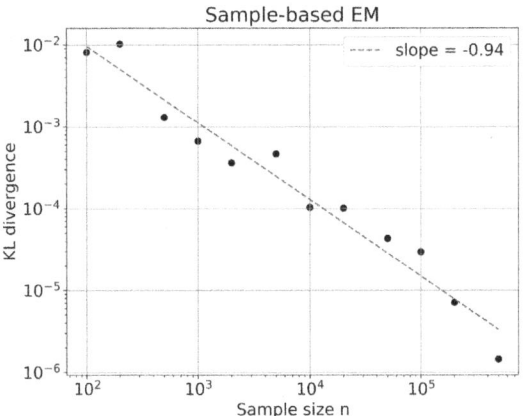

Fig. 3. Sample-Based EM Performance: The figure plots the final KL divergence against the sample size n on a log-log scale. It demonstrates how increasing the number of samples improves the accuracy of the EM estimate by reducing the divergence between the fitted mixture and the true $\mathcal{N}(0, I)$ distribution.

Notation. Lowercase letters (x) denote vectors in $\mathbb{R}^d$, uppercase letters (A, X) denote matrices and random vectors. The Euclidean norm is denoted by $\|x\| := \sqrt{x^\top x}$. We denote $\{1, 2, \ldots, k\}$ with $[k]$.

The probability density function of $Z \sim \mathcal{N}(0, I)$, where I is a $d \times d$ identity matrix, is denoted by $\phi(z)$. The cumulative distribution function of $Z \sim \mathcal{N}(0, 1)$ is denoted by $\Phi(z)$.

Given $f : \mathbb{R} \to \mathbb{R}$ and $g : \mathbb{R} \to \mathbb{R}_+$, we write $f \precsim g$ if there exist $x_0 \in \mathbb{R}$, $c \in \mathbb{R}_+$ such that for all $x > x_0$ we have $|f(x)| \leq cg(x)$. When $f : \mathbb{R} \to \mathbb{R}_+$, we write $f \asymp g$

if $f \precsim g$ and $g \precsim f$. We use c, c_1, c_2, etc. to denote some universal constants (which might change in value each time they appear).

Related Work

Research on the Expectation-Maximization (EM) algorithm and its convergence behavior in Gaussian mixture models has advanced rapidly. Balakrishnan et al. [3] introduced a framework to delineate the region of convergence in terms of distribution parameters. Their work contrasted a population-level analysis with the sample-based implementation commonly used in practice, focusing specifically on the well-specified case of $k = 2$ components and addressing both balanced and unbalanced scenarios.

Within this context, significant effort has been devoted to developing initialization strategies that guarantee convergence to the global optimum. Klusowski and Brinda [12] demonstrated that local convergence can occur over a broader region than previously identified for the two-component case, while Zhao et al. [19] investigated how initialization affects mixtures with an arbitrary number of well-separated components. In addition, Daskalakis et al. [6] provided global convergence guarantees for a two-component model with symmetrically positioned mean vectors. For mixtures with k well-separated components, Segol and Nadler [16] proved that convergence is assured even when the algorithm is initialized near the midpoint between clusters, refining the estimation error bounds and extending the analysis to Gradient EM—a variant of the classical EM algorithm. Moreover, Yan et al. [18] further analyzed the convergence rate and local contraction radius of Gradient EM for an arbitrary number of mixture components.

Another major line of inquiry has focused on model misspecification. Dwivedi et al. [10] examined an underspecified scenario, where a two-component Gaussian mixture is fitted to data generated by a three-component mixture, and characterized the resulting bias while also exploring the influence of initialization on convergence. The benefits of overspecified mixture models have been recognized by Dwivedi et al. [9], Dwivedi et al. [8], Chen et al. [4], and others. In particular, Dwivedi et al. [9] and Dwivedi et al. [8] studied the case of fitting two Gaussian components to data from a single Gaussian distribution. They compared balanced and unbalanced scenarios, demonstrating that in sample-based EM the unbalanced case converges at a statistical rate of $O(1/\sqrt{n})$, in contrast to $O(\sqrt[4]{1/n})$ for the balanced case when estimating mean vectors under both known and estimated isotropic covariance structures. They further showed that the algorithmic convergence rate is exponentially faster in the unbalanced setting.

Bayesian approaches to model overspecification, as discussed in [15], have revealed that the estimated mixture weights can vary greatly, often causing some components to become redundant and allowing for model refinement by discarding those with very small weights. In addition, Chen et al. [4] found that even spurious local minima of the negative log-likelihood retain structural information that is valuable for identifying component means, highlighting the advantages of overspecification over underspecification—a contrast often described as "many-fit-one" versus "one-fit-many." Furthermore, Dasgupta and Schulman [5] proposed a method for finite mixture overspecification by recommending that models be deliberately initialized with $\frac{\log(k)}{w_{\min}}$

clusters, where $w_{\min}$ denotes the smallest weight, to substantially accelerate convergence.

While much of the literature has focused on convergence in terms of distribution parameters, investigations measuring the quality of fit using the Kullback-Leibler (KL) divergence are relatively few. Ghosal and van der Vaart [11] derived a statistical convergence rate of $(\log n)^{\kappa}/\sqrt{n}$ in Hellinger distance, which translates to a lower bound of $(\log n)^{2\kappa}/n$ in KL divergence; however, their analysis was confined to well-specified models and did not consider algorithmic factors. Dwivedi et al. [10] also employed KL divergence in the context of underspecified mixtures, but, to our knowledge, the use of KL divergence in overspecified mixtures was first explored by Xu et al. [17]. They obtained KL divergence bounds for the population version of Gradient EM applied to a k-component mixture with known variances. In contrast, our work extends these results by analyzing both population and sample-based EM under a structured configuration of mixture centers and weights, and importantly, we establish an *exponentially faster* algorithmic convergence rate in KL divergence than that reported by Xu et al. [17].

2 Initialization with k-Means

Initialization is a critical step in the ExpectationMaximization (EM) algorithm, particularly in overspecified settings where the number of mixture components exceeds the true number. A common strategy is to first run the $k$means algorithm (i.e., Lloyd's algorithm) on the data and then use the resulting cluster centers to initialize the EM algorithm.

When the data are generated from a single Gaussian distribution $\mathcal{N}(0, I)$, one observes that Lloyd's algorithm exhibits a natural fixedpoint property under a symmetric configuration. In particular, consider initializing the k centers at the vertices of a regular $(k-1)$-simplex centered at the origin. That is, let

$$\mu_i = r\,v_i, \quad i = 1, \ldots, k,$$

where the vectors $v_1, \ldots, v_k \in \mathbb{R}^d$ (with $d \geq k-1$) are unit vectors forming the vertices of a regular simplex, and $r > 0$ is a scaling factor.

A key observation is that the Voronoi partition induced by these centers depends only on the directions v_i and not on the scalar r. Consequently, the conditional expectations computed in the Lloyd update—i.e., the new centers—are also determined solely by the angular configuration. In fact, one may show that the Lloyd update maps the configuration to

$$\mu_i' = R_0\,v_i, \quad i = 1, \ldots, k,$$

where $R_0 > 0$ is determined by the radial integrals of the Gaussian density. Thus, the fixedpoint condition $\mu_i' = \mu_i$ for all i is equivalent to choosing $r = R_0$.

This fixedpoint property suggests that initializing the EM algorithm with a regular simplex (properly scaled) is natural in the context of overspecified Gaussian mixtures. In the proof of the following proposition (Sect. A), we rigorously analyze this phenomenon by first characterizing the Voronoi partition induced by a regular simplex and then proving that there exists a unique scaling $r > 0$ such that the configuration

$$\{\mu_i = r\,v_i : i = 1, \ldots, k\}$$

remains invariant under the populationlevel Lloyd update.

Proposition 1. *Let $d \geq k - 1$, and suppose that*

$$v_1, \ldots, v_k \in \mathbb{R}^d$$

are unit vectors that form the vertices of a regular simplex in some $(k-1)$-dimensional subspace of $\mathbb{R}^d$,

$$\|v_i\| = 1, \quad \text{for } i = 1, \ldots, k, \quad \text{with} \quad \sum_{i=1}^{k} v_i = 0,$$

with the pairwise inner products being constant for $i \neq j$. For any $r > 0$, define centers

$$\mu_i = r\, v_i, \quad i = 1, \ldots, k,$$

and let the Voronoi cells be

$$V_i = \{\, x \in \mathbb{R}^d : \|x - \mu_i\| \leq \|x - \mu_j\| \text{ for all } j \neq i \,\}.$$

Then there exists a unique $r > 0$ such that if one performs the population-level Lloyd update

$$\mu_i' = \frac{\int_{V_i} x\, \phi(x)\, dx}{\int_{V_i} \phi(x)\, dx},$$

one obtains $\mu_i' = \mu_i$ for all $i = 1, \ldots, k$. That is, the configuration

$$\{\mu_i = r\, v_i : i = 1, \ldots, k\}$$

is a fixed point of Lloyd's algorithm.

3 Population-Level Analysis

We begin by analyzing the behavior of the so-called *population EM*, a theoretical construct that isolates algorithmic complexity from sample complexity. Population EM assumes direct access to the data-generating distribution $\mathcal{N}(0, I)$ and, instead of maximizing the sample-based log-likelihood in Eq. (2), optimizes the population log-likelihood:

$$\mathcal{L}(\theta) := \mathbb{E}_{Z \sim \mathcal{N}(0, I)}[\log f(Z; \theta)]. \tag{4}$$

The algorithm proceeds iteratively by applying the following two steps:

– *Expectation step*: Given the current estimate θ_t, compute the function

$$Q(\theta, \theta_t) := \mathbb{E}_{Z \sim \mathcal{N}(0, I)} \left[\sum_{j=1}^{k} w_j(Z; \theta_t) \log \left(\pi_j \cdot \phi \left(Z - R^{j-1} \theta \right) \right) \right],$$

where

$$w_j(Z; \theta_t) = \frac{\pi_j \cdot \phi(Z - R^{j-1} \theta_t)}{\sum_{\ell=1}^{k} \pi_\ell \cdot \phi(Z - R^{\ell-1} \theta_t)}.$$

- *Maximization step*: Update the parameters by solving the optimization problem:

$$\theta_{t+1} \in \arg\max_\theta Q(\theta, \theta_t).$$

In this specific case, where the population EM algorithm is used to fit the mixture Eq. (1) to $\mathcal{N}(0, I)$, the recurrence relations governing the parameter updates can be explicitly derived (Sect. B.1). The parameter updates follow the recursion $\theta_{t+1} = M(\theta_t)$, where

$$M(\theta) := \mathbb{E}_{Z \sim \mathcal{N}(0,I)} \left[\sum_{j=1}^k w_j(Z;\theta)(R^{j-1})^\top Z \right]. \quad (5)$$

The mapping $M(\theta)$ is referred to as the *population EM operator*. Notably, it is closely related to the population negative log-likelihood, as stated in the following equation (Sect. B.2):

$$\nabla_\theta[-\mathcal{L}(\theta)] = \theta - M(\theta). \quad (6)$$

Denote $L(\theta) := -\mathcal{L}(\theta)$. The equation Eq. (6) implies that

$$\theta_{t+1} = \theta_t - \nabla_\theta[L(\theta_t)],$$

which means that in the given setting, the EM algorithm is equivalent to gradient descent (GD) on $L(\theta)$ with a step size 1. This suggests that standard techniques used in the analysis of GD can be applied to study the convergence of the EM algorithm. One such technique is the Polyak-Łojasiewicz inequality, a sufficient condition for the exponential convergence of GD. We establish this property for $L(\theta)$ in the following lemma.

Lemma 1 (Local PL Inequality). *Let $\mathcal{L}(\theta)$ be the population log-likelihood function defined by Eq. (4). Suppose $\pi_1, \ldots, \pi_k > 0$ are positive real numbers whose discrete Fourier transform has no zero entries. Then there exists $\delta > 0$ such that $L(\theta) := -\mathcal{L}(\theta)$ satisfies the following local Polyak–Łojasiewicz (PL) inequality in $\{\theta : \|\theta\| \leq \delta\}$:*

$$\|\nabla L(\theta)\|^2 \geq \lambda_{\min} \Big(L(\theta) - L(0) \Big), \quad (7)$$

where $\lambda_{\min} \leq 1$ is the smallest eigenvalue of $\nabla^2 L(0)$.

A key step in establishing the local Polyak –Ł ojasiewicz (PL) inequality around $\theta^* = 0$ is to show that the Hessian $\nabla^2 L(\theta)$ remains positive definite in a sufficiently small neighborhood of $\theta^* = 0$. Concretely, we need the Jacobian of the EM operator at $\theta^* = 0$ to have spectral properties that ensure strong convexity of the population negative log-likelihood L.

In our setup, this boils down to proving that the matrix $A = \sum_{j=1}^k \pi_j R^{j-1}$ is invertible (cf. Lemmas 2 and 3 in Sect. 5), since one can then show $I - \frac{\partial M}{\partial \theta}(0) = A^\top A$ is positive definite. The invertibility of A follows from the assumption that the π_j's have a discrete Fourier transform with no zero entries. Intuitively, if the discrete Fourier transform of $\{\pi_j\}$ vanished at one of the k-th roots of unity, then certain "rotational symmetries" in the update equations would cause degeneracies, preventing A from being invertible. By ruling out such degeneracies, the condition $\hat{\pi}(\ell) \neq 0$ for all ℓ guarantees the necessary full rank of A.

Under these conditions, the Hessian $\nabla^2 L(\theta)$ remains uniformly positive definite in a neighborhood of $\theta^* = 0$, which yields the strong convexity of L around $\theta^* = 0$. From strong convexity, the usual argument then gives the local PL inequality Eq. (7) demonstrating the sharpness of the landscape near the stationary point $\theta^* = 0$.

Since the local PL inequality plays a central role in our convergence analysis, we present the proof of Lemma 1 in the main text (Sect. 5) to ensure the core argument remains transparent. The proofs of the remaining supporting lemmas are deferred to the Appendix.

We are ready to prove the exponential decay of the KL divergence between the true distribution and the sequence of fitted mixtures.

Proof (Proof of Theorem 1). We start by noting that

$$\mathrm{D_{KL}}\big[\mathcal{N}(0,I) \,\big\|\, \mathcal{G}(\theta_t)\big] = L(\theta_t) - L(0).$$

Equation Eq. (6) implies that the Hessian of L is given by

$$\nabla^2 L(\theta) = I - \frac{\partial M}{\partial \theta}.$$

Furthermore, we can show (see Lemma 2 in Sect. 5) that at $\theta^* = 0$, we have

$$\nabla^2 L(0) = AA^\top, \quad \text{where} \quad A := \sum_{j=1}^{k} \pi_j R^{j-1}.$$

Since R is an orthogonal matrix, its eigenvalues are among the k-th roots of unity $\{e^{2\pi i \ell / k}\}_{\ell=0}^{k-1}$, implying $\|R\|_{\mathrm{op}} = 1$. Hence, by the triangle inequality,

$$\|\nabla^2 L(0)\|_{\mathrm{op}} \leq \left(\sum_{j=1}^{k} \pi_j \|R^{j-1}\|_{\mathrm{op}}\right)^2 = \left(\sum_{j=1}^{k} \pi_j\right)^2 = 1.$$

By smoothness of $L(\theta)$, there is therefore a neighborhood of $\theta^* = 0$ in which $\|\nabla^2 L(\theta)\|_{\mathrm{op}} \leq 3/2$. Consequently, for θ and θ' in that neighborhood,

$$L(\theta') \leq L(\theta) + \nabla L(\theta)^\top (\theta' - \theta) + \tfrac{3}{4} \|\theta' - \theta\|^2.$$

In particular, applying this to θ_{t+1} and θ_t yields

$$\begin{aligned}
L(\theta_{t+1}) &\leq L(\theta_t) + \nabla L(\theta_t)^\top (\theta_{t+1} - \theta_t) + \tfrac{3}{4} \|\theta_{t+1} - \theta_t\|^2 \\
&= L(\theta_t) + \nabla L(\theta_t)^\top (M(\theta_t) - \theta_t) + \tfrac{3}{4} \|M(\theta_t) - \theta_t\|^2 \\
&= L(\theta_t) - \|\nabla L(\theta_t)\|^2 + \tfrac{3}{4} \|\nabla L(\theta_t)\|^2 \\
&= L(\theta_t) - \tfrac{1}{4} \|\nabla L(\theta_t)\|^2.
\end{aligned}$$

Next, using the Polyak–Lojasiewicz inequality Eq. (7), we obtain

$$L(\theta_{t+1}) \leq L(\theta_t) - \tfrac{\lambda_{\min}}{4}\left(L(\theta_t) - L(0)\right).$$

Subtracting $L(0)$ from both sides gives

$$L(\theta_{t+1}) - L(0) \leq \left(1 - \tfrac{\lambda_{\min}}{4}\right)\left(L(\theta_t) - L(0)\right).$$

Applying this inequality recursively completes the proof.

4 Finite-Sample Analysis

When the sample-based averaged log-likelihood in Eq. (2) is maximized via the EM algorithm, the parameter updates can be expressed explicitly by replacing the expectation $\mathbb{E}$ in Eq. (5) with the empirical average over the sample:

$$\hat{\theta}_{t+1} = M_n(\hat{\theta}_t),$$

$$\text{where} \quad M_n(\theta) := \frac{1}{n}\sum_{i=1}^{n}\sum_{j=1}^{k} w_j(Z_i;\theta)(R^{j-1})^\top Z_i. \tag{8}$$

The following perturbation bound (Sect. C) relates the sample-based EM operator to its population-level counterpart:

$$\Pr\left[\sup_{\|\theta\|\leq r} \|M_n(\theta) - M(\theta)\| \leq cr\sqrt{\frac{d + \log(1/\delta)}{n}}\right] \geq 1 - \delta, \tag{9}$$

for any radius $r > 0$, threshold $\delta \in (0, 1)$, and sufficiently large n.

Due to the strict contractivity of the population EM operator in a neighborhood of $\theta^* = 0$ (Lemma 4 in Sect. 5) and the perturbation bound above, we can establish that the sequence of EM iterates $\hat{\theta}_t$ satisfies, with probability at least $1 - \delta$,

$$\|\hat{\theta}_T\| \lesssim \|\theta_0\|\sqrt{\frac{\log(1/\delta)}{n}}, \tag{10}$$

for $T \gtrsim \log\left(\frac{n}{\log(1/\delta)}\right)$, provided that θ_0 lies within the contraction neighborhood (see the proof of Theorem 2 in [3]).

With this, we are ready to establish our key result on convergence in KL distance for the finite-sample case.

Proof (Proof of Theorem 2). By the convexity of L in a neighborhood of $\theta^* = 0$ (Lemma 5 in Sect. 5), we have

$$L(\hat{\theta}_t) - L(0) \leq \nabla L(\hat{\theta}_t)^\top \hat{\theta}_t. \tag{11}$$

From Eq. (6), it follows that

$$\nabla L(\hat{\theta}_t)^\top \hat{\theta}_t = \|\hat{\theta}_t\|^2 - [M(\hat{\theta}_t)]^\top \hat{\theta}_t \lesssim \|\hat{\theta}_t\|^2, \tag{12}$$

where we used the contraction property of M near $\theta = 0$ (Corollary 1 in Sect. 5). The theorem follows directly from Eqs. (10), (11), and (12).

5 Proof of the Local PL Inequality

In this section, we prove the local Polyak–Lojasiewicz (PL) inequality for the negative log-likelihood $L(\theta)$ of our overspecified Gaussian mixture model. By analyzing the Jacobian of the population EM operator $M(\theta)$ at $\theta^* = 0$, we show that $M(\theta)$ is locally contractive, which implies that the Hessian of $L(\theta)$ is uniformly positive definite near $\theta^* = 0$.

The subsequent lemmas establish these properties and lead directly to the local PL inequality, ensuring the exponential convergence of the EM algorithm in terms of the KL divergence.

Lemma 2. *Let $M(\theta)$ be the EM operator defined by Eq. (5). Then the Jacobian of $M(\theta)$ at $\theta^* = 0$ is given by $\frac{\partial M}{\partial \theta}(0) = I - \left(\sum_{j=1}^{k} \pi_j R^{j-1}\right) \left(\sum_{j=1}^{k} \pi_j R^{j-1}\right)^\top$.*

Proof. Let $S(\theta, Z) = \sum_{\ell=1}^{k} \pi_\ell \exp\left((R^{\ell-1}\theta)^\top Z\right)$. Then

$$w_j(Z;\theta) = \frac{\pi_j \exp\left((R^{j-1}\theta)^\top Z\right)}{S(\theta, Z)}.$$

At $\theta^* = 0$, each exponential term is $\exp(0) = 1$, so $S(0, Z) = \sum_{\ell=1}^{k} \pi_\ell = 1$, $w_j(Z; 0) = \pi_j$. Since

$$\nabla_\theta \left((R^{j-1}\theta)^\top Z\right) = (R^{j-1})^\top Z,$$

$$\nabla_\theta S(\theta, Z) = \sum_{\ell=1}^{k} \pi_\ell \exp\left((R^{\ell-1}\theta)^\top Z\right) \left[(R^{\ell-1})^\top Z\right],$$

using the quotient rule for $\nabla_\theta w_j(Z; \theta)$, and then evaluating it at $\theta^* = 0$, we get

$$\nabla_\theta w_j(Z;\theta)\big|_{\theta^*=0} = \pi_j \left[(R^{j-1})^\top Z - \sum_{\ell=1}^{k} \pi_\ell (R^{\ell-1})^\top Z\right].$$

Define $g(\theta, Z) = \sum_{j=1}^{k} w_j(Z; \theta) (R^{j-1})^\top Z$. Then

$$\frac{\partial g}{\partial \theta}(\theta, Z) = \sum_{j=1}^{k} (R^{j-1})^\top Z \left[\nabla_\theta w_j(Z;\theta)\right]^\top.$$

At $\theta^* = 0$,

$$\frac{\partial g}{\partial \theta}(\theta, Z)\big|_{\theta^*=0} = \sum_{j=1}^{k} \pi_j (R^{j-1})^\top Z \left[(R^{j-1})^\top Z - \sum_{\ell=1}^{k} \pi_\ell (R^{\ell-1})^\top Z\right]^\top.$$

Then the sought Jacobian of $M(\theta)$ at $\theta^* = 0$ is

$$\frac{\partial M}{\partial \theta}(0) = \mathbb{E}_Z \left[\nabla_\theta g(0, Z)\right].$$

Since $Z \sim \mathcal{N}_d(0, I)$, we have $\mathbb{E}[ZZ^\top] = I$. Each R^{j-1} is orthogonal, hence

$$\mathbb{E}\left[(R^{j-1})^\top Z Z^\top R^{j-1}\right] = (R^{j-1})^\top I R^{j-1} = I.$$

Collecting terms, the result is

$$\frac{\partial M}{\partial \theta}(0) = I - \left(\sum_{j=1}^k \pi_j R^{j-1}\right)\left(\sum_{j=1}^k \pi_j R^{j-1}\right)^\top,$$

which completes the proof.

Lemma 3. *Let $R \in \mathbb{R}^{d \times d}$ be a (real) matrix whose eigenvalues lie among the k-th roots of unity (except 1), i.e., $\mathrm{spec}(R) \subseteq \{e^{i\frac{2\pi\ell}{k}} : \ell = 1, 2, \ldots, k-1\}$. Let $\pi_1, \ldots, \pi_k > 0$ be positive real numbers whose discrete Fourier transform $\widehat{\pi}(\ell) = \sum_{j=0}^{k-1} \pi_{j+1} e^{i\frac{2\pi\ell}{k}j}$, $\ell = 0, 1, \ldots, k-1$, has no zero entries (i.e. $\widehat{\pi}(\ell) \neq 0$ for all ℓ). Define the matrix $A := \sum_{j=1}^k \pi_j R^{j-1}$. Then A is invertible.*

Proof. Since all eigenvalues of R lie among the k-th roots of unity (except 1), we can work over $\mathbb{C}$ and bring R into a Jordan (or block-diagonal) form. Concretely, there exists an invertible matrix $V \in \mathbb{C}^{d \times d}$ such that $R = V \Lambda V^{-1}$, where Λ is block-diagonal and each block corresponds to an eigenvalue of the form $e^{i\frac{2\pi\ell}{k}}$ (with $1 \leq \ell \leq k-1$). In particular, $R^{j-1} = V \Lambda^{j-1} V^{-1}$ for all $j = 1, \ldots, k$. Thus we can rewrite A as

$$A = \sum_{j=1}^k \pi_j R^{j-1} = \sum_{j=1}^k \pi_j (V \Lambda^{j-1} V^{-1}) = V\left(\sum_{j=1}^k \pi_j \Lambda^{j-1}\right) V^{-1}.$$

Since V is invertible, A is invertible if and only if $\sum_{j=1}^k \pi_j \Lambda^{j-1}$ is invertible.

Now, Λ is block-diagonal with Jordan blocks corresponding to eigenvalues $\lambda \in \{e^{i\frac{2\pi\ell}{k}} : \ell = 1, \ldots, k-1\}$. Consider a single eigenvalue λ. The diagonal entry of the diagonal block of $\sum_{j=1}^k \pi_j \Lambda^{j-1}$ is $\sum_{j=1}^k \pi_j \lambda^{j-1} = \sum_{j=0}^{k-1} \pi_{j+1} \lambda^j$. Since $\lambda^j = e^{i\frac{2\pi\ell}{k}j}$ for some $\ell \in \{1, \ldots, k-1\}$, this sum is precisely the discrete Fourier transform of $(\pi_1, \ldots, \pi_k)$: $\sum_{j=0}^{k-1} \pi_{j+1} e^{i\frac{2\pi\ell}{k}j} = \widehat{\pi}(\ell)$. By hypothesis, $\widehat{\pi}(\ell) \neq 0$ for all $\ell = 0, \ldots, k-1$, hence each diagonal entry is nonzero. Therefore, every diagonal block of $\sum_{j=1}^k \pi_j \Lambda^{j-1}$ is invertible, so the entire block-diagonal matrix is invertible.

Lemma 4. *Under the conditions of Lemmas 2 and 3, the matrix $I - \frac{\partial M}{\partial \theta}(0)$ is positive definite.*

Proof. From Lemma 2, the Jacobian of the EM operator at $\theta^* = 0$ is given by $\frac{\partial M}{\partial \theta}(0) = I - AA^\top$, where $A = \sum_{j=1}^k \pi_j R^{j-1}$. Rearranging this equation, we obtain $I - \frac{\partial M}{\partial \theta}(0) = AA^\top$. By Lemma 3, the matrix A is invertible. Since $AA^\top$ is the product of A and $A^\top$, it follows that $AA^\top$ is symmetric and positive definite. To see this, note that for any nonzero vector $x \in \mathbb{R}^d$, $x^\top AA^\top x = (A^\top x)^\top (A^\top x) = \|A^\top x\|^2 > 0$, since A is invertible and thus $A^\top x \neq 0$ for $x \neq 0$. Therefore, the matrix $I - \frac{\partial M}{\partial \theta}(0) = AA^\top$ is positive definite.

Corollary 1. *All eigenvalues of $\frac{\partial M}{\partial \theta}(0)$ lie strictly below 1, which in turn implies that M is a contraction near $\theta^* = 0$.*

Lemma 5. *Let $\mathcal{L}(\theta)$ be the population log-likelihood function defined by Eq. (4). Suppose $\pi_1, \ldots, \pi_k > 0$ are positive real numbers whose discrete Fourier transform has no zero entries. Then there exists $\delta > 0$ such that L is strongly convex in $\{\theta : \|\theta\| \leq \delta\}$:*

Proof. Since $\nabla L(\theta) = \theta - M(\theta)$, its Hessian is given by $\nabla^2 L(\theta) = I - \frac{\partial M}{\partial \theta}(\theta)$. By Lemma 4, $S := I - \frac{\partial M}{\partial \theta}(0)$ is positive definite. Let $\lambda_{\min} = \lambda_{\min}(S) > 0$ be the smallest eigenvalue of S.

Next, by continuity of $\frac{\partial M}{\partial \theta}(\theta)$ at $\theta = 0$, for any $\varepsilon > 0$ there exists a $\delta > 0$ such that

$$\|\theta\| < \delta \implies \left\|\frac{\partial M}{\partial \theta}(\theta) - \frac{\partial M}{\partial \theta}(0)\right\|_{\text{op}} < \varepsilon,$$

where $\|\cdot\|_{\text{op}}$ denotes the operator norm.

Choose $\varepsilon = \frac{1}{2}\lambda_{\min}$. Then for $\|\theta\| < \delta$, $\left\|\frac{\partial M}{\partial \theta}(\theta) - \frac{\partial M}{\partial \theta}(0)\right\|_{\text{op}} < \frac{1}{2}\lambda_{\min}$. Thus, for any vector $v \in \mathbb{R}^d$ with $\|v\| = 1$,

$$v^\top \left(I - \frac{\partial M}{\partial \theta}(\theta)\right)v = v^\top \left(I - \frac{\partial M}{\partial \theta}(0)\right)v - v^\top \left(\frac{\partial M}{\partial \theta}(\theta) - \frac{\partial M}{\partial \theta}(0)\right)v$$

$$\geq v^\top \left(I - \frac{\partial M}{\partial \theta}(0)\right)v - \left\|\frac{\partial M}{\partial \theta}(\theta) - \frac{\partial M}{\partial \theta}(0)\right\|_{\text{op}}$$

$$\geq \lambda_{\min} - \frac{1}{2}\lambda_{\min} = \frac{1}{2}\lambda_{\min}.$$

Therefore, $I - \frac{\partial M}{\partial \theta}(\theta) \succeq \frac{1}{2}\lambda_{\min} I$ for all $\|\theta\| < \delta$. Since $\nabla^2 L(\theta) = I - \frac{\partial M}{\partial \theta}(\theta)$, we deduce $\nabla^2 L(\theta) \succeq \frac{1}{2}\lambda_{\min} I$ whenever $\|\theta\| < \delta$. Hence $L(\theta)$ is $\left(\frac{1}{2}\lambda_{\min}\right)$-strongly convex in the ball $\{\theta : \|\theta\| < \delta\}$.

Proof (Proof of Lemma 1). By Lemma 5, L is $\frac{\lambda_{\min}}{2}$-strongly convex in a neighborhood of $\theta^* = 0$, i.e. there exists $\delta > 0$ such that for $\theta, \theta' \in \{\theta : \|\theta\| \leq \delta\}$

$$L(\theta') \geq L(\theta) + \nabla L(\theta)^T(\theta' - \theta) + \frac{\lambda_{\min}}{4}\|\theta' - \theta\|^2.$$

Minimizing both sides with respect to θ', we get

$$L(0) \geq L(\theta) - \frac{1}{\lambda_{\min}}\|\nabla L(\theta)\|^2.$$

Re-arranging the terms we have the PL inequality.

Acknowledgments. This research has been funded by the Science Committee of the Ministry of Science and Higher Education of the Republic of Kazakhstan (Grant No. AP27510283). Artur Pak's work was supported by Nazarbayev University under Faculty-development competitive research grants program for 2023–2025 Grant #20122022FD4131, PI R. Takhanov. Zhenisbek Assylbekov's work was supported by Purdue University Fort Wayne under Summer Research Grant Program 2024, and he would like to thank Igor Melnykov and Francesco Sica for useful discussions.

Disclosure of Interests. The authors have no competing interests to declare that are relevant to the content of this article.

A Proof of Proposition 1

Proof. See the full version [2].

B Population EM Properties

B.1 Population EM Updates

We begin by providing additional details on the EM algorithm. It is convenient to represent the mixture distribution Eq. (1) using a latent categorical random variable K, which identifies the mixture components. Given the mixture weights $(\pi_1, \ldots, \pi_k)$, we assume that
$$\Pr[K = j] = \pi_j.$$
The conditional distribution of X given $K = j$ is then defined as
$$(X \mid K = j) \sim \mathcal{N}_d(R^{j-1}\theta, I), \quad \text{for } j \in [k].$$
This specifies the joint distribution of the tuple (X, K), ensuring that the marginal distribution of X corresponds to the Gaussian mixture $\mathcal{G}(\theta)$ in Eq. (1). The Population EM algorithm maximizes the expected log-likelihood Eq. (4) through the following iterative steps:

- *E-step:* Given the current estimate θ_t, compute the soft assignment of any $x \in \mathbb{R}^d$ to component $K = j$, i.e., evaluate the posterior probability:
$$w_j(x; \theta_t) = \frac{\pi_j \cdot \phi(x - R^{j-1}\theta_t)}{\sum_{\ell=1}^{k} \pi_\ell \cdot \phi(x - R^{\ell-1}\theta_t)}, \tag{13}$$
and use it to compute the Q-function:
$$Q(\theta, \theta_t) := \mathbb{E}_{Z \sim \mathcal{N}(0,I)} \left[\sum_{j=1}^{k} w_j(Z; \theta_t) \log\left(\pi_j \cdot \phi(Z - R^{j-1}\theta)\right) \right].$$

- *M-step:* Update the parameter by solving the following optimization problem:
$$\theta_{t+1} \in \arg\max_\theta Q(\theta, \theta_t). \tag{14}$$

Lemma 6. *Let the population EM algorithm maximize the expected log-likelihood Eq. (4). Then, the parameter updates follow the recursion $\theta_{t+1} = M(\theta_t)$, where*
$$M(\theta) := \mathbb{E}_{Z \sim \mathcal{N}(0,I)} \left[\frac{\sum_{j=1}^{k} \pi_j \cdot \exp\left((R^{j-1}\theta)^\top Z\right)(R^{j-1})^\top Z}{\sum_{\ell=1}^{k} \pi_\ell \cdot \exp\left((R^{\ell-1}\theta)^\top Z\right)} \right].$$

Proof. See the full version [2].

B.2 Population EM Operator and Log-Likelihood

Lemma 7. *The population log-likelihood $\mathcal{L}(\theta)$ defined in Eq. (4) and the population EM operator $M(\theta)$ are related by the equation:*

$$\nabla_\theta[-\mathcal{L}(\theta)] = \theta - M(\theta).$$

Proof. See the full version [2].

C Perturbation Bound

Lemma 8. *There exist universal constants $c, c' > 0$ such that for any radius $r > 0$, confidence level $\delta \in (0, 1)$, and sample size $n \geq c' \left(d + \log(1/\delta)\right)$, the following holds with probability at least $1 - \delta$:*

$$\sup_{\|\theta\| \leq r} \| M_n(\theta) - M(\theta) \| \leq cr \sqrt{\frac{d + \log(1/\delta)}{n}}.$$

Proof. See the full version [2].

References

1. Polyak, B.T.: Gradient methods for the minimisation of functionals. USSR Comput. Math. Math. Phys. **3**(4), 864–878 (1963)
2. Assylbekov, Z., Legg, A., Pak, A.: Learning overspecified Gaussian mixtures exponentially fast with the EM algorithm. arXiv preprint arXiv:2506.11850 (2025)
3. Balakrishnan, S., Wainwright, M.J., Yu, B.: Statistical guarantees for the EM algorithm: from population to sample-based analysis. Ann. Stat. **45**(1), 77–120 (2017)
4. Chen, Y., Song, D., Xi, X., Zhang, Y.: Local minima structures in Gaussian mixture models. IEEE Trans. Info. Theory **70**(6), 4218–4257 (2024)
5. Dasgupta, S., Schulman, L.J.: A two-round variant of EM for Gaussian mixtures. In: Proceedings of the Sixteenth Conference on Uncertainty in Artificial Intelligence, pp. 152–159 (2000)
6. Daskalakis, C., Tzamos, C., Zampetakis, M.: Ten steps of EM suffice for mixtures of two Gaussians. In: Conference on Learning Theory, pp. 704–710. PMLR (2017)
7. Dempster, A.P., Laird, N.M., Rubin, D.B.: Maximum likelihood from incomplete data via the EM algorithm. J. Roy. Stat. Soc. Ser. B Methodol. **39**(1), 1–22 (1977)
8. Dwivedi, R., Ho, N., Khamaru, K., Wainwright, M., Jordan, M., Yu, B.: Sharp analysis of expectation-maximization for weakly identifiable models. In: International Conference on Artificial Intelligence and Statistics, pp. 1866–1876. PMLR (2020)
9. Dwivedi, R., Ho, N., Khamaru, K., Wainwright, M.J., Jordan, M.I., Yu, B.: Singularity, misspecification and the convergence rate of EM. Ann. Stat. **48**(6), 3161–3182 (2020)
10. Dwivedi, R., Khamaru, K., Wainwright, M.J., Jordan, M.I., et al.: Theoretical guarantees for EM under misspecified Gaussian mixture models. Adv. Neural Info. Process. Syst. **31** (2018)
11. Ghosal, S., Vaart, A.W.: Entropies and rates of convergence for maximum likelihood and bayes estimation for mixtures of normal densities. Ann. Stat. **29**(5), 1233–1263 (2001)

12. Klusowski, J.M., Brinda, W.: Statistical guarantees for estimating the centers of a two-component gaussian mixture by EM. arXiv preprint arXiv:1608.02280 (2016)
13. Lloyd, S.P.: Least squares quantization in PCM. IEEE Trans. Inf. Theory **28**(2), 129–136 (1982)
14. Lojasiewicz, S.: A topological property of real analytic subsets. Coll. du CNRS, Les équations aux dérivées partielles **117**(87–89), 2 (1963)
15. Rousseau, J., Mengersen, K.: Asymptotic behaviour of the posterior distribution in overfitted mixture models. J. Roy. Stat. Soc. Ser. B Stat. Meth. **73**(5), 689–710 (2011)
16. Segol, N., Nadler, B.: Improved convergence guarantees for learning Gaussian mixture models by EM and gradient EM. Electron. J. Stat. **15**(2), 4510–4544 (2021)
17. Xu, W., Fazel, M., Du, S.S.: Toward global convergence of gradient EM for overparamterized Gaussian mixture models. In: The Thirty-Eighth Annual Conference on Neural Information Processing Systems (2024)
18. Yan, B., Yin, M., Sarkar, P.: Convergence of gradient EM on multi-component mixture of Gaussians. Adv. Neural Info. Process. Syst. **30** (2017)
19. Zhao, R., Li, Y., Sun, Y.: Statistical convergence of the EM algorithm on gaussian mixture models. Elect. J. Stat. **14**, 632–660 (2020)

Missing but Not Missed: On Learnability Under Imputation

Andrea Campagner[✉]

IRCCS Ospedale Galeazzi Sant'Ambrogio, Milan, Italy
andrea.campagner@unimib.it

Abstract. Missing data represents one of the most ubiquitous data quality issues, and also one of the most impactful on machine learning (ML) pipelines. Indeed, not only most commonly applied ML methods cannot directly employ incomplete data, but also the techniques employed to manage this issue can impact on the performance and evaluation of ML models. Among such techniques to manage missing data, *imputation*, that is filling in the missing values using information from the observed data, remains among the most popular and effective in practice. Yet, from a theoretical point of view, it is still not clear under which conditions it is possible to learn effectively after imputation. In this article we address this gap by studying learnability under imputation in the framework of statistical learning theory. After giving a general definition of learnability under imputation, we show three main contributions: 1) we introduce a novel stability condition, called *noise risk stability*, which we prove to be both sufficient and, under weak assumptions, necessary for learnability under imputation; 2) we show that a large class of ML models (including linear and kernel methods) satisfies noise risk stability; 3) we characterize the learning-theoretic properties of two common imputation methods (constant and regression imputation). Our results set the stage for a rigorous study of imputation and missing data management in the framework of statistical learning theory, by also describing relevant open questions.

Keywords: Imputation · Missing Data · Learnability · Statistical Learning Theory

1 Introduction

Missing data is one of the most commonly occurring data quality issues in real-world datasets. In fact, in many practical settings, facing missing data is the norm more than the exception, and failure to account for this issue can have profound consequences on the development and evaluation of machine learning (ML) models [1,34], especially since most commonly used ML algorithms do not have a way to directly use missing data in the training process.

Consequently, a variety of approaches have been developed to manage missing data and enable the development of downstream ML tasks [21]. Among them, imputation (i.e., filling in the missing data with some replacement values) is one of the most popular approaches, with a variety of techniques ranging from constant imputation (encompassing commonly used approaches such as mean imputation) to regression imputation [43,44], to multiple imputation [7,38].

Nonetheless, the conditions under which missing data imputation is expected to work—i.e., it does not negatively impact the learnability of downstream ML tasks—are yet unclear. As such, the exploration of imputation methods is still mostly guided by empirical experimentation and ad-hoc strategies. Indeed, despite extensive empirical validation and comparisons [18,24,29,35], often providing conflicting results, there is no consensus on when and how imputation should be applied [31], and when learning is still possible despite the potential noise introduced by imputation [27]. Most relevantly, from a theoretical point of view, there is still a lack of research studying the impact of missing data imputation on learnability in the statistical learning theory framework, especially in regard to the development of practical finite-sample guarantees that ensure the feasibility of learning after imputation.

Research on the interaction between missing data, imputation, and learnability has been carried out mainly within the algorithmic learning theoretic framework of *learning under partial observability* [13,14,22,33,39]. While these approaches can provide finite-sample guarantees, most work in the area has focused on model classes (e.g., propositional formulas) and settings (e.g., concept learning) which, while interesting from the point of view of exploring the computational limits to learnability with missing data, are rather distant from the current practice of ML. In contrast, research in the statistical learning framework has been primarily concerned with asymptotic consistency or optimality guarantees [8,25,27,28,40], especially so for specific classes of ML models such as linear predictors, which despite being closer to the methodology most commonly adopted in modern ML do not provide finite-sample guarantees. More recently, Ayme et al. [4–6,37] have investigated finite-sample (as well as optimality) guarantees for learning after imputation: however, this line of research has focused only on linear models under specific imputation strategies (constant and pattern-by-pattern imputation), and does not provide general conditions for learnability in this setting that can be applied for general learning models.

In this paper, we start to address this gap by studying conditions under which learning under imputation is feasible. In particular, we provide three main contributions. First, we introduce a condition for learnability under imputation, called *noise stability*, which we show to be sufficient and, under weak assumptions, also necessary. Intuitively, this condition guarantees that a learning algorithm is stable under noisy variations of the real data introduced by an imputation mechanism. Second, we study two common imputation strategies (namely, constant and regression imputation), providing bounds on the noise they may introduce in learning problems. Finally, we show that a large class of ML models are noise stable, and provide finite-sample guarantees for learnability with missing data using these model classes.

2 Background and Mathematical Notation

Let X be the instance space: we assume that X is a (subset of a) d-dimensional real vector space. Given any vector $x \in X$, $x^{(i)}$ denotes the i-th dimension of x. Let Y be the target space. Y can be either discrete (finite or countable), in which case we consider a classification task, or also continuous (that is, uncountable), in which case we consider a regression task. Let $\mathcal{D}$ be a probability measure over $X \times Y$, called *data-generating process*. $\mathcal{D}$ represents the process that generates the complete, possibly unobserved, data samples. We also assume the existence of d probability measures $\mathcal{M}_1, \ldots, \mathcal{M}_d$, where, for each i, $\mathcal{M}_i$ is a probability measure over $X \times Y \times \tilde{X}^{(i)}$, where $\tilde{X}^{(i)} = X^{(i)} \cup \{\bot\}$. In particular, the symbol $\bot$ denotes a missing value. Let $\mathcal{M} = \Pi_i \mathcal{M}_i$ and $\tilde{X} = \Pi_i \tilde{X}^{(i)}$. We will assume that data is generated according to the following process: first, a sample (x, y) is drawn from $\mathcal{D}$; subsequently, an *incomplete* sample $(x', y) \in \tilde{X} \times Y$ is drawn from the conditional $\mathcal{M}(\cdot|(x,y))$. The conditional distributions $\mathcal{M}_i(\bot|x^{(1)}, \ldots, x^{(i)}, \ldots, x^{(d)})$ are of particular interest since, based on the dependency structure of the conditionals, one can distinguish different types of missingness mechanisms: as we will not discuss further this categorization, we refer the interested reader to [30].

We will represent the action of imputation methods by the abstract definition of an *imputation mechanism*. A imputation mechanism is a randomized algorithm Impute : $(\tilde{X} \times Y)^m \times (\tilde{X} \times Y) \to X$ that takes as input a training set S, a (partially observed) instance (x, y) and gives as output an imputed, possibly corrupted, instance x'. Given a missing data mechanism $\mathcal{M}$ and an imputation mechanism Impute, we define a randomized algorithm Corrupt : $(X \times Y)^m \times (X \times Y) \to X$: Corrupt takes as input a dataset S, an instance (x, y), applies the missingness mechanism $\mathcal{M}$ to both S and (x, y), and then returns the result of Impute$(S, (x, y))$. We will use the notation Corrupt$_S(x, y)$ to denote the action of Corrupt on an instance (x, y) for a given dataset S. We call the probability measure defined by Corrupt a *corruption mechanism*. We say that Corrupt satisfies the *small noise condition*, with noise function $\epsilon_{\text{Corrupt}} : \mathbb{N} \times \mathbb{R} \to \mathbb{R}$, if, for each $m > 0, \delta > 0$, with probability larger than $1 - \delta$ over the sampling of a dataset $S \sim \mathcal{D}^m$ and $T = \{Corrupt_S(x, y)|(x, y) \in A\}$, it holds that:

$$\mathbb{E}[\|Corrupt_S(x, y) - x\|_X] \leq \epsilon_{\text{Corrupt}}(m, \delta), \quad (1)$$

where $\epsilon_{\text{Corrupt}}$ is non-increasing in its arguments and $\|\cdot\|_X$ is a norm on X.

Let $\mathcal{H}$ be a set of models, that are, functions $h : X \to Z$, where Z is a set[1]. A *learning algorithm* is a function $A : \bigcup_{m \in \mathbb{N}^+}(X \times Y)^m \to \mathcal{H}$. A loss function is a map $l : X \times Y \times \mathcal{H} \to \mathbb{R}$. A loss function l is L-Lipschitz if $\mathcal{H}$ has a norm $\|\cdot\|_{\mathcal{H}}$ and $\forall x \in X, y \in Y, h_1, h_2 \in \mathcal{H}, |l(x, y, h_1) - l(x, y, h_2)| \leq L\|h_1 - h_2\|$. l is μ-strongly convex if $\forall h_1, h_2 \in \mathcal{H}, \alpha \in [0, 1], \alpha h_1 + (1 - \alpha)h_2$ exists and is in $\mathcal{H}$ and it holds that $l(x, y, \alpha h_1 + (1-\alpha)h_2) \leq \alpha l(x, y, h_1) + (1-\alpha)l(x, y, h_2) - \frac{\mu}{2}\alpha(1-\alpha)\|h_1 - h_2\|^2$. l is convex if the previous requirement holds only for $\mu = 0$. If l is differentiable,

---

[1] In general, Z can be different from Y: for example, in the case of binary classification (where $Y = \{-1, 1\}$), Z is often set equal to $\mathbb{R}$.

then l is M-smooth if $\forall x \in X, y \in Y, h_1, h_2 \in \mathcal{H}, \|\nabla l(x,y,h_1) - \nabla l(x,y,h_2)\|_* \leq M\|h_1 - h_2\|$, where $\|\cdot\|_*$ is the dual norm.

Given a data-generating distribution $\mathcal{D}$ and a model $h \in \mathcal{H}$, we define the *true risk* of h as $R(h) = \mathbb{E}_{(x,y)\sim\mathcal{D}}[l(x,y,h)]$. Given a finite sample $S = \{(x_1, y_1), \ldots, (x_m, y_m)\} \in (X \times Y)^m$, we define the *empirical risk* of h as $\hat{R}_S(h) = \frac{1}{m}\sum_{i=1}^m l(x_i, y_i, h)$. We define empirical risk minimization (ERM) to be any learning algorithm A s.t. $A(S) \in \inf_{h\in\mathcal{H}} \hat{R}_S(h)$. We say that a model class $\mathcal{H}$ is *(agnostic) learnable*[2] if there exists a learning algorithm $A : \bigcup_{m\in\mathbb{N}^*}(X \times Y)^m \to \mathcal{H}$ and a function $\epsilon_L^{\mathcal{H},A} : \mathbb{N} \times \mathbb{R} \to \mathbb{R}$ s.t., for each data-generating mechanism $\mathcal{D}$, $\delta > 0$ and sample size m, with probability larger than $1 - \delta$ over the sampling of $S \sim \mathcal{D}^m$ it holds that:

$$|R(A(S)) - \hat{R}_S(A(S))| \leq \epsilon_L^{\mathcal{H},A}(m,\delta), \tag{2}$$

with $\lim_{m\to\infty} \epsilon_L^{\mathcal{H},A}(m,\delta) = 0$. We say that $\mathcal{D}$ is *realizable* (w.r.t. $\mathcal{H}$) if $\exists h \in \mathcal{H}$ s.t. $R(h) = 0$. Finally, $\mathcal{H}$ satisfies *uniform convergence* if there exists a function $\epsilon_{UC}^{\mathcal{H}} : \mathbb{N} \times \mathbb{R} \to \mathbb{R}$ s.t., for all data-generating mechanisms $\mathcal{D}$, $\delta > 0$ and sample sizes $m > 0$, with probability larger than $1 - \delta$ over the sampling of $S \sim \mathcal{D}^m$, it holds that $\sup_{h\in\mathcal{H}} |R(h) - \hat{R}_S(h)| \leq \epsilon_{UC}^{\mathcal{H}}(m,\delta)$, with $\lim_{m\to\infty} \epsilon_{UC}^{\mathcal{H}}(m,\delta) = 0$.

3 Learnability with Missing Data

As a first step, we extend the definition of learnability to the case of learning with missing data using imputation.

Definition 1. *Let $\mathcal{H}$ be a class of models. Then, $\mathcal{H}$ is* learnable under imputation *if there exists a learning algorithm $A : \bigcup_{m\in\mathbb{N}}(X \times Y)^m \to \mathcal{H}$ and two functions $\epsilon_1^{\mathcal{H},A} : \mathbb{N} \times \mathbb{R} \to \mathbb{R}$ and $\epsilon_2^{\mathcal{H},A} : \mathbb{N} \times \mathbb{R}^2 \to \mathbb{R}$ s.t. for any $\delta, \epsilon > 0$, $m \in \mathbb{N}^+$, data-generating mechanism $\mathcal{D}$, corruption mechanism Corrupt with $\epsilon_{Corrupt}(m,\delta) \leq \epsilon$, it holds with probability larger than $1 - \delta$ (over the sampling of $S \sim \mathcal{D}^m$ and $T = \{\text{Corrupt}_S(x,y)|(x,y) \in S\}$) that:*

$$R(A(T)) \leq \hat{R}_T(A(T)) + \epsilon_1^{\mathcal{H},A}(m,\delta) + \epsilon_2^{\mathcal{H},A}(m,\epsilon,\delta), \tag{3}$$

with $\epsilon_1^{\mathcal{H},A}, \epsilon_2^{\mathcal{H},A}$ decreasing in all of their arguments, and $\lim_{m\to\infty} \epsilon_1^{\mathcal{H},A}(m,\delta) = 0$ and $\lim_{m\to\infty, \epsilon\to 0} \epsilon_2^{\mathcal{H},A}(m,\epsilon,\delta) = 0$.

Definition 1 is a natural generalization of the notion of *agnostic learnability* in the classical PAC learning framework. Indeed, for a model class to be learnable under imputation means that the generalization gap can be bounded as

---

[2] The definition of agnostic learnability we provide is sometimes called *generalizability* in the literature, whereas (strict) learnability (also called, universal consistency) is defined by replacing Eq. (2) with $|R(h^*) - R(h(S))| \leq \epsilon_L^{\mathcal{H},A}(m,\delta)$, with $h^* \in \arg\inf_{h\in\mathcal{H}} R(h)$. Since, under weak assumptions (in particular, under uniform convergence), generalizability is both necessary and sufficient for strict learnability, in this paper we focus on the former notion, and term it learnability.

a quantity that vanishes with the noise introduced by the considered imputation mechanism (and increasing data). Thus, if the imputation is approximately faithful to the real, unobserved data, the empirical risk on the imputed data should be (with high probability) close to the true risk. Specifically, note that Definition 1 requires that if we are able to make the noise due to imputation ϵ arbitrarily small, we recover exactly the definition of agnostic learnability. In contrast, when the noise due to imputation is too large, we cannot expect a model to work as well, as the data used for training will essentially be out-of-distribution compared to the data-generating mechanism $\mathcal{D}$ w.r.t. which the true risk is computed: nonetheless, the penalty in performance can be upper bounded by a quantity that only depends on the noise itself.

As an additional comment, we note that Definition 1 also implies that a good learning algorithm could be obtained by minimizing the right side of Eq. (3). While in standard supervised learning such an algorithm exists (e.g., in both binary classification and regression, ERM), it is not similarly easy to identify such an optimal algorithm in the setting of learning under imputation, as the learning algorithm A affects not only the empirical risk $\hat{R}_T$ but also the term $\epsilon_2^{\mathcal{H},A}$: as a consequence, it is not clear whether ERM minimizes the bound in Eq. 3, even under uniform convergence (in which case, the term $\epsilon_2^{\mathcal{H}}$ is independent of A). This situation is not unexpected, as also in the setting of general learning there exist natural learning tasks for which ERM is not always an optimal strategy [41]. For this reason, in the following, we allow arbitrary learning algorithms A.

We now introduce the central definition in our mathematical development, which we will use to provide a characterization of learnability under imputation.

Definition 2. *Let $\mathcal{H}$ be a set of models, l a loss function and A a learning algorithm for $\mathcal{H}$. We say that A is* noise risk stable *(NRS) if there exists a function $\epsilon_{NRS}^A : \mathbb{N} \times \mathbb{R}^2 \to \mathbb{R}$ s.t., for every $\delta, \epsilon > 0, m > 0$ and corruption mechanism Corrupt with $\epsilon_{Corrupt}(m, \delta) \leq \epsilon$, with probability larger than $1 - \delta$ over the sampling of $S \in (X \times Y)^m$ and $T = \{Corrupt_S(x,y) : (x,y) \in S\}$, it holds that:*

$$\hat{R}_S(h) - \hat{R}_T(h) \leq \epsilon_{NRS}^A(m, \epsilon, \delta) \tag{4}$$

where $h = A(T)$, and $\limsup_{m \to \infty, \epsilon \to 0} \epsilon_{NRS}^A(m, \epsilon, \delta) \leq 0$.

Intuitively, a learning algorithm is NRS if the losses of the models trained on the complete (unobserved) data and the data corrupted by the imputation mechanism are close. Thus, when the imputation does not introduce an excessive amount of noise, a NRS algorithm will not amplify this noise by more than a negligible quantity (that goes to 0 as the noise itself goes to 0). Then, we prove our main result: model classes for which there exists a NRS algorithm are learnable even under corruptions introduced by imputation.

Theorem 1. *Let $\mathcal{H}$ be a model class and l be a loss function bounded in $[0, b]$. Assume that $\mathcal{H}$ is learnable, and define $\mathcal{A}_{\mathcal{H}} = \{A : \bigcup_{m \in \mathbb{N}^+}(X \times Y)^m \to \mathcal{H} | \mathcal{H}$ is learnable using $A\}$. For each $A \in \mathcal{A}_{\mathcal{H}}$, let $\epsilon_L^{\mathcal{H},A}$ be the generalization gap* as defined in Eq. (3). Then, a sufficient condition for learnability under imputation is that there exists $A \in \mathcal{A}_\mathcal{H}$ that is NRS. Furthermore, when such an A exists, then, with probability larger than $1 - \delta$ over the sampling of $S \sim \mathcal{D}^m$ and $T = \{Corrupt_S(x,y)|(x,y) \in S\}$, it holds that $R(A(T))$ can be upper bounded by $\hat{R}_T(A(T)) + \epsilon_L^{\mathcal{H},A}(m, \frac{\delta}{3}) + \epsilon_{NRS}^{\mathcal{H},A}(m, \epsilon_{Corrupt}(m, \frac{\delta}{3}), \frac{\delta}{3})$.

Under the assumption that $\mathcal{H}$ satisfies uniform convergence, the existence of a NRS $A \in \mathcal{A}_\mathcal{H}$ is also necessary for learnability under imputation.

Theorem 1 provides a tight characterization of the notion of learnability under imputation, as it shows that, under weak assumptions, it is equivalent to the notion of noise risk stability. Thus, if the gap in empirical risk $(\hat{R}_S(A(T)) - \hat{R}_T(A(T)))$ introduced by imputation can be controlled, then also the generalization gap $R(A(T)) - \hat{R}_T(A(T))$ can be controlled: in particular, if we can make the noise $\epsilon_{Corrupt}$ arbitrarily small (as a function of m), then we can make the generalization gap also arbitrarily small. Note that, under uniform convergence and with probability larger than $1 - \delta$, this also implies that $R(A(T)) - \inf_{h \in \mathcal{H}} R(h)$ can be made arbitrarily small[3]: this guarantees that, in particular and despite the presence of noise introduced by imputation, it is possible to get a model that (with high probability) will be arbitrarily close to the optimal Bayes predictor $h^* = \inf_{h \in \mathcal{H}} R(h)$. Note that this result is considerably stronger than agnostic learnability, as in the case of learning under imputation the learning algorithm A is not able to observe the real data sampled from $\mathcal{D}$ but only an out-of-distribution sample drawn from Corrupt. Nonetheless, we note that Theorem 1 only provides an upper bound on the generalization gap. In general, a lower bound could easily be obtained by using a lower bound for learnability, however it is not clear whether this bound is tight: that is, there may exist learning problems for which, despite the presence of imputation, we can recover the same generalization gap as if the data were completely observed. We leave the search for lower bounds (as well as to understand whether there exist matching lower and upper bounds) as future work.

Before proceeding further, we make some further comments on Theorem 1 and highlight some potential related open questions. Firstly, a known result from statistical learning theory implies that a class of models $\mathcal{H}$ is (agnostic) learnable if and only if there exists a uniform replace-one (RO) stable[4] asymptotic ERM[5] algorithm A that learns it [41]. Thus, in a sense, stability is already a necessary condition for (conventional) learnability. However, even though both definitions

---

[3] Indeed, $R(A(T)) - \inf_{h \in \mathcal{H}} R(h) = R(A(T)) - \hat{R}_T(A(T)) + \hat{R}_T(A(T)) - \inf_{h \in \mathcal{H}} R(h)$. If uniform convergence holds, then, without loss of generality, A can be set to be an ERM [41]. Hence, letting $h^* = \inf_{h \in \mathcal{H}} R(h)$, it holds that $R(A(T)) - R(h^*) \leq R(A(T)) - \hat{R}_T(A(T)) + \hat{R}_T(h^*) - R(h^*) \leq \epsilon_{NRS}^A(m, \epsilon_{Corrupt}(m, \frac{\delta}{4}), \frac{\delta}{4}) + \epsilon_L^{\mathcal{H},A}(m, \frac{\delta}{4}) + \epsilon_{UC}^{\mathcal{H}}(m, \frac{\delta}{4}) \to 0$, as $\epsilon_{Corrupt} \to 0$ and $m \to \infty$.

[4] A is uniform RO stable if there exists $\epsilon_{stable} : \mathbb{R} \to \mathbb{R}$ s.t. for all possible $S = \{(x_1, y_1), \ldots, (x_m, y_m)\} \in (X \times Y)^m$ and $(x,y) \in (X \times Y)$ it holds that $\frac{1}{m}\sum_{i=1}^m |l(x,y,A(S)) - l(x,y,A(S^i))| \leq \epsilon_{stable}(m)$, where $S^i = \{(x_1, y_1), \ldots, (x_{i-1}, y_{i-1}), (x,y), (x_{i+1}, y_{i+1}), \ldots, (x_m, y_m)\}$.

[5] A is an asymptotic ERM if $\lim_{m \to \infty} \mathbb{E}_{S \sim \mathcal{D}^m}[|\hat{R}_S(A(S)) - \inf_{h \in \mathcal{H}} \hat{R}_S(h)|] = 0$.

of stability require that the risk of a learning algorithm does not change too much under small variations of the data, the constraints they impose on a learning algorithm are rather different from an intuitive point of view. Indeed, while uniform RO stability requires the loss being stable under arbitrary changes to a single instance, noise risk stability requires stability under constrained changes to the entire data-generating distribution. We leave the problem of further characterizing the relationships among these two notions of stability (and, in particular, the identification of conditions under which they are equivalent) as future work.

Second, while Theorem 1 shows that noise risk stability is necessary for learnability under imputation, the proof of this fact relies on uniform convergence. Such an assumption is reasonable for many commonly occurring learning tasks: e.g., for both binary classification [12,45] and bounded regression [3], uniform convergence is equivalent to learnability, and, more generally, uniform convergence is equivalent to learnability whenever the loss function l is bounded, has linear dependence on $h \in \mathcal{H}$ and $\mathcal{H}$ itself is bounded [42]. However, uniform convergence may also fail to hold in many natural scenarios in which learnability is nevertheless possible [19,41]. In these scenarios, noise risk stability is still sufficient for learnability under imputation, but the proof of necessity in Theorem 1 fails. Therefore, a more general proof technique should be adopted to understand whether noise risk stability characterizes learnability under imputation also in these more general settings: we leave this open question as future work.

Finally, while in this work we focus solely on learnability under imputation, the small noise condition in Eq. (1) only requires that the average distance between instances sampled from $\mathcal{D}$ and instances sampled from a different distribution $\mathcal{L}$ can be bounded from above by a quantity that is monotonically decreasing (in m). While in our setting $\mathcal{L}$ is the distribution derived by the corruption mechanism Corrupt, in principle one could set $\mathcal{L}$ arbitrarily as long as it satisfies the above-mentioned condition. In this sense, learnability under imputation can be seen as a special case of *domain adaptation* [36] and *credal learning* [15,16]. That is, given a set of data sampled from $\mathcal{L}$, we want to control the out-of-distribution (OOD) risk on data sampled from $\mathcal{D}$, under the constraint that both $\mathcal{D}$ and $\mathcal{L}$ are contained in a set of probability distributions which, by the small noise condition, is not too large: hence information about $\mathcal{L}$ can be used as a proxy for information about $\mathcal{D}$. We leave studying the relationships between learning under imputation and OOD learnability as future work.

4 Linear-In-Parameter Models are Learnable Under Imputation

While in the previous section we established that noise risk stability is equivalent to learnability under imputation, we have not yet proved the existence of NRS algorithms. The following Theorem establishes this fact.

Theorem 2. *Let* $l : X \times Y \times \mathcal{H} \to \mathbb{R}$ *be a loss function that is L-Lipschitz in its first argument, and assume that X is s.t.* $\sup_{x \in X} \|x\|_X = B$. *Then, any learning* algorithm $A : \bigcup_{m=1}^{\infty} (X \times Y)^m \to \mathcal{H}$ is NRS and:

$$\epsilon_{NRS}^A(m, \epsilon_{Corrupt}, \delta) \leq L\epsilon_{Corrupt}(m, \frac{\delta}{2}) + 2BL\sqrt{\frac{\log(2/\delta)}{2m}}. \quad (5)$$

In particular, assume $l(x, y, h) = g(\langle h, \phi(x) \rangle_K)$, where $g : \mathbb{R} \to \mathbb{R}$ is L-Lipschitz, K is a Reproducing Kernel Hilbert Space, $\langle \cdot, \cdot \rangle_K$ is an inner product on K and $\| \cdot \|_K$ the derived norm, $\mathcal{H} \subseteq K$ is s.t. $\sup_{h \in \mathcal{H}} \|h\|_K = H$, $\phi : X \to K$, and $\phi(X) = \{\phi(x) : x \in X\}$ is s.t. $\sup_{k \in \phi(X)} \|k\|_K = B$. Then, any learning algorithm A is NRS and:

$$\epsilon_{NRS}^A(m, \epsilon_{Corrupt}, \delta) \leq LH\epsilon_{Corrupt}(m, \frac{\delta}{2}) + 2BHL\sqrt{\frac{\log(2/\delta)}{2m}}. \quad (6)$$

Assume that $l(x, y, h) = g(\langle h, \phi(x) \rangle_K) + r(\|h\|_K^2)$, with g as defined above, g and $r : \mathbb{R} \to \mathbb{R}$ differentiable and M_g-smooth, M_r-smooth respectively. Assume that l is b-bounded and $\mu(m)$-strongly convex in $\mathcal{H}$, with $\mu : \mathbb{N} \to \mathbb{R}$ being a function monotone increasing with m. Then, assuming $\inf_{h \in \mathcal{H}} \hat{R}_S(h) \leq \hat{R}_T(A(T))$ with S and T defined as above, there exists an algorithm A for which it holds, with probability larger than $1 - \delta$, that:

$$\epsilon_{NRS}^A(m, \epsilon_{Corrupt}, \delta) \leq b(1 - \frac{1}{2(B^2 M_g + 2M_r)})^T + \frac{\psi^2}{\mu(m)}, \quad (7)$$

where $\psi = HL\epsilon_{Corrupt}(m, \frac{\delta}{2}) + 2BHL\sqrt{\frac{\log(2/\delta)}{2m}} + \delta BHL$. The algorithm A is gradient descent with step size $\gamma \leq \min\{\frac{1}{(B^2 M_g + 2M_r)}, \frac{1}{\mu(m)T}\}$ and executed for T iterations. The result above holds, in expectation, also for stochastic gradient descent (with the same step size and the same number of iterations) as long as for all $h \in \mathcal{H}$ the noisy gradient estimates $g(h)$ satisfy $\mathbb{E}[g(h)] = \nabla \hat{R}_T(h)$.

Theorem 2 shows that when the loss function is Lipschitz w.r.t. X, any algorithm in $\mathcal{A}_\mathcal{H}$ (and, in particular if uniform convergence holds, ERM) is NRS. Hence, not only ERM w.r.t. such a loss function provides an algorithm for learning under imputation but, under these assumptions, learnability under imputation is equivalent to learnability. In particular, as a consequence of Eq. (6), the result holds for linear-in-parameter models (which include any kernel method), as long as the models have bounded norm. Nevertheless, we note that this does not imply that learning under imputation is as easy as conventional learning. Indeed, the bound in Eqs. (5) and (6) encompass also the $\epsilon_{Corrupt}$ term. Thus, fixed a particular class of imputation mechanisms and a class of models $\mathcal{H}$, if the term $\epsilon_{Corrupt}$ does not converge to 0 as $m \to \infty$, it may be that ϵ_{NRS} (and, thus, the generalization gap $R(A(T)) - \hat{R}_T(A(T))$) does not converge to 0, even though $\mathcal{H}$ is learnable under imputation using A. The reason behind this seemingly paradoxical phenomenon is that the definition of learnability under imputation guarantees the above-mentioned convergence only when we consider a class of imputation mechanisms whose small noise constant also converges to 0 as the sample size grows. In this sense, learnability under imputation is in general strictly harder than learnability, as the former requires not only a good learning algorithm, but also a good imputation mechanism.

Notably, however, under the stronger assumptions on the learning problem required for Eq. (7), learnability under imputation is always possible, regardless of the specific imputation mechanism adopted. Indeed, even for asymptotically inconsistent imputation mechanisms for which $\lim_{m \to \infty} \epsilon_{\text{Corrupt}}(m, \delta) > 0$, Eq. (7) guarantees that ϵ_{NRS} converges to 0 as m grows, since the learning algorithm (gradient descent) ensures that the noise due to imputation is attenuated at a rate $\frac{1}{\mu(m)}$. Nonetheless, also in this setting, not all imputation mechanisms are equally good: indeed, the guarantee in Eq. (7) is particularly favorable when it is possible to find a class of imputation mechanisms that is consistent (i.e., $\lim_{m \to \infty} \epsilon_{\text{Corrupt}}(m, \delta) > 0$) as, in this case, the generalization gap can decrease exponentially fast in the size of the training set. Also, we note that, though stronger than the assumptions of Eqs. (5) and (6), the assumptions required for Eq. (7) to hold (with the exception of the requirement that $\inf_{h \in \mathcal{H}} \hat{R}_S(h) \leq \hat{R}_T(A(T))$, which is intuitively reasonable[6] but not testable, as S is not available) are naturally satisfied by several natural learning problems, such as (regularized) kernel logistic regression as well as kernel ridge regression. As we discuss in the next section, this result provides a generalization of the main result in [5].

Before proceeding to the next section, we provide some further discussion of the previous result, also highlighting some open questions. First, we note that Theorem 2 requires that the loss function be Lipschitz w.r.t. X: this is different from the usual definition of a Lipschitz loss function, which requires Lipschitzness w.r.t. $\mathcal{H}$. Nonetheless, whenever the loss function is symmetric w.r.t. X and $\mathcal{H}$ (this happens, e.g., for linear-in-parameter models, as in Eq. (6)) the two requirements are equivalent (though with different parameters).

Secondly, Theorem 2 only provides a necessary condition for noise risk stability, and furthermore only provides an upper bound on ϵ_{NRS}. In particular, this implies that even though under the assumptions of Theorem 2 learnability and learnability under imputation are equivalent, there may be learning problems for which this equivalence does not hold. We leave the analysis of noise risk stability for other algorithms, as well as possibly the computation of lower bounds (as well as tighter upper bounds) on ϵ_{NRS}, to future work.

Thirdly, while Eq. (7) provides better guarantees than both Eqs. (5) and (6), it also enforces the selection of a learning algorithm: indeed, while Eqs. (5) and (6) hold for any learning algorithm A, Eq. (7) is guaranteed to hold only for (stochastic) gradient descent. While this is generally not a problem, as descent methods are among the most commonly employed ML algorithms and can be usually implemented efficiently, the previous observation implies that when it is not possible to use gradient descent (e.g., for non-differentiable functions, or also for black-box problems in which only a zero-th order oracle is available), Eq. (7) cannot be applied. As our analysis strictly relies on the possibility to use a gradient descent procedure, it is therefore not clear whether it would be

---

[6] For example, the assumption holds when the original distribution $\mathcal{D}$ is realizable.

possible to achieve similar convergence guarantees, that hold irrespective of the imputation mechanism and its (in)consistency, also for other learning algorithms.

Finally, our proof of Eq. (7) relies on previous results on the convergence gradient descent with biased oracles [2]. Other papers have investigated the properties of descent-based algorithms with inexact gradient oracles [9,10,20,23]. In particular, Chen et al. [17] studied convergence of (sub)gradient descent under a noise model according to which a biased but asymptotically consistent estimator of the gradient is available: at each iteration of the descent procedure, the estimator is computed on the basis of multiple samples, and the estimator is required to converge (in probability) to the actual gradient. This setting seems to be of particular relevance to learnability under imputation: indeed, there exist imputation mechanisms that allow the construction of multiple filled-in datasets, so-called multiple imputation methods [38], and these alternative imputations could, in turn, be used to obtain the multiple gradient approximations required for the procedure described in [17]. As in this paper we do not discuss multiple imputation methods, we leave the investigation of such a scenario to future work.

5 Characterizing the Small Noise Condition

In this section we provide a characterization of the small noise condition in Eq. (1) for two commonly used imputation strategies, namely constant imputation and regression imputation. These results provide computable certificates for the small noise condition and thus, together with Theorem 2, also provide a way to explicit finite-sample guarantees from the bounds in Theorem 1.

Theorem 3. *Let FV_v, with $v : (\tilde{X} \times Y)^m \to X$, be the imputation mechanism defined coordinate-wise by:*

$$FV_v(S,(x,y))_i = \begin{cases} x_i & x_i \neq \bot \\ v_i(S) & otherwise \end{cases}. \qquad (8)$$

Then, for every ℓ_p norm it holds, with probability 1, that: $\mathbb{E}[\|x - Corrupt_S(x,y)\|_X] \leq Tr(\Sigma) + \mathbb{E}[\|v(T) - \mu\|_X] \leq \sup_{x_1,x_2 \in X} \|x_1 - x_2\|_X$, where Σ is the covariance matrix of $\mathcal{D}_X = \int_Y \mathcal{D}$ and $\mu = \mathbb{E}[x]$. Let avg be defined coordinate-wise by $avg_i(S) = \frac{1}{|S_i^C|} \sum_{(x_j, y_j) \in S} x_j^{(i)} \mathbb{1}_{x_j^{(i)} \neq \bot}$. Then, if $\|\cdot\|_X$ is the ℓ_2 norm, then it holds with probability 1, that $c \cdot Tr(\Sigma) \leq \mathbb{E}[\|x - Corrupt_S(x,y)\|_X]$.

Additionally, if $\mathcal{M}$ is s.t. $\forall i, \mathcal{M}_i(\bot | (x,y)) = c$ and $\sup_{x \in X} \|x\|_X = D$, then, with probability larger than $1 - \delta$ over the sampling of $S \sim \mathcal{D}^m$ and $T = \{Corrupt_S(x,y) : (x,y) \in S\}$ it holds that $c \cdot Tr(\Sigma) \leq \mathbb{E}[\|x - Corrupt_S(x,y)\|_X] \leq Tr(\Sigma) + 2D \sum_{i=1}^{d} \sqrt{\frac{\log(1/\delta)}{2|S_i^C|}}$.

Theorem 4. *Let $\mathcal{R}_i$ be a set of regression models $r : X^{-i} \to \mathbb{R}$, where $X^{-i} = \Pi_{i' \neq i} X^{(i')}$. Let $Fill : \cup_{m=1}^{\infty} \Pi_{i=1}^{d} \tilde{X}^{-i} \to \cup_{m=1}^{\infty} \Pi_{i=1}^{d} \tilde{X}^{-i}$ be an arbitrary function satisfying: 1) $|Fill(S)| = |S|$; 2) $Fill(S)_j^{(i)} = S_j^{(i)}$ iff $S_j^{(i)} \neq \bot$. For each feature i,* assume that l_i is a loss function bounded in $[0, b_i]$ on $X^{(i)}$ and s.t. there exists a $\nu : \mathbb{R} \to \mathbb{R}$ with $\|x_1 - \Pi_{i=1}^d r_i(x_2^{-i})\|_X = \nu(\sum_{i=1}^d l_i(x^{-i}, x^{(i)}, r(x^{-i})))$[7]. Assume that $\mathcal{R}_i$ is learnable over $(\Pi_{i=1}^d X^{-i}) \times X^{(i)}$ through an algorithm A_i with $\epsilon_L^{\mathcal{R}_i, A_i}$. We set Reg to be the imputation mechanism defined coordinate wise by:

$$Reg(S, (x, y))_i = \begin{cases} x^{(i)} & x^{(i)} \neq \bot \\ A_i(T_C^i)(Fill(T^{-i})_j) & otherwise \end{cases}, \quad (9)$$

where $T_C^i = \{(Fill(T^{-i})_j, x_j^{(i)}) : x_j \in T \wedge x_j^{(i)} \neq \bot\}$.

Then, with probability larger than $1 - \delta$ over the sampling of $S \sim \mathcal{D}^m$ and $T = \{(Corrupt_S(x, y) : (x, y) \in S\}$, it holds that $\mathbb{E}[\|x - Corrupt_S(x, y)\|_X]$ can be upper bounded by $\nu(\phi(T, l, \mathcal{R}_1, \ldots, \mathcal{R}_d))$, with $\phi(T, l, \mathcal{R}_1, \ldots, \mathcal{R}_d)$ being:

$$\sum_{i=1}^d 2Rad(l_i \circ \mathcal{R}_i \circ T_C^i) + \frac{1}{S_i^C} \sum_{j=1}^m l_1(x^{-i}, x^{(i)}, A_i(T_C^i)) \mathbb{1}_{x_j^{(i)} \neq \bot} + 4b_i \sqrt{\frac{2\log(4d/\delta)}{|S_i^C|}}, \quad (10)$$

where $T_C^i = \{(Fill(T^{-i})_j, x_j^{(i)}) : x_j \in T \wedge x_j^{(i)} \neq \bot\}$ and Rad is the empirical Rademacher complexity.

Corollary 1. *Assume the same setting as in Theorem 4. Let $\mathcal{L}$ be the distribution over X induced by the composition of $\mathcal{D}$, $\mathcal{M}$ and Fill. Assume, further, that: 1) $\mathcal{L}$ is realizable; 2) $Rad(l_i \circ \mathcal{R}_i \circ T_C^i) \to 0$ as $|T_C^i| \to \infty$[8]; 3) ν is monotone increasing and $\lim_{z \to 0^+} \nu(z) = 0$. Then $\lim_{m \to \infty} \epsilon_{Corrupt}(m, \delta) = 0$.*

Finally, we prove instantiantions of Theorem 4 for two concrete class of regression models, namely linear models (used, for example, by the MICE library [44]) and tree ensembles (used, for example, by the missForest library [43]).

Corollary 2. *Assume the same setting as in Theorem 4. Assume that each of the loss functions l_i is L-Lipschitz and can be written as $g_i(\langle h, \phi(x) \rangle_K)$, where g, $\langle \cdot, \cdot \rangle_K$ and K are defined as in Theorem 2. Assume further that the derived norm $\| \cdot \|_K$ is the ℓ_2 norm over K and $\sup_{h \in \mathcal{H}} \|h\|_K = B$. Then, it holds that Eq. (10) can be upper bounded by $\sum_{i=1}^d \hat{R}_{Fill}(A_i(T_C^i)) + 2 \sup_{x \in X} \frac{LB\|\phi(x)\|_K}{\sqrt{|S_i^C|}} + 4b_i \sqrt{\frac{2\log(4d/\delta)}{|S_i^C|}}$, where $\hat{R}_{Fill}(h) = \frac{1}{S_i^C} \sum_{j=1}^m l_1(Fill(T^{-i})_j, x_j^{(i)}, h(T_C^i)) \mathbb{1}_{x_j^{(i)} \neq \bot}$. Similarly, under the same assumptions as above but requiring that the derived norm $\| \cdot \|_K$ is the ℓ_1 norm over K, it holds that Eq. (10) can be upper bounded by $\sum_{i=1}^d \hat{R}_{Fill}(A_i(T_C^i)) + 2LB \sup_{x \in X} \|\phi(x)\|_\infty \sqrt{\frac{2\log(2(d-1))}{|S_i^C|}} + 4b_i \sqrt{\frac{2\log(4d/\delta)}{|S_i^C|}}$.*

---

[7] For example, if $\| \cdot \|_X^{\ell_2}$, then, setting $l_i(x, y, r) = (y - r(x))^2$ and $\nu(x) = \sqrt{x}$ satisfies the mentioned condition. Indeed, $\|x - \Pi_i r_i(x^{-i})\|_X^{\ell_2} = \sqrt{\sum_i (x^{(i)} - r_i(x^{-i}))^2} = \nu(\sum_i l_i(x_i, y_i, r_i))$. Similarly, if $\| \cdot \|_X^{\ell_1}$ then setting $l_i(x, y, r) = l_1(x, y, r) = |y - r(x)|$ and ν the identity, also satisfies the mentioned condition.

[8] This condition holds, in particular, for both the class of linear models bounded in ℓ_1 or ℓ_2 norm, as well as the class of ensembles of regression trees.

Corollary 3. *Assume the same setting as in Theorem 4. Assume that, for each i, $X^{(i)}$ is bounded in $[-B, B]$. Assume, further, that for each i, $\mathcal{R}_i$ is the class of ensembles composed by at most r regression trees with depth at most k. Then, it holds that Eq. (10) can be upper bounded by $\sum_{i=1}^{d} \hat{R}_{Fill}(A_i(T_C^i)) + 4b_i\sqrt{\frac{2\log(4d/\delta)}{|S_i^C|}} + O\left(b_i\sqrt{\frac{r2^{k+1}\log(d \cdot 2^{k+1})\log(Br)}{|S_i^C|}}\right)$*

Theorems 3 and 4 provide a bound on the noise introduced by constant and regression imputation. Theorem 3 reveals that noise risk stability is not sufficient as a condition for learnability under imputation if we restrict the imputation mechanism to be mean imputation, as this latter does not provide a consistent estimator for the real (unobserved) data, even in the best case. Indeed, in such a situation, one would need the stronger condition $\lim_{m\to\infty} \epsilon_{NRS}(m, \epsilon, \delta) = 0$, irrespective of ϵ, because the small noise constant ϵ will be lower bounded by the trace of the covariance matrix. This fact is a manifestation of the issue we mentioned in the previous section wherein for a fixed class of imputation mechanisms (in this case, mean imputation), it may not be possible to have a vanishing generalization gap, even for a class of models that is learnable under imputation. At the same time, if the conditions for Eq. (7) are satisfied, and using gradient descent as a learning algorithm, learning is possible even while using such an inconsistent imputation mechanism. This allows deriving the following:

Corollary 4. *Let FV_v be defined as in Theorem 3. Let $\mathcal{H}, X \subseteq K$, with K being a Reproducing Kernel Hilbert Space with $\|\cdot\|_K$ being the corresponding norm, that is H-bounded on $\mathcal{H}$ and B-bounded on X. Assume that $l(x, y, h) = g(\langle h, \phi(x)\rangle_K) + \frac{\lambda(m)}{2}\|h\|_K^2$, with g differentiable, M-smooth, b-bounded and satisfying the assumptions required for Eq. (6) to hold. Let $A = GD$ be gradient descent with step-size as defined in Theorem 2 and executed for T steps. Then, with probability larger than $1 - \delta$ over the sampling of $S \sim \mathcal{D}^m$ and $T = \{(Corrupt_S(x, y), y) : (x, y) \in S\}$, and requiring $\lambda(m) \leq \sqrt{m}$ and increasing in m, it holds that $R(GD(T)) - \hat{R}_T(GD(T))$ goes to 0 as $m \to \infty$, and is upper bounded by $\frac{2B\max\{HL, \lambda(m)H^2\}}{\sqrt{\min_i |S_i^C|}} + 4(b + \frac{\lambda(m)}{2}H^2)\sqrt{\frac{2\log(8/\delta)}{\min_i |S_i^C|}} + (b + \frac{\lambda(m)}{2}H^2)\left(1 - \frac{1}{2(B^2M + \lambda(m))}\right)^T + \frac{HL(Tr(\Sigma) + \mathbb{E}[\|v(T) - \mu\|_X]) + 2BHL\sqrt{\frac{\log(4/\delta)}{2m}} + \frac{\delta}{2}BHL}{\lambda(m)}$.*

In particular, the previous bound holds for (kernel) ridge regression (i.e., $g(z) = (y - z)^2$) with $M = 2$, $L = 2BH$, and for (kernel) shrinked logistic regression (i.e., $g(z) = \log(1 + e^{-yz})$) with $M \leq \frac{1}{4}$, $L = 1$.

Corollary 4 is related to and, in some sense, generalizes the main result in [5]. Indeed, while the results in [5] are only applicable to linear ridge regression in the realizable setting, using naive imputation (i.e., constant imputation with 0), and assuming that $\mathcal{M}$ satisfies $\forall i, \mathcal{M}_i(\perp|(x, y)) = c$, in contrast, Corollary 4 can be applied to a larger class of regularized linear-in-parameters models, any form of constant imputation, no assumptions on the missingness mechanism and also in the agnostic setting. On the other hand, the results in [5] provide tighter finite-sample bounds for learnability under imputation of linear ridge regression. In this sense, the two results provide a complementary perspective on the generalization properties of linear models in learning under imputation: we leave to future work the study of additional conditions under which tighter bounds in the style of [5] for the class of models discussed in Corollary 4.

Even though the previous Corollary illustrates that learnability under imputation is still possible even when considering only inconsistent imputation mechanisms, in general the convergence of the generalization gap could be much slower than optimal. Indeed, as previously shown in [25], one can expect regression imputation to provide better generalization guarantees in general scenarios. For example, as a consequence of Theorem 4, whenever the features are not uncorrelated and the regression models are consistent, the small noise constant $\epsilon_{Corrupt}$ for regression imputation vanishes as the sample size grows to infinity. This holds, in particular, for regression models that are universal approximators (e.g., kernel regression model [32], studied in Corollary 2, or also model ensembles [11]), studied in Corollary 3). We note, however, that the assumptions mentioned in Theorem 4 are rather strong, as they imply that features are not just merely strongly correlated under the data generating distribution $\mathcal{D}$, but are so also under the perturbed distribution determined by the missingness mechanism $\mathcal{M}$ and the Fill function. In practice, Fill may itself depend on the corrupted sampled dataset T [7,27,43], making the study of correlation particularly hard. Therefore, precisely characterizing the conditions under which regression imputation provides an asymptotically optimal imputation strategy, remains an open question. We leave to future work the study of more general conditions under which the noise introduced by regression imputation vanishes, as well as the study of other imputation strategies and their properties.

6 Illustrative Experiments

In this section we illustrate our results by means of two simple experiments. In the first example we demonstrate the application of Theorem 2, for both mean and regression imputation, in the simplified (but practically relevant) setting of (regularized) linear regression (as previously studied in [4]). In the second example, by contrast, we demonstrate the application of Theorems 3 and 4.

For the first experiment, we first generated a 10-dimensional vector w. Then, given a sample size m, we generated a dataset X of dimensionality 10, which was subsequently split into a training set T and a validation set V, with sizes, respectively, equal to $0.8m$ and $0.2m$. The target variable was generated as $y = Xw$. Data were generated uniformly at random between 0 and 1, and then instances were normalized[9]. 20% of the entries, randomly selected, in both X and V were set to missing. We then applied, respectively, mean imputation and regression imputation (using Ridge regression as the regression model): by construction, $\epsilon_{Corrupt} \sim \frac{1}{2}$, regardless of the imputation mechanism. Then, we fitted

---

[9] By construction, he covariance matrix Σ is the identity matrix.

a ridge regression model[10], using regularization coefficient $\lambda = \log(|T|)$, on the imputed training set, reconstructing a regularized linear model w'. In the experiment, we varied the sample size m from 100 to 10000 and assessed the error of the reconstructed model w' in terms of the l_2 loss on the validation set: i.e., $\frac{1}{|V|}\sum_{(x,y)\in V}(y - \langle w', x\rangle)^2$. The empirical error was compared with the theoretical estimates given by Theorem 2, Eq. (7). To account for uncertainty due to randomization, the above simulations were repeated 10 times, and we report the average error and 95% confidence intervals resulting from the experiments.

The results of the first experiment are illustrated in Fig. 1. First of all, we note that there were no significant differences between mean and regression imputation. This result is not surprising: indeed, by construction, regression imputation cannot be expected to outperform mean imputation, as no information in the features can reliably be used to predict the missing data[11]. More generally, in both cases, the results provide a confirmation of Theorem 2 since, in all cases, the empirical error is upper bounded by the generalization curve predicted by the proven results. In general, the theoretical bounds become tighter with increasing sample size: indeed, as shown in Fig. 1, the theoretical generalization curve rapidly (in fact, exponentially) decreases, approaching the observed empirical error. At the same time, the results of the experiment show that the proven bounds are not the tightest possible (at least in the simple setting of independent features and missing completely at random data, as assumed in the experiments), and hence finding tighter bounds (as well as matching lower bounds) could be of significant practical interest.

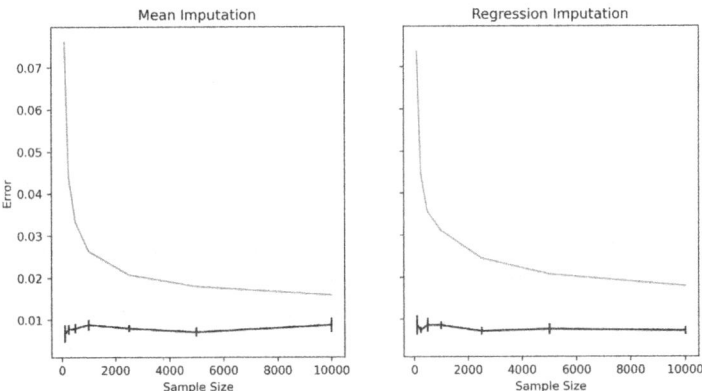

Fig. 1. Results of the experiment illustrating Theorem 2. The blue curve represents the empirical error, the orange one the theoretical bound given by Eq. (7).

---

[10] We note that ridge regression with the above regularization setting defines a $||w'||$-Lipschitz learning problem satisfying the additional assumptions for Eq. (7), with $M_g = M_r = 2$, $b = 1$, $B = 1$, and $\mu(m) = 2\log(m)$.

[11] Indeed, the data-generating distribution adopted in the experiment ensures independence of the features and missing completely at random data [30].

As for the second experiment, given a sample size m, we generated a dataset of dimensionality 10, which was subsequently split into a training set T and a validation set V, with sizes, respectively, equal to $0.8m$ and $0.2m$. The dataset was generated according to a random probabilistic graphical model [26]: first, we selected, uniformly at random between 1 and 10, a number of features (root features) to be generated uniformly at random; each subsequent feature f was generated by first randomly selecting a subset of the already generated features (the parents of f) and then defining f as a random linear combination of its parents. The instances in the generated dataset were then normalized. For the root features, 20% of the entries, randomly selected, were set to missing. By contrast, for each other feature f, we generated a random logistic regression model based on the parents of f, setting to missing values for which the logistic regression model predicted a target smaller than 0.5. We then applied, respectively, mean imputation and regression imputation (using ridge regression as the regression model), fitting the model on the training set and then evaluating imputation error on the validation set. These empirical error estimates were compared with the theoretical upper bounds given by Theorems 3 and 4. To account for uncertainty due to randomization, the simulations were repeated 10 times, and we report the average error and 95% confidence intervals resulting from the experiments.

The results of the experiment are illustrated in Fig. 2. In contrast with the previously described experiment, regression imputation reported on average a smaller imputation error: in several cases, the observed differences were significant. This result shows that, in general, regression imputation can be more effective than mean imputation (more generally, constant imputation) whenever the data is not missing completely at random[12]. More in general, we observe that the theoretical upper bound given by Theorem 3 provides a tight approximation to the expected imputation error of constant imputation, as the predicted value was almost always in the 95% confidence interval for the actual imputation error (only for $m = 2500$ the theoretical guarantee strictly upper bounded the imputation error): this shows that, in general, the given result for constant imputation may be tight. By contrast, the guarantee in Theorem 4 always strictly upper bounded the imputation error of regression imputation: while the deviation between theoretical and actual imputation error rapidly decreased with increasing sample size, the upper approximation is not the tightest possible, showing that the bound in Theorem 4 could be further improved.

7 Conclusion

In this article, we studied the interplay between learnability and imputation within the framework of statistical learning theory. In particular, we provided a necessary and sufficient condition for learnability under imputation, and showed that a large class of ML models satisfies this condition. Finally, we studied the

---

[12] By construction, the adopted experimental design ensures that the data is missing at random [30].

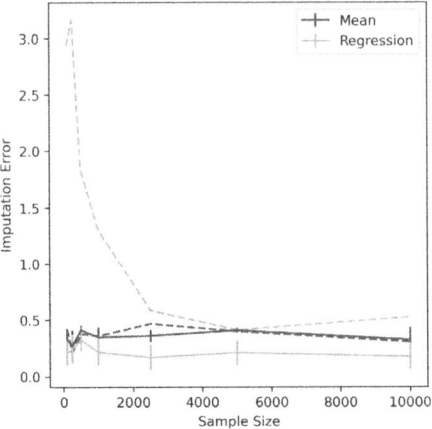

Fig. 2. Results of the experiment illustrating Theorems 3 and 4. For each imputation method, the solid line represents the empirical imputation error, while the dashed one represents the theoretical estimate.

behaviour of two commonly employed imputation strategies. Taken together, our results establish finite-sample guarantees and computable generalization certificates for learning with missing data. Our results set the stage for further formal exploration of missing data: to this aim, we discussed several open questions as well as highlighted relevant connections with other ML settings.

Code and Proof Availability. Proofs of all the results, as well as the code employed in the illustrative experiments, are available on GitHub at the following link: https://github.com/AndreaCampagner/missing_ecml.

References

1. Ahmad, A.F., Sayeed, M.S., Alshammari, K., Ahmed, I.: Impact of missing values in machine learning: a comprehensive analysis. arXiv preprint arXiv:2410.08295 (2024)
2. Ajalloeian, A., Stich, S.: Analysis of SGD with biased gradient estimators. arXiv preprint arXiv:2008.00051 (2020)
3. Alon, N., Ben-David, S., Cesa-Bianchi, N., Haussler, D.: Scale-sensitive dimensions, uniform convergence, and learnability. J. ACM **44**(4), 615–631 (1997)
4. Ayme, A., Boyer, C., Dieuleveut, A., Scornet, E.: Near-optimal rate of consistency for linear models with missing values. In: International Conference on Machine Learning, pp. 1211–1243. PMLR (2022)
5. Ayme, A., Boyer, C., Dieuleveut, A., Scornet, E.: Naive imputation implicitly regularizes high-dimensional linear models. In: International Conference on Machine Learning, pp. 1320–1340. PMLR (2023)
6. Ayme, A., Boyer, C., Dieuleveut, A., Scornet, E.: Random features models: a way to study the success of naive imputation. In: International Conference on Machine Learning, pp. 2108–2134. PMLR (2024)

7. Azur, M.J., Stuart, E.A., Frangakis, C., Leaf, P.J.: Multiple imputation by chained equations: what is it and how does it work? Int. J. Methods Psychiatr. Res. **20**(1), 40–49 (2011)
8. Bertsimas, D., Delarue, A., Pauphilet, J.: Simple imputation rules for prediction with missing data: theoretical guarantees vs. empirical performance. Trans. Mach. Learn. Res .(2024)
9. Bhaskara, A., Cutkosky, A., Kumar, R., Purohit, M.: Descent with misaligned gradients and applications to hidden convexity. In: The Thirteenth International Conference on Learning Representations (2025)
10. Bhavsar, N., Prashanth, L.: Nonasymptotic bounds for stochastic optimization with biased noisy gradient oracles. IEEE Trans. Autom. Control **68**(3), 1628–1641 (2022)
11. Biau, G., Devroye, L., Lugosi, G.: Consistency of random forests and other averaging classifiers. J. Mach. Learn. Res. **9**(9) (2008)
12. Blumer, A., Ehrenfeucht, A., Haussler, D., Warmuth, M.: Learnability and the vapnik-chervonenkis dimension. J. ACM **36**(4), 929–965 (1989)
13. Bouthinon, D., Soldano, H.: Learning first order rules from ambiguous examples. In: 2014 IEEE 26th International Conference on Tools with Artificial Intelligence, pp. 39–46. IEEE (2014)
14. Bouthinon, D., Soldano, H., Ventos, V.: Concept learning from (very) ambiguous examples. In: Machine Learning and Data Mining in Pattern Recognition: 6th International Conference, MLDM 2009, Leipzig, Germany, July 23-25, 2009. Proceedings 6, pp. 465–478. Springer (2009)
15. Campagner, A.: Credal learning: weakly supervised learning from credal sets. In: ECAI 2023, pp. 327–334. IOS Press (2023)
16. Caprio, M., Sultana, M., Elia, E., Cuzzolin, F.: Credal learning theory. arXiv preprint arXiv:2402.00957 (2024)
17. Chen, J., Luss, R.: Stochastic gradient descent with biased but consistent gradient estimators. arXiv preprint arXiv:1807.11880 (2018)
18. Cismondi, F., Fialho, A.S., Vieira, S.M., Reti, S.R., Sousa, J.M., Finkelstein, S.N.: Missing data in medical databases: impute, delete or classify? Artif. Intell. Med. **58**(1), 63–72 (2013)
19. Daniely, A., Shalev-Shwartz, S.: Optimal learners for multiclass problems. In: Conference on Learning Theory, pp. 287–316. PMLR (2014)
20. d'Aspremont, A.: Smooth optimization with approximate gradient. SIAM J. Optim. **19**(3), 1171–1183 (2008)
21. Enders, C.K.: Applied Missing Data Analysis. Guilford Publications (2022)
22. Goldman, S.A., Kwek, S.S., Scott, S.D.: Learning from examples with unspecified attribute values. Inf. Comput. **180**(2), 82–100 (2003)
23. Hu, X., Prashanth, L., György, A., Szepesvari, C.: (bandit) convex optimization with biased noisy gradient oracles. In: Artificial Intelligence and Statistics, pp. 819–828. PMLR (2016)
24. Jäger, S., Allhorn, A., Bießmann, F.: A benchmark for data imputation methods. Front. big Data **4**, 693674 (2021)
25. Josse, J., Chen, J.M., Prost, N., Varoquaux, G., Scornet, E.: On the consistency of supervised learning with missing values. Stat. Pap. **65**(9), 5447–5479 (2024)
26. Koller, D., Friedman, N.: Probabilistic Graphical Models: Principles and Techniques. MIT Press (2009)
27. Le Morvan, M., Josse, J., Scornet, E., Varoquaux, G.: What'sa good imputation to predict with missing values? Adv. Neural. Inf. Process. Syst. **34**, 11530–11540 (2021)

28. Le Morvan, M., Prost, N., Josse, J., Scornet, E., Varoquaux, G.: Linear predictor on linearly-generated data with missing values: non consistency and solutions. In: International Conference on Artificial Intelligence and Statistics, pp. 3165–3174. PMLR (2020)
29. Lenz, O.U., Peralta, D., Cornelis, C.: No imputation without representation. In: Benelux Conference on Artificial Intelligence, pp. 1–21. Springer (2023)
30. Little, R.J., Rubin, D.B.: Statistical Analysis with Missing Data. John Wiley & Sons (2019)
31. Lodder, P., et al.: To impute or not impute: that's the question. Adv. Res. Meth. Sel. Top. **2013** (2013)
32. Micchelli, C.A., Xu, Y., Zhang, H.: Universal kernels. J. Mach. Learn. Res. **7**(12) (2006)
33. Michael, L.: Partial observability and learnability. Artif. Intell. **174**(11), 639–669 (2010)
34. Nijman, S.W., et al.: Missing data is poorly handled and reported in prediction model studies using machine learning: a literature review. J. Clin. Epidemiol. **142**, 218–229 (2022)
35. Perez-Lebel, A., Varoquaux, G., Le Morvan, M., Josse, J., Poline, J.B.: Benchmarking missing-values approaches for predictive models on health databases. GigaScience **11**, giac013 (2022)
36. Redko, I., Morvant, E., Habrard, A., Sebban, M., Bennani, Y.: Advances in Domain Adaptation Theory. Elsevier (2019)
37. Reyero Lobo, A.D., Ayme, A., Boyer, C., Scornet, E.: Harnessing pattern-by-pattern linear classifiers for prediction with missing data. arXiv preprint arXiv:2405-091096 (2024)
38. Rubin, D.B.: Multiple Imputation for Nonresponse in Surveys. Wiley (1987)
39. Schuurmans, D., Greiner, R.: Learning to classify incomplete examples. In: Computational Learning Theory and Natural Learning Systems: Addressing Real World Tasks, pp. 87–105 (1995)
40. Sell, T., Berrett, T.B., Cannings, T.I.: Nonparametric classification with missing data. Ann. Stat. **52**(3), 1178–1200 (2024)
41. Shalev-Shwartz, S., Shamir, O., Srebro, N., Sridharan, K.: Learnability, stability and uniform convergence. J. Mach. Learn. Res. **11**, 2635–2670 (2010)
42. Sridharan, K., Shalev-Shwartz, S., Srebro, N.: Fast rates for regularized objectives. Adv. Neural Info. Process. Syst. **21** (2008)
43. Stekhoven, D.J., Bühlmann, P.: Missforest–non-parametric missing value imputation for mixed-type data. Bioinformatics **28**(1), 112–118 (2012)
44. Van Buuren, S., Groothuis-Oudshoorn, K.: Mice: multivariate imputation by chained equations in r. J. Stat. Softw. **45**, 1–67 (2011)
45. Vapnik, V., Červonenkis, A.: On the uniform convergence of relative frequencies of events to their probabilities. In: Doklady Akademii Nauk USSR, vol. 181, pp. 781–787 (1968)

The Vanishing Empirical Variance in Randomly Initialized Deep ReLU Networks

Michał Grzejdziak-Zdziarski[1], David M.J. Tax[2], and Marco Loog[3](✉)

[1] Nomagic, Warsaw, Poland
[2] Delft University of Technology, Delft, The Netherlands
[3] Radboud University, Nijmegen, The Netherlands
marco.loog@ru.nl

Abstract. Neural networks are typically initialized such that the hidden pre-activations' theoretical variance remains constant to avoid the vanishing and exploding gradient problem. This condition is necessary to train very deep networks, but numerous analyses show this to be insufficient. We explain this behavior by analyzing the *empirical* variance, which is more meaningful in the practical setting that deals with data sets of finite size. We demonstrate its discrepancy with the theoretical variance, which grows with depth. We study the output distribution of neural networks at initialization and find that its kurtosis grows to infinity with increasing depth, even if the theoretical variance stays constant. As a result, the empirical variance vanishes: its asymptotic distribution converges in probability to zero. Our analysis focuses on fully connected ReLU networks with He-initialization, but we hypothesize that many more random weight initialization methods suffer from vanishing or exploding empirical variance. We support this hypothesis experimentally and demonstrate the failure of state-of-the-art random initialization methods in very deep regimes.

Keywords: vanishing gradient · empirical variance · kurtosis · ReLU

1 Introduction

The main heuristic for deriving initialization methods for deep neural networks is to keep the theoretical variance of the output or gradient distribution constant over all hidden layers. The idea is that this ensures proper propagation of the input signal through the network and therefore mitigates the vanishing gradient problem [3,13]. This approach has been used to derive two initialization methods: so-called Glorot [8] and He-initialization [11]. However, these methods are still not sufficient to train arbitrarily deep networks. Other statistical properties have

---

Supplementary Information The online version contains supplementary material available at https://doi.org/10.1007/978-3-032-06078-5_21.

been shown to explode or vanish even under constant variance [5,9,10,24], while in the meantime, still no initialization method has been demonstrated to work for very deep networks.

Here, we take another look at the consequences of keeping the theoretical variance constant and analyze distributional properties that go beyond this second central moment. Specifically, with a focus on He-initialization [11], we analyze the dynamics of the kurtosis, the fourth standardized moment, as a signal is propagated through a neural network that is He-initialized. Under mild assumptions, we prove that the kurtosis of the output distribution grows to infinity with increasing depth. As we will show, the surprising effect of this is that the *empirical* variance has to go to zero (in probability), despite the constant theoretical variance. Consequently, almost all outputs are mapped to zero by an arbitrarily deep network. We call this problem the vanishing empirical variance.

Our analysis suggests that the problem of vanishing empirical variance may concern many more random initialization schemes. We demonstrate this empirically for state-of-the-art random initialization methods for fully connected ReLU networks. We also show that ZerO [27], which is a deterministic method that keeps empirical variance constant, can train very deep and narrow networks, a fact not realized by its authors.

In Sect. 2, we recall the literature related to our work. In Sect. 3, we define the basic setup we consider, nuancing the original analysis of He-initialization from [11]. In Sect. 4, we analyze this setting and come to our main theoretical result. In Sect. 5, we show its practical consequences for the empirical variance of the output distribution at initialization. In Sect. 6, we present our experimental results. Finally, in Sect. 7, we discuss how our analysis extends to other types of layers and other activation functions.

2 Related Work

The idea to initialize the weights by sampling them i.i.d. from a zero-mean symmetric distribution such that the variance is kept constant over all layers is known at least since the work by [4]. It was popularized as a "trick" by [19]. [8] extended it to balance the need to keep the output variance and the gradient variance constant, while [11] analyzed the specific case of ReLU activation. Further extensions of this work to the specific case of highly popular ResNets [12] have been given by [26] and [1]. Other approaches to random weight initialization include orthogonal initialization [22], delta-orthogonal initialization [25], data-dependent LSUV [20] or MetaInit initialization [6], and GSM initialization [5]. Another approach is to initialize the weights deterministically. Examples are identity initialization [2] and ZerO initialization [27]. Although our focus is He-initialization [11], we hypothesize that our claims extend to other random initialization methods, which we corroborate in our experiments.

Various results indicate that controlling the variance is not sufficient to mitigate gradient problems. [9] showed that the empirical variance of gradients grows exponentially with increasing depth, while [10] and [5] showed the same for the empirical variance of the lengths of activations and pre-activations, respectively. [24] demonstrated that with increasing depth, the output distribution has increasingly heavy tails. We add to this line of research by studying kurtosis of the output distribution, which directly relates to its *empirical* variance. Our analysis shows that even if we keep the theoretical variance constant, the empirical variance will tend to zero.

Proper initialization of neural networks is only a prerequisite to ensure fast convergence to a good solution of the given optimization problem. [23] showed that for standard random weight initialization methods, the number of iterations required to converge grows exponentially in depth. [7] reached a similar conclusion, while [15] showed that the convergence speed is independent of depth for the case of orthogonal initialization. However, our work questions the possibility of convergence of very deep randomly initialized networks in practice, even with initialization schemes designed to overcome the problem of large depth, such as orthogonal initialization [22] or GSM initialization [5].

3 Preliminaries

We consider fully connected networks with leaky ReLU nonlinearities. For an input $\mathbf{x} \in \mathbb{R}^{w_0}$, and a neural network with depth $d \in \mathbb{N}$, widths $(w_l)_{l=0}^d \subset \mathbb{N}$, and negative slope $a \in \mathbb{R}$, the output $\mathbf{y}^{(l)} \in \mathbb{R}^{w_l}$ of the lth layer is recursively defined as[1]

$$\mathbf{y}^{(0)} = \mathbf{x}, \quad \mathbf{y}^{(l)} = \mathbf{W}^{(l)} \phi_a(\mathbf{y}^{(l-1)})$$

where for all $l = 1, ..., d$ $\mathbf{W}^{(l)} \in \mathbb{R}^{w_l \times w_{l-1}}$ is a weight matrix and $\phi_a : \mathbb{R} \to \mathbb{R}$ is leaky ReLU with the negative slope parameter $a \in \mathbb{R}$, applied entry-wise

$$\phi_a(x) = \begin{cases} ax, & \text{if } x < 0, \\ x, & \text{otherwise.} \end{cases}$$

We treat $\mathbf{x}$ and $(\mathbf{W}^{(l)})_{l=1}^d$ as random variables and analyze distributional properties of $\mathbf{y}^{(d)}$ with increasing d. We study tHe-initialization method by [11] which takes the entries of each weight matrix $\mathbf{W}^{(l)}$ to be i.i.d. symmetric variables with variance $\frac{2}{w_l(a^2+1)}$. This method preserves several distributional properties of the input random vectors.

Definition 1 (He random vector). *We say that a random vector $\mathbf{x} \in \mathbb{R}^w$ is a He random vector if all variables in $\mathbf{x}$ have mean zero, symmetric[2], uncorrelated, and homoscedastic with some variance σ_x^2.*

---

[1] Throughout the paper, for vectors and matrices we use upper indices to indicate the layer, and lower indices to refer to entries. For scalars, we use the lower indices to indicate the layer. For the function ϕ_a we use the lower index to indicate the negative slope parameter a.

[2] By a symmetric random variable we mean a random variable with a probability distribution symmetric around its mean.

Proposition 1 (He-initialization). *If for all $l = 1, ..., d$ weight matrices $\boldsymbol{W}^{(l)}$ are i.i.d., zero-mean, and symmetric with variance equal to $\frac{2}{w_l(a^2+1)}$, then for an input He random vector $\boldsymbol{x}$ with variance σ_x^2 the output random vector $\boldsymbol{y}^{(d)}$ is a He random vector with variance σ_x^2.*

A proof for Proposition 1 has been given by [11] under the stronger assumption of preservation of independence of vector entries. For simplification, [11] assumed that independence is preserved through the network, but for our analysis it is important to realize that what actually is preserved is uncorrelatedness. We provide a proof with this modification in the supplementary material.

One may ask how to make sure that the properties of He random vector are satisfied at the input. The Proposition 2 below shows that if we include an additional weight matrix before the first activation, it transforms any input random vector to a He random vector.

Proposition 2 (Any random vector can be transformed to a He random vector). *For any finite-variance random vector $\boldsymbol{x} \in \mathbb{R}^w$, if $\boldsymbol{W} \in \mathbb{R}^{w \times w}$ is a random matrix of i.i.d. zero-mean, symmetric variables with finite variance such that $\boldsymbol{W}$ and $\boldsymbol{x}$ are mutually independent, then $\boldsymbol{z} = \boldsymbol{W}\boldsymbol{x}$ is a He random vector with some variance σ_z^2.*

Proof. Consider a specific entry z_i in $\mathbf{z}$, $z_i = \sum_{k=1}^{w} W_{ik}x_k$. For any i, k, W_{ik} is symmetric and zero-mean, and so must be $W_{ik}x_k$. Because z_i is a sum of zero-mean and symmetric random variables, it is zero-mean and symmetric. All entries of $\mathbf{z}$ have the same variance because it is expressed with the same formula, so they are homoscedastic with some variance σ_z^2. Lastly, we will show that z_i, z_j are uncorrelated for any $i, j, i \neq j$. Consider covariance of two entries z_i, z_j

$$\text{Cov}[z_i, z_j] = \mathbb{E}[z_i z_j] - \mathbb{E}[z_i]\mathbb{E}[z_j].$$

Because $\mathbb{E}[z_i]$ is equal to zero, it simplifies to

$$\text{Cov}[z_i, z_j] = \mathbb{E}[z_i z_j] = \mathbb{E}[(\sum_{k=1}^{w} W_{ik}x_k)(\sum_{k=1}^{w} W_{jk}x_k)]$$

$$= \mathbb{E}[\sum_{k_1=1}^{w}\sum_{k_2=1}^{w} W_{ik_1}x_{k_1}W_{jk_2}x_{k_2}] = \sum_{k_1=1}^{w}\sum_{k_2=1}^{w} \mathbb{E}[W_{ik_1}]\mathbb{E}[x_{k_1}W_{jk_2}x_{k_2}] = 0.$$

We will assume that inputs are always He random vector and that networks are initialized according to Proposition 1. Effectively, the outputs for each hidden layer will be He random vectors too.

4 Theory

We present our main theoretical results. We derive the relation between input and output kurtosis in a neural network (Proposition 3) and prove that for bounded-width networks, it goes to infinity with increasing depth (Theorem 1). Here, kurtosis of a random variable x is defined as $Kurt[x] = \mathbb{E}[\frac{(x-\mathbb{E}[x])^4}{Var[x]^2}]$. We will analyze the case with $\mathbb{E}[x] = 0$ which simplifies it to $Kurt[x] = \frac{1}{Var[x]^2}\mathbb{E}[x^4]$.

First, we prove Proposition 3 in which we will derive the exact recursive formula for the dynamics of kurtosis over consecutive layers. The derived formula tracks two statistical properties in a linear matrix difference equation: kurtosis and covariance of squared outputs. We take the mild assumption, which is satisfied with Proposition 2 that the covariance of squared outputs is equal for any two outputs.

In the proof of Proposition 3, we will use two lemmas 1 and 2 that are given first.

Lemma 1. *Let x be a zero-mean, symmetric random variable with $Var[x] = \sigma_x^2$ and $Kurt[x] = \kappa_x$. Then $\mathbb{E}[\phi_a^4(x)] = \frac{(a^4+1)}{2}\sigma_x^4\kappa_x$.*

Proof.

$$\mathbb{E}[\phi_a^4(x)] = \int_{-\infty}^{\infty} \phi_a^4(x)p(x)dx = \int_{-\infty}^{0} a^4x^4 p(x)dx + \int_{0}^{\infty} x^4 p(x)dx$$

$$= \frac{1}{2}a^4 \int_{-\infty}^{\infty} x^4 p(x)dx + \frac{1}{2}\int_{-\infty}^{\infty} x^4 p(x)dx = \frac{a^4+1}{2}\mathbb{E}[x^4] = \frac{a^4+1}{2}\sigma_x^4\kappa_x.$$

Lemma 2. *Let x, y be identically distributed, uncorrelated, zero-mean, symmetric random variables with variances σ_x^2, kurtoses κ_x and $Cov[x^2, y^2] = c$. Then $\mathbb{E}[\phi_a^2(x)\phi_a^2(y)] = \frac{(a^2+1)^2}{4}(\sigma_x^4 + c)$.*

Proof.

$$\mathbb{E}[\phi_a^2(x)\phi_a^2(y)] = \int_{\mathbb{R}^2} \phi_a^2(x)\phi_a^2(y)p(x,y)dxdy$$

$$= \int_{\mathbb{R}_+^2} x^2 y^2 p(x,y)dxdy + 2a^2 \int_{\mathbb{R}_+ \times \mathbb{R}_-} x^2 y^2 p(x,y)dxdy$$

$$+ a^4 \int_{\mathbb{R}_-^2} x^2 y^2 p(x,y)dxdy = \frac{1}{4}(a^2+1)^2 \mathbb{E}[x^2 y^2]$$

Recall that $Cov[x^2, y^2] = \mathbb{E}[x^2 y^2] - \mathbb{E}[x^2]\mathbb{E}[y^2]$ so $\mathbb{E}[x^2 y^2] = Cov[x^2, y^2] + \mathbb{E}[x^2]\mathbb{E}[y^2]$. We get as a result

$$\mathbb{E}[\phi_a^2(x)\phi_a^2(y)] = \frac{(a^2+1)^2}{4}(\sigma_x^4 + c).$$

Proposition 3. *Consider a network that is He-initialized with a distribution that has kurtosis κ_w and that has output random vectors $\boldsymbol{y}^{(l)}$ at every layer l with variance σ_x^2. Let*

$$c_l = Cov[(y_i^{(l)})^2, (y_j^{(l)})^2]$$

be the covariance between any two squared entries from $\boldsymbol{y}^{(l)}$ and let $\kappa_l = Kurt[y_i^{(l)}]$ be the kurtosis of every entry i in $\boldsymbol{y}^{(l)}$, then the kurtoses of consecutive layers are recursively related through the linear matrix difference equation

$$\boldsymbol{k}^{(l+1)} = \boldsymbol{A}^{(l)} \boldsymbol{k}^{(l)}$$

where $\boldsymbol{k}^{(l)} = [\kappa_l, c_l, 1]^T$ and

$$\boldsymbol{A}^{(l)} = \begin{bmatrix} \frac{2(a^4+1)\kappa_w}{w_l(a^2+1)^2} & \frac{3(w_l-1)}{w_l \sigma_x^4} & \frac{3(w_l-1)}{w_l} \\ \frac{2(a^4+1)\sigma_x^4}{w_l(a^2+1)^2} & \frac{w_l-1}{w_l} & -\frac{\sigma_x^4}{w_l} \\ 0 & 0 & 1 \end{bmatrix}.$$

Consequently, the relation between the input kurtosis and the output kurtosis at depth $d+1$ is

$$\boldsymbol{k}^{(d+1)} = \left(\prod_{l=0}^{d} \boldsymbol{A}^{(d-l)} \right) \boldsymbol{k}^{(0)}.$$

Proof. We will derive the formula for κ_{l+1}, then for c_{l+1}. We have $\mathbb{E}[y_i^{(l+1)}] = 0$, $Var[y_i^{(l+1)}] = \sigma_x^2$, so $\kappa_{l+1} = Kurt[y_i^{(l+1)}] = \frac{1}{\sigma_x^4}\mathbb{E}[(y_i^{(l+1)})^4]$. We can expand $\mathbb{E}[(y_i^{(l+1)})^4] = \mathbb{E}[(\sum_{j=1}^{w_l} W_{ij}^{(l+1)} \phi_a(y_j^{(l)}))^4]$ using the multinomial theorem. Because the weight matrix entries are i.i.d., zero-mean and symmetric, the terms with the odd powers vanish. We get

$$\mathbb{E}[(y_i^{(l+1)})^4] = \sum_{j=1}^{w_l} \mathbb{E}[(W_{ij}^{(l+1)} \phi_a(y_j^{(l)}))^4]$$
$$+ \sum_{\substack{j,k=1 \\ j \neq k}}^{w_l} \binom{4}{2,2} \mathbb{E}[(W_{ij}^{(l+1)} \phi_a(y_j^{(l)}))^2 (W_{ik}^{(l+1)} \phi_a(y_k^{(l)}))^2].$$

Using Lemma 1, we find that

$$\mathbb{E}[(W_{ij}^{(l+1)} \phi_a(y_j^{(l)}))^4] = \frac{4}{w_l^2(a^2+1)^2} \kappa_w \frac{(a^4+1)}{2} \sigma_x^4 \kappa_l = \frac{2(a^4+1)}{w_l^2(a^2+1)^2} \kappa_w \sigma_x^4 \kappa_l.$$

We can get a closed-form formula for $\mathbb{E}[(W_{ij}^{(l+1)} \phi_a(y_j^{(l)}))^2 (W_{ik}^{(l+1)} \phi_a(y_k^{(l)}))^2]$ using Lemma 2

$$\mathbb{E}[(W_{ij}^{(l+1)} \phi_a(y_j^{(l)}))^2 (W_{ik}^{(l+1)} \phi_a(y_k^{(l)}))^2] =$$
$$= \left(\frac{2}{w_l(a^2+1)} \right)^2 \frac{(a^2+1)^2}{4} (\sigma_x^4 + c_l) = \frac{\sigma_x^4 + c_l}{w_l^2}.$$

Putting the two above to the multinomial expansion of $\mathbb{E}[(y_i^{(l+1)})^4]$ given in the beginning, we get

$$\mathbb{E}[(y_i^{(l+1)})^4] = \frac{2(a^4+1)}{w_l(a^2+1)^2}\kappa_w \sigma_x^4 \kappa_l + 6\binom{w_l}{2}\frac{\sigma_x^4+c_l}{w_l^2}$$

$$= \frac{2(a^4+1)}{w_l(a^2+1)^2}\kappa_w \sigma_x^4 \kappa_l + 3w_l(w_l-1)\frac{\sigma_x^4+c_l}{w_l^2}$$

Finally, we should divide $\mathbb{E}[(y_i^{(l+1)})^4]$ by σ_x^4 to get

$$\kappa_{l+1} = \frac{2(a^4+1)\kappa_w}{w_l(a^2+1)^2}\kappa_l + \frac{3(w_l-1)}{w_l\sigma_x^4}c_l + \frac{3(w_l-1)}{w_l}.$$

Next, consider $c_{l+1} = Cov[(y_i^{(l+1)})^2, (y_j^{(l+1)})^2]$ for any $i,j, i \neq j$

$$c_{l+1} = Cov[(y_i^{(l+1)})^2, (y_j^{(l+1)})^2] = \mathbb{E}[(y_i^{(l+1)})^2(y_j^{(l+1)})^2] - \mathbb{E}[(y_i^{(l+1)})^2]\mathbb{E}[(y_j^{(l+1)})^2]$$

$$= \mathbb{E}[(\sum_{k=1}^{w_l} W_{ik}^{(l+1)}\phi_a(y_k^{(l)}))^2(\sum_{k=1}^{w_l} W_{jk}^{(l+1)}\phi_a(y_k^{(l)}))^2] - \sigma_x^4$$

$$= \frac{4}{w_l^2(a^2+1)^2}\sum_{k_1=1}^{w_l}\sum_{k_2=1}^{w_l}\mathbb{E}[\phi_a^2(y_{k_1}^{(l)})\phi_a^2(y_{k_2}^{(l)})] - \sigma_x^4$$

where the sum $\sum_{k_1=1}^{w_l}\sum_{k_2=1}^{w_l}\mathbb{E}[\phi_a^2(y_{k_1}^{(l)})\phi_a^2(y_{k_2}^{(l)})]$ is

$$\sum_{k_1=1}^{w_l}\sum_{k_2=1}^{w_l}\mathbb{E}[\phi_a^2(y_{k_1}^{(l)})\phi_a^2(y_{k_2}^{(l)})] = \sum_{\substack{k_2=1 \\ k_2 \neq k_1}}^{w_l}\frac{(a^2+1)^2}{4}(\sigma_x^4+c_l) + \sum_{k=1}^{w_l}\frac{a^4+1}{2}\sigma_x^4\kappa_l$$

$$= \frac{w_l(w_l-1)(a^2+1)^2}{4}(\sigma_x^4+c_l) + \frac{w_l(a^4+1)}{2}\sigma_x^4\kappa_l.$$

Putting it all together, we get

$$c_{l+1} = \frac{2(a^4+1)\sigma_x^4}{w_l(a^2+1)^2}\kappa_l + \frac{w_l-1}{w_l}c_l - \frac{\sigma_x^4}{w_l}.$$

and $\mathbf{k}^{(l+1)} = [\kappa_{l+1}, c_{l+1}, 1]^T$ is of the desired form.

Now, we will show in Theorem 1, that with the dynamics derived in Proposition 3, for any valid $\mathbf{k}^{(0)}$, κ_d will grow to infinity. To this end, we will first prove three lemmas that describe the properties of matrices $\mathbf{A}^{(l)}$ and their products. In Lemma 3, we will show that any product of such matrices is of a form parameterized with four positive parameters. Next, in Lemma 4, we will show that any matrix $\mathbf{A}^{(l)}$ has a positive eigenvalue that is strictly larger than 1. The proof of

Lemma 4 uses the Perron theorem, which we provide with a reference to a proof in the appendix in the supplement. We combine these two properties in Lemma 5 to show that for any $\mathbf{A} = \mathbf{A}^{(l)}$ raised to a power m, all its positive parameters will tend to infinity with $m \to \infty$ and so its norm tends to infinity. We use this property in the proof of Theorem 1.

Lemma 3. *Consider the product of matrices* $\mathbf{B} = \prod_{l=0}^{d} \mathbf{A}^{(d-l)}$ *as given in Proposition 3, with $w > 1$. $\mathbf{B}$ is of the form*

$$\mathbf{B} = \begin{bmatrix} \alpha & \frac{\beta}{\sigma_x^4} & \beta \\ \gamma \sigma_x^4 & \delta & \sigma_x^4(\delta - 1) \\ 0 & 0 & 1 \end{bmatrix} \quad (1)$$

with $\gamma > 0$, $\alpha \geq \gamma$, $\delta > 0$, $\beta \geq \delta$.

Proof. We prove the lemma by induction on d. For $d = 0$ we have $\mathbf{B} = \mathbf{A}^{(0)}$, which is satisfied by the definition of $\mathbf{A}^{(0)}$. Assume that (1) is satisfied for some $d \in \mathbb{N}$. Denote $\mathbf{C} = \prod_{l=0}^{d} \mathbf{A}^{(d-l)}$ and $\mathbf{B} = \mathbf{A}^{(d+1)} \mathbf{C}$. We can write

$$\mathbf{A}^{(d+1)} = \begin{bmatrix} \alpha_1 & \frac{\beta_1}{\sigma_x^4} & \beta_1 \\ \gamma_1 \sigma_x^4 & \delta_1 & \sigma_x^4(\delta_1 - 1) \\ 0 & 0 & 1 \end{bmatrix},$$

$$\mathbf{C} = \begin{bmatrix} \alpha_2 & \frac{\beta_2}{\sigma_x^4} & \beta_2 \\ \gamma_2 \sigma_x^4 & \delta_2 & \sigma_x^4(\delta_2 - 1) \\ 0 & 0 & 1 \end{bmatrix}$$

with $\forall_{i=1,2}$, $\gamma_i > 0$, $\alpha_i \geq \gamma_i$, $\delta_i > 0$, $\beta_i \geq \delta_i$. $\mathbf{A}^{(d+1)} \mathbf{C}$ is

$$\begin{bmatrix} \alpha_1 \alpha_2 + \beta_1 \gamma_2 & \frac{\alpha_1 \beta_2 + \beta_1 \delta_2}{\sigma_x^4} & \alpha_1 \beta_2 + \beta_1 \delta_2 \\ (\gamma_1 \alpha_2 + \delta_1 \gamma_2)\sigma_x^4 & \gamma_1 \beta_2 + \delta_1 \delta_2 & \sigma_x^4(\gamma_1 \beta_2 + \delta_1 \delta_2 - 1) \\ 0 & 0 & 1 \end{bmatrix}.$$

If we set $\alpha = \alpha_1 \alpha_2 + \beta_1 \gamma_2$, $\beta = \alpha_1 \beta_2 + \beta_1 \delta_2$, $\gamma = \gamma_1 \alpha_2 + \delta_1 \gamma_2$, $\delta = \gamma_1 \beta_2 + \delta_1 \delta_2$, we get that $\mathbf{B} = \mathbf{A}^{(l+1)} \mathbf{C}$ is of the desired form with

$$\gamma = \gamma_1 \alpha_2 + \delta_1 \gamma_2 > 0, \quad \alpha = \alpha_1 \alpha_2 + \beta_1 \gamma_2 \geq \gamma > 0,$$
$$\delta = \gamma_1 \beta_2 + \delta_1 \delta_2 > 0, \quad \beta = \alpha_1 \beta_2 + \beta_1 \delta_2 \geq \delta > 0.$$

Lemma 4. *The largest eigenvalue of any matrix $\mathbf{A}^{(l)}$ from Proposition 3 is larger than 1.*

Proof. Consider the matrix $\mathbf{A}^{(l)}$ for some $l = 0, ..., d$. Its characteristic polynomial is of the form

$$\det(\mathbf{A}^{(l)} - \lambda I) = (\lambda^2 + b\lambda + c)(1 - \lambda)$$

where $\lambda^2 + b\lambda + c$ is the characteristic polynomial of a matrix $\mathbf{A}_-^{(l)}$ equal to $\mathbf{A}^{(l)}$ but with row 3 and column 3 removed. $\mathbf{A}_-^{(l)}$ is positive and by the Perron theorem it has two distinct real eigenvalues λ_{max} and λ_{min} such that $\lambda_{max} > 0$ and $\lambda_{max} > |\lambda_{min}|$. We will show that $\lambda_{max} > 1$.

Express λ_{max} using trace and determinant of $\mathbf{A}_-^{(l)}$, $\lambda_{max} = \frac{\text{tr}(\mathbf{A}_-^{(l)}) + \sqrt{\text{tr}^2(\mathbf{A}_-^{(l)}) - 4\det(\mathbf{A}_-^{(l)})}}{2}$, with $\text{tr}(\mathbf{A}_-^{(l)})$ and $\det(\mathbf{A}_-^{(l)})$:

$$\text{tr}(\mathbf{A}_-^{(l)}) = \frac{2(a^4+1)\kappa_w}{w_l(a^2+1)^2} - \frac{1}{w_l} + 1,$$

$$\det(\mathbf{A}_-^{(l)}) = \frac{2(a^4+1)(w_l-1)(\kappa_w-3)}{w_l^2(a^2+1)^2}.$$

We consider two cases for $\text{tr}(\mathbf{A}_-^{(l)})$ and show that in both of them $\lambda_{max} > 1$. If $\text{tr}(\mathbf{A}_-^{(l)}) \geq 2$, then $\lambda_{max} > 1$ because $\lambda_{max} > \frac{\text{tr}(\mathbf{A}_-^{(l)})}{2}$. Otherwise, if $1 \leq \text{tr}(\mathbf{A}_-^{(l)}) < 2$, then

$$\lambda_{max}(\mathbf{A}_-^{(l)}) > 1$$
$$\Leftrightarrow \sqrt{\text{tr}^2(\mathbf{A}_-^{(l)}) - 4\det(\mathbf{A}_-^{(l)})} > 2 - \text{tr}(\mathbf{A}_-^{(l)})$$
$$\Leftrightarrow \text{tr}^2(\mathbf{A}_-^{(l)}) - 4\det(\mathbf{A}_-^{(l)}) > 4 - 4\text{tr}(\mathbf{A}_-^{(l)}) + \text{tr}^2(\mathbf{A}_-^{(l)})$$
$$\Leftrightarrow \text{tr}(\mathbf{A}_-^{(l)}) > \det(\mathbf{A}_-^{(l)}) + 1$$

which is always satisfied, because for $\kappa_w < 3$, we have $\det(\mathbf{A}_-^{(l)}) + 1 < 1 \leq \text{tr}(\mathbf{A}_-^{(l)})$, and for $\kappa_w \geq 3$

$$\det(\mathbf{A}_-^{(l)}) = \frac{2(a^4+1)(w_l-1)(\kappa_w-3)}{w_l^2(a^2+1)^2}$$
$$< \frac{2(a^4+1)(\kappa_w-3)}{w_l(a^2+1)^2} < \frac{2(a^4+1)(\kappa_w-1)}{w_l(a^2+1)^2} \leq \text{tr}(\mathbf{A}_-^{(l)}) - 1.$$

This proves that $\lambda_{max} > 1$.

Lemma 5. *Consider the matrix $\mathbf{A} = \mathbf{A}^{(l)}$ from Proposition 3 raised to the power m. If $m \to \infty$, then $\alpha_m, \beta_m, \gamma_m, \delta_m$ from the representation of $\mathbf{A}^m$ in the form from Lemma 3 go to infinity.*

Proof. By Lemma 4 $\lambda_{max}(\mathbf{A}) > 1$ so $\lim_{m \to \infty} ||\mathbf{A}^m|| = \infty$, so it must be that at least one of $\alpha_m, \beta_m, \gamma_m, \delta_m$ goes to infinity. Consider four cases:

1. Assume α_m tends to infinity. From the proof of Lemma 3, $\gamma_{m+1} = \gamma_1 \alpha_m + \delta_1 \gamma_m > \gamma_1 \alpha_m$, so γ_m must tend to infinity. In the same way, $\delta_{m+1} = \gamma_m \beta_1 + \delta_m \delta_2 > \gamma_m \beta_1$, so δ_m must tend to infinity too. Because $\beta_m > \delta_m$, β_m must tend to infinity as well.

2. Assume β_m tends to infinity. From the proof of Lemma 3, $\alpha_{m+1} = \alpha_m \alpha_1 + \beta_m \gamma_1$, so α_m must tend to infinity, and so γ_m and δ_m as shown above in 1.
3. Assume γ_m tends to infinity. Then α_m must tend to infinity because $\alpha_m \geq \gamma_m$ for any m, and so β_m and δ_m must tend to infinity as shown above in 1.
4. Assume δ_m tends to infinity. Then β_m must tend to infinity because $\beta_m \geq \delta_m$ for any m, and so α_m and γ_m must tend to infinity as shown above in 2.

Theorem 1. *For any He-initialized network with widths bounded from below by 2 and from above by some w_{max}, the output-distribution kurtosis grows to infinity with increasing depth for any input He random vector.*

Proof. We can express the vector $\mathbf{k}^{(d+1)}$ at depth $d+1$ as $\mathbf{k}^{(d+1)} = \mathbf{B}^{(d)} \mathbf{k}^{(0)}$ with $\mathbf{B}^{(d)} = \prod_{l=0}^{d} \mathbf{A}^{(d-l)}$ parameterized by $\alpha_d, \beta_d, \gamma_d, \delta_d$ from Lemma 3. We can write that

$$\kappa_{d+1} = \alpha_d \kappa_0 + \frac{\beta_d}{\sigma_x^4} c_0 + \beta_d.$$

Note that it must be that $c_0 \geq -\sigma_x^4$, because

$$c_0 = Cov[(y_i^{(0)})^2 (y_j^{(0)})^2]$$
$$= \mathbb{E}[(y_i^{(0)})^2 (y_j^{(0)})^2] - \mathbb{E}[y_i^{(0)}]^2 \mathbb{E}[y_j^{(0)}]^2 = \mathbb{E}[(y_i^{(0)})^2 (y_j^{(0)})^2] - \sigma_x^4 \geq -\sigma_x^4.$$

We can consider the output of the first layer as the actual input, so we can even say that $c_0 = \sigma_x^4(-1+\epsilon)$ for some $\epsilon > 0$, because $c_1 = \gamma_1 \sigma_x^4 \kappa_0 + \delta_1 c_0 + \sigma_x^4(\delta_1 - 1) > \gamma_1 \sigma_x^4 \kappa_0 - \sigma_x^4$ for some $\gamma_1 > 0$ and $\delta_1 > 0$.
We can write then that

$$\kappa_{d+1} = \alpha_d \kappa_0 + \frac{\beta_d}{\sigma_x^4} c_0 + \beta_d = \alpha_d \kappa_0 + \beta_d \epsilon.$$

To know that κ_{d+1} goes to infinity with $d \to \infty$, it is enough to show that $\lim_{d \to \infty} ||\mathbf{B}^{(d)}|| = \infty$, because it would imply that one of $\alpha_d, \beta_d, \gamma_d$ or δ_d goes to infinity, in which case κ_{d+1} goes to infinity. We will show that $\lim_{d \to \infty} \lambda_{max}(\mathbf{B}^{(d)}) = \infty$, which implies that $\lim_{d \to \infty} ||\mathbf{B}^{(d)}|| = \infty$. Because for any two matrices $\mathbf{M}_1$ and $\mathbf{M}_2$ $\lambda_{max}(\mathbf{M}_1 \mathbf{M}_2) = \lambda_{max}(\mathbf{M}_2 \mathbf{M}_1)$, we can consider λ_{max} of a rearranged matrix product

$$\lambda_{max}(\mathbf{B}^{(d)}) = \lambda_{max}\left(\prod_{l=0}^{d} \mathbf{A}^{(l)}\right) = \lambda_{max}\left(\prod_{w=2}^{w_{max}} \mathbf{A}_w^{m_w}\right),$$

where $\mathbf{A}_w$ denotes a matrix $\mathbf{A}^{(l)}$ from Proposition 3 for a specific width w, and m_w the number of occurrences of such matrices until depth d. With $d \to \infty$, there is at least one w for which $m_w \to \infty$. For such widths w, $\mathbf{A}_w^{m_w}$ behaves according to Lemma 5. The product $\prod_{w=2}^{w_{max}} \mathbf{A}_w^{m_w}$ consists of a finite number of matrices of the form from Lemma 3 and at least one matrix with all positive parameters from Lemma 3 going to infinity. In effect, the positive parameters from Lemma 3 for this product goes to infinity, which implies that $\lambda_{max}(\prod_{w=2}^{w_{max}} \mathbf{A}_w^{m_w})$ goes to infinity. As a result, with $d \to \infty$, $\lambda_{max}(\mathbf{B}^{(d)}) \to \infty$.

We set the width to satisfy $w > 1$, but the same can be proven by allowing for $w = 1$. This requires an additional assumption that either $|a| \neq 1$ or $\kappa_w \neq 1$.

5 Vanishing Empirical Variance

Theorem 1 has important consequences for He-initialized networks. That the kurtosis grows to infinity implies that, for any finite sample size, the observed empirical variance will converge in probability to zero. Combined with the other properties preserved through He-initialization, this practically means that virtually all outputs map arbitrarily close to zero for a sufficiently deep network. And this happens despite the theoretical variance being constant.

Let us explain this implication more formally.[3] For variance of the empirical variance S_n^2 and the kurtosis, it holds that $Var[S_n^2] = \left(\kappa - \frac{n-3}{n-1}\right)\frac{\sigma^4}{n}$, where n is the sample size, κ is the kurtosis and σ^2 is the theoretical variance. For large n, we can approximate distribution of the ratio $\frac{S_n^2}{\sigma^2}$ by $\frac{\chi^2(DF_n)}{DF_n}$, where $DF_n = \frac{2\sigma^4}{Var[S_n^2]} = \frac{2n}{\kappa - \frac{n-3}{n-1}}$. This can alternatively be expressed in terms of the gamma distribution $\frac{S_n^2}{\sigma^2} \sim \Gamma(k = \frac{DF_n}{2}, \theta = \frac{2}{DF_n})$. With kurtosis κ growing to infinity, DF_n shrinks to zero for any $n \in \mathbb{N}$, so the shape parameter k shrinks to zero and the scale parameter $\theta = \frac{1}{k}$ grows to infinity. The probability density function for this distribution is given as $f(x; k, \theta) = f(x; k, \frac{1}{k}) = \frac{x^{k-1}e^{-kx}k^k}{\Gamma(k)}$. For any $x > 0$, with $k \to 0$, this converges to zero because the numerator converges to a constant and the denominator grows to infinity. The speed of convergence is faster for large x.

When training sufficiently deep networks on machines with finite precision using finite datasets, we will observe outputs to be zeroed out. As a result, propagated gradients will be zeros and the weights of the network will remain at their initialization values.

6 Experiments

Theorem 1 shows that He-initialization suffers from the vanishing empirical variance problem. We now hypothesize that problems with empirical variance concern all fully random initialization methods that initialize weight matrices with off-diagonal entries, because this induces increased dependence of outputs. If the theoretical variance is kept constant or decreases, the empirical variance vanishes, otherwise it explodes. Here, we present empirical evidence supporting

---

[3] We refer to [21] for a detailed treatment and proofs.

this hypothesis. We verify it experimentally for five state-of-the-art random initialization methods: Glorot by [8], He by [11], orthogonal by [22], GSM by [5], and MetaInit by [6]. We also show that ZerO proposed by [27] is superior to all these methods in very deep regimes.

All experiments are performed on constant-width ReLU networks on MNIST [18] and CIFAR10 [17]. The inputs are preprocessed so that the means of all channels are zero and the variances are one. The experiments were run on a machine with a single Intel i7-11850H CPU. The code is available at https://github.com/Grzejdziok/vanishing-empirical-variance.

6.1 The Necessity of Small Kurtosis for He-Initialization

We performed experiments to illustrate the negative impact of high output kurtosis at initialization on training. In the case of He-initialization, it is possible to calculate the theoretical output kurtosis recursively applying the formula from Proposition 4.3, given κ_0 and c_0 for the input He random vector.

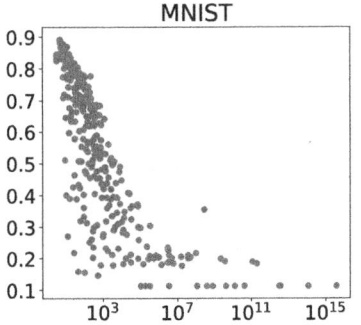 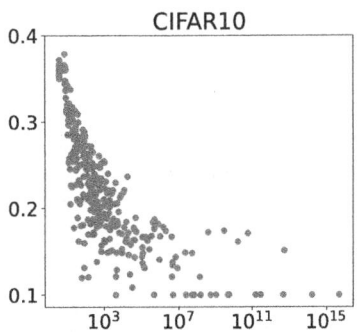

Fig. 1. Test accuracy after 500 gradient steps vs output distribution kurtosis at initialization for networks of varying widths, depths, and initialization distributions trained on MNIST and CIFAR10. Results for 330 experiments per dataset.

We estimated the values for MNIST and CIFAR10 using 10^7 random samples. For MNIST we got $c_0 = 0.71$, $\kappa_0 = 3.95$ and for CIFAR10 we got $c_0 = 0.10$, $\kappa_0 = 3.28$. We trained networks of various depths and widths to observe the relation between different values of kurtosis at initialization and test accuracy. We trained constant-width He-initialized networks twice for each of all tuples (width, depth, initialization distribution) for widths and depths from 5 to 50 with step of 5, and the weight initialization distributions Bernoulli ($\kappa_w = 1$), uniform ($\kappa_w = 1.8$), normal ($\kappa_w = 3$). We used Adam optimizer [16] with learning rate of 10^{-4}, $\beta_1 = 0.9$, $\beta_2 = 0.999$ and no weight decay.

We plotted test accuracy after 500 gradient steps over output kurtosis at initialization. The results are given in Fig. 1. From the plots, we can see that networks with large output kurtosis at initialization cannot be effectively trained.

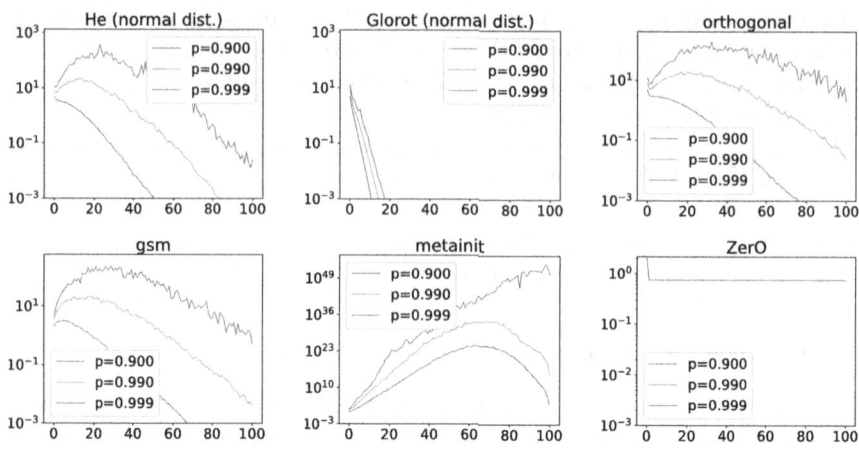

Fig. 2. Estimated quantiles of the output empirical variance distribution over depth given the whole CIFAR10. The plots use a logarithmic scale. ZerO is deterministic, so all its quantiles are equal.

6.2 SOTA Initialization and Empirical Variance Problem

To see whether the problems with empirical variance occur for other state-of-the-art initialization methods, we performed an experiment to estimate the empirical variance distribution at the output.

For all random initialization methods considered, we initialized 10,000 neural networks (1,000 for MetaInit) of constant width $w = 10$ and depth $d = 100$ and calculated the empirical variance of a single output given the whole CIFAR10 training set as input. We then calculated quantiles at 0.9, 0.99, and 0.999 over all different initializations and plotted these against layer depth in Fig. 2.

We observe that for all random initialization methods except MetaInit 90% networks will have empirical variance lower than 10^{-3} after 80 layers and all quantiles monotonously decrease after 40 layers. For MetaInit, empirical variances explode. We observe a different behavior for ZerO, which initializes most layers to identities. It keeps the empirical variance constant after the first layer.

6.3 Empirical Variance Problem: Practical Significance

To evaluate the practical significance of the problems with empirical variances observed in the previous section, we trained neural networks of varying depths on CIFAR10 and evaluated their test accuracy after 500 gradient steps. We used Adam [16] as an optimizer with $\beta_1 = 0.9$, and $\beta_2 = 0.999$ without weight decay. We trained networks for two widths: 1) width 10 and depths from 0 to 100 with a step of 10 and learning rate of 10^{-4}, 2) width 200 and depths from 0 to 500 with a step of 50 and learning rate of 10^{-5}.

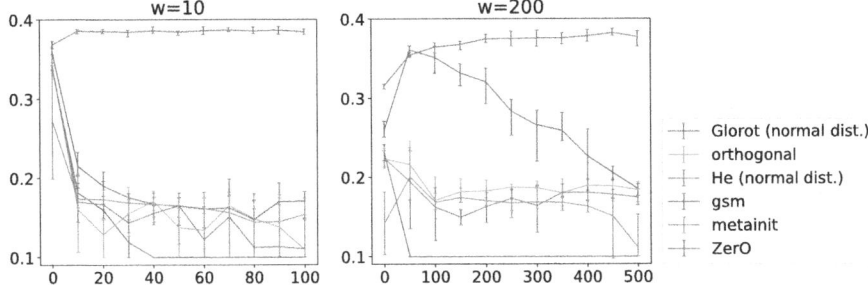

Fig. 3. Test accuracy after 500 gradient steps over network depth for fully connected constant-width ReLU networks trained on CIFAR10. The curves indicate the means and the bars indicate the minima and maxima over 5 repetitions.

The results are given in Fig. 3. We can see that all random initialization methods fail to train in very deep regimes and are inferior to ZerO, which does not suffer from the problems with empirical variance.

7 Discussion

By analyzing the dynamics of the output's kurtosis in He-initialized networks, we identified two new problems in very deep neural networks: the exploding kurtosis and the vanishing empirical variance problems. Our experiments show that issues with exploding or vanishing empirical variance concern not only He-initialization but also other state-of-the-art random initialization methods such as Glorot [8], GSM [5], or MetaInit [6]. All of these methods fail to train very deep networks, while our experiments show that with deterministic initialization methods like ZerO [27], successful training is possible.

Our contribution is primarily theoretical and, in our experiments, we analyzed a toy architecture of constant-width fully connected ReLU networks that illustrated our theoretical results. However, we hypothesize that our main result about exploding kurtosis extends to setups that are commonly used in practice, like transformers or convolutional networks. The addition of skip connections cannot stop the growth of kurtosis because kurtosis explodes even for networks without activation function, which is equivalent to setting the negative slope parameter a to 1 in our analysis. Moreover, convolutional layers will induce even more dependency of layer outputs due to parameter sharing, so we expect the output kurtosis to grow even faster.

It is unclear whether using activation functions other than ReLU could mitigate this issue. Bounded activation functions like tanh or sigmoid reduce the theoretical variance of their inputs, yet their impact on kurtosis is unclear.

A Proof of Proposition 3.2

We first prove the following lemma.

Lemma 6. *Let x be a zero-mean, symmetric random variable with $Var[x] = \sigma_x^2$. Then $\mathbb{E}[\phi_a^2(x)] = \frac{(a^2+1)}{2}\sigma_x^2$.*

Proof.

$$\mathbb{E}[\phi_a^2(x)] = \int_{-\infty}^{\infty} \phi_a^2(x)p(x)dx = \int_{-\infty}^{0} a^2 x^2 p(x)dx + \int_{0}^{\infty} x^2 p(x)dx$$

$$= a^2 \int_{-\infty}^{0} x^2 p(x)dx + \int_{0}^{\infty} x^2 p(x)dx = \frac{1}{2}a^2 \int_{-\infty}^{\infty} x^2 p(x)dx + \frac{1}{2}\int_{-\infty}^{\infty} x^2 p(x)dx$$

$$= \frac{a^2+1}{2}\sigma_x^2$$

Below, we prove Proposition 3.2.

Proposition 4 (He-initialization). *If for all $l = 1,...,d$ weight matrices $\mathbf{W}^{(l)}$ are i.i.d., zero-mean, and symmetric with variance equal to $\frac{2}{w_l(a^2+1)}$, then for an input He random vector $\mathbf{x}$ with variance σ_x^2 the output random vector $\mathbf{y}^{(d)}$ is a He random vector with variance σ_x^2.*

Proof. Consider a He random vector $\mathbf{x}$ with variance σ_x^2 as input. We prove the proposition by induction on d starting from the base case of $d = 0$ which is satisfied by assumptions on the input vector. Assume that it holds for some l. For $l + 1$, we have $\mathbf{y}^{(l+1)} = \mathbf{W}^{(l+1)}\phi_a(\mathbf{y}^{(l)})$. Consider a specific entry $y_k^{(l+1)} = \sum_{i=1}^{w_l} W_{ki}^{(l+1)}\phi_a(y_i^{(l)})$. It is symmetric as it is a sum of symmetric random variables. As it is a sum of uncorrelated variables, its variance is sum of variances of the summands

$$Var[y_k^{(l+1)}] = \sum_{i=1}^{w_l} Var[W_{ki}^{(l+1)}\phi_a(y_i^{(l)})]$$

$$= \sum_{i=1}^{w_l} \mathbb{E}[(W_{ki}^{(l+1)})^2]\mathbb{E}[\phi_a^2(y_i^{(l)})] - \mathbb{E}[W_{ki}^{(l+1)}]^2 \mathbb{E}[\phi_a(y_i^{(l)})]^2$$

$$= \sum_{i=1}^{w_l} Var[W_{ki}^{(l+1)}]\frac{(a^2+1)}{2}\sigma_x^2 = \sum_{i=1}^{w_l} \frac{2}{(a^2+1)w_l}\frac{(a^2+1)}{2}\sigma_x^2$$

$$= \sum_{i=1}^{w_l} \frac{\sigma_x^2}{w_l} = \sigma_x^2.$$

Lastly, consider $Cov[y_k^{(l+1)}, y_j^{(l+1)}]$ for $k \neq j$

$$\begin{aligned}
Cov[y_k^{(l+1)}, y_j^{(l+1)}] &= \mathbb{E}[y_k^{(l+1)} y_j^{(l+1)}] - \mathbb{E}[y_k^{(l+1)}]\mathbb{E}[y_j^{(l+1)}] \\
&= \mathbb{E}[(\sum_{i=1}^{w_l} W_{ki}^{(l+1)} \phi_a(y_i^{(l)}))(\sum_{i=1}^{w_l} W_{ji}^{(l+1)} \phi_a(y_i^{(l)}))] \\
&= \mathbb{E}[\sum_{i_0=1}^{w_l} \sum_{i_1=1}^{w_l} W_{ki_0}^{(l+1)} \phi_a(y_{i_0}^{(l)}) W_{ji_1}^{(l+1)} \phi_a(y_{i_1}^{(l)})] \\
&= \sum_{i_0=1}^{w_l} \sum_{i_1=1}^{w_l} \mathbb{E}[W_{ki_0}^{(l+1)} \phi_a(y_{i_0}^{(l)}) W_{ji_1}^{(l+1)} \phi_a(y_{i_1}^{(l)})] \\
&= \sum_{i_0=1}^{w_l} \sum_{i_1=1}^{w_l} \mathbb{E}[W_{ki_0}^{(l+1)}] \mathbb{E}[\phi_a(y_{i_0}^{(l)}) W_{ji_1}^{(l+1)} \phi_a(y_{i_1}^{(l)})] = 0.
\end{aligned}$$

So all entries in $\mathbf{y}_{l+1}$ are uncorrelated.

B Perron Theorem

We provide the Perron theorem as given in [14]. We refer to this book for further details and proofs.

Theorem 2 (Perron). *Let $\mathbf{A}$ be a $n \times n$ matrix which is irreducible and non-negative and $n \geq 2$. Let $\rho(\mathbf{A})$ denote the spectral radius of $\mathbf{A}$. Then:*

1. *$\rho(\mathbf{A}) > 0$,*
2. *$\rho(\mathbf{A})$ is an algebraically simple eigenvalue of A,*
3. *there is a unique real vector $\mathbf{x}$ such that $\mathbf{A}\mathbf{x} = \rho(\mathbf{A})\mathbf{x}$ and $x_1 + x_2 + ... + x_n = 1$; this vector is positive,*
4. *there is a unique real vector $\mathbf{y}$ such that $\mathbf{y}^T \mathbf{A} = \mathbf{y}^T \rho(\mathbf{A})$ and $y_1 + y_2 + ... + y_n = 1$; this vector is positive,*
5. *$|\lambda| < \rho(\mathbf{A})$ for every eigenvalue λ of $\mathbf{A}$ such that $\lambda \neq \rho(\mathbf{A})$,*
6. *$(\rho(\mathbf{A})^{-1}\mathbf{A})^m \to \mathbf{x}\mathbf{y}^T$ as $m \to \infty$.*

References

1. Bachlechner, T., Majumder, B.P., Mao, H., Cottrell, G., McAuley, J.: Rezero is all you need: fast convergence at large depth. In: de Campos, C., Maathuis, M.H. (eds.) Proceedings of the Thirty-Seventh Conference on Uncertainty in Artificial Intelligence. vol. 161, pp. 1352–1361. PMLR 2021). https://proceedings.mlr.press/v161/bachlechner21a.html
2. Bartlett, P., Helmbold, D., Long, P.: Gradient descent with identity initialization efficiently learns positive definite linear transformations by deep residual networks. In: Dy, J., Krause, A. (eds.) Proceedings of the 35th International Conference on Machine Learning. vol. 80, pp. 521–530 (2018). https://proceedings.mlr.press/v80/bartlett18a.html

3. Bengio, Y., Simard, P., Frasconi, P.: Learning long-term dependencies with gradient descent is difficult. IEEE Trans. Neural Networks **5**(2), 157–166 (1994). https://doi.org/10.1109/72.279181
4. Bishop, C.M.: Neural Networks for Pattern Recognition. OUP, USA (1995)
5. Burkholz, R., Dubatovka, A.: Initialization of Relus for dynamical isometry. In: Wallach, H., Larochelle, H., Beygelzimer, A., d'Alché-Buc, F., Fox, E., Garnett, R. (eds.) Advances in Neural Information Processing Systems. vol. 32. Curran Associates, Inc. (2019). https://proceedings.neurips.cc/paper/2019/file/d9731321ef4e063ebbee79298fa36f56-Paper.pdf
6. Dauphin, Y.N., Schoenholz, S.: Metainit: initializing learning by learning to initialize. In: Wallach, H., Larochelle, H., Beygelzimer, A., d'Alché-Buc, F., Fox, E., Garnett, R. (eds.) Advances in Neural Information Processing Systems. vol. 32. Curran Associates, Inc. (2019). https://proceedings.neurips.cc/paper/2019/file/876e8108f87eb61877c6263228b67256-Paper.pdf
7. Du, S., Hu, W.: Width provably matters in optimization for deep linear neural networks. In: Chaudhuri, K., Salakhutdinov, R. (eds.) Proceedings of the 36th International Conference on Machine Learning. vol. 97, pp. 1655–1664. PMLR (2019). https://proceedings.mlr.press/v97/du19a.html
8. Glorot, X., Bengio, Y.: Understanding the difficulty of training deep feedforward neural networks. In: Teh, Y.W., Titterington, M. (eds.) Proceedings of the Thirteenth International Conference on Artificial Intelligence and Statistics, vol. 9, pp. 249–256. PMLR, Chia Laguna Resort, Sardinia, Italy (2010). https://proceedings.mlr.press/v9/glorot10a.html
9. Hanin, B.: Which neural net architectures give rise to exploding and vanishing gradients? In: Bengio, S., Wallach, H., Larochelle, H., Grauman, K., Cesa-Bianchi, N., Garnett, R. (eds.) Advances in Neural Information Processing Systems. vol. 31. Curran Associates, Inc. (2018). https://proceedings.neurips.cc/paper/2018/file/13f9896df61279c928f19721878fac41-Paper.pdf
10. Hanin, B., Rolnick, D.: How to start training: the effect of initialization and architecture. In: Bengio, S., Wallach, H., Larochelle, H., Grauman, K., Cesa-Bianchi, N., Garnett, R. (eds.) Advances in Neural Information Processing Systems. vol. 31. Curran Associates, Inc. (2018). https://proceedings.neurips.cc/paper/2018/file/d81f9c1be2e08964bf9f24b15f0e4900-Paper.pdf
11. He, K., Zhang, X., Ren, S., Sun, J.: Delving deep into rectifiers: surpassing human-level performance on Imagenet classification. In: 2015 IEEE ICCV, pp. 1026–1034 (2015). https://doi.org/10.1109/ICCV.2015.123
12. He, K., Zhang, X., Ren, S., Sun, J.: Deep residual learning for image recognition. In: 2016 IEEE Conference on Computer Vision and Pattern Recognition, pp. 770–778 (2016). https://doi.org/10.1109/CVPR.2016.90
13. Hochreiter, S.: Untersuchungen zu dynamischen neuronalen netzen. Master's thesis, Institut fur Informatik, Technische Universitat, Munchen **1**, 1–150 (1991)
14. Horn, R.A., Johnson, C.R.: Matrix Analysis, 2nd edn. Cambridge University Press, Cambridge (2013)
15. Hu, W., Xiao, L., Pennington, J.: Provable benefit of orthogonal initialization in optimizing deep linear networks. In: International Conference on Learning Representations (2020). https://openreview.net/forum?id=rkgqN1SYvr
16. Kingma, D.P., Ba, J.: Adam: A method for stochastic optimization. In: International Conference on Learning Representations (2015)
17. Krizhevsky, A.: Learning multiple layers of features from tiny images. Technical Report, University of Toronto (2009). https://www.cs.toronto.edu/~kriz/learning-features-2009-TR.pdf

18. LeCun, Y., Bottou, L., Bengio, Y., Haffner, P.: Gradient-based learning applied to document recognition. Proc. IEEE **86**(11), 2278–2324 (1998). https://doi.org/10.1109/5.726791
19. LeCun, Y., Bottou, L., Orr, G.B., Müller, K.R.: Efficient backprop. In: Orr, G.B., Müller, K.R. (eds.) Neural Networks: Tricks of the Trade, pp. 9–50. Springer Berlin Heidelberg, Berlin, Heidelberg (1998). https://doi.org/10.1007/3-540-49430-8_2
20. Mishkin, D., Matas, J.: All you need is a good init. In: International Conference on Learning Representations (2016)
21. O'Neill, B.: Some useful moment results in sampling problems. American Stat. **68**(4), 282–296 (2014). https://doi.org/10.1080/00031305.2014.966589
22. Saxe, A., McClelland, J., Ganguli, S.: Exact solutions to the nonlinear dynamics of learning in deep linear neural networks. In: International Conference on Learning Representations (2014)
23. Shamir, O.: Exponential convergence time of gradient descent for one-dimensional deep linear neural networks. In: Beygelzimer, A., Hsu, D. (eds.) Proceedings of the Thirty-Second Conference on Learning Theory. vol. 99, pp. 2691–2713. PMLR (2019). https://proceedings.mlr.press/v99/shamir19a.html
24. Vladimirova, M., Verbeek, J., Mesejo, P., Arbel, J.: Understanding priors in Bayesian neural networks at the unit level. In: Chaudhuri, K., Salakhutdinov, R. (eds.) Proceedings of the 36th International Conference on Machine Learning. vol. 97, pp. 6458–6467. PMLR (2019). https://proceedings.mlr.press/v97/vladimirova19a.html
25. Xiao, L., Bahri, Y., Sohl-Dickstein, J., Schoenholz, S., Pennington, J.: Dynamical isometry and a mean field theory of CNNs: How to train 10,000-layer vanilla convolutional neural networks. In: Dy, J., Krause, A. (eds.) Proceedings of the 35th International Conference on Machine Learning. vol. 80, pp. 5393–5402. PMLR (2018). https://proceedings.mlr.press/v80/xiao18a.html
26. Zhang, H., Dauphin, Y.N., Ma, T.: Residual learning without normalization via better initialization. In: International Conference on Learning Representations (2019). https://openreview.net/forum?id=H1gsz30cKX
27. Zhao, J., Schaefer, F.T., Anandkumar, A.: Zero initialization: initializing neural networks with only zeros and ones. Trans. Mach. Learn. Res. (2022). https://openreview.net/forum?id=1AxQpKmiTc

Bandit Max-Min Fair Allocation

Tsubasa Harada[1(✉)], Shinji Ito[2], and Hanna Sumita[1]

[1] Institute of Science Tokyo, Tokyo, Japan
harada.t.30af@m.isct.ac.jp , sumita@comp.isct.ac.jp
[2] The University of Tokyo, Tokyo, Japan
shinji@mist.i.u-tokyo.ac.jp

Abstract. In this paper, we study a new decision-making problem called the *bandit max-min fair allocation* (BMMFA) problem. The goal of this problem is to maximize the minimum utility among agents with additive valuations by repeatedly assigning indivisible goods to them. One key feature of this problem is that each agent's valuation for each item can only be observed through the semi-bandit feedback, while existing work supposes that the item values are provided at the beginning of each round. Another key feature is that the algorithm's reward function is not additive with respect to rounds, unlike most bandit-setting problems. Our first contribution is to propose an algorithm that has an asymptotic regret bound of $O(m\sqrt{T}\ln T/n + m\sqrt{T\ln(mnT)})$, where n is the number of agents, m is the number of items, and T is the time horizon. This is based on a novel combination of bandit techniques and a resource allocation algorithm studied in the literature on competitive analysis. Our second contribution is to provide the regret lower bound of $\Omega(m\sqrt{T}/n)$. When T is sufficiently larger than n, the gap between the upper and lower bounds is a logarithmic factor of T.

Keywords: Fair allocation · Max-min fairness · Bandit feedback

1 Introduction

In this paper, we introduce a new sequential decision-making problem, the *bandit max-min fair allocation* (BMMFA) problem, in which some indivisible goods are divided among some agents in a fair manner. The problem is motivated by a problem of designing a subscription service as follows: the company rents items (e.g., clothes, watches, cars, etc.) to users for a certain period, collects the items when the period ends, receives feedback from users, and, based on that feedback, decides which items to rent to whom in the next period. In such a service, the company would like to make all the users as happy as possible. How can we ensure such a fair allocation?

This problem can be regarded as an online variant of the fair allocation problem, which has been a central problem in algorithmic game theory. The classical settings of the fair allocation problem [15] assume that the valuation of each agent for items is known in advance. However, this is not necessarily the case in practice. In the above subscription service, even agents may not recognize their own valuations until they receive items. Therefore, this paper aims to maximize the agents' utilities while learning the valuations of agents through repeatedly allocating items.

We briefly introduce the BMMFA problem. Let $[n] := \{1, \ldots, n\}$ be a set of n agents with additive valuations, M be a set of m items and T be the time horizon. The value of each agent $i \in [n]$ for each item $e \in M$ follows an unknown distribution D_{ie} over $[0, 1]$ with the expected value μ_{ie}. For each round $t = 1, \ldots, T$, the value v_{ie}^t of agent i with respect to an item e is sampled from D_{ie} independently of the round t. We denote by a matrix $a \in \{0,1\}^{n \times m}$ an allocation of items to agents, where $a_{ie} = 1$ if and only if agent i receives item e. In each round, the algorithm decides an allocation a^t of M based only on the past feedback, and observes values v_{ie}^t only for (i, e) such that $a_{ie}^t = 1$. The utility of agent i obtained at round t (denoted by X_i^t) is the sum of the values for items which are allocated to agent i, i.e., $X_i^t := \sum_{e \in M} v_{ie}^t a_{ie}^t$. The utility of agent i at the end of round T is $X_i := \sum_{t=1}^T X_i^t$.

As a fairness notion, we adopt the *max-min fairness*, which is a prominent notion in the fair allocation literature [3,15,24]. Then, the sequence of allocation $a^1, \ldots, a^T$ is said to be fair if the *egalitarian social welfare*, which is the smallest cumulative utility among agents $\min_{i \in [n]} X_i$, is maximized.

The performance of the algorithm is evaluated by an expected regret R_T, which is the expected difference between the egalitarian social welfare of an optimal policy and that of the algorithm. We assume that an optimal policy chooses a sequence of allocations $x^1, \ldots, x^T$ such that $\min_{i \in [n]} \sum_{t=1}^T \sum_{e \in M} \mu_{ie} x_{ie}^t$ is maximized. Therefore, the expected regret R_T is explicitly defined to be

$$R_T := \mathbb{E}\left[\min_{i \in [n]} X_i - \min_{i \in [n]} \sum_{t=1}^T \sum_{e \in M} v_{ie}^t x_{ie}^t\right].$$

We have two features in the definition of the regret compared with most other bandit problems: (a) an optimal policy knows all the expected values $\mu_{ie} = \mathbb{E}[v_{ie}^t]$ for all $(i, e) \in [n] \times M$ but may make different allocations across the T rounds, and (b) an algorithm's expected reward is $\mathbb{E}\left[\min_{i \in [n]} X_i\right]$, which is *not additive* with respect to rounds.

To be more specific about (a), a naive definition of an optimal policy would be choosing a fixed allocation $\tilde{x}$ that maximizes $\min_{i \in [n]} \sum_{t=1}^T \sum_{e \in M} \mu_{ie} \tilde{x}_{ie}$. However, this fixed-allocation policy may not be reasonable for our problem. To see this issue, consider the case where $m < n$ and all agents have value 1 for any items. Any fixed-allocation policy has zero egalitarian social welfare since at least one agent receives nothing in every round, while we can achieve positive value by allocating items depending on the round.

For the point (b), $\min_i X_i$ is the fairness measure to be maximized. The problem is that analyzing $\mathbb{E}\left[\min_{i \in [n]} X_i\right]$ is difficult if we naively use the existing bandit techniques. Our model is similar to the combinatorial multi-armed bandit (CMAB) problems [18]. However, even in the most general setting of CMAB, the algorithm's reward is the sum of the per-round rewards ($\min_{i \in [n]} X_i^t$ in our setting), and the optimal policy selects a fixed action for all rounds. This implies that the CMAB framework does not cover our setting.

Another similar allocation problem is studied in the context of competitive analysis [22,26,31]. Roughly speaking, in each round, one item arrives and agents reveals the values for the item, and then the algorithm decides who to receive the item so that the overall egalitarian social welfare is maximized. However, those resource allocation problems assume that the *full* information $(v_{ie}^t)_{i \in [n], e \in M}$ are given at the *beginning* of each round, whereas only semi-bandit feedback $(v_{ie}^t)_{i,e:a_{ie}^t=1}$ is given at the end of each round in BMMFA. An optimal policy is assumed to know the realization of all the item values in advance, and the performance metrics are defined differently (see Appendix A of the full version [27] for the detail). Therefore, the existing results do not carry to our setting.

1.1 Our Contributions

In this paper, we first define a regret that is suitable for BMMFA. Next, we propose an algorithm that achieves a regret bound of $O(m\sqrt{T} \ln T/n + m\sqrt{T \ln(mnT)})$ when T is sufficiently large. In addition, we provide a lower bound of $\Omega(m\sqrt{T}/n)$ on the regret. The gap between these bounds is $O(\max\{\ln T, n\sqrt{\ln(mnT)}\})$, which is a logarithmic factor of T. Although this paper mainly addresses the case of a known time horizon T, we note that the same regret bound can be achieved even when T is unknown, by using the well-known doubling trick [11]. In the following, we describe the techniques used in the analysis of the regret upper and lower bounds.

Upper Bound. Due to the features of our regret definition, it is hard to naively apply the existing approaches. We propose an algorithm by combining techniques of regret analysis and competitive analysis. For this, we employ an idea similar to the resource allocation algorithm proposed in [22] in the context of competitive analysis. This is similar to the multiplicative weight updated method [2]. To estimate the item values given by the semi-bandit feedback, we incorporate upper confidence bounds (UCB) [32] on μ_{ie} for each (i, e), and adopt the error analysis used in [6] for the bandits with knapsacks problem. Our algorithm simply allocates each item to an agent with the largest UCB, discounted by a factor depending on the past allocations. However, the regret analysis is challenging. If we directly analyze the regret, we need to connect the algorithm's choice (depending on UCBs) to the algorithm's reward (in terms of μ_{ie}^t's). This is not easy because the reward is non-additive and UCBs do not imply future item values. We bypass this issue by introducing a *surrogate* regret, defined with expected item values. We show that the original regret and the surrogate differ by at most $O(m\sqrt{T \ln T})$, and the surrogate regret has a bound of $O(m\sqrt{T} \ln T/n + m\sqrt{T \ln(mnT)} + m \ln T \ln(mnT))$. These facts imply an upper bound on R_T. We remark that our algorithm runs in $O(mn)$ time per round.

By this analysis, the average egalitarian social welfare $\mathbb{E}\left[\min_{i\in[n]} X_i/T\right]$ of our algorithm achieves per-round fairness up to an additive error of $o(1)$ when m is fixed. Here, we refer to per-round fairness[1] as maximizing the expected minimum utility per round through a stochastic allocation.

Lower Bound. The proof of the lower bound primarily follows the standard method for the multi-armed bandit (MAB) problem by [5]. We first lower bound the regret by averaging over a certain class of instances for BMMFA. Then, by using Pinsker's inequality, we reduce the problem of lower bounding the regret to computing the Kullback-Leibler divergence of certain distributions. The main difference from the standard method for MAB is that we "divide" the problem into m/n subproblems, each with n agents and n items, by treating m/n as an integer. Intuitively, the lower bound $\Omega(m\sqrt{T}/n)$ arises from the number of subproblems times the lower bound of $\Omega(\sqrt{T})$ for each subproblem. This idea of dividing the problem is similar to the proof of the lower bound for the online combinatorial optimization problem [4].

Furthermore, our results are valid for variants of our setting. We will explain this in Sect. 4.1 of the full version [27].

1.2 Relation to Multi-player Bandits

The situation of multiple agents choosing items has been actively studied in the context of multi–player bandits (MPB). In this problem, n agents repeatedly choose one of K items (or arms). In the following, we explain the difference between MPB and BMMFA from three perspectives.

The first difference is the correspondence between agents and items: in MPB, each agent chooses exactly one item per round, and there may be items that are not chosen by any agent. In BMMFA, on the other hand, each item is assigned to an agent, and there may be agents who receive no items or multiple items.

The second difference is the objective function: most MPB studies aim to maximize the sum of agents' utilities and do not consider fairness among the agents. See a survey [14] for details. However, some recent studies address the fairness issues [13,28,30,37]. These studies aim to maximize an objective function of the form $\sum_{t=1}^{T} F((X_i^t)_{i\in[n]})$, where $F((X_i^t)_{i\in[n]})$ represents a fairness measure at round t (e.g. *Nash social welfare* [37] or the minimum expected utility over agents [13]). With such objective functions, the algorithm prioritizes per-round fairness rather than overall fairness. In fact, this approach can hinder the achievement of overall fairness because the algorithm lacks an incentive to

---

[1] Alternative choices are maximizing the minimum expected ex-ante utility $\min_{i\in[n]} \mathbb{E}[X_i]$ or using only deterministic allocations. In fact, the same guarantee holds for any choice.

eliminate the disparity in cumulative utility among agents[2] On the other hand, in our setting, even if a disparity in utility occurs during the learning process, the algorithm adaptively allocates items to make an agent with small utility happier.

The third perspective involves the differences in the "optimal" policy used as a benchmark for evaluating regret. In the context of bandit problems, including prior studies addressing fairness among agents such as [13,28], the optimal policy typically consists of repeatedly making a single fixed decision. In contrast, in BMMFA, the optimal policy can vary its allocation at each round. In other words, we assume a stronger optimal policy than in similar problems.

These distinctions make it impossible to directly compare the challenges of BMMFA with that of related problems.

1.3 Other Related Work

In the MAB problem, there are K arms, and the algorithm chooses one arm in each round and receives a reward corresponding to the chosen arm. In recent years, there has been research into how to choose an arm that satisfies a certain constraint representing fairness. A commonly used constraint for fairness is that "the ratio of the number of rounds each arm has been drawn to the number of rounds must be greater than a certain value" [19,20,34,36]. In BMMFA, we can view an allocation as an arm. However, as the above notion ignores the utility of agents, it is not suitable for our purpose.

There is a vast body of literature on online fair allocation in combinatorial optimization and algorithmic game theory. Recent studies include problems with a fairness notion such as envy-freeness [10], maximum Nash social welfare [7], p-mean welfare [9,21]. They are just a few examples; see also a survey [1]. Offline sequential allocation problems have also been studied [29,35]. In this context, the goal is to obtain a sequence of allocations with both overall and per-round fairness guarantees.

The one-short, offline version of BMMFA has been studied in combinatorial optimization under the name of the *Santa Clause problem* [12,17,23–25]. The problem is NP-hard even to approximate within a factor of better than $1/2$ [33]. [8] proposed an $\Omega(\frac{\ln \ln \ln n}{\ln \ln n})$-approximation algorithm for a restricted case. [3] provided the first polynomial-time approximation algorithm for the general problem and this was improved by [25].

Finally, we note that BMMFA can also be viewed as a repeated two-player zero-sum game [16]. Further details can be found in Appendix B of the full version [27].

---

[2] Consider an instance with two agents and two goods a and b. The value of a is 1 and that of b is $\varepsilon \ll 1$ for both agents. Any sequence of allocations that gives one item for one agent maximizes $\sum_{t=1}^{T} \min_{i \in [2]} X_i^t$. However, to maximize the minimum of cumulative utilities, we need to assign a to either agent once per two rounds.

2 Model

The bandit max-min fair allocation problem is represented by a quadruple $([n], M, T, (D_{ie})_{i \in [n], e \in M})$, where $[n] := \{1, \ldots, n\}$ is a set of n agents, $M = \{1, \ldots, m\}$ is a set of m items, T is the time horizon, and D_{ie} is a probability distribution over $[0, 1]$ representing the value of agent i for an item e. For each $i \in [n]$ and $e \in M$, let μ_{ie} be the expected value of D_{ie}. Assume that $[n]$, M and T are known in advance, while $(D_{ie})_{i \in [n], e \in M}$ is not.

Each allocation of items to agents is expressed as an n-row by m-column 0-1 matrix $a \in \{0,1\}^{n \times m}$, where $a_{ie} = 1$ if and only if agent i receives item e in the allocation. Let $\mathcal{A} \subseteq \{0,1\}^{n \times m}$ be a set of allocations, i.e.,

$$\mathcal{A} = \left\{ a \in \{0,1\}^{n \times m} : \sum_{i \in [n]} a_{ie} = 1 \text{ for all } e \in M \right\}.$$

For each round $t = 1, \ldots, T$, let v_{ie}^t be a random variable drawn from D_{ie}. Note that the random variables $\{v_{ie}^t : i \in [n], e \in M, t = 1, \ldots, T\}$ are mutually independent and are unknown to the algorithm in this step. In round t, the algorithm chooses an allocation $a^t \in \mathcal{A}$ depending only on the previous allocations $(a^s)_{s=1}^{t-1}$ and the feedback obtained by the beginning of round t. Then, the algorithm receives semi-bandit feedback: the algorithm is given the values v_{ie}^t for all (i, e) such that $a_{ie}^t = 1$. The reward of an algorithm ALG is defined by

$$\text{ALG} := \min_{i \in [n]} \sum_{t=1}^T \sum_{e \in M} v_{ie}^t a_{ie}^t.$$

The expected regret R_T is defined to be the expectation of the difference between the egalitarian social welfares of an optimal policy and an algorithm. We assume that an optimal policy takes a sequence of allocations $x^1, \ldots, x^T \in \{0,1\}^{n \times m}$ that maximizes the egalitarian social welfare $\min_{i \in [n]} \sum_{t=1}^T \sum_{e \in M} \mu_{ie} x_{ie}^t$ with respect to the expected values, i.e., $\min_{i \in [n]} \sum_{t=1}^T \sum_{e \in M} \mu_{ie} x_{ie}^t$. Formally, we define

$$\text{OPT} := \min_{i \in [n]} \sum_{t=1}^T \sum_{e \in M} v_{ie}^t x_{ie}^t,$$
$$R_T := \mathbb{E}\left[\text{OPT} - \text{ALG}\right].$$

For the regret analysis, we introduce surrogate values of OPT and ALG as

$$\text{OPT}_\mu := \min_{i \in [n]} \sum_{t=1}^T \sum_{e \in M} \mu_{ie} x_{ie}^t,$$
$$\text{ALG}_\mu := \min_{i \in [n]} \sum_{t=1}^T \sum_{e \in M} \mu_{ie} a_{ie}^t$$

and a *surrogate* regret

$$R_T^\mu := \mathbb{E}\left[\text{OPT}_\mu - \text{ALG}_\mu\right].$$

In fact, R_T^μ is not so far from R_T as the following lemma shows. The proof is found in Lemma 1 of the full version [27].

Lemma 1. $|R_T - R_T^\mu| = O(m\sqrt{T \ln T})$.

Furthermore, OPT_μ is upper bounded by the optimal value of the following LP:

$$\begin{aligned}
\max_{P,x} \; & T \cdot P \\
\text{s.t.} \; & P \leq \sum_{e \in M} \mu_{ie} x_{ie} && (\forall i \in [n]), \\
& \sum_{i \in [n]} x_{ie} = 1 && (\forall e \in M), \\
& 0 \leq x_{ie} \leq 1 && (\forall i \in [n], \forall e \in M).
\end{aligned} \quad \text{(LP)}$$

Indeed, if we set $\hat{x}_{ie} = \sum_{t=1}^T x_{ie}^t / T$ $(i \in [n], e \in M)$, then $\hat{x}$ is a feasible solution to (LP). Let (P^*, x^*) be an optimal solution of (LP). We will see $T \cdot P^* - \mathbb{E}[\text{ALG}_\mu]$ to obtain an upper bound on R_T^μ.

Note that (LP) can be interpreted as maximizing the minimum expected per-round utility when a stochastic allocation is allowed. Since P^* upper bounds the maximum "expected minimum" per-round utility, bounding $T \cdot P^* - \mathbb{E}[\text{ALG}_\mu]$ leads to per-round fairness on average; see Remark 1.

In what follows, we assume $P^* > 0$ because otherwise $R_T^\mu = 0$. Moreover, intuitively, if P^* is sufficiently small, then a per-round utility $\sum_{e \in M} \mu_{ie} a_{ie}^t$ of any agent i is not far less than P^*, and hence ALG_μ is also close to P^*T. Therefore, the difficulty of our problem lies in the case when P^* is large. This is a nature of max-min fair allocation problems. Indeed, existing results in [22,31] for competitive analysis also assume that the offline optimal value is sufficiently large.

3 Algorithm

In this section, we describe an algorithm that has a regret bound of $O(m\sqrt{T} \ln T/n + m\sqrt{T \ln(mnT)} + m \ln T \ln(mnT))$. The regret bound will be shown in the next section. The algorithm is based on the resource allocation algorithm in [22,31]. The brief description of (a multiple-item variant of) the algorithm is as follows. It is assumed that the values v_{ie}^t for all (i,e) are given at the beginning of each round. Let $\varepsilon > 0$ be a parameter, which will be set later. We denote by u_i^t the cumulative utility of agent i at the end of round t. In each round t, the algorithm chooses an allocation a^t that maximizes a total sum of utilities with respect to item values discounted with u_i. More specifically, a^t achieves $\max_{a \in \mathcal{A}} \sum_{i \in [n], e \in M} (1-\varepsilon)^{u_i^{t-1}/m} v_{ie}^t a_{ie}$.

Due to the feedback model, a direct application of the above resource allocation algorithm is impossible in our setting. It is also not clear whether the existing result carries to due to the different definition of OPT.

To address those issues, we estimate each value using an *upper confidence bound* (UCB), and reconstruct the performance evaluation by incorporating the error analysis used in [6].

Algorithm 1. Allocation algorithm

Parameter: $\varepsilon \in (0, 1)$.
1: **for** $t = 1, \ldots, n$ **do**
2: Assign all items to agent t and receive values v_{te}^t for each $e \in M$.
3: **end for**
4: Set $\bar{v}_{ie}^{n+1}$ as in Eq. 1 for each $i \in [n]$ and $e \in M$.
5: Let $u_i^n = 0$ for each $i \in [n]$.
6: **for** $t = n+1, \ldots, T$ **do**
7: Let a^t be an allocation $a \in \mathcal{A}$ maximizing

$$\sum_{i \in [n]} \sum_{e \in M} (1-\varepsilon)^{\frac{1}{m} u_i^{t-1}} \bar{v}_{ie}^t \cdot a_{ie}.$$

8: Receive values v_{ie}^t for each (i,e) such that $a_{ie}^t = 1$.
9: Set $u_i^t \leftarrow u_i^{t-1} + \sum_{e \in M} \bar{v}_{ie}^t a_{ie}^t$ for each $i \in [n]$.
10: Set $\bar{v}_{ie}^{t+1}$ accordingly as in Eq. 1.
11: **end for**

For $v \in \mathbb{R}_+$ and $N \in \mathbb{Z}_+$, let $\text{r}(v, N) = \sqrt{C_{\text{rad}} \cdot v/N} + C_{\text{rad}}/N$, where C_{rad} is a positive constant independent of v and N. For each round t and $(i,e) \in [n] \times M$, we define

$$\bar{v}_{ie}^t = \hat{v}_{ie} + \text{r}(\hat{v}_{ie}, N_{ie,t}) \tag{1}$$

as a UCB of v_{ie}^t, where $N_{ie,t}$ is the number of rounds in which item e is assigned to agent i in the first $t-1$ rounds and $\hat{v}_{ie}$ is the average of the $N_{ie,t}$ samples of v_{ie}^t. For this setting of UCBs, the following useful result is known.

Theorem 1 ([6]). *Let $\hat{\nu}$ be the average of N independent samples from a distribution over $[0,1]$ with expectation ν. For each $C_{\text{rad}} > 0$, it holds that $\Pr[|\nu - \hat{\nu}| \leq \text{r}(\hat{\nu}, N)] \leq 3\text{r}(\nu, N)] \geq 1 - e^{-\Omega(C_{\text{rad}})}$. This holds even if $X_1, \ldots, X_N \in [0,1]$ are random variables, $\hat{\nu} = \frac{1}{N}\sum_{t=1}^N X_t$ is the sample average, and $\nu = \frac{1}{N}\sum_{t=1}^N \mathbb{E}[X_t \mid X_1, \ldots, X_{t-1}]$.*

We will set the constant $C_{\text{rad}} = \Theta(\ln(mnT))$. Then, by using the union bound, we have

$$\mu_{ie} \in [\hat{v}_{ie}^t - \text{r}(\hat{v}_{ie}^t, N_{ie,t}), \hat{v}_{ie}^t + \text{r}(\hat{v}_{ie}^t, N_{ie,t})]$$

for any $(i,e) \in [n] \times M$ and round t with probability at least $1 - \frac{1}{T}$. We call this event a *clean execution* [6] and denote it by $\mathcal{E}$.

Our algorithm is summarized in Algorithm 1. We devote the first n rounds to collect one sample of each item value. At the subsequent rounds t, assuming $\bar{v}_{ie}^t$ as an estimation of μ_{ie}, we choose an allocation a^t maximizing $\sum_{i \in [n], e \in M}(1-\varepsilon)^{u_i^{t-1}/m} \bar{v}_{ie}^t \cdot a_{ie}^t$. We can obtain a^t easily just by allocating each item e to the agent with the largest discounted UCB for e.

4 Regret Analysis

The goal of this section is to prove the following theorems, which provides an asymptotic guarantee on R_T.

Theorem 2. *The regret R_T for Algorithm 1 is bounded as*

$$R_T \leq m + \varepsilon W' + n \cdot e^{-\frac{\varepsilon^2}{2m} W'} W' + P^* + O(err),$$

where $W' = P^*(T - n)$, $err = O(\sqrt{C_{\text{rad}} m^2 T} + C_{\text{rad}} m \ln T)$ and $C_{\text{rad}} = \Theta(\ln(mnT))$. If $T \geq e^{\frac{2m}{P^*}} + n$, by setting $\varepsilon = \ln(T - n)/\sqrt{T - n}$, we have $R_T = O(m\sqrt{T} \ln T/n + err)$.

Weakening the assumption on T to $T \geq n$ yields another regret bound.

Theorem 3. *The regret R_T for Algorithm 1 is also bounded as*

$$R_T \leq \frac{m\varepsilon T}{n} + \frac{m \ln n}{\varepsilon} + O(err).$$

If $T \geq n$, by setting $\varepsilon = \sqrt{n \ln n / T}$, we have $R_T = O(m\sqrt{T \ln n / n} + err)$.

By Lemma 1, we have $R_T \leq R_T^\mu + O(m\sqrt{T \ln T}) = R_T^\mu + O(err)$. Then, to prove Theorems 2 and 3, it suffices to show the upper bound on the surrogate regret R_T^μ.

First, we prove Theorem 2. As described before, $R_T^\mu \leq TP^* - \mathbb{E}[\text{ALG}_\mu]$. For each agent i, let X_i^t be random variables representing the reward of the agent i at round t with respect to the expected item values, i.e., $X_i^t = \sum_{e \in M} \mu_{ie} a_{ie}^t$. For notational convenience, let $W' = P^*(T - n)$ and let $\text{ALG}'_\mu = \min_{i \in [n]} \sum_{t=n+1}^T X_i^t$. The following simple calculations allow us to ignore regret in the first n rounds:

$$R_T^\mu \leq P^*T - \mathbb{E}\left[\min_{i \in [n]} \sum_{t=n+1}^T X_i^t\right]$$
$$= P^*n + W' - \mathbb{E}[\text{ALG}'_\mu] \leq m + W' - \mathbb{E}[\text{ALG}'_\mu]. \quad (2)$$

Then, in the rest of this section, we bound $W' - \mathbb{E}[\text{ALG}'_\mu]$.

For each agent i, let $\bar{X}_i^t$ be a random variable representing the reward of the agent i at round t if values are replaced with their UCBs, i.e., $\bar{X}_i^t = \sum_{e \in M} \bar{v}_{ie}^t a_{ie}^t$. In addition, let $\overline{\text{ALG}'} := \min_{i \in [n]} \sum_{t=n+1}^T \bar{X}_i^t$ be the total reward of Algorithm 1 after round n with respect to the UCBs. We first claim that $\mathbb{E}\left[\overline{\text{ALG}'}\right]$ is not far from $\mathbb{E}[\text{ALG}'_\mu]$ in the follwing lemma. Let $err := \mathbb{E}\left[\overline{\text{ALG}'}\right] - \mathbb{E}[\text{ALG}'_\mu]$.

Lemma 2. $err = \mathbb{E}\left[\overline{\text{ALG}'}\right] - \mathbb{E}[\text{ALG}'_\mu] = O(\sqrt{C_{\text{rad}} m^2 T} + C_{\text{rad}} m \ln T)$.

The proof of Lemma 2 is similar to the proof of Lemma 5.6 in [6] and is given in Lemma 2 of the full version [27]. Lemma 2 implies that we only need to evaluate $W' - \mathbb{E}\left[\overline{\mathrm{ALG}'}\right]$. We proceed based on the idea in [22,31].

By the union bound and Markov's inequality, the probability that $\overline{\mathrm{ALG}'}$ is at most $(1-\varepsilon)W'$ is

$$\Pr\left[\min_{i \in [n]} \sum_{t=n+1}^{T} \bar{X}_i^t \leq (1-\varepsilon)W'\right]$$

$$\leq \sum_{i \in [n]} \Pr\left[\sum_{t=n+1}^{T} \bar{X}_i^t \leq (1-\varepsilon)W'\right]$$

$$= \sum_{i \in [n]} \Pr\left[(1-\varepsilon)^{\frac{1}{m}\sum_{t=n+1}^{T} \bar{X}_i^t} \geq (1-\varepsilon)^{\frac{(1-\varepsilon)W'}{m}}\right]$$

$$\leq \sum_{i \in [n]} \mathbb{E}\left[(1-\varepsilon)^{\frac{1}{m}\sum_{t=n+1}^{T} \bar{X}_i^t}\right] / (1-\varepsilon)^{\frac{(1-\varepsilon)W'}{m}}. \quad (3)$$

If the rightmost value in Eq. 3 is sufficiently small, then we can bound the regret by $m + O(\varepsilon W')$ with high probability. For $s = n, n+1, \ldots, T$, let us define $\Phi(s)$ as

$$\Phi(s) := \sum_{i \in [n]} (1-\varepsilon)^{\frac{1}{m}\sum_{t=n+1}^{s} \bar{X}_i^t} \cdot \left(1 - \frac{\varepsilon P^*}{m}\right)^{T-s}.$$

We note that the rightmost value in Eq. 3 is equal to $\mathbb{E}[\Phi(T)]/(1-\varepsilon)^{(1-\varepsilon)W'/m}$.

Lemma 3. *In a clean execution of Algorithm 1, $\Phi(s)$ is monotone non-increasing in s.*

Proof. Since the feasible region of (LP) is a subset of the convex hull of some integral allocations of M to $[n]$, we can decompose x^* as a convex combination of integral allocations $y^1, \ldots, y^k$ so that $x^* = \sum_{j \in [k]} \lambda_j y^j$, where $\lambda_j \geq 0$ ($\forall j \in [k]$) and $\sum_{j \in [k]} \lambda_j = 1$. We note that $y^1, \ldots, y^k$ are not necessarily optimal solutions to (LP). Then, for $s = n+1, \ldots, T-1$, letting $\alpha_i = (1-\varepsilon)^{\frac{1}{m}\sum_{t=n+1}^{s} \bar{X}_i^t}$, we can see that

$$\Phi(s+1) = \sum_{i \in [n]} \alpha_i \cdot (1-\varepsilon)^{\frac{1}{m}\bar{X}_i^{s+1}} \cdot \left(1 - \frac{\varepsilon}{m}P^*\right)^{T-s-1}$$

$$\leq \sum_{i \in [n]} \alpha_i \cdot \left(1 - \frac{\varepsilon}{m}\bar{X}_i^{s+1}\right) \cdot \left(1 - \frac{\varepsilon}{m}P^*\right)^{T-s-1}$$

$$\leq \sum_{i \in [n]} \alpha_i \cdot \left(1 - \frac{\varepsilon}{m}P^*\right) \cdot \left(1 - \frac{\varepsilon}{m}P^*\right)^{T-s-1}$$

$$= \sum_{i \in [n]} \alpha_i \cdot \left(1 - \frac{\varepsilon}{m}P^*\right)^{T-s} = \Phi(s).$$

Here, the first inequality holds by $\bar{X}_i^{s+1}/m \in [0,1]$ and $(1-\varepsilon)^x \leq 1 - \varepsilon x$ for any $x \in [0,1]$. As for the second inequality,

$$\sum_{i \in [n]} \alpha_i \cdot \bar{X}_i^{s+1} \geq \sum_{j=1}^k \lambda_j \sum_{i \in [n]} \alpha_i \sum_{e \in M} \bar{v}_{ie}^{s+1} y_{ie}^j$$
$$= \sum_{i \in [n]} \alpha_i \sum_{e \in M} \bar{v}_{ie}^{s+1} x_{ie}^*$$

holds for each $i \in [n]$ by the choice of a^t in line 1. Since we assume a clean execution, it further holds that $\sum_{e \in M} \bar{v}_{ie}^{s+1} x_{ie}^* \geq \sum_{e \in M} \mu_{ie} x_{ie}^* \geq P^*$.

The proof of Lemma 3 requires a connection between a utility with respect to the UCBs and an optimal policy. This task is made easier if we use the surrogate regret.

Lemma 4. $\Phi(n)/(1-\varepsilon)^{(1-\varepsilon)W'/m} \leq n \cdot e^{-\frac{\varepsilon^2 W'}{2m}}$.

Proof. By Lemma 3 and $1 - x \leq e^{-x}$ for any x, we have

$$\frac{\Phi(n)}{(1-\varepsilon)^{\frac{(1-\varepsilon)W'}{m}}} = \frac{\sum_{i \in [n]}\left(1 - \frac{\varepsilon P^*}{m}\right)^{T-n}}{(1-\varepsilon)^{(1-\varepsilon)\frac{W'}{m}}} \leq \frac{n \cdot e^{-\varepsilon \frac{W'}{m}}}{(1-\varepsilon)^{(1-\varepsilon)\frac{W'}{m}}}.$$

This is bounded by $n \cdot e^{-\frac{\varepsilon^2 W'}{2m}}$ since $\frac{1}{(1-\varepsilon)^{(1-\varepsilon)}} \leq e^{\varepsilon - \varepsilon^2/2}$ for any $\varepsilon \in [0,1)$.

Now we are ready to prove theorems.

Proof. (Proof of Theorem 2). By applying Lemmas 3 and 4 to Eq. 3, we see that

$$\Pr\left[\overline{\text{ALG}'} \leq (1-\varepsilon)W'\right] \leq \Pr\left[\overline{\text{ALG}'} \leq (1-\varepsilon)W' \mid \mathcal{E}\right] + \frac{1}{T}$$
$$\leq \frac{\mathbb{E}[\Phi(T) \mid \mathcal{E}]}{(1-\varepsilon)^{(1-\varepsilon)W'/m}} + \frac{1}{T}$$
$$\leq \frac{\Phi(n)}{(1-\varepsilon)^{(1-\varepsilon)W'/m}} + \frac{1}{T} \leq n \cdot e^{-\frac{\varepsilon^2 W'}{2m}} + \frac{1}{T}.$$

This implies that

$$W' - \mathbb{E}\left[\overline{\text{ALG}'}\right] \leq \varepsilon W' + (n \cdot e^{-\frac{\varepsilon^2 W'}{2m}} + 1/T)W'$$
$$\leq \varepsilon W' + n \cdot e^{-\frac{\varepsilon^2 W'}{2m}} W' + P^*. \tag{4}$$

This together with Eq. 2 and Lemma 2 implies that

$$R_T^\mu \leq m + \varepsilon W' + n \cdot e^{-\frac{\varepsilon^2 W'}{2m}} W' + P^* + O(\text{err}). \tag{5}$$

Let $T' := T - n \; (\geq e^{\frac{2m}{P^*}})$, and we set $\varepsilon = \frac{\ln T'}{\sqrt{T'}}$. Then it follows that $\varepsilon W' + n \cdot e^{-\frac{\varepsilon^2 W'}{2m}} W' = P^* \sqrt{T'} \ln T' + n P^* T'^{1 - \frac{P^*}{2m} \ln T'} \leq P^* \sqrt{T'} \ln T' + n P^*$.

Therefore, from Eq. 5, we finally see that

$$R_T \leq m + P^* \sqrt{T'} \ln T' + n P^* + P^* + O(\text{err}) = O\left(\frac{m}{n} \sqrt{T} \ln T + \text{err}\right).$$

This completes the proof of Theorem 2.

Proof. (Proof of Theorem 3). Let $i^* \in \arg\min_i \sum_{t=n+1}^{T} \bar{X}_i^t$. Under the clean execution $\mathcal{E}$, we have

$$(1-\varepsilon)^{\frac{1}{m}\sum_{t=n+1}^{T} \bar{X}_{i^*}^t} \leq \sum_{i \in [n]} (1-\varepsilon)^{\frac{1}{m}\sum_{t=n+1}^{T} \bar{X}_i^t}$$

$$= \Phi(T) \leq \Phi(n) = n\left(1 - \frac{\varepsilon P^*}{m}\right)^{T-n},$$

where the inequality follows from from Lemma 3. By taking the logarithm of both sides, it follows that $\frac{1}{m}\sum_{t=n+1}^{T} \bar{X}_{i^*}^t \ln(1-\varepsilon) \leq (T-n)\ln\left(1 - \frac{\varepsilon P^*}{m}\right) + \ln n$. As we have $-x - x^2 \leq \ln(1-x) \leq -x$ for $x \leq 1/2$, we obtain

$$(-\varepsilon - \varepsilon^2)\frac{1}{m}\sum_{t=n+1}^{T} \bar{X}_{i^*}^t \leq -(T-n)\frac{\varepsilon P^*}{m} + \ln n = -\frac{\varepsilon W'}{m} + \ln n.$$

Therefore, under the clean execution $\mathcal{E}$, it follows that

$$W' - \overline{\text{ALG}'} = W' - \sum_{t=n+1}^{T} \bar{X}_{i^*}^t \leq \varepsilon \sum_{t=n+1}^{T} \bar{X}_{i^*}^t + \frac{m}{\varepsilon}\ln n \leq \frac{m}{n}\varepsilon T + \frac{m}{\varepsilon}\ln n.$$

Since $\mathcal{E}$ occurs with probability at least $1 - 1/T$, we have

$$W' - \mathbb{E}\left[\overline{\text{ALG}'}\right] \leq \frac{m}{n}\varepsilon T + \frac{m}{\varepsilon}\ln n + P^*(T-n)/T. \tag{6}$$

Applying Eq. 6 to the proof of Theorem 2 instead of Eq. 4 yields Theorem 3.

Remark 1. We observe the outcome of Algorithm 1 almost achieves per-round fairness on average across rounds. Here we mean per-round fairness by attaining the maximum expected minimum utility per round with a stochastic allocation, whose value is bounded by P^*. Indeed, by Eq. 4, we have $P^* - \mathbb{E}\left[\min_{i \in [n]} \frac{1}{T}\sum_{t=1}^{T} X_i^t\right] \leq P^* - \frac{1}{T}\mathbb{E}\left[\text{ALG}'_\mu\right] = P^*(\varepsilon + n \cdot e^{-\frac{\varepsilon^2 W'}{2m}} + \frac{n+1}{T}) + O(\frac{err}{T})$, and this is $o(1)$ under the assumption of Theorem 2.

5 Lower Bound

In this section, we prove a lower bound on R_T^μ and R_T.

Theorem 4. *For bandit max-min fair allocation problem with $m \geq n$, the surrogate regret R_T^μ of any algorithm is at least $\Omega(m\sqrt{T}/n)$.*

If $T \geq \max\{n, m^2\} \geq 2$ and $m/n \geq \lceil 2338 \ln T \rceil$ in addition, then the regret R_T is also at least $\Omega(m\sqrt{T}/n)$.

We first prove this for any deterministic algorithm based on the idea of [4,5], and then extend the proof to any randomized algorithm. In the following, we use ALG to denote both an algorithm and its reward.

Fix any deterministic algorithm. Let b be a positive integer and $m = nb$. We use two index (j,k) ($j = 1, \ldots, n$ and $k = 1, \ldots, b$) to represent one item e. An item (j,k) is called the j-th item in the k-th item block k. Then, we can write the set of allocations as follows:

$$\mathcal{A} = \{a \in \{0,1\}^{n \times n \times b} : \sum_i a_{i,j,k} = 1 \text{ for } \forall j, k\}.$$

Similarly, we define the set of optimal allocations as follows:

$$\mathcal{A}^* = \left\{a \in \{0,1\}^{n \times n \times b} : \begin{array}{l} \sum_i a_{i,j,k} = 1 \text{ for } \forall j, k \\ \sum_j a_{i,j,k} = 1 \text{ for } \forall i, k \end{array}\right\}.$$

For any $\alpha \in \mathcal{A}^*$, $j \in [n]$ and $k \in [b]$, let $I_{\alpha,j,k}$ be the unique i such that $\alpha_{i,j,k} = 1$.

Now we design a hard instance for the problem. Let $\varepsilon \in (0,1)$ be a parameter. We first choose $\alpha \in \mathcal{A}^*$ arbitrarily and set a distribution $D_{i,j,k}$ (of agent i for item (j,k)) to be a Bernoulli distribution $\text{Ber}(1/2 + \varepsilon\alpha_{i,j,k})$. We refer to $(\text{Ber}(1/2 + \varepsilon\alpha_{i,j,k}))_{i,j,k}$ as α-adversary. Moreover, for each $\alpha \in \mathcal{A}^*$ and $k' \in [b]$, we also define another adversary called $(\alpha - k')$-adversary as follows: $D_{i,j,k} = \text{Ber}(1/2)$ if $k = k'$, and $D_{i,j,k} = \text{Ber}(1/2 + \varepsilon\alpha_{i,j,k})$ otherwise. Note that for an allocation $\beta \in \mathcal{A}^*$, the $(\alpha - k')$-adversary is the same as the $(\beta - k')$-adversary if $\alpha_{i,j,k} = \beta_{i,j,k}$ for each $i \in [n]$, $j \in [n]$ and $k \in [b] \setminus \{k'\}$. When we use an α-adversary, for each agent i and each item (j,k), we say that (i,j,k) is a *correct assignment* if $\alpha_{i,j,k} = 1$. We use $\mathbb{P}_\alpha[\cdot]$ and $\mathbb{E}_\alpha[\cdot]$ to denote the conditional probability and expectation when we choose an α-adversary at first.

Let $\alpha^* \in \mathcal{A}^*$ be the most unfavorable adversary that minimize the reward. Let $\mu_{i,j,k}$ be the expected value of each $D_{i,j,k}$. We denote $N_{\alpha,k} := \sum_{t,i,j} \alpha_{i,j,k} a^t_{i,j,k}$. Then we have

$$\mathbb{E}_{\alpha^*}[\text{ALG}_\mu] = \mathbb{E}_{\alpha^*}\left[\min_i \sum_{t,j,k} \mu_{i,j,k} a^t_{i,j,k}\right] \leq \frac{1}{n|\mathcal{A}^*|} \sum_{\alpha \in \mathcal{A}^*} \mathbb{E}_\alpha\left[\sum_{t,i,j,k} \mu_{i,j,k} a^t_{i,j,k}\right]$$

$$= \frac{1}{2}bT + \frac{\varepsilon}{n|\mathcal{A}^*|} \sum_{k=1}^{b} \sum_{\alpha \in \mathcal{A}^*} \mathbb{E}_\alpha[N_{\alpha,k}], \quad (7)$$

where we substitute $\mu_{i,j,k} = \frac{1}{2} + \varepsilon\alpha_{i,j,k}$ in the last equality. Next, we show the following lemma.

Lemma 5. *For each $0 < \varepsilon \leq 1/4$, $\mathbb{E}_\alpha[N_{\alpha,k}] \leq \mathbb{E}_{\alpha-k}[N_{\alpha,k}] + 2\varepsilon nT\sqrt{\mathbb{E}_{\alpha-k}[N_{\alpha,k}]}$.*

Proof. Let $\sigma^t \in \{0,1\}^{n \times b}$ denote the feedback that the algorithm observes at round t, i.e., the (j,k) entry of σ^t is $v^t_{i',j,k}$ where i' is the agent who receives (j,k). In addition, for $t = 1, \ldots, T$, we denote by $S_t = (\sigma^1, \ldots, \sigma^t) \in \{0,1\}^{n \times b \times t}$.

all feedback observed up to round t. In the rest of the proof, we use the following notation on the KL-divergence:

$$K_t := \sum_{S_t \in \{0,1\}^{n \times b \times t}} \mathbb{P}_{\alpha-k}[S_t] \ln \frac{\mathbb{P}_{\alpha-k}[S_t]}{\mathbb{P}_{\alpha}[S_t]},$$

$$K'_t := \sum_{S_t \in \{0,1\}^{n \times b \times t}} \mathbb{P}_{\alpha-k}[S_t] \ln \frac{\mathbb{P}_{\alpha-k}[\sigma^t | S_{t-1}]}{\mathbb{P}_{\alpha}[\sigma^t | S_{t-1}]}.$$

By the chain rule, we have $K_T = \sum_{t=1}^{T} K'_t$. Since the algorithm is assumed to be deterministic, we can treat $N_{\alpha,k}$ as a function f of S_T. Then, the following holds:

$$\mathbb{E}_{\alpha}[N_{\alpha,k}] - \mathbb{E}_{\alpha-k}[N_{\alpha,k}] = \mathbb{E}_{\alpha}[f(S_T)] - \mathbb{E}_{\alpha-k}[f(S_T)]$$

$$= \sum_{S_T} f(S_T)(\mathbb{P}_{\alpha}[S_T] - \mathbb{P}_{\alpha-k}[S_T])$$

$$\leq \sum_{S_T : \mathbb{P}_{\alpha}[S_T] > \mathbb{P}_{\alpha-k}[S_T]} f(S_T)(\mathbb{P}_{\alpha}[S_T] - \mathbb{P}_{\alpha-k}[S_T])$$

$$\leq nT \sum_{S_T : \mathbb{P}_{\alpha}[S_T] > \mathbb{P}_{\alpha-k}[S_T]} (\mathbb{P}_{\alpha}[S_T] - \mathbb{P}_{\alpha-k}[S_T])$$

$$= \frac{nT}{2} \sum_{S_T} |\mathbb{P}_{\alpha}[S_T] - \mathbb{P}_{\alpha-k}[S_T]|$$

$$\leq \frac{nT}{2} \sqrt{2K_T} = \frac{nT}{2} \sqrt{2 \sum_{t=1}^{T} K'_t}, \quad (8)$$

where $N_{\alpha,k} := f(S_T)$, the first inequality is due to $N_{\alpha,k} \leq nT$ and the last inequality is due to the Pinsker's inequality. K'_t is computed as follows.

Claim. Fix any S_{t-1} and let $P(S_{t-1})$ be the number of correct assignments (i, j, k') in a^t such that $k' = k$, i.e., $P(S_{t-1}) := \sum_{i,j=1}^{n} \alpha_{i,j,k} a^t_{i,j,k}$. Then, we have $K'_t = \frac{1}{2} \ln \frac{1}{1-4\varepsilon^2} \mathbb{E}_{\alpha-k}[P(S_{t-1})]$.

The proof of the claim can be found in Claim 3 of the full version [27]. By applying the claim to Eq. 8, it follows that

$$\mathbb{E}_{\alpha}[N_{\alpha,k}] - \mathbb{E}_{\alpha-k}[N_{\alpha,k}] \leq \frac{nT}{2} \sqrt{\ln \frac{1}{1-4\varepsilon^2} \sum_{t=1}^{T} \mathbb{E}_{\alpha-k}[P(S_{t-1})]}$$

$$= \frac{nT}{2} \sqrt{\ln \frac{1}{1-4\varepsilon^2} \mathbb{E}_{\alpha-k}[N_{\alpha,k}]} \leq 2\varepsilon nT \sqrt{\mathbb{E}_{\alpha-k}[N_{\alpha,k}]},$$

where the last inequality follows from the convexity of $-\ln(1-x)$ and $0 < \varepsilon \leq 1/4$. This completes the proof.

By the definition of an $(\alpha - k)$-adversary, we obtain

$$\sum_{\alpha \in \mathcal{A}^*} \mathbb{E}_{\alpha-k}[N_{\alpha,k}] = \frac{1}{n!} \sum_{\beta \in \mathcal{A}^*} \sum_{\alpha:(\alpha-k)=(\beta-k)} \mathbb{E}_{\alpha-k}[N_{\alpha,k}]$$

$$= \frac{1}{n!} \sum_{\beta \in \mathcal{A}^*} \mathbb{E}_{\beta-k} \left[\sum_{\alpha:(\alpha-k)=(\beta-k)} \sum_{t,i,j} a_{i,j,k}^t \alpha_{i,j,k} \right]$$

$$= \frac{1}{n!} \sum_{\beta \in \mathcal{A}^*} \mathbb{E}_{\beta-k} \left[\sum_{t,i,j} a_{i,j,k}^t \sum_{\alpha:(\alpha-k)=(\beta-k)} \alpha_{i,j,k} \right]$$

$$= \frac{1}{n!} \sum_{\beta \in \mathcal{A}^*} (nT \cdot (n-1)!) = |\mathcal{A}^*|T.$$

By this result, Lemma 5 and the Cauchy-Schwartz inequality, it follows that

$$\sum_\alpha \mathbb{E}_\alpha[N_{\alpha,k}] \leq |\mathcal{A}^*|T + 2\varepsilon nT\sqrt{|\mathcal{A}^*| \cdot |\mathcal{A}^*|T}$$

and then, $\frac{\varepsilon}{n|\mathcal{A}^*|}\sum_{k=1}^b \sum_{\alpha \in \mathcal{A}^*} \mathbb{E}_\alpha[N_{\alpha,k}] \leq \varepsilon bT\left(\frac{1}{n} + 2\varepsilon\sqrt{T}\right)$. Note that $\mathrm{OPT}_\mu = (1/2+\varepsilon)bT$. By tuning $\varepsilon = 1/(8\sqrt{T})$, we finally have the following lower bound:

$$\mathrm{OPT}_\mu - \mathbb{E}_{\alpha^*}[\mathrm{ALG}_\mu] \geq \varepsilon bT\left(1 - \frac{1}{n} - 2\varepsilon\sqrt{T}\right) \geq \frac{1}{32}b\sqrt{T} = \Theta\left(\frac{m}{n}\sqrt{T}\right). \quad (9)$$

By Yao's principle, the lower bound also applies to randomized algorithms. This concludes the proof of the first part of Theorem 4.

Lower Bound for R_T

Next we show a lower bound on R_T. Under the assumptions $T \geq \max\{n, m^2\}$ and $m/n \geq \lceil 2338 \ln T \rceil$, we claim that OPT_μ is close enough to $\mathbb{E}[\mathrm{OPT}]$, whose proof is found in Lemma 6 of the full version [27].

Claim. $\mathrm{OPT}_\mu \leq \mathbb{E}[\mathrm{OPT}] + (\frac{1}{32} - \frac{1}{1000})b\sqrt{T}$.

Since we can show that $\mathbb{E}_{\alpha^*}[\mathrm{ALG}] \leq \frac{1}{2}bT + \frac{\varepsilon}{n|\mathcal{A}^*|}\sum_{k=1}^b \sum_{\alpha \in \mathcal{A}^*} \mathbb{E}_\alpha[N_{\alpha,k}]$ in a way similar to Eq. 7, the lower bound $b\sqrt{T}/32$ established in the first part of Theorem 4 is also a lower bound of $\mathrm{OPT}_\mu - \mathbb{E}[\mathrm{ALG}]$. This holds also for randomized algorithms. Plugging the clam into Eq. 9, we finally see that $\mathbb{E}[\mathrm{OPT}] - \mathbb{E}_{\alpha^*}[\mathrm{ALG}] \geq \frac{1}{1000}b\sqrt{T} = \Theta\left(\frac{m}{n}\sqrt{T}\right)$. Then we see that the second part of Theorem 4 holds.

6 Conclusion and Discussion

In this paper, we introduced the bandit max-min fair allocation problem. We have proposed an algorithm with a regret bound of $O(m\sqrt{T}\ln T/n +$

$m\sqrt{T\ln(mnT)})$ when T is sufficiently large, and showed a lower bound $\Omega(m\sqrt{T}/n)$ on the regret. Thus, when T is sufficiently large, the bounds matches up to a logarithmic factor of T.

We remark that the regret bounds also apply to variations of our problem. One such case is maximizing the minimum "expected" utility: $\text{ALG}_\text{E} = \min_i \mathbb{E}\left[\sum_{t,e} \mu_{ie} a_{ie}^t\right]$ where the regret is defined as $\text{OPT}_\mu - \text{ALG}_\text{E}$. In this setting, we have $\text{ALG}_\text{E} \geq \text{ALG}_\mu$ and then similar proofs work to derive the same bounds.

For another, our algorithm works even when each agent's bundle in each round must satisfy a matroid constraint. We detail this in the full version [27].

One future work is to close the gap between the upper and lower bounds on R_T. An upper bound with a weaker assumption on T and a lower bound using $\mathbb{E}[\text{OPT}]$ directly are also open. Another potential future work is to extend the problem setting to reflect practical situations. For example, in a subscription service, the rental period can be different depending on situations. It would be possible to improve a regret if users let us know what they probably dislike (i.e., item e with μ_{ie} being almost zero). We believe that such an extension of the problem provides insight into real-world applications.

Acknowledgments. This work was partially supported by the joint project of Kyoto University and Toyota Motor Corporation, titled "Advanced Mathematical Science for Mobility Society", JST ERATO Grant Number JPMJER2301, JST ASPIRE Grant Number JPMJAP2302, and JSPS KAKENHI Grant Numbers JP21K17708, JP21H03397, and JP25K00137.

Disclosure of Interests. The authors have no competing interests to declare that are relevant to the content of this article.

References

1. Aleksandrov, M., Walsh, T.: Online fair division: a survey. Proc. AAAI Conf. Artif. Intell. **34**(09), 13557–13562 (2020)
2. Arora, S., Hazan, E., Kale, S.: The multiplicative weights update method: a meta-algorithm and applications. Theor. Comput. **8**(1), 121–164 (2012)
3. Asadpour, A., Saberi, A.: An approximation algorithm for max-min fair allocation of indivisible goods. SIAM J. Comput. **39**(7), 2970–2989 (2010)
4. Audibert, J.Y., Bubeck, S., Lugosi, G.: Regret in online combinatorial optimization. Math. Oper. Res. **39**(1), 31–45 (2014)
5. Auer, P., Cesa-Bianchi, N., Freund, Y., Schapire, R.E.: The nonstochastic multi-armed bandit problem. SIAM J. Comput. **32**(1), 48–77 (2002)
6. Badanidiyuru, A., Kleinberg, R., Slivkins, A.: Bandits with knapsacks. J. ACM **65**(3), 13:1–13:55 (2018)
7. Banerjee, S., Gkatzelis, V., Gorokh, A., Jin, B.: Online nash social welfare maximization with predictions. In: Proceedings of the 2022 Annual ACM-SIAM Symposium on Discrete Algorithms, pp. 1–19 (2022)
8. Bansal, N., Sviridenko, M.: The santa claus problem. In: Proceedings of the 38th Annual ACM Symposium on Theory of Computing, pp. 31–40 (2006)

9. Barman, S., Khan, A., Maiti, A.: Universal and tight online algorithms for generalized-mean welfare. In: Proceedings of the AAAI Conference on Artificial Intelligence, vol. 36, pp. 4793–4800 (2022)
10. Benade, G., Kazachkov, A.M., Procaccia, A.D., Psomas, C.A.: How to make envy vanish over time. In: Proceedings of the 2018 ACM Conference on Economics and Computation, pp. 593–610 (2018)
11. Besson, L., Kaufmann, E.: What doubling tricks can and can't do for multi-armed bandits. arXiv preprint arXiv:1803.06971 (2018)
12. Bezáková, I., Dani, V.: Allocating Indivisible Goods. ACM SIGecom Exchanges **5**(3), 11–18 (2005)
13. Bistritz, I., Baharav, T.Z., Leshem, A., Bambos, N.: One for all and all for one: distributed learning of fair allocations with multi-player bandits. IEEE J. Sel. Areas Inf. Theor. **2**(2), 584–598 (2021)
14. Boursier, E., Perchet, V.: A survey on multi-player bandits. J. Mach. Learn. Res. **25**(137), 1–45 (2024)
15. Bouveret, S., Chevaleyre, Y., Maudet, N.: Fair allocation of indivisible goods. In: Brandt, F., Conitzer, V., Endriss, U., Lang, J., Procaccia, A.D. (eds.) Handbook of Computational Social Choice, chap. 12, pp. 284–310. Cambridge University Press (2016)
16. Cesa-Bianchi, N., Lugosi, G.: Prediction and playing games. In: Prediction, Learning, and Games, chap. 7, pp. 180–232. Cambridge University Press (2006)
17. Chakrabarty, D., Chuzhoy, J., Khanna, S.: On allocating goods to maximize fairness. In: Proceedings of the 50th Annual IEEE Symposium on Foundations of Computer Science, pp. 107–116 (2009)
18. Chen, W., Wang, Y., Yuan, Y.: Combinatorial multi-armed bandit: general framework and applications. In: Proceedings of the 30th International Conference on Machine Learning, pp. 151–159 (2013)
19. Chen, Y., Cuellar, A., Luo, H., Modi, J., Nemlekar, H., Nikolaidis, S.: The fair contextual multi-armed bandit. In: Proceedings of the 19th International Conference on Autonomous Agents and MultiAgent Systems, pp. 1810–1812 (2020)
20. Claure, H., Chen, Y., Modi, J., Jung, M., Nikolaidis, S.: Multi-armed bandits with fairness constraints for distributing resources to human teammates. In: Proceedings of the 2020 ACM/IEEE International Conference on Human-Robot Interaction, pp. 299–308 (2020)
21. Cohen, S., Agmon, N.: Near-optimal online resource allocation in the random-order model. In: Proceedings of the 23rd International Conference on Autonomous Agents and Multiagent Systems, pp. 2219–2221 (2024)
22. Devanur, N.R., Jain, K., Sivan, B., Wilkens, C.A.: Near optimal online algorithms and fast approximation algorithms for resource allocation problems. J. ACM **66**(1), 7:1–7:41 (2019)
23. Feige, U.: On allocations that maximize fairness. In: Proceedings of the 19th Annual ACM-SIAM Symposium on Discrete Algorithms, pp. 287–293 (2008)
24. Golovin, D.: Max-min fair allocation of indivisible goods. Technical Report CMU-CS-05-144, Carnegie Mellon University (2005)
25. Haeupler, B., Saha, B., Srinivasan, A.: New constructive aspects of the lovász local lemma. J. ACM **58**(6), 28:1–28:28 (2011)
26. Hajiaghayi, M., Khani, M., Panigrahi, D., Springer, M.: Online algorithms for the Santa Claus problem. In: Advances in Neural Information Processing Systems 35, vol. 35, pp. 30732–30743 (2022)
27. Harada, T., Ito, S., Sumita, H.: Bandit max-min fair allocation. arXiv preprint arXiv:2505.05169 (2025)

28. Hossain, S., Micha, E., Shah, N.: Fair algorithms for multi-agent multi-armed bandits. Adv. Neural. Inf. Process. Syst. **34**, 24005–24017 (2021)
29. Igarashi, A., Lackner, M., Nardi, O., Novaro, A.: Repeated fair allocation of indivisible items. In: Proceedings of the 38th AAAI Conference on Artificial Intelligence, pp. 9781–9789 (2024)
30. Jones, M., Nguyen, H., Nguyen, T.: An efficient algorithm for fair multi-agent multi-armed bandit with low regret. Proc. AAAI Conf. Artif. Intell. **37**(7), 8159–8167 (2023)
31. Kawase, Y., Sumita, H.: Online max-min fair allocation. In: Proceedings of International Symposium on Algorithmic Game Theory, pp. 526–543 (2022)
32. Lai, T., Robbins, H.: Asymptotically efficient adaptive allocation rules. Adv. Appl. Math. **6**(1), 4–22 (1985)
33. Lenstra, J.K., Shmoys, D.B., Tardos, É.: Approximation algorithms for scheduling unrelated parallel machines. Math. Program. **46**, 259–271 (1990)
34. Li, F., Liu, J., Ji, B.: Combinatorial sleeping bandits with fairness constraints. IEEE Trans. Netw. Sci. Eng. **7**(3), 1799–1813 (2019)
35. Micheel, K.J., Wilczynski, A.: Fairness in repeated house allocation. In: Proceedings of the 23rd International Conference on Autonomous Agents and Multiagent Systems, pp. 2390–2392 (2024)
36. Patil, V., Ghalme, G., Nair, V., Narahari, Y.: Achieving fairness in the stochastic multi-armed bandit problem. J. Mach. Learn. Res. **22**(174), 1–31 (2021)
37. Zhang, M., Deo-Campo Vuong, R., Luo, H.: No-regret learning for fair multi-agent social welfare optimization. In: Advances in Neural Information Processing Systems, vol. 37, pp. 57671–57700 (2024)

Weight-Rounding Error in Deep Neural Networks

Jiří Šíma(✉) and Petra Vidnerová

Institute of Computer Science of the Czech Academy of Sciences, Prague 8, Czechia
{sima,petra}@cs.cas.cz

Abstract. Current AI technologies based on deep neural networks (DNNs) are computationally extremely demanding, which limits their widespread deployment in embedded devices with constrained energy resources (e.g. battery-powered smartphones). One possible approach to solving this problem is to reduce the precision of weight parameters, which can save an enormous amount of energy for computation and data transfer at the cost of only a small loss in inference accuracy. In this paper, we provide a theoretical analysis of the effect of any weight rounding (e.g. reduced bitwidth) in a trained DNN on its output. We first derive a global upper bound on the output error of DNN (under the L_1 norm) caused by the weight rounding for all inputs from a bounded domain in the worst case, which turns out to be overestimated for practical use. We prove that computing this maximum error is NP-hard for a given weight rounding even for two layers, which follows from the NP-hardness of neuron state domains. Based on the concept of so-called shortcut weights, we propose a method called AppMax that estimates this error using linear programming on convex polytopes around test/training data points, which works for any approximation of DNN (e.g. including pruning). The AppMax method was extensively tested on fully connected and convolutional neural networks (trained on the MNIST database) for decreasing bitwidth of weights. The experiments demonstrate a clear improvement in the error guarantees provided by this method, which can be used to evaluate different approximation strategies and identify those that best balance accuracy and energy efficiency.

Keywords: Deep neural networks · Weight rounding · Maximum error bounds · NP-hardness · Linear programming

1 Introduction

Deep neural networks (DNN) stands at the forefront of both research and practical applications in artificial intelligence (AI), including large language models, image recognition, computer vision, speech recognition, robotics, etc. An increasing number of embedded devices rely on DNNs to deliver sophisticated services, such as autonomous surveillance systems utilizing advanced object recognition, personal assistants employing machine translation, smart healthcare applications. Nevertheless, remarkable performance on these tasks comes with increased computational demands, posing significant challenges for deploying DNNs on resource-constrained edge devices. The escalated computational requirements of DNNs which typically consist of tens of layers, hundreds of thousands of neurons, and tens of millions of weight parameters, naturally lead to increased battery consumption, which is a major bottleneck to the development of smart wearable electronics, such as smartphones, smart glasses, or voice assistants. In light of these considerations, addressing the energy consumption of DNN implementations emerges as a topic of paramount importance.

Recent research has focused on developing methods that enable energy-efficient processing of DNNs [26]. There are basically two main approaches to reduce energy costs of DNNs. First, computational requirements are addressed by *hardware design* utilizing specialized accelerators tailored for DNN inference [11,23] that employ massive parallelism. DNNs are implemented on various hardware platforms including GPUs [32], FPGAs [18], in-memory computing architectures [19], etc. which share asymptotic energy complexity bounds [24,25].

The second approach is suitable for error-tolerant applications such as image classification where enormous amount of energy can be saved at the cost of only a small loss in accuracy by using *approximate computing* methods [2,6,15-17,27]. One possibility is to reduce the number of operations and model size which is based on techniques such as compression [4], pruning [31], and compact network architectures [12]. Another possibility is to reduce the precision of the used arithmetics which includes conversion from floating point to fixed point [30], reducing the bitwidth [20], nonuniform quantization [14], weight sharing [8], and approximate multiplication circuits [1]. For example, an 8-bit fixed-point multiply consumes 15.5 or 18.5 times less energy than a 32-bit fixed-point or floating-point multiply, respectively [9].

It has been empirically observed that the energy consumption for DNN inference is predominantly due to both numerical computation and data moves in memory where the later can achieve 70% of the total energy cost [31]. Both these energy components can be significantly decreased by reducing the precision of DNN weight parameters. In this paper, we theoretically analyze the effect of weight rounding in a trained DNN on its output. This post-training rounding is specified by individual weight deviations and can thus be generated by any method, such as those referenced above (e.g., reduced bitwidth, quantization). For the purposes of error analysis, we formalize a model of feedforward (acyclic) DNNs composed of ReLU gates employing the rectified linear unit activation function (Sect. 2), which appears also to cover a widespread important DNN class of convolutional neural networks (CNNs).

First, we derive a global worst-case upper bound on the DNN output error that is caused by a given weight rounding, which is valid for all inputs from a bounded domain (Sect. 3). The error of DNN outputs is measured by the L_1 norm which makes the analysis applicable to regression tasks. The main idea is that the output error of any individual neuron is bounded for *all* its inputs taken from a previously estimated interval state domains, which is propagated feedforwardly through the network. Nevertheless, our experiments show that this worst-case upper bound on the DNN output error turns out to be overestimated for practical tasks. It could be improved by refining the estimation of neuron state domains, which, however, are shown to be NP-hard to compute even for two-layer networks (Sect. 4). Since the maximum of the DNN output can be attained at any interior point of the input domain, we prove this result for both binary and real inputs. As a consequence, we obtain NP-hardness also for computing the global maximum error for a given weight rounding even for two layers.

Furthermore, we introduce a concept of so-called shortcut weights which are coefficients of the linear dependence of DNN outputs on its inputs for fixed saturations of neuron states, due to the ReLU activation function is piecewise linear. Based on these shortcut weights, we propose a method called AppMax that estimates the maximum error for a given weight rounding using linear programming on convex polytopes surrounding test/training data points (Sect. 5). The method is also adapted to classification tasks and it is applicable not only to weight rounding but it provides the maximum error for any approximation of a DNN by another network, e.g., created by pruning. We have tested the AppMax method on fully connected and convolutional neural networks trained on the MNIST database for decreasing bitwidth of weights (Sect. 6). The presented experiments demonstrate that the AppMax method provides more confident estimates of the maximum error than those on the test data points only, which is already achieved with fewer data.

A related recent study [3] develops a theoretical framework for analyzing the numerical stability of DNNs with differentiable activation functions (e.g., hyperbolic tangent) under floating-point arithmetic, using backward error analysis and condition numbers. While its focus is on global perturbation models, our work complements this by introducing the practically applicable AppMax method for estimating approximation errors of piecewise linear DNNs under arbitrary post-training modifications, including but not limited to weight rounding. The proposed AppMax method enables systematic comparison of approximation strategies and helps identify those that offer the best trade-off between accuracy and performance. Further research in this direction could facilitate the development of techniques for identifying DNN components suitable for approximation or removal, aiming to reduce energy consumption while maintaining explicit and reliable error guarantees.

2 A Formal Model of NNs and Weight Rounding

For the error analysis of weight rounding, we define a formal model of (artificial) feedforward neural networks (NNs) with the ReLU (rectified linear unit) activation function, which covers commonly used DNNs such as convolutional neural networks (CNNs). The architecture of a NN $\mathcal{N}$ is a connected directed acyclic graph (V, E) where $E \subset V \times V$, which is composed of units, called neurons, whose real states (outputs) are denoted as y_j for $j \in V$. This includes a set of n input neurons $X = \{1, \ldots, n\} \subseteq V$ that serve only for presenting an external real input $(x_1, \ldots, x_n) \in \mathbb{R}^n$ to $\mathcal{N}$, that is $y_j = x_j$ for $j \in X$, whereas a set of m

output neurons, $Y \subseteq V' = V \setminus X$ provides the output $\mathcal{N}(x_1,\ldots,x_n) \in \mathbb{R}^m$ from $\mathcal{N}$ for this input. For any neuron $j \in V$, we denote by $j_\leftarrow = \{i \in V \mid (i,j) \in E\}$ the set of units in $\mathcal{N}$ from which connections (edges) lead to j, which represent the inputs to j. Thus, we assume $j_\leftarrow = \emptyset$ for $j \in X$, and $j_\leftarrow \cap Y = \emptyset$ for $j \in V$.

For any non-input neuron $j \in V'$ and its input $i \in j_\leftarrow$, let $w_{ji} \in \mathbb{R}$ be a real weight associated with the connection $(i,j) \in E$, whereas formally $w_{ji} = 0$ for $i \in V \setminus j_\leftarrow$. In addition, $w_{j0} \in \mathbb{R}$ denotes its real bias, which, as usual, can be viewed as a weight of an edge $(0,j) \in E$ leading from an additional formal input neuron $0 \in X$ to j, whose state $y_0 = 1$ is constantly one and $0 \in j_\leftarrow$ for every $j \in V'$ such that $w_{j0} \neq 0$. Then the excitation ξ_j of neuron $j \in V'$ is evaluated as a weighted sum of its inputs:

$$\xi_j = \sum_{i \in j_\leftarrow} w_{ji} y_i, \tag{1}$$

provided that the states y_i have already been computed for all units $i \in j_\leftarrow$, after an external input $(x_1,\ldots,x_n)$ to $\mathcal{N}$ was given at the beginning. Then the output y_j from neuron $j \in V'$ is computed by applying the ReLU activation function $R : \mathbb{R} \to \mathbb{R}$ to its excitation ξ_j,

$$y_j = R(\xi_j) = \max(0, \xi_j). \tag{2}$$

Alternatively, for *classification* tasks, the states y_j of at least two output neurons $j \in Y$ normalize their excitations into a categorical probability distribution by using the softmax function

$$y_j = \frac{e^{\xi_j}}{\sum_{k \in Y} e^{\xi_k}} \in (0,1). \tag{3}$$

while the identity $y_j = \xi_j$ for $j \in Y$ can be employed for *regression* (to allow negative outputs).

The convolutional layers in CNNs are at times interlaced by max pooling layers whose units j implement the maximum of its inputs, $y_j = \max_{i \in j_\leftarrow} y_i$. Note that $y_i \geq 0$ for $i \in V'$ due to (2), and we will assume $y_i \geq 0$ for $i \in X$ without loss of generality (see below). Then such a max pooling unit can be replaced in $\mathcal{N}$ by a subnetwork composed of neurons that compute their states according to (1) and (2), since the maximum of two numbers $\max(x,y) = R(x-y) + y$ for $x, y \geq 0$, can be used for evaluating the maximum of $|j_\leftarrow|$ nonnegative inputs (e.g., the maxima of pairs is used to compute the maxima of fours, eights, sixteens, etc.). The alternative average pooling unit j that computes the average of its nonnegative inputs, $y_j = \frac{1}{|j_\leftarrow|} \sum_{i \in j_\leftarrow} y_i$, can be viewed as a neuron $j \in V'$ with the bias $w_{j0} = 0$ and weights $w_{ji} = 1/|j_\leftarrow|$ for $i \in j_\leftarrow \setminus \{0\}$. Thus, we will hereafter assume without loss of generality that $\mathcal{N}$ does not contain pooling layers.

Suppose that the weights (including the biases) in $\mathcal{N}$ are rounded, e.g. to a given number of binary digits in their floating-point representations, which can be expressed as

$$\widetilde{w_{ji}} = w_{ji} + \delta_{ji} \quad \text{for } j \in V' \ \& \ i \in j_\leftarrow \tag{4}$$

where $\delta_{ji} \in \mathbb{R}$ is a real rounding error of weight w_{ji}. Denote by $\widetilde{\xi}_j$ and $\widetilde{y}_j$ the excitation and output of $j \in V'$, respectively, that are computed by using the rounded weights (4). We will be interested in the effect of this weight rounding on the output of $\mathcal{N}$, which is measured for regression tasks by the L_1 norm as the sum of excitation deviations of output neurons for given external inputs:

$$E(x_1,\ldots,x_n) = \sum_{j \in Y} \left|\xi_j - \widetilde{\xi}_j\right|. \tag{5}$$

3 The Worst-Case Error Bounds for Weight Rounding

For an unbounded external input $(x_1,\ldots,x_n) \in \mathbb{R}^n$ to $\mathcal{N}$, the output error (5) caused by weight rounding (4) can be arbitrarily large. In practical applications, however, this input is usually taken from some bounded interval domain:

$$a_i \leq x_i \leq b_i \quad \text{for } i \in X \tag{6}$$

(particularly, $a_0 = x_0 = b_0 = 1$ for the formal input $0 \in X$ corresponding to biases w_{j0} for $j \in V'$) which ensures $a_i \leq y_i \leq b_i$ for $i \in X$. In addition, we assume without loss of generality that $a_i = 0$ and $b_i = 1$ for each input neuron $i \in X \setminus \{0\}$, since external inputs can be linearly mapped onto $[0,1]^n$ by appropriately adjusting the corresponding weights.

Then we can estimate the state intervals $[a_j, b_j]$ also for non-input neurons $j \in V'$ by propagating the input domain (6) through $\mathcal{N}$ so that

$$a_j \leq y_j \leq b_j \quad \text{for } j \in V', \tag{7}$$

provided that $a_i \leq y_i \leq b_i$ for all its inputs $i \in j_\leftarrow$. This can be ensured by

$$a_j = R(a'_j), \quad b_j = R(b'_j) \quad \text{for } j \in V', \quad \text{where} \tag{8}$$

$$a'_j = \sum_{\substack{i \in j_\leftarrow \\ w_{ji} < 0}} w_{ji} b_i + \sum_{\substack{i \in j_\leftarrow \\ w_{ji} > 0}} w_{ji} a_i, \quad b'_j = \sum_{\substack{i \in j_\leftarrow \\ w_{ji} < 0}} w_{ji} a_i + \sum_{\substack{i \in j_\leftarrow \\ w_{ji} > 0}} w_{ji} b_i \quad \text{for } j \in V'. \tag{9}$$

Furthermore, we assume without loss of generality that $a_j = 0$ and $b_j > 0$ for $j \in V \setminus (Y \cup \{0\})$, since any non-input neuron $j \in V'$ with $a_j > 0$ or $b_j = 0$ can be eliminated from $\mathcal{N}$ as its output is linear, $y_j = \xi_j$, or zero, $y_j = 0$, respectively, due to (7) and (2). Note that the interval bounds (9) represent the possible worst case only for one neuron while they are overestimated when combined for more consecutive neurons in deep $\mathcal{N}$ where their states usually cannot reach the interval endpoints (8) for any external input satisfying (6). We will show in Sect. 4 that it is actually NP-hard to find the tight bounds in (7) already for two-layer $\mathcal{N}$.

For weight rounding (4), the states $\widetilde{y}_i$ of inputs $i \in j_\leftarrow$ to a non-input neuron $j \in V'$ are supposed to be within intervals around their precise values y_i as

$$y_i + \alpha_i \leq R(y_i + \alpha_i) \leq \widetilde{y}_i \leq y_i + \beta_i \quad \text{for } i \in j_\leftarrow, \tag{10}$$

where $\alpha_i \leq 0 \leq \beta_i$. Clearly, the states $y_i = \widetilde{y}_i$ of input units $i \in X$ are not affected by weight rounding, which means $\alpha_i = \beta_i = 0$ for $i \in X$. The main idea of estimating the impact of weight rounding on the non-input neuron $j \in V'$ in the worst case, is to bound $\widetilde{y}_j$ so that for some $\alpha_j \leq 0 \leq \beta_j$,

$$y_j + \alpha_j \leq R(y_j + \alpha_j) \leq \widetilde{y}_j \leq y_j + \beta_j \tag{11}$$

for every $\widetilde{y}_i \in [R(y_i + \alpha_i), y_i + \beta_i]$ in (10), over all $y_i \in [a_i, b_i]$ (where $a_i = 0$ and $b_i > 0$) given by (6) for $i \in j_- \cap X$ or by (8) for $i \in j_- \cap V'$. This can be achieved by

$$\alpha_j = \min(0, \alpha'_j) \leq 0, \quad \beta_j = \max(0, \beta'_j) \geq 0 \tag{12}$$

where $\xi_j + \alpha'_j \leq \widetilde{\xi}_j \leq \xi_j + \beta'_j$ is ensured by

$$\alpha'_j = \delta_{j0} + \sum_{\substack{i \in j_- \\ \delta_{ji} < 0}} \delta_{ji} b_i + \sum_{\substack{i \in j_- \\ \widetilde{w}_{ji} > 0}} \widetilde{w}_{ji} \alpha_i + \sum_{\substack{i \in j_- \\ \widetilde{w}_{ji} < 0}} \widetilde{w}_{ji} \beta_i \tag{13}$$

$$\beta'_j = \delta_{j0} + \sum_{\substack{i \in j_- \\ \delta_{ji} > 0}} \delta_{ji} b_i + \sum_{\substack{i \in j_- \\ \widetilde{w}_{ji} < 0}} \widetilde{w}_{ji} \alpha_i + \sum_{\substack{i \in j_- \\ \widetilde{w}_{ji} > 0}} \widetilde{w}_{ji} \beta_i \tag{14}$$

for $j \in V'$.

We show that (12)–(14) meets (11). It follows from (10) and (4) that

$$\widetilde{\xi}_j = \sum_{i \in j_-} \widetilde{w}_{ji} \widetilde{y}_i \geq \sum_{\substack{i \in j_- \\ \widetilde{w}_{ji} \geq 0}} \widetilde{w}_{ji}(y_i + \alpha_i) + \sum_{\substack{i \in j_- \\ \widetilde{w}_{ji} < 0}} \widetilde{w}_{ji}(y_i + \beta_i)$$

$$= \sum_{i \in j_-} (w_{ji} + \delta_{ji}) y_i + \sum_{\substack{i \in j_- \\ \widetilde{w}_{ji} > 0}} \widetilde{w}_{ji} \alpha_i + \sum_{\substack{i \in j_- \\ \widetilde{w}_{ji} < 0}} \widetilde{w}_{ji} \beta_i \geq \xi_j + \alpha'_j \tag{15}$$

according to (6), (7), $a_i = 0$ for $i \in j_- \setminus \{0\}$, and (13), which gives

$$\widetilde{y}_j = R(\widetilde{\xi}_j) \geq R(\xi_j + \alpha'_j) \geq R(\xi_j + \alpha_j) \geq R(\xi_j) + \alpha_j = y_j + \alpha_j \tag{16}$$

due to (12). Similarly, $\widetilde{\xi}_j \leq \xi_j + \beta'_j$, which implies $\widetilde{y}_j \leq y_j + \beta_j$. This completes the proof of (11).

The theoretical estimates (12)–(14) including (8) and (9), can be used to compute an upper bound on the weight-rounding error (5) of $\mathcal{N}$ in the worst case, which is valid for any external input from the interval domain (6):

$$\max_{(x_1,\ldots,x_n) \in [0,1]^n} E(x_1, \ldots, x_n) \leq \sum_{j \in Y} \max(-\alpha'_j, \beta'_j). \tag{17}$$

Nevertheless, practical experiments show that these bounds are very conservative. For example, we tested a NN (see Net1 in Sect. 6) with only three fully connected layers whose weights were rounded to be represented by 16 bits. The experiment has shown that the intervals $[\alpha_j, \beta_j]$ for $j \in V$, tend to get larger by magnitude every next layer (see Table 1). For comparison, the actual values of error (5) are shown in Sect. 6 to be less than 0.1 for all test data points. Therefore, this approach turns out to be infeasible for practical usage, since the interval bounds are highly overestimated.

Table 1. The smallest and widest intervals $[\alpha_j, \beta_j]$ according to (12)–(14) for each of the three layers of the fully-connected NN Net1.

Layer	Smallest $[\alpha_j, \beta_j]$	Widest $[\alpha_j, \beta_j]$
1	[−0.0016, 0.0028]	[−0.0142, 0.0157]
2	[−2.0662, 2.0615]	[−2.6336, 2.6642]
3	[−57.5910, 58.6081]	[−84.9428, 85.1832]

4 Computing the Maximum Error Is NP-Hard

In Sect. 3, the worst-case error bound (17) computed by (12)–(14) is overestimated also because it is based on the very conservative estimates of the interval boundaries of neuron states (8), (9). Thus, there is a natural issue whether these estimates could be improved. This can be formulated as the problem of finding the maximum output for a given NN. Namely, we are given $\mathcal{N}$ with one output ($|Y| = 1$) and $|X| = n$ input neurons, and a positive real constant $M > 0$. The *maximum output* problem (MO) is to decide whether there is an external input $(x_1, \ldots, x_n) \in [0, 1]^n$ to $\mathcal{N}$ such that $\mathcal{N}(x_1, \ldots, x_n) \geq M$. However, this problem is proven to be computationally hard by reduction from the *Boolean satisfiability* problem SAT (proof omitted):

Theorem 1. *MO is NP-hard for two-layer NNs with binary inputs from $\{0, 1\}^n$.*

Nevertheless, the maximum output value of NNs can also be attained at any interior point of the external input domain $[0, 1]^n$. Consider a simple example of a NN $\mathcal{N}_\mu$ with a real parameter $\mu \in (0, 1)$, that is composed of two layers with one input neuron ($n = 1$) for external inputs $x \in [0, 1]$, one unit in the first layer, and one output neuron which computes the function $\mathcal{N}_\mu(x) = R(x - R(\frac{x}{\mu} - 1))$. Observe that $\mathcal{N}_\mu(x) = x$ for every x such that $0 \leq x \leq \mu$ due to $R(\frac{x}{\mu} - 1) = 0$ in this case. On the other hand, for every x satisfying $\mu < x \leq 1$ we have $R(\frac{x}{\mu} - 1) = \frac{x}{\mu} - 1$ which, for $\mathcal{N}_\mu(x) > 0$, implies $\mathcal{N}_\mu(x) = R(x - (\frac{x}{\mu} - 1)) = \frac{\mu-1}{\mu} x + 1 < \mu$ due to $x > \mu$ and $0 < \mu < 1$. It follows that the maximum output value $\max_{x \in [0,1]} \mathcal{N}_\mu(x) = \mu$ is attained at the interior point $x = \mu \in (0, 1)$. Therefore, we generalize Theorem 1 to the *real* external input domain.

Theorem 2. *MO is NP-hard for two-layer NNs with real inputs from $[0, 1]^n$ (remains NP-hard even if the excitation of the output neuron is nonnegative).*

Proof. We will use a reduction from the known NP-complete *Exactly-1 Positive 3-SAT* problem (1-in-3-SAT+) [22] which is a variant of SAT restricted to Boolean formulas in conjunctive normal form with 3 positive literals (i.e. variables) per clause, to decide whether there exists an assignment to the variables so that each clause has 1 assigned to exactly one variable (and thus 0 assigned to exactly two variables). For any such 1-in-3-SAT+ instance φ over n variables $y_1, \ldots, y_n \in \{0, 1\}$ with r clauses $C_1, \ldots, C_r \subseteq \{y_1, \ldots, y_n\}$ where $|C_j| = 3$ for all $j \in \{1, \ldots, r\}$, we will construct a NN $\mathcal{N}_\varphi^M$ so that there exists an assignment to variables $y_i = x_i \in \{0,1\}$ for every $i \in \{1,\ldots,n\}$, satisfying φ such that $|\{y_i \in C_j \mid x_i = 1\}| = 1$ for all $j \in \{1,\ldots,r\}$ iff the output of $\mathcal{N}_\varphi^M$ reaches a given real bound $M > 0$ for some external real input.

The NN $\mathcal{N}_\varphi^M$ is composed of two layers with n input neurons for external real inputs $(x_1,\ldots,x_n) \in [0,1]^n$, representing the n Boolean variables $y_1,\ldots,y_n \in \{0,1\}$ of φ, $3r$ units in the first layer corresponding to the 3 variables per each of the r clauses $C_1,\ldots,C_r$ in φ, and one output neuron on the top which computes the function $\mathcal{N}_\varphi^M(x_1,\ldots,x_n) = R(\sum_{j=1}^r \frac{M}{r} Y_j)$ where

$$Y_j = R(x_{j1} - x_{j2} - x_{j3}) + R(x_{j2} - x_{j1} - x_{j3}) + R(x_{j3} - x_{j1} - x_{j2}) \geq 0 \quad (18)$$

for $C_j = \{y_{j1}, y_{j2}, y_{j3}\} \subseteq \{y_1,\ldots,y_n\}$, for every $j \in \{1,\ldots,r\}$.

For each $j \in \{1,\ldots,r\}$, suppose at least two of the 3 terms $x_{j1} - x_{j2} - x_{j3}$, $x_{j2} - x_{j1} - x_{j3}$, and $x_{j3} - x_{j1} - x_{j2}$ in (18) are nonnegative, say $x_{j1} - x_{j2} - x_{j3} \geq 0$ and $x_{j2} - x_{j1} - x_{j3} \geq 0$ (similarly for the other pairs of terms), which sums to $-2x_{j3} \geq 0$ implying $x_{j3} = 0$ and hence, $x_{j1} - x_{j2} = x_{j2} - x_{j1} = 0$. Thus, we have $Y_j = R(-x_{j1} - x_{j2}) = 0$ according to (18). On the other hand, if all these 3 terms are negative, then clearly $Y_j = 0$. Thus, consider the remaining case when only one of these 3 terms is nonnegative, say $x_{j1} - x_{j2} - x_{j3} \geq 0$ (similarly for the other terms), then $Y_j = x_{j1} - x_{j2} - x_{j3}$ attains its maximum 1 for $x_{j1} = 1$ and $x_{j2} = x_{j3} = 0$. It follows that if the Boolean formula φ is satisfied by an assignment $x_1,\ldots,x_n \in \{0,1\}$ such that each clause C_j has 1 assigned exactly to one variable, that is, $|\{y_i \in C_j \mid x_i = 1\}| = 1$, then $Y_j = 1$ for every $j \in \{1,\ldots,r\}$ when $(x_1,\ldots,x_n)$ is presented to $\mathcal{N}_\varphi^M$ as an external input. This implies that $\mathcal{N}_\varphi^M(x_1,\ldots,x_n) = r \cdot \frac{M}{r} \cdot 1 = M$ reaches its maximum M at $(x_1,\ldots,x_n)$. Conversely, if $\mathcal{N}_\varphi^M(x_1,\ldots,x_n) \geq M$ for some external input $(x_1,\ldots,x_n) \in [0,1]^n$, then for the same reason, $x_1,\ldots,x_n \in \{0,1\}$ must be an assignment satisfying φ that meets $|\{y_i \in C_j \mid x_i = 1\}| = 1$ for every $j \in \{1,\ldots,r\}$. This completes the proof that the reduction of 1-in-3-SAT+ to MO is correct for the real external input domain $[0,1]^n$. Finally, note that the excitation of the output neuron of $\mathcal{N}_\varphi^M$ is nonnegative according to (18) which proves the NP-hardness of MO also for this case. □

The NP-hardness of MO has negative consequences on the complexity of finding the maximum error (5) of a given NN caused by rounding its weights even for two layers. Namely, given $\mathcal{N}$ with n input neurons, weight-rounding errors δ_{ji} for $j \in V'$ and $i \in j_\leftarrow$, from (4), and a positive real constant $M > 0$, then the *maximum weight-rounding error* problem (MWRE) is to decide whether there is an external input $(x_1,\ldots,x_n) \in [0,1]^n$ to $\mathcal{N}$ such that $E(x_1,\ldots,x_n) \geq M$.

Corollary 1. *MWRE is NP-hard for two-layer NNs.*

Proof. We reduce MO with nonnegative output neuron excitations, which is NP-hard according to Theorem 2, to MWRE. For a given MO instance $\mathcal{N}$ with two layers, n input neurons, and one output neuron e (i.e. $Y = \{e\}$) such that $\xi_e \geq 0$, and a real bound $M > 0$, it is sufficient to round only the weights w_{ei} of the output neuron e to $\widetilde{w_{ei}} = 0$ for its inputs $i \in e_\leftarrow$, which means $\delta_{ei} = -w_{ei}$

for $i \in e_\leftarrow$, whereas $\delta_{ji} = 0$ for $j \in V' \setminus Y$ and $i \in j_\leftarrow$. Hence, $\widetilde{\xi}_e = 0$ and $E(x_1, \ldots, x_n) = |\xi_e| = \xi_e = R(\xi_e) = y_e = \mathcal{N}(x_1, \ldots, x_n)$ from (5) due to $\xi_e \geq 0$, which ensures the correct reduction of MO to MWRE. □

5 Approximating the Maximum Weight-Rounding Error

We have shown in Sect. 4 that it is computationally hard to compute the maximum of weight-rounding error (5) in the worst case over the whole input domain $[0, 1]^n$ of $\mathcal{N}$. Nevertheless, this maximum can simply be approximated by the maximum or average over a finite sample $T \subset [0, 1]^n$ which is usually a training or test data chosen according to some input domain distribution, as

$$E_T = \max_{(x_1, \ldots, x_n) \in T} E(x_1, \ldots, x_n), \quad \overline{E_T} = \frac{1}{|T|} \sum_{(x_1, \ldots, x_n) \in T} E(x_1, \ldots, x_n). \quad (19)$$

In this section, we improve this approximation by proposing a method called AppMax that computes the maximum weight-rounding error on a certain convex polytope of $[0, 1]^n$ which surrounds a data point from T in the input domain.

To this end, we first introduce the concept of so-called shortcut weights. Given an external input $(x_1, \ldots, x_n) \in [0, 1]^n$ to $\mathcal{N}$, some neurons may receive negative excitation and thus remain inactive, i.e., produce zero output. We define

$$S = S(x_1, \ldots, x_n) = \{j \in V' \mid \xi_j < 0\} \quad (20)$$

to be the subset of non-input neurons whose states are *saturated* at $y_j = 0$ according to (2). The complement of this set, $U = V \setminus S$, consists of *unsaturated* units, including both the input neurons $X \subset U$ and any non-input neurons with nonnegative excitation (i.e. $\xi_j \geq 0$ for $j \in V'$). Clearly, fixing a particular pattern of saturation S uniquely determines a corresponding set of active neurons U. Under this fixed activation pattern, $\mathcal{N}$ operates linearly: for each non-input neuron $j \in V'$, the ReLU activation simplifies to either $y_j = 0$ if $j \in S$, or $y_j = \xi_j$ if $j \in U \setminus X$. This turns the entire computation into a linear function of the input values $y_i = x_i$ for $i \in X$. Hence, we can express each excitation ξ_j as:

$$\xi_j = \sum_{i \in X} W_{ji} y_i, \quad (21)$$

where $W_{ji} \in \mathbb{R}$ are the so-called *shortcut weights* (including the shortcut bias W_{j0}), capturing the total effect of input neuron $i \in X$ on the excitation of neuron $j \in V'$, under the assumption that the saturation pattern S is fixed. This representation (21) allows us to characterize the saturation condition (20) in terms of shortcut weights:

$$\sum_{i \in X} W_{ji} y_i \begin{cases} < 0 & \text{if } j \in S \\ \geq 0 & \text{if } j \in U. \end{cases} \quad (22)$$

Each shortcut weight W_{ji} represents the cumulative influence from input neuron $i \in X$ to unit $j \in V'$ through all unsaturated paths in $\mathcal{N}$. More precisely, it can be expanded from (1) and (2) as

$$W_{ji} = \sum_{\substack{\text{paths } i=j_0,j_1,\ldots,j_m=j \text{ in } (V,E) \\ j_1,\ldots,j_{m-1} \in U}} \prod_{\ell=1}^{m} w_{j_\ell,j_{\ell-1}}, \qquad (23)$$

i.e., the sum over all directed paths $i = j_0, j_1, \ldots, j_m = j$ from i to j in the graph (V, E) (i.e. $(j_\ell, j_{\ell-1}) \in E$ for every $\ell \in \{1, \ldots, m\}$) that pass only through unsaturated units $j_1, \ldots, j_{m-1} \in U$, with each path contributing the product $w_{j_1,j_0} w_{j_2,j_1} \cdots w_{j_m,j_{m-1}}$ of edge weights along the path. The shortcut weights can be computed efficiently by propagating the weight values forward through $\mathcal{N}$, in topological order. A formal initialization is performed for input neurons $j \in X$ by:

$$W_{ji} = \begin{cases} 1 & \text{if } j = i \\ 0 & \text{otherwise} \end{cases} \quad \text{for every } i \in X. \qquad (24)$$

Then, for any non-input neuron $j \in V'$, the shortcut weight is recursively computed as:

$$W_{ji} = \sum_{k \in j_- \cap U} w_{jk} W_{ki} \quad \text{for each } i \in X, \qquad (25)$$

assuming the shortcut weights W_{ki} have already been computed for all its predecessors $k \in j_-$ and $i \in X$.

Furthermore, we construct a NN $\mathcal{N}^*$ that evaluates the weight-rounding error (5) for a given NN $\mathcal{N}$. The NN $\mathcal{N}^*$ is composed of $\mathcal{N}$ and its parallel copy $\widetilde{\mathcal{N}}$ with rounded weights (4), that share the input neurons $X^* = X = \widetilde{X}$ and their originally output units are replaced one by one by new hidden neurons $Y \cup \widetilde{Y} \subset V^*$ in $\mathcal{N}^*$ which have additional connections to the other network with the opposite weights so that

$$\xi_j^* = \xi_j - \widetilde{\xi}_j = \sum_{i \in j_-} w_{ji} y_i - \sum_{i \in j_-} \widetilde{w}_{ji} \widetilde{y}_i \quad \text{for } j \in Y \qquad (26)$$

$$\xi_j^* = \widetilde{\xi}_j - \xi_j = \sum_{i \in j_-} \widetilde{w}_{ji} \widetilde{y}_i - \sum_{i \in j_-} w_{ji} y_i \quad \text{for } j \in \widetilde{Y}. \qquad (27)$$

In addition, we add one new output unit e in $\mathcal{N}^*$ (i.e. $Y^* = \{e\}$) on the top of these new neurons with the unit weights and zero bias, which computes

$$\mathcal{N}^*(x_1, \ldots, x_n) = y_e^* = \xi_e^* = \sum_{j \in Y} y_j^* + \sum_{j \in \widetilde{Y}} y_j^* = \sum_{j \in Y} R(\xi_j^*) + \sum_{j \in \widetilde{Y}} R(\xi_j^*)$$

$$= \sum_{j \in Y} \left(R\left(\xi_j - \widetilde{\xi}_j\right) + R\left(\widetilde{\xi}_j - \xi_j\right) \right) = \sum_{j \in Y} \left| \xi_j - \widetilde{\xi}_j \right| = E(x_1, \ldots, x_n) \qquad (28)$$

according to (2), (26), (27), and (5).

Finally, we calculate the shortcut weights W_{ji} of units $j \in V^*$ for input neurons $i \in X$ of $\mathcal{N}^*$, according to (24) and (25). Thus, for any fixed set $S \subset V^*$ of saturated units in $\mathcal{N}^*$, which induces $U = V^* \setminus S$, we can formulate a linear program of finding the states $y_1, \ldots, y_n$ of its input neurons $X \setminus \{0\}$ that

$$\text{maximize} \quad W_{e0} + \sum_{i=1}^{n} W_{ei} y_i \tag{29}$$

$$\text{subject to} \quad W_{j0} + \sum_{i=1}^{n} W_{ji} y_i \leq 0 \quad \text{for every } j \in S \tag{30}$$

$$W_{j0} + \sum_{i=1}^{n} W_{ji} y_i \geq 0 \quad \text{for every } j \in U \setminus X \tag{31}$$

$$0 \leq y_i \leq 1 \quad \text{for every } i \in \{1, \ldots, n\}. \tag{32}$$

By solving this program we obtain the maximum of weight-rounding error (28) for the original $\mathcal{N}$ on the convex polytope $\Xi_S \subseteq [0,1]^n$ in its input domain, that is defined by (30)–(32) for a given $S \subset V^*$ according to (22) where zero excitations are allowed for saturated units without loss of generality:

$$E_{\Xi_S} = \max_{(y_1,\ldots,y_n) \in \Xi_S} E(y_1, \ldots, y_n). \tag{33}$$

Hence, in our AppMax method, we can improve the maximum error approximation (19) as

$$E_{\Xi_{S(T)}} = \max_{(x_1,\ldots,x_n) \in T} E_{\Xi_{S(x_1,\ldots,x_n)}}, \quad \overline{E_{\Xi_{S(T)}}} = \frac{1}{|T|} \sum_{(x_1,\ldots,x_n) \in T} E_{\Xi_{S(x_1,\ldots,x_n)}} \tag{34}$$

which takes the maximum or average not only over data points $(x_1, \ldots, x_n)$ from T but over the convex polytopes $\Xi_{S(x_1,\ldots,x_n)}$ around these data points.

For classification tasks, the regression error (5) under the L_1 norm can be replaced by the cross-entropy between the output categorical probability distributions (3) of $\mathcal{N}$ and $\widetilde{\mathcal{N}}$, respectively,

$$L(x_1, \ldots, x_n) = -\sum_{k \in Y} y_k \ln \widetilde{y}_k = \sum_{k \in Y} y_k \ln \left(1 + \sum_{j \in \widetilde{Y} \setminus \{k\}} e^{\widetilde{\xi}_j - \widetilde{\xi}_k} \right). \tag{35}$$

We interpret the output from $\mathcal{N}$ to be the class with the maximum excitation of output neurons which discretizes the softmax probabilities (3) by the winner-take-all principle. For each input $(x_1, \ldots, x_n) \in T$, the correct class inferred by the trained $\mathcal{N}$ is thus $c = \arg\max_{k \in Y} \xi_k$, which means that $y_c \geq 1/m$ by (3), where $m = |Y|$ is the number of classes. Hence, we can lower bound the cross-entropy loss (35), subject to $\xi_c \geq \xi_k$ for all $k \in Y \setminus \{c\}$, as

$$L(x_1, \ldots, x_n) \geq \frac{1}{m} \ln \left(1 + \exp \left(\max_{j \in \widetilde{Y} \setminus \{c\}} \left(\widetilde{\xi}_j - \widetilde{\xi}_c \right) \right) \right). \tag{36}$$

In this case, contrary to (26)–(27), the original unmodified units from $Y \cup \widetilde{Y}$ create the output neurons of $\mathcal{N}^*$ instead of the removed e. The convex polytope $\Xi_S \subseteq [0,1]^n$ in (33) is then defined by (30)–(32) for the saturated units $S = S(x_1, \ldots, x_n) \subset V^* \setminus (Y \cup \widetilde{Y})$ in this new $\mathcal{N}^*$, inducing $U = V^* \setminus (S \cup Y \cup \widetilde{Y})$, which is further constrained by conditions:

$$W_{c0} + \sum_{i=1}^{n} W_{ci} y_i \geq W_{k0} + \sum_{i=1}^{n} W_{ki} y_i \quad \text{for every } k \in Y \setminus \{c\}. \tag{37}$$

We replace the argmax of (35) on a feasible convex set $\Xi_{S(x_1,\ldots,x_n)}$ for $(x_1, \ldots, x_n) \in T$, that meets $\xi_c \geq \xi_k$ for all $k \in Y \setminus \{c\}$, due to (37), by the argument of

$$\max_{j \in \widetilde{Y} \setminus \{c\}} \max_{\substack{(y_1,\ldots,y_n) \in \Xi_{S(x_1,\ldots,x_n)} \\ \widetilde{\xi}_c \leq \widetilde{\xi}_j}} (\widetilde{\xi}_j - \widetilde{\xi}_c), \tag{38}$$

according to (36), which is computed by solving the $|Y|-1$ linear programs that maximize $\widetilde{\xi}_j - \widetilde{\xi}_c$ subject to (30)–(32), (37), and $\widetilde{W}_{c0} + \sum_{i=1}^{n} \widetilde{W}_{ci} y_i \leq \widetilde{W}_{j0} + \sum_{i=1}^{n} \widetilde{W}_{ji} y_i$, for each $j \in \widetilde{Y} \setminus \{c\}$ separately. Clearly, if the nonnegative error $\widetilde{\xi}_j - \widetilde{\xi}_c \geq 0$ is feasible, then $\widetilde{\mathcal{N}}$ does not infer the correct class produced by $\mathcal{N}$.

Note that the proposed AppMax method of computing the maximum error can be used for any approximation of $\mathcal{N}$ by $\widetilde{\mathcal{N}}$, which can be an arbitrary DNN with the same number of input and output neurons, e.g. created by pruning hidden neurons and connections in $\mathcal{N}$.

6 Experiments

We have tested the AppMax method introduced in Sect. 5 on two NNs trained on the MNIST database [7] of handwritten digits (28 × 28 grayscale pixels) categorized into 10 classes (0–9). We carried out our experiments using the deep learning library PyTorch [21] and the SciPy linear programming routine scipy.optimize.linprog [10,29]. The source code is publicly available [28].

The first Net1 is a NN of three fully connected layers with 784–2000–1000–10 neurons (including $784 = 28^2$ input units), respectively. The second Net2 is a CNN composed of two convolutional layers with 32 and 64 3 × 3-kernels (stride 1, padding 1), respectively, followed by one max pooling layer with 64 2 × 2-kernels (stride 2), and topped by two fully connected layers with 1024–10 neurons, respectively. The convolutional and max-pooling layers in Net2 are

Table 2. Accuracy on the test set.

	32b	16b	12b	8b	6b	4b
Net1	98.30	98.30	98.30	98.30	98.30	24.85
Net2	99.25	99.25	99.25	99.25	99.25	99.14

Table 3. The worst-case maximum error estimates E_T and $E_{\Xi_{S(T)}}$ and their averaged variants $\overline{E_T}$ and $\overline{E_{\Xi_{S(T)}}}$ for the weight rounding to 16 bits.

	E_T	$E_{\Xi_{S(T)}}$	$\overline{E_T}$	$\overline{E_{\Xi_{S(T)}}}$
Net1	0.032854	0.099374	0.007629	0.030884
Net2	0.013466	0.014763	0.006127	0.006777

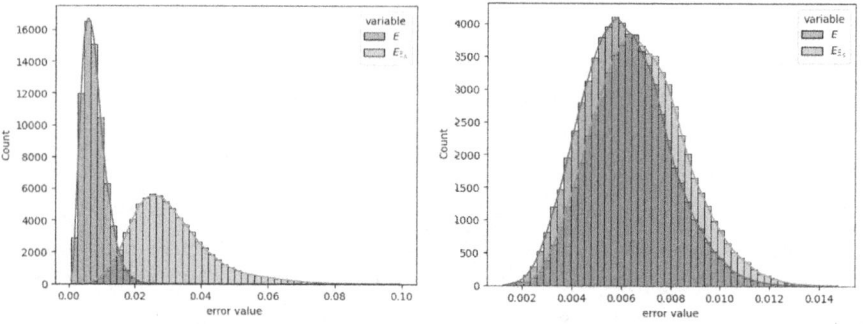

Fig. 1. The histograms of weight-rounding errors E on T (blue) and E_{Ξ_S} over convex polytopes Ξ_S on T (orange) according to (19) and (33), respectively, for Net1 (left) and Net2 (right) with 16-bitwidth for weights. (Color figure online)

transformed to eight fully connected layers with 784–25088–50176–50176–25088–25088–12544–1024–10 neurons (see Sect. 2) where sparse matrices are used to fit the weights into the memory. Both NNs employ the ReLU activation function (2) and were originally trained with 32-bitwidth for weights. Table 2 lists accuracies of Net1 and Net2 on the test set (i.e. the percentage of correctly classified data points) for weights that are rounded to 16, 12, 8, 6, and 4 bits, showing their high robustness in terms of accuracy only.

We applied the AppMax method to approximate the maximum of regression error (5) under L_1 norm for Net1 and Net2 whose weights are rounded to 16 bits. All available (training and test) 70,000 data points were first used as a sample T in the maximum error estimates (19) and (34), where the latter thus involves solving 70,000 linear programs (29)–(32). The results of this experiment are listed in Table 3 and graphically depicted using histograms in Fig. 1. We can observe a clear shift in the weight-rounding errors E on T and E_{Ξ_S} over convex polytopes Ξ_S on T according to (19) and (33), respectively. This shift is less pronounced in Net2 due to its higher number of neurons, which results in smaller convex polytopes. This effect could be mitigated by also considering the convex polytopes adjacent to those containing the test data points, thereby expanding the region in which the maximum error is searched for. The AppMax method clearly improves the estimation of the maximum weight-rounding error. For illustration, the worst-case points found by the AppMax method (33) in cor-

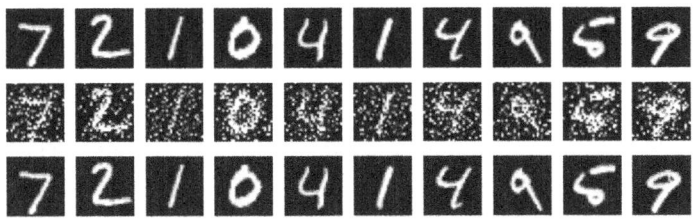

Fig. 2. The first line shows a few examples of original data points $(x_1, \ldots, x_n) \in T$, whereas the second and third lines depict the points $(y_1, \ldots, y_n) \in \Xi_{S(x_1,\ldots,x_n)}$ with the maximum error $E_{\Xi_{S(x_1,\ldots,x_n)}}$ found by the AppMax method in the convex polytopes $\Xi_{S(x_1,\ldots,x_n)}$ for Net1 and Net2, respectively, with 16-bitwidth for weights.

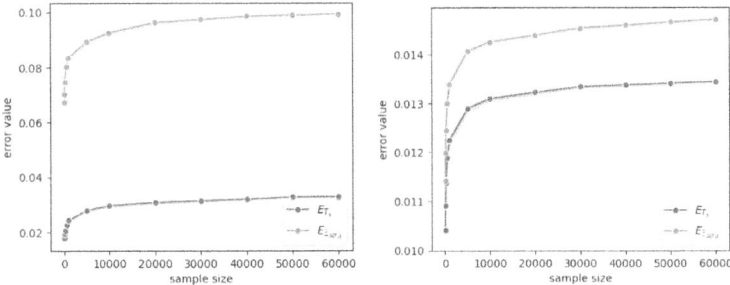

Fig. 3. Estimates of errors E_{T_s} (blue) and $E_{\Xi_{S(T_s)}}$ (orange) for increasing size of data samples T_s for Net1 (left) and Net2 (right) with 16-bitwidth for weights.

responding convex polytopes around several data points are depicted in Fig. 2. They include noise, which is quite visible for Net1, while negligible for Net2.

The AppMax method, which is based on solving large linear programs for each data point in the sample T, turns out to be computationally intensive. For example, the presented experiments performed on 70,000 data points required several days using tens of parallel processors. Specifically, the average computation time per one data point was approximately 8 s for Net1 and 250 s for Net2 on an Intel® Xeon® E5-2620 v4 processor running at 2.10 GHz. In the next experiment, we try to answer the question, how many data points do we need to get reliable estimate of $E_{\Xi_{S(T)}}$. We sampled randomly sets $T_s \subset T$ from the available data points, ranging from 50 to 60,000 sample size, repeating each sample hundred times. For each sample, the approximate maximum errors E_{T_s} and $E_{\Xi_{S(T_s)}}$ were evaluated according to (19) and (34), respectively, as depicted in Fig. 3. The results show that it is not necessary to employ the whole data to get reasonable error estimates because the improvement using tens of thousands data points is not significant. This brings the required computation time down to a reasonable level—on the order of several hours in our setting.

Table 4. The error estimates E_T and $E_{\Xi_{S(T)}}$ and their averaged variants $\overline{E_T}$ and $\overline{E_{\Xi_{S(T)}}}$ for Net1 with decreasing bitwidth of weights.

	E_T	$E_{\Xi_{S(T)}}$	$\overline{E_T}$	$\overline{E_{\Xi_{S(T)}}}$
16 bits	0.024727	0.093156	0.007558	0.030998
12 bits	0.613171	1.049668	0.135616	0.384750
8 bits	8.191886	17.585771	2.138221	6.070758
6 bits	40.410836	85.562221	10.226672	25.475516
4 bits	301.230476	479.39271	81.117751	153.583925

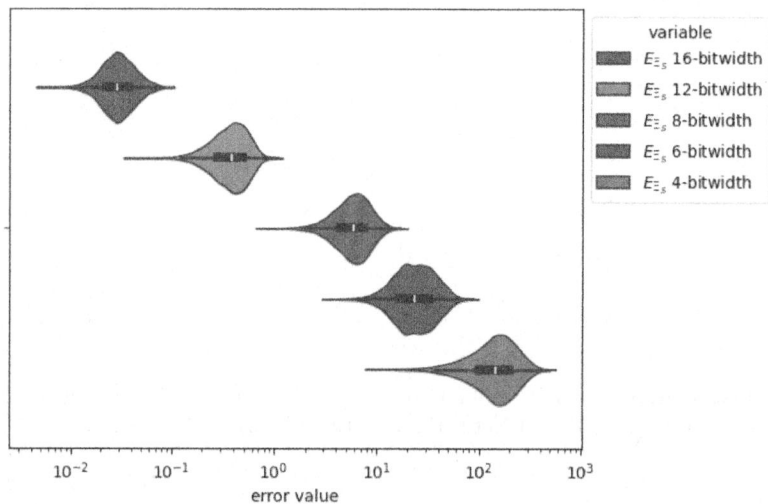

Fig. 4. The violin plots showing E_{Ξ_S} for different bitwidths of weights in Net1.

Furthermore, we demonstrate the effect of decreasing bitwidth on the weight-rounding errors (19) and (34). We used 10000 and 2000 randomly chosen test data points as a sample T for Net1 and Net2, respectively, due to the larger Net2 is slower to evaluate. We summarize the results only for Net1 in Table 4, as Net2 shows similar trends. Moreover, Fig. 4 depicts graphically the increase of error E_{Ξ_S} (on a logarithmic scale) for decreasing bitwidth of weights in Net1. Clearly, the AppMax method improves the error guarantees for different bitwidths.

Finally, we test the AppMax variant (38) for the classification by Net1 with decreasing bitwidth of weights on a sample T of 5000 randomly chosen data points. For each $(x_1, \ldots, x_n) \in T$ which is classified by Net1 as a digit class $c \in Y$, the AppMax method found the argument of (38) in the convex polytope $\Xi_{S(x_1,\ldots,x_n)}$ (by solving 9 linear programs) whose all points are classified by Net1 as the same digit class c due to (37), if it exists. This argmax is a point misclassified by weight-rounded Net1 as another digit class $g \in Y \setminus \{c\}$. Table 5

Table 5. The percentage of data points in T that are surrounded by misclassified polytopes including the arguments of (38), for which the output probabilities $\widetilde{y_c}$ and $\widetilde{y_g}$ of the correct and wrong classes, respectively, averaged over these points, are listed, which were provided by Net1 with decreasing bitwidth for weights, and compared to those by the original Net1.

bitwidth	percentage of misclassified polytopes	rounded Net1 $\widetilde{y_c}$	$\widetilde{y_g}$	original Net1 $\overline{y_c}$	$\overline{y_g}$
16 bits	0.91	0.28	0.28	0.28	0.28
12 bits	0.91	0.27	0.30	0.29	0.29
8 bits	0.91	0.15	0.39	0.31	0.30
6 bits	0.88	0.14	0.51	0.40	0.32
4 bits	0.89	0.08	0.44	0.57	0.16

lists the percentage of data points in T that are surrounded by convex polytopes containing misclassified points (shortly, misclassified polytopes), which seems to be not affected by the bitwidth for weights. The next columns of Table 5 present the output probabilities $\widetilde{y_c}$ and $\widetilde{y_g}$ of correct and wrong classes, respectively, averaged over T (restricted to data points surrounded by misclassified polytopes) that were provided by Net1 with rounded weights using the softmax function (3) for the argument of (38) as its input, where $c, g \in Y$ may differ for each of these points. In Table 5, these are further compared to the analogous averaged output probabilities $\overline{y_c}$ and $\overline{y_g}$ of correct and wrong classes, respectively, by the original Net1 for the same inputs. It turns out that the AppMax method reveals the increase of the cross-entropy restricted to the correct and wrong classes for decreasing bitwidth of weights although the percentage of misclassified polytopes surrounding the data points from T seems to be not affected by the weight rounding.

7 Conclusion

In this paper, we theoretically analyzed the effect of any weight rounding in a trained DNN on its output. We derived an upper bound on the worst-case output regression error for bounded input domains, which appears to be overestimated for practical use. We proved that it is in fact NP-hard to determine this error precisely. We introduced the AppMax method that approximates the weight-rounding error by computing its maxima in convex polytopes around the data points. This method can be used for any DNN approximation. We tested the AppMax method on fully connected and convolutional NNs trained on the MNIST database for decreasing bitwidth of weights, showing a clear improvement in error guarantees as compared to those for test data points only. The proposed AppMax method enables systematic comparison of approximation strategies to identify those with optimal accuracy-performance trade-offs, paving the way for techniques that reduce energy consumption by approximating or removing suitable DNN components with reliable error guarantees.

The AppMax method has only been partially generalized to classification based on the softmax function. In future research, we plan to explore the possibility of approximating the cross-entropy loss using a piecewise linear function or addressing the underlying nonlinear optimization problem using techniques such as the Karush-Kuhn-Tucker conditions. Another open problem concerns approximating the weight-rounding error on a global scale by estimating the probabilities of considered convex polytopes in terms of their volumes. We also plan to extend the error analysis to modern architectures such as ResNet, Transformers. One of the most important challenges is to identify components in a given DNN that can be neglected (e.g. specific weights to be rounded) at the cost of an explicitly bounded increase in the output error. We will also extend our experiments with the AppMax method to other test datasets including CIFAR-100 [13] and ImageNet [5].

Acknowledgments. This research was institutionally supported by RVO: 67985807, J. Šíma was partially supported by the Czech Science Foundation grant GA25-15490S, and P. Vidnerová was partially supported by the Strategy AV21 project "AI: Artificial Intelligence for Science and Society."

Disclosure of Interests. The authors have no competing interests to declare that are relevant to the content of this article.

References

1. Ansari, M.S., et al.: Improving the accuracy and hardware efficiency of neural networks using approximate multipliers. IEEE Trans. Very Large Scale Integr. VLSI Syst. **28**, 317–328 (2020). https://doi.org/10.1109/TVLSI.2019.2940943
2. Armeniakos, G., et al.: Hardware approximate techniques for deep neural network accelerators: A survey. ACM Comput. Surv. **55**, 83 (2023). https://doi.org/10.1145/3527156
3. Beuzeville, T., Buttari, A., Gratton, S., Mary, T.: Deterministic and probabilistic backward error analysis of neural networks in floating-point arithmetic. Manuscript (2024). https://hal.science/hal-04663142
4. Chen, Y., et al.: Eyeriss: An energy-efficient reconfigurable accelerator for deep convolutional neural networks. IEEE J. Solid-State Circuits **52**, 127–138 (2017). https://doi.org/10.1109/JSSC.2016.2616357
5. Deng, J., Dong, W., Socher, R., Li, L.J., Li, K., Fei-Fei, L.: ImageNet: A large-scale hierarchical image database. In: Proceedings of the CVPR 2009, pp. 248–255 (2009). https://doi.org/10.1109/CVPR.2009.5206848
6. Deng, L., et al.: Model compression and hardware acceleration for neural networks: A comprehensive survey. Proc. IEEE **108**, 485–532 (2020). https://doi.org/10.1109/JPROC.2020.2976475
7. Deng, L.: The MNIST database of handwritten digit images for machine learning research. IEEE Signal Process. Mag. **29**, 141–142 (2012). https://doi.org/10.1109/MSP.2012.2211477

8. Han, S., Mao, H., Dally, W.J.: Deep compression: Compressing deep neural network with pruning, trained quantization and Huffman coding. In: Proceedings of the ICLR 2016 (2016). https://doi.org/10.48550/arXiv.1510.00149
9. Horowitz, M.: 1.1 Computing's energy problem (and what we can do about it). In: Proceedings of the ISSCC 2014, pp. 10–14 (2014). https://doi.org/10.1109/ISSCC.2014.6757323
10. Huangfu, Q., Hall, J.A.J.: Parallelizing the dual revised simplex method. Math. Program. Comput. **10**, 119–142 (2018). https://doi.org/10.1007/S12532-017-0130-5
11. Jouppi, N.P., et al.: A domain-specific architecture for deep neural networks. Commun. ACM **61**, 50–59 (2018). https://doi.org/10.1145/3154484
12. Kim, Y., et al.: Compression of deep convolutional neural networks for fast and low power mobile applications. In: Proceedings of the ICLR 2016 (2016). https://doi.org/10.48550/arXiv.1511.06530
13. Krizhevsky, A., Nair, V., Hinton, G.: CIFAR (Canadian Institute for Advanced Research). http://www.cs.toronto.edu/~kriz/cifar.html
14. Lee, E.H., et al.: LogNet: Energy-efficient neural networks using logarithmic computation. In: Proceedings of the ICASSP 2017, pp. 5900–5904 (2017). https://doi.org/10.1109/ICASSP.2017.7953288
15. Li, Z., Li, H., Meng, L.: Model compression for deep neural networks: A survey. Computers **12**, 60 (2023). https://doi.org/10.3390/COMPUTERS12030060
16. Lyu, Z., et al.: A survey of model compression strategies for object detection. Multimedia Tools Appl. **83**, 48165–48236 (2024). https://doi.org/10.1007/S11042-023-17192-X
17. Mittal, S.: A survey of techniques for approximate computing. ACM Comput. Surv. **48**, 62 (2016). https://doi.org/10.1145/2893356
18. Mittal, S.: A survey of FPGA-based accelerators for convolutional neural networks. Neural Comput. Appl. **32**, 1109–1139 (2020). https://doi.org/10.1007/S00521-018-3761-1
19. Mittal, S., et al.: A survey of SRAM-based in-memory computing techniques and applications. J. Syst. Archit. **119**, 102276 (2021). https://doi.org/10.1016/J.SYSARC.2021.102276
20. Moons, B., Verhelst, M.: An energy-efficient precision-scalable ConvNet processor in 40-nm CMOS. IEEE J. Solid-State Circuits **52**, 903–914 (2017). https://doi.org/10.1109/JSSC.2016.2636225
21. Paszke, A., et al.: PyTorch: An imperative style, high-performance deep learning library. CoRR arXiv:1912.01703 (2019). https://doi.org/10.48550/arXiv.1912.01703
22. Schaefer, T.J.: The complexity of satisfiability problems. In: Proceedings of the STOC 1978, pp. 216–226 (1978). https://doi.org/10.1145/800133.804350
23. Silvano, C., et al.: A survey on deep learning hardware accelerators for heterogeneous HPC platforms. CoRR arXiv:2306.15552 (2023). https://doi.org/10.48550/arXiv.2306.15552
24. Šíma, J., Cabessa, J., Vidnerová, P.: On energy complexity of fully-connected layers. Neural Netw. **178**, 106419 (2024). https://doi.org/10.1016/J.NEUNET.2024.106419
25. Šíma, J., Vidnerová, P., Mrázek, V.: Energy complexity of convolutional neural networks. Neural Comput. **36**, 1601–1625 (2024). https://doi.org/10.1162/NECO_A_01676

26. Sze, V., et al.: Efficient Processing of Deep Neural Networks. Synthesis Lectures on Computer Architecture, Morgan & Claypool Publishers (2020). https://doi.org/10.2200/S01004ED1V01Y202004CAC050
27. Tang, Y., et al.: A survey on transformer compression. CoRR arXiv:2402.05964 (2024). https://doi.org/10.48550/arXiv.2402.05964
28. Vidnerová, P.: Source code for experiments. (2024). https://github.com/PetraVidnerova/RoundingErrorEstimation
29. Virtanen, P., et al.: SciPy 1.0: Fundamental algorithms for scientific computing in Python. Nat. Methods **17**, 261–272 (2020). https://doi.org/10.1038/s41592-019-0686-2
30. Wang, P., Cheng, J.: Fixed-point factorized networks. In: Proceedings of the CVPR 2017, pp. 3966–3974 (2017). https://doi.org/10.1109/CVPR.2017.422
31. Yang, T., Chen, Y., Sze, V.: Designing energy-efficient convolutional neural networks using energy-aware pruning. In: Proceedings of the CVPR 2017, pp. 6071–6079 (2017). https://doi.org/10.1109/CVPR.2017.643
32. Zhou, G., Zhou, J., Lin, H.: Research on NVIDIA deep learning accelerator. In: Proceedings ASID 2018, pp. 192–195 (2018). https://doi.org/10.1109/ICASID.2018.8693202

The Local Convexification Method and Its Application to Learning Weakly Convex Boolean Functions

Eike Stadtländer[1,2], Tamás Horváth[1,2,3(✉)], and Stefan Wrobel[1,2,3]

[1] Department of Computer Science, University of Bonn, Bonn, Germany
{stadtlaender,horvath,wrobel}@cs.uni-bonn.de
[2] Lamarr Institute for Machine Learning and Artificial Intelligence, Bonn, Germany
[3] Fraunhofer IAIS, Sankt Augustin, Germany

Abstract. We study the problem of finding consistent hypotheses over finite metric spaces, focusing on hypothesis classes formed by weakly convex subsets of the domain. These hypotheses are closed under geodesics of length below a given threshold and exhibit a natural partitioning. Their generalization performance is strongly correlated with the number of blocks in the partition: fewer blocks yield greater generalization power. We prove that finding consistent weakly convex hypotheses with a minimum number of blocks is NP-hard. To address this negative result, we propose a novel greedy heuristic for computing compact solutions across a broad class of metric spaces and analyze its formal properties. Unlike standard approaches that calculate a single global distance threshold, our heuristic dynamically adjusts multiple local thresholds to seek compact hypotheses. To evaluate our method, we consider the specific case where the underlying metric space is the Hamming space, corresponding to learning weakly convex Boolean functions. Our empirical results demonstrate that our general-purpose algorithm outperforms the method specifically designed for learning this kind of Boolean functions in both model compactness and predictive performance. In fact, our approach generates hypotheses that are near-optimal with respect to the number of blocks in most cases.

Keywords: concept learning · consistent hypothesis finding · finite metric spaces · convexity · k-convex Boolean functions

1 Introduction

One of the core problems of supervised learning is the *consistent hypothesis finding* (CHF) problem. This problem involves identifying a hypothesis within a predefined hypothesis space that achieves zero empirical error on a given set of training examples. The CHF problem has been studied for numerous concept learning problems over different domains, including tabular data, propositional logic, first-order logic, graphs, and geometric concepts (see, e.g., [1, 2, 17, 18, 20–22, 24]). In this work we propose a *generic* heuristic that efficiently solves the CHF problem for a *broad* class of concept learning problems defined over finite *metric spaces*. Building on the fact that metric spaces admit the notion of weak convexity, our algorithm solves the CHF problem by computing consistent weakly convex hypotheses as in [14,23]. Unlike [14,23], however, our approach produces more compact hypotheses with better generalization performance. These hypotheses are subsets of the domain, consisting of pairwise disjoint blocks that are distant from one another. They are closed under geodesics between specific point pairs. More precisely, for any pair of points with a distance below a threshold *specific* to the pair, all points on all geodesics between the two points are included in the subset.

The idea of using weakly convex hypotheses was coined in [14] for learning *Boolean functions*. Specifically, [14] restricts the hypothesis space to Boolean functions with a particular property: Their true points (those satisfying the function) can be partitioned into subcubes of the d-dimensional Boolean cube such that each pair of subcubes has a Hamming distance greater than a positive integer k. Such Boolean functions can be can be represented by disjunctive normal forms (DNFs) in which the subcubes corresponding to the conjunctive terms are pairwise disjoint. One of the main results of [14] is that the CHF problem can be solved in *polynomial* time for hypothesis spaces formed by these so-called k-*convex* Boolean functions. The key insight is that, for some $k \geq 0$, there always exists a largest k-convex hull of the positive examples that is disjoint from the negative examples. Building on this, [23] generalizes the concept of k-convex Boolean functions and the associated CHF algorithm, extending them to weakly convex hypotheses over a broader class of metric spaces.

The generalization power of weakly convex hypotheses is strongly correlated with the number of their blocks. Specifically, hypotheses with fewer blocks exhibit higher generalization performance. This raises an important question: Can consistent weakly convex hypotheses with the *minimum* number of blocks be found in polynomial time? As a first contribution, we answer this question *negatively*, proving that the problem is NP-complete.

In line with this negative result, both algorithms in [14] and [23] fail to effectively optimize the number of blocks. A closer examination reveals that these approaches determine a *global* distance threshold for the output hypothesis. This threshold is defined as the minimum distance between two blocks across *all* block pairs (e.g., pairs of subcubes of the Boolean cube in the case of k-convex Boolean functions) that cannot be merged without violating consistency. However, the global nature of this threshold has a detrimental effect: it can force block pairs to remain separate, even if they could be merged into a single block at a larger distance threshold without violating consistency.

As a second contribution, we propose the LOCAL CONVEXIFICATION METHOD (LCM) to address this problem. It constructs *compact* weakly convex hypotheses by greedily merging blocks in order of increasing distance, while maintaining consistency and dynamically adjusting distance thresholds. A distinguishing feature of LCM, compared to [14,23], is its ability to compute multiple *local* thresholds that vary across different pairs of points. Applying LCM requires implementing certain operations (e.g. the join operation for blocks) specific to the underlying metric space. To illustrate this, we consider k-convex Boolean functions as an example, demonstrating that this step generally does not present significant challenges. Importantly, we emphasize that LCM is a *general* method applicable to CHF problems across various finite metric spaces, not just the Hamming space.

We study some formal properties of LCM. In particular, we show that it is *sound* (i.e., it returns a consistent weakly convex hypothesis). Moreover, LCM is *efficient* whenever the abovementioned functions specific to the underlying metric space can be computed in polynomial time. Regarding *optimality* in terms of the number of blocks, the hypotheses generated by LCM are at least as compact as those produced by the algorithm in [23]. Additionally, LCM can achieve an exponential-size compression ratio compared to the hypotheses returned by [23]. As a further contribution, we conduct an experimental evaluation of LCM, our *general-purpose* heuristic, in the special case of Hamming spaces. We compare its performance against the CHF algorithm designed for k-convex Boolean functions in [14] and against DNFs extracted from Boolean decision trees. Our results demonstrate that LCM significantly outperforms both baselines in terms of model compactness and predictive performance. Furthermore, the number of terms in the DNFs produced by LCM is very close to the optimal value.

The rest of the paper is organized as follows. Section 1.1 reviews related work, while Sect. 2 introduces the necessary background notions. Section 3 defines locally constrained block systems, which constitute the hypotheses of the hypothesis class explored in this study. The negative result concerning the complexity of finding block-minimum consistent weakly convex hypotheses, along with the proposed heuristic, is presented in Sect. 4. The experimental results are presented and discussed in Sect. 5. Finally, Sect. 6 concludes the paper and suggests potential directions for future research.

Due to space limitations, we omit most proofs and offer a simplified adaptation of our approach–originally developed for *interval convexity* [4]–to the case of geodesic convexity. Full formal statements and their proofs will be provided in an extended version of this work.

1.1 Related Work

Closure systems (resp. closed sets) [11] can be regarded as a generalization of the family of all convex subsets of $\mathbb{R}^d$ (resp. convex sets in $\mathbb{R}^d$). Abstract closure systems have been studied also in the context of the CHF problem, e.g., in [17,21]. Recently, there is an increasing interest in *geodesic* or *shortest-path* convexity [25] in machine learning, e.g., for vertex classification in graphs [12,22–24] and recovering clusterings [3].

The relaxation of convexity to *weak convexity* and to similar notions was studied before for *discrete* metric spaces (see, e.g., [6–9]). In machine learning, k-convex Boolean functions were first investigated in [14]. In our general results, we utilize abstract interval functions [4] to extend the concept of weak convexity to weak interval convexity. Our notion of *locally constrained block systems* generalizes the concept of θ-decompositions of *weakly convex sets* defined in [23]. In particular, the CHF problem for learning weakly convex sets is solved in [23] (see, also, [14]) by finding the largest θ-convex *hull* of the positive examples over all $\theta \geq 0$ that is consistent with the negative examples. We are interested in consistent locally constrained block systems, i.e., consistent hypotheses formed by unions of weakly (interval) convex sets, that are more compact in terms of their number of blocks. This is due to the property that the number of blocks is inversely correlated with the block system's generalization power.

2 Preliminaries

This section collects the necessary concepts and defines the notation. Unless otherwise stated, all sets and metric spaces are assumed to be *finite*. Special attention will be given to the *Hamming space*, denoted by $\mathcal{M}_H = (\mathbf{B}_d, D_H)$, where $\mathbf{B}_d = \{0,1\}^d$ is the d-dimensional Boolean cube and D_H denotes the Hamming distance.

The *power set* of a set X is denoted by 2^X. A *closure system* (see, e.g., [11]) $\mathcal{C}$ over a set X is a collection of subsets of X that contains X and is closed under arbitrary intersections. It has a corresponding *closure operator* $\rho : 2^X \to 2^X$ that is *extensive* (i.e., $A \subseteq \rho(A)$ for all $A \in 2^X$), *monotone* (i.e., $\rho(A) \subseteq \rho(B)$ for all $A, B \in 2^X$ with $A \subseteq B$), and *idempotent* (i.e., $\rho(\rho(A)) = \rho(A)$ for all $A \in 2^X$) and which satisfies $C \in \mathcal{C}$ iff $C = \rho(C)$ for all $C \subseteq X$. The fixpoints of ρ are referred to as *closed* sets.

Ordinary and abstract *convexity* are used explicitly or implicitly by many learning algorithms. Examples include support vector machines [10] (half-spaces are convex subsets of $\mathbb{R}^d$) or learning separating half-spaces in graphs [22] (half-spaces are defined by abstract convexity over the vertex set of a graph). For a metric space $\mathcal{M} = (X, D)$, $C \subseteq X$ is *geodesically convex* or simply, *convex* if for all $x, y \in C$ and $z \in X, z \in C$ whenever z lies on a geodesic between x and y, i.e., $D(x,y) = D(x,z) + D(z,y)$. The family of all convex subsets of a metric space $\mathcal{M} = (X, D)$ is denoted by $\mathcal{C}$. As an example, consider the function over $\mathbf{B}_d$ that maps all subsets A of $\mathbf{B}_d$ to the smallest subcube C of $\mathbf{B}_d$ that contains A. It is elementary to check that C is convex for $\mathcal{M}_H$. Note that C can be represented by a conjunction over $2d$ Boolean literals.

Hypothesis classes formed by convex subsets of the domain can be disadvantageous for machine learning, as they cannot capture *multiple well-separated* regions of interest. This limitation is addressed in [23] by generalizing the notion of convexity to that of *weak convexity*: A subset C of a metric space (X, D) is *weakly convex* (or θ-*convex*) for some $\theta \geq 0$ if, for all $x, y \in C$ and $z \in X$, $z \in C$ whenever $D(x,y) \leq \theta$ and $D(x,y) = D(x,z) + D(z,y)$. The collection of all θ-convex subsets of X is denoted by $\mathcal{C}_\theta$.

Our focus will be on hypotheses formed by pairwise disjoint "contiguous" blocks. To this end, we need to define the notion of "contiguity" for metric spaces. Specifically, a sequence $x_1, \ldots, x_\ell$ of pairwise distinct elements of X forms a θ-*path* for some $\theta \geq 0$, if $D(x_i, x_{i+1}) \leq \theta$ for all $i = 1, \ldots, \ell - 1$. A set $A \subseteq X$ is θ-*connected* if for all $x, y \in A$, there exists a θ-path in A connecting x and y (i.e., $x_1 = x$ and $x_\ell = y$). Clearly, A is $\text{diam}(A)$-connected, where $\text{diam}(A) = \max\{D(x,y) : x, y \in A\}$ is the *diameter* of A. The proof of the proposition below is immediate from the definitions.

Proposition 1. *Let (X, D) be a metric space and $A \subseteq X$. Then for all $\theta \geq 0$,*

(i) *if A is θ-connected then A is θ'-connected for all $\theta' \geq \theta$,*
(ii) *A has a unique θ-partitioning defined by θ-connectivity, i.e., for all $x, y \in A$, x and y are in the same θ-connected component if and only if they are θ-connected.*

The *connectivity index* of A in the above proposition, denoted by $\text{CI}(A)$, is defined as the smallest value θ for which A is θ-connected. This is well-defined, as X is finite.

Theorem 1 below, a decomposition result from [23], provides a characterization of θ-convex sets. Specifically, it states that $\mathcal{C}_\theta$, the collection of θ-convex sets, forms a closure system. Moreover, every θ-convex set can be expressed as a family of θ-connected and θ-convex sets that are pairwise θ-distant from each other.

Theorem 1. *Let $\theta \geq 0$ and $\mathcal{M} = (X, D)$ be a metric space. Then (i) $\mathcal{C}_\theta$ forms a closure system and (ii) for all $C \subseteq X$, $C \in \mathcal{C}_\theta$ if and only if there exists a family $\mathcal{P} = \{B_j\}_{j \in J}$ for some index set J with $C = \bigcup_{j \in J} B_j$ that satisfies the following properties for all $j \in J$:*

(α) B_j is θ-convex,
(β) B_j is θ-connected, and
(γ) for all $i \in J$ with $i \neq j$, $D(B_i, B_j) > \theta$.

As a consequence of Proposition 1, $\mathcal{P}$ in the theorem above forms a *unique* partition of C. We will therefore refer to $\mathcal{P}$ as the θ-*convex decomposition* of C. The B_js will be called θ-*convex blocks*, or simply *blocks* of C. Furthermore, (i) of Theorem 1 implies that there exists a *closure operator* $\rho_\theta : 2^X \to 2^X$ with $A \mapsto \bigcap\{C \in \mathcal{C}_\theta : A \subseteq C\}$ for all $A \subseteq X$. In other words, ρ_θ maps A to the (unique) smallest θ-convex set in $\mathcal{C}_\theta$ that contains A. Henceforth, it will be referred to as the θ-*convex hull* of A.

The fundamental properties of weak convexity, as stated in Lemma 1 below, will be used frequently throughout the remainder of this paper.

Lemma 1. *Let $\mathcal{M} = (X, D)$ be a metric space, $\theta \geq \theta' \geq 0$, and $S \subseteq X$. Then*

(i) $\mathcal{C} \subseteq \mathcal{C}_\theta \subseteq \mathcal{C}_{\theta'}$, i.e., convexity implies θ-convexity, which in turn implies θ'-convexity,
(ii) $\rho_{\theta'}(S) \subseteq \rho_\theta(S)$, and
(iii) if $C = \rho_\theta(S)$ and $\mathcal{P} = \{B_j\}_{j \in J}$ is the θ-convex decomposition of C, then $B_j = \rho_\theta(S \cap B_j)$ for all $j \in J$.

Properties (i) and (ii) of Lemma 1 establish that monotonicity for the θ-convex hulls holds not only with respect to the input set but also to the distance threshold θ. This result, when combined with the decomposition theorem (Theorem 1), implies that the generators of a θ-convex set C determine its blocks, as stated in Property (iii).

3 Locally Constrained Block Systems

This paper is concerned with the *consistent hypothesis finding* (CHF) problem for learning weakly convex concepts. We first consider the following CHF problem:

Problem 1. Given a metric space $\mathcal{M} = (X, D)$ and $E^+, E^- \subseteq X$, find a $\theta \geq 0$ and a θ-convex set $H \in \mathcal{C}_\theta$ that is *consistent* with E^+ and E^- (i.e., $E^+ \subseteq H$ and $E^- \cap H = \emptyset$); or return "NO" if there is no such H.

To solve Problem 1, [23] (cf. [14]) employs the decomposition theorem (Theorem 1). Specifically, the solution involves computing the *largest* θ-convex hull of E^+ over all $\theta \geq 0$ that remains disjoint from E^-. Since $\rho_0(A) = A$ for all $A \subseteq X$, a consistent hypothesis is guaranteed to exist when E^+ and E^- are disjoint. Depending on the context, this hypothesis will be referred to as the *consistent globally constrained θ-convex hypothesis*, or simply the *consistent θ-GC hypothesis*.

Example 1. To illustrate the above concepts, consider the Hamming space $\mathcal{M}_H = (\mathbf{B}_d, D_H)$ for $d = 8$. Let $E^+ = \{u_1, u_2, v_1, \ldots, v_4\}$ and $E^- = \{w\}$ with

$$u_1 = (00001111), \quad u_2 = (00010111)$$
$$v_1 = (11111000), \quad v_2 = (11111011), \quad v_3 = (11111101), \quad v_4 = (11111110)$$
$$w = (00100111) \ .$$

The consistent θ-GC hypothesis is attained for $\theta = 2$. To seee this, note first that $\rho_2(E^+)$, which can be represented by the DNF $\phi = \overline{x}_1 \overline{x}_2 \overline{x}_3 x_6 x_7 x_8 \lor x_1 x_2 x_3 x_4 x_5$, is consistent, as it is not satisfied by the negative example w. Furthermore, $w \in \rho_\theta(E^+) = \mathbf{B}_8$ for all $\theta > 2$. Notice that the two subcubes represented by the terms in ϕ fulfill all properties required in (ii) of Theorem 1 for the blocks of a 2-convex decomposition of $\rho_\theta(E^+)$. Notably, they are separated by a distance of 3 from each other. □

A major limitation of the approach in [23] is that the consistent θ-GC hypothesis may contain an excessively high number of blocks. This can lead to an overly specific solution, potentially resulting in overfitting. The issue arises from a fundamental property of the approach: Although the value of θ corresponding to the θ-GC hypothesis is determined by *local* regions induced by the training examples, it is applied *globally* across the entire training set. The following example illustrates this problem.

Example 2. Consider the set E^+ of positive examples in Example 1. Let $E^- = \{w'\}$, where $w' = (00011111)$. Since the negative example w' satisfies the conjunction $\overline{x}_1 \overline{x}_2 \overline{x}_3 x_6 x_7 x_8$, which represents $\rho_2(\{u_1, u_2\})$, we have $w' \in \rho_2(\{u_1, u_2\}) \subset \rho_2(E^+)$. Consequently, given that $\rho_0(E^+) = \rho_1(E^+) = E^+$, the consistent θ-GC hypothesis is identical for $\theta = 0$ and $\theta = 1$, comprising $|E^+|$ singleton blocks. The local distance constraint defined by u_1, u_2, and w' prevents the algorithm from generalizing the positive examples $v_1, \ldots, v_4$ for all $\theta > 1$. However, they can be generalized for $\theta = 2$ without violating consistency. Specifically, $\rho_2(\{v_1, \ldots, v_4\})$, represented by $x_1 x_2 x_3 x_4 x_5$, does not contain w' and is at a distance of $4 > 2$ from both u_1 and u_2. □

To address this limitation, we consider other weakly convex sets as potential candidate hypotheses. The above observations motivate the following definition.

Definition 1 (Locally Constrained Block Systems). *Let $\mathcal{M} = (X, D)$ be a metric space and $\theta \geq 0$. A set $\mathcal{B} = \{(B_j, \theta_j)\}_{j \in J}$ with $\theta_j \geq \theta$ for some index set J is a locally constrained block system for θ, or θ-LC block system for short, if the following properties hold for all $j \in J$:*

(α') B_j *is θ_j-convex,*
(β') B_j *is θ_j-connected,*
(γ') *for all $i \in J$ with $i \neq j$, $D(B_i, B_j) > \max\{\theta_i, \theta_j\}$.*

A set $A \subseteq X$ is *covered* by $\mathcal{B}$ in Definition 1 if $A \subseteq \mathrm{dom}(\mathcal{B})$, where $\mathrm{dom}(\mathcal{B}) = \bigcup_{j \in J} B_j$ denotes the *domain* of $\mathcal{B}$. Definition 1 is inspired by the characterization of weakly convex sets in (ii) of Theorem 1. The key distinctions between (α) and (α') and between (β) and (β') lie in the *relaxation* of the distance thresholds from the global θ in Theorem 1 to some local $\theta_j \geq \theta$. Consequently, the pairwise distance constraints in (γ)

must hold for the maximum of the blocks' distance thresholds in (γ'). It is worth noting that the θ_j values in the definition are not required to be pairwise distinct. Furthermore, different θ-LC block systems can share the same domain.

Example 3. For E^+ in Example 2 we have that $\mathcal{B} = \{(T_1, 0), (T_2, 0), (T_3, 2)\}$ is a 0-LC block system, where $T_1 = \overline{x}_1\overline{x}_2\overline{x}_3\overline{x}_4 x_5 x_6 x_7 x_8, T_2 = \overline{x}_1\overline{x}_2\overline{x}_3 x_4 \overline{x}_5 x_6 x_7 x_8$, and $T_3 = x_1 x_2 x_3 x_4 x_5$ represent $\rho_0(\{u_1\}) = \{u_1\}, \rho_0(\{u_2\}) = \{u_2\}$, and $\rho_2(\{v_1,\ldots,v_4\})$, repectively. □

We note that $\mathrm{dom}(\mathcal{B})$ of a θ-LC block system $\mathcal{B}$ is the union of pairwise distant weakly convex sets, each discretely connected for some (local) distance threshold (see Example 3). The decomposition result in Theorem 1 suggests that $\mathrm{dom}(\mathcal{B})$ itself is a weakly convex set. Proposition 2 below addresses this observation (cf. (ii)). However, although each block B_j of $\mathcal{B}$ is θ_j-connected (cf. (iii)), the θ-convex decomposition of $\mathrm{dom}(\mathcal{B})$ might comprise even more blocks, as θ_j may be strictly larger than θ.

Proposition 2. *Let* $\mathcal{M} = (X, D)$ *be a metric space,* $\theta \geq 0$, *and* $\mathcal{B} = \{(B_j, \theta_j)\}_{j \in J}$ *a θ-LC block system over* $\mathcal{M}$. *Then*

(i) $\mathrm{dom}(\mathcal{B}) \subseteq X$,
(ii) $\mathrm{dom}(\mathcal{B})$ *is θ-convex,*
(iii) for all $j \in J$, B_j *is a θ_j-convex block, and*
(iv) for every $J' \subseteq J$ *with* $J' \neq \emptyset$, $\mathcal{B}' = \{(B_j, \theta_j)\}_{j \in J'}$ *is a θ-LC block system.*

Conversely, Proposition 4 below asserts that the θ-convex decomposition of a θ-convex set $C \subseteq X$ can be regarded as a θ-LC block system in a straightforward manner. Moreover, this *canonical* θ-LC block system is the "finest" among all possible θ-LC block systems covering C, in the following sense: A θ-LC block system $\mathcal{B} = \{(B_j, \theta_j)\}_{j \in J}$ over a metric space $\mathcal{M} = (X, D)$ for some $\theta \geq 0$ is considered *coarser* than a θ-LC block system $\mathcal{B}' = \{(B'_k, \theta'_k)\}_{k \in K}$ for some $\theta' \geq 0$, denoted $\mathcal{B} \preccurlyeq \mathcal{B}'$ (or equivalently, $\mathcal{B}'$ is *finer* than $\mathcal{B}$, denoted $\mathcal{B}' \succcurlyeq \mathcal{B}$), if for every $k \in K$ there exists $j \in J$ such that $B'_k \subseteq B_j$. Clearly, $\mathcal{B} \preccurlyeq \mathcal{B}'$ implies $\mathrm{dom}(\mathcal{B}) \supseteq \mathrm{dom}(\mathcal{B}')$. Our focus will be on θ-LC block systems that contain *no* irrelevant blocks with respect to the set of positive examples, meaning that every block contains at least one positive example. Specifically, $\mathcal{B}$ is *S-relevant* for some $S \subseteq X$ if $S \subseteq \mathrm{dom}(\mathcal{B})$ and for every $j \in J$, $S \cap B_j \neq \emptyset$. We restrict the $\preccurlyeq$ relation to this type of block systems. In particular, $\mathcal{B} \preccurlyeq_S \mathcal{B}'$ denotes that $\mathcal{B} \preccurlyeq \mathcal{B}'$ and both $\mathcal{B}$ and $\mathcal{B}'$ are S-relevant. As mentioned earlier, S will later be restricted to the set of positive examples. Clearly, $\mathcal{B} \preccurlyeq_S \mathcal{B}'$ implies that all blocks of $\mathcal{B}$ contain a block of $\mathcal{B}'$, leading to the following claim.

Proposition 3. *Let* $\mathcal{M} = (X, D)$ *be a metric space,* $S \subseteq X$, *and let* $\mathcal{B} = \{(B_j, \theta_j)\}_{j \in J}$ *and* $\mathcal{B}' = \{(B_k, \theta_k)\}_{k \in K}$ *be θ-LC and θ'-LC block systems, respectively, for some* $\theta, \theta' \geq 0$. *If* $\mathcal{B} \preccurlyeq_S \mathcal{B}'$, *then* $|J| \leq |K|$, *i.e., the number of blocks in $\mathcal{B}$ is bounded by that in $\mathcal{B}'$.*

We employ the notation $\succ_S$ and $\prec_S$ when $|J| < |K|$. In the following proposition, we establish a relationship between the θ-convex decomposition of a θ-convex set $C \subseteq X$ and the θ-LC block systems that cover C.

Proposition 4. *Let $\mathcal{M} = (X, D)$ be a metric space, $\theta \geq 0$, $\mathcal{B} = \{(B_i, \theta_i)\}_{j \in J}$ a θ-LC block system, $C \subseteq X$ a θ-convex set covered by $\mathcal{B}$, and $\mathcal{P} = \{P_k\}_{k \in K}$ the θ-convex decomposition of C. Then*

(i) *$\mathcal{B}' = \{(P_k, \theta)\}_{k \in K}$ is a θ-LC block system with $\mathrm{dom}(\mathcal{B}') = C$,*
(ii) *$\mathcal{B} \preccurlyeq \mathcal{B}'$, i.e., any θ-LC block system covering C is coarser than the θ-convex decomposition of C, and*
(iii) *if $\mathcal{B}$ is C-relevant then $|J| \leq |K|$, i.e., the number of blocks in a C-relevant θ-LC block system is bounded by that in the θ-convex decomposition of C.*

Proposition 4 (iii) suggests that θ-LC block systems can cover the consistent θ-GC hypothesis studied in [23], potentially using fewer blocks. In Sect. 5, we provide experimental evidence demonstrating that the consideration of this broader hypothesis class for the CHF problem results in a substantial reduction in the number of blocks.

4 The Local Convexification Method

Under some natural assumptions, the consistent θ-GC hypothesis can be found in polynomial time [23]. As discussed earlier, it is not optimal in terms of the number of blocks compared to consistent θ-LC block systems; a θ-LC block system $\mathcal{B}$ is *consistent* with the sets E^+ and E^- of positive and negative examples if $E^+ \subseteq \mathrm{dom}(\mathcal{B})$ and $E^- \cap \mathrm{dom}(\mathcal{B}) = \emptyset$. The following theorem demonstrates, in the specific case of k-convex Boolean functions, that a consistent θ-LC block system can be *exponentially* more compact than the consistent θ-GC block system considered in [14,23].

Theorem 2. *For all sufficiently large positive integers d, there exist $E^+, E^- \subseteq \mathbf{B}_d$ and a θ-LC block system $\mathcal{B}$ consistent with E^+ and E^- such that the size of the consistent θ-GC block system $\mathcal{B}_c$ relative to $\mathcal{B}$ satisfies*

$$\frac{|\mathcal{B}_c|}{|\mathcal{B}|} = 2^{\Omega(d)} .$$

Proof. Let $d' = d - 7$ and let S be a largest subset of $\mathbf{B}_{d'}$ such that the pairwise Hamming distance between any two elements of S is at least 3. By the Gilbert-Varshamov bound (see, e.g., Chap. 8 in [16]), a fundamental result in coding theory, we have

$$|S| \geq \frac{2^{d'}}{\sum_{j=0}^{2} \binom{d'}{j}} = 2^{\Omega(d)} . \quad (1)$$

Let $E^+ = \{x, y\} \cup S'$ and $E^- = \{z\}$, where $x = 0^3 0^4 0^{d-7}$, $y = 1^3 0^4 0^{d-7}$, $z = 001 0^4 0^{d-7}$, and $S' = \{0^3 1^4 \oplus s : s \in S\}$. Here, a^ℓ and $\oplus$ denote the ℓ-fold repetition of the symbol a and the string concatenation, respectively.

Since $D_H(x, y) = D_H(x, z) + D_H(z, y)$ and $D_H(x, y) = 3$, there is no consistent 3-convex Boolean function. In contrast, there exists a consistent hypothesis for $\theta = 2$. On the one hand, the consistent globally constrained θ-convex hypothesis $\mathcal{B}_c$ for $\theta = 2$ contains $|S| + 2 = 2^{\Omega(d)}$ blocks by (1), each of which is a singleton. On the other hand, utilizing the fact that the convex hull of a set of at least 3 points of $\mathbf{B}_d$ is always 2-connected [13], the 2-LC block system $\mathcal{B} = \{(\{x\}, 2), (\{y\}, 2), (\text{convex hull of } S, 2)\}$ is consistent and contains only three blocks. □

Using the notion of optimality in terms of number of blocks, Theorem 2 gives rise to the following CHF problem.

Problem 2 (Block-Minimum CHF Problem). *Given* a metric space $\mathcal{M} = (X, D)$ and $E^+, E^- \subseteq X$, *find* a $\theta \geq 0$ and a consistent θ-LC block system $\mathcal{B} = \{(B_i, \theta_i)\}_{i \in \{1,...,k\}}$ with the *smallest* k, or return "NO" if there are no such θ and $\mathcal{B}$.

The following theorem presents a negative result on the complexity of Problem 2.

Theorem 3. *Problem 2 is NP-complete.*

Proof. Given a finite set $\mathcal{B} \subseteq 2^X \times [0, \infty)$ over a metric space $\mathcal{M} = (X, D)$ and $\theta \geq 0$, it can be decided in polynomial time whether $\mathcal{B}$ is a θ-LC block system that is consistent with E^+ and E^-. Thus, Problem 2 is in NP. To show that it is NP-hard, we use a reduction from the disjoint version of the *boxes class cover* (BCC) problem [19] defined as follows: Given disjoint finite sets B of blue and R of red points in the plane, find a *minimum cardinality* set $\mathcal{H}$ of pairwise disjoint axis-aligned rectangles such that every blue point is contained in a rectangle and none of the red points belongs to any of the rectangles in $\mathcal{H}$. This problem is NP-complete [19, Theorem 4.10].

The main idea behind the reduction is that for an instance B, R of the disjoint version of the BCC problem, we construct a finite rectangular grid graph $G = (V, E)$ with vertices containing $B \cup R$ such that the shortest path between any two vertices in $B \cup R$ is at least 3, where the distance between the vertices is defined by the shortest-path distance. We have that a subset C of V is θ-convex for all $\theta \geq 2$ iff the subgraph of G induced by C is a grid graph. This property allows us to establish the connection between solutions of the disjoint version of the BCC problem containing k rectangles and those of Problem 2 containing k blocks.

More precisely, for an instance B, R of the disjoint version of the BCC problem with $|B \cup R| = n$, construct a graph $G = (V, E)$ as follows: For all $p \in B \cup R$, take a vertical and a horizontal line through p. Sort the points in $B \cup R$ according to their x-coordinates and for each adjacent points $(x, y), (x', y')$ with $x < x'$, select three values x_1, x_2, x_3 satisfying $x < x_1 < x_2 < x_3 < x'$ and take the three vertical lines through $(x_1, 0), (x_2, 0), (x_3, 0)$, respectively. In a similar way, sort the points in $B \cup R$ according to their y-coordinates and for each adjacent points with different y-coordinates take three pairwise different horizontal lines. In this way we obtain a grid in the plane with vertices defined by the set of pairwise intersections of the horizontal and vertical lines. Define V by the set of vertices of this grid and add edge $\{u, v\}$ to E iff they are adjacent in the grid. For any $u, v \in V$, define their distance $D(u, v)$ by their shortest-path distance in G. By construction, G is a rectangular grid graph with $B \cup R \subseteq V$ and $D(u, v) > 2$ for all $u, v \in R \cup B$ with $u \neq v$.

It holds that if $C \subseteq V$ induces a connected subgraph of G and C is θ-convex for some $\theta \geq 2$ then C is θ-convex for *all* $\theta \geq 2$ (i.e., C is convex) and that C induces a rectangular subgrid graph of G. Since the size of G is $\mathcal{O}(n^2)$, the reduction is polynomial.

It is easy to check that for all $k > 0$, there exists a hypothesis $\mathcal{H}$ containing k pairwise disjoint axis-aligned rectangles in $\mathbb{R}^2$ that is consistent with $B \cup R$ iff there exists a θ-LC block system $\mathcal{B}$ over $\mathcal{M}$ for $\theta = 2$ that consists of k blocks and is consistent with $E^+ = B$ and $E^- = R$. This completes the proof of the NP-hardness. □

Algorithm 1. LOCAL CONVEXIFICATION METHOD

Require: metric space $\mathcal{M} = (X, D)$ and threshold $\tau \geq 0$
Input: $E^+, E^- \subseteq X$
Output: θ-LC block system $\mathcal{B}$ for some $\theta \geq \tau$ which is consistent with E^+ and E^- if such θ and $\mathcal{B}$ exist; otherwise "NO"

1: $\mathcal{B} \leftarrow \{(B, \tau) : B \in \text{WEAKLYCONVEXHULL}(\tau, E^+)\}, \mathcal{F} \leftarrow \emptyset$
2: **if** $\exists (B, \theta_B) \in \mathcal{B}, e \in E^-$ such that $\text{MEMBERSHIP}(e, B) = \text{TRUE}$ **then return** "NO"
3: **while** $\mathcal{A} := \{((R, \theta_R), (S, \theta_S)) \in \mathcal{B}^2 : R \neq S, \{R, S\} \notin \mathcal{F}\} \neq \emptyset$ **do**
4: $\quad \lambda \leftarrow \min\{\text{DISTANCE}(R, S) : ((R, \theta_R), (S, \theta_S)) \in \mathcal{A}\}$
5: $\quad$ choose $((R, \theta_R), (S, \theta_S)) \in \mathcal{A}$ such that $\text{DISTANCE}(R, S) = \lambda$
6: $\quad \mathcal{D} \leftarrow \{(R, \theta_R), (S, \theta_S)\}$
7: $\quad B \leftarrow \text{JOIN}(\max\{\tau, \lambda\}, R, S), \theta_B \leftarrow \max\{\tau, \text{CONNECTIVITYINDEX}(B)\}$
8: $\quad$ **while** $\exists (Q, \theta_Q) \in \mathcal{B} \setminus \mathcal{D}$ with $\text{DISTANCE}(B, Q) \leq \max\{\tau, \theta_B, \theta_Q\}$ **do**
9: $\quad\quad B \leftarrow \text{JOIN}(\max\{\tau, \theta_B, \theta_Q\}, B, Q), \mathcal{D} \leftarrow \mathcal{D} \cup \{(Q, \theta_Q)\}$
10: $\quad\quad \theta_B \leftarrow \max\{\tau, \text{CONNECTIVITYINDEX}(B)\}$
11: $\quad$ **if** $\exists e \in E^-$ such that $\text{MEMBERSHIP}(e, B) = \text{TRUE}$ **then** $\mathcal{F} \leftarrow \mathcal{F} \cup \{\{R, S\}\}$
12: $\quad$ **else** $\mathcal{B} \leftarrow (\mathcal{B} \setminus \mathcal{D}) \cup \{(B, \theta_B)\}$
13: **return** $\mathcal{B}$

4.1 The Algorithm

Motivated by the aforementioned negative result, we present a *greedy heuristic* called the LOCAL CONVEXIFICATION METHOD (LCM; see Algorithm 1) for finding *compact* consistent θ-LC block systems. The main idea of Algorithm 1 is to greedily *join* pairs of blocks in *ascending* order of their distance until any further join would result in an inconsistency.

Algorithm 1 operates on a finite metric space $\mathcal{M}$ and requires a threshold $\tau \geq 0$. Regarding τ, a user-specified lower bound on θ for the consistent θ-LC block system computed by the algorithm, it has been shown in [23] that certain metric spaces permit a *compact representation* of the blocks in θ-convex decompositions of θ-convex sets. In particular, some representation schemes make use of the fact that blocks are *convex sets*. For instance, the terms of a DNF representing a weakly convex Boolean function correspond to convex subsets of $\mathbf{B}_d$. This property can also be leveraged for θ-LC block systems. However, this requires the value of θ for a block to exceed a certain threshold τ, which is *intrinsically* tied to the underlying metric space. More precisely, a metric space is *blockwise convex* for some $\theta \geq 0$ if every θ-convex block (i.e., θ-connected and θ-convex set) is convex. For representation languages restricted to convex blocks, τ should be at least the smallest value of θ for which the metric space is blockwise convex. As an example, k-convex Boolean functions can be represented by DNFs whose conjunctive terms correspond precisely to the blocks in their respective decompositions [14]. In this specific case, $\tau = 2$, since the blocks of 2-convex subsets of $\mathcal{M}_H$ are convex [13].

In each iteration of the outer loop, Algorithm 1 computes a strictly coarser consistent θ-LC block system from the current consistent θ-LC block system $\mathcal{B}$ by joining block pairs in their increasing distance order. This is an iterated process that is repeated as long as the resulting block is consistent with the negative examples and does not violate any of the blocks' local distance constraints. If a join operation results in an inconsistency, the algorithm does *not* stop the computation. Instead, it returns to the state before the invalid join, adds the pair of blocks that led to the inconsistency to a set of *forbidden* pairs, and continues with the next pair of blocks.

We do not provide the pseudocode of the *subroutines* in Algorithm 1. Semantically, they are defined as follows: For $E^+ \subseteq X$, $e \in X$, blocks $B, R \subseteq X$, and $\theta \geq \tau$,

- WEAKLYCONVEXHULL(θ, E^+) computes the set of blocks of $\rho_\theta(E^+)$.
- MEMBERSHIP(e, B) decides whether or not $e \in B$.
- DISTANCE(B, R) computes the distance $D(B, R) = \min_{b \in B, r \in R} D(b, r)$.
- CONNECTIVITYINDEX(B) calculates the connectivity index CI(B) of B (i.e., the smallest θ' such that B is θ'-connected).
- JOIN(θ, B, R) computes the join of B and R defined by $\rho_\theta(B \cup R)$. Note that $\rho_\theta(B \cup R)$ constitutes a single block whenever $\theta \geq D(B, R)$, a condition that is always fulfilled during the entire execution of Algorithm 1.

Algorithm 1 starts by calling WEAKLYCONVEXHULL(τ, E^+) and initializing $\mathcal{F}$ as an empty set. It is used to store forbidden pairs of blocks, i.e., which cannot be joined. According to Proposition 4 (ii), this initial step produces the finest θ-LC block system containing E^+ for some $\theta \geq \tau$. If the resulting hypothesis is inconsistent with the negative examples E^-, the algorithm must return "NO", as there is no consistent hypothesis. This consistency check is performed in line 2. It follows from the definition of weakly convex hulls and Lemma 1 (iii) that the initial hypothesis $\mathcal{B}$ in line 1 is E^+-relevant.

When entering the main loop of Algorithm 1 (line 3), the properties of θ-LC block systems (see Definition 1) are preserved. Among the block pairs in $\mathcal{B}$ that are not in $\mathcal{F}$, a pair with the smallest distance, denoted λ, is selected (lines 4–5). However, the new block B, obtained by joining the two selected blocks (line 7), may violate local distance constraints with other blocks in relation to the updated connectivity index. To address this, further joins of violating blocks with B are computed in the inner loop (lines 8–10), if necessary. During this process, the connectivity index is updated to ensure that the properties of θ-LC block systems remain satisfied. Additionally, the join operation could potentially cause an inconsistency with E^-; this is checked in line 11. If an inconsistency is detected, the initial pair of blocks is added to the set $\mathcal{F}$ of forbidden joins. Otherwise, the data structure $\mathcal{B}$ is updated by removing the blocks that were joined into B and by adding B, along with the maximum of τ and its connectivity index θ_B. In each iteration of the main loop that modifies $\mathcal{B}$, the update results in a consistent *coarsening* of $\mathcal{B}$. This guarantees a consistent hypothesis for both E^+ and E^- while ensuring that it remains E^+-relevant. The following theorem addresses the soundness and computational complexity of Algorithm 1.

Theorem 4. *The following properties hold for Algorithm 1:*

(i) *It returns a consistent E^+-relevant θ-LC block system $\mathcal{B}$ for some $\theta \geq \tau$, or "NO" if such θ and $\mathcal{B}$ do not exist.*
(ii) *It runs in time polynomial in $|E^+|$, $|E^-|$, and the parameters of the underlying metric space $\mathcal{M}$, provided that all five functions called by the algorithm also run in time polynomial in $|E^+|$ and the parameters of $\mathcal{M}$.*

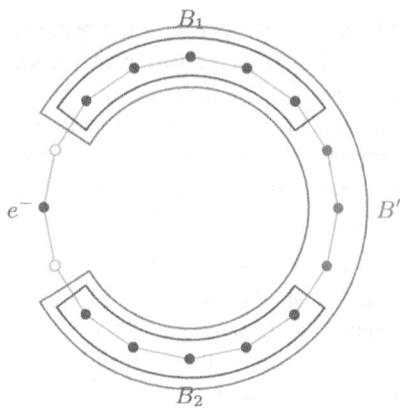

Fig. 1. An example for which Algorithm 1 returns a consistent θ-LC block system that is *not* block-minimal consistent. The output is $\mathcal{B} = \{(B_1, 1), (B_2, 1)\}$. However, $\mathcal{B} = \{(B', 1)\}$ is a consistent E^+-relevant 1-LC block system with $\mathcal{B} \succ_{E^+} \mathcal{B}'$. (Color figure online)

It remains to ask whether Algorithm 1 *always* returns at least a *block-minimal consistent* θ-LC block system. Specifically, a θ-LC block system $\mathcal{B}$ with $\theta \geq \tau$ is considered block-minimal consistent if it is consistent with E^+ and E^-, E^+-relevant, and there exists no consistent E^+-relevant θ'-LC block system $\mathcal{B}'$ for some $\theta' \geq \tau$ such that $\mathcal{B}' \prec_{E^+} \mathcal{B}$. Recall that E^+-relevance guarantees that $\mathcal{B}$ has no block that is disjoint with E^+. Note further that block-minimal consistency of a θ-LC block system does not imply that its number of blocks is minimum across all consistent θ-LC block systems. Example 4 below demonstrates that the answer to the above question is *negative*.

Example 4. We present an example which shows that the output of Algorithm 1 is *not* block-minimal consistent in general. The underlying metric space in this example is formed by the vertex set of an (unweighted) connected graph and the shortest-path distance. To this end, note first that $\mathrm{CI}(B) = 1$ for every $\theta \geq 1$ and for every θ-convex block B. Indeed, if B is a θ-convex block and $u, v \in B$, then there is a θ-path $u = p_1, p_2, \ldots, p_\ell = v$ between u and v that lies in B. Furthermore, since $D(p_i, p_{i+1}) \leq \theta$, all shortest paths between p_i and p_{i+1} are contained in B, for all $i = 1, \ldots, \ell - 1$. Choose one such shortest path between p_i and p_{i+1}, for all i. The concatenation of these paths is a 1-path between u and v. Hence, B is 1-connected implying $\mathrm{CI}(B) \leq 1$. Since $\mathrm{CI}(B) \geq 1$, $\mathrm{CI}(B) = 1$.

For the example, let $G = (V, E)$ denote the cycle consisting of 16 vertices given in Fig. 1. Let the positive examples E^+ consist of the points depicted in **red** and the negative example $E^- = \{e^-\}$ be the single point depicted in **blue**. Consider the subgraphs B_1 and B_2 consisting of 5 positive examples each, as shown in the figure. Using $\mathrm{CI}(B_1) = \mathrm{CI}(B_2) = 1$, one can easily check that the output of Algorithm 1 will be $\mathcal{B} = \{(B_1, 1), (B_2, 1)\}$.

Now consider the 1-LC block system $\mathcal{B}' = \{(B', 1)\}$, where B' consists of the 10 **red** and 3 **purple** points as shown in Fig. 1. It is an 1-LC block system, E^+-relevant, consistent, and $\mathcal{B} \succ_{E^+} \mathcal{B}'$. Hence, $\mathcal{B}$ is not block-minimal consistent. □

Note that B' in the example is not convex. In the theorem below, we give a sufficient condition for Algorithm 1 to return block-minimal consistent hypohteses. It requires, among others, that the underlying metric space is blockwise convex. However, whether this condition is also necessary remains an open question.

Theorem 5. *Let $\mathcal{M} = (X, D)$ be a blockwise convex metric space for some $\tau \geq 0$. If there exists some constant $\sigma > 0$ such that $\mathrm{CI}(B) = \sigma$ for all θ'-convex blocks $B \subseteq X$ with $\theta' \geq \tau$, then the output of Algorithm 1 is block-minimal consistent.*

5 Application: Learning Weakly Convex Boolean Functions

To demonstrate the performance of our general-purpose heuristic LCM in practice, we consider the CHF problem for the special case where the underlying metric space is the Hamming space $\mathcal{M}_H = (\mathbf{B}_d, D_H)$. This case gives rise to weakly convex Boolean functions, i.e., whose sets of true points are θ-convex [14]. As previously discussed, such functions can be represented by DNFs, where the terms correspond to the θ-convex blocks of their sets of true points. The CHF problem for this class of Boolean functions was studied and solved in [14], using a *domain-specific* algorithm that computes consistent θ-GC hypotheses.[1] One can verify that $\mathcal{M}_H$ is *blockwise convex* for all $\theta \geq 2$ (cf. [13]) and that $\mathrm{CI}(B) = 1$ for all $\theta \geq 2$ and all θ-convex convex blocks B, leading to the following result by Theorem 5:

Corollary 1. *For $\mathcal{M} = \mathcal{M}_H$ and $\tau = 2$, all θ-LC block systems returned by Algorithm 1 are block-minimal consistent.*

For all experiments, we set $\tau = 2$ based on the rationale discussed above. The application of Algorithm 1 to weakly convex Boolean functions involves the implementation of the following subroutines for (irredundant) terms B and R over variables $x_1, \ldots, x_d$ ($m_\oplus$ and $m_\ominus$ below denote $|E^+|$ and $|E^-|$ in Algorithm 1, respectively):

- WEAKLYCONVEXHULL(θ, E^+) computes a set of conjunctive terms representing the blocks of $\rho_\theta(E^+)$ in $\mathcal{O}(dm_\oplus^2)$ time (see [14] for details).
- MEMBERSHIP(e, B) determines in $\mathcal{O}(d)$ time whether $e \in \mathbf{B}_d$ satisfies B.
- DISTANCE(B, R) computes the distance between the two subcubes of $\mathbf{B}_d$ represented by B and R in $\mathcal{O}(d)$ time.
- CONNECTIVITYINDEX(B) returns 1 in constant time (see the remark above).
- JOIN(θ, B, R) computes the conjunction representing the *smallest* subcube of $\mathbf{B}_d$ containing the subcubes represented by B and R in $\mathcal{O}(d)$ time.

Since all functions run in time polynomial in $m_\oplus$ and the parameter d, Algorithm 1 runs in time polynomial in $m_\oplus$, $m_\ominus$, and d by Theorem 1 (ii).

---

[1] In [14], the authors use the notation k instead of θ and refer to k-convex Boolean functions.

5.1 Experimental Results

In this section, we present our experimental results on learning θ-convex Boolean functions. We empirically compare the *number of blocks* and the *predictive accuracy* of the output of Algorithm 1 with those of two baseline methods. The first one is the algorithm in [14], developed specifically for this task. It computes a DNF representing the consistent θ-GC hypothesis. As the second baseline method, we compare the results with the DNFs extracted from Boolean decision trees learned on the same training data. The rationale for considering this baseline is that Boolean decision trees represent DNFs.

Datasets. For each DNF learning task, we first generated t conjunctions, each with the following procedure for parameters $\tilde{d}, \theta_{\min}, \theta_{\max} \in \mathbb{N}$: Tossing a biased coin $\tilde{d}$ times independently and with success probability $\ell/\tilde{d}$ for some random integer $0 \leq \ell \leq \tilde{d}$, we have generated a subset V of the Boolean variables $x_1, \ldots, x_{\tilde{d}}$. For each $x_i \in V$, we then tossed an unbiased coin and, depending on the outcome, added either x_i or $\overline{x}_i$ to the conjunction. For each pair of the t conjunctions, a distance $\theta' \in \mathbb{N}$ is generated uniformly at random within the interval $[\theta_{\min}, \theta_{\max}]$. It determines the number of conflicting new variables–distinct from those in V–that must be added to both terms. Thus, after processing all pairs, we obtain a θ-convex DNF over $d \geq \tilde{d}$ Boolean variables for some $\theta \geq \theta_{\min}$, consisting of t terms. This DNF was used as the *unknown* target weakly convex Boolean function. Finally, the positive (resp. negative) training examples E^+ (resp. E^-) of varying sizes were chosen *uniformly* from this DNF's true (resp. false) points.

Parameters. We considered all combinations of $t \in \{4, 5\}$, $\tilde{d} \in \{10, 15, 20\}$, and $\ell \in \{4, 5\}$. $\theta_{\min} = 3$ and $\theta_{\max} = 6$ were constant as a compromise between variability of the distances and dimensionality of the underlying Hamming space. Regarding the training examples, we considered two cases, the *balanced* with $|E^+| = |E^-|$ and the *imbalanced* one with $|E^-| = 150000 \gg |E^+|$. In both cases, $|E^+| \in \{10, 20, \ldots, 100, 200, \ldots, 1000, 1500, 2000, \ldots, 5000\}$. In order to estimate mean and standard deviation of the performance measures, the experiment was repeated $i = 50$ times, independently for each parameter combination.

Limitations. The experimental design described above has some inherent *limitations*. Most importantly, due to the addition of conflicting variables during the concept generation, the *dimension* d of the underlying Hamming spaces is also determined randomly. However, as the VC-dimension of weakly convex Boolean functions is tied to the dimension of the surrounding space, this has a direct impact on learnability. In particular, none of the parameter combinations we considered satisfies any bounds for efficient PAC-learnability [14]. This limits the number of terms that can be considered, as in this case *much* more training examples are needed. Interestingly, the number of *negative* examples appears to govern this effect, which was investigated in the *imbalanced* case described above. Furthermore, it is known that there is an inherent imbalance between true and negative points in weakly convex Boolean functions [14]. This is reflected neither in the balanced nor in the imbalanced cases described above, as otherwise we would end up with high probability with none or only very few positive examples. Notice that the DNF generation is biased also in the sense that the conflicting variables are disjoint

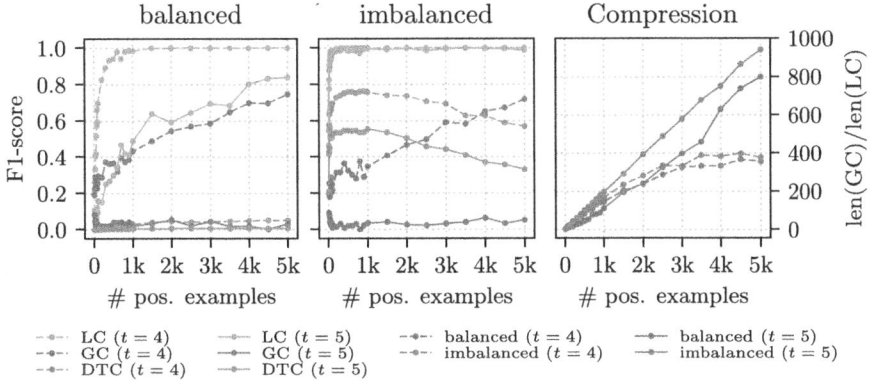

Fig. 2. Mean F1-score obtained by θ-LC (orange lines), θ-GC (**blue** lines), and DTC hypotheses (**purple** lines) depending on the number $|E^+|$ of positive examples drawn from target concepts with $t = 4$ (dashed lines) and $t = 5$ terms (solid lines). The *balanced* case (left plot) with $|E^-| = |E^+|$ is distinguished from the *imbalanced* case (center plot) where $|E^-| = 150000 \gg |E^+|$ is constant. The compactness (right plot) is the ratio of the θ-GC over θ-LC hypotheses' number of blocks (i.e., terms in the output DNFs). All values are averaged over 50 independent iterations. (Color figure online)

for distinct term pairs, except for the initial $\tilde{d}$ common variables. Increasing the overlap of common conflicting variables results in smaller blocks, further emphasizing the imbalance between true and negative points of the generated DNFs. As mentioned, the goal of our experiments is to examine, as a proof-of-concept, Algorithm 1 in terms of *compactness* (number of blocks) and *predictive* performance by comparing its output hypotheses to those of the two baseline algorithms. Accordingly, since our general-purpose algorithm does not utilize any domain-specific knowledge, except for setting $\tau = 2$, a comparison with state-of-the-art algorithms specific to learning DNFs is out of the scope of this work. For all learning tasks and iterations, the decision tree model's hyperparameters were individually optimized using cross-validated grid search.

Results. For each learning task, the three algorithms are called with E^+ and E^-, using $\tau = 2$ for the first two algorithms. The corresponding three DNFs are denoted by ϕ_{GC} (consistent θ-GC hypothesis, i.e., the largest consistent θ-convex hull of E^+ [14]), ϕ_{LC} (consistent θ-LC block system produced by Algorithm 1), and ϕ_{DTC} (decision tree). The hypotheses are compared with each other by their number of terms (i.e., blocks) and F1-score. The results[2] for $t \in \{4,5\}$ and $\tilde{d} = 15$ are shown in Fig. 2. Notice that the output hypotheses of all three algorithms show higher predictive performance for target concepts with $t = 4$ terms (dashed lines) compared to $t = 5$ (solid lines). This is expected because a) there are more examples *per block* for $t = 4$ than for $t = 5$, and b) the dimension d of the Hamming space increases with t due to the addition of

---

[2] The algorithms and the experiments were implemented in Python 3.11 using the sortedcontainers package for managing the underlying data structures of Algorithm 1 and the θ-convex baseline algorithm [23]. For the decision tree models, we used the implementation of the sklearn package.

conflicting variables to the terms. Specifically, d ranged from 27 to 48 (mean 37.84, std. dev. 3.82) for $t = 4$ and from 36 to 66 (mean 52.92, std. dev. 5.29) for $t = 5$.

Notice that the DNFs extracted from decision tree classifiers (DTC) for the balanced case (left plot) performed very poorly, regardless of t and the number of examples. However, $|E^+| = |E^-| \geq 1000$ examples suffice for Algorithm 1 to return excellent θ-LC hypotheses with a stable F1-score of almost 1.0 (mean 0.998, std. dev. 0.037) for target concepts with $t = 4$ terms (dashed lines). For $t = 4$ and $|E^+| \geq 1000$, the returned hypotheses even coincide *exactly* with the unknown target concepts in more than 95.4% of the cases; for $t = 5$ and $|E^+| \geq 1000$, in about 52.89% of the cases. The average F1-score also drops substantially in the latter case ($t = 5$) but was still 0.84 (std. dev. 0.32) for $|E^+| = |E^-| = 5000$ positive and negative examples. In contrast, the θ-GC hypotheses performed far worse than θ-LC hypotheses. In particular, they coincided with the unknown target concepts exactly only in 19.6% of the cases with an average F1-score of 0.75 (std. dev. 0.39) for $t = 4$ and not even once with an average F1-score of only 0.03 (std. dev. 0.15) for $t = 5$, for $|E^+| \geq 1000$ in both cases. It is worth mentioning that the θ-GC hypotheses have a very high precision (near 1.0 almost all the time) but a poor mean recall of 0.03 (std. dev. 0.13). This is a direct consequence of the effect of the global distance constraint θ, which prevents the necessary join operations leading to hypotheses with several very small blocks, often even only singletons. In other words, the θ-GC hypotheses do *not* generalize at all from the training data.

A comparison between the balanced (left plot) and the imbalanced case (center plot) reveals that the predictive performance of θ-GC hypotheses is not affected by the additional negative examples. This is to be expected because, as discussed before, θ-GC hypotheses appear to often overfit E^+. In contrast, since Algorithm 1 greedily joins blocks until inconsistency with E^-, it benefits more from the additional negative examples. It is remarkable, that it obtains an excellent F1-score of 0.99 (std. dev. 0.09) even for $t = 5$ terms when provided with $|E^+| \approx 1000$ positive and $|E^-| = 150000$ negative examples. Another difference to the balanced case is that the DNFs extracted from decision tree classifiers also appear to benefit from the additional negative examples. Still, they perform significantly worse than the θ-LC hypotheses for both $t = 4$ (mean 0.68, std. dev. 0.22) and $t = 5$ (mean 0.48, std. dev. 0.32).

The right plot in Fig. 2 shows the mean ratio of the lengths (i.e., number of blocks) of θ-GC hypotheses over θ-LC hypotheses. θ-GC hypotheses have up to almost *three* orders of magnitudes more terms than θ-LC hypotheses. On average, the factor is 141.13 (std. dev. 245.38) for unknown target concepts with $t = 4$ and 230.04 (std. dev. 293.29) with $t = 5$ terms.

In summary, our experiments show that Algorithm 1 solves the CHF problem for weakly convex DNFs with *significantly less* blocks and with a (much) *better* average predictive performance compared to the related baseline decision tree and weakly convex DNF learning algorithms [14,23].

6 Concluding Remarks

Weak convexity [14,23] has proven to be a powerful parameterized tool for solving the CHF problem for hypotheses composed of pairwise separated blocks. A major limitation of the approaches in [14,23] is that the pairwise distances between blocks of consistent θ-GC hypotheses are often determined by the local configuration of only a few training examples. As our experimental results in Sect. 5.1 demonstrate, this can lead to *poor* generalization performance. To address this issue, we introduced and studied LC block systems, a general framework for discontiguous hypothesis classes that extends weakly convex hulls in finite metric spaces. Motivated by the negative complexity result in Theorem 3, we proposed a greedy heuristic to compute consistent and compact LC block systems.

For simplicity, this short version restricts the discussion to geodesic convexity, a special case of *interval convexity* [4]. In addition to the Hamming space considered in this paper, this special case covers other metric spaces commonly used in machine learning, such as those formed by the vertex set of a graph equipped with the shortest-path or weighted shortest-path distance (see, e.g., [3,12,22,24]).

In the special case of learning weakly convex Boolean functions, our heuristic LCM is optimal, meaning that no coarser consistent LC block system exists with fewer blocks than the output of our algorithm. Our experimental results clearly show that the hypotheses generated by our *general-purpose* heuristic achieve *significantly better* predictive performance compared to those produced by the domain-specific method in [14] and by Boolean decision tree learning algorithms. The improvement over [14] can largely be attributed to the *compactness* of the output hypotheses: our approach generates hypotheses with significantly fewer blocks than those produced by the method in [14]. In fact, they are *near-optimal* in terms of the number of blocks in most cases.

The approach and results of this paper raise several questions for further research. For instance, is the sufficient condition of block-minimal consistency in Theorem 5 also necessary? If not, what properties characterize this kind of optimality? Another interesting question is whether our heuristic can be adapted to *unsupervised* learning problems. This question is motivated by the strong relationship between LC block systems and *density-based clusters* [5,15], which share similar definitions of connectedness, global parameters that limit expressivity, and similar algorithmic strategies for greedily joining blocks or clusters by ascending distance.

Another promising avenue for future research could involve *relaxing* the strictness of LC block systems to tolerate a certain amount of misclassifications, akin to soft margin support vector machines [10]. Additionally, motivated by various learning problems over infinite domains, extending the results of this paper from finite to *infinite* metric spaces presents an important and challenging task. This extension is nontrivial, requiring a careful integration of concepts from topology, computational complexity, and machine learning.

Acknowledgements. We are grateful to Victor Chepoi for insightful discussions on abstract convexity.

References

1. Bereg, S., Cabello, S., Díaz-Báñez, J.M., Pérez-Lantero, P., Seara, C., Ventura, I.: The class cover problem with boxes. Comput. Geom. **45**(7), 294–304 (2012)

2. Blumer, A., Ehrenfeucht, A., Haussler, D., Warmuth, M.K.: Learnability and the Vapnik-Chervonenkis dimension. J. ACM **36**(4), 929–965 (1989)
3. Bressan, M., Cesa-Bianchi, N., Lattanzi, S., Paudice, A.: Exact recovery of clusters in finite metric spaces using oracle queries. In: Belkin, M., Kpotufe, S. (eds.) Proceedings of Thirty Fourth Conference on Learning Theory. Proceedings of Machine Learning Research, Boulder, Colorado, USA, vol. 134, pp. 775–803. PMLR (2021)
4. Calder, J.R.: Some elementary properties of interval convexities. J. London Math. Soc. **s2-3**(3), 422–428 (1971)
5. Campello, R.J.G.B., Moulavi, D., Zimek, A., Sander, J.: Hierarchical density estimates for data clustering, visualization, and outlier detection. ACM Trans. Knowl. Discov. Data **10**(1), 5:1–5:51 (2015)
6. Chalopin, J., Chepoi, V., Moran, S., Warmuth, M.K.: Unlabeled sample compression schemes and corner peelings for ample and maximum classes. J. Comput. Syst. Sci. **127**, 1–28 (2022)
7. Chepoi, V.: Classification of graphs by means of metric triangles. Metody Diskretnogo Analiza **96**, 75–93 (1989)
8. Chepoi, V.: Basis graphs of even delta-matroids. J. Comb. Theory Ser. B **97**(2), 175–192 (2007)
9. Chepoi, V., Knauer, K., Marc, T.: Hypercellular graphs: partial cubes without Q3- as partial cube minor. Discret. Math. **343**(4), 111678 (2020)
10. Cortes, C., Vapnik, V.: Support-vector networks. Mach. Learn. **20**(3), 273–297 (1995)
11. Davey, B.A., Priestley, H.A.: Introduction to Lattices and Order, 2nd edn. Cambridge University Press, Cambridge (2002)
12. Araújo, P.H.M., Campêlo, M.B., Corrêa, R.C., Labbé, M.: The geodesic classification problem on graphs. Electron. Notes Theor. Comput. Sci. **346**, 65–76 (2019)
13. Ekin, O., Hammer, P.L., Kogan, A.: On connected Boolean functions. Discret. Appl. Math. **96–97**, 337–362 (1999)
14. Ekin, O., Hammer, P.L., Kogan, A.: Convexity and logical analysis of data. Theoret. Comput. Sci. **244**(1), 95–116 (2000)
15. Ester, M., Kriegel, H.P., Sander, J., Xu, X.: A density-based algorithm for discovering clusters in large spatial databases with noise. In: Proceedings of the Second International Conference on Knowledge Discovery and Data Mining, pp. 226–231. AAAI Press (1996)
16. Hill, R.: A First Course in Coding Theory. Oxford Applied Mathematics and Computing Science Series. Clarendon Press, Oxford (1986)
17. Horváth, T., Turán, G.: Learning logic programs with structured background knowledge. Artif. Intell. **128**(1–2), 31–97 (2001)
18. Kietz, J., Dzeroski, S.: Inductive logic programming and learnability. SIGART Bull. **5**(1), 22–32 (1994)
19. Lantero, P.P.: Geometric Optimization for Classification Problems. Ph.D. theis, Universidad de Sevilla (2010)
20. Mitchell, T.M.: Generalization as search. Artif. Intell. **18**(2), 203–226 (1982)
21. Natarajan, B.K.: On learning Boolean functions. In: Proceedings of the Nineteenth Annual ACM Symposium on Theory of Computing, STOC 1987, pp. 296–304. Association for Computing Machinery, New York City (1987)
22. Seiffarth, F., Horváth, T., Wrobel, S.: Maximal closed set and half-space separations in finite closure systems. Theoret. Comput. Sci. **973**, 114105 (2023)
23. Stadtländer, E., Horváth, T., Wrobel, S.: Learning weakly convex sets in metric spaces. In: Oliver, N., Pérez-Cruz, F., Kramer, S., Read, J., Lozano, J.A. (eds.) Machine Learning and Knowledge Discovery in Databases. Research Track. LNCS, vol. 12976, pp. 200–216. Springer, Cham (2021)

24. Thiessen, M., Gärtner, T.: Online learning of convex sets on graphs. In: Amini, M.R., Canu, S., Fischer, A., Guns, T., Kralj Novak, P., Tsoumakas, G. (eds.) Machine Learning and Knowledge Discovery in Databases, pp. 349–364. Springer, Cham (2022)
25. van de Vel, M.L.J.: Theory of Convex Structures, North-Holland Mathematical Library, vol. 50. North-Holland, Amsterdam (1993)

Gathering and Exploiting Higher-Order Information when Training Large Structured Models

Pierre Wolinski(✉)

LAMSADE, Paris-Dauphine University, PSL University, CNRS, Paris 75016, France
`pierre.wolinski@dauphine.psl.eu`

Abstract. When training large models, such as neural networks, the full derivatives of order 2 and beyond are usually inaccessible, due to their computational cost. Therefore, among the second-order optimization methods, it is common to bypass the computation of the Hessian by using first-order information, such as the gradient of the parameters (e.g., quasi-Newton methods) or the activations (e.g., K-FAC).

In this paper, we focus on the exact and explicit computation of projections of the Hessian and higher-order derivatives on well-chosen subspaces relevant for optimization. Namely, for a given partition of the set of parameters, we compute tensors that can be seen as "higher-order derivatives according to the partition", at a reasonable cost as long as the number of subsets of the partition remains small.

Then, we give some examples of how these tensors can be used. First, we show how to compute a learning rate per subset of parameters, which can be used for hyperparameter tuning. Second, we show how to use these tensors at order 2 to construct an optimization method that uses information contained in the Hessian. Third, we show how to use these tensors at order 3 (information contained in the third derivative of the loss) to regularize this optimization method. The resulting training step has several interesting properties, including: it takes into account long-range interactions between the layers of the trained neural network, which is usually not the case in similar methods (e.g., K-FAC); the trajectory of the optimization is invariant under affine layer-wise reparameterization. Our code is available on GitHub: https://github.com/p-wol/GroupedNewton.

Keywords: Optimization · Newton's method · Deep Learning

1 Introduction

In machine learning, computing the derivatives of the loss at various orders is challenging when using large models, such as neural networks. While the first-order derivative is relatively cheap to compute and easy to use to train neural networks, things get difficult when it comes to higher-order derivatives. In particular, Hessian-based training algorithms such as Newton's method are very expensive to use on large models. Therefore, the study of the Hessian of a loss according to many parameters has become a research area in its own right. For derivatives of order 3 and higher, the situation is even worse: their exact computation is far more expensive than the Hessian, and only a few optimization algorithms use them.

Main Contribution: Extracting Higher-Order Information. Formally, we study a loss $\mathcal{L}$ to be minimized according to a vector of parameters $\boldsymbol{\theta} \in \mathbb{R}^P$. Thus, the order-$d$ derivative of $\mathcal{L}$ at a given point is a tensor of order d with P^d coefficients. Usually, such tensors cannot be computed exactly and explicitly with $d \geq 2$ (which includes the Hessian) for medium-sized models ($P \gtrsim 10^6$).

Instead of trying to approximate these tensors, we propose to compute their projections along well-chosen directions, that are relevant for optimization. This computation can be done efficiently by taking advantage of the practical implementation of the vector of parameters $\boldsymbol{\theta}$ as a tuple of tensors $(\mathbf{T}^1, \cdots, \mathbf{T}^S)$. Such a projection of the order-d derivative yields a tensor of order d with S^d coefficients, instead of P^d. Thus, the Hessian of a model of size $P = 10^6$ represented by a tuple of $S = 20$ tensors can be reduced to a matrix of size $S^2 = 400$, instead of $P^2 = 10^{12}$. More generally, whenever $S \ll P$, the projected order-d derivative of $\mathcal{L}$ is significantly smaller and easier to compute than the full order-d derivative.

Application: Computing per-Layer Learning Rates. Then, we show that such projections of the order-1 and order-2 derivatives can be used to compute the optimal learning rates to choose for each one of the S tensors (or subsets of parameters). The procedure we propose to compute per-layer learning rates is both theoretically well-grounded and usable in practice (as long as the number of layers is not too large). In particular, our computation does not neglect long-range interactions between layers.

Application: Second-Order Optimization Method. Finally, we show that the information contained in the 1st, 2nd, and 3rd order derivatives is not only accessible at reasonable cost, but can also be used for optimization. In particular, we propose an optimization method that exploits higher-order information about the loss obtained by using the main contribution. For simplicity, our optimization method and Newton's method look similar: in both cases, a linear system $\mathbf{H}_0 \mathbf{x} = \mathbf{g}_0$ has to be solved (w.r.t. $\mathbf{x}$), where $\mathbf{g}_0$ and $\mathbf{H}_0$ contain respectively first-order and second-order information about $\mathcal{L}$. Despite this formal resemblance, the difference is enormous: with Newton's method, $\mathbf{H}_0$ is equal to the Hessian $\mathbf{H}$ of $\mathcal{L}$ of size $P \times P$, while with ours, $\mathbf{H}_0$ is equal to a matrix $\bar{\mathbf{H}}$ of size $S \times S$. Thus, $\bar{\mathbf{H}}$ is undoubtedly smaller and easier to compute than $\mathbf{H}$ when $S \ll P$. Nevertheless, since $\bar{\mathbf{H}}$ is a dense matrix, it still contains information about the interactions between the tensors $\mathbf{T}^s$ when they are used in $\mathcal{L}$. This point is crucial because most second-order optimization methods applied to neural networks use a simplified version of the Hessian (or its inverse), usually a diagonal or block-diagonal approximation, ignoring interactions between layers.

Additionally, we propose an anisotropic version of Nesterov's cubic regularization [24], which uses order-3 information to regularize $\bar{\mathbf{H}}$ and avoid instabilities when computing $\bar{\mathbf{H}}^{-1}\bar{\mathbf{g}}$. In particular, the resulting training trajectory is invariant by layer-wise affine reparameterizations, so our method preserves some interesting properties of Newton's method.

Structure of the Paper. First, we show the context and motivation of our work in Sect. 2. Then, we provide in Sect. 3 our core method, and in Sects. 4 and 5 its applications. In Sect. 6, we present experimental results showing that the developed methods are usable in practice. Finally, we discuss the results in Sect. 7.

2 Context and Motivation

2.1 Higher-Order Information

It is not a novel idea to extract higher-order information about a loss at a minimal computational cost to improve optimization. This is typically what is done by [6], although it does not go beyond the second-order derivative. In this line of research, the *Hessian-vector product* [28] is a decisive tool, that allows to compute the projection of higher-order derivatives in given directions at low cost (see Appendix A). For derivatives of order 3, Nesterov's cubic regularization of Newton's method [24] uses information of order 3 to avoid too large training steps. Incidentally, we develop an anisotropic variant of this in Sect. 5. In the same spirit, the use of derivatives of any order for optimization has been proposed [3]

2.2 Using and Estimating the Hessian in Optimization

The Hessian $\mathbf{H}$ of the loss $\mathcal{L}$ according to the vector of parameters $\boldsymbol{\theta}$ is known to contain useful information about $\mathcal{L}$. Above all, the Hessian is used to develop second-order optimization algorithms. Let us denote by $\boldsymbol{\theta}_t$ the value of $\boldsymbol{\theta}$ at time step t, $\mathbf{g}_t \in \mathbb{R}^P$ the gradient of $\mathcal{L}$ at step t and $\mathbf{H}_t$ its Hessian at step t. One of the most widely known second-order optimization method is Newton's method, whose step is [25, Chap. 3.3]:

$$\boldsymbol{\theta}_{t+1} := \boldsymbol{\theta}_t - \mathbf{H}_t^{-1}\mathbf{g}_t. \tag{1}$$

Under certain conditions, including strong convexity of $\mathcal{L}$, the convergence rate of Newton's method is quadratic [25, Th. 3.7], which makes it very appealing. Besides, other methods use second-order information without requiring the full computation of the Hessian. For instance, Cauchy's steepest descent [4] is a variation of the usual gradient descent, where the step size is tuned by extracting very little information from the Hessian:

$$\boldsymbol{\theta}_{t+1} := \boldsymbol{\theta}_t - \eta_t^* \mathbf{g}_t, \quad \text{where} \quad \eta_t^* := \frac{\mathbf{g}_t^T \mathbf{g}_t}{\mathbf{g}_t^T \mathbf{H}_t \mathbf{g}_t}, \tag{2}$$

where the value of $\mathbf{g}_t^T \mathbf{H}_t \mathbf{g}_t$ can be obtained with little computational cost (see Appendix A). However, when optimizing a quadratic function f with Cauchy's steepest descent, $f(\theta_t)$ is known to decrease at a rate $(\frac{\lambda_{\max}-\lambda_{\min}}{\lambda_{\max}+\lambda_{\min}})^2$, where $\lambda_{\max}$ and $\lambda_{\min}$ are respectively the largest and the smallest eigenvalues of the Hessian of f [19, Chap. 8.2, Th. 2]. If the Hessian of f is strongly anisotropic, then this rate is close to one and optimization is slow. For a comparison of the two methods, see [9,19,25].

Finally, there should be some space between Newton's method, which requires the full Hessian $\mathbf{H}$, and Cauchy's steepest descent, which requires minimal and computationally cheap information about $\mathbf{H}$. The optimization method presented in Sect. 5 explores this in-between space.

Quasi-Newton Methods. When the parameter space is high-dimensional, computation of the Hessian $\mathbf{H}_t$ and inversion of the linear system $\mathbf{g}_t = \mathbf{H}_t \mathbf{x}$ are computationally intensive. Quasi-Newton methods are designed to avoid any direct computation of the Hessian, and make extensive use of gradients and finite difference methods to approximate the direction of $\mathbf{H}_t^{-1} \mathbf{g}_t$. For a list of quasi-Newton methods, see [25, Chap. 8]. However, [25] argue that, since it is easy to compute the Hessian by using Automatic Differentiation (AutoDiff), quasi-Newton methods tend to lose their interest.

Applications to Deep Learning. Many methods overcome the curse of the number of parameters by exploiting the structure of the neural networks. It is then common to neglect interactions between layers, leading to a (block)-diagonal approximation of the Hessian. A first attempt has been made by [32]: they divide the Hessian into blocks, following the division of the network into layers, and its off-diagonal blocks are removed. From another perspective, [27] keeps this block-diagonal structure, but performs an additional approximation on the remaining blocks.

More recently, K-BFGS has been proposed [10], which is a variation of the quasi-Newton method BFGS with block-diagonal approximation and an approximate representation of these blocks. In a similar spirit, the Natural Gradient method TNT [29] also exploits the structure of neural networks by performing a block-diagonal approximation. Finally, AdaHessian [34] efficiently implements a second-order method by approximating the Hessian by its diagonal.

Kronecker-Factored Approximate Curvature (K-FAC) is a method for approximating of the Hessian proposed in [20] in the context of neural network training. K-FAC exploits the specific architecture of neural networks to output a cheap approximation of the true Hessian. Despite its scalability, K-FAC suffers from several problems. First, the main approximation is quite rough, since "[it assumes] statistical independence between products [...] of unit activities and products [...] of unit input derivatives" [20, Sec. 3.1]. Second, even with an approximation of the Hessian, one has to invert it, which is computationally intensive even for small networks. To overcome this difficulty, a block-(tri)diagonal approximation of the inverse of the Hessian is made, which eliminates many of the interactions between the layers.

Summarizing the Hessian. In Sect. 5, we propose to summarize the Hessian to avoid the expensive computation of the full Hessian. This idea is not new. For instance, [18] proposes to approximate the Hessian with a matrix composed of blocks in which all coefficients are identical. A more broadly used technique to compress the Hessian is to perform *sketching* on it, that is, project it on randomly chosen directions. This idea is used for solving linear systems [35], as well as for minimizing functions [11], and can be further adapted to Newton's method with cubic regularization [13]. Finally, it is also possible to choose the directions of the projection by using available information [26]. This is the strategy that we have adopted in Sect. 5.

Invariance by Affine Reparameterization. Several optimization methods, such as Newton's, have an optimization step invariant by affine reparameterization of $\boldsymbol{\theta}$ [1] [23, Chap. 4.1.2]. Specifically, when using Newton's method, it is equivalent to optimize $\mathcal{L}$ according to $\boldsymbol{\theta}$ and according to $\tilde{\boldsymbol{\theta}} = \mathbf{A}\boldsymbol{\theta} + \mathbf{B}$ ($\mathbf{A} \in \mathbb{R}^{P \times P}$ invertible, $\mathbf{B} \in \mathbb{R}^P$). This affine-invariance property holds even if the function $\mathcal{L}$ to minimize is a negative log-likelihood, and one chooses to minimize $\boldsymbol{\theta}$ by the *natural gradient* method [1]. This method is still being studied for its invariance property [37] (which is also a feature of K-FAC), but it requires computing the Hessian of $\mathcal{L}$ at some point.

Methods Based on the Moments of the Gradients. Finally, many methods acquire geometric information on the loss by using only the gradients. For instance, Shampoo [12] uses second-moment information of the accumulated gradients.

2.3 Motivation

What are we Really Looking for? The methods that aim to estimate the Hessian matrix $\mathbf{H}$ or its inverse $\mathbf{H}^{-1}$ in order to imitate Newton's method implicitly assume that Newton's method is adapted to the current problem. This assumption is certainly correct when the loss to optimize is strongly convex. But, when the loss is not convex and very complicated, e.g. when training a neural network, this assumption is not justified. Worse, it has been shown empirically that, at the end of the training of a neural network, the eigenvalues of the Hessian are concentrated around zero [30], with only a few large positive eigenvalues. Therefore, Newton's method itself does not seem to be recommended for neural network training, so we may not need to compute the full Hessian at all, which would relieve us of a tedious, if not impossible, task.

To avoid such problems, it is very common to regularize the Hessian by adding a small, constant term $\lambda \mathbf{I}$ to it [25, Chap. 6.3]. Also, trust-region Newton methods are designed to handle non-positive-definite Hessian matrices [25, Chap. 6.4] [22].

Importance of the Interactions Between Layers. Also, some empirical works have shown that the role and the behavior of each layer must be considered along its interactions with the other layers, which emphasize the importance of off-diagonal blocks in the Hessian or its inverse. We give two examples. First, [36] has shown that, at the end of their training, many networks exhibit a strange feature: some (but not all) layers can be reinitialized to their initial value with little loss of the performance. Second, [15] has compared the similarity between the representations of the data after each layer: changing the number of layers can qualitatively change the similarity matrix of the layers [15, Fig. 3]. Among all, these results motivate our search for mathematical objects that show how layers interact.

Per-layer Scaling of the Learning Rates. A whole line of research is concerned with building a well-founded method for finding a good scaling for the initialization distribution of the parameters, and for the learning rates, which can be chosen layer-wise. For instance, a layer-wise scaling for the weights was proposed and theoretically justified in the paper introducing the Neural Tangent Kernels [14]. Also, in the "feature learning" line of work, [33] proposes a relationship between different scalings related to weight initialization and training. Therefore, there is an interest in finding a scalable and theoretically grounded method to build per-layer learning rates.

Unleashing the Power of AutoDiff. Nowadays, several libraries provide easy-to-use automatic differentiation packages that allow the user to compute numerically the gradient of a function, and even higher-order derivatives. [1] Ignoring the computational cost, the full Hessian could theoretically be computed numerically without any approximation. To make this computation feasible, one should aim for an simpler goal: instead of computing the Hessian, one can consider a smaller matrix, consisting of projections of the Hessian.

Moreover, one might hope that such projections would "squeeze" the close-to-zero eigenvalues of the Hessian, so that the eigenvalues of the projected matrix would not be too close to zero.

3 Summarizing Higher-Order Information

Let us consider the minimization of a loss function $\mathcal{L} : \mathbb{R}^P \to \mathbb{R}$ according to a variable $\boldsymbol{\theta} \in \mathbb{R}^P$.

Notation. Let us consider a tensor $\mathbf{A} \in \mathbb{R}^{P^d}$. $\mathbf{A}$ contains P^d coefficients denoted by $A_{i_1,\cdots,i_d}$, indexed by a multi-index $(i_1, \cdots, i_d) \in \{1, \cdots, P\}^d$. The tensor $\mathbf{A}$ can be regarded as a multi-linear form on $\mathbf{R}^{P^d}$: for a tuple of vectors $(\mathbf{u}^1, \cdots, \mathbf{u}^d) \in \mathbb{R}^P \times \cdots \times \mathbb{R}^P$, the application of $\mathbf{A}$ to $(\mathbf{u}^1, \cdots, \mathbf{u}^d)$ is defined as follows:

$$\mathbf{A}[\mathbf{u}^1, \cdots, \mathbf{u}^d] := \sum_{i_1=1}^{P} \cdots \sum_{i_d=1}^{P} A_{i_1,\cdots,i_d} u_{i_1}^1 \cdots u_{i_d}^d \in \mathbb{R}, \qquad (3)$$

where $u_{i_k}^k$ is the i_k-th coordinate of $\mathbf{u}^k$. This operation is also called *tensor contraction*.

---
[1] With PyTorch: torch.autograd.grad.

Full Computation of the Derivatives. The order-d derivative of $\mathcal{L}$ at a point $\boldsymbol{\theta}$, that we denote by $\frac{d^d \mathcal{L}}{d\boldsymbol{\theta}^d}(\boldsymbol{\theta})$, can be viewed as either a d-linear form (see [7] and Appendix L) or as an order-d tensor belonging to $\mathbb{R}^{P^d}$. For convenience, we will use the latter: the coefficients of the tensor $\mathbf{A} = \frac{d^d \mathcal{L}}{d\boldsymbol{\theta}^d}(\boldsymbol{\theta}) \in \mathbb{R}^{P^d}$ are $A_{i_1,\cdots,i_d} = \frac{\partial^d \mathcal{L}}{\partial \theta_{i_1}\cdots \partial \theta_{i_d}}(\boldsymbol{\theta})$, where $(i_1,\cdots,i_d) \in \{1,\cdots,P\}^d$ is a multi-index. The order-d derivative $\frac{d^d \mathcal{L}}{d\boldsymbol{\theta}^d}(\boldsymbol{\theta}) \in \mathbb{R}^{P^d}$ contains P^d scalars. But, even when considering its symmetries [2], it is computationally too expensive to compute it exactly for $d \geq 2$ in most cases. For instance, it is not even possible to compute numerically the full Hessian of $\mathcal{L}$ according to the parameters of a small neural network, i.e., with $P = 10^5$ and $d = 2$, the Hessian contains $P^d = 10^{10}$ scalars.

Terms of the Taylor Expansion. At the opposite, one can obtain cheap higher-order information about $\mathcal{L}$ at $\boldsymbol{\theta}$ by considering a specific direction $\mathbf{u} \in \mathbb{R}^P$. The Taylor expansion of $\mathcal{L}(\boldsymbol{\theta} + \mathbf{u})$ gives:

$$\mathcal{L}(\boldsymbol{\theta} + \mathbf{u}) = \mathcal{L}(\boldsymbol{\theta}) + \sum_{d=1}^{D} \frac{1}{d!} \frac{d^d \mathcal{L}}{d\boldsymbol{\theta}^d}(\boldsymbol{\theta})[\mathbf{u},\cdots,\mathbf{u}] + o(\|\mathbf{u}\|^D). \quad (4)$$

The terms of the Taylor expansion contain higher-order information about $\mathcal{L}$ in the direction $\mathbf{u}$. In particular, they can be used to predict how $\mathcal{L}(\boldsymbol{\theta})$ would change if $\boldsymbol{\theta}$ was translated in the direction of $\mathbf{u}$. Additionally, computing the first D terms has a complexity of order $D \times P$, which is manageable even for large models. The trick that allows for such a low complexity, the *Hessian-vector product*, was proposed by [28] and is recalled in Appendix A.

An Intermediate Solution. First, we define the partial tensor contractions of the order-d derivative of $\mathcal{L}$ at $\boldsymbol{\theta}$ applied to one vector $\mathbf{u}$. We express $\boldsymbol{\theta} \in \mathbb{R}^P$ and $\mathbf{u} \in \mathbb{R}^P$ as tuples of S tensors: $(\mathbf{T}^1,\cdots,\mathbf{T}^S)$ for $\boldsymbol{\theta}$ and $(\mathbf{U}^1,\cdots,\mathbf{U}^S)$ for $\mathbf{u}$. In other words, for any $i \in \{1,\cdots,P\}$, there exist $s \in \{1,\cdots,S\}$ and an index j such that the parameter θ_i is located at T_j^s, and, similarly, u_i is located at U_j^s. We can now define the partial tensor contraction $\mathbf{D}_{\boldsymbol{\theta}}^d(\mathbf{u}) \in \mathbb{R}^{S^d}$, which is a tensor with coefficients:

$$(\mathbf{D}_{\boldsymbol{\theta}}^d(\mathbf{u}))_{s_1,\cdots,s_d} = \frac{\partial^d \mathcal{L}}{\partial \mathbf{T}^{s_1}\cdots \partial \mathbf{T}^{s_d}}(\boldsymbol{\theta})[\mathbf{U}^{s_1},\cdots,\mathbf{U}^{s_d}] \quad (5)$$

$$= \sum_{i_1=1}^{P_{s_1}} \cdots \sum_{i_d=1}^{P_{s_d}} \frac{\partial^d \mathcal{L}}{\partial T_{i_1}^{s_1}\cdots \partial T_{i_d}^{s_d}}(\boldsymbol{\theta}) U_{i_1}^{s_1}\cdots U_{i_d}^{s_d}, \quad (6)$$

where P_s is the number of coefficients of the tensor $\mathbf{T}^s$. Thus, $\mathbf{D}_{\boldsymbol{\theta}}^d(\mathbf{u})$ is a tensor of order d and size S in every dimension resulting from a partial contraction of the full derivative $\frac{d^d \mathcal{L}}{d\boldsymbol{\theta}^d}(\boldsymbol{\theta})$.

---

[2] If $\mathcal{L}$ is smooth, then, for any permutation σ of $\{1,\cdots,d\}$, $\frac{\partial^d \mathcal{L}}{\partial \theta_{i_1}\cdots \partial \theta_{i_d}} = \frac{\partial^d \mathcal{L}}{\partial \theta_{\sigma(i_1)}\cdots \partial \theta_{\sigma(i_d)}}$.

Now, let us assume that, in the practical implementation of a gradient-based method of optimization of $\mathcal{L}(\boldsymbol{\theta})$, $\boldsymbol{\theta}$ is represented by a tuple of tensors $(\mathbf{T}^1, \cdots, \mathbf{T}^S)$. So, each Taylor term can be expressed as:

$$\frac{d^d \mathcal{L}}{d\boldsymbol{\theta}^d}(\boldsymbol{\theta})[\mathbf{u}, \cdots, \mathbf{u}] = \sum_{s_1=1}^{S} \cdots \sum_{s_d=1}^{S} \frac{\partial^d \mathcal{L}}{\partial \mathbf{T}^{s_1} \cdots \partial \mathbf{T}^{s_d}}(\boldsymbol{\theta})[\mathbf{U}^{s_1}, \cdots, \mathbf{U}^{s_d}]$$
$$= \mathbf{D}_{\boldsymbol{\theta}}^d(\mathbf{u})[\mathbb{1}_S, \cdots, \mathbb{1}_S], \quad (7)$$

where $\mathbb{1}_S \in \mathbb{R}^S$ is a vector full of ones, the tuple of tensors $(\mathbf{U}^1, \cdots, \mathbf{U}^S)$ represents $\mathbf{u}$.[3] In this case, the trick of [28] applies to the computation of $\mathbf{D}_{\boldsymbol{\theta}}^d(\mathbf{u})$, which is then much less expensive to compute than the full derivative (see Appendix A).

Properties of $\mathbf{D}_{\boldsymbol{\theta}}^d(\mathbf{u})$. We show a comparison between the three techniques in Table 1. If S is small enough, computing $\mathbf{D}_{\boldsymbol{\theta}}^d(\mathbf{u})$ becomes feasible for $d \geq 2$. For usual multilayer perceptrons with L layers, there is one tensor of weights and one vector of biases per layer, so $S = 2L$. This allows to compute $\mathbf{D}_{\boldsymbol{\theta}}^d(\mathbf{u})$ in practice for $d = 2$ even when $L \approx 20$.

Table 1. Comparison between three techniques extracting higher-order information about $\mathcal{L}$: size of the result and complexity of the computation.

Technique	Size	Complexity
Full derivative $\frac{d^d \mathcal{L}}{d\boldsymbol{\theta}^d}(\boldsymbol{\theta})$	P^d	P^d
Taylor term $\mathbf{D}_{\boldsymbol{\theta}}^d(\mathbf{u})[\mathbb{1}_S, \cdots, \mathbb{1}_S]$	1	$d \times P$
Tensor $\mathbf{D}_{\boldsymbol{\theta}}^d(\mathbf{u})$	S^d	$S^{d-1} \times P$

According to Eq. (7), the Taylor term can be obtained by full contraction of $\mathbf{D}_{\boldsymbol{\theta}}^d(\mathbf{u})$. However, $\mathbf{D}_{\boldsymbol{\theta}}^d(\mathbf{u})$, is a tensor of size S^d, and cannot be obtained from the Taylor term, which is only a scalar. Thus, the tensors $\mathbf{D}_{\boldsymbol{\theta}}^d(\mathbf{u})$ extract more information than the Taylor terms, while keeping a reasonable computational cost. Moreover, their off-diagonal elements give access to information about one-to-one interactions between tensors $(\mathbf{T}^1, \cdots, \mathbf{T}^S)$ when they are processed in the function $\mathcal{L}$.

4 Application: Computing per-Layer Learning Rates

To build per-layer (or per-subset-of-parameters) learning rates, we partition the set of indices of parameters $\{1, \cdots, P\}$ into S subsets $(\mathcal{I}_s)_{1 \leq s \leq S}$, we assign for all $1 \leq s \leq S$ the same learning rate η_s to the parameters $(\theta_p)_{p \in \mathcal{I}_s}$, and we find the vector of learning rates $\boldsymbol{\eta} = (\eta_1, \cdots, \eta_S)$ optimizing the decrease of the loss

---
[3] $(\mathbf{U}^1, \cdots, \mathbf{U}^S)$ is to $\mathbf{u}$ as $(\mathbf{T}^1, \cdots, \mathbf{T}^S)$ is to $\boldsymbol{\theta}$.

$\mathcal{L}$ for the current training step t, by using its order-2 Taylor approximation.[4] Formally, given a direction $\mathbf{u}_t \in \mathbb{R}^P$ in the parameter space (typically, $\mathbf{u}_t = \mathbf{g}_t$, the gradient) and $\mathbf{U}_t := \text{Diag}(\mathbf{u}_t) \in \mathbb{R}^{P \times P}$, we consider the training step: $\boldsymbol{\theta}_{t+1} := \boldsymbol{\theta}_t - \mathbf{U}_t \mathbf{I}_{P:S} \boldsymbol{\eta}_t$, that is a training step in a direction based on $\mathbf{u}_t$, distorted by a subset-wise step size $\boldsymbol{\eta}_t$. Then, we minimize the order-2 Taylor approximation of $\mathcal{L}(\boldsymbol{\theta}_{t+1}) - \mathcal{L}(\boldsymbol{\theta}_t)$: $\boldsymbol{\Delta}_2(\boldsymbol{\eta}_t) := -\mathbf{g}_t^T \mathbf{U}_t \mathbf{I}_{P:S} \boldsymbol{\eta}_t + \frac{1}{2}\boldsymbol{\eta}_t^T \mathbf{I}_{S:P} \mathbf{U}_t \mathbf{H}_t \mathbf{U}_t \mathbf{I}_{P:S} \boldsymbol{\eta}_t$, which gives:

$$\boldsymbol{\theta}_{t+1} = \boldsymbol{\theta}_t - \mathbf{U}_t \mathbf{I}_{P:S} \boldsymbol{\eta}_t^*, \qquad \boldsymbol{\eta}_t^* := (\mathbf{I}_{S:P} \mathbf{U}_t \mathbf{H}_t \mathbf{U}_t \mathbf{I}_{P:S})^{-1} \mathbf{I}_{S:P} \mathbf{U}_t \mathbf{g}_t, \qquad (8)$$

where $\mathbf{I}_{S:P} \in \mathbb{R}^{S \times P}$ is the *partition matrix*, verifying $(\mathbf{I}_{S:P})_{sp} = 1$ if $p \in \mathcal{I}_s$ and 0 otherwise, and $\mathbf{I}_{P:S} := \mathbf{I}_{S:P}^T$. Alternatively, $\boldsymbol{\eta}_t^*$ can be written (details are provided in Appendix B):

$$\boldsymbol{\eta}_t^* = \bar{\mathbf{H}}_t^{-1} \bar{\mathbf{g}}_t, \quad \text{where:} \quad \bar{\mathbf{H}}_t := \mathbf{I}_{S:P} \mathbf{U}_t \mathbf{H}_t \mathbf{U}_t \mathbf{I}_{P:S} \in \mathbb{R}^{S \times S}, \quad \bar{\mathbf{g}}_t := \mathbf{I}_{S:P} \mathbf{U}_t \mathbf{g}_t \in \mathbb{R}^S. \qquad (9)$$

With the notation of Sect. 3, $\bar{\mathbf{H}}_t = \mathbf{D}^{(2)}_{\boldsymbol{\theta}_t}(\mathbf{u}_t)$ and $\bar{\mathbf{g}}_t = \mathbf{D}^{(1)}_{\boldsymbol{\theta}_t}(\mathbf{u}_t)$. Incidentally, computing $\bar{\mathbf{H}}$ is of complexity SP, and solving $\bar{\mathbf{H}}\mathbf{x} = \bar{\mathbf{g}}$ is of complexity S^2.

5 Application: Optimization Method

5.1 Presentation

Now that we can compute per-layer learning rates, we decide to incorporate them into an optimization method. However, computing them requires to compute $\bar{\mathbf{H}}^{-1}\bar{\mathbf{g}}$. Usually, inverting such a linear system at every step is considered as hazardous and unstable. Therefore, when using Newton's method, instead of computing descent direction $\mathbf{u} := \mathbf{H}^{-1}\mathbf{g}$, it is very common to add a regularization term: $\mathbf{u}_\lambda := (\mathbf{H} + \lambda \mathbf{I})^{-1} \mathbf{g}$ [25, Chap. 6.3].

However, the theoretical ground of such a regularization technique is not fully satisfactory. Basically, the main problem is not having a matrix $\bar{\mathbf{H}}$ with close-to-zero eigenvalues: after all, if the loss landscape is very flat in a specific direction, it is better to make a large training step. The problem lies in the order-2 approximation of the loss made in the training step (8), as well as in Newton's method: instead of optimizing the true decrease of the loss, we optimize the decrease of its order-2 approximation. Thus, the practical question is: does this approximation faithfully model the loss at the current point $\boldsymbol{\theta}_t$, in a region that also includes the next point $\boldsymbol{\theta}_{t+1}$?

To answer this question, one has to take into account order-3 information, and regularize $\bar{\mathbf{H}}$ so that the resulting update remains in a region around $\boldsymbol{\theta}_t$ where the cubic term of the Taylor approximation is negligible. In practice, we propose an anisotropic version of Nesterov's cubic regularization [24].

---

[4] With the notation of Sect. 3, $\mathcal{I}_s$ is the set of indices p of the parameters θ_p belonging to the tensor $\mathbf{T}^s$, so the scalars $(\theta_p)_{p \in \mathcal{I}_s}$ correspond to the scalars belonging to $\mathbf{T}^s$. So, everything is as if a specific learning rate η_s is assigned to each $\mathbf{T}^s$.

Anisotropic Nesterov Cubic Regularization. By using the technique presented in Sect. 3, the diagonal coefficients $(D_1, \cdots, D_S)$ of $\mathbf{D}_{\theta}^{(3)}(\mathbf{u}) \in \mathbb{R}^{S \times S \times S}$ are available with little computational cost. Let $\mathbf{D} := \mathrm{Diag}(|D_1|^{1/3}, \cdots, |D_S|^{1/3}) \in \mathbb{R}^S$.

We modify the method of [24] by integrating an anisotropic factor $\mathbf{D}$ into the cubic term. Thus, our goal is to minimize according to $\boldsymbol{\eta}$ the function $T \colon T(\boldsymbol{\eta}) := -\boldsymbol{\eta}^T \bar{\mathbf{g}} + \frac{1}{2} \boldsymbol{\eta} \bar{\mathbf{H}} \boldsymbol{\eta} + \frac{\lambda_{\mathrm{int}}}{6} \| \mathbf{D} \boldsymbol{\eta} \|^3$, where λ_{int} is the *internal damping* coefficient, which can be used to tune the strength of the cubic regularization. Under conditions detailed in Appendix D, this minimization problem is equivalent to finding a solution $\boldsymbol{\eta}_*$ such that:

$$\boldsymbol{\eta}_* = \left(\bar{\mathbf{H}} + \frac{\lambda_{\mathrm{int}}}{2} \| \mathbf{D} \boldsymbol{\eta}_* \| \mathbf{D}^2 \right)^{-1} \bar{\mathbf{g}}, \qquad (10)$$

which is a regularized version of (8). Finally, this multi-dimensional minimization problem boils down to a scalar root finding problem (see Appendix D).

5.2 Properties

The final method is a combination of the learning rate computed in Eq. (8) with regularization (10):

Method 1 *Training step* $\boldsymbol{\theta}_{t+1} = \boldsymbol{\theta}_t - \mathbf{U}_t \mathbf{I}_{P:S} \boldsymbol{\eta}_t^*$, *where* $\boldsymbol{\eta}_t^*$ *is the solution with the largest norm* $\| \mathbf{D}_t \boldsymbol{\eta} \|$ *of the equation:* $\boldsymbol{\eta} = \left(\bar{\mathbf{H}}_t + \frac{\lambda_{\mathrm{int}}}{2} \| \mathbf{D}_t \boldsymbol{\eta} \| \mathbf{D}_t^2 \right)^{-1} \bar{\mathbf{g}}_t$.

Encompassing Newton's Method and Cauchy's Steepest Descent. Without the cubic regularization ($\lambda_{\mathrm{int}} = 0$), Newton's method is recovered when using the *discrete partition*, that is, $S = P$ with $\mathcal{I}_s = \{s\}$ for all s, and Cauchy's steepest descent is recovered when using the *trivial partition*, that is, $S = 1$ with $\mathcal{I}_1 = \{1, \cdots, P\}$. See Appendix C for more details.

No Need to Compute or Approximate the Full Hessian. The full computation of the Hessian $\mathbf{H}_t \in \mathbb{R}^{P \times P}$ is not required. Instead, one only needs to compute the $S \times S$ matrix $\bar{\mathbf{H}}_t := \mathbf{I}_{S:P} \mathbf{U}_t \mathbf{H}_t \mathbf{U}_t \mathbf{I}_{P:S}$, which can be done efficiently by computing $\mathbf{u}^T \mathbf{H}_t \mathbf{v}$ for a number $S \times S$ of pairs of well-chosen directions $(\mathbf{u}, \mathbf{v}) \in \mathbb{R}^P \times \mathbb{R}^P$. This property is especially useful when $S \ll P$. When optimizing a neural network with $L = 10$ layers and $P = 10^6$ parameters, one can naturally partition the set of parameters into $S = 2L$ subsets, each one containing either all the weights or all the biases of each of the L layers. In this situation, one has to solve a linear system of size $2L = 20$ at each step, which is much more reasonable than solving a linear system of $P = 10^6$ equations. We call this natural partition of the parameters of a neural network the *canonical partition*.

No Need to Solve a Large Linear System. Using Equations (8) or (10) requires solving only a linear system of S equations, instead of P in Newton's method. With the cubic regularization, only a constant term is added to the complexity, since it is a matter of scalar root finding.

The interactions Between Different Tensors are not Neglected. The matrix $\bar{\mathbf{H}}_t$, which simulates the Hessian $\mathbf{H}_t$, is basically dense: it does not exhibit a (block-)diagonal structure. So, the interactions between subsets of parameters are taken into account when performing optimization steps. In the context of neural networks with the canonical partition, this means that interactions between layers are taken into account during optimization, even if the layers are far from each other. This is a major advantage over many existing approximations of the Hessian or its inverse, which are diagonal or block-diagonal.

Invariance by Subset-Wise Affine Reparameterization. As showed in Appendix E, under a condition on the directions $\mathbf{u}_t$, [5] the trajectory of optimization of a model trained by Method 1 is invariant by affine reparameterization of the subvectors of parameters $\boldsymbol{\theta}_{\mathcal{I}_s} := \text{vec}(\{\theta_p : p \in \mathcal{I}_s\})$. Let $(\alpha_s)_{1 \leq s \leq S}$ and $(\beta_s)_{1 \leq s \leq S}$ be a sequence of nonzero scalings and a sequence of offsets, and $\tilde{\boldsymbol{\theta}}$ such that, for all $1 \leq s \leq S$, $\tilde{\boldsymbol{\theta}}_{\mathcal{I}_s} = \alpha_s \boldsymbol{\theta}_{\mathcal{I}_s} + \beta_s$. Then, the training trajectory of the model is the same with both parameterizations $\boldsymbol{\theta}$ and $\tilde{\boldsymbol{\theta}}$. This property is desirable in the case of neural networks, where one can use either the usual or the NTK parameterization, which consists of a layer-wise scaling of the parameters. The relevance of this property is discussed in Appendix E.1.

Compared to the standard regularization $\bar{\mathbf{H}} + \lambda \mathbf{I}$ and Nesterov's cubic regularization, the anisotropic Nesterov regularization does not break the property of invariance by subset-wise scaling of the parameters of (8). This is mainly due to our choice to keep only the diagonal coefficients of $\mathbf{D}_{\boldsymbol{\theta}}^{(3)}(\mathbf{u})$ while discarding the others. In particular, the off-diagonal coefficients contain cross-derivatives that would be difficult to include in an invariant training step.

6 Experiments

6.1 Empirical Computation of $\bar{\mathbf{H}}$ and η_*

As recalled in Sect. 2, many works perform a diagonal, block-diagonal or block-tridiagional [20] approximation of the Hessian or its inverse. Since a summary $\bar{\mathbf{H}}$ of the Hessian and its inverse $\bar{\mathbf{H}}^{-1}$ are available and all their off-diagonal coefficients have been computed and kept, one can to check if these coefficients are indeed negligible.

Setup. We have trained LeNet-5 and VGG-11' [6] on CIFAR-10 using SGD with momentum. Before each epoch, we compute the full-batch gradient, denoted by $\mathbf{u}$, which we use as a direction to compute $\bar{\mathbf{H}}$, again in full-batch. We report submatrices of $\bar{\mathbf{H}}$ and $\bar{\mathbf{H}}^{-1}$ at initialization and at the epoch where the validation loss is the best in Fig. 1a (LeNet) and Fig. 1b (VGG-11').

For the sake of readability, $\bar{\mathbf{H}}$ has been divided into blocks: a weight-weight block $\bar{\mathbf{H}}_{\text{WW}}$, a bias-bias block $\bar{\mathbf{H}}_{\text{BB}}$, and a weight-bias block $\bar{\mathbf{H}}_{\text{WB}}$. They represent the interactions between the layers: for instance, $(\bar{\mathbf{H}}_{\text{WB}})_{l_1 l_2}$ represents the

---

[5] It holds if $\mathbf{u}_t$ is the gradient or a moving average of the gradients (momentum).
[6] VGG-11' is a variant of VGG-11 with 1 final fully-connected layer instead of 3.

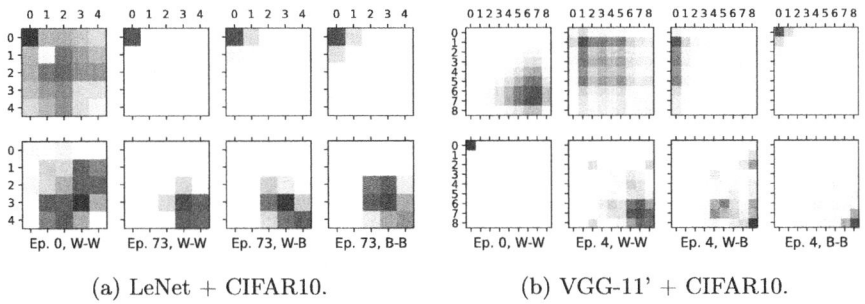

Fig. 1. Setup: models trained by SGD on CIFAR-10. Submatrices of $\bar{\mathbf{H}}$ (1st row) and $\bar{\mathbf{H}}^{-1}$ (2nd row), where focus is on interactions: weight-weight, weight-bias, bias-bias of the different layers, at initialization and before best validation loss.

interaction between the tensor of weights of layer l_1 and the vector of biases of layer l_2.

Results on $\bar{\mathbf{H}}$. First, the block-diagonal approximation of the Hessian is indeed very rough, while the block-diagonal approximation of the inverse Hessian seems to be more reasonable (at least in these setups), which has already been shown by [20]. Second, there seem to be long-range interactions between layers, both at initialization and after several epochs. For LeNet, all the layers (except the first one) seem to interact together at initialization (Fig. 1a). In the matrix $\bar{\mathbf{H}}^{-1}$ computed on VGG, the last 3 layers interact strongly and the last 6 layers also interact, but a bit less.

According to these observations, a neural network should also be considered as a whole, in which layers can hardly be studied independently from each other. To our knowledge, this result is the first scalable representation of interactions between distant layers, based on second-order information.

Results on $\boldsymbol{\eta}_*$. The evolution of the learning rates η_* computed according to (10) in LeNet and VGG is shown in Fig. 2. First, the learning rates computed for the biases are larger than those computed for the weights. Second, even if only the weights are considered, the computed η_* can differ by several orders of magnitude. Finally, the first two layers of LeNet (which are convolutional) have smaller η_* than the last three layers (which are fully-connected). Conversely, in VGG, the weights of the last (convolutional) layers have a smaller η_* than those of the first layers.

6.2 Training Experiments

To show that the projections of the 2nd and 3rd order derivatives of the loss defined in Sect. 3 can be practically used to train neural networks, we test our optimization method 1 (summarized in Algorithm 1) on simple vision tasks. All the implementation details are available in Appendix G. In particular, we have

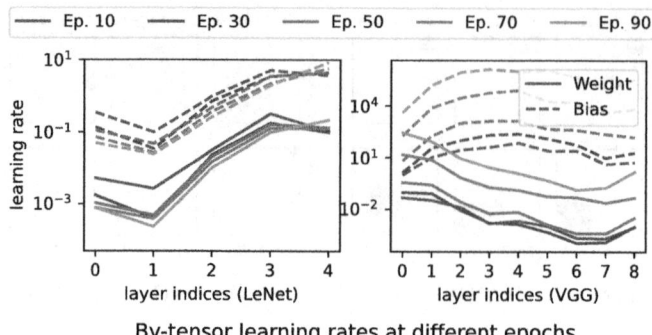

By-tensor learning rates at different epochs

Fig. 2. Setup: LeNet, VGG-11' trained by SGD on CIFAR-10. Learning rates η_* computed according to (10), specific to each tensor of weights and tensor of biases of each layer. For each epoch $k \in \{10, 30, 50, 70, 90\}$, the reported value has been averaged over the epochs $[k-10, k+9]$ to remove the noise.

introduced a step size λ_1 that leads to the following modification of the training step (8): $\boldsymbol{\theta}_{t+1} = \boldsymbol{\theta}_t - \lambda_1 \mathbf{U}_t \mathbf{I}_{P:S} \boldsymbol{\eta}_t^*$.

Algorithm 1. Informal description of the 2nd-order method described in Sec. 5. Let $u_t(\cdot)$ be a function computing a direction of descent $\mathbf{u}_t$ from a gradient $\mathbf{g}_t$ and $\mathbf{U}_t = \mathrm{Diag}(\mathbf{u}_t)$.

Hyperparameters: $\lambda, \lambda_{\mathrm{int}}$
$\mathcal{D}_{\mathrm{g}}, \mathcal{D}_{\mathrm{newt}}$: independent samplers of minibatches
for $t \in [1, T]$ **do**
  $Z_t \sim \mathcal{D}_{\mathrm{g}}, \tilde{Z}_t \sim \mathcal{D}_{\mathrm{newt}}$ (sample minibatches)
  $\mathbf{g}_t \leftarrow \frac{d\mathcal{L}}{d\boldsymbol{\theta}}(\boldsymbol{\theta}_t, Z_t)$ (backward pass)
  $\mathbf{u}_t \leftarrow u_t(\mathbf{g}_t)$ (custom direction of descent)
  $\bar{\mathbf{g}}_t \leftarrow \mathbf{D}^{(1)}_{\boldsymbol{\theta}_t}(\mathbf{u}_t) = \mathbf{I}_{S:P} \mathbf{U}_t \frac{d\mathcal{L}}{d\boldsymbol{\theta}}(\boldsymbol{\theta}_t, \tilde{Z}_t)$
  $\bar{\mathbf{H}}_t \leftarrow \mathbf{D}^{(2)}_{\boldsymbol{\theta}_t}(\mathbf{u}_t) = \mathbf{I}_{S:P} \mathbf{U}_t \frac{d^2\mathcal{L}}{d\boldsymbol{\theta}^2}(\boldsymbol{\theta}_t, \tilde{Z}_t) \mathbf{U}_t \mathbf{I}_{P:S}$
  $\mathbf{D}_t \leftarrow \mathrm{Diag}(|\mathbf{D}^{(3)}_{\boldsymbol{\theta}_t}(\mathbf{u}_t)|^{1/3}_{iii} : i \in \{1, \cdots, S\}) \in \mathbb{R}^{S^2}$
  $\boldsymbol{\eta}_t \leftarrow$ sol. of $\boldsymbol{\eta} = \left(\bar{\mathbf{H}}_t + \frac{\lambda_{\mathrm{int}}}{2} \|\mathbf{D}_t \boldsymbol{\eta}\| \mathbf{D}_t^2\right)^{-1} \bar{\mathbf{g}}_t$ with max. norm $\|\mathbf{D}_t \boldsymbol{\eta}\|$ (Method 1)
  $\boldsymbol{\theta}_{t+1} \leftarrow \boldsymbol{\theta}_t - \lambda \mathbf{U}_t \mathbf{I}_{P:S} \boldsymbol{\eta}_t$ (training step)
end for

Setup. We consider 4 image classification setups:

- **MLP**: multilayer perceptron trained on MNIST with layers of sizes 1024, 200, 100, 10, and tanh activation;
- **LeNet**: LeNet-5 [16] model trained on CIFAR-10 with 2 convolutional layers of sizes 6, 16, and 3 fully connected layers of sizes 120, 84, 10;

- **VGG**: VGG-11' trained on CIFAR-10. VGG-11' is a variant of VGG-11 [31] with only one fully-connected layer at the end, instead of 3, with ELU activation function [5], without batch-norm;
- **BigMLP**: multilayer perceptron trained on CIFAR-10, with 20 layers of size 1024 and one classification layer of size 10, with ELU activation function.

And we have tested 3 optimization methods:

- **Adam**: learning rate selected by grid-search;
- **K-FAC**: learning rate and damping selected by grid-search;
- **NewtonSummary** (ours): λ_1 and λ_{int} selected by grid search.

Results. The evolution of the training loss is plotted in Fig. 3 for each of the 3 optimization methods, for 5 different seeds. In each set of experiments, the training is successful, but slow or unstable at some points (e.g., see BigMLP + CIFAR-10). Anyway, the minimum training loss achieved by Method 1 (NewtonSummary) is comparable to the minimum training loss achieved by K-KAC or Adam in all the series except for MLP, whose training is slower. We provide the results on the test set in Appendix I and a comparison of the training times in Appendix M.

Some runs have encountered instabilities due to very large step sizes η_*. In fact, we did not use any safeguards, such as a regularization term $\lambda \mathbf{I}$ added to $\bar{\mathbf{H}}$, or clipping the learning rates to avoid increasing the number of hyperparameters. So, the training process is vulnerable to the rare situations where $\bar{\mathbf{H}}^{-1}$ has very small or negative eigenvalues and $\mathbf{D}$ has very small coefficients on the diagonal.

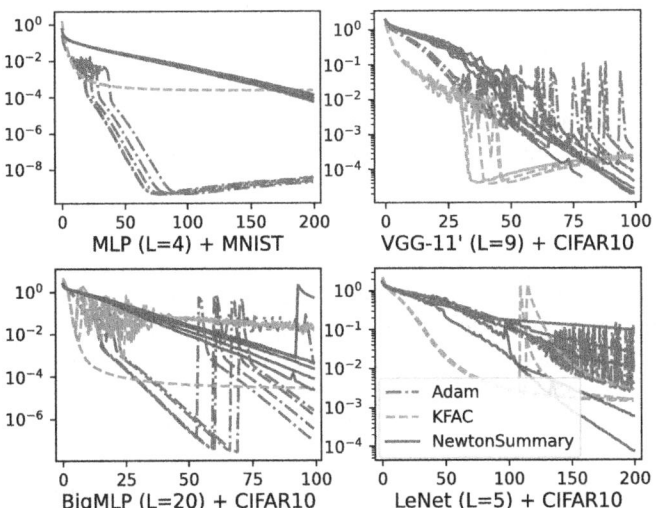

Fig. 3. Training curves in different setups. The reported loss is the negative log-likelihood computed on the training set.

Extension to Very Large Models. Since the matrix $\bar{\mathbf{H}}$ can be computed numerically as long as S remains relatively small, this method may become unpractical for very large models. However, Method 1 is flexible enough to be adapted to such models: one can regroup tensors "of the same kind" to build a coarser partition of the parameters, and thus obtain a small S, which is exactly what is needed to compute $\bar{\mathbf{H}}$ and invert it. The difficulty would then be to find a good partition of the parameters, by grouping all the tensors that "look alike". We provide an example in Appendix H with a very deep multilayer perceptron.

Choice of the Partition. We propose in Appendix J an empirical study and a discussion about the choice of the partition of the parameters. We show how it affects the training time and the final loss.

Importance of the Interactions Between Layers. We show in Appendix K that the interactions between layers cannot be neglected when using our method: Method 1 outperforms its *diagonal approximation* on LeNet and VGG11', showing the importance of off-diagonal coefficients of $\bar{\mathbf{H}}$.

7 Discussion

We have shown that it is possible to obtain 2nd and 3rd order information about the loss, and that this information can be used to construct per-layer learning rates and an optimization method with interesting properties. However, this optimization method can only be seen as a proof of concept, showing that higher-order derivatives are accessible and can be used to train neural networks, and not as a generic optimizer with excellent results on a wide range of tasks and models. Therefore, we propose future research directions.

Convergence Rate. Method 1 does not come with a precise convergence rate. The rate proposed in Appendix F (Theorem 1) gives only a heuristic. Given the convergence rates of Newton's method and Cauchy's steepest descent, we can expect to find some in-between convergence rates. Since Cauchy's steepest method is vulnerable to a highly anisotropic Hessian, it would be valuable to know how much this weakness is overcome by our method.

Accounting for the Noise During Training. Our optimization method remains subject to instabilities during training, which is expected for a second-order method, but not acceptable for the end user. In fact, it is very likely that our algorithm would achieve better performance if it were designed from the beginning to work in a stochastic context. Currently, it is designed as if training was done in full batch.

Acknowledgments. The project leading to this work has received funding from the French National Research Agency (ANR-21-JSTM-0001 and ANR-19-CHIA-0021). This work was granted access to the HPC resources of IDRIS under the allocation 2024-AD011013762R2 made by GENCI. We thank Julyan Arbel, Michael N. Arbel, Gilles Blanchard and Christophe Giraud for their support.

Disclosure of Interests. The authors have no competing interests to declare that are relevant to the content of this article.

References

1. Amari, S.: Natural gradient works efficiently in learning. Neural Comput. **10**(2), 251–276 (1998)
2. Arora, S., Du, S., Hu, W., Li, Z., Wang, R.: Fine-grained analysis of optimization and generalization for overparameterized two-layer neural networks. In: International Conference on Machine Learning, pp. 322–332 (2019)
3. Birgin, E.G., Gardenghi, J., Martínez, J.M., Santos, S.A., Toint, P.L.: Worst-case evaluation complexity for unconstrained nonlinear optimization using high-order regularized models. Math. Program. **163**, 359–368 (2017)
4. Cauchy, A.L.: Méthode générale pour la résolution des systèmes d'équations simultanées. Comptes rendus hebdomadaires des séances de l'Académie des sciences, Paris **25**, 536–538 (1847)
5. Clevert, D.A., Unterthiner, T., Hochreiter, S.: Fast and accurate deep network learning by exponential linear units (ELUS). arXiv preprint arXiv:1511.07289 (2015)
6. Dangel, F.J.: Backpropagation beyond the gradient. Ph.D. thesis, Universität Tübingen (2023)
7. Dieudonné, J.: Foundations of Modern Analysis. No. 10 in Pure and Applied Mathematics, Academic press (1960)
8. Du, S., Lee, J., Li, H., Wang, L., Zhai, X.: Gradient descent finds global minima of deep neural networks. In: International Conference on Machine Learning, pp. 1675–1685 (2019)
9. Gill, P.E., Murray, W., Wright, M.H.: Practical Optimization. Academic Press, San Diego (1981)
10. Goldfarb, D., Ren, Y., Bahamou, A.: Practical quasi-Newton methods for training deep neural networks. In: Advances in Neural Information Processing Systems, vol. 33, pp. 2386–2396 (2020)
11. Gower, R., Kovalev, D., Lieder, F., Richtárik, P.: RSN: randomized subspace Newton. In: Advances in Neural Information Processing Systems, vol. 32 (2019)
12. Gupta, V., Koren, T., Singer, Y.: Shampoo: preconditioned stochastic tensor optimization. In: International Conference on Machine Learning, pp. 1842–1850 (2018)
13. Hanzely, F., Doikov, N., Nesterov, Y., Richtarik, P.: Stochastic subspace cubic Newton method. In: International Conference on Machine Learning, pp. 4027–4038 (2020)
14. Jacot, A., Gabriel, F., Hongler, C.: Neural tangent kernel: convergence and generalization in neural networks. In: Advances in Neural Information Processing Systems, vol. 31 (2018)
15. Kornblith, S., Norouzi, M., Lee, H., Hinton, G.: Similarity of neural network representations revisited. In: International Conference on Machine Learning, pp. 3519–3529 (2019)
16. LeCun, Y., Bottou, L., Bengio, Y., Haffner, P.: Gradient-based learning applied to document recognition. Proc. IEEE **86**(11), 2278–2324 (1998)
17. Lee, J., et al.: Wide neural networks of any depth evolve as linear models under gradient descent. In: Advances in Neural Information Processing Systems, vol. 32 (2019)

18. Lu, Y., Harandi, M., Hartley, R., Pascanu, R.: Block mean approximation for efficient second order optimization. arXiv preprint arXiv:1804.05484 (2018)
19. Luenberger, D.G., Ye, Y.: Linear and Nonlinear Programming. Springer, 4th edn. (2008). https://doi.org/10.1007/978-0-387-74503-9
20. Martens, J., Grosse, R.: Optimizing neural networks with Kronecker-factored approximate curvature. In: International Conference on Machine Learning, pp. 2408–2417 (2015)
21. Mei, S., Montanari, A.: The generalization error of random features regression: precise asymptotics and the double descent curve. Commun. Pure Appl. Math. **75**(4), 667–766 (2022)
22. Nash, S.G.: Newton-type minimization via the Lanczos method. SIAM J. Numer. Anal. **21**(4), 770–788 (1984)
23. Nesterov, Y.: Introductory Lectures on Convex Optimization: A Basic Course, vol. 87. Springer Science & Business Media (2003). https://doi.org/10.1007/978-1-4419-8853-9
24. Nesterov, Y., Polyak, B.T.: Cubic regularization of newton method and its global performance. Math. Program. **108**(1), 177–205 (2006)
25. Nocedal, J., Wright, S.J.: Numerical optimization. Springer (1999). https://doi.org/10.1007/978-0-387-40065-5
26. Nonomura, T., Ono, S., Nakai, K., Saito, Y.: Randomized subspace newton convex method applied to data-driven sensor selection problem. IEEE Signal Process. Lett. **28**, 284–288 (2021)
27. Ollivier, Y.: Riemannian metrics for neural networks I: feedforward networks. Inf. Inference J. IMA **4**(2), 108–153 (2015)
28. Pearlmutter, B.A.: Fast exact multiplication by the hessian. Neural Comput. **6**(1), 147–160 (1994)
29. Ren, Y., Goldfarb, D.: Tensor normal training for deep learning models. In: Advances in Neural Information Processing Systems, vol. 34, pp. 26040–26052 (2021)
30. Sagun, L., Evci, U., Guney, V.U., Dauphin, Y., Bottou, L.: Empirical analysis of the Hessian of over-parametrized neural networks. In: International Conference on Learning Representations (2018)
31. Simonyan, K., Zisserman, A.: Very deep convolutional networks for large-scale image recognition. arXiv preprint arXiv:1409.1556 (2014)
32. Wang, Y.J., Lin, C.T.: A second-order learning algorithm for multilayer networks based on block hessian matrix. Neural Netw. **11**(9), 1607–1622 (1998)
33. Yang, G., Hu, E.J.: Tensor programs iv: Feature learning in infinite-width neural networks. In: International Conference on Machine Learning, pp. 11727–11737 (2021)
34. Yao, Z., Gholami, A., Shen, S., Mustafa, M., Keutzer, K., Mahoney, M.: ADAHESSIAN: an adaptive second order optimizer for machine learning. In: Proceedings of the AAAI Conference on Artificial Intelligence, vol. 35, no. 12, pp. 10665–10673 (2021)
35. Yuan, R., Lazaric, A., Gower, R.M.: Sketched newton-Raphson. SIAM J. Optim. **32**(3), 1555–1583 (2022)
36. Zhang, C., Bengio, S., Singer, Y.: Are all layers created equal? J. Mach. Learn. Res. **23**(67), 1–28 (2022)
37. Zhang, G., Martens, J., Grosse, R.B.: Fast convergence of natural gradient descent for over-parameterized neural networks. In: Advances in Neural Information Processing Systems, vol. 32 (2019)

Gradient Boosting Versus Mixed Integer Programming for Sparse Additive Modeling

Fan Yang[1]([✉]), Pierre Le Bodic[1], and Mario Boley[1,2]

[1] Department of Data Science and AI, Monash University, Clayton, VIC 3800, Australia
{fan.yang1,pierre.lebodic,mario.boley}@monash.edu
[2] Department of Information Systems, University of Haifa, Haifa 3498838, Israel

Abstract. Gradient boosting is a widely used algorithm for fitting sparse additive models over flexible classes of basis functions. Despite its popularity, the performance of gradient boosting as an approximation algorithm to the empirical risk minimizing model with a specific number k of selected basis functions is poorly understood. We provide a theoretical lower bound of $1/2 - 1/(4k-2)$ on the worst-case approximation ratio for the risk reduction that gradient boosting achieves relative to the optimal model when both are limited to k terms. This result reveals an inherent limitation in boosting's ability to approximate the best possible sparse additive model, raising the question of how tight and representative this bound is in practice. To empirically answer this question, we employ mixed integer programming (MIP) to approximate the optimal additive models on 21 real datasets. The experimental results do not show larger gaps than the theoretical analysis, indicating that the theoretical lower bound is tight. Moreover, for twelve datasets, the approximation gaps are of the same order of magnitude as the theoretical lower bound, which shows the representativeness of the theoretical bound. To that end, the study also has the practical implication that the presented MIP approach frequently offers notable improvements over gradient boosting.

Keywords: Gradient boosting · Mixed integer programming · Approximation gap · Additive model · Rule learning

1 Introduction

Gradient boosting is a widely used algorithm for training additive models [10], particularly in tasks that require a balance between predictive accuracy and model complexity. By iteratively fitting weak learners to residual errors, boosting builds powerful predictive models while maintaining a level of interpretability

---

Supplementary Information The online version contains supplementary material available at https://doi.org/10.1007/978-3-032-06078-5_26.

often lacking in more complex machine learning approaches [1,4,16,21]. However, a fundamental limitation arises due to its greedy nature: at each iteration, boosting selects the basis function that most reduces the empirical risk in the immediate step, rather than making globally optimal selections over all iterations [7]. This property leads to an approximation gap, defined as the relative difference between the risk achieved by models generated by boosting and the theoretical optimum for a given model class and number of terms [16].

To better understand the approximation gap of greedy approaches like boosting, prior work has analyzed the performance of greedy algorithms relative to optimal models. For instance, according to [7], the ratio between the risk reductions of models generated by greedy approaches and the optimal model is lower bounded by $1 - \exp(-\lambda_{min})$, where λ_{min} is the smallest eigenvalue of the covariance matrix of input variables, i.e. it shows an upper bound of the gap between risks of greedy approaches and optimal models. However, in general, this upper bound can be arbitrarily large, indicating that the potential for improvement over boosting for general inputs remains unknown.

In this work, we show that there exists datasets for which k-term models generated by boosting have an approximation gap of $1/2 - 1/(4k-2)$. Since there may be datasets for which boosting performs worse, we can state that the worst-case approximation gap of boosting is at least $1/2 - 1/(4k-2)$. This bound formalizes a fundamental limitation of boosting and quantifies its suboptimality. Furthermore, to evaluate the bound empirically, we employ Mixed Integer Programming (MIP) to attempt to improve the additive models generated by boosting on real-world datasets. Our experiments confirm that the observed approximation gaps align with the theoretical bound, indicating practical relevance.

A key goal of our study is to evaluate whether the theoretical bound on the boosting approximation gap established is both tight (i.e., accurately characterizing the worst-case gap) and representative (i.e., aligning with typical empirical cases). Figure 1 shows the cumulative distribution of the empirical risk gaps across 21 datasets, along with reference lines that partition the space into four interpretive quadrants. As shown in Fig. 1, for twelve out of 21 datasets, the approximation gaps have the same magnitude as the theoretical worst-case bound (Optimistic), and for the eleven datasets where the optimal additive models are achieved by MIP (Conservative), there are seven datasets whose approximation gaps are of the same magnitude as the theoretical analysis. This result shows the representativeness and tightness of the theoretical analysis. These results suggest that the theoretical analysis captures not only the worst-case behavior but also reflects typical empirical scenarios.

The remainder of this paper is structured as follows: Sect. 2 provides background on gradient boosting and additive models. Section 3 presents the lower bound of the worst-case approximation gap of boosting. Section 4 uses a MIP approach to approximate the optimal additive models. With the empirical evaluation using 21 real-world datasets, we show the tightness and the representativeness of our theoretical analysis. Section 4.2 concludes the paper with key takeaways and future research directions.

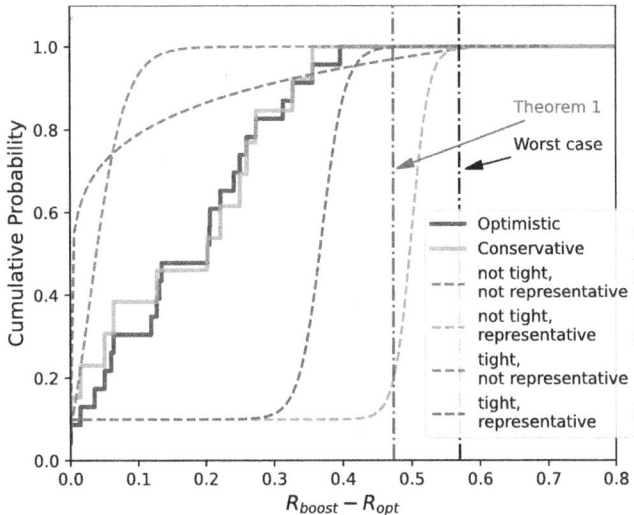

Fig. 1. The cumulative probabilities of the distribution of risk differences between models generated by boosting and MIP where MIP provides a feasible solution (Optimistic) and MIP obtains optimal solutions (Conservative). The dashed curves depict four scenarios regarding the analysis in Theorem 1 and possible worst-case gaps: whether the bound is tight or not to the actual worst-case gap, and whether the worst case is representative of real-world datasets or not.

2 Background

Throughout this paper we denote by Y the target random variable and by X the input variable that take values in $\mathcal{Y} \subseteq \mathbb{R}$ and $\mathcal{X} \subseteq \mathbb{R}^d$, respectively. Moreover, we assume a dataset $\{(\mathbf{x}_1, y_1), \ldots, (\mathbf{x}_n, y_n)\}$ drawn from the joint distribution of Y and X. A set of basis functions $\mathcal{H} \subseteq \mathbb{R}^d \to \mathbb{R}$ and an activation or inverse link function $\mu: \mathbb{R} \to \mathbb{R}$ define a family of additive models for predicting Y given X, where an individual model correspond to a finite sub-selection $H = \{h_1, \ldots, h_k\} \subseteq \mathcal{H}$. The H defines an **additive model** as a linear function

$$f(\mathbf{x}) = \sum_{i=1}^{k} \beta_i h_i(\mathbf{x}) = \boldsymbol{\beta}^T \mathbf{h}(x) \tag{1}$$

parameterized by $(\beta_1, \ldots, \beta_k) \in \mathbb{R}^k$ that defines $\hat{y}(\mathbf{x}) = \mu(f(\mathbf{x}))$ as a prediction for Y given $X = \mathbf{x}$.

As an instance of additive models, an **additive rule ensemble** [9,11], or a **rule set** has basis functions in the space of boolean query functions $\mathcal{H}_{\text{query}}$. An additive rule ensemble can be represented as a set of "IF ... THEN ..." rules, which can be easily understood by humans. These additive rule ensembles can be interpretable if the number of rules is not large [14].

2.1 Measurements of Performance of Machine Learning Models

Given a loss function $l \colon \mathbb{R} \times \mathbb{R} \to \mathbb{R}_+$ that quantifies the cost of misprediction and a prescribed number of terms k, our goal is then to select a model $H = (h_1, \ldots, h_k)$ and estimate optimal corresponding parameters $\beta_1, \ldots, \beta_k$ that minimize the **expected loss** or prediction **risk** $R(\beta; H) = \mathbf{E}[l(Y, \hat{y}(X))]$. Absent any further information about the joint distribution of X and Y, this goal is typically pursued by minimizing the **regularized empirical risk**:

$$\hat{R}_\lambda(z\beta; H) = \sum_{i=1}^n l(y_i, \hat{y}(\mathbf{x}_i))/n + \lambda\Omega(\beta)$$

as a surrogate, where $\lambda \in \mathbb{R}_+$ is a regularization parameter and Ω is a positive penalty function that penalizes model parameters according to their magnitude.

An important special case are loss functions that are derived as deviance functions when modeling the target variable as member of a canonical exponential family [13] with natural parameter f, i.e., when considering the probabilistic additive model where the target variable $Y \mid X = \mathbf{x}$ follows a probability density or mass function given by

$$p(y \mid f(\mathbf{x})) = \exp\left(\frac{yf(\mathbf{x}) - b(f(\mathbf{x}))}{\phi} - c(y, \phi)\right)$$

with some positive dispersion parameter ϕ and scaled log normalizer $b \colon \mathbb{R} \to \mathbb{R}$. In this case, the loss function

$$l(y, \hat{y}) = \log p(y \mid \mu^{-1}(y)) - \log p(y \mid \mu^{-1}(\hat{y})) \qquad (2)$$

is convex in $\hat{y} = f(\mathbf{x})$ [13].

2.2 Forward Selection and Boosting

To learn additive models, forward selection and boosting approaches are commonly used [3,5,10,18]. Forward selection methods construct model sequences $H_0 \subset H_1 \subset \cdots \subset H_k$ with $H_0 = \{\}$ and $H_{t+1} \setminus H_t = \{h_{t+1}\}$ via greedily optimizing a selection score $\mathfrak{S}(\cdot; H_t, \beta^{(t)})$ depending on the previous model and parameter fit:

$$h_{t+1} = \arg\max\{\mathfrak{S}(h; H_t, \beta^{(t)}) \colon h \in \mathcal{H}\}$$
$$\beta^{(t+1)} = \arg\min\{\hat{R}_\lambda(\beta; H_t \cup \{h_{t+1}\}) \colon \beta \in \mathbb{R}^{t+1}\} \ .$$

The traditional forward selection methods [3] assume finite sets of basis functions that are small enough to explicitly compute a model fit for each candidate $h \in \mathcal{H} \setminus H_t$, i.e., they use

$$\mathfrak{S}_{\mathrm{fs}}(\varphi; \Phi_t) = -\min\{\hat{R}_\lambda([\Phi_t; \phi]\beta) \colon \beta \in \mathbb{R}^{t+1}\} \ . \qquad (3)$$

Gradient boosting [10] instead implicitly searches $\mathcal{H}$ by exactly or approximately optimizing a score that quantifies the alignment of the output vector of

Algorithm 1 Boosting for Additive Models

Input: dataset $(\mathbf{X}, \mathbf{y}) = (x_i, y_i)_{i=1}^n$, number of terms k,
Initialize $f_0 = 0$, $\Phi_0 = []$.
for $t = 1 \cdots k$ **do**
  $h_t = \arg\max_{\mathbf{h}} \mathrm{obj}(\mathbf{h})$
  $\Phi_t = [\Phi_{t-1}; \mathbf{h}_t(\mathbf{X})]$
  $\boldsymbol{\beta}^{(t)} = \mathrm{WeightCalculate}(\Phi_t)$
  $f_t(x) = \boldsymbol{\beta}^{(t)T} \mathbf{h}(x)$
Output the additive model f_k

$h \in \mathcal{H}$ defined by $\mathbf{h} = (h(\mathbf{x}_1), \ldots, h(\mathbf{x}_n))$ with the empirical risk gradient vector $\mathbf{g}$ of the current model fit, i.e., at iteration t

$$g_i = \frac{\partial}{\partial f_t(\mathbf{x}_i)} l(y_i, \mu(f_t(\mathbf{x}_i))) \ , \ i = 1, \ldots, n \ . \tag{4}$$

Starting with an empty model $f_0(\mathbf{x}) = 0$, **idealized boosting** adds a basis function $h_t^* \in \mathcal{H}$ into the additive model to achieve the largest decrease in (regularized) empirical risk for the training dataset in the t-th iteration. Then an updated weight vector $\boldsymbol{\beta}^{(t)}$ is calculated, resulting in a sequence of models $f_1, \cdots, f_k$, where

$$f_t(x) = \sum_{j=1}^t \beta_j^{(t)} h_j(x) \quad , \text{ for } t \in \{1, \ldots, k\}. \tag{5}$$

To efficiently choose basis functions, the commonly-used boosting variants approximate h_t^* based on an objective function $\mathrm{obj}(\mathbf{h}) : \mathbb{R}^n \to \mathbb{R}$, which is a function of the output vector of the basis function $\mathbf{h} = (h(x_1), \cdots, h(x_n))$. For instance, we have the gradient boosting [10] objective $\mathrm{obj}_{\mathrm{gb}}(\mathbf{h}) = |\mathbf{h}^T \mathbf{g}|/\|\mathbf{h}\|_2$ and the gradient sum [6,9] objective function $\mathrm{obj}_{\mathrm{gs}}(\mathbf{h}) = |\mathbf{h}^T \mathbf{g}|$.

To calculate the weight vector $\boldsymbol{\beta}$, the **stepwise weight update** method calculates the weight only for the last basis function added into the model [9,10].

$$\boldsymbol{\beta}^{(t)} = \left[\boldsymbol{\beta}^{(t-1)}; \arg\min_{\beta} \hat{R}_\lambda (f_{t-1} + \beta h_t)\right]. \tag{6}$$

The stepwise weight update method keeps the weight of the previously-generated basis functions unchanged. The **corrective weight update** method [17,21] recalculates the weights of all queries:

$$\boldsymbol{\beta}^{(t)} = \arg\min_{\boldsymbol{\beta}} \hat{R}_\lambda (\Phi_t \boldsymbol{\beta}), \tag{7}$$

where $\Phi_t = [\mathbf{h}_1, \ldots, \mathbf{h}_t]$ is the $n \times t$ **output matrix** of selected basis functions. The corrective weight update method further reduces the risk of the models, yielding models with higher accuracy for given number of terms. We summarize the general framework of boosting for learning additive models in Algorithm 1.

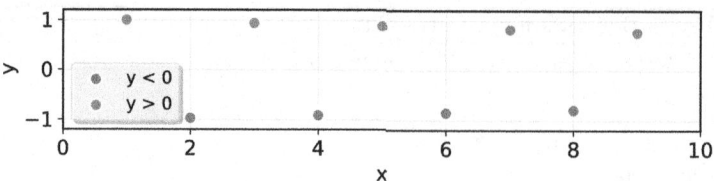

Fig. 2. An example alternating regression dataset with $k = 5$ and $\Delta = 0.03$.

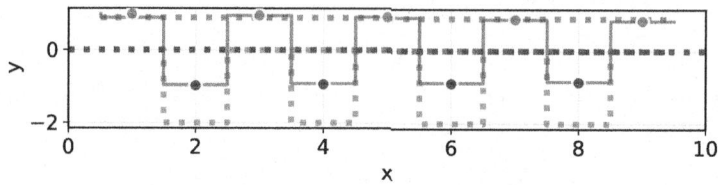

Fig. 3. The reference rule ensemble for $D_{5,0.03}$. The blue dotted line is the rule covering all data points, and the green dotted curves are the other rules. The red curve shows the predicted values of the additive rule ensemble. (Color figure online)

3 Lower Bound on Boosting Risk Gap

In this section, we give a lower bound to the risk difference between the optimal k-term additive model and the boosting model f_k, i.e., the **approximation gap** $R_\lambda(f_k) - R_\lambda(f_k^*)$, in the worst-case across all input datasets. In particular, this bound will apply to the special case of rule base-learners, i.e., $\mathcal{H} = \mathcal{H}_\text{rules}$, and the squared loss $l(y, \hat{y}) = l_\text{sq}(y, \hat{y}) = (y - \hat{y})^2$. It turns out that the bounds can be proved using a simple construction of datasets with an alternating sequence of positive and negative data points with target values of decreasing magnitude (see Fig. 2 for an illustration). Formally, for a positive integer k, the alternating regression dataset $D_{k,\Delta} \subseteq (\mathbb{R} \times \mathbb{R})^{2k-1}$ is defined by

$$D_{k,\Delta} = \{(x_1, y_1), \ldots, (x_{2k-1}, y_{2k-1})\} \tag{8}$$
$$x_i = i \tag{9}$$
$$y_i = (-1)^{i-1}(a_i) \tag{10}$$
$$a_i = 1 - (i-1)\Delta \tag{11}$$

where $1 \leq i \leq 2k-1$ is the index of data points, and $\Delta > 0$ is used for controlling the sequence of selected queries. For $D_{k,\Delta}$, we can construct a reference rule ensemble f_k^* with k rules as follows: The first rule $w_1 q_1(x)$ has the query $q_1(x_i) = 1$, where $i = 1, \ldots, 2k-1$; for $j = 2, \ldots, k$, the rules $w_j q_j$ are defined as $q_j(x_i) = \mathbb{1}(i = 2(j-1))$, as shown in Fig. 3. With this reference rule ensemble, we have the following lemma:

Lemma 1. For $D_{k,\Delta}$, there exists an additive rule ensemble $f_k^\dagger$ containing k rules whose risk is

$$R(f_k^\dagger) = \frac{\Delta^2 k(k^2-1)}{3(2k-1)} \ .$$

Proof. We calculate the risk of the reference rule ensemble f_k^* as

$$\min_\beta R(f_k^*) = \min_\beta \frac{1}{2k-1}\left(\sum_{i=1}^{k}(\beta_1 - y_{2i-1})^2 + \sum_{i=1}^{k-1}(\beta_1 + \beta_{i+1} - y_{2i})^2\right)$$

setting $\beta_{i+1} = y_{2i} - \beta_1$ minimizes term i of the second sum, hence we get

$$= \min_{\beta_1} \frac{1}{2k-1}\left(\sum_{i=1}^{k}(\beta_1 - (1-(2i-2)\Delta))^2\right)$$

$$= \min_{\beta_1} \frac{k\left((\beta_1-1)^2 + 2\Delta(\beta_1-1)(k-1) + \frac{2}{3}\Delta^2(k-1)(2k-1)\right)}{2k-1}$$

which is a quadratic function in $\beta_1 - 1$ which is minimised at $\beta_1 - 1 = -\Delta(k-1)$

$$= \frac{\Delta^2 k(k^2-1)}{3(2k-1)} \ . \tag{12}$$

Therefore, f_k^* satisfies the condition in the lemma. □

Next, we show the behavior of boosting algorithms on the dataset $D_{k,\Delta}$. The following lemma shows the risk of a rule ensemble generated by boosting for $D_{k,\Delta}$ with k rules. Using the risks of the reference rule ensemble and the risk of the rule ensemble generated by boosting, we are able to obtain the lower bound of the worst case approximation gap of the boosting algorithm.

Lemma 2. For any $D_{k,\Delta}$ with $0 < \Delta < 1/(2k - 4 + \sqrt{2}/2)$, the total loss of an ensemble f_k of k basis functions fitted by idealized boosting is

$$R(f_k) = (k-1)\left(\frac{(1-\Delta(3k-2))}{2k-1} + \frac{\Delta^2(6 - 19k + 14k^2)}{6(2k-1)}\right) \ .$$

Proof. We start by examining the matrix Q_t with entries $q_{i,j} = q_i(x_j)$ of the rule ensemble f_k produced by boosting at iteration $t \in \{0, 1, \ldots, 2k-1\}$. Specifically, for $0 < \Delta < 1/(2k - 4 + \sqrt{2}/2)$, we will prove that the matrix Q_t has the form

$$Q_t = \begin{pmatrix} 1 & 0 & \cdots & & \cdots & \cdots & 0 \\ b_{21} & 1 & 0 & & \cdots & \cdots & 0 \\ b_{31} & b_{32} & 1 & 0 & & \cdots & 0 \\ \cdots & \cdots & \cdots & & \cdots & \cdots & \\ b_{t1} & b_{t2} & \cdots & b_{t,t-1} & 1 & 0 & \cdots & 0 \end{pmatrix}, \tag{13}$$

for all $1 \leq i \leq t$, $0 \leq b_{i,j} \leq b_{i,t+1} \leq 1$ and $b_{i,j} \in \{0,1\}$. Once this statement is proven, we can readily show that f_t covers the first t data points with a loss of 0, and that the other data points are uncovered. Formally,

1. For $i \leq t$, the loss $l(f_t(x_i), y_i) = 0$;
2. For $i > t$, the loss $l(f_t(x_i), y_i) = (1 - (i-1)\Delta)^2$.

For Property 1, since the matrix Q_t has full rank, the equation system $Q_t\beta = \mathbf{y}$ always has a unique solution, hence the corrective weight update ensures that $f_t(x_i) = y_i$ for $1 \leq i \leq t$. For Property 2, if $i > t$, $q_{i,j} = 0$ for all $j \in \{1, \ldots, 2k-1\}$, so $f_t(x_i) = 0$, thus $l(f_t(x_i), y_i) = (1 - (i-1)\Delta)^2$.

We now prove by induction that (13) holds. In the base case $t = 0$, the model is empty. Therefore, the matrix Q_0 is empty, so the base case is true. The induction hypothesis is that (13), and therefore Properties 1 and 2, hold at the t-th iteration. We denote β the weight of the $(t+1)$-th rule generated by boosting, and the ordered set A (resp. B) the indices of positive (resp. negative) data points uncovered by rules q_1 to q_t, and covered by rule q_{t+1}, ordered by increasing x_i. (Note that data points covered by rule $t+1$ can include data points already covered, but Property 1 will ensure that their loss remain 0.) Formally, we define A and B as following:

$$A = \{i | q_{t+1}(x_i) = 1, y_i > 0, q_j(x_i) = 0, \text{ for all } j = 1, \ldots, t\}, \quad (14)$$
$$B = \{i | q_{t+1}(x_i) = 1, y_i < 0, q_j(x_i) = 0, \text{ for all } j = 1, \ldots, t\}, \quad (15)$$

and A_t (resp. B_t) represents the t-th element of A (resp. B).

We denote $\alpha = |A|$ and $\gamma = |B|$. Since a rule can only cover contiguous data points, and that positive and negative points alternate, we have $|\alpha - \gamma| \leq 1$.

For idealized boosting, the risk reduction of the i-th data point is $(a_i)^2 - (a_i - \beta)^2 = -\beta^2 + 2\beta a_i$ if $y_j > 0$, and $(-a_i)^2 - (-a_i - \beta)^2 = -\beta^2 - 2\beta a_i$ if $y_i < 0$. Then, the total risk reduction produced by the $(t+1)$-th rule is

$$\max_\beta n(R(f_t) - R(f_{t+1})) = \max_\beta \sum_{k=1}^{\alpha} (-\beta^2 + 2\beta a_{A_k}) + \sum_{k=1}^{\gamma} (-\beta^2 - 2\beta a_{B_k})$$

$$= \max_\beta -(\alpha + \gamma)\beta^2 + 2\beta \left(\sum_{k=1}^{\alpha} a_{A_k} - \sum_{k=1}^{\gamma} a_{B_k} \right)$$

which is a quadratic function in β whose maximizer is $\beta = \dfrac{\sum_{k=1}^{\alpha} a_{A_k} - \sum_{k=1}^{\gamma} a_{B_k}}{\alpha + \gamma}$

$$= \frac{1}{\alpha + \gamma} \left(\sum_{k=1}^{\alpha} a_{A_k} - \sum_{k=1}^{\gamma} a_{B_k} \right)^2,$$

where $n = 2k - 1$. Since $a_i = 1 - (i-1)\Delta$,

$$\max n(R(f_t) - R(f_{t+1})) = \max \frac{(\alpha a_{A_1} - \gamma a_{B_1} - \alpha(\alpha-1)\Delta + \gamma(\gamma-1)\Delta)^2}{\alpha + \gamma}$$

If $\alpha = \gamma$, then $|a_{A_1} - a_{B_1}| = \Delta$, and

$$\max n(R(f_t) - R(f_{t+1})) = \frac{\alpha \Delta^2}{2}. \quad (16)$$

Since the first t data points are already covered, the maximum of the risk reduction in the case $\alpha = \gamma$ is $(k - \lfloor(t+1)/2\rfloor)\Delta^2/2$.

If $\alpha = \gamma + 1$, then $B_1 = A_1 - 1$, $a_{B_1} = a_{A_1} - \Delta$, $\alpha \geq 1$, and

$$\max n(R(f_t) - R(f_{t+1})) = \max \frac{(a_{A_1} - (\alpha-1)\Delta)^2}{2\alpha - 1} \quad (17)$$

In this expression, the numerator increases if α decreases, and the denominator decreases if α decreases. Therefore, the maximum value of the risk reduction in the case $\alpha = \gamma + 1$ is $a_{A_1}^2$, and it is achieved when $\alpha = 1$. It means that the query which covers only one positive data point reduces the most risk. The maximum risk reduction is achieved at (x_i, y_i) where $i = \min\{j : j > t, y_j > 0\}$.

If $\alpha = \gamma - 1$, then $B_1 = A_1 + 1$, $a_{B_1} = a_{A_1} + \Delta$, $\alpha \geq 0$, and

$$\max n(R(f_t) - R(f_{t+1})) = \max \frac{(a_{B_1} - \alpha\Delta)^2}{2\alpha + 1} \quad (18)$$

Similar to the case of $\alpha = \gamma + 1$, the maximum value of the risk reduction in the case $\alpha = \gamma - 1$ is $a_{B_1}^2$, which is achieved when $\gamma = 1$. Therefore, the query which covers only one negative data point reduces the most risk, and its maximum value is achieved at (x_i, y_i) where $i = \min\{j : j > t, y_j < 0\}$. From the above discussion, if $|\alpha - \gamma| = 1$, then the query covering only (x_{t+1}, y_{t+1}) reduces the most risk, and the maximum risk reduction is $(1 - t\Delta)^2$. If

$$\Delta < \sqrt{2}/(k + \sqrt{2}(t-1) - \lfloor(t+1)/2\rfloor) , \quad (19)$$

i.e. $(1-t\Delta)^2 > (k - \lfloor(t+1)/2\rfloor)\Delta^2/2$, the query selected by boosting covers the data points (x_i, y_i) with largest $|y_i|$, which is the $(t+1)$-th data point. To make sure (19) is satisfied for all iterations until the whole dataset is covered, we need

$$0 < \Delta < \frac{1}{2k - 4 + \sqrt{2}/2} . \quad (20)$$

According to Properties 1 and 2, with t iterations, the losses of data points $(x_1, y_1), \ldots, (x_t, y_t)$ are 0. Therefore, the risk of the t-term rule ensemble is

$$R(f_t) = \frac{1}{2k-1} \sum_{i=t+1}^{2k-1} (1 - (i-1)\Delta)^2$$

$$= \frac{(2k-t-1)(6 - 6\Delta(2k+t-2) + \Delta^2(2t^2 + 4kt + 8k^2 - 5t - 14k + 6))}{6(2k-1)} .$$

If $t = k$, then

$$R(f_k) = \frac{(k-1)(6 - 6\Delta(3k-2) + \Delta^2(14k^2 - 19k + 6))}{6(2k-1)} .$$

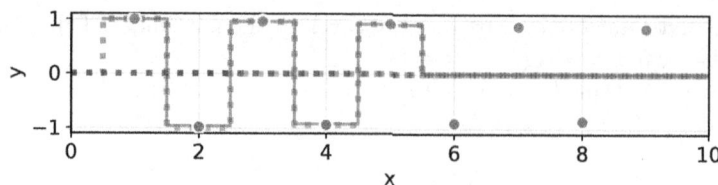

Fig. 4. The additive rule ensemble generated by boosting for $D_{5,0.03}$. The dotted lines represent each rule generated by boosting, and the red solid line represent the output of the model. (Color figure online)

□

Lemma 2 highlights a key observation regarding the structure of rule ensembles generated by boosting for the alternating dataset $D_{k,\Delta}$. Specifically, the rule ensembles produced by boosting tend to cover only individual data points rather than capturing the broader structure of the dataset. As shown in Fig. 4, the rules generated by boosting focus on minimizing the local risk for each point rather than modelling the overall pattern, leading to suboptimal performance when compared to the reference rule ensemble.

With Lemmas 1 and 2, we can calculate the gap between the risks of the models generated by boosting and the reference solution. Formally, the lower bound to the worst-case additive risk gap is given by the following theorem.

Theorem 1. *For $k > 0$ and any $\epsilon > 0$, the worst case additive approximation gap between the k-term optimal model f_k^* and boosting model f_k satisfies*

$$R(f_k) - R(f_k^*) \geq \frac{1}{2} - \frac{1}{4k-2}. \tag{21}$$

Proof. Using Lemmas 1 and 2, we obtain for the approximation gap for $D_{k,\Delta}$

$$\begin{aligned} R(f_k) - R(f_k^*) &= \frac{(k-1)(2 - \Delta(6k-4) + \Delta^2(4k^2 - 7k + 2))}{2(2k-1)} \\ &= \frac{1}{2} - \frac{1}{4k-2} - \underbrace{\frac{(k-1)(\Delta(6k-4) - \Delta^2(4k^2 - 7k + 2))}{2(2k-1)}}_{\xi(\Delta)}. \end{aligned} \tag{22}$$

For $k = 1$, $\xi(\Delta)$ is the constant zero function, hence, the claim is true. For $k > 1$, ξ is a concave quadratic function in Δ with maximum value at $\Delta^* = (3k-4)/(4k^2 - 7k + 2) > 0$. The claim is true for $\epsilon \geq \xi(\Delta^*)$. For $0 < \epsilon < \xi(\Delta^*)$, we observe that $\xi(0) = 0$. Therefore, we can find a positive Δ' such that $\xi(\Delta') = \epsilon$ by the intermediate value theorem, which concludes the proof. □

Note that this result is consistent with the optimality of boosting in the special case of $k = 1$. For $k = 2$, we obtain a lower bound to the approximation gap of 1/3. In the limit, for arbitrarily large k, the bound converges to 1/2. Further, it is worth noting that, while the proof of the result uses idealized boosting (forward selection), it can be adapted to the other discussed variants.

4 Empirical Evaluation of the Boosting Risk Gap via MIP

In Sect. 3, we analyze the lower bound of the worst-case gap between the risks of boosting and optimal models theoretically. However, to answer the question of how tight this bound is, and how representative the worst case is for the real-world datasets, we need to explore alternative approaches of generating rule ensembles with lower risks. In this section, we adopt a MIP approach to approximate the optimal models for different datasets.

MIP involves modelling a problem into a formulation containing decision variables, constraints and an objective function, and solving the formulation using existing solvers like Gurobi [2,12]. In a typical MIP setting, a part of variables are constrained to be integers or discrete values, while others can take continuous values [20]. MIP allows us to find the optimal solution by maximizing or minimizing an objective function subject to a set of constraints. MIP is particularly well-suited for problems where decisions (such as whether a query is selected) are binary or integer-based, while other parameters, like rule weights, are continuous, making it commonly used to obtain or approximate the optimal additive models [8,17,19].

A MIP formulation consists of several key components [20]. First, *decision variables* represent the choices to be made, with some restricted to integers (e.g., binary decisions) and others take continuous values. The *objective function* is a mathematical expression that the MIP seeks to optimize (either minimize or maximize), often involving a cost or risk function. The problem is subject to *constraints*, which are typically linear equations or inequalities that limit the possible values of the decision variables, ensuring that solutions are feasible. Previous works presented in literatures [12,15,17] solve the machine learning problem using MIP solvers, but they usually adopt column generation approaches to model the problem, such as IPBoost [15]. Instead, in our approach, we model the problem of learning additive rule ensembles directly.

4.1 The MIP Formulation

First, we introduce the MIP formulation for approximating optimal additive rule ensembles. Below is a list of variables used in this formulation:

- $l_{t,j}$ (resp. $u_{t,j}$): the lower (resp. upper) bound of t-th rule on j-th dimension ($t = 1, \ldots, k$, $j = 1, \ldots, d$, same below) demonstrated in Fig. 5.
- β_t: the weight of the t-th rule, as shown in Fig. 5.
- $s_{i,t,j}$: A binary variable indicating whether the i-th data point is between the lower bound and the upper bound on the j-th dimension of the t-th rule ($i = 1, \ldots, n$, same below).

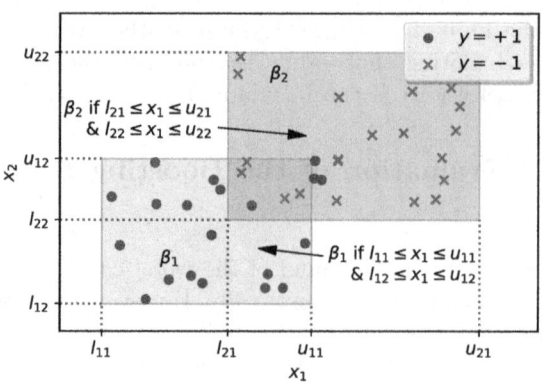

Fig. 5. An illustration of the decision variables used in the MIP formulation for learning additive rule ensembles, including the lower and upper bounds and weights of rules. There are two rules, and the query of each rule is a conjunction of two propositions.

- $z_{i,t}$: A binary variable indicating whether the i-th data point is selected by the t-th rule. Figure 6 demonstrates the usage of the variables $s_{i,t,j}$ and $z_{i,t}$.
- $r_{i,t,j}$ (resp. $p_{i,t,j}$): a binary variable indicating whether the j-th coordinate value of the i-th data point is greater (resp. less) than $l_{t,j}$.

The auxiliary variables $r_{i,t,j}$ and $p_{i,t,j}$ facilitate the expressing of $s_{i,t,j}$ as linear functions of other variables. Specifically, $r_{i,t,j}$ (resp. $p_{i,t,j}$) indicates whether the i-th data point is greater (resp. less) than the lower (resp. upper) bound on the dimension j. The value of $s_{i,t,j}$ is 1 only if both $r_{i,t,j}$ and $p_{i,t,j}$ are 1, meaning the point is within the specified range. A data point is covered by the t-th rule if $s_{i,t,j} = 1$ for all dimensions, in which case $z_{i,t} = 1$. Totally, there are $O(ndk)$ decision variables in this formulation.

To reduce the number of constraints, rather than directly using lower and upper bounds for each rule in every dimension, we represent rules based on the data points they cover. The dataset is sorted along each dimension, and a point is selected by a rule if it has a neighboring point that is also selected. Specifically: If a selected data point exists to the left (resp. right) of the i-th data point on dimension j, then $r_{i,t,j}$ (resp. $p_{i,t,j}$) is 1. If both $r_{i,t,j}$ and $p_{i,t,j}$ are 1, the i-th data point is covered by the t-th rule on dimension j.

The list of constraints is described below:

- On dimension j, if both neighboring points of the i-th data point are covered by the t-th rule, then the i-th data point is also covered by the t-th rule:

$$s_{i,t,j} \geq s_{i_<,t,j} + s_{i_>,t,j} - 1 \qquad \forall t, j,$$

where $i_<$ (resp. $i_>$) refer to the data point whose value is smaller (resp. greater) on dimension j, if any.

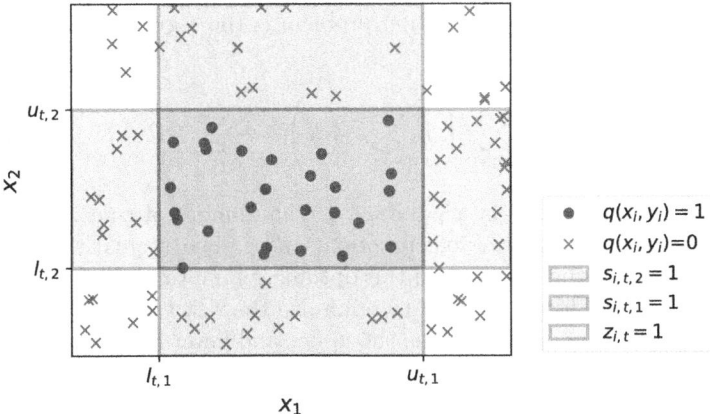

Fig. 6. The constraints in the MIP Formulation for learning rule ensembles. These constraints guarantee that data points satisfying the condition of a query are covered by the query. In this figure, the query q is represented as a conjunction of two propositions: "$l_{t,1} \leq x_1 \leq u_{t,1}$ and $l_{t,2} \leq x_2 \leq u_{t,2}$".

- If neither neighbors of the i-th data point are covered by the t-th rule on dimension j, the i-th data point is not, either:

$$s_{i,t,j} \leq s_{i_<,t,j} + s_{i_>,t,j} \qquad \forall t,j.$$

- If two points i and $i_=$ have the same coordinate on dimension j, then

$$s \text{ (resp. } r, p)_{i,t,j} = s \text{ (resp. } r, p)_{i_=,t,j} \qquad \forall t,j \ .$$

- $r_{i,t,j}$ and $p_{i,t,j}$ are no less than $s_{i,t,j}$:

$$r \text{ (resp. } p)_{i,t,j} \geq s_{i,t,j} \qquad \forall i,t,j.$$

- $r_{i,t,j}$ (resp $p_{i,t,j}$) is monotonically non-decreasing:

$$r_{i,t,j} \geq r_{i_<,t,j} \ , \quad p_{i,t,j} \leq p_{i_<,t,j} \qquad \forall i,t,j.$$

- $s_{i,t,j} = 1$ if and only if both $r_{i,t,j} = 1$ and $p_{i,t,j} = 1$:

$$s_{i,t,j} = r_{i,t,j} + p_{i,t,j} - 1 \qquad \forall i,t,j.$$

This constraint ensures that if a data point is between the lower bound and upper bound of a proposition, then it satisfies the condition of the proposition.
- The data point x_i is in the box of the t-th rule if

$$z_{i,t} \leq s_{i,t,j}, \quad \forall j \ ,$$
$$z_{i,t} \geq \sum_j s_{i,t,j} - d - 1 \ .$$

This constraint indicates that if a data point satisfies all the propositions in a query, then it is covered by this query, as demonstrated in Fig. 6.

The objective of this optimization problem is the regularized empirical risk, which is calculated as:

$$\hat{R}_\lambda = \frac{1}{n}\sum_{i=1}^{n} l\left(y_i, \sum_{t=1}^{k} z_{i,t}\beta_t\right) + \frac{\lambda}{n}\sum_{t=1}^{k} \Omega(\beta_t), \tag{23}$$

where n is the number of data points, k is the number of rules, λ is the regularization parameter, l is the loss function, and Ω is a regularization function. The risk function is the objective in this optimization formulation. The objective of this optimization formulation is to minimize the risk value. After solving the optimization problem, we determine the upper and lower bounds of the t-th rule on the j-th dimension according to the values of $s_{i,t,j}$ for all $i=1,\ldots,n$.

Based on this MIP formulation, we can easily implement the idealized boosting algorithm (MIP-boosting). In the m-th iteration, we fix the weights $\beta_t^{(m)}$, lower and upper bounds $l_{t,j}^{(m)}$ and $u_{t,j}^{(m)}$, $s_{i,t,j}^{(m)}$ and $z_{i,t}^{(m)}$ of the t-th rule ($t<m$) generated in previous iterations as constants. We take $s_{i,t,j}^{(m)}$ as an example:

$$s_{i,t,j}^{(m)} = s_{i,t,j}^{(m-1)}, t<m.$$

Only the decision variables with $t=m$, such as $\beta_m^{(m)}$, $s_{i,m,j}^{(m)}$ and $z_{i,m}^{(m)}$, related to the new rule to be generated in the m-th iteration are included as variables in the MIP formulation in the m-th iteration. Therefore, in such a configuration, only one more rule is generated by the optimization solver. There are totally $O(nd)$ decision variables and $O(nd)$ constraints in this formulation. With the MIP-boosting implementation, the problem of learning additive rule ensembles generated by boosting are easily solved optimally, where the MIP bounds of the training risks are the same as the solutions. In each iteration, this implementation adds one rule which minimizes the empirical risk into the model.

4.2 Experiments

To answer the question whether the lower bound of the worst-case approximation gap of boosting shown in Theorem 1 is tight and representative, we compare the risks of models generated by MIP-boosting and the original MIP formulation. To obtain the optimal models, the original MIP formulations are solved using starting values provided by the boosting implementation. With this setting, the models generated by MIP are always better than boosting models. All the experiments use Gurobi to solve the MIP formulations. The time budget for generating each rule for MIP and boosting are set as 600 s for all datasets. All experiments in this paper are conducted on a computer with "Intel(R) Core(TM) i5-10300H CPU @ 2.50 GHz" and memory of 72 GB. All code and datasets used in our experiments are provided in the supplementary materials and in the GitHub repository https://github.com/fyan102/MIPRule to ensure full reproducibility .

We compare the empirical risks of additive rule ensembles with 10 rules generated by boosting for 21 datasets, and the optimal model implemented using

Table 1. Comparison of training risks of additive rule ensembles trained via boosting (b, implemented with MIP) and globally optimal models obtained via the MIP approach (M) for both classification ($^+$) and regression tasks. The middle section shows the maximum difference in training risk between the two approaches (bolded), the iteration k^* where this occurs, and the corresponding risks. The right section reports the training risks of both approaches, objective bounds (bnd) of MIP, and runtimes (t, in seconds) for 10 rules. Optimal MIP risk values and their bounds are the same.

dataset	d	n	Max risk difference				Training 10 rules				
			diff$_{\max}$	k^*	R_{b,k^*}	R_{M,k^*}	$R_{b,10}$	$R_{M,10}$	bnd$_{M,10}$	$t_{b,10}/s$	$t_{M,10}/s$
tic-tac-toe$^+$	27	958	**.397**	9	.835	.438	.793	.422	.000	2579	5082
salary	1	30	**.357**	2	.501	.144	.050	.050	.050	.214	3.08
study time	1	96	**.328**	2	.669	.341	.069	.069	.069	.654	75.2
demog.	13	6876	**.313**	10	.919	.606	.919	.606	.000	3061	5814
iris$^+$	4	150	**.274**	2	.490	.216	.095	.028	.028	133	4081
IBM HR$^+$	32	1470	**.260**	10	.848	.587	.847	.587	.587	340	1779
student marks	2	100	**.250**	2	.636	.386	.050	.045	.045	1.48	1762
titanic$^+$	7	1043	**.241**	1	.788	.547	.593	.387	.000	1767	4728
income	2	20	**.222**	2	.512	.290	.018	.016	.016	.371	1757
happiness	8	315	**.206**	2	.628	.421	.093	.071	.000	49.2	2059
used cars	4	1770	**.206**	3	.622	.417	.216	.202	.000	1045	2903
gdp	1	35	**.203**	2	.687	.484	.385	.385	.385	.964	141
boston	13	506	**.135**	2	.695	.560	.326	.307	.000	261	2364
headbrain	3	237	**.131**	2	.743	.612	.395	.387	.000	3.918	1800
fitness	3	30	**.128**	2	.573	.446	.115	.108	.1078	.641	1755
mobile	20	2000	**.119**	2	.842	.722	.602	.542	.000	2617	5340
wine$^+$	13	178	**.063**	3	.145	.082	.031	.013	.013	4719	5606
insurance	6	1338	**.060**	3	.383	.323	.196	.185	.000	1166	3547
social media	2	63	**.050**	4	.585	.535	.500	.490	.490	.871	1761
wage	5	1379	**.036**	3	.756	.720	.614	.594	.000	1109	2903
breast$^+$	30	569	**.015**	10	.392	.378	.392	.378	.378	240	4590

MIP approach in Table 1, as well as the MIP bounds. The *MIP bound* is the lower bound of the objective value that can be achieved by the MIP solver, indicating how close the solution found by the solver is to the true optimum. In the table, we observe that for eleven datasets, such as IBM HR, gdp, fitness, and salary, the MIP bound matches the training risk achieved by MIP, indicating that the solver has successfully proved optimality for these models. For these datasets, the solution obtained is guaranteed to be the global optimum, which highlights the effectiveness of the MIP approach in learning optimal rule ensembles for datasets with a small size and dimensions. However, there are ten datasets with large number of data points and features (like titanic, tic-tac-toe and insurance) where the optimality of the solutions cannot be guaranteed. For these datasets, the optimal models may still have a lower risk than the risks shown in Table 1.

In Table 1, we show the maximum difference between the risks of rule ensembles generated by boosting and MIP over all the iterations between 1 and 10 in the middle part of the table, as well as the iteration number the maximum difference occurs and their risk values. We plot the distribution of the largest risk differences between the boosting and optimal models in Fig. 1. There are totally twelve datasets where the largest risk gaps are of the same magnitude as the theoretical lower bound, indicating that the worst-case scenario we analyze is representative. Furthermore, since we have not found any datasets whose largest risk difference between boosting and MIP models are larger than the theoretical analysis, the experimental results show that the actual approximation gaps are usually less than the theoretical bound, suggesting that the lower bound of the worst-case approximation gap is tight. This implies that boosting generally provides a good approximation to the optimal solutions, with performance significantly better than the worst-case bound in most real-world cases.

Notably, the MIP approach generally incurs a higher computational cost compared to boosting. This is primarily due to its increased complexity: the number of decision variables and constraints in the full MIP formulation scales as $O(nkd)$. In contrast, the MIP-boosting implementation only involves $O(nd)$ variables and constraints, since it incrementally adds one rule at a time. As the number of rules increases, solving the full MIP formulation becomes increasingly time-consuming, often reaching the pre-specified time limit. Nevertheless, as shown in Table 1, for nine datasets the running times of the MIP and MIP-boosting methods are of the same order of magnitude, demonstrating that MIP can remain tractable for moderate-sized problems.

5 Conclusion

This paper examines the approximation gap by boosting to generate additive models theoretically and empirically. We provide a constructive proof showing the lower bound of the worst-case risk gap between boosting and the optimal solutions, which is approximately 50% of the initial risk. This gap arises from the greedy nature of boosting, highlighting the need for alternative approaches to obtain better accuracy-complexity trade-offs. To empirically explore the gap, we introduce MIP formulations to approximate optimal additive models. By reducing redundancy in candidate solutions, MIP finds optimal models for small datasets. The experimental results confirm that the observed risk gap aligns with our theoretical analysis, suggesting the tightness and representative of the worst-case bound. Future work may further explore the theoretical upper bound of the risk gap of boosting. Another interesting direction is to improve the scalability of MIP formulations to learn additive models for larger, more complex datasets.

Acknowledgements. This work was supported by the Australian Research Council (DP210100045).We thank the anonymous reviewers for their valuable feedback that led to a substantial improvement of this work.

References

1. Bénard, C., Biau, G., Da Veiga, S., Scornet, E.: Interpretable random forests via rule extraction. In: International Conference on Artificial Intelligence and Statistics, pp. 937–945. PMLR (2021)
2. Bertsimas, D., Dunn, J.: Optimal classification trees. Mach. Learn. **106**(7), 1039–1082 (2017). https://doi.org/10.1007/s10994-017-5633-9
3. Blanchet, F.G., Legendre, P., Borcard, D.: Forward selection of explanatory variables. Ecology **89**(9), 2623–2632 (2008)
4. Boley, M., Teshuva, S., Le Bodic, P., Webb, G.I.: Better short than greedy: interpretable models through optimal rule boosting. In: Proceedings of the 2021 SIAM International Conference on Data Mining (SDM), pp. 351–359. SIAM (2021)
5. Chen, T., Guestrin, C.: XGBoost: a scalable tree boosting system. In: Proceedings of the 22nd Acm Sigkdd International Conference on Knowledge Discovery and Data Mining, pp. 785–794 (2016)
6. Cohen, W.W., Singer, Y.: A simple, fast, and effective rule learner. AAAI/IAAI **99**(335–342), 3 (1999)
7. Das, A., Kempe, D.: Approximate submodularity and its applications: subset selection, sparse approximation and dictionary selection. J. Mach. Learn. Res. **19**(3), 1–34 (2018)
8. Dash, S., Gunluk, O., Wei, D.: Boolean decision rules via column generation. In: Advances in Neural Information Processing Systems, vol. 31 (2018)
9. Dembczyński, K., Kotłowski, W., Słowiński, R.: Ender: a statistical framework for boosting decision rules. Data Min. Knowl. Disc. **21**(1), 52–90 (2010)
10. Friedman, J.H.: Greedy function approximation: a gradient boosting machine. Ann. Stat. **29**, 1189–1232 (2001)
11. Friedman, J.H., Popescu, B.E.: Predictive learning via rule ensembles. The annals of applied statistics, pp. 916–954 (2008)
12. Günlük, O., Kalagnanam, J., Li, M., Menickelly, M., Scheinberg, K.: Optimal decision trees for categorical data via integer programming. J. Global Optim. **81**(1), 233–260 (2021). https://doi.org/10.1007/s10898-021-01009-y
13. McCullagh, P., Nelder, J.A.: Generalized Linear Models. Routledge (2019)
14. Murdoch, W.J., Singh, C., Kumbier, K., Abbasi-Asl, R., Yu, B.: Definitions, methods, and applications in interpretable machine learning. Proc. Natl. Acad. Sci. **116**(44), 22071–22080 (2019)
15. Pfetsch, M., Pokutta, S.: IPBOOST–non-convex boosting via integer programming. In: International Conference on Machine Learning, pp. 7663–7672. PMLR (2020)
16. Shalev-Shwartz, S., Srebro, N., Zhang, T.: Trading accuracy for sparsity in optimization problems with sparsity constraints. SIAM J. Optim. **20**(6), 2807–2832 (2010)
17. Shen, C., Li, H., Van Den Hengel, A.: Fully corrective boosting with arbitrary loss and regularization. Neural Netw. **48**, 44–58 (2013)
18. Sutter, J.M., Kalivas, J.H.: Comparison of forward selection, backward elimination, and generalized simulated annealing for variable selection. Microchem. J. **47**(1–2), 60–66 (1993)

19. Wei, D., Dash, S., Gao, T., Gunluk, O.: Generalized linear rule models. In: International Conference on Machine Learning, pp. 6687–6696. PMLR (2019)
20. Wolsey, L.A.: Mixed integer programming. In: Wiley Encyclopedia of Computer Science and Engineering, pp. 1–10 (2007)
21. Yang, F., Le Bodic, P., Kamp, M., Boley, M.: Orthogonal gradient boosting for simpler additive rule ensembles. In: International Conference on Artificial Intelligence and Statistics, pp. 1117–1125. PMLR (2024)

Multimodal Data

ChitroJera: A Regionally Relevant Visual Question Answering Dataset for Bangla

Deeparghya Dutta Barua[1], Md Sakib Ul Rahman Sourove[1], Md Fahim[1,2],
Fabiha Haider[1], Fariha Tanjim Shifat[1], Md Tasmim Rahman Adib[1],
Anam Borhan Uddin[1], Md Farhan Ishmam[1,3(✉)], and Md Farhad Alam[1]

[1] Research and Development, Penta Global Limited, Dhaka, Bangladesh
deeparghya.csedu@gmail.com,fariha.tanjim.shifat@gmail.com,pdcsedu@gmail.com,
{mdsakibulrahman-2018425350,fabiha-2018325342,mdtasmimrahman-2018425314,
anamborhan-2017514983}@cs.du.ac.bd
[2] CCDS Lab, Independent University, Dhaka, Bangladesh
fahimcse381@gmail.com
[3] Kahlert School of Computing, University of Utah, Salt Lake City, UT, USA
farhan.ishmam@gmail.com

Abstract. Visual Question Answer (VQA) poses the problem of answering a natural language question about a visual context. Bangla, despite being a widely spoken language, is considered low-resource in the realm of VQA due to the lack of proper benchmarks, challenging models known to be performant in other languages. Furthermore, existing Bangla VQA datasets offer little regional relevance and are largely adapted from their foreign counterparts. To address these challenges, we introduce a large-scale Bangla VQA dataset, ChitroJera, totaling over 15k samples from diverse and locally relevant data sources. We assess the performance of text encoders, image encoders, multimodal models, and our novel dual-encoder models. The experiments reveal that the pre-trained dual-encoders outperform other models of their scale. We also evaluate the performance of current large vision language models (LVLMs) using prompt-based techniques, achieving the overall best performance. Given the underdeveloped state of existing datasets, we envision ChitroJera expanding the scope of Vision-Language tasks in Bangla. Our code and data are available at: http://github.com/farhanishmam/ChitroJera.

Keywords: Visual Question Answering · Low Resource Languages · Multimodal Models

1 Introduction and Related Work

Visual Question Answering (VQA) has gained relevance lately with the onset of transformer-based models, facilitating a better understanding of language and

---

D. D. Barua, M. S. U. R. Sourove, and M. Fahim—Equal Contribution.

Supplementary Information The online version contains supplementary material available at https://doi.org/10.1007/978-3-032-06078-5_27.

context in different modalities [25]. This has led to the focus in VQA research shifting from the perception of language and vision to understanding the reasoning of these opaque systems [46]. VQA systems are also being used to aid in visual impairment [19], enhance robotic systems [47], expedite the screening of medical conditions from relevant imagery [36], and so on. The performance of these systems is strongly coupled with the quality of the datasets they are trained on [18,41]. With that in mind, VQA datasets in English are being designed with increasing complexity, leaning more towards advanced reasoning instead of simple answers [40,46]. However, the landscape for most low-resource languages speaks differently, with the major pain point being the lack of substantial datasets that can address even the most basic of answers.

Table 1. Comparison between existing datasets based on the number of questions (#Q), answers (#A), and images (#I), source of images (Img Src.), annotation (Annot.) and Validation (Val.) methods, Question Type (QT), and categorical metadata availability (CMA). gTrans means Google Translate.

Datasets	#Q	#A	#I	Img Src.	Annot.	Val.	QT	CMA
Bengali VQA v1	5000	2	500	English	gTrans	Authors	Binary	✗
Bengali CLEVR	12291	1600	1271	English	gTrans	Authors	WH	✗
Bengali VQA 2.0	13046	2	3280	English	Manual	N/A	Binary	✗
CVQA (Bengali subset)	286	780	136	Bangla	Manual	Natives	WH	✓
ChitroJera (Ours)	15292	5542	15147	Bangla	GPT-4 Turbo	Experts	WH	✓

Despite being a language with around 284 million[1] speakers, Bangla has received limited exposure to the domain of visual question answering. The issues are multifaceted, with one aspect being the lack of pre-trained vision language models (VLMs) to entertain the idiosyncrasies of the language, and the other being the lack of datasets tailored for this particular purpose, further compounding the issue of VLM unavailability.

Presently, only four instances of VQA datasets have been compiled for Bangla [26,43,45], all of which have certain limitations as per Tab. 1. The first work presents two datasets, Bengali-VQA-v1 and Bengali CLEVR, built on top of the existing English VQA datasets — VQA v1 [4] and CLEVR [27] respectively. The second work presents Bengali-VQA-2.0, compiled from the English VQA v2.0 dataset. Among these, Bengali-VQA-v1 and Bengali-VQA-2.0 offer limited applicability to non-trivial VQA tasks, as the questions are restricted to binary answers. While the answers in Bengali CLEVR encompass multiple classes, the issue with all these datasets is that the source images and texts are derived from English datasets, which lack the geographical context associated with Bangla. Also, Bengali VQA 2.0 magnifies its scale by relying on tactics that yield repetitive samples with minor differences. Lastly, CVQA [45] addresses some of these issues, but as it explores 26 languages, the focus on Bangla is quite thin, yielding only 286 samples.

---

[1] https://www.ethnologue.com/insights/ethnologue200/ (Current as of writing; figures are subject to change.)

With the intent of addressing the shortcomings within the existing space of Bangla VQA, our contributions are as follows:

ChitroJera Dataset: We propose a new dataset for Bangla VQA, named ChitroJera, comprising 15k images and questions, synthesized using OpenAI GPT-4 Turbo with curated prompting and validated by linguistic experts. The images and text have a Bangla regional flavor, *i.e.* that they capture the connotations associated with the Bangla-speaking region. We ensure diversity by imposing restrictions on the number of questions per image. For better analysis, we provide a categorical breakdown of the samples based on the subject of the questions. Comparison between ours and existing datasets is given in Table 1.

Dual Encoder Models: Due to the lack of VLMs that are aligned on Bangla text with regional images, we introduce novel dual encoder-based models that outperform existing unimodal models and VLMs trained on English data sources, showing promising performance at its scale.

Extensive Experimentation: We conduct experiments on our dataset using state-of-the-art and widely adopted text encoders, visual encoders, and multimodal models fine-tuned for this task. We observe the performance of dual encoder models with and without pretraining, with ablations on different pretraining objectives and batch sizes. Finally, we assess both open and closed-source LVLMs via zero-shot prompting and compare them. Experiments demonstrate that the dual encoder-based models we propose outperform all open-source LVLMs in zero-shot evaluations across all metrics.

2 ChitroJera Dataset

The ChitroJera dataset is meticulously curated and annotated for regionally relevant Bangla VQA. We source the data from internet content representative of the Bengali communities (Fig. 1).

2.1 Dataset Collection

The question-answer pairs in the dataset have been collected from existing Bangla images and image captions found in the BanglaLekhaImageCaptions [44], Bornon [48], and BNATURE [17] datasets. These sources contain images from the internet, which have been collected using keywords relevant to Bangladesh and its vicinity, transitively ensuring that our dataset is regionally relevant. A detailed breakdown of the source distribution is given in Table 2.

2.2 Data Preprocessing

We corrected image-caption mismatches, deduplicated images, and removed erroneous ICC color profiles. A single image can have multiple captions. For images

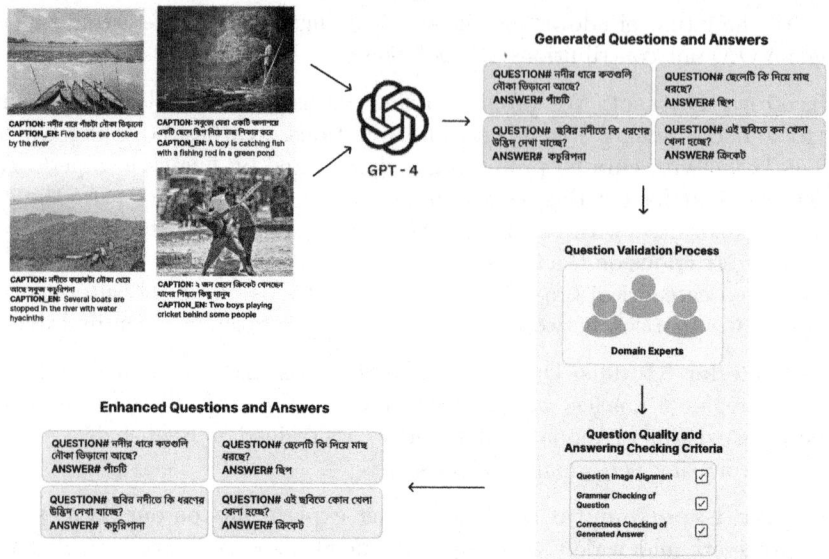

Fig. 1. Overview of the dataset generation pipeline. The image-caption pairs are passed to GPT-4 Turbo using a curated prompt to generate QA pairs, then validated and corrected by the domain experts.

with more than 3 captions, we choose the longest and the shortest captions, and a third caption having the highest BERTScore with the former two. The reason behind this choice is to capture a diverse depiction of the image. While shorter captions typically convey the broader context, longer captions tend to include finer details. These three (or fewer) captions are concatenated to form the textual ground truth context for the question generation.

2.3 QA Pair Generation

We compared QA pairs generated by GPT-4 Turbo and Google Gemini 1.5 Pro over 1,000 imagecaption pairs, and relied on two domain experts to choose the superior output for each instance. Since the evaluation criteria were binary and there were exactly two annotators, we measured inter-annotator agreement using Cohen's κ between the annotators, obtaining a score of 89.27%. GPT-4 Turbo was preferred in most of the cases, and is therefore used for question synthesis. We prompt the model in such a manner to generate complex and diverse questions while constraining answers to one to three words, ensuring the response remains concise and minimizes irrelevant information. The prompt used for QA pair generation has been reported in Sect. 8.

Table 2. Dataset statistics of ChitroJera.

Source Distribution		
BanglaLekhaImageCaptions	8600	
Bornon	4292	
BNATURE	2400	
Splits		
Train	12231	
Validation	1529	
Test	1532	
General Statistics		
Samples	15292	
Captions	14927	
Images	15147	
Questions	13299	
Answers	5542	
WH-words	11	
Categories/Types	17	
QA Statistics	**Q**	**A**
Mean character length	33.50	7.10
Max character length	105	45
Min character length	11	1
Mean word count	5.86	1.43
Max word count	17	4
Min word count	3	1
QA Pair LLM Selection		
#Samples		1000
Cohen's κ coefficient		89.27%
QA Pair Validation		
#Samples		2500
Accuracy	**#**	**%**
Annotator 1	2462	98.48
Annotator 2	2476	99.04

2.4 Dataset Annotation

We verify the quality and consistency of the synthesized QA pairs by defining a few evaluation criteria, namely caption-question alignment, image-question alignment, question correctness, and answer correctness. Our approach to data validation is methodological. We employ two experts in Bangla linguistics to evaluate the dataset on the aforementioned criteria over a subset of 2500 randomly selected samples due to resource constraints. Both experts are native Bangla speakers, accredited in linguistic proficiency, possess strong cultural awareness, and conform to the same principles in assessing grammatical correctness. We hired them on an hourly basis. The rationale for hiring domain experts instead of general annotators lies in their deeper understanding of the linguistic nuances of Bangla, enabling them to uphold the quality of the dataset. Since the overhead of cross-checking between two annotators is low, any inter-annotator disagreement is disputed directly via discussion. If no consensus is reached, we discard the ambiguous sample. However, such cases are rare, with only 5 samples being flagged. The annotation statistics are shown in Table 2.

2.5 Dataset Statistics

We randomly split the dataset into training, validation, and test sets with a ratio of 80:10:10. To capture a more diverse representation of different contexts, we restrict the number of questions for each image to one or, at most, two. The number of unique questions is lesser than the total number of question, i.e., the same question has been asked on different images. This enables the models to generalize effectively, even when the visual context significantly differs. While the ratio of unique questions to unique answers is approximately 2.4, it does not necessarily indicate a sparsity in the training distribution. This is due to the inclusion of suffixes in the answers, i.e., the same root word can take multiple forms. The statistics of ChitroJera are shown in Table 2.

Question Statistics. The questions generated by GPT-4 Turbo range from a minimum of 3 words to a maximum of 17 words, with a mean of 6 words. To assess the diversity of the questions, we chose a set of 11 wh-question words in Bangla that comprehensively cover all the grammatically correct questions. These are — "কি"(what/tag questions), "কোন" (which), "কত"(how many/much), "কোথায়"(where), "কখন" (how many/much), "কার" (who), "কে" (singular whose), "কয়" (when), "কিভাবে" (how), "কাদের" (plural whose) and "কবে" (when).

Figure 2a offers an overview of the distribution of the keywords, respectively. We hypothesize that the low sample count of questions using "কখন"(singular whose), "কার" (when), "কাদের" (plural whose), and "কবে" (when) is due to the difficulty in assessing temporal and possessive qualities from still images and captions that are unassuming of their subjects.

Answer Statistics. The prompt used to generate the QA pairs limits the answers to short phrases, with most being single-word answers. For gauging the distribution of the answers in terms of content, we employ a keyword-based method to classify them into the discrete and exclusive categories of "Numeric", "Food", "Place", "Weather", "Animal", "Color", "Plant", "Material", "Activity", Emotion", "Cloth", "Direction", "Human", "Vehicle", "Time" and "Object"; outlined in Figure 2b .

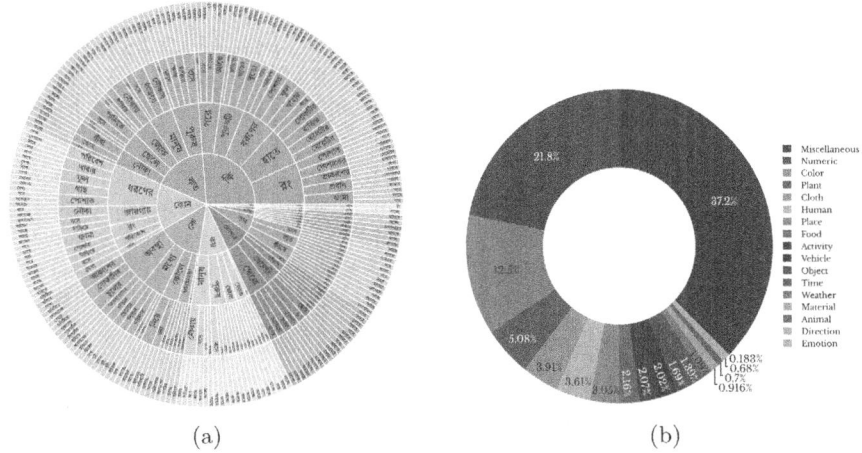

Fig. 2. (a) Question keyword and (b) Answer category distribution of ChitroJera dataset.

3 Baselines

We evaluate image-only, text-only, and multimodal (image + text) settings, and compare the performance of LLMs and VLMs. For evaluation, we consider exact match accuracy, BERTScore [54], and LAVE score [39].

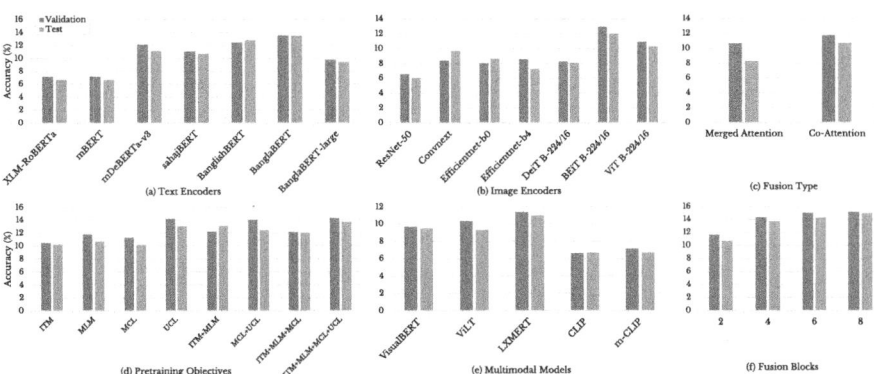

Fig. 3. Validation and test accuracy across different text encoders, image encoders, multimodal models, fusion types, number of fusion blocks, and pretraining objectives.

3.1 Fine-tuning

We evaluate the dataset on models fine-tuned with our train split. The problem is treated as a multi-class classification task, following other close-ended

VQA approaches [40,46]. Unimodal fine-tuning is performed on text and image modalities separately. In this case, the text models involve multilingual models like XLM-Roberta [11], mBERT [35], and mDeBERTa-v3 [23], and Bangla language models such as sahajBERT[2], BanglishBERT and BanglaBERT [8], where BanglaBERT achieves the best performance (Fig. 3a). Here, the input, $x_t =$ Ques: {question} [SEP] Caption: {caption}. For the visual modality, we run our experiments on ResNet [22], Convnext [38], Efficientnet, [50], DeiT [51], BEiT, [6], and ViT [14], where BEiT and ViT outperform the others (Fig. 3b). We also fine-tune multimodal models (VLMs), such as VisualBERT [33], ViLT [29], LXMERT [49], CLIP [42], and m-CLIP [9], where LXMERT has the best standing. The formal representation of the [CLS] token (denoted as $\mathbf{h}$) extraction is as follows:

Text encoders: $\mathbf{h} = f_T(x_t)$ and image encoders: $\mathbf{h} = f_I(x_{img})$.
For VisualBERT and ViLT: $\mathbf{h} = f_{VL}(x_t, x_{img})$.

For LXMERT, CLIP, m-CLIP: $\begin{cases} \mathbf{h}_T, \mathbf{h}_I = f_{VL}(x_t, x_{img}) \\ \mathbf{h} = [\mathbf{h}_T; \mathbf{h}_I]. \end{cases}$

If there are multiple [CLS] tokens for each modality, we simply concatenate them to have a single representation, $\mathbf{h}$. As per the definition of a multi-class classification problem, $\mathbf{h}$ is then passed to an MLP. To fine-tune the model, the system calculates cross-entropy loss by evaluating MLP outputs against the ground truth labels.

3.2 Pretrained Dual Encoders

From the discussion in Section 3.1, pre-trained multimodal models are typically trained on image-English text pairs, resulting in a limited semantic understanding of Bangla text. To address this gap, we adopt a dual-encoder approach to extract semantic features. However, these unimodal models initially lack alignment between modalities, which we address by training a multi-modal fusion network on a pretraining dataset with specific pretraining objectives.

Following the experimental results, we utilize the best-performing models from each modality: BanglaBERT for text, and both BEiT and ViT separately for the image. For pretraining datasets, we consider the image-caption dataset to align the dual encoders for both modalities. As described in Section 2.1, we use BanglaLekhaImageCaptions, Bornon, and BNATURE to generate our VQA dataset. Therefore, we omit these datasets for our pretraining tasks and instead use the BanCap [28] dataset.

Pretraining Mechanism. During the pretraining stage, the image x_{img} and its corresponding captions are fed x_t into image encoder f_I and text encoder f_T separately, to extract image representations $\mathbf{h}_I$ and text representations $\mathbf{h}_T$ where $\mathbf{h}_I = f_I(x_{img}); \mathbf{h}_T = f_T(x_t)$. Here, $\mathbf{h}_I \in \mathbb{R}^{n_v \times d_v}$ and $\mathbf{h}_T \in \mathbb{R}^{n_t \times d_t}$, where n_v and n_t are the number of visual and textual tokens, respectively, and d_v and d_t are

---
[2] https://github.com/tanmoyio/sahajbert.

their dimensionalities. A fusion module is employed to align the image and text representations. We explore two types of fusion modules: merged attention and co-attention like [15,24].

Merged Attention: Merged attention integrates information from both modalities into a single attention mechanism. We concatenate both representations $\mathbf{h}_{VL} = [\mathbf{h}_I; \mathbf{h}_T] \in \mathbb{R}^{(n_v+n_t)\times d}$. $\mathbf{h}_{VL}$ is passed into B different fusion blocks which is typically the transformer-encoder blocks [52].

Co-Attention: In the co-attention module, the features are processed through D separate transformer blocks, utilizing techniques like cross-attention for cross-modal interaction. For each block i, the representations are calculated as follows:

$$Q_I^i, K_I^i, V_I^i = W_{Q_I}^i \mathbf{h}_I^i, W_{K_I}^i \mathbf{h}_I^i, W_{V_I}^i \mathbf{h}_I^i; \quad Q_T^i, K_T^i, V_T^i = W_{Q_T}^i \mathbf{h}_T^i, W_{K_T}^i \mathbf{h}_T^i, W_{V_T}^i \mathbf{h}_T^i$$
$$\mathbf{h}_I^i = \text{Self-Attn}(Q_I^i, K_I^i, V_I^i); \quad \mathbf{h}_T^i = \text{Self-Attn}(Q_T^i, K_T^i, V_T^i)$$
$$\mathbf{h}_I'^i = \text{Cross-Attn}(Q_I^i, K_T^i, V_T^i); \quad \mathbf{h}_T'^i = \text{Cross-Attn}(Q_T^i, K_I^i, V_I^i)$$
$$\mathbf{h}_I^{i+1} = \text{MLP}(\mathbf{h}_I'^i); \quad \mathbf{h}_T^{i+1} = \text{MLP}(\mathbf{h}_T'^i).$$

Pretraining Objectives: We utilize four different losses, namely Masked Language Modeling (MLM) [13,55], Image-Text Matching (ITM) [32], Multimodal Contrastive Loss (MCL) [21], and Unimodal Contrastive Loss (UCL) [34], for the pretraining process. These are the most common and widely used pretraining objectives in the multimodal domain. From Figure 3d, combining all pretraining objectives as $\mathcal{L}_{PT} = \mathcal{L}_{ITM} + \mathcal{L}_{MLM} + \mathcal{L}_{MCL} + \mathcal{L}_{UCL}$.

Fusion Type: Following Fig. 3c, the Co-Attention fusion outperforms the Merged Attention fusion. Hence, we choose Co-Attention as the type of fusion for further experimentation.

Table 3. Evaluation of dual-encoder pre-training with $\mathcal{L}_{PT}$ training objectives using accuracy and BERTScore.

Dual Encoders	Performance Metrics			
	Validation		Test	
	Accuracy	BERTScore	Accuracy	BERTScore
w/o Pretraining				
BanglaBERT + ViT-224	11.45	89.01	10.64	88.71
BanglaBERT + BEiT-224	12.68	89.87	11.11	89.26
with Pretraining				
BanglaBERT + ViT-224	14.26	90.78	13.64	90.59
BanglaBERT + BEiT-224	14.45	89.50	13.12	89.56

Effect of Pre-training: Table 3 presents the performance results of the selected dual-encoders with and without pretraining. It indicates that pretraining enhances the dual encoder accuracy by approx. 2-3% on both the validation and test datasets. Given that our pretraining dataset contains only 44k samples, the improvement is modest and is likely to improve with more training.

Feature Aggregation based Fine-tuning. When employing a co-attention-based network for modality fusion, we get image-aware text representations $\mathbf{h}'_L$ and text-aware image representations $\mathbf{h}'_I$ after pre-training. While fine-tuning for VQA classification, we extract the [CLS] token representations, denoted as $h'^{[CLS]}_T$ and $h'^{[CLS]}_I$. To derive the ultimate representation for classification, we explore two aggregation techniques.

- **Concat-based:** The final representation z is calculated as follows:

$$z = \texttt{MLP}([h'^{[CLS]}_T; h'^{[CLS]}_I]).$$

- **Summed-based:** In this case, the final representation z is calculated using:

$$z = \texttt{MLP}([h'^{[CLS]}_T + h'^{[CLS]}_I]).$$

This aggregated representation z is then fed into the classification head, followed by a linear layer for prediction.

3.3 LLM Prompting

We also investigate the performance of LLMs & V-LLMs using our dataset through zero-shot prompting techniques. For this, we input an image x_{img} along with a question x_t along with the proper instruction and ask the LVLMs to generate the answer based on the image and question. The selection of the models considers a few criteria: whether they are monolingual and multilingual or not, and whether the model is open weights/source or closed weights/source.

The monolingual open weights/source include BLIP-2 [31], InstructBLIP [12], LLaVa-1.5-7B [37], and LLaVa-OneVision-7B [30]. For open weights/source multilingual models, we chose PaliGemma-3B [7], Pangea-7B [53], Qwen2.5-VL-7B [5], Phi-3.5-Vision [1], and InternVL2-8B [10]. The closed weights/source offerings include commercial models with vision capabilities, namely Gemini 2.0 Flash, Claude 3.7 Sonnet, GPT-4 Turbo, and GPT-4o. The prompts used for our experiments are reported in Sect. 8.

4 Benchmarking and Analysis

Following Table 4, our evaluation largely focuses on the effectiveness of large language models, and to a smaller extent, the performance of our pretrained dual-encoder models at different configurations.

Table 4. The performance of dual-encoder models using different modality aggregation techniques and large language models on the ChitroJera dataset.

Models	Validation			Test		
	Acc	BScore	LAVE	Acc	BScore	LAVE
Dual Encoder Fusion Type						
BanglaBERT-ViT [Concat]	14.26	90.78	15.83	13.64	90.59	16.08
BanglaBERT-BEiT [Concat]	14.45	89.50	20.60	13.12	89.56	20.10
BanglaBERT-ViT [Sum]	14.08	89.71	18.88	13.61	89.32	23.46
BanglaBERT-BEiT [Sum]	14.03	89.76	18.58	14.45	90.22	20.44
Open Source LLMs [Monolingual]						
BLIP-2	11.74	87.29	19.74	10.35	86.92	19.71
InstructBLIP	5.29	70.25	6.68	5.67	71.14	7.24
LLaVa-1.5-7B	7.93	74.86	8.80	6.73	73.75	7.93
LLaVA-OneVision-7B	7.89	73.64	8.79	6.68	71.64	7.88
Open Source LLMs [Multilingual]						
PaliGemma-3B	8.44	79.26	9.37	8.98	80.72	10.59
Pangea-7B	11.26	86.28	17.94	10.28	86.26	18.88
Qwen2.5-VL-7B	12.31	88.04	18.36	12.04	87.93	18.45
Phi-3.5-Vision	10.67	83.57	19.01	10.31	83.26	19.97
InternVL2-8B	11.98	87.33	17.22	11.24	87.01	16.85
Closed Weights/Source LLMs						
Gemini 2.0 Flash	23.07	90.15	**62.31**	26.58	89.15	**66.08**
Claude 3.7 Sonnet	21.55	88.72	52.76	28.09	89.48	63.82
GPT-4o	31.58	92.01	56.28	30.22	91.79	58.54
GPT-4 Turbo	**33.35**	**92.28**	61.30	**32.83**	**92.18**	57.79

Dual Encoder Models: As shown in Table 4, the concat-based fusion technique outperforms the sum-based approach, with BEiT paired with BanglaBERT yielding better performance than the BanglaBERT-ViT combination. Concat-based fusion increased accuracy by 0.18% and 0.42% compared to their sum-based counterparts for BanglaBERT paired with ViT and BEiT encoders, respectively. Using the BEiT encoder increased accuracy by 0.19% compared to ViT for concat-based fusion, but saw a 0.5% decline for sum-based fusion.

Monolingual vs. Multilingual LLMs: It can be seen from the benchmarks that models that have an explicit focus on multilingualness, which are models that have been trained on multilingual data, perform better on our dataset compared to monolingual models, largely focused on English. The viability of the tokenizers in a monolingual or multilingual setting also plays an important role [3].

Most of the monolingual models have sub-10% accuracy and LAVE scores, while nearly all the multilingual models make it past that.

Closed Source LVLMs: Among the closed source LVLMs, the GPT family outperforms Gemini and Claude with a margin of around 10% in terms of accuracy. Besides accuracy, the performances of Gemini 2.0 Flash, Claude 3.7 Sonnet, GPT-4o, and GPT-4 Turbo are comparable in terms of BERTScore and LAVE, with Gemini having an edge in LAVE. For a rigid metric like accuracy, GPT-4 has a bigger advantage due to the exactness between the answers it generated during QA pair synthesis and the blind answer generation. In open-ended answer generation, metrics like accuracy do not paint the full picture [39].

Dual Encoder vs. Open Source: Our dual encoder models outperform all open-source LVLMs, including multilingual ones, across all evaluation metrics. The best-performing model, BanglaBERT-BEiT[Concat], achieves 14.45% accuracy and 20.60% LAVE on the validation set, and 13.10% accuracy and 20.10% LAVE on the test set. These results surpass those of the top-performing zero-shot open-source LVLM, Qwen2.5 VL, which achieves 12.31% accuracy and 17.94% LAVE on the validation set, and 12.04% accuracy and 18.45% LAVE on the test set. While this comparison may not be entirely fair, it suggests that open-source LVLMs lack sufficient Bangla regional data in their pretraining, indicating the need for fine-tuning to achieve better performance.

Open Source vs. Closed Source LVLMs: Based on the benchmarks, the proprietary LLMs surpass the results of open-source models in every evaluation metric. Among the open-source models, Qwen2.5-VL-7B attains the best performance in accuracy and BERTScore. Phi-3.5-Vision, on the other hand, offers the best LAVE score, suggesting that while it does not get the answers as exact as Qwen2.5, it has a more holistic idea of what the correct answer might be, having considered semantic equivalence, synonyms, and variations in verbosity. Proprietary models, such as Gemini 2.0 Flash, Claude 3.7 Sonnet, GPT-4o, and GPT-4 Turbo, are trained on multilingual data. The scale of their training is reflected in the performance improvement over the open-source models.

5 Error Analysis

From Fig. 4, it can be reasonably inferred that implicit answers can affect the V-LLM performance. In the first image, GPT-4o struggles with the ability to differentiate between two similar-looking objects, failing to tell a "টায়ার" (tire) apart from a "চাকা" (wheel) as both objects are circular. The second example showcases an example of these models lacking regional context in their training data, where the model is unable to recognize the action of drying paddy through manual labor, a common practice in rural Bengal. Finally, the third image shows that using accuracy as a metric treats answers too rigidly, as semantic equivalence is not assessed. The answers from GPT-4o, GPT-4 Turbo, and Gemini 2.0 Flash are technically acceptable but are considered an error as the ground truth is "কাঁচা বাজার" (fresh market).

Fig. 4. Error Analysis of LLMs in Our Dataset using

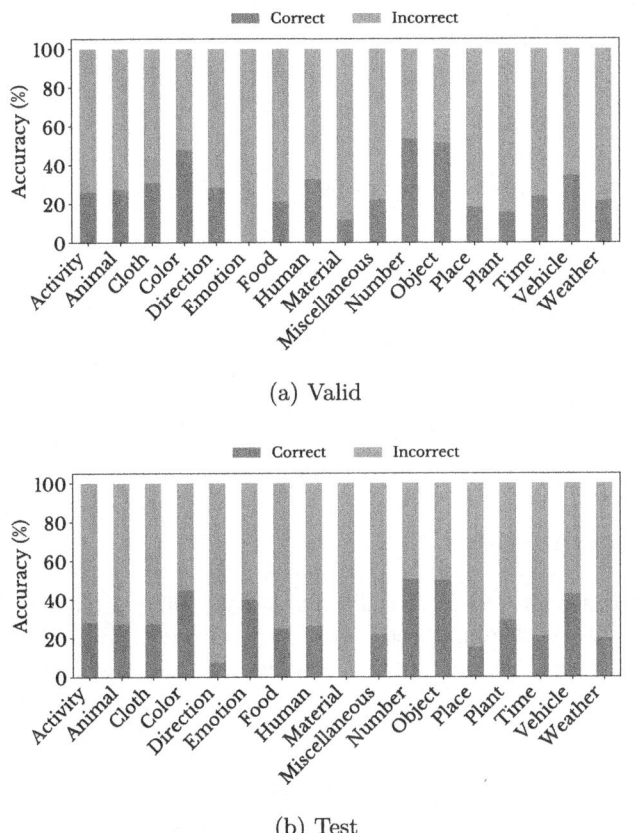

Fig. 5. Category-based accuracy by GPT-4 Turbo on valid and test sets.

Fig. 5 exhibits that for some of the categories, such as "Color", "Human", "Number", "Object", and "Vehicle", the performance is consistently well across both the validation and test splits. These categories can easily be reasoned with from the images alone, as their presence is explicit. On the other hand, the more abstract or implicit the category is, the harder it gets for the LLM to reason from the visual information alone. This is reflected in categories such as "Emotion", "Direction", and "Time". It should be noted that the performance disparity in "Emotion" is likely due to the low sample count.

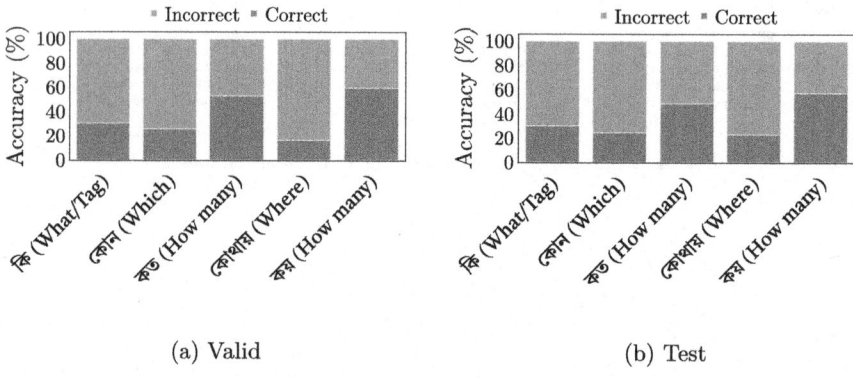

(a) Valid   (b) Test

Fig. 6. WH-word-based accuracy by GPT-4 Turbo on valid and test sets.

For WH-words, GPT-4 Turbo attains 50% or more accuracy on counting questions on both test and validation splits, as seen in Fig. 6. For WH-words such as কি(what/tag question) and কোন(which), the accuracy is close to the model average. Performance is comparatively poor for কোথায়(where), as spatial reasoning from a still image can be challenging. These findings resemble the explicit/implicit subject trend from the categorical breakdown. Note that Fig. 6 only lists the top 5 WH-words (in terms of sample count) for brevity.

6 Future Directions

With the growing interest in transliterated text [20], a promising extension of our work is VQA with romanized [16] or code-mixed [2] Bangla. A benchmark incorporating cultural understanding of images, similar to CVQA [45], can also be a potential direction. Finally, our work does not account for regional variations within the Bengal region, which future works can investigate.

7 Conclusion

We introduce ChitroJera, a VQA dataset deeply rooted in the geography, culture, and norms of the Bangla-speaking region. To our knowledge, ChitroJera is the first VQA benchmarking with images relevant to the Bengal region, filling a crucial gap in the Bangla vision-language landscape. We anticipate that our work will foster improvements in future models, enabling better modality alignment with low-resource contexts and thereby, overall improved performance.

8 Prompts

The prompts used in our literature have been reported here.

Prompt to Generate the Question-Answer Pairs

You are an expert in generating Bangla visual question-answer pairs. Given an image and its captions, follow these guidelines:
1. Questions must align with both the image and the captions.
2. Answers should be one or two words, never more than three.
3. Both question and answer must be in Bangla.

⟨CAPTION⟩
Based on the caption and image, generate one pair:
Q: ⟨QUESTION⟩, A: ⟨ANSWER⟩

Prompt to Generate Answers using GPT-3.5 (Text only model)

You are an expert Bangla QA assistant. Given a caption and a question, follow these rules:
1. Answer in one or two words (never more than three).
2. Answer must be in Bangla.

⟨CAPTION⟩, ⟨QUESTION⟩
Generate an answer in this format:
A: ⟨ANSWER⟩

Prompt to Generate Answers with caption	Prompt to Generate Answers without caption
You are an expert Bangla visual QA assistant. Given an image, its caption, and a question, follow these rules: 1. Answer in one or two words (never more than three). 2. Answer must be in Bangla. ⟨CAPTION⟩, ⟨QUESTION⟩ Generate an answer in this format: A: ⟨ANSWER⟩	You are an expert Bangla visual QA assistant. Given an image and a question, follow these rules: 1. Answer in one or two words (never more than three). 2. Answer must be in Bangla. ⟨QUESTION⟩ Generate an answer in this format: A: ⟨ANSWER⟩

CO_2 Emission

With a carbon efficiency of 0.432 kgCO_2eq/kWh (OECD average), a total of 150 hours of computation was performed using Tesla P100 hardware (TDP of 250W) for the unimodal, multimodal, and dual encoder models. Total emissions of those experiments are estimated to be 16.2 kgCO_2eq.

Acknowledgments. We sincerely appreciate the generous support of our sponsor, Penta Global Limited, Bangladesh, for funding this project.

References

1. Abdin, M., et al.: Phi-3 technical report: a highly capable language model locally on your phone. arXiv preprint arXiv:2404.14219 (2024)
2. Alam, S., Ishmam, M.F., Alvee, N.H., Siddique, M.S., Hossain, M.A., Kamal, A.R.M.: Bnsentmix: a diverse Bengali-English code-mixed dataset for sentiment analysis. arXiv preprint arXiv:2408.08964 (2024)
3. Ali, M., et al.: Tokenizer choice for LLM training: negligible or crucial? In: Duh, K., Gomez, H., Bethard, S. (eds.) Findings Of Naacl 2024, pp. 3907–3924. Association for Computational Linguistics, Mexico City, Mexico (2024)
4. Antol, S., et al.: VQA: visual question answering. In: In the IEEE International Conference on Computer Vision (ICCV), pp. 2425–2433 (2015)
5. Bai, S., Chen, K., Liu, X., Wang, J., Ge, W., et al.: Qwen2.5-vl technical report. arXiv preprint arXiv:2502.13923 (2025)
6. Bao, H., Dong, L., Piao, S., Wei, F.: Beit: BERT pre-training of image transformers. arXiv (2021)
7. Beyer, L., Steiner, A., Pinto, A.S., Kolesnikov, A., Wang, X., et al.: Paligemma: a versatile 3B VLM for transfer (2024)

8. Bhattacharjee, A., et al.: BanglaBERT: language model pretraining and benchmarks for low-resource language understanding evaluation in Bangla. arXiv (2021)
9. Chen, G., et al.: mCLIP: multilingual CLIP via cross-lingual transfer. In: Rogers, A., Boyd-Graber, J., Okazaki, N. (eds.) In the 61st ACL (2023)
10. Chen, Z., et al.: Expanding performance boundaries of open-source multimodal models with model, data, and test-time scaling (2025)
11. Conneau, A., et al.: Unsupervised cross-lingual representation learning at scale. arXiv (2019)
12. Dai, W., et al.: Instructblip: towards general-purpose vision-language models with instruction tuning. NIPS '23 (2023)
13. Devlin, J., Chang, M.W., Lee, K., Toutanova, K.: BERT: pre-training of deep bidirectional transformers for language understanding. In: In NAACL (2019)
14. Dosovitskiy, A., et al.: An image is worth 16x16 words: transformers for image recognition at scale. arXiv (2020)
15. Dou, Z.Y., et al.: An empirical study of training end-to-end vision-and-language transformers. In: In CVPR, pp. 18166–18176 (2022)
16. Fahim, M., et al.: Banglatlit: a benchmark dataset for back-transliteration of Romanized Bangla. In: Findings of the Association for Computational Linguistics: EMNLP 2024, pp. 14656–14672 (2024)
17. Faruk, A.M., Faraby, H.A., Azad, M.M., Fedous, M.R., Morol, M.K.: Image to Bengali caption generation using deep CNN and bidirectional gated recurrent unit. In: ICCIT (2020)
18. Gong, Y., Liu, G., Xue, Y., Li, R., Meng, L.: A survey on dataset quality in machine learning. Inf. Softw. Technol. **162**, 107268 (2023)
19. Gurari, D., et al.: Vizwiz grand challenge: answering visual questions from blind people. In: 2018 CVPR, pp. 3608–3617 (2018)
20. Haider, F., et al.: Banth: a multi-label hate speech detection dataset for transliterated Bangla. arXiv preprint arXiv:2410.13281 (2024)
21. He, K., Fan, H., Wu, Y., Xie, S., Girshick, R.: Momentum contrast for unsupervised visual representation learning. In: In the IEEE/CVF Conference on Computer Vision and Pattern Recognition, pp. 9729–9738 (2020)
22. He, K., Zhang, X., Ren, S., Sun, J.: Deep residual learning for image recognition. In: CVPR (2016)
23. He, P., Gao, J., Chen, W.: Debertav3: improving deberta using electra-style pretraining with gradient-disentangled embedding sharing. arXiv (2021)
24. Hendricks, L.A., Mellor, J., Schneider, Alayrac, J., Nematzadeh, A.: Decoupling the role of data, attention, and losses in multimodal transformers. TACL (2021)
25. Ishmam, M.F., Shovon, M.S.H., Mridha, M., Dey, N.: From image to language: a critical analysis of visual question answering (VQA) approaches, challenges, and opportunities. Inf. Fusion, 102270 (2024)
26. Islam, S., et al.: Note: towards devising an efficient VQA in the Bengali language (2022)
27. Johnson, J., Hariharan, B., van der Maaten, L., Fei-Fei, L., Lawrence Zitnick, C., Girshick, R.: Clevr: a diagnostic dataset for compositional language and elementary visual reasoning. In: CVPR (2017)
28. Khan, M.F., Shifath, S.S.U.R., Islam, M.S.: BAN-cap: a multi-purpose English-Bangla image descriptions dataset. In: LREC (2022)
29. Kim, W., Son, B., Kim, I.: Vilt: vision-and-language transformer without convolution or region supervision. In: ICML. PMLR (2021)
30. Li, B., et al.: LLaVA-onevision: easy visual task transfer. TMLR (2025)

31. Li, J., Li, D., Savarese, S., Hoi, S.: Blip-2: bootstrapping language-image pre-training with frozen image encoders and large language models. In: ICML (2023)
32. Li, J., Li, D., Xiong, C., Hoi, S.: Blip: bootstrapping language-image pre-training for unified vision-language understanding and generation. In: International Conference on Machine Learning, pp. 12888–12900. PMLR (2022)
33. Li, L.H., Yatskar, M., Yin, D.: Visualbert: a simple and performant baseline for vision and language. arXiv (2019)
34. Li, P., Liu, G., He, J., Zhao, Z., Zhong, S.: Masked vision and language pre-training with unimodal and multimodal contrastive losses for medical visual question answering. In: International Conference on Medical Image Computing and Computer-Assisted Intervention, pp. 374–383. Springer (2023)
35. Libovický, J., Rosa, R., Fraser, A.: How language-neutral is multilingual BERT? arXiv preprint arXiv:1911.03310 (2019)
36. Lin, Z., et al.: Medical visual question answering: a survey. AI Med. **143**, 102611 (2023)
37. Liu, H., Li, C., Li, Y., Lee, Y.J.: Improved baselines with visual instruction tuning. In: CVPR (2024)
38. Liu, Z., Mao, H., Wu, C.Y., Feichtenhofer, C., Darrell, T., Xie, S.: A convnet for the 2020s. In: CVPR (2022)
39. Mañas, O., Krojer, B., Agrawal, A.: Improving automatic VQA evaluation using large language models. In: The AAAI, vol. 5 (2024)
40. Marino, K., Rastegari, M., Farhadi, A., Mottaghi, R.: Ok-VQA: a visual question answering benchmark requiring external knowledge. In: The CVPR, pp. 3190–3199 (2019)
41. Quionero-Candela, J., Sugiyama, M., Schwaighofer, A., Lawrence, N.: Dataset shift in machine learning (2009)
42. Radford, A., et al.: Learning transferable visual models from natural language supervision. In: ICML. PMLR
43. Rafi, M., Islam, S., Labib, S.H.I., Hasan, S.S., Shah, F., Ahmed, S.: A deep learning-based Bengali visual question answering system (2022)
44. Rahman, M., Mohammed, N., Mansoor, N., Momen, S.: Chittron: an automatic Bangla image captioning system. In: The ICICT Procedia Computer Science (2019)
45. Romero, D., Lyu, C., Wibowo, H.A., Aji, A.F., et al.: CVQA: culturally-diverse multilingual visual question answering benchmark (2024)
46. Schwenk, D., Khandelwal, A., Clark, C., Marino, K., Mottaghi, R.: A-okvqa: a benchmark for visual question answering using world knowledge (2022)
47. Sermanet, P., Ichter, T.D.B., Cao, Y.: Robovqa: multimodal long-horizon reasoning for robotics (2023)
48. Shah, F., Humaira, M., Jim, M., Ami, A., Paul, S.: Bornon: Bengali image captioning with transformer-based deep learning approach. SN Comput. Sci. **3** (2022)
49. Tan, H., Bansal, M.: Lxmert: learning cross-modality encoder representations from transformers. arXiv preprint arXiv:1908.07490 (2019)
50. Tan, M., Le, Q.: Efficientnet: rethinking model scaling for convolutional neural networks. In: ICML. PMLR (2019)
51. Touvron, H., Cord, M., Douze, M., Massa, F., Sablayrolles, A., Jégou, H.: Training data-efficient image transformers & distillation through attention. In: International Conference on Machine Learnin, pp. 10347–10357. PMLR (2021)
52. Vaswani, A., et al.: Attention is all you need. Adv. Neural Inf. Process. Syst. **30** (2017)
53. Yue, X., Song, Y., Asai, A., Kim, S., et al.: Pangea: a fully open multilingual multimodal LLM for 39 languages. In: ICLR (2025)

54. Zhang, T., Kishore, V., Wu, F., Weinberger, K.Q., Artzi, Y.: Bertscore: evaluating text generation with BERT. arXiv preprint arXiv:1904.09675 (2019)
55. Zhuang, L., Wayne, L., Ya, S., Jun, Z.: A robustly optimized BERT pre-training approach with post-training. In: CNCCL (2021)

Revisiting Cross-Modal Knowledge Distillation: A Disentanglement Approach for RGBD Semantic Segmentation

Roger Ferrod[1,4](✉)[iD], Cássio F. Dantas[2,3][iD], Luigi Di Caro[1][iD], and Dino Ienco[2,3][iD]

[1] University of Turin, Turin, Italy
luigi.dicaro@unito.it
[2] INRAE, UMR TETIS, Univ. Montpellier, Montpellier, France
{cassio.fraga-dantas,dino.ienco}@inrae.fr
[3] EVERGREEN, Univ. Montpellier, Inria, Montpellier, France
[4] LIPADE, Univ. Paris Cité, 75006 Paris, France
roger.ferrod@unito.it

Abstract. Multi-modal RGB and Depth (RGBD) data are predominant in many domains such as robotics, autonomous driving and remote sensing. The combination of these multi-modal data enhances environmental perception by providing 3D spatial context, which is absent in standard RGB images. Although RGBD multi-modal data can be available to train computer vision models, accessing all sensor modalities during the inference stage may be infeasible due to sensor failures or resource constraints, leading to a mismatch between data modalities available during training and inference. Traditional Cross-Modal Knowledge Distillation (CMKD) frameworks, developed to address this task, are typically based on a teacher/student paradigm, where a multi-modal teacher distills knowledge into a single-modality student model. However, these approaches face challenges in teacher architecture choices and distillation process selection, thus limiting their adoption in real-world scenarios. To overcome these issues, we introduce CroDiNo-KD (Cross-Modal Disentanglement: a New Outlook on Knowledge Distillation), a novel cross-modal knowledge distillation framework for RGBD semantic segmentation. Our approach simultaneously learns single-modality RGB and Depth models by exploiting disentanglement representation, contrastive learning and decoupled data augmentation with the aim to structure the internal manifolds of neural network models through interaction and collaboration. We evaluated CroDiNo-KD on three RGBD datasets across diverse domains, considering recent CMKD frameworks as competitors. Our findings illustrate the quality of CroDiNo-KD, and they suggest reconsidering the conventional teacher/student paradigm to distill information from multi-modal data to single-modality neural networks. Source code is available here.

Keywords: Knowledge Distillation · Cross-modal · Disentanglement Learning · RGBD · Semantic Segmentation

1 Introduction

Multi-modal information, such as RGB and Depth (RGBD) imagery, is becoming predominant in a plethora of diverse domains including robotics, autonomous driving, augmented reality, healthcare and remote sensing. The combination of these complementary sources of information significantly enhances environmental perception by enriching traditional 2D images with 3D spatial context provided by the Depth modality.

Despite the advantages of multi-modal learning, real-world deployment faces practical challenges. While multi-modal data may be available during training, operational constraints often limit modality availability at inference time due to sensor failures or budget restrictions. This can result in a mismatch between training and testing data, which can impede the practical deployment of an RGBD multi-modal model. To address this challenge, it is essential to design frameworks that are resilient to missing modalities at test time, transferring multi-modal knowledge available during training into single-modality models that operate solely on either RGB or Depth information at inference time. To this purpose, Cross-Modal Knowledge Distillation (CMKD) frameworks have been introduced [1]. Conversely to traditional knowledge distillation techniques, which typically transfers knowledge from a large model to a smaller one using the same input data [2], CMKD enables the transfer of information across modalities. Existing CMKD frameworks typically adopt a teacher/student paradigm, transferring knowledge from a multi-modal teacher to a single-modality student. However, these methods are sensitive to design choices such as teacher architecture, fusion mechanisms and knowledge distillation techniques. Moreover, they require substantial computational resources associated with the training of multiple neural network models: a multi-modal teacher and separate single-modality students, one for each target modality.

With the aim to advance cross-modal knowledge distillation for RGB and Depth imagery, we introduce CroDiNo-KD (Cross-Modal Disentanglement: a New Outlook on Knowledge Distillation), a novel framework that goes beyond conventional teacher/student paradigm, dominant in the CMKD field. Rather than relying on a multi-modal teacher model to guide single-modality RGB or Depth models, CroDiNo-KD relaxes the need for a teacher model through a collaborative training strategy where single-modality models interact with each other via carefully designed loss functions. Our approach removes design decisions related to the teacher architecture and fusion mechanism and teacher/student knowledge distillation techniques. Furthermore, CroDiNo-KD reduces training resources in terms of computational time and parameter size while achieving superior results to recent approaches based on the common teacher/student paradigm.

Specifically, CroDiNo-KD jointly trains two single-modality neural networks using disentangled representation and contrastive learning. This process structures each model's internal manifold into modality-invariant and modality-specific features, capturing both shared and unique information from RGB and Depth modalities. Finally, the training process enables a flexible data augmentation strategy, eliminating the constraints of conventional CMKD framework that require paired augmentation techniques between modalities.

In summary, our contributions are threefold:

(i) We introduce a novel framework for cross-modal knowledge distillation based solely on the joint training of two single-modality models, offering an alternative to the traditional multi-modal teacher/student paradigm;
(ii) We are the first to explore disentanglement representation learning jointly with contrastive learning for RGBD cross-modal knowledge distillation, demonstrating the benefits of structuring internal models manifold into modality-invariant and modality-specific information;
(iii) We provide insights and discussion on the advantages of our framework beyond classification results, analyzing resource efficiency in terms of both computational training time and model size (parameters count).

We validate the effectiveness of CroDiNo-KD on three RGBD benchmarks for semantic segmentation across different application domains, demonstrating superior performance compared to recent state-of-the-art methods especially designed for semantic segmentation under cross-modal knowledge distillation.

2 Related Work

Knowledge Distillation (KD) is the process of transferring information from a large model (teacher) to a smaller one (student). Originally envisioned in [2] for classification tasks with the aim to provide a compact, smaller and faster model, yet performing comparably to the wider teacher model, it has been further refined and formalized by [3], where KD has been commonly implemented via a Kullback-Leibler (KL) divergence between teacher and student predictions. The KD framework can be formulated as follows:

$$\mathcal{L} = \alpha \mathcal{L}_{task} + (1 - \alpha)\mathcal{L}_{KD} \tag{1}$$

where $\mathcal{L}_{task}$ is the task-specific loss and $\mathcal{L}_{KD}$ the KL divergence between student and teacher predictions. By changing the way the KD loss is used, one could distill different kinds of knowledge: response-based [4], feature-based [5] or relation-based [6].

Beyond traditional approaches, KD has also been successfully applied to multi-modal learning [1]. Taking inspiration from the standard KD process, one can distill the knowledge from a multi-modal teacher to single-modality students [7], or from a single-modality teacher to a student working on a different modality [8]. Considering semantic segmentation, cross-modal KD has been proven to be effective over different applications [9]. For example, studies such as [10–16] explored RGBD segmentation with standard KD frameworks, while [17,18] performed similar experiments on RGBT (RGB+Thermal) dataset. Following works extended the standard cross-modal knowledge distillation approach by adding a generative task [19], via prototype learning [20] or by decomposing the KD loss function into magnitude and angular terms [21].

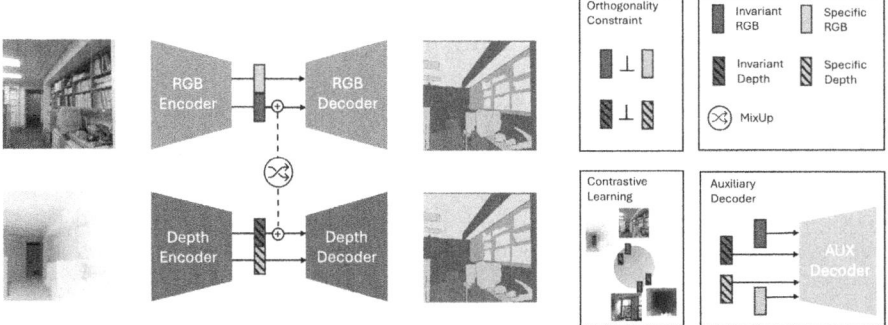

Fig. 1. Overview of the CroDiNo-KD architecture, composed by two encoder-decoder models, for both RGB and Depth modalities. In addition, an auxiliary decoder and a set of loss functions are adopted to enforce the desired disentanglement properties between modalities, i.e., modality-invariant and modality-specific features for both RGB and Depth information.

Differently from standard learning processes, disentanglement representation learning aims to explicitly decompose the feature representation into semantic factors carrying explainable and meaningful information [22]. Leveraged also in multi-modal scenarios (e.g., [23,24]) it can be used to learn modality-specific and modality-invariant features for the downstream task [25–27]. In particular, in [28] the authors successfully exploited disentanglement —together with adversarial learning— for cross-modal knowledge distillation in the context of scene classification. Inspired by this pioneering work, we further extended this research path onto dense classification, more precisely semantic segmentation.

3 Method

With the objective to overcome the limitations of current teacher/student paradigm, here we introduce CroDiNo-KD, a new cross-modal knowledge distillation framework that combines disentanglement representation learning, contrastive learning and decoupled data augmentation. Our approach simultaneously trains two single-modality models – one for RGB and another for Depth imagery – by exploiting modality interaction and collaboration during the training stage.

3.1 Proposed Framework

The overall framework, depicted in Fig. 1, consists of: i) two separate encoder-decoder models and ii) an auxiliary decoder, all trained with a set of carefully designed loss functions to structure the internal manifold representation of the single-modality models into modality-invariant and modality-specific features.

Given a batch of RGB images X_{RGB} and the corresponding Depth images X_D, with $X_{RGB} \in \mathbb{R}^{B \times H \times W \times 3}$ and $X_D \in \mathbb{R}^{B \times H \times W \times 1}$, we first encode them, via convolutional neural networks, into embedding representations Z_{RGB} and Z_D, respectively. Denoting generically $Z_m \in \mathbb{R}^{B \times h \times w \times F}$ with $m \in \{RGB, D\}$ we have:

$$Z_m = Enc_m(X_m) \qquad (2)$$

where B is the batch size, $H \times W$ the spatial dimension of the RGB and Depth images, $h \times w$ the spatial dimension of the embedding representations and F the number of output channels.

For each modality, once the encoded representation Z_m is obtained, we divide it into two separate embeddings Z_m^{inv} and Z_m^{spc}, with $Z_m^{inv}, Z_m^{spc} \in \mathbb{R}^{B \times h \times w \times F/2}$. During training, we then encourage Z_m^{inv} (resp. Z_m^{spc}) to encode modality-invariant (resp. modality-specific) information.

To generate segmentation outputs, the decoder takes as input the concatenated representation $[Z_m^{inv} : Z_m^{spc}]$, where $[:]$ denotes concatenation along the feature dimension. The auxiliary decoder, used only during training, follows a similar architecture but takes only half the channel dimension as input. While the decoder included in the main model relies on $[Z_m^{inv} : Z_m^{spc}]$ as input, the auxiliary one works separately on Z_{RGB}^{inv}, Z_{RGB}^{spc}, Z_D^{inv} and Z_D^{spc} to enforce every individual embedding representation to encode relevant information for the segmentation task.

With the aim to encourage invariant representation across modalities, we introduce a feature mixup strategy [29]. Precisely, we blended the RGB and Depth invariant embeddings, following the equations below, with $\lambda \in [0, 1]$:

$$\tilde{Z}_{RGB}^{inv} = \lambda Z_D^{inv} + (1-\lambda) Z_{RGB}^{inv}$$
$$\tilde{Z}_D^{inv} = \lambda Z_{RGB}^{inv} + (1-\lambda) Z_D^{inv} \qquad (3)$$

The augmented images $\tilde{Z}_m^{inv}$ are then processed by the main decoder and contribute to the final loss computation together with the original ones.

Losses: To enhance the performance of single-modality models through mutual interaction and collaboration, we design a set of loss functions that shape the models' internal manifold. The first term is a task-specific segmentation loss, modeled through Cross Entropy. More formally, we have:

$$\mathcal{L}_{seg}^m = CE\left(Dec_m([Z_m^{inv} : Z_m^{spc}]), Y\right) \qquad (4)$$

where CE denotes the pixel-wise cross-entropy loss, $Y \in \{1, \ldots, C\}^{B \times H \times W}$ is the ground-truth segmentation map over C classes and Dec_m the decoder for the modality $m \in \{RGB, D\}$.

Then, to explicitly constrain embeddings to encode complementary information (i.e., modality-invariant and modality-specific) we enforced orthogonality between the modality-invariant and modality-specific embeddings of the same modality $m \in \{RGB, D\}$ as follows:

$$\mathcal{L}_\perp^m = \frac{1}{B} \sum_{b=1}^{B} \sum_{i=1}^{h} \sum_{j=1}^{w} sim(Z_m^{inv}[b,i,j,:], Z_m^{spc}[b,i,j,:]) \quad (5)$$

where $Z_m[b,i,j,:] \in \mathbb{R}^{F/2}$ is the feature vector at spatial location ij in the feature map corresponding to the b-th sample in the batch and $sim(u,v) = \frac{u \cdot v}{||u||_2 ||v||_2}$ denotes the cosine similarity between vectors u and v.

Furthermore, we introduce a contrastive term to bring Z_{RGB}^{inv} and Z_D^{inv} closer together, to force the representation to be invariant with respect to the modality. To this end, we relied on the InfoNCE loss [30] with a negative Euclidean distance, contrasting a positive example (i.e., an RGB-Depth pair of the same instance) with in-batch negatives (i.e., all the remaining invariant embeddings inside the batch, both RGB and Depth). Let $p_m^{(b)} \in \mathbb{R}^{F/2}$ be the L2 normalized feature vector of the b-th instance obtained via spatial average pooling from Z_m^{inv}, that is:

$$p_m^{(b)} = \frac{\rho_m^{(b)}}{||\rho_m^{(b)}||_2}, \quad \text{with } \rho_m^{(b)} = \frac{1}{hw} \sum_{i=1}^{h} \sum_{j=1}^{w} Z_m^{inv}[b,i,j,:], \quad (6)$$

the contrastive loss is then formulated as:

$$\mathcal{L}_{con}^{RGB} = -\frac{1}{B} \sum_{i=1}^{B} \log \frac{exp(-||p_{RGB}^{(i)} - p_D^{(i)}||_2/\tau)}{\sum_{m \in \{RGB,D\}} \sum_{j \neq i} exp(-||p_{RGB}^{(i)} - p_m^{(j)}||_2/\tau)}$$
$$\mathcal{L}_{con}^{D} = -\frac{1}{B} \sum_{i=1}^{B} \log \frac{exp(-||p_D^{(i)} - p_{RGB}^{(i)}||_2/\tau)}{\sum_{m \in \{RGB,D\}} \sum_{j \neq i} exp(-||p_D^{(i)} - p_m^{(j)}||_2/\tau)} \quad (7)$$

where τ is the temperature parameter. In the first equation, the RGB modality serves as the anchor, while in the second equation, the Depth modality takes this role. In both cases, the numerator represents the positive pair, which corresponds to the embeddings of the same instance across different modalities. The denominator contains the negative samples, comprising all other invariant embeddings from both modalities within the batch, excluding the anchor itself.

To ensure that the embeddings independently encode relevant information for the segmentation task, we added an auxiliary segmentation loss that processes each embedding individually:

$$\mathcal{L}_{aux}^m = CE\left(Dec_{Aux}(Z_m^{inv}), Y\right) + CE\left(Dec_{Aux}(Z_m^{spc}), Y\right) \quad (8)$$

with Dec_{Aux} the auxiliary decoder.

Finally, the loss optimized by CroDiNo-KD is an unweighted combination of all the loss terms previously introduced:

$$\mathcal{L}_{tot} = \sum_{m \in \{RGB,D\}} \mathcal{L}_{con}^m + \mathcal{L}_{seg}^m + \mathcal{L}_\perp^m + \mathcal{L}_{aux}^m \quad (9)$$

Algorithm 1: CroDiNo-KD training procedure

input: RGB-Depth labeled dataset $\mathcal{D} = \{(X_{RGB}, X_D, Y)^{(i)}\}_{i=1}^{N}$

1 **for** epoch $\in \{1, \ldots, N_{ep}\}$ **do**
2   **forall the** batches $(X_{RGB}, X_D, Y) \in \mathcal{D}$ **do**
        // Decoupled Augmentations
3        $X_{RGB} = \text{Aug}(X_{RGB})$;
4        $X_D = \text{Aug}(X_D)$;
        // Encoder
5        $Z_{RGB}^{inv}, Z_{RGB}^{spc} \leftarrow Enc_{RGB}(X_{RGB})$;
6        $Z_D^{inv}, Z_D^{spc} \leftarrow Enc_D(X_D)$;
7   **for** $m \in \{RGB, D\}$ **do**
           // Define complementary modality
8           $\overline{m} = D$ **if** $m = RGB$ **else** $\overline{m} = RGB$
           // Feature mixup
9           $\tilde{Z}_m^{inv} \leftarrow \lambda Z_{\overline{m}}^{inv} + (1-\lambda)Z_m^{inv}$;
           // Main Semantic Segmentation task
10          $S_m \leftarrow Dec_m([Z_m^{inv} : Z_m^{spc}])$;
11          $\tilde{S}_m \leftarrow Dec_m([\tilde{Z}_m^{inv} : \tilde{Z}_m^{spc}])$;
12   Compute $\mathcal{L}_{seg}^m$ using $(S_m, \tilde{S}_m, Y)$ with Eq. (4);
           // Auxiliary Semantic Segmentation task
13          $A_m^{inv} \leftarrow Dec_{Aux}(Z_m^{inv})$;
14          $A_m^{spc} \leftarrow Dec_{Aux}(Z_m^{spc})$;
15   Compute $\mathcal{L}_{aux}^m$ using $(A_m^{inv}, A_m^{spc}, Y)$ with Eq. (8);
           // Disentanglement contrainsts
16   Compute $\mathcal{L}_\perp^m$ using (Z_m^{inv}, Z_m^{spc}) with Eq. (5);
17   Compute $\mathcal{L}_{con}^m$ using $(Z_m^{inv}, Z_{\overline{m}}^{inv})$ with Eqs. (6)–(7);
18   **end**
19        $\mathcal{L}_{tot} = \sum_{m \in \{RGB, D\}} \mathcal{L}_{seg}^m + \mathcal{L}_\perp^m + \mathcal{L}_{con}^m + \mathcal{L}_{aux}^m$
20   Update weights of $(Enc_{RGB}, Enc_D, Dec_{RGB}, Dec_D, Dec_{Aux})$ by back-propagating $\mathcal{L}_{tot}$
21   **end**
22 **end**
23 **return** $(Enc_{RGB}, Enc_D, Dec_{RGB}, Dec_D)$

Training Procedure: The training process, outlined in Algorithm 1, runs over a predefined number of epochs (N_{ep}). For each batch in an epoch, it starts by augmenting the RGB and Depth images, as commonly done in prior works [10,31]. However, unlike conventional CMKD frameworks, which enforce paired transformations for both RGB and Depth images, our approach relaxes this constraint by allowing independent per-modality augmentations, a strategy we term as *decoupled augmentation* (lines 3–4). Since RGB and Depth losses are computed separately, this strategy enables greater augmentation flexibility compared to approaches based on the standard teacher/student paradigm, where augmentation consistency across modalities is required.

Next, we extract both domain-invariant and domain-specific embeddings for RGB and Depth images using their respective encoders (lines 5–6). To enhance domain-invariant representations, we leverage feature mixup (line 9), which blends RGB and Depth features, enriching the decoder's training samples (lines 10–12). Additionally, an auxiliary decoder is used to enforce task discrimination for both modality-invariant and modality-specific feature representations, independently (lines 13–15).

To accommodate disentanglement representation learning properties, we use an orthogonality constraint between domain-invariant and domain-specific embeddings (line 16) and we rely on a contrastive loss (line 17) to encourage the RGB and Depth representations of the same instance to be closer to each other while ensuring separation from other instances within the same batch, regardless of the modality. Finally, the total loss is computed as an unweighted sum of all the previously computed losses across RGB and Depth modalities (line 19), back propagating the signal and updating the framework components accordingly.

4 Experiment

To assess the behavior of our framework, CroDiNo-KD, we conducted a comprehensive experimental evaluation using three RGBD benchmarks, comparing our approach against recent competitors in Cross-Modal Knowledge Distillation for semantic segmentation. Furthermore, we performed an ablation study to examine the contributions of individual CroDiNo-KD components and a sensitivity analysis on the hyperparameter λ, which controls the feature mixup strategy across modalities. Finally, we analyze and discuss the computational requirements of competing methods in terms of both training time and model size (parameter counts), emphasizing the advantages provided by CroDiNo-KD over competitors based on the conventional teacher-student paradigm.

Benchmarks: We selected three RGBD semantic segmentation datasets spanning diverse domains to ensure a broad evaluation: indoor scene segmentation, aerial imagery and synthetic drone flight data. Specifically, we considered the following benchmarks:

- **NYU Depth v2** [32]: dataset consisting of 1,449 pairs of indoor RGB and Depth images, labeled with 40 semantic classes. Each image has a resolution of 480 × 640 and is captured using Microsoft's Kinect. Following prior works [10,31,33], we split the dataset into 795 training pairs and 654 test pairs;
- **Potsdam** [34]: a remote sensing dataset comprising 38 scenes of true orthophotos with a ground resolution of 5 cm, annotated with 6 semantic classes. The dataset includes four-channel visual images (R-G-B-IR) and corresponding Digital Surface Models (DSM). For our experiments, we used IR-G-B images and the provided normalized DSMs. Each high-resolution 6,000 × 6,000 scene was divided into 500 × 500 crops with stride 1 and further resized to 256 × 256 due to computational constraints. This resulted in a total of 5,472 images. We followed the same training/test split as described in [35];

- **Mid-Air** [36]: a synthetically generated dataset designed for low-altitude drone flight segmentation, containing 79 min of flight data across different weather and seasonal conditions. It includes RGB images and stereo disparity depth maps annotated with 13 semantic classes. Given the large dataset size (over 400k frames) and computational limitations, we selected only a subset of images generated using Unreal Engine's PLE plugin during the spring season. We further subsampled the dataset by selecting one frame every 8 and downscaling the resolution from 1,024 × 1,024 to 256 × 256. This resulted in 6,859 images, which were split into training and test sets following the original benchmark.

Competing Methods: We compare our approach against several baselines and state-of-the-art CMKD methods for semantic segmentation. Specifically, we evaluate:

- Single-modality, either RGB or Depth, models which do not receive any distillation supervision (referred to as single-modality);
- A full multimodal architecture, corresponding to the teacher model (referred to as *multimodal*);
- Two standard knowledge distillation (KD) baselines [1] (referred to as $KDv1$ and $KDv2$);
- Four state-of-the-art CMKD frameworks, especially tailored for semantic segmentation in multi-modal scenario.

For KD baselines, we adopt the approaches proposed in [1]. These follow a standard KD framework (Eq. 1), where α controls the balance between task-specific loss and knowledge distillation. In particular, $KDv1$ sets $\alpha = 0$, meaning the student model learns exclusively from the teacher's soft labels, whereas $KDv2$ uses $\alpha = 0.5$, combining both the original ground-truth labels and the teacher's soft labels equally.

Regarding state-of-the-art CMKD competing frameworks, we consider the following approaches from the recent literature:

- **KD-Net** [9]: originally designed for medical imaging, KD-Net transfers knowledge from a multimodal teacher network to a single-modal student to handle missing modalities. It employs a generalized KD framework [37], utilizing both the teacher's soft labels and bottleneck logits alongside a task-specific loss (binary cross-entropy and Dice loss).
- Masked Generative Distillation (**Masked Dist.**) [19]: introduces a generative distillation task where the student learns to reconstruct a corrupted feature map using the teacher's features as a reference. The final loss consists of a task-specific segmentation loss and a generative distillation term. For the experimental evaluation, we use the encoders output as feature map to reconstruct.
- **ProtoKD** [20]: combines prototype learning with traditional knowledge distillation and segmentation loss. This method captures semantic correlations across the entire dataset by modeling intra- and inter-class feature variations,

transferring similarity maps from the teacher to the student. For the experimental evaluation, we consider the features of the decoder just before the logits computation.
- Layer-wise Angular Distillation (**LAD**) [21] and Channel-wise Angular Distillation (**CAD**) [21]: these methods extend conventional KD approaches by incorporating angular constraints on features. Similar to KD-Net, they perform distillation on both bottleneck features and logits. However, LAD applies layer-wise angular constraints, while CAD operates on channel-wise angular representations.

Experimental Settings: We adopted a consistent training setup across all methods and experiments, with 140 training epochs and batch size of 8. Optimization was performed using the AdamW optimizer with a staring learning rate of 10^{-8} and a learning rate schedule with 10 linear warmup epochs, reaching a target learning rate of 10^{-4}, followed by polynomial decay with power 0.9. Regarding CroDiNo-KD, the temperature τ and the feature mixup λ hyperparameters were set to 0.07 and 0.35, respectively. For data augmentation, we use random flipping, scaling, and cropping for both RGB and Depth images and color jittering only for RGB images, following common practices from previous research [10,31]. Model performance on the test set has been evaluated using the mean Intersection over Union (mIoU) metric. All experiments were conducted on a single NVIDIA A40 GPU with 48 GB of memory.

Implementation Details: To ensure a fair comparison, all the competing approaches share the same architecture, which follows a convolutional encoder-decoder design. For each modality, the encoder is based on a ResNet-50 network with dilated convolutions[1] and initialized with ImageNet-pretrained weights. In the Depth single-modality model, the first-layer weights are initialized by averaging the three-channel pretrained weights into a single-channel representation.

Segmentation outputs are generated using the DeepLabV3+ model [38], which integrates Atrous Spatial Pyramid Pooling (ASPP) and a skip connection linking the second convolutional layer of the ResNet backbone to the decoder.

The teacher model follows the ACNet [10] architecture, a commonly adopted multi-modal semantic segmentation framework for RGBD data. It consists of two ResNet-50 branches dedicated to RGB and Depth modalities, alongside a third ResNet-50 branch for fusing per-modality features. The fusion process is further refined through an Attention Complementary Module (ACM), which applies attention pooling, a 1×1 convolution followed by a sigmoid activation function, as introduced in ACNet. The DeepLabV3+ decoder then processes the fused representation. Figure 2 provides an overview of the teacher model architecture.

---

[1] The final pooling operation is removed and replaced with a $conv_{1 \times 1}$ projection, followed by batch normalization and a ReLU activation, reducing the feature dimensionality from 2048 to 1024.

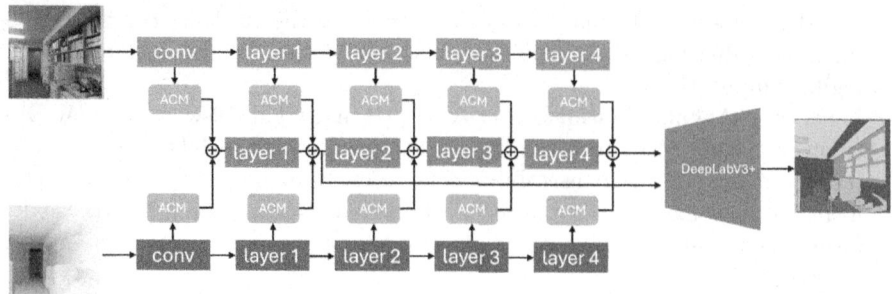

Fig. 2. Teacher model architecture used for the competing methods. It consists of ResNet50 branches for i) RGB ii) Depth and iii) fused representation encoding with an Attention Complementary Module (ACM) as proposed in ACNet [10]. A DeepLabV3+ decoder is added to generate semantic segmentation predictions.

4.1 Results

We present in Table 1 a comparison between the performances achieved by CroDiNo-KD and the competing methods described in the previous section, in terms of mIoU score. Specifically, we include the multi-modal teacher, single-modality models, standard KD baselines (Eq. 1) and state-of-the-art competitors. We highlight models that outperform the single-modality baseline with a green arrow and those that underperform the same baseline with a red arrow. To ensure a comprehensive evaluation, we assess each benchmark in two cross-modal distillation scenarios, transferring knowledge from multi-modal RGBD data to either the RGB or Depth modality.

We observe that CroDiNo-KD consistently outperforms all competitors across all benchmarks in both RGB and Depth cross-modal distillation scenarios. For the NYUDepth and Mid-Air datasets, the single-modality models are outperformed by the multimodal teacher. However, in the Postdam benchmark, both CroDiNo-KD and Masked Dist. produce RGB-based models that surpass the multimodal approach, achieving mIoU scores of 76.13 and 76.09, respectively, compared to the 74.98 mIoU achieved by the multimodal teacher. Notably, our framework stands out as the only one that consistently demonstrates improvements (green arrows) over the single-modality baselines across all cross-modal scenarios, delivering results that surpass the state-of-the-art methods in Cross-Modal Knowledge Distillation for the considered RGBD benchmarks.

Ablation. Table 2 presents the results of our ablation study, examining the contribution of individual components and loss terms in CroDiNo-KD. Our analysis reveals that the most significant performance drops occur when removing the auxiliary loss ($\mathcal{L}aux$) and the contrastive loss ($\mathcal{L}con$), indicating their crucial role in the framework. The impact of other components and loss terms remains comparable, with variations depending on the dataset. Overall, the highest performance is consistently achieved when all components are included, highlighting the rationale behind CroDiNo-KD.

Table 1. Mean Intersection over Union (mIoU) performances over the three considered benchmarks, comparing our model with the multi-modal teacher and single-modality models, as well as state-of-the-art competitors for CMKD semantic segmentation; green and red arrows indicate, respectively, improvement or reduction of scores with respect to the single-modality model.

Model	NYUDepth		Potsdam		Mid-Air	
	RGB	Depth	RGB	Depth	RGB	Depth
multimodal	46.92		74.98		51.21	
single-modality	42.64	36.01	75.73	42.47	47.84	47.07
KDv1 [39]	43.43 (↑)	36.44 (↑)	66.32 (↓)	39.20 (↓)	47.36 (↓)	45.80 (↓)
KDv2 [39]	43.86 (↑)	36.91 (↑)	66.24 (↓)	39.38 (↓)	47.62 (↓)	45.88 (↓)
KD-Net [9]	42.78 (↑)	36.36 (↑)	73.82 (↓)	41.85 (↓)	48.32 (↑)	46.22 (↓)
Masked Dist. [19]	40.97 (↓)	34.93 (↓)	76.09 (↑)	42.43 (↓)	47.60 (↓)	47.40 (↑)
ProtoKD [20]	43.82 (↑)	37.28 (↑)	66.64 (↓)	39.27 (↓)	47.11 (↓)	45.45 (↓)
LAD [21]	43.62 (↑)	36.86 (↑)	66.80 (↓)	39.31 (↓)	48.01 (↑)	46.98 (↓)
CAD [21]	43.48 (↑)	37.16 (↑)	66.43 (↓)	38.89 (↓)	48.21 (↑)	47.09 (↑)
CroDiNo-KD	**44.85** (↑)	**37.60** (↑)	**76.13** (↑)	**42.78** (↑)	**48.37** (↑)	**47.91** (↑)

Table 2. Analysis of the contributions of all the components of CroDiNo-KD in terms of mIoU.

	NYUDepth		Potsdam		Mid-Air		Avg
	RGB	Depth	RGB	Depth	RGB	Depth	
w/o $\mathcal{L}_\perp$	43.98	37.24	75.88	42.48	48.15	47.58	49.22
w/o $\mathcal{L}_{con}$	43.10	**37.96**	75.53	42.31	48.46	47.26	49.11
w/o $\mathcal{L}_{aux}$	44.84	37.62	75.55	**42.99**	47.08	46.44	49.09
w/o mixup	44.82	37.48	75.52	42.36	48.19	47.47	49.31
w/o dec. aug.	43.62	37.49	75.92	42.37	48.31	47.30	49.17
Original	**44.85**	37.60	**76.13**	42.78	**48.37**	**47.91**	**49.61**

Sensitivity Analysis. We explored the impact of varying the mixup hyperparameter λ (Eq. 3) from 0.05 to 0.5, adjusting the degree of feature mixup between domain-invariant RGB and Depth features. As shown in Table 3, performance remains relatively stable across this range, with no significant variation as highlighted by the standard deviation.

Segmentation Examples. Some qualitative segmentation examples on the Potsdam dataset are presented in Fig. 3. Here, we compare our method with best performing competitors (KD-Net and Masked Dist.) and the single-modality baseline. The analysis focuses on the RGB modality, as it provides greater visual detail. The results clearly show that all the CMKD frameworks provide a more precise and reliable segmentation mask compared to the one produced by the single-modality baseline. Among the different approaches, we can observe that the quality of segmentation examples is consistent with the quantitative results we have reported above.

Table 3. Sensitivity analysis on the feature mixup hyperparameter λ.

λ	NYUDepth		Potsdam		**Mid-Air**	
	RGB	Depth	RGB	Depth	RGB	Depth
0.05	44.55	37.66	75.90	42.66	48.16	46.82
0.1	44.67	37.72	76.09	42.71	47.95	46.96
0.2	44.64	37.82	76.06	42.59	48.17	47.04
0.35	44.85	37.60	76.13	42.78	48.37	47.91
0.5	44.53	37.50	75.99	42.39	48.13	47.41
std	0.13	0.12	0.09	0.15	0.15	0.44

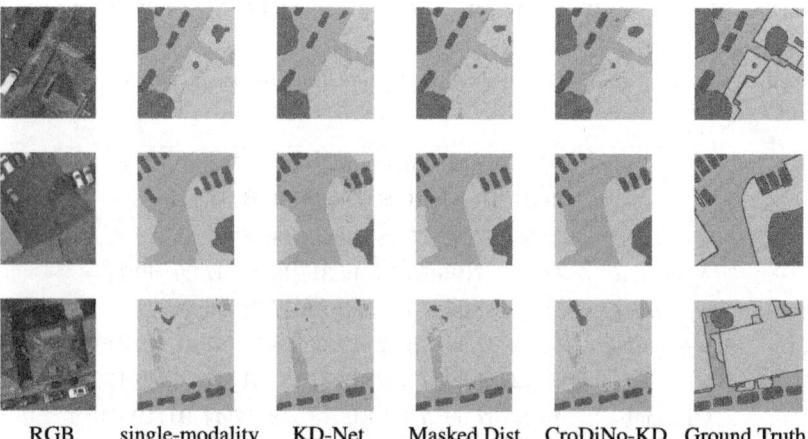

RGB single-modality KD-Net Masked Dist. CroDiNo-KD Ground Truth

Fig. 3. Example of qualitative results from Potsdam dataset.

To further inspect the behavior of our model, in Fig. 4 we depict the output of each per-modality branch, separately, on a few samples coming from the MidAir dataset. It could be noted that the input features may provide complementary information for the segmentation task, for example, in the second row the road is perfectly detected via the RGB sensor, while in the third row the Depth map provides useful information given the lack of visibility, due to fog, on the RGB image.

Table 4. Training time in GPU hours.

Model	GPU hours		
	Main	Teacher	Tot.
Single-Modality	14 h 52 m	–	14 h 52 m
KDv1/KDv2	22 h	14 h	36 h
KD-Net	22 h 46 m	14 h	36 h 46 m
Masked Dist.	47 h 22 m	14 h	61 h 22 m
ProtoKD	25 h 02 m	14 h	39 h 02 m
LAD	22 h 26 m	14 h	36 h 26 m
CAD	38 h 24 m	14 h	52 h 24 m
CroDiNo-KD	20 h 30 m	–	20 h 30 m

Table 5. Models' size in terms of parameters counts at training time.

Model	Num. of Params.			
	Main	Aux	Teacher	Tot.
Single-Modality	80M	–	–	80M
KDv1/KDv2	80M	–	98M	178M
KD-Net	80M	–	98M	178M
Masked Dist.	80M	150M	98M	328M
ProtoKD	80M	–	98M	178M
LAD/CAD	80M	–	98M	178M
CroDiNo-KD	68M	5M	–	73M

Training Time and Model Size. To further emphasize the advantages of CroDiNo-KD, we compare models performance in terms of total training time and model size (parameters count). Table 4 presents the complete training time for all competing methods on the MidAir dataset for training both RGB and Depth single-modality models. We report the training time[2] for the distillation process (referred as **Main**), the one for the teacher training (referred as **Teacher**) and the total one (referred as **Tot.**) CroDiNo-KD exhibits the shortest training time for the distillation process, completing both RGB and Depth single-modality models training in less than twenty-one hours. Furthermore, unlike our approach, all CMKD methods require pre-training a teacher model, adding an extra 14 h overhead to the total training time. Such analysis clearly demonstrates the advantage, in terms of training time, of CroDiNo-KD over standard teacher/student CMKD frameworks.

Table 5 compares the number of parameters required by competing frameworks during training. We categorize the parameters into: those required for the main architecture (**Main**), those used for auxiliary tasks which are discarded during inference such as the generative decoder in the *Masked Dist.* model (**Aux**), the parameters of the teacher model (**Teacher**) and the total per framework parameters (**Tot.**). CroDiNo-KD has fewer parameters in its main architecture compared to competing models, due to the practical choice to reduce the encoder's extracted features to accommodate the disentanglement representation process. The auxiliary parameters in CroDiNo-KD, associated with the auxiliary decoder, remain negligible compared to the overall model size. Furthermore, by eliminating the need for a computationally demanding multi-modal teacher, our approach requires less than half the parameters of the second smallest CMKD framework, thus highlighting the parameter-efficient design of CroDiNo-KD.

---

[2] Training times are reported in GPU hours, meaning the equivalent training duration without parallelization.

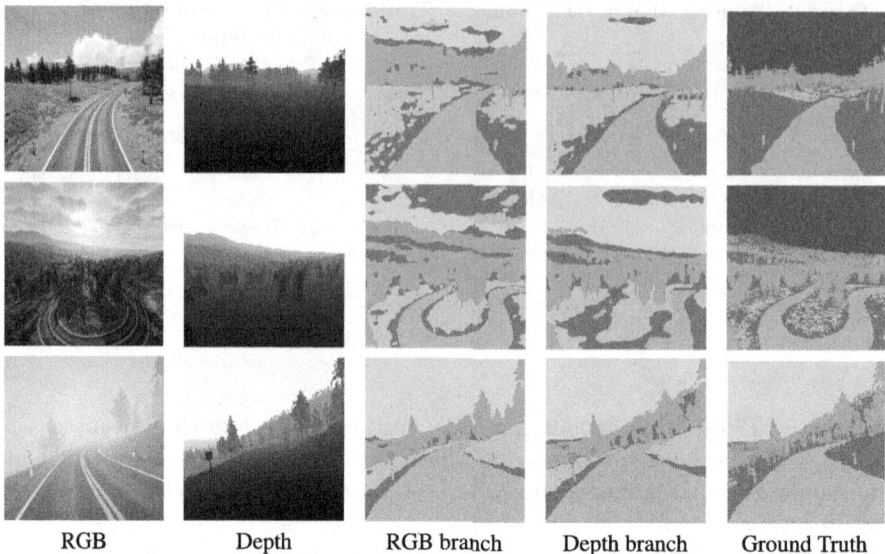

Fig. 4. Example of qualitative results from CroDiNo-KD predictions over the MidAir dataset.

5 Conclusion

In this paper, we propose CroDiNo-KD, a novel framework for RGBD Cross-Modal Knowledge Distillation (CMKD). Unlike conventional teacher/student approaches, our framework facilitates knowledge transfer between single-modality models without requiring a multi-modal teacher. This is achieved by leveraging disentanglement representation learning, contrastive learning and decoupled data augmentation. Through carefully designed loss functions, our method structures the internal manifolds of the single-modality models to account for both modality-invariant and modality-specific features. This approach harnesses the synergy between RGB and Depth modalities to enhance semantic segmentation performance in scenarios where mismatches exist between the data modalities accessible during training and inference. Our evaluation demonstrates the quality of CroDiNo-KD over baselines and state-of-the-art CMKD frameworks, considering both classification performance and computational efficiency during training. Furthermore, our findings invite reconsidering the traditional teacher/student paradigm for distilling information from multi-modal data to single-modality neural networks in the context of semantic segmentation.

References

1. Xue, Z., Gao, Z., Ren, S., Zhao, H.: The modality focusing hypothesis: towards understanding crossmodal knowledge distillation. In: ICLR (2022)
2. Bucila, C., Caruana, R., Niculescu-Mizil, A.: Model compression. In: KDD (2006)
3. Hinton, G.E., Vinyals, O., Dean, J.: Distilling the knowledge in a neural network. ArXiv, vol. abs/1503.02531 (2015)
4. Jin, Y., Wang, J., Lin, D.: Multi-level logit distillation. In: CVPR, pp. 24276–24285 (2023)
5. Guo, Z., Yan, H., Li, H., Lin, X.L.: Class attention transfer based knowledge distillation. CVPR, pp. 11868–11877 (2023)
6. Huang, T., You, S., Wang, F., Qian, C., Xu, C.: Knowledge distillation from a stronger teacher. ArXiv, vol. abs/2205.10536 (2022)
7. Liu, B., et al.: Lite-MKD: a multi-modal knowledge distillation framework for lightweight few-shot action recognition. In: ACM Multimedia (2023)
8. Hafner, F.M., Bhuyian, A.H., Kooij, J.F.P., Granger, E.: Cross-modal distillation for RGB-depth person re-identification. Comput. Vis. Image Underst. **216**, 103352 (2018)
9. Hu, M., et al.: Knowledge distillation from multi-modal to mono-modal segmentation networks. ArXiv, vol. abs/2106.09564 (2020)
10. Hu, X., Yang, K., Fei, L., Wang, K.: ACNet: attention based network to exploit complementary features for RGBD semantic segmentation. In: ICIP, pp. 1440–1444 (2019)
11. Xu, X., Kong, L., Shuai, H., Liu, Q.: FRNet: frustum-range networks for scalable lidar segmentation. ArXiv, vol. abs/2312.04484 (2023)
12. Hazirbas, C., Ma, L., Domokos, C., Cremers, D.: FuseNet: incorporating depth into semantic segmentation via fusion-based CNN architecture. In: Lai, S.-H., Lepetit, V., Nishino, K., Sato, Y. (eds.) ACCV 2016. LNCS, vol. 10111, pp. 213–228. Springer, Cham (2017). https://doi.org/10.1007/978-3-319-54181-5_14
13. Couprie, C., Farabet, C., Najman, L., LeCun, Y.: Indoor semantic segmentation using depth information. arXiv (2013)
14. Yang, J., Bai, L., Sun, Y., Tian, C., Mao, M., Wang, G.: Pixel difference convolutional network for RGB-D semantic segmentation. IEEE Trans. Circ. Sys. Video Tech. **34**, 1481–1492 (2023)
15. Lee, S., Park, S.J., Hong, K.S.: RDFNet: RGB-D multi-level residual feature fusion for indoor semantic segmentation. In: ICCV, pp. 4990–4999 (2017)
16. Jiang, J., Zheng, L., Luo, F., Zhang, Z.: RedNet: residual encoder-decoder network for indoor RGB-D semantic segmentation. ArXiv, vol. abs/1806.01054 (2018)
17. Lv, Y., Liu, Z., Li, G.: Context-aware interaction network for RGB-T semantic segmentation. IEEE Trans. Multimed. **26**, 6348–6360 (2024)
18. Sun, Y., Zuo, W., Yun, P., Wang, H., Liu, M.: FuseSeg: Semantic segmentation of urban scenes based on RGB and thermal data fusion. IEEE Trans. Autom. Sci. Eng. **18**(3), 1000–1011 (2021)
19. Yang, Z., Li, Z., Shao, M., Shi, D., Yuan, Z., Yuan, C.: Masked generative distillation. In: ECCV (2022)
20. Wang, S., Yan, Z., Zhang, D., Wei, H., Li, Z., Li, R.: Prototype knowledge distillation for medical segmentation with missing modality. In: ICASSP (2023)
21. Liu, T., Chen, C., Yang, X., Tan, W.: Rethinking knowledge distillation with raw features for semantic segmentation. In: WACV, pp. 1144–1153 (2024)

22. Wang, X., Chen, H., Wu, Z., Zhu, W., et al.: Disentangled representation learning. IEEE Trans. Pattern Anal. Mach. Intell. (2024)
23. Tsai, Y.H.H., Pu Liang, P., Zadeh, A, Morency, L.P., Salakhutdinov, R.: Learning factorized multimodal representations. ArXiv, vol. abs/1806.06176 (2018)
24. Zhang, Y., Zhang, Y., Guo, W., Cai, X., Yuan, X.: Learning disentangled representation for multimodal cross-domain sentiment analysis. IEEE Trans. Neural Net. Learn. Syst. **34**(10), 7956–7966 (2023)
25. Xu, Z., et al.: Predict, prevent, and evaluate: Disentangled text-driven image manipulation empowered by pre-trained vision-language model. In: CVPR, pp. 18208–18217 (2021)
26. Yu, Y., et al.: Towards counterfactual image manipulation via CLIP. In: ACM Multimedia (2022)
27. Materzyńska, J., Torralba, A., Bau, D.: Disentangling visual and written concepts in CLIP. In: CVPR (2022)
28. Ienco, D., Dantas, C.F.: Discom-kd: cross-modal knowledge distillation via disentanglement representation and adversarial learning. In: BMVC (2024)
29. Zhang, H., Cissé, M., Dauphin, Y., Lopez-Paz, D.: Mixup: beyond empirical risk minimization. ArXiv, vol. abs/1710.09412 (2017)
30. van den Oord, A., Li, Y., Vinyals, O.: Representation learning with contrastive predictive coding. ArXiv, vol. abs/1807.03748 (2018)
31. Wan, Z., et al.: Sigma: siamese mamba network for multi-modal semantic segmentation. ArXiv, vol. abs/2404.04256 (2024)
32. Kohli, P. Silberman, N., Hoiem, D., Fergus, R.: Indoor segmentation and support inference from RGBD images. In: ECCV, 2012
33. Girdhar, R., Singh, M, Ravi, N., van der Maaten, L., Joulin, A., Misra, I.: Omnivore: A single model for many visual modalities. In: CVPR, pp. 16081–16091 (2022)
34. ISPRS. Urban modelling and semantic labelling benchmark (2024). https://www.isprs.org/education/benchmarks/UrbanSemLab/default.aspx
35. Kieu, N. Nguyen, K., Sridharan, S., Fookes, C.: General-purpose multimodal transformer meets remote sensing semantic segmentation. ArXiv, vol. abs/2307.03388 (2023)
36. Fonder, M., Droogenbroeck, M.: Mid-air: a multi-modal dataset for extremely low altitude drone flights. In: CVPRW (2019)
37. Lopez-Paz, D., Bottou, L., Scholkopf, B., Naumovich Vapnik, V.: Unifying distillation and privileged information. ArXiv, vol. abs/1511.03643 (2015)
38. Chen, L.C., Zhu, Y., Papandreou, G., Schroff, F., Adam, H.: Encoder-decoder with atrous separable convolution for semantic image segmentation. In: ECCV (2018)
39. Xue, Z., Gao, Z., Ren, S., Zhao, H.: The modality focusing hypothesis: towards understanding crossmodal knowledge distillation. In: ICLR (2023)

Revisiting Multi-modal Emotion Learning with Broad State Space Models and Probability-Guidance Fusion

Yuntao Shou[1], Tao Meng[1(✉)], Wei Ai[1], and Keqin Li[2]

[1] College of Computer and Mathematics, Central South University of Forestry and Technology, Changsha 410004, Hunan, China
shouyuntao@stu.xjtu.edu.cn, {mengtao,aiwei}@hnu.edu.cn
[2] Department of Computer Science, State University of New York, New Paltz, New Paltz, NY 12561, USA
lik@newpaltz.edu

Abstract. Multi-modal Emotion Recognition in Conversation (MERC) has received considerable attention in various fields, e.g., human-computer interaction and recommendation systems. Most existing works perform feature disentanglement and fusion to extract emotional contextual information from multi-modal features. After revisiting the characteristic of MERC, we argue that long-range contextual semantic information should be extracted in the feature disentanglement stage and the inter-modal semantic information consistency should be maximized in the feature fusion stage. Inspired by recent State Space Models (SSMs), Mamba can efficiently model long-distance dependencies. Therefore, in this work, we fully consider the above insights to further improve the performance of MERC. Specifically, on the one hand, in the feature disentanglement stage, we propose a Broad Mamba, which does not rely on a self-attention mechanism for sequence modeling, but uses state space models to compress emotional representation, and utilizes broad learning systems to explore the potential data distribution in broad space. Different from previous SSMs, we design a bidirectional SSM convolution to extract global context information. On the other hand, we design a multi-modal fusion strategy based on probability guidance to maximize the consistency of information between modalities. Experimental results show that the proposed method can overcome the computational and memory limitations of Transformer when modeling long-distance contexts, and has great potential to become a next-generation general architecture.

Keywords: Multi-modal Emotion Recognition · State Space Models · Multi-modal Fusion

1 Introduction

Emotion recognition in conversation [36–38,43] has received considerable research attention and has been widely used in various fields, e.g., emotion analysis [14] and public opinion warning [44], etc. Recently, research on Multi-modal Emotion Recognition in Conversation (MERC) has mainly focused on multimodality, i.e., text, video and audio [3,25]. As shown in Fig. 1, MERC aims to identify emotion labels in sentences with text, video, and audio information. Unlike previous work [17] that only uses text information for emotion recognition, MERC improves the model's emotion understanding capabilities by introducing audio and video information. The introduction of audio and video alleviates the limitation of insufficient semantic information caused by relying solely on text features.

Many existing works [24,35,40] improve the performance of MERC by effectively extracting contextual semantic information of different modalities and fusing inter-modal complementary semantic information. By revisiting the characteristics of MERC, we argue that the core idea of MERC includes a feature disentanglement step and a feature fusion step.

Fig. 1. An illustrative example of multi-modal emotion recognition in conversation. For each given sentence, it contains three modal information about the speaker, i.e., text, video and audio. The task of MERC is to identify the emotional labels contained in the three modal information.

Specifically, the goal of feature disentanglement is to extract the contextual semantic information most relevant to emotional features in multi-modal features [42]. Recent work on Transformers [21] has achieved great success in modeling long-range contextual semantic information. Compared with traditional Recurrent Neural Networks (RNNs) [20,27], the advantage of Transformer is that it can effectively provide global contextual semantic information through the attention mechanism in parallel. However, the quadratic complexity of the self-attention mechanism in Transformers poses challenges in terms of speed and memory when dealing with long-range context dependencies. Inspired by the state space models, Mamba with linear complexity is proposed to achieve efficient training and inference. Mamba's excellent scaling performance shows that it is a promising Transformer alternative for context modeling. Therefore, to efficiently extract long-distance contextual semantic information, we designed the broad Mamba, which incorporates the SSMs for data-dependent global emotional context modeling, and a broad learning system to explore the potential data distribution in the broad space. Different from previous SSMs, we design a bidirectional SSM convolution to extract global context information. In addition, we also introduce position encoding information to improve SSMs' ability to understand sequences at different positions.

After completing feature disentanglement, the model needs to perform feature fusion to maximize the consistency of information between different modalities. The core idea of feature fusion is to assign different weights by determining the importance of different modal features to downstream tasks. Many cross-modal feature fusions have been proposed in existing MERC research, e.g., tensor fusion network [45], graph fusion network [34,46], attention fusion [32]. However, the feature fusion process in previous works is relatively coarse-grained and cannot actually determine the contribution of each modal feature to downstream tasks. We argue that label information plays an important role in guiding multi-modal information fusion. Therefore, how to properly fuse multi-modality and determine the contribution of multi-modal features to downstream tasks in a fine-grained manner remains a challenge.

To tackle the above problems, we propose an effective probability-guided fusion mechanism to achieve multi-modal contextual feature fusion, which utilizes the predicted label probability of each modal feature as the weight vectors of the modal features. Compared with other feature fusion models for emotion recognition tasks, the proposed fusion method can utilize the predicted label probability information in a fine-grained manner to actually determine the contribution of different modal features to the emotion prediction task.

To evaluate the effectiveness and efficiency of our proposed method, we conduct extensive experiments on two widely used benchmark datasets, IEMOCAP and MELD. In fact, the proposed method achieves state-of-the-art performance with low computational consumption, and experimental results demonstrate its effectiveness and efficiency.

Overall, our main contributions can be summarized as follows:

- We propose a Broad Mamba, which combines a broad learning system for searching abstract emotional features in a broad space and a SSM for data-dependent global emotional context information extraction. Different from previous SSMs, we design a bidirectional SSM convolution to extract global context information.
- We propose an effective probability-guided fusion mechanism to achieve multi-modal contextual feature fusion, which utilizes the predicted label probability of each modal feature as the weight vectors of the modal features.
- We conduct extensive experiments on the IEMOCAP and MELD datasets. Experimental results show that our proposed method achieves superior performance compared with the well-established Transformer or GNN architectures.

2 Related Work

2.1 Multi-modal Emotion Recognition in Conversation

In the early eras, GRU [5] and LSTM [13] are the de-facto standard network designs for Natural Language Processing (NLP). Many recurrent neural network architectures [10,11,20,27] have been proposed for various Multi-modal Emotion Recognition in Conversation (MERC). The pioneering work, Transformer changed the landscape by enabling efficient parallel computing under the premise of long sequence modeling. Transformer treats text as a series of 1D sequence data and applies an attention architecture to achieve sequence modeling. Transformer's surprising results on long sequence modeling and its scalability have encouraged considerable follow-up work for MERC [4,22,33]. One line of works focus on achieving intra-modal and inter-modal information fusion. For example, CTNet [23] proposes a single Transformer and cross Transformer. CKETF [7] constructs a Context and Knowledge Enriched Transformer. TL-ERC applies the Transformer with the transfer learning. Another pioneering work,

Graph Neural Network (GNN) further improved the performance of ERC. The core idea of GNN is to learn the representation of nodes or graphs through the feature information of nodes and the connection relationships in the graph structure [46]. For instance, DialogueGCN [6] proposes to use context information to build dialogue graphs. DER-GCN [1] fuses event relationships into speaker relationship graphs.

2.2 State Space Models

The State Space Models (SSMS) is used to describe the dynamic change process consisting of observed values and unknown internal state variables. Gu et al. [9] proposes a Structured State Space Sequence (S4) model, an alternative to the Transformer architecture that models long-range dependencies without using attention. The property of linear complexity of state space sequence lengths has received considerable research attention. Smith et al. [39] improves S4 by introducing MIMO SSM and efficient parallel scanning into the S4 layer to achieve parallel initialization and state reset of the hidden layer. He et al. [12] proposes introducing dense connection layers into SSM to improve the feature representation ability of shallow hidden layer states. Mehta et al. [28] improves the memory ability of the hidden layer by introducing gated units on S4. Recently, Gu et al. [8] proposes the general language model Mamba, which has better sequence modeling capabilities than Transformers and is linearly complex. Zhu et al. [47] introduces bidirectional SSM based on Mamba to improve the context information representation of the hidden layer.

3 Preliminary Information

3.1 Multi-modal Feature Extraction

Following previous work [26], we use RoBerta in this paper to obtain context-embedded representations of text. For video and audio features, following previous work [19], we utilize DenseNet and openSMILE for feature extraction and obtain video embedding features ξ_v and audio embedding features ξ_a, respectively.

3.2 State Space Model

The State Space Model (SSMs) is an efficient sequence modeling model that can capture the dynamic changes of data over time. A typical SSM consists of a state equation and an observation equation, where the state equation describes the dynamic changes within the system, and the observation equation describes the connection between the system state and observations. Given an input $x(t) \in \mathbb{R}$ and a hidden state $h(t) \in \mathbb{R}$, $y(t)$ is obtained mathematically through a linear ordinary differential equations (ODE) as follows:

$$h'(t) = \mathbf{A}h(t) + \mathbf{B}x(t), y(t) = \mathbf{C}h(t) \tag{1}$$

where $\mathbf{A} \in \mathbb{R}^{N \times N}$ is the evolution parameter and $\mathbf{B} \in \mathbb{R}^{N \times 1}, \mathbf{C} \in \mathbb{R}^{1 \times N}$ are the projection parameters, and N is the latent state size.

Inspired by SSM, Mamba discretizes ODEs to achieve computational efficiency. Mamba discretizes the evolution parameter **A** and the projection parameter **B** by introducing a timescale parameter Δ to obtain $\overline{\mathbf{A}}$ and $\overline{\mathbf{B}}$. The formula is defined as follows:

$$\overline{\mathbf{A}} = \exp(\Delta \mathbf{A}), \overline{\mathbf{B}} = (\Delta \mathbf{A})^{-1}(\exp(\Delta \mathbf{A}) - \mathbf{I}) \cdot \Delta \mathbf{B} \tag{2}$$

In practice, we use a first-order Taylor series to obtain an approximation of $\overline{\mathbf{B}}$ as follows:

$$\overline{\mathbf{B}} = (e^{\Delta \mathbf{A}} - \mathbf{I})\mathbf{A}^{-1}\mathbf{B} \approx (\Delta \mathbf{A})(\Delta \mathbf{A})^{-1}\Delta \mathbf{B} = \Delta \mathbf{B} \tag{3}$$

After obtaining the discretized $\overline{\mathbf{A}}$ and $\overline{\mathbf{B}}$, we rewrite Eq. 1 as follows:

$$h_t = \overline{\mathbf{A}} h_{t-1} + \overline{\mathbf{B}} x_t, y_t = \mathbf{C} h_t + \mathbf{D} x_t \tag{4}$$

and then the output is computed via global convolutiona as follows:

$$\overline{\mathbf{K}} = (\mathbf{C}\overline{\mathbf{B}}, \mathbf{C}\overline{\mathbf{A}}\overline{\mathbf{B}}, \ldots, \mathbf{C}\overline{\mathbf{A}}^M \overline{\mathbf{B}}), \mathbf{y} = \mathbf{x} * \overline{\mathbf{K}} + \mathbf{x} * \mathbf{D} \tag{5}$$

We adopted Mamba as a sequence modeling method in this work since Mamba can efficiently process sequence data without significant performance degradation.

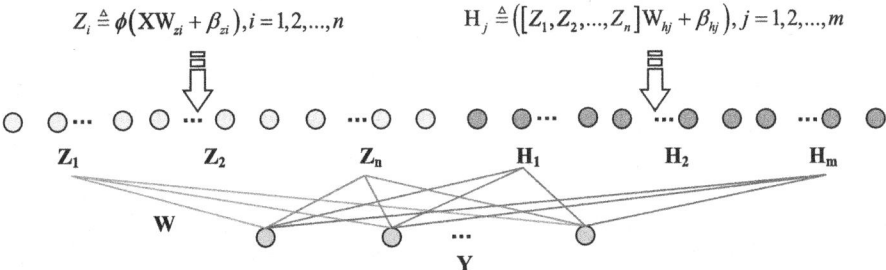

Fig. 2. The overall architecture of Broad Learning System (BLS). $\mathbf{Z}_i$ represents the feature nodes, $\mathbf{H}_i$ represents the enhancement nodes, and $\mathbf{Y}$ represents the predicted labels.

3.3 Broad Learning System

Broad Learning System (BLS) is different from traditional deep learning methods that it mainly focuses on discovering the relationship between features in the input data, rather than extracting features through multi-level nonlinear transformations. The core idea of BLS is to jointly solve the optimization problem by integrating the semantic information of feature nodes and enhancement nodes. The overall process of the BLS algorithm is shown in the Fig. 2.

Specifically, for a given input data $\mathbf{X} \in \mathbb{R}^{N \times M}$, where N represents the number of samples and M represents the dimension of the feature. The generated feature nodes are defined as follows:

$$\mathbf{Z}_i \triangleq \phi(\mathbf{X}\mathbf{W}_{z_i} + \beta_{z_i}), i = 1, 2, \ldots, n \tag{6}$$

where $\mathbf{W}_{z_i} \in \mathbb{R}^{M \times d_z}$ and $\beta_z \in \mathbb{R}^{1 \times d_z}$ are the learnable parameters. d_z is the embedding dimensions of generated features and ϕ is the activation function. The set of

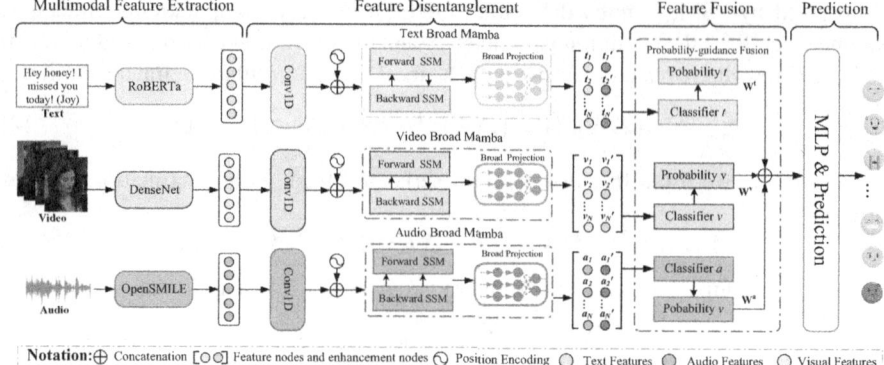

Fig. 3. The overall framework of the proposed model. Specifically, we first input the extracted multi-modal features into a 1-D convolutional layer for multi-scale feature extraction and introduce position encoding information to consider the position information of the series in the context. Then we input the obtained multi-modal features with multi-scale information into Broad Mamba to extract contextual semantic information and explore the potential data distribution in the broad space. Finally, we use a probability-guidance fusion model to complete the fusion of multi-modal features and achieve emotion prediction.

generated feature nodes is represented as $\mathbf{Z}^n \triangleq [\mathbf{Z}_1, \ldots, \mathbf{Z}_n]$, n is the size of the set of generated feature nodes. Similarly, enhancement node features are defined as follows:

$$\mathbf{H}_j \triangleq \phi(\mathbf{Z}\mathbf{W}_{h_j} + \beta_{h_j}), j = 1, 2, \ldots, m \tag{7}$$

where $\mathbf{W}_{h_i} \in \mathbb{R}^{d_z \times d_h}$ and $\beta_z \in \mathbb{R}^{1 \times d_h}$ are the learnable parameters. d_h is the embedding dimensions of enhancement features. The set of enhancement feature nodes is represented as $\mathbf{H}^m \triangleq [\mathbf{H}_1, \ldots, \mathbf{H}_m]$.

The final model output by concatenating feature nodes and enhancement nodes is as follows:

$$\mathbf{Y} = [\mathbf{Z}_1, \ldots, \mathbf{Z}_n | \mathbf{H}_1, \ldots, \mathbf{H}_m]\mathbf{W} = [\mathbf{Z}^n | \mathbf{H}^m]\mathbf{W} \tag{8}$$

where $\mathbf{W}$ are the learnable parameters (Fig. 3).

4 The Proposed Method

4.1 Feature Disentanglement

1D-Conv. To capture features of different scales and abstraction levels in multi-modal features (e.g., information such as the relationship between words and the importance of utterance), we input text features $\boldsymbol{\xi}_t$, video features $\boldsymbol{\xi}_v$ and audio features $\boldsymbol{\xi}_a$ into a 1D convolutional network (Conv1D) as follows:

$$\hat{\boldsymbol{\xi}}_t/\hat{\boldsymbol{\xi}}_a/\hat{\boldsymbol{\xi}}_v = Conv1D_{t/a/v}(\boldsymbol{\xi}_t, \boldsymbol{\xi}_a, \boldsymbol{\xi}_v) \tag{9}$$

where $\hat{\boldsymbol{\xi}}_t \in \mathbb{R}^{T_t \times d_m}$, $\hat{\boldsymbol{\xi}}_a \in \mathbb{R}^{T_a \times d_m}$, and $\hat{\boldsymbol{\xi}}_v \in \mathbb{R}^{T_v \times d_m}$, T_t, T_a, T_v represent the feature dimensions of text, audio, and video respectively, d_m represents the output feature dimensions.

Furthermore, to facilitate the model to capture the dependencies between long-distance positions in the sequence, we introduce sine and cosine position encoding embedding as follows:

$$PE_{(pos,2i)} = \sin\left(\frac{pos}{10000^{2i/d}}\right), PE_{(pos,2i+1)} = \cos\left(\frac{pos}{10000^{2i/d}}\right) \quad (10)$$

where pos represents the position in the sequence. i represents the dimension index of position encoding, $i = 0, 1, ..., D-1$. D represents the embedded dimension. We input $\hat{\xi}_t, \hat{\xi}_a, and \hat{\xi}_v$ ($\hat{\xi}_t, \hat{\xi}_a, \hat{\xi}_v = Conv1D_{t/a/v}(\xi_t, \xi_a, \xi_v) + PE$) that encodes position information at each time step into Broad Mamba.

Broad Mamba. The overall architecture of the proposed Broad Mamba is shown in Fig. 4. In order to aggregate the contextual semantic information from the forward and backward directions, we build a bidirectional SSM convolution module. Specifically, the first kernel $\overleftarrow{\kappa}$ performs a 1D convolution operator to obtain forward context information. The second kernel $\overrightarrow{\kappa}$ performs a 1D convolution operator to obtain the mutual information associated with emotional information, and we add the two convolved results. The overall operating process is formally defined as follows:

$$\bar{\xi}_j^{t/a/v} = \sum_{l \leq j} \overleftarrow{\kappa}_{j-l}^{t/a/v} \odot \hat{\xi}_l^{t/a/v} + \sum_{l \geq j} \overrightarrow{\kappa}_{l-j}^{t/a/v} \odot \hat{\xi}_l^{t/a/v} + d^{t/a/v} \odot \hat{\xi}_j^{t/a/v} = \text{BiSSM}(\hat{\xi}_j^{t/a/v}) \quad (11)$$

where $\overleftarrow{\kappa}$, and $\overrightarrow{\kappa}$ are obtained via Eq. 5.

To explore the potential data distribution of multi-modal data in the broad space and improve the performance of Mamba, we use Broad Learning Systems (BLS) to enhance the emotional representation ability of features. Specifically, we map the features output by BiSSM to a random broad space and obtain feature nodes and enhancement nodes, and concatenate the feature nodes and enhancement nodes as the input of the feature fusion layer. Specifically, feature nodes can be formally defined as follows:

$$\mathbf{Z}_i^{t/a/v} \triangleq \text{BiSSM}(\hat{\xi}_j^{t/a/v})\mathbf{W}_{z_i}^{t/a/v} + \beta_{z_i}^{t/a/v}, \ i = 1, 2, \ldots, n \quad (12)$$

and the enhancement nodes can be computed as:

$$\mathbf{H}_j^{t/a/v} \triangleq \text{ReLU}(\mathbf{Z}_{t/a/v}^n \mathbf{W}_{h_j}^{t/a/v} + \beta_{h_j}^{t/a/v}), j = 1, 2, \ldots, m \quad (13)$$

Furthermore, we introduce l2 regularization into the loss function to avoid the overfitting phenomenon of BLS, which is formally defined as follows:

$$\mathcal{L}_{norm} = \|[\mathbf{Z}_{t/a/v}^n | \mathbf{H}_{t/a/v}^m]\mathbf{W}_b^{t/a/v} - \mathbf{Y}^{t/a/v}\|_2^2 + \lambda \|\mathbf{W}_b^{t/a/v}\|_2^2 \quad (14)$$

where λ is the weight decay coefficient, $\mathbf{W}_b^{t/a/v}$ is the learnable parameters, $\mathbf{Y}^{t/a/v} = [\mathbf{Z}_1^{t/a/v}, \ldots, \mathbf{Z}_n^{t/a/v}, \ldots, \mathbf{H}_1^{t/a/v}, \ldots, \mathbf{H}_n^{t/a/v}]$.

By deriving and solving the Eq. 14, the solution to $\mathbf{W}_b^{t/a/v}$ can be calculated as follows:

$$\mathbf{W}_b^{t/a/v} = \left([\mathbf{Z}_{t/a/v}^n | \mathbf{H}_{t/a/v}^m]^\top [\mathbf{Z}_{t/a/v}^n | \mathbf{H}_{t/a/v}^m] + \lambda \mathbf{I}\right)^{-1} [\mathbf{Z}_{t/a/v}^n | \mathbf{H}_{t/a/v}^m]^\top \mathbf{Y}^{t/a/v} \quad (15)$$

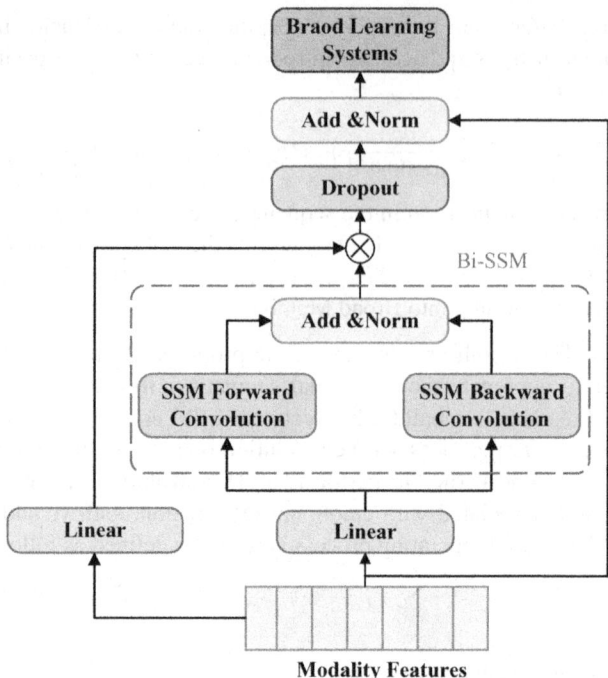

Fig. 4. The overall architecture of Broad Mamba. We use a bidirectional SSM to encode forward and reverse contextual semantic information.

Computation-Efficiency. SSM and the self-attention mechanism in Transformer both plays an important role in modeling global contextual semantic information. However, the self-attention mechanism is quadratic in complexity and is very time-consuming in training and inference. On the contrary, the computational complexity of SSM is $O(LlogL)$, so it can accelerate model inference in modeling long sequences.

4.2 Feature Fusion

Probability-Guided Fusion Model. Many studies have proven that different modalities have different contributions to the prediction of emotional labels, so modal features with higher contributions need to be given greater weight in the multi-modal feature fusion process. Different from previous works that fuse modal features at a coarse-grained level without using label information for guidance, we design a probability-guided fusion model (PFM) that dynamically assigns weights to each modality by using the predicted emotion label probabilities of the modalities. Specifically, we build an emotion classifier for the feature representation of each modality to obtain the predicted probability of the label as the weight of the modal features in the fusion process. The fusion process is formally defined as follows:

$$\omega^{t/a/v} = \text{Sigmoid}\left(\text{MLP}^{t/a/v}\left(Y^{t/a/v}\right)\right) \tag{16}$$

and then we can obtain the fused multi-modal feature representations as follows:

$$h^f = \omega^t Y^t + \omega^a Y^a + \omega^v Y^v \tag{17}$$

4.3 Training Loss

During the optimization phase of the model, the overall training loss function is defined as follows:

$$\mathcal{L} = \mathcal{L}_{norm} + \mathcal{L}_{emo} \tag{18}$$

5 Experiments

In comparative experiments, our experimental results are the average of 10 runs with different weight initializations. The results of our experiments are statistically significant (all $p < 0.05$) under paired t-tests.

5.1 Implementation Details

In the experiments, the number of feature nodes n and the number of enhancement node features m are set to 10 and 30 respectively. Following previous work, we use the same split ratio of training, test, and validation sets for model training and inference.

5.2 Datasets and Evaluation Metrics

We conduct experiments using two popular MERC datasets, IEMOCAP [2] and MELD [30], which include three modal data: text, audio, and video. IEMOCAP contains 12 h of conversations, each containing six emotion labels. The MELD dataset contains conversation clips from the TV show Friends and contains seven different emotion labels. In addition, in the experiments we report the F1 of the proposed method and other baseline methods on each emotion category and weighted average F1 (W-F1).

5.3 Overall Results

Tables 1 show the experimental results on the IEMOCAP and MELD data sets. Experimental results show that our method significantly improves the performance of emotion recognition. The performance improvement may be attributed to the effective extraction of contextual semantic information and efficient integration of underlying data distribution.

Furthermore, our method is optimal compared with other multi-modal fusion methods in experimental results. The results demonstrate the effectiveness of our model in achieving multi-modal semantic information fusion. We also give W-F1 for each emotion. Specifically, on the IEMOCAP data set, our model's W-F1 is optimal on happy, neutral, and frustrated. On the MELD data set, our model's W-F1 is optimal on happy, neutral, and frustrated.

Table 1. Comparison with other baselines on the IEMOCAP and MELD dataset. The best result in each column is in bold.

Methods	IEMOCAP								MELD						
	Params.	Happy	Sad	Neutral	Angry	Excited	Frustrated	W-F1	Neutral	Surprise	Fear	Sadness	Joy	Disgust	Anger	W-F1
bc-LSTM [29]	1.28M	34.4	60.8	51.8	56.7	57.9	58.9	54.9	73.8	47.7	5.4	25.1	51.3	5.2	38.4	55.8
A-DMN [43]	-	50.6	76.8	62.9	56.5	77.9	55.7	64.3	78.9	55.3	8.6	24.9	57.4	3.4	40.9	60.4
DialogueGCN [6]	12.92M	42.7	**84.5**	63.5	64.1	63.1	66.9	65.6	72.1	41.7	2.8	21.8	44.2	6.7	36.5	52.8
RGAT [15]	15.28M	51.6	77.3	65.4	63.0	68.0	61.2	65.2	78.1	41.5	2.4	30.7	58.6	2.2	44.6	59.5
CoMPM [18]	-	60.7	82.2	63.0	59.9	78.2	59.5	67.3	82.0	49.2	2.9	32.3	61.5	2.8	45.8	63.0
EmoBERTa [16]	499M	56.4	83.0	61.5	69.6	78.0	68.7	69.9	**82.5**	50.2	1.9	31.2	61.7	2.5	46.4	63.3
CTNet [23]	8.49M	51.3	79.9	65.8	67.2	**78.7**	58.8	67.5	77.4	50.3	10.0	32.5	56.0	11.2	44.6	60.2
LR-GCN [31]	15.77M	55.5	79.1	63.8	69.0	74.0	68.9	69.0	80.8	57.1	0	36.9	**65.8**	11.0	54.7	65.6
AdaGIN [41]	6.3M	53.0	81.5	71.3	65.9	76.3	67.8	70.7	79.8	60.5	15.2	43.7	64.5	**29.3**	56.2	66.8
DER-GCN [1]	78.59M	58.8	79.8	61.5	**72.1**	73.3	67.8	68.8	80.6	51.0	10.4	41.5	64.3	10.3	**57.4**	65.5
Our Model	1.73M	**65.5**	81.6	**73.5**	70.1	76.3	**69.8**	**73.3**	79.7	**65.6**	**16.9**	**48.9**	63.0	27.0	57.1	**67.6**

We also report the model parameter quantities of the proposed method and the baseline method. The results show that the parameter amount of our model is 1.73M, which is far lower than other methods. The model complexity of other baseline methods is relatively high, but the emotion recognition effect is relatively poor. Experimental results demonstrate that the proposed method is an effective and efficient MERC model.

5.4 Running Time

In this section, we report the inference time of different baselines and our proposed method on the IEMOCAP and MELD datasets. As shown in Table 2, the inference time of our method is below 10 s, which is much lower than some GCN-based methods and RNN-based methods. Experimental results demonstrate the high efficiency of SSMs. In addition, we also counted the Flops of each method, and the results showed that our method was only slightly higher than bc-LSTM.

Table 2. We tested the running time of the proposed method and other comparative methods.

Methods	FLOPs(G)	Running time (s)	
		IEMOCAP	MELD
bc-LSTM	0.46	8.3	10.4
DialogueRNN	5.03	61.7	138.2
RGAT	6.87	68.5	146.3
DialogueGCN	4.81	58.1	127.5
LR-GCN	6.98	87.7	142.3
DER-GCN	20.83	125.5	189.7
Ours	0.71	3.5	6.6

5.5 Ablation Studies

Ablation Studies for PE, BLS, PFM. As shown in Table 3, we found that the performance of the model will decrease after removing PE, which indicates that positional encoding information is quite important for understanding contextual semantic information. Furthermore, without BLS, the performance of the model also degrades. The performance degradation is attributed to the underlying contextual data distribution which is also crucial for emotion prediction. Finally, when the PFM module is removed, the performance of the model drops sharply. Experimental results demonstrate the necessity of each proposed module.

Table 3. Ablation studies for PE, BLS, PFM

Methods	IEMOCAP		MELD	
	W-Acc.	W-F1	W-Acc.	W-F1
Ours	73.1	73.3	68.0	67.6
w/o PE	72.4(↓0.7)	72.0(↓1.3)	66.7(↓1.3)	66.3(↓1.3)
w/o BLS	71.5(↓1.6)	72.1(↓1.2)	65.5(↓2.5)	64.9(↓2.7)
w/o PFM	70.3(↓2.8)	70.7(↓2.6)	65.8(↓2.2)	65.3(↓2.3)

Ablation Studies for Multi-modal Features. To show the impact of different modal features on experimental results, we conducted ablation experiments to verify the combination of different modal features. From the experimental results in Table 4, it is found that: (1) In the single-modal experimental results of the model, the accuracy of emotion recognition in text mode is far better than the other two modes, indicating that text features play a dominant role in emotion recognition effect. (2) The emotion recognition effect using bimodal features is better than its own single-modality result. (3) The emotion recognition effect using three modal features is optimal. Experimental results prove the necessity of fusion of multi-modal features for emotion recognition.

Table 4. The effect of our method using unimodal features, bimodal and multi-modal features, respectively.

Modality	IEMOCAP		MELD	
	W-Acc.	W-F1	W-Acc	W-F1
T+A+V	73.1	73.3	68.0	67.6
T	65.5(↓7.6)	65.7(↓7.6)	64.6(↓3.4)	63.9(↓3.7)
A	58.6(↓14.5)	58.8(↓14.5)	52.7(↓15.3)	52.0(↓15.6)
V	49.4(↓23.7)	49.7(↓23.6)	40.1(↓27.9)	41.4(↓26.2)
T+A	71.3(↓1.8)	70.2(↓3.1)	65.2(↓2.8)	65.6(↓2.0)
T+V	68.7(↓4.4)	67.4(↓5.9)	65.0(↓3.0)	63.7(↓3.9)
V+A	62.1(↓11.0)	62.2(↓11.1)	51.3(↓16.7)	51.9(↓15.7)

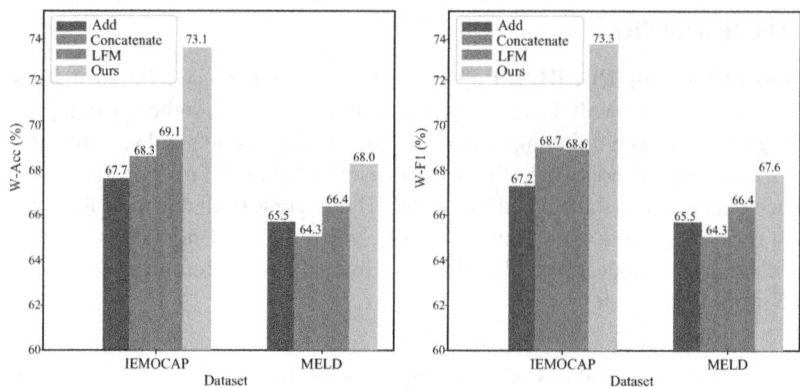

Fig. 5. Emotion recognition effects of different fusion methods. The experimental results are statistically significant (t-test with $p < 0.05$).

Effect of Different Fusion Strategies. To study the effectiveness of the probability-guided fusion method proposed in this paper, we compare it with some previous multi-modal fusion strategies.

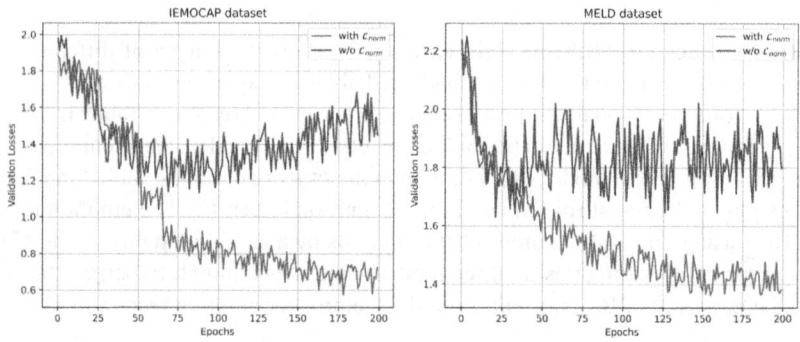

Fig. 6. Loss trends on IEMOCAP and MELD datasets.

As shown in Fig. 5, compared with other fusion methods, the probability-guided fusion strategy we proposed has better emotion recognition effects on the two data sets. The results show that the emotion recognition effect of directly adding or concatenating multi-modal features to achieve multi-modal information fusion is relatively poor. The multi-modal information fusion effect of LMF is better than the adding method and the concatenating method. The probabilistic fusion strategy we propose introduces label information to guide the fusion of multi-modal information and further achieves parameter optimization of the model.

Effect of $\mathcal{L}_{norm}$. To illustrate the impact of $\mathcal{L}_{norm}$ on the experimental results, we conducted experiments on the IEMOCAP and MELD datasets to prove that $\mathcal{L}_{norm}$ can alleviate the problem of model overfitting. The experimental results are shown in Fig. 6. The loss curves on two datasets show that when $\mathcal{L}_{norm}$ is not introduced as a constraint, the model will overfit.

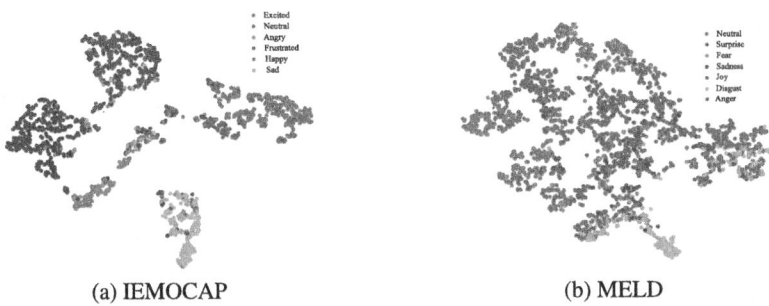

(a) IEMOCAP (b) MELD

Fig. 7. Visualizing feature embeddings for the multi-modal emotion on the IEMOCAP (**Left**) and MELD (**Right**) datasets. Each dot represents an utterance, and its color represents an emotion.

5.6 Multi-modal Representation Visualization

To intuitively demonstrate the classification results of our proposed method on the two data sets, we use t-SNE to project the high-dimensional multi-modal feature representation into a two-dimensional space, as shown in Fig. 7. The results show that the proposed method is able to effectively separate different emotion categories from each other.

Turn	Speaker	Visual	Audio	Text	Dialogue RNN*	MM GCN*	SDT (only text)	SDT	Ground Truth
1	Joey			Oh my god, you're back!	surprise	surprise	surprise	surprise	surprise
2	Phoebe			Ohh, let me see it! Let me see your hand!	surprise	surprise	surprise	surprise	surprise
3	Monica			Why do you want to see my hand?	*surprise*	*surprise*	neutral	neutral	neutral
4	Phoebe			I wanna see what's in your hand. I wanna see the trash.	disgust	disgust	*neutral*	disgust	disgust
5	Phoebe			Eww! Oh, it's all dirty. You should throw this out.	disgust	disgust	disgust	disgust	disgust

Fig. 8. An illustrative example of multi-modal emotion recognition in the MELD dataset.

5.7 Error Analysis

As shown in Fig. 8, we test the emotion classification results of DialogueRNN, DialogueGCN and the proposed method on the MELD dataset. In the disgust emotion category, the classification results of DialogueRNN and DialogueGCN are very poor, and they are all misclassified as neutral emotions. When the proposed method only uses text features, the emotion classification effect on the disgust category is unstable, but when multi-modal features are used, it can better classify disgust category emotions.

6 Conclusions

In this work, we introduce a novel MERC method that comprehensively considers both feature disentanglement and multi-modal feature fusion. Specifically, during the feature disentanglement, we designed the broad Mamba, which incorporates the SSMs for data-dependent global emotional context modeling, and a broad learning system to explore the potential data distribution in the broad space. During the multi-modal feature fusion, we propose an effective probability-guided fusion mechanism to achieve multi-modal contextual feature fusion, which utilizes the predicted label probability of each modal feature as the weight vectors of the modal features. Extensive experiments conducted on two widely used benchmark datasets, IEMOCAP and MELD demonstrate the effectiveness and efficiency of our proposed method.

Acknowledgments. This work is supported by the National Natural Science Foundation of China (Grant No. 62372478), the Research Foundation of Education Bureau of Hunan Province of China (Grant No. 22B0275), and the Hunan Provincial Natural Science Foundation Youth Project (Grant No. 2025JJ60420).

References

1. Ai, W., Shou, Y., Meng, T., Li, K.: DER-GCN: dialog and event relation-aware graph convolutional neural network for multimodal dialog emotion recognition. IEEE Trans. Neural Netw. Learn. Syst. (2024)
2. Busso, C., et al.: Iemocap: interactive emotional dyadic motion capture database. Lang. Resour. Eval. **42**, 335–359 (2008)
3. Chen, F., Sun, Z., Ouyang, D., Liu, X., Shao, J.: Learning what and when to drop: adaptive multimodal and contextual dynamics for emotion recognition in conversation. In: Proceedings of the 29th ACM International Conference on Multimedia, pp. 1064–1073 (2021)
4. Chudasama, V., Kar, P., Gudmalwar, A., Shah, N., Wasnik, P., Onoe, N.: M2fnet: multi-modal fusion network for emotion recognition in conversation. In: Proceedings of the IEEE/CVF Conference on Computer Vision and Pattern Recognition, pp. 4652–4661 (2022)
5. Chung, J., Gulcehre, C., Cho, K., Bengio, Y.: Empirical evaluation of gated recurrent neural networks on sequence modeling. In: NIPS 2014 Workshop on Deep Learning, December 2014 (2014)
6. Ghosal, D., Majumder, N., Poria, S., Chhaya, N., Gelbukh, A.: Dialoguegcn: a graph convolutional neural network for emotion recognition in conversation. In: Proceedings of the 2019 Conference on Empirical Methods in Natural Language Processing and the 9th International Joint Conference on Natural Language Processing (EMNLP-IJCNLP), pp. 154–164 (2019)

7. Ghosh, S., Varshney, D., Ekbal, A., Bhattacharyya, P.: Context and knowledge enriched transformer framework for emotion recognition in conversations. In: 2021 International Joint Conference on Neural Networks (IJCNN), pp. 1–8. IEEE (2021)
8. Gu, A., Dao, T.: Mamba: linear-time sequence modeling with selective state spaces. arXiv preprint arXiv:2312.00752 (2023)
9. Gu, A., Goel, K., Re, C.: Efficiently modeling long sequences with structured state spaces. In: International Conference on Learning Representations (2021)
10. Hazarika, D., Poria, S., Mihalcea, R., Cambria, E., Zimmermann, R.: Icon: interactive conversational memory network for multimodal emotion detection. In: Proceedings of the 2018 Conference on Empirical Methods in Natural Language Processing, pp. 2594–2604 (2018)
11. Hazarika, D., Poria, S., Zadeh, A., Cambria, E., Morency, L.P., Zimmermann, R.: Conversational memory network for emotion recognition in dyadic dialogue videos. In: Proceedings of the conference. Association for Computational Linguistics. North American Chapter. Meeting, vol. 2018, p. 2122. NIH Public Access (2018)
12. He, W., et al.: Densemamba: state space models with dense hidden connection for efficient large language models. arXiv preprint arXiv:2403.00818 (2024)
13. Hochreiter, S., Schmidhuber, J.: Long short-term memory. Neural Comput. 9(8), 1735–1780 (1997). https://doi.org/10.1162/neco.1997.9.8.1735
14. Hu, J., Liu, Y., Zhao, J., Jin, Q.: MMGCN: multimodal fusion via deep graph convolution network for emotion recognition in conversation. In: Proceedings of the 59th Annual Meeting of the Association for Computational Linguistics and the 11th International Joint Conference on Natural Language Processing (Volume 1: Long Papers), pp. 5666–5675 (2021) convolution network for emotion recognition in conversation. In: Proceedings of the 59th Annual Meeting of the Association for Computational Linguistics and the 11th International Joint Conference on Natural Language Processing (Volume 1: Long Papers). pp. 5666–5675 (2021)
15. Ishiwatari, T., Yasuda, Y., Miyazaki, T., Goto, J.: Relation-aware graph attention networks with relational position encodings for emotion recognition in conversations. In: Proceedings of the 2020 Conference on Empirical Methods in Natural Language Processing (EMNLP), pp. 7360–7370 (2020)
16. Kim, T., Vossen, P.: Emoberta: speaker-aware emotion recognition in conversation with roberta. arXiv preprint arXiv:2108.12009 (2021)
17. Kim, Y.: Convolutional neural networks for sentence classification. In: Proceedings of the 2014 Conference on Empirical Methods in Natural Language Processing (EMNLP), pp. 1746–1751. Association for Computational Linguistics (2014)
18. Lee, J., Lee, W.: Compm: context modeling with speaker's pre-trained memory tracking for emotion recognition in conversation. In: Proceedings of the 2022 Conference of the North American Chapter of the Association for Computational Linguistics: Human Language Technologies, pp. 5669–5679 (2022)
19. Li, B., et al.: Revisiting disentanglement and fusion on modality and context in conversational multimodal emotion recognition. In: Proceedings of the 31st ACM International Conference on Multimedia, pp. 5923–5934 (2023)
20. Li, W., Shao, W., Ji, S., Cambria, E.: Bieru: bidirectional emotional recurrent unit for conversational sentiment analysis. Neurocomputing **467**, 73–82 (2022)
21. Li, W., Zhu, L., Mao, R., Cambria, E.: Skier: a symbolic knowledge integrated model for conversational emotion recognition. In: Proceedings of the AAAI Conference on Artificial Intelligence, vol. 37, pp. 13121–13129 (2023)
22. Li, Z., Tang, F., Zhao, M., Zhu, Y.: Emocaps: emotion capsule based model for conversational emotion recognition. In: Findings of the Association for Computational Linguistics: ACL 2022, pp. 1610–1618 (2022)

23. Lian, Z., Liu, B., Tao, J.: CTNet: conversational transformer network for emotion recognition. IEEE/ACM Trans. Audio Speech Lang. Process. **29**, 985–1000 (2021)
24. Liu, S., Gao, P., Li, Y., Fu, W., Ding, W.: Multi-modal fusion network with complementarity and importance for emotion recognition. Inf. Sci. **619**, 679–694 (2023)
25. Lu, X., Zhao, Y., Wu, Y., Tian, Y., Chen, H., Qin, B.: An iterative emotion interaction network for emotion recognition in conversations. In: Proceedings of the 28th International Conference on Computational Linguistics, pp. 4078–4088 (2020)
26. Ma, H., Wang, J., Lin, H., Zhang, B., Zhang, Y., Xu, B.: A transformer-based model with self-distillation for multimodal emotion recognition in conversations. IEEE Trans. Multimedia (2023)
27. Majumder, N., Poria, S., Hazarika, D., Mihalcea, R., Gelbukh, A., Cambria, E.: Dialoguernn: an attentive RNN for emotion detection in conversations. In: Proceedings of the AAAI Conference on Artificial Intelligence, vol. 33, pp. 6818–6825 (2019)
28. Mehta, H., Gupta, A., Cutkosky, A., Neyshabur, B.: Long range language modeling via gated state spaces. In: International Conference on Learning Representations (2023)
29. Poria, S., Cambria, E., Hazarika, D., Majumder, N., Zadeh, A., Morency, L.P.: Context-dependent sentiment analysis in user-generated videos. In: Proceedings of the 55th Annual Meeting of the Association for Computational Linguistics (Volume 1: Long Papers), pp. 873–883 (2017)
30. Poria, S., Hazarika, D., Majumder, N., Naik, G., Cambria, E., Mihalcea, R.: Meld: a multimodal multi-party dataset for emotion recognition in conversations. In: Proceedings of the 57th Annual Meeting of the Association for Computational Linguistics, pp. 527–536 (2019)
31. Ren, M., Huang, X., Li, W., Song, D., Nie, W.: LR-GCN: latent relation-aware graph convolutional network for conversational emotion recognition. IEEE Trans. Multimedia **24**, 4422–4432 (2021)
32. Ren, M., Huang, X., Shi, X., Nie, W.: Interactive multimodal attention network for emotion recognition in conversation. IEEE Signal Process. Lett. **28**, 1046–1050 (2021)
33. Shen, W., Chen, J., Quan, X., Xie, Z.: Dialogxl: all-in-one XLNet for multi-party conversation emotion recognition. In: Proceedings of the AAAI Conference on Artificial Intelligence, vol. 35, pp. 13789–13797 (2021)
34. Shou, Y., Lan, H., Cao, X.: Contrastive graph representation learning with adversarial cross-view reconstruction and information bottleneck. Neural Netw. **184**, 107094 (2025)
35. Shou, Y., Liu, H., Cao, X., Meng, D., Dong, B.: A low-rank matching attention based cross-modal feature fusion method for conversational emotion recognition. IEEE Trans. Affect. Comput. (2024)
36. Shou, Y., Meng, T., Ai, W., Li, K.: Adversarial representation with intra-modal and inter-modal graph contrastive learning for multimodal emotion recognition. arXiv preprint arXiv:2312.16778 (2023)
37. Shou, Y., Meng, T., Ai, W., Yang, S., Li, K.: Conversational emotion recognition studies based on graph convolutional neural networks and a dependent syntactic analysis. Neurocomputing **501**, 629–639 (2022)
38. Shou, Y., Meng, T., Ai, W., Yin, N., Li, K.: A comprehensive survey on multi-modal conversational emotion recognition with deep learning. arXiv preprint arXiv:2312.05735 (2023)
39. Smith, J.T., Warrington, A., Linderman, S.: Simplified state space layers for sequence modeling. In: The Eleventh International Conference on Learning Representations (2022)
40. Sun, J., et al.: Layer-wise fusion with modality independence modeling for multi-modal emotion recognition. In: Proceedings of the 61st Annual Meeting of the Association for Computational Linguistics (Volume 1: Long Papers), pp. 658–670 (2023)
41. Tu, G., Xie, T., Liang, B., Wang, H., Xu, R.: Adaptive graph learning for multimodal conversational emotion detection. In: Proceedings of the AAAI Conference on Artificial Intelligence, vol. 38, pp. 19089–19097 (2024)

42. Wang, Y., Li, D., Shen, J.: Inter-modality and intra-sample alignment for multi-modal emotion recognition. In: ICASSP 2024-2024 IEEE International Conference on Acoustics, Speech and Signal Processing (ICASSP), pp. 8301–8305. IEEE (2024)
43. Xing, S., Mai, S., Hu, H.: Adapted dynamic memory network for emotion recognition in conversation. IEEE Trans. Affect. Comput. **13**(3), 1426–1439 (2020)
44. Yan, C., Liu, J., Liu, W., Liu, X.: Research on public opinion sentiment classification based on attention parallel dual-channel deep learning hybrid model. Eng. Appl. Artif. Intell. **116**, 105448 (2022)
45. Zadeh, A., Chen, M., Poria, S., Cambria, E., Morency, L.P.: Tensor fusion network for multimodal sentiment analysis. In: Proceedings of the 2017 Conference on Empirical Methods in Natural Language Processing, pp. 1103–1114 (2017)
46. Zhang, D., Chen, F., Chen, X.: Dualgats: dual graph attention networks for emotion recognition in conversations. In: Proceedings of the 61st Annual Meeting of the Association for Computational Linguistics (Volume 1: Long Papers), pp. 7395–7408 (2023)
47. Zhu, L., Liao, B., Zhang, Q., Wang, X., Liu, W., Wang, X.: Vision mamba: efficient visual representation learning with bidirectional state space model. arXiv preprint arXiv:2401.09417 (2024)

AMST: Alternating Multimodal Skip Training

Hugo Manuel Alves Henriques e Silva[1,2](✉), Hongguang Chen[1,2], and Selpi[1,2]

[1] Chalmers University of Technology, 41296 Gothenburg, Sweden
[2] University of Gothenburg, Gothenburg, Sweden
{hugoalv,chenhon,selpi}@chalmers.se

Abstract. Multimodal Learning is one of the many fields in Machine Learning where models leverage the combination of various modalities to enhance learning outcomes. However, modalities may differ in data representation and complexity, which can lead to learning imbalances during the training process. The time it takes for a certain modality to converge during training is a crucial metric to determine modality imbalance. Given differences in convergence rates, different modalities may harmfully interfere with each other's learning process when simultaneously trained, as is commonly done in a multimodal scenario. To mitigate this negative impact, we propose Alternating Multimodal Skip Training (AMST) where the training frequency is adjusted for each specific modality. This novel method not only improves performance in conventional multimodal models that learn with fused modalities but also enhances alternating models that train each modality separately. Additionally, it outperforms state-of-the-art models while reducing training times.

Keywords: Multimodal Learning · Modality Imbalance · Modality Convergence Rate · Modality Bias · Skip Training · Training Frequency

1 Introduction

Multimodal Machine Learning aims to mimic how humans rely on different senses to analyse, judge, and act in distinct situations. Inspired by this aspect of human perception, multimodal models leverage diverse sensory inputs to improve learning outcomes. However, with multimodal learning comes its challenges. A key difficulty in recent multimodal approaches is the integration of information from multiple modalities, without having them negatively interfere with each other, in a way where rich modality-specific information is lost. Studies such as [14,15] have previously confirmed that some modalities tend to be more "dominant" than others, which causes the learning process to focus disproportionately on them, thereby limiting the contribution of other, potentially richer, modalities. Even though the "dominance" of one modality over another does not measure its informativeness or discriminative power, it affects the overall model performance.

Generally, raw data produced from different sensors and the way it is represented may differ in complexity when processing it. Consequently, more complex

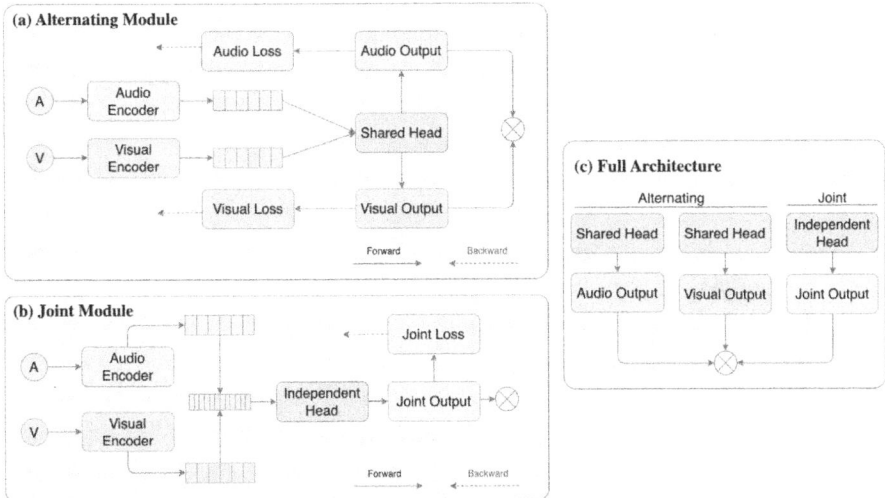

Fig. 1. Example of AMST's pipeline for 2 modalities (Audio and Visual): The Alternating Module (**a**) comprises both audio and visual encoders. The Shared Head predicts for audio and visual modalities individually. The Joint Module (**b**) consists of audio and visual encoders that produce a fused concatenated representation. The Independent Head predicts with the joint representation. The Full Architecture (**c**) averages the visual and audio outputs from the Alternating Module and the joint output from the Joint Module for a prediction.

data may require longer training times than data with simpler representations. For example, when representing a video in both audio and visual modalities, it is relatively straightforward to create a single representation for the entire audio of the video. In contrast, generating a single representation for the visual modality often requires concatenating frames from various time steps, resulting in a more complex data representation overall. Recent methods do not address the issue of modality imbalance related to convergence rates, which leads to inefficient training and negatively affects the overall model performance. Neglecting differences in modality convergence rates allows certain modalities to overfit at different stages, resulting in the under optimisation of those that learn more slowly. When a modality overfits to the training data earlier than others, the multimodal model tends to prioritise it, causing premature convergence.

We address the problem of modality dominance related to convergence rates, by allowing the model to train more frequently on the data with the highest complexity, i.e., the slowest learning modalities, while periodically training it on the fastest learning ones. Inspired by human perception, the proposed method emulates how people allocate more effort to a more challenging task while still occasionally practising the simpler one. This uneven focus ultimately yields comparable performance across all tasks despite their different complexities.

Our approach, as illustrated in Fig. 1, is built upon two modules, **Alternating** and **Joint**, both including skip training (see Fig. 2). This approach led to

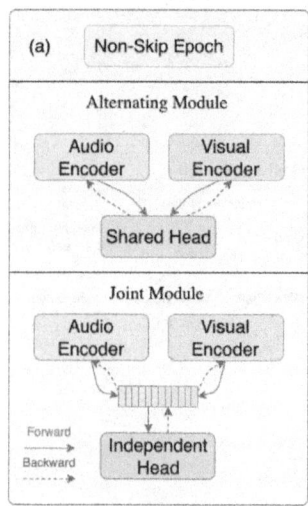 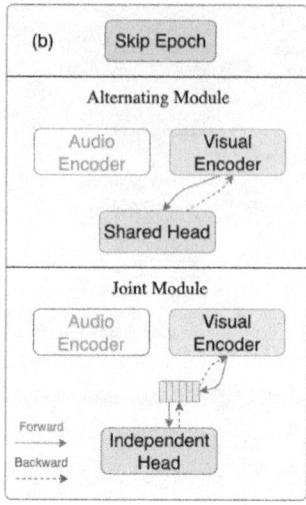 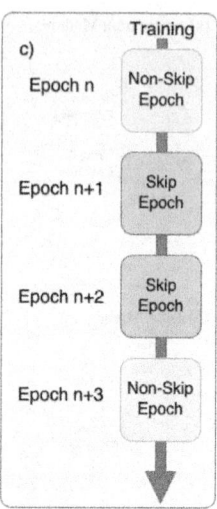

Fig. 2. AMST's training framework with skip parameter set to 3 for the audio modality and 1 for visual. (**a**) represents an epoch in which audio is not skipped and both modalities are updated. (**b**) represents an epoch in which the audio is skipped and only visual is updated. (**c**) represents how the training should proceed: 2 consecutive skip epochs as in (**b**) for every non-skip epoch as in (**a**).

the creation of the **A**lternating **M**ultimodal **S**kip **T**raining (**AMST**) method. The contribution of this paper is summarised as follows:

- We introduce Alternating Multimodal Skip Training (AMST), a novel method that (1) optimises the multimodal learning process without compromising the modality-specific information, and (2) addresses modality imbalance due to different convergence rates across modalities.
- We conduct experiments to show that AMST is able to (1) decrease the dominance gap related to convergence rates between the different modalities through skip training, (2) outperform the closest state-of-the-art methods, (3) increase the performance compared to when any of its key components are removed, and (4) greatly reduce overall computational expenses compared to the fastest existing methods.

The remainder of this paper is structured as follows: Sect. 2 introduces the related work. Our method AMST is presented in Sect. 3. The experiments are detailed in Sect. 4 and the results are discussed in Sect. 5. We conclude our work in Sect. 6. We provide the code at https://github.com/CXianRen/AMST.

2 Related Work

Modality convergence rate has previously been studied in works such as [7,14,15]. In [14], the authors demonstrated that different modalities overfit and generalise at different rates, which makes conventional joint training of multimodal data not optimal, compared to the best unimodal counterpart. The finding that joint training of multimodal data is not optimal was also demonstrated in [12].

Several methods have been proposed to mitigate the impact of different convergence rates on the learning process. [11] proposed "on-the-fly gradient modulation", where the authors dynamically adjusted the gradient contributions of each modality during training. Inspired by [6,11] developed an adaptive gradient modulation. Similarly, [7] took a comparable approach, while [3] introduced Prototypical Modal Rebalance (PMR). Here, prototypes were created. These represent centroids in the feature space for each class and serve as targets for each modality to cluster around, encouraging the alignment of slow-learning modalities. In [14], the authors proposed the gradient blending method to compute "an optimal blending of modalities based on their overfitting behaviours". Further, in [15], a metric called conditional learning speed was proposed to measure the learning speed of an individual modality relative to the other modalities. [12] suggested balancing the learning rates across modalities such that the modality nearing convergence would be given a lower learning rate so other modalities could catch up. The idea of adapting the learning rate was also proposed by [17].

In addition to balancing the learning rate, [12] also suggested separating the unimodal network from the multimodal network to allow modality-specific optimisation. Modality-specific optimisation is also promoted in a recent method called MLA [18] with its alternating approach. The aim of MLA is to provide each modality with an independent learning process in which they can fully leverage their information, without being disturbed by any other modality. Furthermore, cross-modal information is captured through a shared head between all modalities.

Our work builds on the alternating approach in MLA [18]. Despite MLA's efforts to minimise modality imbalance, we hypothesise that, similar to conventional multimodal joint training approaches, the model may remain biased toward the faster-learning modality, potentially compromising overall performance.

3 Alternating Multimodal Skip Training (AMST)

This section presents our proposed method. We describe both implemented modules, **Alternating** and **Joint**, explaining how they complement each other and how skip training is established in each of them, as displayed in Fig. 2.

The Alternating Module, Fig. 1(a), aims to reframe the conventional multimodal joint training practice, where modalities are first fused and trained together. With the introduction of the alternating framework in [18], we allow each modality to train independently and learn a complete representation from its data by having modality-specific losses. Despite the training being done independently, we rely on a single head that is shared among all modalities. This shared head, which is simply a classification layer, aims to capture the cross-modal information while minimising the learning disturbance caused by the modalities' interaction.

The pipeline in the Alternating Module flows as shown in Fig. 1(a). A dedicated encoder is designed for each modality to generate its distinct latent representation. These representations are then processed by the shared head where different predictions are obtained per modality. For each modality, the model's parameters are optimised according to its modality-specific loss. Even though the training of a modality does not influence the encoders of other modalities, the shared head is always optimised, allowing minimal inter-modal communication.

Contrary to the Alternating Module, the Joint Module, Fig. 1(b), implements the conventional joint training practice, where full communication between the modalities is allowed, fusing them at a much earlier stage. However, scenarios that adopt this approach are more susceptible to modality imbalance related to convergence rates. This occurs because a single loss function is optimised, which inherently favours the faster learning modalities. As these modalities overfit and achieve near-perfect training performance, the overall model also attains near-perfect performance on the training data. Consequently, the premature convergence of the loss to near-zero values diminishes the effectiveness of gradient updates, hindering the learning of slower-learning modalities.

As displayed in Fig. 1(b), the Joint Module has its own encoders, which follow the same encoder structure as the Alternating Module. Each modality-specific encoder generates latent embeddings, which are subsequently fused into a single representation via concatenation. This fused representation is then processed by a classification layer, referred to as the independent head, as it operates separately from the Alternating Module's classification head.

3.1 The Motivation for Skip Training

We observed that each modality learns at different rates, converging at distinct time steps. Figure 3's (a) and (c) show the training accuracies of audio and visual modalities and the overall prediction on the CREMA-D dataset [2], for the Alternating and Joint Modules, respectively. In both plots, the audio and overall accuracy curves are closely aligned with each other, suggesting a bias towards the audio modality in both modules.

In the Alternating Module, Fig. 3(a), by epoch 25, the audio modality achieves near-perfect accuracy, whereas the visual modality remains at 40%. However, the overall prediction, derived from averaging the logits of both modalities' outputs from the shared head, closely follows the audio accuracy curve, suggesting a bias toward the audio modality in this module. Nevertheless, the visual modality continues to learn, albeit at a slower pace. Since rapid convergence of the audio modality does not hinder the learning of the visual modality in this module, we further examine the impact of not balancing modality convergence rates in an alternating setup. Figure 4 presents the average entropy values of each modality's predictions for each class in the CREMA-D dataset in different experiments. Lower entropy values indicate greater confidence in the corresponding modality's predictions. Figure 4(a) shows the entropy values of both modalities in all classes in the default scenario (i.e., when no measures are applied to mitigate imbalances caused by differing convergence rates). One

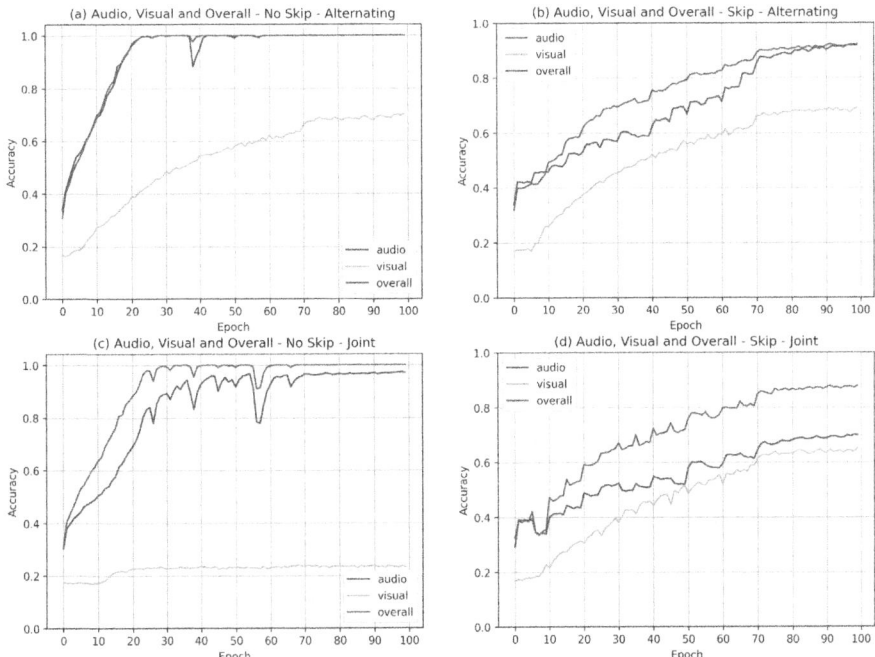

Fig. 3. Accuracies, for both Alternating and Joint modules, on CREMA-D dataset for audio and visual modalities as well as the overall case considering both modalities: (a) Alternating Module without skip training. (b) Alternating Module including skip training. (c) Joint Module without skip training. (d) Joint Module including skip training. The skip parameter for audio is 5 and for visual is 1.

can see that the observed entropy values for the audio modality are considerably lower than the visual ones, demonstrating the model's overconfidence in the audio modality. This further reinforces the notion that a bias is introduced in favour of the audio modality.

A potential way to mitigate overtraining of faster-learning modalities is the use of the early stopping technique (for neural networks) for a modality's training. However, as demonstrated in Fig. 4(b), where the training of the audio modality is halted around epoch 30 (5–10 epochs after approaching 100% accuracy), the gap in average entropy values observed in Fig. 4(a) remains. This indicates that entirely discontinuing a modality's training shortly after convergence does not eliminate the bias formed in its favour. Furthermore, these findings suggest that the early stages of training play a critical role in establishing this bias towards the faster-learning modalities. Thus, early stopping alone is insufficient to address the imbalance due to differing convergence rates.

For the Joint Module, Plot (c) in Fig. 3 shows a pattern similar to the Alternating Module, where the overall joint accuracy closely follows the audio accuracy. By epoch 30, the overall accuracy reaches a near-perfect 100%, once again

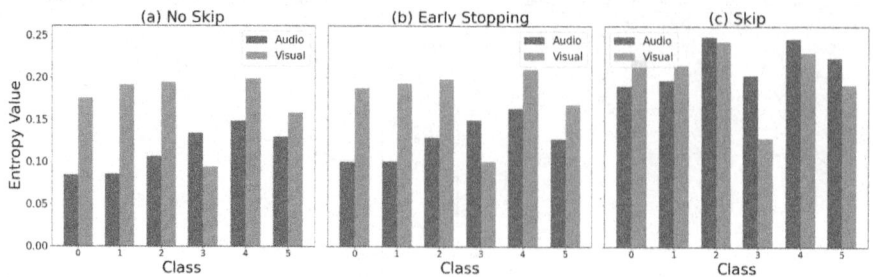

Fig. 4. Average entropy values for each class in the CREMA-D Dataset for 3 different methods in the Alternating Module. **(a)** - default method without skipping; **(b)** - early stopping. **(c)** - AMST's skip training. Each plot corresponds to the results of the best-performing model over 100 epochs of training.

indicating a bias toward the audio modality due to its faster convergence. Yet, unlike in the Alternating Module, the visual accuracy stagnates as soon as the overall accuracy attains this near-perfect value. This occurs because, with a joint loss, as the loss approaches zero, gradient updates become progressively smaller, eventually reaching a point of insignificance. As a result, the visual modality fails to learn due to the absence of meaningful gradient updates.

Failing to address the bias in both scenarios can reduce overall model performance. To mitigate this, skip training is proposed as a solution to counteract the bias introduced by faster-learning modalities and their rapid convergence.

3.2 Skip Training in the Alternating Module

In this module, despite only the final layer being shared across modalities, given the learning curves observed in Fig. 3(a) and the substantial gap in average entropy values across modalities shown in Fig. 4(a), we hypothesised that a bias could develop in favour of the fastest-learning modalities. Were this to be the case, it would hinder the performance of the slow-learning ones, limiting their contribution and causing the model to overfit to the faster-learning counterparts.

Therefore, Skip Training is introduced in the Alternating Module. As shown in Fig. 2(b), the approach prioritises the learning process for slow-learning modalities, by skipping the optimisation of the faster-learning ones. This means that, during training, we determine with the help of an integer hyperparameter per modality, whether or not each modality should be optimised in the current epoch. Despite needing fine-tuning, a reasonable initial estimate for this integer hyperparameter can be obtained by analysing the rate of change in accuracy across all modalities during the initial epochs. Specifically, the skip parameter for each modality should be assigned in proportion to its accuracy rate of change relative to the slowest learning modality. For example, if a modality demonstrates an accuracy rate of change three times greater than that of the slowest learning modality in the early stages, its initial skip parameter should be set to three.

Algorithm 1. Alternating Skip Method

```
1: Input: Skip hyperparameters s₁,...,sₘ, Total epochs E, Modalities M
2: // Training Stage
3: for e = 1 to E do                               ▷ Iterate over epochs
4:   for each modality m in M do                   ▷ Iterate over modalities
5:     if e mod sₘ = 0 then                        ▷ Check skip schedule
6:       out := predModality(encode(m))   ▷ Generate prediction for modality m
7:       Backprop(Loss(out))                       ▷ Backpropagate
8:     end if
9:   end for
10: end for
11: return trained_model

12: // Inference Stage
13: Init predictions P ← []                        ▷ List to store modality predictions
14: for each modality m in M do                    ▷ Iterate over modalities for inference
15:   out := predModality(encode(m))               ▷ Generate prediction for modality m
16:   Append out to P                              ▷ Store prediction
17: end for
18: return Softmax(Average(P))                     ▷ Compute final prediction by averaging
```

Given a modality M with respective integer skip parameter s_m, and current training epoch e, the decision to train M follows Eq. (1). Algorithm 1 presents the pseudo-code for the alternating skip method mechanism. For inference, the default no-skip approach is used.

$$\text{Train}(M) = \begin{cases} True, & \text{if } e \bmod s_m = 0, \\ False, & \text{otherwise.} \end{cases} \quad (1)$$

This approach not only mitigates the overfitting of faster-learning modalities but also allows sufficient time for the model to learn from slower-learning ones. Furthermore, it alleviates some of the influence that the dominant modalities have on the updates of the shared head's parameters. During inference, the Alternating Module produces logit outputs for each modality which are then averaged to generate the final prediction.

To demonstrate the importance of having skip training in the alternating module, we compare Plots (b) and (a) of Fig. 3, which illustrate the learning curves for the audio, visual, and overall module accuracies for the Alternating Module in the CREMA-D dataset, with and without skip training, respectively. As shown in Fig. 3(b), the audio and the overall accuracy curves exhibit a more iterative path compared to Fig. 3(a), while both plots' visual modality curves follow a similar trend. By epoch 70 in Fig. 3(b), all modalities and the overall accuracies begin to converge. This indicates a more balanced learning scenario, where modalities begin to converge at similar time steps, enabling the models to better utilise the multimodal setting. Furthermore, in Fig. 4, we observe a significant reduction in the gap between the average entropy values of the audio and visual modalities in (c) compared to (a) and (b). This indicates that the model has become nearly equally confident in both modalities. These results strongly support our initial hypothesis that there was a bias towards the faster-learning modality and demonstrate that skip training effectively mitigates this bias.

3.3 Skip Training in the Joint Module

To address the issue of modality imbalance related to convergence rate in joint architectures, skip training is applied similarly to how it is used in the Alternating Module. Figure 2(b) illustrates the joint skip method. The same hyperparameters that define how many epochs each modality's optimisation is skipped during the alternating phase are reused to govern the joint skip method. Moreover, the initial skip parameter estimates from the Alternating Module apply similarly here. Like the Alternating Module, given a modality M with an associated integer skip parameter s_m and the current training epoch e, M is trained according to Eq. (1).

A standard joint training approach concatenates modalities' embeddings in a fixed order. As defined in Eq. (1), in skip training, a modality's latent representation is only used for prediction if its skip parameter divides the current training epoch. As a result, only the weights of the independent head and the encoders corresponding to these modalities are updated. At each epoch, a sub-head is derived from the independent head, retaining the weights of the modalities that are not skipped. The non-skipped modalities are then concatenated and fed into this sub-head to compute the final joint loss for that training epoch. This approach ensures that only the encoders of the non-skipped modalities, along with the corresponding weights of the independent head, are updated.

Figure 3(d) illustrates the learning curves for the audio, visual, and overall module accuracies for the Joint Module in the CREMA-D dataset, incorporating skip training. With skip training, the audio modality and the overall accuracies undergo a more gradual learning process, allowing the visual modality to learn, since the overall joint loss does not reach zero in the early training stages. As in the Alternating Module, all modalities and the overall accuracies begin to converge around epoch 70.

During inference, the joint representation is formed by concatenating the latent embeddings of all modalities and feeding them into the independent head to generate the final prediction. Algorithm 2 presents the pseudo-code for the joint skip method.

3.4 Complementary Module Interaction

The Alternating and Joint Modules follow two different approaches. The former minimises inter-modal communication, while the latter maximises it. Both approaches have their advantages and drawbacks depending on the specific application. Notably, they operate independently, and skip training is not reliant on their co-existence, as each module is trained separately. By integrating skip

Algorithm 2. Joint Skip Method

1: **Input:** Skip hyperparameters $s_1, \ldots, s_m$, Total epochs E, Modalities M
2: **// Training Stage**
3: **for** $e = 1$ to E **do** ▷ Iterate over epochs
4:     Init $R \leftarrow []$ ▷ Store embeddings of active modalities
5:     Init active_modalities $\leftarrow []$ ▷ Track which modalities are active
6:     **for** each modality m in M **do** ▷ Determine active modalities
7:         **if** $e \bmod s_m = 0$ **then** ▷ Check skip condition
8:             Append encodeModality(m) to R
9:             Append m to active_modalities
10:         **end if**
11:     **end for**
12:     Init reduced_head $\leftarrow$ Weights(independent_head, active_modalities)
13:     joint_representation := Concatenate(R) ▷ Form reduced joint representation
14:     out := reduced_head(joint_representation) ▷ Generate prediction
15:     Backprop(Loss(out)) ▷ Backpropagate
16: **end for**
17: **return:** trained_model
18: **// Inference Stage**
19: joint_representation := Concatenate({encodeModality(m) **for** $m \in M$})
20: **return:** independent_head(joint_representation) ▷ Generate final prediction

---

training with the full communication benefits of the joint approach and the independent training structure of the alternating method, the resulting fusion can generate more confident and aligned predictions. With skip training's reduced computational costs, employing both modules concurrently may become a feasible option depending on the task. When both modules are used simultaneously, the final prediction corresponds to a mean of the logit outputs of each modality from the Alternating Module and the logit output from the Joint Module.

4 Experiments

4.1 Data

To assess the performance of the proposed method, we utilised two audio-visual datasets: **CREMA-D** [2], **AVE** [13]; one visual-text dataset: **MVSA** [10]; and two audio-visual-text datasets: **IEMOCAP** [1] and **UR-FUNNY** [4].

CREMA-D [2] consists of 7,442 original clips displaying one of six different emotions (Anger, Disgust, Fear, Happy, Neutral, and Sad). The AVE dataset [13] comprises 4143 10-second video clips of common actions and events. The dataset contains 28 different classes. MVSA-Single [10] is a multimodal sentiment analysis dataset that comprises 5129 image-text pairs collected from Twitter, labelled in 3 classes (positive, neutral and negative). The IEMOCAP dataset [1] comprises approximately 12 h of audiovisual data, including video, speech, facial motion capture, and text transcriptions, labelled in angry, excited, frustrated, neutral and sad. Finally, UR-FUNNY [4] consists of 16514 video segments with 8257 labelled as humorous and 8257 as non-humorous.

4.2 Experimental Setup

For AVE, the data was split into train, test, and validation sets following [13]. For the rest of the datasets, we randomly allocate 80% of the data for training, 10% for the validation, and 10% for the testing as no previous split is given. The MVSA-single dataset was processed as in [16]. ResNet18 [5] was used as the backbone encoder for both audio and visual modalities. For the text modality, RoBERTa [8] was used as the encoder with five unfrozen encoder layers. For the visual modality, for all datasets we extracted one frame per second from each video and selected three images as done in [18]. For MVSA, the single provided image per sample was used as the visual modality. For audio, we converted the raw audio samples into fbank (filterbank) [9] features. Regarding text, we tokenised the raw sample text with the RoBERTa tokeniser. To ensure complete fairness among all models, they were all trained for 100 epochs using a mini-batch size of 64, SGD optimiser and the exact same backbones. Given the nature of the MSLR method [17], different learning rates for each modality were used: 0.001 for audio, 0.01 for visual, and 8e-5 for text. For the rest of the methods, including AMST and its sub-modules, a learning rate of 0.001 was used for all modalities. Moreover, all SOTA methods were evaluated using the exact parameters specified in their original works, and their official code was used whenever available. All modalities' skip parameters require fine-tuning and their optimal values may differ depending on each modality's informativeness and task at hand. The visual skip parameter was set to 1 in all datasets (i.e., we do not skip its training). Concerning audio, its skip parameter was set to 5 for CREMA-D, 2 for AVE, 4 for IEMOCAP and 6 for UR-FUNNY. For text, we set the text skip parameter to 10 for MVSA, IEMOCAP and UR-FUNNY. Moreover, all modality skip parameters were the same for both the alternating and joint skip methods. Regarding the final prediction, we followed a standard even split approach for all methods that adopted late fusion prediction (MLA and AMST).

Experiments were conducted to compare the performance of AMST, state-of-the-art methods, and their unimodal counterparts. We further make comparisons of the performances of AMST, by excluding its key components, i.e., **(1)** Baseline Joint Module, **(2)** Skip Training in Joint Module (AMST-Joint), **(3)** Baseline Alternating Module, **(4)** Skip Training in Alternating Module (AMST-Alt), **(5)** Alternating and Joint Modules Without Skip Training and **(6)** Skip Training in the Complete Architecture (AMST-Full). All experiments were performed on an A100 GPU and the average training time per epoch is shown in Table 3. Finally, in Table 1 and Table 3, we include a baseline Naïve method, which uses a joint sum fusion approach without any optimisation, where modality embeddings are summed before being used in the classification head. This baseline serves as a reference point for performance comparisons across all datasets.

Table 1. Comparison of accuracies of unimodal models, state-of-the-art methods, and AMST architectures on the used test sets. Results are reported as the average over 3 random seeds, with standard error. The best results for each dataset are displayed in bold, and the second-best are underlined.

Method	CREMA-D	AVE	MVSA	IEMOCAP	URFUNNY
Audio	59.1 ± 0.49	55.3 ± 0.56	-	49.2 ± 1.41	59.7 ± 0.64
Visual	60.5 ± 0.75	28.5 ± 0.64	57.7 ± 1.21	46.5 ± 0.53	49.2 ± 0.78
Text	-	-	70.8 ± 0.10	62.3 ± 0.30	68.9 ± 0.05
Naïve	62.9 ± 1.24	55.9 ± 0.46	71.1 ± 0.10	67.3 ± 1.20	70.0 ± 0.26
OGM-GE	65.5 ± 1.46	56.1 ± 1.24	72.7 ± 0.55	67.5 ± 0.44	70.3 ± 0.38
PMR	67.5 ± 1.65	58.8 ± 1.55	**73.6 ± 0.20**	-	-
MSLR	71.6 ± 0.82	61.1 ± 0.70	71.0 ± 0.10	61.1 ± 0.70	69.0 ± 0.58
MLA	74.8 ± 0.30	61.9 ± 0.44	71.8 ± 0.10	63.9 ± 0.62	65.6 ± 0.24
AMST-Alt	<u>79.0</u> ± 0.55	62.1 ± 0.76	72.5 ± 0.31	67.5 ± 0.20	70.8 ± 0.34
AMST-Joint	78.2 ± 0.03	<u>63.2</u> ± 0.46	72.5 ± 0.79	<u>67.6</u> ± 0.99	**72.1 ± 0.46**
AMST-Full	**80.5 ± 0.77**	**65.8 ± 0.38**	72.6 ± 0.43	**68.4 ± 0.54**	<u>71.6</u> ± 0.13

5 Results and Discussion

5.1 Comparison with State-of-the-Art Methods

Table 1 shows the performance of AMST against state-of-the-art methods and unimodal models. We separate the AMST architecture into three components: **AMST-Alt**, Fig. 1(a), corresponds to the Alternating Module; **AMST-Joint**, Fig. 1(b), corresponds to the Joint Module; **AMST-Full**, Fig. 1(c), consists of using both modules in a complementary fashion. For clearer comparisons, it is important to note that only MLA and AMST-Alt utilise an alternating architecture with separately optimised modality-specific losses. In contrast, AMST-Joint, MSLR, PMR, OGM-GE, and the Naïve methods follow a joint training approach, relying on a single multimodal loss. Moreover, PMR does not provide an implementation for more than two modalities, which explains why its results are missing for IEMOCAP and UR-FUNNY.

As evident from the results, all methods outperform their unimodal counterparts, except for MSLR in IEMOCAP and UR-FUNNY, and MLA in UR-FUNNY. AMST's alternating and joint architectures consistently surpass their respective alternatives under the same conditions across all datasets, except for MVSA-Single. In CREMA-D, AVE, and IEMOCAP, the full AMST architecture achieves the best performance, with both the alternating (AMST-Alt) and joint (AMST-Joint) variants performing similarly while still outperforming other methods. For the UR-FUNNY dataset, AMST-Joint emerges as the best-performing architecture, with AMST-Alt and AMST-Full following closely behind.

The primary reason AMST architectures do not outperform other methods on the MVSA-Single dataset is that the visual modality is less informative than the

Table 2. Average accuracies over 3 random seeds with standard error for AMST, with and without its main components, across datasets. CREMA-D and AVE use audio-visual modalities, MVSA uses visual-text, while IEMOCAP and UR-FUNNY incorporate all three. In the "Alt." (alternating), "Joint," and "Skip" columns, a tick indicates inclusion of the respective method. For each dataset, the best result is in bold and the second-best is underlined.

Exp	Alt.	Joint	Skip	CREMA-D	AVE	MVSA	IEMOCAP	UR-FUNNY
1	-	✓	-	64.0 ± 1.45	59.6 ± 1.76	71.7 ± 0.90	65.3 ± 0.35	68.3 ± 0.25
2	-	✓	✓	78.2 ± 0.03	63.2 ± 0.46	72.5 ± 0.79	67.6 ± 0.99	**72.1 ± 0.46**
3	✓	-	-	74.8 ± 0.35	61.9 ± 1.13	71.0 ± 0.93	65.5 ± 1.69	66.1 ± 0.53
4	✓	-	✓	<u>79.0 ± 0.55</u>	62.1 ± 0.76	72.5 ± 0.31	67.5 ± 0.20	70.8 ± 0.34
5	✓	✓	-	75.9 ± 1.39	<u>64.3 ± 0.58</u>	72.6 ± 0.07	<u>67.7 ± 1.27</u>	68.4 ± 0.21
6	✓	✓	✓	**80.5 ± 0.77**	**65.8 ± 0.38**	**72.6 ± 0.43**	**68.4 ± 0.54**	<u>71.6 ± 0.13</u>

textual one. A possible explanation for this discrepancy in modality informativeness, compared to other datasets, is that in MVSA, the visual modality consists of a single image per sample, rather than multiple frames of a video. Additionally, training the visual modality is a significantly prolonged process, requiring substantial time to reach convergence. Consequently, models that favour a bias toward the faster learning modality may achieve superior results as the inherent imbalance, in this case, tends to be advantageous. Although AMST is not the best-performing model for MVSA, all methods exhibit similar performance on this dataset, approaching the baseline unimodal text accuracy.

In contrast, AMST-Alt demonstrates a clear advantage over the standard MLA alternating architecture. In a three-modality scenario, as seen in IEMOCAP and UR-FUNNY, the MLA method underperforms compared to other approaches, highlighting its limitations in handling more complex multimodal interactions. With the introduction of skip training and the mitigation of bias toward faster-learning modalities, AMST-Alt demonstrates that the alternating architecture can achieve performance comparable to joint models on these datasets.

In conclusion, AMST-Alt outperforms MLA in every scenario, highlighting the effectiveness of skip training in alternating and joint training approaches.

5.2 Ablation Study

Table 2 shows results from including and excluding key components of the full AMST architecture. These experiments used audio, visual, and text modalities.

Rows 1 & 2 of Table 2 present the results of the joint method without and with skip training, respectively. Across all datasets, we observe a significant improvement in performance with the incorporation of skip training. Notably, in the CREMA-D dataset, the model's accuracy increases by 14.2% points. This substantial improvement highlights the effectiveness of balancing modalities based on convergence rates in joint architectures, particularly in scenarios

Table 3. Comparisons on average training time per epoch (in seconds, on GPU, averaged over 100 epochs) between state-of-the-art methods and AMST architectures. The percentage of performance improvements or degradations between AMST architectures and the Naïve baseline are reported with (+x%) or (−x%) respectively in the last three rows.

Method	CREMA-D	AVE	MVSA	IEMO-CAP	UR-FUNNY
Naïve	20.3	14.2	27.3	36.9	53.0
MSLR	20.3	14.2	27.3	37.7	53.3
OGM	20.9	15.0	28.0	37.8	54.5
PMR	41.0	65.0	34.2	-	-
MLA	20.8	16.5	27.4	37.6	52.8
AMST-Alt	15.4(**+24%**)	12.4(**+13%**)	16.9(**+38%**)	26.1(**+29%**)	34.1(**+36%**)
AMST-Joint	14.7(**+28%**)	12.2(**+14%**)	17.0(**+38%**)	25.4(**+31%**)	33.9(**+36%**)
AMST-Full	25.1(−24%)	17.1(−20%)	32.0(−17%)	45.7(−24%)	63.6(−20%)

where modalities provide comparable levels of informativeness. Prior to introducing skip training, the underutilised visual modality was unable to fully contribute its informative potential to the final prediction.

A notable improvement is also observed in the alternating architecture (rows 3 & 4 of Table 2, without and with skip training, respectively). The alternating approach facilitates the learning of all modalities by optimising separate modality-specific losses. However, by further mitigating the imbalance caused by varying convergence rates, skip training proves advantageous over scenarios without it.

With the inclusion of skip training, the Alternating and Joint architectures achieve similar performance (rows 2 & 4), closing the gap where joint architectures previously underperformed, especially in the CREMA-D dataset (rows 1 & 3). This further highlights the benefits of skip training.

Finally, rows 5 & 6 of Table 2 present the results of integrating Alternating and Joint Modules, without and with skip training, respectively. Row 5 highlights the advantages of combining these architectures, consistently outperforming the standalone Alternating and Joint cases (rows 1 & 3). Furthermore, as expected, the inclusion of skip training in both modules enhances performance, yielding the best overall results across all datasets, except for the UR-FUNNY dataset.

5.3 Computational Expenses

Table 3 presents the training times for every experiment. We can observe that, compared to the baseline (the Naïve method), most approaches introduce minimal overhead, except for the PMR method, which nearly doubles the training time due to the additional cost of computing prototypes. Notably, our proposed methods, both AMST-Alt and AMST-Joint, significantly reduce the average training time with improvements ranging from around **13%** to **38%** (AMST-Alt and AMST-Joint rows of Table 3) compared to the fastest method (Naïve), while achieving superior results. Moreover, our **Full** architecture (AMST-Full), despite incorporating **4 encoders** (2x as many as other methods), only increases the training time by approximately **17–25%** (AMST-Full row of Table 3) compared to the fastest method (Naïve), demonstrating skip training's efficiency.

6 Conclusion

In this work, we proposed a novel method called AMST to address one aspect of modality imbalance, indicated by different convergence rates across modalities. AMST optimises the multimodal learning process without compromising modality-specific information by having (1) independent training for each of the modalities in the Alternating Module, (2) conventional joint training in the Joint Module, and (3) skip training in both Alternating and Joint Modules.

Our experiments demonstrated that skip training in AMST decreases the dominance gap between modalities in terms of convergence rate, reduces the overall training cost, and provides the complementary benefits of alternating and conventional multimodal joint training practices. Furthermore, we demonstrate AMST's efficacy in scenarios with up to three modalities.

As a consequence of the implementation of skip training in the learning process, an additional hyperparameter, the skip parameter, is created per modality. Currently, fine-tuning each skip parameter is necessary. A future direction is to quantify the convergence rate disparities between modalities and automate the skipping process during training by dynamically adjusting each modality's skip parameter. Finally, it is important to note that improper skip parameter settings may result in suboptimal outcomes, as excessive skipping can lead to under-optimisation of the modalities.

References

1. Busso, C., et al.: Iemocap: interactive emotional dyadic motion capture database. Lang. Resour. Eval. **42**, 335–359 (2008)
2. Cao, H., Cooper, D.G., Keutmann, M.K., Gur, R.C., Nenkova, A., Verma, R.: CREMA-D: crowd-sourced emotional multimodal actors dataset. IEEE Trans. Affect. Comput. **5**(4), 377–390 (2014). https://doi.org/10.1109/TAFFC.2014.2336244
3. Fan, Y., Xu, W., Wang, H., Wang, J., Guo, S.: PMR: prototypical modal rebalance for multimodal learning. In: 2023 IEEE/CVF Conference on Computer Vision and Pattern Recognition (CVPR), pp. 20029–20038 (2023). https://doi.org/10.1109/CVPR52729.2023.01918
4. Hasan, M.K., et al.: Ur-funny: a multimodal language dataset for understanding humor. arXiv preprint arXiv:1904.06618 (2019)
5. He, K., Zhang, X., Ren, S., Sun, J.: Deep residual learning for image recognition. In: Proceedings of the IEEE Conference on Computer Vision and Pattern Recognition, pp. 770–778 (2016)

6. Li, H., Li, X., Hu, P., Lei, Y., Li, C., Zhou, Y.: Boosting multi-modal model performance with adaptive gradient modulation. In: 2023 IEEE/CVF International Conference on Computer Vision (ICCV), pp. 22157–22167 (2023). https://doi.org/10.1109/ICCV51070.2023.02030
7. Lin, X., et al.: Suppress and rebalance: towards generalized multi-modal face anti-spoofing. In: Proceedings of the IEEE/CVF Conference on Computer Vision and Pattern Recognition (CVPR), pp. 211–221 (2024)
8. Liu, Y., et al.: Roberta: a robustly optimized BERT pretraining approach. arXiv preprint arXiv:1907.11692 (2019)
9. McFee, B., et al.: librosa: audio and music signal analysis in python. In: Proceedings of the 14th Python in Science Conference,Proceedings of the Python in Science Conference (2014). https://doi.org/10.25080/majora-7b98e3ed-003
10. Niu, T., Zhu, S., Pang, L., Saddik, A.: Sentiment analysis on multi-view social data. In: Tian, Q., Sebe, N., Qi, G.-J., Huet, B., Hong, R., Liu, X. (eds.) MMM 2016. LNCS, vol. 9517, pp. 15–27. Springer, Cham (2016). https://doi.org/10.1007/978-3-319-27674-8_2
11. Peng, X., Wei, Y., Deng, A., Wang, D., Hu, D.: Balanced multimodal learning via on-the-fly gradient modulation. In: 2022 IEEE/CVF Conference on Computer Vision and Pattern Recognition (CVPR), pp. 8228–8237. IEEE Computer Society, Los Alamitos (2022). https://doi.org/10.1109/CVPR52688.2022.00806
12. Sun, Y., Mai, S., Hu, H.: Learning to balance the learning rates between various modalities via adaptive tracking factor. IEEE Signal Process. Lett. **28**, 1650–1654 (2021). https://doi.org/10.1109/LSP.2021.3101421
13. Tian, Y., Shi, J., Li, B., Duan, Z., Xu, C.: Audio-visual event localization in unconstrained videos. In: Proceedings of the European Conference on Computer Vision (ECCV) (2018)
14. Wang, W., Tran, D., Feiszli, M.: What makes training multi-modal classification networks hard? In: 2020 IEEE/CVF Conference on Computer Vision and Pattern Recognition (CVPR), pp. 12692–12702 (2020). https://doi.org/10.1109/CVPR42600.2020.01271
15. Wu, N., Jastrzebski, S., Cho, K., Geras, K.J.: Characterizing and overcoming the greedy nature of learning in multi-modal deep neural networks. In: Chaudhuri, K., Jegelka, S., Song, L., Szepesvari, C., Niu, G., Sabato, S. (eds.) Proceedings of the 39th International Conference on Machine Learning. Proceedings of Machine Learning Research, vol. 162, pp. 24043–24055. PMLR (2022)
16. Xu, N., Mao, W.: Multisentinet: a deep semantic network for multimodal sentiment analysis. In: Proceedings of the 2017 ACM on Conference on Information and Knowledge Management, pp. 2399–2402 (2017)
17. Yao, Y., Mihalcea, R.: Modality-specific learning rates for effective multimodal additive late-fusion. In: Muresan, S., Nakov, P., Villavicencio, A. (eds.) Findings of the Association for Computational Linguistics: ACL 2022, Dublin, Ireland, pp. 1824–1834. Association for Computational Linguistics (2022). https://doi.org/10.18653/v1/2022.findings-acl.143
18. Zhang, X., Yoon, J., Bansal, M., Yao, H.: Multimodal representation learning by alternating unimodal adaptation. In: 2024 IEEE/CVF Conference on Computer Vision and Pattern Recognition (CVPR), pp. 27446–27456. IEEE Computer Society, Los Alamitos (2024). https://doi.org/10.1109/CVPR52733.2024.02592

Cross-Modal Causal Scheduling for Enhancing Target-Oriented Multi-modal Sentiment Classification

Pengyu Zhao[1], Chaoyang Li[1,2], Lingzhi Wang[1], and Qing Liao[1,2(✉)]

[1] Harbin Institute of Technology, Shenzhen, China
{23S151160,22b951022}@stu.hit.edu.cn
[2] Peng Cheng Laboratory, Shenzhen, China
{wanglingzhi,liaoqing}@hit.edu.cn

Abstract. Target-oriented multi-modal sentiment classification (TMSC) aims to identify sentiment polarity towards specific targets by considering multiple modalities, e.g., text and images. However, current methods often ignore spurious correlations within the data, which can cause models to learn irrelevant features that misrepresent the sentiment of targets. To address this issue, we propose a novel *Cross-Modal Causal Scheduling* framework (CMCS) that prioritizes learning multi-modal features with fewer spurious correlations. Specifically, we first design a *Multi-modal Feature Selection* model (MFS) that utilizes causal intervention to select relevant features. Second, we construct a *Causal cross-Modal Scheduler* (CMS) to assess the causal effects of selected features, which further optimize the multi-modal learning process based on these effects. Finally, we formulate the CMS and the multi-modal learning process as a bi-level optimization problem. In the lower optimization, the MFS is updated with the scheduled gradient, while in the upper optimization, the CMS is updated with the implicit gradient. Extensive experiments demonstrate that our method outperforms existing baseline methods on TMSC and can effectively schedule the learning process of multi-modal features based on causal effects.

Keywords: Multi-modal Sentiment Analysis · Target-oriented multi-modal sentiment classification · Causal Inference

1 Introduction

Target-oriented multi-modal sentiment classification (TMSC) [19,27,47] is a challenging fine-grained sentiment analysis task that determines the sentiment polarity of opinion targets by considering various modalities, such as text and images. Taking Fig. 1(a) as an example, in the sentence *"Pat celebrating her 90th birthday with Emily Roux in Chez Roux at the Newmarket Guineas Festival"*, three distinct targets can be identified: *"Pat"*, *"Emily Roux"*, and *"Newmarket Guineas Festival"*. The corresponding

---

P. Zhao and C. Li—The first two authors contributed equally to this work.

Supplementary Information The online version contains supplementary material available at https://doi.org/10.1007/978-3-032-06078-5_31.

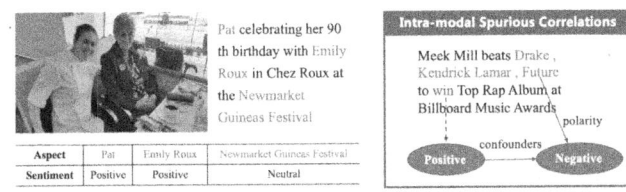

Fig. 1. The example and spurious correlations in the TMSC task. In (b), the left side depicts intra-modal spurious correlations, where the sentiment of the blue target may be influenced by the word *"win"*. The right side shows inter-modal spurious correlations, where the irrelevant visual features may interfere with the sentiment of the red target. (Color figure online)

sentiment polarities for these targets are *"positive"*, *"positive"*, and *"neutral"*, respectively. TMSC has gained notable attention in multi-modal sentiment analysis due to the challenges of simultaneously handling different modalities [11,24,53]. Most existing works on TMSC primarily focus on effectively fusing multi-modal information, including methods like feature concatenation [25,41], cross-modal alignment of image regions with text sequences [11,47,55], and using Energy-Based Models [15,30] to enhance TMSC performance.

Despite progress in the TMSC field, most existing works overlook the spurious correlations within the multi-modal data, easily learning features irrelevant to the sentiment polarities of targets and degrading TMSC performance [37]. On the one hand, for a text sentence, a correlation bias (i.e., intra-modal spurious correlation) often exists between targets and co-occurring contextual words, which may lead the model to focus on words irrelevant to the sentiment of the targets, harming sentiment classification performance [54]. As shown in Fig. 1(b), the word *"win"* is typically associated with positive sentiment, which may interfere with the negative sentiment polarity of targets (i.e., blue-marked words). On the other hand, given text-image pairs, images often contain information irrelevant to the text, leading models to erroneously associate irrelevant visual features with sentiment labels during training (i.e., inter-modal spurious correlations) [52]. As shown in Fig. 1(b), the text *"Benicia High baseball clinches a playoff berth with 10-0 win over Fairfield"* lacks meaningful correlation with its corresponding image, which can cause the model to learn irrelevant visual features mistakenly.

To identify the causes of spurious correlations and suggest solutions, we construct a Structural Causal Model (SCM) (Fig. 2), where T, I, C and Y represent the text sentence, image, confounding factors and the sentiment predictions of targets, respectively. Here, $T \rightarrow Y$ and $I \rightarrow Y$ denote the desired causal effect, enabling the model to predict label Y directly from image T and I. However, not all features in T and I are relevant to Y. The confounding factors C, stemming from data bias, can interfere between T and Y, as well as between I and Y, creating spurious cor-

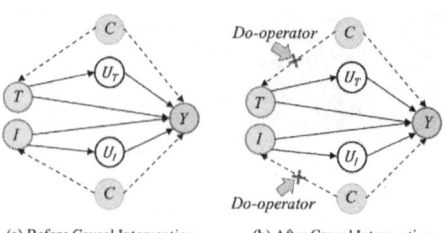

(a) Before Causal Intervention   (b) After Causal Intervention

Fig. 2. The SCMs of TMSC. T, I, C, U_T, U_I, Y denote text, image, confounders, textual/visual features, and predictions. Solid and dotted arrows indicate causal relationships and spurious correlations. $Do - operator$ is an intervention operation.

relations with irrelevant features [13]. To address this, we aim to mitigate spurious correlations via causal intervention (i.e., $Do - operator$), extracting relevant textual features U_T and relevant visual features U_I to learn beneficial causal effects (i.e., $T \rightarrow U_T \rightarrow Y$ and $I \rightarrow U_I \rightarrow Y$). Notely, different modal features can introduce varying degrees of spurious interference on sentiment labels, with samples exhibiting strong spurious correlations presenting greater challenges for model learning and hindering the convergence of multi-modal feature learning. This motivates us to explore a method that adaptively optimizes the learning process of multi-modal features based on causal effects, ultimately enhancing TMSC performance.

To achieve the above goal, we propose a novel *Cross-Modal Causal Scheduling* framework (CMCS), which prioritizes the learning of multi-modal features based on their susceptibility to spurious correlations. Our framework consists of three main components. First, we introduce the *Multi-modal Feature Selection* model (MFS), which leverages causal interventions to identify key features across modalities. Second, we design the *Causal cross-Modal Scheduler* (CMS), which employs counterfactual reasoning to assess the causal effects of selected features and schedule them for learning accordingly. Lastly, we implement a bi-level optimization strategy that determines the optimal cross-modal scheduling. The lower-level optimization updates the MFS using the scheduled gradient, while the upper-level optimization updates the CMS by implicit gradient updates. The key contributions are summarized as follows:

- We propose a novel *Cross-Modal Causal Scheduling* framework (CMCS) that optimizes multi-modal feature learning from a causal perspective, enhancing the performance of TMSC.
- We design a multi-modal feature selection model, which selects relevant multi-modal features with targets by simple yet effective causal intervention, alleviating spurious correlations.
- We construct a causal cross-modal scheduler that manages multi-modal learning processes by assessing the causal effects of features, incorporating a bi-level optimization to determine the optimal scheduling adaptively.

– Extensive experiments on two benchmark datasets show the superiority of our proposed framework over several baselines in terms of TMSC.

2 Related Work

2.1 Target-Oriented Sentiment Classification

Sentiment analysis, also known as opinion mining, is a key research area in natural language processing and data mining [20,45]. It focuses on systematically identifying affective states in textual data, enabling computational evaluation of emotions, opinions, and attitudes in written or spoken language [9].

Over the past decade, Target-Oriented Sentiment Classification (TSC), also known as Aspect-Based Sentiment Analysis (ABSA) [21], has become a key subfield of sentiment analysis, primarily focusing on identifying the sentiment polarity of target words in textual data [4,26]. Early studies in target-oriented sentiment classification primarily focused on modeling the structural relationships between target words and their contextual environments. For instance, introducing multi-grained attention architectures [6] to explicitly capture fine-grained linguistic dependencies between target words and their surrounding context. Others leverage graph convolutional networks, utilizing syntactic dependency trees and semantic role labeling frameworks to represent the bidirectional interdependencies between target words and their contextual descriptors [16,17,28].

More recently, causal inference has been incorporated into target-oriented sentiment classification to address issues related to data biases and spurious correlations between target words and their context. For example, some studies have introduced Structural Causal Models (SCMs) to disentangle confounding factors [54], while others have employed prompt-enhanced Large Language Models (LLMs) to generate counterfactually augmented training samples, effectively mitigating dataset biases [38].

2.2 Target-Oriented Multi-modal Sentiment Classification

In recent years, with advancements in multimedia technology, social media data has exhibited a multi-modal trend, leading to widespread research interest in multi-modal sentiment analysis [1,11,51]. This has led to growing interest in target-oriented multi-modal sentiment classification (TMSC), which seeks to utilize both visual and textual content for more accurate sentiment predictions.

Most works in TMSC focus on fusing multi-modal information to improve sentiment analysis accuracy. For example, [2] bridges the gap between text and images using image attributes, while ESAFN [48] applies LSTM for entity-level sentiment analysis. [49] leverages BERT [5] for aspect-sensitive representations, offering deeper insights into sentiment in specific contexts. Additionally, [12] translates images into text to improve sentiment prediction, and [39] introduces multi-modal retrieval to refine text-image integration. [44] translates facial expressions into emotional semantics, connecting visual cues to emotional understanding. [18] advances vision-language pre-training for richer modality representations. [55] introduces an aspect-aware attention module that enhances the model's ability to focus on relevant features tied to specific sentiment aspects. [50] captures image-target relationships. [30] integrates Energy-Based Models [15] into TMSC, refining the fusion process and boosting sentiment classification by modeling energy-based relationships between modalities.

Differences. Existing works primarily focus on fusion and alignment across modalities, often overlooking spurious correlations within multi-modal data. In contrast, we propose a novel cross-modal causal scheduling framework that extracts multi-modal features and assigns weights based on causal effects, reducing spurious correlations.

2.3 Causal Inference

Causal inference has gained attention for improving predictions by focusing on causal relationships rather than mere statistical correlations. For instance, structural causal models and do-calculus formalize causal relationships and guide interventions [29]. Neural networks can estimate causal effects between input variables and output targets [10,34]. [8] mitigate the spurious association problem in the sarcasm detection task through causal interventions. [46] alleviate the problem of spurious correlations of visual modalities through causal interventions. Although few works apply causal inference to sentiment analysis, such as [54] for text-aspect-based sentiment and [35,36,43] for traditional multi-modal sentiment, research on causal inference in TMSC is limited. Our method not only measures the causal effects of different modal features but also adaptively schedules them based on these effects, a consideration missing in existing approaches.

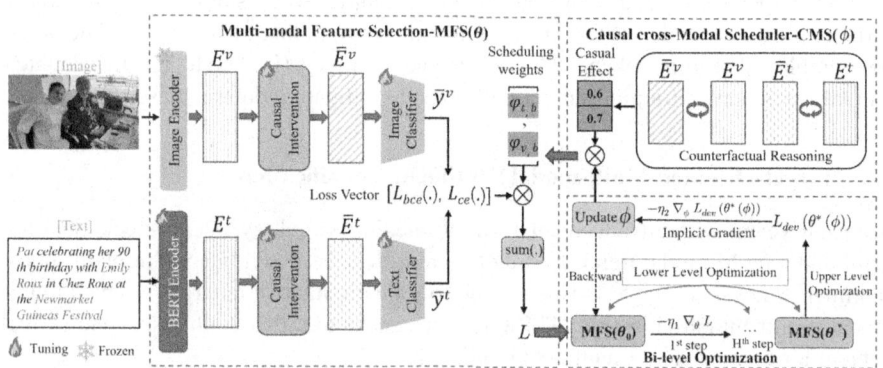

Fig. 3. An overview of CMCS training. First, the MFS selects relevant features with targets via causal interventions. These selected features are further input into classifiers for sentiment prediction. Second, the CMS assesses the causal effects of features using counterfactual reasoning, dynamically assigning learning weights based on causal effects. Last, the bi-level optimization is to solve optimal scheduling weights for enhanced multi-modal feature learning.

3 Methodology

3.1 Overview

Task Definition. Given a set of multi-modal samples $\mathcal{X}$, each sample $X \in \mathcal{X}$ contains a text sentence X_t with n words and its corresponding image X_v, as well as the l opinion targets $\mathcal{T} = (T_1, T_2, ..., T_l)$ referring to a span in the sentence X_t. TMSC aims to predict the sentiment label y of each opinion target mentioned in the text-image pair $X = (X_t, X_v)$, where y can be either positive, negative, or neutral.

Our Framework. Figure 3 illustrates our proposed CMCS training framework. Specifically, to reduce the interference from spurious features, we first introduce the *Multi-modal Feature Selection* model (MFS), employing causal intervention to select relevant multi-modal features with targets. These selected features are then fed into the classifiers to generate predictions. Considering that different modal features exhibit varying levels of spurious interference with sentiment labels, we also develop a *Causal cross-Modal Scheduler* (CMS) that uses counterfactual reasoning to assess the causal effects of selected features and assigns learning weights accordingly. Finally, bi-level optimization is implemented to adaptively find the optimal weights for scheduling multi-modal learning.

3.2 Multi-modal Feature Selection

Spurious correlations may mislead the model into learning irrelevant textual and visual features to sentiment labels, further degrading TMSC effectiveness. To address these issues, we propose the *Multi-modal Feature Selection* model (MFS) that utilizes simple yet effective causal intervention to identify relevant features with targets' labels.

Textual Feature Selection. Given the sentence X_t, we use the BERT [5] to obtain its textual embedding from the [CLS] token $E^t \in \mathbb{R}^{m \times d}$ by $E^t = \Phi_t(X_t)$, where Φ_t is the BERT encoder and $m \times d$ is the dimensions of the textual embedding. To mitigate intra-modal spurious correlations in the text data, we design a causal intervention network with learnable masks $M^t \in \mathbb{R}^{m \times d}$. The values of M^t range between $(0, 1)$ and are used to filter textual features by training the corresponding parameters. $\odot$ means element-wise multiplication and M^t assigns weights to each feature to implement the do-operator. Through the causal intervention network, we can derive the counterfactual textual features $\overline{E}^t$ as follows:

$$M^t = \text{Sigmoid}(\text{MLP}(E^t)), \tag{1}$$

$$\overline{E}^t = \text{MLP}(M^t \odot E^t + \text{MLP}(M^t \odot E^t)), \tag{2}$$

where MLP is the multi-layer perception.

The $\overline{E}^t$ are designed to predict the correct sentiment label accurately. Thus, we use the Cross-Entropy loss function L_{ce} to guide the model to learn label-relevant textual features as follows,

$$L_t = L_{ce}\left(\overline{y}^t, y^t\right), \tag{3}$$

where $\overline{y}^t = f_t(\overline{E}^t)$ is the prediction of the counterfactual textual features, f_t represents the textual classifier, and y^t denotes the textual ground truth.

Visual Feature Selection. The image information may interfere with predicting the target sentiment due to inter-modal spurious correlations. To address this issue, we also design a causal intervention network to capture relevant visual features with targets' labels. Given the image $X_v \in \mathbb{R}^{c \times h \times w}$ with the dimensions of $c \times h \times w$, we use the CLIP [31] image encoder Φ_v to obtain the image embedding $E^v = \Phi_v(X_v) \in \mathbb{R}^{m \times d}$. The causal intervention network for selecting relevant visual features by training learnable masks $M^v \in \mathbb{R}^{m \times d}$, which has the same structure as the textual causal intervention network. The counterfactual visual features $\overline{E}^v$ can be obtained using Eq. (5),

$$M^v = \text{Sigmoid}(\text{MLP}(E^v)), \tag{4}$$

$$\overline{E}^v = \text{MLP}(M^v \odot E^v + \text{MLP}\left(M^v \odot E^v\right)). \tag{5}$$

To better align images with their corresponding sentiment labels of targets, we formulate the task as a multi-class classification problem. In practice, the sentiment labels can be marked by a triple $(negative, neutral, positive)$. For instance, if the text associated with an image contains both *"neutral"* and *"positive"* sentiments, its label is defined as $(0, 1, 1)$. We use Binary Cross-Entropy Loss L_{bce} to constrain predictions of counterfactual visual features. Therefore, the training loss of visual features is formulated by Eq. (6),

$$L_v = L_{bce}\left(\overline{y}^v, y^v\right), \tag{6}$$

where $\overline{y}^v = f_v(\overline{E}^v)$ denotes the prediction of counterfactual visual features, f_v represents the image classifier, and y^v denotes the image ground truth.

3.3 Causal Cross-Modal Scheduler

An intuitive way for joint learning of selected multi-modal features is to train the sum of L_t and L_v. However, this can be sub-optimal as it ignores the fact that varying degrees of spurious correlations in the multi-modal data impact model training differently. To enhance multi-modal learning, we propose a *Causal cross-Modal Scheduler* (CMS) that adapts training based on the perceived causal effects of selected features, assigning greater learning weights to those with stronger causal effects. Inspired by the granger-causal objective [32,33] for mining causal relationships (illustrations are provided in the Appendix A.1), we propose a novel counterfactual reasoning method to measure the causal effect by computing the loss difference between the counterfactual features and the original features.

Causal Effect of Textual Feature. Specifically, the causal effect $\Delta\epsilon(\overline{E}^t)$ is computed by comparing the losses of $\overline{E}^t$ and E^t, which is formulated by Eq. (7),

$$\Delta\epsilon(\overline{E}^t) = \exp\left(L_{ce}\left(y^t, \widehat{y}^t\right) - L_{ce}\left(y^t, \overline{y}^t\right)\right), \tag{7}$$

where $\widehat{y}^t = f_t(E^t)$ denotes the prediction of original textual features, $\overline{y}^t$ is the prediction of the counterfactual textual features, and y^t denotes the textual ground truth.

Causal Effect of Visual Feature. Given the counterfactual visual features $\overline{E}^v$ and the original visual features E^v, we also introduce counterfactual reasoning to measure the causal effect of selected visual features. It is formulated by Eq. (8),

$$\Delta\epsilon(\overline{E}^v) = \exp\left(L_{bce}\left(y^v, \widehat{y}^v\right) - L_{bce}\left(y^v, \overline{y}^v\right)\right), \tag{8}$$

where $\widehat{y}^v = f_v(E^v)$ represents the prediction of the original visual features, $\overline{y}^v$ denotes the prediction of counterfactual visual features, and y^v is the image ground truth.

When $\Delta\epsilon(\overline{E}^t)$ or $\Delta\epsilon(\overline{E}^v)$ is greater than 1, it indicates that $\overline{E}^t$ or $\overline{E}^v$ generates smaller task loss compared to E^t or E^v, suggesting the selected features positively impact sentiment prediction. Conversely, if $\Delta\epsilon(\overline{E}^t)$ or $\Delta\epsilon(\overline{E}^v)$ is less than 1, the selected features negatively affect the task. As the model trains, the causal effect is expected to increase or remain stable, allowing the model to learn more relevant features aligned with the target.

Casual Scheduling Objective. The larger the causal effect of features, the greater their causal contribution to predicting correct sentiment labels. Based on the causal effects, we then design learnable scheduling weights $\varphi_{t,b} = \sigma\left(\alpha \cdot \Delta\epsilon(\overline{E}^t)\right)$ and $\varphi_{v,b} = \sigma\left(\beta \cdot \Delta\epsilon(\overline{E}^v)\right)$ (detailed explanation is provided in the Appendix A.2), where b is the batch index, σ is the softplus function, α and β are the learnable parameters. φ_t and φ_v aim to perceive the causal effects of the extracted textual and visual features, respectively. Then, we use these learnable scheduling weights to perform a weighted summation of the multi-modal joint training losses to obtain the final scheduled objective, as follows,

$$L = \sum_{b \in D_{train}} (\varphi_{t,b} \cdot L_t + \varphi_{v,b} \cdot L_v), \tag{9}$$

where D_{train} is the training dataset.

3.4 Solving Scheduler via Bi-Level Optimization

The scheduler is to optimize the learnable parameters set $\phi = \{\alpha, \beta\}$ to minimize Eq. (9). Considering the high computational cost of searching for optimal scheduling parameters for multi-modal features in each batch, this approach demands substantial resources. To address this, we introduce a small developing dataset $D_{dev} = \{(x_b^{dev}, y_b^{dev})\}_b^B$, which is a small subset sampled from the validation set D_v [3]. We utilize the objective loss on D_{dev} to optimize the parameters ϕ to achieve the optimal scheduling weights for multi-modal loss on D_{dev}. Given the ϕ and MFS model parameter θ, our problem can be formulated as a bi-level optimization problem shown as Eq. (11),

$$L_{dev}(\theta^*(\phi)) = \sum_{b \in D_{dev}} (\varphi_{t,b} \cdot L_t + \varphi_{v,b} \cdot L_v), \tag{10}$$

$$\phi^* = \arg\min_{\phi} L_{dev}(\theta^*(\phi)),$$
$$s.t.\ \theta^* = \arg\min_{\theta} L(\theta, \phi), \tag{11}$$

where $L_{dev}(\theta^*(\phi))$ is the scheduled training loss in Eq. (9) on D_{dev}. It is noted that $\varphi_{t,b}$ and $\varphi_{v,b}$ are parameterized by ϕ.

In the lower-level optimization, we update the MFS parameter θ with the fixed parameter ϕ. θ is updated by using the weighted gradient sum of the different modalities as follows,

$$\nabla_\theta L(\theta, \phi) = \sum_{b \in D_{train}} (\varphi_{t,b} \cdot \nabla_\theta L_t + \varphi_{v,b} \cdot \nabla_\theta L_v). \tag{12}$$

In the upper-level optimization, it is expected to compute the gradient $L_{dev}(\theta^*(\phi))$ to ϕ. Given the indirect dependency of $L_{dev}(\theta^*(\phi))$ on ϕ through θ, we use implicit differentiation to obtain this implicit gradient [22]. Inspired by the *Cauchy-based Implicit Function Theorem* [22], we can leverage the chain rule to systematically derive the gradient of $L_{dev}(\theta^*(\phi))$ to ϕ,

$$\begin{aligned}\nabla_\phi L_{dev}(\theta^*(\phi)) &= \nabla_\theta L_{dev} \cdot \nabla_\phi \theta^* \\ &= -\nabla_\theta L_{dev} \cdot \left(\nabla_\theta^2 L\right)^{-1} \cdot \nabla_\phi \nabla_\theta L|_{(\phi, \theta^*(\phi))}.\end{aligned} \tag{13}$$

The detailed derivation of the implicit gradient is in Appendix A.3. However, directly computing the inverse of the Hessian matrix for deep neural models is often computationally intractable due to its immense size and complexity. To address this, we employ the *K-truncated Neumann* series [3] to approximate this inverse, i.e., $\left(\nabla_\theta^2 L\right)^{-1} \approx \sum_{j=0}^{K} \left(I - \nabla_\theta^2 L\right)^j$ where I is the identity matrix. Thus, the implicit gradient $\nabla_\phi L_{dev}(\theta^*(\phi))$ can be calculated as in Eq. (14).

$$\nabla_\phi L_{dev} = -\nabla_\theta L_{dev} \cdot \sum_{j=0}^{K} \left(I - \nabla_\theta^2 L\right)^j \cdot \nabla_\phi \nabla_\theta L. \tag{14}$$

Algorithm 1 outlines the comprehensive process for optimizing the MFS (θ) and the CMS (ϕ) based on their gradients. During the lower-level optimization phase, ϕ remains fixed while θ is updated using the gradient specified in Eq. (12) at a learning rate of η_1. Rather than aiming for full convergence of θ, we employ an efficient H-step optimization approach, inspired by [22], where θ undergoes H iterations of updates before shifting to the upper-level optimization of ϕ. We first evaluate L_{dev} according to Eq. (14) and then leverage the implicit gradient to update ϕ with a learning rate of η_2. Given N modalities, the truncated Neumann series number as K, the time complexity for the gradient backward of CMCS is $O(N + (K + N)/H)$. Details are provided in the Appendix A.4.

3.5 Model Inference

Cross-modal feature fusion may be suboptimal because images often contain a significant amount of information that may be irrelevant to the sentiment of the target words in the text [52]. To address this, we integrate the prediction scores from both the image and text modalities to make the final sentiment classification during the inference stage. Following previous works [30], we design prompts for images. Specifically, the prompt corresponding to an image is *"it's a picture of with a target of [label]"*, where [label]

Algorithm 1. CMCS Algorithm

1: **Input:** datasets: D_{train}, D_{dev}; hyperparameters: H, K, η_1, η_2
2: **Initialization:** $\theta, \phi, \theta_{opt}$
3: **while** not converge **do**
4:    // lower-level optimization (update θ with fixed ϕ)
5:    **for** $t = 0$ to $H - 1$ **do**
6:      Calculate the causal effect of textual features by Eq. (7)
7:      Calculate the causal effect of visual features by Eq. (8)
8:      Update model parameters θ by
       $\theta = \theta - \eta_1 \nabla_\theta L(\theta, \phi)$
9:    **end for**
10:    // upper-level optimization (update ϕ with current θ)
11:    Obtain the $L_{dev}(\theta^*(\phi))$ on D_{dev} by Eq. (14)
12:    Update scheduling parameters ϕ by
       $\phi = \phi - \eta_2 \nabla_\phi L_{dev}$
13: **end while**
14: **Return** θ_{opt}
---

is the target term from the text. For the text prompt X_P, we use the CLIP [31] text encoder Φ_p and prompt embedding $E^p = \Phi_t(X_P) \in \mathbb{R}^{m \times d}$. The similarity scores $\theta = \cos(E^t, E^p)$ can be used to ensemble prediction scores from the two modalities. If the similarity is higher, the image and the text are more relevant, so the proportion of the image will be larger in the final fusion. Finally, the prediction is obtained by computing the weighted sum of the image and text predictions, formulated by Eq. (15),

$$y^h = (1 - \theta) \cdot \overline{y}^t + \theta \cdot \overline{y}^v. \qquad (15)$$

4 Experiment

4.1 Experimental Settings

Dataset. Following previous works [42,55], we conduct experiments on two well-known benchmark datasets: Twitter2015 [23] and Twitter2017 [47]. Basic statistics for datasets are summarized in Appendix A.5.

Table 1. Results of different methods for TMSC. * denotes the results from VEMP [42]. ♣ denotes the results from AoM [55].

Methods	Twitter2015		Twitter2017	
	Acc	F1	Acc	F1
Text-based				
AE-LSTM*	70.3	63.4	61.7	58.0
MGAN*	71.2	64.2	64.8	61.5
BERT	77.1	71.1	70.2	68.2
Multimodal				
ESAFN♣	73.4	67.4	67.8	64.2
TomBERT♣	77.2	71.8	70.5	68.0
CapTrBERT♣	78.0	73.2	72.3	70.2
JML♣	78.7	-	72.7	-
FITE*	78.5	73.9	70.9	68.7
ITM	78.3	74.2	72.6	72.0
CLUE	77.8	72.6	71.7	70.3
GEAR	78.5	73.8	73.1	72.2
VEMP	78.6	74.1	73.0	72.4
AoM	78.3	72.9	73.6	72.0
DQPSA	76.5	-	70.3	-
CMCS(ours)	**79.7**	**75.5**	**74.3**	**73.5**

Implementation Details. Our method is built on BERT [5] and CLIP [31], trained for 30 epochs with a batch size of 32 on TMSC. The learning rate is set to 2e-5, and the hidden sizes of BERT and CLIP are both 1024. All instruction-tuning experiments are conducted using PyTorch on an NVIDIA Tesla V100 GPU.

Evaluation Metrics. Following previous studies, we evaluate the performance of our model on the TMSC task by Micro-F1 score (F1) and accuracy (Acc) and report the average of 5 independent training runs as results. To prevent overfitting of the model, the dropout is set to 0.1.

4.2 Baselines

We compare our proposed CMCS with the twelve baselines, including AE-LSTM [40], MGAN [7], BERT [5], ESAFN [48], TomBERT [49], CapTrBERT [12], JML [11], FITE [44], ITM [50], CLUE [36], GEAR [35], VEMP [42], AoM [55], and DQPSA [30]. Due to the space limit, details of baselines are in the Appendix A.6.

4.3 Main Results and Analysis

Performance. Table 1 presents performance metrics for TMSC. Our proposed CMCS outperforms all text-based models, highlighting the advantages of using multi-modal information. Existing multi-modal sentiment analysis methods often require extensive pre-training on image datasets to align image and text features. In contrast, CMCS does not require such pre-training. Even without pre-training, CMCS exceeds previous multi-modal models in several metrics, achieving 1.0% and 0.9% improvements in accuracy and 1.5% and 0.5% improvements in F1 scores on the Twitter2015 and Twitter2017 datasets, respectively. The accuracy change curves of CMCS compared to the sub-optimal methods in Appendix A.7 show that CMCS achieves a higher accuracy more quickly. The computational efficiency analysis in Appendix A.8 shows that CMCS achieves optimal TMSC performance without significantly increasing training and inference overhead.

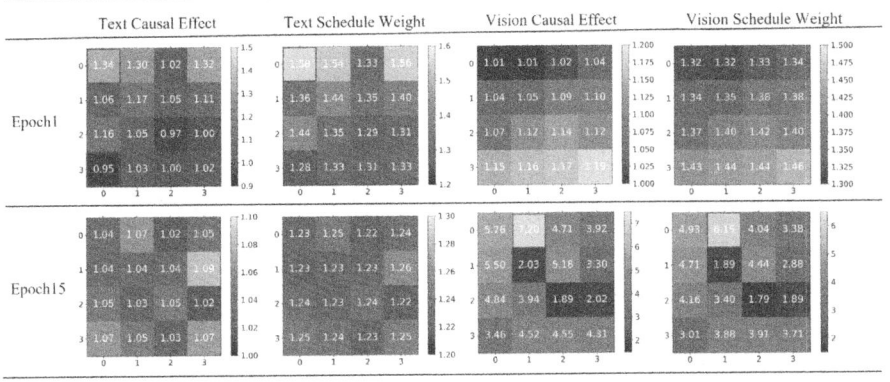

Fig. 4. Visualization of causal effect and scheduling weights.

4.4 Ablation Study

We study the effectiveness of each component in CMCS, the results are shown in Table 2.

W/o Visual Modality shows that after removing the visual modality, the performance declines by 0.6% and 0.9% in accuracy on Twitter2015 and Twitter2017, but 0.4% in F1 on Twitter2015 and 2.4% on Twitter2017. It underscores the importance of the visual modality.

Table 2. Ablation results.

Method	Twitter2015		Twitter2017	
	Acc	F1	Acc	F1
ours	**79.7**	**75.5**	**74.3**	**73.5**
w/o Visual Modality	79.1	75.1	73.5	71.2
w/o CMS	78.2	73.4	72.4	71.2
w/o MFS	78.3	72.8	72.9	71.6
w/o (MFS & CMS)	78.4	72.5	73.1	71.5

W/o CMS indicates that removing the causal cross-modal scheduler results in performance drops of 1.5% and 1.2% in accuracy on Twitter2015 and Twitter2017, respectively. This underscores that measuring the causal effects of different samples helps prioritize those that are easier to learn, ultimately enhancing model performance.

W/o MFS. We set the learnable mask values in MFS to a fixed value of 0.5 and tested its ablation results, and it shows that MFS plays a significant role in TMSC.

W/o (MFS & CMS) shows that cross-modal causal scheduling is essential; merely extracting features without measuring their effects does not benefit model improvement.

4.5 Further Analysis

To investigate the effectiveness of the causal scheduling, we show the causal effects and scheduling weight of 16 batches at Epoch 1 and Epoch 15, presented in Fig. 4. First, within the same epoch, batches with greater causal effects correspond to larger scheduling parameters, demonstrating that our causal cross-modal scheduler effectively adjusts to different samples based on their causal effects. Second, for text features, some causal effects are less than 1 in Epoch 1, while in Epoch 15, almost all exceed 1,

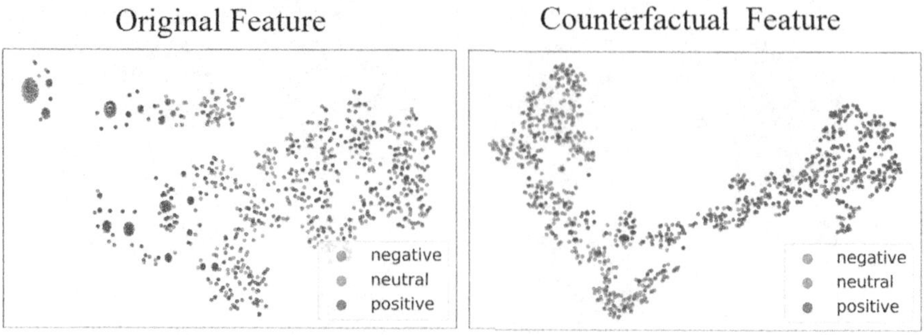

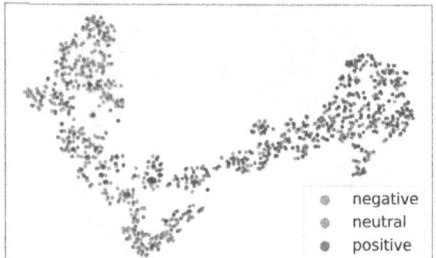

Fig. 5. Textual feature visualization in Twitter2017.

Image		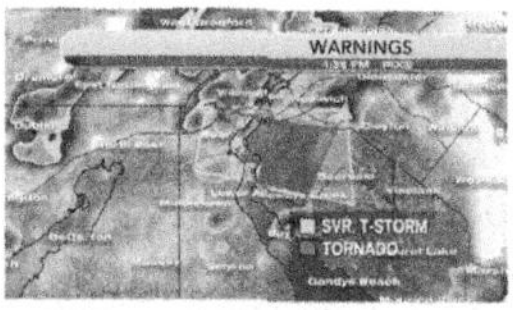	
Sentence	(a) RT @ dailynation : NBK suspends CFO over alleged links to [Mumias]$_{negative}$ fiasco	(b) Tornado Warning for Salem County in [Southern NJ]$_{neutral}$ until 5pm . @ PIX11News	(c) 17 Awesome # [Facebook]$_{positive}$ # Business Page Post Ideas for Small Businesses
BERT	Neutral ×	Negative ×	Neutral ×
ITM	Positive ×	Negative ×	Positive √
AoM	Positive ×	Neutral √	Positive √
VEMP	Negative √	Negative ×	Neutral ×
CMCS	Negative √	Neutral √	Positive √

Fig. 6. Comparison of BERT, ITM, AoM, VEMP, and CMCS on three test samples.

suggesting the model becomes more adept at selecting relevant features over time. For image features, a noticeable increase in causal effects with more epochs indicates the presence of irrelevant features in the image data, allowing the model to identify relevant features more easily.

We also use the t-SNE [14] to visualize textual features of test datasets, as shown in Fig. 5 and Fig. 2 (in the Appendix A.7). These two figures illustrate that some original instances are misclassified into other categories. In contrast, CMCS effectively distinguishes the three sentiment polarities through textual causal intervention. This indicates that textual causal intervention can enhance textual sentiment classification.

4.6 Case Study

To intuitively demonstrate the advantage of our method, we compare the predictions of BERT [5], ITM [50], AoM [55], VEMP [42], and CMCS on three test samples, as shown in Fig. 6. In sample (a), BERT misjudges the sentiment by ignoring important words relevant to the target *"Mumias"* while ITM and VEMP errors seem to arise from interference from the visual modality. In sample (b), BERT, VEMP, and ITM incorrectly classify the sentiment of *"Southern NJ"* as negative due to a spurious correlation between the word "Warning" and negative sentiment. In sample (c), both BERT and VEMP misclassify the sentiment of *"Facebook"* as neutral, influenced by surrounding neutral sentiment words. These examples highlight CMCS's effectiveness in identifying important features related to the target through causal intervention and causal cross-modal scheduling.

5 Conclusion

In this paper, we propose a novel *Cross-Modal Causal Scheduling* framework (CMCS) for TMSC, aiming to tackle spurious correlations in multi-modal data. By implementing a *Multi-modal Feature Selection* model (MFS), a *Causal cross-Modal Scheduler* (CMS), and the bi-level optimization strategy, CMCS can prioritize relevant multi-modal features. Experimental results on two public datasets validate the effectiveness of our framework in improving sentiment classification.

Limitations

Since existing datasets for the TMSC task primarily include only the image and text modalities, our method considers information from these two modalities and does not account for other modalities such as audio and video. In the future, we will explore how to effectively utilize additional modalities and investigate multi-modal target sentiment analysis in incremental scenarios.

Acknowledgments. This work was supported in part by the National Key Research and Development Program of China under Grant 2023YFB3107000.

References

1. Asgari-Chenaghlu, M., Feizi-Derakhshi, M.R., Farzinvash, L., Balafar, M.A., Motamed, C.: A multimodal deep learning approach for named entity recognition from social media. Neural Comput. Appl. 1905–1922 (2022)
2. Cai, Y., Cai, H., Wan, X.: Multi-modal sarcasm detection in twitter with hierarchical fusion model. In: Proceedings of the 57th Annual Meeting of the Association for Computational Linguistics (2019)
3. Chen, H., Wang, X., Guan, C., Liu, Y., Zhu, W.: Auxiliary learning with joint task and data scheduling. In: International Conference on Machine Learning, ICML, pp. 3634–3647 (2022)
4. Chen, Z., Qian, T.: Relation-aware collaborative learning for unified aspect-based sentiment analysis. In: Proceedings of the 58th Annual Meeting of the Association for Computational Linguistics (2020)

5. Devlin, J., Chang, M., Lee, K., Toutanova, K.: BERT: pre-training of deep bidirectional transformers for language understanding. CoRR abs/1810.04805 (2018)
6. Fan, F., Feng, Y., Zhao, D.: Multi-grained attention network for aspect-level sentiment classification. In: Proceedings of the 2018 Conference on Empirical Methods in Natural Language Processing (2018)
7. Fan, F., Feng, Y., Zhao, D.: Multi-grained attention network for aspect-level sentiment classification. In: Proceedings of the 2018 Conference on Empirical Methods in Natural Language Processing (2018)
8. Jia, M., Xie, C., Jing, L.: Debiasing multimodal sarcasm detection with contrastive learning. In: AAAI Conference on Artificial Intelligence (2023)
9. Jim, J.R., Talukder, M.A.R., Malakar, P., Kabir, M.M., Nur, K., Mridha, M.F.: Recent advancements and challenges of NLP-based sentiment analysis: a state-of-the-art review. Nat. Lang. Process. J. 100059 (2024)
10. Johansson, F.D., Shalit, U., Sontag, D.: Learning representations for counterfactual inference. In: Proceedings of the 33rd International Conference on Machine Learning (ICML), pp. 3020–3029 (2016)
11. Ju, X., et al.: Joint multi-modal aspect-sentiment analysis with auxiliary cross-modal relation detection. In: Proceedings of the 2021 Conference on Empirical Methods in Natural Language Processing, pp. 4395–4405 (2021)
12. Khan, Z., Fu, Y.: Exploiting BERT for multimodal target sentiment classification through input space translation. In: Proceedings of the 29th ACM International Conference on Multimedia (2021)
13. Kim, J., Lee, B.K., Ro, Y.M.: Demystifying causal features on adversarial examples and causal inoculation for robust network by adversarial instrumental variable regression. In: 2023 IEEE/CVF Conference on Computer Vision and Pattern Recognition (CVPR), pp. 12032–12042 (2023)
14. Maaten, L.V.D., Hinton, G.: Visualizing data using t-SNE. J. Mach. Learn. Res. **9**(2605), 2579–2605 (2008)
15. LeCun, Y., Chopra, S., Hadsell, R., Ranzato, A., Huang, F.: A tutorial on energy-based learning. Predicting structured data (2006)
16. Li, R., Chen, H., Feng, F., Ma, Z., Wang, X., Hovy, E.: Dual graph convolutional networks for aspect-based sentiment analysis. In: Proceedings of the 59th Annual Meeting of the Association for Computational Linguistics and the 11th International Joint Conference on Natural Language Processing (Volume 1: Long Papers) (2021)
17. Liang, S., Wei, W., Mao, X.L., Wang, F., He, Z.: BiSyn-GAT+: bi-syntax aware graph attention network for aspect-based sentiment analysis (2022)
18. Ling, Y., Yu, J., Xia, R.: Vision-language pre-training for multimodal aspect-based sentiment analysis. arXiv preprint arXiv:2204.07955 (2022)
19. Liu, B.: Sentiment Analysis and Opinion Mining. Synthesis Lectures on Human Language Technologies. Morgan & Claypool Publishers (2012)
20. Liu, B.: Sentiment analysis and opinion mining. Springer Nature (2022)
21. Liu, D., Li, L., Tao, X., Cui, J., Xie, Q.: Descriptive prompt paraphrasing for target-oriented multimodal sentiment classification. In: Findings of the Association for Computational Linguistics: EMNLP 2023, Singapore, 6–10 December 2023, pp. 4174–4186. Association for Computational Linguistics (2023)
22. Lorraine, J., Vicol, P., Duvenaud, D.: Optimizing millions of hyperparameters by implicit differentiation. In: The 23rd International Conference on Artificial Intelligence and Statistics, AISTATS. Proceedings of Machine Learning Research, vol. 108, pp. 1540–1552. PMLR (2020)
23. Lu, D., Neves, L., Carvalho, V., Zhang, N., Ji, H.: Visual attention model for name tagging in multimodal social media, pp. 1990–1999 (2018)

24. Lv, Y., et al.: Aspect-level sentiment analysis using context and aspect memory network. Neurocomputing 195–205 (2021)
25. Moon, S., Neves, L., Carvalho, V.: Multimodal named entity recognition for short social media posts. In: Proceedings of the 2018 Conference of the North American Chapter of the Association for Computational Linguistics: Human Language Technologies, Volume 1 (Long Papers) (2018)
26. Oh, S., et al.: Deep context- and relation-aware learning for aspect-based sentiment analysis. In: Proceedings of the 59th Annual Meeting of the Association for Computational Linguistics and the 11th International Joint Conference on Natural Language Processing (Volume 2: Short Papers) (2021)
27. Pang, B., Lee, L.: Opinion mining and sentiment analysis. Found. Trends Inf. Retr. 2(1–2), 1–135 (2007)
28. Pang, S., Xue, Y., Yan, Z., Huang, W., Feng, J.: Dynamic and multi-channel graph convolutional networks for aspect-based sentiment analysis. In: Findings of the Association for Computational Linguistics: ACL-IJCNLP 2021 (2021)
29. Pearl, J.: Causality: Models, Reasoning, and Inference. Cambridge University Press (2000)
30. Peng, T., Li, Z., Wang, P., Zhang, L., Zhao, H.: A novel energy based model mechanism for multi-modal aspect-based sentiment analysis. In: Proceedings of the AAAI Conference on Artificial Intelligence, vol. 38, pp. 18869–18878 (2024)
31. Radford, A., et al.: Learning transferable visual models from natural language supervision. In: International Conference on Machine Learning, pp. 8748–8763. PMLR (2021)
32. Schwab, P., Karlen, W.: Cxplain: causal explanations for model interpretation under uncertainty. In: Advances in Neural Information Processing Systems 32: Annual Conference on Neural Information Processing Systems, pp. 10220–10230 (2019)
33. Schwab, P., Miladinovic, D., Karlen, W.: Granger-causal attentive mixtures of experts: learning important features with neural networks. In: The Thirty-Third AAAI Conference on Artificial Intelligence, pp. 4846–4853 (2019)
34. Shalit, U., Johansson, F.D., Sontag, D.: Estimating individual treatment effect: generalization bounds and algorithms. In: Proceedings of the 34th International Conference on Machine Learning (ICML), pp. 3076–3085 (2017)
35. Sun, T., Ni, J., Wang, W., Jing, L., Wei, Y., Nie, L.: General debiasing for multimodal sentiment analysis. In: Proceedings of the 31st ACM International Conference on Multimedia (2023)
36. Sun, T., Wang, W., Jing, L., Cui, Y., Song, X., Nie, L.: Counterfactual reasoning for out-of-distribution multimodal sentiment analysis. In: Proceedings of the 30th ACM International Conference on Multimedia (2022)
37. Wang, Q., Ding, K., Liang, B., Yang, M., Xu, R.: Reducing spurious correlations in aspect-based sentiment analysis with explanation from large language models. In: Findings of the Association for Computational Linguistics: EMNLP 2023, pp. 2930–2941 (2023)
38. Wang, Q., Ding, K., Liang, B., Yang, M., Xu, R.: Reducing spurious correlations in aspect-based sentiment analysis with explanation from large language models. In: Findings of the Association for Computational Linguistics: EMNLP 2023, pp. 2930–2941. Association for Computational Linguistics, Singapore (2023)
39. Wang, X., Cai, J., Jiang, Y., Xie, P., Tu, K., Lu, W.: Named entity and relation extraction with multi-modal retrieval. Cornell University - arXiv, Cornell University - arXiv (2022)
40. Wang, Y., Huang, M., Zhu, X., Zhao, L.: Attention-based LSTM for aspect-level sentiment classification. In: Proceedings of the 2016 Conference on Empirical Methods in Natural Language Processing (2016)
41. Xu, N., Mao, W., Chen, G.: Multi-interactive memory network for aspect based multimodal sentiment analysis. In: Proceedings of the AAAI Conference on Artificial Intelligence, pp. 371–378 (2019)

42. Yang, B., Li, J.: Visual elements mining as prompts for instruction learning for target-oriented multimodal sentiment classification. In: Findings of the Association for Computational Linguistics: EMNLP 2023, pp. 6062–6075 (2023)
43. Yang, D., et al.: Towards multimodal sentiment analysis debiasing via bias purification. In: Leonardis, A., Ricci, E., Roth, S., Russakovsky, O., Sattler, T., Varol, G. (eds.) Computer Vision - ECCV 2024, pp. 464–481. Springer, Cham (2025)
44. Yang, H., Zhao, Y., Qin, B.: Face-sensitive image-to-emotional-text cross-modal translation for multimodal aspect-based sentiment analysis. In: Proceedings of the 2022 Conference on Empirical Methods in Natural Language Processing, pp. 3324–3335 (2022)
45. Yang, M., Wang, Z., Xu, Q., Li, C., Xu, R.: Leveraging hierarchical semantic-emotional memory in emotional conversation generation. CAAI Trans. Intell. Technol. **8**(3), 824–835 (2023)
46. Yang, X., Feng, F., Ji, W., Wang, M., Chua, T.S.: Deconfounded video moment retrieval with causal intervention. In: Proceedings of the 44th International ACM SIGIR Conference on Research and Development in Information Retrieval (2021)
47. Yu, J., Jiang, J.: Adapting BERT for target-oriented multimodal sentiment classification. In: Proceedings of the Twenty-Eighth International Joint Conference on Artificial Intelligence (2019)
48. Yu, J., Jiang, J., Xia, R.: Entity-sensitive attention and fusion network for entity-level multimodal sentiment classification. IEEE/ACM Trans. Audio Speech Lang. Process. **28**, 429–439 (2020)
49. Yu, J., Jiang, J., Yang, L., Xia, R.: Improving multimodal named entity recognition via entity span detection with unified multimodal transformer. In: Meeting of the Association for Computational Linguistics (2020)
50. Yu, J., Wang, J., Xia, R., Li, J.: Targeted multimodal sentiment classification based on coarse-to-fine grained image-target matching. In: Raedt, L.D. (ed.) Proceedings of the Thirty-First International Joint Conference on Artificial Intelligence, IJCAI 2022, pp. 4482–4488. International Joint Conferences on Artificial Intelligence Organization (2022)
51. Zhang, Q., Fu, J., Liu, X., Huang, X.: Adaptive co-attention network for named entity recognition in tweets. In: Proceedings of the AAAI Conference on Artificial Intelligence (2022)
52. Zhao, F., Li, C., Wu, Z., Ouyang, Y., Zhang, J., Dai, X.: M2DF: multi-grained multi-curriculum denoising framework for multimodal aspect-based sentiment analysis. In: Proceedings of the 2023 Conference on Empirical Methods in Natural Language Processing, pp. 9057–9070. Association for Computational Linguistics, Singapore (2023)
53. Zhao, F., Wu, Z., Long, S., Dai, X., Huang, S., Chen, J.: Learning from adjective-noun pairs: a knowledge-enhanced framework for target-oriented multimodal sentiment classification. In: Proceedings of the 29th International Conference on Computational Linguistics, COLING 2022, Gyeongju, Republic of Korea, 12–17 October 2022, pp. 6784–6794. International Committee on Computational Linguistics (2022)
54. Zhou, J., Lin, Y., Chen, Q., Zhang, Q., Huang, X., He, L.: Causalabsc: causal inference for aspect debiasing in aspect-based sentiment classification. IEEE/ACM Trans. Audio Speech Lang. Process. **32**, 830–840 (2024)
55. Zhou, R., Guo, W., Liu, X., Yu, S., Zhang, Y., Yuan, X.: AOM: detecting aspect-oriented information for multimodal aspect-based sentiment analysis. arXiv preprint arXiv:2306.01004 (2023)

Author Index

A
Ai, Wei   509
Alam, Md Farhad   473
Ashkenazi, Maor   187
Assylbekov, Zhenisbek   327

B
Barua, Deeparghya Dutta   473
Belcastro, Loris   290
Biecek, Przemysław   94
Boley, Mario   453
Bonchi, Francesco   78
Brenner, Ofir   187

C
Campagner, Andrea   344
Cascione, Alessio   3
Charland, Philippe   130
Chen, Hongguang   526
Chen, Huan   273
Cheng, Zhenrong   224
Cosentino, Cristian   290

D
Dantas, Cássio F.   492
de Souza Loureiro, André   205
Di Caro, Luigi   492
Ding, Steven H. H.   130
Domańska, Joanna   22
Dong, Yushun   307

E
e Silva, Hugo Manuel Alves Henriques   526
Escarcega, David   205

F
Fahim, Md   473
Fan, Xuanbo   224
Fedele, Andrea   3
Ferrod, Roger   492

Filho, Rômulo Férrer   149
Filus, Katarzyna   22
Fragkathoulas, Christos   41
Freitas, Stenio   149
Fung, Benjamin C. M.   130

G
Gezici, Gizem   149
Giannotti, Fosca   149
Grzejdziak-Zdziarski, Michał   362
Guidotti, Riccardo   3, 94
Guo, Shengnan   240

H
Haider, Fabiha   473
Harada, Tsubasa   380
He, Qiang   257
Horváth, Tamás   417

I
Ienco, Dino   492
Ifrim, Georgiana   60
Ishmam, Md Farhan   473
Ito, Shinji   380

K
Kotowski, Krzysztof   94

L
Lan, Long   273
Landi, Cristiano   3
Le Bodic, Pierre   453
Legg, Alan   327
Li, Chaoyang   542
Li, Kaiyuan   224
Li, Keqin   509
Li, Mengyuan   307
Li, Zhaoye   273
Liao, Qing   542

© The Editor(s) (if applicable) and The Author(s), under exclusive license to Springer Nature Switzerland AG 2026
R. P. Ribeiro et al. (Eds.): ECML PKDD 2025, LNAI 16016, pp. 559–560, 2026.
https://doi.org/10.1007/978-3-032-06078-5

Liò, Pietro 290
Loog, Marco 362

M
Maghsudi, Setareh 257
Marcacini, Ricardo 205
Marozzo, Fabrizio 290
Marques-Silva, Joao 166
Meng, Tao 509

N
Nerini, Francesco Paolo 78
Nguyen, Thach Le 60
Noguez, Julieta 205
Ntagiou, Evridiki Vasileia 94

P
Pak, Artur 327
Panisson, André 78
Papanikou, Vasiliki 41
Peng, Boci 224
Pitoura, Evaggelia 41
Planes, Jordi 166
Plantevit, Marc 113
Płudowski, Dawid 94

R
Ragno, Alessio 113
Rahman Adib, Md Tasmim 473
Raimondi, Franco 149
Ren, Jing 273
Robardet, Céline 113
Rossi, Ryan 307

S
Santos, Alexandre 149
Saqib, Mohd 130
Selpi, 526
Serafim, Paulo Bruno 149
Shifat, Fariha Tanjim 473
Shohet, Tal Furman 187
Shou, Yuntao 509
Šíma, Jiří 398

Siala, Mohamed 166
Sourove, Md Sakib Ul Rahman 473
Spinnato, Francesco 94
Stadtländer, Eike 417
Sui, Yize 273
Sumita, Hanna 380
Sun, Hao 224

T
Tan, Huibin 273
Tax, David M. J. 362
Terzi, Evimaria 41
Treister, Eran 187

U
Uddin, Anam Borhan 473

V
Valverde-Rebaza, Jorge 205
Vidnerová, Petra 398

W
Wang, Lingzhi 542
Wang, Zhangyi 240
Wang, Ziyi 307
Wilczyński, Piotr 94
Wolinski, Pierre 436
Wrobel, Stefan 417

X
Xu, Haoyan 307

Y
Yang, Fan 453
Yao, Zhengtao 307

Z
Zhai, Yuchen 240
Zhang, Shenyi 240
Zhang, Yan 224
Zhao, Lingchen 240
Zhao, Pengyu 542
Zhao, Yue 307